A MONETARY HISTORY OF
THE UNITED STATES
1867–1960

NATIONAL BUREAU OF ECONOMIC RESEARCH
Studies in Business Cycles

(Titles 1 through 12 that are not listed below in the series are available through the National Bureau of Economic Research.)

A Monetary History
of the
United States

1867-1960

MILTON FRIEDMAN

ANNA JACOBSON SCHWARTZ

A STUDY BY THE
NATIONAL BUREAU OF ECONOMIC RESEARCH, NEW YORK

PUBLISHED BY
PRINCETON UNIVERSITY PRESS, PRINCETON
1963

Printed in the United States of America
by Princeton University Press, Princeton, N. J.

RELATION OF THE DIRECTORS
TO THE WORK AND PUBLICATIONS
OF THE NATIONAL BUREAU OF ECONOMIC RESEARCH

1. The object of the National Bureau of Economic Research is to ascertain and to present to the public important economic facts and their interpretation in a scientific and impartial manner. The Board of Directors is charged with the responsibility of ensuring that the work of the National Bureau is carried on in strict conformity with this object.

2. To this end the Board of Directors shall appoint one or more Directors of Research.

3. The Director or Directors of Research shall submit to the members of the Board, or to its Executive Committee, for their formal adoption, all specific proposals concerning researches to be instituted.

4. No report shall be published until the Director or Directors of Research shall have submitted to the Board a summary drawing attention to the character of the data and their utilization in the report, the nature and treatment of the problems involved, the main conclusions, and such other information as in their opinion would serve to determine the suitability of the report for publication in accordance with the principles of the National Bureau.

5. A copy of any manuscript proposed for publication shall also be submitted to each member of the Board. For each manuscript to be so submitted a special committee shall be appointed by the President, or at his designation by the Executive Director, consisting of three Directors selected as nearly as may be one from each general division of the Board. The names of the special manuscript committee shall be stated to each Director when the summary and report described in paragraph (4) are sent to him. It shall be the duty of each member of the committee to read the manuscript. If each member of the special committee signifies his approval within thirty days, the manuscript may be published. If each member of the special committee has not signified his approval within thirty days of the transmittal of the report and manuscript, the Director of Research shall then notify each member of the Board, requesting approval or disapproval of publication, and thirty additional days shall be granted for this purpose. The manuscript shall then not be published unless at least a majority of the entire Board and a two-thirds majority of those members of the Board who shall have voted on the proposal within the time fixed for the receipt of votes on the publication proposed shall have approved.

6. No manuscript may be published, though approved by each member of the special committee, until forty-five days have elapsed from the transmittal of the summary and report. The interval is allowed for the receipt of any memorandum of dissent or reservation, together with a brief statement of his reasons, that any member may wish to express; and such memorandum of dissent or reservation shall be published with the manuscript if he so desires. Publication does not, however, imply that each member of the Board has read the manuscript, or that either members of the Board in general, or of the special committee, have passed upon its validity in every detail.

7. A copy of this resolution shall, unless otherwise determined by the Board, be printed in each copy of every National Bureau book.

(Resolution adopted October 25, 1926,
as revised February 6, 1933, and February 24, 1941)

Contents

Tables

Charts

Experience in controversies such as these brings out the impossibility of learning anything from facts till they are examined and interpreted by reason; and teaches that the most reckless and treacherous of all theorists is he who professes to let facts and figures speak for themselves, who keeps in the background the part he has played, perhaps unconsciously, in selecting and grouping them, and in suggesting the argument post hoc ergo propter hoc.

ALFRED MARSHALL

Preface

THIS book had its origin in a conversation one of us had more than a decade ago with the late Walter W. Stewart. That conversation was about a statistical study of monetary factors in the business cycle, then proposed as one of the National Bureau's cyclical studies. Stewart stressed the desirability of including an "analytical narrative" of post–Civil War monetary developments in the United States as a background for the statistical work, arguing that such a narrative was not currently available and would add a much needed dimension to the numerical evidence.

His suggestion led us to include a chapter on the historical background of the money stock in our planned monograph. The chapter, which we began to write only after we had completed a first draft of the remaining chapters, took on a life of its own. The one chapter became two, then a separate part, and has now become a separate book. But, though separate, it is not entirely independent. Some statistical series we use in this book are explained in full in the forthcoming companion volume, "Trends and Cycles in the Stock of Money in the United States, 1867–1960," which though first into draft will be later into print. The prescience of Stewart's advice has been impressed upon us repeatedly as we have revised the chapters of the companion volume. Our foray into analytical narrative has significantly affected our statistical analysis.

The National Bureau's interest in the cyclical behavior of monetary factors dates back to the inception of its studies in business cycles. The first product lineally related to the present study was Technical Paper 4 on currency and vault cash, published in 1947.[1] The estimates there presented, now superseded, were the first step in the development of the money series which form the statistical backbone of the present study and of Phillip Cagan's forthcoming volume, "Determinants and Effects of Changes in the U.S. Money Stock, 1875–1955." Some early results were published in two occasional papers on the demand for money, and a by-product on problems of interpolation appeared as a technical paper.[2]

[1] Anna .Jacobson Schwartz and Elma Oliver, *Currency Held by the Public, the Banks, and the Treasury, Monthly, December 1917–December 1944,* New York, National Bureau of Economic Research, Technical Paper 4, 1947.

[2] Phillip Cagan, *The Demand for Currency Relative to Total Money Supply,* New York, NBER, Occasional Paper 62, 1958; Milton Friedman, *The Demand for Money: Some Theoretical and Empirical Results,* New York, NBER, Occasional Paper 68, 1959; idem, *The Interpolation of Time Series by Related Series,* New York, NBER, Technical Paper 16, 1962.

Despite the length to which this volume has grown, we are painfully aware of its restricted scope. Money touches every phase of the economic life of an enterprise-exchange economy and in consequence cannot fail to affect its politics as well. A full-scale economic and political history would be required to record at all comprehensively the role of money in the United States in the past century. Needless to say, we have not been so ambitious. Rather, we have kept in the forefront the initial aim: to provide a prologue and background for a statistical analysis of the secular and cyclical behavior of money in the United States, and to exclude any material not relevant to that purpose.

We have accumulated numerous and heavy debts during the many years that this book has been in the making. An earlier draft of the manuscript was duplicated some years ago and circulated among a number of scholars from whose comments and suggestions we have profited greatly. We owe an especially heavy debt to Clark Warburton. His detailed and valuable comments on several drafts have importantly affected the final version. In addition, time and again, as we came to some conclusion that seemed to us novel and original, we found he had been there before. Among the many others to whom we are indebted for valuable criticism are Moses Abramovitz, Gary S. Becker, Arthur F. Burns, Phillip Cagan, Lester V. Chandler, C. A. E. Goodhart, Gottfried Haberler, Earl J. Hamilton, Bray Hammond, Albert J. Hettinger, Jr., James K. Kindahl, David Meiselman, Lloyd Mints, Geoffrey H. Moore, George R. Morrison, Jay Morrison, Edward S. Shaw, Matthew Simon, and George J. Stigler.

Because the Federal Reserve System since its establishment has played so central a role in the monetary history of the United States, we have of necessity examined its operations in great detail. We have often had to rely on secondary sources, since much primary source material is not in the public domain. Accordingly, the penultimate version of this book was sent for criticism to the Board of Governors of the Federal Reserve System and to a number of present and former officials of the System. We are grateful to the three individuals who sent comments on the manuscript: Clay Anderson, currently economic adviser, Federal Reserve Bank of Philadelphia; W. Randolph Burgess, from 1930 to 1938 a deputy governor and vice-president, Federal Reserve Bank of New York; and Allan Sproul, from 1940 to 1954 president, Federal Reserve Bank of New York. The final version of this book has been appreciably altered in consequence. In addition, Mr. Sproul's comments brought to our attention the George Leslie Harrison Papers on the Federal Reserve System, in the Columbia University Library, of which we have made extensive use in our final version. Together with the Diary of Charles S. Hamlin, member of the Federal Reserve Board from 1914 to 1936, the Harrison

Papers have been our major primary source of information about the operations of the System during a critical part of its history.

A number of scholars have been good enough to furnish unpublished material: Phyllis Deane, a price index for Great Britain; Raymond W. Goldsmith, United States net international capital movements from the turn of the century until 1919, the year when Department of Commerce figures become available; Simon Kuznets, annual net national product figures.

We owe a special debt to David C. Mearns, chief of the Manuscript Division of the Library of Congress, which controls all rights of publication, for permission to cite and quote from the Charles S. Hamlin Diary. We are also grateful to Roland Baughman, head of Special Collections at the Columbia University Library, for authorizing us to cite and quote from the writings of George L. Harrison in the Harrison Papers described above. Permission to cite and quote from other material in the Harrison Papers was kindly given us by the Federal Reserve Bank of New York. We wish to express our gratitude also to Mrs. E. A. Goldenweiser for permission to cite and quote from the unpublished writings of her late husband, in the Goldenweiser Papers, in the Manuscript Division of the Library of Congress.

This book has required an extremely large amount of statistical computation. Most of that work has been done at the National Bureau of Economic Research, chiefly by Mark L. Wehle, who also made useful criticisms of the manuscript. In addition, we have had assistance at various stages of our study from Edith Hanover, Juanita Johnson, Phyllis A. Wallace; also Nadeschda Bohsack, John Helbok, Martha S. Jones, David Laidler, Esther D. Reichner, Sophie Sakowitz, Hanna Stern, Judie Tomkins, and Tom Teng-pin Yu. Harry Eisenpress and Millard Hastay contributed valuable advice and assistance in connection with problems of computation. In addition, statistical assistance was provided by the Center for Advanced Study in the Behavioral Sciences, where Milton Friedman was a Fellow during part of the preparation of the earlier draft, and by the Money and Banking Workshop and the Economic Research Center at the University of Chicago. We are indebted to these institutions, to the late Mary Girschik and her assistants at the Center for Advanced Study, and to Lilly Monheit and her assistants at Chicago. Last but not least, Janet Friedman cheerfully sacrificed parts of a number of summers to run a computing machine for her father.

The Center for Advanced Study provided many other facilities in addition to computing assistance during a most fruitful year. Discussion of the earlier draft of the manuscript at a number of seminars with other Fellows was most valuable, as were more informal discussions. The draft was also discussed at sessions of the Money and Banking Workshop at

Chicago, and suggestions made there have left their mark on the final manuscript.

We have made much use of the library facilities of Columbia University and the University of Chicago, of the Baker Library and the Library of the Tuck School at Dartmouth College, and of the New York Public Library. The librarians of all these institutions have been most cooperative and helpful.

H. Irving Forman has turned in his usual outstanding performance in drawing the charts. Margaret T. Edgar has made editorial suggestions for which not only we but also the readers of this book are in her debt.

Finally, we cannot forbear saying a word of appreciation to the National Bureau as an institution and to the two successive directors of research, Arthur F. Burns and Solomon Fabricant, under whom this study has been conducted. True to the spirit of dedication to the pursuit of truth, they have encouraged and assisted us to follow our path where it led, even though that meant repeated postponements of completion and a first major product very different indeed from the one initially contemplated.

MILTON FRIEDMAN
ANNA JACOBSON SCHWARTZ

A MONETARY HISTORY OF
THE UNITED STATES
1867–1960

CHAPTER 1

Introduction

THIS book is about the stock of money in the United States. It traces changes in the stock of money for nearly a century, from just after the Civil War to 1960, examines the factors that accounted for the changes, and analyzes the reflex influence that the stock of money exerted on the course of events.

We start with 1867 because that is the earliest date at which we can begin a continuous series of estimates of the stock of money in the United States. When the National Banking Act was passed during the Civil War, it was believed that state banks would shortly go out of existence. As a result, organized federal collection of statistics for state banks ceased, though, as it happens, state banks suffered only a temporary and never a complete eclipse. Accordingly, there is a serious hiatus in statistical data. Better data are available for the period before the Civil War than for the years from 1863 to 1867.

Money played an important role in economic and political developments in the United States during the period we cover—as it so often has in other periods and other places. We have therefore been led to examine some of these developments in considerable detail, so much so that this book may read in part like a general economic history. We warn the reader that it is not; it is highly selective. Throughout, we trace one thread, the stock of money, and our concern with that thread explains alike which episodes and events are examined in detail and which are slighted.

The estimates of the stock of money we have constructed give for the first time a continuous series covering more than nine decades.[1] These estimates, graphed in Chart 1 (and given numerically in Table A-1), show clearly the impress of most of the major episodes in U.S. history since the Civil War.

The most notable feature of the stock of money is its sharp upward trend. In 1867, the first year for which we have an estimate, the public[2]

NOTE: Albert J. Hettinger, Jr., a Director of the National Bureau, has prepared a comment on this book which appears on pp. 809–814.

[1] For a full description of these estimates and their derivation, see our companion volume, "Trends and Cycles in the Stock of Money in the United States, 1867–1960," a National Bureau study, in preparation.

[2] The public, as we use the term, includes all holders of U.S. currency or deposits located in the continental United States, except banks, offices of the

3

held about $585 million of currency—consisting at the time mostly of "greenbacks" issued to help finance the Civil War, plus national bank notes and subsidiary coinage[3]—and $729 million of deposits in commercial banks[4] or a total of $1,314 million of what by one definition—and the one we use here—may be called *money*. In addition, the public held $276 million in deposits at mutual savings banks, or a total of $1,590 million of what, by a broader definition, may about as reasonably be called money. Our figures do not classify deposits in commercial banks at this early date into demand and time deposits, because this distinction had little meaning, either for banks or their customers. Reserve requirements for banks were levied against deposits, without distinction between demand and time. Demand deposits, like time deposits, frequently paid interest; and time deposits, like demand deposits, were frequently transferable by check. The distinction became of major importance to banks (and so reliable data became available on a continuous basis for the two categories separately) only after 1914, when the Federal Reserve Act introduced differential requirements for demand and time deposits. Accordingly, we have no estimate for 1867 for a third and narrower possible definition of money, namely, currency plus demand deposits alone.[5]

In mid-1960, the last year for which estimates are presented in

---

Treasury Department (for deposits; for currency, only the Washington, D.C., offices), and mint and assay offices of the U.S. It includes individuals, partnerships, corporations, states, counties, municipalities, and government corporations and credit agencies. For a more detailed description, see "Trends and Cycles."

[3] In accordance with our definition of the public, this figure excludes currency in bank vaults and in the U.S. Treasury.

[4] Again, in accordance with our definition of the public, this figure excludes interbank deposits and U.S. government deposits. It is also adjusted to exclude items in the process of collection from recorded total deposits to avoid double counting.

We consider a financial institution to be a bank if it provides deposit facilities for the public, or if it conducts principally a fiduciary business—in accordance with the definition of banks agreed upon by federal bank supervisory agencies. Of these two classes, fiduciaries are negligible in importance. Banks are classified as either commercial or mutual savings banks. Commercial banks include national banks, incorporated state banks, loan and trust companies, stock savings banks, industrial and Morris Plan banks if they provide deposit facilities, special types of banks of deposit—such as cash depositories and cooperative exchanges in certain states—and unincorporated or private banks. Mutual savings banks include all banks operating under state banking codes applying to mutual savings banks. See Federal Deposit Insurance Corporation (FDIC), *Annual Report*, 1956, pp. 88–89.

By this definition savings and loan associations and credit unions are not banks. Holders of funds in these institutions are for the most part technically shareholders, not depositors, though clearly they may regard such funds as close substitutes for bank deposits, as we define them.

[5] See our forthcoming volume, "Trends and Cycles," for a discussion of the reasons we use the term money to refer to currency plus all deposits in commercial banks.

4

Chart 1, the public held about $29 billion of currency (consisting mostly of Federal Reserve notes but with an appreciable residue of silver certificates and subsidiary coinage as well as a number of other relics of earlier monetary history), $110 billion of demand deposits, and $67 billion of time deposits in commercial banks, or a total of $206 billion of money by the terminology we use. In addition, it held some $35 billion of deposits in mutual savings banks and under $1 billion of postal savings deposits, or a total of $242 billion of money plus such deposits. The public held 50 times as many dollars of currency at the end of the 93 years spanned by our figures as at the beginning; 243 times as many dollars of commercial bank deposits; and 127 times as many dollars of mutual savings deposits.

The total we designate as money multiplied 157-fold in the course of these more than nine decades, or at the annual rate of 5.4 per cent.[6] Since the population of the United States nearly quintupled over the same period, the stock of money per capita multiplied some 32-fold, or at the annual rate of 3.7 per cent. We can break this total into three components: 1.9 percentage points, which is the rate of rise in output per capita; 0.9 percentage points, which is the rate of rise in prices; and a residual of 0.9 percentage points, which is the rate of rise in the amount of money balances, expressed as a fraction of income, that the public chose to hold.[7] So great is the power of compound interest that this residual small rate of growth corresponds to a rise in the public's holdings of money from a sum equal to less than 3 months' income in 1869 to a sum equal to more than 7 months' income in 1960. Of course, as Chart 2 shows, these developments did not proceed steadily; and it is with the vicissitudes along the way that this study is mostly concerned.

In discussing these vicissitudes, we frequently find it convenient to mark off periods by dates at which business activity reached a cyclical peak or trough. We use for this purpose the reference cycle chronology

[6] These rates, and all other annual rates cited hereafter, assume continuous compounding; i.e., they are the difference between the natural logarithms of the stock of money at the terminal and initial dates divided by the number of years separating those dates.

Continuously compounded rates of growth are lower than rates compounded for discrete intervals—annually or semiannually or quarterly. For example, the rate of growth of money, which is 5.38 per cent compounded continuously, is 5.43 per cent compounded quarterly, 5.46 per cent compounded semiannually, 5.53 per cent compounded annually.

[7] Income, here and throughout this study unless otherwise specified, is defined as net national product, variant III, computed by Simon Kuznets in *Capital in the American Economy: Its Formation and Financing,* Princeton for NBER, 1961.

The measure for output per capita, cited in the text, is net national product in 1929 prices; the measure for prices is the index of implicit prices obtained by dividing net national product in current prices by net national product in 1929 prices.

CHART 2

Number of Months' Income Held as Money in Each Year, 1869–1960

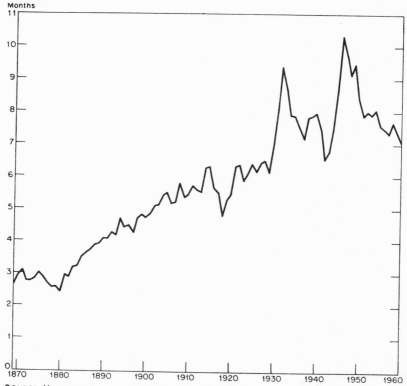

SOURCE: Money stock was multiplied by 12 and divided by money income.

Money stock, figures in col. 8 of Table A-1 were averaged to center on June 30; before 1908, annual averages were obtained from that source, interpolated by the step method (see Table 25, col. 1, for description).

Money income, same as for Chart 62.

established by the National Bureau of Economic Research. Our extensive use of this chronology perhaps justifies an explicit caveat that we do not present a comprehensive history of cyclical movements in economic activity in the United States. Monetary factors played a major role in these movements, and conversely, nonmonetary developments frequently had a major influence on monetary developments; yet even together the matters that concern the historian of money do not exhaust those that are relevant to the historian of cyclical movements.

The years from 1867 to 1879 were dominated by the financial

aftermath of the Civil War. Early in 1862, convertibility of Union currency into specie was suspended as a result of money creation in the North to help finance the Civil War, disturbances in foreign trade, the general financial uncertainty arising out of the war, and the borrowing techniques of the Treasury. From then until resumption of specie payments on January 1, 1879, the United States was legally on a fiduciary standard—the greenback standard as it has come to be called. The dollar was linked with other currencies through exchange rates determined in the market and fluctuating from day to day. The dollar was inconvertible in the older sense of not being exchangeable at fixed parity for specie; it was not inconvertible in the modern sense of being subject to legal restrictions on its purchase or sale. For domestic payments, gold was in the main simply a commodity like any other, with a variable market price. For foreign payments, gold was equivalent to foreign exchange, since Great Britain maintained a gold standard throughout the period, and several other important countries did so during the latter part of the period.

Despite support for inconvertible currency by many business groups both during and after the war, and growing farm support after the war, as agricultural prices fell, suspension of payments was generally regarded as temporary. The major announced aim of financial policy was a resumption of specie payments at the prewar parity. This aim was finally achieved on January 1, 1879. The whole episode, discussed in detail in Chapter 2, is clearly reflected in the series in Chart 1. The decline in the stock of money from 1875 to 1878—one of the few absolute declines in the whole history of the series and next to the largest—was a necessary prelude to successful resumption. The extremely sharp rise thereafter was partly a reaction to success.

Another aftermath of the Civil War was an extremely rapid growth in banking institutions, which produced a sharp rise in the ratio of deposits to currency. The financial measures of the war included establishment of the National Banking System and, effective July 1, 1866, a prohibitive tax on state bank notes. Initially, few national banks were created, while the prospective tax measure was a strong deterrent to state banks. The result was that the major effect of the National Banking Act came after the end of the war, and, along with a revival of state banks, helped to produce the sharp rise in deposits recorded in Chart 1.

The success of resumption did not end uncertainty about the monetary standard. For nearly two decades thereafter, the U.S. financial scene was dominated by controversy, which had started in the seventies, over the place of silver in the monetary system.

The rapid expansion of output in the Western world during those decades and the adoption of a gold standard over an area far wider

7

than before added substantially to the demand for gold for monetary purposes at any given price level in terms of gold. That expansion in demand more than offset a contemporary expansion in supply, as a result both of increased production of gold and improvement of financial techniques for erecting a larger superstructure of money on a given base of gold. The result was a slow but rather steady downward tendency in product prices that prolonged and exacerbated the political discontent initiated by the rapid decline in prices after the end of the Civil War. "Greenbackism" and "free silver" became the rallying cries. The silver forces were strong enough to obtain concessions that shook confidence in the maintenance of the gold standard, yet they were not strong enough to obtain the substitution of silver for gold as the monetary standard. The monetary history of this period is therefore one of repeated crises and of legislative backing and filling. The defeat of William Jennings Bryan in the Presidential election of 1896 marks in retrospect the end of the period (Chapter 3).

Bryan's defeat marks the end of the period, rather than simply a minor setback on the road to ultimate success, because it happened to follow gold discoveries in South Africa and Alaska and the perfection of the cyanide process for extracting gold. These developments doomed Bryan to political failure, far more than any waning in the effectiveness of his oratory or any shortcomings in his political organization. They produced a rapid expansion of the world's production of gold, sufficiently large to force an upward price movement over the next two decades despite a continued growth in world output. In the United States, the stock of money was approximately constant from 1890 to 1896. During those years, uncertainty about the monetary standard and associated banking and international payment difficulties prevented any expansion in the U.S. stock of gold despite a moderate acceleration in the growth of the world's stock of gold. The money stock then rose over the next two decades at a rate decidedly above that from 1881 to 1896 (Chart 1). The accompanying gradual rise in prices rendered the gold standard secure and unquestioned in the United States until World War I.

The elimination of controversy about the monetary standard shifted the financial and political spotlight to the banking structure. Dissatisfaction had been generated by recurrent banking difficulties. The most severe of these occurred in 1873, 1884, 1890, and 1893, when bank failures, runs on banks, and widespread fears of further failures produced banking crises and, on several occasions, most notably 1893, suspension by most banks of convertibility of deposits into currency. The 1893 episode is reflected in Chart 1 in the concomitant rise in currency and decline in deposits, as well as in the decline in total currency and deposits. The dissatisfaction with the banking structure was brought to a head by the banking panic of 1907. That panic was a repetition of earlier episodes, including the suspension of convertibility of deposits into currency. It is marked in Chart 1 by the only decline in the stock of money during the period 1897–1914, accompanied as in 1893 by a rise in currency and hence a still sharper decline in deposits. The result was the enactment by Congress of the Aldrich-Vreeland Act in 1908 as a temporary measure, a searching examination of the monetary and banking structure by a National Monetary Commission in 1910, the publication by the Commission of some notable scholarly works on money and banking, and the adoption by Congress of the Federal Reserve Act of 1913 as a permanent measure (Chapter 4).

The Federal Reserve System began operations in 1914. This far-reaching internal change in the monetary structure of the United States happened to coincide with an equally significant external change—the loosening of links between external conditions and the internal supply of money which followed the outbreak of World War I—destined to become permanent. Taken together, the two changes make 1914 a major watershed in American monetary history.

Important as they were, both changes were changes of degree. The Treasury had long exercised central banking powers that were no less potent because they were not so labeled, and, as Chapter 4 documents, it had been doing so to an increasing extent. The growing size of the U.S. economy relative to the world economy and the declining importance of U.S. foreign trade relative to domestic trade had long been increasing the importance of internal changes in the United States for world monetary conditions and introducing ever greater play in the links between the two.

Though independent in their inception, the two changes were destined to become closely related. The weakening of the international gold standard gave the Federal Reserve System both greater freedom of action and wider responsibilities. In turn, the manner in which the Federal Reserve System exercised its powers had an important effect on the fate of the gold standard. One who did not know the subsequent history of money in the United States would very likely conjecture that the two changes reinforced one another in reducing the instability in the stock of money. The weakening of external links offered the possibility of insulating the domestic stock of money from external shocks. And the Reserve System, established in response to monetary instability, had the power to exercise deliberate control over the stock of money and so could take advantage of this possibility to promote monetary stability.

That conjecture is not in accord with what actually happened. As is clear to the naked eye in Chart 1, the stock of money shows larger

9

fluctuations after 1914 than before 1914 and this is true even if the large wartime increases in the stock of money are excluded. The blind, undesigned, and quasi-automatic working of the gold standard turned out to produce a greater measure of predictability and regularity—perhaps because its discipline was impersonal and inescapable—than did deliberate and conscious control exercised within institutional arrangements intended to promote monetary stability. Here is a striking example of the deceptiveness of appearances, of the frequently dominant importance of forces operating beneath the surface.

The rapid rise in the stock of money during World War I, when the Federal Reserve System served as an engine for the inflationary financing of government expenditures, continued for some eighteen months after the end of the war, at first as a continued accompaniment of government expenditures, then as a result of the almost inadvertent financing of private monetary expansion by the System. The monetary expansion was abruptly reversed in early 1920 by Federal Reserve action—the first major deliberate and independent act of monetary policy taken by the System and one for which it was severely criticized (Chapter 5).

The rest of the twenties were in many ways the high tide of the Federal Reserve System. The stock of money grew at a highly regular rate, and economic activity showed a high degree of stability. Both were widely attributed to the beneficent actions of the System. Within the System, there was much sophisticated and penetrating research on the operation of the financial markets and the role of the System. The result was a deepened understanding of its own operations and tools. Outside the System, bankers and businessmen at home regarded its powers with awe, and foreign countries sought its assistance in mending their own monetary arrangements. Cooperation with the great central banks of Britain, France, and Germany was close; and the belief arose that, through such cooperation, the central bankers could assure not only domestic but also international economic stability (Chapter 6).

That era came to an abrupt end in 1929 with the downturn which ushered in the Great Contraction. In its initial stages, the contraction was not unlike earlier ones in its monetary aspects, albeit the money stock did decline slightly. Severe contractions aside, the money stock rises on the average during contraction and expansion alike, though at a slower rate during contraction. The monetary character of the contraction changed drastically in late 1930, when several large bank failures led to the first of what were to prove a series of liquidity crises involving runs on banks and bank failures on a scale unprecedented in our history. Britain's departure from gold in 1931 and the Federal Reserve's reaction to that event sharply intensified the banking collapse, if indeed they did not nip a potential revival in the bud. By early 1933, when the monetary collapse terminated in a banking holiday, the stock of money had fallen by one-third—the largest and longest decline in the entire period covered by our series. The banking holiday was a panic of the genus that the founders of the Federal Reserve System had expected it to render impossible. It was, however, of a different species, being far more severe than any earlier panic. In addition, whereas in earlier panics, restriction of payments came before many banks had failed and served to reduce the number of subsequent failures, the 1933 banking holiday occurred only after an unprecedentedly large fraction of the banking system had already failed, and many banks open before the holiday never reopened after it. One-third of the banks had gone out of existence through failure or merger by 1933 (Chapter 7).

The drastic decline in the stock of money and the occurrence of a banking panic of unprecedented severity did not reflect the absence of power on the part of the Reserve System to prevent them. Throughout the contraction, the System had ample powers to cut short the tragic process of monetary deflation and banking collapse. Had it used those powers effectively in late 1930 or even in early or mid-1931, the successive liquidity crises that in retrospect are the distinctive feature of the contraction could almost certainly have been prevented and the stock of money kept from declining or, indeed, increased to any desired extent. Such action would have eased the severity of the contraction and very likely would have brought it to an end at a much earlier date. Such measures were not taken, partly, we conjecture, because of the fortuitous shift of power within the System from New York to other Federal Reserve Banks and the weakness of the Federal Reserve Board in Washington, partly because of the assignment—by the community at large as well as the Reserve System—of higher priority to external than to internal stability (Chapter 7).

Major changes in both the banking structure and the monetary system resulted from the Great Contraction. In banking, the major change was the enactment of federal deposit insurance in 1934. This probably has succeeded, where the Federal Reserve Act failed, in rendering it impossible for a loss of public confidence in some banks to produce a widespread banking panic involving severe downward pressure on the stock of money; if so, it is of the greatest importance for the subsequent monetary history of the United States. Since the establishment of the Federal Deposit Insurance Corporation, bank failures have become a rarity. The Federal Reserve System itself was reorganized, greater power being concentrated in the Board and less in the Banks. The System was also given additional powers, of which the power to vary reserve requirements was by far the most important. In the monetary system, the dollar was devalued in terms of gold, and

11

the character of the gold standard was changed. Gold coinage was discontinued and the holding of gold coin or bullion made illegal. The Treasury continued to buy gold freely at a fixed price at the Mint but sold it freely at a fixed price only for purposes of foreign payment. With the departure from the gold standard of country after country during and after World War II and the widespread introduction of exchange controls by other countries, the United States came to be effectively on a fiduciary standard. Gold is currently a commodity whose price is legally supported, rather than in any meaningful sense the base of our monetary system (Chapter 8).

The changes in men's ideas were no less important than the changes in institutions. The collapse of the banking system during the contraction and the failure of monetary policy to stem the contraction undermined the faith in the potency of the Federal Reserve System that had developed in the twenties. In the worlds of scholarship and policy alike, these events led, rightly or wrongly, to the relegation of money to a minor role, and to the assignment of major emphasis to governmental fiscal actions and direct interventions.

One result of these changes in ideas was that the Reserve System was led to adopt a largely passive role, adapting itself in an orderly manner to changes as they occurred rather than serving as an independent center of control. With one exception, the Treasury rather than the Reserve System originated and executed such monetary policy measures as were taken. The rapid rise in the stock of money after 1933 reflected two factors: first, the measures taken to repair the monetary structure, which produced a return of confidence in banks and so a rise in the ratio of deposits to currency; second, a large gold inflow, resulting initially from the lowering of the gold content of the dollar and later from the flight of capital from Europe after Hitler's accession to power began to engender fears of war. The Reserve System did nothing either to offset or to increase the effect of these factors until 1936. It then used its newly acquired powers to double reserve requirements in the course of six months—this is the exception referred to above. The result was the one significant interruption in the rise in the money stock during that period. The interruption accompanied the brief but sharp recession of 1937–38, added to its severity, and may have contributed to its occurring when it did (Chapter 9).

Federal Reserve policy continued to be subordinated to Treasury policy after the outbreak of World War II in Europe in 1939 and even more after the entry of the United States in 1941. The Federal Reserve System, as in World War I, became virtually the agent of the Treasury in its financial operations. It established a fixed pattern of rates of interest on government securities and permitted the stock of money to become an indirect consequence of the taxing and spending activities of government and of the real resources the community was willing to use to buy government securities at these fixed rates. The result was that from 1939 to 1945, the money stock was multiplied 2½-fold (Chapter 10).

The money stock grew at a much reduced rate in the early postwar years, yet indexes of prices rose rapidly. That outcome was widely regarded as, at least partly, a delayed reaction to the large wartime increases in the stock of money. The Federal Reserve System was impotent to control the stock of money by the usual means so long as it continued to support the prices of government securities at fixed levels. It was therefore led to experiment with a variety of expedients, none of which proved effective. As a result, controversy arose over the bond-support program itself. Finally, the rapid upward surge of prices after the outbreak of war in Korea dramatized the inhibiting effect of the bond-support policy on control of the money stock and led to the Treasury–Federal Reserve Accord of 1951, which made the support policy less rigid and, two years later, was followed by the abandonment of the policy.

These strictly domestic events were reinforced by experience abroad. Many countries pursued "cheap money" policies in the postwar period. Every such country experienced either open inflation or a network of partly effective, partly ineffective, controls designed to suppress the inflationary pressure. No country succeeded in curbing inflation without adopting measures that made it possible to restrain the growth of the stock of money. The result of these events and of the changing currents of thought in academic halls was a revival of interest in monetary matters and a renewed emphasis on monetary policy. This renewed emphasis, in its turn, stimulated renewed attention to alleged limitations of monetary policy.

These changes in attitude are more dramatic and manifest in pronouncements than in records of action. The graph of the money stock in Chart 1 shows the clear impress of neither the Treasury–Federal Reserve Accord nor of any subsequent statement about the direction and course of monetary policy, unless it be through the absence of movements that would otherwise have occurred. The distinctive feature of the rise in the money stock in the decade after 1947 is the high degree of stability, by comparison with earlier periods, in the year-to-year rate of change. In this respect, the postwar period resembles most the years 1903–13 and 1923–29. All three were periods of relative stability of both the rate of change in the money stock and of the state of business (Chapter 11).

Perhaps the most puzzling feature of postwar monetary developments is the coincidence of a relatively slow rate of rise in the stock of money with a fairly rapid rate of growth of money income. As noted at the outset, the stock of money has tended to grow more rapidly than money income over the more than nine decades covered by our data (see Chart 2). By contrast, from 1948 to 1960, the money stock grew at the rate of 2.9 per cent per year and money income grew at the rate of 5.0 per cent; which is to say, the velocity of money rose. Of the various explanations of this phenomenon that have been offered, we are inclined to believe that the most fundamental is that it reflects changes in the public's expectations about the degree of future economic stability (Chapter 12).

CHAPTER 2

The Greenback Period

THE PERIOD from the end of the Civil War to the resumption of gold payments in 1879 is of unusual interest to the student of money. These were the formative years of the National Banking System and, more generally, of a banking structure that was to remain largely unchanged until the establishment of the Federal Reserve System.

The monetary standard of the period had unique features, some not to recur for many decades, others not at all. It was a fiduciary standard under which no agency of the government was committed to selling gold at a fixed price to all who offered legal tender. It involved freely floating exchange rates between U.S. currency and the currencies of other countries. A fiduciary standard did not recur until 1933. Freely floating rates between the dollar and such other major currencies as the pound sterling and the French franc did not recur until World War I. On no occasion since have they prevailed so long as they did after the Civil War. This was probably the only period of floating rates during which official U.S. transactions played no significant part in either the gold or exchange markets.[1] It was certainly the only period in which two kinds of money exchanging at a fluctuating rate—greenbacks and gold—were used domestically side by side to any considerable extent.[2]

Finally, the price level fell to half its initial level in the course of less than fifteen years and, at the same time, economic growth proceeded at a rapid rate. The one phenomenon was the seedbed of controversy about monetary arrangements that was destined to plague the following decades; the other was a vigorous stage in the continued economic expansion that was destined to raise the United States to the first rank among the nations of the world. And their coincidence casts serious doubts on the validity of the now widely held view that secular price deflation and rapid economic growth are incompatible.

A good starting point for the analysis of both the period covered in this chapter and the longer period covered by this book is the composition of the money stock in 1867, the year our money series starts. The

---

[1] One possible exception is the refunding of Civil War debt at lower rates of interest by the Treasury in 1877–79 (see sect. 5, below).

[2] During banking panics, currency and deposits have for brief periods sometimes constituted dual monies exchanging at a fluctuating rate (see Chaps. 3 and 4).

15

various types of money then in circulation mirror the Civil War financial developments and foreshadow future developments (section 1). The changes in the stock of money, in income, and in prices to 1879 (section 2) reveal some features that we shall find recurring again and again, others that are special to this period. Section 3 examines the politics of resumption; section 4, the factors accounting for the changes in the stock of money, and the concluding section, three problems special to this period: the premium on gold, the factors determining the stock of gold, and the economic bases for successful resumption of gold payments.

1. Composition of the Stock of Money in 1867

DIVISION BETWEEN CURRENCY AND DEPOSITS

Throughout our analysis, we shall have occasion to divide the money stock into two major components: currency and deposits. The reason for the primacy of this division is clear. Since the Civil War, currency has consisted in the main either of specie or of a direct or indirect obligation of the government (for qualifications see below); deposits have been an obligation of privately owned and operated banks that have been legally required to hold assets in the form of currency or its equivalent equal to a fraction of their liabilities. As a result, the lending and investing activities of banks have been linked with the stock of money through deposit creation. In addition, under such a system of fractional reserve banking, the total amount of money is likely to be sensitive to the division of the total between currency and deposits. As we shall see in the course of this chronicle, changes in the public's attitude toward these two forms of money and the resulting changes in the proportion in which it has desired to hold them have at times played a critical role in monetary developments.

In 1867, the public divided its stock of money almost equally between deposits and currency: it held about $1.20 of deposits for each dollar of currency (Table 1). In the five years after 1867, deposits rose to $2 for each dollar of currency. That increase reflects the rapid post–Civil War growth and spread of commercial banking. The deposit-currency ratio fluctuated around this level until 1880, and then began to rise again—a rise that was destined to continue, albeit with numerous short-term reversals, until 1929, when the public held about $12 of deposits for each dollar of currency. The ratio then fell. In 1960, it was about 6 to 1.

DIVISION OF DEPOSITS BETWEEN NATIONAL AND OTHER BANKS

Of the total of commercial bank deposits held by the public, roughly 60 per cent were liabilities of banks that were part of the Civil War-created

16

TABLE 1

COMPOSITION OF CURRENCY AND COMMERCIAL BANK DEPOSITS, END OF JUNE 1867
(millions of dollars)

	Total	Treasury	Held by Banks	Public
Currency (lines 1–9)				
1. Gold coin	142	94		48
2. Gold certificates	19	0		19
3. State bank notes	4	0		4
4. National bank notes	292	12		280
5. U.S. notes	372	53		319
6. Subsidiary silver	8	1		7
7. Fractional currency	18	2		16
8. Other U.S. currency	124	0		124
9. Total (lines 1–8)	979	162	247	570
Adjusted commercial bank deposits (lines 10–12)				
10. National		33		411
11. State and private		0		280
12. Total (line 10 plus line 11)		33		691
13. Total currency and deposits (line 9 plus line 12)		195		1,261
14. Total money stock at nominal value				1,261
15. Excess over nominal value of market value of gold coin, gold certificates, and gold deposits held by public				26
16. Total money stock valued in greenbacks (line 14 plus line 15)				1,287

SOURCE, BY LINE

TOTAL

1. *Annual Report* of the Secretary of the Treasury, 1928, p. 552, less $19 million held against gold certificates (line 2), and less $25 million of gold coin assumed exported or used in the arts and manufactures.
2. *Ibid.*, p. 550.
3, 5, 6, 8. *Ibid.*, p. 552.
4. *Ibid.*, less $7 million in vaults of issuing banks (difference between national bank notes outstanding, from A. P. Andrew, *Statistics for the United States, 1867–1909*, National Monetary Commission, 1911, Vol. 21, p. 43; and national bank note liabilities of those banks, from *Annual Report* of the Comptroller of the Currency, 1918, Vol. II, p. 248).
7. *Annual Report* (Treasury), 1928, p. 552, less $10 million estimated to have been lost by that date.

HELD BY TREASURY

1–9. Total, less amounts held by banks and public.
10. *Annual Report* (Comptroller), 1918, Vol. II, p. 249.
11. No Treasury deposits were held at nonnational banks at that time.

(continued)

17

NOTES to Table 1 (concluded)

HELD BY BANKS AND PUBLIC

1. *Historical Statistics of the United States, Colonial Times to 1957*, Bureau of the Census, 1960 (*Historical Statistics*, 1960), Series X-285, less the $25 million deduction made in the "total" column.
2–8. *Ibid.*, Series X-286, X-290, X-291, X-296–X-298, with same deductions that are made in the "total" column.
9. Banks: Sum of figures for national banks, nonnational commercial banks, and mutual savings banks. Vault cash of national banks, from *Annual Report* (Comptroller), 1918, Vol. II, p. 248, July 1, 1867 figures. For composition of national bank vault cash, see Table A-2, notes to col. 1. Vault cash of nonnational commercial banks was interpolated along a straight line between Jan. figures for 1867 and 1868 in James K. Kindahl, "Estimates of Nonnational Bank Deposits for the United States, 1867–1875" (unpublished Ph.D. dissertation, U. of Chicago, 1958). Vault cash in mutual savings banks was estimated as described for 1867–75 in Table A-2, col. 1.
9. Public: Currency outside the Treasury, minus currency in the banks.
10. *Annual Report* (Comptroller), 1900, p. 583.
11. Kindahl, "Estimates of Nonnational . . . ."
14. Repeats line 13.
15. The sum of gold coin plus gold certificates, held by banks and the public, times $38\frac{5}{16}$, the premium on gold, from W. C. Mitchell, *Gold, Prices, and Wages under the Greenback Standard*, U. of California Press, 1908, p. 304. Gold coin and gold certificates held by the banks are assumed to equal gold deposits held by the public (see text).

National Banking System. The rest were liabilities either of banks that were chartered under the laws of the several states or of private banks.

The national banks grew rapidly immediately after the Civil War. First authorized in February 1863 to provide a uniform national currency and to aid in financing the Civil War by issuing bank notes secured by government bonds, few national banks were established until defects in the original act had been removed in the act of June 3, 1864.[3] Shortly thereafter, in February 1865, a tax of 10 per cent was imposed on note issues of state banks paid out after July 1, 1866 (later changed to

[3] See Bray Hammond, "The North's Empty Purse," *American Historical Review*, Oct. 1961, pp. 8–11, for a discussion of the three-part program adopted to finance the Civil War, which included greenback issues, taxes, and borrowings, the latter "to be facilitated by a national system of banks whose demand would greatly enlarge the market for government bonds." Many of the ideas embodied in the National Banking Act were copies of features of the New York free banking system established in 1838, and the Massachusetts Banking Act of 1858. See Fritz Redlich, *The Molding of American Banking*, New York, Hafner, 1951, Vol. II, Part II, pp. 99–105.

See also Simon Newcomb's penetrating criticism of and vigorous attack on the establishment of the National Banking System as a means of contributing to the financing of the war (*A Critical Examination of Our Financial Policy during the Southern Rebellion*, New York, Appleton, 1865, pp. 199–222). His little book contains the most sophisticated, original, and profound analysis of the theoretical issues involved in Civil War finance that we have encountered, regardless of date of publication.

August 1, 1866), denying state banks *de facto* the privilege of note issue. At the time, such great importance was attached to the privilege of note issue that state banks converted to national banks in droves, and state banks were widely believed to be on the way to near extinction. The growing importance of deposits relative to currency and the less restrictive conditions imposed by state than by federal legislation combined to reverse the trend in very short order. By 1867, the decline in the deposits of state and private banks had ceased. These banks then expanded so rapidly that by 1871 the deposits of nonnational commercial banks roughly equaled national bank deposits. From then until now, the two classes of banks have remained roughly equal in the size of their deposits. Indeed, national banks have more frequently had the smaller total.

Private banks are chartered by neither the state nor the national government; they operate as individual proprietorships or partnerships. Once numerous and including some of the most influential banking institutions (J. P. Morgan and Company was probably the most widely known), private banks have played a negligible role in recent years.

The preceding comments all refer to currency and deposits held by the public, including in that term state and local governments but not the U.S. Treasury. In addition, in 1867 the Treasury held deposits totaling $33 million, or about 4½ per cent as much as the deposits of the public in commercial banks, and currency totaling $162 million, or nearly 30 per cent of the public's holdings. The Treasury clearly held a much lower ratio of deposits to currency than the public, 20 cents in deposits for each dollar of currency compared to the $1.20 held by the public. The reason is twofold. First, as a monetary authority issuing currency, the Treasury's balances were in part "inventory" and could at times be increased simply by printing more currency without issuing it to the public. Second, the low level of deposits was a consequence of the Independent Treasury System, which was first adopted in 1840 as a legacy of the Bank War over the renewal of the charter of the Second Bank of the United States, was discontinued in 1841, and was re-established in 1846. In the form that the Independent Treasury had assumed by 1867, disbursing officers were permitted to use national banks as depositories and the Treasury was permitted to deposit receipts from internal revenues in national banks provided the banks furnished security by depositing United States and other bonds with the U.S. Treasurer. However, the Treasury was prohibited from depositing customs receipts (which were paid in gold). The Treasury's deposits remained small relative to either its currency holdings or the public's deposits until near the end of the century, except for isolated occasions when they were built up as a deliberate act of monetary policy. For some years after the turn of the century, they remained relatively high as part of a deliberate policy of continuous Treasury intervention in the money market. They then relapsed until they rose to unprecedented levels as a result of the bond-selling drives of World War I.

Commercial banks also held deposits for one another. These interbank deposits are not recorded in Table 1. Since one bank's asset is another bank's liability, interbank deposits cancel when the accounts of banks are consolidated into the accounts of the banking system as a whole. The deposits recorded in Table 1 represent the liabilities of the commercial banking system as a whole to the public and the Treasury. The system as a whole can have no net liability to itself.

COMPOSITION OF THE CURRENCY

The banking system as a whole did, of course, hold currency. In June 1867, it held $247 million of currency, nearly half as much as the public held and equal to over a third of its net liabilities to the public. Currency constituted the whole of the banking system's net cash assets, and we shall refer to it as the banking system's "reserves", recognizing that we are using this term in a sense that corresponds neither to an individual bank's view of its cash assets—which would clearly include the amount due from other banks—nor to funds acceptable as satisfying legal reserve requirements—which generally included deposits at other banks within specified limits and sometimes did not include all types of currency.[4] Unfortunately, available data do not permit division of each of the various kinds of currency between the banks and the public. So we have to deal with the combined totals (Table 1, lines 1 to 8).

The impress of the Civil War was even sharper on currency than on deposits: the three largest items in the list (national bank notes, U.S. notes, and other U.S. currency) and one of the smaller items (fractional currency) were all creations of the Civil War. Taken together, these four items account for over 90 per cent of the total currency in the hands of the public and in banks in 1867. If we apply the same percentage to the public's holdings alone, nearly three-quarters of the total money stock—these items plus national bank deposits—was of Civil War origin, types of money that had not existed only six or seven years earlier.

The national bank notes were liabilities of the national banks, which could issue them by depositing with the U.S. Treasurer specified government bonds equal in face value to 111 per cent of the value of the notes issued.[5] After 1874, the banks were also required to deposit with

[4] For a more extended discussion, see Appendix B.
[5] This requirement was later reduced to 100 per cent: the act of Mar. 14, 1900, entitled national banks to receive circulating notes from the Comptroller of the Currency equal in amount to the par value of bonds deposited.

the Treasury a redemption fund in lawful money equal to 5 per cent of the value of their notes.[6] In addition, the amount of notes a bank could issue was limited to nine-tenths of its capital until 1900 and the whole of its capital thereafter. First issued in 1864, the amount outstanding grew rapidly to nearly $300 million in 1866 and then increased more slowly but fairly steadily to $340 million in 1874.[7] National bank notes played an important part in our monetary system for some six decades until 1935, when all United States bonds bearing the circulation privilege were called for redemption.

Though national bank notes were nominally liabilities of the banks that issued them, in effect they were indirect liabilities of the federal government thanks to both the required government bond security and the conditions for their redemption. Hence, their value did not depend on the financial condition of the issuing bank. If a bank failed, the law provided for the immediate redemption of all its notes at the Treasury and authorized the Comptroller of the Currency to declare the bonds securing the circulation to be forfeited to the United States. The Treasury was given a first lien upon the assets of the bank and upon the personal liability of the stockholders in order to make good any possible deficiency between the amount of notes it redeemed and the sum of the 5 per cent cash redemption fund which the issuing bank maintained with the Treasury (after 1874) and the proceeds from the sale by the Comptroller of the forfeited bonds.

National bank notes differed in usefulness from currency issued directly by the U.S. government in only one respect. Federal law did not permit them to be used to meet the legal reserve requirements of national banks, though most state laws did permit them to be used for this purpose by state banks. Only "lawful money" was acceptable for national banks and national bank notes were not lawful money. But inasmuch as the public at large regarded national bank notes as equivalent to other notes and other types of currency were always a multiple of bank vault cash, that restriction was of no great practical importance. We know of no episode after 1874 in which it raised any significant problems for banks.[8] Consequently, national bank notes after that date circulated

---

[6] The 5 per cent redemption fund was introduced in the act of June 20, 1874, which freed national banks from the requirement previously in effect to maintain reserves against their circulation.

[7] The aggregate issue of national bank notes was originally restricted to $300 million. The limit was raised to $354 million by the act of July 12, 1870. The Resumption Act of 1875 eliminated this restriction altogether.

[8] In early 1873, New York City national banks sold national bank notes at a discount for greenbacks (*Commercial and Financial Chronicle,* Jan. 18, 1873, quoted by O. M. W. Sprague, *History of Crises Under the National Banking System,* National Monetary Commission, GPO, 1910, p. 29).

The reason was that the seasonal movement of currency from the interior to

at parity with other currency; and we shall have little occasion subsequently to distinguish them from currency issued directly by the Treasury. There was no recurrence of the pre-Civil War phenomena of notes of different banks circulating at discounts or premiums with respect to one another, and at different discounts or premiums depend-

---

New York at the time included a large fraction of national bank notes issued by country banks. These notes were less useful to New York City national banks than greenbacks were because of two institutional arrangements then in effect: (1) The rules of the New York Clearing House, unlike those of clearing houses in other cities, required settlement of deficits in lawful money. (2) Before 1874, national bank notes were redeemable only at the issuing bank's counter or at the counter of its designated redemption agent—in a reserve city or in New York— with which it kept deposits to satisfy legal reserve requirements.

New York City banks could have redeemed the notes of issuing banks for which they were redemption agents simply by canceling deposits of those banks equal to the dollar value of the notes retired, a course, which Sprague argues, the New York banks "might have been reasonably expected to resort to" on occasion. Such redemption would have reduced required reserves of New York banks, thereby releasing 25 cents of lawful money for each dollar of notes redeemed. Redemption in this way, however, would have entailed loss of legal reserves to the issuing banks, with the onus upon their city correspondents, so there seems nothing unreasonable in the decision of the New York banks to avoid such action. Instead, they sold the notes to brokers at one-quarter of 1 per cent discount— the brokers reselling them to country banks at one-eighth of 1 per cent discount— and obtained greenbacks in payment.

It is not clear whether the discount on national bank notes occurred regularly before the change in redemption procedures in 1874, or whether it was unusual. James Buell, president of a New York City national bank, testified in Feb. 1874 that the city banks refused to receive national bank notes for deposit when they became "redundant," but "there is not . . . chronic difference in value between the national currency and greenbacks." He referred to a premium of "two, three, and four per cent" on greenbacks "during the panic [Sept. 1873]; since then, nothing" (see his *Statement to the Committee on Banking and Currency of the House of Representatives,* Feb. 9, 1874, reprinted from the official report, New York, 1879, pp. 5–9). Sprague described "the currency premium" that resulted from the banks' refusal to maintain convertibility of deposits and currency during Sept. and Oct. 1873, as applying equally to both greenbacks and national bank notes. Oct. 22 is the last date for which he presented quotations. A note attached to the quotation for that date states: "Bank notes at par."

After the change in redemption procedures in June 1874, national bank notes were always redeemable at par at the Treasury. The Treasury paid out lawful money from funds each national bank deposited with it for redemption purposes in amounts equal to at least 5 per cent of that bank's circulation. Since the 5 per cent fund also counted as part of the reserves required against deposits, a bank's reserves were reduced, of course, by redemption of its notes. An issuing bank, however, had no way of identifying banks that returned its notes to the Treasury for redemption; hence its New York City correspondents could do so with impunity.

Writing in the 1880's, C. B. Patten, cashier of a Boston national bank, stated: "The National bank bill is redeemable at a central bureau in Washington—and over the counter of the issuing bank—in lawful money . . . ; their market value is therefore the same as the legal tender Treasury note," i.e., greenback (*The Methods and Machinery of Practical Banking,* 7th ed., New York, Bradford Rhodes, 1896, p. 37).

ing on the distance from the issuing bank, or of bank-note detectors to enable merchants and others to determine the value of particular notes. In this respect the Civil War and immediately post–Civil War legislation succeeded in one of its primary objectives—the provision of a uniform national currency.

National bank notes were like explicit Treasury currency, not only because they were obligations of the federal government at one remove, but also because the maximum possible amount outstanding was determined, also at one remove, largely by federal action, either administrative or legislative. This amount was determined by the volume of government securities bearing the circulation privilege. The fraction of this maximum issued might be expected to depend on the financial incentive to do so and this in turn to hinge partly on the terms on which bonds bearing the circulation privilege could be acquired on the market.

These expectations are not fully confirmed by the evidence. Before 1890 the amount outstanding ranged around 20 per cent of the possible maximum, by 1900 it had risen to about 28 per cent, and by World War I to about 80 per cent. The maximum was in fact approached only in the twenties, when for the first time U.S. bonds deposited to secure circulation and government deposits (which also required such security) nearly equaled the total of eligible bonds. Before 1905, the capital stock of national banks set narrower limits to their maximum possible note issue than did the total of eligible bonds, but the actual issue did not approach this lower limit either. Thereafter, the capital stock of national banks exceeded the total of eligible bonds and hence was not the effective limit on note issue. Yet, despite the failure to use fully the possibilities of note issue, the published market prices of government bonds bearing the circulation privilege were apparently always low enough to make note issue profitable except in the years 1884 to 1891. The fraction of the maximum issued fluctuated with the profitability of issue, but the fraction was throughout lower than might have been expected. We have no explanation for this puzzle.[9]

[9] See also the discussion in Phillip Cagan's forthcoming monograph on the determinants and effects of changes in the money stock in the United States since 1875, a National Bureau study. The remarks in the text about the profit on note issue are based on Cagan's calculations. He expresses the rate of return as the ratio of the income from the bonds securing the notes minus the expenses of note issue to the bank's capital tied up in acquiring the bonds. Capital tied up is simply the difference between the market price of the bond and the amount of notes issued on the basis of it. The Comptroller of the Currency on the other hand treated the capital tied up as equal to the full market price of the bond (see his *Annual Report,* 1873, p. xxxiii, and subsequent reports), a procedure which yields much lower rates of return, and his procedure was adopted by others. See *Report of the Monetary Commission of the Indianapolis Convention,*

The United States notes are the "greenbacks" of Civil War fame. First issued to supplement tax and loan receipts in the financing of war expenditures, the total outstanding (in and outside the Treasury) reached a maximum of $449 million in January 1864. Under the terms of the act of April 12, 1866, the amount outstanding was reduced to $356 million by the end of 1867 and was then legally fixed at that level until 1873–74, when additional amounts were issued that raised the total outstanding to $382 million. As part of the Resumption Act of 1875, the retirement of the greenbacks was linked to the increase in national bank notes—for every five dollar increase in national bank notes the Treasury retired four dollars in greenbacks—and was to cease when the amount outstanding fell to $300 million. However, further retirement was suspended by an act of May 31, 1878, which established as a permanent issue the amount then outstanding, $347 million, the level at which the total issue of U.S. notes stands today. These repeated legal changes from 1865 to 1878 are a symptom of the political

---

University of Chicago Press, 1898, pp. 186–196; J. Laurence Laughlin, *Money and Prices*, New York, Scribner, 1924, pp. 239–245 and 270–271. Laughlin's calculation treats the *face* value of the bond as the amount of capital tied up, and deducts the excess of the market price over the face value of the bond from "loanable circulation." Both the Comptroller and Laughlin compare the interest earned on the bond, plus the interest on lending the circulation at, say, 6 per cent, minus the expenses of note issue, with the amount that the tied-up capital, as each defined it, would yield if directly loaned at 6 per cent. Laughlin's calculation would yield the same net figure as the Comptroller's except that he also deducts from "loanable circulation" the 5 per cent redemption fund on notes deposited with the Treasury by issuing banks, and so obtains lower rates of return, than does the Comptroller. Since this fund counted as part of the required reserves against deposits, there is no need to consider it in calculating the return on note issues.

In testifying before the House Committee on Banking and Currency in Dec. 1894, Secretary of the Treasury Carlisle cited low profit figures on note issue computed according to the Comptroller's method. His method would show profits of between $6.52 and $7.83 per $100 of market prices of bonds deposited to secure circulation, profits that were compared to $6.00 said to be available from lending $100 of the tied-up capital directly. According to Cagan's calculations for that year, the return on note issue was 9.2 per cent compared to 4.2 per cent earned on other assets. Bankers testifying before the House Committee followed the Comptroller. The president of a New Haven national bank asserted that the bank's $50,000 circulation "is not worth one stiver to us." The president of a Buffalo, N.Y., state bank said that his bank kept its state charter not out of sentiment but "because there is no profit in the national bank system." Carlisle summed up the prevailing view: "It is well known, of course, that the profits of the circulation of a national bank constitute a very small item of the total profits of the institution." See *National Currency and Banking System*, Report and Hearings before the House Committee on Banking and Currency, Dec. 1894, H. Rept. 1508, 53d Cong., 3d sess., Report, pp. 7–9; Hearings, pp. 49, 154, 176.

Either bankers did not recognize a profitable course of action simply because the net return was expressed as a percentage of the wrong base, which is hard to accept, or we have overlooked some costs of bank note issue that appeared large to them, which seems much more probable.

controversy about the greenbacks and about their role in the accompanying price decline, on which we shall comment further, below.

"Other U.S. currency" (Table 1, line 8) is a total of various Civil War issues that circulated as currency. It includes interest-bearing legal tender notes—one of the few instances we know of in which hand-to-hand currency paid interest—government demand notes, and other obligations that were not a legal tender.[10] These issues reached a maximum of almost $240 million in 1865; by 1867, they had been cut in half. Their retirement was substantially achieved by 1872 and only negligible amounts were outstanding thereafter.

Gold aside, the only other items of any size are fractional currency and subsidiary silver. The former, as noted, dates from the Civil War, when coins were exported because subsidiary silver became more valuable as metal than as money. Postage stamps and privately issued "shinplasters" came into use as a substitute until the Treasury began to issue fractional currency in the denominations previously used for subsidiary silver.

THE ROLE OF GOLD

The final item in the inventory is gold coin and certificates,[11] the estimates for which during that period of a fiduciary currency are most unreliable. This statistical uncertainty is matched by uncertainty about

[10] From Jan. 1868 through Feb. 1873 our figures for other U.S. currency include "three per cent certificates," an obligation created to retire "compound-interest notes," both of which national banks were authorized to count as part of their lawful money holdings. Compound-interest notes were a legal tender while three per cent certificates were not.

[11] By the act of Mar. 3, 1863, the Secretary of the Treasury was empowered to issue gold certificates not in excess of 20 per cent above the amount of gold left on deposit with him as cover for these certificates. First issued in Nov. 1865, the certificates were a convenience to customs officers, the Treasurer, banks, and traders on the New York Gold Exchange. In 1878, when preparations for resumption were under way, Secretary Sherman halted their issue. An act of July 12, 1882, authorized the issue of gold certificates which were simply warehouse receipts.

It is not certain that the certificates issued from 1865 on were in fact partly fiduciary rather than simply warehouse receipts. To judge by figures shown in the *Annual Report* of the Secretary of the Treasury, 1928, pp. 550 and 554, the amount of gold held in trust by the Treasury against gold certificates, at June dates, 1866–82, was always equal to the value of gold certificates outside the Treasury.

It is curious that Mitchell does not refer to the authorization to issue gold certificates in his description of the act of Mar. 3, 1863 (W. C. Mitchell, *A History of the Greenbacks*, University of Chicago Press, 1903, pp. 110–118). He discusses (pp. 225–226) a futile attempt by Secretary Chase in 1864, when the Treasury's gold receipts from customs duties exceeded its requirements for meeting the interest on the public debt, to sell gold certificates to importers for greenbacks at a rate a trifle below the current premium. These sales were made under the authority of a joint resolution of Congress. The market refused to recognize different quotations on gold coin and gold certificates, and the attempt was abandoned.

the economic role of gold and about the appropriate way to treat it for monetary analysis.

The major monetary use of gold was for foreign transactions. For foreign payments, gold was equivalent to foreign exchange since a number of important countries, notably Great Britain, maintained a gold standard. The leading traders in foreign exchange quickly adopted the practice of hedging against exchange fluctuations by buying and selling gold to offset changes in their liabilities in foreign currencies.[12] (The risk to be hedged was particularly great before the completion in 1866 of the first successful trans-Atlantic cable.[13] Before cable transfers were possible, it took about two weeks for dealers in New York to learn exchange rates on the London market and for dealers in London to learn New York rates. The completion of the cable made it possible to reduce the information lag to a matter of minutes or hours.)

Dealers as well as others having extensive foreign transactions therefore found it convenient to maintain gold balances as well as greenback balances. To accommodate them, New York banks, and perhaps others as well, had two kinds of deposit accounts: the usual deposits payable in greenbacks or their equivalent, and special deposits payable in gold. The gold deposits were expressed in "dollars" like the greenback deposits, but that dollar meant a very different thing. It stood for the physical amount of gold that had corresponded to a dollar before the Civil War and was to again after 1879. During the period of suspension, this physical amount of gold was worth more than a dollar in greenbacks—it was worth well over two dollars in greenbacks from mid-1864 to early 1865, and about $1.383 in June 1867, the date to which Table 1 refers (see the dashed line on Chart 5 below, which gives the greenback price of gold from 1861 to 1879. The line shows the prices in current paper money of the weight of gold which cost $100 before the Civil War and after resumption).

Gold also retained an appreciable, though minor, role in domestic

---

[12] J. C. Brown, *A Hundred Years of Merchant Banking,* New York, privately printed, 1909, pp. 281–282; A. H. Cole, "Evolution of the Foreign Exchange Market of the United States," *Journal of Economic and Business History,* May 1929, pp. 417–418.

[13] Cole (see footnote 12), pp. 414–415, judges from the fact cable transfers are first mentioned in the *Commercial and Financial Chronicle* in 1879 that they were not used until then and remarks that exchange dealers were surprisingly slow in adopting cable communication. It seems incredible that there should have been such a long delay, and two nineteenth-century writers confirm that there was not. Henry Clews (*Fifty Years in Wall Street,* New York, Irving Publishing Company, 1908, p. 508) referred to transmission by cable of London quotations from August 1866 on, and Henry M. Field (*The Story of the Atlantic Telegraph,* New York, Scribner, 1893, p. 391), to the commercial revolution the cable wrought in this country within the space of a few months—"Lombard Street and Wall Street talked with each other as two neighbors across the way."

payments. Customs duties were payable in gold. In addition, throughout the suspension period, the Treasury made virtually all interest and principal payments on its debt in gold at the pre–Civil War monetary value, though there was some dispute about whether it was legally required to do so.[14] Some private debt instruments required payment of interest or principal in gold. Finally, the West Coast remained largely on a specie basis. In the rest of the country, prices were quoted in greenbacks, and gold offered in payment was valued at its current market premium in greenbacks. On the West Coast, by contrast, prices were quoted in gold, and greenbacks offered in payment were valued at their current market discount in gold.[15]

In essence, there was a dual monetary standard—the greenback dollar and the gold dollar—the one official, the other unofficial, and the price of the one in terms of the other determined in a free market—the market for gold, or, equivalently, British sterling. The two kinds of money were not interchangeable at a fixed rate. That is why they could coexist side by side without either driving the other out.[16] The total of the two obtained by treating one greenback dollar as equal

[14] There is one minor exception of a 6 per cent bond that paid currency interest and accounted for one per cent of the long-term debt of the government in 1867.

Beginning with suspension, legislation authorizing government borrowing specified whether payment of interest would be in "coin." Coin as used in these laws was then understood to mean gold, although later the word gave rise to much controversy. Greenback advocates argued that since the bonds specified only that the interest be paid in gold, the government could pay the principal in greenbacks. To allay any doubts in investors' minds on this score, the "public credit act" of Mar. 18, 1869, declared the purpose of the U.S. to pay its notes and bonds in coin or the equivalent, pledging the faith of the nation to such payment. Silver proponents thereupon claimed that payment in silver rather than gold would satisfy the legal commitment to pay in coin (see Joseph Dorfman, *The Economic Mind in American Civilization*, New York, Viking, 1949, Vol. III, pp. 4–20).

[15] Mitchell noted that a "specific contract act" was passed in California in 1863 providing that contracts for the payment of specific kinds of money should be enforceable. "Greenbacks were not prevented from circulating, but when they were passed it was usually at their gold, not at their nominal, value" (Mitchell, *A History of the Greenbacks*, p. 144).

[16] As this example illustrates, Gresham's law, that cheap money drives out dear money, applies only when there is a fixed rate of exchange between the two. It therefore explains how greenbacks drove out subsidiary silver and required the introduction of fractional currency, since subsidiary silver retained its monetary usefulness only so long as it exchanged at its nominal value—which means a fixed rate of exchange between it and greenbacks. Once the market value of silver exceeded its monetary value, silver could still have stayed in circulation, as gold could and did, by being accepted at its market rather than its nominal value, but this clearly would have rendered it useless for its initial purpose of facilitating transactions of low value.

Gresham's law is often misunderstood and therefore misused, especially when it is applied by analogy in nonmonetary contexts, because the requirement that there be a fixed rate of exchange is forgotten.

to one gold dollar, as is done in calculating entries in Table A-1, in lines 9–14 of Table 1, and in every other summary of monetary statistics for the greenback period we know of, is, strictly speaking, meaningless: it is like adding current Canadian or Hong Kong dollars to U.S. dollars on a one-for-one basis. In order to get the total greenback value of the money stock in the hands of the public, the public's holdings of gold coin and gold certificates and also of deposits payable in gold should be raised by the premium on gold, approximately 38.3 per cent at the end of June 1867, the date to which the figures in Table 1 refer. Unfortunately, we cannot make this correction at all accurately, even if we assume that the gold stock figures in Table 1 are correct, because there are no adequate data on either the subdivision of the gold stock outside the Treasury between the banks and the public or the division of total deposits between greenback and gold deposits. The correction entered in line 15 of Table 1 assumes implicitly that the banks held one dollar in gold coin or certificates for each dollar of gold deposits. One might expect this to be an underestimate of the correction, since at first glance there seems no reason for banks that held fractional reserves against greenback deposits to hold an amount of gold equal in value to the deposit liabilities payable in gold. However, some empirical evidence suggests this is roughly what they did, and banking practice and legal requirements suggest some reasons it might have been sensible for them to do so.[17]

[17] The 1873 *Annual Report* of the Comptroller of the Currency gives a breakdown of gold assets and liabilities, as well as currency assets and liabilities, of New York national banks on Oct. 3, 1872, and on Sept. 3, 1873. The special deposits of those banks payable in gold on those two dates are $6,171,000 and $12,102,000, respectively, and the gold coin held by those banks, $6,375,000 and $14,586,000, respectively. This amounts to approximately $1 in gold for $1 in gold deposits.

Banks could legally count gold as reserves against greenback deposits as well as gold deposits, but they had no incentive to hold them for that purpose alone. Why hold an amount of gold worth more than a dollar in greenbacks when a dollar in greenbacks would do as well? This is the reason that the bulk of the gold held by the banks was apparently held by New York banks, which also had the bulk of the gold deposits.

Given that gold was held as a reserve against gold deposits, it was also, of course, counted as legal reserves in reports to the Comptroller of the Currency, since the statements of the national banks and the enforcement of legal reserve requirements, like most monetary statistics for the period, all proceeded on the fiction that a dollar is a dollar for all that. Hence, a bank that was legally required to hold, say, a 25 per cent reserve, had no excess legal reserves, and received an additional gold deposit of $100 in nominal value had to add to its legal reserves an amount equal to $25 in nominal value, either in greenbacks or their equivalent or in gold.

The following hypothetical example will illustrate how holding $1 in gold for each $1 in gold deposits would be compatible with fractional reserve banking. Suppose a bank in New York City subject to a 25 per cent legal reserve ratio and with no excess legal reserves received a $100 gold deposit. Its required

The correction required to allow for the excess value in greenbacks of gold counted as money almost certainly declined over time along with the greenback price of the gold dollar. Gold deposits may have increased as the premium on gold declined, because that reduced the risk of holding liquid funds in the form of gold as a reserve for liabilities expressed in greenbacks.[18] However, it seems unlikely that any such increase, if indeed there was one, could have been large enough to offset the decline in the premium. In consequence, while our estimates of the stock of money from 1867 to 1879 underestimate the economically relevant total throughout, they probably do so by successively smaller amounts.[19] The understatement, while appreciable, cannot at any time be substantial, as the smallness of our approximate correction in Table 1 shows, which is why we have felt no serious compunction about making no such correction in the figures entered in Table A-1.

2. Changes in Money, Income, Prices, and Velocity

The stock of money in January 1867, when our series starts, was probably lower than it had been in the North at the end of the Civil

---

reserves would be raised by $25 in nominal value, which it could hold either in greenbacks or gold. Suppose it held it in gold. This leaves $75 in gold in excess of legal requirements. Suppose it used this $75 to replace $75 of greenbacks formerly held as reserves against other deposits, and used the greenbacks so liberated to buy interest-earning assets. At a premium on gold of, say, $37\frac{1}{2}$ per cent these operations, evaluated in terms of the market value in greenbacks of assets and liabilities, involved adding $137.50 to its deposits, $62.50 to its reserve funds (the market value of the $100 in gold minus the $75 of greenbacks taken from reserves), and $75 to its interest-earning assets. This is fractional reserve banking for gold deposits as well as greenback deposits, though with a higher reserve ratio (in our example 62.50/137.50 or 45.5 per cent), yet it involves holding gold equal in value to the deposit liabilities payable in gold.

One reason it might have been sensible for the banks to proceed in roughly this way was that there were few legally permitted investments that were in gold dollars. Loans payable in gold to New York City national banks represented 55 and 36 per cent, respectively, of the banks' special deposits payable in gold on the dates in 1872 and 1873 for which gold assets and liabilities of these banks are shown. To the extent that the demand for gold loans was limited, the only way the banks could protect themselves against differential changes in the value of their assets and liabilities as a result of changes in the gold premium was by holding gold itself.

[18] The risk involved in holding balances in the one form or the other depends on the liabilities in connection with which the balances are held. If the liabilities were in gold, then any risk of a change in the premium could be hedged by holding gold balances.

[19] The existence of two kinds of money would presumably increase, other things being the same, the money balances people would want to hold, i.e., would tend to make the velocity of the combined money total lower than if all elements of the money stock were perfect substitutes. To some unknown extent, this effect offsets the statistical error of counting the two kinds of money at their nominal values.

CHART 3
Money Stock, Income, Prices, and Velocity, in Reference Cycle Expansions and Contractions, 1867–79

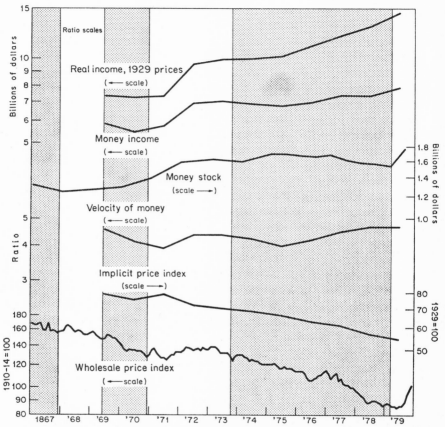

NOTE: Shaded areas represent business contractions; unshaded areas, business expansions.
SOURCE: Wholesale prices, *Historical Statistics of the United States, 1789–1945*, Bureau of the Census, 1949 (*Historical Statistics, 1949*), p. 344. Other data, same as for Chart 62.

War. It continued to decline to January 1868, according to the annual figures for those years plotted in Chart 3, then rose, at first mildly, then sharply, then mildly again, to a temporary peak in 1873. After a mild relapse and mild further rise, the stock of money reached a peak in 1875 from which it declined by some 9 per cent to a trough in early 1879.

This behavior is in one respect most unusual. There are 5 calendar years in which the money stock declined and 7 in which it rose. The rises were on the average larger than the declines, but even so the money stock in February 1879 was only 17 per cent above its level 12 years earlier in January 1867. By comparison with later experience, this is an extraordinarily high ratio of declines to rises and a small total rise. One must go more than half a century forward from 1879 all the way to 1933 to find another 12-year period within which the money stock declined in as many as 5 calendar years. In the whole 81 years from 1879 to 1960 there are only 13 single years of decline.[20] As to the size of the rise, the only other period in our subsequent history when the money stock was as little as 17 per cent above its level twelve years earlier is from 1931 to 1939, reflecting the sharp decline in the stock of money from 1929 to 1933.

As this final comment suggests, although the fraction of years of decline from 1867 to 1879 is atypical, the circumstances under which the declines occurred are not. Most of the declines during that period came during the contraction of 1873 to 1879 (designated in Chart 3 by the shaded area), one of the longest on record and generally regarded as one of the more severe. All except three succeeding declines also took place during unusually severe business cycle contractions.[21] In the remaining business cycle contractions, the stock of money continued to grow though at a slower rate than during expansions. The contrast between the slow rate of growth from January 1868 to January 1870—which is to be associated with the business contraction from June 1869 to December 1870—and the more rapid rate of growth from January 1870 to January 1872—which is to be associated with the business expansion from December 1870 to October 1872—is rather typical of subsequent experience.

The timing of the rate of change in the stock of money in relation to the cyclical movements is fairly typical of later experience: the rate of growth of the stock of money accelerated well before the cyclical trough in December 1870, decelerated well before the cyclical peak in October 1873, and accelerated well before the trough in March 1879. For the 1879 trough, the acceleration consisted of a slower rate

[20] In making this count, we compared Feb. of one year with Feb. of the preceding year for the period 1879 to 1881; Feb. 1881 with June 1882; June with June, for the period 1882 to 1906 for which we have only one observation a year; and Dec. with Dec. thereafter. We assumed that the Dec. figure for 1906, which we do not have, would have been higher than the recorded Dec. figure for 1907. We treated 1926 as a year of no change.

[21] The exceptions are: Aug. 1926–Dec. 1926, a decline of 1.2 per cent; Jan. 1948–Nov. 1949, a decline of 1.3 per cent; and Sept. 1959–June 1960, a decline of 1.1 per cent. In the two world wars, sharp one- and two-month declines also occurred during bond drives, which occasioned transfers from private deposit accounts to government war loan accounts. Payments by the government to the public subsequently reduced government deposits and restored private deposit accounts.

31

of decline than earlier, so that the absolute trough in the level of the money stock just about coincided with the trough in business, so far as we can tell from our semiannual figures (see Chart 3). We shall find these phenomena of acceleration of the money stock preceding a cyclical trough and deceleration preceding a cyclical peak, both by sizable intervals, repeated time and again in subsequent experience.[22] We shall find also in subsequent deep depressions that the absolute trough in the money stock often coincided with the cyclical trough as, for example, it did in 1933.

The unusually slow rate of rise in the money stock and the unusually large fraction of declines from 1867 to 1879 are paralleled by and connected with the unusual behavior of prices. As Chart 3 shows, wholesale prices fell sharply from 1867 to 1879. The decline was interrupted significantly only during the cyclical expansion beginning December 1870, the interruption following by a year the one segment of the period (1870–72) when the money stock rose sharply. And the decline in prices was especially sharp from 1873 to 1879, the period when the money stock first rose very mildly and then fell for some four years. There is no subsequent period of comparable length during which wholesale prices fell fairly continuously at a rate approaching the average rate of 6½ per cent per year at which they fell in the fourteen years from 1865 to 1879.[23]

Though the movements in both money and prices differ in the same way from subsequent experience, there is a sharp contrast between their absolute behavior. From January 1867 to February 1879, the money stock at nominal value *rose* at the rate of 1.3 per cent per year; the price index *fell* at the rate of 5.4 per cent per year. Part of this contrast probably reflects statistical defects in our estimates. We have seen that our money figures overstate the rise in the money stock by failing to allow for the excess of market over nominal value of gold. But this would have only a minor effect in bridging the gap between the changes in money and in prices, at most reducing the estimate of the rate of rise in money from 1.3 to 1.1 per cent per year. We shall

---

[22] The detailed timing of peaks and troughs in the *rate of change* in the money stock is presented in our forthcoming "Trends and Cycles." We note there that, before the Oct. 1873 peak in business, there are no turns in the rate of change series to match with three earlier turns in business that fall in the period covered by our money series: the business trough of Dec. 1867, peak of June 1869, and trough of Dec. 1870. The absence of a turn in the rate of change series to match with the Dec. 1867 business trough may simply result from the fact that our series does not go back far enough in time. For the other two business turns, we conjecture that the annual data for successive Januarys—all we have for that period—may conceal by their crudeness turns that monthly data would reveal.

[23] Calculated from the average Warren-Pearson index number for the first quarters of 1865 and 1879 (see source notes to Chart 62).

assume that the lower figure measures the true rate of growth of the money stock over this period.

Probably more serious are defects in the plotted index as a measure of wholesale prices in general, let alone as a measure of a broader concept of the price level. The unavailability of monthly data limited sharply the commodities included in the index, and enforced disproportionate emphasis on farm products and raw materials.[24] But this was a period when improvements in transportation were reducing prices of such products by lowering the cost of shipment from areas cultivated earlier and, even more, by making it feasible to cultivate commercially new areas containing highly fertile land. In addition, technological improvements were probably producing a decline in the price of commodities in general relative to services that would have considerable weight in a consumer price index. Alternative indexes available on an annual basis suggest decidedly smaller price declines—of the order of 2.3 to 3.9 per cent per year rather than 5.4 per cent.[25] We shall assume that a 3.5 per cent annual rate of decline in prices is a reasonable estimate of the change from January 1867 to February 1879.

The rest of the contrast, that between a rise of 1.1 per cent per year in the money stock and a decline of 3.5 per cent per year in prices, must, as a matter of arithmetic, reflect either a rise in output and so in the "work" to be done by the money stock, or a rise in the amount of money balances in real terms that the public held per unit of output,

[24] "The indexes of wholesale prices that have been carried back into years before 1890 are almost inevitably overweighted with farm products" (Wesley C. Mitchell, *What Happens During Business Cycles: A Progress Report,* New York, NBER, 1951, p. 270).

[25] The Hoover consumer price index for all items declines at the rate of 3.1 per cent per year from 1867 to 1879. The group index for clothing shows the greatest decline (4.7 per cent per year), followed by the fuel and light group index (3.5 per cent per year) and food (3.3 per cent per year). Rent declined 0.8 per cent per year, services and other items, 0.6 per cent per year (Ethel D. Hoover, "Retail Prices After 1850," *Trends in the American Economy in the Nineteenth Century,* Studies in Income and Wealth, Vol. 24, Princeton for NBER, 1960, p. 143).

Over the same period the Snyder-Tucker annual index of the general price level declines at the rate of 3.5 per cent per year; the Federal Reserve Bank of New York cost-of-living index number, which for this period is based on Mitchell's index in *Gold, Prices, and Wages Under the Greenback Standard* (University of California Press, 1908), p. 91, at the rate of 2.1 per cent per year (*Historical Statistics of the United States, 1789–1947,* Bureau of the Census, 1949, Series L-1, p. 231; L-36, p. 235).

However, because based on annual figures, these indexes understate the rate of decline from Jan. 1867 to Feb. 1879. We can make a rough correction by noting that the annual version of the Warren-Pearson monthly index number plotted in Chart 3 declines at the annual rate of 4.9 per cent per year from 1867 to 1879. This compares with a 5.4 per cent per year decline from Jan. 1867 to Feb. 1879. We have used the ratio of 5.4 to 4.9 to raise the rates of change for the aggregate indexes cited in this footnote to those given in the text.

which is to say, a decline in the velocity of money, defined as the ratio of money income to the stock of money. As a matter of economics, there can be little doubt that it reflects primarily a rise in output.

A rough guess of the size of the rise can be obtained by estimating on the basis of later data the change in velocity from 1867 to 1879. As we shall see in later chapters, velocity is a relatively stable magnitude that has declined secularly as real income has risen, and that has a fairly regular cyclical pattern, falling during contractions and rising—or falling at a lower rate—during expansions. Later experience suggests that the relevant secular decline for the period 1867–79 is about 1 per cent per year, whether estimated crudely or in a more refined way.[26] Both 1867 and 1879 contain cyclical troughs. Even so, some allowance for the influence of cyclical factors should in principle be made, since 1867 is the trough of a mild depression cycle and 1879 is the trough of a deep depression cycle. However, we made no such allowance, since our estimate of what it should be turns out to be negligible—about one-tenth of 1 per cent per year.[27] One might therefore infer that of the 4.6 percentage point gap to be explained, about 1 percentage point can be attributed to velocity, leaving 3.6 percentage points to be accounted for by a rise in output.

We need not rely solely on this indirect inference since there is much direct evidence of a rapid rise in output from 1867 to 1879 to confirm the inference. Population rose by more than 30 per cent or at the unusually high rate of 2.3 per cent per year, so that it alone

[26] See Milton Friedman, "Monetary Data and National Income Estimates," *Economic Development and Cultural Change*, Apr. 1961, pp. 277, 279–280.

[27] According to p. 277, *ibid.*, cyclical factors would have made the 1879 velocity 4.6 per cent less than its trend value. According to Table 1, p. 278, *ibid.*, the 1867 value could be expected to be 3.1 per cent below trend. Therefore, the different cyclical position would account for a decline over the interim at the rate of $1.5/12 = .125$ per cent per year.

Special factors associated with this period point in different directions with respect to velocity. (1) The shift from a period of rising prices, as during the Civil War, to falling prices, as after it, means a reduction in the cost of holding money, since in the first case, money depreciates in purchasing power, whereas in the second, it appreciates. This might be expected to lower velocity. However, a continuation of a given rate of decline in prices, while a reason for a low velocity, is not a reason for a falling velocity, once adaptation is made to it. Adaptation can be expected to be gradual and might not have been completed in 1867, in which case this would be a reason for a further decline in velocity. (2) Prices fell less rapidly after 1867 than before which, for the preceding reasons, would work in the direction of a higher velocity. (3) The spread of the money economy, relative to production by families for their own use, might have been proceeding more rapidly than later, which would be a reason for a decline in velocity. (4) Uncertainty about the monetary standard might be a reason for a rise in velocity.

It is not easy to see any reason these factors should have produced a significant departure from the later trend.

accounted for half of the gap of 4.6 per cent to be explained, and output per capita was surely rising. The population rise is itself indirect if somewhat ambiguous testimony; it seems probable the wave of immigration that contributed to it was attracted by *rising* per capita income, though it is possible it was attracted simply by *higher* per capita income in the United States than in the country of origin. The latter part of the period was after all regarded as a period of depression throughout the world.

There are many other signs of rapid economic growth. This was a period of great railroad expansion dramatized by the linking of the coasts by rail in 1869. The number of miles of track operated more than doubled from 1867 to 1879, a rate of expansion not matched subsequently.[28] In New York State, for which figures are readily available, the number of ton miles of freight carried on railroads nearly quintupled and, for the first time since the figures began, exceeded the number of ton miles carried on canals and rivers.[29] The outcome of the Civil War terminated the political controversies that had raged about the manner of settlement and development of the great plains west of the Mississippi. The political developments combined with the great cheapening in transportation to produce a rapid extension of the area under cultivation. The number of farms rose by over 50 per cent from 1870 to 1880 for the U.S. as a whole. The average value per acre apparently increased despite the sharp decline in the price of farm products—clear evidence of a rise in economic productivity. The output of coal, pig iron, and copper all more than doubled and that of lead multiplied sixfold.

Manufacturing shared in the expansion. The Census reported 33 per cent more wage earners engaged in manufacturing in 1879 than in 1869, though 1879 was a year containing a cyclical trough and one following an unusually long contraction, while 1869 was a year containing a cyclical peak. An index of basic production compiled by Warren and Pearson nearly doubled from 1867 to 1879 (since 1867 also contained a cyclical trough, comparisons between 1867 and 1879 are freer from distortion by cyclical change than comparisons between 1869 and 1879). The rapid progress of the United States in manufacturing was clearly reflected in international trade statistics. Despite a decline in prices, exports of finished manufactures were nearly 2½ times as large in gold values and 1¾ times as large in greenback values in 1879 as in 1867. These increases are certainly not too small to be consistent with the rise of 3.6 per cent per year in total output— equivalent to a 54 per cent increase in total output over the 12-year

[28] *Historical Statistics,* 1949, Series K-1, p. 200.
[29] *Historical Statistics,* 1949, Series K-168 and -169, p. 218.

period—and of about 1.3 per cent per year in per capita output suggested by indirect inference from the rates of change in money and in prices.

Beginning with 1869, annual estimates are available of net national product, in both current and constant prices, constructed by Simon Kuznets (worksheets underlying his *Capital in the American Economy*).[30] These estimates, plotted in Chart 3, are admittedly highly tenuous for this early period, which is why we have not wished to rely on them alone. Indeed, Kuznets himself has been most reluctant to use them except in the form of averages for groups of years, and even then only for the study of secular trends.[31] He notes that a major reason for questioning the accuracy of the figures for the early decades is the extraordinarily large increase in estimated real income from 1869–78 to 1879–88. "The rise in gross and in net national product is close to 40 per cent of the mid-decade base. No comparable rises occur in any other decade in the period."[32] Kuznets points out that "this large rise is directly traceable to that shown for the 1869–79 decade" by the series on commodity output constructed by Shaw and incorporated in Kuznets' estimates.[33] He cites the opinions of Shaw and Francis A. Walker that the 1869 *Census of Manufactures* was understated relative to the 1879 *Census*, quoting estimates of the extent of understatement ranging from 5 per cent to 13 per cent; but he concludes, "We did not make the adjustment [for understatement] here, because we had no firm basis for 10 per cent in 1869 and 0 per cent in 1879, and because the effect on the *decade* averages was relatively minor."[34]

[30] Most of the rest of this section is based on Friedman, "Monetary Data and National Income Estimates," pp. 273–282.

[31] "For the early years of the period, 1869–1888, the derived annual series, even for the comprehensive aggregates—gross and net national product—did not seem sufficiently reliable as *annual* measures to warrant their presentation. For the next twenty years, 1889–1908, acceptable annual estimates could be derived only for the broader aggregates—national product, capital formation, and flow of goods to consumers.

"For the specific uses of our study of secular trends in capital formation and financing these annual estimates are of interest only as raw material in the calculation of five-year or more complicated moving averages which serve to cancel the short-term fluctuations while revealing the underlying secular movements and any longer swings in them with sufficient accuracy" (Simon Kuznets, *Capital in the American Economy: Its Formation and Financing*, Princeton for NBER, 1961, pp. 534 and 535).

See also two other works by Kuznets: *National Product Since 1869*, New York, NBER, 1946, especially pp. 59–90; and "Long-Term Changes in the National Income of the United States of America Since 1870," *Income and Wealth of the United States: Trends and Structure, Income and Wealth*, Series II, Cambridge, Eng., Bowes and Bowes, 1952, especially pp. 34–38.

[32] Kuznets, "Long-Term Changes," p. 37.

[33] Quotation from "Long-Term Changes," p. 37; see also, William H. Shaw, *Value of Commodity Output Since 1869*, New York, NBER, 1947.

[34] Kuznets, "Long-Term Changes," p. 38.

According to these annual estimates, net national product in current prices rose at the rate of 3.0 per cent per year from 1869 to 1879,[35] and net national product in constant prices rose at the rate of 6.8 per cent per year, implying a decline in prices at the rate of 3.8 per cent per year (Table 2, lines 2–4). Since population grew over the

TABLE 2
KEY ECONOMIC VARIABLES IN 1869 AND 1879

	Value of Indicated Variable		Rate of Change (per cent per year)
	1869	1879	
1. Stock of money, valued in greenbacks, middle of year ($billion)	1.298	1.698	2.7
2. Net national product, current prices ($billion)	5.82	7.89	3.0
3. Net national product, 1929 prices ($billion)	7.36	14.52	6.8
4. Implicit price index (1929 = 100)	79.1	54.3	−3.8
5. Velocity of money[a]	4.48	4.65	0.4
6. Population at midyear (millions)	39.1	49.2	2.3
7. Net national product per capita, 1929 prices (dollars)	188	295	4.5

NOTE: Annual rates of change are continuously compounded.

[a] Differs from velocity figures used elsewhere in this study, which are based on nominal values of money stock.

SOURCE, BY LINE

1. Straight-line interpolation to end of June between figures in Table A-1, col. 8, with addition for 1869 of the sum of gold coin (corrected) and gold certificates outside the Treasury, times the premium on gold (Mitchell, *Gold, Prices, and Wages*, p. 310).
2–4. Same as for Chart 62.
5. Line 2 divided by line 1.
6. *Historical Statistics*, 1960, Series A-2, p. 7.
7. Line 3 divided by line 6.

decade at the rate of 2.3 per cent per year, the implied rate of growth of real per capita income is no less than 4.5 per cent (Table 2, lines 6–7). The qualitative conclusion is the one we reached before, but the quantitative result is far more extreme. The result is rendered even more surprising by the cyclical characteristics of the initial and terminal years. According to National Bureau monthly reference dates, June 1869 was a cyclical peak and March 1879 a cyclical trough, though the subsequent upturn was so rapid that 1878 is listed as the trough year in the annual reference dates. Moreover, the contraction terminating

[35] Because of the important role played by the decennial censuses in the construction of the estimates, the estimates for census years like 1869 and 1879 are presumably considerably more reliable and involve less interpolation than other individual years.

in 1879 was the longest experienced by the United States from at least the Civil War to the present. In consequence, a comparison between 1869 and 1879 might be expected to understate the secular rate of growth. These are among the considerations that have led Kuznets and others to question the accuracy of his estimates for the early decades.[36]

Our money estimates provide some evidence on the possible error in the net national product figures for the decade 1869–79. We earlier derived from these figures the estimate that real income grew from January 1867 to February 1879 at the rate of 3.6 per cent per year—or by a total of 54 per cent in the 12-year period. Since there was a cyclical upswing from 1867 to 1869, real income must have grown during those years. Hence, on this score, 54 per cent is an overestimate of the growth from 1869 to February 1879, and probably also, though less certainly, to calendar 1879. Yet Kuznets' estimates show a growth of 97 per cent from calendar 1869 to calendar 1879.

Instead of drawing an inference from the 1867–79 estimates, we can use the money and price figures to derive corresponding estimates directly for calendar 1869 to calendar 1879. This time crude and refined estimates of velocity yield somewhat more divergent results (see Table 3).[37] For net national product in current prices, these estimates imply a rise of 12 or of 5 per cent from 1869 to 1879; Kuznets' estimates show a rise of 35 per cent. For net national product in constant prices, these estimates imply a rise of 63 or of 54 per cent; Kuznets' figures, as just noted, show a rise of 97 per cent. The lower of these estimates is identical with the one we extracted crudely from our 1867 to 1879 money and price data.

It should be emphasized that the crude monetary estimate of the annual rate of change in net national product in current prices, 1.1 per cent (Table 3, line 1, column 2), is statistically completely independent of the net national product figures indicating a rate of growth of

[36] One other study covering this period also shows very rapid growth in output. According to Gallman's estimates of commodity output, the decennial percentage rate of change in output per capita from 1869 to 1879 was higher than in the two pre–Civil War decades, and was exceeded only from 1879 to 1889 during the nineteenth century and from 1919 to 1929 and 1939 to 1949 during the twentieth century (Robert E. Gallman, "Commodity Output, 1839–1899," *Trends in the American Economy in the Nineteenth Century,* Studies in Income and Wealth, Vol. 24, Princeton for NBER, 1960, pp. 16, 19).

On the other hand, the evidence in A. F. Burns, *Production Trends in the United States Since 1870* (New York, NBER, 1934) suggests that the decade of the seventies was one of average rather than of unusually rapid growth. The medians of the trend cycles of all four of the comprehensive groups of production series he examined are close to the exponential curves fitted to their decade percentage rates of growth, three being slightly above and one slightly below (p. 181).

[37] The details of these estimates are given in Friedman, "Monetary Data and National Income Estimates," pp. 273–280.

3.0 per cent. With but a negligible exception, not a single number used in the calculation of the net national product figures for the decade 1869 to 1879 has been used in computing the crude estimates.[38] For the refined estimate of 0.5 per cent, the price index implicit in the net national product series was used in the derivation of velocity, so that estimate is not completely independent of the net national product series. But it is completely independent of any of the quantity data entering into the net national product series. This is equally true of the other estimates based on the monetary figures in the table.

TABLE 3

ALTERNATIVE ESTIMATES OF CHANGE IN NET NATIONAL PRODUCT FROM 1869 TO 1879

		Percentage Change per Year According to:	
	NNP Estimate	Crude Monetary Estimate	Refined Monetary Estimate
1. Aggregate NNP (current prices)	3.0	1.1	0.5
2. Aggregate NNP (constant prices)	6.8	4.9	4.3
3. Per capita NNP (constant prices)	4.5	2.6	2.0

SOURCE: Friedman, "Monetary Data and National Income Estimates," p. 280, Table 2.

The estimates based on the monetary figures confirm one striking finding of the Kuznets estimates, namely, that the decade from 1869 to 1879 was characterized by an extraordinarily rapid growth of output: at a rate of 4.3 or 4.9 per cent per year in total output, and 2.0 or 2.6 per cent per year in per capita output. Such rapid growth from a year at the peak of a cycle to a year following an extremely long cyclical contraction is no mean accomplishment. In this respect, the monetary estimates confirm the general reliability of the Kuznets estimates for precisely the use for which Kuznets designed them.

At the same time the monetary estimates also indicate that the rate of growth was appreciably lower than that shown by the net national product estimates, and that the margin of error in the latter may well have been higher than the maximum estimate of error cited by Kuznets. If they are taken as entirely accurate, the monetary estimates in Table 3

[38] The negligible exception is that the 1878 and 1879 net national product figures determine the velocity figures for the first two years of the cycle 1878–85, which is one of the 12 cycles averaged in computing the cyclical component for mild depression cycles.

imply that the ratio of the 1869 to 1879 net national product estimate understates the "true" ratio by 18 per cent, according to the crude estimate, or by 22 per cent, according to the refined estimate. The maximum estimate of error cited by Kuznets is 13 per cent.

The monetary estimates so far cited give no basis for distributing the indicated error between 1869 and 1879. So far as they go, the error may arise entirely from underestimation of the 1869 net national product, and the 1879 figure may be correct; or the 1869 figure may be correct and the error arise entirely from overestimation of the 1879 net national product; or any of an infinite number of other combinations may be valid. However, a similar analysis for the next decade suggests that the 1879 net national product figure is high relative to the 1889 figure.[39] If we suppose the 1889 figure to be accurate, this would imply that the 1879 figure is too high. Hence, a division of the indicated error between 1869 and 1879, so as to raise the 1869 figure and lower the 1879 figure, could render the income figures consistent simultaneously with the monetary figures for the decades 1869–79 and 1879–89.

The monetary figures for 1869 to 1879 give reason to question not only the change in income shown by Kuznets' figures but also the pattern within that decade as depicted in Chart 3. Consider the velocity series on that chart. Velocity declines from 1869 to 1871, rises to 1873, and declines to 1875. So far, so good. June 1869 marked a cyclical peak, December 1870, a cyclical trough, and October 1873, a cyclical peak, so these movements conform to the cycle in the same direction as later movements. But then comes a serious discrepancy. Velocity rose some 17 per cent from 1875 to 1879, bringing the terminal velocity to a level 4 per cent higher than in 1869 and 8 per cent higher than in 1873, both cyclical peak years. Such a rise in velocity during the later stages of a contraction is unique in the statistical record from that time to the present: in subsequent contractions, velocity rose in only one out of twenty contractions (1899–1900) and then by less than 2 per cent. Even this exception may reflect only the defect of annual data for such a short contraction.

The movements of velocity suggest that much of the overstatement of the rate of growth may be concentrated in the net national product estimates for the years 1875 to 1879. And this is also the impression given by the annual net national product estimates themselves. In constant prices, these show no decline at all during the contraction of 1873 to 1879, only a slowing down of the rate of growth during the initial years from 1873 to 1875. The estimates show a very rapid rate

---

[39] Velocity for this decade falls at a more rapid rate than would be expected from the indicated rate of increase of real income.

of growth from 1875 to 1879—indeed, that rate of growth was exceeded in the whole decade only from 1871 to 1872. During those final four years of the supposed contraction the indicated rate of growth was nearly 9 per cent per year. The only other four-year period in the peacetime record showing a more rapid rate of growth of real income is 1933–37, the recovery period after the severe 1929–33 contraction.

Of course, the monetary estimates, too, are subject to error and cannot be taken as entirely accurate. Errors in the figures on the stock of money or the failure of velocity to behave during this decade as it did during others may have produced an overestimate of the error in the net national product figures. But, equally, they may have produced an underestimate. The fact that the monetary estimates indicate an error in the net national product figures in the same direction, and of roughly the same order of magnitude, as that suggested by independent evidence is some testimony to both the accuracy of the underlying monetary data, and the validity of the relations used to convert the rate of change in the money stock into an estimate of the rate of change in income.

Whichever estimate of net national product one accepts, the major conclusion is the same: an unusually rapid rise in output converted an unusually slow rate of rise in the stock of money into a rapid decline in prices. We have dwelt on this result and sought to buttress it by a variety of evidence, because it runs directly counter both to qualitative comment on the period and to some of the most strongly held current views of economists about the relation between changes in prices and in economic activity. Contrast, for example, this result with the widely accepted interpretation of British experience in the 1920's, when Britain resumed specie payments at prewar parity. The prewar parity, it was said, overvalued the pound by some 10 per cent or so at the price level that prevailed in 1925 at the time of resumption (prices by then having fallen about 50 per cent from the postwar price peak); hence, the successful return to gold at the prewar parity required a further 10 per cent deflation of domestic prices; the attempt to achieve such further deflation produced, instead, stagnation and widespread unemployment, from which Britain was unable to recover until it finally devalued the pound in 1931. On this interpretation, the chain of influence ran from the attempted deflation to the economic stagnation.

In the greenback episode, a deflation of 50 per cent took place over the course of the decade and a half after 1865. Not only did it not produce stagnation; on the contrary, it was accompanied and produced by a rapid rate of rise in real income. The chain of influence ran from expansion of output to price decline. From 1869 to 1873, the money stock rose on the average by more than enough to match the estimated rise in population and presumably also the rise in the labor

41

force, so money wages did not have to fall. This doubtless eased the process of adjustment, since it required flexibility only in product prices in response to rising output per worker. After 1873, the stock of money rose less rapidly and then fell, while population continued to rise, so money wage rates did fall; and this was connected with the severe contraction beginning in 1873. But even so, wages apparently fell fast enough to avoid continued severe unemployment or industrial stagnation.[40]

Though declining prices did not prevent a rapid rise in real income over the period as a whole, they gave rise to serious economic and social problems. The price declines affected different groups unevenly and introduced additional elements of uncertainty into the economic scene to which adjustment was necessary. Moreover, as we have seen, neither the decline in prices nor the rise in real income proceeded regularly. The beginning of cyclical contraction in 1873 was accompanied by a financial panic in September 1873[41] and by numerous business failures, and was followed by a resumption of the decline in prices—which had been interrupted briefly during the expansion of 1870–73. The business contraction did not end until March 1879.

Accustomed as we are to viewing economic affairs through a monetary

[40] Rendigs Fels (*American Business Cycles, 1865–1897*, University of North Carolina Press, 1959, pp. 107–108) presents evidence in support of our view.

It should perhaps be noted explicitly that our account begs the crucial analytical question. Did the rapid rise in output occur despite the relatively constant stock of money per capita, and hence despite the necessity for the rise in output per capita to be manifested in falling prices? Or was the relatively constant stock of money per capita one of the factors accounting for the rapid rise in output per capita, so that a more expansionary monetary environment would have meant a slower rise in output per capita? Or do both of these overestimate the influence of monetary factors, so that the factors determining the rate of growth were largely independent of monetary influences?

The tendency of modern economic thinking would clearly favor the first interpretation. Yet recent empirical evidence now available for both the United States and Great Britain is mixed. Kuznets' figures for the United States give no clear indication whether output per capita grew more or less rapidly during the generally deflationary period before 1896 than during the generally inflationary period thereafter; the result obtained depends critically on the particular initial and terminal years used for comparison (see Chap. 3 below). According to available estimates of income per head in constant prices for the United Kingdom, the deflationary period was characterized by a definitely higher rate of growth than the later inflationary period. (See James B. Jefferys and Dorothy Walters, "National Income and Expenditure of the United Kingdom, 1870–1952," *Income and Wealth*, Series V, Cambridge, Eng., Bowes and Bowes, 1955, Tables III and XVI. These national income estimates are based on A. R. Prest, "National Income of the United Kingdom, 1870–1946," *Economic Journal*, Mar. 1948, pp. 58–59.)

[41] The National Bureau reference peak is Oct. 1873. However, considerable evidence places the date of the peak some months earlier, which is why our statement about the timing relation between the peak and the panic cannot be precise. We are indebted to Clark Warburton for calling this point to our attention. See also Fels, *American Business Cycles*, pp. 98–99.

veil, the steady decline in prices from 1873 to 1879 probably led contemporary observers and has certainly led later observers to overstate the severity of the contraction in terms of real output. As we have seen, Kuznets' estimates show no decline in net national product in constant prices at all, only a slowing up of the rate of growth in 1874 and 1875, and an exceedingly rapid rate of growth thereafter. Although these estimates almost surely paint too rosy a picture, only retinting, not repainting, is needed. Some physical-volume series decline during 1874 and 1875, but some rise throughout the contraction and most do so after 1875.[42]

The contraction was severe. Yet an analyst who assessed the con-

[42] See the annual data for physical-volume series in *Historical Statistics of the United States, Colonial Times to 1957*, Bureau of the Census, 1960 [*Historical Statistics*, 1960], pp. 357, 360–361, 366–368, 370, 415–417, 428, 448, 451, 455, and *ibid.*, 1949, pp. 149, 218; also the annual data in Burns, *Production Trends*, pp. 288 ff.

The evidence on the behavior of construction during the business contraction is mixed. Construction in current prices, as measured by Kuznets, shows a slight decline, 1875–78; in constant prices, it shows virtually continuous mild growth. On the other hand, building permit data, both in dollar value and in numbers, show a marked decline in the later seventies. Number of miles built of railroads reached a trough in 1875, rebounded in 1876, declined again in 1877, and then turned up in 1878 and 1879. Gross capital expenditures for plant and equipment of regulated public utilities (mainly railroads in the 1870's), in current prices, reached a trough in 1876 and rose only slightly thereafter; in constant prices they reached a trough in 1875 and then rose more strongly than the current prices series. Moses Abramovitz concludes that the foregoing evidence and other series he has examined definitely establish a retardation in growth of construction activity in the seventies and suggest that a decline in absolute level of construction activity may have occurred (see his "Evidences of Long Swings in Aggregate Construction Since the Civil War," a National Bureau study, in preparation).

The severe decline in monetary series from 1873 to 1879 is beyond question: prices, clearings, railway revenues, value of imports. It is the behavior of these series which has largely colored the description of the contraction. A. R. Eckler ("A Measure of the Severity of Depressions, 1873–1932," *Review of Economic Statistics*, May 1933, p. 79) described 1873–79 as severe mainly because of the three monetary series he used in addition to two physical-volume series and a sixth, which is not clearly one or the other. David A. Wells (*Recent Economic Changes*, New York, Appleton, 1889) regarded the whole period 1873–89 as characterized by "a most curious and, in many respects, unprecedented disturbance and depression of trade" (p. 1). Yet a detailed reading of his comments makes it clear that the decline in prices was the feature that Wells emphasized, and indeed that he attributed the decline in prices to an enormous expansion in both the capacity to produce goods and actual production (for example, see comments on pp. 11, 12, 25, 49, 62, 82, 338, 432).

How much of the indisputable discontent during the contraction reflected decline in wage rates rather than increase in unemployment, it is impossible to say. In 1878, Carroll D. Wright, chief of the Massachusetts Bureau of Labor estimated unemployment in the entire country at less than a half-million, although current estimates by presumably less qualified observers were as high as three million (Samuel Rezneck, "Distress, Relief, and Discontent in the United States During the Depression of 1873–78," *Journal of Political Economy*, Dec. 1950, p. 498). The labor disturbances of 1877 were provoked by a series of wage cuts and introduction of laborsaving devices.

traction on the basis of physical-volume series alone would regard it as shorter in length and far less severe than it has generally been judged. The decline in prices and the monetary uncertainty from 1873 through 1878 converted it into an episode regarded by contemporaries as the onset of the Great Depression, and influenced the choice of dates assigned to the contraction in the National Bureau chronology.

Contemporary discussion of that difficult period attributed falling prices and depressed conditions largely to the behavior of the stock of money—and rightly so in the sense that, given the rapid rate of economic growth, the price decline could have been avoided only by a more rapid rate of rise in the stock of money. Attention centered almost entirely on greenbacks, as our earlier listing of legislation indicates, and hardly any notice was taken of the decline in deposits after 1875.[43]

3. The Politics of Resumption

The political agitation for expansion of the currency which was to mark the last three decades of the century had its inception in the period immediately after the Civil War.

At the close of the Civil War, the Administration, Congress, and the public at large were all generally committed to resumption of specie payments, and regarded contraction of the currency as a necessary step toward that end. In his annual report issued in December 1865, Secretary of the Treasury Hugh McCullough wrote that "The present legal-tender acts . . . ought not to remain in force one day longer than shall be necessary to enable the people to prepare for a return to the constitutional currency,"[44] and recommended measures directed toward the early retirement of the greenbacks. The House of Representatives promptly resolved by a vote of 144 to 6 that it cordially concurred in these views,[45] and a few months later Congress passed the act of April 12, 1866, which was intended to put into effect the policies recommended by McCulloch. As to the public, bankers and business men—later to be deeply divided on the question—were at the time as one in favor of resumption; and labor and agrarian groups—later to be in the forefront of the drive for expansion of the greenback issue and for free silver—were at the time still committed to hard money, as they had been since at least the Bank War.[46]

The sharp decline in prices and the business contraction that fol-

---

[43] See Charles F. Dunbar, *Economic Essays*, New York, 1904, p. 213; Dorfman, *The Economic Mind*, Vol. III, pp. 15–18. However, it may have been recognized that, since greenbacks were also usable for bank reserves, an increase in greenbacks would encourage deposit expansion as well.

[44] *Annual Report on the Finances*, 1865, p. 4.

[45] See Mitchell, *A History of the Greenbacks*, p. 128.

[46] R. P. Sharkey, *Money, Class, and Party*, Baltimore, Johns Hopkins University Press, 1959, *passim*.

lowed the end of the Civil War produced, after some lag, a marked change in sentiment. In February 1868, Congress suspended the retirement of greenbacks. Prominent, though ultimately unsuccessful, candidates for both the Republican and Democratic Presidential nominations proposed that government bonds be paid in greenbacks instead of gold. Indeed, the Democratic platform contained a provision to that end —"one currency for the government and the people, the laborer and the office-holder, the pensioner and the soldier, the producer and the bond holder"—though its nominee, Horatio Seymour, was strongly opposed.[47] The Republican platform opposed this step and, after the Republican victory, Congress passed the act of March 18, 1869, pledging repayment in specie, except only for securities issued with an express provision for some other payment.

Needless to say, public controversy continued. Currency contraction was strongly advocated as a step toward immediate resumption, especially by persons engaged in foreign trade, eastern bankers, and some manufacturers, predominantly New England textile men. Currency expansion was just as strongly advocated, to offset the baleful effects of deflation, by an even more mixed lot—agrarian groups that had initially been strong proponents of currency contraction, spokesmen for labor groups, western merchants and bankers, Pennsylvania ironmasters, and business-

---

[47] For the Democratic party platform, see K. H. Porter and D. B. Johnson, *National Party Platforms, 1840–1956,* Urbana, University of Illinois Press, 1956, pp. 37–39.

See John Stuart Mill's comments regarding the Democratic party's stand:

A plea which imposes upon some people who would shrink from anything which they themselves regarded as repudiation, is this: Greenbacks, however they may be depreciated, are legal tender, are the lawful currency of the United States; other persons are obliged to receive this currency in payment of all their dues and why should the public creditor be an exception? . . . But the answers to it are manifold . . . If those who lent their savings to the United States had been told, at the time, that every thousand dollars they lent should be repaid to them in greenbacks, which might then be worth not more than a thousand cents (the depreciation of the French assignats amounted to that and more), nobody, unless he could afford to make the nation a present of his money, would have parted with it unless at a rate of interest sufficient to assure against the extreme risk. The United States obtained these sums of money, in their extreme necessity, at an interest (all things considered) not very much exceeding what the high value of capital in a new country compels them to pay in ordinary times; and after having reaped the benefit, having by that indispensable help saved their national existence, they are now exhorted to withhold the price, at the cost of the national honor (in a letter to a friend in England, printed in the *Nation,* Oct. 15, 1868, pp. 308–309, as "John Stuart Mill on National Faith").

Though Mill's logic is unassailable, his factual assumptions are not. As we shall see below in sect. 5, the market prices of government bonds during the Civil War suggest that purchasers treated them as greenback obligations and did not in fact expect the government to pay principal and interest in gold.

men with interests in western real estate and transportation.[48] Still others favored leaving the currency alone—in the phrase used by George Opdyke, of this group, "masterly inactivity" with respect to the currency—with resumption as an ultimate albeit distant goal.[49]

In Washington, the bone of controversy was the right of the Secretary of the Treasury to reissue the $44 million of greenbacks that had been retired by 1868. While Democrats tended to support that right and Republicans to deny it, there were no hard and fast lines dividing the parties, and Republican-appointed secretaries from time to time exercised the right.[50]

While these disputes raged, a related issue was under consideration in the courts: Was it constitutional for Congress to make greenbacks a legal tender in payment of all debts, public and private, even those contracted before the Legal Tender Acts (the name for the acts authorizing the greenback issues) were passed? In the first of the famous greenback cases, *Hepburn v. Griswold,* decided on February 7, 1870, a majority of the Supreme Court declared it was not constitutional. Perhaps the most fascinating aspect of this decision is that it was delivered by Chief Justice Salmon P. Chase, who had been Secretary of the Treasury when the first greenbacks were issued. Not only did he not disqualify himself, but in his capacity as Chief Justice convicted himself of having been responsible for an unconstitutional action in his capacity as Secretary of the Treasury!

[48] Irwin Unger, "Businessmen and Specie Resumption," *Political Science Quarterly,* Mar. 1959, pp. 36–70.

[49] See his *Letter on National Finances,* New York, Sun Job Print, 1869, pp. 19, 44. In a varied career, including a term as mayor of New York, Opdyke had been a commercial banker with links to the private banking firm of Jay Cooke.

[50] In Oct. 1872, Secretary Boutwell increased greenbacks outstanding by $4.6 million and the House challenged his authority (E. B. Patten, "Secretary Shaw and Precedents as to Treasury Control over the Money Market," *Journal of Political Economy,* Feb. 1907, p. 73. The *Annual Report on the Finances* does not allude to this or other reissues. They show up in monthly public debt statements). In reply, he claimed that the retired notes were a reserve on which he could draw to relieve seasonal pressure. The Senate Finance Committee also considered the matter and in a majority report denied the Secretary's power, while a minority report upheld it. No further action was taken on the right of reissue and, by Mar. 1873, all of the $4.6 million had been retired. A $2.5 million reissue of greenbacks was made that month, however, to meet current expenditures, and retired in May. In the fall, the panic of 1873 intensified the pressure on the Treasury by the financial community to provide relief by reissuing greenbacks. President Grant and Secretary Richardson met Wall Street representatives in New York on Sunday, Sept. 21—the Stock Exchange having closed the previous day not to reopen for ten days—but they opposed the financiers' plan. Instead, the Treasury bought bonds with greenbacks it held as cash and the *Annual Report* for 1873 states that those purchases were made "without the use of any part of the forty-four millions of United States notes, generally known as the reserve." The report did not, however, mention that, from Oct. 1873 to Mar. 1874, the Treasury, faced with inadequate cash holdings, reissued $26 million in greenbacks to meet ordinary expenses.

The first decision caused little stir because, at the time it was delivered, it was assumed that it applied merely to contracts made before the war—the question at issue in *Hepburn v. Griswold*—but soon it was realized that the reasoning of the majority made the Legal Tender Acts unconstitutional also for contracts entered into after the war. To obtain a reversal of what was believed to be a disastrous decision, a drive was undertaken to get the Court to review the whole question on argument of other legal-tender cases pending on its docket. Supporters of that drive were encouraged by the fact that two vacancies on the Court had been filled sinced the decision.[51] In *Knox v. Lee*, decided on May, 1, 1871, which gave the enlarged Court the opportunity to rule on the question, it affirmed that making greenbacks a legal tender was constitutional, reversing the earlier decision by a majority of five to four, with Chief Justice Chase as one of the dissenting justices.

The banking panic in September 1873 and the subsequent economic contraction stimulated renewed attempts to expand the greenback issue. In 1874, a bill initially designed to require specie resumption by January 1, 1876, was converted into a bill to expand the greenback issue, known as the Inflation Bill. It was passed by both Houses of Congress under Republican sponsorship, was then vetoed by President Grant, and was followed by the act of June 20, 1874, fixing the maximum greenback issue at the amount then outstanding.

[51] An act of Mar. 3, 1863, increased the number of associate justices to nine, with the Chief Justice as the tenth member of the Court. Because of Congressional distrust of both the Court and President Andrew Johnson, the membership of the Court was reduced to seven by the act of July 23, 1866, which deprived the President of the opportunity to fill expected vacancies.

A month after Grant's accession to the Presidency in 1869, Congress increased the number of the Court to nine, and authorized the President to nominate an additional judge at the next session of the Senate. Eight justices heard the case of *Hepburn v. Griswold*, but the decision of only seven was recorded, one having retired the week before the decision was given, in accordance with a public announcement some months earlier. Because of the Senate's refusal to confirm the nominee for the new judgeship whose name the President had submitted in 1869, he had two vacancies to fill in 1870 after that retirement. On Feb. 7, 1870, the day of the decision in the first greenback case, he sent the Senate the names of two nominees. That coincidence gave rise to a charge that Grant packed the Court in order to obtain a reversal. Charles Warren, author of the definitive history of the Court, denied the validity of the charge (*The Supreme Court in United States History*, Boston, Little Brown, 1935 ed., Vol. II, pp. 517–518). On Mar. 25, four days after Grant's appointees were confirmed, the U.S. Attorney General moved in the Supreme Court that two legal tender cases then pending, which involved contracts made after the passage of the Legal Tender Acts, be taken up for argument. The Court agreed, but the litigants withdrew their cases on Apr. 18, to the general relief, Warren adds, "since it seemed apparent that, if the decision should be reversed, a political movement might be initiated to reverse this second decision by adding still more Judges to the Court" (p. 524). The act of 1869 was the chief historical precedent for President Roosevelt's unsuccessful 1937 proposal to enlarge the Supreme Court, which gave rise to the famous court-packing controversy.

The Republicans were badly beaten in the Congressional elections of 1874, losing control of the House for the first time since 1860. In the final weeks of the legislative session, before the new Congress took office, the "lame duck" Congress reversed course and passed the Resumption Act of January 14, 1875, which announced the intention to resume specie payments at the prewar parity on January 1, 1879, and authorized the Secretary of the Treasury both to use surplus revenue and to sell bonds in order to accumulate a gold reserve. At the time, the act was little more than the expression of a pious hope and, insofar as it had any contemporary effect, it was to heighten the opposition to resumption.[52]

The importance of the currency issue was reflected in the organization in 1875 of the Greenback party, which captured third parties formed in different states during the early seventies under various titles—Independent, Anti-Monopoly, Reform, and Farmers. Greenbackism had spread rapidly after the panic of 1873. Its goals included a plentiful supply of currency, destruction of the "money monopoly," elimination of foreign capitalists as investors in the United States, and reduction of the burden of debt. The party adopted the view that resumption was a bankers' conspiracy to contract the money supply, and nominated Peter Cooper for President in 1876 to run on a platform demanding unconditional repeal of the Resumption Act.[53] The party got few votes—less than one per cent of the total cast for President—but greenback agitation provoked concern among business groups that had earlier favored currency expansion. Pennsylvania ironmasters, for example, reversed their views. The fortunes of the Greenback party were at a high point in the elections of 1878, when it polled about 10 per cent of the votes and won 14 seats in Congress. By 1880, denunciation of the Resumption Act was no longer a live issue; instead the party platform called for a government monopoly of paper currency and for unlimited coinage of silver. Thereafter Greenback party agitation waned, although its financial program lived on.

The much-disputed Presidential election of 1876, in which Samuel J. Tilden received a majority of the popular vote but Rutherford B. Hayes was elected President by a margin of one electoral vote, left the Republicans in command of the White House, the House with a Democratic majority, and the Senate with thirty-eight Republicans, thirty-seven

[52] The act contained a variety of provisions designed to appeal to silver advocates (replacement of fractional currency by silver coins) ; paper-money advocates (removal of all limits on the aggregate issue of national bank notes and linking the retirement of greenbacks—the aggregate outstanding not to fall below $300 million—to the increase in national bank notes) ; gold standard advocates (its main provisions).

[53] See Richard Hofstadter, *The Age of Reform*, New York, Knopf, 1955, pp. 73 ff.

Democrats, and one Independent (a Greenbacker).[54] Late in 1877, the House passed a bill to repeal the Resumption Act. The bill was defeated in the Senate by one vote. This paper-thin decision turned out to be politically decisive. The subsequent act of May 31, 1878, which forbade any further retirement of greenbacks, did not alter the legal commitment to resume on January 1, 1879, though it was widely doubted at the time that the commitment could be honored.

Side-by-side with the controversy over the greenbacks and resumption, there arose, from about 1875 on, pressure to give silver a larger place in the monetary system and to establish a bimetallic rather than a gold standard. The United States had been on a nominal bimetallic standard until 1873, when silver was demonetized by the Coinage Act of 1873 (to be discussed in more detail in the following chapter). At the time, demonetization occasioned little comment, but the subsequent decline in the price of silver created a political issue about its enactment. In 1876, Congress established a monetary commission to hold hearings and report on the role of silver and related issues. The eight-man commission included three members each from the House and the Senate, and two nongovernment experts. Its majority report, submitted in 1877, favored the adoption of bimetallism but opposed greenback issues. George S. Boutwell, then Senator from Massachusetts, submitted a minority report favoring bimetallism only if international, and opposing unilateral action by the United States. Professor Francis Bowen of Harvard and Representative R. L. Gibson of Louisiana submitted a second minority report opposing bimetallism as impractical because the market ratio would diverge from the mint ratio, with the result that one or the other would in fact become the standard.[55] These three reports fairly accurately represented the range of contemporary opinion.

The near-success of the "free silver" movement of the national bimetallists is discussed at length in the following chapter. The international bimetallists never matched their record. They won appropriations from Congress over the next two decades for the conduct of negotiations with foreign governments for international remonetization of silver. They organized international conferences with the hope of establishing a common set of mint ratios in the countries participating. They never came close, however, to achieving effective international monetary cooperation.

As is clear from this account, the politics of resumption was confused

[54] Horace White, *Money and Banking,* Boston, Ginn, 1935, p. 259. According to *Historical Statistics,* 1949, Series P-53-56, in the 45th session of Congress, the Senate was composed of 39 Republicans, 36 Democrats, and 1 Independent. The classification of party membership at that time is difficult, because of the existence of offshoots of the major parties.

[55] *Report and Accompanying Documents of the United States Monetary Commission,* organized under Joint Resolution of Aug. 15, 1876, 2 vols., 44th Cong., 2d sess., S. Rept. 703, GPO, 1877.

and contradictory. Moreover, the political measures taken bore a rather tenuous relation to the economic factors that ultimately made resumption possible, as we shall see when we discuss the economics of resumption toward the end of this chapter.

4. *Factors Accounting for Changes in the Stock of Money*

So far, we have taken for granted the movements in the stock of money. We turn now to an analysis of the factors that account for these movements.

Ever since the Civil War, the United States has had a monetary system in which hand-to-hand currency consists of specie or of fiduciary money which is a direct or indirect liability of the government,[56] and deposits held by the public consist of promises to pay hand-to-hand currency on the part of fractional-reserve commercial banks. In such a system, it is useful to distinguish three major channels through which any changes in the stock of money must, as a matter of arithmetic, occur.[57]

1. *High-powered money:* The total amount of hand-to-hand currency held by the public plus vault cash plus, after 1914, deposit liabilities of the Federal Reserve System to banks. The two final items constitute bank reserves, which, in our terminology, exclude interbank deposits and before 1914 consist only of vault cash.[58] This total is called high-powered money because one dollar of such money held as bank reserves may give rise to the creation of several dollars of deposits. Other things being the same (namely, the items to be specified below), any increase in the total of high-powered money involves an equal percentage increase in the stock of money.[59]

2. *The ratio of commercial bank deposits to bank reserves:* The higher this ratio, the larger the amount of deposits that is outstanding for a given amount of reserves. However, the quantitative effect on the money

---

[56] See sect. 1 above for the reasons we regard national bank notes as liabilities of the government rather than as liabilities of the banks comparable to their deposits.

[57] For a full analysis of this framework, see Appendix B.

[58] Note that this definition does not require that all kinds of money contained in the total be usable for both hand-to-hand currency and reserves. For example, in the greenback period, national bank notes could not be used for both by national banks. Currently, deposits at Federal Reserve Banks cannot be used for hand-to-hand currency (see Appendix B).

[59] The term high-powered money is not original with us. See W. R. Burgess, *The Reserve Banks and the Money Market*, New York, Harper, 2d. ed., 1936, pp. 5–8; 3rd ed., 1946, pp. 5–8 ("The central bank deals in high-powered money . . ."); see also Board of Governors of the Federal Reserve System, *The Federal Reserve System: Purposes and Functions*, 2d ed., Nov. 1947, p. 16 ("Federal Reserve dollars are often called high-powered dollars as compared with ordinary deposit dollars . . ."); 3rd ed., Apr. 1954, pp. 20, 27; 4th ed., Feb. 1961, pp. 19, 27.

stock of a change in this ratio cannot be stated as simply as can the effect of a change in high-powered money because, other things being the same, any increase in the ratio of deposits to reserves tends to drain currency into public circulation and hence changes the amount of reserves. The effect of a change in this ratio is, therefore, connected with the size of the next ratio.

3. *The ratio of commercial bank deposits to currency held by the public:* The higher this ratio, the larger the fraction of high-powered money that will be in use as bank reserves, and hence the larger the money stock, given the other two items. The quantitative effect of a change in this ratio is connected with the size of the preceding ratio.

These three items determine the stock of money in the arithmetic sense that knowledge of their numerical values permits computation of the numerical value of the money stock.[60] For this reason, we shall call them the proximate determinants of the money stock.

This particular triplet of proximate determinants is economically useful because it corresponds to a classification of more basic factors affecting the money stock into three separate and largely, though not entirely, independent sets of forces influenced by or under the control of different economic actors.

1. Under a fiduciary standard, as from 1862 to 1879, the amount of high-powered money is determined by governmental action. The government may not formulate any explicit policies with respect to high-powered money; the amount outstanding may be the net result of many other actions affecting taxes and expenditures, borrowing and repayment of debt. Yet, ultimately, government has the power to make total high-powered money anything it wishes by its decisions about how much fiduciary money to issue to the public and the banks. In this respect, the Greenback party and its predecessors were right in their emphasis on greenbacks.

As we shall see in more detail in the next chapter, a specie standard offers a sharp contrast to a fiduciary standard. Under an international specie standard, the amount of money in any one country must be whatever is necessary to maintain international balance with other

[60] The formula connecting them with the money stock is

$$M = H \cdot \frac{\frac{D}{R}\left(1 + \frac{D}{C}\right)}{\frac{D}{R} + \frac{D}{C}}$$

where H is total high-powered money, D is commercial bank deposits, R is commercial bank reserves, and C is currency held by the public, so that D/R is item 2 above and D/C item 3 (see Appendix B, sect. 5).

countries on the same standard, and the amount of high-powered money will alter through imports and exports of specie in order to produce this result. Under a specie standard confined to a single country, or for the world as a whole under an international standard, the existing amount of specie is determined by the available physical stock plus the relative demand for monetary and other uses; and changes in the amount of specie, by relative costs of production of specie and other goods and services. In either case, the amount of high-powered money is a dependent rather than an independent variable, and is not subject to governmental determination. The flexible exchange rates between the dollar and other currencies in the greenback period cut the mechanical link between external conditions and the stock of money, and permitted high-powered money and the stock of money to be determined by domestic considerations alone. The link that remained was not mechanical but political: a governmental policy of seeking restoration of a specie standard at the prewar parity.

2. The ratio of deposits to reserves is, in the first instance, determined by the banking system—not, of course, through concerted action but through the combined effect of the actions of individual banks. Each bank may pay explicit attention to the absolute volume of its deposits and its reserves separately rather than to their ratio; and any one bank can make the volume of its reserves, at least, anything it wants within limits set only by its total assets. The situation is quite different for banks taken as a whole. The total reserves available to all together are limited by the amount of high-powered money available for banks and the public, and the share the banks can acquire will depend not only on their own actions but also on the willingness of the public to hold deposits rather than currency. What the banking system as a whole can determine is any ratio of deposits to reserves. It can achieve any ratio that is the implicit or explicit objective of its component units regardless of what the two other sets of actors—the government and the public—do. The level at which the banks will seek to maintain that ratio is linked to the government by the requirements imposed by law; and is linked to the public by the expectations of bankers about likely variations in the public's desire to add to or withdraw deposits, which is to say, to change the ratio of deposits to currency. In addition, of course, the desired reserve ratio will be affected by the profitability of alternative uses of assets.

3. The ratio of deposits to currency is, in the first instance, determined by the public—again, not through concerted action, but through the combined effect of the actions of individual holders of money. The public as a whole cannot determine the absolute volume of either its deposits or its currency, though each individual separately can, since these will

52

depend on the willingness of the banks to create deposits relative to their reserves and on the amount of high-powered money available. The public can determine only the ratio of its deposits to its currency. The level at which it will seek to maintain this ratio is linked to the other two sets of actors: to the government, by the legal conditions under which currency and deposits may be issued, insofar as these affect their relative desirability; and to the banks, through the terms they offer depositors, in the form of services rendered and of interest paid on deposits.

The joint determination of the two ratios reflects the necessity for the reserves and currency in their denominators to add up to the quantity of high-powered money. The terms on which banks can make loans or acquire investments, their costs of operation, and the competitive conditions they face will combine to induce them to offer some rate of interest and some free services in order to attract deposits. In response to these terms the public will seek some deposit-currency ratio. If the public's adherence to this ratio leaves less high-powered money in the banks than the banks desire to hold under the stated conditions, banks will dispose of assets in the attempt to acquire reserves, which will reduce total deposits and thereby lead the public to hold less currency at the given deposit-currency ratio. If the deposit-currency ratio leaves more high-powered money in the banks than banks desire, banks will use the extra reserves to acquire assets which will expand deposits and thereby lead the public to hold more currency. Under equilibrium conditions, banks will have that volume of deposits and that volume of reserves which will make the marginal cost of a dollar of deposits equal to the marginal yield, as they value it, from a dollar of nonreserve assets or from a dollar of reserves, where both cost and yield include, of course, both direct and indirect costs and yields.

As these brief comments suggest, and as we hope the rest of the book will demonstrate, this framework of proximate determinants is designed to facilitate analysis of the simultaneous interaction of the various forces determining the money stock, not to separate them into watertight compartments.

Chart 4 plots the stock of money and the three proximate determinants for the period 1867–79. The most striking feature of this graph is the mild and almost horizontal movement in high-powered money up to the cyclical trough in February 1879 (the movements after the turn are considered along with the subsequent expansion, in the following chapter). The rise in the stock of money from 1867 to this trough reflected the behavior of the two deposit ratios and occurred in spite of a decline in high-powered money. From January 1867 to February 1879, high-powered money fell by 1 per cent per year. That is how fast the stock

53

of money would have fallen if the two deposit ratios had remained the same. In fact, the stock of money rose 1.3 per cent per year. The two deposit ratios contributed about equally to the conversion of the decline in high-powered money to a rise in the stock of money.[61]

The impact of high-powered money is clearest from 1867 to 1868, when its decline was offset only partly by a rise in the two ratios and so produced a decline in the stock of money. For the rest of the period, high-powered money leaves less of an imprint on the stock of money than do the deposit ratios. The stock of money moves in the same direction as high-powered money only in those years when the deposit ratios do also (1870 to 1873, 1878 to 1879) or when the deposit ratios are roughly constant (1875 to 1876).

The initial decline in high-powered money from 1867 to 1870 was produced by the retirement of the miscellaneous remnants of Civil War financing, listed in Table 1 under "Other U.S. currency" held by banks and the public, and therefore reflected the final and quasi-automatic liquidation of these highly transitory wartime expedients. The rise from 1870 to 1874 was produced by roughly equal rises in national bank notes and greenbacks, and the subsequent decline, primarily by retirement of greenbacks. The fluctuations in greenbacks were partly a result of the legislative measures mentioned above—the act of 1874 that authorized additional issues, the Resumption Act that specified a limited retirement, and the act of May 1878 that suspended further retirement. But they were also partly a result of the exigencies of the Treasury's needs and the policies of its officers that determined how much of the amount authorized was held in the Treasury. In particular, the final reduction from August 1878 to February 1879 in the greenbacks held by banks and the public resulted from an increase in the greenbacks held by the Treasury; the fixed total amount authorized remained unchanged. The fluctuations in high-powered money mirror the political struggle over

---

[61] See Appendix B for the method used to determine the contribution of each determinant to a change in the stock of money. For Jan. 1867 to Feb. 1879, the numerical contributions are:

Change in Money Stock That Would Have Been
Produced by Indicated Determinant, if It Alone
Had Changed

Proximate Determinant	Rate of Change Per Year (per cent)	Fraction of Total Change
High-powered money	−1.03	−0.77
Deposit-reserve ratio	1.06	0.80
Deposit-currency ratio	.93	0.70
Interaction of two ratios	.37	0.28
All	1.33	1.00[a]

[a] Detail does not add to 1.00 because of rounding.

CHART 4
The Stock of Money and Its Proximate Determinants, 1867–79

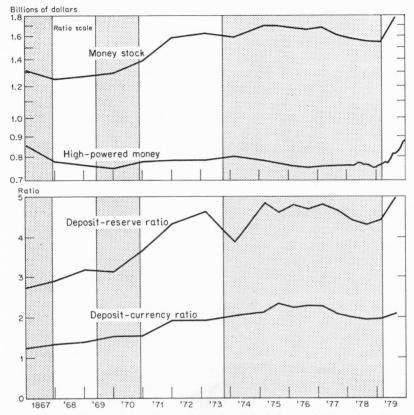

NOTE: Shaded areas represent business contractions; unshaded areas, business expansions.
SOURCE: Tables A-1 (col. 8) and B-3; monthly figures for high-powered money beginning June 1878 from same source as for Table B-3.

greenbacks and resumption. The mildness of the fluctuations and the rough constancy of the total show how close and relatively stable was the political balance.

The balance might not have been so close, and political imperatives might have produced a very different behavior of high-powered money, if rises in the deposit ratios had not permitted a rise in the stock of money, despite the rough constancy or decline in high-powered money. These rises in the deposit ratios owed little to contemporaneous governmental action. They were linked mainly to the prior governmental measures that affected the development of the banking structure. The one appreciable

55

exception is a change in 1874 in the provisions governing national bank notes which reduced national bank reserve requirements.

The initial rise in the deposit-currency ratio doubtless reflected the rapid spread of commercial banking and hence the greater usefulness of bank deposits. The tapering off of the rise from 1872 to 1874 probably helped to produce and then was intensified by the banking difficulties in 1873, which culminated in the banking panic of September, set off by the failure of a number of banking houses. The most important house that failed was Jay Cooke and Company, which had become nationally famous through its role in pioneering the widespread public distribution of government bonds during the Civil War. Annual data are too crude to reveal accurately the reaction to such an episode. In general, however, any widespread banking difficulties that weaken the public's confidence in banks can be expected to be followed by a fall in the ratio of deposits to currency, as the public seeks to convert the one into the other, and this is quite clearly what happened after subsequent episodes for which we have monthly data. The decline after 1876 may very well have a similar explanation. In 1877–78, there was a notable increase in commercial bank suspensions.

The rise in the deposit-reserve ratio from 1867 to 1873 reflects partly a rise in the ratio for national banks, partly a sharp increase in the relative importance of nonnational banks measured by their share of total reserves. Though the ratio for nonnational banks was roughly constant, it was, throughout, two to four times as high as the ratio for national banks, hence an increase in the relative importance of nonnational banks tended to raise the average ratio for both groups combined. The ratio for national banks roughly doubled, from 2.0 to 3.8, their deposits rising 12.5 per cent, and their reserves falling 41 per cent. This change was presumably part of the maturation of national banks. As their rapid growth tapered off and they were able to adjust to their experience, they found it possible and profitable to operate with a smaller volume of reserves relative to their deposits. The much higher ratio for nonnational than for national banks reflected mainly differences in the legal reserve requirements to which each was subject. As of 1879, only six states had legal reserve requirements against deposits, and only three required total reserves as large as those specified in the National Banking Act.[62] From 1867 to 1873 the share of total bank reserves held by non-

[62] R. G. Rodkey, *Legal Reserves in American Banking,* Michigan Business Studies, Vol. VI, No. 5, University of Michigan, 1934, p. 32.
The laws imposing reserve requirements antedated the National Banking Act in two states (Lousiana, 1842; Massachusetts, 1858 and re-enacted, 1865), and were passed afterwards in four (Michigan, 1871; Connecticut, 1872; New Hampshire, 1874; Minnesota, 1878). A number of other states imposed reserve requirements in the period before the Civil War, but these applied to note issues only.
Under the National Banking Act, banks in so-called central reserve cities had

national banks rose from 13 to 33 per cent. Of the two factors producing
the rise in the deposit ratio from 1867 to 1873, the rise in the ratio for
national banks was somewhat more important quantitatively than the
rise in the relative importance of nonnational banks.

The sharp decline in the deposit-reserve ratio from 1873 to 1874 is
almost surely a response to the banking panic of 1873. In its initial stages
such a panic is accompanied by a reduction in bank reserves as the public
seeks to convert deposits into currency, which by itself would make for a
rise in the deposit-reserve ratio. But banks very quickly seek to strengthen
themselves by acquiring greater liquid resources and succeed in doing so,
so that their reserves generally rise relative to their deposits shortly after
a panic. For some time thereafter, their reserves generally remain at a
higher level than one would expect from earlier experience. For example,
from 1873 to 1874, banks absorbed an increase in high-powered money
plus the currency released by a decline in the public's holdings, while
deposits decreased slightly.

The sharp rise in the deposit-reserve ratio from 1874 to 1875 is no
doubt partly a reaction to the prior search for liquidity on the part of
the banks. But it probably owes more to a change in the provisions of the
law governing the issue of national bank notes. Before 1874, national
banks were required to apply the legally specified reserve percentages
to the sum of their deposits and note circulation; thereafter, only to their
deposits. This reduction in legal reserve requirements led the banks to
raise the deposit-reserve ratio to a new and higher level after 1874 than
they had maintained earlier.

The decline in the deposit-reserve ratio after February 1877 was an
indirect consequence of the banking suspensions referred to earlier. These
were concentrated among nonnational banks, and were accompanied by a
decline in the relative importance of deposits in such banks which, as we
have seen, would tend to lower the average ratio for all banks because
of the high deposit-reserve ratio of nonnational banks. In addition, the
suspensions induced nonnational banks to achieve greater liquidity
and so led to a decline in their deposit-reserve ratio.

---

to keep reserves in lawful money equal to 25 per cent of their deposits; banks in
reserve cities had to keep total reserves as large as central reserve city banks, but
could keep up to half as deposits at banks in those cities; and banks in other
cities had to keep total reserves of 15 per cent, but could keep up to 60 per cent
as deposits at banks in reserve or central reserve cities.

We exclude from our total of reserves for the consolidated banking system the
legally required reserves that banks held in the form of deposits at other banks
(see Appendix B).

We also exclude the redemption fund, consisting of lawful money equal to at
least 5 per cent of note circulation, which national banks were required from 1874
on to deposit with the Treasury.

To summarize: The sharp rise in the stock of money from 1868 to 1872 was primarily a consequence of the spread of deposit banking. This both induced the public to hold a larger ratio of deposits to currency and enabled the banking system to create more dollars of deposits per dollar of vault cash. The decline in the stock of money from 1877 to 1879 was primarily a consequence of a series of nonnational bank failures that produced a reverse movement in these ratios. The monetary authorities contributed to and lengthened both the rise and the decline in the money stock: the first, by an increase in high-powered money that began in 1870 and continued to 1874; the second, by a decline in high-powered money that began in 1874. In addition the monetary authorities were entirely responsible for the initial decline in the money stock from 1867 to 1868.

5. *Special Problems Connected with the Greenback Period*

THE PREMIUM ON GOLD

From 1862 to 1879, gold was a commodity in the domestic economy. But it was also more than a commodity: for external and some internal purposes it was a second species of money; and it was recognized as the legitimate, if temporarily dethroned, sovereign. In consequence, special monetary significance attached to its price, or the premium on gold, as the difference between its market price in greenbacks and its prewar nominal monetary value was always referred to in a community that regarded any such differences as a temporary hang-over from wartime.

The key to understanding the behavior of the premium on gold during the greenback period is that the price of gold was to all intents and purposes the dollar-pound exchange rate. It was therefore determined by the forces underlying the international balance of payments, and its movements reflected changes in those forces: the comparative advantage of the United States (the northern states during the war) and the outside world in various lines of production; the relative price levels in the U.S. and the outside world; and movements of capital between the U.S. and the outside world. These are not the forces stressed by either contemporary or most subsequent writers. They have tended rather to stress the shifting expectations about the prospect of eventual redemption of the greenbacks in gold. Those expectations certainly played a role but not as a factor in addition to the ones just listed. Such shifting expectations could affect the price of gold *only* as they affected the demand for or supply of foreign exchange; for example, by producing a greater or lesser willingness on the part of foreigners to hold assets whose value was fixed in terms of greenbacks, or on the part of U.S. citizens to hold assets fixed in terms of foreign currencies.

At the outbreak of the Civil War, the price of the pound sterling in

58

terms of the dollar varied in a narrow interval around $4.86. This was the price that the U.S. Treasury was willing to pay or receive for the amount of gold for which the Bank of England would pay or receive one pound sterling; it was, that is, the mint par.[63] The interval about the mint par was determined by the cost of exporting or importing gold; these determined the so-called gold points. Any tendency of the exchange rate to move outside this range would lead to the import or export of gold and set in motion the classical gold standard adjustment mechanism involving both capital movements and changes in prices and incomes in the U.S. and the rest of the world.

The unwillingness or inability of the United States to permit the adjustments required to keep the exchange rate within the former gold points made departure from the gold standard inevitable.[64] Once the U.S.

[63] According to Mitchell, the mint par was 109.45⅝ cents = 54d., which works out to $4.8647 a pound sterling. He notes that the former "style of quoting sterling exchange arose in colonial days when the Spanish dollar was worth approximately 54d. in English silver coin. The present style of quoting the British pound in dollars and cents (£1 = $4.86.65) was not introduced until January 1, 1874" (Mitchell, *Gold, Prices, and Wages*, p. 252).

[64] There is much discussion in the literature about the details of the relations between the Treasury and the banks preceding suspension. The main writers attribute much of the responsibility for suspension to the methods used by the U.S. Treasury under Secretary Salmon P. Chase in borrowing funds to finance war expenditures in 1861—in particular, to the failure of Secretary Chase to suspend the provision of the Independent Treasury System that required proceeds of loans to be paid at once into the Treasury in specie. See Mitchell, *A History of the Greenbacks*, pp. 23–27, 42–43; and Don C. Barrett, *The Greenbacks and Resumption of Specie Payments, 1862–1879,* Harvard Univeristy Press, 1931, especially Chap. II.

Detailed mistakes of policy of this kind may indeed have led to suspension earlier and in a different manner than a more sophisticated policy would have done. In our opinion, however, their effect has been grossly overrated for the usual reason that, though they deal with superficials, they are newsworthy and prominent in the records of the period, whereas the basic forces at work are concealed from view. In view of the effect of the war on the foreign trade of the U.S., discussed below, the prevention of suspension required a decline in domestic prices in the U.S. This in turn would have required that the government refrain from financing any war expenditures by the tax on money balances implicit in the inflationary creation of money for government purposes. Indeed, the prevention of suspension would have required that the government use funds raised in other ways—from taxation in other forms and from borrowing at home and abroad at whatever interest rates were necessary—not only to finance war expenditures but also to force down the price level. Given the obvious unwillingness or inability to follow so Spartan a policy, suspension was inevitable sooner or later.

We do not, incidentally, mean to imply that so Spartan a policy, even if technically feasible, would necessarily have been desirable. On the contrary, in contrast to most earlier writers, we are inclined to believe that suspension itself was probably desirable, though an optimum financial policy would have involved more taxation and less inflation than was experienced. At the same time, in light of the U.S. experience in two world wars, especially World War I, the financing of the Civil War involved surprisingly little inflation, thanks more to accident than to policy. The tendency in the literature before World War I—of which Mitchell's

went off gold in 1862, the exchange rate was free to move outside these limits and, of course, did so. The dollar depreciated, which meant that the greenback price of the pound rose and hence so did the greenback price of gold, since the pound price of gold was fixed within gold points by the Bank of England's buying and selling rates. Thereafter, until resumption in 1879, the exchange rate—and hence the premium on gold—was determined by the demand for and supply of foreign exchange.[65]

We stress the identity of the premium on gold with the exchange rate because there has been so much confusion and misunderstanding about the relation between changes in the domestic demand for and supply of gold and changes in the premium on gold. Because gold was primarily a commodity for internal purposes and not money, there is a temptation to try to explain variations in its price by changes in its domestic demand and supply conditions—to analyze its price as one would analyze house rents or the price of bricks. This approach is wrong, not primarily because it treats gold as a commodity, but because it treats gold as a domestic commodity rather than an internationally traded commodity. Like many another internationally traded commodity, the domestic stock of gold was small relative to the world stock. Hence, as for such other commodities, changes in domestic demand and supply had a negligible effect on its value in terms of internationally traded goods. This value depended on world demand and supply, and world demand was mostly for monetary use.

---

work is by far the most important part—to regard the financing of the Civil War as a disgracefully inflationary episode reflects the implicit application of standards of monetary rectitude that, to the modern student, seem almost utopian in light of the monetary vagaries of the past half-century. See Friedman, "Prices, Income and Monetary Changes in Three Wartime Periods," *American Economic Review,* May 1952, pp. 623–625.

The most persuasive argument against the use of inflationary finance that we have encountered is in Newcomb, *Financial Policy during the Southern Rebellion.* Newcomb explicitly recognized the distinction between borrowing at a zero rate of interest through currency issue—to the extent that it displaced gold and did not raise prices or force suspension—and imposing a tax through a still larger issue. He estimated the amount that could have been borrowed at a zero rate through currency issue at about $250 million (p. 161). Implicitly approving of such an issue and explicitly deploring issues beyond that amount, he argued that it would promote the war effort and raise fewer problems for the future to finance the remaining war expenses by explicit taxation and by borrowing at whatever interest rate was necessary to avoid suspension. Given the probably greater flexibility of wages and prices at that time than in World Wars I and II, Newcomb's conclusions may well have been correct for the Civil War, even if they would not be for the later wars.

[65] Here and throughout the rest of the book we use the terms demand and supply to refer to schedules expressing the quantity demanded or supplied as a function of price—in this case, of the exchange rate—and not to the quantities demanded and supplied.

Further, since the British maintained the gold standard, changes in domestic demand for or supply of gold had no effect at all on its price in terms of sterling—except within the narrow limits set by the British official buying and selling prices of gold. They affected the greenback price of gold *only* insofar as they affected the pound-dollar exchange rate. In this respect, such changes were strictly on a par with changes in the supply of any other export or in the demand for any other import. They had special significance because, and only because, gold was a U.S. export. An increase in the quantity of U.S. wheat exported, for example, had exactly the same effect on the greenback price of gold as an increase in the quantity of U.S. gold exported of equal value in pounds sterling. The only feature not shared by other internationally traded goods was that gold was one form in which it was convenient to hold foreign exchange. In consequence, a change in the demand for or supply of foreign exchange for capital or speculative purposes often took the form of an offer to buy or sell gold. In these cases, gold was the medium through which speculative forces affecting international capital movements expressed themselves.

THE PREMIUM AND PURCHASING-POWER PARITY

The demand for and supply of foreign exchange, which determined the exchange rate, reflected the U.S. demand for goods and services from abroad, the supply of goods and services in the United States for export, the demand abroad for U.S. goods and services, the supply abroad of goods and services for export to the United States, the desire of foreigners to transfer capital or make unilateral transfers to the United States, and of U.S. residents to transfer capital or make unilateral transfers abroad. Each of these in its turn was critically dependent on the relative level of internal prices at home and abroad. A doubling of the internal price level in the United States, for example, with no change in internal prices within Britain would make U.S. goods twice as expensive in Britain at any given exchange rate and so reduce the amount the British would desire to import from the United States. It would make British goods half as expensive in the U.S. relative to domestic goods and so increase the amount the U.S. desired to import from Britain. It would mean that a given number of dollars transferred by immigrants, for example, to their families abroad would constitute only half as large a fraction of the immigrants' wages and so would tend to increase the amount sent. Conversely, it would mean that a given number of pounds sterling intended for capital investment in the United States would buy only half as much physical capital while still commanding an unchanged amount at home and so would discourage capital investment in the U.S. And so on, for other items in the balance of payments. A simul-

61

taneous doubling of the greenback price of sterling would exactly offset these effects and leave the real amounts demanded and supplied unchanged. Other things being the same, the exchange rate would tend to vary with relative internal prices—this is the famous purchasing-power parity theory of exchange rates. Of course, other things were not the same during the greenback period and, as we shall see, they produced significant deviations from the changes in exchange rates that would have been strictly in accord with changes in purchasing-power parity. However, as in most periods of widely varying prices, the relative movement of internal price levels in the United States and in gold-standard countries was, far and away, the most important factor affecting exchange rates with the currencies of such countries and hence the premium on gold.[66]

[66] The price indexes that would be optimum for computation of purchasing-power parity would presumably be indexes of the prices of the factors of production employed in each country. These seem preferable to indexes of product prices because their use implicitly classifies differential changes in productivity as a "real" rather than a "monetary" factor affecting exchange rates, as seems appropriate. Needless to say, satisfactory factor price indexes are not available for the period in question and are generally far less readily available and less comprehensive than product price indexes. Hence most students of purchasing-power parity and exchange rates have been led to use product price indexes.

Since internationally traded goods have a single world price, the ratio of their prices in domestic currencies must, shipping costs aside, move with exchange rates simply as a matter of arithmetic. This does not mean that they should be excluded from the relevant price index, as can be seen by considering the simplified textbook case of two countries each producing only a single product, part of which it exports to the other. All products are then international, and there are no strictly domestic products (though there are of course domestic factors), so exclusion of international products would make any comparisons impossible. As this example suggests, for each country, products exported should be included in the price index as reflecting the movement of domestic factor prices, but products imported should not be; and the weights for products exported by each country are volume of domestic production as a proxy for volume of resources employed, which means of course that "products exported" should not include "re-exports" but only domestic "value added."

In practice, the chief problems raised by internationally traded goods are, first, that indexes include exported and imported goods indiscriminately; second, that, for a period like the greenback period when data are scanty, the available indexes tend to be dominated by raw materials with a broad market, and these in turn are mostly internationally traded goods, so that internationally traded goods are heavily overweighted in the available indexes. Because of these defects and the difficulty of overcoming them satisfactorily, indexes of domestic goods only might be preferable to the actually available indexes, even though not preferable to an optimum index. Rough indexes of this kind could be constructed by pulling out of existing indexes those items that are predominantly domestic. However, the probable return seems unlikely to justify the great amount of labor involved. For the United States, in any event, it seems clear from work already done that domestic prices moved roughly in harmony with the prices of internationally traded goods. See analyses of Frank D. Graham ("International Trade Under Depreciated Paper. The United States, 1862–79," *Quarterly Journal of Economics*, Feb. 1922, pp. 253–254) and James K. Kindahl ("Economic Factors in Specie Resumption: The United States, 1865–79," *Journal of Political Economy*, Feb. 1961, pp. 34–35), based on data collected by Mitchell (*Gold*

In order to see how much of the movement in the greenback price of gold can be accounted for by movements in relative price levels, we have approximated purchasing-power parity by the ratio of the Warren-Pearson wholesale price index for the United States to the Sauerbeck wholesale price index for Great Britain. The ratio was adjusted so that the average value of the resulting purchasing-power parities for the period 1861 through 1879 would equal the average value of the actual price of gold in terms of greenbacks for the same period.[67] The resulting pur-

---

Prices, and Wages, pp. 256 ff.). For Britain, which we have taken to represent the gold-standard world, the situation is rather different because of the weight attached in most indexes to imported articles. Cotton, for example, rose sharply in price relative to other goods during the Civil War, because the supply from the South, a major producer, was cut off. For Britain, cotton was wholly imported and should be excluded. However, for Britain regarded as representative of the rest of the world, cotton should be included with a weight equal to the amounts produced outside of the U.S. (see note 67, below).

As is clear from the preceding, the price indexes that are relevant for the present purpose are very different from those relevant for such other purposes as comparisons of international standards of living. For that purpose, items should be weighted according to consumption, not production, and it may be desirable to use identical baskets of goods, with the usual index-number problem that alternative baskets or consumption patterns in different countries will give different results. For the present purpose, the use of identical goods has nothing to recommend it, as is clear from the simplified textbook example of the second preceding paragraph. There is the usual index-number problem, but it is connected with the particular year or years from which the weights are derived for each country separately, not with the difference between the weights for different countries.

[67] The Warren-Pearson index is available monthly and so is the greenback price of gold. The Sauerbeck index, which is perhaps the best known and most widely used index for Britain for that period, is annual (Augustus Sauerbeck, "Prices of Commodities and the Precious Metals," *Journal of the Royal Statistical Society*, Sept. 1886, p. 648). It would be highly desirable to have data for more frequent intervals to permit a more sensitive comparison between the actual and the purchasing-power parity price of gold. Hence, we considered the possibility of using the *Economist* price index, which is available on June and December dates (*Economist*, London, Aug. 26, 1911, pp. 421–425; Feb. 4, 1911, pp. 206–207). Neither index comes close to the optimum outlined in the preceding note, since both are weighted arbitrarily (being simple averages of relative prices, the base being 1867–77 for Sauerbeck and 1845–50 for the *Economist*), and over half their weight is given to imported goods. However, the *Economist* index gives much greater relative weight than the Sauerbeck index does to cotton and tobacco: 5 out of 22 commodities reflect the prices of these items directly or indirectly (India raw cotton, cotton wool, cotton yarn, cotton cloth, and tobacco) and these five items accounted for 42 per cent of the aggregate of the relatives in Dec. 1863. Two out of 45 items in the Sauerbeck index are cotton (tobacco is not included). Whereas some weight should be given to cotton and tobacco for the non-U.S. world as a whole, the weight given them by the *Economist* index seems so clearly excessive that we decided to use the Sauerbeck index despite its availability only annually during the greenback period.

The two indexes behave very differently during the Civil War period. The Sauerbeck index reaches a peak in 1864, some 7 per cent above its value in 1861. A comparable average for 1864 computed from the *Economist* index (a weighted average of the values for Dec. 1863, June 1864, and Dec. 1864 with

chasing-power parity price of gold is plotted along with the actual price of gold in the lower part of Chart 5, and the ratio of the actual price to the hypothetical price in the upper part.[68]

We use Britain as the basis of comparison primarily because of its importance in U.S. trade, and partly also because it was the only major country that was on gold throughout the period. For the years 1861–78, over one-third of U.S. imports came from Britain and over one-half of U.S. exports went to Britain.[69] The area under the gold standard widened notably during the greenback period: Germany adopted gold in 1871–73; the Latin Monetary Union (France, Italy, Belgium, Switzerland), in 1873–74; the Scandinavian Union (Denmark, Norway, and Sweden) and the Netherlands, in 1875–76; and this list is not exhaustive, though it does include the major changes.[70]

It is clear from Chart 5 that movements in relative price levels account for the greater part of the movement in the price of gold. Whereas the price of gold varies over a range of more than 2 to 1, the ratio of the actual to the hypothetical price varies over a range of only 1.3 to 1. To some extent, this residual variation may reflect the crudeness of our calculation of purchasing-power parity. It seems most unlikely, however, that it can be wholly accounted for by such statistical errors.[71]

---

weights ¼, ½, and ¼) is 38 per cent above a corresponding average for 1861. To judge from some tentative calculations, most but not all of the difference is attributable to the greater weight attached to cotton and tobacco in the *Economist* index.

In a continuation of purchasing-power parity computations for subsequent periods presented in the next and later chapters, we use the ratio of the price index for the U.S. implicit in the conversion of national income at current prices to national income at constant prices, to a general price index for Britain instead of the ratio of wholesale price indexes. The U.S. implicit price index and the British general price index are much broader in scope and give more nearly the appropriate weight to domestic relative to international goods, which is why we prefer them. Unfortunately, such indexes are not available for the Civil War period.

[68] Because the sum of the denominators of the ratios in the upper part of Chart 5 was adjusted so as to equal the sum of the numerators, the ratios themselves average out to a figure that is close to unity. This is the only meaning of the base line of 100 in the upper part of the chart.

[69] *Historical Statistics*, 1960, Series U-134, U-142, U-116, U-124.

[70] In some of these countries, notably the Latin Union, silver as well as gold remained legally a monetary metal but the amount of silver that was coined was limited, hence the standard was in effect a gold standard.

[71] If the *Economist* index is used and a similar calculation made for semi-annual dates, the range of the price of gold is 2.3 to 1, of the ratio of the actual to the hypothetical price, 1.8 to 1, so that by this computation movements in relative price levels account for a much smaller share of the movement in the price of gold than according to the computation in the text. The difference is attributable mainly to the greater weight attached to cotton and tobacco by the *Economist* index and reflects mostly, therefore, the defects of that index for our purpose. For example, for the period 1866 to 1879, when the wartime effects on the relative price of cotton and tobacco are no longer important, the

CHART 5
Actual and Hypothetical Purchasing-Power Parity Price of Gold in Greenbacks, 1861–79

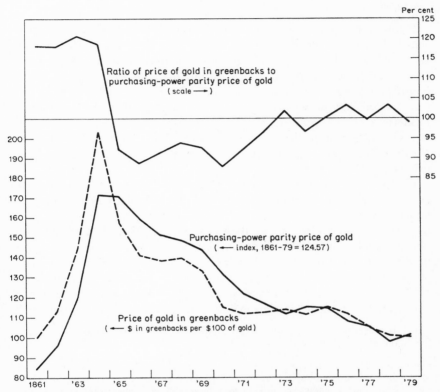

SOURCE: Price of gold in greenbacks, Mitchell, *Gold, Prices, and Wages,* p. 4.
Purchasing-power parity price of gold, U.S. wholesale price index, in greenbacks, for all commodities (from *Historical Statistics,* 1949, p. 232, Series L-2), was divided by Sauerbeck's index of wholesale commodity prices in Great Britain (from Sauerbeck, "Prices of Commodities," p. 648). The quotient was converted to the base 1861–79 = 100 and multiplied by 124.57, the average price of gold in greenbacks in the period.

DISCREPANCIES BETWEEN ACTUAL AND HYPOTHETICAL PURCHASING-POWER PARITY PRICE OF GOLD

There are two major discrepancies between the actual and the hypothetical purchasing-power parity price of gold: the relatively high

range of the price of gold is 1.41 to 1 based on annual averages, and 1.45 to 1 based on June and Dec. dates; the range of the ratio of the actual to the hypothetical price is 1.17 to 1 based on the Sauerbeck annual figures, and 1.20 to 1 based on the *Economist* index, so that the two computations attribute roughly the same share of the movement in the price of gold to changes in purchasing-power parity.

actual price of gold during the Civil War itself, and the relatively low actual price of gold from then through 1871. Both are readily accounted for.

1861–64

Before the Civil War, cotton was the United States' major export commodity and it alone accounted for something like one-half the total value of merchandise exports. The typical pattern of trade was that the North had a deficit abroad and a surplus in trade with the South, the South had a surplus abroad and a deficit in trade with the North. The war cut off almost wholly the foreign exchange that the North had formerly received indirectly from cotton exports without curtailing to any similar extent its demand for imports. The war therefore left the North with an exchange deficit at the former exchange rate and relative price levels.[72]

Under a gold standard and stable foreign prices, the result would have been internal deflation produced by an outflow of gold. Under the actual fiduciary standard, the result was a greater rise in the price of gold (i.e., the price of foreign exchange) than in domestic prices. Indeed, it seems remarkable that so sizable a decline in the supply of goods for export produced a rise of only about 20 per cent at most in the ratio of the price of gold to its purchasing-power parity, especially when political attitudes of the ruling groups in England were on the whole unfavorable to the North and so inhibited foreign loans.[73] Part of the explanation may well

[72] It is tempting to add: even if no allowance is made for increased demand for imports arising from the war. However, it is by no means clear that this addendum is justified, and it would take much more detailed analysis than is appropriate for our purposes to determine whether it is. The government *instead of* private individuals used real resources. It acquired them by taxation, including the tax on money balances implicit in inflationary currency issue, and by borrowing. The effect on the foreign trade situation depends on whether the government or the individuals who released the resources had a larger or smaller demand for imports per unit of total resources employed. The answer is by no means obvious.

[73] From fiscal 1860 to fiscal 1865, exports of U.S. merchandise valued in prewar gold dollars fell $179 million, or from $316 million to $137 million. Exports of crude materials alone, reflecting mostly cotton, fell by $183 million, or from $217 million to $34 million (*Historical Statistics*, 1960, Series U-10, U-62, and U-75). We use fiscal 1860 rather than fiscal 1861, because the recorded figures for the latter already show a substantially reduced level of exports, owing to the omission of returns on cotton exports from Southern ports (*Annual Report* of the Secretary of Treasury, 1864, p. 246; *Statistics of the Foreign and Domestic Commerce of the United States*, Treasury Dept., 1864, p. 40). Our basis for describing these figures as in prewar gold dollars is a comparison with *Monthly Summary of Commerce and Finance of the United States*, Treasury Dept., Apr. 1903, pp. 3315–3316 (cited in *Historical Statistics*, 1960, p. 533).

Matthew Simon's failure to recognize the faulty character of the merchandise export figures for 1861 results in a residual figure for net capital imports of $104.4 million in that year, according to his calculations ("The United States Balance of Payments, 1861–1900," *Trends in the American Economy in the*

be that we underestimate the extent of the depreciation because of defects in the price indexes.[74] But correction for even a substantial understatement would not change the general tenor of the results.

One possible explanation for a relatively small exchange depreciation is that suspension reduced domestic monetary demand for gold and so added to the supply of goods for export, offsetting to some extent the loss of cotton. However, the recorded figures do not support this explanation. They show no sustained rise in gold exports over prewar levels.[75] Apparently, the small depreciation reflected, rather, a combination of highly elastic demands for and supplies of commodity imports and exports and an elastic supply of capital.

The role played by capital movements is particularly interesting, because of the light it throws on both the behavior of interest rates during the war and the character of speculative capital movements under floating exchange rates. A capital inflow might have been induced in either of two ways: first, by high interest rates in the United States; second, by an expectation that the price of gold in terms of greenbacks, which is to say, the price of foreign exchange, would fall, thereby making it profitable for foreigners to hold greenback funds.

It is clear from Chart 6 that interest rates could hardly have been an

---

Nineteenth Century, Studies in Income and Wealth, Vol. 24, Princeton for NBER, 1960, pp. 699–700). This is an unlikely result. The largest capital import in the preceding forty years, according to Douglass C. North, was $62.2 million in fiscal 1836 ("The United States Balance of Payments, 1790–1860," p. 621). Is it likely that, in the year the war broke out between the North and the South, foreigners would have sent more than $100 million here?

See also R. A. Kessel and A. A. Alchian, "Real Wages in the North during the Civil War: Mitchell's Data Reinterpreted," *Journal of Law and Economics,* Oct. 1959, pp. 95–113.

[74] The alternative calculation using the *Economist* index gives both a different magnitude and a different time pattern of depreciation. The depreciation increases markedly from 1861 to June 1864, reaching a peak of 55 per cent, then falls sharply. The greater magnitude seems not implausible as implied by the text, but the different pattern seems most implausible except as a reflection of the overweighting of cotton and tobacco. It is hard to see why the "true" depreciation should have increased sharply over the period, especially in late 1863 and early 1864, when apparently there was an increased inflow of capital. The implausibility of this pattern was a major factor in our rejecting the *Economist* calculation in favor of the Sauerbeck.

As to magnitude, the truth is probably between the two estimates, though also probably closer to that given by the Sauerbeck index.

[75] *Historical Statistics,* 1960, Series U-6, shows a total of net gold exports of $256 million in the five fiscal years from 1856 through 1860, of $205 million in the next five. There is an increase in the course of these last five years from a net import in 1861 to a level of exports in the final three years slightly above the average of the five prewar years. The difference even then is not large. The figures before 1864 include domestic exports of silver as well as of gold; thereafter only of gold. However, to judge from the small increase in recorded silver exports that results from this reclassification (*ibid.,* Series U-7), the exclusion of domestic exports of silver from our figures before 1864 would hardly affect the above calculation.

CHART 6

Bond Yields in Gold and Greenbacks, and Price of Gold in Greenbacks, Monthly, 1861–78

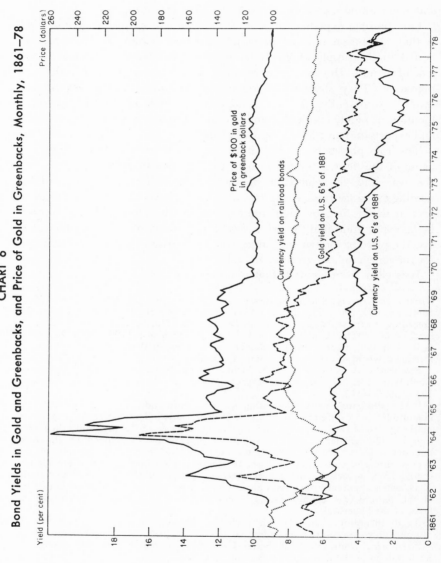

See opposite page for notes.

68

attracting force during the Civil War. On the contrary, yields on rail-road bonds fell from the end of 1861 to early 1863, and were decidedly lower throughout 1863 and 1864 than either before or after the Civil War. Call loan rates (not shown on this chart) show a slight rise in 1863 and 1864, but even so these rates were not at an unprecedentedly high level. Government bond yields are more difficult to describe because of the ambiguity about whether to regard the bonds as gold bonds, as they ultimately turned out to be, or as bonds whose principal at least and perhaps interest coupon as well would be paid in greenbacks, as was widely anticipated at the time. We shall return to them subsequently. For the moment, it will suffice to note that if regarded as greenback bonds, their yields, too, were relatively low.

The relevant consideration for capital movements is not the absolute level of interest rates in the United States but the difference between U.S. rates and foreign interest rates. However, examination of British rates does not alter the picture just drawn. Long-term rates in London were stable or, if anything, rising over the period; they certainly show no decided fall such as would have been required to make the American capital market more attractive relative to the London market than it had been earlier.[76]

The behavior of interest rates in the United States is one of the most

[76] Cf. the monthly prices of consols (*Statistical Abstract of the United Kingdom, 1852–1866, Parliamentary Papers*, 1867, Vol. LXXI, p. 113). The monthly average discount rate charged by the Bank of England fell from 8.0 per cent in early 1861 to 2 per cent in mid-1862 and then rose to a peak of 9 per cent in the fall of 1864. The ease in the London money market in the summer of 1862 was attributed to the gold inflow from the U.S. produced by the liquidation of American securities by British holders (*Economist*, July 26, 1862, cited by Simon, "Cyclical Fluctuations and the International Capital Movements of the United States, 1865–1897," unpublished Ph.D. dissertation, Columbia University, 1955, p. 82), and the pattern of Bank of England rates is indeed consistent with a capital inflow from the U.S. from 1861 until late 1862. The pattern is also consistent with a capital outflow from the U.S. from late 1862 to 1864, but, in fact, there was no capital outflow from Britain to the U.S. during that period. The Dutch and Germans bought American securities, 1863–64; the British did not until later, when Union victory was assured.

Notes to Chart 6.
SOURCE: Price of gold in greenbacks, same as for Chart 5.
Currency yield on railroad bonds, F. R. Macaulay, *The Movements of Interest Rates, Bond Yields, and Stock Prices in the United States since 1856*, New York, NBER, 1938, pp. A143–A147; all bonds in the index in those years were currency bonds.
Currency yield on U.S. bonds of 1881, from quarterly yield tables, using averages of monthly high and low prices in *Annual Report* of the Comptroller of the Currency, 1902, pp. 129–131. June 1, 1881, maturity was used through July 1861, June 30 thereafter, maturity date for bulk of issue authorized at that time.
Gold yield on U.S. bonds of 1881, same, except that the monthly average price of the bond was divided by the monthly average price of gold in greenbacks. A nomograph was used instead of yield tables for part of the period.

interesting features of the Civil War period and has puzzled most of its historians.[77] A priori, one might expect the rapid rise in prices during the Civil War—a more than doubling of prices within less than four years—to have produced, after some lag, a substantial rise in money interest rates as lenders sought to protect themselves against inflation, and as borrowers were willing to pay higher rates in the expectation of further inflation. In addition, the government was acquiring a large fraction of the nation's resources for war purposes and was financing the great bulk of the corresponding expenditures by borrowing rather than by either explicit taxation or the taxation implicit in money creation. The resulting demand for loan funds must surely have been larger than any private demand that was suppressed by the diversion of resources to war use. Surely, the combination of these forces might have been expected to produce a substantial rise in interest rates. Yet interest rates were unusually low.

Far from explaining the capital movements, the level of interest rates is, in our view, itself explained by speculative capital movements induced by the rise in the greenback price of gold, i.e., the depreciation in the foreign exchange value of the dollar. Such a depreciation can have very different effects according to the expectations about future exchange rates that it generates. If an initial rise in the greenback price of gold had produced expectations of further rises, the result would have been to establish an incentive to convert greenbacks into gold or foreign exchange in order to benefit from the subsequently higher price. On the other hand, if a rise in the greenback price of gold produced an expectation of a return to an earlier level, if the emphasis was on the fact that the price was high rather than that it was rising, the result would be to establish an incentive to convert gold or foreign exchange into greenback funds in order to benefit from the subsequently lower price of gold. It seems likely that the latter kind of expectation was generated and hence that the rise in the greenback price of gold produced speculative capital inflows, which helped to finance a deficit in the balance of trade and which explain why the depreciation in the exchange value of the dollar, over and beyond that to be expected from purchasing-power parity, was so mild—given the drastic change in the North's international trade position. Such capital inflows would also have constituted a demand for U.S. securities, which explains why interest rates were so low despite the rise in commodity prices and the extensive government borrowing.

[77] Mitchell, *A History of the Greenbacks,* pp. 360–379; and Irving Fisher, "Appreciation and Interest," *Publications of the American Economic Association,* Vol. XI, No. 4, Aug. 1896, pp. 38–45. Mitchell offers a series of possible explanations, but it is clear that he himself is extremely skeptical that they are at all satisfactory, as in fact they are not.

A strong piece of indirect evidence favoring this interpretation is the movement of the yield on railroad bonds. A foreigner who expected the greenback price of gold to be lower at a later date had an incentive to convert assets which were fixed in terms of gold-standard currencies into assets fixed in greenbacks. He could have done so by selling his assets for foreign currencies, using the foreign currencies to buy gold in, say, New York, and the gold to buy greenbacks. But there was no necessity for him to keep the proceeds in cash or as deposits in commercial banks. It was more profitable to acquire assets such as railroad bonds which paid a much higher rate of interest than he could earn on bank deposits. He could then sell these and use the proceeds to repurchase gold or foreign exchange when and if his expectations were realized and the price of gold fell.[78] An inflow of speculative capital induced by an expectation of a subsequent fall in the price of gold, therefore, constituted a demand for U.S. securities and tended to raise their prices and depress their yields; an outflow of speculative capital had the opposite effects. Insofar as expectations about the future price of gold were linked to the *level* rather than the *direction of change* of the price of gold, this factor would tend to produce an inverse relation between the greenback price of gold and the yield on, say, railroad bonds. As Chart 6 shows, this is precisely the relationship that prevailed throughout the war, and, to a much lesser extent, some years thereafter. The greenback price of gold reached its peak in July 1864 and the yield on railroad bonds, its trough in the same month; and the lesser ups and downs in the greenback price of gold left an equally clear impress on the yield of railroad bonds. Moreover, this interpretation is also consistent with the different behavior of short- and long-term interest rates from mid-1862 to mid-1864, the period of the rise in the greenback price of gold. Call money and commercial paper rates were rising during that period, as might have been expected from the concurrent inflation and the large government borrowing. At the same time, yields on railroad bonds and currency yields on government bonds were falling, which would be understandable if they were the means used for investing speculative funds, but hardly otherwise.

[78] At the time, private securities were entirely "paper" rather than "gold" securities, i.e., both interest and principal were payable in legal tender and did not contain what came to be known as "gold clauses." The introduction of gold clauses was a consequence of the greenback experience. In Macaulay's list of 150 railroad bonds, 32 issued before 1865 were all payable in currency. The first one payable in gold was issued in 1865, but until after resumption, payment in gold was the exception. Of 24 issued in 1865–78, only 6 were payable in gold. Gold clauses then became the rule. Of 22 bonds issued in 1879–86, 14 were payable in gold; and all but 2 of the remaining 72 bonds issued thereafter were (F. R. Macaulay, *Movements of Interest Rates, Bond Yields, and Stock Prices*, pp. A5-A16).

As already noted, U.S. government bonds raise a special problem. As we have seen, both interest and principal were in fact paid in gold. If this outcome had been completely anticipated at the time, the greenback prices of government bonds should have fully reflected the premium on gold. For example, consider the 6 per cent U.S. coupon bonds of 1881.[79] Suppose the market is pricing comparable greenback bonds to yield 6 per cent, i.e., a $100 bond with a 6 per cent coupon is priced at $100 in greenbacks. Then an equivalent price for the government bond would be $100 in gold since this would mean a yield of $6 in gold. The greenback price of the government bond would then be 100 times the greenback price of gold. If, for example, the price of gold in greenbacks is $1.50, then the price of the government bond would be $150 in greenbacks. This bond would yield $6 in gold, worth $9 in greenbacks; hence its current yield would be 6 per cent whether calculated in gold or greenbacks.[80] Under these circumstances, government bonds would have been useless as a means of speculating on a future fall in the price of gold. Holding government bonds would have been equivalent to holding gold, not to holding greenbacks.

If the actual situation had conformed to that described, the market gold yield on government bonds (i.e., the yield calculated by expressing interest, the final principal payment, and the current market price all in gold) would have roughly approximated the market greenback yield on comparable securities with interest and principal payable in greenbacks.[81] But, in fact, the gold yield deviated widely from greenback yields. At the peak of the premium on gold, when railroad bonds were yielding less than 6 per cent, the gold yield on the 6 per cent government bonds of 1881 exceeded 16 per cent. Throughout the period from 1862 to about 1866 or 1867 the gold yield fluctuated in strict accordance with the premium on gold whereas, under the conditions of the preceding paragraph, it would have been entirely independent of the premium. It

---

[79] Continuous quotations on this bond are available throughout the greenback period. The 5's of 1862 (date of issue) were the bonds foreigners particularly favored, but were not quoted continuously.

[80] There is a subtle problem here in calculating yield to maturity in greenbacks, since it depends on what happens to the greenback price of gold at the dates when interest payments are made and the principal repaid. The yield is 6 per cent only if the price of gold remains unchanged.

This consideration means that the statement in the text about the greenback price of the gold bond, while literally correct, is incomplete. Arbitrage would, of course, assure that the price of the gold bond in greenbacks would equal its gold price times the price of gold. But the gold bond and the currency bond might not sell for "equivalent" yields. Holding currency bonds is a way to speculate on a future fall in the price of gold; holding gold bonds, on a future rise. If the market, on the average, expects a fall, it will price currency bonds at a lower currency yield than the gold yield at which it will price gold bonds, and conversely.

[81] "Roughly," because of the considerations in the preceding footnote.

72

tended to become increasingly independent of the premium after 1867, as expectations that payments would be in gold grew stronger (see Chart 6).

The explanation, of course, is that during the war and for some time thereafter there was little confidence that the government would in fact pay principal and interest in gold.[82] The bonds were being treated as if they were predominantly paper bonds. There is no easy way to compute the market yield under those expectations. Since current interest coupons were being paid in gold, investors must surely have had different expectations for coupon payments in the near future and for coupon and principal payments in the distant future. The extreme is to suppose that, at the time of purchase, investors expected the very next coupon and all future coupons and principal payments to be in greenbacks, i.e., that they treated the bond as a greenback security. The yield calculated on this assumption must have been below the yield expected by purchasers when they bought the securities. Yet Chart 6 shows that the yield so calculated was only slightly below the yield on railroad greenback bonds in 1863–64. The actual situation in these years must therefore have been very close indeed to the extreme. But this means that government bonds were as good a vehicle for speculating in gold as were securities that were explicitly greenback obligations.

The fall in the price of gold in 1864–65 narrowed the difference between the gold and currency yields on government bonds. The accompanying shift in expectations about the payment of government bonds in gold is reflected in the relation of those two yields to the currency yield on railroad bonds. As we have seen, until late 1864, the currency yield on government bonds was only slightly lower than the currency yield on railroad bonds. After 1864, as expectations shifted, the yield on railroad bonds rose markedly above the currency yield on government bonds and settled at a level only slightly below the gold yields on government bonds. As Republican victory became certain in 1868, on a platform that

[82] Note that this is not inconsistent with an expectation on the part of foreign or domestic speculators that the greenback price of gold would fall, for these reasons: (1) a fall could occur without taking the price back to prewar par; (2) even if it took it back to par, that might occur after the repayment of the bond, and even if it occurred before, the coupon payments in the interim might be in greenbacks; (3) the purchasers of government securities were a much more mixed and broader group than the speculators in foreign exchange were, so we are dealing with the expectations of two very different groups.

See Newcomb for a parallel analysis (*Financial Policy during the Southern Rebellion*, pp. 108–111). For each month from Mar. 1862 through Dec. 1864 he shows the price of gold in greenbacks, the gold value of $100 in greenbacks, and the gold value of $100 of par value of 20-year 6 per cent government bonds. He interprets the low value of the bonds as reflecting a lack of confidence in their repayment in gold, citing the "much higher price commanded by Massachusetts bonds of similar character" as conclusive evidence for his interpretation.

CHART 7
U.S. Net International Capital Movement and Purchasing-Power Parity, 1861–79

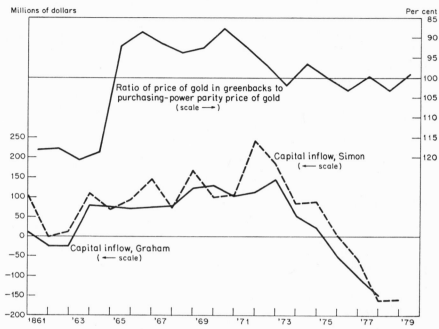

NOTE: Capital movement is in gold values. Capital inflow is plotted as plus.
SOURCE: Ratio, same as for Chart 5. Capital movement, Graham, "International Trade," p. 231; Simon, "The United States Balance of Payments, 1861–1900," Table 27, line 30.

promised repayment of bonds in specie, the gold yield on government bonds dropped sharply relative to the currency yield on railroad bonds, the two coming together just about election time. After the turn of the year, and more especially after the act of March 18, 1869, pledging repayment in specie, gold yields on government bonds fell increasingly below currency yields on railroad bonds. After about 1867, the currency yield on government bonds began to move inversely to the premium on gold, just as the gold yields had earlier moved in the same direction.

The indirect evidence from bond yields is largely supported by such direct evidence as exists on capital inflows. The evidence based on capital movements for fiscal 1863 is mixed. Though the dollar depreciated and interest rates fell during most of the year, estimates of capital flows by Frank Graham show a capital outflow that persisted from the preceding year. (See Chart 7, which gives two estimates of U.S. net international capital inflows or outflows and also the ratio of the actual price of gold

74

to the purchasing-power parity price. This ratio is plotted invertedly—compare Chart 5—to make its expected movements in the same direction as that of capital inflows, for easier reading of the chart.) Later estimates by Matthew Simon, however, show a small capital inflow in fiscal 1863, which is consistent with our interpretation of the premium on gold and of interest rate movements. Simon's estimate, moreover, is supported by direct evidence that, as early as February 1863, Dutch bankers began small-scale purchases of Union securities. Both estimates of capital movements agree that there was a substantial increase in capital inflows from the year ending June 30, 1863, to the year ending June 30, 1864. Since fiscal 1864 corresponded with the greatest depreciation of the dollar, that increase in capital inflows is consistent with our interpretation. Dutch and German investors were heavy net purchasers in that year of U.S. government bonds and to a lesser extent of railroad bonds payable in greenbacks.[83] The victories of Grant, Sherman, and Sheridan in late 1864, which seemed to herald a swift end of the war and the complete defeat of the Confederacy, must have greatly stimulated the willingness of these and other investors to acquire greenback assets despite the rapid rise in the premium on gold in 1864, which otherwise might well have produced expectations of still further rises. Simon reports that these events were particularly important in restoring the attractiveness of the Union as an outlet for investment to English investors, who had been antagonistic to the North during the conflict. These capital inflows provided the North with needed foreign exchange, long before victory and reconstruction again made available the proceeds from cotton.

If this analysis is correct, the depreciation of the exchange rate manifested in the rise in the greenback price of gold contributed to resolving the North's balance of payment difficulties in two very different ways: by affecting the "real" terms of trade and so fostering exports and discouraging imports; by stimulating a speculative inflow of capital, which limited the depreciation, holding it to only some 20 per cent in excess of that required to compensate for internal price level changes, and kept the terms of trade from turning even more strongly against the North.

It is interesting to note that a very similar sequence of events accompanied the early stages of German inflation after World War I.[84] As the mark depreciated, foreigners at first were persuaded that it would subsequently appreciate and so bought a large volume of mark assets, which helped to keep the mark at a higher value in terms of foreign currency

[83] Simon, "Cyclical Fluctuations," pp. 83–84, 87, 110.
[84] See Graham, *Exchange, Prices, and Production in Hyper-inflation: Germany, 1920–23*, Princeton University Press, 1931, pp. 49–56; Cagan, "The Monetary Dynamics of Hyperinflation," *Studies in the Quantity Theory of Money*, Milton Friedman, ed., University of Chicago Press, 1956, p. 91.

than purchasing-power parity would have dictated. The capital inflow provided a substantial volume of resources to Germany. As the German inflation went on, expectations were reversed, the inflow of capital was replaced by an outflow, and the mark depreciated more rapidly than purchasing-power parity would have dictated. The difference, of course, is that, in the Civil War, the speculators were ultimately correct and their speculation in retrospect was "stabilizing"; in Germany, they were ultimately wrong and so their speculation was "destabilizing." But this is a retrospective judgment. As of, say, late 1864 in the one case and late 1922 in the other, it would have been far more difficult to predict that the outcomes would prove so different.

1865–71

Capital continued to flow in after the war ended, capital seeking permanent investment presumably replacing in part the speculative capital that had been attracted by the high premium on gold. In addition, the end of the war meant an improvement in the supply of exports relative to imports, as the South was once again integrated into the Union economically. The result was a sharp shift in the price of gold relative to purchasing-power parity from a level some 20 per cent above purchasing-power parity to a level some 10 per cent below. This appreciation of some 30 per cent in the exchange value of the greenback dollar is a measure of the pressure that the wartime disturbance of trade relations had imposed on the balance of payments.

The price of gold remained some 10 per cent below the hypothetical purchasing-power parity in 1865–71, producing the second major discrepancy noted above, and then rose relative to purchasing-power parity until 1873, after which it fluctuated around the purchasing-power parity. As Graham has documented in an excellent analysis of the movement of the premium from the end of the war to resumption,[85] the relatively low price of gold—which is to say, high value of the greenback dollar—from 1865 through 1871 can be attributed to the capital inflow from abroad. During that period foreign investors initially bought government bonds in preference to railroad securities, then about 1870 shifted to the latter.[86] The shift reflected the decreasing relative attractiveness of government bonds, which were bid up by banks because of the demand for them as collateral for national bank notes and government deposits, and which no longer were useful for holding funds in expectation of a fall in the greenback price of gold since they had become gold bonds in fact as well as in name. As Chart 6 shows, the currency yield on railroad bonds moved permanently above the gold yield on the government bond early

[85] Graham, "International Trade," pp. 242–244.
[86] Simon, "Cyclical Fluctuations," p. 150.

in 1869, and maintained a 2 percentage point gap from late 1870 on. The decline in European-held U.S. government debt that began at that time continued for a decade as a result of refunding operations of the government, and of a trans-Atlantic movement of those securities here for replacement by the more lucrative railroad bonds.[87]

The subsequent depreciation of the dollar from 1871 to 1873 is something of a puzzle, since both Graham's estimates and Simon's more recent ones in general show a high level of capital inflows up to 1873. A plausible explanation is that the depreciation resulted from a combination of a domestic boom, which raised the demand for imports sharply, and a poor cotton crop in 1871, which reduced the supply of exports.[88] Since these phenomena were temporary, they may have been met partly by depreciation and partly by a temporary accommodating short-term capital inflow. An influx of short-term foreign capital, extended in the form of call loans in the stock market and sterling loans in the New York money market, was in fact reported, beginning in the summer of 1872 and continuing through September 1873.[89]

The persistence of the lower value of the dollar after 1873, like the higher value from 1865 to 1871, is readily attributable to capital movements. Capital inflows declined drastically after 1873 and were soon replaced by net outflows, according to both sets of estimates. If the preceding explanation of the 1871–73 movements is correct, the decline reflected partly the necessity of repaying the temporary accommodating short-term capital advances of those years. The decline in capital inflows reflected also the widening financial difficulties of railroads and the default of some roads on their obligations. These contributed importantly to banking

[87] The repatriation of American government securities after 1870, of itself, would have raised no difficulties in the U.S. securities markets, if it had continued to be a transfer of funds from government to railroad and other bonds. In addition to the continuing demand for government securities by national banks, in 1876–78, those savings banks that did not succumb during the runs on them (particularly in Rhode Island, Massachusetts, Pennsylvania, and New York) shifted from mortgages to government bonds for greater safety; and former depositors who withdrew balances from those banks also bought government bonds (Simon, "Cyclical Fluctuations," p. 237). However, after 1873, the demand abroad for railroad bonds declined, so there was a net reduction in foreign demand for all U.S. securities.

[88] From fiscal 1871 to fiscal 1872, general imports rose by $107 million, or 21 per cent, and continued to rise moderately until 1873, thereafter falling sharply. From fiscal 1871 to fiscal 1872, total exports stayed almost exactly constant, whereas they had been rising, and exports of crude materials fell; in fiscal 1873, total exports rose by $78 million (see *Historical Statistics*, 1960, Series U-10, U-13, K-302, and U-62).

[89] Simon, "Cyclical Fluctuations," pp. 146–149. As Simon notes, this short-term capital movement may in part account for the fact that the difference between Graham's net long-term loans floated, estimated directly, and his own net total capital movements, estimated indirectly from balance of payment figures, reaches a peak in fiscal 1872.

failures that set off the financial panic of 1873.[90] In its turn, one consequence of the panic was to intensify the difficulties of the railroads.

If this period offers any problem of interpretation, it is why the dollar did not depreciate to a still lower level in view of the exceedingly adverse capital movement. One possible explanation, which, however, we have not tested, is that rapid agricultural and industrial growth during the Civil War and in the following decade had improved the competitive position of the United States in exports more than it had expanded its demand for imports, which is to say, had increased the demand for U.S. dollars by foreigners (to buy U.S. exports) more than it had increased the demand for foreign currency by U.S. residents (to buy imports). The effect of such a shift in comparative advantage would be to raise the value of U.S. currency in terms of foreign currencies at which trade would balance. To put this explanation in terms of Chart 7, it implies that the price of gold relative to purchasing-power parity that might be expected to prevail in the absence of capital movements would be declining over time, or in terms of the inverted scale of that chart, would be represented by a rising curve. Deviations from such a curve, rather than from the horizontal line in the chart, are then the appropriate magnitudes to compare with capital movements. For the last few years, at least, such deviations would clearly be more highly correlated with the capital movements than deviations from the horizontal line would be. Chart 9 in Chapter 3, showing the relation between relative prices and capital movements for a much longer period, supports this interpretation, since over the whole period the level of U.S. prices relative to foreign prices that is consistent with any given capital movement tends to rise.

THE STOCK OF GOLD

Just as for any other export commodity with a fixed world price whose domestic price therefore varies with the exchange rate, the relatively high price of gold in greenbacks during the Civil War might be expected to have encouraged its production, the relatively low price from 1865 to 1871 to have discouraged it, and the higher price thereafter to have encouraged it again. And this is roughly what happened, although with a sizable lag, due partly to conditions of production, partly to the isolation of California from the rest of the country. From a trough of 1.9 million ounces in 1862, output rose to a peak of 2.6 million ounces in 1866, then declined erratically to a trough of 1.6 million ounces in 1875, then rose sharply to a peak of 2.5 million ounces in 1878.

Net exports of gold followed a rather different pattern. From 1862 to 1876, they varied erratically from year to year around a level roughly that which had prevailed in the decade before the war, then de-

[90] See O. M. W. Sprague, *History of Crises*, pp. 35–38.

clined drastically in 1877 and became negative in 1878 and 1879. During the final years of the greenback period, therefore, production was increasing but exports decreasing.

The movements of gold exports resulted primarily from changes in the demand for gold for domestic purposes. The short-term year-to-year fluctuations from 1862 to 1876 must largely reflect short-term movements in foreign trade and, therefore, in short-term balances of foreign exchange or their equivalent. The shift that took place in 1877, on the other hand, undoubtedly reflects a change in the monetary situation. So long as resumption of payments was in the indefinite future, the main incentive to hold gold was either to speculate on its value or to acquire the equivalent of foreign exchange to pay for imports. As we pointed out in section 1 (the role of gold), the latter was undoubtedly the primary motive for holding gold.[91] The demonetization of gold must therefore have led to an initial reduction in the demand for it. The consequent export of existing stocks of gold allowed total exports of gold to remain relatively constant, despite the decline in production, and so prevented the decline in production from putting still further pressure on the greenback price of gold. Once resumption of specie payments was likely at a reasonably close date, gold became a more attractive way to hold domestic funds, and there was probably an increase in demand for it for this purpose on private account. In addition, as we shall see, the Treasury entered the market on a large scale after 1877 to accumulate gold. The combined effect of the increase in demand for gold on the part of the public and the Treasury was to reduce exports of gold drastically and to raise the greenback price of gold relative to purchasing-power parity.[92]

THE ECONOMICS OF RESUMPTION

One of the most interesting questions about the period is the relative importance of various factors in permitting the successful resumption of

[91] It should be noted, however, that the existence of a free market in foreign exchange eliminated one motive for holding gold that has been important in recent years, namely, as a way to get around foreign exchange controls.

[92] Graham states at one point, "During the period of heavy borrowing the net export of gold was large. This was to be expected, inasmuch as the borrowing tended to depress the premium on gold and thus to make it relatively cheap. Note that just the opposite trend would be expected under a gold regime" ("International Trade," p. 232).

This is clearly wrong: the lower premium on gold, by making it relatively cheap, would depress production, and so tend to reduce exports of gold, precisely as a relatively cheap price for gold would under a gold regime. If exports were nonetheless large, it was because the reduction in supply out of production was more than offset by an increase in supply out of stock and by a reduction in demand for domestic use, both of which reflected the demonetization of gold.

This is the one flaw we have noted in Graham's excellent analysis of the period, from which the above discussion has benefited greatly.

specie payments at the pre-Civil War parity in 1879. The earlier sections of this chapter provide the factual and analytical basis for an answer to this question. It is only necessary to select the relevant elements.

As we have seen, before the Civil War the exchange rate between the U.S. dollar and the British pound varied around $4.86 within a narrow interval determined by the costs of shipping gold. From 1862 on, the exchange rate was not so limited and did, of course, move far outside these limits. It was determined, as explained in the first pages of section 5, by the demand for and supply of foreign exchange, and there were no legal commitments on the part of the United States that prevented it from taking any value that was necessary to balance international payments. The essential requirement for a return to the prewar parity was that the exchange rate so determined be within the initial range determined by the gold points. An attempt to return to the prewar parity before the greenback price of the pound sterling had fallen to that level would have meant a "pound shortage" strictly comparable with the post-World War II "dollar shortage" associated with the maintenance by other countries of official exchange rates that overvalued their own currencies. And since exchange controls and the associated restrictions on imports and exports that contained the post-World War II dollar shortage had not yet been invented—or perhaps one should say perfected—in the greenback period, the "pound shortage" would have meant a loss of gold at a rate that would have forced renewed suspension.

The factors determining the exchange rate between the dollar and the pound sterling were numerous and complex. It is clear, however, from the discussion of the premium on gold in the first part of section 5, that the most important factor, once the Civil War was over, was the movement of internal prices in the United States relative to prices in gold-standard countries which we may represent by the most important among them, Great Britain. As a first approximation, therefore, the major requirement for resumption was that prices in the United States in greenbacks bear about the same relation to prices in Britain in pounds sterling as U.S. prices did before suspension, say, in 1861. Prices in Great Britain were 15 per cent lower in 1879 than in 1861, as measured by Sauerbeck's wholesale price index.[93] Wholesale prices in the United States, to judge from the Warren-Pearson monthly index, reached their peak in August-September 1864, and an only slightly lower peak in January 1865—at both peaks being 2½ times the average level in 1861. And for 1865 as a whole they averaged just a little over twice the 1861 level. In order for resumption to be achieved at the prewar parity, therefore, prices had to fall to less than half of their 1865 level. And this is, of course, what they did: the price index averaged 185 (with 1910–14 = 100) for 1865; it

[93] The *Economist* index shows the same change from June 1861 to June 1879.

was 86 in December 1878, and 87 in January 1879, or about 3 per cent less than its average value in 1861.

We have seen in section 2, above, that the drastic and sustained price decline occurred, despite a mild rise in the stock of money, because of an exceedingly rapid rise in output, with perhaps a mild assist from a fall in velocity, i.e., an increase in the demand for money per unit of output. The primary factor producing the decline in prices that made resumption possible was, therefore, the rapid growth in real income—the economy grew up to its money stock.[94]

Specie resumption was throughout a major political objective, and the question whether the government was proceeding toward this objective too rapidly or too slowly was a major political issue, as we saw in section 3, which perhaps reached its peak in the controversy about the Resumption Act of 1875. It is therefore of interest to note that this account of the factors explaining successful resumption assigns government action only a minor, if nonetheless crucial, supporting role. Government action may have contributed to the rapid expansion of output through its policies on sale of public land, land grants to railroads, and other similar measures which contributed to the expansion of the West. But such government action was not of the kind that anyone at the time or since would have regarded as explicitly directed toward achieving resumption.

Government action had mixed effects on the mild rate of growth of the money stock. On the one hand, federal and state legislation laid the foundation for the rapid growth of commercial banking—after 1867, particularly by state banks—that, as we have seen, produced rises in the ratios of deposits to reserves and of deposits to currency for most of the period after the Civil War. In addition, the elimination of reserve requirements against national bank notes in 1874 liberated reserves that encouraged a rise in the deposit-reserve ratio. The rises in the deposit ratios tended to increase the money stock, and thereby to inhibit price declines and to postpone the achievement of the prerequisites for successful resumption. On the other hand, the government did succeed in bringing about a minor reduction in the stock of high-powered money, mostly through use of government surpluses and debt refunding operations to retire "other United States currency" from 1865 to 1869, and it thereby helped offset to a limited extent the effect of the rises in the deposit ratios.

In view of the recurrent political pressures to expand the greenback issues—to which the government in fact yielded in 1873–74—and the political difficulty then as now of obtaining budget surpluses to retire debt, the achievement of even a minor decline in high-powered money was

---

[94] Or, as Schumpeter put it, "the economic organism was allowed to grow into its monetary coat" (J. A. Schumpeter, *Business Cycles,* New York, McGraw-Hill, 1939, Vol. I, p. 315).

by no means a negligible accomplishment.[95] But it was an accomplishment of omission, as it were, not of commission.

Interestingly enough, the decline in the stock of money in the last few years before resumption, which helped foster the particularly rapid price decline of those years, owed less, as we have seen, to any Treasury action under the influence of the Resumption Act than to the decline in the two deposit ratios, a decline that we have attributed to a rise in bank suspensions.

In 1877–79, the Treasury refunded about half the average outstanding interest-bearing public debt, to take advantage of lower rates of interest. For foreign holders of securities, calls of old bonds were so timed that one collection of securities was replaced by another or, if offsetting sales of new bonds were not possible, surplus from current account was available to pay for old bonds retired without export of U.S. gold. In fact, during those years, the United States was a net importer of over $5 million in gold, despite a repatriation of over $300 million of U.S. government securities by foreigners.[96]

---

[95] This terminology takes for granted the objective of resumption at prewar parity and is not intended to imply that we regard that objective as desirable. Our own judgment in retrospect is that, given that a gold standard was to be reestablished, it would have been preferable to have resumed at a parity that gave a dollar-pound exchange rate somewhere between the pre-Civil War rate and the rate at the end of the war.

We initially wrote that this judgment was "heavily influenced by current attitudes," but then Gottfried Haberler reminded us of Ricardo's views on the wisdom of Britain's resumption of specie payments at prewar parity in 1821, following the depreciation of its currency during the Napoleonic war period. "I perceive that you rather misconceive my opinions on this question [the reduction in prices 1813–19]—I never should advise a government to restore a currency, which was depreciated 30 pc^t., to par; I should recommend, as you propose, but not in the same manner, that the currency should be fixed at the depreciated value by lowering the standard, and that no further deviations should take place. It was without any legislation that the currency from 1813 to 1819 became of an increased value, and within 5 pc^t. of the value of gold,—it was in this state of things, and not with a currency depreciated 30 pc^t., that I advised a recurrence to the old standard" (Ricardo to John Wheatley, Sept. 18, 1821, *The Works and Correspondence of David Ricardo,* ed. by Piero Sraffa with the collaboration of M. H. Dobb, Cambridge U. Press for Royal Economic Society, 1952, Vol. IX, p. 73).

[96] In the two years 1877–79, the Treasury refunded $845 million (John Sherman, *Recollections of Forty Years in the House, Senate, and Cabinet,* Chicago, Werner, 1895, Vol. II, p. 723) of $1,790 million outstanding interest-bearing public debt (*Historical Statistics,* 1949, Series P-136, p. 306). On the Treasury's refunding operations, see *Specie Resumption and Refunding of the National Debt,* Letter from the Secretary of the Treasury, dated Dec. 2, 1879 (accompanying the *Annual Report on the Finances,* with documents relating to resumption and refunding), 46th Cong., 2d sess., H. Exec. Doc. 9. For the estimate of the volume of government securities repatriated by foreigners, see Simon, "Cyclical Fluctuations," p. 378. We cite an estimate for 1876–78, which, if anything, is too low for 1877–79, since 1876 was a year of virtually no capital movement and 1879 was a year of a large capital outflow.

Both before and immediately after resumption, the Treasury in its refunding operations went to great lengths to avoid the introduction of even temporary disturbances of any magnitude in the foreign exchange market. Here again, a mishandling of the operations might have interfered with resumption, so the Treasury deserves much credit.

The Resumption Act of 1875 itself, like the rest of governmental actions, had mixed effects on the achievement of resumption. Little was done under the act until John Sherman became Secretary of the Treasury in March 1877 and began serious attempts to accumulate a specie reserve. The act, and the borrowing and accumulation of a specie reserve under its provisions, had three effects, working in different directions, on resumption.

1. Insofar as the act and the specie reserve instilled confidence in the prospective maintenance of specie payments, it inhibited either a speculative withdrawal of funds from the United States or a speculative accumulation of specie, and enhanced the willingness of foreigners to hold U.S. dollar balances. Had there been no Resumption Act, repatriation by foreigners of U.S. securities in 1876–78 might well have been even greater than it actually was. More important, by setting a definite exchange rate that was to be attained and a definite date at which it was to be attained, the act offered those speculators with confidence that the government would in fact succeed in achieving these aims an incentive to proceed so as to achieve the specified exchange rate at an earlier date and to hold it there. In fact, the monthly average premium on gold dropped below 2 per cent by March 1878 and never thereafter rose above that level. This effect clearly favored resumption.

2. The sale of bonds was an open market operation. If the bonds had been sold for domestic currency and the proceeds added to the currency holdings of the Treasury, the effect, as of any other open market sale, would have been to reduce the high-powered money base of the monetary system and so enforce monetary contraction. In fact, the bonds were sold not for currency but for gold. The sale of bonds at home for gold was equivalent to selling bonds for greenbacks and then using the proceeds to purchase gold. In a nongold system, the purchase of gold with currency newly issued or taken from the currency holdings of the monetary authorities is an open market purchase that is expansionary in its monetary effect. The sale of bonds for gold thus had the effect of an open market purchase combined with an equivalent open market sale, the two together leaving the total monetary base unaffected. In practice, although gold was not the legal standard, it was, as we have noted, used for monetary purposes alongside greenbacks. In consequence, insofar as the gold purchased came from gold held for monetary purposes by either the domestic public or the domestic banks, it did, in the first instance, reduce

83

the reserve basis of the system. However, the banks and others could always replace gold holdings, if they so wished, by purchasing gold or its equivalent, sterling, in the free market at home or abroad, and in fact, that is what happened. The increase in the Treasury's gold reserves was not appreciably at the expense of the high-powered money holdings of the public or the banks.[97] Hence this consideration does not alter the conclusion that the sale of bonds for gold either at home or abroad was essentially neutral in its effects on the monetary base. It does mean that the operation might affect the gold premium in the manner noted in point 3, which follows.

3. Since gold was the equivalent of foreign exchange, the Treasury's purchase of gold constituted an increase in the demand for foreign exchange.[98] Insofar as it borrowed abroad resources that would otherwise not have been available for loans to this country, it increased the supply correspondingly. But some of its borrowing abroad must surely have been at the expense of other lending to this country (lending was going on even though the net capital movement from this country was outward); to that extent, the supply was increased less than the demand even by foreign borrowing. Borrowing at home had this effect to an even greater extent. By borrowing at home, the Treasury acquired resources that would have been used in other ways, some of which might have involved a demand for foreign exchange. At most, however, only part of the resources would have been used to purchase foreign exchange, whereas the Treasury used all of them in this way. The result of the greater increase in demand than in supply was to make the greenback price of sterling higher than it otherwise would have been. This effect therefore made resumption more difficult; it required, that is, a decline in domestic prices sufficient not only to balance foreign payments on current account at the desired exchange rate but also to produce a large enough surplus to finance the accumulation of the specie reserve. Whether the Resumption Act on balance hindered or helped resumption therefore depends on

[97] The Treasury's balances rose notably only after 1877, from $101 million in Feb. 1877 to $196 million in Feb. 1879. Over the same period, total high-powered money, which is to say, currency in the hands of the public plus bank reserves, was almost constant, falling only from $757 million to $752 million. Holdings of specie by the national banks actually rose rather than fell in that period. The rise in the holdings of national banks and of the government was roughly equal to domestic gold output. Hence one can treat the operation as if domestic bond purchasers used domestic currency to buy gold at home and transferred the gold to the Treasury in return for bonds. This would involve a transfer of currency from bond purchasers to gold miners with no change in the total. Of course, this description of the operation is only figurative, since there is no way to identify the particular source of a particular transaction.

[98] It may be well to repeat that demand and supply are being used to refer to schedules expressing quantity demanded or supplied as a function of price, in this case, the exchange rate.

whether this effect was more or less important than the effects on confidence and speculation.

Whatever the conclusion on this score, the cessation of government borrowing to build up a gold reserve, once resumption had taken place, removed a source of pressure on the exchange rate and permitted domestic prices to rise sharply immediately after resumption without producing balance-of-payment problems, as we shall see in more detail in the next chapter.

If this account makes the successful achievement of resumption on the date specified in the Resumption Act appear to be pure coincidence, two considerations may make this result seem less surprising. (1) The date was not set until the premium had already fallen to roughly one-tenth of its peak level, so most of the adjustment required for resumption had already taken place. (2) Numerous studies suggest that there is considerable leeway in the balance of payments, so long as there is reasonable confidence in the maintenance of an official exchange rate—that speculation and accommodating capital movements grant time for adjustment. This meant that the conditions for successful resumption were not a razor's edge but a broad band. Resumption might well have been successful a year or more earlier than the date set and certainly could have occurred later.

6. *Summary*

From 1862 to 1879, there was no official link between the U.S. dollar and gold, and hence no fixed parity between U.S. currency and the pound sterling, which was throughout rigidly linked to gold. The price of gold in terms of greenbacks was in effect the dollar price of sterling.

The average monthly price of gold, hence of sterling, varied widely over the period, reaching a peak in 1864 of over $2.50 in greenbacks for the amount of gold that had been worth a dollar before the war. This corresponded to a price of more than $12 per pound sterling, or two and one-half times the prior and subsequent parity of $4.86. The price of gold and sterling then declined irregularly to parity by the time of resumption on January 1, 1879. The changes in the price of gold were produced primarily by changes in relative prices of goods and services in the U.S. and abroad, and these in turn mainly by changes in U.S. prices. Wholesale prices more than doubled during the Civil War and then fell irregularly over the next fifteen years to their initial level. The price decline was a necessary condition for successful resumption at prewar parity.

During the Civil War, the dollar depreciated by a greater amount (i.e., the dollar price of sterling rose by more) than can be explained by commodity price movements alone. The explanation is the severing of the links that had connected the South, the North, and the rest of the world:

85

the South exporting cotton and using part of the proceeds to import from the North, which in turn used its surplus with the South to pay for goods from abroad. The foreign exchange loss to the North was partly made up by a speculative inflow of capital from abroad in the expectation of a subsequent appreciation of the dollar. As a result, the depreciation in excess of that attributable to price level changes was only about 20 per cent. The speculative capital inflow contributed also to unusually low rates of interest in 1863 and 1864.

For some five or six years after the Civil War, the dollar price of sterling was less than might have been expected from commodity price movements alone. The explanation is a sizable capital inflow from abroad for investment—up to 1870, particularly in U.S. government securities, and after that, in railroad bonds. When the capital inflow declined sharply, as it did in 1873–79, the dollar price of sterling first rose by comparison with the ratio of U.S. to British prices, then moved in accord with that ratio.

The initial price rise in the United States during the Civil War accompanied a sizable increase in the stock of money as a result of the issuance of greenbacks and other forms of legal tender to help pay for governmental expenditures, and the associated expansion in bank deposits. Unfortunately, we have no satisfactory data on the stock of money corresponding to either the wartime price rise or to the immediate postwar decline. Our continuous series begins only in 1867, by which time prices had already declined by more than 25 per cent from their wartime peak.

From January 1867 to February 1879, the date for which we have an estimate of the stock of money closest to the date of resumption, the stock rose 17 per cent or at the annual rate of 1.1 per cent per year. Most of the rise occurred from 1870 to 1872. From 1875 on, the money stock actually declined. Prices show a comparable pattern: they actually rose from 1871 to early 1873, and fell most sharply from 1876 to 1879. The behavior of the money stock was unusual by subsequent standards; the rise was unusually small for so long a period, and the number of years of actual decline was unusually large. However, as in later periods, the rate of rise tended to decelerate well before a cyclical peak and to accelerate well before a cyclical trough.

The reason for the small rise in the money stock was the virtual constancy from 1868 to 1878 in the amount of high-powered money— the sum of currency held by the public plus the reserves held by banks in the form of cash in vault. This total first decreased shortly after the Civil War, as a result of the retirement of emergency governmental legal-tender obligations, then varied about a constant level in response to the closely balanced political controversy that raged about resumption, greenbacks, and silver. Not until after resumption was a settled fact did controversy about its desirability cease and then only to be replaced by the silver issue.

The initial constancy in high-powered money was converted into a rise in the total stock of money by a rise in the number of dollars of deposits held by the public per dollar of their currency holdings and also a rise in the number of dollars of deposits created by banks per dollar of their vault cash holdings. The rise in the deposit-currency ratio probably reflected the spread of commercial banking. The rise in the deposit-reserve ratio reflected the combined effect of a near-doubling of the ratio for national banks and a sharp increase in the relative importance of non-national banks with a ratio higher than that of national banks. The rise in both deposit ratios was concentrated in the years up to 1873; both fell somewhat after 1875, which is why the stock of money shows the same pattern.

The mild rise in the stock of money was converted into a sharp decline in prices by a rapid rise in output. We cannot measure this rise in output at all accurately. The only available comprehensive measure—net national product in constant prices—begins in 1869 and there is strong reason to believe that the available estimates seriously overestimate the rate of growth of output during the subsequent decade. But there is much evidence that, while the growth of output was not so phenomenal as the net national product estimates alone would suggest, it was very rapid indeed.

The inadequacies of income estimates preclude any firm conclusion about velocity. The available data show a slight rise from 1869 to 1879. More accurate estimates would probably show a decline but we cannot say by how much.

The period from 1873 to 1878 or 1879 is of especial interest. Contemporary observers regarded these years as a period of marked "depression and disturbance of industry."[99] The National Bureau dates a reference peak in October 1873 and a trough in March 1879, making this the longest contraction in the U.S. record, and there is little doubt that these dates correspond to the qualitative impressions of contemporary observers. Yet if the evidence from physical-volume series can be believed, at least the later years of that contraction were years of expanding output. In terms of output measures alone, the trough may have come not later than 1877.

The obvious explanation for the apparent contradiction is the behavior of prices, which unquestionably fell sharply from 1877 to early 1879, and the continuing state of monetary uncertainty up to the successful achievement of resumption. The contraction was long and it was severe—of that there is no doubt. But the sharp decline in financial magnitudes, so much more obvious and so much better documented than the behavior of a

[99] The phrase is from David A. Wells, *Recent Economic Changes,* p. 6.

host of poorly measured physical magnitudes, may well have led contemporary observers and later students to overestimate the severity of the contraction and perhaps even its length. Observers of the business scene then, no less than their modern descendants, took it for granted that sharply declining prices were incompatible with sharply rising output. The period deserves much more study than it has received precisely because it seems to run sharply counter to such strongly held views.

CHAPTER 3

Silver Politics and the Secular Decline
in Prices, 1879–97[1]

THE RETURN of the United States to the gold standard in 1879, at a time
when the most important nations with which it traded were also on a
gold standard, in principle inverted the role of the stock of money. Under
the prior flexible exchange rate system, the stock of money was, or could
be, an independent variable controlled by domestic considerations. The
major channel of influence was from the stock of money to the level of
money income to the level of prices, and thence to the rate of exchange
between the dollar and other currencies, though undoubtedly some influences ran in the other direction. The objective of returning to specie
payments at the pre–Civil War parity had implications for the required
behavior of the stock of money. But this required behavior had to be
achieved by political measures, implicit or explicit; economic forces would
not "automatically" bring it about, though, as we have seen, they did
dominate the actual course of events, making adequate for the purpose
political measures that, under other circumstances, would have been
completely inadequate.

Under a gold standard with fixed exchange rates, on the other hand,
the stock of money is ultimately a dependent factor controlled primarily
by external influences—at least for a country which is an economically
minor part of the gold-standard world.[2] The major channel of influence

[1] According to the National Bureau's monthly reference dates, the cyclical trough
came in June 1897 but the expansion during the balance of 1897 was so rapid that
the annual dates designate 1896 rather than 1897 as the trough year. Although
many of our data are annual, we shall take 1897 as the terminal date of this
segment.

It should be noted that Rendigs Fels would put the monthly trough in Oct. 1896
(*American Business Cycles, 1865–1897*, University of North Carolina Press, 1959,
pp. 204–205).

[2] At the time of resumption, the U.S. held just over 5 per cent of the world's
monetary gold stock, and perhaps 8 per cent of that part of the gold stock which
served as monetary reserves; a year later these percentages were 9 and 13; and
for the rest of the century both percentages were probably below 20. This is one
rough measure of the relative importance of the U.S. economy in the gold-
standard world and one that almost surely overstates its importance, since both the
unit banking system in the U.S. and the absence of a central bank probably worked
to make the ratio of the gold stock to the money stock higher than in most other
important gold-standard countries.

It is impossible to document this statement adequately, since we have not even
passably reliable gold-stock figures for other important gold-standard countries
(see National Monetary Commission, *Statistics for Great Britain, Germany and*

is from the fixed rates of exchange with other currencies through the balance of payments to the stock of money, thence to the level of internal prices that is consistent with those exchange rates. Once again, there are undoubtedly some influences running in the other direction. Moreover, as is also true under a fiduciary standard, the links have much play in them, so that domestic policies can produce sizable short-term deviations in the stock of money from the level dictated by external influences. This slippage aside, domestic policies can affect the stock of money only by changing either the level of prices consistent with the fixed exchange rates (for example, by tariffs that affect the flow of trade or by measures that influence capital movements) or the stock of money consistent with the level of prices (for example, by measures that affect the incentive to hold money balances), so long, that is, as the gold standard is maintained.

Though the United States has been on the gold standard since 1879 except for part of World War I and a few months in 1933,[3] these considerations are especially relevant to the period before 1914. Much of the time since then, many other countries have not been on the gold standard or, if nominally on it, on a standard that was less automatic and controlling than that of the pre–World War I period, and the relative economic importance of the U.S. had become so great by the end of World War I that it could no longer be regarded as an economically minor part of the gold-standard world. Since 1934, the U.S. has been on the gold standard in little but name.[4]

The period from 1879 to 1914, in turn, breaks into two nearly equal parts that differ in important economic characteristics, both international

---

France, 1867–1909, Vol. XXI, 1910, 61st Cong., 2d sess., S. Doc. 578, p. 75, for available estimates for the U.K. and their shortcomings) ; some data are, however, available on the distribution of the gold reserves of central banks and governments. In December 1913, the earliest date for which figures are available, the U.K. held 3.4 per cent and the U.S. 26.6 per cent of those gold reserves of the world (*Banking and Monetary Statistics,* Board of Governors of the Federal Reserve System, 1943, pp. 544, 551. Although the figure for the U.S. in this source is described as the total U.S. gold stock, it is actually only gold in the Treasury, including the cover for gold certificates outstanding, and probably understates the aggregate of gold coin and certificate holdings of national and nonnational banks and the Treasury's net holdings.) Yet the U.S. was surely not nearly 7.8 times as important economically as the U.K. as judged by such measures as national income, world trade, and the like. To cite one figure, Simon Kuznets' estimate (worksheets underlying his *Capital in the American Economy: Its Formation and Financing,* Princeton for National Bureau of Economic Research, 1961) of U.S. national income for 1913 is 2.9 times that of the U.K., as estimated by Jefferys and Walters and converted to dollars at the official exchange rate (see James B. Jefferys and Dorothy Walters, "National Income and Expenditure of the United Kingdom, 1870–1952," *Income and Wealth,* Series V, Cambridge, Eng., Bowes and Bowes, 1955, p. 8). In world trade, the ratio undoubtedly was decidedly lower yet.

[3] From Sept. 1917 to June 1919, gold exports were embargoed unless authorized by the Federal Reserve Board, though gold continued to circulate domestically. A temporary departure from gold in Mar. 1933 was followed by a period of flexible and depreciating exchange rates ending in Jan. 1934.

[4] See Chap. 8, the first part of sect. 2, below.

90

and domestic. A combination of events, including a slowing of the rate of increase of the world's stock of gold, the adoption of the gold standard by a widening circle of countries, and a rapid increase in aggregate economic output, produced a secular decline from the 1860's almost to the end of the century in the world price level measured in gold, despite the rapid extension of commercial banking and of other devices for erecting an ever larger stock of money on a given gold base. That trend was reversed in the 1890's by fresh discoveries of gold in South Africa, Alaska, and Colorado combined with the development of improved methods of mining and refining, especially the introduction of the cyanide process. These occurred during a period when there were few further important extensions of the gold standard yet a continued development of devices for "economizing" gold. In consequence, the prior declining trend in world prices was replaced by a rising trend despite a continued rapid increase in physical output.

The decline and subsequent rise in world prices in terms of gold were naturally reflected in U.S. prices, and the different price trends in turn were reflected in domestic monetary politics. The preceding chapter recorded the beginning of the political agitation for an expansion of the money stock. That agitation continued from 1879 to the end of the century. The only difference was that silver instead of greenbacks became the popular means for expansion. The ebb and flow of political agitation during those two decades were an important source of short-term monetary uncertainty which affected the links between external and internal prices. After 1897, "cheap" gold achieved the objectives that had been sought by the silver advocates. The economic basis for the silver movement was thereby eliminated. The gold standard became securely enshrined. Uncertainty about its maintenance did not again play a significant role in our monetary experience until the 1930's.

According to our estimates, the stock of money grew both from 1879 to 1897 and from 1897 to 1914. But the rate of growth during the earlier period, though large by present-day standards and much larger than during the greenback period, was decidedly smaller than during the later period. It averaged about 6 per cent per year from 1879 to 1897, about 7½ per cent from 1897 to 1914. The different rates of monetary growth were associated with a corresponding difference in the behavior of prices. Prices fell at the rate of over 1 per cent a year from 1879 to 1897 and rose at the rate of over 2 per cent a year from 1897 to 1914.[5] The rate of growth of the money stock was not only lower but also decidedly more uneven during the earlier period; it was extraordinarily high from 1879 to 1881—over 19 per cent per year—and essentially zero from 1892 to 1897. The greater unevenness of monetary growth in the earlier period

[5] Fels, following Rostow, whom he cites on this point, believes that the secular decline of interest rates during the period 1879–97 demonstrates that a higher rate

waş associated with a more uneven pace of economic activity. The business cycle contraction from 1882 to 1885 was unusually long and fairly severe; and two relatively severe contractions succeeded one another in the 1890's separated by only an unusually brief expansion. By contrast, the period from 1897 to 1914 was interrupted by only one sharp contraction, in 1907, and that relatively brief.[6] The qualitative evidence assembled by economic historians and other students of the period is perhaps even more striking than these statistical indicators. The decades of the 1880's and the 1890's were notable for political unrest, protest movements, and unsettled conditions; the early part of the twentieth century, for relative political stability and widespread confidence in the rapid economic progress of the country.

These monetary differences, though strikingly reflected in the political climate, leave surprisingly little impress on records of physical performance. Both the earlier and the later periods were characterized by rapid economic growth. The two final decades of the nineteenth century saw a growth of population of over 2 per cent per year, rapid extension of

---

of growth of the money stock would not have eliminated the secular price decline (Fels, *American Business Cycles*, pp. 68–70, 81). D. Coppock similarly asserts that "The behaviour of interest rates is the crucial argument against the monetary theory of the price decline" ("The Causes of the Great Depression 1873–96," *Manchester School of Economic and Social Studies*, Sept. 1961, p. 209).

We do not accept this conclusion. On the contrary, even on the most extreme and naive liquidity preference theory of the interest rate, the fact that interest rates did decline meant that the liquidity preference was not absolute, i.e., that the liquidity preference schedule was not infinitely elastic at the going interest rate. Hence, a more rapid increase in the money stock, even on that theory, would have meant a more rapid decrease in interest rates, and hence, again reasoning in terms of the most extreme and rigid income-expenditure theory, would have meant an expansion in investment and so in money income.

On any other theory of the determination of interest rates, the declining interest rates may very plausibly be interpreted as in part a reflection of the declining prices and as in turn increasing the rate of growth of the money stock required to keep the price decline at any given level. The first follows from the discrepancy between the "real" and "money" rates of interest produced by anticipated changes in prices. Insofar as lenders and borrowers anticipate changes in the purchasing power of money, bond prices will tend to be higher and nominal yields lower when commodity prices are falling than when commodity prices are rising, since the increase in the real value of the principal is a return in addition to the nominal interest. Insofar as anticipations of falling prices lag behind the actual fall in prices, as they generally seem to do, interest rates will fall together with prices in the process of adjusting interest rates to the price decline. The lower interest rates, in turn, will make money more attractive as an asset relative to other fixed nominal value assets and so tend to mean that a larger rate of growth of the money stock is required to keep the price decline at any given level.

See also Phillip Cagan's discussion of the Gibson Paradox in his forthcoming monograph on the determinants and effects of changes in the money stock in the United States since 1875, a National Bureau study, in preparation, Chap. 6.

[6] If all business-cycle contractions 1882–1914 are ranked in order of increasing severity, the average for the period 1882–97 is well above that for 1899–1914 (Arthur F. Burns and Wesley C. Mitchell, *Measuring Business Cycles*, New York, NBER, 1946, p. 403).

the railway network, essential completion of continental settlement, and an extraordinary increase both in the acreage of land in farms and the output of farm products. The number of farms rose by nearly 50 per cent, and the total value of farm lands and buildings, by over 60 per cent—despite the price decline.[7] Yet at the same time, manufacturing industries were growing even more rapidly, and the Census of 1890 was the first in which the net value added by manufacturing exceeded the value of agricultural output. A feverish boom in western land swept the country during the eighties. "The highest decadal rate [of growth of real reproducible tangible wealth per head from 1805 to 1950] for periods of about ten years was apparently reached in the eighties with approximately 3.8 per cent."[8]

During the first decade of the twentieth century, population, the number of farms, and agricultural output all grew at a somewhat slower rate than in the preceding two decades. Manufacturing output, however, maintained its earlier high rate of expansion, as the country continued to shift from agriculture to industry.

Was economic growth more rapid during the earlier period of declining prices or during the later period of rising prices? Unfortunately, the readily available figures do not yield a simple, clear-cut answer. Kuznets' aggregate net national product in constant prices rises at the rate of 3.7 per cent per year from 1879 to 1897, and at the rate of 3.2 per cent from 1897 to 1914. This implies a rise in per capita net national product of 1.5 per cent a year for the earlier period, of 1.4 per cent for the later. However, the results of such a calculation are extraordinarily sensitive to the choice of dates: the use of 1880, 1896, and 1913, instead of 1879, 1897, and 1914, gives a rise in aggregate net national product of 2.6 per cent per year from 1880 to 1896 and of 4.4 per cent from 1896 to 1913. Inspection of the graph of net national product (see Chart 8, below) suggests little significant change in the rate of growth over the period as a whole, but rather a sharp retardation from something like 1892 to 1896 and then a sharp acceleration from 1896 to 1901, which just about made up for lost time. If this be right, generally declining or generally rising prices had little impact on the rate of growth, but the period of great monetary uncertainty in the early nineties produced sharp deviations from the longer-term trend. This evidence reinforces the tentative conclusion reached in the preceding chapter that the forces making for economic growth over the course of several business cycles are largely independent of the secular trend in prices.

[7] *Historical Statistics of the United States, Colonial Times to 1957*, Bureau of the Census, 1960 (*Historical Statistics*, 1960), Series K-1 and K-4, p. 278.

[8] R. W. Goldsmith, "The Growth of Reproducible Wealth of the United States of America from 1805 to 1950," *Income and Wealth of the United States, Trends and Structure, Income and Wealth*, Series II, Cambridge, Eng., Bowes and Bowes, 1952, p. 247.

CHART 8
Money Stock, Income, Prices, and Velocity, in Reference Cycle Expansions and Contractions, 1879–1914

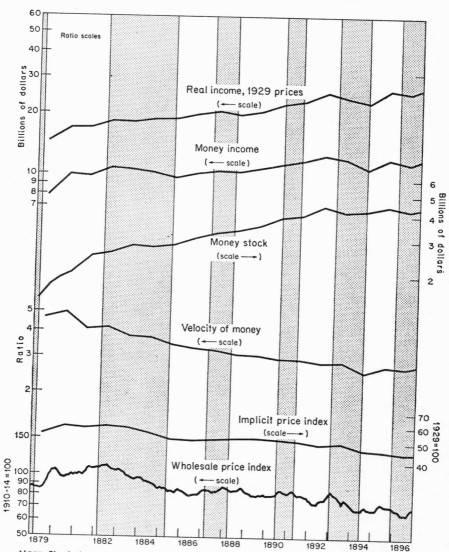

NOTE: Shaded areas represent business contractions; unshaded areas, business expansions.
SOURCE: Wholesale prices, George F. Warren and Frank A. Pearson, *Prices*, New York, Wiley, 1933, p. 13. Other data, same as for Chart 62.

94

CHART 8 (Concluded)

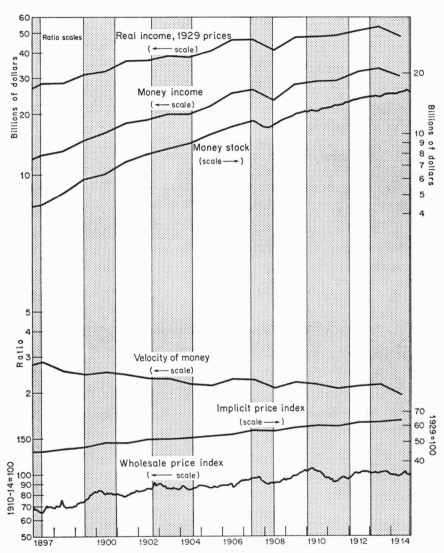

We turn now to a more detailed examination of the movements in money, income, prices, and velocity from 1879 to 1897.

1. *Movements in Money, Income, Prices, and Velocity*

Chart 8 plots for the period from 1879 to 1914 the series we examined in the preceding chapter for the greenback period: (a) the money stock,

(b) net national product in current prices and (c) in constant prices, (d) velocity or the ratio of net national product in current prices to the money stock, and two indexes of prices, one (e) the price index implicit in Kuznets' net national product in constant prices, on an annual basis, the other (f) the Warren and Pearson wholesale price index, on a monthly basis. As before, the shaded areas correspond to the periods designated "contraction" by the National Bureau reference dates, i.e., the period between the reference peak and the reference trough.

One striking fact for the years 1879–97 that is added by this chart is the sizable and highly regular decline in velocity—it fell at an average rate of nearly 3 per cent per year. During this period, an increase in money income required a decidedly larger increase in the stock of money, as reflected in the divergent slopes of the series on the stock of money and on net national product in current prices.

This period is generally regarded as one in which prices declined secularly. And so it is taken as a whole. But both of the price series in Chart 8 show that the decline proceeded unevenly. There was an initial decided rise in prices from 1879 to 1882—by almost a fifth for wholesale prices—then an even sharper fall to 1886, then rough constancy to 1891, then another rather sharp decline interrupted by a brief spurt in 1892–93 and followed by a much slower decline during the final years of the period.

The intervals of different price movements, which are reflected in our other series as well, serve to divide the period from 1879 to 1897 into four reasonably well defined segments.

1. The initial cyclical expansion from 1879 to 1882. This segment was characterized by an unusually rapid rise in the stock of money and in net national product in both current and constant prices. The stock of money rose over 50 per cent, net national product in current prices over 35 per cent, and net national product in constant prices nearly 25 per cent, or at annual rates of 16, 10, and 7 per cent per year, respectively.[9]

2. The subsequent cyclical contraction from 1882 to 1885. This was an unusually long contraction during which the stock of money and net national product in constant prices continued to rise but at drastically reduced rates—by roughly 9 and 4 per cent, respectively, or at annual rates of 3 and 1 per cent, and net national product in current prices fell about a tenth.

3. The period from 1885 to 1891. This segment contains two reference cycles, both rather mild with brief contractions, and is characterized

[9] For the stock of money, the rise is calculated for the period from Feb. 1879 to June 1882, for the net national product series, from calendar 1879 to calendar 1882.

96

by a fairly steady rate of growth of the money stock and of net national product in both current and constant prices—at annual rates of about 6, 3, and 3½ per cent, respectively.

4. The period from 1891 to 1897. This segment, too, contains two reference cycles. Both contractions were fairly severe and the expansion that separated them was mild and relatively brief, so that these six years are generally regarded as one of the economically most troubled periods of our history. The money stock, after an initial spurt from 1891 to 1892, declined 5 per cent from 1892 to 1896, resulting in an increase of only 6 per cent for the five years from 1891 to 1896; even the appreciable increase in the stock of money in 1897 raised the average annual rate from 1891 to 1897 to less than 2 per cent per year. From 1891 to 1896 net national product in current prices fell at an average rate of roughly 1 per cent per year, and in constant prices rose at a rate of roughly 2 per cent per year. The rapid rebound from 1896 to 1897 raised net national product in current as well as constant prices to a level above that in 1891; from 1891 to 1897 they rose at average rates of 1 and 3 per cent per year, respectively.

In broad terms, the explanation for the different experience during these periods is fairly clear.

THE CYCLICAL EXPANSION FROM 1879 TO 1882

The initial rapid expansion reflected a combination of favorable physical and financial factors. On the physical side, the preceding contraction had been unusually protracted; once it was over, there tended to be a vigorous rebound; this is a rather typical pattern of reaction.[10] On the financial side, the successful achievement of resumption, by itself, eased pressure on the foreign exchanges and permitted an internal price rise without external difficulties, for two reasons: first, because it eliminated the temporary demand for foreign exchange on the part of the Treasury to build up its gold reserve, referred to in section 5 of the preceding chapter; second, because it promoted a growth in U.S. balances held by foreigners and a decline in foreign balances held by U.S. residents, as confidence spread that the specie standard would be maintained and that the dollar would not depreciate again.[11] These forces were powerfully reinforced

[10] See our forthcoming "Trends and Cycles in the Stock of Money in the United States, 1867–1960," a companion volume to this book, also a National Bureau study.

[11] An offset to this was the fact that appreciation of the dollar in the years before resumption established an incentive to hold speculative balances, but that incentive was eliminated by resumption, since it was clear that thereafter, if the dollar varied at all relative to the pound, it would *depreciate,* not appreciate. However, since the dollar was within 1 per cent of parity from Apr. 1878 on, it seems

by accidents of weather that produced two successive years of bumper crops in the United States and unusually short crops elsewhere.[12] The result was an unprecedentedly high level of exports. Exports of crude foodstuffs, in the years ending June 30, 1880 and 1881, reached levels roughly twice the average of either the preceding or the following five years. In each year they were higher than in any preceding year, and neither figure was again exceeded until 1892.[13]

The resulting increased demand for dollars meant that a relatively higher price level in the United States was consistent with equilibrium in the balance of payments. Pending the rise in prices, it led to a large inflow of gold. The estimated stock of gold in the United States rose from $210 million on June 30, 1879, to $439 million on June 30, 1881. In classical gold-standard fashion, the inflow of gold helped produce an expansion in the stock of money and in prices. The implicit price index for the U.S. rose 10 per cent from 1879 to 1882 while a general index of British prices was roughly constant, so that the price level in the United States relative to that in Britain rose from 89.1 to 96.1.[14]

In classical gold-standard fashion, also, the outflow of gold from other countries produced downward pressure on their stock of money and their prices. The Bank of England reserve in the Banking Department declined by nearly 40 per cent from mid-1879 to mid-1881. In response, Bank rate was raised by steps from 2½ per cent in April 1881 to 6 per cent in January 1882. The resulting effects on both prices and capital movements contributed to the cessation of the gold outflow to the U.S., and, indeed, to its replacement by a subsequent inflow from the U.S. These lags in response to gold movements produced what appears to be a see-saw movement between the U.S. and Great Britain that deserves much closer study than we have given to it and that may well help to account for the particular pattern of cyclical turning points in the two countries.[15]

---

unlikely that this could have been a major factor in the final year before resumption.

[12] As J. K. Kindahl has pointed out, the underlying conditions for successful resumption were met during fiscal 1879, and no help from the fortuitous grain exports in fiscal 1880–81 was needed in order to maintain specie payments. What the grain exports accomplished was to permit a rise in U.S. prices, relative to British prices, that was greater than would have otherwise happened ("Economic Factors in Specie Resumption," *Journal of Political Economy*, Feb. 1961, p. 38.)

[13] *Historical Statistics*, 1960, Series U-63. In addition to foodstuffs, there were also abnormally high exports of cotton because of the failure of the Indian cotton crop.

[14] We are indebted to Phyllis Deane of the Department of Applied Economics of Cambridge University for the British price index, which she has constructed for 1871–1913. It is based on the Board of Trade wholesale price index with an allowance for rents and wages.

For ratios of U.S. to British prices, see Table A-4, col. 1.

[15] We are indebted to Clark Warburton both for calling our attention to

These gold movements and those before resumption have contrasting economic significance. As mentioned in the preceding chapter, the inflow into the U.S. before resumption was deliberately sought by the Treasury and represented an increased demand for foreign exchange. It required a surplus in the balance of payments sufficient to finance the gold inflow. The surplus could be generated only by a reduction in U.S. prices relative to foreign prices or in the price of the dollar in terms of foreign currencies and was, in fact, generated by a relative reduction in U.S. prices. The gold inflow was, as it were, the active element to which the rest of the balance of payments adjusted. After resumption, on the other hand, the active element was the increased demand for dollars resulting largely from the crop situation. The gold inflow was a passive reaction which temporarily filled the gap in payments. In its absence, there would have had to be an appreciation of the dollar relative to other currencies—a solution ruled out by the fixed exchange rate under the specie standard—or a more rapid rise in internal U.S. prices. At the same time, the gold inflow provided the basis and stimulus for an expansion in the stock of money and thereby a rise in internal prices at home and downward pressure on the stock of money and prices abroad sufficient to bring an end to the necessity for large gold inflows. It would be hard to find a much neater example in history of the classical gold-standard mechanism in operation.

THE CYCLICAL CONTRACTION FROM 1882 TO 1885

The level of prices and money income reached in the United States by the end of 1882 was higher than could be maintained at the fixed ex-

---

this see-saw movement and for the term. Note that the reaction mechanism alluded to is one that would convert a random shock affecting conditions of international trade into a series of cycles. Note also that the cycles on the two sides of the Atlantic would have predictable differences in phase.

For the reserve position of the Bank of England, and Bank rate, see R. G. Hawtrey, *A Century of Bank Rate,* London, Longmans, Green, 1938, pp. 289, 74–75.

While the gold inflow to the U.S. was in process, the long-term interest rate differential in favor of the United States, which was at a peak in Mar. 1877, declined gradually to a trough in mid-1881 (see the New York–London, New York–Paris, and New York–Berlin data in Oskar Morgenstern, *International Financial Transactions and Business Cycles,* Princeton for NBER, 1959, fold-in charts between pp. 472 and 473). These interest rate changes must be largely a consequence of the measures induced by the gold inflow. In principle, they could also reflect forces making capital investment in the United States relatively less attractive than capital investment abroad, hence reflect an independent corrective force. However, it seems rather implausible that the shift in the United States from a period of at least financial difficulties to a period of expansion should have been associated with a reduction in the attractiveness of the United States as a place for capital investment.

change rates. To some extent, the reason was that prices and income were adjusted to the abnormally favorable export situation of the preceding few years. The mere cessation of that abnormal situation meant that some reaction was inevitable. However, apparently only a minor reaction was required on this score alone. Our purchasing-power parity index, which, as noted above, reached 96.1 in 1882, fell to 95.1 in 1885. That shift, in itself, would have required only a 1 to 2 per cent decline in U.S. prices if foreign prices had remained unchanged.[16] And if both domestic and foreign prices had adjusted fully to the abnormal export situation, foreign prices might be expected to rise once that situation ceased. In fact, however, British prices not only failed to rise but rather fell appreciably— by over 12 per cent from 1882 to 1885. This fall was at least partly a delayed reaction to the loss of gold to the United States in the preceding years. The major reason, therefore, prices had to fall in the United States was that there had not been a full adjustment to the abnormal export situation. In order to achieve a 1 per cent decline in the U.S. price level relative to the British, absolute prices in the United States, therefore, had to fall 13 per cent in the course of the three years from 1882 to 1885.

The required price and income fall during the contraction was further intensified by a decline in capital inflows. This decline too was partly a delayed effect of the measures taken by the Bank of England in response to the loss of gold. In addition, foreigners lost confidence in railway and financial management and began to question the ability of the United States to stay on the gold standard. Accordingly, instead of continuing to add to their holdings, they reduced them.[17] Responsibility for the financial panic in May 1884 has been attributed to an outflow of gold resulting from the sale of foreign-owned securities.[18] The panic, while severe, did

[16] Wholesale price indexes tell a rather different story than the implicit price indexes used in this calculation do. They indicate that a 10 per cent fall in U.S. prices relative to British was required.

[17] Foreign holdings of railroad issues apparently quadrupled between 1876 and 1883 (from $375 million to $1.5 billion). From 1882 to 1885 foreigners disposed of securities at a net rate of about $25 million a year, creating a shift from net foreign purchases of $200 million a year to net sales of $25 million a year (M. G. Myers, *The New York Money Market*, Columbia University Press, 1931, pp. 290–291). By the mid-1880's, foreign holdings of American securities other than railroad issues were negligible, according to Matthew Simon, "The United States Balance of Payments, 1861–1900," *Trends in the American Economy in the Nineteenth Century*, Studies in Income and Wealth, Vol. 24, Princeton for NBER, 1960, pp. 696–697.

Recurrent rate wars and mismanagement of individual lines from 1882 on undermined public confidence in railroad securities. At the same time, silver purchases under the Bland-Allison Act of 1878 and the resulting growth of the Treasury's balances at the expense of its gold holdings created disquiet about the likely maintenance of the gold standard.

[18] O. M. W. Sprague, *History of Crises Under the National Banking System*, National Monetary Commission, GPO, 1910, p. 109; Fels, *American Business Cycles*, p. 131.

not lead to restriction of the convertibility of deposits into currency and was largely confined to New York.[19]

Arithmetically, the required decline in U.S. prices was achieved by sharp reductions in the rate of growth of the stock of money (from 16 per cent per year to 3 per cent) and of real output (from 7 per cent per year to 1 per cent), and a continued rapid decline in the velocity of money. Economically, these were the channels whereby a necessary adjustment was worked out. They were not the forces determining what adjustment was necessary. Given that the United States was to remain on the gold standard and given that prices and incomes moved as they did in the rest of the world, a sizable price or income decline, or both, had to occur in the United States, one way or another. If, for example, velocity had been constant or rising instead of declining, then the stock of money would have had to rise less rapidly or to decline, since there is no reason to expect that output would in such an eventuality have risen still more rapidly. The less rapid rise or decline in the stock of money would have been brought about by actual or threatened balance of payments deficits and gold drains. The factors accounting for the behavior of velocity and of real output are extremely important in explaining why the adjustment took the form it did—i.e., why velocity, real output, and hence the money stock behaved as they did—but they are of only secondary importance in explaining why the adjustment in prices and income was what it was. The discipline of the balance of payments under the gold standard enforced that adjustment and determined its size.

We shall examine in section 2 below the factors accounting for changes in the money stock. There, too, we shall find the same contrast between the arithmetic and the economics of the situation. If the required change in the money stock had not occurred in one way, it would have occurred in another. In 1882–85, however, there was one particular secondary effect of the way in which the change in the money stock took place that was of especial significance in affecting the size of the required adjustment in prices and income. The secondary effect was the tendency of

[19] A decline in security values, attributed at the time to foreign orders to sell, resulted in the failure on May 8 of a brokerage firm. Its failure, in turn, led to the failure of a New York national bank that had illegally certified a check for the bankrupt firm. A defalcation in another New York national bank thereupon came to light, several other brokerage firms and private banks failed, and a national bank with large bankers' deposits was suspended as a result of its president's speculations. The prompt issue of clearing house loan certificates by the New York Clearing House Association, starting on May 15, relieved the strain upon the money market, and no restriction of cash payments occurred. The maximum amount of certificates outstanding at any one time was $22 million. There were few failures among country banks, and out-of-town banks took over loans in the New York market which the local banks liquidated. New York's loss of reserves to the interior was thus limited (see Sprague, *History of Crises*, pp. 108–123, 353).

silver purchases to weaken confidence in the maintenance of the gold standard and thereby stimulate capital outflows or reduce capital inflows. As we shall see more fully below, silver agitation had its major economic impact through this effect on expectations rather than through the direct contribution that silver purchases made to the expansion of the money stock.

RELATIVE STABILITY FROM 1885 TO 1891

There is little that requires special mention about this segment, which is to say that the fluctuations within it seem attributable to no special "disturbing" factors, and hence that, in the absence of a tested theory of cyclical movements, we do not know how to explain them.[20] The fluctuations were relatively mild so that the period is one of fairly steady growth of output and income and of gently falling prices. British prices, as measured by a general price index, rose about 2½ per cent. There was first a rise and then a decline in the ratio of U.S. prices to British—our purchasing-power parity index rose from 95.1 in 1885 to 100.0 in 1887, fell slightly to 99.1 in 1888 and then more sharply to 91.0 in 1891— so that over the period as a whole there was a decline in the relative demand for dollars. These relative price movements are paralleled by the changes in net capital flows and net international gold flows to the United States (see Chart 9, which plots the purchasing-power parity index against [1] net international capital movements to the U.S.; [2] the sum of [1] and net international gold movements from the U.S., each expressed as a ratio to net national product; these ratios are for fiscal years which are plotted at the beginning of the same calendar years).[21] Capital imports rose substantially from fiscal 1885 through fiscal 1888, and then declined by fiscal 1892 to about their level in fiscal 1885. In addition, there were substantial gold exports from the United States from 1888 through 1891. Both the decline in capital imports and the gold exports are very likely early stages of a capital flight induced by distrust of the intention of the United States to maintain the gold standard—an interpretation that is supported by the behavior of relative interest rates.[22] However, the consequent decline that was called for in the ratio of U.S.

[20] One possibility is that they reflect partly the secondary and tertiary waves from the reaction mechanism referred to in footnote 15 above.

[21] The reason for adding capital inflows to gold exports is that both constitute a source of foreign currency, available to pay for imports or make other foreign payments. Similarly, both capital outflows and gold imports must be paid for with foreign currency acquired from exports or other sources of foreign funds.

[22] The long-term interest rate differential in favor of the United States widened from a trough in mid-1889 to a peak about mid-1891 (Morgenstern, *International Financial Transactions*, charts between pp. 472 and 473). Since the widening was accompanied by a decline in the volume of capital imports, it must have resulted from a relative shift to the left of the supply schedule of capital to the U.S.

CHART 9

U.S. Net International Capital Movement as a Ratio to National Income, and Purchasing-Power Parity, 1879–1914

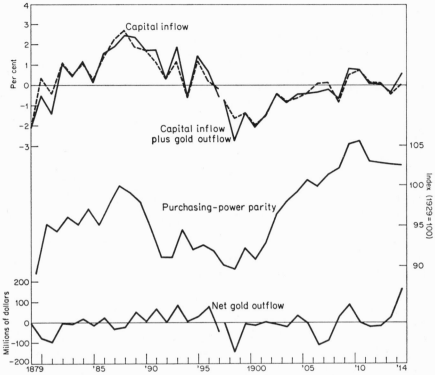

NOTE: Calendar years are shown. Movements in a fiscal year are plotted at the beginning of the calendar year. Capital inflow and gold outflow are plotted as plus.
SOURCE: Table A-4. For net gold outflow, see source notes to that table.

to British prices from 1885 to 1891 did not involve serious deflationary pressure. Thanks to the rise in British prices, it could be achieved by an absolute decline of only some 2 per cent in U.S. prices.

Precisely because it is so unremarkable, this segment provides a good bench mark in terms of which to judge monetary requirements for stable prices at this epoch of American history. The money stock grew at the rate of nearly 6 per cent per year, of which a bit less than half was absorbed by a decline in velocity, a bit more than half, by rising money income. Since prices fell slightly, monetary growth of a bit more than 6 per cent per year apparently would have been required for stable prices.

103

The most interesting, because most puzzling, component of this total is the large allowance required for declining velocity.

The brief business contraction from July 1890 to May 1891, which terminated that period, was accompanied by severe money market disturbances. A shift of British investment to the Argentine in mid-1890 caused a loss of gold from New York just at the beginning of the crop-moving season, which typically meant a drain of reserves from New York to the interior. Treasury open market bond purchases relieved the stringency only temporarily. The money market disturbance reached a height in early November, when a number of brokers and bankers failed as a result of a decline in security prices. The announcement on November 15 that Baring Brothers had suspended in London touched off a final display of panic. There were numerous additional bank failures but restriction of payments did not occur and, within a month, the New York money market was again stable.

THE DISTURBED YEARS FROM 1891 TO 1897

This segment is by far the most interesting for the historian of money, and we shall accordingly examine it in much greater detail. The serious difficulties of those years arose mainly from the combination of two forces. In the first place, world gold prices fell sharply: to judge from an index of general prices in Britain, by 11 per cent from 1891 to 1897. This alone would have required something like comparable price or income reductions in the United States. In the second place, agitation over silver reached its peak, and the political forces in favor of free silver came closest to victory. The effect was to create a lack of confidence both at home and abroad in the maintenance of the gold standard and to lead to something of a "flight" from the dollar—or rather a series of flights and returns as views altered. (See the sharp fluctuations in the capital movement estimates in Chart 9.) The financing of the adverse capital movement put still further pressure on prices and on income; it was either financed by gold outflows which put pressure on the money stock or by an excess of earnings abroad made possible by relatively low prices or incomes.[23]

---

[23] To avoid misunderstanding, we should perhaps emphasize that we do not regard lack of confidence in the maintenance of the gold standard as the only factor accounting for the decline in net capital imports during that period, although we are inclined to believe that in the nineties it was the most important factor accounting for the great instability in capital flows, since speculative funds flowed both in and out as confidence in the maintenance of the standard waxed and waned.

As we shall see in the next chapter, the figures show a continued decline in capital imports after the election of 1896, which presumably calmed the worst fears about the gold standard. That alone is persuasive evidence that forces other than fears about the gold standard were at work. Such forces

The U.S. experience in 1891–97 was similar to British post-World War II exchange crises. In both cases, a government was seeking to maintain a fixed exchange parity. In both cases, it was uncertain whether the government would succeed. In both cases, it was clear that, if there were any change, it would be a depreciation of the relevant currency. Hence, in both cases, there was an incentive to reduce the balances held of the currency in question, and this incentive varied in intensity as the chances of the maintenance of fixed parity varied. The result was in both cases rapid fluctuations in short-term balances and serious economic disturbances. Of course, there were also important differences: the commitment of Britain to a full employment policy gave it much less leeway in domestic monetary policy; the development of direct exchange and trade controls gave it means of affecting its balance of payments other than through movements in prices and incomes; foreign trade was of greater relative importance to Britain; and, finally, Britain did devalue. Yet the comparison is instructive in providing a

---

were the Baring crisis in 1890 and the subsequent severe contraction in England; the factors cited by A. K. Cairncross (*Home and Foreign Investment, 1870–1913*, Cambridge, University Press, 1953) and Brinley Thomas (*Migration and Economic Growth*, Cambridge, University Press, 1954) in accounting for the low level of total British capital exports from 1891 to 1904; U.S. commercial and bank failures in 1893, and so on. But whatever these other forces may have been, lack of confidence in the maintenance of the gold standard certainly made capital inflows lower or capital outflows higher than they otherwise would have been. And indeed, some of the effects of these other forces were postponed to after 1896 by the actions taken to stay on gold (see below).

Fels (*American Business Cycles*, pp. 195, 203), while acknowledging that foreigners believed that silver constituted a threat to the gold standard in the U.S., adds:

> At no time during the nineties, not even in 1896, did majority opinion among investors, at home or abroad, hold that the United States would actually leave the gold standard. If the threat to the gold standard had really been considered dangerous, the outflow of gold would have assumed proportions great enough to have forced its abandonment. Capital tended to flow in or out of the country depending on whether short-run conditions turned favorable or unfavorable. This should not be blamed entirely on the threat to the gold standard. The extraordinary failures of 1893, which in part are attributable to other causes, made American securities unattractive.

This judgment is not at all inconsistent with our position. It was only necessary for a minority—and a small minority, at that—to "hold that the U.S. would actually leave the gold standard," or even for a somewhat larger minority simply to believe that the likelihood of the U.S. leaving the gold standard had risen from, say, 1 per cent to 30 per cent, to produce a substantial outflow of capital. And, of course, the governmental measures taken to stay on the gold standard— chiefly the sale of bonds by the Treasury to get gold—encouraged capital inflows through their deflationary effect. What is important, here as in so many instances, is the threatened capital outflow, capital outflow ex ante rather than ex post, or, to put it still differently, the shift in a schedule rather than in the quantity coordinate of the point of equilibrium.

105

contemporary example of the volatility of "speculative" balances under a fixed exchange-rate standard whose maintenance is in doubt.[24]

The proximate origin of the distrust of the maintenance of the gold standard—or perhaps better, of the drastic increase in distrust—was probably the Sherman Silver Purchase Act, passed on July 14, 1890, by a Republican Congress as a purported concession to the West for the support of the protectionist McKinley Tariff Act of 1890, sought by the industrial East. The Sherman Act stipulated that the Treasury should purchase 4.5 million ounces of silver per month, or roughly twice the amount the Treasury had been purchasing under the Bland-Allison Act of 1878. Payment was to be made in a new currency, the so-called Treasury notes of 1890, which were to be a full legal tender redeemable in either gold or silver at the discretion of the Secretary of the Treasury.

The higher import duties imposed by the McKinley Tariff reduced the demand for imports of the protected commodities and hence for foreign currency to pay for them. In this respect, it offset to a slight extent the impact of the silver legislation on the speculative demand for dollars. But in another respect, it intensified that impact. The tariff put sugar, a great revenue producer, on the free list and so reduced total customs receipts. At the same time, Congress authorized increased expenditures for pensions and rivers and harbors. The combined result was to threaten the conversion of a Treasury surplus into a deficit, and this was taken to mean, rightly or wrongly, that the government would be less able to maintain the gold standard.

In the spring of 1891, there was an abnormally large outflow of gold. The Treasury's gold reserve was sharply reduced and the Treasury adopted a sequence of short-sighted expedients to obtain and retain gold.[25] It seems reasonable to attribute the outflow of gold and the associ-

[24] See Milton Friedman, *Essays in Positive Economics,* University of Chicago Press, 1955, p. 163; also Simon, "The Hot Money Movement and the Private Exchange Pool Proposal of 1896," *Journal of Economic History,* Mar. 1960, pp. 31–50.

[25] Earlier, in Aug. 1890 the New York Subtreasury changed its practice of settling its clearing house balances almost exclusively in gold coin or certificates and began using the Treasury notes of 1890 and United States notes instead. Previously the banks had paid out gold to customers who had custom dues to pay so that customs receipts in New York had been largely in gold coin and certificates. With the change in the subtreasury's settlement practices, the proportion of gold coin and certificates in customs receipts fell drastically and the United States notes and Treasury notes of 1890 replaced them ("Annual Report of the Treasurer," *Annual Report on the Finances,* 1891, p. 49).

In Mar. 1891 the Treasury imposed a charge of 40 cents per $1,000 on gold bars taken for export, although it had a plentiful supply. As a result most of the net gold export from the United States through 1893 was of American coin. In the summer of 1891 it sold legal tender western exchange at a price 60 cents per $1,000 less than the normal rates, on condition of being paid in gold (A. D. Noyes, "The Banks and the Panic of 1893," *Political Science Quarterly,* Mar. 1894, p. 27, n. 2; J. DeWitt Warner, "The Currency Famine of 1893," in *Sound Currency,* Feb. 15, 1895, p. 3). Cf. Frank Fetter's

ated continued British sales of American securities to growing distrust of the maintenance of the gold standard. If this be so, it is likely that the mild contraction of 1890–91, characterized as it was by financial strain and by failures of banks and brokers in the fall of 1890, would have been intensified and protracted by a further flight from the dollar if it had not been for another accident of weather like the one that occurred in 1879–81. European grain crops failed in the summer of 1891, while American production was the largest on record. The result was that exports of crude foodstuffs were 2½ times as large in the year ending June 30, 1892, as in the preceding year, exceeding the exports in 1881 for the first time and nearly equaling the record exports of 1880. The increased demand for dollars temporarily reversed the gold movement. The gold inflow fostered a spurt in the stock of money from 1891 to 1892, followed by a rise in wholesale prices from mid-1892 to February 1893, a month after the cyclical peak.

This surcease, however, was bound to be temporary and may well have made the subsequent reaction even sharper than it would otherwise have been. Both the fall in world gold prices and the decline in capital inflows continued.[26] Gold exports were resumed, and the Treasury's gold reserve declined after December 1892. No political developments occurred to still the fears and hopes that silver would topple gold. On the contrary, the Senate's approval in July 1892 of a free silver coinage bill, which never became law, must have reinforced such fears. Public misgivings about the maintenance of the gold standard became widespread and were further intensified by attempts by both banks and the Treasury to accumulate gold. And, of course, protestations by the Treasury of its intentions to maintain gold redemption only served to feed suspicion.[27]

---

remarks on the importance of Treasury impartiality towards different forms of currency ("The Gold Standard; Its Function and Its Maintenance," *Political Science Quarterly*, June 1896, pp. 245–246).

[26] It has been estimated that of $3 billion American securities held abroad in 1890, $300 million were returned to this country in 1890–94, so that there was a change from annual average net purchases by foreigners of perhaps $200–$300 million, 1885–89, to annual average net sales by foreigners here of $60 million, 1890–94 (Myers, *New York Money Market*, p. 291).

[27] Banks began to insert clauses in notes and mortgages requiring payment in gold coin or its equivalent. In Feb. 1893, the Secretary of the Treasury prevailed on the New York banks to give the Treasury about $6 million in gold in exchange for legal-tender notes. This was gold the banks had obtained by presenting legal-tender notes for redemption. The run on the Treasury did not, however, cease after that exchange (New York *Tribune*, Feb. 10, 11, 1893).

The new administration that took office on Mar. 4, 1893, found $101 million in gold in the Treasury and barely $25 million in other forms of currency. In Mar. and Apr. the banks voluntarily returned $25 million in gold to the Treasury for notes (*Annual Report on the Finances*, 1893, p. lxxii; 1896, p. 130). On Apr. 15, the Secretary of the Treasury gave notice that issue of Treasury gold certificates would be suspended in conformity with the law of July 12, 1882. A rumor then spread that the Treasury would thenceforth redeem Treasury notes

The commercial failure of a stock market favorite in May 1893, after months of depressed stock market prices, touched off the panic for which the stage had been set by the general uneasiness about the currency. There had been no distrust of the banks up to this time. A month following the stock market collapse, however, the movement of currency from the interior to New York, normal at this season of the year, was abruptly reversed by withdrawals of currency from New York. Runs led to the failure and suspension of many banks, national, state, and private, predominantly in the West and South. The proximate cause of the runs was distrust of the solvency of the banks, rather than dissatisfaction with the currency. A large number of mercantile failures during the first half of 1893 had excited alarm concerning the quality of bank loans. As in many such cases, however, a deeper cause was doubtless the preceding price deflation. Loans that would have been good and banks that would have been solvent if prices had been stable or rising became bad loans and insolvent banks under the pressure of price deflation. And doubtless, also, the collapse of some banks caused runs on others and their suspension, in turn, even though many would have remained fully solvent in the absence of the runs. At this point, in June 1893, the external drain of gold ceased temporarily as information was made public that the administration would press for the repeal of the purchase clause in the Sherman Silver Act.[28]

---

of 1890 in silver rather than gold, now that its reserve had fallen below the legal limit. On Apr. 20, the Secretary in a public interview tried unsuccessfully to still the misgivings which the rumor had fed, but the disturbance in the money market was not allayed even when the President left no doubt that the notes were redeemable in gold (Allan Nevins, *Grover Cleveland*, New York, Dodd, Mead, 1944, p. 525).

[28] Due to a filibuster, the purchase clause in the Silver Act of 1890 was not actually repealed until Nov. 1, although Congress was called into special session for that purpose on Aug. 7.

The distinction between external and internal drains made here seems a more satisfactory explanation of events leading up to the crisis of 1893 and of the crisis itself than is offered either by Sprague (*History of Crises*, pp. 153 ff.) or by A. D. Noyes (*Forty Years of American Finance*, New York, Putnam, 1909, pp. 159–173, 182–206).

Sprague, in general, minimizes the importance of silver in accounting for the crisis (see pp. 162, 165, 169, 179), despite its unmistakable influence upon the extraordinary gold outflows from this country, 1891–93. Noyes explains the crisis largely in terms of the silver issue, but in consequence is at a loss in describing the run on western banks, and the public's desire to shift from other assets to Treasury notes and silver certificates. Thus, he states, "Panic is in its nature unreasoning; therefore, although the financial fright of 1893 arose from fear of depreciation of the legal tenders, the first act of frightened bank depositors was to withdraw these very legal tenders from their banks" (p. 190). Sprague's rebuttal is more to the point:

In the eastern money centers bank failures and suspensions were attributed almost entirely to the silver influence. But it is to be noted that they occurred

The run on the banks reinforced the effect of the gold outflow on the stock of money by leading the public to desire a higher ratio of currency to deposits: currency held by the public was 6 per cent higher at the end of June 1893 than a year earlier, whereas deposits were 9½ per cent lower, so that the ratio of deposits to currency fell sharply (see Chart 10, below).[29] The total money stock fell by some 6 per cent—the first substantial decline since 1875–79. Thereupon, a second wave of distrust of banks spread over the West and South with consequent withdrawals of cash reserves from the New York banks. Later in July the Erie Railroad went into receivership, and the stock market suffered the worst decline of the year.[30] Bank suspensions occurred in the East as well as in the South and West.[31] Banks throughout the country, starting with those in New York, partly restricted cash payments, which is to say, the con-

---

principally in the West and Southwest, where there is no evidence that people were distrustful of silver money. Had the monetary influence been potent, we should expect to find numerous failures in the eastern States and also some discrimination on the part of depositors between the different kinds of money in circulation. Distrust of the solvency of banks rather than dissatisfaction with the circulating medium was clearly the direct cause which brought about runs upon banks and the numerous failures and suspensions (p. 169).

In short, two sets of forces were responsible for the two different drains: distrust of the Treasury's ability to maintain silver at parity with gold caused the external drain; distrust of the solvency of banks, particularly western institutions, caused the internal drain. The link between them was the effect on the solvency of banks of the additional deflation that was produced by a decline in capital inflow arising out of doubt about the maintenance of the gold standard.

[29] Unfortunately, we have no monthly data for that period for the money stock as a whole; so we cannot trace more precisely the connection between the fall in the deposit-currency ratio and the runs on banks. Data on national bank deposits and on currency outside the Treasury are available for call dates, and it is clear from these that the deposit-currency ratio did not begin to fall until the interval between May 4, 1893, and July 12, 1893, the period of the first stock market crash and the first bank runs. The deposit-currency ratio, as judged from national bank data, reached a low at the call date on Oct. 3, 1893. In all likelihood, however, the low probably occurred in Sept., when restriction of cash payments ended, the Oct. call date figure marking a point on a rising deposit-currency ratio curve. By June 1894, our figure for the ratio for all banks had almost regained its level of June 1892, although the July 1894 ratio based on national bank data was still about 5 per cent below the July 1892 ratio.

[30] The break in stock prices stimulated foreign purchases, since repeal of silver purchase was considered a foregone conclusion.

[31] Out of 360 national and state banks suspended during 1893, with liabilities of $110 million, 343 suspensions with liabilities of $96 million occurred west or south of Pennsylvania. In addition, 250 private and savings banks with liabilities of $42 million suspended, 224 of them with liabilities of $36 million outside of New England and the Middle Atlantic States (Noyes, "The Banks and the Panic of 1893," pp. 15–16). Many of these banks were perfectly solvent and were embarrassed on account of runs only for the length of time it took shipments of money from New York to reach them.

vertibility of deposits into currency, apparently because of the deficiency in the reserves of particular banks that had the bulk of bankers' deposits, rather than because of the inadequacy of total reserves.

Restriction of cash payments[32] brought to an end the stream of bank failures. But it also in effect created a dual monetary system—currency and deposits not interchangeable at a fixed rate. Currency sold at a premium for certified checks from the beginning of August to the beginning of September, when the currency premium ended, as enormous gold imports restored reserves. The currency premium was, of course, equivalent to a depreciation of the deposit dollar in terms of gold or foreign exchange; and, since it was not expected to last, gave an incentive to convert foreign balances, i.e., gold, into deposit dollars, though it should be noted that the gold inflow has been attributed to other factors in earlier accounts.[33]

By creating a dual monetary system, restriction of cash payments also reduced the usefulness of deposits. This made the given nominal stock of money equivalent to a smaller stock with free interchangeability. It also led the public to desire to decrease its ratio of deposits to currency, even aside from any doubts about the solvency of banks. That is the meaning of the "dearth of currency" so much complained of. Additions to national bank circulation and imported gold were supplemented by emergency currency issues of various types, estimated at roughly $80 million.[34] Notes called "clearing house certificates" were frequently issued in denominations from 25 cents to $500 by temporary committees of banks in towns, principally in the Southeast, where no clearing house existed. Certified checks drawn on themselves were sold by banks everywhere in currency denominations. In addition, wherever banks could not supply currency, factory pay checks and a variety of miscellaneous notes and certificates, issued by corporations and individuals, became acceptable as currency.

Regarding that panic, it is worth emphasizing once again the difference between what we have called the arithmetic and the economics of the situation. The panic had important effects on the banking structure, then and subsequently, and on the climate of political opinion; and it undoubtedly affected the detailed timing, form, and impact of the economic adjustment. At the same time, it was at bottom simply the way in which

[32] The concerted refusal of banks to convert deposits into currency on demand is generally referred to in the literature as a "suspension of payments by banks." We use instead either the term "restriction of cash payments" or "restriction of convertibility of deposits into currency" in order to avoid confusion with two very different kinds of "suspension": suspension of specie payments by monetary authorities, as in 1862 and 1933; and suspension of an individual bank, involving the temporary closing of a bank and discontinuance of its operations, which may be followed either by subsequent reopening or permanent disappearance of the bank through failure or merger.

[33] See Noyes, "The Banks and the Panic of 1893," p. 24; Sprague, *History of Crises*, pp. 191–195.

[34] Warner, "The Currency Famine of 1893," p. 8.

an adjustment, forced by other considerations, worked itself out. The price decline abroad and the distrust of the maintenance of the gold standard by the United States meant that there were only two alternatives: (1) a sizable decline in U.S. prices and a decline or a reduced rate of rise in money income; or (2) the abandonment of the gold standard and the depreciation of the dollar relative to other currencies. Given the maintenance of the gold standard, the adjustments in prices and income were unavoidable. If they had not occurred through the banking panic and the accompanying deepening of the recession under way, they would have taken place in some other way. Indeed, this is clear from contemporary suggestions of a "remedy" for the banking difficulties, namely, earlier loan contraction by banks through the maintenance of a "higher" quality of loans. That remedy would have produced by design much the same financial adjustments produced inadvertently by the panic.

It should perhaps be noted explicitly that we do not intend to suggest that the alternative involving abandonment of the gold standard was economically undesirable. On the contrary, our own view is that it might well have been highly preferable to the generally depressed conditions of the 1890's. We rule it out only because, as it turned out, it was politically unacceptable.

Though restriction of cash payments ended in September 1893, the next three years were characterized by dragging deflation, interrupted only by a brief cyclical revival from June 1894 to December 1895. This is one of the few revivals in the cyclical history of the United States in which aggregate output probably did not reach the level of the preceding cyclical peak, and in which per capita output almost surely did not. World gold prices continued to fall, the British general price index reaching its trough in 1896. Speculative pressure on the dollar continued, as political agitation proceeded apace. The Treasury's gold reserve fell to a low of $45 million in January 1895, and the Treasury adopted one expedient after another to replenish it. The fact that such measures were taken is important, though the details of the measures taken are not.[35] In the first place, the

[35] Successive bond issues of $50 million, sold to New York banks, in Jan. and Nov. 1894, under the terms of the Resumption Act, were unsuccessful in restoring Treasury gold reserves. Most of the proceeds were needed for current government expenditures, and most of the gold coin needed for the subscription was obtained by redemption of legal tenders at the Treasury.

On Feb. 8, 1895, the Treasury signed a contract with a syndicate of bankers, headed by J. P. Morgan and August Belmont, who agreed to sell the government 3.5 million ounces of gold ($65 million)—one-half to be obtained and shipped from Europe—under the terms of an act of Mar. 17, 1862, for 30-year 4 per cent bonds at 104½. The bonds were marketed by the syndicate at 112¼, and the contract was later modified by mutual consent, so that only $14.5 million in gold was shipped from Europe, the remainder of the bonds that were sold in Europe having been resold in the United States. The syndicate also undertook to protect the Treasury against gold withdrawals pending completion of the

111

measures were a link in the transmission of the external pressure to the domestic money stock and thence to prices and income; as we shall see in more detail later, they contributed to keeping the money stock essentially constant from 1892 to 1897. In the second place, the Treasury's willingness to take the measures served to reassure holders of dollar balances that the U.S. government was determined to remain on gold. It thereby reduced the speculative pressure on the dollar. At almost any time, the Treasury could clearly have forced a suspension of specie payments simply by inaction, let alone by positive steps.

During the second quarter of 1896, renewed gold exports, stimulated by the apparently rising political strength of the pro-silver forces, produced a serious decline in the government's gold reserves. After Bryan's nomination by the Democratic convention on July 10, the flight of short- and long-term capital sharply accelerated, as alarmed American and foreign investors increased their demand for foreign exchange. The financial community, itself thoroughly alarmed by the political prospects, closed ranks; and New York, Boston, Philadelphia, and Chicago banks transferred part of their gold holdings to the Treasury after July 20. In addition, a syndicate of foreign exchange and gold-shipping houses agreed to block gold outflows.[36] Economically speaking, this meant that the members of the syndicate committed themselves to use their credit standing abroad to borrow funds in foreign currencies, which they could sell to domestic investors wishing to buy foreign exchange, or to foreign holders

---

actions stipulated by the contract. As one step, the syndicate offered their own drafts on London, at or below the price accepted by gold-exporting houses, and did not cover their own sales by remittances of specie. The syndicate then took pains to eliminate competition from the foreign exchange market by allotting a share of the new government loan to practically every New York banking house with foreign connections, on condition that it would ship no gold and sell no exchange except at a price above the gold-export point. During the 5 months after the contract was signed, no gold was withdrawn from the Treasury, confidence was restored, and European demand for American securities rebounded. London debtors now sought drafts on New York, which the syndicate supplied, thus repaying most of its London borrowings. During July 1895, the syndicate rates were fixed at a minimum of $4.90, one cent above the point at which drafts on London could be profitably covered by specie shipments. The syndicate collapsed, however, after a New York coffee importing firm with European connections offered exchange 1 point below the syndicate's, and shipped gold, withdrawn from the Treasury, to cover its sterling drafts, remitting first on its own behalf and later for the benefit of others. On the whole episode, see A. D. Noyes, "The Treasury Reserve and the Bond Syndicate," *Political Science Quarterly*, Dec. 1895, pp. 573–602. The allegedly onerous contract terms, arranged secretly through agents long identified in Populist literature as "the conspiracy of international bankers," became an issue in the campaign of 1896.

In Jan. 1896 the Treasury publicly advertised a $100 million 4 per cent bond issue, which was heavily oversubscribed. Again, the subscription was made mainly with gold withdrawn from the Treasury for the purpose.

[36] See Simon, "The Hot Money Movement," pp. 31–50.

of dollar balances who wished to transfer them into foreign currencies. This would enable holders of dollar balances to convert them into foreign currency without first converting them to gold. Put differently, the members of the syndicate committed themselves to create an accommodating capital inflow to offset any speculative capital outflow. The mere formation of the syndicate was a sufficiently striking demonstration of confidence in the exchange value of the dollar to bring the flight of short- and long-term capital to a halt. At the end of August, when the regular seasonal flow of agricultural exports and associated inflow of gold had gotten under way, the syndicate was dissolved without having made a single transaction. From that time on, the gold reserves were never again in danger. But, in the fall, there was evidence of deliberate shifts by individuals to assets specifically payable in gold or foreign exchange, gold went to a premium, and bank loans were difficult to obtain at the previously prevailing interest rates, gold imports notwithstanding. Once the Republicans won the election, domestic accumulation of gold ceased; and the pressure on the dollar eased, this time permanently, thanks to the factors that were making for a rapid increase in world gold supplies. A decided improvement in business activity, however, waited until the middle of 1897.

2. *The Politics of Silver*

A notable feature of the last three decades of the nineteenth century, and particularly, of course, the years after 1890, was the political importance of the "money" issue which, as we have seen, was partly the cause of the disturbed economic conditions of the early 1890's and in its turn was exacerbated by the conditions it had helped to create.

Even before the formation of the national Greenback party in 1875, the seed had been sown from which the silver agitation of the 80's and 90's was to grow. The seed was the so-called "crime of 1873," a law passed on February 12, 1873, "revising and amending the laws relative to the mints, assay-offices, and coinage of the United States." The law discontinued the coinage of the standard 412.5-grain silver dollar containing 371.25 grains of fine silver.[37]

[37] The act of Feb. 12, 1873, specified that the silver coins of the U.S. were to consist of a trade dollar of 420 grains (378 grains of fine silver), newly authorized, and subsidiary coins—a half-dollar, a quarter-dollar, and a dime—with "a legal tender at their nominal value for any amount not exceeding five dollars in any one payment." The act of 1873 also specified the minor coins: a 5-cent piece, a 3-cent piece, and 1-cent piece.

Section 3586 of the Revised Statutes, adopted in June 1874, restricted to sums not exceeding 5 dollars the legal-tender power not merely of the silver coins enumerated in the act of 1873 but of all silver coins of the U.S. It thus included the standard silver dollar of 412.5 grains, though no such standard silver dollars were reported in circulation at the time.

The trade dollar was introduced for use in settling trade balances with the Orient. It was designed to supersede the Mexican dollar, which contained

113

Because the market price of silver had been higher than the mint price, the silver dollar had not been in circulation since 1836, and was an unknown coin to Americans. In 1873 it seems to have been generally accepted that the demonetization of standard silver dollars simply gave legal recognition to that fact, and silver spokesmen in Congress did not oppose the legislation. However, the price of silver began to fall in 1872, a fall which turned out to be the beginning of a sharp secular decline. The reasons for the price decline seem fairly clear: on the supply side, rich new mines were opened in the American West, and there was a worldwide increase in productivity; on the demand side, a number of European countries shifted from a silver or bimetallic to a gold standard and sharply reduced their monetary use of silver. By 1875, U.S. silver producers discovered to their distress that, while it would then have been profitable to bring silver to the mints for coinage under earlier legislation, they were debarred from doing so by the act of 1873. They branded the act a crime, alleging that the provision for dropping the standard silver dollar had been secretly introduced into the act as a result of a conspiracy of Eastern bankers and legislators. Historians of the period have denied the charge,[38] although the most recent writer on the issue concludes that the draftsman of the act included the critical provision in full knowledge that the price of silver was likely to fall, and with the definite intention of assuring that gold would be the basis of the U.S. monetary system.[39] Whatever be the

---

377.25 grains of fine silver, and which American merchants in the China trade bought from banks in the U.S., usually at a premium, for remittance to the Far East. It was not intended to circulate in the U.S.; and according to Laughlin, its inclusion in the list of coins to which a legal-tender power was given in sums not exceeding 5 dollars was inadvertent. The fall in the price of silver, however, made it profitable to put trade dollars into circulation in California, where gold was the chief money in use, but not in the rest of the country, where there was still a premium on silver valued in greenbacks. To discourage domestic circulation, the act of July 22, 1876, removed the legal tender quality from the trade dollar and empowered the Secretary of the Treasury to suspend its coinage at his discretion. By 1877 the price of silver was low enough for trade dollars to circulate at a discount from greenbacks in the U.S. outside of California, and when money brokers sent large amounts into remote districts at full value, despite their lack of legal tender power, the Secretary of the Treasury ordered the discontinuance of their coinage. Speculators thereupon reimported them from China in the expectation that the trade dollars would be redeemed at their face value in gold. Congress fulfilled the expectation by passing a bill to redeem at par all trade dollars presented within six months. This act, passed on Mar. 3, 1887, became law without President Cleveland's signature (J. Laurence Laughlin, *The History of Bimetallism in the United States,* New York, Appleton, 1901, pp. 102–105, 256–258).

[38] D. R. Dewey, *Financial History of the U.S.,* 7th ed., New York, Longmans, 1920, pp. 403–405; Noyes, *Forty Years of American Finance,* pp. 35–36; Laughlin, *History of Bimetallism,* pp. 95–101.

[39] In a thoughtful and interesting note, Paul M. O'Leary has argued that there was indeed a crime of 1873, because H. R. Linderman, the draftsman of the

final verdict on this question, a generation of silver orators certainly portrayed the demonetization of silver as a conspiracy. One version, popular as an explanation of resumption, was that demonetization of silver was planned by the British in order to raise the value of U.S. government bonds they held by insuring payment in gold only.[40]

Silver producers demanded as a remedy the free and unlimited coinage of silver at the ratio of sixteen to one. Debtor farmers in the Middle West and South, who had no interest in a higher price for silver, joined the silver producers, in the belief that "free coinage" or "free silver," as they termed it, would increase the money supply and thereby lower the real burden of their debt. Greenback party adherents also accepted this argument; putting new silver dollars into circulation would be just as effective in increasing the money stock as issuing more greenbacks.

In the summer of 1876 a number of silver bills were introduced in the House but were not considered by the Senate. The next year the Senate amended a House bill that was sent up by striking out a provision for free coinage, and the House reluctantly accepted the change. The bill,

---

act of 1873, was aware of the secular forces at work to increase the supply of silver and to decrease the demand, and deliberately excluded the standard silver dollar from the U.S. monetary system in an effort to eliminate the possibility of "a *de facto* silver standard if and when resumption of specie payments was undertaken" ("The Scene of the Crime of 1873 Revisited: A Note," *Journal of Political Economy*, Aug. 1960, p. 392). Although O'Leary is most persuasive about Linderman's knowledge and aims, it may be that he reads into Linderman's account of the act, written in 1877 after silver spokesmen awoke to their error in acquiescing in its passage, omniscience and too much prevision on the part of its author. Linderman and John Jay Knox, then Comptroller of the Currency, were appointed in 1869 to consider the revision of all the coinage laws. The report they submitted in 1870 recommended that the silver dollar be dropped. Linderman was unlikely to have been influenced at that early date by the prospective change in the price of silver. No one will quarrel with O'Leary's final comment that an interesting chapter in history-as-it-might-have-been could be written on the consequences that would have followed the inclusion in the act of 1873 of provision for the coinage of the standard silver dollar.

[40] Richard Hofstadter, *The Age of Reform*, Knopf, 1955, pp. 74–77. In silverite and Populist literature on currency and monetary problems, the three favorite symbols of the conspiracy of the plutocracy were Wall Street, the British, and the Jewish bankers. "Wall Street was by far the most popular and has remained so ever since among politicians of agrarian and Populist tradition. Populist agitators used the ethnic symbols more or less indiscriminately, British along with Jewish, although some of them bore down with peculiar viciousness on the Semitic symbol" (C. Vann Woodward, "The Populist Heritage and the Intellectual," *The American Scholar*, Winter 1959–60, p. 64).

Woodward argues that emphasis on the irrational and evil doctrines of Populism by recent critics, of whom Hofstadter is one, overlooks "hysterical responses and apocalyptic delusions" in other quarters during the political crises of the nineties. "An intensive study of the nineties can hardly fail to leave the impression that this decade had rather more than its share of zaniness and crankiness, and that these qualities were manifested in the higher and middling as well as the lower orders of American society" (pp. 68–69).

115

passed on February 28, 1878, after having been vetoed by President Hayes, became known as the Bland-Allison Act (see below). Free silver forces were dissatisfied with that legislation because it did not provide for unlimited coinage. From that time forward, agitation for free silver was carried on with a religious fervor. The theme of "the crime of 1873" was echoed and re-echoed in the pro-silver speeches of the next two decades. The disappearance of the Greenback party, after a weak performance in local elections in 1882 and national elections in 1884, left no organized political expression for silver agitation until the formation during the eighties of new farmers' organizations known as "Alliances." At first these were nonpolitical in character, but they drifted into political activity in 1890 following the collapse of the western land boom in the latter part of the eighties.[41]

The People's—or Populist—party of the U.S.A., an agrarian party formed out of a union of the Northwestern Alliance and a minority of the Southern Alliance, was formally organized in 1892, with a platform that among other items demanded free and unlimited coinage of silver, an increase in the circulation to equal $50 per capita, and government issue of all currency. Its candidate polled one million out of the 12 million votes cast in the Presidential election of 1892. The repeal in 1893 of the purchase clause in the Sherman Silver Act and the money panic of that year both seemed further evidence to the Populists of what they regarded as a betrayal of agrarian debtors to mortgage holders in the East.

Labor groups were restive as well. From mid-1892 to February 1893 there were notable and unsuccessful strikes at the Carnegie mills and at the Buffalo railroad yards, and, in the spring of 1894, at coal mines and the Great Northern Railroad. In May 1894, a strike against the Pullman Company developed into a general railroad strike that was not settled until federal troops established martial law and Eugene Debs was imprisoned for disobeying a blanket injunction. "General" Jacob S. Coxey, a Greenbacker and a Populist, led a march of unemployed men—Coxey's army—on Washington, seeking an issue of $500 million in legal tender notes as one among a long list of demands for action by the government.

In 1894 a bill providing for the coinage of the seigniorage silver then in the Treasury—uncoined silver representing the difference between $1.29 an ounce (the official monetary value of silver and hence its nominal value in the form of coins) and the price paid for silver under the Sherman Act—was passed by both Houses of Congress but vetoed by President

[41] The Alliances were not the principal backers of the Sherman Silver Purchase Act of 1890. Its supporters were chiefly American silver producers and a combination of owners of silver in New York, London, and on the Continent who engaged in a gigantic speculation in silver to raise the price to $1.29 an ounce, during the week after the act was passed. The speculation failed and the price of silver collapsed (Laughlin, *History of Bimetallism,* p. 264).

Cleveland. The sale of bonds by the Treasury in 1895 by secret negotiation to a syndicate, because a public offering seemed doomed to failure, was interpreted as proof of a conspiracy between the administration and the bankers to maintain the costly gold dollar.[42] The decision of the Supreme Court upholding the injunction against Debs aroused many labor groups. Although these resentments were directed against the economic system as a whole, the dominant issue became the money stock, and the chief demand of the critics was the free coinage of silver. Agitation was widespread. The National Bimetallic Union, which was established in 1895 and published a weekly, *The Bimetallist,* joined forces in 1896 with the American Bimetallic League and the National Silver Committee, a political league.

William H. Harvey dramatized the argument for silver and against the gold standard in the form of a novel entitled *Tale of Two Nations* and a presentation, enlivened by cartoons, entitled *Coin's Financial School.* The opponents of silver countered by forming the National Sound Money League, under banker aegis, with its own weekly, *Sound Money.* Horace White replied to Harvey in *Coin's Financial Fool.* Many members of the antisilver group did not oppose international bimetallism. So its arguments were not categorically in opposition to the monetization of silver.

The opponents of silver recognized, of course, many of the defects of the monetary system demonstrated by recurrent money panics, of which the silver advocates complained. The solution offered by the opponents of silver[43] was reform of note issue. A plan for an asset-backed currency, unconditionally guaranteed by the federal government, the so-called "Baltimore Plan," was proposed by the American Bankers Association at its Baltimore convention in October 1894.[44] Another proposal was the

[42] See footnote 35 above. Also see Grover Cleveland, *Presidential Problems,* New York, Century, 1904, pp. 132–159, for an interesting discussion of this episode and its immediate antecedents.

[43] See, for example, the pamphlets on note reform included in *Sound Currency,* an antisilver publication, issued semimonthly, afterwards quarterly (1891; 1894–1900) by the New York Reform Club.

[44] Comptroller of the Currency Eckels (in his *Annual Report,* 1894, pp. 32–36) and Secretary of the Treasury Carlisle (in his *Report* that year, pp. lxxvi–lxxxii) both recommended the repeal of all laws requiring the deposit of U.S. bonds as security for circulation, and the substitution of an asset-backed currency. Their specific proposals differed: the Comptroller suggested that national bank issues, limited to the amount of the banks' capital, be secured in part by general assets, in part by a fund of legal tenders to be deposited with the Secretary of the Treasury, the notes secured by legal tenders to be eligible as reserves against deposits; the Secretary suggested that the notes, limited to 75 per cent of the banks' capital, be secured by a legal tender reserve of 30 per cent, the note issues to constitute a first lien upon all the assets of the banks.

Carlisle further proposed repeal of legal reserve requirements against deposits.

Every prudently managed bank, if left free to conduct its deposit and discount business in the manner most advantageous to its own interests and the interests

117

repeal of the prohibitive tax on state bank issues. The silver party was willing to support the latter but not the Baltimore Plan.

The political campaign of 1896 on these issues was conducted with notorious bitterness involving both class and sectional conflicts. Fear and smear techniques were freely used on all sides. The free-silver advocates succeeded in capturing Democratic state conventions and in maneuvering the adoption of a free-silver plank in the Democratic national convention, which chose William Jennings Bryan as candidate. The National Silver party and the People's party, deflected from its more extensive reform program by the hope of victory on the silver issue, also nominated Bryan. A Conservative Democratic group seceded, held an independent convention, and nominated its own candidate (John M. Palmer). The Republican party nominated McKinley who was persuaded to accept along with the nomination a platform favoring the gold standard until "international agreement with the leading commercial nations of the earth . . . can be obtained" for coining gold and silver at a fixed ratio.[45] A rump group seceded from that convention and went over to the Democrats.

The election was won by the Republicans, largely, it has been claimed, because the farm vote swung to the party as a result of the rise in price and quantity of farm-product exports during the fall of 1896. Once the party was in power, Republican political action for monetary or banking reform was restrained. Although a group of Indianapolis businessmen organized a conference of leading bankers and businessmen, which appointed a monetary commission in 1897, its report received no Congressional support. Bryan's strength at the polls, however, compelled the

---

of its patrons, will undoubtedly keep on hand a reasonable reserve to meet not only all the ordinary demands upon it, but to provide for such emergencies as are liable to occur in the community where it is located; but it ought not to be prohibited by law from using such reserve for the only purposes it was designed to accomplish . . . . To provide for a reserve which can not be utilized even at a time of the greatest stringency and distrust without incurring the penalties of forfeiture, affords a most striking illustration of the impolicy of legislative interference with the natural laws of trade and finance (p. lxxx).

See also his testimony, *National Currency and Banking System,* House Committee on Banking and Currency, Dec. 10, 1894, H. Rept. 1508, 53d Cong., 3d sess., Hearings, pp. 13–56.

At that time and for at least the next half-century, the U.S. was the only major country in the world that had legal reserve requirements for commercial bank deposits (R. G. Rodkey, *Legal Reserves in American Banking,* Michigan Business Studies, VI, no. 5, University of Michigan, 1934, p. 4). The 8 per cent cash ratio agreed upon by the London clearing banks, in consultation with the Bank of England at the end of 1946, is not a statutory requirement (U.K. Committee on the Working of the Monetary System [Radcliffe Committee], *Report,* Cmnd. 827, Aug. 1959, p. 119, para. 351).

[45] For the text of the Republican money plank, see K. H. Porter and D. B. Johnson, *National Party Platforms,* Urbana, University of Illinois Press, 1956, p. 108.

Republicans to keep a campaign promise to propose another international conference in Europe in 1897 to remonetize silver. The defeat of the silver inflationists had improved the United States' bargaining position, but by that time rising gold output had snatched from silver advocates the chance of achieving an international bimetallic standard.

Not until March 14, 1900, however, was the Gold Standard Act passed. It declared the gold dollar to be the monetary standard of the country and prescribed a reserve of $150 million in the Treasury for the redemption of paper money. The gold standard had finally triumphed in the United States, and Bryan's second defeat in the Presidential election in the fall of 1900 sealed the doom of silver as a major issue dominating national politics. The price reversal, which farmers had sought to achieve with silver, was produced after 1897 by the prodigious increase in the international supply of monetary gold. The "money" issue retreated from the center of political controversy.

3. Factors Accounting for Changes in the Money Stock

Changes in the total money stock were ultimately determined, as we have seen, largely by factors outside the domestic monetary structure, primarily, the behavior of prices abroad, the coincidence of good crops at home and poor ones abroad, and attitudes about the maintenance of the gold standard by the United States. The particular channels through which changes in the money stock were achieved, however, and some of the shorter-term movements in it reflected domestic monetary influences.

Chart 10 plots the money stock over the period from 1879 to 1897 and the three proximate determinants of the stock that we introduced in the last chapter: the total of high-powered money, the ratio of deposits to reserves, and the ratio of deposits to currency. In addition, the chart shows the currency in the Treasury (Treasury cash)—which reflected the influence of Treasury actions on the money stock and thus had considerable short-run significance—and the sum of high-powered money plus Treasury cash.

The most notable feature of this chart is the fairly close parallelism between the money stock and high-powered money. It was disturbed mainly by the rise in the ratio of deposits to reserves and of deposits to currency, which produced a widening spread between the money stock and high-powered money, and by the decided cyclical fluctuations in the deposit-reserve ratio, which are mirrored in corresponding cyclical perturbations of a much milder amplitude in the money stock. As we saw earlier, the money stock grew very rapidly in the reaction after resumption. It grew almost as much in total in the two and one-half years from February 1879 to August 1881 (62 per cent) as in the remaining sixteen years until June 1897 (79 per cent). The contemporaneous rise in high-

119

CHART 10

The Stock of Money and Its Proximate Determinants, and
Treasury Cash, 1879–97

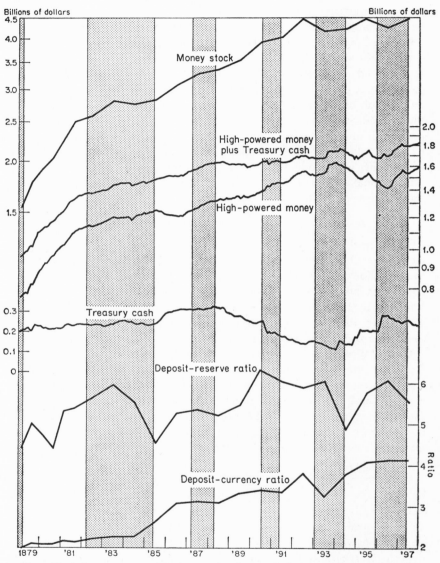

NOTE: Shaded areas represent business contractions; unshaded areas, business expansions.
The top three curves are plotted on a ratio scale, the bottom three on an arithmetic scale.

SOURCE: Money stock, Table A-1, col. 8. High-powered money, same as for Table B-3. Ratios,
Table B-3. Treasury cash, Jan. 1879–Feb. 1887, from *Annual Report* of the Secretary of the
Treasury, 1898, pp. 124–133; Mar. 1887–Jan. 1898, from *Circulation Statement of U.S. Money*
(Treasury Dept.), averaged to the middle of the month and seasonally adjusted by ratio-to-
moving-total method.

powered money accounted for 81 per cent of the initial rapid increase, in the sense that, had the two deposit ratios remained unchanged, the stock of money would have grown at 81 per cent of the rate at which it did (see Table 4).[46] The remaining sixteen years comprised eleven years,

TABLE 4
CONTRIBUTION OF PROXIMATE DETERMINANTS TO CHANGES IN THE
MONEY STOCK, 1879–97

Proximate Determinant	Change in Money Stock That Would Have Been Produced by Indicated Determinant, if It Alone Had Changed			
	Feb. 1879 to Aug. 1881	Aug. 1881 to June 1892	June 1892 to June 1897	Feb. 1879 to June 1897
	RATE OF CHANGE PER YEAR (per cent)			
1. High-powered money	15.7	2.9	−0.1	3.9
2. Deposit-reserve ratio	2.3	0.2	−0.5	0.4
3. Deposit-currency ratio	1.2	2.1	0.6	1.4
4. Interaction of ratios	0.1	0.1	0.0	0.2
5. All	19.3	5.4	0.1	5.8
	FRACTION OF TOTAL CHANGE			
1. High-powered money	0.81	0.55		0.66
2. Deposit-reserve ratio	0.12	0.04		0.06
3. Deposit-currency ratio	0.06	0.39		0.24
4. Interaction of ratios	0.00	0.02		0.04
5. All	1.00	1.00		1.00

NOTE: Annual rates of change are continuously compounded. Because of rounding, components may not add to totals shown. Because of the small size of the actual change in the money stock, 1892–97, fraction of change figures for that period would be absurdly large and so are not computed.

The money stock reached its trough in June 1896. Figures for the subperiods separated by this date, by line, are:

June 1892–June 1896

Rate of change per year
(per cent)   (1) −2.2   (2) 0.3   (3) 0.8   (4) 0.0   (5) −1.2
Fraction of total change   1.91   −0.22   −0.68   −0.01   1.00

June 1896–June 1897

Rate of change per year
(per cent)   (1) 8.6   (2) −3.7   (3) 0.0   (4) 0.0   (5) 4.9
Fraction of total change   1.74   −0.75   0.0   0.0   1.00

SOURCE: Table B-3. See also App. B, sect. 7.

from 1881 to 1892, of fairly steady growth in the stock of money, and five years of near-constancy. High-powered money accounted for 55 per cent of the growth from 1881 to 1892, and the rise in the deposit-currency ratio for most of the rest. In 1892–97 taken as a whole, the stock of

[46] See Appendix B for a description of how these percentages were computed. Note that, here as elsewhere, the rate referred to is an annual rate of growth compounded continuously.

money changed but little. This period, however, breaks down into two subperiods. From 1892 to 1896 the decline in the stock of money reflected the decline in high-powered money, almost half of which was offset by a rise in the deposit ratios. In the final year of the period, the money stock grew thanks to a rise in high-powered money which more than offset a decline in the deposit-reserve ratio, with the deposit-currency ratio remaining unchanged.

In discussing the movements in these determinants in somewhat more detail, we shall consider first the two deposit ratios, then high-powered money.

RATIO OF DEPOSITS TO CURRENCY

Taken as a whole, 1879–97 was a period of rapid extension of the commercial banking system. At the outset of the period, the public held under $2 of deposits for each dollar of currency; at the end, more than $4. The rapid rise in deposits relative to currency probably resulted in part from the more widespread availability of checking facilities, which is to say, it was partly a response to a reduction in the effective cost of holding deposits. A more important factor, however, was probably the growing real income per capita. Deposits are apparently regarded by holders of appreciable sums as superior to currency as a way of holding money balances. When their incomes rise they tend to substitute deposits for currency.[47]

But the rise in the deposit-currency ratio did not proceed evenly through the period. A slow but fairly steady rise from 1879 to 1883 ceased entirely from 1883 to 1884. The cessation of the rise presumably reflected the banking crisis in the spring of 1884, although it may also have reflected a general tendency of the ratio to fall relative to its trend in at least the early stages of contraction. The next two years saw by far the most rapid rise of the period, a movement for which we have no adequate explanation. The subsequent much slower rise ceased during the business contraction from 1887 to 1888 and again from 1890 to 1891 in the aftermath of the banking difficulties in the second half of 1890. The most significant interruption was from 1892 to 1893, undoubtedly associated with the banking difficulties of 1893, which produced a panic and a restriction of cash payments in the summer of that year.

Each of the three banking crises of the 18-year period thus left its mark even on these annual data. If monthly data were available, in all likelihood they would show the impress of the banking difficulties much more clearly and, indeed, enable us to follow their evolution with considerable precision. As we shall see in later chapters covering periods for

---

[47] See Phillip Cagan, *The Demand for Currency Relative to Total Money Supply,* New York, NBER, Occasional Paper 62, 1958, p. 4.

which we have monthly data, until the establishment of federal deposit insurance in 1934, there was no more sensitive indicator of the state of public confidence in the banks than the deposit-currency ratio.

RATIO OF DEPOSITS TO RESERVES

The deposit-reserve ratio fluctuated about a gradually rising level. The mildness of the trend reflects the absence of any substantial changes in legal reserve requirements, in the relative importance of national and nonnational banks with their different reserve requirements in terms of high-powered money, and apparently in any other secular factor affecting the reserves which banks thought it prudent to keep over and above legal requirements.[48]

The deposit-reserve ratio has a clearly marked cyclical pattern, tending to rise during business expansion and to fall during business contraction. In large part, the pattern was produced by the reactions to the three banking crises referred to in connection with the deposit-currency ratio, all of which came during the contraction phase of the cycle. The banking crisis of 1884 was followed by a sharp decline in the deposit-reserve ratio from 1884 to 1885; the crisis of 1890, by a mild decline from 1890 to 1891; and the panic of 1893, by the sharpest decline of all.

In the 1893 panic, the decline in the deposit-reserve ratio occurred a year after the decline in the deposit-currency ratio. A similar, though less-marked, pattern is evident in the banking crisis of 1884, when stability in the deposit-currency ratio from 1883 to 1884 was followed by a decline in the deposit-reserve ratio from 1884 to 1885. In the 1890 crisis, both ratios declined from 1890 to 1891. These deviations from the 1893 pattern occurred partly because the earlier panics were less severe, partly because their dating happens not to coincide with our annual June data. The sharp decline in the deposit-currency ratio from 1892 to 1893 reflects

---

[48] The only change in legal reserve requirements affecting national banks that occurred during the period was the shift of Chicago and St. Louis banks from reserve city to central reserve city status and of banks in some ten other cities from country district to reserve city status, under the terms of the act of Mar. 3, 1887. The act provided that cities with a minimum population of 50,000 (reduced to 25,000 by the act of Mar. 3, 1903) might, upon the application of three-fourths of the national banks established in them, become reserve cities, and that cities with a minimum population of 200,000 might similarly become central reserve cities. Inasmuch as these shifts affected at most only about 10 per cent of the deposits in national banks, they could not have materially lowered the national bank deposit-reserve ratio.

Nine states, in addition to the six that had imposed such requirements by 1879, imposed reserve requirements against deposits up to 1897, most of them setting high-powered money reserve and total reserve requirements lower than under the National Banking Act (R. G. Rodkey, *Legal Reserves*, pp. 30–35). During those years the level of the deposit-reserve ratio of nonnational banks was about twice as high as that of national banks. The share of bank reserves held by nonnational banks varied from a little less to a little more than a third.

the runs on banks that were to produce a restriction of cash payments in July 1893. At the same time, the deposit-reserve ratio rose slightly, probably reflecting the depletion of bank reserves by customer withdrawals despite the banks' attempt to build them up. Once the panic was past and confidence in the banks restored, the deposit-currency ratio rose and at the same time the banks were able to achieve the greater liquidity the crisis had led them to believe they needed. So the deposit-reserve ratio fell. It will be recalled that in the preceding chapter we described a similar decline in the deposit-reserve ratio in the year following the panic of 1873. In that case, however, the deposit-currency ratio was nearly constant in the panic year rather than declining, presumably because the available estimates for 1873 are for a date seven months before the panic.

Aside from the effects of the panics, the deposit-reserve ratio shows also a mild cyclical movement that reflects less the changing desired reserves of individual banks than a growth in nonnational bank deposits relative to national bank deposits during expansions and a decline during contractions. The changing relative importance of the two classes of banks during the cycle imparted a cyclical pattern to the deposit-reserve ratio and thereby contributed to a cyclical pattern in the money stock itself.

CHANGES IN HIGH-POWERED MONEY

Given the two deposit ratios, the total of high-powered money was, as we have seen, ultimately under the sway of external conditions which could produce an increase, if that were called for, by gold inflows, or a decrease by gold outflows. The adjustment mechanism was, of course, not instantaneous, leaving considerable leeway for domestic forces to affect the total in short periods. Moreover, domestic forces affected international trade and, in the process, the domestic position that was consistent with the international position. One example was considered at the end of the last chapter. The Treasury's accumulation of a gold reserve before resumption made necessary a larger surplus or smaller deficit in the balance of payments than would otherwise have been required. The Treasury's action therefore made for a lower level of prices in the United States relative to world prices than would otherwise have prevailed.

From 1879 to 1897, the main domestic sources of change in high-powered money were connected with Treasury cash, either directly or indirectly through the effect on national bank notes of Treasury actions, or with the Treasury's purchase of silver under the two silver acts. Under many circumstances, Treasury cash is not a useful total, because it can be so easily altered by what are simple bookkeeping transactions. During this period, however, it so happens that the legislative enactments govern-

124

ing it left the Treasury little possibility of affecting its reported balances through bookkeeping entries. There was no category of fiduciary currency that it was legally free to issue and simply add to its balances. The only fiduciary currency issued was the fiduciary element in minor coins and silver currency.[49] Purchase of bronze, copper, nickel, and silver for the sake of coining the seigniorage to add to Treasury cash was neither contemplated nor made. Treasury cash could be increased by either a surplus of revenue or by borrowing, either of which subtracted from high-powered money, or could be decreased by deficits or repayment of debt, either of which added to high-powered money.

Treasury Cash

As is clear from Chart 10, Treasury cash was at all times a minor fraction of high-powered money. It fluctuated between 9 and 27 per cent of high-powered money and for much of the period varied relatively little. Yet it is clear also that those variations in Treasury cash accounted, at least proximately, for most of the shorter-term movements in high-powered money: high-powered money alone is much more unstable than the total of high-powered money plus Treasury cash.

It is difficult to judge the net effect of the variations in Treasury cash on the stability of the money stock. Some of the changes produced by Treasury cash may have been called for by international trade conditions. In the absence of the changes in Treasury cash, the movement now recorded in high-powered money, hence in the money stock, would have been produced by gold movements and would have been recorded in the total of high-powered money and Treasury cash as well as in high-powered money alone. But inasmuch as changes in Treasury cash were in the main short-term, it is equally plausible that they introduced deviations from the pattern called for by international trade conditions and so fostered gold movements that would otherwise have been unnecessary. This interpretation is rather strongly supported by Chart 11, which shows the changes in Treasury cash from June 30 to June 30 and the net international movement of gold in the corresponding fiscal year. There is a clearly marked inverse relation for the years 1880–84 and 1888–92 between the short-term movements in the two series. There is a

[49] The fiduciary element in minor coins and silver is the excess of the monetary value of bronze, copper, nickel, and silver purchased over the sum expended by the Treasury in purchasing them. This seigniorage profit was added to the Treasury's General Fund. But it did not add to recorded Treasury cash. Silver held as security for Treasury notes of 1890 was valued at its monetary value, the fiduciary element therein equaling the excess of the monetary value over the cost of the bullion, but this silver cover is not included in our figures of Treasury cash. Since uncoined silver was not currency, it again is also not included as part of Treasury cash. The silver in Treasury cash consists of silver certificates, coined silver, and Treasury notes of 1890.

125

CHART 11
Net Gold Outflow and Year-to-Year Change in Treasury Cash,
Fiscal Years, 1879–97

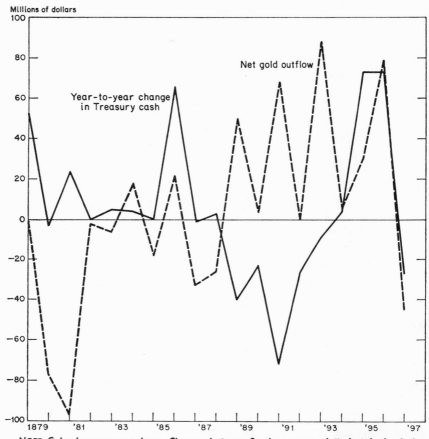

NOTE: Calendar years are shown. Changes between fiscal years are plotted at the beginning of the calendar year.

SOURCE: *Historical Statistics*, 1960, Series U-6, pp. 537–538; Table 5, col. 6, below, and for 1878, same source as for 1879 in that table.

clear positive relation for the years 1884–88. If we omit the final years, which were dominated by the silver problem, it therefore appears that the gold movements were exaggerated by the movements in Treasury cash about twice as often as they were minimized.[50]

[50] Presumably there was a lag in reaction. However, the annual figures are for too long a time unit to permit analysis of lags that were presumably a few months in duration. Monthly and quarterly figures, in seasonally adjusted form, give some indication of a lag of one to three quarters in the reaction of gold movements.

126

If this conclusion is right, it means that in this respect the movements in Treasury cash were destabilizing. In their absence, the total of high-powered money plus Treasury cash might have been less stable than it was, but high-powered money alone, hence the money stock, would have been more stable. However, this effect may have been offset, or more than offset, by the relation between changes in Treasury cash and the two other determinants of the money stock, the two deposit ratios. The sharp increase in Treasury cash from 1885 to 1886 offset to some extent the sharp rises in both deposit ratios in that year, in their rebound from the earlier impact of the banking crisis of 1884, and thus helped to moderate the rise in the stock of money, which even so was at a higher rate than in either the preceding or the following year. Again, the decrease in Treasury cash from 1890 to 1891 helped to offset the decline in the two deposit ratios in those years, and so helped to convert what otherwise might have been an absolute decline in the money stock into a retardation in the rate of growth. On the other hand, the further decrease from 1891 to 1892 contributed to the sharp spurt in the money stock in that year, destined to be followed by a decline in the next.

These judgments take for granted the movements in the two deposit ratios. In the absence of the fluctuations in Treasury cash, however, the deposit ratios might themselves have been different. If, as our tentative judgment suggests, more stable Treasury cash would have meant a more stable total of high-powered money, that stability might in its turn have affected the position of banks and thereby both of the deposit ratios. There seems no simple way, however, of estimating the magnitude or even the direction of such indirect effects.

Whatever may be the correct conclusion about whether the fluctuations in Treasury cash had a stabilizing or destabilizing effect on the money stock, one thing is clear. The fluctuations in Treasury cash could be kept as small as they were only by explicit and deliberate action by the Treasury. Under the Independent Treasury System, customs receipts, the largest source of revenue, could not be kept in banks but, until paid out, had to be kept in the form of currency in the Treasury. During most of the period, the government was running a surplus. That surplus was small relative to total national income but not negligible relative to high-powered money. At its peak, the annual surplus was well over 10 per cent of high-powered money, and the cumulated surplus from 1879 to 1892 amounted to two-thirds of the high-powered money at the end of the period. Had the surplus simply been allowed to accumulate in the Treasury, it would have forced sufficient monetary contraction to have produced gold imports large enough to replace it. In order to prevent that result, the surplus was used to redeem the debt or to prepay interest on it, or forms of revenue other than customs were allowed to accumulate on

127

deposit at banks. These measures, in turn however, had offsetting effects, since debt redemption reduced the amount and raised the price of bonds available to serve as backing for national bank notes, and so led to a reduction in national bank notes from a peak of some $350 million in 1882 to a trough of some $160 million in 1891. They also had the effect of disposing the Treasury toward similar open market operations at times of financial strain, so that the Treasury assumed central bank functions, though it did so erratically and unpredictably. In consequence, the detailed monetary history of the period is replete with references to Treasury interventions in the money market.

From 1888 to 1893, Treasury cash declined steadily and sizably as a result of debt redemptions in excess of the surplus. The Treasury was, as it were, engaging in net open market purchases. The result shows up partly in the temporary spurt in the money stock from 1891 to 1892 referred to above, but perhaps mainly in larger gold exports, or smaller imports, than would otherwise have occurred. That effect was intensified from 1890 to 1893 by the simultaneous expansion in the monetization of silver under the Sherman Silver Act. From 1893 through 1896, Treasury cash rose, despite the emergence of a deficit, because of even larger borrowings—the Treasury engaged in open market sales of securities. From its point of view, it did so to protect and build up its gold reserve. But the effect was to enforce the monetary contraction that was necessary to produce a balance of payments permitting the export of capital.

Silver Legislation

Silver legislation had its direct influence on the composition of high-powered money (see Chart 12 and Table 5; the latter also shows the composition of Treasury cash). Silver legislation is manifested in the growth of silver and Treasury notes of 1890.

As Chart 12 makes clear, until 1886, silver grew fairly slowly and the greater part of the increase in high-powered money consisted of gold. From then until 1893, silver grew rapidly, replacing gold almost entirely as a source of *additional* high-powered money. Thereafter, both silver and gold as well as total high-powered money fluctuated about a nearly constant level.

From 1879 to 1893, the total of silver and Treasury notes of 1890 outside the Treasury grew some $500 million, which is a measure of the strength of the silver forces. These purchases added to high-powered money and so contributed to an expansion of the stock of money. This is the effect that contemporaries pointed to as constituting a threat to the gold standard. But it is clear that the direct effect of the silver purchases on the stock of money did not, in fact, threaten the maintenance of the gold standard. In the first place, the growth in silver

128

CHART 12
Composition of High-Powered Money, 1879–97

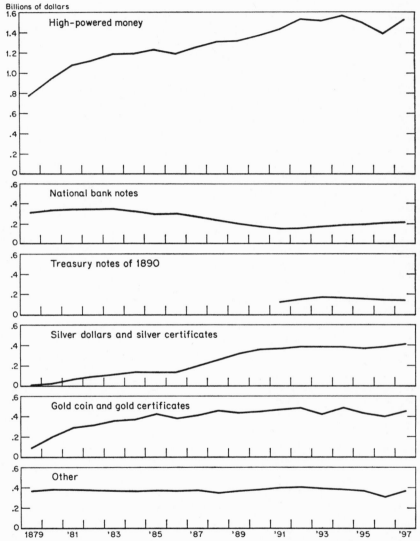

SOURCE: Table 5, cols. 7–12. "Other" consists of U.S. notes, subsidiary silver, and currency certificates.

129

TABLE 5
CURRENCY IN AND OUTSIDE THE TREASURY, BY KIND, 1879–97
(millions of dollars)

End of June	Gold (1)	Silver (2)	Treasury Notes of 1890 (3)	National Bank Notes (4)	Other (5)	Total (6)
		CURRENCY IN THE TREASURY (TREASURY CASH)				
1879	120	28		8	54	210
1880	118	39		7	43	207
1881	157	23		5	46	231
1882	143	33		6	49	231
1883	138	39		8	51	236
1884	134	39		9	58	240
1885	120	64		10	46	240
1886	157	93		4	52	306
1887	187	69		2	47	305
1888	194	43		7	64	308
1889	187	22		4	55	268
1890	190	16		4	35	245
1891	118	17	10	6	22	173
1892	114	5	4	5	19	147
1893	95	6	7	4	26	138
1894	65	15	18	7	37	142
1895	108	29	30	5	43	215
1896	102	36	34	11	105	288
1897	141	31	31	5	53	261
	(7)	(8)	(9)	(10)	(11)	(12)
	CURRENCY OUTSIDE THE TREASURY (HIGH-POWERED MONEY)					
1879	90	8		313	368	779
1880	198	25		331	383	937
1881	282	68		341	381	1,072
1882	319	87		341	377	1,124
1883	359	108		342	375	1,184
1884	365	136		327	362	1,190
1885	421	140		298	374	1,233
1886	384	140		301	368	1,193
1887	414	198		275	373	1,260
1888	457	256		240	356	1,309
1889	438	311		204	366	1,319
1890	449	353		178	386	1,366
1891	469	365	40	159	400	1,433
1892	483	384	98	162	401	1,528
1893	424	383	141	178	394	1,520
1894	482	378	135	192	382	1,569
1895	439	372	116	200	375	1,502
1896	400	383	95	208	312	1,398
1897	450	410	84	216	364	1,524

(continued)

TABLE 5 (concluded)

End of June	Gold (13)	Silver (14)	Treasury Notes of 1890 (15)	National Bank Notes (16)	Other (17)	Total (18)
	CURRENCY IN AND OUTSIDE THE TREASURY					
1879	210	36		322	423	991
1880	316	64		339	426	1,145
1881	439	91		346	427	1,303
1882	463	119		348	427	1,357
1883	497	147		350	427	1,421
1884	499	175		336	421	1,431
1885	541	204		308	420	1,473
1886	541	234		305	420	1,500
1887	601	267		277	420	1,565
1888	651	299		247	421	1,618
1889	625	334		208	421	1,588
1890	640	369		182	421	1,612
1891	587	382	50	165	421	1,605
1892	598	388	102	168	420	1,676
1893	519	390	147	182	420	1,658
1894	547	394	153	198	419	1,711
1895	547	401	146	205	419	1,718
1896	502	419	130	219	418	1,688
1897	591	441	115	221	417	1,785

NOTE: On account of rounding differences there may be minor discrepancies between the sums of kinds of currency in and outside the Treasury and the figures shown in cols. 13–18. Cols. 6 and 12 are unadjusted for seasonal variations, and so differ from col. 1 in Tables A-3 and B-3. Gold consists of gold coin and gold certificates. Silver consists of silver dollars and silver certificates. Other consists of U.S. notes, currency certificates, and subsidiary silver. Minor coin is omitted. Cols. 1 through 6 are unrevised Treasury figures, i.e., holdings, so far as the Treasury Dept. in Washington was informed, on the last day of the month when the statement was compiled.
SOURCE: Same as for col. 1 of Tables A-1 and A-3.

currency was offset to some extent by a reduction in national bank notes outstanding, a reduction enforced by debt retirement. In the second place, and more important, total high-powered money grew from 1879 to 1893 by $740 million or by $240 million more than the silver currency. In the absence of the silver purchases, the gold stock—or perhaps some other component of the money stock—would have risen more than it did.

The threat to the gold standard came from the effects of the silver purchases on the willingness of foreigners to hold dollars. This evidence of the power of the silver forces discouraged the inflow of capital or produced speculative capital outflows of substantial magnitude and kept alive the possibility of very much larger outflows. The smaller inflows or actual outflows made for a lower rise in high-powered money than would otherwise have occurred, so that in their absence the growth in silver currency would have been a still smaller fraction of the total growth

131

in high-powered money. Together with the measures taken in fear of potential outflows, they enforced monetary deflation to produce the requisite adjustments in the balance of payments. Paradoxically, therefore, the monetary damage done by silver agitation was almost the opposite of that attributed to it at the time. It kept the money stock from rising as much as it otherwise would have, rather than producing too rapid an increase in the money stock.[51]

Another paradox is that a major concern of the Treasury was how to keep silver out of the Treasury and in circulation, a problem that was finally solved by the authorization of silver certificates in small denominations. Yet keeping silver in circulation was adverse to the Treasury's objective of maintaining the gold standard. The accumulation of silver in the Treasury, in the form of a net addition to Treasury cash, would have prevented silver purchases from adding to the stock of money outside the Treasury, and so from promoting an unfavorable trade balance and gold export. The purchase of silver would have been simply a government expenditure like the purchase of coal for furnaces and would have had no direct monetary effects. It would have had to be financed by taxation or borrowing, either of which would have reduced the resources at the disposal of some by the same amount that the purchases of silver increased the resources available to others. The silver-purchase program would have been simply a stockpiling operation or a price-support program of the kind with which we have become familiar in recent decades.

The silver purchases fall into three well-defined periods. From the spring of 1878 to August 1890, purchases were made under the Bland-Allison Act of 1878, which instructed the Secretary to buy between $2 million and $4 million of silver a month. Actual purchases tended to be near the lower limit. So the increment of silver dollars varied between $27 million and $35 million a year. Over the same period, as already noted, national bank note circulation declined because of the use of the surplus to retire the debt. For the fiscal years 1880–90 (June 1879–June 1890), silver dollars added to the silver stock totaled $333 million, the reduction in national bank notes totaled $140 million, and the Treasury increased its cash by $35 million, so that the net contri-

[51] If we abstract from the effect on confidence in the monetary standard and the associated economic uncertainty and difficulties—which is admittedly abstracting from the major effects in fact—whether the purchase of silver involved costs or gains to the community depends on the alternative mode of increasing the money stock. If the alternative had been gold imports, the silver purchases involved gains since, given the difference between the market and monetary prices of silver, the production of the silver used fewer resources than the production of the exports to replace gold exports or to finance gold imports. If the alternative had been a fiduciary currency—which under the circumstances seems unlikely—the reverse would be the case.

bution of Treasury monetary actions to high-powered money amounted to only $158 million over the eleven years, or an average of $14 million a year. High-powered money grew by $587 million, or by nearly 3¾ times as much. True, the net contribution of the Treasury varied from year to year, mostly because of the fluctuations in Treasury cash that we have already considered. Even so, it is clear that, over this period, the net monetary impact of Treasury operations, including silver purchases, was of secondary importance.

From fiscal 1891 through fiscal 1893, silver purchases were stepped up drastically under the Sherman Silver Purchase Act, and additions to silver dollars and Treasury notes of 1890 amounted to $168 million in the three years. At the same time, the reduction in national bank notes ceased, and Treasury cash declined by $107 million, rather than increasing. In consequence, in those three years, the net contribution of Treasury monetary actions to high-powered money amounted to a total of $275 million or nearly twice the total for the preceding eleven years—$118 million in fiscal 1891; $87 million, in fiscal 1892; and $70 million, in fiscal 1893. In the same years, total high-powered money went up only $154 million, the difference taking the form of net gold exports over and above gold production. During those three years, then, Treasury action was on a scale large enough to be highly significant, in the sense that it was on a scale which, if indefinitely maintained, would have driven the United States off the gold standard entirely by its direct effects on the money stock. But note that even in those years, over a third of the effect was through reduced Treasury cash balances. Monetary additions by silver alone were at a rate of about $60 million a year. If that had been the sole source of increased currency and if it had had no indirect effects upon confidence in the maintenance of the gold standard, it could almost surely have been absorbed indefinitely without seriously threatening the gold standard.

Finally the years from 1893 to 1897 saw an increase in the silver stock of only about $19 million (due to purchases made between June 30, 1893, and the repeal of the silver purchase clause), a rise in national bank notes of $53 million, and a rise in the Treasury cash balance of $123 million, so Treasury action was a deflationary factor to the net extent of $51 million. That was, therefore, the period when the direct effect of silver purchases was negligible, yet it may well have been the period when the indirect effect was at its maximum.

This entire silver episode is a fascinating example of how important what people think about money can sometimes be. The fear that silver would produce an inflation sufficient to force the United States off the gold standard made it necessary to have a severe deflation in order to stay on the gold standard. In retrospect, it seems clear that either acceptance of a silver standard at an early stage or an early commitment to gold would have been preferable to the uneasy compromise that was maintained, with the uncertainty about the ultimate outcome and the consequent wide fluctuations to which the currency was subjected.[52]

[52] As between the early adoption of silver as the standard at the nominal monetary value of $1.29 an ounce and an early commitment to gold, it seems likely that on the whole the adoption of silver would have been preferable, though this is clearly a difficult and complex judgment.

Adoption of silver by the United States would certainly have moderated or eliminated deflationary tendencies here. It would also have moderated and might have eliminated deflation in the world at large. The U.S. monetary demand for gold would have been sharply reduced and, in addition, the U.S. example might have encouraged other countries to stay on silver or convert to it and so still further have reduced the pressure on the gold supply.

For the period before 1897, therefore, the choice between silver and gold hinges mainly on one's judgment about the desirable price trends. If one regards the deflationary price trend as an evil and a horizontal price trend as preferable, as we do, though with some doubts, silver would on this account and for that period have been preferable to gold. The only other effect of any importance for the period was on the system of international exchange rates. The adoption of silver by the U.S. would have meant rigid exchange rates between it and other silver countries, but flexible rates between that group and the gold-standard countries. This effect too we are inclined to regard as an advantage of silver rather than a disadvantage. A striking, more recent, example of how much of an advantage it can be is furnished by China's experience from 1929 to 1931. Because it was on a silver standard, it avoided almost entirely the adverse consequences of the first two years of the worldwide depression, which began in 1929 (see Chap. 8, sect. 2, below).

The gold price of silver fell rapidly from the 1870's and by the end of the century was less than half its initial level. Does this mean that the substitution of silver for gold by the U.S. would simply have replaced the deflationary price trend by an even sharper inflationary trend? The answer is clearly negative. The decline in the gold price of silver itself reflected the demonetization of silver and the widening adoption of the gold standard. The adoption of silver by the U.S. would have reduced the monetary demand for gold and increased the monetary demand for silver and in both respects would have contributed toward a higher gold price of silver. And this would have been intensified by the effects of American action on other countries. A rough examination of the magnitudes involved suggests that the adoption of silver instead of gold by the U.S. in 1879 might well have largely eliminated the decline that actually occurred in the gold price of silver and have permitted roughly stable prices in both gold and silver countries.

The more troublesome argument against silver concerns the effects for the period after 1897 when gold alone produced an inflationary trend. Would not this trend have been intensified, at least in the gold part of the world, if the U.S. had been on silver? Here again, the answer is less clear than might at first appear. The deflation in terms of gold before 1896 was an important factor stimulating gold exploration and efforts to develop improved techniques of refining ore. In its absence, there might not have been a comparable outpouring of gold.

CHAPTER 4

Gold Inflation and Banking Reform, 1897–1914

PRICES in the United States rose between 40 and 50 per cent from 1897 to 1914: nearly 50 per cent or at the average rate of 2½ per cent per year according to the wholesale price index, 40 per cent or at the average rate of 2 per cent per year according to the implicit index used to deflate net national product (see Chart 13). The rise brought prices in 1914 just about back to the level reached in 1882 at the peak of the immediate postresumption expansion.

This price behavior is probably unique in the history of the United States. So far as we can judge from available data, no other peacetime period of equal or greater length has been characterized by a persistent upward trend in prices, though if the 1948–60 trend is not reversed the post–World War II period will in time provide another example.[1] Price rises of larger total magnitude have occurred in U.S. history, but all have been during or immediately after wars—the rough doubling of prices in the Revolutionary War, the Civil War, and the two world wars. The only peacetime rise comparable in total magnitude followed the California gold discoveries in the early 1850's, when prices rose at a faster rate than from 1897 to 1914 but for less than half as long.

The price rise in the United States after 1897 was part of a worldwide movement. British wholesale prices, which may be taken as reasonably representative of prices in the rest of the western world linked together by a common monetary standard, rose by 26 per cent from 1897 to 1914 according to the Board of Trade index.[2]

[1] For the post–World War II period, the jump in price indexes after the war was presumably a delayed reflection of the war. To avoid the immediate aftereffects, we may date the postwar price rise as beginning in 1948. By 1960, the wholesale price index had risen 15 per cent, the consumer price index, 23 per cent, and the implicit price index, 27 per cent, or at annual rates of 1.1, 1.7, and 2.0 per cent, respectively. Between 39 and 59 per cent of this rise, depending on the index, occurred in the two Korean War years, 1950–52. In the eight peacetime years from 1952 to 1960, the wholesale price index rose 7 per cent, the consumer price index, 11 per cent, and the implicit price index, 14 per cent, or at annual rates of 0.9, 1.4, and 1.6 per cent, respectively. What happened in the post-World War II period, therefore, as of 1960, fell considerably short of matching what happened in the 1897–1914 period with respect to either duration or rate of price rise.

[2] *Board of Trade Journal*, Jan. 13, 1921, p. 34.

CHART 13

Money Stock, Income, Prices, and Velocity, in Reference
Cycle Expansions and Contractions, 1897–1914

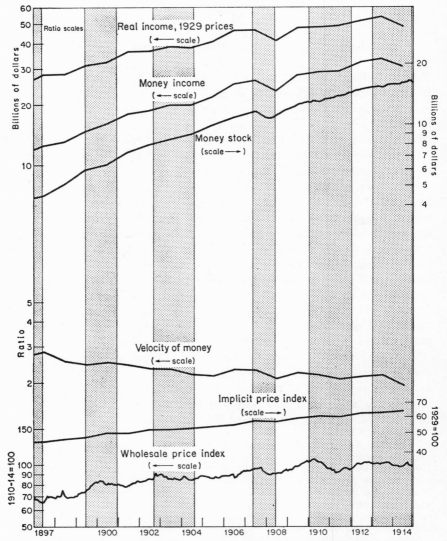

NOTE: Shaded areas represent business contractions; unshaded areas, business expansions.
SOURCE: Same as for Chart 8.

The proximate cause of the world price rise was clearly the tremendous outpouring of gold after 1890 that resulted from discoveries in South Africa, Alaska, and Colorado and from the development of improved methods of mining and refining. The gold stock of the world is estimated to have more than doubled from 1890 to 1914, growing at an average rate of 3½ per cent a year. By contrast, it rose about 40 per cent during the preceding twenty-four years, or at an average rate of 1½ per cent per year.[3] And even this comparison understates the difference. The earlier period 1866–90 was marked by a return to gold in the United States (1879) and the substitution of gold for gold and silver, or for silver, as the monetary standard in Germany (1871–73), the Latin Monetary Union (1873), and the Netherlands (1875–76). There was no counterpart in the later period of this major source of demand for gold. An offsetting factor in the earlier period was the rise in the ratio of deposits to currency, which reduced the demand for gold in the U.S. But the rise continued during the period after 1890 at something like the same percentage rate. So it did not affect the two periods differently.

Because of the monetary difficulties in the United States arising out of the silver agitation, the stock of gold started to increase in the U.S. rather later than 1891, the date when its rate of growth accelerated in the world at large. From a level of $640 million in June 1890, the U.S. monetary gold stock (inside and outside the Treasury) fell to a low of $502 million in June 1896 and had recovered only to $591 million by June 1897. But once the gold stock started to rise, it rose much faster in the United States than in the rest of the world—at an average rate of 6.8 per cent per year. By 1914 it was $1,891 million or more than triple its 1897 level. In 1897, the United States held 14 per cent of the world's gold stock; by 1914, it held nearly one-quarter.

The total stock of money in the United States rose at only a slightly higher rate than the gold stock (7½ per cent per year) despite sizable rises in both the deposit-currency and the deposit-reserve ratios (see Chart 14, below), both of which might be expected to produce a more rapid rate of rise in the money stock than in gold. The explanation is that almost the entire increase in high-powered money came in the form of gold and national bank notes. The other chief components of high-powered money—silver and silver certificates, Treasury notes of 1890,

[3] See *Interim Report of the Gold Delegation of the Financial Committee,* League of Nations, Geneva, 1930, estimates by Joseph Kitchin, pp. 83–84. There is some evidence that Kitchin's estimate for 1913 (and presumably for 1914) is too low by something like 14 per cent (see *ibid.,* p. 114; and C. O. Hardy, *Is There Enough Gold?* Washington, Brookings, 1936, pp. 205–207). However, we do not know how much of a similar correction is required in Kitchin's earlier figures and hence cannot judge the effect of such a correction on the rates of growth.

137

and U.S. notes—grew hardly at all (see Chart 15, below). Gold and national bank notes comprised only 44 per cent of high-powered money in 1897, 68 per cent in 1914.

Of the 7½ per cent per year increase in the stock of money, price rises, as we have seen, absorbed some 2 per cent per year. Something over 3 per cent was absorbed by a growth in the real output of goods and services, something under 2½ per cent by a decline in the velocity of money—that is, a rise in money balances relative to income.

These average figures for the period as a whole conceal nearly as much as they reveal. As Chart 13 brings out, the years from 1897 to 1914 were by no means uniform. The initial years from 1897 to 1901 or 1902 represented a rebound from the depressed conditions of the preceding four or five years: the money stock, real output, and prices all grew at extraordinary rates. From 1901 or 1902 to 1914, the economy experienced relatively steady growth, interrupted seriously only by the banking panic of 1907, with its associated severe but brief business contraction. That panic is important for our purposes because it produced the strong demand for banking reform which finally led to the passage of the Federal Reserve Act. We shall therefore find it desirable to consider separately (1) the rebound from 1897 to 1902; (2) the period from 1902 to 1907; (3) the panic of 1907; (4) the movement for banking reform in the wake of the restriction of cash payments by the banks; (5) the remaining years from 1907 to 1914.

1. *The Rebound, 1897 to 1902*

CHANGES IN MONEY, INCOME, PRICES, AND VELOCITY

The final years of the century saw a dramatic reversal of economic conditions. The stock of money had fluctuated about a roughly constant level from 1892 to 1897; in June 1896 it was lower than in June 1892, in June 1897 about the same as in June 1892. From then on it bounded upward at an extraordinary rate: by 15 per cent from 1897 to 1898, 17 per cent from 1898 to 1899, 6 per cent from 1899 to 1900, 15 per cent from 1900 to 1901, and 9 per cent from 1901 to 1902—a cumulative increase of nearly 80 per cent in five years.

Prices had been declining from early 1893 to 1896, not only absolutely but also relative to prices in Great Britain. Beginning in mid-1897, wholesale prices rose somewhat erratically to early 1900, and then declined only briefly before rising again to a peak in the final months of 1902 and early months of 1903 that was not to be exceeded for some four years. From the reference trough in June 1897 to the reference peak in September 1902, wholesale prices rose 32 per cent; from then to the reference trough in December 1914, by 13 per cent, as judged by average values for the three months centered on the reference turn. Of the total price rise (so measured) of 49 per cent in the seventeen and a half years between the reference troughs of 1897 and 1914, two-thirds occurred in the first five years. Until 1900, the price rise in the United States was at almost the same rate as in Britain. Our purchasing-power parity index (see Chart 9) is 90.1 for 1897, 90.8 for 1900. In the next two years, U.S. prices advanced further while British prices declined, so the purchasing-power parity index rose to 96.3.

Stagnation in the money stock and declining prices from 1893 to 1896 had been accompanied by a generally depressed level of business activity. Here, too, there was a sharp reversal. From 1896 to 1902, net national product in constant prices rose by 45 per cent, or at a rate in excess of 6 per cent per year. Population was rising at a rate of less than 2 per cent per year, so per capita output rose at a rate of nearly $4\frac{1}{2}$ per cent per year. This was clearly a period of vigorous expansion on all fronts. According to the National Bureau's business cycle chronology, it was interrupted by a business contraction running from a peak in June 1899 to a trough in December 1900. That contraction is mirrored in the lower rate of increase in the money stock from 1899 to 1900, recorded above. But it was an extremely mild contraction and shows up in net national product in constant prices as only a moderate slackening in the rate of growth. The rapid expansion of physical output after 1896 is very much like that which occurred after 1879 and is another example of the tendency, noted in connection with that episode, of a severe contraction to be followed by a vigorous rebound.[4]

In view of the important role that uncertainty about the U.S. monetary standard apparently played in producing the troubled conditions of the early 1890's, a key issue is the improvement in financial conditions that permitted revival on the physical level. Here, too, there is much in common with the postresumption episode.

The defeat of Bryan and his free-silver platform in the Presidential election of 1896 is a convenient and dramatic date to mark the turning point. And undoubtedly, it had some effect in allaying uncertainty about the monetary standard and so in reducing speculation against the dollar. It is doubtful, however, that that political event was at all decisive. After all, McKinley's victory, while clear-cut, was by no means a landslide—his popular vote exceeded Bryan's by less than 10 per cent. Had economic circumstances been favorable to free silver, the issue could easily

---

[4] See Tables 9 and 22 below, and the serial correlation analysis in our forthcoming "Trends and Cycles in the Stock of Money in the United States, 1867–1960," a study of the National Bureau of Economic Research.

have been as unsettling in the four years after 1896 as it was in the preceding four years.

Two economic factors were of far greater significance in producing the sharp reversal after 1896. One, already referred to, was the rapid expansion of the world's output of gold. World gold prices, as represented by an index of British prices, reached their trough in 1896 and rose steadily thereafter. This meant that a rise in the stock of money and in prices in the United States was consistent with equilibrium in the balance of payments, even if capital flight due to monetary uncertainty continued at its prior level. And indeed, as already noted, the rise in U.S. prices just about kept pace with the rise in British prices up to 1900. Put differently, had the U.S. stock of money and prices not risen, the result would have been a surplus, or an even larger surplus than did occur, in the balance of payments.

The worldwide price rise unquestionably would have produced a rise in both the stock of money and prices in the United States sooner or later. But the rise in both might well have come later and certainly would have proceeded at a slower pace if it had not been for a second factor: another one of those fortuitous combinations of good harvests at home and poor harvests abroad that were so critical from time to time in nineteenth-century American economic history, in particular in the immediate postresumption period. The European wheat crop was smaller in 1897 than in 1896 by more than a fifth. At the same time, the U.S. crop was decidedly larger than in the year before. U.S. exports of wheat and wheat products doubled. Further, the Dingley Tariff of July 1897 raised duties sharply on imports. These events were accompanied by a major shift in the recorded balance of merchandise trade. For the twelve months ending June 30, 1896, the value of exports from the United States was reported to exceed the value of imports by $103 million; for the next twelve months, by $286 million; for the next, by no less than $615 million. The largest excess of exports over imports previously recorded was $265 million, for the twelve months ending June 30, 1879; that value was exceeded in every fiscal year from 1897 through 1909, and the lowest values in that period were in the initial and final years—the $286 million already noted for the initial year and $351 million for the final. Indeed, the shift in the recorded balance of trade is so sudden, so large, and so long continued that it raises doubts in our minds about the accuracy of the figures. However, despite considerable effort, we have been unable to find any changes in the method of compiling the figures or any other source of differential error that would explain the sudden shift in level.[5]

[5] Wesley C. Mitchell (*Business Cycles,* Berkeley, University of California Press,

The sharp rise in the excess of merchandise exports over merchandise imports was promptly reflected in gold movements. In the twelve months ending June 30, 1896, the United States exported some $79 million in gold in excess of gold imports; in the three succeeding fiscal years it imported, net, $45, $105, and $51 million, respectively; thereafter through fiscal 1903 net movements were very small.

From the point of view of the stock of money, these sums are very large indeed. The total monetary gold stock in the United States on June 30, 1896, was $502 million. Net imports of gold during the next three years amounted to $201 million or 40 per cent of the initial stock. In addition, domestic gold production was at the rate of some $60 million a year. Additions from abroad and at home raised the monetary gold stock to $859 million by June 30, 1899.

From the point of view of the balance of payments, the gold movements are much smaller. The change in annual gold movement absorbed two-thirds of the change in the merchandise balance from fiscal year 1896 to fiscal year 1897, a little more than one-third from fiscal 1896 to fiscal 1898, a little less than one-third from fiscal 1896 to fiscal 1899, and a negligible fraction from fiscal 1900 to fiscal 1903.

Under the gold standard, an unusually favorable balance of payments would be expected to produce a gold inflow (or reduce an outflow); the gold inflow, to produce a rise in the stock of money at home and a fall abroad (or a rise at home relative to abroad); the changes in the stock of money, to produce a rise in domestic income and prices relative to foreign income and prices; and the changes in relative income and prices, to produce a reduction in exports and an increase in imports tending to restore the balance of payments. This is precisely the sequence which occurred in 1880 and 1881. Chart 9 (which gives the ratio of U.S. to British prices, capital movements expressed as a ratio to net national product, and gold movements) shows a marked rise in the ratio of U.S. to British prices in 1880 and 1881, during which—fiscal—years there was a heavy inflow of gold into the United States. In the present instance, however, the sequence was interrupted in mid-passage: the gold inflows occurred, and they raised the domestic stock of money absolutely and almost certainly also relative to the stock abroad. But here the sequence ended. While prices rose in absolute level, they apparently did not rise relative to prices abroad until about 1901 (see Chart 9). Substantial net gold inflows petered out by 1899. Yet the balance of trade remained favorable and indeed reached a higher level in the twelve months ending June 30,

---

1913, p. 69) comments on the shift and notes sources of errors in the figures but does not consider whether these are greater or in a different direction after 1897 than before. His comments, however, lend themselves to the interpretation that he was somewhat suspicious of the statistical accuracy of the recorded shift.

1901, than in any other fiscal year from 1896 through 1902. Similarly, such estimates as we have for capital movements (the trade balance adjusted for "invisible" items in the balance of payments) indicate that capital exports were roughly zero in 1896, became sizable in 1897, and remained sizable all the way to 1906. They were largest in 1900 and declined thereafter, most sharply from 1901 to 1902 (see Chart 9).

WHY SHOULD CAPITAL EXPORTS HAVE OCCURRED?

This course of events is most puzzling. Why should the United States have been a net exporter of capital during 1897–1906, let alone on so large a scale?[6] The explanation generally given for the favorable trade balance, and implicitly for the export of capital, is that after the unusually favorable agricultural exports of 1897 and 1898, imports were held down by the Dingley Tariff while exports of manufactured goods rose as a result of the United States' growing industrial strength.[7] But this is no answer at all. An improvement in the United States' competitive position in exports might tend in the first instance to produce a piling up of U.S.–owned foreign balances, but there is no reason the owners of these balances should invest them abroad. Unless the improvement in competitive position should happen to coincide with some independent factor making foreign investment or the holding of foreign funds relatively more attractive than before compared to domestic investment or the holding of domestic funds, the effect would be the sequence of gold flows and monetary and price changes summarized in the preceding paragraph. In consequence, an improvement in the U.S. external competitive position would produce, perhaps after some delay, a rise in domestic prices relative to foreign prices—presumably this is the explanation for the rise that did occur after 1901 when recorded capital exports declined sharply (see Chart 9)—but it alone would not produce capital exports. Indeed, it might well have precisely the opposite effect. Our

[6] For simplicity of exposition, we speak in absolute terms for that period by itself. This is in one respect an oversimplification. The puzzle relates to the difference between the behavior in that and other periods. For example, suppose the statistical estimates of capital movements had a common bias in the direction of understating capital imports so that correction would show the U.S. to have been importing capital during the period. The puzzle would still remain, since the figures would show the U.S. to be importing capital during the period at a decidedly lower rate than earlier. On the other hand, suppose—as we to some extent suspect—that there is a differential bias, so that the earlier figures are biased in the direction of overstating capital imports *relative* to the later (this does not say which set of figures is in error—the earlier or the later). This might remove the puzzle, whether corrected figures showed capital exports or imports in 1897–1906.

[7] See A. D. Noyes, *Forty Years of American Finance,* New York, Putnam, 1909, pp. 269–276, 280–283.

growing industrial strength presumably meant increasingly attractive investment opportunities in the United States.

Uncertainty about the monetary standard makes foreign funds more attractive than domestic and hence is a factor tending to produce capital outflows—a "forced" export of capital, as it were. But this can hardly be the explanation in the present instance. The uncertainty was surely greater before than after 1896. Yet despite a net gold outflow before 1896, there apparently was no net capital outflow. According to the estimates in Chart 9, large capital exports emerged only after the 1896 election which gave, if anything, reason for greater confidence in the dollar.

One other factor that has been assigned an important role in producing capital exports is the growth of immigrant remittances and tourist expenditures. However, insofar as these played a role, they must have constituted a gradually growing amount over the entire period 1897 to 1914 and can hardly explain the sudden shift of capital exports to a new level after 1896 or the bulge in capital exports from 1896 to 1902.[8]

Three events during the period may have made for capital exports.

1. Stock market prices were declining before 1896. Beginning in late summer 1896, there was a revival, at first slow, and then at a more rapid pace. Stock market indexes show a rise of close to 70 per cent from August 1896 to August 1899. At the same time, bond yields, which had been falling since 1893, continued to fall until 1899, so that bond prices rose along with stock prices. It could be that capital export from the United States—in the form of sales here of securities owned by foreigners—though in process in the period before 1896 and encouraged by rising bond prices, was inhibited by declining stock prices. The capital, held reluctantly in the United States, may have been repatriated subsequently after stock prices boomed, while the continued rise in bond prices encouraged continued sales of bonds. There is some contemporary

---

[8] Charles J. Bullock, John H. Williams, and Rufus S. Tucker, in their article, "The Balance of Trade of the United States" (*Review of Economic Statistics,* July 1919, p. 228), give this explanation for the shift in level of the balance of trade. However, since they gave figures only for the period 1896–1914 as a whole, they were not faced directly with the problem of the time pattern of the shift.

Simon's estimates of total passenger payments, including U.S. tourist expenditures, immigrants' remittances, and emigrants' funds, increase from $116 million in 1897 to $162 million in 1900. This is the highest figure reached during the period 1861–1900 that his estimates cover. A change of this magnitude in total passenger payments is much too small to account for the shift in the balance of trade from 1897 to 1900 (see Matthew Simon, "The United States Balance of Payments, 1861–1900," *Trends in the American Economy in the Nineteenth Century,* Studies in Income and Wealth, Vol. 24, Princeton University Press for NBER, 1960, p. 704).

evidence that high stock prices did induce some foreigners to dispose of their holdings.[9]

2. The declaration of war on Spain in April 1898 probably had little direct effect on the capital flow, though it did briefly upset financial markets.[10] But it had some indirect effects that may have contributed to capital exports. The Treasury prepared for the war expenditures by floating a bond issue of $200 million in June 1898.[11] Since the war expenses were met only gradually, the bond sale raised Treasury balances and had an initial deflationary effect, which is reflected in wholesale commodity prices. After a sudden jump in May 1898, wholesale prices fell for some months—indeed, until after the armistice in August 1898—to a level below that reached before the declaration of war. Although, later on, government expenditures more than counteracted the

[9] Some contemporary commentators attributed considerable importance to this explanation. For example, in its annual "Retrospect of the Year" article, the *Commercial and Financial Chronicle* said of 1897: "The European public held firmly to the opinion that unless there is a complete rehabilitation of our currency and financial system, the country's future cannot be regarded as assured. They have consequently refused to make new capital investments here of any considerable amount, while on the other hand they have at times returned large quantities of our securities, taking advantage of the high prices prevailing to dispose of the same" (Jan. 1, 1898, p. 5). It said of 1899, "By our wild speculation on the stock market we favored a return of large amounts of our European-held securities. All through the early months sales of gilt-edged securities for foreign account were recorded, the inducement being the high prices prevailing here for this class of investments" (Jan. 6, 1900, p. 4). It said of 1900, ". . . with the great advance in our Stock Exchange prices following the November elections, European holders of our securities and bonds disposed of them in enormous amounts" (Jan. 5, 1901, p. 6). See also, C. A. Conant, "Securities as Means of Payment," *Annals of the American Academy of Political Science,* Vol. XIV, 1899, pp. 193–194.

Of course, these comments are also consistent with a shift of capital not on speculative grounds of distrust of the U.S. currency, but simply to earn a higher rate of return abroad than here.

[10] Secretary of the Treasury Gage described the public reaction as follows:

The morbidly timid along our eastern and northern coast were in a state of more or less alarm. The simpler-minded depositors in savings banks made withdrawals of their funds; the commercial banks in the larger cities sympathetically suffered through loss of cash reserves to savings institutions. The rate of interest rose; the price of securities declined. Even old issues of United States bonds fell to a point where they would yield to the investor from 3.1 to 3.25 per cent per annum upon an investment then made. Such was the condition of the financial market in the latter part of April and the earlier part of May last (*Annual Report on the Finances,* 1898, p. xciii).

Even the expected direction of the direct effect is not at all clear. The rise in domestic interest rates would attract capital; any uncertainty about monetary stability would repel it; the desire of domestic banks or financial institutions to strengthen their position might lead to a return of funds held abroad.

[11] This was a 3 per cent issue that sold at par, largely because it was attractive to national banks as security for national bank notes (see *Annual Report on the Finances,* 1898, p. xciii).

deflationary effect of the bond sale, the Treasury's immediate steps to offset it probably did not do so completely.[12] Insofar as the bond sale and increased taxes kept prices lower in the United States than they would otherwise have been, they promoted exports relative to imports. However, it is doubtful that the deflationary effects were at all sizable. After all, despite the bond sale, the stock of money rose by no less than 17 per cent from June 30, 1898 to June 30, 1899, and wholesale prices rose steadily from October 1898 through March 1900 at a rate of 13 per cent per year. Moreover, whatever the effect on imports and exports, and hence on short-term capital movements, there remains the question why such short-term capital accumulations were not repatriated.

Other wartime effects were an indemnity of $20 million paid Spain in April 1899 for the Philippines, Guam, and Puerto Rico, and expenditures to maintain our forces in the Philippines. These represented autonomous increases in the demand for foreign currency that directly contribute a mite to explain the capital exports.

3. The outbreak of the Boer War in October 1899 had special monetary significance because it threatened, and in the event produced, a sizable drop in gold production in the Transvaal, output which had been going in the first instance to Britain. The threat to gold production undoubtedly led to a sharper reaction on the part of the financial community in London than would otherwise have occurred, since the war itself was generally expected to be short. When that expectation was disappointed, the burden of carrying on the war replaced the monetary impact in importance. Contemporary observers assert that the reverses of the war led to a recall of British investments in this country in late 1899.[13] If this is correct, it presumably reflected a desire on the part of British financial institutions to increase their liquidity in preparation for possible demands on them by their creditors arising out of the uncertainty engendered by the war, especially as a result of the reduced gold inflow. That is, it may have meant not a net capital import into Britain but simply a sale of assets in one area to reduce liabilities elsewhere.[14] However, for the United States, which was a net debtor with

[12] Gage prepaid interest and the principal of maturing government bonds and increased government deposits with national banks in Sept. and Oct. 1898. The level of government deposits remained high throughout the rest of 1898 and 1899, because the war with Spain required less outlay than had been provided for.
[13] See "The Financial Situation," *Commercial and Financial Chronicle,* Dec. 16, 1899, p. 1216.
[14] This conjecture is borne out for 1900, when British net export of capital is estimated to have been slightly higher than in 1899. In 1901 and 1902, when the financial costs of carrying on the war became the most important factor, capital exports fell to about one-half their 1899–1900 level (A. K. Cairncross, *Home and Foreign Investment, 1870–1913,* Cambridge, University Press, 1953, p. 180).

respect to Britain, it meant a withdrawal of capital. The initial effect was probably less important than subsequent effects arising out of the British government's flotation of loans to finance the war. It is estimated that some $300 million of British government loans were floated in the New York market from 1900 to 1902. In order to be sold, the bonds had to be made attractive to purchasers. Hence the bond flotations involved a rise in the rate of return on foreign investment relative to that on domestic investment. Contemporary observers certainly judged that interest rates were decidedly higher abroad than at home.[15]

These factors, particularly the first and third, may contribute toward explaining the puzzle. But even all together they seem inadequate. Capital export in the calendar years 1897 through 1901 is estimated to total about $1.1 billion. Even if we offset against this sum a round figure of $0.3 billion of U.S. purchases of British government loans floated in New York plus U.S. loans to Canada, Mexico, Cuba, and European borrowers, and as much again of direct investments in U.S.–controlled commercial and industrial ventures located abroad, about half of the total remains unexplained.[16] Moreover, two further factors make this residuum a decided understatement of the total requiring explanation. First, the reduction in uncertainty about the maintenance of the gold standard could be expected to be a factor at least as important as any of those mentioned, and working in the opposite direction; second, the U.S. was typically an importer of capital before 1896.[17]

[15] "With dearer money abroad than here, the prevailing condition during the greater part of the year . . . " (*Commercial and Financial Chronicle,* Jan. 5, 1901, p. 8).

[16] Cleona Lewis (*America's Stake in International Investments,* Washington, Brookings, 1938, pp. 335–340) summarizes the known changes during those years in the American portfolio of foreign securities. Available information—often not quantitative—on American direct investments, 1897–1901, in companies located abroad engaged in trade and banking, gold and silver mining, production of oil, copper, and other industrial minerals, agricultural enterprises, public utilities, and other enterprises is scattered through pp. 173–329.

[17] According to our annual capital movement data, the United States was a net exporter of $1.7 billion of capital from 1897 to 1908. One might therefore expect a reduction in U.S. net foreign obligations over that period. The available estimates, however, move in the opposite direction: U.S. net foreign obligations increased $1.2 billion; although U.S. foreign investments increased $1.8 billion, U.S. foreign obligations increased $3.0 billion, 1897–1908 (Lewis, *America's Stake in International Investments,* p. 455).

According to Goldsmith's published data covering the period 1900–12, the United States was a net exporter of $1.3 billion of capital, with no net change in U.S. net foreign obligations: U.S. assets abroad increased $2.4 billion, and foreign assets in the U.S. increased $2.3 billion (R. W. Goldsmith, *A Study of Saving in the United States,* Princeton University Press, 1955, Vol. I, Tables K-6, K-7, and K-1, col. 8, pp. 1089, 1093, 1079).

Such discrepancies between flows and stocks in international financial statistics might arise even if both sets of estimates were wholly accurate. Some factors affect stocks but not flows, e.g., reinvestment of interest and dividends

To put the puzzle in a different way, Chart 9 shows from 1879 to 1914 an index of the relative prices in the United States and Britain and estimates of U.S. capital flows, expressed as ratios to net national product. The two series show the very considerable agreement in their broader movements that economic analysis would lead us to expect, but the whole level of the capital movement series for the period after 1896 seems lower compared with the relative prices series than the level before 1896 does, so that the puzzle is not removed, even when the bulge in recorded capital exports ceased around 1902.

Data on interest rate differentials between Britain and the United States are consistent with a decline in the relative attractiveness of investment in the United States. In the decade ending in 1897, U.S. railroad bond yields exceeded yields on British consols by about 0.9 percentage points. A decline set in after 1897 which reduced the differential to a low of about 0.2 percentage points in 1901. It then recovered and fluctuated around 0.5 percentage points until World War I, if allowance is made for a discontinuity in the consol series.[18] The unusually low level around 1901 is presumably the effect of the Boer War, referred to earlier.

The shift in the interest rate differential is confirmatory evidence that a shift in capital movements like that revealed by our data did take place. It is therefore a relevant piece of evidence on what did happen. It adds little, however, to our understanding of why it happened, since the change in the interest rate differential is but another aspect of the puzzle.[19] If the magnitude as well as the direction of the shift in capital movements is correctly measured by the estimates we use, the small change in the interest rate differential suggests a rather high elasticity of supply of capital for foreign investment at the time.

If the shift in level after 1896 is accepted as statistically valid, the only interpretation we have been able to construct to rationalize the shift is that fortuitously large exports of agricultural crops in 1897 and

---

earned abroad, and revaluation of stocks. In addition, constituents of stocks may not be strictly comparable with those of flows—e.g., the change in the gold stock is included in Goldsmith's flows, but the U.S. gold stock is not included in U.S. claims on foreigners.

Unexplained discrepancies between flows and stocks exist even for more recent and presumably more accurate data than are available for the first decade of this century. The flow data are usually considered more reliable.

[18] Oskar Morgenstern, *International Financial Transactions and Business Cycles,* Princeton for NBER, 1959, Chart 58, facing p. 472.

[19] Our earlier discussion is concerned with factors that might account for shifts in the demand and supply curves of capital for foreign investment. The discussion is phrased in terms of the quantity axis of such curves, in effect considering quantity shifts for given prices. Alternatively it could have been phrased in terms of the price axis, in this case, interest rates. We could have asked why the interest rate differential should have been reduced, rather than why capital exports occurred.

1898 plus the Dingley Tariff plus the three special events cited above account for the export surpluses of the early years, up to, say, 1902; and that that provided time for the growth of immigrant remittances and tourist expenditures to produce those of the later years. The preceding discussion explains why this rationalization is most unsatisfactory. In consequence, we are inclined to believe that there are either some other important economic factors at work that we have overlooked or some errors in the figures that we have been unable to discover.

The behavior of relative prices in the United States and Britain, considered independently of the level but not of the year-to-year changes in capital movement, is more readily explained. One would expect the period following the heavy gold imports to see a rise in U.S. prices relative to British, and such a rise got under way in 1898, according to the indexes used in computing the relative price series in Chart 9. Relative prices were then at their lowest level since 1879 and did not again fall so low in the rest of the period up to World War I. Simultaneously, the capital movement series was then at its lowest level for the whole period 1861–1914.

The rise was interrupted by a fall from 1899 to 1900, which carried the relative price series halfway back to its level in 1898. Presumably that interruption reflects the coincidence of a mild business recession in the United States (beginning June 1899) and the outbreak of the Boer War (in October 1899). There followed a monetary stringency in the fall of 1899, a panic in the stock market, and a number of failures of banks and financial institutions.[20] From June 1899 to June 1900, the money stock grew but, as noted earlier, at a decidedly lower rate than for the preceding or following year, and it may well be that these annual figures conceal a brief intervening fall. Wholesale prices showed a distinct retardation in the rate of rise in late 1899. They reached a peak in early 1900, from which they declined to a low in mid-1901, six months after the reference trough in December 1900. At the same time, wholesale prices in Britain rose sharply from 1899 to 1900. From the trough in 1900 in U.S. prices relative to British prices, the price ratio rose rapidly up to 1902, a rise which was a resumption of the movement begun in 1898.

It is tempting to associate the rapid rise in relative prices from 1900 to 1902 with domestic political events that might affect speculation. In March 1900, the Gold Standard Act was passed, and in the fall Bryan,

[20] To relieve the money market tension in Nov. 1899, Secretary of the Treasury L. J. Gage purchased $18.4 million of government bonds between Nov. 15 and 30 at a premium of $2.3 million and about a million more from Dec. 1 to Dec. 23. In Dec., when further difficulties arose and New York City banks formed a pool to lend $10 million on the New York Stock Exchange, Gage announced that he would deposit between $30 million and $40 million of current Treasury receipts in national bank depositories.

148

on a free-silver platform, was defeated by McKinley a second time, this time by larger popular and electoral majorities. By strengthening confidence in the U.S. monetary standard, these events would certainly operate to permit a higher domestic price level than otherwise. However, it seems dubious that they were of much quantitative importance; they probably only served to reinforce a movement already under way, that had been temporarily interrupted from 1899 to 1900.

CENTRAL-BANKING ACTIVITIES OF THE TREASURY

On the domestic side, two developments deserve special mention for their monetary importance. One is the growth in the relative importance of nonnational banks, particularly loan and trust companies. The mushrooming trust companies in New York City, where they could operate with lower reserves and looser supervision than other commercial banks, were destined to play a notable part in the panic of 1907. A second is the growing tendency on the part of the Treasury to intervene frequently and regularly in the money market. The central-banking activities of the Treasury were being converted from emergency measures to a fairly regular and predictable operating function.

Treasury intervention occurred in the period of monetary stringency at the end of 1899; again in mid-1901, after the collapse of the stock market that followed the separate attempts of the Morgan and Harriman interests to corner Northern Pacific stock and the discovery on May 9 that more shares had been sold than were in existence;[21] and again in the fall of 1901, when a stock market panic was feared as a result of the assassination of President McKinley.[22]

Treasury intervention reached its peak after Leslie M. Shaw was appointed Secretary of the Treasury in 1902. He was a vigorous and explicit advocate of using Treasury powers to control the money market and had great confidence in the Treasury's ability to do so. In his final report to the Congress, written at the end of 1906, after four years of experience and less than a year before the panic of 1907, he wrote: "If the Secretary of the Treasury were given $100,000,000 to be deposited with the banks or withdrawn as he might deem expedient, and if in addition he were clothed with authority over the reserves of the several banks, with power to contract the national-bank circulation at pleasure, in my judgment no

---

[21] Between Apr. 2 and June 30, 1901, the Secretary of the Treasury purchased $14.4 million of government bonds at a premium of $1.9 million for the sinking fund (*Annual Report on the Finances,* 1901, p. 20).

[22] On that occasion, the Secretary purchased $7.7 million of bonds, at a premium of $2.1 million, increased government deposits in banks by $5 million, and prepaid interest due Oct. 1 on government bonds (*see Annual Report on the Finances,* 1901, pp. 20, 152; *Commercial and Financial Chronicle,* Sept. 14, 1901, p. 535).

panic as distinguished from industrial stagnation could threaten either the United States or Europe that he could not avert. No central or Government bank in the world can so readily influence financial conditions throughout the world as can the Secretary under the authority with which he is now clothed."[23] It is tempting to laugh this statement off as a prize example of bureaucratic megalomania. It is that, but not only that. Though overdrawn, it contains much truth. The Treasury's monetary powers were very great indeed. If they had been expanded as Shaw requested, the Treasury would have been clothed with effective power different from but not clearly inferior to that later assigned to the Federal Reserve System.[24]

[23] *Annual Report on the Finances,* 1906, p. 49. See also A. Piatt Andrew, "The Treasury and the Banks under Secretary Shaw," *Quarterly Journal of Economics,* Aug. 1907, pp. 554–556.

[24] The Treasury's debt management powers were then and are now comparable to the Federal Reserve System's ability to conduct open market operations. The power to deposit or withdraw funds from commercial banks is equivalent to the existing possibility of affecting commercial bank reserves by transferring government deposits from commercial banks to Federal Reserve Banks, or by disbursements from government deposits at Federal Reserve Banks.

Shaw described the power he requested to vary reserve requirements against deposits as follows: ". . . a better plan, in my judgment, would be to clothe the Secretary of the Treasury with authority to require all banks, at certain times fixed by him, to slightly and gradually increase their reserves and hold the same within their own vaults, with corresponding authority to release the same from time to time as in his judgment will best serve the business interests of the country" (*Annual Report on the Finances,* 1906, p. 48). That power is equivalent to the Federal Reserve System's current power to vary reserve requirements, granted permanently in 1935.

Shaw also desired power to control note issues. One measure of control he suggested was the power to vary the limit on the amount of lawful money banks could deposit in any one month to reduce their notes outstanding: ". . . it would be wise to clothe the Secretary of the Treasury with discretion whether he will allow retirement of circulation at any given time, and to place such limitation thereon as in his judgment will best conserve the business interests of the country" (*ibid,* p. 46). Another measure was to vary the redemption fund requirement: "Suppose the Secretary of the Treasury had authority to order the national banks to make deposit to the credit of the redemption fund of an amount equal to 1 per cent of their circulation every fifteen days [during the summer]. This would result in a contraction of national-bank circulation amounting to sixty millions, and by requiring the bonds to remain on deposit this amount could again be issued during the fall and winter as necessity required" (*ibid.,* p. 49). Another measure was to increase the flexibility of the requirement that national bank notes be secured by government bonds, so that banks could issue in excess of the par value of the bonds on deposit: "By eliminating the words 'secured by United States bonds deposited with the Treasury of the United States' from the present bank note, the additional circulation issue need contain no distinguishing feature" (*ibid.,* p. 44). A final measure was to determine the tax rate, depending on changing conditions, at which banks could issue emergency currency: ". . . authority might be given the Secretary of the Treasury to specify the rate at which . . . credit currency should be issued" (Leslie M. Shaw, *Current Issues,* New York, Appleton, 1908, p. 306). These controls over note issue would have been inferior to the Reserve System's power to issue

Shaw's first opportunity to apply his philosophy came at the very close of the period from 1897 to 1902. In September 1902, the expansion that began in December 1900 reached its peak, according to the National Bureau's chronology. There was severe stringency in the money market as the ratio of cash reserves to net deposits of New York City banks reached the lowest point experienced at any call date since 1883. Secretary Shaw made unprecedented efforts to bring relief to the banks. He anticipated the November payment of interest on outstanding bonds, purchased bonds for the sinking fund at abnormally high premiums (37¾ per cent and interest to date of purchase) and increased government deposits in national banks (waiving reserve requirements)—in total adding $57 million to funds available to the money market.[25]

These measures did not prevent a contraction. Tension in the money market continued in November and December, with heavy liquidation in the stock market, as banks began to call the loans of underwriting syndicates which had guaranteed the numerous Wall Street promotions of the preceding two years. The syndicates were forced to sell older high-grade stocks and bonds as well as unsold underwritten securities. The market broke under their sales—the so-called rich man's panic—and the decline continued through most of 1903. The great new industrial combinations presently gave indications of distress, notably U.S. Steel, which stopped paying dividends on its common stock. Railroads found difficulty in bor-

---

Federal Reserve notes, but they might well have given the Treasury nearly as effective indirect control over the volume of notes outstanding.

The main difference between the powers of the Treasury then, if extended as Shaw desired, and of the Reserve System after World War I would have been less in the explicit instruments of control available to each than in the narrower limits imposed by the gold standard on any national monetary authority before World War I than after it.

We are grateful to C.A.E. Goodhart for his comments on an earlier version of this footnote, as well as on several other points in this chapter.

[25] *Annual Report on the Finances,* 1906, p. 37.

In addition, at the height of the stringency, he was responsible for an increase of $26 million in national bank circulation. During the preceding summer he suggested to eighteen of the larger national banks in central reserve cities that they increase their circulation, in anticipation of fall needs. Fifteen responded with orders for printing $12 million of which $7 million were actually issued. Additional government deposits were made at banks that agreed to increase the circulation by an amount equal to, and sometimes double, the deposit. In this way a further addition of $4 million to national bank circulation was arranged.

He also permitted the acceptance of certain state and municipal bonds as security for government deposits, on condition that government bonds thus released would be used to secure additional national bank note circulation. Within a few weeks the banks deposited $20 million of state and municipal bonds as security, and the note circulation was increased $15 million (*Annual Report on the Finances,* 1902, p. 58; 1903, p. 138).

The New York City Clearing House Association continued to include government deposits in calculating reserve requirements, despite their exemption by the Secretary of the Treasury, until 1908 (see footnote 57, below).

151

rowing on usual terms, and as a result their demand for iron and steel declined. Other companies failed and some financial houses went bankrupt.

These events did not lead Shaw to regard his intervention as a failure. "These operations," he wrote, "were not begun, however, until a condition existed which in the opinion of many leading bankers of New York City justified the issuance of clearing-house certificates, and when a resort thereto was being seriously considered."[26] He may well have been correct in his conclusion that they prevented a severe banking panic. Despite the cyclical contraction, there was no banking panic and bank suspensions in 1903 were apparently unchanged from the preceding year.

2. *Relatively Stable Growth, 1903–07*

The contraction that began in the fall of 1902 lasted twenty-three months, from September 1902 to August 1904, according to the National Bureau chronology. Though the contraction was rather on the long side, as contractions go, it was relatively mild; it was followed by an expansion that was both vigorous and the most protracted since the postresumption expansion of 1879–82. As Chart 13 shows, wholesale prices were affected only mildly by the contraction. They fluctuated about a nearly constant level from 1902 to late 1906, then rose fairly sharply, continuing to rise for some months after the reference peak, and reaching a level in September 1907 some 10 per cent above that at the end of 1902. While the annual implicit price index shows a more regular behavior, rising in every year from 1902 to 1907, its total rise over the period was about the same as in wholesale prices.

Relative to British prices, U.S. prices continued to rise from 1902 to 1905, though at a slower rate than from 1900 to 1902. The rise was accompanied by an irregular rise in the ratio of U.S. capital imports to net national product, which is to say, reduction in capital exports, continuing the general parallelism between capital movements and relative prices, noted earlier.

The pattern was interrupted from 1905 to 1906. Although U.S. prices rose absolutely, British prices rose even more, so that U.S. prices fell relative to British prices, and this despite a shift from capital exports to minor capital imports in 1906 and 1907. That interruption in the upward movement in U.S. relative prices probably reflected an incomplete adjustment in the U.S. to the world price rise; full adjustment would have required an even larger rise in U.S. prices. Gold movements strongly support this view. Net gold movement had fluctuated about a zero level from 1899 to 1904. In early 1905, a fairly definite trend toward imports emerged: of the eight quarters from the second quarter of 1905 through

[26] *Annual Report on the Finances,* 1906, p. 37.

the first quarter of 1907, only one shows a gold outflow; in these eight quarters as a whole, the net gold inflow totaled $143 million. Doubtless this gold inflow helped to produce the stringency in London in 1906, which, as we shall have occasion to note, in its turn contributed to the termination of U.S. monetary expansion—another see-saw movement like the one in the years after resumption.

Net national product on an annual basis rose fairly sharply from 1902 to 1903—by 6 per cent in current prices and 5 per cent in constant prices —despite the onset of contraction in late 1902. It was unchanged from 1903 to 1904 in current prices and declined by only 2 per cent in constant prices. It then rose vigorously in the next three years—by 33 per cent in current prices and 23 per cent in constant prices.

The years from 1902 to 1907 were characterized by industrial growth— of which the most obvious signs were rapid growth of the output of coal and iron and of the volume of railroad traffic—by speculative activity in the stock market, and by a wave of immigration. From a low in 1898, the number of immigrants rose every year up to 1907, except for a slight drop from 1903 to 1904, exceeded 1 million for the first time in 1905, and remained above 1 million in 1906 and 1907—the only three successive years on record in each of which over 1 million immigrants were admitted.

The stock of money rose steadily and by June 1907 was 45 per cent above its level five years earlier. Because of the relatively steady growth exhibited during that period, it is interesting to use it, as in section 1 of the preceding chapter we used the period 1885–91, to es- timate the rate of growth of the stock of money consistent with stable prices, even though the period departed further from stability than the earlier one had (see Table 6). From 1902 to 1907, the money stock grew at an annual rate of a little over 7 per cent, and this figure does not seem to be an accident of the particular dates chosen. The rate of growth is roughly the same if 1901 is substituted for 1902, or 1906 for 1907, or both substitutions are made. From 1902 to 1907, prices rose at the average rate of 2 per cent per year, as judged by annual figures for either the wholesale or implicit price index. The implication is that a rate of growth of the stock of money of about 5 per cent per year was required for stable prices.

This estimate is fairly close to the estimate of a bit over 6 per cent based on 1885–91. But there is an important difference. Nearly half of the earlier 6 per cent, but less than a tenth of the later 5 per cent, was accounted for by a decline in velocity. The later figure is close to the earlier because the rate of rise in real income, according to the particular numerical estimates we use, was greater for the later five- year period than for the earlier six years. The difference in the division between velocity and real income change may well be an accident of the particular figures; or of the fact that the earlier comparison is between two cyclical troughs, and the later, between two cyclical peaks; or even of differences in the dating of the cyclical turns within the particular years. However, the difference in the size of the velocity change can also be plausibly explained by the difference in price trends. In the earlier period prices were falling; insofar as people were still adjusting to that phenomenon, velocity would be expected to fall faster than otherwise. In the later period, prices were rising; insofar as people were still adjusting to that phenomenon, velocity would be expected to rise or to fall less rapidly than otherwise.[27] This may be why velocity was falling at a rate of nearly 3 per cent per year from 1885 to 1891, and of less than ½ per cent per year from 1902 to 1907.

TABLE 6

RATE OF GROWTH OF STOCK OF MONEY CONSISTENT WITH STABLE PRICES
DURING THE PERIODS 1885–91 AND 1902–07

	1885–91	1902–07
Annual percentage rate of change in:		
1. Stock of money	5.8	7.3
2. Implicit price index	−0.3	2.1
3. Stock of money required for stable prices, with given changes in velocity	6.1	5.1
4. Velocity of money	−2.6	−0.4
5. Stock of money required for stable prices, if velocity had not changed (equal to actual change in real income)	3.5	4.7

NOTE: Real income is assumed to have changed as it actually did.

SOURCE, BY LINE

1, 2, and 4.   From same source as for Chart 62.
     3.   Line 1 minus line 2.
     5.   Either from same source as for Chart 62; or line 3 plus line 4 (with rounding error).

Secretary Shaw continued to manifest his central-banking proclivities. During 1903, despite the absence of any special monetary difficulties of the kind that had earlier tended to call forth Treasury intervention, he took steps to tighten the market in the summer and ease it in the fall,

[27] The emphasis on "still adjusting" is required because full adjustment to a price level falling at a particular rate would mean a lower velocity than full adjustment to a price level rising at a particular rate, but there is no reason year-to-year changes in velocity in response, say, to changes in real income should be larger in the one case than in the other.

It may seen unlikely that people were "still adjusting" to falling prices in 1885–91 when, from a broad view, prices had been falling since about 1865. However, resumption in 1879 presumably had a decided effect on expectations about price behavior that were confirmed by a fairly sharp price rise from 1879 to 1882, so the price decline that is relevant probably dates from 1882 rather than 1865.

a usual period of seasonal strain.[28] Shaw kept out of the money market in late 1905, despite severe strain in it.[29] One reason may have been his reluctance to intervene in what he regarded as a stringency produced by speculative activity in the stock market. Another was that he could intervene only by altering Treasury balances or using a revenue surplus. Treasury deficits, partly as a result of heavy disbursements for the Panama Canal, had reduced Treasury balances to unusually low levels.[30] An increase in the Treasury's receipts in 1906 facilitated its re-entry into the market, and Shaw acted to ease the market in February and April, withdrew funds in the summer and again eased the market in the fall, when extreme tightness developed. Both in the spring and fall he tried to multiply the effect of his easing measures by using government deposits as an inducement to banks to import gold.[31] As noted earlier, the

[28] Since the Treasury was prohibited by law from depositing customs receipts in banks, the only U.S. funds available to Shaw for deposit were internal revenue and miscellaneous receipts. On Aug. 27, Shaw announced that he had sequestered $38.5 million of the latter two classes of receipts, with which he intended to replenish the money market. Although it was contrary to existing procedure to transfer to the banks money that had already been turned in to the Treasury, Shaw ruled that the depositories were actually a part of the Treasury and that the transfer of funds to them was merely a change of place from one part of the Treasury to another. In the fall, he deposited $14 million in national banks and purchased an approximately equal amount of government bonds in order to forestall seasonal strain in the market (Andrew, "The Treasury and the Banks," pp. 540–541; *Annual Report on the Finances,* 1906, pp. 37–38).

[29] Call money rates rose as high as 25 per cent in Nov. and even higher in Dec., when reserves of New York City banks fell below requirements (*Commercial and Financial Chronicle,* Jan. 6, 1906, pp. 19–20).

[30] Andrew, "The Treasury and the Banks," p. 543; idem, "The Partial Responsibility of Secretaries Gage and Shaw for the Crisis of 1907," *Publications of the American Economic Association,* 3rd series, Vol. IX, 1908, p. 224; and unsigned "Note from Washington," *Journal of Political Economy,* Jan. 1908, p. 31.

[31] In Feb., Shaw deposited $10 million in seven principal cities on security other than government bonds, announcing that the deposits would be called in July. Early in Apr. 1906, New York reserves were deficient, and the Secretary increased government deposits at national banks that pledged to import an equivalent amount of gold. The sum deposited was to be regarded as a temporary loan, to be returned to the Treasury as soon as the gold arrived. One bank was allowed to count the gold in transit as part of its reserves. The gold import arrangement with the Treasury was in effect from Apr. 14 to May 29. About $50 million in gold was imported in this way, although net gold imports during the second quarter amounted to only $41 million.

In Sept., New York bank reserves were again below requirements and call loan rates rose to 40 per cent (*Commercial and Financial Chronicle,* Jan. 5, 1907, pp. 17–18). On Sept. 5, Shaw announced that beginning Sept. 10 he would again deposit government funds with banks against gold engagements, and in the succeeding month deposited $46.6 million. On Sept. 27, he offered an additional $26 million of government deposits to banks located in 26 different cities, to be recalled after Feb. 1, 1907; and on Dec. 5, an additional $10 million to be returned between Jan. 20 and Feb. 1 (*Annual Report on the Finances,* 1906, pp. 8, 39–40; Andrew, "The Treasury and the Banks," pp. 547, 551–552).

Andrew states (p. 544) that Shaw tried to make it profitable for banks to im-

155

international payments position was one that would have produced gold imports in any event, and it is doubtful that Shaw's measures had much effect on their volume, though they may have had some on their timing.

During September and October 1906, when the New York money market was relieved by gold imports, mainly from Great Britain and Germany, the London money market was in turmoil. On September 13 the Bank of England raised its discount rate from 3½ to 4 per cent, on October 11 to 5 per cent, and on October 19 to 6 per cent. The Reichsbank made similar increases in its rate. At the same time the Bank of England served notice on the London private banks that it would not look with favor upon the continued negotiation of American finance bills. Thereafter, finance bills had to be paid as they matured, unless by previous arrangement a single renewal had been stipulated. These measures served first to reduce, then to reverse, the flow of gold to the United States, and in this and other ways contributed to a change in the economic situation in the United States. The effect showed up first in the financial markets. Severe price declines occurred on the stock exchange early in March 1907. Union Pacific stock, which had been extensively used as collateral in finance bill operations, fell by 30 per cent within less than two weeks.[32] Despite easing action undertaken by the Treasury,[33] and a temporary reversal in stock prices, the boom had come to an end, the National Bureau dating the cyclical peak in May 1907.

3. The Panic of 1907

The business contraction from May 1907 to June 1908, though relatively brief, was extremely severe, involving a sharp drop in output and employment. Even the annual net national product figures show a fall of over 11 per cent in both constant and current prices from 1907 to 1908, and monthly figures would undoubtedly show a decidedly larger decline. Though the annual implicit price index shows no change, the monthly wholesale price index declines by 5 per cent. Various other indicators all

---

port gold without waiting for sterling exchange to fall to the normal import point. Shaw denied that banks had profited. He claimed that sterling had fallen sufficiently to insure the import of gold if banks had been in a position to buy the exchange with which to obtain it. Hence his loan of government funds (*Annual Report on the Finances,* 1906, p. 39). In general Andrew was unsympathetic to Shaw's innovations directed toward seasonal relief of the money market.

[32] O. M. W. Sprague, *History of Crises Under the National Banking System,* National Monetary Commission, GPO, 1910, p. 241

[33] The government deposits of Sept. 1906, which were due to be recalled on Feb. 1, 1907, were not withdrawn until June or July because of "unfavorable conditions" (*Annual Report on the Finances,* 1907, pp. 50–52). Between Mar. 14 and June 24 the Treasury redeemed $25 million of the 4 per cent loan due that year, with interest prepaid to July 1. After Mar. 4, 1907, all collectors of customs except those in cities with subtreasuries deposited receipts directly in national bank depositories when located in the same town (*ibid.*).

agree in ranking the contraction among the five or six most severe in our cyclical history since 1879.[34]

The contraction is sharply divided into two parts by the banking panic that occurred in October 1907. From May to September, the contraction showed no obvious signs of severity. Prices continued to rise; production in various lines flattened out but did not decline seriously, and freight car loadings behaved similarly; bank clearings held fairly steady, and there was no drastic rise in the liabilities of commercial failures. The one significant change was the reversal noted earlier in gold movements from net imports to net exports. In October came the banking panic, culminating in the restriction of payments by the banking system, i.e., in a concerted refusal, as in 1893, by the banking system to convert deposits into currency or specie at the request of the depositors. The contraction simultaneously became much more severe. Production, freight car loadings, bank clearings, and the like all declined sharply and the liabilities of commercial failures increased sharply. Restriction of payments by banks was lifted in early 1908, and a few months thereafter recovery got under way.

Our estimates of the stock of money become monthly just at the outset of the contraction, so that we can trace the course of events more closely than for earlier episodes.[35] From May 1907 on, the stock of money, seasonally adjusted, declined in every month until February 1908—mildly until the panic, then sharply. From May to the end of September, the money stock fell by 2½ per cent, from September to February by 5 per cent. Though mild, the decline before the panic is worth noting. It gives some evidence of unusually strong downward pressure, at least in the monetary field. Thanks to its strong upward trend, the stock of money typically rises during mild contractions, declining at most for an occasional month or two. There are only three subsequent contractions in which the estimated money stock in *any* month of the contraction was below its previous peak by a larger percentage than the 2½ per cent decline from May to September 1907 alone. These three exceptions, significantly enough, are 1920–21, 1929–33, and 1937–38, the only three subsequent

[34] See A. F. Burns and W. C. Mitchell, *Measuring Business Cycles*, New York, NBER, 1946, p. 403, Table 156, and a revision and extension of that table in *Business Cycle Indicators*, G. H. Moore, ed., Vol. I, Princeton University Press for NBER, 1961, p. 104.

[35] It is not simply a coincidence that our estimates become monthly at this point. The key role played by monetary forces in the contraction contributed to the improvement in the data for all banks, which permitted us to shift to a monthly basis. The first comprehensive balance sheet of nonnational banks, by states, compiled by the National Monetary Commission, is dated Apr. 28, 1909. After the panic, nonnational bank reports to state supervisory authorities were greatly improved. These data, combined with national bank figures, made it possible for us to construct call-date estimates between the annual all-bank data, as a preliminary to monthly estimates (see source notes to Table A-1).

contractions that rival 1907–08 in severity. In the ten other reference contractions from then through the 1960–61 contraction, the estimated stock of money never fell as much as 2½ per cent below its previous peak, and in some showed no decline at all. In view of the margin of error of our monthly estimates, this result cannot be regarded as firmly established; it certainly suggests that something more than a typical mild contraction was already in train before the financial panic.

The proximate sources of the initial and subsequent decline in the stock of money are strikingly different. The initial decline of about 2½ per cent (from May to September 1907) reflected in part a decline in high-powered money by about 1 per cent, largely the result of the gold exports. The rest of the initial decline reflected a fall in the ratio of deposits to reserves, as banks increased their high-powered money holdings by some 5 per cent despite the decline in total high-powered money. The public offset the fall in the deposit-reserve ratio to some extent by permitting the ratio of deposits to currency to rise. Although the absolute amount of both deposits and currency fell, deposits fell by 2 per cent, currency by 5 per cent. These changes in the deposit ratios have the appearance of a fairly passive response to a business decline, with banks strengthening their reserve position and holders of money showing no distrust of banks.

The subsequent decline in the money stock from September 1907 to February 1908, on the other hand, has all the earmarks of an active scramble for liquidity on the part of both the public and the banks. The stock of high-powered money rose by 10 per cent over that five-month period, yet the money stock fell by 5 per cent. As in 1893, the public's distrust of the banks and the reduced usefulness of deposits after the restriction of their convertibility were reflected in the combination of a rise in currency in the hands of the public, this time by 11 per cent, and a decline in deposits, this time by 8 per cent. The two together produced a decline in the ratio of deposits to currency from 6.0 to 5.0. At the same time, the banks sought to improve their capacity to meet the demands of the public by raising their currency holdings. They were unable to do so in the panic month of October itself and suffered instead a slight decrease. Thereafter they succeeded so well that, despite the decline in deposits, the absolute amount of reserves was 8 per cent higher at the end of February 1908 than at the end of September 1907. The result was a decline in the ratio of deposits to reserves from 8.2 to 7.0. Taken by itself, each of the changes in the deposit ratios would have produced a decline of 7–8 per cent in the stock of money and, together, of nearly 14 per cent. The actual decline was kept to 5 per cent only because of the accompanying 10 per cent rise in high-powered money, which itself resulted partly from gold imports, partly from the reduction of Treasury cash balances.

The first direct signs of the financial crisis occurred during the week of October 14 when five banks that were members of the New York Clearing House and three outside banks required assistance, which was given them by a group of Clearing House banks.[36] Order seemed to have been restored by Monday, October 21, when the Knickerbocker Trust Company, the third largest trust company in New York with deposits of $62 million, began to experience unfavorable clearing house balances as a result of connections with the banks that were initially in trouble.[37] A run on the company the next day forced it to suspend. Had the Knickerbocker been a member of the Clearing House, it probably would have been helped, and the further crisis developments might thereby have been prevented.[38]

On October 23, a run began on the second largest trust company in the city, with deposits of $64 million, and on the following day on still another trust company. Those companies were given assistance, because it was now clear that the entire credit structure was in danger. However, assistance was granted slowly and without dramatic effect; the assistance saved those two companies from failure but did not allay general alarm outside New York.

During the heavy runs on the trust companies, October 21 to 23, the New York Clearing House banks had to furnish currency required by the trust companies whose reserves were deposited with them, and were also shipping currency to interior banks and paying it out over their counters to their own frightened depositors. On October 24 the Secretary of the Treasury—since March, George Cortelyou—came to their aid by depositing $25 million with the chief central reserve city banks in New York.[39]

[36] Four were national banks, three state banks, and one a trust company. Their combined deposits totaled $71 million.
The banks were controlled through stock ownership on margin by a few men of no great financial standing, who used the banks to further speculation in the stocks of copper-mining companies. When the prices of those stocks declined sharply, depositors became alarmed and runs were started (see Sprague, *History of Crises,* pp. 246–251; Mitchell, *Business Cycles,* pp. 515–516).

[37] The president of the Knickerbocker Trust Company had some business connections with the enterprises of one of the men in control of the banks that were in difficulty. On Oct. 21 the member bank of the Clearing House that cleared for the Knickerbocker announced it would discontinue doing so the following day. The Knickerbocker president immediately resigned, but this did not allay distrust.

[38] Sprague, *History of Crises,* p. 252. Until June 1911 trust companies were not members of the New York Clearing House. It adopted a rule in 1903 which required all trust companies clearing through members of the Association to accumulate reserves, smaller than those of the banks but larger than those held by most of the trust companies. The Knickerbocker was one of the few trust companies that accepted that requirement in order to maintain its clearing arrangements.

[39] *Response of the Secretary of the Treasury to Senate Res. No. 33 of Dec. 12, 1907,* S. Doc. 208, 60th Cong., 1st sess., 1908, pp. 8–9, 23, 227. In effect those deposits furnished the banks with the funds for local withdrawals. Between Oct. 19 and 31 a total of $36 million was deposited in New York banks by the Secretary of the Treasury. In addition, $28 million had already been deposited mainly in outside banks, from Aug. 28 through Oct. 14.

Despite this step, New York was threatened with panic, loans were obtainable only with great difficulty, and stock market prices collapsed.[40] To prevent a further price decline on the exchange, J. P. Morgan organized a money pool of $25 million to which some leading banks and financiers subscribed. A similar pool of $10 million was formed the next day. The savings banks demanded legal notice of withdrawal from all depositors. By the end of the week, however, the local runs appeared to have subsided.

By the time the panic in New York was under control, alarm had spread throughout the country. Although there were runs on some banks in scattered parts of the country due to local causes, loss of confidence was displayed less by the public than by country banks. Past experience had taught country banks the difficulty of obtaining currency from their city correspondents in times of crisis. Country banks therefore demanded currency for the funds on deposit or on call in New York. At that point, October 26, the New York Clearing House began issuing clearing house loan certificates, a device that had been developed in earlier crises as a means of providing a substitute for currency at least for settling local interbank balances.[41]

Even though New York banks were now in a position to extend loans to borrowers, and their available reserves, though unevenly distributed, were far from exhausted, they immediately restricted the convertibility of deposits into currency. An attempt to maintain payments by pooling reserves and satisfying the country banks' demands for currency might have ended the demands promptly without seriously reducing reserves. If it had, the seasonal return flow of currency to New York, which typically began around mid-December, might have shortly restored the reserve position of New York banks. Restriction of payments came when it did because the banks were loath to risk a drain on their reserves.[42]

[40] Sprague, the leading student of the episode, argued that at this point the Clearing House banks should have issued clearing house loan certificates to enable banks to extend loans more freely to borrowers and also to prevent the weakening of particular banks with unfavorable clearing house balances. He attributed the inactivity of the Clearing House Association to the mistaken belief that an issue of clearing house loan certificates would cause restriction of specie payments (see Sprague, *History of Crises*, pp. 257–258, 272–273).

[41] Clearing house loan certificates, obligations of Clearing House banks, which members and other banks agreed to accept in lieu of currency in settling adverse clearing balances, were issued to individual banks in return for their own obligations secured by assets acceptable to a committee of bankers. "Clearing house certificates" were issued by banks as currency for the public's use.

[42] During the week following restriction, New York City Clearing House member banks lost $31 million in currency, but during the three weeks thereafter only $8 million. After Nov. 23, regular increases in vault cash were shown. Although the banks claimed that they were losing currency by "shipment to out of town customers and for payment over to (*sic*) the counter to those needing it for payrolls, etc., also to meet the demand for extension of credits, usually large at this time of year" (*Response of the Secretary of the Treasury*, p. 215), interior banks

160

As soon as the New York banks restricted payments, countrywide restrictions followed, legally sanctioned by a few states,[43] and tolerated in the rest.

With restriction, currency went to a premium over deposits, the premium ranging as high as 4 per cent. This reflected the fact that, despite the increase in the ratio of currency to deposits, the desired ratio was still higher. Deposits became a less desirable asset than before, not only because of distrust of banks, but also because deposits were no longer so useful for transaction purposes. Hence, there was an attempted shift from deposits to currency that has been termed "hoarding" of currency.[44] The premium on currency in turn gave an incentive to import gold, which was only partly dissipated in an increase in the deposit-dollar

---

complained that they could not obtain currency from New York during Nov. (*Refusal of National Banks in New York City to Furnish Currency for Needs of Interior Banks*, S. Doc. 435, 60th Cong., 1st sess., 1908, p. 2). Secretary Cortelyou pointed out that on Dec. 3, of the 43 complainants, only 8 held reserves (in vault and with reserve agents) that were below requirements (*Refusal of National Banks*).

However, this evidence is hardly conclusive on the amount of currency the New York banks would have had to supply in the absence of restriction. On the one hand, restriction may have dramatized the situation and so have led to a greater demand than otherwise. On the other, since it was followed by restriction elsewhere, it may have choked off a great increase in demand that would have grown out of a series of unsuccessful attempts by country banks to maintain payments (see further discussion below).

New York City Clearing House banks increased their loans on call—not commercial loans—through the week ending Nov. 30, taking over loans that the trust companies and outside banks were no longer willing to carry. National banks elsewhere contracted their loans by more than the New York banks increased theirs. After Nov., New York also contracted.

[43] Actually, the governor of Nevada had declared a legal holiday on Oct. 24, which was renewed through Nov. 4. This had no general importance. It was New York's action that affected the whole country. On Oct. 28, the governor of Oregon declared a legal holiday, which was renewed until Dec. 16; in California, legal holidays were declared from Oct. 31 to Dec. 21.

In all these states, the banks kept open during the holiday, making loans and paying out substitutes for cash. The whole judicial system, however, was brought to a standstill by the declaration of holidays; not even criminal cases could be tried. "Special" holidays were therefore proclaimed, during which only civil actions based on contracts for the payment of money were prohibited. In Indiana the attorney general authorized banks to restrict depositors "to a limited amount of money in cash and settle the balance due by issuing certified checks, or drafts on correspondents." The South Dakota Superintendent of Banks suggested that cash withdrawals be limited to $10 and cashiers' checks be issued in place of currency. In Iowa and Oklahoma there was also official sanction of a limitation of cash payments. (A. P. Andrew, "Substitutes for Cash in the Panic of 1907," *Quarterly Journal of Economics*, Aug. 1908, p. 498 and Table I; A. L. Mills, "The Northwest in the Recent Financial Crisis," *Annals of the American Academy of Political and Social Science*, 1908, p. 414.)

[44] Andrew, "Hoarding in the Panic of 1907," *Quarterly Journal of Economics*, Feb. 1908, pp. 290–299.

161

price of foreign exchange.[45] The premium reinforced the effect of high interest rates and of a rise in exports and a fall in imports, producing an inflow of over $100 million of gold in November and December alone. Government deposits and additional issues of banknotes supplemented these gold imports, so that $239 million was added to high-powered money from the end of September until the end of December.[46]

As in previous periods of restriction, substitutes for currency were issued. Clearing house loan certificates were issued to the banks for payments to each other. The amount issued totaled $256 million, compared with $69 million in 1893, although of course the whole sum was not in use at any one time. In addition, small clearing house checks and certificates, cashiers' checks, and manufacturers' pay checks totaled over $250

[45] Suppose the exchange rate of deposit dollars against sterling to be at par: £1 = $4.86. Then through the exchange market £1 will purchase $4.86 in deposits. Let the premium on currency over deposits be 4 per cent. By shipping gold, and exchanging this at the Treasury, £1 would purchase $4.86 in currency and this in turn would purchase $5.05 in deposits (4.86 × 1.04). Hence, so long as the deposit-dollar exchange rate remained at $4.86, it was profitable to ship gold. Of course, this meant that the deposit-dollar price of a pound tended to rise. It rose as high as $4.88¾, "well above the gold export point in normal times, and still gold imports continued upon an enormous scale" (Sprague, *History of Crises*, p. 283).

[46] According to the Treasury's calculations, its "available working balance" had been reduced to approximately $5 million by the middle of Nov. (*Annual Report on the Finances*, 1908, p. 21). To determine that balance, from total Treasury assets, including the cover for gold and silver certificates, four items were deducted: (1) the Treasury's liability for all outstanding gold and silver certificates and Treasury notes of 1890—including such certificates and notes in its own General Fund; (2) Treasury liabilities that were termed "agency account," including the 5 per cent redemption fund, outstanding checks and warrants, the account due to the Post Office, etc.; (3) a reserve fund of $150 million in gold set aside as cover for greenbacks; (4) deposits in national banks and in the treasury of the Philippines. The figures for Treasury cash in Table A-3, which include all unduplicated Treasury cash holdings, bear no relation to the Treasury definition of "available working balance."

Given the small size of the working balance so defined, the usual techniques of Treasury intervention by deposits in banks, purchases of bonds, etc. were unavailable. In lieu thereof, Cortelyou on Nov. 17 offered an issue of $50 million of 2 per cent bonds and $100 million of 3 per cent certificates with the object of providing banks with additional securities as a basis for bank note issue. The banks were authorized to keep on deposit 90 per cent of their purchases of bonds, 75 per cent of certificates. Only $24.6 million of bonds and $15.4 of certificates were sold (*Annual Report on the Finances*, 1908, pp. 21–22). An increase of $34 million in national bank notes outstanding was attained in Dec.

The Secretary defended his action on the ground that a crisis could be averted by making it plain that the banks had adequate resources of currency (see *Response of the Secretary of the Treasury*, p. 17). However, his action was too late to achieve this objective; it would have been much more to the point if it had been taken in Oct.

The Treasury withdrew from the banks $6 million in Dec., $10 million in Jan., because of the increase in bank vault cash, although there was no net decline in the unprecedently high level of government deposits until Mar. 1908.

million.[47] These substitutes may have amounted in all to something like half our estimated absolute decline in the money stock. Payroll difficulties apparently were less conspicuous than in 1893, for banks generally supplied their customers' requirements for this purpose in one way or another. The dislocation of the domestic exchanges, of course, caused delay in remittances between different parts of the country.

Although the Treasury required all payments to it to be made in currency after December 4, the end of restriction was not fully achieved until the beginning of January 1908. The public continued to add to its currency holdings during January, with not much change in the banks' holdings. Deposits continued to decline at the same rate as in November and December. The figures for the end of February clearly indicate the end of the crisis: an increase of $81 million in bank vault cash represented a return flow of currency from the public's holdings, while deposits declined only $28 million. From that point on, the money stock climbed steadily, rising 4 per cent up to the reference trough in June. Regained confidence in banks and renewed usefulness of deposits were reflected in a 5 per cent decline in the public's holdings of currency and a 6 per cent rise in its deposits, these movements serving to restore the public's deposit-currency ratio to a level somewhat short of that at the reference peak in May 1907. The banks, however, contrived not only to add to their reserves of high-powered money but also to maintain a relatively low ratio of deposits to reserves. It was 7.0 in June, about the same as in February.

The contemporary, and still standard, interpretation of this episode is that an apparently rather mild contraction was converted into a severe contraction by the banking panic and the associated restriction of payments by the banking system. It was this interpretation of the episode that provided the prime impetus for the monetary reform movement that culminated in the Federal Reserve Act.

In the light of more recent experience, particularly the contraction beginning in 1929 and ending in the banking panic of 1933, we are inclined to believe that this interpretation is too simple, failing to distinguish between the banking panic per se and the restriction of payments that accompanied it. There can be little doubt that the banking panic served to intensify and deepen the contraction: its occurrence coincides with a notable change in both the statistical indicators and the qualitative comment. If it had been completely avoided, the contraction would almost surely have been milder. On the other hand, given the occurrence of the banking panic and the spread of distrust of the banks, the fairly prompt restriction of payments was a therapeutic measure that almost surely kept the contraction from being even more severe and much more protracted than it was.

[47] "Substitutes for Cash," p. 515; *Annual Report,* Comptroller, 1915, I, p. 90.

In this kind of judgment, everything depends on the alternative with which the experienced state of affairs is contrasted. One possibility is the avoidance of restriction of payments by measures both early enough and effective enough to prevent the emergence of any serious doubts about the soundness of the banking system. Such measures would have prevented both the attempted conversion by the public of deposits into currency and the associated attempted strengthening by the banks of their cash position. This result would clearly have been preferable to the actual course of events. Sprague, the leading critic of the action of the New York banks, implies that early assistance to the Knickerbocker Trust Company might have had this effect, but even he concludes that "the failure of the clearing-house authorities to take any action [to save Knickerbocker] was doubtless the most natural course, and though unfortunate in its consequences, can hardly be regarded as blameworthy."[48]

A more likely possibility is the avoidance of restriction of payments by measures taken at a later date after a shift by the public from deposits to currency had already set in and after country banks had already been led to try to strengthen their reserves. Sprague's chief criticism of the New York banks is that they failed to act at that stage, delaying the issue of clearing house loan certificates and resorting to restriction of payments while their own reserves were still ample. "The six large banks [in New York] acting in concert," he wrote, "could have sustained the local situation by making loans and at the same time could have supplied the demands of outside banks for money. Had that course been followed, alarm could have been speedily allayed in the country at large, as it was already being allayed in New York City before the discreditable step of restricting payments was taken."[49] Sprague may well have been correct in believing that those measures could have postponed and perhaps prevented restriction of payments altogether. But with the experience of 1929–33 before us, it is far less clear to us now than it was to him in 1910 that the result would have been preferable to the actual course of events.

The banking system was highly vulnerable to a shift in the liquidity preferences of the public in 1907, much more so than at any earlier time, for two reasons. In the first place, the ratio of deposits to currency had been growing steadily: from $2 in deposits for every $1 of currency in 1879, to nearly $6 in deposits in June 1907. The potential reduction in the stock of money as a result of an attempted shift on the part of the public from deposits to currency was correspondingly greater. In the second place, the ratio of deposits to currency in bank vaults—to bank reserves of high-powered money—had been rising irregularly and slowly until about 1898 and then at a much accelerated pace: from 4.4 in

[48] *History of Crises*, p. 253.
[49] *History of Crises*, p. 273.

February 1879 to 5.9 in June 1898 to 8.9 in June 1907. The final rapid rise may well have been partly the result of the increased adoption by the Treasury of responsibility for money market conditions, which reduced the incentives of banks to keep reserves for themselves. Whatever its cause, the rise in the ratio of deposits to reserves intensified the effect of any attempted shift on the part of the public to currency.

The quantitative importance of these changes in the deposit ratios can be illustrated by a numerical example. In the course of the 1893 panic, the public lowered the ratio of deposits to currency by an amount that would have forced a 6.3 per cent reduction in the ratio of the stock of money to the stock of high-powered money, if the 1892 deposit-reserve ratio had been kept unchanged. Had a shift of the same magnitude occurred in 1907, it would have forced a 7.8 per cent reduction in the ratio of the stock of money to the stock of high-powered money at the 1892 deposit-reserve ratio and a 9.8 per cent reduction at the 1907 deposit-reserve ratio.[50] The combined effect of the changes since 1892 in the deposit ratios was thus to increase the vulnerability of the money stock to a change in the deposit-currency ratio by more than 50 per cent. Even that is not the whole story. It allows only for the effect of the desire of depositors to convert deposits into currency and assumes that the banks remain passive in the sense of simply holding their deposit-reserve ratios constant. In fact, the increased ratio of deposits to reserves was an important additional source of vulnerability because of its likely effects on the attitudes of bankers, though this is an effect to which we cannot readily attach a numerical measure. By reducing the extent of any shift from deposits to currency that banks could meet out of their reserves of high-powered money (i.e., by letting the ratio of deposits to reserves rise still further), the higher deposit-reserve ratios made banks more susceptible to failure through runs. It thereby gave them a greater incentive to seek to strengthen their cash positions at the slightest sign of possible demands on them.

Under these circumstances, suppose the actual restriction of payments had been avoided by New York banks after the initial panic involving the suspension of the Knickerbocker Trust and the accompanying

[50] There is no unambiguous way of defining a shift of the same magnitude in the ratio of deposits to currency. In the above computations we have expressed the 1892 to 1893 shift in terms of the percentage of deposits that would have had to be converted into currency to produce the observed shift with a constant total stock of money. This was 3.459 per cent, since the ratio of deposits to currency declined from 3.81 to 3.25. We then computed the shift in the ratio of deposits to currency that would have been produced in June 1907 by a conversion of 3.459 per cent of 1907 deposits into currency with a constant total. The answer is that the observed ratio of 5.84 would have been reduced to 4.69. Using these ratios, plus the observed ratios of deposits to reserves in 1892 and 1907, respectively, in equation 12 of Appendix B gave the above results.

financial failures. Is it not likely that elements of distrust would have remained that would have led to a continuing drain on the banks? If so, unrestricted payments could have been preserved only by a steady contraction of the money stock. This would in turn have forced failures of banks that were financially "sound" but not immediately liquid—the Knickerbocker Trust Company itself resumed business in March 1908. These successive failures would have fed the distrust and intensified the desire of the public to shift from deposits to currency and of the banks to accumulate reserves. The ultimate result would very likely have been a much more severe contraction than actually occurred, and restriction of payments might in the end have been only postponed until after much more harm had been done.

As it was, the fact of relatively early restriction of payments cut short this hypothetical train of events. Bank suspensions in the final quarter of 1907 and in the first half of 1908, it is true, were at a considerably higher annual rate than in the preceding and succeeding years. Yet, expressed as a ratio to the total number of banks, they were not at an exceptionally high level. According to annual statistics, the number of commercial bank suspensions in preceding years had been running between 0.33 and 0.50 of 1 per cent of the number of those banks, except for 1904 when it reached 0.74 of 1 per cent; in 1907, the recorded figure was only 0.50 of 1 per cent, well within the usual range; in 1908, it rose to 0.73 of 1 per cent; thereafter, it dropped back to its earlier level. Number of suspensions, however, may understate the banking difficulties.[51] Though moderate, the deposit liabilities of the banks that suspended show a more sizable contrast: for 1900–06, they were between one-fifth and two-fifths of 1 per cent of total deposits in commercial banks; in 1907, the recorded figure was 1.22 per cent; in 1908, it dropped back to 0.65 of 1 per cent, somewhat above the earlier level. If the comparison is based on loss to depositors, the effect of the panic is equally apparent, yet equally moderate. In preceding years, the loss had ranged between 2 and 6 cents per $100 of deposits, except for 1904, when it reached 10 cents. In 1907, it was 18 cents and in 1908, 14 cents.[52]

These figures suggest that the panic had a remarkably small effect on

---

[51] Commercial bank suspensions are unpublished FDIC revisions of FDIC, *Annual Report*, 1934, p. 93 (see source notes to Part I of Table 16, below); number of commercial banks from *All-Bank Statistics, United States, 1896–1955*, Board of Governors, FRS, 1959, p. 37. *Dun's Review* showed quarterly figures of number and liabilities of suspended banks beginning 1894. Because of differing definitions of a bank and of a suspension, Dun's series and the FDIC series are apparently not comparable. Except in 1904–05 and 1915–24 (1924 is the last year of Dun's series), the annual totals of the quarterly figures of number of suspensions are larger than the FDIC series.

[52] Deposit liabilities of suspended banks and loss to depositors are unpublished estimates of the FDIC (see footnote 51).

the banking structure. It is probable that new bank formations exceeded suspensions throughout, so that the number of banks increased despite the panic. Thanks to restriction of payments, few banks suspended simply because they were not momentarily liquid. Banks failed now, as earlier, primarily because they were "unsound" banks; and the failure of one bank did not set in train a chain reaction. Restriction of payments thus protected the banking system and gave time for the immediate panic to wear off, as well as for additional currency to be made available. Restriction of payments was not removed until all danger of widespread runs had passed; recovery could then begin rapidly.

This interpretation is, of course, suggested by the striking contrast between the 1907–08 experience and the 1929–33 experience, which we shall examine in detail in Chapter 7. In both cases, the financial climax was the restriction of payments by the banking system. But in the 1907–08 episode, the climax occurred early before the banking structure had been seriously affected and, if our analysis is correct, served to prevent widespread bank failures, to cut short a possible major deflation, and to keep the maximum decline in the stock of money to less than 8 per cent. In the 1929–33 episode, the climax occurred after more than three years of dragging deflation, after bank failures had cut the number of banks by more than a quarter and after the stock of money had fallen by nearly a third, and served only to close the stable door after the horse had been stolen. Finally, the climax itself was much more severe. The 1907 restriction involved the refusal of banks to convert deposits into currency at the demand of the depositor; it did not involve, on any large scale, even the temporary closing of banks or the cessation of their financial operations, let alone the permanent failure of any substantial number. It lasted for several months, and once adjustment was made to the use of two only partly convertible media of payment—currency and deposits—could have continued for a much longer period, as in some earlier episodes, without producing an economic breakdown and indeed could have continued in conjunction with economic revival. The 1933 restriction involved the closing of all banks for a week, the complete cessation of their financial operations, the reopening after that period of most but by no means all of the closed banks, and the permanent failure or liquidation of more than two thousand banks. It disrupted financial transactions more extensively than ever before and it is hard to see how it could have continued for very long without producing almost utter economic chaos.

As we shall see in Chapter 7, the 1929–33 episode shows much similarity in its early phases to the 1907–08 contraction. If the 1907 banking system had been in operation in 1929, restriction of payments might have come in October 1929 when the stock market crashed. If

167

not, it would surely have come at the latest at the end of 1930—probably on the occasion of the failure of the Bank of United States on December 11, 1930. Had restriction come then, it seems likely in retrospect that it would have produced an immediate shock and reaction much more severe than the unspectacular worsening of conditions that occurred in the fall of 1930, but would also have prevented the collapse of the banking system and the drastic fall in the stock of money that were destined to take place, and that certainly intensified the severity of the contraction, if they were not indeed the major factors converting it from a reasonably severe into a catastrophic contraction.[53]

This is, of course, conjectural history—the tale of "what might have been." There is no way to repeat the experiment precisely and so to test these conjectures in detail. That is equally true of the analysis suggesting that it would have been preferable to have avoided restriction of payments in 1907—that, too, is what might have been. Indeed, all truly analytical history, history that seeks to interpret and not simply record the past, is of this character, which is why history must be continuously rewritten in the light of new evidence as it unfolds. In the present instance, our conjectures about 1929–33 lead us to question Sprague's conjectures about 1907–08 and to judge more favorably than he the restriction of payments by the banking system.

4. Banking Reform in the Wake of Restriction of Payments

Though restriction of payments may have been preferable in 1907 to the alternatives then available, that very fact betokened a serious weakness in the financial structure. The weakness had long been recognized in the banking literature, if by no means adequately understood or analyzed. It took the dramatic experience of 1907 to make some measure of reform politically imperative.

Contemporary criticism centered on the alleged "inelasticity" of the stock of money.[54] This term was used in two different senses, one clearly valid; the other highly dubious. The valid sense referred to the absence of effective interconvertibility between currency and deposits. Currency in hand-to-hand circulation consisted mainly of national bank notes, specie, U.S. notes, and silver certificates; these same items served also as till money for banks and as ultimate reserves against deposit liabilities (see Appendix B). The total of what we term high-powered money was

[53] To avoid misunderstanding, we should note explicitly that there were other and preferable measures that could have been taken in 1929–33, under the banking system then in operation, to prevent the banking collapse and the fall in the stock of money. The comparison with 1929–33 is introduced here solely to throw light on the 1907 episode (see Chap. 7).

[54] See Clark Warburton, "Monetary Control under the Federal Reserve Act," *Political Science Quarterly*, Dec. 1946, pp. 509–513.

fairly rigidly fixed within short periods; the only item that could be varied rapidly was specie, through imports from abroad, and it could be varied on a large scale only by drastic changes in the balance of payments.[55] Yet, for a fixed total of high-powered money, any attempt by the public at large to change the form of money it held from deposits to currency would initially drain bank reserves, which in turn would force banks operating with fractional reserves to contract their outstanding liabilities by a multiple of the loss in reserves, thereby reducing the total amount of money available to be held. In a unit banking system with some 20,000 independent banks, the impact was bound to be uneven, to force some banks into suspension, and to threaten a chain reaction involving a cumulative increase in the desire on the part of the public to convert deposits into currency. Short-period "elasticity" in one component of the money stock—currency—was therefore desirable in order to prevent undesired "elasticity" in the total money stock.

The dubious sense in which "inelasticity" was regarded as a defect was with respect to the money stock as a whole. There was a widespread feeling that the money stock should conform to the "needs of trade," that it should expand during periods of active business and contract during periods of dull business. That view was partly a confused version of the first sense of inelasticity arising from a failure to recognize fully the significance of deposits as money, partly a particular manifestation of the ubiquitous "real bills" doctrine.[56] The influence of the view is attested by its partial incorporation in the Federal Reserve Act.

Effective interconvertibility could be fostered by action along any of three main lines. (1) The establishment of some central reserve of currency which would be made available to meet the demand for currency whenever it arose but would be held idle in ordinary times, which means that it would have to be held for purposes other than currently profitable use. This solution was implicit in Treasury operations at the time and earlier, was recommended explicitly by Secretary Shaw, and was envisaged by some proponents of a central bank. (2) The provision of

---

[55] An increase in national bank notes in circulation required time (1) for national banks to purchase government bonds to serve as security against the note issue; (2) for transfer of the bonds to the Treasurer of the United States; (3) for notification of the Comptroller of the Currency to forward notes to the banks; and (4) for transit. There was a statutory limit on the amount of U.S. notes outstanding. With the repeal of the silver-purchase program in late 1893, coinage of silver dollars from the bullion purchased before repeal and the issue of silver certificates depended in part on the amount of bullion in the Treasury, in part on administrative procedures. An act of June 13, 1898, directed the Secretary of the Treasury to coin into standard silver dollars all the silver bullion then in the Treasury, as rapidly as the public interest required, to an amount, however, of not less than $1.5 million in each month.

[56] See L. W. Mints, *A History of Banking Theory*, University of Chicago Press, 1945, pp. 9–10.

some method of issuing currency on a fractional reserve basis to meet emergency needs. The simplest plan would be to have the currency backed by the same kind of assets held by banks as the counterpart to their deposit liabilities. In the extreme, if all hand-to-hand currency were issued by banks under the same conditions as deposit liabilities, there could be no problem of interconvertibility. The principle was embodied in a number of bills presented to Congress shortly after the panic. Two provided for the issue of currency with the same reserve requirements as commercial bank deposits: in the Fowler bill, issue by clearing house associations; in the bill sponsored by the American Bankers Association, which was similar to an earlier plan of the New York Chamber of Commerce, issue by national banks. A third provided for the establishment of a central bank which could issue its own notes by discounting bank assets. (3) A guarantee of bank deposits to make it less likely that a few failures would start a chain reaction involving a widespread attempt by the public to convert from deposits to currency. Such a guarantee would do nothing by itself to enable deposits in fact to be converted into currency without a decline in the stock of money. Its effectiveness would depend entirely on its success in persuading the public that it need have no fears for its deposits and hence in preventing any widespread attempt by the public to reduce the ratio of deposits to currency.

It turned out that some measures were adopted along each of the three lines. Treasury actions along the first line have been noted. The immediate action along the second line on a federal level was the Aldrich-Vreeland Act, approved May 30, 1908, and intended as a temporary stopgap. The act provided for the issuance of an emergency currency by groups of banks, on the basis of usual banking assets, with penalty provisions designed to force retirement after the emergency.[57]

[57] Ten or more national banks, which individually had unimpaired capital and surplus of at least 20 per cent of their liabilities and collectively an aggregate capital and surplus of at least $5 million, might form a National Currency Association to issue to their members emergency currency up to 75 per cent of the value of commercial paper they deposited with the association, and up to 90 per cent of the market value of approved state and local government bonds. Individual national banks might be authorized by the Secretary of the Treasury to issue similar currency against the deposit of such approved bonds with him. In order to speed the retirement of the notes after the emergency had passed, all banks issuing currency were to be taxed at the rate of 5 per cent per annum for the first month, with an additional tax of 1 per cent per annum for each succeeding month until the rate of tax reached 10 per cent per annum. (The Federal Reserve Act of Dec. 23, 1913, reduced those rates to 3 per cent for the first three months, with an additional one-half per cent for each succeeding month up to 6 per cent per annum.) Aggregate emergency circulation was limited to $500 million and the individual bank's emergency circulation, to its capital and surplus. (By the act of Aug. 4, 1914, the Secretary of the Treasury was empowered to suspend the limit on aggregate circulation and to raise the maximum for individual banks to 125 per cent of capital and surplus.)
Since the plan of emergency circulation was not considered a permanent solu-

One clause of the Aldrich-Vreeland Act provided for the appointment of a National Monetary Commission, consisting of nine Senators and nine Representatives. The chairman was Senator Nelson W. Aldrich, the vice-chairman, Representative Edward B. Vreeland. The Commission conducted hearings and arranged for a large number of special studies. Its report was submitted to Congress in 1912.[58] After extensive Congressional debate, in which the report of the Commission provided the point of departure, the Federal Reserve Act was passed December 23, 1913, establishing a system very similar in general structure to, and identical in many details with, the specific plan of reform recommended by the Commission.[59]

As for action along the third line mentioned above, laws setting up

---

tion of existing defects, the act expired by limitation on June 30, 1914. It was, however, extended to June 30, 1915, by the act establishing the Federal Reserve System, by which time the district Federal Reserve Banks were expected to be in operation.

The Aldrich-Vreeland Act also required payment of interest on government deposits at not less than 1 per cent per annum and formally exempted banks from keeping a reserve against those deposits (informal exemption dated from Secretary Shaw's ruling of Sept. 1902).

[58] The Commission's report—the last of 24 volumes of publications—summarized the defects of the existing banking system and recommended the incorporation of a National Reserve Association to remedy them. The plan of reform was known as the Aldrich Plan, after the chairman of the Commission.

The Commission is better known for the other 23 volumes prepared by economists and financial experts it employed here and abroad. About two-thirds of the contents of those volumes is concerned with banking in foreign countries. The material on the United States includes digests of U.S. financial laws and of state banking laws; financial statistics over the forty-year period from 1867; financial diagrams; descriptive monographs on clearing house methods and the use of credit instruments in the U.S.; historical studies of the First Bank and Second Bank of the United States, state banking practices before the Civil War, the Safety Fund banking system in New York State, the Independent Treasury System, the origins of the national banking system and national bank currency; and an investigation of the growth of state banks and trust companies after the Civil War. Major analytical contributions were made by E. W. Kemmerer in *Seasonal Variations in the Relative Demand for Money and Capital in the United States,* George Paish in *The Trade Balance of the United States,* and O. M. W. Sprague in *History of Crises under the National Banking System.*

Although the National Monetary Commission did not attempt a systematic review of American financial experience, many of the individual monographs have had a lasting value.

[59] The National Monetary Commission was appointed by a Republican Congress and its chairman was a Republican. The Federal Reserve Act was passed by a Democratic Congress. Its chief Congressional sponsor, Representative (later, Senator) Carter Glass, naturally tried to differentiate the Democratic product from the Republican proposal, and insisted then and later that the Federal Reserve Act had little in common with the Aldrich Plan. The near-identity of the two is documented in Paul M. Warburg, *The Federal Reserve System, Its Origins and Growth,* New York, Macmillan, 1930, Vol. I, Chaps. 8 and 9, which compare in parallel columns provisions of the bill proposed by the National Monetary Commission and of the Federal Reserve Act.

deposit guaranty funds were enacted by eight western, midwestern, and southern states between December 1907 and March 1917.[60]

The Aldrich-Vreeland Act was used on only one occasion before it expired June 30, 1915. That occasion was the outbreak of World War I, when fears of financial difficulties were exacerbated by the closing of the New York Stock Exchange on July 31, 1914, in order to prevent a demoralized market as a result of wholesale unloading of securities by Europeans.[61] Country banks began to withdraw currency from city banks, the New York Clearing House issued clearing house loan certificates on August 3, and clearing houses in other cities followed suit shortly thereafter. A total of $212 million in clearing house loan certificates was issued in the whole country. As soon as depositors began runs on banks, the emergency currency provided for in the Aldrich-Vreeland Act was put into circulation. By the end of November, nearly $400 million had been issued and about a third of that total redeemed. The maximum amount outstanding on any one date was $364 million, which was nearly one-quarter of the total amount of currency in the hands of the public before the outbreak of war, and nearly one-eighth of total high-powered money.[62] The availability of the emergency issue probably prevented a monetary panic and the restriction of payments by the banking system.

To judge by that one episode, the Aldrich-Vreeland Act provided an effective device for solving a threatened interconvertibility crisis without monetary contraction or widespread bank failures. The episode strengthens our own view, based primarily on other considerations, that it would have been equally effective on the occasion of the next threat of an interconvertibility crisis which arose in late 1930. As noted above, we conclude in Chapter 7 that restriction of payments would almost surely have been preferable on that occasion to the actual course of events under the more far-reaching alteration of the monetary system achieved under the Federal Reserve Act. It seems highly likely that the Aldrich-Vreeland device would have been preferable to either, though not necessarily to measures that could have been but were not taken under the later system.

[60] Proposals for deposit guaranty anteceding these state plans are discussed in Fritz Redlich, *The Molding of American Banking*, New York, Hafner, 1951, Vol. 2, Part II, pp. 215–217.

[61] The stock exchange opened for restricted trading on Dec. 12 after an "outlaw" market, in operation on the Wall Street sidewalk since the closing of the official market, published quotations equal to or above those of July 30. On Apr. 1, 1915, all restrictions were removed. Dealings in bonds, with fixed minimum prices, were resumed on Nov. 28, 1914.

[62] Most of the Aldrich-Vreeland currency was doubtless in the hands of the public, but some was held in bank vaults on any given date. It should be noted that, unlike the emergency issues of 1893 and 1907, Aldrich-Vreeland currency is included in our estimates of the money stock. See also *Annual Report,* Comptroller of the Currency, 1915, Vol. I, pp. 45, 49, 103.

One more banking reform deserves mention. A system of government-owned banks was converted from a radical nostrum, long a Populist demand, to a hallowed institution by the opening in January 1911 of postal savings banks.[63] The Postal Savings System was of negligible importance until the 1929–33 contraction, when the general distrust of the banking system led to an eightfold increase in its deposits in the course of a few years. Even after that growth, it remained a minor factor.[64]

5. *The Postpanic Period, 1908 to 1914*

Aside from the banking reforms just discussed, the period contains little of interest for our purposes. Though real output shows reasonably steady if unspectacular growth, an unusually high fraction of the period is characterized by business cycle analysts as cyclical contraction. On the average, the United States experienced 1.57 months of cyclical expansion per month of contraction from 1854 to 1961. Of the 78 months covered by the 1908–12 and 1912–14 cycles, only 31 were in the two expansion phases, 47 in the two contraction phases, or only 0.66 months of expansion per month of contraction.

A vigorous rebound from the sharp contraction of 1907–08 in the stock of money, money income, real income, and prices, culminated in a cyclical peak dated January 1910. The protracted recession that followed lasted until January 1912, was preceded by a retardation in the rate of growth of the money stock, and was accompanied by a fairly sharp drop in the level of wholesale prices. To judge from Chart 9 the behavior of both money and prices reflects an overreaction to the large gold imports of 1906 to 1907. Once the panic was over, and the deposit-currency ratio rose, those gold imports permitted a sharp rise in the stock of money and thence in the ratio of U.S. prices to British prices, which reversed the movement of gold. If our figures on capital movements can be trusted,

[63] Under the authority of the act of June 25, 1910, an amount equal to 5 per cent of the deposits was to be kept as a reserve in the Treasury; the remainder of the funds of the banks could be redeposited in national or state banks at a rate of interest not less than 2¼ per cent. Alternatively, an amount equal to not more than 30 per cent of the deposits might be invested by the trustees in government bonds. By direction of the President, the remaining funds could also be invested in government bonds. Interest on deposits was payable at the rate of 2 per cent. From July 1911 to July 1935, a depositor had the option of exchanging his deposit for an equal amount of tax-exempt postal savings 2½ per cent bonds, redeemable in one year, and payable in twenty years from date of issue, with interest payable semiannually. The first issue was made in July 1911, and was followed by additional issues semiannually through July 1935. A fall in the market price of postal savings bonds in Nov. 1911 led the trustees to announce their readiness to repurchase these bonds at par before maturity.

[64] Postal savings deposits grew to a peak of 4 per cent of savings deposits in mutual savings banks in 1919, declined to 2 per cent in 1929, then rose to 13 per cent in 1933, and remained in that neighborhood until World War II. They then rose to 20 per cent in 1947. By the end of 1960 they had fallen back to 2 per cent.

capital imports were very high during 1909 and 1910. This may have been either a transitory reaction to the relatively high level of U.S. prices—an accommodating capital movement—or the independent force that permitted prices in the United States to rise so high. In either event, the sharp decline in capital imports from 1910 to 1911 was accompanied by a sharp absolute decline in U.S. prices, required in order to lower U.S. prices relative to British prices.

Though protracted, the contraction was relatively mild. Kuznets' net national product series in constant prices shows no decline, only a retarded rate of rise; and the mildness of the contraction is confirmed by other indicators of the physical level of activity.

The cyclical trough was reached in January 1912 and succeeded by one of the briefest expansions on record, terminating just 12 months later in January 1913. The expansion was preceded by a sharp rise in wholesale prices, which had reached their trough in mid-1911. Wholesale prices rose until October 1912 and from then until late 1915 fluctuated about a roughly constant level. Until after the outbreak of war in 1914, the price movement paralleled that in Britain (as did also the movement of the index of U.S. implicit prices and an index of British prices), so relative prices changed little from 1911 on. The money stock rose fairly steadily throughout the period from 1909 to 1914, interrupted only by brief retardations in rate of growth in 1910 and again in 1913.

Net national product in constant prices rose fairly vigorously from 1911 to 1913, then fell sharply to 1914 as the contraction that began in January 1913 was intensified by the uncertainty and disorganization resulting from the outbreak of war in Europe.

6. *The Arithmetic of Changes in the Money Stock*

Chart 14 shows the behavior from 1897 to 1914 of the money stock and of its three proximate determinants: (1) total high-powered money, (2) the ratio of commercial bank deposits to reserves of high-powered money, and (3) the ratio of deposits to currency held by the public.

All three factors clearly contributed to the increase in the stock of money that took place. Table 7 shows for the period as a whole and for two subperiods the rate of change in the money stock that would have been produced by each factor alone, and the fraction of the total rate of change in the money stock accounted for by each. The two subperiods are the initial years of exceedingly rapid monetary growth from 1897 to 1902, and the subsequent years of fairly steady growth from 1902 to 1914 (except for the 1907 panic). In addition, for comparative purposes, the table repeats the corresponding figures presented in Table 4 for the earlier period.

The relative importance of the different factors is strikingly similar in

174

CHART 14
The Stock of Money and Its Proximate Determinants, and Treasury Cash, 1897–1914

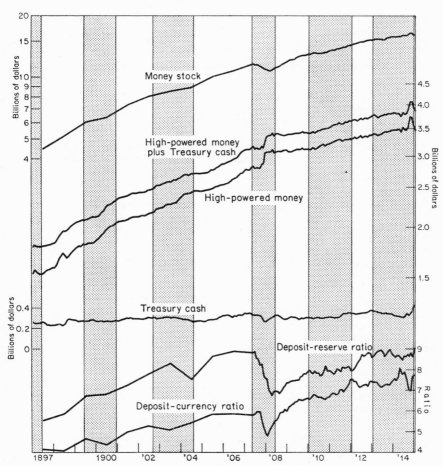

NOTE: Shaded areas represent business contractions; unshaded areas, business expansions. The top three curves are plotted on a ratio scale, the bottom three on an arithmetic scale.

SOURCE: Money stock, Table A-1, col. 8. High-powered money, 1897–Apr. 1907, monthly figures from same source as annual figures for those years in Table B-3; May 1907 on, Table B-3. Ratios, Table B-3. Treasury cash, 1897–Apr. 1907, monthly figures from same source as annual figures for those years in Table A-3; May 1907 on, Table A-3.

accounting for the 5.8 per cent per year increase in the money stock from 1879 to 1897 and the 7.5 per cent per year increase from 1897 to 1914.[65] In the later as in the earlier period, the change in the total stock of high-powered money was the dominant factor, and the rising ratio of deposits to the public's currency holdings was second in importance. The one significant difference is the greater contribution in the second than in the first period of the rise in the ratio of deposits to reserves, i.e., the decline in the reserves maintained by the banks relative to their deposits.

TABLE 7

CONTRIBUTION OF PROXIMATE DETERMINANTS TO CHANGES IN THE
MONEY STOCK, 1879–1914

Proximate Determinant	Change in Money Stock That Would Have Been Produced by Indicated Determinant, if It Alone Had Changed			
	Feb. 1879 to June 1897	June 1897 to June 1902	June 1902 to June 1914	June 1897 to June 1914
	RATE OF CHANGE PER YEAR (per cent)			
1. High-powered money	3.9	6.8	4.0	4.9
2. Deposit-reserve ratio	0.4	2.6	0.4	1.0
3. Deposit-currency ratio	1.4	1.8	1.4	1.3
4. Interaction of ratios	0.2	0.4	0.1	0.4
5. All	5.8	11.6	5.8	7.5
	FRACTION OF TOTAL CHANGE			
1. High-powered money	0.66	0.59	0.69	0.64
2. Deposit-reserve ratio	0.06	0.23	0.06	0.13
3. Deposit-currency ratio	0.24	0.15	0.23	0.17
4. Interaction of ratios	0.04	0.04	0.01	0.05
5. All	1.00	1.00	1.00	1.00

NOTE: Because of rounding, detail may not add to totals.
SOURCE: Table B-3. See also Table 4 and App. B, sect. 7.

Though the change in high-powered money was of major importance for the period as a whole, it was much less so for the shorter-run movements within the period. Total high-powered money grew fairly regularly, except for the hump in 1908 caused by the large increase in currency through gold imports and other means arising out of the panic of 1907, and the briefer hump in late 1914 produced by the issue of Aldrich-Vreeland currency. The earlier hump, which by itself would have produced an increase in the stock of money, is associated with and follows a decline in the stock of money, thanks to the associated reductions in the deposit-reserve ratio and the deposit-currency ratio—a train of events discussed above in connection with the panic. The second hump is ac-

[65] See Appendix B for an explanation of how these percentages are calculated.

176

companied by a minor increase in the stock of money, despite a simultaneous sharp drop in the deposit-currency ratio of brief duration. This contrast with the 1907 episode attests to the effectiveness of the emergency currency issue. Had there been no provisions for such an issue, the decline in the deposit-currency ratio would probably have had to produce a decline in the stock of money, as in 1907, in order to have stimulated a growth in high-powered money. Given the international situation, it might not have done so even then. The consequent bank difficulties might have intensified the decline in the deposit-currency ratio and spread it over a longer period, so converting the brief dip in the ratio, as plotted, into a much deeper and broader valley more like that of 1907–08, with further effects on the stock of money. As it was, the prompt satisfaction of the public's demand for additional currency cut the process short at the outset.

The two deposit ratios show considerable variations throughout the period, not only at the time of the 1907 panic. It will be recalled that in the period 1879–97 the deposit-reserve ratio shows a fairly clear cyclical pattern. In the later period, it also rises during expansions and rises at a reduced rate or falls during contractions. Once again, the panic greatly exaggerates the size of the movement without noticeably changing its pattern. Except for the panic, the movements in the deposit-currency ratio are much less regularly cyclical, though it too shows some tendency to rise during expansions and to rise at a smaller pace or fall during contractions.

There are two interesting differences in the behavior of the deposit ratios that are worth note. In the first place, the panic produced a notable absolute decline in both ratios and an even more sizable decline relative to trend. The deposit-currency ratio rebounded rapidly and within less than a year seems to have resumed its earlier trend. The deposit-reserve ratio resumed its rate of rise after 1908 but at a lower level rather than at the level of the earlier trend. A minor part of the explanation is the concentration of failures during the panic among banks with high ratios of deposits to high-powered money. More important, the experience of the panic apparently raised the liquidity preference of the commercial banks for a considerably longer period than it did that of their depositors. The same contrast in the behavior of the two ratios is noticeable after the monetary crises of 1884 and again after the troubled period of 1890 to 1893 (see Charts 10 and 14). We shall see it occur again after the panic of 1933 (Chapter 8). The different reaction of bankers and their depositors need not mean that bankers have a longer memory or that they are more sluggish in reacting, but simply that they have more at stake and hence more reason to remember.

The second interesting difference between the two deposit ratios is in their comparative behavior in 1897–1914 and 1879–97. The deposit-currency ratio rose at roughly the same percentage rate in both periods. As Table 7 shows, by itself it would have produced roughly the same rate of increase in the stock of money in 1897–1914 and in each of the two segments distinguished in the table as in the earlier period.[66] Evidently, we can attribute its rise to common factors acting with roughly the same force in both periods, of which rising real income and rising convenience (i.e., falling costs) of bank services are probably the most important. The deposit-reserve ratio, on the other hand, rose decidedly more rapidly from 1897 to 1907 than it did from 1879 to 1897. Table 7 alone might suggest that the whole of this difference is concentrated in the 1897–1902 segment, but a glance at Chart 14 shows that this is not so. The reason the period 1902–14 exhibits no greater rate of rise attributable to the deposit-reserve ratio than the period 1879–97 is not the reversion of the deposit-reserve ratio to its pre-1897 rate of rise but its sharp drop after 1907. From 1902 to 1906 and again from 1908 to 1914, the deposit-reserve ratio rose at a more rapid rate than it did from 1879 to 1897. A minor reason for the accelerated rate of rise is a relatively more rapid rate of growth after 1897 than before of the fraction of deposits in banks with a high deposit-reserve ratio—nonnational banks plus national banks outside the central reserve cities.[67] The major reason is an accelerated tendency of banks to reduce the margin between high-powered money held at their discretion and the high-powered money they were required by law to hold—to reduce their "prudential" reserves. That tendency may have reflected in part the rising rates of interest, which increased the cost of holding high-powered reserves and encouraged

[66] The reason the rate of increase is 1.8 in the first of the two segments of the period and 1.4 in the second, yet only 1.3 in the period as a whole, is connected with the index-number problem of the base used in calculating the numbers and is reflected in the size of the interaction term for the period as a whole. Had we used the later rather than the earlier year as the base, the percentages would have been 2.2, 1.5, and 1.7 (see Appendix B, sect. 7).

[67] It will be recalled that our deposit-reserve ratio counts as reserves only high-powered money. Both nonnational banks and national banks outside reserve cities were permitted by law to keep a large fraction of legally required reserves as deposits with other banks, which is to say, legally required high-powered reserves were relatively low.

If the ratio of deposits to reserves for each class of banks separately (nonnational banks, central reserve city national banks, reserve city national banks, and country national banks) had been the same from 1879 to 1914 as it was in 1914, the changing distribution of deposits among them would have raised the deposit-reserve ratio at the rate of 0.4 per cent per year from 1879 to 1897, and of 0.8 per cent per year from 1897 to 1914. In fact, the deposit-reserve ratio rose at the rate of 1.10 per cent per year from 1879 to 1897 and of 2.55 per cent per year from 1897 to 1914.

These results would no doubt be changed if the calculation were made for the deposit-reserve ratios in years other than 1914, but hardly by enough to change the quantitative conclusion in the text.

TABLE 8

CURRENCY IN AND OUTSIDE THE TREASURY, BY KIND, 1897–1914

(millions of dollars)

End of June	Gold (1)	Silver and Treasury Notes of 1890 (2)	Sub- sidiary Silver (3)	U.S. Notes (4)	National Bank Notes (5)	Total Plus Minor Coin[a] (6)
			CURRENCY IN THE TREASURY (TREASURY CASH)			
1897	141	62	16	37	5	261
1898	167	13	12	34	5	231
1899	241	7	6	15	4	273
1900	221	17	7	26	9	280
1901	249	24	11	14	9	307
1902	252	25	14	10	11	312
1903	252	27	9	10	13	311
1904	215	26	12	12	16	281
1905	217	29	13	14	15	288
1906	285	12	7	10	12	326
1907	300	10	9	4	14	339
1908	213	22	24	6	66	334
1909	223	14	27	6	23	296
1910	237	13	20	10	29	310
1911	227	37	21	6	37	330
1912	263	25	29	9	40	368
1913	251	23	20	9	43	348
1914	241	16	22	8	33	322
	(7)	(8)	(9)	(10)	(11)	(12)
		CURRENCY OUTSIDE THE TREASURY (HIGH-POWERED MONEY)				
1897	450	494	54	310	216	1,524
1898	587	547	59	313	216	1,722
1899	619	558	65	332	232	1,806
1900	696	549	70	321	291	1,953
1901	753	545	73	332	340	2,071
1902	814	546	76	336	341	2,143
1903	870	546	85	337	392	2,262
1904	981	548	88	334	425	2,410
1905	1,007	539	93	333	471	2,478
1906	1,053	556	103	336	542	2,628
1907	1,166	558	113	343	584	2,805
1908	1,405	547	114	340	623	3,067
1909	1,419	554	123	341	650	3,127
1910	1,399	555	136	336	675	3,146
1911	1,526	530	138	341	682	3,266
1912	1,555	542	141	338	695	3,322
1913	1,620	545	155	338	702	3,414
1914	1,650	551	160	339	705	3,461

(continued)

TABLE 8 (concluded)

End of June	Gold (13)	Silver and Treasury Notes of 1890 (14)	Sub-sidiary Silver (15)	U.S. Notes (16)	National Bank Notes (17)	Total Plus Minor Coin[a] (18)
		CURRENCY IN AND OUTSIDE THE TREASURY				
1897	591	556	70	347	221	1,785
1898	754	559	71	347	221	1,952
1899	859	565	71	347	235	2,077
1900	916	567	76	347	301	2,233
1901	1,001	568	84	347	349	2,377
1902	1,067	570	90	347	352	2,456
1903	1,122	573	95	347	406	2,575
1904	1,198	573	99	347	440	2,691
1905	1,226	568	107	347	487	2,770
1906	1,342	568	110	347	554	2,959
1907	1,466	568	122	347	598	3,142
1908	1,618	568	138	347	689	3,401
1909	1,642	568	150	347	673	3,423
1910	1,636	569	155	347	703	3,456
1911	1,753	568	160	347	719	3,596
1912	1,818	568	171	347	735	3,690
1913	1,871	569	175	347	745	3,762
1914	1,891	568	182	347	738	3,783

NOTE: On account of rounding differences there may be minor discrepancies between the sums of kinds of currency in and outside the Treasury and the figures shown in cols. 13–18. Cols. 6 and 12 are unadjusted for seasonal variations, and so differ from col. 1 in Tables A-3 and B-3. Gold consists of gold coin and gold certificates, silver of silver dollars and silver certificates. U.S. notes include currency certificates.

[a] Minor coin is not shown separately. The amount in the Treasury never exceeded $3.2 million; the amount outside the Treasury rose from $26 million, when figures first became available in 1900, to $57 million in 1914.

SOURCE: Same as for col. 1 of Tables A-1 and A-3.

banks that were legally permitted to do so to build up the proportion of reserves held in the form of interest-earning deposits with other banks. As already suggested, the tendency may in part also have resulted from the increasing readiness of the Treasury to intervene in the money market and to assume responsibility for money market conditions.

Table 8 shows Treasury cash, high-powered money, and the total of the two, each classified by type, and Chart 15 the composition of high-powered money. The increase in the total stock of high-powered money came primarily from gold (coins and certificates) and national bank notes. Of the total increase from 1897 to 1914, these two account for 87 per cent—gold for 62 per cent, national bank notes for 25 per cent. Silver, which had been so critical an element in the preceding period, accounted for only 3 per cent, and was exceeded in importance by subsidiary silver,

CHART 15
Composition of High-Powered Money, 1897–1914

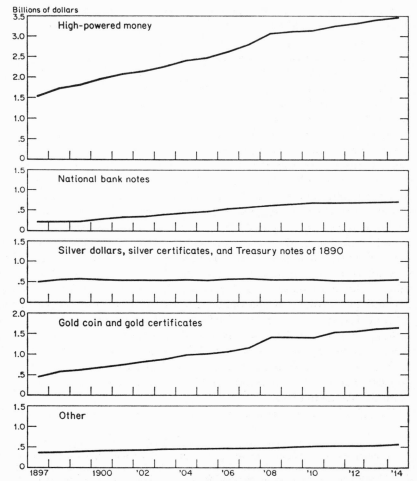

SOURCE: Table 8, cols. 7–12. "Other" consists of U.S. notes, subsidiary silver and, from 1900 on, minor coin.

which accounted for 5 per cent. U.S. notes and minor coin accounted for the remaining 5 per cent.

The absence of substantial growth in types of currency other than gold and national bank notes reflects the conditions under which they were issued: U.S. notes inside and outside the Treasury stayed at the fixed maximum specified in the act of 1878; Treasury notes of 1890 were retired and silver certificates issued in their place; silver dollars and certificates increased to the extent that silver bullion purchased by the Treasury before 1893 was coined; subsidiary silver and minor coin (the latter is included in Table 8, beginning 1900) were issued as demanded, so that the amounts in circulation grew at rates intermediate between those of currency held by the public and of commercial bank deposits.

The fairly rapid growth of national bank notes dates from 1900, when the Gold Standard Act of 1900 made the conditions of issue more profitable for banks.[68] A minor change in 1907 had similar effects.[69]

Though Treasury cash remained roughly constant in absolute amount, it declined sharply relative to the stock of high-powered money. The passing of the crisis about the monetary standard made the size and composition of Treasury cash less critical—the amount of gold in the Treasury was no longer the subject of frequent newspaper comment and minor changes no longer stimulated speculative flurries. The passing of the crisis also reduced the possibility that particular types of Treasury cash would be subjected to sudden and unexpected drains to redeem legal tender notes. Despite the greater degree of Treasury intervention in the money market, Treasury cash fluctuated less from one year to the next than it had during the earlier period, although in certain years, intra-yearly fluctuations were greater.[70] Both were partly a consequence of that very intervention, which was designed to prevent revenue surpluses from simply adding to balances and also to offset seasonal variations in the demand for currency by the public. Mostly, however, the decline in the ratio of Treasury cash to total high-powered money reflected the use of techniques enabling the Treasury to hold sizable deposits at commercial banks and to vary the size of such deposits as an instrument of control. In consequence, such deposits were larger relative to commercial bank deposits, particularly from 1900 to 1909, than earlier and display much more sizable fluctuations.

Though changes in high-powered money were the dominant factor ac-

[68] The act entitled national banks to receive from the Comptroller of the Currency notes equal in amount to the par value of the bonds deposited—instead of only 90 per cent as formerly. In addition it repealed the prohibition—in effect since 1882—of an increase in circulation for a period of six months after a bank had deposited lawful money with the Treasurer of the United States, in order to decrease its circulation. The act also contributed to the growth in national bank circulation by authorizing the formation of national banks with a capital as low as $25,000.

[69] By raising the monthly limit on retirement of national bank notes from $3 million to $9 million, the act of Mar. 4, 1907 reduced the banks' reluctance to make temporary increases in circulation.

[70] The difference in intra-yearly fluctuations of Treasury cash is not observable in Charts 15 and 10, since seasonally adjusted figures are shown there. The average deviation of the seasonal index computed for the years 1899–1913 is, however, 11 per cent greater than that of the seasonal index computed for the years 1879–92.

counting—in an arithmetic sense—for the increase in the stock of money from 1897 to 1914, other factors were by no means negligible even over the period as a whole, let alone in the shorter movements. A hypothetical calculation may bring out their importance in perhaps a more striking way than the numbers in Table 8 do. For the time being, ignore the reflex influence of the manner in which the United States increased its money stock on the stock of money and on prices in the rest of the world. The total increase in the U.S. stock of money would then have been much the same, however it was brought about. Assume that the two deposit ratios had remained unchanged from 1897 to 1914. To achieve the actually attained increase in the stock of money, the total stock of high-powered money would have had to be 3.60 instead of 2.28 times as large in 1914 as in 1897, that is, in 1914 it would have had to be $5,489 million instead of $3,482 million—an increase from 1897 to 1914 of $3,965 million instead of $1,958 million. If gold had accounted for the same fraction of this hypothetical larger increase in high-powered money as it did of the actual increase, the stock of gold outside the Treasury would have had to grow by $2,430 million instead of by $1,200 million. The latter figure was itself nearly one-third of the estimated growth of the world's monetary stock of gold from 1897 to 1914; the larger hypothetical figure would have been over three-fifths of the increase in the world's gold stock. Under these conditions, to ignore the reflex influence on the rest of the world of the way in which the U.S. money stock grew, however satisfactory as a first approximation under conditions close to those experienced, would have been clearly untenable. Both the rise in deposits of commercial banks relative to reserves and the rise in deposits held by the public relative to currency clearly had an appreciable impact on the worldwide growth of the stock of money and on the movements of world prices expressed in gold. Consequently, they also had an appreciable effect on the movements of money and prices that could and did occur in the United States.

7. A Retrospective Comparison

We may summarize the broader features of the period dealt with in this and the two preceding chapters by using a rather different division of the period than the one we have so far employed. This alternative division is suggested by the extraordinary parallelism between the two decades preceding and the two decades following the cyclical peak dated January 1893 in the National Bureau's chronology. Both started with unusually protracted economic difficulties: the serious business contraction from 1873 to 1879 and the turbulent period from 1893 to 1896 or 1897. Although the NBER reference cycle chronology labels the eighteen months from June 1894 to December 1895 as a period of expansion, the expansion was mild and the 1895 peak well below the level corresponding to full utilization of the productive potentialities of the economy. And in both these troubled periods—troubled in many countries abroad as well as in the United States—the U.S. difficulties were greatly intensified by monetary uncertainty, attendant on the move toward resumption in the one case and, in the other, on the possibility that the United States would replace the gold by a silver standard.

In both cases, the termination of the uncertainty was marked by a political event—the official resumption of gold payments in 1879 and the defeat of Bryan in 1896—and insured by an accidental coincidence of good harvests here and poor harvests abroad. In both cases, there followed an extraordinarily rapid upsurge in the stock of money, in prices, and in output, in what appears to be a rebound from the prior difficulties. And finally, in both cases, the rebound was succeeded by something like a decade of moderately steady economic growth, interrupted by banking difficulties, which did not create protracted disturbances because they reflected primarily domestic conditions not seriously complicated by an external drain—in the first period, in 1884; in the second, in 1907. Perhaps the only difference in the behavior of output important enough to note is the unusually protracted and severe contraction of 1882 to 1885, which has no counterpart in the later period, unless it be the large fraction of the years from 1908 to 1914 characterized by cyclical contraction. In addition, of course, prices behaved very differently—generally declining during the earlier period, generally rising during the later period.

Table 9 documents this parallelism in terms of the behavior of various magnitudes during the corresponding segments of the two periods. The dates chosen for the segments are to some extent arbitrary. To provide some objective criterion, we have used the dates in the National Bureau reference chronology. The initial segment of monetary uncertainty runs from a reference peak to a reference trough—though not in both cases the immediately following trough; the segment labeled rebound runs from a reference trough to a reference peak; the segment of moderately steady growth, from a reference peak to a reference peak. In principle, there is an element of arbitrariness in deciding which reference peak or trough to use to mark the beginning or end of a segment. In practice, these historical episodes are so clearly differentiated that there is little doubt which turning point to use. A more troublesome problem is whether to use the NBER monthly or annual dates, since these give different results in at least one instance.[71] The monthly dates seem indicated for our money series, the annual dates for the other series. After 1907, the money data are monthly. For 1882–1906, the money series gives

[71] On the basis of the monthly dates, the successive segments are 1873–79, 1879–82, 1882–93, 1893–97, 1897–1902, 1902–13.

TABLE 9

COMPARISON OF TWO SIMILAR PERIODS IN AMERICAN MONETARY HISTORY: RATES OF CHANGE IN VARIOUS MAGNITUDES DURING SEGMENTS OF THE PERIODS 1873–92 AND 1892–1913

SERIES AND PERIOD	SEGMENT OF:		
	Monetary Uncertainty or Monetary Contraction 1873–78 1892–96	Rebound 1878–82 1896–1903	Moderately Stable Growth 1882–92 1903–13
	NUMBER OF YEARS		
Duration of segment			
1873–92	5	4	10
1892–1913	4	7	10
	RATE OF CHANGE (per cent per year)		
Stock of money			
1873–92	−0.6	12.6	5.4
1892–1913	−1.0	9.9	6.0
Money income			
1873–92	0.9	9.6	1.5
1892–1913	−2.3	8.0	5.2
Wholesale prices			
1873–92	−7.6	4.3	−3.5
1892–1913	−2.9	3.5	1.6
Price index implicit in real income			
1873–92	−4.3	1.2	−2.0
1892–1913	−2.2	2.0	2.0
Real income			
1873–92	5.2	8.4	3.5
1892–1913	−0.1	6.0	3.3
Real income per capita			
1873–92	2.9	6.2	1.3
1892–1913	−2.1	4.1	1.4
Velocity of money			
1873–92	1.5	−3.0	−3.9
1892–1913	−1.3	−1.9	−0.8

NOTE: Rate of change is from initial to terminal value assuming continuous compounding; computed by dividing the difference between the natural logarithms of the terminal and initial values by the time interval between them.

SOURCE: Money stock: annual averages of data in Table A-1, col. 8, centered on June 30. Wholesale prices: *Historical Statistics of the United States, Colonial Times to 1957*, Bureau of the Census, 1960, Series E-1, E-13, pp. 115–117. Population: *ibid.*, Series A-2, p. 7. Other series: from same sources as for Chart 62.

the stock on June 30 of successive years; for that period, the use of the year in which the monthly reference date falls would mean the least difference between the date of the money figure and the reference turning point. For 1875–81, when the money data are available for end of February and end of August, this procedure would introduce even less of a discrepancy. For the income series, however, the only data available are annual totals, and, for comparability, we have used annual averages for the price series. We have let these series decide the issue and so have used annual reference dates. Throughout the table we have accommodated the money series to the annual dates by using annual averages of whatever data are available. Except for one point, mentioned below, the general picture is much the same whichever set of dates is used.

The use of 1903 in Table 9 to terminate the period of the rebound instead of 1902 as in Table 7 is a mechanical result of the use of the annual reference date rather than of the year in which the monthly reference date falls. But, unfortunately, it violates an economic reality we have commented on earlier, namely, the tendency of the money stock to diminish its rate of growth well before the onset of contraction. The money stock grew at a decidedly lower rate from 1901 to 1902 than from 1900 to 1901 and at a still lower rate from 1902 to 1903.

The table brings out the striking parallelism between the two decades before and the two decades after 1893. That parallelism is particularly marked for the rebound, as noted earlier (see section 1, above). For the segment of monetary uncertainty, price behavior is more similar than is behavior of real income: according to these figures, real income, both total and per capita, rose at a very rapid rate during the 1873–78 contraction, whereas both fell during the 1892–96 period. However, as we saw in Chapter 2, the income figures for the earlier period are very rough approximations and almost surely overstate considerably the rate of rise in real income during the contraction period. Hence this result probably reflects more on the accuracy of our evidence than on a valid difference between the periods.

Perhaps the most interesting result in the table is the contrast between the behavior of real and monetary magnitudes during the two decades of moderately steady growth. The rate of increase in both total and per capita real income is roughly identical in 1882–93 and in 1903–13. On the other hand, prices fell at the rate of 2 to 4 per cent—depending on which price index is used—in the first period and rose at the rate of 2 per cent in the second. In terms of the figures given here, this differential reflects primarily a difference in the behavior of velocity; the stock of money grew at only a slightly smaller rate during the earlier decade than during the later. However, this is the point mentioned earlier at which the exact date chosen makes an appreciable difference. According to our estimates, the stock of money was decidedly higher in 1892 than in either 1891 or 1893. If 1893, the year that contains the monthly cyclical peak, is used to terminate the segment of relatively steady growth, the rate of change in the stock of money is 4.4 instead of 5.4; on the other hand, use of the years containing the monthly dates for the second period (1902–13 instead of 1903–13) raises the rate of growth a trifle—from 6.00 to 6.02. Accordingly, the stock of money grew noticeably more rapidly than the table shows during the later than during the earlier decade of relatively steady growth, if years containing the monthly reference dates are substituted for those containing annual reference dates. This is also the impression given by examination of Charts 8 and 13 for the two decades as a whole rather than solely for selected initial and terminal values.

The comparison of real and monetary magnitudes is relevant to two major issues that are closely connected with monetary phenomena though not our direct concern here. In the first place, it bears on an issue that we have referred to earlier: the connection between secular price change and the secular growth of real output. It has been widely believed that rising prices over a period covering several business cycles stimulate economic growth and falling prices inhibit growth. The present comparison is another piece of evidence calling this simple connection in question. The decades of 1882–92 and 1903–13 appear to have been characterized by roughly similar rates of growth of real output, yet in the one, prices declined at a rate of 2 per cent or more, and in the other, prices rose at a rate of about 2 per cent. If these figures can be trusted, the rate of price change over several cycles had little or no connection with the associated rate of growth of output. May it be that the rate of change in prices has a stronger effect on what contemporaries regard the rate of growth to be rather than on what the actual rate of growth is?

The second major issue is the existence or interpretation of so-called "long cycles" or long swings in economic activity. Looking at matters as we do from the monetary side, we are tempted to regard these periods of roughly twenty years in length as not cyclical in character. The interpretation embodied in the table is rather of a relatively stable rate of growth interrupted by two monetary episodes from which the system rebounded to approximately its initial path. This is a point to which we return in later chapters. But it is worth emphasizing here that there is an alternative interpretation which would designate 1879 or thereabouts as the trough of a long cycle, some date in the 1880's as the peak and in the mid-1890's as a second trough, and something like 1906 as the next peak. And this interpretation is based not alone on the evidence for these four decades, but also on data that suggest the existence of swings of roughly the same duration for a much longer period before and since. On this alternative

187

interpretation, the monetary difficulties are in part the product of the underlying cyclical process, and the periodization in Table 9 is simply equivalent to approximating a smooth curvilinear function by a series of connected straight-line segments.[72]

We have described these interpretations as if they were mutually exclusive. Of course, they are not. One can regard the monetary events partly as shocks that trigger a cyclical reaction mechanism; partly as consequences of prior cyclical reactions. For example, there can be no doubt that the long period of declining prices before the 1890's was an important factor in stimulating the search for gold and for economical techniques for extracting gold from low-grade ore. And the subsequent rapid rate of growth of the world's gold stock was bound to taper off after a time because of exhaustion of the newly discovered fields, but more fundamentally, because of the rise in prices which reduced the incentive to mine gold. Similarly, for the United States, the movements of capital from and to the outside world played an important role in monetary changes, and they too can be regarded as moving in long swings and as reflecting the fundamental factors giving rise to coordinated long swings in a variety of economic activities.

[72] See Moses Abramovitz, statement in *Employment, Growth, and Price Levels,* Hearings before Joint Economic Committee, Part 2, 86th Cong., 1st sess., 1959; and *idem,* "The Nature and Significance of Kuznets Cycles," *Economic Development and Cultural Change,* Apr. 1961, pp. 225–248. See also the contributions of Abramovitz in NBER, *Annual Report,* 38th, 1958, to 41st, 1961.

CHAPTER 5

Early Years of the Federal Reserve System, 1914–21

ENACTED in years of relative calm, the Federal Reserve Act had its first trial in years of economic turmoil. The widespread abandonment or relaxation of the gold standard accompanying World War I made the circumstances under which the act came into effect very different from those anticipated by its framers. Further alterations in the money and banking structure were produced by legislative enactments designed to adapt the System to wartime service.

These changes in the monetary and banking structure, sketched in section 1, contributed mildly to the more than 45 per cent increase in the U.S. stock of money which accompanied the price inflation during the period of U.S. neutrality, and played a major role in the further increase by nearly a half in the stock of money which accompanied the inflation during the war and after the Armistice (section 2). The actions of the monetary authorities established by the new law largely determined the timing and character of the sizable decline in the stock of money from 1920 to 1921 associated with a sharp cyclical contraction and an unprecedentedly rapid decline in the price level (section 3).

1. *Changes in the Monetary and Banking Structure*

The fundamental change made by the Federal Reserve Act was, in the words of the title of the act, "to furnish an elastic currency."[1] Hitherto, high-powered money had consisted of gold, national bank notes, subsidiary silver and minor coin, and an assemblage of assorted relics of earlier monetary episodes—greenbacks, silver dollars, silver certificates, and Treasury notes of 1890. Henceforth, Federal Reserve notes were available for use as hand-to-hand currency or as vault cash for banks; and deposits to the credit of banks on the books of Federal Reserve Banks were available to satisfy legal reserve requirements and were equivalent, from the point of view of the commercial banking system as a whole, to Federal Reserve notes or other currency as a means of meeting demands of

[1] The title in full reads as follows: "An Act to provide for the establishment of Federal reserve banks, to furnish an elastic currency, to afford means of rediscounting commercial paper, to establish a more effective supervision of banking in the United States, and for other purposes."

depositors for cash.[2] We shall treat both Federal Reserve notes and Federal Reserve deposits as high-powered money,[3] terming their total Federal Reserve money.

Just as the exigencies of the Civil War had rapidly elevated one new form of high-powered money, the greenback, to a dominant place in the total, so World War I produced a correspondingly rapid growth of Federal Reserve money. By 1920, 69 per cent of high-powered money consisted of Federal Reserve notes and deposits.

Federal Reserve money was designed to differ from other forms of money by being "elastic," that is, subject to substantial change in quantity over short periods for reasons other than immediate profit to either the issuer, or, in the case of specie, the importer or exporter or producer. This required (1) some body or bodies to supervise or control the creation and retirement of Federal Reserve money and to handle the mechanical details; (2) some means for creating and retiring Federal Reserve money; (3) some criteria to replace profit in determining the amount to be created or retired.

1. The Federal Reserve Board and the Federal Reserve Banks were the bodies established to exercise jointly the functions both of controlling creation and retirement of Federal Reserve money and of handling the mechanical details. How the functions were initially divided between the two is complex and of no special importance for our present purpose. The fact of division was, however, important and gave rise to numerous conflicts within the System, the most notable being the continual struggle for power between the Federal Reserve Bank of New York and the Federal Reserve Board, with the balance shifting from time to time depending largely on the personalities involved. We shall have occasion to revert to this struggle in our later discussion of the 1920's and the early 1930's (Chapters 6 and 7). Initially, the New York Bank was dominant. But in the course of time, the general trend has been toward greater centralization in the hands of the Board, so that by the late 1930's the role of the Banks had become largely mechanical and advisory. Able and persuasive men at the Reserve Banks exert influence by the weight their views carry in the decisions of the Board or the System as a whole, rather than directly through independent action by the Banks.

2. Receipt of gold, rediscounting of "eligible" paper, discounting of foreign trade acceptances, and open market purchases of government securities, bankers' acceptances, and bills of exchange were the means

---

[2] Though not equivalent for satisfying legal reserve requirements. During most of the period since 1914, only Federal Reserve deposits could be used for this purpose.

[3] See Appendix B, sect. 2, for our reasons for treating them as equivalent despite the difference mentioned in the preceding note.

190

initially provided for creating Federal Reserve money, and the converse for retiring it. These were supplemented in 1916 by an amendment authorizing advances to member banks on their own 15-day notes, secured either by paper eligible for rediscount or by government securities. A 1917 amendment authorized the issuance of Federal Reserve notes against these 15-day collateral notes of member banks.[4]

3. Two criteria for determining the amount of Federal Reserve money to be created or retired are implicit in the original act: first, a gold standard rule incorporated in gold reserve requirements for Federal Reserve liabilities—the gold standard ruled supreme when the act was passed, and its continued supremacy was taken for granted; second, a "real bills" doctrine according to which the amount issued would be linked to "notes, drafts, and bills of exchange arising out of actual commercial transactions" (section 13), offered for discount at rates to be established "with a view of accommodating commerce and business" (section 14 d).[5] Both were regarded as quasi-automatic in their operation.

Taken literally, and regarded as criteria for determining the total amount of money—both deposit money and currency—the two criteria are of course contradictory. As we have repeatedly emphasized, maintenance of the gold standard means that the stock of money must be whatever is necessary to balance international payments. On the other hand, the real bills criterion sets no effective limit to the quantity of money.[6] However, this contradiction is more apparent than real. While the gold standard determines the longer-term movements in the total stock of money, it leaves much leeway in shorter-run movements. Gold reserves and the international capital market provide cushions for temporary imbalances. More important, the gold standard does not determine the division of the total stock of money between currency and deposits,

[4] Widening of the collateral on which Federal Reserve Banks could advance funds was completed in 1932, when the Banks were authorized to make advances to member banks on any asset. The authorization was granted on an emergency basis in the Glass-Steagall Act of Feb. 27, 1932, and permanently in the Banking Act of 1935. The only other later addition worth noting—and it has been of little importance—is direct lending to domestic borrowers in a limited class of circumstances, enacted in 1934 (see Chap. 8).

Similarly, widening of collateral on which Federal Reserve notes could be issued was also completed by the Glass-Steagall Act, which provided that government securities in the Reserve Banks' portfolios were eligible as part of the 60 per cent collateral other than gold required against Federal Reserve notes.

[5] Federal Reserve Act, as reproduced in Federal Reserve Board, *Annual Report* for 1914, pp. 34, 36.

[6] See L. W. Mints, *A History of Banking Theory*, University of Chicago Press, 1945, pp. 9–10. On the role of the real bills doctrine in the formulation of the Federal Reserve Act, see also Clark Warburton, "Co-ordination of Monetary, Bank Supervisory, and Loan Agencies of the Federal Government," *Journal of Finance*, June 1950, pp. 153–155; and his "Monetary Control under the Federal Reserve Act," *Political Science Quarterly*, Dec. 1946, pp. 507–509.

whereas the real bills criterion was linked to this division. The Federal Reserve System was created by men whose outlook on the goals of central banking was shaped by their experience of money panics during the national banking era. The basic monetary problem seemed to them to be banking crises produced by or resulting in an attempted shift by the public from deposits to currency. In order to prevent such shifts from producing either widespread bank failures or the restriction of cash payments by banks, some means were required for converting deposits into currency without a reduction in the total of the two. This in turn required the existence of some form of currency that could be rapidly expanded—to be provided by the Federal Reserve note—and some means of enabling banks to convert their assets readily into such currency —to be the role of discounting.[7] Since commercial banks then held a large fraction of their assets in the form of "notes, drafts, and bills of exchange arising out of actual commercial transactions," limiting the "lender of last resort" to the rediscounting of only such paper was not a serious limitation, though it is hard to see any advantage in it. Its imposition doubtless reflected, on the one hand, a disapproval of "speculative" as opposed to "commercial" activities, on the other, confusion between "elasticity" of one component of the money stock relative to others and "elasticity" of the total[8]—a disapproval and a confusion that have plagued the Reserve System throughout its history and are still with us in nearly undiminished strength.

The act was no sooner passed than the conditions taken for granted ceased to hold. Before the System began operations, World War I had begun. Very soon the belligerents effectively left the gold standard and a flood of gold started coming to the United States to pay for purchases by the Allies. By the end of the war, the U.S. had imposed an embargo on gold exports. The gold standard criterion set a largely ineffective

[7] J. Laurence Laughlin testifying in 1913 (*Banking and Currency Reform*, Hearings before a subcommittee [Carter Glass, Chairman] of the House Banking and Currency Committee, 62d Cong., 3d sess., Jan. 7–Feb. 28, 1913) stated that what the country urgently needed was credit reform: currency reform would then take care of itself:

> . . . it is primarily a question of the organization of credit rather than a question of creating essentially a medium of exchange . . . the organization of credit is more important than the question of bank notes (p. 108) . . .

> . . . the organization of credit by discounting institutions must be the core of the whole reform, and the elasticity of currency would follow it (p. 110).

[8] See above, Chap. 4, sect. 4. "Flexibility (elasticity) in currency—*not in total bank credit*—was the aim of the founders of the Federal Reserve System, and this flexibility was desired as a means of producing stability in total bank credit by providing stability in bank reserves," according to Warburton, "Co-ordination of Monetary," pp. 154–155.

limit on the total money stock. A worldwide gold standard was re-established for a brief period in the twenties and this fact had important effects on Federal Reserve policy; yet the gold standard never again played the role that the framers of the act took for granted.

The real bills criterion fared no better. Once the United States entered the war, loans on government securities began to rival commercial paper as collateral for Reserve Bank rediscounts. As mentioned above, the Reserve System was authorized to issue notes against rediscounted assets other than commercial paper, mainly member banks' 15-day notes secured by government bonds.

The Federal Reserve System therefore began operations with no effective legislative criterion for determining the total stock of money. The discretionary judgment of a group of men was inevitably substituted for the quasi-automatic discipline of the gold standard. Those men were not even guided by a legislative mandate of intent—unless the purpose of the act described as "to furnish an elastic currency, to afford means of rediscounting commercial paper" or the instruction to set discount rates "with a view of accommodating commerce and business" can be so considered—and were hardly aware of the enlarged powers and widened responsibilities the change in circumstances had thrust upon them. Little wonder, perhaps, that the subsequent years saw so much backing and filling, so much confusion about purpose and power, and so erratic an exercise of power.

Although the real bills criterion in fact provided no effective limit to the amount of money, this was by no means widely recognized—any more than it is today—and its incorporation in the Federal Reserve Act, albeit in limited form, had important effects. For years, the Reserve System emphasized the rediscounting facilities it offered. The road to elasticity of the money stock, it was believed, was paved with commercial paper that member banks would present for rediscounting. The eligibility of particular kinds of commercial paper became a specialized field of research. Conflicting monetary policies were sometimes pursued, because it was not clear to the Federal Reserve that the rediscounting of any security, open market purchases, and gold inflows all had precisely the same effects on the money stock as the rediscounting of eligible paper.[9]

So far, we have not mentioned the institutional reorganization of the banking system which is the most prominent feature of the Federal Reserve System: the relation between member banks and the System; and the requirement that member banks hold, at first, some, later, all, and still later again, some of their reserves in the form of deposits with

[9] For example, in the second half of 1928 the Systems permitted increases in its holdings of bankers' acceptances while attempting to restrict rediscounts.

Federal Reserve Banks.[10] Important as this reorganization was, it was in no way essential for the provision of an "elastic currency," as is demonstrated by the example of the Aldrich-Vreeland emergency currency as well as that of the Bank of England and other central banks. It was enacted partly to provide more effective supervision of commercial banks, partly to centralize reserves in order to "economize" gold. It had only one significant relation to an elastic currency. It was the means adopted for providing the Federal Reserve System with a gold reserve that could enable it to meet the rather curious double requirement initially imposed on the issuance of Federal Reserve notes: on the one hand, a gold reserve of 40 per cent; on the other, collateral in the form of commercial paper, equal dollar for dollar to the amount of notes issued. The initial deposits to the credit of member banks were established by the literal deposit of "lawful money," consisting of gold or of money that the Treasury would exchange for gold.[11] Since the Federal Reserve was required to keep a gold (or lawful money) reserve of 35 per cent of its deposits, it could use any excess over that amount received from member banks to meet the 40 per cent requirement for notes. The double requirement for notes was later changed: in addition to the 40 per cent gold reserve, only 60 per cent of collateral was required, satisfied by either gold or eligible paper.[12] The enactment of

[10] The Federal Reserve Act of 1913 required member banks to hold a specified part of their reserves with Federal Reserve Banks, another part in their vaults, and the remainder either in their own vaults or at the Reserve Banks. It authorized reserve city and country member banks to keep the remainder until Nov. 1917, at their option, also with national banks in central reserve and reserve cities but provided that after Nov. 1917 balances with other banks would no longer count as reserves. Provision was made for the immediate transfer (i.e., in 1914) of part of the reserves required to be held in the Reserve Banks; the balance, after a year, in a series of three subsequent instalments at six-month intervals. Federal Reserve Board, *Annual Report* for 1916, p. 22, erroneously refers to a transfer of reserves on May 16, 1915; the second transfer occurred on Nov. 16, 1915 (*Commercial and Financial Chronicle,* Nov. 6, 1915, p. 1515). A revision of the act, approved Sept. 7, 1916, permitted member banks to transfer to Federal Reserve Banks immediately any part of their reserves then required to be held in their own vaults but few, if any, member banks responded. An amendment to the act, dated June 21, 1917, provided that vault cash could no longer be counted as meeting legal reserve requirements; thereafter only deposits with Federal Reserve Banks could be so counted.

An amendment to the act, dated July 28, 1959, authorized the Board of Governors to permit member banks to treat vault cash as reserves. The Board granted permission to count a fraction of vault cash in Dec. 1959, an increased fraction in Sept. 1960, and all vault cash after Nov. 1960.

[11] This was true of the first instalment of reserves paid into the Federal Reserve Banks by member banks under the terms of Circular No. 10 (dated Oct. 28, 1914) from the Federal Reserve Board to member banks (*Annual Report* for 1914, p. 167). Up to one-half of each subsequent instalment was receivable by the Banks in eligible paper, in accordance with sect. 19 of the Federal Reserve Act.

[12] Amendment dated June 21, 1917.

the double requirement in its initial form as well as the differential gold reserve requirement for notes and deposits are instances of the inappropriate differentiation of deposits from notes that has played so large a part in monetary history.[13] As pointed out above, Federal Reserve notes and deposits have always been interconvertible for banks and hence essentially equivalent, both as liabilities of the Federal Reserve System and in their function as high-powered money.[14] Yet the reserve requirements for their creation were not made uniform until an amendment of 1945.[15]

The banking reorganization was significant for the stock of money mainly through its effect on the ratio of deposits to reserves of the banking system. The centralization of legally required reserves was accompanied by a substantial lowering of legal requirements (see section 2, below), which raised the ratio of deposits to reserves that the banking system wished to maintain and thereby also raised the stock of money that was consistent with any given amount of high-powered money. Further, it paved the way for granting, at a much later date, of power to the Federal Reserve System to change legal reserve requirements as an instrument for control of the stock of money. During its early years, the Federal Reserve System generally viewed member bank reserve requirements as mostly a device for enhancing the convertibility of bank deposits into currency, rather than for controlling the stock of money. Because member banks had originally transferred cash to Federal Re-

[13] J. Laurence Laughlin in his testimony before the House subcommittee, referred to in footnote 7 above, advocated conditions of issue for notes separate and distinct from those for deposits on grounds that: "The note issue passes out from the hands of the bank into the hands of the public. It thereby differs from a deposit account in that the note gets a quasi-public function . . . A private contract between a bank and its depositors stands on an entirely different level" (p. 138). According to Laughlin, the way to protect deposits was "to improve the kind of paper you take in the assets" (p. 139).

[14] See Appendix B.

[15] Of course, viewed as ultimate means of payment, they differ since one can be held by the nonbanking public, the other, only by banks. From this point of view, currency in the hands of the public and commercial bank deposits are interchangeable. Maintenance of the same ultimate gold reserve behind these two forms of media of payment would require a much smaller fractional gold reserve behind Federal Reserve notes than behind Federal Reserve deposits, enough smaller so that the former when multiplied by the number of dollars of commercial bank deposits per dollar of Federal Reserve deposits would equal the latter. For example, if there were $7 of commercial bank deposits per dollar of Federal Reserve deposits, and a 35 per cent gold (or lawful money) reserve for the latter, this would amount to a 5 per cent gold reserve per dollar of commercial bank deposits. The gold reserve for Federal Reserve notes would then have to be 5 per cent in order that the conversion by the public of a dollar of commercial bank deposits into a dollar of currency, taken to be in the form of a Federal Reserve note, would leave the legal gold position unchanged.

serve Banks, member bank reserves were considered balances deposited by the banks rather than a creation of the System, thereby perpetuating the initial failure to recognize the essential equivalence of notes and deposits.

The banking reorganization greatly reduced the importance of the distinction between national and nonnational banks. A more important distinction became that between member and nonmember banks. But of course, in typical governmental fashion, the new distinction did not replace the old; it was superimposed upon it. Every member bank became technically subject to supervision by two nominally independent authorities: all by the Federal Reserve, national banks also by the Comptroller of the Currency and state banks also by the state banking authorities. And from September 1933, a third was superimposed—the Federal Deposit Insurance Corporation (see Chapter 8, section 1).

2. *Wartime and Postwar Inflation*

World War I began while the United States was in the contraction phase of a business cycle. As noted in the preceding chapter, the initial effect was to intensify the contraction, particularly in the financial markets. By the time the Federal Reserve Banks opened for business in the middle of November 1914, the country had recovered from the immediate shock of the declaration of war in Europe, thanks in no small part to the availability of Aldrich-Vreeland emergency currency.

The National Bureau dates the end of the contraction in December 1914, though rapid expansion did not get under way until well into 1915, when the full impact was felt of urgent demands by the belligerents for munitions, foodstuffs, and shipping services, and by neutrals for manufactured goods previously purchased from the belligerents. As Chart 16 shows, wholesale prices were roughly constant until the final quarter of 1915. Then they began a rapid climb that was to continue with only minor interruptions until May 1920, when wholesale prices stood at nearly two and one-half times their level in September 1915. The rise was particularly rapid in 1916 and the first half of 1917, before the entry of the United States into the war; and again from mid-1919 on. The only appreciable decline—from September 1918 to February 1919—corresponds with the August 1918–March 1919 business cycle contraction, and that decline was only 5½ per cent.

Net national product in current prices (money income) showed a similar pattern, rising mildly from 1914 to 1915 and then rapidly and uninterruptedly to a peak in 1920, nearly two and a half times its level in 1914. Net national product in constant prices (real income) rose fairly sharply from 1914 to 1916 and, after a pause, again from 1917 to 1919. A decline from 1919 to 1920 brought it back to a level slightly higher

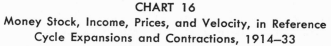

CHART 16

Money Stock, Income, Prices, and Velocity, in Reference
Cycle Expansions and Contractions, 1914–33

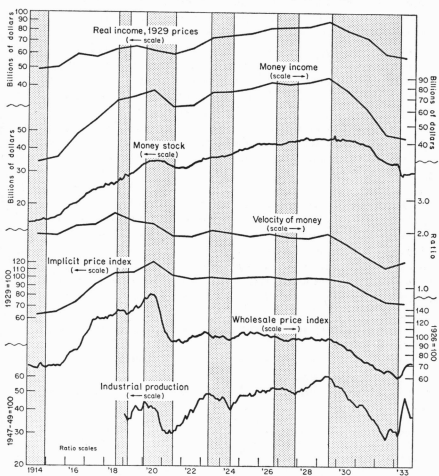

NOTE: Shaded areas represent business contractions; unshaded areas, business expansions.
SOURCE: Industrial production, seasonally adjusted, from *Industrial Production, 1959 Revision*,
Board of Governors of the Federal Reserve System, 1960, p. S-151 (manufacturing and mining
production only). Other data, same as for Chart 62.

than in 1916.[16] As a result, the implicit price index rose less than net
national product in current prices did and hence less than wholesale
prices did, not quite doubling from 1914 to 1920.

The stock of money, which had been rising at a moderate rate through-

[16] The net national product figures shown for 1917–19 modify Kuznets' esti-

197

out 1914, started to rise at an increasing rate in early 1915, rose most rapidly, as prices did, from late 1915 to mid-1917, and then resumed its rapid rise before the end of 1918, rather sooner than prices did. At its peak, in June 1920, the stock of money was roughly double its September 1915 level and more than double the level of November 1914, when the Federal Reserve Banks opened for business.

For a comparably rapid and extended rise in prices and in the stock of money, one must either go back in time over half a century to the Civil War or forward in time a quarter of a century to World War II.

In analyzing these movements, we must alter the emphasis of the preceding two chapters dealing with the period since resumption. There, we treated the maintenance of balance in external financial relations as the dominant factor determining the stock of money. We treated internal forces as controlling short-term movements only or as operating through the balance of payments or as having their main effects on the way in which changes in the stock of money came about—what we called the arithmetic of the money supply. For this wartime and postwar period, the balance—or perhaps one should say imbalance—in external financial relations continued to have much to do with both the amount of change in the stock of money and the way in which the change came about. But internal factors, mostly connected with the banking changes under the Federal Reserve Act, began to have their main effects on the amount of change in the total stock of money, and indeed from some points of view can be regarded as the dominant factor in determining that change. In this respect, the situation was close to that during the greenback period.

The reason for the altered emphasis is the wartime change in the character of international trade and financial arrangements. In the belligerent nations, private individuals reacting to price incentives were

---

mates, which, for wartime periods, we believe, are misleading for our purpose. According to his definition, the value of government services to consumers is measured by direct taxes. Government spending, which increased much more sharply than direct taxes during 1917–19, is, in effect, not fully included for those years in his estimates (Simon Kuznets, worksheets underlying *Capital in the American Economy: Its Formation and Financing*, Princeton for NBER, 1961).

John W. Kendrick has adjusted Kuznets' estimates from 1889 on, annually, by adding national security outlays to obtain what he calls the "national security version" of net national product (see Kendrick's *Productivity Trends in the United States*, Princeton for NBER, 1961, pp. 235 ff.; Table A-I, col. 7, pp. 290–292, shows the series in 1929 dollars; figures in current dollars were obtained by us from Kendrick's unpublished worksheets).

We used "national security version" in current dollars as an interpolator of Kuznets' estimates. For 1917, 1918, and 1919, we computed the difference between the logarithm of the national security version and a matching value obtained from the logarithms of the national security version for 1916 and 1920 by linear interpolation. We added the differences to values for 1917, 1918, and 1919, obtained by linear interpolation between the logarithms of the 1916 and 1920 Kuznets estimates, to derive our adjusted estimates of net national product for those years.

largely replaced as the major traders on international markets by governments controlling their own financial machinery. They exercised an insistent and pressing demand for American goods; created an excess of exports for the United States over imports; and paid for the excess during the period of U.S. neutrality by shipping more than $1 billion in gold, selling for dollars $1.4 billion of American securities owned by their citizens and transferred under compulsion to government control, reducing by $0.5 billion short-term loans by their citizens to the United States, and by borrowing about $2.4 billion in U.S. financial markets, a total of no less than $5.3 billion.[17] After U.S. entry into the war, the excess of exports continued but was financed primarily by credits which the U.S. government extended to its Allies rather than by either gold or the liquidation of privately held dollar securities. Those capital movements transformed the international investment position of the United States from a net debtor on short- and long-term of $3.7 billion in 1914 to a net creditor of the same amount by the end of 1919.[18]

The gold movements to and the capital exports from the United States during the period of U.S. neutrality had essentially the same domestic economic and monetary effects as they would have had under usual peacetime circumstances. Although the Federal Reserve System was later to be in a position to offset gold inflows, at that time it had no power to do so. It could intensify their effects, and did so to a minor extent. The gold movements did not, however, have the same monetary effects abroad as they had in peacetime. The governments losing gold did not permit the loss to exercise any deflationary influence on internal prices: gold did not flow automatically in response to a deficit in payments and as a first step in a corrective mechanism; it was rather a highly liquid asset which could be mobilized by governments, like foreign securities to pay for imports. One example of departure from the usual pattern was that prices in Britain and France rose decidedly more rapidly than in the United States, although Britain and France were losing gold and the United States was gaining gold. By April 1917, British wholesale prices had risen 100 per cent since July 1914, and French wholesale prices, 150 per cent, whereas U.S. prices had risen 70 per cent. Another example was the relation between movements of capital and of gold. A country that increases its capital exports can generally be expected to lose gold, at least in the transition period, and a country that imports capital, to gain gold. Yet in that episode, the United States both exported capital and gained gold.

Under gold-standard conditions, capital imports into the United States tend to be associated with a price level in this country that is high

[17] W. A. Brown, Jr., *The International Gold Standard Reinterpreted, 1914–1934,* New York, NBER, 1940, Vol. I, p. 65.

[18] *Historical Statistics of the United States, 1789–1945,* Bureau of the Census, 1949, Series M-1, p. 242.

relative to that in other gold-standard countries; capital exports, with a price level that is relatively low. Under nongold-standard conditions, as during the greenback period, the same statement holds, provided price movements are adjusted for movements in exchange rates. In this respect, the wartime experience corresponds with earlier patterns: the United States was exporting capital, and its price level was relatively low. The correspondence is the other side of the two departures listed in the preceding paragraph: the lack of correspondence of gold movements with price movements on the one hand and with capital movements on the other—two negatives make a positive. But the correspondence is more than an accidental arithmetic result of two correlated departures. It was required by the economics of the situation. The Allies were purchasing goods in this country by shipping gold, realizing on their investments, and borrowing— these constitute the capital and gold movements—precisely because they wanted to use domestic resources for wartime purposes rather than to produce exports. The goods they usually exported were therefore relatively scarce to the outside world and tended to be bid up in price in terms of foreign currency. No less in wartime than in peacetime, if a country is in a position to sell little, the prices of the goods it sells will be relatively high, in terms of foreign currency, compared with the prices of goods produced in the outside world.

In judging relative prices, allowance must of course be made for changes in exchange rates. It so happens that not much allowance is needed on this account with respect to Britain during World War I. The dollar price of the pound sterling, after rising sharply on the outbreak of the war to a peak of $7, fell to a low of $4.50 in September 1915, and in January 1916 was stabilized by the British government at $4.76⅞₆, or only 2 per cent below prewar parity.[19] In the absence of free gold movements, the British government used official and unofficial means to control the foreign exchange transactions of British residents in order to facilitate the maintenance of the rate as well as to acquire exchange for wartime purposes. However, the controls were fairly limited, certainly in the early years of the war, and even if they had been much more extensive and rigorous than they were, it is doubtful that they would have enabled the fixed exchange rate to be maintained for long, if the relative internal price levels had been greatly out of line with those consistent with the capital and gold movements.

Similarly, the French franc did not deviate widely from its prewar parity of 19.30 cents. In terms of monthly averages, the lowest price reached was 16.74 cents in April 1916. The British and French governments then agreed to stabilize the price of the franc. It rose to 17.51 cents in April 1917, the month the United States entered the war, and remained fairly stable at that level until the summer of 1918. As the end

[19] J. P. Morgan and Company was the agent of the British Treasury in the U.S.

CHART 17

U.S. Net International Capital Movement and Unilateral
Transfers as a Ratio to National Income, and
Purchasing-Power Parity, 1914–33

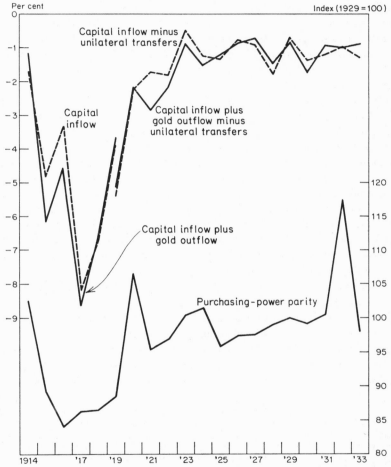

NOTE: Calendar years are shown. Capital inflow, minus unilateral transfers, is plotted as plus.
Gold outflow is plotted as plus.

SOURCE: Table A-4.

of the war approached, speculation that exchange rates would soon
return to normal raised the price of the franc to 18.37 cents in November
1918.[20]

[20] *Banking and Monetary Statistics,* Board of Governors of the Federal Reserve
System, 1943, p. 670; Brown, *International Gold Standard,* Vol. I, pp. 50–70.

It is clear from Chart 17, which is a continuation after 1914 of Chart 9, that relative price levels during the war were not far out of line with capital and gold movements. The combined capital export from and gold import into the United States was far larger in absolute magnitude than in any year since 1860. Relative to national income, the capital and gold movements were more than twice as large for most of the war as in any prior year since 1873. And, as one would expect, the ratio of U.S. to British prices, corrected for changes in the exchange rate, was throughout the war lower than in any prior year since the Civil War (compare with Charts 7 and 9). Further, capital movements and the price ratio display similar temporal patterns.

The large capital export from the United States, primarily to Britain and France, would have enabled those countries, at the exchange rates that prevailed, to have maintained internal prices that were high relative to U.S. prices compared with historical levels, even without the exchange controls they employed. Alternatively, without those controls and given the movement of internal prices, the capital exports would have enabled them to maintain the dollar price of their currencies at a higher level than would in the past have been consistent with their own and U.S. internal prices. And without the combined effect of capital exports from and gold shipments to the United States, it is doubtful that exchange controls alone would have enabled Britain and France to reduce imports sufficiently to keep both internal prices and the dollar price of their currencies at the levels that prevailed. One or the other would have had to be lower.

Calculations based on prior experience suggest that the capital and gold movements were sufficiently large to account for the relatively high internal prices in Britain and France (or, alternatively, for the maintenance of the exchange rates at not much below prewar levels) without making any allowance for the effect of exchange controls.[21] The calcu-

---

[21] Two sets of calculations were made with the series on capital plus gold flows relative to net national product, and U.S. prices relative to British prices (as in Table A-4; however, for comparability with the 1871–1913 data, the capital flow data used for 1914–19 include errors and omissions; the latter are excluded in Table A-4 and Chart 17, 1914–19, for comparability with the 1919–60 data).

1. We first dated the major peaks and troughs in the capital plus gold series. These were as follows:

Peak	Trough
Fiscal 1872	Fiscal 1878
Fiscal 1888	Fiscal 1898 and calendar 1898
Calendar 1909	Calendar 1913

We then computed the difference between the recorded capital plus gold movements from one turning point to the next, the difference between the logarithms of the adjusted relative price ratios (for fiscal years, we averaged the ratios for the

lations are not sufficiently reliable to justify the conclusion that exchange controls had no influence, but they do at least mean that their presence did not produce a relation between prices and capital movements drastically out of line with previous experience.

---

two relevant calendar years), and the ratio of the latter difference to the former. The results, based on the Table A-4 series, are shown in the following tabulation.

Shift	Change in Capital plus Gold Movements (1)	Change in Logarithm of Relative Price Ratio (2)	(2) ÷ (1) (3)
Fiscal Years			
1872 to 1878	−6.734	−0.0667	0.00990
1878 to 1888	+4.751	+0.0538	0.01132
1888 to 1898	−5.469	−0.0445	0.00814
Calendar Years			
1898 to 1909	+3.542	+0.0692	0.01955
1909 to 1913	−1.167	−0.0207	0.01775

The average of the entries in the final column, weighted by the duration of the shifts, is 0.01317.

The shift in the capital plus gold movements from calendar 1914 to calendar 1916 is −7.360. The product of this and 0.01317, or −0.0969, is the change in the logarithm of the adjusted price ratio that might have been expected on the basis of prior experience. The actual change was −0.0864. On the basis of earlier experience, therefore, the decline in the adjusted price ratio would have been about one-eighth larger than it actually was. Or, to express the comparison in another way, the entry like those in the final column above for calendar 1914 to calendar 1916 would be 0.01174, well within the range of earlier experience.

2. We computed multiple correlations among purchasing-power parity x, capital inflow plus gold outflow y, and time t, for the years 1871 through 1913. The results were:

(i)	$x = 94.89 + 2.122y + 0.3327t$	$R^2 = .52$
(ii)	$y = 15.42 + 0.1646x − 0.085t$	$R^2 = .45'$

where R^2 is the square of the multiple correlation coefficient, (i) is the regression of x on the other variables, (ii) is the regression of y on the other variables. Solving (ii) for x gives

$$(iii) \qquad x = + 93.67 + 6.075y + 0.5166t.$$

Under a fairly wide range of assumptions, (i) and (iii) may be expected to bound the "true" relation between x and y that prevailed between figures free of error and adjusted for other variables that affected the relation.

We then used (i) and (iii) to estimate values for the years 1914 through 1919. The actual and estimated values are shown in the following tabulation.

		Purchasing-Power Parity	
		Computed from	
	Actual	(i)	(iii)
1914	102.6	103.4	105.3
1915	89.1	92.7	77.5
1916	84.1	88.5	64.9
1917	86.3	90.2	69.3
1918	86.5	96.6	67.3
1919	88.5	92.2	74.3

The actual values are between the two estimates and very much closer to the higher of the two. So this calculation gives the same result as the first.

CHART 18

The Stock of Money and Its Proximate Determinants, 1914–21

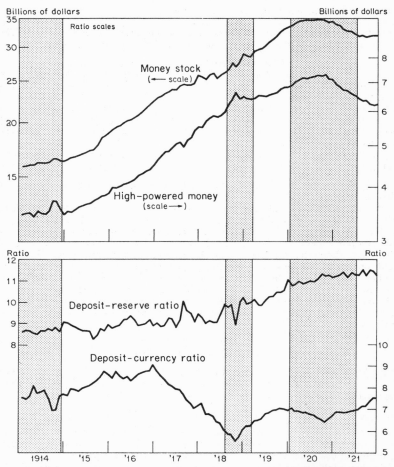

NOTE: Shaded areas represent business contractions; unshaded areas, business expansions.
SOURCE: Tables A-1 (col. 8) and B-3.

Though the money stock grew throughout the period from 1914 to 1920, the factors accounting for the rise were quite different (1) before U.S. entry into the war on April 6, 1917; (2) during the period of active U.S. participation in the war, when government expenditures greatly exceeded tax receipts; and (3) during the price boom that occurred subsequently, when government receipts equaled or exceeded expenditures.

Chart 18 summarizes the major factors accounting for changes in the stock of money and Table 10 summarizes their effects for the three periods just distinguished.

The first period is sharply demarcated at both ends. It begins with the outbreak of war in Europe and extends to the United States' declaration of a state of war with Germany on April 6, 1917. We have used statistical data for June 1914 as reflecting conditions at the outset of the period and for March 1917, at the end. Over that interval of not quite three years, the stock of money rose by 46 per cent and wholesale prices by 65 per cent. Real income also rose, and so did velocity. Over the subsequent period of somewhat more than three years to the price peak in May 1920 (a period not shown separately in Table 10), the stock of money rose a further 49 per cent and wholesale prices a further 55 per cent. Real income and velocity changed little. The U.S. entry into the war therefore comes not only roughly midway in time between the outbreak of war and the postwar price peak, but also roughly midway in terms of monetary expansion and more than midway in terms of price rise.

The arithmetic of the changes in the money stock in the period of neutrality is unusually simple: 90 per cent of the total increase is accounted for by the increase in high-powered money; the rest by moderate rises in the two deposit ratios. And 87 per cent of the change in high-powered money consists of an increase in the gold stock (see Table 10). This was a straightforward gold inflation.

Deposit-Currency Ratio

The ratio of deposits to currency held by the public continued to rise during the period of neutrality at roughly the same rate as in preceding years. It contributed only 3 per cent to the increase in the stock of money, not primarily because it was less important in absolute magnitude than formerly, but because the increase in high-powered money was at so much more rapid a rate.

Deposit-Reserve Ratio

One minor puzzle is why the ratio of deposits to reserves (vault cash plus commercial bank deposits at the Federal Reserve Banks) does not show a rising trend from December 1914 to March 1917 like that which was so consistent a feature of the prewar period—especially in view of the sizable lowering of reserve requirements under the Federal Reserve Act. Part of the answer is the difference between the ratio relevant to the stock of money—of deposits to high-powered reserves—and the ratio relevant to the individual bank. The Federal Reserve Act not only

TABLE 10

CHANGES IN PRICES AND IN STOCK OF MONEY, AND SOURCE OF CHANGES IN STOCK OF MONEY, DURING THREE SEGMENTS OF THE PERIOD JUNE 1914–MAY 1920

	U.S. Neutrality June 1914 Through Mar. 1917	War or Wartime Deficits		To Postwar Price Peak		Period as a Whole June 1914 Through May 1920
		Mar. 1917 Through Nov. 1918	Mar. 1917 Through May 1919	Nov. 1918 Through May 1920	May 1919 Through May 1920	
Number of months	33	20	26	18	12	71
Percentage change in:						
1. Wholesale prices	65	23	22	22	23	147
2. Stock of money	45	18	27	26	16	115
3. High-powered money	40	33	35	12	10	107
Per cent change per year in:						
4. Wholesale prices	18	12	9	13	21	15
5. Stock of money	14	10	11	15	15	13
6. High-powered money	12	17	14	7	9	12
Fraction of change in stock of money (total change = 1.00) attributable to change in:						
7. High-powered money	0.90	1.72	1.25	0.48	0.60	0.95
8. Ratio of commercial bank deposits to vault cash plus deposits at Federal Reserve Banks	0.03	0.34	0.20	0.13	0.26	0.13
9. Ratio of commercial bank deposits to currency held by the public	0.07	−0.98	−0.42	0.37	0.14	−0.07
10. Interaction of ratios	0.00	−0.07	−0.02	0.01	0.01	−0.01

Fraction of change in high-powered money
(total change = 1.00) consisting of change in:

11. Monetary gold stock	0.87	0.04	0.04	−0.41	−0.51	0.26
12. F.R. claims on the public and banks	0.15	1.24	1.26	1.44	1.41	0.87
13. Other physical assets and fiat of monetary authorities	−0.02	−0.28	−0.31	0.03	0.10	−0.13

SOURCE, BY LINE

1. *Historical Statistics*, 1949, p. 344.
2. Table A-1.
3. Table B-3.
4-6. Continuously compounded: the change in the natural logarithm of the variable over each period was divided by the number of months and multiplied by 1,200.
7-10. Computed as described in App. B, sect. 7. Money stock, deposits, and currency, Table A-1. High-powered money and deposit ratios, Table B-3. Detail may not add to 1.00 because of rounding.
11-12. Computed as described in App. B, sect. 8. Gold stock at end of month, from *Banking and Monetary Statistics*, p. 536, plus $287 million deducted by the Federal Reserve in each month, 1914–33, and restored by us (see Chap. 8, footnote 45); adjusted for seasonal by Shiskin-Eisenpress method (see Julius Shiskin and Harry Eisenpress, *Seasonal Adjustments by Electronic Computer Methods*, New York, NBER, Technical Paper 12, 1958). Federal Reserve claims on the public and banks: Federal Reserve credit and U.S. government securities held, from *Banking and Monetary Statistics*, pp. 373–374, were each corrected for seasonal by the Shiskin-Eisenpress method and the latter subtracted from the former.
13. 1.00, minus line 11, minus line 12.

lowered reserve requirements but also changed the form in which the reserves could be held. Before passage of the act, national banks outside central reserve cities (New York, Chicago, and St. Louis) could hold a large fraction of their required reserves in the form of deposits with other banks that qualified as reserve agents.[22] The act in its initial form provided that all reserves would ultimately be either vault cash or deposits at Federal Reserve Banks, both of which we count as high-powered money. It provided for a transition period, starting a year after the opening of the Federal Reserve Banks, during which the fraction kept as deposits increased at six-month intervals. The required ratio of high-powered money to demand deposits plus time deposits was therefore initially lowered along with the corresponding ratio to those deposits of all funds acceptable as meeting legal reserve requirements.[23] But after the transition period the required ratio of high-powered money was higher for both country and reserve city banks than before the Federal Reserve Act. By the end of 1916, the change in the form of required reserves had approximately offset the effect of the change in their level on the required ratio of high-powered money to deposits. A net reduction in that required ratio occurred only after an amendment to the act which further reduced reserve requirements, effective June 21, 1917, to the level at which they were to stand for nearly two decades (for demand deposits: 7 per cent for country banks, 10 per cent for reserve city banks, and 13 per cent for central reserve city banks; for time deposits: 3 per cent for all banks). The amendment also specified that as of the same date only deposits at

[22] Up to three-fifths of the 15 per cent required reserve for country banks and one-half of the 25 per cent required reserve for reserve city banks. Central reserve city banks had to keep the entire 25 per cent required reserve in the form of lawful money in their vaults (see Chap. 2, footnote 62).

In addition, until Jan. 13, 1914, national banks could count the 5 per cent redemption fund for national bank notes as part of their required reserves (*Annual Report* of the Comptroller of the Currency, 1914, Vol. II, p. 191). In practice, they did so by deducting a multiple of the redemption fund from net deposits requiring reserves, central reserve and reserve city banks deducting 4 times and country banks 6⅔ times the redemption fund. The Comptroller permitted the inclusion of the item for the last time on the call date immediately following Dec. 23, 1913, the date on which the Federal Reserve Act was passed, although sect. 20 of the act repealed as of the date of passage the 1874 provision which authorized the inclusion of the redemption fund as part of lawful reserves. In the subsequent discussion of the effect of the Federal Reserve Act on required reserves, we ignore the effect of the change in the treatment of the redemption fund since the quantitative effect is negligible. The redemption fund amounted to about one-half of 1 per cent of total deposits held by the public in national banks at the end of 1913.

The redemption fund is never included in our figures of bank reserves, since we treat it as part of Treasury, not bank vault, cash. By disallowing its inclusion, the act made the desired ratio of deposits to high-powered money held by banks—as we calculate that total—a trifle lower than it otherwise would be.

[23] See footnote 10, above.

Federal Reserve Banks could be counted as meeting those requirements.[24] As Chart 18 shows, the ratio of deposits to high-powered reserves rose temporarily immediately after that change. However, it then declined again to prior levels by mid-1918 before starting a more sustained upward movement that continued until 1929.

While these changes in reserve requirements help to account for the behavior of the deposit-reserve ratio, they do not explain it in full. A sizable amount of high-powered reserves was released in late 1914 and not fully taken up by transfers to the Federal Reserve Banks until late in 1916. Yet the ratio stayed roughly constant from 1914 to 1915, rose slightly to 1916, and then was roughly constant to mid-1917. We suspect the reason for this behavior is twofold. First, the financial uncertainties attendant on the outbreak of the war, which led to runs on banks and the issuance of emergency currency, must have given banks an incentive to be unusually liquid. As in earlier episodes of this kind, the effect must have lasted for some time. Second, the inflow of gold eased reserve positions substantially, and there may well have been a lag before the slack was fully taken up in the presence of a continuing inflow.

High-Powered Money

Because of the intervention of the Federal Reserve System, there are several possible ways to break down the total of high-powered money into components.

(1) The most direct, yet in our view not the most illuminating, is to classify it according to the form in which it is held by the public or banks: Federal Reserve notes, Treasury currency, Federal Reserve deposits, gold coin and certificates, etc. (Chart 19A). This is essentially the method we used in earlier chapters. The difficulty with it is that it does

---

[24] This amendment excluded from reserves deposits with other banks five months earlier than provided in the original act.

The exact effect of the changes in reserve requirements is complicated by the introduction by the Federal Reserve Act of separate requirements for time deposits. Phillip Cagan has made a detailed study of the effect of these changes with full allowance for this and other complications, and the statements in the text are based on his findings. He estimates that the immediate effect (other than the exclusion of the redemption fund) of the changes in reserve requirements introduced by the Federal Reserve Act was to reduce high-powered reserve requirements of national banks as of Nov. 16, 1914, by 13 per cent; that the effect of subsequently required transfers of reserves to Federal Reserve Banks on Nov. 16, 1915, May 16, 1916, and Nov. 16, 1916, was to raise these requirements by 14 per cent; and that the final change on June 21, 1917, reduced them by 21 per cent (see Cagan's forthcoming study of the determinants and effects of changes in the money stock in the United States since 1875, a National Bureau study).

The final reduction overstates the effect of the change for our purposes. Though vault cash no longer counted as satisfying legal reserve requirements, banks clearly had to retain cash in their vaults for operating purposes, and we count such cash in the total we call reserves.

CHART 19

High-Powered Money, by Assets and Liabilities of the Treasury
and Federal Reserve Banks, November 1914–December 1921

A. Liabilities

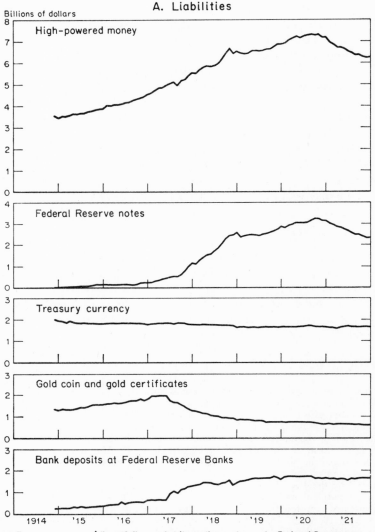

NOTE: Treasury currency (silver dollars, subsidiary silver, minor coin, Federal Reserve notes, and national bank notes) and other currency issues are outside the Treasury and Federal Reserve Banks.

SOURCE: High-powered money, Table B-3. Federal Reserve notes, Treasury currency, gold coin and gold certificates, same as for Table A-1, col. 1, seasonally corrected by index used for currency outside the Treasury and Federal Reserve Banks. Bank deposits at Reserve Banks, Table A-2, col. 2. Monetary gold stock, F.R. claims, "other," same as in notes to Table 10.

CHART 19 (Concluded)

B. Assets

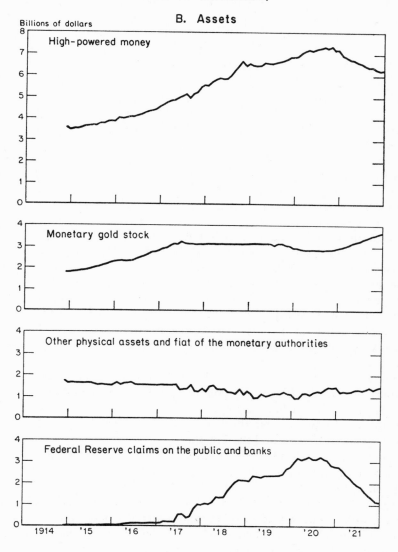

Billions of dollars

High-powered money

Monetary gold stock

Other physical assets and fiat of the monetary authorities

Federal Reserve claims on the public and banks

1914 '15 '16 '17 '18 '19 '20 '21

not distinguish between the fiduciary and nonfiduciary elements in the total. To illustrate: gold inflow which finds its way to the Federal Reserve and is matched by an increase in Federal Reserve deposits of member and nonmember banks is treated as exactly equivalent to a purchase of securities by the Federal Reserve matched by the same numerical increase in Federal Reserve deposits of member and nonmember banks. This method would conceal what seems to us the essential difference between the first and second periods in Table 10; the increase in high-powered money was produced by a gold inflow in the first period and by an increase in Federal Reserve credit outstanding in the second, but in both it took the form primarily of an increase in Federal Reserve notes and deposits. This difficulty is present for prewar years as well but to a much smaller extent because of the small size of Treasury balances.

(2) Another way is to view high-powered money in terms of the assets that correspond to it on the books of the monetary authorities. The variant of this alternative we have adopted treats all gold, valued at cost to the Treasury, as if it corresponded dollar for dollar to high-powered money in the hands of the public and the banks. This treatment would be precisely correct, if gold certificates had been issued to the public and the banks in exchange for gold, and all gold had been acquired solely in exchange for such gold certificates. The variant treats the remainder of high-powered money either as a contribution of the Federal Reserve System through its claims on the public and the banks (i.e., bills discounted, bills bought, and other Federal Reserve Bank credit other than holdings of government securities); or as a contribution of both the Federal Reserve System and the Treasury based on their holdings of physical assets (bank premises for the Reserve System, the silver stock for the Treasury); or finally, as a fiduciary contribution of the Treasury based on its fiat (see Appendix B, section 8). Hence we show the change in high-powered money (Chart 19B) as consisting of changes in the monetary gold stock, valued at its cost to the Treasury—this means that we exclude the excess valuation of gold appropriated by the Treasury upon the devaluation of gold in January 1934, since this is a fiduciary element (see Chapter 8); Federal Reserve claims on the public and the banks; other physical assets and the fiat of the Federal Reserve and the Treasury.

In its initial years, the Federal Reserve System was essentially powerless to offset the monetary influence of the gold inflow—in the terminology of the 1920's, to "sterilize" the gold inflow. In order to do so, it would have had to impound and thereby keep out of bank reserves and public circulation a sum of gold or other high-powered money equal in amount to the gold inflow; or, alternatively, to induce banks to lower the ratio of deposits to reserves by enough to offset the effect of the inflow on the stock of money; or, finally, to induce the public to lower the ratio of deposits to currency by enough to do so. It could do none of these. In order to impound gold or other high-powered money it had to be able to accumulate funds to acquire the gold or high-powered money without creating high-powered money to do so, else it would be undoing with one hand what it did with the other. But at the outset, the

212

Federal Reserve System had no bonds or other assets to sell to accumulate funds. Neither did it have the power, then or later, to issue its own securities or to borrow in some other way on the open market, which in principle are alternative possibilities.[25] And it had no direct way to influence the deposit-reserve or deposit-currency ratio.[26]

The Reserve System was thus in an asymmetrical position. It had the power to create high-powered money and to put it in the hands of the public or the banks by rediscounting paper or by purchasing bonds or other financial assets. It could therefore exert an expansionary influence on the money stock. At the same time, it had no effective power to contract the money stock. Under the circumstances, the most it could have done was to avoid creating any additional high-powered money. But even this required that the Federal Reserve Banks simply accumulate in their vaults the gold and other lawful money transferred to them as reserves by member banks, acquire no earning assets, and finance their expenditures solely by assessments on member banks. They were understandably reluctant to follow fully so ascetic a policy. They wanted to acquire portfolios so that they could, on the one hand, "be in the market" continuously, and, on the other hand, use the income from the portfolios to become independent of assessments on member banks.[27] They were therefore led to acquire portfolios. Rediscount rates, which were set at 6 to 6½ per cent when the Federal Reserve Banks opened in November 1914, were generally lowered to 4 per cent in 1915 and maintained at that level until September 1916, when the New York and St. Louis Banks lowered their rates to 3 per cent, with the rate in other

[25] Various writers have at times suggested that the Federal Reserve System be given the power to borrow on the open market so as to be capable of contractionary action even when its portfolio is bare (see Jacob Viner, "Recent Legislation and the Banking Situation," *American Economic Review*, Mar. 1936, Suppl., p. 118). In sect. 2 of a bill (H.R. 10517) introduced by Rep. Goldsborough in 72d Cong., 1st sess. (1932), but never enacted, "to stabilize the purchasing power of money," the System would have been given the right to issue new debentures if in selling securities it exhausted its holdings.

[26] In principle, of course, the gold inflow could have been sterilized by raising reserve requirements by legislative action. In Dec. 1916, the Federal Reserve Board asked Congress for authority to raise reserve requirements (*Annual Report* for 1916, pp. 28, 140), but the authority was not granted. The one thing the Federal Reserve System could do to reduce any part of the money stock was to purchase bonds carrying the circulation privilege, but this only substituted Federal Reserve notes for national bank notes.

[27] "The Reserve Banks have expenses to meet, and while it would be a mistake to regard them merely as profit-making concerns and to apply to them the ordinary test of business success, there is no reason why they should not earn their expenses, and a fair profit besides, without failing to exercise their proper functions and exceeding the bounds of prudence in their management. Moreover, the Reserve Banks can never become the leading and important factor in the money market which they were designed to be unless a considerable portion of their resources is regularly and constantly employed" (Federal Reserve Board, *Annual Report* for 1914, p. 18).

213

CHART 20

Discount Rates of the Federal Reserve Bank of New York, 1914–21

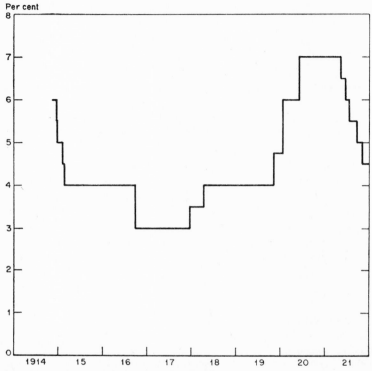

SOURCE: *Banking and Monetary Statistics*, pp. 439–440.

districts ranging from 3½ to 4 per cent (see Chart 20 for rates at the New York Bank).[28] But even at these rates, the amount of paper offered for rediscount was small. The Banks were therefore led to purchase bills and acceptances, U.S. government securities, and municipal warrants to earn income (Chart 21). In all, Federal Reserve credit outstanding on March 31, 1917, was $286 million, approximately 6 per cent of total high-powered money and 21 per cent of the increase since 1914. Federal Reserve activity thereby made a minor though not negligible contribution to the expansion in the money stock.

[28] Before 1921 there were different rates for various maturities and types of paper. Rates shown here applied to the type of paper and maturity for which the rate was lowest—31- to 60-day commercial, agricultural, or livestock paper through Aug. 1916; 15-day paper or under 15 for dates from Sept. 1916 to Dec. 1920. Preferential rates on paper secured by government obligations were in existence from 1917 through Nov. 1921 at some Reserve Banks, but are not quoted here. The range shown covers the 12 district Banks.

CHART 21
Federal Reserve Credit Outstanding, by Types,
November 1914–December 1921

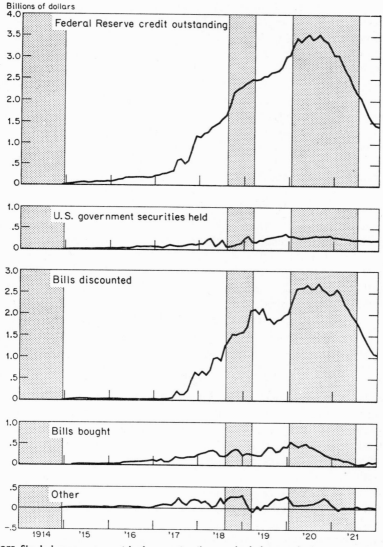

NOTE: Shaded areas represent business contractions; unshaded areas, business expansions.
SOURCE: Federal Reserve credit outstanding; U.S. government securities held; bills discounted; and bills bought, end-of-month data from *Banking and Monetary Statistics*, pp. 373–374, adjusted for seasonal by Shiskin-Eisenpress method (Julius Shiskin and Harry Eisenpress, *Seasonal Adjustments by Electronic Computer Methods*, N.Y., NBER, Technical Paper 12, 1958). "Other," obtained as a residual.

During the period of U.S. neutrality, there was a major shift in composition of high-powered money viewed as liabilities of the monetary authorities. That shift was produced primarily by the inflow of gold, which raised its ratio to the total, and by the change in the form in which member banks held their reserves from entirely vault cash to mainly deposits at the Federal Reserve Banks. In November 1914, Treasury currency (including national bank notes) constituted 56 per cent of total high-powered money, gold coin and certificates in circulation, 37 per cent, Federal Reserve notes, a negligible percentage, deposits at Federal Reserve Banks, 7 per cent. By March 1917, the retirement of $330 million of national bank notes, which was not fully offset by a slight increase in other components of Treasury currency, plus the rise in total high-powered money reduced the share of Treasury currency to 38 per cent; the gold inflow raised the share of gold coin and certificates to 41 per cent; Federal Reserve notes rose to 7 per cent and Federal Reserve deposits to 14 per cent (see Chart 19A).

PERIOD OF WARTIME DEFICITS

Our entry into the war on April 6, 1917, brought a major change in apparent financial conditions. Purchases in the United States by our new allies, heretofore financed largely by shipments of gold, sales of foreign-held securities, and flotation of loans on private capital markets, were henceforth financed by U.S. government credits to their accounts.[29] In addition, the United States began to mobilize its resources explicitly for war. Initial government expenditures to pay for purchases by the Allies were shortly supplemented by expenditures for U.S. forces. Though taxes were raised, ordinary receipts fell far short of expenditures during the period of active warfare and continued to do so after the Armistice in November 1918 and through the remainder of fiscal 1919. The large federal government deficits, totaling in all some $23 billion, or nearly three-quarters of total expenditures of $32 billion from April 1917 to June 1919, were financed by explicit borrowing and by money creation.[30] The Federal Reserve became to all intents and purposes the bond-selling window of the Treasury, using its monetary powers almost exclusively to that end. Although no "greenbacks" were printed, the same result was achieved by more indirect methods using Federal Reserve notes and Federal Reserve deposits. At the beginning of U.S. participation in the war, Federal Reserve notes accounted for 7 per cent of high-powered money and bank deposits at Federal Reserve Banks for 14

---

[29] From U.S. entry into the war until the Armistice, the U.S. Treasury advanced $7.3 billion to the Allies; in the next two years, an additional $2.2 billion.

[30] *Annual Report* of the Secretary of the Treasury, 1919, p. 213; also Chap. 10, pp. 557 and 574.

per cent; by the Armistice, Federal Reserve notes and deposits accounted for 38 and 21 per cent, respectively. The share of gold coin and certificates, on the other hand, fell from 41 per cent to 14 per cent, and the share of Treasury currency fell from 38 per cent to 27 per cent.[31]

The change in financial conditions after our entry into the war was more striking in appearance than in effect, and it was accompanied by little alteration in the direction of the underlying changes in the allocation of real resources. Foreign demands had set in motion a massive adaptation of resources to the production of armaments and other wartime needs. Domestic demands continued the process once the United States became a belligerent. The major effect was on the sources of financing rather than on the rate at which expenditures for war purposes were growing. Although the change in the sources of financing stopped the gold inflows, it did not stop a continued expansion in the stock of high-powered money or in the total money stock.

Somewhat surprisingly, our entry into the war brought, if anything, a slowing down of the pace of inflation rather than the speeding up one might a priori expect. And perhaps equally surprising, the end of wartime deficit financing saw a speeding up of the pace of inflation. Apparently the pattern was more than an accident, since it recurred in World War II.

Table 10 shows the percentage rise in prices and the money stock for two different periods: from March 1917, just before the declaration of war, to November 1918, the month of the Armistice; and from March

[31] The withdrawal of over $1 billion of gold coin and certificates from circulation was effected as part of the policy of concentrating gold in the Federal Reserve System and was achieved by asking the banks to cooperate by "sorting out of your incoming cash the gold certificates, not paying out any such certificates over your counter unless especially requested, but instead, forwarding to this [New York Federal Reserve] bank all you may accumulate in excess of those you think it advisable to carry as part of your vault money" (*Federal Reserve Bulletin,* Sept. 1917, p. 660). The banks were asked to pay out Federal Reserve notes instead, and the public was discouraged from requesting gold coins for gifts (*ibid.,* Dec. 1917, pp. 931, 951).

The decline in Treasury currency, unlike the decline during the period of U.S. neutrality, did not result primarily from the retirement of national bank notes. Great Britain desired silver bullion for shipment to India, which was on a silver standard and where there was much war activity. Under terms of the Pittman Act, passed in Apr. 1918, it purchased silver for that purpose from the U.S. Treasury. The mechanics of the transaction involved the accumulation of silver certificates by the Federal Reserve Banks, and their transfer to the Treasury in exchange for Pittman certificates of indebtedness, an asset item included in Federal Reserve Bank credit; the cancellation of the silver certificates by the Treasury, which released the silver bullion shipped to India; and, to replace the silver certificates, the issue by the Federal Reserve Banks of Federal Reserve Bank notes secured by Pittman certificates. Up to the Armistice, $185 million of silver certificates had been withdrawn from circulation but only $75 million of such Federal Reserve Bank notes had been issued. Those notes were at a maximum of $259 million at the end of 1920.

217

1917 to May 1919, the date at which the net government interest-bearing debt reached $25 billion, a level around which it fluctuated moderately, and hence the date that marks the end of heavy wartime fiscal deficits.[32] For both periods and for both prices and money, the percentage rise was not only much smaller in total than during the longer prior period of U.S. neutrality, it was also decidedly smaller per year. By comparison with the shorter final segment distinguished in Table 10, the percentage rise in prices and money during the period of war or of wartime deficits was roughly the same in total and decidedly smaller per year.

It is by no means clear why the pace of inflation slowed after our entry into the war, though one contributory factor, monetary in character, is suggested by the figures in Table 10.[33] The stock of money rose less than in proportion to the rise in high-powered money during the wartime period, whereas it rose more than in proportion during both the preceding and succeeding periods. The annual rate of growth of the stock of money was less during that period than during either the preceding or succeeding period; yet the annual rate of growth of high-powered money was higher. The reason for the divergence between the stock of money and high-powered money during the wartime period is clear from the part of the table that shows the factors accounting for the changes in the stock of money. Up to the Armistice, a decline in the ratio of deposits to currency offset about half the expansionary influence exerted by rises in high-powered money and in the ratio of deposits to reserves. The public held over $8 of deposits per dollar of currency when war was declared; it held only about $6 of deposits per dollar of currency shortly after the Armistice. We have no fully satisfying explanation for the sharp increase in demand for currency relative to deposits. Cagan argues that the corresponding increase during World War II reflected in part an increase in currency transactions as a means of avoiding tax, in part, other factors such as increased mobility which rendered currency

---

[32] The Victory Loan, the final bond issue of World War I, was floated Apr.-May 1919.

[33] A number of other possible factors can be mentioned, but a full analysis would carry us too far afield: (1) Only a minor part of war expenditures was financed by taxation, but such taxation as there was did absorb funds that would otherwise have been available for private expenditures, and there was no tax counterpart at all to the expenditures made by the Allies during the period of neutrality. (2) The bond drives may have stimulated voluntary savings, in the relevant sense of increasing the fraction of their income individuals would save in the absence of price changes. (3) There was a steady rise in interest rates. (4) Price controls, voluntary controls over capital issues, compulsory foreign exchange controls, and other wartime measures may have curtailed some expenditures that would otherwise have been made and so diverted resources to wartime use. (5) Immediately after the Armistice, uncertainty about the future, reconversion, and demobilization must all have been deflationary in their impact.

relatively more useful, and foreign demand for U.S. currency.[34] These factors may well be the main explanation for the World War I movement as well. Whatever the explanation, the effect was clear: the drain of currency into circulation was a deflationary factor, offsetting the expansionary influence of Federal Reserve credit creation, helping to slow down the pace of inflation, and enabling a given number of dollars of money creation by the federal government through the Federal Reserve to command more real resources than it otherwise would have.[35]

[34] See Phillip Cagan, *The Demand for Currency Relative to the Total Money Supply*, New York, NBER, Occasional Paper 62, 1958 (reprinted from *Journal of Political Economy*, Aug. 1958, pp. 303–328); and his forthcoming volume on determinants and effects of changes in the U.S. money stock, 1875–1955, a National Bureau study.

[35] We can express the effect of the drain of currency on the pace of inflation in terms of the financing of government expenditures. Let us regard the Federal Reserve as a government agency and consolidate its accounts with those of the Treasury. Let us also, for the present purpose, set aside the composition of high-powered money shown in Table 10, and treat high-powered money as consisting of two components having different significance in the period in question: gold and fiduciary currency issued directly or indirectly by the government. For every dollar of such fiduciary currency, the government acquires control over one dollar of resources. (Strictly speaking, national bank notes and, less clearly, silver currency should perhaps be separated out, since this statement may not be valid for them. But there was virtually no change in national bank notes during the war. The major change in silver currency was the replacement of part by Federal Reserve Bank notes [see footnote 31], which had no net effect on resources available to the U.S. government. Hence the inclusion of national bank notes and silver currency with other fiduciary currency not only makes for simplicity in exposition but also for greater accuracy.) This is equivalent to borrowing resources at zero interest rate, to the extent that it is accomplished without a price rise, and to imposing a tax on money balances, to the extent that it occurs through a price rise (see Milton Friedman, *Essays in Positive Economics*, University of Chicago Press, 1955, pp. 254–255). If there were no fractional reserve banking, so that all money consisted of what we call high-powered money, this would be the end of the story. But with fractional reserve banking it is not. For every dollar created by the government, several dollars can be created by the banking system, since only part of the extra dollars of high-powered money go into circulation, and part go into bank reserves. In effect, as it were, the government engages in a sharing arrangement with the banking system whereby the two divide between them the amount the public is willing to lend at zero interest rate (or in the case of deposits bearing interest, at an interest rate below that on other types of loans) and also the proceeds of the implicit tax on money balances involved in a price rise. The sharing formula, i.e., the number of dollars the banking system can create per dollar created by the government, depends on the banks' reserve ratio (in terms of high-powered money) and the public's deposit-currency ratio. The public's shift to currency reduces the share of the banking system and increases the share of the government, which thereby acquires resources with less of an increase in the money stock.

In terms of magnitudes, the fiduciary component of high-powered money increased by about $1.5 billion from U.S. entry into the war to the Armistice. This is the amount of war expenditures financed by either a zero interest rate loan or the proceeds of an implicit tax on money balances. If the public had not shifted from deposits to currency, but the deposit-reserve ratio had risen as it in fact did,

As the bottom half of Table 10 shows, more than the entire increase in the stock of money can be attributed to an expansion in Federal Reserve private claims (see also Chart 19B). Had Federal Reserve private claims alone changed and other assets contributing to high-powered money remained constant, high-powered money would have increased more than it did. And even the actual change in high-powered money would have produced a change in the money stock larger than the change which occurred, if it had not been offset by a decline in the deposit-currency ratio. The main source of the increase in Federal Reserve private claims was the discounting of bills secured by government war obligations. Member banks made loans to their customers who used them to purchase government securities, and banks in need of reserves in turn rediscounted at a Federal Reserve Bank the customer loans or their own collateral notes secured by government war obligations. This process contrasts with that in World War II, when the increase in Federal Reserve credit outstanding was primarily the result of the direct purchase of government securities by the Reserve Banks.

The monetary gold stock contributed little during the war period to the change in high-powered money. The declaration of war brought a prompt end to gold inflows and a tendency toward outflows. Since the U.S. government in effect assumed financial responsibility for the foreign trade deficits of its Allies, dollars were no longer in short supply. On the contrary, they were plentiful. What mattered was the foreign trade position of the Allies as a whole vis-à-vis the rest of the world and, left to itself, that position would surely have been in deficit, gold movements aside. After the tendency toward outflows manifested itself, the President (on September 7, 1917) prohibited all gold exports without permission of the Federal Reserve Board and the Treasury and brought foreign exchange transactions under explicit control. Those and other devices sufficed to keep the gold stock roughly constant.

The negative contribution to the change in high-powered money of other physical assets and fiat of the Treasury and Federal Reserve Banks (Table 10, line 13) is a sign of how completely new methods of money

---

this component could have increased only $0.6 billion without an increase in the money stock larger than occurred. It would have required the government to raise an additional $1 billion some other way. Alternatively, if the public had not shifted to currency, the $1.5 billion actually issued by the government would have raised the money stock about 40 per cent instead of 18 per cent. But in that case, prices would surely have risen more than they did. In consequence, for the government to have raised the same amount of real resources from fiduciary issue would have required an increase in high-powered money of more than $1.5 billion, with an additional inflationary impact. It is clear from these figures that the effects in question are by no means negligible (see Friedman, "Price, Income, and Monetary Changes in Three Wartime Periods," *American Economic Review,* May 1952, pp. 612–625).

creation had replaced old. The creation of new money through Federal Reserve loans and discounts to the banks and the indirect absorption of that money by government through its operations were sufficient to enable the Treasury actually to reduce its net direct fiduciary issue; cash balances which it accumulated served to offset Treasury currency and other liabilities outstanding.

The total increase in high-powered money excluding gold was approximately $1.5 billion from March 1917 through November 1918, and $1.6 billion from March 1917 through May 1919. This is roughly the amount of fiduciary currency issued by the government to pay for war-time expenses.[36] For the period through May 1919, it was about one-fifth as large as the $7.3 billion collected in explicit taxes, one-fifteenth as large as the $24 billion borrowed explicitly. Stated differently, total federal government expenditures during that period were $32 billion and additions to Treasury cash balances $2 billion. Of that total of $34 billion, approximately 25 per cent was financed by explicit taxes plus nontax receipts; 70 per cent by explicit borrowing; and 5 per cent by direct money creation, which may be regarded for that period as largely an implicit tax on money balances levied through the rise in prices.[37] The total money stock increased by $6.4 billion, or some $4.8 billion more than fiduciary currency issued by the government. This was, of course, a consequence of the fractional reserve system, which meant that the banking system was able to create $3 of money per $1 created by the monetary authorities. The ratio was so low only because of the sizable decline in the deposit-currency ratio which, as noted above, was the reason the rise in total money stock was less than in proportion to the rise in high-powered money. Since the increase in bank-created money was matched primarily by an increase in government securities held by the banks or their customers, the rise in bank-created money may be regarded as indirectly associated with the financing of war expenditures.

POSTWAR INFLATION

A temporary peak in wholesale prices reached in September 1918 was followed by a plateau and then a brief decline before prices once again

---

[36] "Roughly" is needed only because of national bank notes, which declined slightly during the period, and which one may or may not wish to term government-issued fiduciary currency (see Appendix B and footnote 35, above), and because of silver currency, which again is subject to alternative interpretations.

[37] Insofar as additional money issued was accepted by the public without a rise in prices, it can be regarded as an implicit loan at zero interest rate. However, the approximate stability of velocity demonstrates that money balances did not increase as a fraction of income, and the rough stability of real income means that no additional real money balances were demanded on that account—hence our conclusion that for that period the issue of additional money was a tax.

221

resumed their upward march. The period of price hesitation corresponds roughly with the reference contraction dated by the National Bureau as running from August 1918 to March 1919. The end of the war brought an immediate termination of orders for munitions and much confusion and uncertainty about both the immediate and the longer-range future. Total output undoubtedly declined fairly sharply. But the decline in both prices and output was brief and was succeeded by a renewed expansion. Beginning in March, prices started to rise at a more rapid pace than during the period of active war, and an intense boom got under way, marked by rapid accumulation of inventories and commodity speculation.

As Table 10 shows, the percentage rise in prices, as in the preceding wartime period, was roughly equal in magnitude to the percentage rise in the stock of money. The rise in the stock of money, however, had a very different relation to the rise in high-powered money. The wartime decline in the ratio of deposits to currency, which offset so large a part of the increase in high-powered money, was succeeded by a rise which had the opposite effect. In addition, deposits continued to rise relative to bank holdings of high-powered money. Consequently, the rise in high-powered money accounts for only about one-half or two-thirds, depending on the period considered, of the rise in the stock of money.

The rise in high-powered money took place despite the net outflow of close to $300 million of gold after the lifting of the embargo in June 1919 (see Chart 19B). The outflow was much more than offset by a continued rise in Federal Reserve credit outstanding, mainly through increased rediscounting, partly through purchase of government securities and of bankers' acceptances originating in the main from foreign trade transactions. The rediscount rate at the Reserve Bank of New York, which had been raised in December 1917 to 3½ per cent and in April 1918 to 4 per cent, was kept unchanged until November 1919 (Chart 20), and the pattern at the other Banks was similar. Those rates were decidedly below market rates. Given the speculative climate, characterized by a strong demand for bank loans—which itself, of course, partly reflected the effect of prior monetary expansion—a continued rise in high-powered money and in the total stock of money was to be expected. Throughout the period, member banks could be regarded as operating entirely on borrowed reserves: from September 1918 through July 1921, the outstanding volume of bills discounted by Federal Reserve Banks exceeded member bank reserve balances.

The Reserve Board was aware that Bank discount rates were below current market rates throughout 1919, that this was contributing to monetary expansion, and that monetary expansion was contributing to the inflation. "In April, 1919, the Board gave serious consideration to the suggestions made by several of the Federal Reserve Banks that the discount rate be advanced,"[38] yet it restricted itself to moral suasion, urging banks to discriminate between "essential and non-essential credits" —a formula that successive use from that time to this has rendered neither less appealing to the Reserve System as a means of shifting responsibility nor more effective as a means of controlling monetary expansion. And, of course, the Board also took the position that the expansion in the stock of money was a result, not a cause, of rising prices.[39] Although in one sense correct, that contention was irrelevant to the question of appropriate Federal Reserve policy. Any particular level of Federal Reserve discount rates may be consistent with either monetary expansion or monetary contraction, depending on the state of demand for loans. In mid-1919, there was a sufficiently strong demand for loans to make it profitable for commercial banks to expand the stock of money at the then existing discount rate. In a less exuberant state of demand for loans, the same discount rate might have meant monetary contraction and deflation: e.g., the 6 per cent discount rates finally attained in early 1920 were accompanied by or produced deflation; they might not have, if they had been introduced in early or mid-1919. It is therefore true that, *given the discount rate,* the demand for goods, reflected in the demand for loans, determined the behavior of the stock of money. But a fixed discount rate can hardly be interpreted as a policy of "neutrality" by the Reserve System—this is the essence of the controversy after World War II about the bond-support program (see Chapters 10 and 11). In the circumstances of 1919, a rise in discount rates could have moderated or, if sufficiently large, have terminated—though perhaps only after some lag—the rise in loans extended, thereby, the rise in the stock of money, and thereby, the rise in prices—precisely the sequence that did in fact occur one year later.

The reason for Federal Reserve inaction was not, as in the earlier period of U.S. neutrality, the absence of technical power to control monetary expansion. On the one hand, there was a gold outflow rather than inflow; on the other, the System had acquired a substantial portfolio. By raising discount rates and selling securities on the open market, the System was clearly in a position to keep down the growth of the stock of money to any desired rate. Nor was the reason, at least after the spring of 1919, Treasury deficit financing. It was rather an alleged necessity for facilitating Treasury funding of the floating debt plus un-

[38] W. P. G. Harding, *The Formative Period of the Federal Reserve System,* Houghton Mifflin, 1925, p. 148.
[39] "The purchasing power of the public growing out of high wages and large profits is greater than it has ever been before; and this purchasing power, competing with export demands arising out of the necessities of Europe, has raised prices to a point that takes no account of prudence. . . . There is practically unlimited demand for credit. . . " *Annual Report* for 1919, p. 3.

willingness to see a decline in the prices of government bonds, while commercial banks still held on their own account substantial amounts of the Victory Loan, floated from April 25 to May 10, 1919, and had extensive loans outstanding to their customers on those securities.[40]

The Diary of Charles S. Hamlin throws much light on the leading personalities in the Federal Reserve System at that time and their influence on the policies followed. Hamlin was a Boston lawyer, who served as Assistant Secretary of the Treasury in the second Cleveland administration and again in the first Wilson administration until his appointment in August 1914 as a member of the Federal Reserve Board for a two-year term, and also as the first governor of the Board. He was succeeded as governor by W. P. G. Harding but received two ten-year reappointments as a member of the Board in 1916 and 1926, serving until 1936, when he was appointed special counsel. Throughout that extended period, Hamlin kept a detailed record of his daily round of activities, including proceedings of the Board. The Diary provides invaluable information on the play of personalities and the pressure of events in the decisions reached by the Board. For the years before 1935, when the annual reports of the Federal Reserve Board contain no full record of policy matters, the Diary is one of the two main primary sources of information we have used.

The other primary source is the George Leslie Harrison Papers on the Federal Reserve System. In 1928 Harrison became governor of the Federal Reserve Bank of New York, having served earlier as a deputy governor. When he resigned at the end of 1940 to become president of the New York Life Insurance Company, he took with him files of material covering the period of his association with the Bank (1920–40), and

---

[40] In the words of the *Annual Report* for 1919, p. 3, ". . . it is evident that an advance in discount rates while the Government had an unwieldy floating debt and Liberty bonds were still largely unabsorbed would have added to the difficulties of government financing. While regulation and control of credit have been as desirable since the war restrictions were removed as before, the Board was convinced that to attempt this control through premature adjustments of rates would be so detrimental to the Treasury's position as to offset, if not prevent entirely, the results sought." Reinforcing the urgings of the Treasury was apparently an understanding with commercial banks that the Reserve Banks would carry both the commercial banks' and their customers' subscriptions to the Victory loan for six months at an interest rate equal to the loan's rate (H. P. Willis, *The Federal Reserve System,* New York, Ronald, 1923, pp. 1395–1396). Another deterrent to raising the Bank rate was an agreement dating from early 1918 between the Reserve Board and the Clearing House banks of New York for the latter to pay $2\frac{1}{4}$ per cent interest on demand bankers' balances, the rate to be increased $\frac{1}{4}$ of 1 per cent for every $\frac{1}{2}$ per cent increase in the New York Reserve Bank rate on 90-day commercial paper, up to a maximum of 3 per cent. In 1919 the Reserve Board was reluctant to see a rise in Reserve Bank rates that would result in a rise in the interest allowed on out-of-town balances and might lead to wholesale shifts of bankers' deposits in search of maximum returns (*Federal Reserve Bulletin,* Apr. 1918, p. 252; Jan. 1920, p. 3).

in 1957 he gave the files to Columbia University, of which he was a trustee. Since the files start at a later date than the Hamlin Diary does and are most valuable for the period after Harrison became governor, our major use of them is in subsequent chapters, but they contain many official memoranda and other documents referring to earlier years as well.[41] The Harrison Papers provide the student a second insider's view of the System as well as much unpublished documentary evidence. The two sources both complement and, to some extent, duplicate one another. The comparisons we have made of them strengthen our confidence in the reliability of both.

The entries in the Hamlin Diary covering the postwar period reveal Benjamin Strong, who was governor of the Federal Reserve Bank of New York from 1914 until his untimely death in 1928, as a leading figure in the System, foremost in the struggle to free it from subservience to the Treasury. Late in September 1919, upon his return from Europe —where he had spent the summer in discussions with central bankers, government officials, and American relief workers—Strong began to argue the case for higher discount rates. At issue were two questions that were to divide the System again in 1928–29: (1) Was it possible for the Federal Reserve Banks to restrain the growth of credit outstanding by the exercise of moral suasion that would deter member banks from

[41] The Harrison Papers provide a wealth of documentary evidence on three broad topics of domestic monetary policy: (1) the controversy within the System during the late twenties over control of the stock market boom; (2) cross-currents affecting System policy from the stock market crash in Oct. 1929 to the bank holiday in Mar. 1933; (3) the role of the System under the New Deal. They partly extend but mostly overlap the period covered by the Hamlin Diary. The documentary evidence includes the minutes of open market committee meetings, official correspondence and memoranda exchanged in connection with those meetings, and minutes of meetings of the board of directors of the New York Federal Reserve Bank at which System policy was reviewed and analyzed. Finally, the Papers contain a full record of Harrison's conversations—on the telephone or face-to-face—with leading figures in the System, in the banking community, in political office, and in foreign central banks, usually dictated immediately afterwards or at most several days later. Of the eight file drawers containing the Harrison Papers, the four holding material devoted mainly to domestic monetary policy (separated from the material on international central bank relations in the other four drawers) were examined.

In subsequent references to the Harrison Papers, items are identified by the titles of sections of the Papers, as follows: Conversations, 1926–40 (cited as Harrison, Conversations), Office Memoranda, 1921–40 (Harrison, Office), both records of conversations, with some duplication; Miscellaneous Letters and Reports, 1920–40 (Harrison, Miscellaneous), copies of correspondence with the Federal Reserve Board and others; Open Market Investment Committee, 1928–40 (Harrison, Open Market), minutes of regular meetings, meetings of the executive committee, memoranda, correspondence, resolutions; Governors Conference, 1921–40 (Harrison, Governors), detailed agenda for meetings; Discussion Notes, 1930–40 (Harrison, Notes), minutes of meetings of the board of directors of the Federal Reserve Bank of New York and of the executive committee; Special Memoranda, 1933–40 (Harrison, Special), discussions of policy questions prepared by the Bank's research staff.

borrowing for speculative purposes, without raising discount rates? (2) If some rise in discount rates was essential, was it possible to restrain speculative borrowing and at the same time maintain a preferential rate for "legitimate" borrowing—which in 1919–20 was paper secured by Treasury obligations? To both these questions, Strong answered, No. Secretary of the Treasury Carter Glass, on the other hand, was certain that the System could discriminate against "undesirable" credit uses without rate increases. In addition, before mid-January 1920, both he and Assistant Secretary Russell C. Leffingwell viewed any plan to tighten the money market as an intolerable interference with their program of Treasury financing. Despite poor health, which shortly forced him to take a year's leave of absence, Strong undertook to oppose the Treasury, though neither the Federal Reserve Board nor most governors of other Banks were ready to support him. The impression emerges from the Diary that Strong was harried and frustrated, and that at times his strength of purpose in driving for higher rates was obscured by tactical retreats.

At a Governors Conference on October 28, 1919, Strong argued that the rate on 15-day paper secured by Treasury certificates should be raised from 4 to $4\frac{3}{4}$, not $4\frac{1}{4}$ per cent, as proposed in a schedule drawn up after discussions between Secretary Glass, ex-officio chairman of the Board, Assistant Secretary Leffingwell, Governor Harding, and Governor Strong. In view of Treasury opposition, however, Strong announced that he would advise his directors to fix a rate of $4\frac{1}{4}$ per cent. Under the schedule, the rate on 90-day paper secured by Liberty bonds was to be raised to $4\frac{3}{4}$ per cent. After the meeting Glass denounced the proposed increase in a private conversation with Hamlin. Two days later, according to Hamlin, Strong telephoned from New York "that his directors feared a $4\frac{3}{4}\%$ rate would depress Liberty bonds to 90 and might cause a panic." Strong said he wanted to reconsider the rate. In Washington on October 31, Strong said "he would have to insist on rate advances, that the reputation of the New York Bank was at stake. . . ." The upshot was that the rate schedule that went into effect on November 4 at New York raised to $4\frac{1}{4}$ per cent the rate on 15-day paper secured by $4\frac{1}{4}$ per cent Treasury certificates, and to $4\frac{1}{2}$ per cent the rate on 15- and 90-day paper secured by Liberty bonds. The rate on commercial paper maturing within 15 days, including member banks' collateral notes secured by such paper, was raised from 4 to $4\frac{3}{4}$ per cent; the rate on 16- to 90-day commercial paper was unchanged at $4\frac{3}{4}$ per cent.

On November 13, Strong told the Board "that last August, when Treasury revenues began to equal expenditures, rates should have been put up, whatever the result on Treasury operations. . . . He said he had loyally carried out Treasury and Board policy of control other than by raising rates and would see this particular crisis through, but after this he would resign rather than continue such a policy. He quoted Bagehot to [the] effect that in every war [the] insidious hand of the Treasury appears, and said they had [the] same struggle last summer in England, and that [the] Bank of England had put up rates so that [the] British loaning rate became 5½%."[42] The Boston and New York Federal Reserve Banks proposed further rate increases on November 24, which the Board rejected because of Treasury opposition.[43]

A few weeks later, as a result of an improvement in its position, the Treasury withdrew its unqualified opposition to a rate increase, and the Federal Reserve Board so informed the Banks. On December 12, 1919, the New York rate on 15-day paper secured by Treasury certificates was raised to 4½ per cent, and on 15- and 90-day paper secured by Liberty bonds to 4¾ per cent. Hamlin reported that certain of the New York Bank directors "had said they were whipped into agreeing to" the increase by Strong. On December 30, after Strong went on leave to recover his health, the former rate was raised to 4¾ per cent at New York, with the result that all discounts by the Bank were at a uniform rate, an objective that Strong cherished.[44]

Despite Strong's vigorous fight to raise discount rates, he apparently began to have some doubts, even while he was in the middle of the battle, about whether the time for such action might not already have passed. Hamlin records that on November 29 Strong "said it would *not* do to increase rates now—should have been done long ago—to do it now

[42] Charles S. Hamlin, Diary (1887–1937, Hamlin Papers, Manuscript Division, Library of Congress), Vol. 5, Oct. 28–Nov. 1 and 12–13, 1919, pp. 41–47, 54–57.

[43] The episode involved Strong in a controversy with Secretary of the Treasury Carter Glass concerning the Board's authority over discount rates. Although the Attorney General supported Glass' view that the Board had authority to initiate rate changes and order their establishment, the legal question posed remained unsettled (Lester V. Chandler, *Benjamin Strong, Central Banker,* Washington, Brookings, 1958, pp. 162–165).

The action by the Boston and New York Reserve Banks came a week after the Federal Advisory Council (of 12 bankers, one elected by each Bank) had recommended "that no further change be made in discount rates at present" (Federal Reserve Board, *Annual Report* for 1919, p. 530).

[44] Hamlin Diary, Vol. 5, Dec. 12, 30, 1919, pp. 82–87, 109–110. Despite his advocacy of a single discount rate, Strong argued that a preferential rate on acceptances was justified "in order to stimulate a necessary banking development in the country and in recognition that this particular type of paper was a better asset than any other line of commercial paper" (quoted in Chandler, *Benjamin Strong,* p. 160). The argument was essentially the same as the Treasury's justification of preferential rates on paper secured by Treasury obligations, which Strong was to refute a few years later (see footnote 66, Chap. 6 below). On Dec. 30, New York also increased its minimum buying rate on acceptances to 4¾ per cent.

would be to bring on a crisis." Almost precisely the same pattern was to be repeated in 1929 when, after a long and bitter battle, the Board finally permitted the New York Bank to raise its discount rate. By that time, however, New York feared the time had passed for restrictive measures.[45]

Federal Reserve policy during 1919 gave rise to much controversy, both at the time and since, and has been severely criticized. The Joint Congressional Commission of Agricultural Inquiry, established in 1921 in response to the sharp break in prices in 1920, concluded and, in our view, correctly:

> The commission believes that a policy of sharp advances in discount rates should have been inaugurated in the first six months of 1919, and can not excuse the action of the Federal Reserve Board and the Federal reserve banks in this period in failing to take measures to restrict the expansion, inflation, speculation, and extravagance, which characterized the period.[46]

Governor Harding's reply, as recorded in his memoirs, was characteristic:

> . . . all legitimate steps were taken by the Federal Reserve Board to restrict expansion, inflation, speculation, and extravagance during the year 1919, except one—a sharp advance in the discount rates; and it is not at all certain that even that expedient would have been effective at a time when the public seemed to care little for expense. In all events . . . the Board felt that it was its duty to cooperate with the Treasury authorities. Failure to cooperate would have been tantamount to an undertaking by the Board to dictate the policies of the Treasury. In such a case I think the Board would have heard something of the Overman Act. Under this act, which at that time was still in effect, the President could, by Executive Order, have transferred any of the functions of the Federal Reserve Board to the Secretary of the Treasury, or to any other officer of the Government.[47]

It seems clear that personal weakness, not mistaken principle, was the major explanation for the Board's inaction.[48]

[45] Hamlin, Diary, Vol. 5, p. 89. Strong's retrospective judgment that rates should have been raised early in 1919 is implicit in his later testimony before the Joint Commission of Agricultural Inquiry (Benjamin Strong, *Interpretations of Federal Reserve Policy*, W. Randolph Burgess, ed., New York, Harper, 1930, pp. xvi, 85–88). On the episode, see also Harold L. Reed, *The Development of Federal Reserve Policy*, New York, Houghton Mifflin, 1922, pp. 298–315; and Chandler, *Benjamin Strong*, pp. 119, 139–160. See also Chap. 6, sects. 3 and 4, below.

[46] *Report of the Joint Commission of Agricultural Inquiry*, 67th Cong., 1st sess., H. Rept. 408, 1922, part II, p. 15.

[47] Harding, *The Formative Period*, p. 223.

[48] The memoirs of a governor of another central bank are an instructive contrast to those of Harding, bringing out dramatically how the personal character of the governor of a central bank can affect its position vis-à-vis the Treasury under essentially identical legal conditions. See Émile Moreau, *Souvenirs d'un Gouverneur de la Banque de France*, Éditions M.-Th. Genin, Librairie de Médicis, Paris, 1954, *passim*. Moreau was governor of the Bank of France during the stabilization of the franc from 1926 to 1928.

As is often the case, the weakness prevented neither criticism of the Board nor the replacement of Harding as governor; indeed, it probably made the criticism more severe and Harding's replacement inevitable. A strong policy in early 1919 would have produced immediate criticism but, by preventing the subsequent inflation, would have obviated the severe deflationary measures the Board was impelled to take in 1920 and the sharp price decline that occasioned so much of the later criticism. A memorandum in the Harrison Papers records the results of the episode: "The criticism aroused and the political animosities which developed, led directly to the failure of reappointment of the Governor of the Federal Reserve Board, upon the expiration of his term of office, and introduced an element of political instability into the Board which could not but affect future credit administration."[49]

The continued expansion in Federal Reserve credit outstanding during 1919 plus the gold outflow after the lifting of the embargo combined to produce a rapid decline in the reserve ratio of the Federal Reserve System. The ratio had fallen sharply during the war, reaching a trough of 48.1 in December 1918. It then recovered irregularly to a high of 50.6 in June 1919. At that point, it began to fall steadily and sizably, reaching a level of 42.7 in January 1920 and 40.6 in March 1920. "Free" reserves—that is, reserves in excess of legal requirements—were reduced from $569 million in June 1919 to $234 million in January 1920 and reached a low of $131 million in March. The declining reserves finally rendered some action imperative. The Board had the power to suspend the legal reserve requirements, but it could hardly have justified doing so when the declining reserves were so clearly the result of internal inflation fed by Federal Reserve credit creation. In consequence, at long last it permitted the Reserve Banks to raise discount rates—first, as already noted, in November and December 1919, to a level of 4¾ per cent at most Banks, then in late January or early February 1920, to a uniform level of 6 per cent at all Banks. The second rise, 1¼ percentage points at

[49] Harrison, Special, No. 2, "Credit Policies of Federal Reserve System, 1914–1934," p. 2a.

We should perhaps note that the memorandum does not make the distinction we do between the probable consequences of action in 1919 and of the actual action in 1920, as illustrated by the sentence preceding the quoted one: "The action of the Federal Reserve System in checking the 1919–20 boom was unpopular with large groups of the community, as such action by central banks usually has been and probably always will be, no matter how beneficial the longer term consequences of the policies adopted."

When Harding was not reappointed governor in 1922, he left the Board, and in January 1923 became governor of the Federal Reserve Bank of Boston at a salary more than twice his prior salary at the Board! The same pattern was repeated in 1930, when Roy A. Young resigned as governor of the Federal Reserve Board and became governor of the Boston Bank. Again, there had been dissatisfaction with Young's performance as governor of the Federal Reserve Board (see footnote 104, Chap. 7, below).

most Banks, was the sharpest single rise in the entire history of the System, before or since. It produced an immediate retardation of the rate of rise in the money stock, though the level of the stock of money continued to rise slowly until September.

Surprisingly, in view of the Treasury's earlier role, the sharp rate increase to 6 per cent was adopted at the Treasury's suggestion, according to Hamlin's Diary. On January 14, 1920, the New York Bank had proposed a uniform rate increase on all paper to $5\frac{1}{2}$ per cent. The Treasury, however, insisted that the rate on certificates be kept at $4\frac{3}{4}$, so New York submitted a revised schedule with the lower rate on certificates. At that point, Assistant Secretary Leffingwell, representing Secretary Glass at a morning meeting on January 21, proposed increasing the rate on commercial paper to 6 per cent, on paper secured by Liberty loans to $5\frac{1}{2}$ per cent, while leaving paper secured by Treasury certificates for a short period at $4\frac{3}{4}$ per cent. Leffingwell "pointed out our low reserve position and said nothing but a drastic increase on commercial paper to 6% would curtail the situation. He said we were dangerously near leaving the gold standard . . . that soon a new gold embargo would have to be put in . . . ." Hamlin writes: "I pointed out that while a 6% rate might be necessary, yet an immediate advance of $1\frac{1}{4}$% was unjust and might give rise to panicky conditions. Leffingwell . . . said if a panic in N.Y. should break out he would be glad of it." In the afternoon Glass participated in the meeting and, to Hamlin's amazement, said he favored the immediate increase. A telephone call to the New York Bank before the morning meeting adjourned had put the Board on notice that the executive committee and J. S. Alexander, a director, "were a unit in opposing such a drastic increase. Mr. Alexander said an immediate 6% rate would cause much uneasiness, that people would think the Federal Reserve Board had lost its head or that conditions must be very critical to call for such drastic increase; he also said there was danger that it might cause panicky conditions." The final motion to raise the rate to 6 per cent on commercial paper passed by a vote of 4 to 3, the ayes being Governor Harding, Adolph Miller, the economist on the Board, Albert Strauss, a member who had been a New York investment banker, and Secretary Glass, casting the tie-breaking vote.[50] When the rate increase was put

[50] Hamlin resented Miller's action.

Before the meeting Dr. Miller told me he should never vote for a 6% rate, and he argued vehemently in the meeting against it and once voted vs. it. On the second vote, however, he weakened and said harmony was necessary, that the *Secretary of Treasury* and Governor Harding favored a 6% rate and therefore he should vote for it! The result was what Miller called harmony. It settled the question by 4 to 3 in favor, while if he had not weakened, it would have been 4 to 2 counter [Secretary Glass would then not have voted]. A queer idea of harmony! Miller has time and time again accused the Board

to the New York, Boston, and Philadelphia Banks the next day, they accepted it; and the schedule went into effect a day later.[51]

For reasons of health, Benjamin Strong was on leave from the Reserve Bank of New York for thirteen months beginning mid-December 1919. He took a trip around the world and was not in close touch with Bank officials. In view of Strong's belief in November 1919 that an increase in rates had been delayed beyond the point when it could be imposed without precipitating a crisis, it seems likely that he would not have agreed to the steep rise in January 1920, had he then been at the helm of the Bank. If there had been opposition on his part, Secretary Glass would probably have reopened the question, for Hamlin reports that Glass regarded his vote as only tentative.

3. The Contraction of 1920–21

The rise in discount rates in January was not only too late but also probably too much. The National Bureau dates the peak of the expansion as occurring in January 1920, simultaneously with the rise in rates and before the higher rates could have taken effect. The contraction, at first mild, became extremely severe in its later stages, when it was characterized by an unprecedented collapse in prices.

There is little sign of any severe decline until past the middle of the year. Indeed, it was not until early fall that contemporary observers were in substantial agreement that a sizable contraction was under way. As noted, the stock of money continued rising at a slow rate until September and wholesale prices until May. Industrial production, manufacturing employment, and payrolls, seasonally adjusted, reached their peaks in January but declined only very moderately until fall.

Beginning sometime about the middle of the year, the contraction changed its character. From a mild decline or sidewise movement, it became one of the most rapid declines on record. From their peak in May, wholesale prices declined moderately for a couple of months, and then

---

of being dominated by the Treasury and yet today he publicly announced that he changed his vote, against his convictions, because the *Secretary of Treasury* and Governor Harding wanted the 6% rate. (He is a time server!!!)

At a dinner party later that evening Glass confessed to Hamlin that "he was not so sure he had voted correctly . . . . He seemed much disturbed and worried" (Hamlin Diary, Vol. 5, Jan. 21, 1920, pp. 134–142).

[51] After they accepted the schedule of rates the Board had voted, the New York directors obtained an opinion from a Wall Street law firm on the power of the Board to determine discount rates. The opinion sustained the Board: "Our conclusion, therefore, is that the Banks alone have the power to initiate rates but the Board has the power to change those so established" (Chandler, *Benjamin Strong*, p. 167). Chandler comments on the Board's action, "What fireworks there would have been if the Board had done this while Strong was on duty!"

collapsed (see Chart 16). By June 1921, they had fallen to 56 per cent of their level in May 1920. More than three-quarters of the decline took place in the six months from August 1920 to February 1921. This is, by all odds, the sharpest price decline in the period covered by our money series, either before or since that date and perhaps also in the whole history of the United States. The only possible "competitors" are the price declines that followed the War of 1812 and the Civil War.

What was true of prices was true also of many physical magnitudes. Industrial production, employment in manufacturing, and similar series show a precipitous increase in the rate of decline in the autumn of 1920. The result is that although this contraction was relatively brief—the National Bureau dates the trough in July 1921—it ranks as one of the severest on record. Its brevity makes annual data misleading guides to its severity. Yet even so, Kuznets' net national product in current prices is more than 18 per cent lower in 1921 than in 1920; and in constant prices, more than 4 per cent lower.

From the peak reached in September 1920, the stock of money declined fairly steadily until the reference trough in July 1921, then flattened out, and reached bottom in January 1922. The total decline was 9 per cent. Although the magnitude of decline was much less than in prices or value of output, it was a major decline in terms of the historical behavior of the stock of money, which tends ordinarily to rise during mild business contractions as well as during business expansions. It was, indeed, the largest percentage decline recorded in our series up to that time, though only slightly larger than that before resumption in 1879. True, our data before 1907 are annual and semiannual and so understate the amplitude of change but it is extremely doubtful that monthly data would alter this conclusion. Furthermore, there is only one larger decline in the subsequent record—that accompanying the contraction of 1929–33.

As Chart 18 shows, the initial rise in the stock of money from January 1920 to September 1920 paralleled the change in high-powered money: from January to September the total stock of money rose by over 3 per cent and high-powered money by about 6 per cent. Banks continued to expand the ratio of their deposits to their high-powered reserves, but that was more than offset in its effect on the stock of money by a decline in the ratio of deposits to currency in the hands of the public.

The increase in high-powered money was accounted for primarily by a rise in bills discounted by Federal Reserve Banks in excess of a decline in bills bought. Since member banks were heavily in debt and apparently close to their minimum legal reserve requirements, the sharp rise in discount rates in January 1920 gave them an immediate and strong incentive to reduce the rate of expansion of their loans and investments and perhaps to contract them. But it took time for the effect of the change in discount rates to take hold. Member banks sustained a slight reduction in their high-powered money holdings over the period, despite a rise in total deposits, partly by a shift in deposits from demand to time accounts. Demand deposits reached a peak in March, while time deposits continued to increase throughout 1920. Member banks reduced their investments, both in government and in other securities, in the first half of 1920, but they continued to expand their loans, though at a much slower pace. Their loans rose 18 per cent in the final six months of 1919 and only 8 per cent in the next six months. Presumably, banks were willing to borrow for a time from the Federal Reserve at 6 per cent even at a loss in order to keep commitments entered into and to maintain favorable relations with their customers.

Moreover, in the conditions of early 1920, when prices were still rising, and there was much uncertainty whether the turn had come, the demand for loans was still strong. So it may have paid the banks to borrow from the Reserve System, even at 6 per cent, to make additional loans. At that time there had developed no tradition against continuous borrowing at the Federal Reserve Banks. For more than a year before the 6 per cent rate went into effect, member bank borrowings were continuously higher than their total reserve balances. It was of course less profitable for member banks to borrow at 6 per cent than at the former discount rates, and it seems doubtful that it would have continued to be profitable for long. Just as it took time for the higher discount rate to affect member banks, so it must have taken time for the higher open market rates and the higher rates charged by banks to affect commercial and other borrowers. In consequence, it seems highly likely that had the January rates been maintained, they alone would have produced a decline in the total stock of money before very long.

That result was rendered certain by a further rise in rates. On June 1, New York raised the rediscount rate to 7 per cent, and most other Banks either did the same or adopted other measures involving higher rates.[52] It is the highest rate that has ever been imposed by the System, before or since. The increase in rates came nearly six months after the cyclical

[52] Boston, Chicago, and Minneapolis raised the rediscount rate to 7 per cent in June. A progressive rate schedule was adopted by Atlanta, St. Louis, Kansas City, and Dallas during Apr. and May as a means of curbing borrowing by member banks. The System had sponsored that scheme in 1919, when it would not raise Bank rates. The Phelan Act of Apr. 1920 permitted the Reserve Banks with the approval of the Board, first, to determine the normal maximum rediscount line of each member bank; and second, to fix graduated rates on an ascending scale applicable equally and ratably to all member banks rediscounting on a scale in excess of the normal line. The progressive rate schedules were abandoned late in 1920 or in 1921, and Atlanta and Dallas adopted a flat 7 per cent rate. Weaker banks in agricultural areas complained particularly of the progressive rate schedule. The Agricultural Credits Act of Mar. 4, 1923, repealed the provisions of the Phelan Act.

peak, roughly coincided with the peak in wholesale prices and in the money stock, and was followed shortly by the collapse in prices already noted.

The discount policy was apparently dominated by concern over the Reserve System's own reserve position. As noted above, the ratio of the System's reserves to its deposit and note liabilities fell to a low of 40.6 per cent in March 1920 and hovered not much above that point throughout the rest of 1920, though it began to climb fairly steadily toward the end of the year. Despite the collapse in prices in the final months of 1920, the discount rate was lowered to $6\frac{1}{2}$ per cent at the New York Bank only in May 1921, when the reserve percentage had climbed to 56.4 per cent.[53] That was sixteen months after the cyclical peak and only two months before the cyclical trough. Four additional reductions were made in the balance of the year, bringing the rate down to $4\frac{1}{2}$ per cent in November.

From Hamlin's Diary it is clear that Governor Strong, who had resumed active control of the New York Bank in mid-January 1921, was opposed to reducing rates in the spring of 1921. On March 29, Secretary of the Treasury Mellon said the "time has nearly come for a reduction of discount rates from 7 to 6 per cent." The Board discussed the matter on April 4 without reaching a decision on a request from the Reserve Bank of Boston to institute a 6 per cent rate. Later that week in Washington, Strong "violently opposed lowering of Boston rates" on the ground that public opinion would demand that New York do the same, and that it would cause violent speculation in the stock market. Strong wanted to wait until wage rates were lower. He noted that deposits had fallen off considerably, retail prices had fallen moderately, wholesale prices precipitously, but wages had hardly been affected. Lower discount rates would force up wholesale prices, and prices and wages would be stabilized at too high a level. Strong proposed waiting to reduce discount rates until the "curve of wages, deposits and prices, wholesale and retail, were more nearly together—on a much lower basis."[54] At a Governors Conference on April 12, "every Governor opposed any decrease except Boston and Atlanta."[55] In the meantime President Harding told reporters "that the Federal Reserve Board has to lower rates generally and help the farmers," with the result that the only two New York directors who favored a decrease felt they had to oppose it lest it appear they were subject to Presidential influence. Hamlin noted on April 28 that "the

[53] The Boston Bank, which lowered the rate to 6 per cent on Apr. 15, was the only one to act before the New York Bank did.

[54] Ten days earlier, Strong suggested the earmarking of gold in the Bank of England "to keep it out of the Federal Reserve bank reserves, thus lowering the pressure for lower discount rates based on our high reserve percentage."

[55] Boston won approval for the rate reduction, as noted, but Atlanta had to wait until May 6.

Bank of England has reduced to 6½% . . . this may influence Governor Strong."[56]

Despite the sharp rise in discount rates in January and June 1920, Federal Reserve credit outstanding, seasonally adjusted (Chart 21), continued to rise until August 1920 (until October in the unadjusted data) as a result of a continued increase in discounts, then declined drastically, being halved in less than a year. The decline was produced by a sharp decrease in member bank borrowing from the Federal Reserve Banks, which in turn produced a sharp curtailment in customer loans by member banks. From the last week in October 1920 to the end of 1921, weekly reporting member banks cut their loans (unadjusted for seasonal) by one-sixth.[57] The reduction in Federal Reserve credit was offset in part by gold inflows that began in the second quarter of 1920 but, even so, total high-powered money fell some 11 per cent from September 1920 to the cyclical trough in July 1921.

The monetary contraction brought in its train a sharp increase in bank failures from 63 in 1919 to 155 in 1920 to 506 in 1921. But there seem to have been no signs of a liquidity crisis, of a general fear of bank deposits, or of a general attempt to convert deposits into currency. The ratio of deposits to currency held by the public, in fact, rose slightly from 6.52 in September 1920 to 7.00 in July 1921 (Table B-3), and the banks strengthened their own liquidity only negligibly, the ratio of deposits to reserves declining from 11.29 to 11.24. The rise in the deposit-currency ratio served to convert an 11 per cent decline in high-powered money into an 8 per cent decline in the total stock of money.

[56] Hamlin Diary, Mar. 29, Apr. 4, 9, 12, 28, May 5, 1921, pp. 66–72, 81, 87–90.

The Diary confirms Chandler's judgment that Strong would not have disagreed much with the policy followed in 1920–21 (Chandler, *Benjamin Strong,* pp. 169–170), despite evidence that in Dec. 1920, when Strong was in London, he apparently favored some relaxation of the tight money policy (see also Strong, *Interpretations,* pp. xvi and 133). Chandler points out that Strong was under the misapprehension that the System was following Bagehot's rule of lending freely but at high rates and ignored Bagehot's application of the rule to brief periods of panic in the money market, not to extended periods of business contraction (*Benjamin Strong,* pp. 173–174).

[57] It was easier to liquidate loans in the East than in agricultural areas. Much of the rediscounting during 1920–21 reflected this fact: to keep their reserve ratios above the legal minimum, Reserve Banks in agricultural areas turned for aid mainly to those in the industrial East. The drastic fall in agricultural prices began in Jan. 1920, some four months before the peak in the price index as a whole, largely because foreign demand declined as European agricultural output was restored. With bank loans hard to get, farmers sought aid in the fall of 1920 through the familiar device of the deposit of Treasury funds for crop loans or through the resumption of activities of the War Finance Corporation, which had suspended operations in May 1920. By a joint resolution, passed Jan. 4, 1921, over the President's veto, Congress revived the War Finance Corporation to finance the export of agricultural and other products. The volume of direct loans made annually by the War Finance Corporation rose from $45 million in 1920 to $112 million in 1921 and $196 million in 1922.

High-powered money continued to fall after the cyclical trough to January 1922, though a bit more slowly than before. All told, from its peak in October 1920 to its trough in January 1922, high-powered money fell 17 per cent. The only other declines of even roughly comparable magnitude in our series occurred from 1867 to 1870, as a result of the retirement of various Civil War currency issues; in 1933, when the public shifted back from currency to deposits after the reopening of the banks (see Chapter 8); and in 1948–49, when member bank reserves were reduced as a result of the Federal Reserve's policy of preventing a rise in the price of government bonds then in process of retirement (see Chapters 10 and 11). However, in each of these episodes the decline was only 11 per cent. No other decline from 1867 to 1960 is even half as large, including the decline from 1929 to 1930, early in the course of the Great Contraction, a contraction in which the fall in the stock of money was much larger. In the episode from October 1920 to January 1922, half the percentage reduction in the money stock that would have been produced by the decline in high-powered money alone was offset by a rise in the deposit-currency ratio. In the 1929–33 episode, the effect on the money stock of an initial decline in high-powered money was multiplied by a subsequent decline in the deposit-currency ratio, and the continued decline in that ratio much more than offset a subsequent rise in high-powered money.

The price and output movements of the post-World War I years in this country were, of course, part of a worldwide movement. Throughout most of the world, for victors, vanquished, and neutral alike, prices rose sharply before or into 1920 and fell sharply thereafter. About the only countries that avoided the price decline were those that were to experience hyperinflation. Though many national currencies—and among them some of the most important, like the pound sterling and the French franc—were not rigidly tied either to gold or to the dollar, central bank policies nevertheless produced linkages sufficiently strong to result in a common movement of prices in most national currencies. Flexible exchange rates were regarded as a transitory expedient pending a return to gold, and monetary authorities everywhere sought to facilitate such a return to fixed parities. The results were therefore similar to those that would have been experienced with fixed parities. The monetary actions, taken by authorities anxious to stabilize exchange rates as a step in the return to gold, transmitted the effect of movements in balances of trade and in capital in much the same way that gold flows would have done under a fully operative gold standard.

The Federal Reserve Board emphasized the international character of the price movements in justifying its own policies during that period.[58]

[58] *Annual Report* for 1920, pp. 6–17; 1921, p. 1.

It argued that changes in U.S. prices were effect rather than cause, that the Reserve Board was powerless to do more than adapt to them, and that the Board's policies had prevented financial panic at home and moderated the price changes. Its position was somewhat disingenuous. The United States had by that time become a substantial factor in the world at large and could no longer be regarded as dancing to the tune of the rest of the world. Moreover, since the dollar was linked to many currencies by flexible exchange rates, U.S. prices could move independently to some extent. Finally, there is evidence that changes in U.S. prices were the source of price changes elsewhere. This is certainly suggested by gold movements. The United States lost gold from mid-1919 to early 1920—the result to be expected if rising prices in this country were a source of price rises elsewhere—and the United States gained gold thereafter, at first slowly, then from the end of 1920 on, more rapidly—again the result to be expected if U.S. price declines were a source of other declines. These gold movements are not decisive, since they were affected also by capital movements, and U.S. capital exports to Europe declined sharply in 1920 and again in 1921, but they are most suggestive.

The extraordinary disturbances of the World War I period certainly induced national and international adjustments in the use of real resources on a far larger scale than is usual, and were unquestionably a source of uncertainty. Those disturbances might well have made it impossible to avoid a more than usually severe cyclical movement in this country, though our experience after World War II demonstrates that this result need not follow. But there can be little doubt that Federal Reserve policy was a further and not unimportant factor contributing to the severity of the movement. An earlier rise in discount rates would, at the very least, have moderated the inflationary price rise in 1919. In and of itself, such a moderation would have lessened the severity of the contraction that followed. Given the mistake in 1919, it was probably another mistake to raise the discount rates a further notch in June 1920, and it was certainly a mistake to maintain those rates so long. Though easier money in the second half of 1920 might not have prevented a sizable price decline, it certainly would have moderated its magnitude. The monetary structure was peculiarly sensitive to Federal Reserve policy, since member bank borrowings exceeded their reserve balances until late 1921. And the price movements were probably also peculiarly sensitive to the state of the money market, given the unusually important role played by inventories in the cycle.

The reserve position of the System seems inadequate justification for the policy followed. In the first place, it would never have become as tight as it did except for the easy money policy of 1919. In the second place, it improved so rapidly after late 1920 that it almost surely would have improved even with a much easier policy. In the third place, the Board had the legal power at any time to suspend the reserve requirements temporarily at only negligible cost.[59]

It is interesting to speculate on what the course of events would have been if the Federal Reserve Act had not been passed.

Up to our entry into the war, there would have been only a minor difference. Most of the monetary expansion of that period was produced by the gold inflow, which would have come in any event. In the absence of the Federal Reserve, gold inflows would not have been supplemented by additional fiduciary money, so that high-powered money would have risen about 10 to 15 per cent less than it did and, presumably, so also would the stock of money and prices.

During the active participation of the United States in the war, some substitute would almost certainly have been found for Federal Reserve credit—some equivalent for greenbacks to finance part of government expenditures. But in the absence of the reduction in reserve requirements produced by the act and amendments to it, a given amount of money creation to finance government expenditures would have had a smaller effect on the total money stock. It seems likely, therefore, that monetary expansion and the associated price rise would have been less from March 1917 to May 1919 than they were in fact. But, again, the difference would not have been very great.

The major difference would have come after the war. Monetary expansion would almost certainly have come to an end when heavy government borrowing ended in the second quarter of 1919, and prices would almost surely have reached their peak about the same time. Under comparable circumstances in the Civil War, prices reached their peak slightly before the end of the war. The final spurt in prices in 1919–20 would therefore not have occurred. It is harder to say what would have happened instead. The final spurt might have been replaced by a more gradual rise if gold movements to this country had occurred; or there might have been a decline in prices if the money stock had remained relatively stable and velocity had declined under the altered circumstances, as it did under the actual ones.

[59] Section 11(c) of the Federal Reserve Act authorized the Federal Reserve Board "to suspend for a period not exceeding thirty days, and from time to time to renew such suspension for periods not exceeding fifteen days, any reserve requirements specified in this Act: *Provided,* That it shall establish a graduated tax upon the amounts by which the reserve requirements of this Act may be permitted to fall below the level hereinafter specified: *And provided further,* That when the gold reserve held against Federal reserve notes falls below forty per centum, the Federal Reserve Board shall establish a graduated tax of not more than one per centum per annum upon such deficiency until the reserves fall to thirty-two and one-half per centum . . . ."

A rough quantitative estimate can be made of these effects. Wholesale prices in May 1920 were 2.48 times their level in June 1914; the stock of money, 2.15 times its level in June 1914. Assume that (1) the increase in gold stock would have been the only source of increase in high-powered money from June 1914 to March 1917; (2) the increase in high-powered money would have been the same as it actually was from March 1917 to May 1919; (3) there would have been no change in high-powered money from May 1919 to May 1920; (4) the ratio of bank deposits to reserves would have remained at the same level as in June 1914; and (5) the ratio of deposits to currency would have behaved precisely as it did. The stock of money in May 1920 would then have been 1.74 times rather than 2.15 times its level in June 1914. If we suppose the 1920–14 price ratio were the same multiple of the money ratio as it was (2.48/2.15), then prices in May 1920 would have been 2.00 times their level in June 1914. The price rise, on these assumptions, would have been about two-thirds as large as it actually was. And this is, if anything, an overestimate. For one thing, a slower price rise would have meant a smaller increase in velocity during the war, hence a lower ratio of the price rise to the money rise. For another, we have not allowed for either the greater economic effectiveness of government money issues with a lower deposit-reserve ratio or for the likelihood that, in the absence of a ready-made new instrument for creating fiduciary money in a less than obvious fashion, there would have been greater pressure on government to refrain from money creation to finance expenditures. The only offset in the other direction suggested to us is the possibly adverse effect on velocity of the direct issue of government money instead of its indirect issue through the Federal Reserve System. Conceivably, the result could have been a more rapid rise in velocity than occurred, though we are inclined to doubt that the effect would have been appreciable.

The business cycle from 1919 to 1921 was the first real trial of the new system of monetary control introduced by the Federal Reserve Act. In its first years, the Federal Reserve System was powerless to offset the inflows of gold. During the active participation of the United States in the war, it could not be a free agent. Its poor performance in that trial is understandable. There was no strictly comparable American experience on which to base policy or judge the effect of actions designed to stimulate or retard monetary expansion. In particular, there was no evidence on the length of lag between action and effect. There was a natural, if regrettable, tendency to wait too long before stepping on the brake, as it were, then to step on the brake too hard, then, when that did not bring monetary expansion to a halt very shortly, to step on the brake yet again. The contemporaneous gold reserve ratio was a simple, easy guide; economic stability, a complex, subtle will-o'-the-wisp.

CHAPTER 6

The High Tide of the Reserve System, 1921–29

THE PERIOD from 1921 through 1929 is of especial interest for our purposes on a number of counts.

(1) It was characterized by fairly rapid economic growth without major contractions. Regarded at the time as a "new era," it seemed even more Elysian in retrospect during the major contractions that succeeded it.

(2) Developments in industry and finance modified the role of commercial banks. The character and distribution of bank assets changed markedly over the decade. Many banks engaged in side lines in addition to making loans and investments—principally fiduciary functions and the underwriting and distributing of securities. These changes affected the number and size of banks. The growing use of automobiles, the declining relative importance of agriculture, and the increasing size of firms impaired the position of small-town banks, and furthered the high rate of bank failures that was the most striking feature of the commercial banking system in this decade.

(3) The Federal Reserve System for the first time felt itself a free agent, relieved alike from the pressures of Treasury needs and of internal liquidity. Moreover, its own gold position plus prevailing international monetary conditions enforced recognition of the difference between its problems and those of earlier central banks. It had to face explicitly the need to develop criteria and standards of monetary policy to replace the automatic operation of the gold standard. One result was a conscious attempt, for perhaps the first time in monetary history, to use central-bank powers to promote internal economic stability as well as to preserve balance in international payments and to prevent and moderate strictly financial crises. In retrospect, we can see that this was a major step toward the assumption by government of explicit continuous responsibility for economic stability. As the decade wore on, the System took—and perhaps even more was given—credit for the generally stable conditions that prevailed, and high hopes were placed in the potency of monetary policy as then administered.

(4) This fact, the newness of the System, its own research activities, and the exclusive reliance on monetary policy to promote stability all

240

combined to produce an unusual amount of scholarly attention to the problems of the System. No other period of its operation has been subjected to such intensive and penetrating analysis.[1]

(5) The close of the period was marked by open conflict between the Federal Reserve Board and the Federal Reserve Banks over the technique for controlling stock market speculation. This was the crucial engagement in a struggle for power within the System that had always been potential and that was to lead in the course of the next few years to a near-complete shift of power from the Banks in general and the New York Bank in particular to the Board.

In discussing the period from 1921 through 1929, we shall first summarize the course of money, income, prices, and velocity; next, changes in commercial bank operations; then, what the Federal Reserve Board said about monetary policy; and finally, what the System did, with special attention to those actions which are recorded in the factors accounting for changes in the stock of money.

1. The Course of Money, Income, Prices, and Velocity

The decline of 1920–21, like earlier severe contractions, was followed by an extremely vigorous expansion. From the reference trough in July 1921 to the peak in May 1923, the Federal Reserve Board index of industrial production rose no less than 63 per cent, wholesale prices, 9 per cent, and the stock of money, 14 per cent (see Chart 16). The rise in industrial production no doubt overstates the rise in total real income. On the other hand, the available estimates of income understate the rise because they are on an annual basis, a particularly serious limitation for a movement that lasted in all only some twenty-two months. Yet even so, net national product in constant prices rose 23 per cent from calendar 1921 to calendar 1923.

The next six years, from 1923 to 1929, were years of relatively steady growth, interrupted by two recessions: one from May 1923 to July 1924, the other from October 1926 to November 1927. Both recessions were mild and moderately brief. Wholesale prices were fairly stable, fluctuating around a horizontal or slightly falling trend. The stock of money grew at a fairly steady rate until early 1928, after which it declined very slightly until the end of 1929 as a result of the restrictive monetary measures arising out of the Federal Reserve System's concern with the con-

[1] Especially noteworthy are: W. R. Burgess, *The Reserve Banks and the Money Market*, New York, Harper, 1927, and Winfield W. Riefler, *Money Rates and Money Markets in the United States*, New York, Harper, 1930, both studies by economists employed within the System; and H. L. Reed, *Federal Reserve Policy, 1921–1930*, New York, McGraw-Hill, 1930, and C. O. Hardy, *Credit Policies of the Federal Reserve System*, Washington, Brookings, 1932, both evaluations of Reserve policy by economists outside the System.

temporaneous stock market boom—a feature of the period which is not reflected in our chart but which had far-reaching effects on the conduct of monetary policy.

All in all, the period from the peak of the postwar inflation in 1920 to the cyclical peak in 1929 repeats with extraordinary fidelity, though in condensed time scale, the course of events of the two periods compared at the end of Chapter 4—1873–92 and 1892–1913. In all three cases, an initial sharp collapse was followed by a vigorous rebound and then a period of moderately steady growth. The similarity of those periods and the differences among them are summarized in Table 11, which repeats the entries for Table 9 and adds corresponding entries for the period 1920–29.

In terms of the rate of change per year, the 1920–21 contraction is by all odds the sharpest. Despite its brevity, it shows a greater decline in monetary magnitudes than do the other two. The much sharper fall in the stock of money was associated with a much sharper fall in money income, prices, and real income as well. The rebound, on the other hand, while more vigorous in real terms, in reaction to the more vigorous decline, was milder in both the stock of money and in prices.

Perhaps the most interesting feature of the comparison, as in our earlier comparison of the first two periods, is the difference between the behavior of money and real magnitudes during the periods of moderately stable growth. The rate of growth of real income, both total and per capita, was very similar; of prices, highly varied. Wholesale prices declined by 3½ per cent per year in the first period, rose by over 1½ per cent in the second, and declined by nearly 1 per cent per year in the third. Implicit prices declined by 2 per cent in the first period, rose by 2 per cent in the second, and were roughly unchanged in the third. Yet in all three stable-growth periods, total real income grew at a rate close to 3½ per cent per year and real income per capita at a rate between 1.3 and 2.0 per cent per year. These results reinforce our earlier conclusion that there seems to be no necessary relation between the direction of movement of prices over a period covering several business cycles and the corresponding secular rate of growth of real output. Apparently the steadiness of the price movement is far more important than its direction.

The difference between 1903–13 and 1923–29 in the behavior of prices is associated with an almost identical difference in the behavior of the stock of money: wholesale prices changed in 1923–29 at a rate 2.5 percentage points less than in 1903–13, and implicit prices at a rate 2.1 percentage points less; the stock of money changed at a rate 2.0 percentage points less.

As Table 11 shows, there is much less close agreement between price and monetary behavior in the first two periods. Though implicit prices

TABLE 11

COMPARISON OF THREE SIMILAR PERIODS IN AMERICAN MONETARY HISTORY: RATES OF
CHANGE IN VARIOUS MAGNITUDES DURING SEGMENTS OF THE PERIODS
1873–92, 1892–1913, AND 1920–29

SERIES AND PERIOD	SEGMENT OF:		
	Monetary Uncertainty or Monetary Contraction 1873–78 1892–96 1920–21	Rebound 1878–82 1896–1903 1921–23	Moderately Stable Growth 1882–92 1903–13 1923–29
	NUMBER OF YEARS		
Duration of segment			
1873–92	5	4	10
1892–1913	4	7	10
1920–29	1	2	6
	RATE OF CHANGE (per cent per year)		
Stock of money			
1873–92	−0.6	12.6	5.4
1892–1913	−1.0	9.9	6.0
1920–29	−5.7	5.4	4.0
Money income			
1873–92	0.9	9.6	1.5
1892–1913	−2.3	8.0	5.2
1920–29	−20.3	9.1	3.3
Wholesale prices			
1873–92	−7.6	4.3	−3.5
1892–1913	−2.9	3.5	1.6
1920–29	−45.9	1.5	−0.9
Price index implicit in real income			
1873–92	−4.3	1.2	−2.0
1892–1913	−2.2	2.0	2.0
1920–29	−16.0	−1.4	−0.1
Real income			
1873–92	5.2	8.4	3.5
1892–1913	−0.1	6.0	3.3
1920–29	−4.3	10.5	3.4
Real income per capita			
1873–92	2.9	6.2	1.3
1892–1913	−2.1	4.1	1.4
1920–29	−6.3	8.9	2.0
Velocity of money			
1873–92	1.5	−3.0	−3.9
1892–1913	−1.3	−1.9	−0.8
1920–29	−14.7	3.7	−0.7

NOTE: Rate of change is from initial to terminal value assuming continuous compounding; computed by dividing the difference between the natural logarithms of the terminal and initial values by the time interval between them.

SOURCE: Same as for Table 9.

changed from 1882 to 1892 at a rate 4.0 percentage points less than from 1903 to 1913, the stock of money changed at a rate only 0.6 percentage points less. The 3.4 percentage point discrepancy is accounted for arithmetically by a 0.2 percentage point higher rate of rise in real income and a 3.1 percentage point faster rate of decline in velocity, 1882–92. The division of the discrepancy between real income and velocity, as was suggested in Chapter 4, partly reflects deficiencies in the income data for the first period, and the size of the discrepancy itself may partly reflect deficiencies in the money and the price data. The close consilience for the two later periods, for which the data are clearly better, is some evidence in this direction.

2. *Changes in Commercial Bank Operations*

Important changes occurred in the role of commercial banks in the financial system during the decade under consideration. These were reflected in the character of their credit operations and in the number and size of banks. In 1914, 53 per cent of the total loans of commercial banks were classified as commercial, 33 per cent as security, and less than 14 per cent as real estate.[2] Real estate loans were so unimportant largely because national banks had not been permitted to make any real estate loans until the Act of 1913 establishing the Federal Reserve System, which even then relaxed restrictions only with respect to loans on farm land.[3] Instalment credit was hardly known. During the twenties, commercial loans declined markedly relative to loans on securities and on real estate. Loans by national banks on nonfarm real estate were encouraged by a 1916 amendment to the Federal Reserve Act and by the McFadden Act of 1927. Instalment finance companies, of which automobile finance companies were the most important, increased their loans received from large commercial banks. Businessmen's reluctance to become indebted to banks after their experience of loan liquidation in 1920–21 may have contributed to the decline in the relative importance of the commercial loan in the twenties. In any event, the combination in the years after 1921 of large profits and an eager demand for new issues by

---

[2] Computed from data in *All-Bank Statistics, United States, 1896–1955*, Board of Governors of the Federal Reserve System, Apr. 1959, p. 34. Loans denoted in source as "all other loans" (see *ibid.*, p. 86, for composition) are here referred to as "commercial loans."

[3] The term of these loans was limited to five years. For loans on farm land exceeding five years in length, the 12 district Federal Land Banks were organized in Feb. and Mar. 1917 under the Federal Farm Loan Act of July 17, 1916, the Treasury originally providing most of their capital of $9 million. Until 1933, the land banks, which were under the supervision of the Federal Farm Loan Board during that period, never financed more than 9 per cent of all new farm mortgage loans.

244

the securities market made possible internal and external financing not involving bank loans. By 1929, 45 per cent of the total loans of commercial banks were classified as commercial, 38 per cent as security, and 17 per cent as real estate.

Investments of commercial banks rose from 29 per cent of their loans in 1914 to 42 per cent in 1919, fell back to 29 per cent in 1920, then rose again to fluctuate around a level of 40 per cent from 1922 to 1929.[4] The rise during World War I occurred despite the financing of the federal government deficit principally through sales of government securities to the nonbanking public rather than directly to banks (see Chapter 5). Banks participated indirectly, by extending loans to customers on the collateral of government securities. Yet they also purchased enough federal government securities themselves to account for the major part of the wartime rise in the ratio of investments to loans. The higher level during the twenties than before the war was accounted for partly by increased holdings of federal government securities, partly by increased holdings of state and municipal, corporate, and foreign securities.

The higher level of investments may have reflected partly the operations of security underwriting and distributing companies that were then affiliated with commercial banks. Through the organization of so-called affiliates, commercial banks in most of the principal cities became, in effect, wholesalers and retailers of stocks and bonds. Affiliates began by issuing bonds, then financed and issued, first, preferred stock and, finally, common stock and also became direct buyers of stock which they held for a speculative rise.

In addition to combining the function of investment distribution with that of credit extension, commercial banks intensified their exercise of fiduciary functions after the Federal Reserve Act and a wartime amendment recognized the right of national banks to engage in any kind of trust function. In an effort to attract banks to their respective jurisdictions, the state and national banking systems engaged in a competitive relaxation of charter requirements and of the limitations imposed on banking activities.

These developments in banking were part of the general surge of financial activity so distinctive of the twenties. The main features of the financial activity, which culminated in the great stock market boom, were the public flotation on a large scale of foreign securities for the first time in U.S. history, and a widening shift by domestic concerns from bank loans to public issue of bonds and stocks as a means of raising funds. One result of these developments was that they apparently led to a reduction in the average quality of credit outstanding, in the sense that the securities

[4] Computed from data in *All-Bank Statistics*, pp. 34–35.

issued and the loans made in the late twenties experienced a larger frequency of default and foreclosure than those issued in the early twenties.[5] Partly, the difference reflected simply the larger number of economically prosperous years available to the early than to the late borrowers for repaying their loans in whole or in part and for using the borrowed funds to strengthen their economic position. But various attempts to allow for this bias suggest that it does not account in full for the difference in subsequent experience.[6] The high prosperity of the twenties and the spreading belief in a new era understandably led to an increasingly optimistic

---

[5] For a summary of the evidence, see Geoffrey H. Moore, "The Quality of Credit in Booms and Depressions," *Journal of Finance,* May 1956, pp. 292, 294–296.

[6] The most persuasive evidence is that for foreign government bonds analyzed by Ilse Mintz (*Deterioration in the Quality of Foreign Bonds Issued in the United States, 1920–1930,* New York, NBER, 1951, esp. pp. 34–40). Mintz allows for the bias by classifying bonds as sound or defaulted according to the status of the borrower in 1937 rather than according to the date of the particular issue. If the borrower had an issue in default in 1937, she treats all bonds issued by that borrower as defaulted in calculating her "default index," even if some issues had in fact been fully repaid at an earlier date. The method is fully satisfactory only if many or most borrowers borrowed in all periods contrasted. For example, if each borrower sold only one bond issue, the adjustment would be meaningless. For foreign government bonds, the number of borrowers was small compared with the number of issues, so the method is feasible. Moreover, the difference in experience is so great in the adjusted data that it cannot easily be attributed to the bias referred to.

In his analysis of domestic corporate bonds, W. Braddock Hickman (*Corporate Bond Quality and Investor Experience,* Princeton for NBER, 1958, pp. 104–107) attempts to adjust for the bias by comparing the default experience of bonds in good standing on Jan. 1, 1930, rather than of all bonds issued. The adjustment is far less satisfactory than the method used by Mintz. Hickman argues that the calculation is biased in the opposite direction to that suggested in the text, because "issues that, by reason of their high quality, were called and refunded during the late twenties are automatically excluded." He gives no evidence, however, to support the assumption implicit in limiting the sample to bonds in good standing on Jan. 1, 1930, as a technique for eliminating the possible bias in using ex post results to judge ex ante differences in quality. The assumption is that for equal ex ante quality, the date of a bond's issue in the twenties, and hence its age during the years 1930–35, made no difference in its ex post performance. To us, on the contrary, it seems not implausible to suppose that the relative default experience of issues of different age would vary in ordinary times, and that under extremely adverse circumstances, such as the Great Contraction, the spread would be much greater. Whatever may be the final verdict on the general effect of the age of a bond on the probability of default under normal conditions, Hickman's adjustment does nothing to correct for the greater opportunity that the earlier borrowers had to use the loans under favorable circumstances to strengthen their economic position. It is as if, in studying mortality during an epidemic, one were to compare the deaths of children 10 years old and 5 years old at its onset by expressing the mortality as a fraction of the number of 10-year olds and 5-year olds living at its onset, rather than by expressing total mortality before and during the epidemic as a fraction of the number born 10 and 5 years earlier. The former calculation would indeed eliminate the effect of the greater exposure of 10-year olds to the risk of death at earlier ages; but it would in no way eliminate the

246

evaluation of the prospects of repayment and hence to an increasing readiness to lend on a given project or collateral.

Of course, hindsight is better than foresight. Given the disastrous collapse from 1929 to 1933, the evaluations of the late twenties were unduly optimistic. Returns to lenders of the time were not high enough to compensate for the risk. But it does not follow that the lenders were wrong in those circumstances any more than the fact that a man loses a wager demonstrates that the wager was a bad one. The collapse from 1929 to 1933 was neither foreseeable nor inevitable. It could, in fact, have been greatly moderated by policies that there was every reason in advance to expect would be followed, as we shall see in the next chapter. If they had been followed, the lenders might well have been justified. Even though loans made during the later twenties might still have experienced a greater frequency of default and foreclosure than those made during the earlier twenties, they might have yielded as much as their purchasers expected them to on the average.[7]

---

difference arising from the different capacity of youngsters of different ages to withstand disease.

Agency ratings cited by Hickman (p. 179) give evidence of a moderate reduction in average quality of bonds issued, primarily for bonds offered in the two years 1928 and 1929. The evidence from ratings might be expected to be biased in the direction opposite to the bias of the evidence from subsequent experience. Hence, it seems to us much more persuasive. It is clear from both kinds of evidence that the decline in quality was notably less in domestic bonds than in foreign government bonds.

[7] Interest rates on high-grade securities fell during the twenties, and so apparently did the risk premium during at least the later twenties (see Mintz, *Deterioration in the Quality of Foreign Bonds*, p. 70). But this need not contradict the statement in the text; it may simply mean that there was a shift of demand on the part of investors involving a change in tastes but not mistaken expectations.

It is a widespread economic fallacy to believe that higher average quality is necessarily better both for society and for the individual lender than lower average quality is. This is no more true of credit than of other services or of commodities. The opposite view that what we always need is more venturesomeness or more risk capital is not true either, though there are many who simultaneously hold both views without recognizing that they are mutually contradictory. Quality must be balanced against quantity or, what is equivalent, against cost. For credit, uniformly high quality can be obtained only by limiting the capital market to an extremely small role in the economy, which would probably greatly reduce the economy's productivity and efficiency. It is at least as plausible to say that the difficulties in the early thirties reflected the unduly high standards of quality then imposed by lenders—especially by the supposed "lender of last resort," the Federal Reserve System—as to say that they were the aftermath of unduly low standards imposed in the late twenties. Or, to put it differently, the effect of the widespread imposition of higher standards during the twenties would have been higher interest rates paid by borrowers and a lower volume of investment. As it was, there was no inflationary pressure during the twenties as judged by commodity prices. The result might therefore have been a lower level of output and a lower rate of growth.

The minutes of meetings of the board of directors of the Federal Reserve Bank

A lowering of credit quality affected assets of the kind acquired by commercial banks as well as those acquired by other lenders—notably, foreign government bonds, domestic municipal and other bonds, and urban mortgages.[8] However, there was a force working in the opposite direction which may have offset the effect. Commercial banks were under heavy reserve pressure during the final years of the twenties and were almost surely extending a decreasing fraction of all credit outstanding. Consequently, an enforced higher selectivity may have offset any decline in the average quality of assets available (see further discussion in Chapter 7, section 3). If the net outcome was indeed a decline in the average quality of commercial bank assets, such a decline may have contributed a mite to the banking collapse of the early thirties, not by making such a collapse inevitable or even likely, but by opening the way for mistakes in monetary policy and by making the monetary system more vulnerable to such mistakes.

Cyclical fluctuations in credit quality, arising out of fluctuations in the standards used by lenders to assess risk and by borrowers to assess the prospects of ventures, may well play a part in the cyclical process. But it is the fluctuations, not the level of credit quality, that play a part; and it is fluctuations in the *standards,* not in the ex post outcome, that alone are a separate contribution of the credit mechanism toward the amplification of disturbances. Fluctuations in the ex post outcome without a change in standards are a consequence of other forces, and will have their impacts in turn elsewhere; they involve simply the transmission of impulses through the credit mechanism. In the 1929–33 episode, changes in the ex post outcome were far more dramatic than in the standards adopted.

---

of New York during the early thirties contain numerous criticisms of commercial banks for their alleged unwillingness to assume risks in investing their funds (see the George Leslie Harrison Papers on the Federal Reserve System, Columbia University Library, described in Chap. 5, footnote 41 and accompanying text, Harrison, Notes, Vols. I–III).

[8] For urban mortgages, Carl F. Behrens shows that foreclosure rates on loans closed in the later twenties were four times greater for number and eight times greater for amount of loans (based on a sample of loans made by 116 commercial banks) than in the early twenties (*Commercial Bank Activities in Urban Mortgage Financing,* New York, NBER, 1952, p. 62). J. E. Morton obtained results roughly similar to those shown by Behrens in the two periods for a somewhat different sample of two classes of commercial bank mortgage loans on nonfarm properties, homes and income-producing properties (*Urban Mortgage Lending: Comparative Markets and Experience,* Princeton for NBER, 1956, pp. 98–101). Fully amortized commercial bank loans of the later twenties on nonfarm homes, however, had a better foreclosure record than similar loans of the early twenties, and only a slightly higher loss rate (pp. 103, 114). The results of both these studies are strongly affected by the bias discussed in footnote 6. The results could be entirely consistent with an absence of change in the ex ante quality of mortgages, the entire difference in results reflecting instead the circumstances of the year in which the mortgage came due. Neither author tests that possibility satisfactorily.

The number of commercial banks rose from 27,000 in 1914 to 30,000 in 1921 but then began to decline, falling below 25,000 in 1929. In part, the decline reflected mergers. In part, however, it also reflected an extremely high failure rate. Whereas about 500 commercial banks suspended from 1915 through 1920, nearly 6,000 did from 1921 through 1929.[9] During the later years there was an average of at least one bank suspension a day in every year and of as many as 2.7 bank suspensions a day in one year (1926). A large fraction of all banks that suspended during the period had capital of $25,000 or less and were located in towns of 2,500 or less, largely situated in seven western grain states.

These failures had no connection with the possible decline in quality of credit just discussed. They were primarily explained by improvements in transportation and increase in urbanization, which benefited the large banks at the expense of the small, and by the agricultural difficulties of the twenties.

3. Development of Monetary Policy

During the contraction of 1920–21, monetary policy was apparently dominated by the gold reserve position of the Federal Reserve System (see Chapter 5, above). The combination of a decline in the stock of money and a large influx of gold relieved the pressure on reserves. By the end of 1921, the System's gold holdings were 65 per cent of its note and deposit liabilities. For the rest of the decade, the only problem about the reserve percentage that concerned the System was how to keep it down by means other than monetary expansion.[10]

The annual reports of the Board from 1921 to the end of the decade contain only two reasonably full-dress discussions of the general role of the Federal Reserve System and of the principles of monetary policy: the first, in the report for 1921; the second, and rightly the more celebrated, in the *Tenth Annual Report* for 1923.

THE 1921 *Annual Report* ON PRINCIPLES OF MONETARY POLICY

The first was clearly defensive and contains little of interest for our purposes. "During the past year," says the report, "many things have been said and written regarding the Federal Reserve System which are cal-

[9] Figures on number of banks, *All-Bank Statistics,* p. 37; on suspensions, unpublished FDIC revisions of FDIC, *Annual Report,* 1934, p. 93, and *Federal Reserve Bulletin,* Sept. 1937, pp. 868, 873 (see source note to Part I of Table 16, below). The number of suspensions before 1921 is not strictly comparable with the number after, because they are from different sources. The figure for the later years includes temporary as well as permanent suspensions, whereas the figure for the earlier years excludes at least some temporary suspensions.

[10] For example, the expedient of paying out gold certificates instead of Federal Reserve notes was adopted with this end in view. See Benjamin Strong, *Interpretations of Federal Reserve Policy,* W. Randolph Burgess, ed., New York, Harper, 1930, pp. 300–302; Lester V. Chandler, *Benjamin Strong, Central Banker,* Washington, Brookings, 1958, pp. 192–193.

culated to create entirely false impressions." Accordingly, a section entitled "Fundamental Principles of the Federal Reserve Act" was included "in order that a clearer idea may be presented of the principles which govern the policies of the Federal Reserve Board and the operations of the Federal Reserve Banks."[11] The section contains much competent material on the details of Federal Reserve operations; very little on the major issues of Federal Reserve policy.

It is hard to escape the conclusion that much of this section is disingenuous, designed to turn aside the criticisms without either meeting them or making explicit misstatements. The device adopted to this end is a selective analysis that concentrates on details and emphasizes the impotence of the System. For example, in the whole nine-page section, neither the words "discount rate" nor any synonyms occur, although there is much sophisticated discussion of discounting, and although an earlier section of the same report dealing with changes in discount rates during 1921 describes "control over discount rates" as "an important and far-reaching power."[12] This omission and the general tone and content were surely intentional.[13]

[11] Federal Reserve Board, *Annual Report* for 1921, p. 90.

[12] *Annual Report* for 1921, p. 30. Consider, as another example, the following excerpt from a subsection, Federal Reserve Note Issues: "There are some who appear to have an impression that the Federal Reserve Board has the power to expand or contract the currency of the country at will . . . . An increase or decrease in the volume of Federal Reserve notes outstanding is not the result of any preordained policy or premeditated design, for the volume of Federal Reserve notes in circulation depends entirely upon the activity of business or upon the kind of activity which calls for currency rather than book credits . . . . The increased volume of Federal Reserve notes in circulation from 1917 to the end of the year 1920 was, in so far as it was not the result of direct exchanges for gold and gold certificates, the effect of advancing wages and prices and not their cause, just as the reduction which has taken place during the past year is the result of lower prices and smaller volume of business, rather than their cause" (*ibid.*, pp. 96–98).

Taken literally, the statement can be defended as correct, but only because it restricts attention to *notes* and says nothing about the total volume of Federal Reserve credit or the connection between deposits and currency.

As implied by the absence of the words discount rate, nothing at all is said in the discussion of Fundamental Principles about the criteria for determining discount rates or about the effect of the level of discount rates on the total level of Federal Reserve credit. Yet, in the earlier section of the report dealing with changes in discount rates during 1921, it is noted that higher discount rates were necessary in 1920 because "it was evident that a continuance of the wartime policy of abnormally low rates would result in disaster to the public, the member banks and the Federal Reserve Banks alike" (p. 32).

A final example is the comment, "As the Federal Reserve Banks are made the sole custodians of the legal reserves of all member banks . . . it is necessary that Federal Reserve Banks should keep themselves in a 'liquid' position; that is, their bills discounted must be of short maturity and should be readily collectible" (pp. 93–94).

[13] It is a natural human tendency to take credit for good outcomes and seek to avoid the blame for bad. One amusing dividend from reading through the annual

THE *Tenth Annual Report* ON PRINCIPLES OF MONETARY POLICY

The discussion in the *Tenth Annual Report* (for 1923) is on an altogether different intellectual level.[14] The discussion of Federal Reserve actions during the year provided the occasion for raising general issues about open market operations, their role in general policy, and their relation to discounting. The report emphasizes the need for relating open market operations to the general credit policy of the System and of coordinating the actions of the separate Banks. It demonstrates, on the basis of experience during 1922 and 1923, the tendency of open market purchases to reduce the volume of discounting and open market sales to increase it—the so-called scissors effect. This was the first explicit recognition of the coordinate importance of open market operations and rediscounting for general credit policy, although the System had earlier recognized the effects of its purchases and sales on the money market. The report provides a rationalization for the open market committee, which had been tentatively organized in 1922, and reorganized in 1923, after purchases by individual Banks to obtain earnings had demonstrated both the general credit effects of such purchases and the need for coordination.[15]

---

reports of the Federal Reserve Board seriatim is the sharpness of the cyclical pattern in the potency attributed to the System. In years of prosperity, monetary policy is said to be a potent instrument, the skillful handling of which deserves credit for the favorable course of events; in years of adversity, monetary policy is said to have little leeway but is largely the consequence of other forces, and it was only the skillful handling of the exceedingly limited powers available that prevented conditions from being even worse.

[14] This annual report covers the first full year (1923) for which Walter W. Stewart was director of research, and it seems likely that he played an important part in formulating it.

[15] From Oct. 1921 to May 1922 the Reserve Banks individually bought approximately $400 million in government securities to obtain earnings without apparent concern for the influence of those purchases on the money market. Their uncoordinated operations disturbed the government securities market, and the Banks organized in May 1922 a committee of governors from eastern Reserve Banks to execute joint purchases and sales and to avoid conflicts with orders for Treasury account. In the spring of 1923 that committee was superseded by the Open Market Investment Committee for the Federal Reserve System, appointed by the Board with the same five members, and future operations were placed under the general supervision of the Board. Beginning Dec. 1923, a System account was established, with pro-rata allocations of transactions to the district Banks. Individual Banks still engaged in independent operations which the Committee executed on their behalf, but they were generally small in amount.

Coordination of open market operations through the new committee was regarded by Governor Strong and the other Bank governors as a voluntary agreement, with individual Banks retaining the legal right to engage in open market operations on their own initiative. That view was shared by some and probably a majority of the members of the Board. However, at least one member, Adolph Miller, expressed the view that the Board had the power to control in detail the open market operations of individual Banks. The issue was never pressed to a final decision (see Chandler, *Benjamin Strong*, pp. 221–228; Charles S. Hamlin,

The most significant part of the report is a ten-page section entitled "Guides to Credit Policy," which presents a highly subtle and sophisticated analysis of the problem of devising criteria to replace the gold-reserve ratio. The section is hard to summarize concisely. It has an indefiniteness befitting its main thesis: that there is no simple test such as the reserve ratio, the exchange rate, or a price-index number that can serve as an adequate guide for policy;[16] that policy "is and must be a matter of judgment,"[17] based on the fullest possible range of evidence about changes in production, trade, employment, prices and commodity stocks. Great emphasis is placed on the distinction between "productive" and "speculative" use of credit. The major test of the "good functioning of the economic system" is "equilibrium" between production of goods and

Hamlin Papers, Manuscript Division, Library of Congress, Diary, Vol. 8, May 29, 1924, pp. 169–170; Vol. 10, Mar. 29, 1925, pp. 134–137; Vol. 11, Mar. 20, 1926, pp. 124–125; Vol. 13, Apr. 24, 1927, pp. 155–157).

The composition of the Committee continued unchanged until Mar. 1930, when interior Banks were successful in broadening it to include a representative from each Reserve Bank, and it was renamed the Open Market Policy Conference (see Chap. 7, sect. 5).

The subordination of earnings needs to general credit considerations for open market operations was formally agreed upon by the Bank governors at the end of 1922, though they continued to regard earnings as relevant. That position was also recommended by the Federal Advisory Council as early as mid-1922. Some members of the Board, however, notably Hamlin, continued for years to urge that earnings needs were relevant, and that it was against the intent of the original Federal Reserve Act to subordinate them. And, from time to time, a Bank would cite earnings needs in connection with some proposed action (see Chandler, *Benjamin Strong*, pp. 213–222; Hamlin Diary, Vol. 7, Oct. 13, 1922, pp. 3–8; Vol. 8, May 7 and 23, 1924, pp. 131–133, 136–137).

The 1924 Federal Reserve *Annual Report* was the last one to refer to Reserve Bank credit as "earning assets" of the System. At the Governors Conference in May 1924, the "importance of conducting open market operations without considering earnings of Reserve Banks as a determining factor" was a topic on the agenda. In Apr. 1925, in connection with the Kansas City Bank's failure at the time to earn its expenses, the question was raised again whether a Bank might buy governments without reference to the Open Market Investment Committee. "Governor Strong then referred to the fact that the Open Market Investment Committee proposed at this conference to recommend a redistribution of its present holdings for the purpose of meeting just such a difficulty" (Harrison, Governors, Vol. I).

[16] It is interesting that one "simple test" omitted from consideration is a steady rate of change in the stock of money. A policy along these lines was apparently urged by Carl Snyder of the New York Federal Reserve Bank ("New Measures in the Equation of Exchange," *American Economic Review*, Mar. 1924, pp. 709, 712–713, implies the desirability of such a policy without explicitly urging it); also by Reed (*Federal Reserve Policy, 1921–1930*, pp. 63, 198–201). It is noteworthy that in his earlier book (*The Development of Federal Reserve Policy*, New York, Houghton Mifflin, 1922), Reed favored a policy and presented an analysis similar to those in the section under discussion of the *Tenth Annual Report*. The main difference is that Reed placed no special emphasis on movements in inventories.

[17] *Tenth Annual Report* (for 1923), p. 32.

their consumption. The danger is that credit will be used to finance the speculative accumulation of commodity stocks, which in turn will produce a disequilibrium between production and consumption and subsequently a contraction in prices and economic activity. "[T]here will be little danger that the credit created and contributed by the Federal reserve banks will be in excessive volume if restricted to productive uses."[18] This marriage of the traditional real bills doctrine and an inventory theory of the business cycle was doubtless inspired by the 1920–21 episode.

Despite the skill and acuity with which this section of the report is written, it is yet most unsatisfactory as a guide to credit policy. The requisite "judgment" cannot be based on factual evidence alone. The evidence must be interpreted and the likely effects of alternative courses of action predicted. On all this the section offers little beyond glittering generalities instructing the men exercising the judgment to do the right thing at the right time with only the vaguest indications of what is the right thing to do. And as Hardy points out, even these vague indications are ambiguous or contradictory. The "needs of trade" doctrine explicit in the section on credit policy pretty clearly implies that the System

. . . should adapt its policy to the changing cyclical situation just as it does to the changing seasonal situation, curtailing credit when business declines and expanding it when business expands . . . . This line of analysis points to the conclusion that it is not the business of the Reserve system to stimulate business by making money artificially cheap in periods of depression or dear in periods of boom, but merely to adapt itself to conditions as it finds them . . . . On the other hand, in a different connection . . . [the view is expressed in the same annual report] that it is the business of the Reserve system to work against extremes either of deflation or inflation and not merely to adapt itself passively to the ups and downs of business.[19]

The ambiguity of the section is illustrated by the contrast between Reed's and Hardy's interpretations of Federal Reserve easing actions in 1924. Reed regarded those actions as an abandonment of the principles set forth in this section; Hardy, in his slightly later analysis, as consistent with them.[20]

Despite the importance assigned to the distinction between speculative and productive uses of credit, little attention is given to the problem that subsequently became the focal point of Federal Reserve policy: stock market speculation. The 1920–21 experience had made speculation in commodities rather than in securities seem to be the chief danger.

Comments on general credit policy are all much briefer and less sys-

[18] *Tenth Annual Report*, p. 34.
[19] Hardy, *Credit Policies*, pp. 78–80. See also Clark Warburton, "Monetary Control Under the Federal Reserve Act," *Political Science Quarterly*, Dec. 1946, pp. 505–534, esp. pp. 523–524.
[20] Reed, *Federal Reserve Policy*, p. 60; Hardy, *Credit Policies*, pp. 79–81.

tematic in subsequent annual reports. (Most other public statements repeat the position expressed in the *Tenth Annual Report*.) The one important addition was the application of the doctrine to speculation in securities and the extraordinary amount of attention devoted to the stock market boom, particularly in 1928 and 1929, though it was not until the 1929 report that emphasis was shifted predominantly to security speculation.

THE DISPUTE OVER CONTROL OF SPECULATION BY "DIRECT PRESSURE"

The stock market boom produced severe disagreement within the System on policy, generally oversimplified as a difference between the Federal Reserve Board and the Federal Reserve Bank of New York.[21] The question at issue between the Board and the New York Bank in 1928–29 had provoked controversy as far back as late 1919, when the Board, at the Treasury's behest, refused to sanction increases in the discount rate and instead urged the Banks to use "direct pressure"—in the language of the 1929 and later annual reports—to prevent overborrowing by member banks (see Chapter 5). The question arose again in October 1925, when Walter W. Stewart, surprisingly in view of his presumed authorship of the *Tenth Annual Report* (for 1923), seems to have recommended direct pressure. Governor Strong disagreed, pointing out that direct pressure could not succeed in New York unless the Federal Reserve Bank refused to discount for banks carrying speculative loans, and that it would mean rationing of credit, "which would be disastrous."[22] In May 1928, Adolph Miller, the economist on the Board, demanded that the presidents of the large New York banks be assembled and warned that speculative activity must be reduced, although a few months later, he was no longer in favor of such a warning.[23]

Both the Board and the Federal Reserve Bank of New York agreed that security speculation was cause for concern. The difference was about the desirability of "qualitative" techniques of control designed to induce banks to discriminate against loans for speculative purposes. The *Tenth Annual Report* section on "guides to credit policy" had emphasized the impossibility of controlling the ultimate use of Reserve credit, and other reports had repeatedly noted the same point. Nevertheless, the view attributed to the Board was that direct pressure was a feasible means of restricting the availability of credit for speculative purposes without unduly

[21] *Operation of the National and Federal Reserve Banking Systems,* Hearings before a subcommittee of the Senate Committee on Banking and Currency pursuant to S. Res. 71 (Jan. 19–30, 1931), 71st Cong., 3d sess., part 1, p. 71, testimony of Governor George L. Harrison of the New York Reserve Bank; Hardy, *Credit Policies,* p. 132.
[22] Hamlin Diary, Vol. 11, Oct. 16 and 27, 1925, pp. 25, 29.
[23] Hamlin Diary, Vol. 14, May 1 and July 28, 1928, pp. 159–160, 193.

restricting its availability for productive purposes, whereas rises in discount rates or open market sales sufficiently severe to curb speculation would be too severe for business in general. The Board's unwillingness to approve a rise in discount rates was partly, no doubt, a reaction to the severe criticism the System had suffered for the 1920–21 deflation. The Board's view prevailed until August 1929, when it finally permitted the New York Bank to raise its discount rate. By then the New York Bank believed the time might have passed for such action.

The dispute between the Board and the New York Bank largely paralyzed monetary policy during almost the whole of the important year 1929. In addition, it was probably the crucial engagement in the struggle for power within the System. Always potential, the struggle became active from time to time. It was ultimately resolved by an almost complete shift of power from the Banks, and particularly the New York Bank, originally the dominant center in the System, to the Board, now still in control. So long as Benjamin Strong was alive, his unquestioned preeminence kept the struggle submerged, though it did not prevent much dissatisfaction and muttering, mostly by members of the Board but to some extent also by representatives of other Banks.[24] Strong's death in October 1928, preceded by a few months of inactivity, triggered a phase of overt conflict. The results were important not only for the year 1929, but also for the conduct of policy during the subsequent economic contraction, as we shall see in more detail in the next chapter.

The active conflict centered on stock market speculation only because that happened to be the most convenient immediate issue. Failing that, some other issue would almost surely have served equally well as the occasion for conflict; indeed, the initial skirmishes were not on the main battleground at all. One skirmish involved the composition and control of the Open Market Investment Committee. The Board proposed to expand the committee from five Bank governors to include all twelve, a proposal approved by at least some of the governors and finally adopted

[24] With respect to initial conflicts between the Banks and the Board in the first several years of the System's operation, see Chandler, *Benjamin Strong*, pp. 68–76. In Oct. 1919, Hamlin reports that Carter Glass, then Secretary of the Treasury and hence ex-officio chairman of the Board, had said that "Governor Strong was trying to dominate [the] Treasury and Federal Reserve Board" (Hamlin Diary, Vol. 5, Oct. 28, 1919, p. 44). On this episode, see also Chandler, p. 163.

In Jan. 1925, George James, a member of the Board, reported Herbert Hoover's telling him that President Coolidge was much disturbed because he feared the Board was dominated in open market policies by the Federal Reserve Bank of New York. Yet when Coolidge reappointed Daniel Crissinger governor of the Federal Reserve Board in May 1925, Governor Harding [former governor of the Federal Reserve Board, then governor of the Boston Federal Reserve Bank] thought Governor Strong got Crissinger his redesignation, because Strong dominated him (Hamlin Diary, Vol. 5, Jan. 27 and June 15, 1925, pp. 65, 141). See also Chap. 7, sect. 5, below.

in March 1930. The Board also announced in effect that it would control the operations of the committee in much more detail than before.[25] A second skirmish involved the power of the New York Bank to make minor changes in its buying rates for bills (i.e., bankers' acceptances—not Treasury bills) without prior approval of the Board. This was apparently the first personal test of strength between George L. Harrison (appointed governor of the New York Bank to succeed Strong in November 1928, after having served as a deputy governor since 1920) and Roy A. Young (governor of the Reserve Board since 1927). Harrison was the clear victor. He stood firm, cited overwhelming precedents, and forced Young to back down.[26] Incidentally, of the Board members, Young himself was one of the least enthusiastic proponents of direct pressure. He was a reluctant follower rather than a prime mover, perhaps because of his earlier experience as governor of the Federal Reserve Bank of Minneapolis.

The main battle was joined on security speculation. The Harrison Papers and the Hamlin Diary make clear the division between the

[25] At the first meetings of the Open Market Investment Committee and the Governors Conference after Strong's death (in mid-Nov. 1928—the committee first met separately and then in a joint session with the other governors), the Board submitted for discussion a proposed revision of the arrangements for conduct of open market operations along lines suggested by the Federal Advisory Council in Sept. 1928 (Federal Reserve Board, *Annual Report* for 1928, p. 229: "The Advisory Council without any intention of criticizing the present arrangements but in order that all governors of the Federal reserve banks may participate in the discussions leading up to actions of the open-market committee suggests to the Federal Reserve Board to consider the advisability of having the membership of the open-market committee consist of all the governors of the Federal reserve banks with an executive committee composed of five members with full power to act"). The Board delayed for nearly two weeks its reply to the recommendations the Open Market Investment Committee made at the Nov. 1928 meeting. Departing from its *pro forma* acknowledgment and approval of earlier recommendations of the committee, the Board disapproved the recommendations. In effect, it asserted its authority to approve or disapprove each individual act of purchase or sale as well as the general program and policy. The committee, at its next meeting, Jan. 7, 1929, expressed great concern about the reply, which it interpreted as a major change in the Board's policies (Harrison, Open Market, Vol. I, documents for Nov. 13, 15, and 27, 1928, and Jan. 7, 1929).

[26] The dispute took place on Jan. 3 and 4, 1929. In accordance with prior practice, Harrison informed Young on Jan. 3 that the directors had approved a change in the buying rate to go into effect the next day. After a sequence of telephone calls, Young asked Harrison to suspend the change pending Board approval. According to Harrison's record of a telephone conversation that evening, Young said "that, ever since being in Washington, he had done his best to cooperate with the Reserve Banks and especially with the Federal Reserve Bank of New York, and that he did not intend any longer to be a rubber stamp. He seemed very much out of temper." The next morning, when Harrison telephoned, Young, after much discussion, retreated (Harrison, Conversations, Vol. I, entry for Jan. 25, 1929).

Commenting on the same incident, Hamlin wrote: "Platt said Governor Young used almost violent language to Harrison" (Hamlin Diary, Vol. 15, Jan. 4, 1929, p. 121).

Board and the rest of the System. The Board believed the way to curb security speculation was to deny rediscounting privileges to member banks making loans on securities. The rest of the System believed: (1) the Reserve Banks had no legal right to refuse to rediscount for member banks that held eligible paper; (2) direct pressure should be exercised only when individual member banks were either borrowing for protracted periods or borrowing far in excess of the amounts borrowed by other banks; (3) the method of correction of a member bank's position at its Federal Reserve Bank—whether through sales of government securities, reduction of business loans, or reduction of collateral loans— was strictly a matter of internal bank management, and not the business of the Federal Reserve Bank; and (4) the way to curb security speculation was to increase the rediscount rate.

The Board's point of view was expressed in a letter written to the Reserve Banks on February 2, 1929, asserting that "a member bank is not within its reasonable claims for rediscount facilities at its Federal reserve bank when it borrows either for the purpose of making speculative loans or for the purpose of maintaining speculative loans." The letter requested a reply from the directors of each Bank addressed to three points: "(a) as to how they keep themselves fully informed of the use made of borrowings by their member banks, (b) what methods they employ to protect their institution against the improper use of its credit facilities by member banks, and (c) how effective these methods have been."[27]

In reponse to this letter, Harrison met with the Board in Washington on February 5 to explain the New York position. There had been, he said, undue credit expansion in the past year—8 per cent as compared to a 3 per cent rise in business. Yet interest rates were too high and represented a threat to the continued expansion of business. The need was for lower interest rates. The way to get lower rates was by "sharp, incisive action" involving a rise in discount rates that would "quickly control the long-continued expansion in the total volume of credit so that we might then adopt a System policy of easing rates."[28] It is by no means

[27] The letter, addressed to Gates W. McGarrah, Federal Reserve agent and chairman of the Federal Reserve Bank of New York, is in Harrison, Miscellaneous, Vol. I. All official correspondence between the Board and the Banks during the twenties was addressed to or signed by the Federal Reserve agent, who was considered the Board's representative at each Bank; for official purposes, the governor was merely a Bank employee. The first few paragraphs of the letter also appear in Federal Reserve Board, *Annual Report* for 1929, p. 3. The second quotation in the text was not included in the printed part of the letter.

[28] Harrison wrote also about this meeting,

I asked specifically whether the Board had in mind anything further that we might properly do other than what we have already done to influence borrowings of our member banks . . . Dr. Miller . . . said that if he were running the

clear, of course, that this tactic would have worked, but it very likely would have hastened the end of the bull market.

To Harrison's consternation, on the day after his meeting with the Board, it released a statement to the press expressing its concern about "the excessive amount of the country's credit absorbed in speculative security loans." No reference to the proposed statement had been made during his discussion with the Board; and he was informed of its proposed release after it was too late for him to stop it, although he tried desperately, going so far as to ask Secretary of the Treasury Mellon to intervene. No doubt his feeling that he had not been dealt with in complete good faith played a part in his willingness to force something of a showdown a week later.[29]

On February 14, Harrison telephoned Governor Young that his directors had unanimously established a 6 per cent rate, which was of course subject to review by the Board. When Young telephoned to report that the Board intended to hold the matter for review, pending the receipt of an answer to the warning letter of February 2, Harrison insisted that the Board approve or disapprove the rate increase that day, stating that his directors would remain in session as late as the Board might want to consider the matter with a view to reaching a decision that day. "No director wanted to leave the directors' room with the private information, unknown to the public, that a higher discount rate established by them today might be made effective at any moment by the Board." Young telephoned a revised statement from the Board, which was neither a flat approval nor a flat disapproval of the rate increase. Thereupon, Charles E. Mitchell, a director of the New York Bank, talked with Young, emphasizing "the impossible position in which he would find himself if he were forced to leave the meeting without the Federal Reserve Board having acted upon the increase in our rate . . . [W]hat course" could he "follow tomorrow as President of the National City Bank of New York in handling their business, especially trans-

---

Federal Reserve Bank of New York and received such a letter as that written by the Board, he would either write a letter to each of the principal member banks in New York or else call them into conference to say that he had been to Washington and had learned that the Federal Reserve Board was opposed to the use of Federal Reserve credit to support speculative credit and that in those circumstances, he would tell them to do 'thus and so.'

Harrison replied that

. . . this so-called direct action, while proper enough to keep individual member banks in line or to avoid their abusing our facilities merely for the sake of a profit, does not have any substantial effect upon the total volume of credit outstanding, but that is a matter which we believe at the last analysis can be controlled properly only through the rate (Harrison, Conversations, Vol. I).

[29] Harrison, Conversations, Vol. I; the press statement, dated Feb. 7, 1929, is in Federal Reserve Board, *Annual Report* for 1929, pp. 2–3.

actions in acceptances and securities, with the knowledge which he would possess if the Board continued to hold the matter in abeyance." Young replied that the New York Bank directors "were trying to force upon the Federal Reserve Board the responsibility of taking action one way or another when they wanted time to think it over, that it was an important question which they needed time to consider." Harrison countered that "it was a function of the Board to take that responsibility of approving or disapproving our action today . . . . Our action today and all the conditions under which it was taken could . . . be no surprise to the Federal Reserve Board requiring more time. They were conditions of which the Board had been currently posted." Finally, three hours after Young received the first call about the rate action, he telephoned Harrison that the Board had reconsidered its previous action and now disapproved the discount rate increase.[30]

One week later, the Reserve Bank of New York replied to the Board's warning letter:

 . . . there is some basis for the conclusion that as one or another bank pays off its debt to the Federal Reserve Bank, it does so by an adjustment of its own position either by selling investments or calling loans, which results in forcing other member banks, either in the country or in New York City, which may not have been on our books at the time, to turn to us for accommodation in order to restore their reserves. This sort of control tends to distribute the pressure and to shuffle borrowings among the different banks, but it is questionable how much, if any, effect it has on the total volume of credit outstanding . . . . The directors believe that, perhaps, the most certain and effective method by which the total volume of credit in the country can successfully be influenced or controlled . . . is the use of the discount rate, supplemented, if necessary, by open market operations.[31]

At ten subsequent meetings, the last on May 23, 1929, the New York Bank directors again voted to raise discount rates, each time requesting the Board to approve or disapprove the same day. Each time, the Board disapproved, though by a steadily narrowing margin—on February 14, the final vote by the Board was unanimously adverse; on May 23, the adverse vote was 5 to 3.[32] In the interim, Harrison repeatedly talked in person and by telephone and wrote to Young and other members of the Board, presenting the case for a rise, and finally persuaded Young himself to vote for a rise. He also enlisted Secretary Mellon's help. Some New York Bank directors met with the Board. The Governors Conference unanimously recommended a higher rate, and so did the

[30] Hamlin Diary, Vol. 15, Feb. 14, 1929, pp. 167–170; Harrison, Conversations, Vol. I.
[31] Letter, dated Feb. 21, 1929, to the Federal Reserve Board, signed by Gates W. McGarrah, in Harrison, Miscellaneous, Vol. I.
[32] Harrison, Conversations, Vol. I; Hamlin Diary, Vol. 15, Feb. 14, 1929, pp. 167–169; Vol. 16, May 24, 1929, pp. 80–81.

Federal Advisory Council. In a memorandum for the files, reporting a long conversation on April 25 with Ogden L. Mills, Under Secretary of the Treasury, Harrison understandably wrote that he felt

> the unanimous opinion of the officers and directors [of the New York Bank] and Federal Advisory Council, as well as the Governors of the twelve Federal reserve banks, that rates should be advanced in the principal Reserve banks . . . should prevail after such a long lapse of time over the views of a small number of men in the Board in Washington.[33]

The Board, on its part, clearly felt, and with some reason, that the New York Bank was not cooperating fully in applying the policy of direct pressure. Harrison tried to establish a record of compliance while at the same time avoiding actions that would produce a money market crisis or panic. One episode highlighted the problem. After a break in stock prices on March 25, Charles E. Mitchell (a director of the Federal Reserve Bank of New York and president of the National City Bank) announced that his bank was ready to lend $25 million on the call market "whatever might be the attitude of the Federal Reserve Board" to avert a sharper price decline, although it was also borrowing at the New York Bank. The announcement was viewed at the time as open defiance of the Board, yet Mitchell's action in lending on the call market had at least the tacit approval of Governor Harrison.[34]

Harrison brought direct pressure on at least two New York City banks in April and May, the First National Bank and the Guaranty Trust Com-

[33] Harrison, Conversations, Vol. I; and Office, Vol. II. Hamlin, in a private talk with Mellon in Apr., argued against an increase in rates on the ground that it would surely be followed by a Congressional investigation; that the Democrats would unite with the Progressive Republicans to carry such a resolution of investigation; and that President Hoover would suffer a decisive defeat at the very beginning of his administration if he fought the resolution. Recollections of the disastrous consequences of the rate increases in 1920 also influenced Hamlin's attitude. He told Paul M. Warburg (a member of the Board, 1914–18), "if we deflated the stock market by increasing discount rates, we would cause a deflation greater than the $2½ billion deflation of 1920." Warburg disagreed (Hamlin Diary, Vol. 16, Apr. 18, May 21, 1929, pp. 24, 68).

[34] On Mar. 26, before Mitchell had done anything, Harrison telephoned to let him know that the "Federal Reserve Bank did not want and could not be in the position of arbitrarily refusing loans on eligible paper to member banks," although Harrison did not want to be understood as either encouraging or discouraging National City's placing money on call at that time. Harrison immediately telephoned Young to report his conversation with Mitchell. A month later, in talking with Secretary Mellon, Harrison recalled:

> . . . on Tuesday, March 26, when money rates went to 20 per cent . . . our position . . . was . . . that the problem of providing funds for the call loan market or determining the rates for call loans was with the New York banks and bankers, not with the Federal reserve bank; that we could not request or suggest that they should or should not put out funds in a period of severe pinch; that that was their problem, but that the necessary corollary of that position was that we should be prepared to lend freely, if necessary, to provide reserves against loans taken over by New York City banks (for Mitchell's state-

pany. Harrison regarded his intervention as successful in curbing action by First National, which had been interpreted in the financial press as open defiance of the Federal Reserve Bank. His intervention with Guaranty Trust had a different origin. Its president represented the New York district on the Federal Advisory Council, and Harrison wanted to be sure he understood the Federal Reserve Bank's position.[35]

On May 1, the Board sent a letter to certain Reserve Banks, listing banks "which have been borrowing more or less continuously from your Federal reserve bank and have not effected any substantial liquidation in

---

ment, see New York *Times,* Mar. 28, 29, 1929; Harrison, Conversations, Vol. I, and Special. Vol. II).

The Reserve Board was much disturbed by Mitchell's statement, and wrote him a letter asking if press reports of his statement were correct, and, if not, what he had said. However, according to Harrison, Governor Young thought Harrison's position was "100% right." Possibly the Board did not disapprove so much of Mitchell's action as of his statement to the press. Senator Carter Glass took strong exception to Mitchell's action and publicly demanded his resignation as a director of the Reserve Bank. Glass was an influential political figure and it may be that his broadside goaded the Board into challenging Mitchell (Harrison, Conversations, Vol. I; New York *Times,* Mar. 29, 1929).

[35] Harrison requested First National to reduce its borrowings from the Reserve Bank because its account was "pretty high in relation to other borrowing banks." George F. Baker, Sr., the chief policy maker at First National, told Harrison in Apr. that he believed the financial health of the country required easier money, and that he intended to produce that outcome by reducing call money rates, for which purpose, he had borrowed $50 million from the Reserve Bank. After outlining his general views on the line between the bank's internal decisions and the Federal Reserve's interest in the relative level and term of its borrowings, Harrison told Baker: "I was afraid that if the First National or other banks should persist in a policy such as he advocated, it would spoil our clean slate in Washington and perhaps invite the very [Congressional] investigation we are all trying to avoid, or else a prohibitive regulation from the Federal Reserve Board."

A month later, Baker told Harrison that if it had not been for their earlier conversation, he would have borrowed not only $50 million—for which his bank was still in debt to the Reserve Bank—but as much as $80 million, $90 million, or even $100 million, in his effort to make call money easier. Harrison concluded:

We both agree that what we want ultimately is easy money. He thinks it is possible to get it by putting money out at the present time. We question whether it is possible just now because of an insatiable demand for credit . . . . [H]e was trying to accomplish, through borrowing from us, what all the rest of us agreed was unwise to try to accomplish just now. He indicated that he did not care about the rest of the banking community; that he felt he was right and that we were wrong . . . .

George F. Baker, Jr., who deferred to his father in policy matters, told Harrison that both of them believed they were entitled to the profit on call loans that was made possible by borrowing from the Federal Reserve Bank on their government bonds. . . .

[T]hey had pursued a policy with respect to government bonds (which meant much less profit to them than if they had invested their funds in call money rather than in government bonds) believing that when the time came, those

their security loans since February 6." The letter concluded: "The Board desires that it be ascertained from each of the member banks concerned, which has not yet readjusted its position, why it should not bring about the readjustment expected by the Board." The letter was drafted while Young was absent from Washington, and he protested vigorously but unsuccessfully by telegraph against sending the letter. To Harrison, "he implied clearly that he did not agree with it or with its being sent to the several banks."[36]

The next day, Harrison informed Edmund Platt, vice-governor of the Board, that he "was surprised and much confused" by the letter because: (1) the Board had not intimated earlier that it had any criticism of the manner in which the New York Bank was operating; and (2) he had been advised that no banks in the New York District were on a "black list" of 100 banks and latterly of 37 banks that Board members discussed. Young had described the test of membership for the black list as continuous borrowing by a bank that had loaned money to brokers and dealers on call—an unsatisfactory test, according to Harrison, because it had the effect of tabooing speculative loans to brokers but not to other customers. Now, Harrison told Platt, "I thought the necessary implication from a reading of the Board's letter by any member bank would be that we are now prepared to ration credit on the basis of the one fact, whether a bank was making security loans; that once member banks got the impression that they could not get money at any price, if needed, it might result in a very critical situation . . . ."[37] At Secretary Mellon's suggestion, the board of directors of the New York Bank on May 10 replied at length to the Board's letter, substantially repeating Harrison's oral remarks and asserting: "We question whether the Federal reserve bank has a right to deny accommodation to a member bank solely on these

government bonds would be eligible for their use with a profit which would compensate them for the loss in subscribing for and carrying the bonds; that that time in his opinion had come . . . ."

Harrison also interviewed William C. Potter, president of the Guaranty Trust Company, about the size of Guaranty's borrowings from the Reserve Bank. Potter explained that his bank had lost deposits as a result of a merger, and in addition was subject to heavy demands from some of its best customers for loans on securities. "He said . . . if we should increase our discount rate, the pressure on these borrowers would be greater all along the line and each bank in itself would be in a better position to discourage further borrowing from such customers without fear that the accounts will go to other less cooperative banks." Potter told Harrison that his bank would sell government bonds at a loss in order not to stay in debt at the Reserve Bank, that it had very little money out on call, sometimes taking over a loan overnight for customers who turned to Guaranty after it was too late to borrow on Wall Street (Harrison, Office, Vol. II).

[36] The letter is in Harrison, Miscellaneous, Vol. I; the comments by Young, in Harrison, Conversations, Vol. I.

[37] Harrison, Conversations, Vol. I.

grounds [i.e., that it has made loans on securities], provided the member bank offers eligible paper for discount to repair its reserves."[38]

By the end of May, the season was approaching when the demand for funds regularly increased, and the directors wrote the Board that ". . . a longer discussion as to the discount rate without a real understanding regarding a future program we regard as futile." They had therefore refrained from rate action at their last meeting until they and the Board could agree on a general policy affecting the prospective seasonal increase in demand for funds. The New York directors were thereupon invited to meet with the Board in Washington on June 5.

The directors and Harrison presented a memorandum prepared by Mitchell, which outlined a program they had discussed for the mid-year period. The program called for the New York Bank: (1) to discount freely for member banks, whether or not they had outstanding collateral loans; (2) to provide monetary ease by purchasing government securities or acceptances, if legitimate demands could not be met adequately by rediscounting; (3) to raise the discount rate, if there was evidence of speculation in securities, real estate, commodities, or inventories; and (4) to reduce rates again promptly as conditions permitted. According to Harrison, the meeting revealed that there was no apparent likelihood of obtaining an increase in the discount rate, so the Bank sought to press the rate question as a future contingency.

On June 12, in Young's absence, Board members drafted a letter to the New York Bank, rejecting its program: "Since February, the policy of the Federal Reserve System has expressed itself primarily through what is called 'direct action' and this position was taken deliberately by the Federal Reserve Board. To this position it holds fast. It is satisfied with the reasonableness of its policy and with its necessity . . . ." The Board informed the Bank that seasonal demands

will be better served by a temporary suspension of a rigid policy of direct pressure, which, however, should not be abandoned but rather tempered in order to permit member banks, that have not found it practicable to readjust their position in accordance with the Board's principle, to avail themselves of the rediscount facilities of the Federal reserve banks for the purpose of avoiding, as far as possible, any undue strain or any unnecessary increase in the cost of credit in meeting the seasonal needs of agriculture, industry, and commerce.

In concluding, the Board conceded that if direct action alone did not operate quickly enough, it "would be glad to consider other corrective measures"—meaning discount rates would be advanced.[39]

[38] Harrison, Miscellaneous, Vol. I.
[39] The letter of May 31, 1929, to Governor Young, from Chairman Gates W. McGarrah, and the Board's letter of June 12 are in Harrison, Miscellaneous, Vol. I.
Hamlin referred to the Board's letter of June 12 as the compromise between the

By the end of July, Harrison was concerned about a program for the fall and early winter: ". . . with the seasonal demand almost upon us, money rates are not apt to relax in the near future unless through a change in Federal reserve policy. The question now is whether there should be such a change." He believed that continuing high money rates would harm U.S. export possibilities and disturb monetary conditions abroad. He proposed a meeting of Bank governors to discuss whether the System should apply more pressure, rock along "as we are now doing," or adopt a policy of ease.

At a meeting with the Federal Reserve Board on August 2, Harrison expressed the opinion that "the time has passed for the adoption of a policy of higher rates" as part of a program of pressure or deflation "looking toward future easier money." Instead, he "suggested an increase in the discount rate to 6% as a warning against the excessive use of credit, with a simultaneous reduction in bill rates to attract acceptances and, possibly, purchases of securities in the event the bill holdings of the System should not increase or increase too slowly."[40] Certain members of the Board questioned the advisability of an increase in the discount rate without a preferential rate on commodity paper, in addition to the lower rate on acceptances. The matter was referred to a conference of representatives of the Banks and the Board on August 7.

The governors at their conference on August 8 passed a resolution calling for an increase in the bill portfolio of Banks that wanted to participate in bill purchases in order to meet the increased seasonal demand for credit. The purchases should be made under "the protection of an effective discount rate in the New York district," i.e., a higher rate. The higher rate would, in their view, necessitate increases by few, if any, of the other Federal Reserve Banks during the period of seasonal business demand. "It is, therefore, recommended that the Reserve Board act favorably on an application that may be made by the Federal Reserve Bank of New York for an increase in its existing rate." On August 9, the Board finally approved a 6 per cent rate in New York.[41]

Board and the Bank and denied the view that the Board was stalling on the discount rate question (Hamlin Diary, Vol. 15, May 21, 23, 28, June 5, 7, 12, 1929, pp. 72–73, 79, 87, 96–97, 99–100, 104, 108–109).

[40] Harrison, Conversations, Vol. I.

[41] See Harrison's letter, dated July 30, 1929, to Governor Calkins of the San Francisco Reserve Bank (Harrison, Miscellaneous, Vol. I). The record of his meeting with the Board is in Harrison, Conversations, Vol. I. The Board's predilection for preferential rates had been expressed a year earlier at a meeting with the Open Market Investment Committee, when the Board proposed a preferential discount rate on agricultural paper, and a preferential buying rate on acceptances drawn for the purpose of seasonal crop movement. The Committee opposed both.

The report of the Governors Conference and the resolution it passed is in Harrison, Conversations, Vol. I. Only Governor Black of Atlanta, "who was committed

After June, Governor Young came to believe that direct pressure was a total failure; but Miller and especially Hamlin persisted in a favorable view of the policy. This difference in the evaluation of the success of direct pressure led to a dispute within the Board in the spring of 1930, when it was time to submit the 1929 *Annual Report* to the Speaker of the House of Representatives. Governor Young at first refused to sign the report because of the favorable references to direct pressure in it. In the end, he broke precedent and signed the report *at the beginning* with formal transmission instead of at the end.[42]

In retrospect, it seems exceedingly doubtful that "direct pressure" had any significant effect on the amount of security loans, though it may have produced some minor changes in their source. With respect to quantitative measures, the outcome, as it so frequently is in disputes of this kind, was a compromise: restrictions that were clearly too easy to stem the bull market and almost surely too tight to permit the continued

---

to his directors not to vote for any action which might lead to an increase in the discount rate in Atlanta," did not vote for the resolution. Harrison voted "yes" without committing himself on whether other Federal Reserve Banks should increase their discount rates. He favored the inclusion of a specification that government securities or foreign exchange be purchased, if enough bills could not be bought to provide Reserve credit adequate to meet seasonal demands or to avoid undue stringency in money rates. (See also Hamlin Diary, Aug. 2, 8, 1929, pp. 146, 155–156.)

[42] The *Annual Report* for 1929, p. 4, referred as follows to direct pressure:

It is not for the Federal Reserve Board to estimate the general expediency or the larger public consequences of its intervention by direct pressure . . . . It may be remarked, however, that the course adopted by the board resulted in a substantial conservation of the credit resources of the banking system of the country, and particularly of the Federal reserve banks, for essential needs which arose later in the year.
The protection of Federal reserve credit against diversion into channels of speculation constitutes the most difficult and urgent problem confronting the Federal reserve system in its effort to work out a technique of credit control that shall bring to the country such steadiness of credit conditions and such maintenance of economic stability as may be expected to result from competent administration of the resources of the system. Whatever method, or combination of methods, of securing these results may eventually win the sanction alike of successful practice and of public opinion, the recent outstanding experience of the Federal reserve system in demonstrating the practicability of direct pressure has clarified the problem and advanced its solution.

The first of these paragraphs, according to Hamlin, was presented by E. A. Goldenweiser, the Board's director of research, in his draft of the annual report. Hamlin complained that the draft contained an inadequate discussion of direct pressure, and Miller added a draft of the second paragraph above. Governor Young protested that Miller's draft did not state the facts correctly. Miller thereupon offered to strike out the following sentence: "Its potentialities and its availability, in dealing with certain types of credit disorder, can no longer be doubted." Miller's draft was then adopted over the protest of Governor Young and Vice-Governor Platt (Hamlin Diary, Vol. 17, Feb. 12, 21, Mar. 17, Apr. 6, 7, 1930, pp. 101–106, 117–118, 127–130).

expansion of business activity without severe downward pressure on prices.

The issues involved in that dispute have recurred several times in the System's history. Whenever the System has felt that external circumstances limit the extent to which it can push quantitative measures of monetary restraint, it has resorted to qualitative measures. It has done so partly in the hope of thereby escaping the external constraints, partly—even though it knew or strongly suspected that this hope was largely in vain—in order to demonstrate to itself and others that it was taking some action to meet clear and pressing problems. This was the story not only in 1929 but also, as we have seen, in 1919 when supposed Treasury needs imposed the external constraint. It was to be so again, as we shall see, in World War II and in the postwar period up to 1951, when the bond-support program was the external constraint. And in all three episodes, any hopes placed in direct pressure and "moral suasion" were doomed to disappointment.

BILLS VERSUS GOVERNMENT SECURITIES

The Board's emphasis on direct pressure was related to a general view of monetary policy which distinguished sharply between discounts, bills (bankers' acceptances), and government securities as sources of credit expansion. From that qualitative, "real bills" point of view, what mattered was the end use of the credit. As Hamlin put it in his Diary in 1923, citing Paul M. Warburg, a former member of the Board, as having expressed agreement, "there was a fundamental difference between putting money into circulation by a) Buying government securities and b) Bills; . . . [M]oney put out for b) went primarily to aid a genuine business transaction, while in the case of a) no one could tell where it might go, e.g., to be loaned on Wall Street, etc." In September 1928, Hamlin reports that Harding, then governor of the Federal Reserve Bank of Boston, told him "the proceeds of acceptances filter into the market more slowly than the proceeds of government securities," and in January 1929, he reports Young as expressing the same view.[43]

That view was, of course, also widely held outside the Board, and was not, in fact, held by all members of the Board. Applied to discounts, it meant that the effect of borrowed funds depended on the specific use to be made of them, hence it was clearly conducive to the support of a policy of direct pressure. However, it was by no means necessarily linked to such a policy. For example, among Board members, Adolph Miller was one of the most consistent and tenacious supporters of the policy of direct pressure, yet apparently he did not accept the real bills view.[44] On the

---

[43] Hamlin Diary, Vol. 7, Apr. 12, 1923, pp. 85–86; Vol. 15, Sept. 7, 1928, and Jan. 4, 1929, pp. 27, 124–125.

[44] Hamlin Diary, Vol. 7, Apr. 12, 1923, p. 86; Vol. 8, Feb. 14, 1924, p. 19.

other hand, Young, who did, was only a lukewarm advocate of direct pressure.

From the quantitative point of view held at the time by many of the technical staff of the System—and that would today be accepted by almost all economists—discounts, bills, and government securities are all credit instruments the acquisition of which adds to Federal Reserve credit outstanding and the sale of which subtracts from Federal Reserve credit outstanding. The composition of Federal Reserve assets matters only as it may affect the attitudes of banks or other participants in the money market. The main distinction called for is between discounts and the other two, because banks generally are more reluctant to make additional loans or acquire additional investments when they are in debt to the Reserve Banks than when they have the same composition of assets but are not in debt to the Reserve Banks. Bills and government securities can, however, be grouped together.

The invalid distinctions drawn between discounts, bills, and government securities were reflected not only in the attitude toward direct pressure but also in many policy decisions of the System—both the Banks and the Board. For example, the Board, in replying to a recommendation of the Open Market Investment Committee in 1928 wrote:

The Board would not care to agree to the purchase of Government securities, except as a last resort. We understand from the discussion had with your committee that you favor easing through the bill market, if possible, and through the Government security market only if unavoidable. With this understanding, the Board approves the purchase of Government securities by the committee, but limits the amount to $100,000,000.[45]

Again, in its letter of June 12, 1929, to the New York Bank, agreeing to a temporary suspension of the policy of direct pressure, the Board expressed its willingness to consider "some release of Federal reserve credit, preferably through the purchase of bills, but if . . . such relief is not adequate or practicable, then . . . through the purchase of short-time Government securities."[46] Similar statements appeared in many other Open Market Investment Committee recommendations and Board communications. Consequently, the System at times undertook actions that in retrospect seem self-defeating, such as increasing acceptance holdings in the last half of 1928 while desperately trying to hold down discounts; lowering acceptance rates in August 1929 while raising discount rates; great unwillingness to expand government security holdings in early 1930 despite a sharp decline in acceptances, and a simultaneous

[45] Harrison, Open Market, Vol. I, letter, dated Aug. 16, 1928, Young to Harrison.
[46] Letter, Young to McGarrah, Harrison, Miscellaneous, Vol. I.

willingness to acquire acceptances, coupled with complaints about their unavailability.

RELATION OF DISCOUNT RATE TO OTHER RATES

A related policy issue that recurred throughout the twenties is the proper relation of the Federal Reserve discount rate to other interest rates. An initial view, based on what was thought to be the British precedent, was that the discount rate should be a penalty rate, set at a level above that received by member banks on the rediscounted paper. It was soon recognized that the rediscount rate could be a penalty rate, even if it were below the rate received by member banks on the bulk of their assets, because of the difference in the credit quality of the member bank loan from the Reserve Bank and the assets the member bank held. Differences in credit quality and in costs led banks to charge different rates on different commercial loans. Clearly, it would not be profitable to a bank to lend at a rate only a trifle above that at which it borrowed if the loan carried any significant degree of risk. In its *Tenth Annual Report* (for 1923), the Board argued that the analogue to London practice was a discount rate above the rate on bankers' acceptances and short-term government bonds, presumably on the grounds that the relevant comparison was not between the discount rate and the rate on commercial loans, but between the discount rate and the rate on securities held as a secondary reserve, since for an individual bank liquidation of the latter was the likeliest alternative to rediscounting as a means of meeting a reserve deficiency.

In practice, the rate was generally set at a level at which it was profitable for banks to borrow continuously at the Federal Reserve since for most of the period the discount rate was appreciably below even the call money rate, which was received on loans with essentially no risk of default. And, as we have seen, after World War I, member bank borrowings exceeded their reserve balances for months on end. Partly, no doubt, because of that experience, continuous borrowing seemed objectionable to the System, which considered itself a "lender of last resort," rather than a source of continuous finance. Accordingly, in lieu of a penalty discount rate, the Reserve System adopted the policy that "continuous indebtedness at the reserve banks, except under unusual circumstances, is an abuse of reserve bank facilities," that "the proper occasion for borrowing at the reserve bank is for the purpose of meeting temporary and seasonal needs."[47] The policy reinforced a pre-World War I tradition against interbank borrowing—then fully justified because of the interdependence of banks in the face of general pressure. The policy was apparently effective in limiting the use of discounting, in the sense that it made the amount of discounting less under any given conditions

[47] The quotations are from *Annual Report* for 1928, p. 8; for 1925, p. 16.

than it otherwise would have been, though it did not, of course, eliminate a dependence between the amount of discounting and the profitability of discounting. In technical parlance, it shifted the demand curve for discounting to the left but did not render it perfectly inelastic and may not even have affected its elasticity.[48]

The decision to rely on a tradition against continuous borrowing rather on a higher discount rate has had important consequences. It helped to make open market operations rather than rediscounting the main instrument for quantitative control.[49] It established relations between member banks and Reserve Banks that facilitated attempts at qualitative control, e.g., over the stock market in 1929. Finally, by making discounting seem a source of weakness of banks, it contributed notably to the problem, which is said to have troubled the Reserve System in the early 1930's, of securing enough eligible paper to serve as collateral for Federal Reserve notes (see Chapter 7, section 6).

INTERNATIONAL CONSIDERATIONS

Federal Reserve literature reflected the great importance attached to the re-establishment of a worldwide gold standard, and the rejoicing over its apparent accomplishment. At the same time, it contained almost no discussion of the policy measures appropriate to achieve the objective. The New York Bank, and in particular its governor, Benjamin Strong, played the leading role in the System's relations with other countries. Perhaps the most important measures taken were agreements to extend credit to Poland, Czechoslovakia, Great Britain, Belgium, Italy, and Rumania. The agreement with Britain was the most important, involving the largest extension of credit.

The System frequently cited foreign considerations as a justification for the general credit policies pursued. We are inclined, however, to agree with Hardy, who concluded that foreign considerations were seldom important in determining the policies followed but were cited as additional justification for policies adopted primarily on domestic grounds whenever foreign and domestic considerations happened to coincide.[50]

BANK SUSPENSIONS

In retrospect, one notable omission from Federal Reserve literature is any policy discussion of bank suspensions, despite the much higher rate of suspensions than during any comparable earlier period. Each year the

[48] For a fuller discussion, see A. J. Meigs, *Free Reserves and the Money Supply,* University of Chicago Press, 1962, pp. 8, 46–48.

[49] See Hardy, *Credit Policies,* pp. 228–232. For one view on the sufficiency of open market operations alone as an efficient tool for monetary policy, and the shortcomings of rediscounting, see Milton Friedman, *A Program for Monetary Stability,* New York, Fordham University Press, 1960, pp. 30–45.

[50] Hardy, *Credit Policies,* p. 108.

Board reported the melancholy figures of suspensions, properly classified as member and nonmember, national and state banks, and confined itself to noting that suspensions were in disproportionate number of nonmember rather than member banks, of banks in small communities rather than in large, and of banks in agricultural rather than industrial areas. It did not discuss methods of mitigating the effect on depositors of the suspensions that did occur, or of reducing the rate of suspensions. And it did not recognize the possibility that a high rate of suspensions might undermine confidence in the banking system and lay the groundwork for subsequent runs.

At a Governors Conference in November 1926, a topic on the agenda was "Discussion of further steps which might be taken by Federal reserve banks to prevent member bank failures." Governor M. B. Wellborn of the Reserve Bank of Atlanta read a memorandum concerning "the responsibilities of the reserve bank in preventing bank failures." The consensus was that "the chief factors which have resulted in failures during the past several years have been bad management and the economic conditions which have resulted from the war."[51] This was apparently a general attitude within the System not only in the twenties, when it had much validity, but also in the early thirties, when the situation had altered radically (see Chapter 7, section 3).

4. *Factors Accounting for Changes in the Money Stock*

In practice, Federal Reserve policy took the form mainly of changes in discount rates and of purchases and sales on the open market. These impinged in the first instance on Federal Reserve credit outstanding: the sum of bills discounted and bought by the System, U.S. government securities held, and "other," consisting mainly of "float" or the excess of credits allowed to member banks for checks and other items in the process of collection over debits to member bank accounts for such items (Chart 22). Changes in Federal Reserve credit outstanding in turn brought about changes in the total volume of high-powered money available for the public to hold as currency and for banks to hold as reserves, which in turn brought about changes in the volume of deposit liabilities.

Other things being the same, an increase in Reserve credit tends to expand the quantity of money and to ease conditions; a decrease, to reduce the quantity of money and to tighten credit conditions. But, of course, other things are seldom the same and Federal Reserve policy must take them into account. Sources of high-powered money other than Federal Reserve credit fluctuated from time to time, most notably the gold stock; and changes in the ratios of deposits to currency and of de-

[51] Harrison, Governors, Vol. I.

CHART 22
Federal Reserve Credit Outstanding, by Types,
July 1921–December 1929

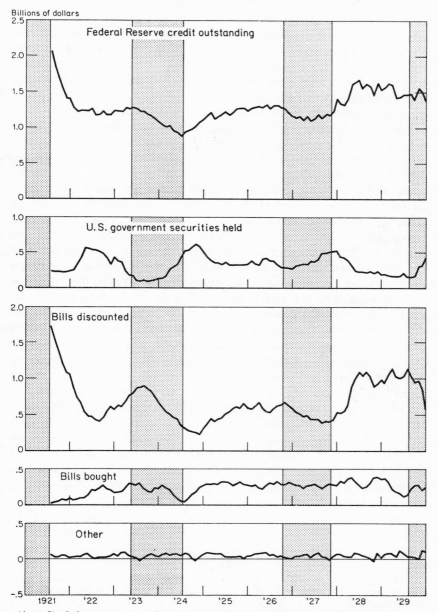

NOTE: Shaded areas represent business contractions; unshaded areas, business expansions.
SOURCE: Same as for Chart 21, except for special supplementary seasonal adjustment of bills bought in 1925–28.

posits to reserves altered the volume of money that could be outstanding for any given volume of high-powered money. The Federal Reserve System had the power to offset or reinforce these factors, and in practice it clearly often attempted to do so. A decline in Federal Reserve credit outstanding might therefore be entirely consistent with a policy of promoting monetary ease, if it were smaller in magnitude than the change required to offset other factors working toward an expansion in the quantity of money, and conversely. In consequence, while simple arithmetic can isolate changes in Federal Reserve credit outstanding, there is no easy way to interpret such changes in terms of the effect either intended or produced on the stock of money and credit conditions.

What is true of Federal Reserve credit outstanding is true also of discount rates. Other things being the same, a rise in discount rates tends to reduce the volume of discounting by member banks, hence to reduce Federal Reserve credit outstanding and to tighten credit conditions, and conversely. But again, other things are seldom the same. In the first place, the Federal Reserve System may itself be undertaking other operations that offset this effect. For example, when the System has wanted to tighten credit conditions it has generally both sold securities and bills and raised discount rates. The sale of securities and bills has reduced reserves of member banks, thereby increasing their desire to discount at any given rate, and conversely. In general, this effect has been stronger than the direct effect of the rise in the rate, so that the level of discounts has generally moved in the same direction as the discount rate rather than in the opposite direction—this is the "scissors effect" of open market operations and discount rates mentioned earlier.[52] In the second place, changes in money market conditions independently of Reserve action may change the desired amount of discounting at any given level of rates. We have already seen that a level of rates that was "easy" and encouraged discounting in 1919 would have been extremely "tight" and would have discouraged discounting in 1920. A rise in rates may therefore be consistent with an easy-money policy if it is less than the rise required to offset other factors making for a higher level of market rates, and conversely. Federal Reserve actions, in short, must be interpreted in the light of all the forces affecting the stock of money and credit conditions.[53]

Chart 23 depicts the behavior of the stock of money and of the three determinants we have used throughout in analyzing the arithmetic of

[52] Burgess, *The Reserve Banks,* pp. 201–202; Hardy, *Credit Policies,* pp. 228–229.

[53] More recently, the same fallacy in interpreting the level of discount rates as easy or tight without regard to other factors affecting the level of market rates has characterized the interpretation of the level of free reserves. See Chap. 11, sect. 2, below, and Friedman, *A Program for Monetary Stability,* pp. 41–42.

CHART 23

The Stock of Money and Its Proximate Determinants, 1921–29

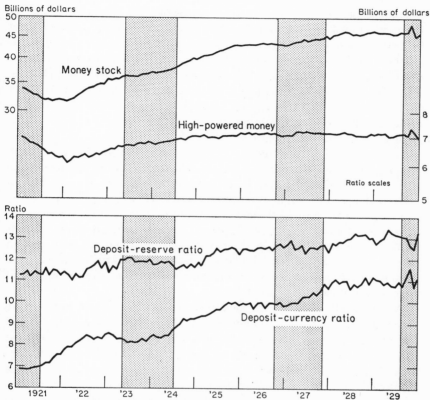

NOTE: Shaded areas represent business contractions; unshaded areas, business expansions.
SOURCE: Tables A-1 (col. 8) and B-3.

the money supply—the stock of high-powered money, the public's deposit-currency ratio, and the banks' deposit-reserve ratio. All are given monthly in seasonally adjusted form (see Appendix B, Table B-3).

Both deposit ratios rose throughout the period in continuation of the pre-World War I trends discussed in the preceding chapter. The deposit-reserve ratio rose at a fairly steady rate, though there was a retardation or minor fall during both the 1923–24 and 1926–27 recessions. This is the kind of cyclical response we have observed in earlier periods. The deposit-currency ratio rose at a faster and more irregular rate. It rose sharply in the earlier stages of the 1921–23 expansion, then fell noticeably before and during the earlier stages of the 1923–24 recession. Most of the remaining rise came during the recession year of 1927. High-

273

powered money shows a rather different behavior: it continued its 1920–21 decline until January 1922, then rose noticeably to 1925 and more mildly to 1927, after which it declined mildly to 1929.

For the period as a whole, from the cyclical trough in July 1921 to the cyclical peak in August 1929, the money stock rose 45 per cent, or at the rate of 4.6 per cent per year. Of this rise, the rise in the deposit-currency ratio accounted for 54 per cent; in the deposit-reserve ratio, for 15 per cent; and in high-powered money, for 27 per cent. The rest was accounted for by interaction between the two deposit ratios. Over the period as a whole, the rise in the deposit-currency ratio was therefore arithmetically by far the most important factor accounting for the changes in the stock of money.

The qualification "arithmetically" is needed in the preceding sentence, because, as always, the arithmetic breakdown does not necessarily explain why the stock of money rose by the amount it did. The Reserve System controlled the stock of high-powered money. Hence, if the deposit-currency ratio had remained unchanged rather than rising, the Reserve System could have increased high-powered money by an amount sufficient to have produced the rise in the money stock that actually occurred. In that case, our arithmetic breakdown would have attributed a larger fraction of the rise in the stock of money to high-powered money, and none of it to the deposit-currency ratio.

Would the Reserve System have behaved in this manner, and can we conclude that the stock of money rose by the amount it did at the will of the System? No easy answer is possible. The Reserve System did not use changes in the money stock as an explicit criterion of policy and apparently paid little direct attention to them. Its explicit criteria were those developed most fully in the *Tenth Annual Report*. As we have seen, those criteria were themselves vague and did not specify at all precisely what actions should be taken under what circumstances. Moreover, we cannot be certain what effect a different behavior of the deposit-currency ratio would have had on the variables to which those criteria referred. Yet there is perhaps some presumption that the answer is between the two extremes: a complete offset to a different behavior of the deposit-currency ratio and also of the deposit-reserve ratio, and no offset to the behavior of either ratio.

Had the deposit-currency ratio been unchanged in 1922, for example, the money stock would have tended to have a downward tilt relative to its actual course; that would have slowed up the expansion of money income in 1922 and imposed downward pressure on prices (or less upward pressure than there was), and so would have made it seem to the System both safe and desirable to allow high-powered money to expand by even more than it did. A similar statement would apply also to subsequent years. Presumably, too, a downward tilt in the money stock would have resulted from greater pressure on bank reserves—which, as it turned out, were expanded by a return of currency from circulation—which, in turn, would have meant higher interest rates in the money market. This, too, or perhaps in the first instance, would have encouraged a more expansionary policy on the part of the Reserve System.

One reason for doubting that the offset would have been complete, and indeed for believing that it might have been very small, is that the later rises in the deposit-currency ratio occurred in periods when the Reserve System was, in any event, engaged in what it regarded as an easy-money policy through purchases of government securities—the later stages of the 1923–24 and 1926–27 recessions and the early stages of the succeeding expansions. (Compare the time pattern of Federal Reserve Bank holdings of U.S. government securities in Chart 22 and of the deposit-currency ratio in Chart 23.) It is possible that the failure of the deposit-currency ratio to rise would have led the System to engage in still larger purchases of securities.[54] However, in view of the experimental nature of the programs and the System's tendency to judge the magnitude of the operation by either the total amount of purchases or by the effect of the purchases on reserves or both, we are inclined to regard any substantial expansion in security purchases on those occasions as unlikely. The offset would have had to come, and to some extent probably would have, either in a lesser decline in bills discounted on those two occasions, or in the cumulative effects of somewhat tighter monetary conditions on later policies.

As these comments indicate, the changes in the proximate determinants of the money stock did not take place evenly from 1921 to 1929. Of the three proximate determinants, changes in high-powered money, despite their minor importance for the period as a whole, impressed their pattern on the changes in the stock of money most strongly. The main effect of the two deposit ratios was to give an upward tilt to the money stock relative to high-powered money—or, perhaps, in terms of the economics

[54] It is possible also, of course, that the particular time pattern of the deposit-currency ratio was produced by the System's operations. The expansionary purchases impinged in the first instance on deposits. It presumably took some time for the community to restore its desired deposit-currency ratio. Consequently, the bunching of the System's purchases may have converted what would otherwise have been a fairly steady rise in the deposit-currency ratio into a rapid rise and then constancy or decline. Under the hypothetical circumstances of no underlying tendency of the deposit-currency ratio to rise, the counterpart to those effects would have been a temporary rise in the ratio coinciding with the System's expansionary actions and a subsequent return to its initial level. That would not affect the main point made in the text. Under such circumstances, it is still true that larger purchases than were actually made would have been required to produce the same increase in the money stock. The effect would be on the requisite timing.

of the changes, to enable the Reserve System to create less high-powered money than would otherwise have been necessary to produce the observed growth in the money stock. The decline in high-powered money from mid-1921 to January 1922 was reflected in a less sharp decline in the stock of money; the fairly rapid rise in high-powered money from then to 1925 was reflected in a relatively rapid growth of the stock of money, though there was a noticeable retardation before and during most of the 1923–24 recession, mirroring partly a corresponding retardation in high-powered money but mostly the contemporaneous decline in the deposit-currency ratio. The slowing up in the rate of rise of high-powered money from 1925 to 1927 was reflected in a slowing up in the rate of rise in the stock of money, though rough constancy of the two deposit ratios also contributed to that result. The mild decline in high-powered money from 1927 to 1929 was reflected in a slight decline in the stock of money from 1928 on.

DEPOSIT-RESERVE RATIO

According to a detailed analysis by Cagan, the two deposit ratios were not directly affected by Federal Reserve policy, though both were affected by the changes in the banking structure produced by the establishment of the Federal Reserve System.[55]

The continued rise in the deposit-reserve ratio reflected the net effect of three partly offsetting changes. The ratio of required reserves to deposits was (1) reduced by a more rapid growth in time deposits than in demand deposits; (2) was raised by a more rapid growth of deposits in member than in nonmember banks; and (3) reserves held fell relative to reserves required. Cagan finds that (1) and (2) roughly offset one another, so that the net rise in the deposit-reserve ratio was about equal to the rise that would have been produced by (3) alone. All three changes can be regarded as at least partly reflecting an adaptation to the changed banking structure.

The clearest example is item 1, the rise in time deposits relative to demand deposits. The Federal Reserve Act instituted lower required reserves for time deposits than for demand deposits. The effect was to give banks a strong incentive to raise the ratio of time deposits to demand deposits, which they could do by making it more attractive for their depositors to hold time rather than demand deposits. Banks increased the differential between interest paid on the two kinds of deposits and offered services in connection with time deposits designed to assimilate them to demand deposits. In the words of a memorandum about the 1920's written within the System (in 1940), "there developed a tendency to induce de-

---

[55] See Phillip Cagan's discussion of the ratios in his forthcoming monograph on the determinants and effects of changes in the money stock in the United States since 1875, a National Bureau study.

276

positors to transfer their funds from checking accounts to savings accounts. Banks frequently not only allowed such a transfer but encouraged it in order to take advantage of lower reserves and to obtain a larger basis for credit expansion . . . . In many cases, particularly in large centers, the aspect of savings was impaired by allowing depositors to draw a limited number of checks against time deposits."[56]

The System was well aware at the time of these tendencies, and many discussions took place about them, but no action was taken.[57] This change in the conditions of supply of time and demand deposits by commercial banks may help to explain why we have found in our own work that a concept of money which includes both categories of deposits in commercial banks often displays a more consistent relation to other economic magnitudes than a concept which excludes time deposits. It may also explain why the relation between the broader total and other economic magnitudes seems not to have been much affected by the establishment of the System.

Item 2, the more rapid growth of deposits in member than in nonmember banks, was mostly a result of the changing distribution of population between rural and urban areas and the disproportionate concentration of nonmember banks in rural areas. Deposit growth was concentrated in larger-sized banks in cities of more than 100,000 population.[58]

---

[56] Harrison, Special, No. 36, Part 2, pp. 98–99.

[57] The following exemplify concern within the System about the problem.

Mar. 1924: ". . . with the tendency shown during the past few years by member banks to convert demand deposits into time deposits, and with the tendency to reduce the percentage of reserve balances maintained by member banks in the Federal Reserve Banks, the Committee believes it is extremely unwise at the present time to make any change in the reserve requirements which might lead to additional expansion" (Report of Federal Reserve Agents Committee on Reserves, in Harrison, Governors, Vol. I).

May 1927: ". . . the Governors of the Federal Reserve Banks view with grave concern the weakening of the reserve position of the banks of the country due to the constantly growing tendency to transfer what are in effect demand deposits into so-called time certificates or savings accounts . . ." (Harrison, Governors, Vol. II).

June 1927: Letter from Federal Reserve Board to Federal Reserve Banks requesting suggestions as to action which can be taken by the Board under the law to deal with the tendency to transfer what are in effect demand deposits into so-called time certificates or savings accounts (Harrison, Governors, Vol. II).

May 1928: ". . . to prevent some of the abuses which have developed, such as the withdrawal by check of savings and time deposits and the lack of a clear distinction between demand and time deposits," Regulation D of the Federal Reserve Board defining deposits should be amplified (Recommendation of the Federal Advisory Council in Federal Reserve Board, *Annual Report* for 1928, p. 228).

[58] Implied by the Federal Reserve Committee on Branch, Group, and Chain Banking, "Changes in the Number and Size of Banks in the United States, 1834–1932," mimeographed, 1932, pp. 19, 35, 48. Size was measured by loans and investments.

Cagan suggests that the most likely explanation for item 3, the decline in actual reserves relative to required reserves, was the existence of the Federal Reserve System as a "lender of last resort," which encouraged banks to trim their reserve balances further than they otherwise would have done. The development of the federal funds market, involving an efficient system for interbank borrowing to repair reserve deficiencies, was partly a consequence of the willingness of banks to trim their reserve balances but in turn facilitated their doing so.[59] These factors, if they are the explanation, had to be sufficiently strong to counterbalance the high level of bank failures. Unlike the failures from 1930 to 1933, those during the twenties did not set off a liquidity crisis or inspire any general distrust of banks. They were correctly attributed to the special problems of agricultural and rural areas. Nonetheless, they might have been expected to make at least the remaining banks in rural areas anxious to strengthen themselves, both by reducing the fraction of their funds in the kinds of loans that were experiencing default and by raising the ratio of their reserves to their deposits.

DEPOSIT-CURRENCY RATIO

Cagan attributes the continued rise in the deposit-currency ratio primarily to the contemporaneous rise in real income per capita. In addition, the rise in the deposit-reserve ratio must have enabled banks to make the holding of deposits more attractive relative to currency than formerly. To that extent, the rise in the deposit-currency ratio can also be attributed to the establishment of the Federal Reserve System.

COMPOSITION OF HIGH-POWERED MONEY

Whatever may have been their ultimate effect on the stock of money, the changes in the deposit ratios had a notable effect on the composition of high-powered money in terms of the form in which it was held by the public and the banks (Chart 24A). The rise in deposits relative to currency made for a rise in Federal Reserve deposits, which member banks were required to hold to meet legal reserve requirements, relative to other forms of high-powered money. The concurrent rise in deposits relative to reserves probably worked in the opposite direction but was much less important quantitatively. As a result, Federal Reserve deposit liabilities to banks rose from 25 per cent of the total of high-powered money in July 1921 to 33 per cent in August 1929.

Federal Reserve notes fell not only for this reason but also because of

---

[59] *The Federal Funds Market,* A Study by a Federal Reserve System Committee, Board of Governors of the Federal Reserve System, 1959, pp. 1–2, 21–29; and also P. B. Willis, *The Federal Funds Market,* Federal Reserve Bank of Boston, 1957, pp. 1–10.

the abandonment in 1922 of the World War I policy of replacing gold certificates in the hands of the public with Federal Reserve notes in order to accumulate gold in the Federal Reserve Banks. The policy was subsequently precisely reversed. Gold certificates were paid out in order to keep the gold reserve percentage of the Reserve System down in the hope of thereby discouraging pressure for monetary expansion. Gold and gold certificates accordingly rose from 10 per cent of total high-powered money in July 1921 to 17 per cent by August 1929.

The 15 percentage-point rise in these two components of high-powered money was mostly absorbed by Federal Reserve notes, which fell from 39 per cent of total high-powered money to 26 per cent. The remaining two percentage points were absorbed by Treasury currency, which rose absolutely but fell from 26 to 24 per cent of total high-powered money.[60]

GOLD MOVEMENTS AND GOLD STERILIZATION

Federal Reserve policy impinged more directly on changes in total high-powered money than on either the deposit ratios or the liability composition of high-powered money. As Chart 24B shows, the major proximate source of increase in high-powered money over the period as a whole was the rise in the gold stock. Federal Reserve claims on the public and banks actually fell from July 1921 to August 1929, though this is a misleading picture for the period as a whole, since it arises entirely from the continued sharp contraction from July 1921 to early 1922, which completed the liquidation after the dramatic wartime and postwar expansion.

Chart 25 isolates the items that contribute most to an understanding of the seasonally adjusted movements in high-powered money; the gold stock and Federal Reserve credit, both monthly in seasonally adjusted form, and the discount rate at the New York Federal Reserve Bank, the relation of which to market rates affected Federal Reserve credit outstanding by altering for member banks the profitability of discounting.

A striking feature of Chart 25 is the inverse relation after 1923 between movements in gold and in Federal Reserve credit. From 1922 to 1923, the increase in gold exerted full effect on high-powered money and for part of the period was even reinforced by an increase in Federal

[60] Treasury currency, which is defined for our purposes as including both national bank notes and Federal Reserve Bank notes, showed a marked change in composition as a result of a reversal of the wartime operation (described in Chap. 5, footnote 31), designed to make silver available to Britain. Silver certificates increased over $200 million and Federal Reserve Bank notes were all but withdrawn from circulation. Federal Reserve Bank notes had been issued from 1918 to 1920 on the security of Pittman Act certificates to replace silver certificates which were retired to release their silver cover for shipment to India. In 1921, the Treasury reversed the process. It coined standard silver dollars from silver bought from domestic producers. The silver dollars were used to retire Pittman Act certificates, and the Federal Reserve Banks thereupon canceled Federal Reserve Bank notes.

CHART 24

High-Powered Money, by Assets and Liabilities of the Treasury and Federal Reserve Banks, 1921–29

A. Liabilities

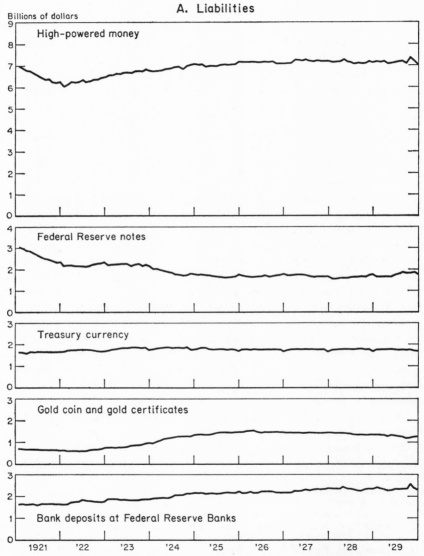

NOTE: Federal Reserve notes, Treasury currency, and gold coin and certificates are outside the Treasury and Federal Reserve Banks.

SOURCE: Same as for Chart 19.

CHART 24 (concluded)

B. Assets

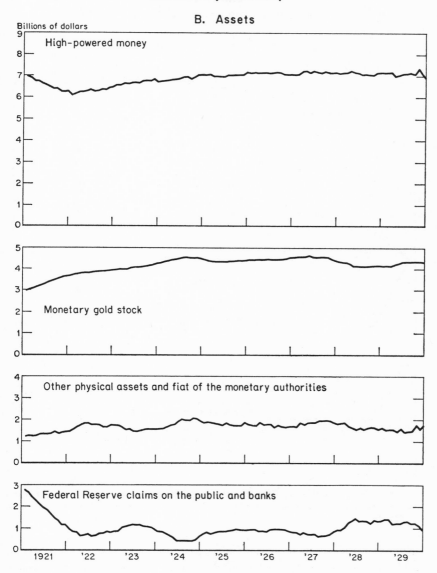

Billions of dollars

Reserve credit. That was partly because an expansion in the money stock seemed clearly desirable after the drastic contraction of 1920–21, as is confirmed by the sharp decline in discount rates, partly because open market operations were not yet coordinated but were being carried out by separate Reserve Banks, which engaged in purchases primarily to increase

281

CHART 25
Major Influences on High-Powered Money, 1921–29

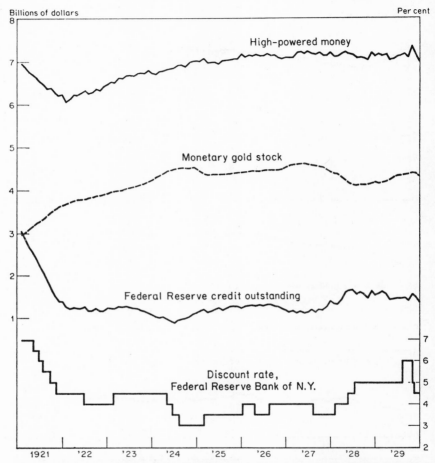

SOURCE: High-powered money, Table B-3. Monetary gold stock, same as for Table 10. Federal Reserve credit outstanding, same as for Chart 22. Discount rate, *Banking and Monetary Statistics,* pp. 440–441.

earnings rather than as part of a general credit policy. From 1923 on, gold movements were largely offset by movements in Federal Reserve credit so that there was essentially no relation between the movements in gold and in the total of high-powered money; the fairly irregular dips and rises in the gold stock were transformed into a horizontal movement in total high-powered money.

The sterilization of gold movements was initially justified by the System on three grounds: first, much of the gold could be regarded as only temporarily in this country pending the re-establishment of gold standards elsewhere; second, with most of the world not on the gold standard, gold movements could not serve their traditional equilibrating role; and third, with respect to sterilization of the inflow, the increase in short-term foreign balances in the United States made a larger gold stock desirable.[61] The third reason was entirely valid; the only question is one of magnitude. The first two reasons were also entirely valid, so long as other countries remained off gold and there was a possibility that they would return to gold at exchange rates that temporarily, at least, undervalued their currencies. Such rates would tend to generate a surplus in their balances of payments and thereby to produce an inflow of gold from the United States without any prior price inflation in the United States. This was in fact the course followed by France.

Once, however, other countries—in particular, Britain in 1925—returned to gold, those reasons were no longer valid, though they continued to be repeated by the System. The sterilization of gold could be justified as a means of insulating internal monetary conditions from external changes. Its international effect, however, was to render the maintenance of the international gold standard more difficult. Suppose all countries linked by a gold standard were to sterilize gold flows. Gold flows would then set in train no forces tending to bring them to a halt or to reverse them. The system could last only so long as the flows resulted from purely temporary imbalances of sufficiently small magnitude to right themselves before draining the countries losing gold of their reserves.[62] The effect would be to insulate the countries from minor adjustments at the cost of letting them accumulate into major ones. Let only some countries—in this case mainly the United States—sterilize gold movements, and the effect is to throw the full burden of adjustment on the other countries involved. In practice, countries are apt to behave asymmetrically, to be willing to sterilize gold inflows more fully than gold outflows, so that a widespread policy of sterilization is likely to mean placing major reliance on the deflationary effects of gold outflows. Yet, paradoxically, the internal pains of adjustment are likely to be more severe when the adjustment required is deflation than when it is inflation.

[61] See Federal Reserve Board, *Annual Report* for 1923, pp. 20–22; for 1925, p. 2; for 1926, p. 16.

[62] Note that even if the countries are and remain in long-run equilibrium in the sense that on the average the net flow of gold would be zero, as the time period lengthens, the probability approaches unity that any given amount of gold reserves will be exhausted by the cumulation of random imbalances. This is a consequence of the so-called law of averages. Given a sequence of random and independent values, the variance of their sum increases without limit as the number of items added increases, while the variance of their *average* decreases. In the present case, it is the sum, not the average, that is relevant.

In the period in question, this problem arose mainly for Britain, which re-established the gold standard in 1925 at a rate that probably overvalued the pound. There was a persistent tendency of Britain to lose gold which it was able to offset only by maintaining almost steady internal deflationary pressure. Rigidities prevented the deflationary pressure from reducing internal prices sufficiently, producing instead generally depressed conditions. There can be little doubt that Britain's problem would have been vastly eased if the United States, and even more France, had permitted a greater degree of monetary expansion—enough in this country, for example, so that wholesale prices would have been stable from 1925 to 1929 instead of falling about 8 per cent.[63] The final result of the policies followed, of course, was the worldwide abandonment of the gold standard.

The United States was in an especially favorable position to sterilize gold movements owing to the small importance of its foreign trade relative to its domestic trade and the high level of its gold reserves. Yet even this country was unwilling or unable to carry out a sterilization policy in full. It did sterilize minor movements during the period under discussion, but we have already seen in the preceding chapter how in 1920 the System felt it necessary to react when its gold reserve ratio fell sharply. We shall have occasion also to note in the next chapter how, when Britain finally went off the gold standard in 1931 and an outflow of gold from the United States first was impending and then occurred, the System again took drastic deflationary action, this time with even more serious consequences. Both actions illustrate the asymmetry that is likely to prevail, since both involved reacting to gold outflows.

In retrospect, it probably would have been better either to have permitted the gold-standard rules to operate fully, once something like an international gold standard was adopted, or to have replaced them completely by an alternative criterion. The compromise of disregarding minor movements but reacting to major ones may have promoted stability during the twenties but, if so, only at the cost of great instability at either end of the decade. The result was that the policy, as carried out, achieved neither the internal objective of domestic stability nor the external objective of a stable international gold standard.

The preceding analysis implies that the gold sterilization program made the flows of gold more unstable than they otherwise would have been. The reason is, of course, that if the gold flows had been permitted to affect

[63] The overvaluation of the pound when the link to gold was re-established has generally been estimated to be of the order of 10 per cent. See *Report of the [Macmillan] Committee on Finance and Industry*, Great Britain, Cmnd. 3897, June 1931, pp. 110–111. Note, however, that Britain's return to the gold standard had been preceded by a 50 per cent decline in prices, so that the total adjustment required of Britain is better described as a price decline of about 55 per cent.

the quantity of money they would thereby have set in motion forces tending to reduce their magnitude. Some evidence that gold flows were in fact more unstable is provided by a comparison of changes in the gold stock in the three periods designated above as periods of relative stability: 1882–92, 1903–13 and 1923–29. As Table 12 shows, the standard deviation of the percentage change from year to year in the gold stock is decidedly higher in the twenties than in either of the earlier periods.[64]

TABLE 12

COMPARATIVE STABILITY OF RATE OF CHANGE IN MONEY STOCK AND IN OTHER MAGNITUDES, IN PERIODS OF RELATIVELY STABLE PRICES AND PERIODS OF FLUCTUATING PRICES, 1869–1929

	Standard Deviation of Year-to-Year Percentage Changes in:					
Period	Monetary Gold Stock (1)	High-Powered Money (2)	Money Stock (3)	Velocity of Money (4)	Wholesale Prices (5)	Real Income (6)
1869–82	20.3	5.7	6.9	8.1	7.0	7.8
1882–92	**4.4**	**2.0**	**3.7**	**3.4**	**4.6**	**3.7**
1892–1903	8.8	4.6	7.1	5.6	5.5	6.9
1903–13	**3.5**	**2.7**	**3.7**	**5.3**	**4.7**	**7.4**
1913–23	10.1	8.9	6.9	9.9	20.3	8.7
1923–29	**5.5**	**1.4**	**2.8**	**4.3**	**3.7**	**2.5**

NOTE: Boldface denotes periods of relative economic stability. The dates are annual reference peaks in the National Bureau chronology.

SOURCE: Table 25, below.

Because of this fact, the actual gold flows cannot be used to estimate the effect on the stock of money of the alternative policy of permitting gold flows to influence the stock of money. There would almost surely have been wider variations in the stock of money under the alternative policy. However, they would not have been so wide as those implied by the actual behavior of the gold stock.

We can perhaps get some idea of the effect of the policy actually followed by comparing the behavior of high-powered money and the stock of money during 1923–29 with their behavior during the earlier relatively

[64] It is not entirely clear that this is the proper basis of comparison, because independent of the change in the monetary adaptation pattern there may have been a change in the amount of gold movement required by the variation in the conditions of international trade. An alternative is to express the change in the gold stock as a ratio to the contemporaneous change in total high-powered money, since this ratio reflects in full the change in the monetary adaptation pattern. As might be expected, this gives an even more striking difference: the standard deviation of these ratios is 1.17 for 1882–92; 0.40 for 1903–13; and 3.38 for 1923–29. However, this comparison may overstate the relevant difference, since the smaller rate of growth of high-powered money in the final period gives small denominators to the ratios and thus renders them statistically unstable.

stable periods of 1882–92 and 1903–13 (see Table 12). The partial in-sulation of the stock of money from gold flows is reflected in smaller variations in both high-powered money and the stock of money. Pre-sumably, the alternative policy of permitting gold-standard rules to operate would have reduced the variability in gold flows to something like its size during the earlier relatively stable periods, which means to something like three-fifths to four-fifths of the magnitude actually experienced. Correspondingly, the alternative policy would have increased the variability in high-powered money and in the stock of money to some-thing like their size in the earlier periods, which means an increase to between 1.4 and 1.9 times the level experienced for high-powered money and 1.3 times for the stock of money.

What effect would the greater variability in the stock of money, in its turn, have had on economic stability? Again we may resort to a com-parison with earlier periods—this time, of the behavior of real income. The comparison is somewhat more difficult to make properly than those for the monetary changes were. Except for real income, all the magnitudes in Table 12 varied decidedly less during the three periods of relative stability than during the three other periods in the table. Real income, on the other hand, varied more from 1903 to 1913 than during one of the other three periods and almost as much as during another. The reason is the severe contraction from 1907 to 1908, which shows up sufficiently even in the annual figures to raise drastically the measure of variability in the table. However, taking all six periods together, there is nonetheless a high correlation between the variability in the stock of money and in real income.[65] And the standard deviations for money and for real income tend not to differ much in magnitude, only the values for 1903–13 dif-fering appreciably. It is therefore reasonable to infer that, if the alterna-tive policy with respect to gold had raised the variability in the stock of money by about a third, it would have had about the same effect on the variability in real income. This would have meant an increase in the variability of real income from 2.5 to about 3.3, still below the level that prevailed in 1882–92.

The behavior of prices is another indication of the degree of economic stability. As might be expected from the preceding comparisons, wholesale prices were less variable during 1923–29 than during any of the other periods distinguished. There is a high correlation between the size of the standard deviation for prices and for money, the one notable deviation

[65] The product-moment correlation coefficient between the standard deviations of the stock of money and real income is .78, a value that, for six observations, would be exceeded (in algebraic value) by chance less than one time in twenty. Adding three additional later periods (1929–39, 1939–48, 1948–60; see Chap. 11) raises the correlation coefficient to .88, a value that, for nine observations, would be exceeded (in algebraic value) by chance less than one time in two thousand.

being the much higher variability of prices from 1913 to 1923 than would be suggested solely by the variability of money. This deviation reflects, of course, the sharp variations in velocity during and after the war. Again, we may infer that if the variability in the stock of money had been 1.3 times as large as it was, so would have been the variability in prices. This would have meant a variability of roughly the same magnitude as during the two earlier periods of relative stability.

Of course this comparison among periods is only suggestive. There were many differences among the periods other than the policy adopted toward gold flows; and the policy adopted toward gold flows was by no means the only factor affecting the variability in the stock of money. Yet the comparison may serve to give some idea of the order of magnitude of the effects in question. And it certainly gives reason for greater confidence in our earlier qualitative reasoning, since the results are in the direction suggested by that reasoning.

OTHER MOVEMENTS IN HIGH-POWERED MONEY

Because of the gold sterilization policy, changes in Federal Reserve credit outstanding are a poor guide to other Reserve policy actions. The movements in Reserve credit are dominated by those that offset the changes in the gold stock. We can come closer to isolating the effects of other Reserve actions by looking at the total of high-powered money, taking it for granted that such movements as did occur were mainly "planned that way," while using other information to insure that we are not led astray by the slip that so often occurs between plan and execution.

Three movements, though appearing minor on the scale of Chart 23, are worth noting: (1) the retardation in the growth of high-powered money in 1923–24; (2) the mild decline in late 1926 and subsequent recovery in 1927; and (3) the generally downward tendency from the end of the first quarter of 1928 to the stock market crash in 1929. The first two require little comment; the third was rather more important.

The rapid rise in economic activity and in prices in 1922, first welcomed as a healthy reaction to the 1920–21 contraction, began to occasion concern early in 1923 and led to a policy of "moderate restraint."[66] As Chart 25 shows, the discount rate in New York was raised at the end of February, some three months before the cyclical peak. Sales of government securities were begun a month or so earlier still. Federal Reserve credit, which had been rising in late 1922 along with the gold stock,

[66] The Treasury opposed this policy. In a letter to the Federal Reserve Bank of New York, a Treasury official suggested that preferential rates for borrowing based on short-term government securities might properly be established in order to strengthen the market. Governor Strong answered with a statement against preferential rates (Harrison, Special, No. 35, Part 4, p. 8; Harrison, Miscellaneous, Vol. II).

reached a peak in May and declined at a substantial rate thereafter. The decline was large enough to offset most of the sizable gold inflow from 1923 to mid-1924 and to produce a noticeable retardation in the growth of high-powered money. The concomitant mild but noticeable recession led to a reversal of policy. From 4½ per cent in April 1924, the discount rate at New York was lowered in three successive steps to 3 per cent by August. Again the change in discount rates was preceded by open market operations. The Reserve System's holdings of government securities were increased from a low of $73 million in November 1923 to $588 million a year later, the greater part of the increase taking place in the seven months from February to September 1924.[67] Federal Reserve credit reached a trough in June 1924; and total high-powered money resumed its earlier rate of growth. The trough of the recession is dated in July 1924.

It is by no means clear how to interpret the close synchronism of Reserve action and business movements during that episode. Doubtless there were effects both ways and common causes as well. But there seems little doubt that the synchronism impressed itself strongly on contemporaries, both inside and outside the System, and strengthened the confidence of both groups in the potency of Reserve System powers. The episode almost surely played an important role in the development of the policy statement in the 1923 report.

The 1926–27 episode is in many respects a repetition. There was a vigorous cyclical revival after the trough in mid-1924, accompanied by a real estate boom that leveled off in 1926 and the beginnings of the great stock market boom. Toward the end of 1926, moderate restraining measures were taken before the cyclical peak which occurred in October 1926. The subsequent contraction was exceedingly mild. Not long before the cyclical trough in November 1927, easing measures were taken. The buying rate on bankers' acceptances was reduced ¼ of 1 percentage point from July to August 1927, and the System's bill holdings rose by $200 million; the discount rate was reduced at all Banks from 4 to 3½ per cent between July and September 1927; and open market purchases of government securities totaling $340 million were made between late June and the middle of November 1927. Both the decline in Federal Reserve credit and the subsequent rise partly offset gold flows so that the net effect on high-powered money was slight. However, the year 1927 saw a decided rise in the ratio of deposits to currency, so there was a much more sizable movement in the total stock of money than in high-powered

[67] The figures cited are seasonally unadjusted figures from the weekly Federal Reserve statements, which give holdings at close of business on Wednesday of each week.

The Board was motivated partly by the desire to help England return to the gold standard through easing credit conditions in the United States relative to England. That motive called for purchases also desirable for internal purposes.

money—a retardation in late 1926 and a resumed rise in 1927. That movement may well have been taken into account, implicitly or explicitly, in the System's action.

As already noted in some detail, few episodes have occasioned so much controversy and discussion as the attempt by the System from early 1928 on to curb the stock market boom. Although business expansion had been resumed only at the very end of 1927, and although commodity prices showed no tendency to rise—they fell from 96.6 in October 1927 to 95.5 in March 1928—the System undertook restrictive action early in 1928.[68] By July, the discount rate had been raised in New York to 5 per cent, the highest since 1921, and the System's holdings of government securities had been reduced from a level of over $600 million at the end of 1927 to $210 million by August 1928, despite an outflow of gold. Federal Reserve credit outstanding nevertheless continued to rise to mid-1928 because of a sharp increase in discounts. The increase in discounts was partly the "scissors" movement in reaction to the open market sales. But it was more than that. The rise in discount rates did not keep pace with the rise in market rates in an environment of rapidly rising stock prices and brisk demand for "street-loans." Hence, discount rates fell relative to market rates, giving banks a stronger incentive to borrow from the System. The System was criticized for not moving even more vigorously; and there was a more or less open feud, as we have seen, between New York, which wanted to take earlier and more drastic action, and the Board.[69] And much of the blame for the stock market boom itself was attributed to the prior "easy" money policy of 1927.

After mid-1928, despite some backing and filling, fairly continuous restraint was maintained, though, as noted, the discount rate in New York was kept constant until August 1929—the National Bureau's reference date for the peak—when it was raised to 6 per cent. However, changes in the buying rate for bills, over which the Federal Reserve Bank of New York had more effective control, served to some extent as a substitute. The minimum buying rate on 60-day acceptances was unchanged at 4½ per cent from July through December 1928, one-half a percentage point below the discount rate, and during that period bill holdings rose sharply, much more than the usual seasonal rise. The rate was then raised five times to 5½ per cent in March 1929, when it was one-half of a percentage point above the discount rate. Bill holdings in the first half of 1929 fell even more sharply than they had risen in the

[68] The Treasury opposed "prompt adoption of a strong policy of restraint," because it was then engaged in refunding operations, but it did not seriously interfere with Federal Reserve policy (Harrison, Special, No. 35, Part 4, p. 8).

[69] See Strong, *Interpretations*, p. xxii; Chandler, *Benjamin Strong*, pp. 454–455. Strong had little influence on Federal Reserve policy from May to Aug. 1928 when he was in Europe. He returned in failing health.

last half of 1928, and accounted for most of the contemporaneous decline in total Federal Reserve credit outstanding. In July, the bill rate was lowered to 5¼ per cent and in August, when the discount rate was increased, again to 5⅛ per cent.

As we have seen, the Board very likely regarded as appropriate the contradictory movements in the discount and bill rates, because of its emphasis on the end use of credit. It is doubtful, however, that Harrison thought it possible to restrain with the discount rate and to ease with the bill rate at the same time. His intention in August 1929 was to ease the money market. It is often said that the decline in the bill rate was the price paid by New York to get the needed increase in the discount rate from the Board. It seems to us that there is at least as much evidence for precisely the opposite interpretation. The course of events had finally led the Board to favor a rise in the discount rate after the need for it had passed. There was not much chance of stopping the ponderous machinery already in motion without a similar long campaign. Harrison therefore accepted the rise in the discount rate because he could offset it by lowering the bill rate.[70]

High-powered money stayed roughly constant or declined a bit during 1928 and 1929. The money stock also declined slightly, being lower at the cyclical peak in August 1929 than 16 months earlier in April 1928. From the time our monthly series starts in 1907, the only previous occasions on which the stock of money was below its level 16 months earlier were during the sharp contractions of 1907–08 and 1920–21. There is on record no prior or subsequent business expansion during which so long a period passed without a rise.

In its famous statement of February 1929 asking for direct restraint on security speculation, the Board said, "The Federal Reserve Board neither assumes the right nor has it any disposition to set itself up as an arbiter of security speculation or values."[71] Nonetheless, there is no doubt that the desire to curb the stock market boom was a major if not dominating factor in Reserve actions during 1928 and 1929. Those actions clearly failed to stop the stock market boom. But they did exert steady deflationary pressure on the economy.[72] Wholesale prices rose during the

[70] See the quotation from the policy suggested by Harrison to the Board on Aug. 2, 1929, p. 264, above.

See also Harrison's letter to Young on Sept. 30, 1929, suggesting that the Open Market Investment Committee be given authority to supplement the purchase of bills with purchases of government securities "at a rate which will permit of a continued reduction in member bank discounts, and thus gradually pave the way for an ultimate ease in interest rates . . . ." (Harrison, Miscellaneous, Vol. I).

[71] See *Annual Report* for 1929, p. 3; and footnote 29 above.

[72] To quote a document of the New York Federal Reserve Bank: "It was suggested that we had encouraged a deflation of credit during most of the years 1928 and 1929, that the rate of increase in total volume of credit in use had been below normal . . . ." (Harrison, Notes, Vol. I, minutes of a meeting of the executive committee of the New York Bank directors, May 19, 1930).

second and third quarters of 1928 but declined from then through 1929. They averaged a trifle lower during the three months centered on the cyclical peak of August 1929 than during the three months centered on the prior trough of November 1927. This was the first cyclical expansion since 1891–93 during which wholesale prices failed to rise, and there have been none to 1960.

In our view, that episode, like the gold sterilization policy, exemplifies the difficulties raised by seeking to make policy serve two masters. Had the Reserve System directed its policy single-mindedly to breaking the stock market boom, it would have refrained from its easing actions in 1927. Instead, it would have started its restraining actions then rather than in 1928 and it would have taken more vigorous action than it did in 1928. There seems little doubt that, had it been willing to take such measures, it could have succeeded in breaking the bull market.[73] On the other hand, if it had single-mindedly pursued the objective implicit in its 1923 policy statement of promoting stable economic growth, it would have been less restrictive in 1928 than it was and would have permitted both high-powered money and the stock of money to grow at something like their usual secular rates. In the event, it followed a policy which was too easy to break the speculative boom, yet too tight to promote healthy economic growth.

In our view, the Board should not have made itself an "arbiter of security speculation or values" and should have paid no direct attention

[73] J. K. Galbraith dismisses the view that the action of the Federal Reserve authorities in cutting rediscount rates in the spring of 1927 and in purchasing government securities in considerable volume had much effect on the speculation and collapse which followed, on the ground that the "explanation obviously assumes that people will always speculate if only they can get the money to finance it. Nothing could be farther from the case. There were times before and there have been long periods since when credit was plentiful and cheap—far cheaper than in 1927–29—and when speculation was negligible. Nor, as we shall see later, was speculation out of control after 1927, except that it was beyond the reach of men who did not want in the least to control it" (*The Great Crash, 1929,* Boston, Houghton Mifflin, 1955, p. 16).

Granted that speculation was not out of control after 1927, surely control would have been less of a problem had the stock market not acquired additional funds in 1927. Speculation would certainly have been hampered if the authorities had substituted a passive or a tight money policy for the expansionary policy that was adopted in 1927.

J. A. Schumpeter (*Business Cycles,* New York, McGraw-Hill, 1939, Vol. II, p. 899) also saw no connection between Reserve policy in 1927 and the stock market boom of 1928–29 or the subsequent breakdown. Yet he claimed that had the Federal Reserve in 1927 forced "banks to withdraw their loans to brokers, whereby other lenders would [have] be[en] induced to retreat" (p. 900), there was no doubt that it would have been successful in preventing the crash. Since virtually the full increase in bank assets from June 1926 to June 1928 as a result of easy money in 1927 was confined to investments and loans on securities, it is hard to see why Schumpeter absolved the Reserve System from fault for making these additional funds available. Simply by withholding them it could have achieved the purpose for which Schumpeter proposed a selective money control.

to the stock market boom, any more than it did to the earlier Florida land boom. At the same time, it seems to us that the final outcome of following the alternative objective single-mindedly would have been preferable to the actual outcome of seeking to serve both objectives. A vigorous restrictive policy in early 1928 might well have broken the stock market boom without its having to be kept in effect long enough to constitute a serious drag on business in general.[74]

SEASONAL MOVEMENTS

The data so far considered in Charts 22–25 are all seasonally adjusted. They have therefore kept out of sight one important facet of Federal Reserve policy, namely, seasonal adjustment of credit to meet the seasonal fluctuation in trade. Before the Federal Reserve System was established, there had been recurrent ease in the money market in the summer and tightness in the fall crop-moving season and in the Christmas season (September through December). One aspect of the seasonal movement was a fluctuation in the ratio of deposits to currency, which produced recurrent ease and tightness in bank reserve positions and a sharp seasonal pattern in call money and other short-term interest rates.[75] That seasonal movement was very much in the minds of the founders of the System and was an important source of their belief in the need for an "elastic" currency.

Chart 26 shows the average seasonal pattern during the twenties in Federal Reserve credit outstanding, in currency outside the Treasury and Federal Reserve Banks (a total that includes both our "currency held by the public" and currency in the vaults of banks), and in member bank deposits at Federal Reserve Banks. The patterns for Reserve credit and currency in circulation are closely alike in both shape and magnitude. The Federal Reserve "sterilized," as it were, seasonal withdrawals and returns of currency and thereby kept deposits of member banks at the Reserve Banks largely, though not entirely, free of seasonal movement.

The effect was to change pre-1914 seasonal patterns notably. The seasonal pattern in currency outside the Treasury was widened, the

---

[74] This was apparently Governor Strong's view (Strong, *Interpretations*, p. xxii). Irving Fisher reported that in 1928, when Strong was in Atlantic City to convalesce, "he paced the floor because he found that his colleagues were not raising the rate of rediscount in order to prevent the crash he saw coming" (*Annals of the American Academy of Political and Social Science*, Jan. 1934, p. 151).

It was also Harrison's view, although, as we have seen, he was unsuccessful in obtaining the Board's support for it (see Harrison, Miscellaneous, Vol. II, letter, dated Apr. 18, 1932, Harrison to Senator Glass, quoted in Chap. 7, footnote 134, below).

[75] E. W. Kemmerer, *Seasonal Variations in the Relative Demand for Money and Capital in the United States,* National Monetary Commission, S. Doc. 588, 61st Cong., 2d sess., 1910, pp. 16, 19, 21, 24–25, 147.

CHART 26
Seasonal Patterns Affected by Federal Reserve Policy, 1922–29

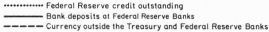

············ Federal Reserve credit outstanding
————— Bank deposits at Federal Reserve Banks
— — — — Currency outside the Treasury and Federal Reserve Banks

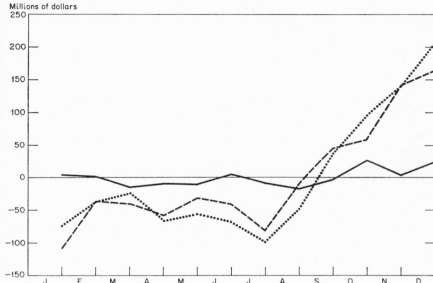

SOURCE: Federal Reserve credit outstanding, seasonal adjustment factors for end-of-month data (*Banking and Monetary Statistics*, pp. 373 ff.) obtained by Shiskin-Eisenpress method (see source, Chart 21) were averaged, 1922–29, for each month of the year and the 12 averages adjusted to add to 1,200. The average monthly value of Federal Reserve credit outstanding, 1922–29, was applied as a constant multiplier to the difference between each of these 12 seasonal indexes and 100.

Bank deposits at Federal Reserve Banks, Table A-2, col. 2. Pattern was computed by method just described.

Currency, end-of-month data (*Banking and Monetary Statistics*, pp. 373 ff.), pattern computed by same method, except that the seasonal adjustment factors, in NBER files, were obtained by the ratio-to-moving-total method.

seasonal pattern in call money rates narrowed.[76] The System was almost entirely successful in the stated objective of eliminating seasonal strain.

[76] Cf. the range of the seasonal indexes for these series computed by the National Bureau of Economic Research:

	High	*Low*
Currency outside the Treasury, 1908–14 (end of month)	100.5 (Nov.)	99.3 (June–July)
Currency outside the Treasury and Federal Reserve Banks, 1922–29 (end of month)	103.6 (Dec.)	97.6 (Jan.)
Call money rates, New York City, 1897–1911 (monthly average of weekly data)	173 (Dec.)	65 (Aug.)
1924–29	112 (Dec.)	94 (Mar.–Apr.)

293

It is important to distinguish analytically two kinds of seasonal movements to which the System adapted and in the process changed in form: first, a movement in the ratio of deposits to currency that would have required a change in high-powered money or in the reserve ratios of commercial banks to permit the same total quantity of money to be outstanding; second, a movement in the total quantity of money (currency and deposits) in the hands of the public. The first raised a problem of "elasticity" in the sense of interconvertibility of deposits and currency; the second, in the quite different sense of variation in the total quantity of money.

Prior to the Federal Reserve System, the first problem was met primarily by changes in bank reserve ratios, themselves largely induced by changes in short-term interest rates; the second, by a seasonal pattern in gold movements. In each case, the extent of the movement was curtailed by the selfsame movement in interest rates that gave banks an incentive to vary reserve ratios: high interest rates at times of a high demand *schedule* for currency or money balances induced economy in their use, and thereby served to reduce the quantity demanded—and conversely.

The Federal Reserve System met the seasonal movements by expanding and contracting high-powered money sufficiently to provide for the changed ratio of deposits to currency and also to permit a seasonal movement in the total stock of money. It thereby largely eliminated the recurrent seasonal ease and tightness in bank reserve positions, and hence the seasonal movement in interest rates. But that in turn eliminated a factor which had curtailed the extent of the movement, so the seasonal variations in currency outside the Treasury and Federal Reserve Banks and, we presume, in the total stock of money were decidedly wider in the 1920's than in earlier periods.

In their empirical manifestation, seasonal and cyclical movements appear similar, and this similarity has been the source of much confusion in thinking about monetary policy, particularly in connection with the much abused notion of "elasticity." In both movements, two kinds of changes can occur: changes in the deposit-currency ratio and changes in the total stock of money. It seems appropriate that seasonal and cyclical movements in the deposit-currency ratio be treated alike, and that both be prevented from affecting the total quantity of money. It is a purely technical result of a fractional reserve banking system that the total stock of money should be affected by a change in the form in which the public wishes to hold its money. It is hard to see how any economic function is performed by permitting a change in the deposit-currency ratio to have that effect. It is simply an unintended and undesired consequence, which it seems eminently proper to eliminate so far as possible.

The second kind of change—a change in the total stock of money—is a different matter. Within the year, there seems little harm and perhaps some merit in permitting the stock of money to decline during the summer months and rise in the fall and winter. Apparently during the summer the community desires smaller money balances relative to income—at any given level of interest rates—and during the fall and winter, higher money balances. Permitting the stock of money to fluctuate accordingly means, in effect, offsetting a rise in desired velocity by a decline in the money stock, and conversely. This kind of "elasticity" of the total money stock is perhaps desirable.[77]

The cyclical counterpart of this seasonal policy appears superficially to be an increase in the stock of money (or better, an increase at more than the secular rate) during cyclical expansion and a decrease (or better, an increase at less than the secular rate) during cyclical contraction. And this is the doctrine enshrined in the view that the money stock should respond to "needs of trade" and in the widespread if erroneous belief in the desirability of "elasticity" of the total money stock. On a deeper level of analysis, however, the correct counterpart of the seasonal policy is precisely the reverse. Desired real money balances apparently fall relative to income during expansion and rise during contraction.[78] Hence, a policy of offsetting movements in velocity with opposite movements in the stock of money—the basic justification for the seasonal monetary reaction described—calls for a reduction in the money stock (or better, a rise at less than the secular rate) during cyclical expansions and a rise (or better, a rise at more than the secular rate) during cyclical contractions.

The policy statements by the Federal Reserve System leave little doubt that this distinction between the appropriate seasonal and cyclical reactions was at least implicitly recognized, at any rate from time to time. But to the best of our knowledge, it was never explicitly emphasized. The failure to do so almost surely played a part in the durability of the "needs of trade" doctrine and in the System's acquiescence in movements in the

[77] Our qualified statement reflects the fact that we see little reason for regarding changes in the stock of money as a better adaptation than a seasonal movement in interest rates. The difficulties giving rise to financial panics in earlier periods resulted much less from the absence of elasticity in the total stock of money than from the absence of interconvertibility of deposits and currency.

In addition, in a system in which the monetary authorities effectively control the money stock, they must decide explicitly how much seasonal change to introduce—a decision depending on uncertain criteria. Should they determine the seasonal change so as to eliminate entirely any seasonal movement in interest rates? If so, which interest rates? Or should they determine the seasonal change to introduce into money by an observed seasonal movement in velocity? On this point, see also Friedman, *A Program for Monetary Stability*, p. 92.

[78] See Friedman, *The Demand for Money: Some Theoretical and Empirical Results*, New York, NBER, Occasional Paper 68, 1959.

money stock that conformed positively to cyclical fluctuations and thereby helped to intensify them, particularly in the years 1930 and 1931 just following the period under consideration.

5. *Summary*

The twenties were, in the main, a period of high prosperity and stable economic growth. An enormous construction boom rebuilt American cities. The automobile reshaped American life. The bull market in stocks mirrored soaring American optimism about the future. From 1921 to 1929, two recessions interrupted economic development, but both were so mild that many if not most of those who lived and worked at the time were unaware that they had occurred. The recessions were clearly registered only on the delicate seismographs economists and statisticians were developing.

On the monetary side, the most notable feature was the close connection in timing between the movements in economic activity and the explicit policy measures taken by the Federal Reserve System. Moderate restraint in early 1923, exercised by sales of government securities and a rise in discount rates, was followed closely by a peak in business and the onset of the 1923–24 recession. A reversal of policy in late 1923 and early 1924 in the direction of ease was followed by a trough in business in July 1924 and a vigorous cyclical revival. Moderate restraint in the third quarter of 1926 was followed by a peak in October, and easing measures in 1927, by a cyclical trough in November.

The close synchronism produced much confidence within and without the System that the new monetary machinery offered a delicate yet effective means of smoothing economic fluctuations, and that its operators knew how to use it toward that end. That confidence was accompanied and in turn strengthened by refinement of the monetary tools available, greater understanding of their operation, and more explicit consideration of criteria for their use. The most important development was surely the rapid spread of understanding within the System of the effects of open market operations on the reserves of member banks and the resulting voluntary coordination of the open market operations of the twelve Federal Reserve Banks through a System account conducted by an open market committee on behalf of all the Banks. A supplementary development was the recognition of the interrelation between discounting and open market operations: the so-called scissors effect, whereby a System sale of securities, by reducing member bank reserves, would lead banks to increase their borrowing from the System through discounting—and conversely—so that a rise in discount rates, if accompanied by open market sales as part of a program of monetary restraint, might actually lead to a rise in the amount of discounting.

The criteria offered for determining the general direction of monetary policy are much less easily summarized. The traditional real bills or needs of trade doctrine received much emphasis, yet it was married to an inventory theory of the business cycle that could be interpreted as requiring action in almost the opposite direction. According to the former, "The Federal reserve supplies the needed additions to credit in times of business expansion and takes up the slack in times of business recession."[79] According to the latter, prevention of a slump requires inhibiting undue inventory expansion; and mitigation of a recession requires inhibiting undue inventory liquidation, and hence resisting the needs of trade toward the latter part of the expansion and fostering "slack" toward the latter part of the contraction. The uneasy compromise was never resolved, and much of the later impasse in deliberations on appropriate monetary policy during the 1929–33 contraction can be traced to failure to resolve it.

On a specific operational level, two more immediate criteria came to play a consistent role. (1) Gold movements were not permitted to affect the total of high-powered money. They were—in the antiseptic term that came into use—sterilized, inflows being offset by open market sales, outflows, by open market purchases. As a result, short-term movements in Federal Reserve credit outstanding after 1923 showed a nice inverse relation to corresponding movements in the gold stock. (2) Seasonal movements in currency held by the public were not permitted to affect member bank reserves. Increases were offset by open market purchases, decreases by open market sales. As a result, member bank reserves showed little seasonal movement, and interest rates showed a seasonal movement of decidedly smaller amplitude than before World War I.

Inevitably, in the absence of any single well-defined statutory objective, conflicts developed between discretionary objectives of monetary policy. The two most important arose out of the re-establishment of the gold standard abroad and the emergence of the bull market in stocks. The gold-standard rules required the United States to permit gold movements to affect the money stock and prices; yet the desire to promote internal stability called for offsetting gold movements. The conflict was resolved by offsetting minor movements during the twenties, as just noted, but also by reacting to the major movements at each end of the decade —in 1920–21 and again in 1931. It seems likely that the offsetting of the minor movements contributed to the development of the later major movement.

The bull market brought the objective of promoting business activity into conflict with the desire to restrain stock market speculation. The conflict was resolved in 1928 and 1929 by adoption of a monetary policy,

[79] Federal Reserve Board, *Tenth Annual Report* for 1923, p. 10.

not restrictive enough to halt the bull market yet too restrictive to foster vigorous business expansion. The outcome was in no small measure a result of the internal struggle for power within the System which followed the death of Benjamin Strong in October 1928. How to restrain speculation became the chief bone of contention: the Banks, led by New York, urged quantitative measures of higher discount rates and open market sales; the Federal Reserve Board urged qualitative measures of direct pressure on banks making security loans. A stalemate persisted throughout most of the crucial year 1929, which not only prevented decisive action one way or the other in that year but also left a heritage of divided counsel and internal conflict for the years of trial that followed.

The economic collapse from 1929 to 1933 has produced much misunderstanding of the twenties. The widespread belief that what goes up must come down and hence also that what comes down must do so because it earlier went up, plus the dramatic stock market boom, have led many to suppose that the United States experienced severe inflation before 1929 and the Reserve System served as an engine of it. Nothing could be further from the truth. By 1923, wholesale prices had recovered only a sixth of their 1920–21 decline. From then until 1929, they fell on the average of 1 per cent per year. The cyclical expansion from 1927 to 1929 is one of the very few in our record during which prices were a shade lower at the three months centered on the peak than at the three months centered on the initial trough. The stock of money, too, failed to rise and even fell slightly during most of the expansion—a phenomenon not matched in any prior or subsequent cyclical expansion. Far from being an inflationary decade, the twenties were the reverse. And the Reserve System, far from being an engine of inflation, very likely kept the money stock from rising as much as it would have if gold movements had been allowed to exert their full influence.

CHAPTER 7

The Great Contraction, 1929–33

THE CONTRACTION from 1929 to 1933 was by far the most severe business-cycle contraction during the near-century of U.S. history we cover and it may well have been the most severe in the whole of U.S. history. Though sharper and more prolonged in the United States than in most other countries, it was worldwide in scope and ranks as the most severe and widely diffused international contraction of modern times. U.S. net national product in current prices fell by more than one-half from 1929 to 1933; net national product in constant prices, by more than one-third; implicit prices, by more than one-quarter; and monthly wholesale prices, by more than one-third.

The antecedents of the contraction have no parallel in the more than fifty years covered by our monthly data. As noted in the preceding chapter, no other contraction before or since has been preceded by such a long period over which the money stock failed to rise. Monetary behavior during the contraction itself is even more striking. From the cyclical peak in August 1929 to the cyclical trough in March 1933, the stock of money fell by over a third. This is more than triple the largest preceding declines recorded in our series, the 9 per cent declines from 1875 to 1879 and from 1920 to 1921. More than one-fifth of the commercial banks in the United States holding nearly one-tenth of the volume of deposits at the beginning of the contraction suspended operations because of financial difficulties. Voluntary liquidations, mergers, and consolidations added to the toll, so that the number of commercial banks fell by well over one-third. The contraction was capped by banking holidays in many states in early 1933 and by a nationwide banking holiday that extended from Monday, March 6, until Monday, March 13, and closed not only all commercial banks but also the Federal Reserve Banks. There was no precedent in U.S. history of a concerted closing of all banks for so extended a period over the entire country.

To find anything in our history remotely comparable to the monetary collapse from 1929 to 1933, one must go back nearly a century to the contraction of 1839 to 1843. That contraction, too, occurred during a period of worldwide crisis, which intensified the domestic monetary uncertainty already unleashed by the political battle over the Second Bank of the United States, the failure to renew its charter, and the speculative activities of the successor bank under state charter. After the lapsing of the Bank's federal charter, domestic monetary uncertainty was further heightened by the successive measures adopted by the government—distribution of the surplus, the Specie Circular, and establishment of an Independent Treasury in 1840 and its dissolution the next year. In 1839–43, as in 1929–33, a substantial fraction of the banks went out of business—about a quarter in the earlier and over a third in the later contraction—and the stock of money fell by about one-third.[1]

The 1929–33 contraction had far-reaching effects in many directions, not least on monetary institutions and academic and popular thinking about the role of monetary factors in the economy. A number of special monetary institutions were established in the course of the contraction, notably the Reconstruction Finance Corporation and the Federal Home Loan Banks, and the powers of the Federal Reserve System were substantially modified. The contraction was shortly followed by the enactment of federal insurance of bank deposits and by further important modifications in the powers of the Federal Reserve System. It was followed also by a brief period of suspension of gold payments and then by a drastic modification of the gold standard which reduced it to a pale shadow of its former self (see Chapter 8).

The contraction shattered the long-held belief, which had been strengthened during the 1920's, that monetary forces were important elements in the cyclical process and that monetary policy was a potent instrument for promoting economic stability. Opinion shifted almost to the opposite extreme, that "money does not matter"; that it is a passive factor which chiefly reflects the effects of other forces; and that monetary policy is of extremely limited value in promoting stability. The evidence summarized in the rest of this chapter suggests that these judgments are not valid inferences from experience. The monetary collapse was not the inescapable consequence of other forces, but rather a largely independent factor which exerted a powerful influence on the course of events. The failure of the Federal Reserve System to prevent the collapse reflected not the impotence of monetary policy but rather the particular policies followed by the monetary authorities and, in smaller degree, the particular monetary arrangements in existence.

The contraction is in fact a tragic testimonial to the importance of monetary forces. True, as events unfolded, the decline in the stock of money and the near-collapse of the banking system can be regarded as a consequence of nonmonetary forces in the United States, and monetary and nonmonetary forces in the rest of the world. Everything depends on

[1] For an interesting comparison of the two contractions, see George Macesich, "Monetary Disturbances in the United States, 1834–45," unpublished Ph.D. dissertation, University of Chicago, June 1958.

how much is taken as given. For it is true also, as we shall see, that different and feasible actions by the monetary authorities could have prevented the decline in the stock of money—indeed, could have produced almost any desired increase in the money stock. The same actions would also have eased the banking difficulties appreciably. Prevention or moderation of the decline in the stock of money, let alone the substitution of monetary expansion, would have reduced the contraction's severity and almost as certainly its duration. The contraction might still have been relatively severe. But it is hardly conceivable that money income could have declined by over one-half and prices by over one-third in the course of four years if there had been no decline in the stock of money.[2]

1. The Course of Money, Income, Prices, Velocity, and Interest Rates

Chart 16, which covers the two decades from 1914 to 1933, shows the magnitude of the contraction in the perspective of a longer period. Money income declined by 15 per cent from 1929 to 1930, 20 per cent the next year, and 27 per cent in the next, and then by a further 5 per cent from 1932 to 1933, even though the cyclical trough is dated in March 1933. The rapid decline in prices made the declines in real income considerably smaller but, even so, real income fell by 11 per cent, 9 per cent, 18 per cent, and 3 per cent in the four successive years. These are extraordinary declines for individual years, let alone for four years in succession. All told, money income fell 53 per cent and real income 36 per cent, or at continuous annual rates of 19 per cent and 11 per cent, respectively, over the four-year period.

Already by 1931, money income was lower than it had been in any year since 1917 and, by 1933, real income was a trifle below the level it had reached in 1916, though in the interim population had grown by 23 per cent. Per capita real income in 1933 was almost the same as in the depression year of 1908, a quarter of a century earlier. Four years of contraction had temporarily erased the gains of two decades, not, of course, by erasing the advances of technology, but by idling men and machines. At the trough of the depression one person was unemployed for every three employed.

In terms of annual averages—to render the figures comparable with the annual income estimates—the money stock fell at a decidedly lower

[2] This view has been argued most cogently by Clark Warburton in a series of important papers, including: "Monetary Expansion and the Inflationary Gap," *American Economic Review*, June 1944, pp. 320, 325–326; "Monetary Theory, Full Production, and the Great Depression," *Econometrica*, Apr. 1945, pp. 124–128; "The Volume of Money and the Price Level Between the World Wars," *Journal of Political Economy*, June 1945, pp. 155–163; "Quantity and Frequency of Use of Money in the United States, 1919–45," *Journal of Political Economy*, Oct. 1946, pp. 442–450.

CHART 27

Money Stock, Currency, and Commercial Bank Deposits,
Monthly, 1929–March 1933

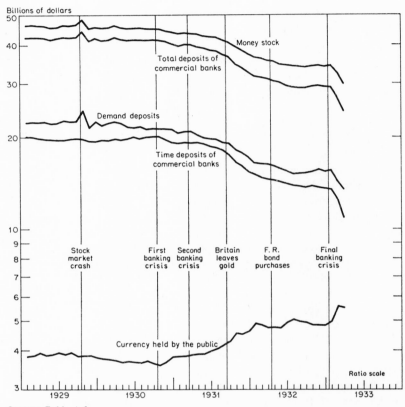

SOURCE: Table A-1.

rate than money income—by 2 per cent, 7 per cent, 17 per cent, and 12 per cent in the four years from 1929 to 1933, a total of 33 per cent, or at a continuous annual rate of 10 per cent. As a result, velocity fell by nearly one-third. As we have seen, this is the usual qualitative relation: velocity tends to rise during the expansion phase of a cycle and to fall during the contraction phase. In general, the magnitude of the movement in velocity varies directly with the magnitude of the corresponding movement in income and in money. For example, the sharp decline in velocity from 1929 to 1933 was roughly matched in the opposite direction by the sharp rise during World War I, which accompanied the rapid rise in the stock of money and in money income; and, in the same direction, by the

CHART 28

Prices, Personal Income, and Industrial Production, Monthly, 1929–March 1933

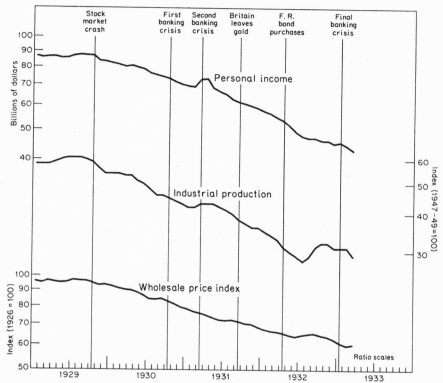

SOURCE: Industrial production, same as for Chart 16. Wholesale price index, same as for Chart 62. Personal income, *Business Cycle Indicators* (Princeton for NBER, G. H. Moore, ed., 1961), Vol. II, p. 139.

sharp fall thereafter accompanying the decline in money income and in the stock of money after 1920. On the other hand, in mild cycles, the movement of velocity is also mild.[3] In 1929–33, the decline in velocity, though decidedly larger than in most mild cycles, was not as much larger as might have been expected from the severity of the decline in income. The reason was that the accompanying bank failures greatly reduced the attractiveness of deposits as a form of holding wealth and so induced the public to hold less money relative to income than it otherwise would have held (see section 3, below). Even so, had a decline

[3] See Milton Friedman, *The Demand for Money: Some Theoretical and Empirical Results*, New York, National Bureau of Economic Research, Occasional Paper 68, 1959, p. 16.

CHART 29

Common Stock Prices, Interest Yields, and Discount Rates of
Federal Reserve Bank of New York, Monthly, 1929–March 1933

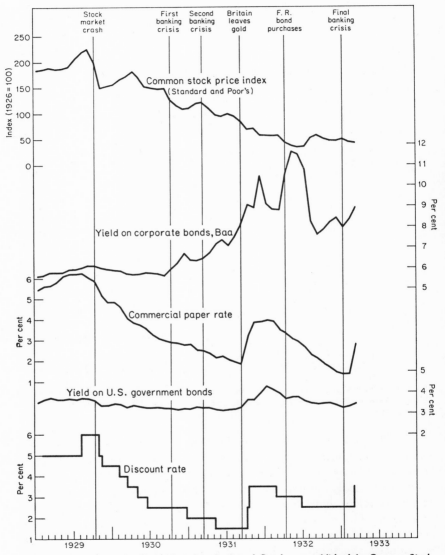

SOURCE: Common stock price index, Standard and Poor's, as published in *Common-Stock Indexes, 1871–1937* (Cowles Commission for Research in Economics, Bloomington, Ind., Principia Press, 1938), p. 67. Discount rates, *Banking and Monetary Statistics*, p. 441. Other data, same as for Chart 35.

in the stock of money been avoided, velocity also would probably have declined less and thus would have reinforced money in moderating the decline in income.

For a closer look at the course of events during these traumatic years, we shift from annual to monthly figures. Chart 27 reproduces on an expanded time scale for 1929 through March 1933 the stock of money, as plotted on Chart 16, and adds series on deposits and currency. Chart 28 reproduces the series on industrial production and wholesale prices, and adds a series on personal income. Chart 29 plots a number of interest rates—of special importance because of the crucial role played during the contraction by changes in financial markets—and also Standard and Poor's index of common stock prices and the discount rates of the Federal Reserve Bank of New York.

It is clear that the course of the contraction was far from uniform. The vertical lines mark off segments into which we have divided the period for further discussion. Although the dividing lines chosen designate monetary events—the focus of our special interest—Charts 28 and 29 demonstrate that the resulting chronology serves about equally well to demarcate distinctive behavior of the other economic magnitudes.

THE STOCK MARKET CRASH, OCTOBER 1929

The first date marked is October 1929, the month in which the bull market crashed. Though stock prices had reached their peak on September 7, when Standard and Poor's composite price index of 90 common stocks stood at 254, the decline in the following four weeks was orderly and produced no panic. In fact, after falling to 228 on October 4, the index rose to 245 on October 10. The decline thereafter degenerated into a panic on October 23. The next day, blocks of securities were dumped on the market and nearly 13 million shares were traded. On October 29, when the index fell to 162, nearly 16½ million shares were traded, compared to the daily average during September of little more than 4 million shares.[4] The stock market crash is reflected in the sharp wiggle in the money series, entirely a result of a corresponding wiggle in demand deposits, which, in turn, reflects primarily an increase in loans to brokers and dealers in securities by New York City banks in response to a drastic reduction of those loans by others.[5] The adjustment was

[4] As in pre-Federal Reserve times, J. P. Morgan and Company assumed leadership of an effort to restore an orderly market by organizing a pool of funds for lending on the call market and for purchase of securities. But the bankers' pool did not stem the tide of selling. By the second week after the crash the phase of organized support of the market was over.

[5] During the two weeks before the panic on Oct. 23, loans to brokers for the account of others by reporting member banks in New York City declined by $120 million, largely as a result of withdrawals of funds by foreigners. From then to the end of the year, those loans declined by $2,300 million, or by no less than 60

orderly, thanks largely to prompt and effective action by the New York Federal Reserve Bank in providing additional reserves to the New York banks through open market purchases (see section 2, below). In particular, the crash left no mark on currency held by the public. Its direct financial effect was confined to the stock market and did not arouse any distrust of banks by their depositors.

The stock market crash coincided with a stepping up of the rate of economic decline. During the two months from the cyclical peak in August 1929 to the crash, production, wholesale prices, and personal income fell at annual rates of 20 per cent, 7½ per cent, and 5 per cent, respectively. In the next twelve months, all three series fell at appreciably higher rates: 27 per cent, 13½ per cent, and 17 per cent, respectively. All told, by October 1930, production had fallen 26 per cent, prices, 14 per cent, and personal income, 16 per cent. The trend of the money stock changed from horizontal to mildly downward. Interest rates, generally rising until October 1929, began to fall. Even if the contraction had come to an end in late 1930 or early 1931, as it might have done in the absence of the monetary collapse that was to ensue, it would have ranked as one of the more severe contractions on record.

Partly, no doubt, the stock market crash was a symptom of the underlying forces making for a severe contraction in economic activity. But partly also, its occurrence must have helped to deepen the contraction. It changed the atmosphere within which businessmen and others were making their plans, and spread uncertainty where dazzling hopes of a new era had prevailed. It is commonly believed that it reduced the willingness of both consumers and business enterprises to spend;[6] or, more pre-

---

per cent. Loans on account of out-of-town banks fell an additional $1 billion. More comprehensive figures show a decline of roughly $4.5 billion in brokers' loans by out-of-town banks and others from Oct. 4 to Dec. 31, and a more than halving of total brokers' loans.

For the data on New York City weekly reporting member bank loans to brokers and dealers in securities, see *Banking and Monetary Statistics,* Board of Governors of the Federal Reserve System, 1943, Table 141, p. 499, and, for quarterly estimates of the total of such loans by all lenders, see *ibid.,* Table 139, p. 494. Although both tables show similar captions for the principal groups of lenders— most of whose funds were placed for them by the New York banks—except for loans by New York City banks for their own accounts, the breakdowns are not comparable. In the weekly series, "out-of-town domestic banks" include member and nonmember banks outside New York City and, to an unknown amount, customers of those banks, whereas in the comprehensive series that category is restricted to member banks outside New York City. Similarly, "others" in the weekly series cover mainly corporations and foreign banking agencies, but in the comprehensive series include also other brokers, individuals, and nonmember banks.

For loans except to brokers and dealers by New York City weekly reporting member banks, which also increased in the week after the crash, see *ibid.,* p. 174. Also see the discussion of that episode in sect. 2, below.

[6] See A. H. Hansen, *Economic Stabilization in an Unbalanced World,* Harcourt,

cisely, that it decreased the amount they desired to spend on goods and services at any given levels of interest rates, prices, and income, which has, as its counterpart, that it increased the amount they wanted to add to their money balances. Such effects on desired flows were presumably accompanied by a corresponding effect on desired balance sheets, namely, a shift away from stocks and toward bonds, away from securities of all kinds and toward money holdings.

The sharp decline in velocity—by 13 per cent from 1929 to 1930—and the turnaround in interest rates are consistent with this interpretation though by no means conclusive, since both declines represent fairly typical cyclical reactions. We have seen that velocity usually declines during contraction, and the more so, the sharper the contraction. For example, velocity declined by 10 per cent from 1907 to 1908, by 13 per cent from 1913 to 1914, and by 15 per cent from 1920 to 1921—though it should be noted that the banking panic in 1907, the outbreak of war in 1914, and the commodity price collapse in 1920 may well have had the same kind of effect on the demand for money as the stock market crash in 1929 had. In contraction years that were both milder and unmarked by such events—1910–11, 1923–24, and 1926–27—velocity declined by only 4 to 5 per cent. It seems likely that at least part of the much sharper declines in velocity in the other years was a consequence of the special events listed, rather than simply a reflection of unusually sharp declines in money income produced by other forces. If so, the stock market crash made the decline in income sharper than it otherwise would have been. Certainly, the coincidence in timing of the stock market crash and of the change in the severity of the contraction supports that view.

Whatever its magnitude, the downward pressure on income produced by the effects of the stock market crash on expectations and willingness to spend—effects that can all be summarized in an independent decline in velocity—was strongly reinforced by the behavior of the stock of money. Compared to the collapse in the next two years, the decline in the stock of money up to October 1930 seems mild. Viewed in a longer perspective, it was sizable indeed. From the cyclical peak in August 1929—to avoid the sharp wiggle in the stock of money produced by the immediate effects of the stock market crash—the money stock declined 2.6 per cent to October 1930, a larger decline than during the whole of all but four preceding reference cycle contractions—1873–79, 1893–94,[7] 1907–08, and

Brace, 1932, pp. 111–112; J. A. Schumpeter, *Business Cycles,* McGraw-Hill, 1939, Vol. II, pp. 679–680; R. A. Gordon, *Business Fluctuations,* Harper, 1952, pp. 377–379, 388; J. K. Galbraith, *The Great Crash, 1929,* Boston, Houghton Mifflin, 1955, pp. 191–192. See also Federal Reserve Board, *Annual Report* for 1929, p. 12.
[7] Since only June estimates of the money stock are available for those years, the

1920–21—and all the exceptions are contractions that were extraordinarily severe by other indications as well. The decline was also larger than in all succeeding reference cycle contractions, though only slightly larger than in 1937–38, the only later contraction comparable in severity to the earlier ones listed.

The decline in the stock of money is especially notable because it took place in a monetary and banking environment that was in other respects free of marked difficulties. There was no sign of any distrust of banks on the part of depositors, or of fear of such distrust on the part of banks. As Chart 27 shows, currency held by the public declined by a larger percentage than deposits—8 per cent compared with 2 per cent—though the reverse relation had been an invariable accompaniment of earlier banking crises. Similarly, the banks made no special effort to strengthen their own liquidity position. Excess reserves—for which no estimates are available before 1929—remained negligible. As we shall see in more detail in the next section, the decline in the stock of money up to October 1930 reflected entirely a decline in Federal Reserve credit outstanding which more than offset a rise in the gold stock and a slight shift by the public from currency to deposits.

ONSET OF FIRST BANKING CRISIS, OCTOBER 1930

In October 1930, the monetary character of the contraction changed dramatically—a change reflected in Chart 30 by the extraordinary rise in the deposits of suspended banks. Before October 1930, deposits of suspended banks had been somewhat higher than during most of 1929 but not out of line with experience during the preceding decade. In November 1930, they were more than double the highest value recorded since the start of monthly data in 1921. A crop of bank failures, particularly in Missouri, Indiana, Illinois, Iowa, Arkansas, and North Carolina, led to widespread attempts to convert demand and time deposits into currency, and also, to a much lesser extent, into postal savings deposits.[8] A contagion of fear spread among depositors, starting from the agricultural areas, which had experienced the heaviest impact of bank failures in the twenties. But such contagion knows no geographical limits. The failure of 256 banks with $180 million of deposits in November 1930 was followed by the failure of 352 with over $370 million of deposits in De-

---

decline was measured from June 1892 to June 1894 rather than from Jan. 1893 to June 1894, the monthly reference dates.

In view of the 5.4 per cent decline in the money stock from Jan. 1867 to Jan. 1868—the earliest dates for which we have estimates—another possible exception is the reference contraction from Apr. 1865 to Dec. 1867.

[8] The growth of postal savings deposits from 1929 to 1933 is one measure of the spread of distrust of banks. In Nov. 1914 postal savings deposits were $57 million. By Aug. 1929 they had grown by only $100 million. By Oct. 1930 they were $190 million; from then to Mar. 1933 they increased to $1.1 billion.

CHART 30

Deposits of Suspended Commercial Banks, Monthly,
1929–February 1933

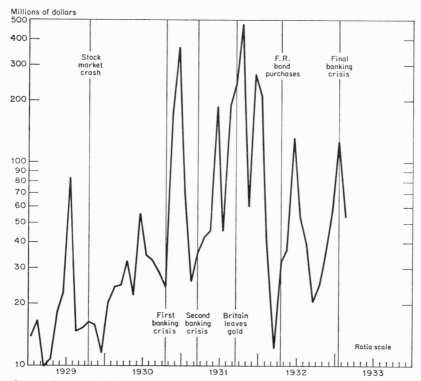

SOURCE: Data from *Federal Reserve Bulletin*, Sept. 1937, p. 909, were adjusted for seasonal variations by the monthly mean method, applied 1921–33.

cember (all figures seasonally unadjusted), the most dramatic being the failure on December 11 of the Bank of United States with over $200 million of deposits.[9] That failure was of especial importance. The Bank of

[9] *Annual Report of Superintendent of Banks,* State of New York, Part I, Dec. 31, 1930, p. 46.

For two and a half months before its closing, Joseph A. Broderick, New York State Superintendent of Banks, had sponsored various merger plans—some virtually to the point of consummation—which would have saved the bank. Governor Harrison devised the final reorganization plan, the success of which seemed so sure that, two days before the bank closed, the Federal Reserve Bank had issued a statement naming proposed directors for the merger. The plan would have become operative had not the Clearing House banks at the last moment withdrawn from the arrangement whereby they would have subscribed $30 million in new capital funds to the reorganized institution. Under Harrison's plan, the Bank of United States would have merged with Manufacturers Trust, Public National, and International Trust—a group of banks that had a majority of stockholders and

United States was the largest commercial bank, as measured by volume of deposits, ever to have failed up to that time in U.S. history. Moreover, though an ordinary commercial bank, its name had led many at

---

directors of the same ethnic origin and social and financial background as most of the stockholders and directors of the Bank of United States—with J. Herbert Case, chairman of the board and Federal Reserve agent of the New York Bank, as head. The decision of the Clearing House banks not to save the Bank of United States was reached at a meeting held at the New York Bank and was not changed despite personal appeals by Broderick and New York State Lieutenant Governor Herbert H. Lehman. Broderick, after waiting in an anteroom for hours despite repeated requests to be allowed to join the bankers in their conference room, was finally admitted through the intercession of Thomas W. Lamont, of J. P. Morgan and Company, and Owen D. Young, a director of the New York Federal Reserve Bank. Broderick's account of his statement of the bankers follows in part:

> I said it [the Bank of United States] had thousands of borrowers, that it financed small merchants, especially Jewish merchants, and that its closing might and probably would result in widespread bankruptcy among those it served. I warned that its closing would result in the closing of at least 10 other banks in the city and that it might even affect the savings banks. The influence of the closing might even extend outside the city, I told them.
>
> I reminded them that only two or three weeks before they had rescued two of the largest private bankers of the city and had willingly put up the money needed. I recalled that only seven or eight years before that they had come to the aid of one of the biggest trust companies in New York, putting up many times the sum needed to save the Bank of United States but only after some of their heads had been knocked together.
>
> I asked them if their decision to drop the plan was still final. They told me it was. Then I warned them that they were making the most colossal mistake in the banking history of New York.

Broderick's warning failed to impress Jackson Reynolds, president of the First National Bank and of the Clearing House Association, who informed Broderick that the effect of the closing would be only "local."

It was not the actual collapse of the reorganization plan but runs on several of the bank's branches, which had started on Dec. 9 and which he believed would become increasingly serious, that led Broderick to order the closing of the bank to conserve its assets. At a meeting with the directors after leaving the conference with the bankers, Broderick recalled that he said: "I considered the bank solvent as a going concern and . . . I was at a loss to understand the attitude of askance which the Clearing House banks had adopted toward the real estate holdings of the Bank of United States. I told them I thought it was because none of the other banks had ever been interested in this field and therefore knew nothing of it." Until that time, he said he never had proper reason to close the bank.

Broderick did succeed in persuading the conference of bankers to approve immediately the pending applications for membership in the Clearing House of two of the banks in the proposed merger, so that they would have the full resources of the Clearing House when the next day he announced the closing of the Bank of United States. As a result, the two banks, which like the Bank of United States had been affected by runs, did not succumb.

The details of the effort to save the bank were revealed in the second of two trials of Broderick upon his indictment by a New York County grand jury for alleged neglect of duty in failing to close the bank before he did. The first proceedings ended in a mistrial in Feb. 1932. Broderick was acquitted on May 28. See *Commercial and Financial Chronicle*, May 21, 1932, pp. 3744–3745 for the quotations; also June 4, 1932, p. 4087, for Harrison's testimony.

home and abroad to regard it somehow as an official bank, hence its failure constituted more of a blow to confidence than would have been administered by the fall of a bank with a less distinctive name. In addition, it was a member of the Federal Reserve System. The withdrawal of support by the Clearing House banks from the concerted measures sponsored by the Federal Reserve Bank of New York to save the bank— measures of a kind the banking community had often taken in similar circumstances in the past—was a serious blow to the System's prestige (see section 3, below).

The change in the character of the contraction is reflected clearly in Chart 27. Currency held by the public stopped declining and started to rise, so that deposits and currency began to move in opposite directions, as in earlier banking crises. Banks reacted as they always had under such circumstances, each seeking to strengthen its own liquidity position. Despite the withdrawal of deposits, which worked to deplete reserves, there was a small increase in seasonally adjusted reserves, so the ratio of deposits to bank reserves declined sharply from October 1930 to January 1931.

We have already expressed the view (pp. 167–168) that under the pre-Federal Reserve banking system, the final months of 1930 would probably have seen a restriction, of the kind that occurred in 1907, of convertibility of deposits into currency. By cutting the vicious circle set in train by the search for liquidity, restriction would almost certainly have prevented the subsequent waves of bank failures that were destined to come in 1931, 1932, and 1933, just as restriction in 1893 and 1907 had quickly ended bank suspensions arising primarily from lack of liquidity. Indeed, under such circumstances, the Bank of United States itself might have been able to reopen, as the Knickerbocker Trust Company did in 1908. After all, the Bank of United States ultimately paid off 83.5 per cent of its adjusted liabilities at its closing on December 11, 1930, despite its having to liquidate so large a fraction of its assets during the extraordinarily difficult financial conditions that prevailed during the next two years.[10]

As it was, the existence of the Reserve System prevented concerted restriction, both directly and indirectly: directly, by reducing the concern of stronger banks, which had in the past typically taken the lead in such a concerted move, since the System provided them with an escape mechanism in the form of discounting; and indirectly, by supporting the general assumption that such a move was made unnecessary by the establishment of the System. The private moves taken to shore up the

---

[10] *Annual Report of Superintendent of Banks,* State of New York, Part 1, 1931–45, Schedule E in each report. Four-fifths of the total recovered by depositors and other creditors was paid out within two years of the bank's closing.

banking system were therefore extremely limited.[11] The result was that the episode, instead of being the climactic phase of the banking difficulties, was only the first of a series of liquidity crises that was to characterize the rest of the contraction and was not to terminate until the banking holiday of March 1933.

The initial crisis did not last long. Bank failures declined sharply in early 1931, and the banks' scramble for liquidity came to a halt. There was a marked rise in the ratio of deposits to reserves from January 1931 to March 1931, the terminal month of the segment we have been discussing and the month of the onset of the second banking crisis. In January and February, the public slackened its demand for additional currency; demand and time deposits, after declining in January, rose a trifle in February and held nearly constant in March.

Interest rates show clearly the effects of the banking crisis. Until September 1930, the month before the first banking crisis, both long- and short-term interest rates had been declining, and so had the yields on corporate Baa bonds. Synchronous with the first crisis, a widening differential began to emerge between yields on lower-grade corporate bonds and on government bonds. The yields on corporate bonds rose sharply, the yields on government bonds continued to fall. The reason is clear. In their search for liquidity, banks and others were inclined first to dispose of their lower-grade bonds; the very desire for liquidity made government bonds ever more desirable as secondary reserves; hence the yield on lower-grade securities rose, which is to say, their prices fell, while the yields on government bonds fell. The decline in bond prices itself contributed, as we shall see in more detail later, to the subsequent banking crises. It made banks more fearful of holding bonds and so fostered declines in prices. By reducing the market value of the bond portfolios of banks, declines in bond prices in turn reduced the margin of capital as evaluated by bank examiners, and in this way contributed to subsequent bank failures.[12] The end of the first banking crisis was registered

---

[11] In some communities financial reconstruction was attempted by arrangements for a strong bank to merge with a weakened bank or, if several weakened banks were involved, by establishing a new institution with additional capital to take over the liabilities of the failing banks, the stockholders of which took a loss (F. Cyril James, *The Growth of Chicago Banks,* New York, Harper, 1938, Vol. II, pp. 994–995).

[12] According to a memorandum, dated Dec. 19, 1930, prepared for the executive committee of the Open Market Policy Conference, banks "dumped securities to make their positions more liquid," thus increasing the pressure on the bond market. Weak bond prices in turn produced "a substantial depreciation in the investment portfolios of many banks, in some cases causing an impairment of capital." In addition, the bond market was almost completely closed to new issues (George L. Harrison Papers on the Federal Reserve System, Columbia University Library, Harrison, Open Market, Vol. I, Dec. 19, 1930; for a full description of the Papers, see Chap. 5, footnote 41 and the accompanying text).

in a sharp improvement in the bond market after the turn of the year; the onset of the next crisis, in renewed deterioration.

The onset of the first liquidity crisis left no clear imprint on the broad economic series shown in Chart 28. However, after the turn of the year, there were signs of improvement in those indicators of economic activity—no doubt partly cause and partly effect of the contemporaneous minor improvement in the monetary area. Industrial production rose from January to April. Factory employment, seasonally adjusted, which had fallen uninterruptedly since August 1929, continued to fall but at a much reduced rate: in all but one month from August 1929 to February 1931, the decline was equal to or greater than the total decline in the three months from February to May 1931. Other indicators of physical activity tell a similar story. Personal income rose sharply, by 6 per cent from February to April 1931, but this is a misleading index since the rise was produced largely by government distributions to veterans.[13] All in all, the figures for the first four or five months of 1931, if examined without reference to what actually followed, have many of the earmarks of the bottom of a cycle and the beginning of revival.

Perhaps if those tentative stirrings of revival had been reinforced by a vigorous expansion in the stock of money, they could have been converted into sustained recovery. But that was not to be. The effects of returning confidence on the part of the public and the banks, which made for monetary expansion by raising the ratios of deposits to currency and to reserves, were largely offset by a reduction in Federal Reserve credit outstanding (see section 5, below). Consequently, the total stock of money was less than 1 per cent higher in March than in January 1931, and lower in March than it had been in December 1930. In March, a second banking crisis started a renewed decline in the stock of money and at an accelerated rate. A month or two later, a renewed decline started in economic activity in general, and the hope of revival that season was ended.

ONSET OF SECOND BANKING CRISIS, MARCH 1931

As Chart 30 shows, deposits of suspended banks began to rise in March, reaching a high point in June. From March on, the public resumed converting deposits into currency, and from April on, banks started strengthening their reserve position, liquidating available assets in order to meet both the public's demand for currency and their own desire for liquidity. Excess reserves, which in January 1931 had for the first time since 1929,

---

[13] U.S. advances to veterans of World War I of up to 50 per cent of the face value of their adjusted service certificates were made possible by legislation of Feb. 27, 1931. These loans totaled $796 million in the first four months after the enactment.

when data become available, reached the $100 million level and had then declined as confidence was restored, again rose, reaching a level of $125–$130 million in June and July.[14] Once bitten, twice shy, both depositors and bankers were bound to react more vigorously to any new eruption of bank failures or banking difficulties than they did in the final months of 1930.

Events abroad still further intensified the financial weakness—a feedback effect, since the events were themselves largely a response to the prior severe economic and monetary decline in the United States which reduced markets for both goods and services and for foreign securities. The failure in May 1931 of the Kreditanstalt, Austria's largest private bank, had repercussions that spread throughout the continent. It was followed by the closing of banks in Germany on July 14 and 15, as well as in other countries, and the freezing of British short-term assets in Germany. A one-year intergovernmental debt moratorium, and a "standstill agreement" among commercial banks not to press for repayment of short-term international credits, both proposed by President Hoover and agreed to in July,[15] gave the countries involved only temporary relief, as did strict control of foreign exchanges by Germany and borrowing by Britain in France and the United States.

These events had mixed effects on the monetary situation in the United States. On the one hand, they stimulated a flight of capital to the United States, which added to the already swollen gold stock. On the other hand, U.S. commercial banks held a large amount of short-term obligations of foreign banks which were now frozen. Furthermore, financial panic is no respecter of national frontiers. The failure of world-famous financial institutions and the widespread closing of banks in a great country could not but render depositors throughout the world uneasy and enhance the desire of bankers everywhere to strengthen their positions.

The downward pressure on the money stock arising from attempts by depositors to convert deposits into currency and by banks to add to their reserves relative to their liabilities was offset to some extent by the gold inflow from abroad. But this was the only offset. Federal Reserve credit outstanding showed only its usual seasonal movements, though minor open market purchases were undertaken, June–August, to ease the market (see section 5, below). In all, from February to mid-August, there was no net change in Federal Reserve credit outstanding, despite an unprecedented liquidation of the commercial banking system.

The result was that the second banking crisis had far more severe effects on the stock of money than the first. In the six months from

---

[14] *Banking and Monetary Statistics*, p. 371.

[15] Herbert Hoover, *Memoirs, The Great Depression, 1929–1941*, Macmillan, 1952, pp. 61–80.

February to August 1931, commercial bank deposits fell by $2.7 billion or nearly 7 per cent, more than in the whole eighteen-month period from the cyclical peak in August 1929 to February 1931. In the seven months from February to September 1931, commercial bank deposits fell by 9 per cent, one percentage point more than the maximum decline in deposits during the whole of the 1920–21 contraction. Currency in the hands of the public increased, absorbing the increase in gold and the decline in reserves, so that the total stock of money fell by a smaller percentage than deposits did. Even so, it fell by nearly 5½ per cent from February to August 1931, or at a rate of 11 per cent per year.

The effects of the banking crisis on interest rates show up clearly in the renewed and far more drastic rise in yields on lower-grade corporate bonds, as banks sought to realize on their portfolios and in the process forced bond prices ever lower. By that time, too, the economic contraction had seriously impaired the earning power of many concerns and sharply raised the chances of default. Yields on long-term government bonds continued to fall and reached extraordinarily low levels in mid-1931; so the yield differential rose as a result of a movement in both low- and high-grade securities. One reason, already cited, was that the very desire for liquidity served to enhance the value of government securities. Another was that those securities could be used as collateral for loans from Federal Reserve Banks, hence the decline in Federal Reserve discount rates served to make them more attractive as a secondary reserve. Yields on commercial paper also fell, keeping nearly a stable relation to discount rates.

BRITAIN'S DEPARTURE FROM GOLD, SEPTEMBER 1931

The climax of the foreign difficulties came on September 21, when, after runs on sterling precipitated by France and the Netherlands, Britain abandoned the gold standard.[16] Anticipating similar action on the part

[16] Some 25 other countries followed Britain's lead within the following year. The currencies of about a dozen—the sterling area within which British financial and economic influence remained dominant—moved in general conformity with sterling.

Because of the weakness in sterling immediately after the departure from gold, there was no internal relaxation of orthodox financial standards for several months: Britain balanced her budget and repaid foreign credits; Bank rate went up to 6 per cent on the date of suspension and was not reduced until February 1932, when it was changed to 5 per cent. From that point on, defense of sterling was in general no longer considered necessary; instead, control was substituted to prevent a rise in sterling exchange that, it was feared, would eliminate the stimulus a low rate was expected to give to British exports. Imports were restricted by a new protective tariff passed in February. Accompanying the protective tariff policy was a cheap money policy, adopted originally to facilitate refunding wartime issues at lower rates. An expansion in bank credit began in the second quarter of 1932; the trough of the British business contraction was reached in August 1932, according to NBER reference cycle chronology.

of the United States, central banks and private holders in a number of countries—notably France, Belgium, Switzerland, Sweden, and the Netherlands—converted substantial amounts of their dollar assets in the New York money market to gold between September 16 and October 28. Because of the low level of money-market interest rates in the United States, foreign central banks had for some time been selling dollar bankers' acceptances previously purchased for their accounts by the New York Reserve Bank, the proceeds of which were credited to their dollar bank deposits. From the week of September 16, the unloading of the bills onto the Federal Reserve assumed panic proportions. Foreign central banks drew down their deposits to increase earmarkings of gold, much of which was exported during the following six weeks. From September 16 to September 30, the gold stock declined by $275 million, from then to the end of October by an additional $450 million. Those losses about offset the net influx during the preceding two years and brought the gold stock back roughly to its average level during 1929.

The onset of the external drain was preceded and accompanied by an intensification of the internal drain on the banking system. In August, deposits of suspended banks rose to a level that had been exceeded only in the month of December 1930, and in September rose higher yet. In those two months alone, banks with deposits of $414 million, or more than 1 per cent of the by-then shrunken total of commercial bank deposits, closed their doors. The outflow of gold in September added to the pressure on bank reserves. Currency was being withdrawn internally by depositors justifiably fearful for the safety of banks, and gold was being withdrawn externally by foreigners fearful for the maintenance of the gold standard. The combination of an external drain and an internal drain, and particularly their joint occurrence in the autumn when the demand for currency was in any event at its seasonal peak, was precisely the set of circumstances that in pre-Federal Reserve days would have produced restriction of convertibility of deposits into currency. If the pre-Federal Reserve banking system had been in effect, all other events had been as they were, and restriction of payments by banks had not taken place in December 1930, restriction almost certainly would have occurred in September 1931 and very likely would have prevented at least the subsequent bank failures.[17]

[17] Men who had experienced the 1907 panic were not unmindful of lessons to be learned from it. Samuel Reyburn (president of Lord and Taylor, a New York City department store, and a director of the New York Federal Reserve Bank) suggested at a board meeting in Dec. 1931 "that if the banking difficulties extended much further, it would be possible for the banks to suspend cash payments as they did in 1907, but still continue in business." He believed there would be a difficulty, "which had not been present in 1907, that the Federal reserve banks cannot suspend cash payments." In Mar. 1933, this turned out not to be a

The Federal Reserve System reacted vigorously and promptly to the external drain, as it had not to the previous internal drain. On October 9, the Reserve Bank of New York raised its rediscount rate to 2½ per cent and on October 16, to 3½ per cent—the sharpest rise within so brief a period in the whole history of the System, before or since. The move was followed by a cessation of the external drain in the next two weeks. The gold stock reached its trough at the end of October, and thereafter rose until a renewed gold drain began at the end of December. But the move also intensified internal financial difficulties and was accompanied by a spectacular increase in bank failures and in runs on banks. In October alone, 522 commercial banks with $471 million of deposits closed their doors, and in the next three months, 875 additional banks with $564 million of deposits. All told, in the six months from August 1931 through January 1932, 1,860 banks with deposits of $1,449 million suspended operations,[18] and the deposits of those banks that managed to keep afloat fell by a much larger sum. Total deposits fell over the six-month period by nearly five times the deposits in suspended banks or by no less than 17 per cent of the initial level of deposits in operating banks.

The rise in currency offset some of the effect on the money stock of the decline in deposits. But the offset was minor. The money stock fell

---

problem; the Reserve Banks joined the other banks in restricting payments. One Bank officer commented that "there is the further difference between 1907 and the present time, that the difficulty of the banks in 1907 was not one of solvency, but inability to continue to pay out currency, whereas at the present time the banks are able to pay out currency in large amounts, if necessary, but there is the danger that they may become insolvent in so doing" (Harrison, Notes, Vol. II, Dec. 7, 1931).

That answer was hardly to the point, confusing the problem of the individual bank with the problem of the banking system. The threat of insolvency arose from the inability of the banking system as a whole to pay out currency without a reduction in total deposits, given the failure of the Federal Reserve System to create sufficient additional high-powered money. The attempted liquidation of assets to acquire the high-powered money drove down their prices and rendered insolvent banks that would otherwise have been entirely solvent. By cutting short this process, the early restriction of payments prevented the transformation of a temporary liquidity problem into a problem of insolvency.

[18] Rumors about the condition of some of the largest and best-known New York City banks spread alarm in Europe (Harrison, Conversations, Vol. I, Oct. 2, 1931). However, Harrison considered their position in October 1931 "stronger and more liquid than for a long time." The 23 New York Clearing House banks were not included in a memorandum, dated Dec. 8, 1931, listing the shrinkage in capital funds of the member banks in the second Federal Reserve District, which Harrison sent to Governor Meyer (Miscellaneous, Vol. I, Dec. 8, 1931). The shrinkage ranged from 56 per cent for the highest quality group of banks to more than double the capital funds for the lowest quality group. One of the reasons New York City banks were said to be reluctant to borrow from the Reserve Bank was the fear that Europeans would interpret borrowings as an indication of weakness.

by 12 per cent from August 1931 to January 1932, or at the annual rate of 31 per cent—a rate of decline larger by far than for any other comparable span in the 53 years for which we have monthly data,[19] and in the whole 93-year period for which we have a continuous series on the money stock.

Why should the gold drain and the subsequent rise in discount rates have intensified the domestic financial difficulties so greatly? They would not have done so, if they had been accompanied by extensive open market purchases designed to offset the effect of the external gold drain on high-powered money, and of the internal currency drain on bank reserves. Unfortunately, purchases were not made. The Reserve System's holdings of government securities were actually reduced by $15 million in the six-week period from mid-September to the end of October, and then kept unchanged until mid-December. Though the System raised bill buying rates along with discount rates, it did buy some $500 million additional bills in the crucial six-week period. However, that amount was inadequate to offset even the outflow of gold, let alone the internal drain. The result was that the banks found their reserves being drained from two directions—by export of gold and by internal demands for currency. They had only two recourses: to borrow from the Reserve System and to dump their assets on the market. They did both, though neither was a satisfactory solution.

Discounts rose to a level not reached since 1929, despite the rise in discount rates. The situation and its effects are well described in a memorandum prepared for a meeting of the Open Market Policy Conference in February 1932. The conditions it described were still much the same as those that had prevailed in October 1931.

. . . The weight of these discounts is falling most heavily on banks outside the principal centers. In fact, the discounts of these groups of banks are considerably larger than they were in 1929 when the reserve system was exerting the maximum of pressure for deflation. The present amount of member bank borrowing has always proved deflationary, except perhaps during the war, and with the present sensitive psychology, an interruption to deflation seems unlikely as long as the weight of discounts is as heavy as at present.[20]

The aversion to borrowing by banks, which the Reserve System had tried to strengthen during the twenties, was still greater at a time when depositors were fearful for the safety of every bank and were scrutinizing balance sheets with great care to see which banks were likely to be the

[19] Excluding only the five 5-month intervals spanning the holiday, Oct. 1932-Mar. 1933—Feb.-July 1933, when the recorded data show a decline of the same order of magnitude as the annual rate of decline, Aug. 1931–Jan. 1932. As we shall see in Chap. 8, sect. 1, the banking holiday produced a discontinuity in the money figures, and the recorded decline may be a statistical artifact.

[20] Harrison, Open Market, Vol. II, memorandum, dated Feb. 23, 1932.

next to go. This is the context of the "sensitive psychology" to which the quotation refers.

The effect of the attempt to realize on assets is vividly displayed in Chart 29. For the first time, yields on long-term government bonds and on commercial paper rose sharply along with the yields on lower-grade corporate securities. Those rises in yields clearly did not reflect the effect of the depression on corporate earnings; they reflected the liquidity crisis and the unwillingness or inability of banks to borrow even more heavily from the Reserve System. There was some discussion at the time, and even more later, attributing the decline in the price of government bonds to the federal deficit (under $0.5 billion in fiscal 1931; $2.5 billion in fiscal 1932), and to the fear of "irresponsible" legislation, but it is hard to believe that those factors had much effect in comparison with the extremely heavy pressure on banks to liquidate their assets. Certainly, the rise in the commercial-paper rate reflected both in timing and amount primarily the movements in the discount rate.

Again, we may draw on a preliminary memorandum for an Open Market Policy Conference, this time in January 1932.

> Within a period of a few months United States Government bonds have declined 10 per cent; high grade corporation bonds have declined 20 per cent; and lower grade bonds have shown even larger price declines. Declines of such proportions inevitably have increased greatly the difficulties of many banks, and it has now become apparent that the efforts of individual institutions to strengthen their position have seriously weakened the banking position in general.[21]

Some measures were attempted or proposed for the relief of banking difficulties, for example, measures sponsored by the New York Reserve Bank to encourage a more liberal evaluation of bank assets, to reduce the pressure on railroad bond prices, and to accelerate the liquidation of deposits in closed banks.[22] These were palliatives that would have

---

[21] *Ibid.*, memorandum, dated Jan. 8, 1932.

[22] (1) The Bank sponsored an attempt to develop a uniform method of valuing bank assets, involving a more liberal procedure to be followed by examiners in estimating depreciation. The Comptroller ruled that national banks would be required to charge off no depreciation on bonds of the four highest ratings, and only 25 per cent of the depreciation on all other bonds, except defaulted issues on which the full depreciation was to be charged off. The rule, however, was applied only to banks whose capital funds would not be wiped out if the entire depreciation of all the investments, together with any losses on other assets, were to be written off. Hence banks most in need of liberal treatment were not helped (Harrison, Notes, Vol. II, Aug. 6, 13, and Dec. 7, 1931). (2) It tried to obtain a revision of the rules governing the list of investments legal for savings banks, insurance companies, and trust funds in New York State. The prospect of the elimination of railroad bonds from the legal list threatened a further decline in their price, as holders bound by the list sold the bonds. As a result, commercial bank holdings of railroad bonds suffered losses (*ibid.*, Aug. 13, 1931). (3) It promoted the formation of a railroad bond pool, to restore bond values, conditional

had little effect, even if they had been fully carried out. More far-reaching proposals came from outside the Reserve System. At the urging of President Hoover, and with only the reluctant cooperation of the banking community, a private National Credit Corporation was created in October 1931 to extend loans to individual banks, associated together in cooperatives in each Federal Reserve district, against security collateral not ordinarily acceptable and against the joint guarantee of the members of the cooperative. The Corporation's loans were, however, limited. In Hoover's words, "After a few weeks of enterprising courage . . . [it] became ultraconservative, then fearful, and finally died. It had not exerted anything like its full possible strength. Its members—and the business world—threw up their hands and asked for governmental action."[23] These arrangements were explicitly patterned after those in the temporary Aldrich-Vreeland Act, which had worked so well in 1914, the one occasion when they were used. On Hoover's recommendation, the Reconstruction Finance Corporation was established in January 1932, with authority to make loans to banks and other financial institutions, as well as to railroads, many of which were in danger of default on their bonded indebtedness.[24] The epidemic of bank failures ended at about the same time as the establishment of the RFC, though the two developments may have been unrelated. In any event, during the rest of 1932, RFC loans to

---

on prior adjustment of railroad costs and income (*ibid.*, Oct. 5, and Dec. 7, 1931; also, Conversations, Vol. I, Dec. 5, 1931). (4) It sought the assistance of a group of member banks to accelerate the liquidation of deposits in closed banks. The going banks were asked to buy the assets of the closed banks, and to make an immediate advance against the assets, so that an agreed percentage of deposits could be paid out promptly to depositors (Harrison, Office, Vol. II, Sept. 11, 1931).

[23] Hoover, *Memoirs*, p. 97. See the copy of the prepared statement—requesting formation of the Corporation—read to a meeting of nineteen New York bankers held at Secretary Mellon's apartment, Sunday, Oct. 4, 1931; Hoover's letter, dated Oct. 5, 1931, to Harrison; and Harrison's answer of Oct. 7 (all in Miscellaneous, Vol. I). Harrison stressed the need for a railroad bond pool, to raise the prices of those bonds in bank assets, as an indispensable measure to help the banks in addition to the formation of the Corporation. Also see Notes, Vol. II. Oct. 5, 12, 15, 1931, for the tepid reception of the Corporation by most of the Bank's directors.

[24] The Emergency Relief and Construction Act of July 21, 1932, which increased the borrowing power of the RFC from $1.5 billion to $3.3 billion in addition to its subscribed capital of $500 million, authorized it to advance up to $300 million at 3 per cent interest to states and territories for unemployment relief; to make loans for self-liquidating public works (little was actually advanced either for relief or public works up to the end of the year); to finance marketing of agricultural products in foreign markets and in the U.S.; and to create a regional credit corporation with capital subscribed by the RFC in any land-bank district. These measures did not prevent the continued fall in farm income and farm land values, the rise in farm foreclosures, and continued forced sales due to tax delinquency.

banks totaled $0.9 billion, and deposits of banks that suspended fluctuated about the level of mid-1930.

The Glass-Steagall Act, passed on February 27, 1932, which had its origins in the Treasury and the White House, was mainly designed to broaden the collateral the Reserve System could hold against Federal Reserve notes, by permitting government bonds as well as eligible paper to serve as collateral.[25] But it also included provisions designed to help individual banks by widening the circumstances under which they could borrow from the System.[26]

In May 1932, a bill to provide federal insurance of deposits in banks was passed by the House of Representatives. It was referred to a sub-committee of the Senate Banking and Currency Committee, of which Carter Glass was chairman, but was never reported out.[27] He had opposed a similar provision at the time of the passage of the original Federal Reserve Act.[28] Glass believed that the solution was reform of the practices of commercial banks and introduced several bills to that end.[29] None received the support of the administration or of the Reserve System, and none was passed.[30]

In July 1932, the Federal Home Loan Bank Act was passed in another attempt to cope with the problem of frozen assets—specifically of home

[25] The provision was to expire on Mar. 3, 1933, but was extended another year on Feb. 3, 1933, and thereafter periodically until made permanent by the act of June 12, 1945.

[26] The Glass-Steagall Act permitted member banks to borrow from the Reserve Banks (at penalty rates) on ineligible assets under specified conditions. With the consent of at least five members of the Federal Reserve Board, notes of groups of five or more member banks with insufficient eligible assets could be discounted. A unit bank with a capital under $5 million was also authorized, in exceptional circumstances, to borrow on ineligible assets with the consent of at least five members of the Federal Reserve Board. The release of funds by these terms was slight. The Emergency Relief and Construction Act of July 21, 1932, therefore permitted the Reserve Banks to discount for individuals, partnerships, and corporations, with no other sources of funds, notes, drafts, and bills of exchange eligible for discount for member banks. Those powers were used to a very limited extent. Discounts for individuals, partnerships, and corporations reached a maximum of $1.4 million in Mar. 1933. Authorization to make those discounts expired July 31, 1936.

[27] House bill 11362 was referred to the Senate Banking and Currency Committee on May 28, 1932 (*Congressional Record,* 72d Cong., 1st sess., p. 11515).

[28] Glass had been chairman of the House Banking and Currency Committee in 1913. The bill that year by the Senate included deposit guaranty; the bill passed by the House did not. In the conference, the House conferees succeeded in eliminating that provision (Paul M. Warburg, *The Federal Reserve System,* New York, Macmillan, 1930, Vol. I, p. 128).

[29] In 71st Cong., 2d sess., June 17, 1930, S. 4723, on national banking associations (*Congressional Record,* p. 10973); in 72d Cong., 1st sess., Jan. 21 and Mar. 17, 1932, S. 3215 and S. 4115, on Federal Reserve Banks (*ibid.,* pp. 2403, 6329), also Apr. 18, 1932, S. 4412, on Federal Reserve Banks and national banking associations.

[30] See also footnote 134, below.

financing institutions (i.e., savings and loan associations, savings banks, insurance companies). The act provided for the organization of federal home loan banks to make advances to those institutions on the security of first mortgages they held.

The broader economic indicators in Chart 28 show little effect of the financial developments that followed Britain's departure from gold. Rather, they show a continuous decline from the onset of the second banking crisis in March 1931 right on through mid-1932. If anything, there is some stepping up of the rate of decline, but any acceleration is less notable than the high rate of decline throughout: an annual rate of 31 per cent for personal income, of 14 per cent for wholesale prices, and of 32 per cent for production.

The severity of the depression stimulated many remedial efforts, governmental and nongovernmental, outside the monetary area. A nation-wide drive to aid private relief agencies was organized in the fall of 1931 by a committee of seventy, appointed by Hoover and named the President's Unemployment Relief Organization. The unemployed in many states formed self-help and barter organizations, with their own systems of scrip. Hoover expanded federal expenditures on public works, but was concerned about incurring deficits for such a purpose. A committee of twelve, representing the public, industry, and labor, appointed by him in September 1931, opposed a construction program financed by public funds. In Congress, however, there was growing support for increased government expenditures and for monetary expansion, proposals widely castigated by the business and financial community as "greenbackism" and "inflationary." On its part, the business and financial community, and many outside it, regarded federal deficits as a major source of difficulty. Pressure to balance the budget finally resulted in the enactment of a substantial tax rise in June 1932. The strength of that sentiment, which, in light of present-day views, seems hard to credit, is demonstrated by the fact that in the Presidential campaign of 1932, both candidates ran on platforms of financial orthodoxy, promising to balance the federal budget.

BEGINNING OF LARGE-SCALE OPEN MARKET PURCHASES, APRIL 1932

In April 1932, under heavy Congressional pressure (see section 5, below), the System embarked on large-scale open market purchases which raised its security holdings by roughly $1 billion by early August. Ninety-five per cent of the purchases were made before the end of June, and no net purchases were made after August 10. The System's holdings then remained almost exactly constant until after the turn of the year when they were reduced in the usual seasonal pattern. Initially, the purchases served mostly to offset a renewed gold outflow but, after June, they were reinforced by a mild gold inflow. From the time the purchases ended until the end of the year, a continued and stronger gold inflow served in their stead to keep high-powered money rising.

The provision of additional reserves reinforced the effect of the tapering off of bank failures in January and February 1932, referred to above, which was accompanied by a return of currency from circulation from February to May. In the absence of the bond purchases, it is possible that the renewed flurry of bank failures in mid-1932, consisting partly of a wave of over 40 failures in Chicago in June, before the RFC granted a loan to a leading Chicago bank, would have degenerated into a major crisis. As it was, bank failures again subsided, so that the rise in the public's currency holdings from May to July was again followed by a decline.

The combination of the more favorable banking situation and of the bond-purchase program is clearly reflected in the behavior of the stock of money. As Chart 27 shows, the decline in both bank deposits and the stock of money moderated. Demand deposits reached a trough in July, total deposits and the money stock, in September; the following rise was mild. In absolute terms, the changes in the stock of money were small; by comparison with the prior sharp declines, the shift was major.

The effect of the purchase program is even clearer in Chart 29, which shows interest rates. In the first quarter of 1932 the rates had fallen from the peaks reached in December 1931 or January 1932. In the second quarter, however, the corporate Baa bond yield soared to a peak (11.63 per cent in May)—unmatched in the monthly record since 1919—and the yield on long-term government bonds rose slightly. Commercial paper rates continued to decline in the second quarter, the reduction in the discount rate in New York on February 26 having led the commercial paper rate. After the purchase program began, a sharp fall occurred in all the rates. The reduction in the discount rate in New York on June 24 again led the commercial paper rate and, in August, the commercial paper rate fell below the discount rate and remained there, a relation without parallel since the beginning of the Reserve System.

The reversal in the relation between the commercial paper rate and the discount rate marked a major change in the role of discounting, about which we shall have more to say in Chapter 9. Except for a spurt in connection with the 1933 banking panic, discounting was not again to be of major importance until long after the end of World War II. Banks were henceforth to seek safety through "excess" reserves, and later, through government securities whose prices were pegged, not through recourse to borrowing. That change was, of course, a major factor in keeping rates from going even lower. Throughout 1932, for example, yields on long-term government bonds were notably higher than at any time between May 1930 and September 1931.

The tapering off of the decline in the stock of money and the beginning of the purchase program were shortly followed by an equally notable change in the general economic indicators shown in Chart 28. Wholesale prices started rising in July, production in August. Personal income continued to fall but at a much reduced rate. Factory employment, railroad ton-miles, and numerous other indicators of physical activity tell a similar story. All in all, as in early 1931, the data again have many of the earmarks of a cyclical revival. Indeed, some students date the cyclical trough in 1932. Burns and Mitchell, although dating the trough in March 1933, refer to the period as an example of a "double bottom."[31]

There is, of course, no way of knowing that the economic improvement reflected the monetary improvement. But it is entirely clear that the reverse was not the case. Aside from the precedence in time of the monetary improvement, the program of large-scale open market purchases was a deliberative action undertaken by the Reserve System. And it was the major factor accounting for the monetary improvement.

The timing relations, previous experience, and general considerations all make it highly plausible that the economic improvement reflected the influence of the monetary improvement, rather than the only other alternative—that it occurred shortly thereafter entirely by coincidence. We have observed that, in the past, an increase in the rate of monetary growth—in the present case, from rapid decline to mild decline and then mild rise—has invariably preceded a trough in general business. After three years of economic contraction, there must have been many forces in the economy making for revival, and it is reasonable that they could more readily come to fruition in a favorable monetary setting than in the midst of continued financial uncertainty.

THE BANKING PANIC OF 1933

As it happened, the recovery proved only temporary and was followed by a relapse. Once again, banking difficulties were a notable feature of the relapse. A renewed series of bank failures began in the last quarter of 1932, mostly in the Midwest and Far West, and there was a sharp spurt in January involving a wider area. The deposit-currency ratio fell; the stock of money ceased growing and began to fall precipitously after January 1933. Statewide bank holidays spread, increasing the demand for currency. Substitutes for currency were introduced as in earlier panics, offsetting to some extent the decline in the money stock shown in our

---

[31] A. F. Burns and W. C. Mitchell, *Measuring Business Cycles,* New York, NBER, 1946, pp. 82–83; *idem, Production during the American Business Cycle of 1927–1933,* New York, NBER, Bulletin 61, Nov. 1936, pp. 2 and 4.

estimates.[32] The monetary difficulties were accompanied by a reversal in the movement of interest rates and by a relapse on the economic front. Physical indexes ceased rising and began to fall once again and so did prices and other indicators of business activity.

This time the availability of RFC loans did not stem the rising tide of bank failures, partly because a provision of an act passed in July 1932 was interpreted as requiring publication of the names of banks to which the RFC had made loans in the preceding month, and such publication began in August. The inclusion of a bank's name on the list was correctly interpreted as a sign of weakness, and hence frequently led to runs on the bank. In consequence, banks were fearful of borrowing from the RFC. The damage was further increased in January 1933 when, pursuant to a House resolution, the RFC made public all loans extended before August 1932.[33] When runs on individual banks in Nevada threatened to involve banks throughout the state, a state banking holiday relieving them of the necessity of meeting their obligations to creditors was declared on October 31, 1932. Iowa followed suit under similar circumstances on January 20, 1933; Louisiana declared a holiday on February 3 to aid the banks of the city of New Orleans; and Michigan, on February 14. Congress freed national banks in February from penalties for restricting or deferring withdrawals according to the terms of holidays in the states where they were located. By March 3, holidays had been declared in about half the states.[34] While the holiday halted withdrawals in a given state, it

[32] It has been estimated that probably as much as $1 billion in scrip was in circulation in the United States up through the bank holiday (H. P. Willis and J. M. Chapman, *The Banking Situation,* New York, Columbia University Press, 1934, p. 15). See also Chap. 8, sect. 1.

[33] Hoover asserts in his memoirs that, before signing the bill in question (the Emergency Relief and Construction Act of July 21, 1932), he was assured that the list of borrowers from the RFC would be treated as confidential and would not be published, and that if it had not been for this assurance, he "would probably have had to veto the bill" (*Memoirs,* pp. 110–111).

The law specified only that the RFC make monthly reports to the President of the United States and the Congress on all loans granted the previous month. It was John N. Garner, then Speaker of the House, who in August instructed the Clerk to make the reports public. The Democrats claimed that publication of RFC loans served as a safeguard against favoritism in the distribution of loans. There was also some resentment against Eugene Meyer, chairman of the RFC until July 1932, and Secretary of the Treasury Mills, a member of the board of directors, for not keeping Democratic directors informed about RFC actions (Jesse Jones, *Fifty Billion Dollars,* Macmillan, 1951, pp. 72, 82–83, 517–520). For the House resolution, see *Congressional Record,* Jan. 6, 1933, p. 1362.

[34] Bank holidays, by legislation or executive order, included the following main types: (1) for a designated time local banks under state jurisdiction were forbidden to pay out funds at depositors' request; (2) individual banks were authorized, either on their own initiative or with the consent of the state banking department, to notify their depositors of their determination to restrict withdrawals to a specified amount or proportion of deposits; (3) a percentage of deposits up to which depositors might draw was specified for all the banks in a state.

increased pressure elsewhere, because the banks that had been given temporary relief withdrew funds from their correspondents in other states in order to strengthen their position. In addition, substitutes for bank money became essential, as in past restrictions of convertibility of deposits, and internal exchanges were disrupted. Currency holdings of the public rose $760 million, or about 16 per cent, in the two months from the end of 1932 to February 1933.

The main burden of the internal drain fell on New York City banks. Between February 1 and March 1, interior banks withdrew $760 million in balances they held with those banks. New York City banks reduced their holdings of government securities by $260 million during February—a measure that tightened the money market—and turned to the Reserve Bank for borrowing funds. The situation produced nervousness among the New York banks with their much intensified aversion to borrowing. At the beginning of March they still held $900 million in interbank balances.

Fear of a renewed foreign drain added to the anxiety of both the commercial banks and the Federal Reserve System. Rumors that the incoming administration would devalue—rumors that were later confirmed by the event—led to a speculative accumulation of foreign currencies by private banks and other holders of dollars and to increased earmarkings of gold. For the first time, also, the internal drain partly took the form of a specific demand for gold coin and gold certificates in place of Federal Reserve notes or other currency. Mounting panic at New York City banks on these accounts was reinforced in the first few days of March by heavy withdrawals from savings banks and demands for currency by interior banks.

The Federal Reserve System reacted to these events very much as it had in September 1931. It raised discount rates in February 1933 in reaction to the external drain, and it did not seek to counter either the external or internal drain by any extensive open market purchases. Though it increased its government security holdings in February 1933, after permitting them to decline by nearly $100 million in January, they were only $30 million higher at the time of the banking holiday than they were at the end of December 1932. Again it raised the buying rates on acceptances along with the discount rate, and again bills bought increased but by far less than the concurrent drain on bank reserves. Again, as in September and October 1931, banks were driven to discount at the higher rates and to dump securities on the market, so that interest rates on all categories of securities rose sharply (see Chart 29).

This time the situation was even more serious than in September 1931 because of all that had gone before. In addition, the panic was far more widespread. In the first few days of March, heavy drains of gold, both internal and external, reduced the New York Bank's reserve percentage

326

below its legal limit. On March 3, Governor Harrison informed Governor Meyer of the Federal Reserve Board that "he would not take the responsibility of running this bank with deficient reserves in the absence of legal sanction provided by the Federal Reserve Act." With some reluctance, the Board suspended reserve requirements for thirty days.[35]

The System itself shared in the panic that prevailed in New York. Harrison was eager for a bank holiday, regarding suspension of reserve requirements as an inadequate solution and, on the morning of March 3, recommended a nationwide holiday to Secretary of the Treasury Mills and Governor Meyer. Despite much discussion between New York and Washington, by evening the declaration of a national holiday was ruled out. Harrison then joined the New York Clearing House banks and the State Superintendent of Banks in requesting New York's Governor Lehman to declare a state banking holiday.[36] Lehman did so, effective March 4. Similar action was taken by the governors of Illinois, Massachusetts, New Jersey, and Pennsylvania. On March 4, the Federal Reserve Banks remained closed as did all the leading exchanges. The central banking system, set up primarily to render impossible the restriction of payments by commercial banks, itself joined the commercial banks in a

[35] Harrison, Notes, Vol. III, Mar. 3, 1933.

[36] Harrison regarded suspension of reserve requirements as the least desirable alternative, because the Reserve Bank would still be obliged to pay out gold and currency to hoarders. Another alternative was suspension of specie payments, which he also considered unattractive, because "hysteria and panic might result and there probably would be a run on the banks of the country." He concluded that the best course was to declare a nationwide holiday "which would permit the country to calm down and which would allow time for the passage of legislation to remedy the situation."

In response to Harrison's recommendation, Secretary Mills and Governor Meyer suggested instead a banking holiday in the State of New York. Harrison refused to make such a request of Governor Lehman on the initiative of the New York Bank, because he believed a state holiday would only result in greater confusion, since the New York Bank would still have to pay out gold to foreigners, and the rest of the country's banking system could not function if New York declared a holiday. The directors of the New York Bank adopted a resolution requesting the Federal Reserve Board to urge the President of the United States to proclaim a nationwide holiday on Saturday, Mar. 4, and Monday, Mar. 6. Harrison talked to President Hoover by telephone, but the President would not commit himself. Later that evening, reports were received from Washington that both the President and President-elect had gone to bed and that there was no chance that a national holiday would be declared.

Harrison left the Bank immediately to join a conference at Governor Lehman's home in New York, at which the decision for a state holiday was finally reached. Lehman had advised Harrison earlier in the day that he would declare the holiday if it seemed desirable, but he had been annoyed with the Clearing House banks because they had induced him to make a statement that he would not. Later that day the Clearing House banks had agreed to cooperate if Lehman declared a holiday but would not request him to. They feared it would hurt their prestige if they were represented as seeking a holiday; in that case, "they would rather stay open and take their beating" (*ibid.*).

more widespread, complete, and economically disturbing restriction of payments than had ever been experienced in the history of the country. One can certainly sympathize with Hoover's comment about that episode: "I concluded [the Reserve Board] was indeed a weak reed for a nation to lean on in time of trouble."[37]

A nationwide banking holiday, which was finally proclaimed after midnight on March 6 by President Roosevelt, closed all banks until March 9 and suspended gold redemption and gold shipments abroad. On March 9, Congress at a special session enacted an Emergency Banking Act confirming the powers assumed by the President in declaring the holiday, provided for a way of dealing with unlicensed banks and authorized emergency issues of Federal Reserve Bank notes to fill currency needs. The President thereupon extended the holiday; it was not terminated until March 13, 14, and 15, depending on the location of the banks, which were authorized to open only if licensed to do so by federal or state banking authorities (for a fuller discussion, see Chapter 8, section 1).

As noted in Chapter 4, section 3, the banking holiday, while of the same species as earlier restrictions of payments in 1814, 1818, 1837, 1839, 1857, 1873, 1893, and 1907, was of a far more virulent genus. To the best of our knowledge, in these earlier restrictions, no substantial number of banks closed down entirely even for a day, let alone for a minimum of six business days.[38] In the earlier restrictions, banks had continued to make loans, transfer deposits by check, and conduct all their usual business except the unlimited conversion of deposits into currency on demand. Indeed, the restriction enabled them to continue such activities and, in some instances, to expand their loans by relieving them from the immediate pressure to acquire currency to meet the demands of their depositors—a pressure that was doomed to be self-defeating for the banking system as a whole except through drastic reduction in the stock of money. True, to prepare themselves for resumption, banks generally tended to reduce the ratio of their deposits to reserves, following restric-

[37] *Memoirs*, p. 212.
[38] Clark Warburton notes: "By the middle 1830's most of the states had adopted or were in the process of developing general banking codes, with the insertion of provisions for severe penalties for failure to pay notes in specie, or had placed such provisions in bank charters when renewing them or granting new ones. Under such provisions, suspension of specie payments meant forfeiture of charters, or at least curtailment of business until specie payments were resumed. In some cases, the latter was permitted by special enactments of state legislatures. Under these conditions, suspension of specie payments provided relief from an immediate banking panic, but led to a process of contraction of the bank-supplied circulating medium" ("Variations in Economic Growth and Banking Developments in the United States from 1835 to 1885," *Journal of Economic History*, Sept. 1958, p. 292). We know of no instance where any legislature or bank supervisory authority declared bank charters to be forfeited as a result of a general restriction of convertibility. Instead, legislation was enacted postponing or relieving banks of the penalties the law imposed for suspension of specie payments.

tion. But the fall in the deposit-reserve ratio and the resulting downward pressure on the money stock were moderate and gradual and could be largely or wholly offset by expansion in high-powered money through specie inflows.[39] As a result, contraction of the stock of money, when it occurred at all, was relatively mild and usually lasted perhaps a year, not several years as in 1929–33. Restriction was, as we remarked earlier, a therapeutic measure to prevent a cumulation of bank failures arising solely out of liquidity needs that the system as a whole could not possibly satisfy. And restriction succeeded in this respect. In none of the earlier episodes, with the possible exception of the restriction that began in 1839 and continued until 1842,[40] was there any extensive series of bank failures after restriction occurred. Banks failed because they were "unsound," not because they were for the moment illiquid.

Restriction of payments was not, of course, a satisfactory solution to the problem of panics. If the preceding description makes it sound so, it is only by comparison with the vastly less satisfactory resolution of 1930–33. Indeed, the pre-World War I restrictions were regarded as anything but a satisfactory solution by those who experienced them, which is why they produced such strong pressure for monetary and banking reform. Those earlier restrictions were accompanied by a premium on currency, which in effect created two separate media of payments; and by charges imposed by banks in one locality on the remission of funds to other banks at a distance, since local substitutes for money would not

[39] See Bray Hammond, *Banks and Politics in America,* Princeton University Press, 1957, p. 713. Referring to the restriction in 1857 which had occurred in the United States but not in Canada, he states: "As usual, the immediate effect of stopping specie payments in the States was ease. The banks, relieved of having to pay their own debts, ceased their harsh pressure on their borrowers. The general understanding that specie payments must sooner or later be resumed impelled a continuance of liquidation but of milder sort."

[40] It is significant that the extensive bank failures of 1839–42 were associated with a restriction of convertibility that was limited mainly to banks in the West and the South. The banks of New York and New England maintained payments. We are doubtful that the 1837 restriction is an exception, although Willard L. Thorp's *Business Annals* (New York, NBER, 1926, p. 122) refers to "over six hundred bank failures" in that year—which may, of course, have occurred before restriction came in May. The reliability of this figure is questionable. The only data available on number of banks for the period 1834–63 are those contained in the reports on the condition of the banks, made annually to Congress in compliance with a resolution of 1832 (the figures are reprinted in *Annual Report* of the Comptroller of the Currency, 1876, Appendix, p. 94). The number of banks, according to this source, rose from 713 in 1836 to 788 in 1837, 829 in 1838, and 840 in 1839. This series shows a continued rise, whereas it almost surely would show a decline if the number of failures had been the more than 600 noted by Thorp. The number of banks is doubtless an underestimate and may entirely exclude unincorporated private banks, whereas failures may have been concentrated among the latter. Even so, it seems unlikely that new banks would have been more numerous than failures in 1837 even among the categories covered, if so many banks of all kinds had in fact failed.

serve as means of payment elsewhere in the country and banks were re-luctant to part with reserve funds that were generally acceptable. To O. M. W. Sprague, "the dislocation of the domestic exchanges" as a result of restriction was a serious disturbance to the trade of the country.[41]

The term suspension of payments, widely applied to those earlier episodes, is a misnomer. Only one class of payments was suspended, the conversion of deposits into currency, and this class was suspended in order to permit the maintenance of other classes of payments. The term suspension of payments is apt solely for the 1933 episode, which did indeed involve the suspension of all payments and all usual activities by the banking system. Deposits of every kind in banks became unavailable to depositors. Suspension occurred after, rather than before, liquidity pressures had produced a wave of bank failures without precedent. And far from preventing further bank failures, it brought additional bank failures in its train. More than 5,000 banks still in operation when the holiday was declared did not reopen their doors when it ended, and of these, over 2,000 never did thereafter (see Chapter 8, section 1). The "cure" came close to being worse than the disease.

One would be hard put to it indeed to find a more dramatic example of how far the result of legislation can deviate from intention than this contrast between the earlier restrictions of payments and the banking holiday under the Federal Reserve System, set up largely to prevent their repetition.

The facts of the banking panic are straightforward. The immediate reasons for its occurrence are not. Why was tentative recovery followed by relapse? Why after some months of quiet was there renewed pressure on the banking system? The answer is by no means clear.

One important factor was the drastically weakened capital position of the commercial banks, which made them extremely vulnerable to even minor drains. The recorded capital figures were widely recognized as overstating the available capital, because assets were being carried on the books at a value higher than their market value.[42] Federal Reserve open market purchases would have improved the capital position by raising market values, but those purchases ended in August 1932. Alternatively, Reconstruction Finance Corporation funds could have improved the capital position if they had been made available in the form of capital.[43]

---

[41] *History of Crises Under the National Banking System,* National Monetary Commission, 1910, pp. 75, 206, 291.

[42] See footnote 22 above for the change at the end of 1931 in the Comptroller of the Currency's valuation of bonds in national bank portfolios. State banking authorities followed the Comptroller's procedure.

[43] RFC loans helped in a measure, but since the RFC took the best of a distressed bank's assets as security for a loan, often little was left to meet any further

They were not, however, until the Emergency Banking Act of March 9, 1933, authorized the RFC to invest in the preferred stock or capital notes of commercial banks.

The election campaign may well have been another factor. It was the occasion for a summing up by the Republicans of all the perils to which the financial system had been exposed and which they claimed to have successfully surmounted, while the Democrats predicted worse perils to come if the Republicans were continued in office. Fears concerning the safety of the banking system were heightened not only by the campaign talk, but also by the January 1933 disclosure, as noted above, of names of banks to which the RFC had made loans before August 1932, and by consideration in the Senate that same month of the Glass bill which proposed reform of questionable practices of the banks.

Uncertainty about the economic and, particularly, the monetary policies to be followed by the new administration also contributed to the relapse.[44] In the course of the election campaign Roosevelt had made ambivalent statements which were interpreted—certainly by Senator Glass, among others—as committing himself to the retention of the gold standard at

---

demands by depositors. Many of the banks helped by the RFC failed by March 1933 for lack of sufficient capital. Owen D. Young remarked to the directors of the New York Federal Reserve Bank, "Under present methods a loan from the Reconstruction Finance Corporation is largely used to pay off certain depositors before the bank ultimately closes, leaving the other depositors out on a limb because the Reconstruction Finance Corporation has gutted the bank of collateral in securing its loan. If this is all that is to be accomplished it might have been better to make no loans" (Harrison, Notes, Vol. II, July 7, 1932).

[44] The election was decided in Nov. 1932 but the new President was not inaugurated until Mar. 1933, and this interregnum coincided almost precisely with the initial halt in the tentative recovery and then the sharp downward slide. In his memoirs, Hoover argues that the final banking panic could have been prevented had Roosevelt disavowed any intention to devalue the dollar or unbalance the budget and had Roosevelt cooperated with him, as he repeatedly requested him to do, in joint measures to stem the rising tide of banking difficulties (*Memoirs*, pp. 206–216; J. M. Burns, *Roosevelt: The Lion and the Fox,* New York, Harcourt, Brace, 1956, p. 147).

Roosevelt's view was that people were withdrawing money from the banks not because of lack of confidence in him, but because of lack of confidence in banks; what was needed was reorganization and reform of the banking system, not optimistic statements by him (A. M. Schlesinger, Jr., *The Age of Roosevelt,* Vol. 1, *The Crisis of the Old Order, 1919–1933,* Boston, Houghton Mifflin, 1957, pp. 476–477).

There were measures Hoover might have taken on his own responsibility, but as his administration approached the end he was understandably unwilling to initiate policy without the approval of the incoming administration. A few days before the inauguration, the Treasury and the Federal Reserve Board pressed him to declare a nationwide bank holiday, but he proposed instead an executive order controlling the foreign exchanges and gold withdrawals if Roosevelt would approve. Roosevelt again refused to take joint action with him.

the then existing gold parity.[45] After the election, rumors spread that the new administration planned to devalue, that Roosevelt had been persuaded by George Warren to follow a policy of altering the gold content of the dollar as a means of "reflating" prices. The rumors became particularly widespread in early 1933 and gained credence when Roosevelt refused to deny them. The effect of the rumors and the failure to deny them was that, for the first time in the course of the contraction, the internal drain in part took the form of a demand for gold coin and certificates thereby reinforcing the external drain arising from speculative accumulation of foreign exchange.

The rumors about gold were only one part of the general uncertainty during the interregnum about future financial and economic policy. Under ordinary circumstances, it would have been doubtful that such rumors and such uncertainty could be a major factor accounting for so dramatic and widespread a financial panic. But these were not ordinary circumstances. The uncertainty came after more than three years of severe economic contraction and after more than two years of banking difficulties in which one wave of bank failures had followed another and had left the banking system in a peculiarly vulnerable position. The Federal Reserve itself participated in the general atmosphere of panic. Once the panic started, it fed on itself.

2. Factors Accounting for Changes in the Stock of Money

The factors accounting for changes in the stock of money during the four years from 1929 to 1933 are strikingly different from those in the other periods we have examined. Generally, the pattern for high-powered money has impressed itself most strongly on the total stock of money, the behavior of the two deposit ratios serving mainly to alter the tilt of the money stock relative to the tilt of high-powered money. That relation holds in Chart 31 only for the period up to October 1930, the onset of the first banking crisis. Thereafter, the two deposit ratios take command. High-powered money moves in a direction opposite to that of the total stock of money, and not even most of its short-term movements leave an impress on the stock of money.

From August 1929 to March 1933 as a whole, the change in high-powered money alone would have produced a rise of 17½ per cent in the stock of money. The change in the deposit-currency ratio alone would

---

[45] Frank B. Freidel, *Franklin Delano Roosevelt*, Vol. 3, *The Triumph*, Boston, Little, Brown, 1956, p. 351; Rixey Smith and Norman Beasley, *Carter Glass*, New York, Longmans, Green, 1939, pp. 321–323. When Roosevelt was authorized to reduce the gold content of the dollar under authority of the Thomas amendment to the Agricultural Adjustment Act of May 12, 1933, Glass, who had made an important speech on behalf of Roosevelt during the election campaign, made a vigorous attack on him in the Senate (Smith and Beasley, pp. 349–356).

CHART 31

The Stock of Money and Its Proximate Determinants, Monthly, 1929–March 1933

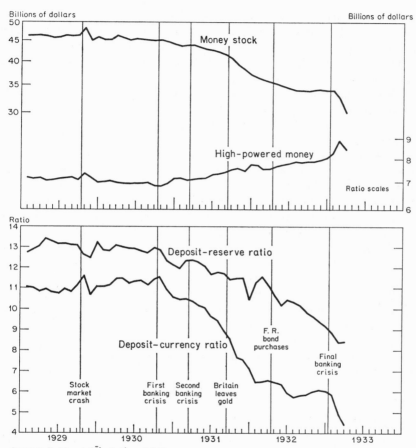

SOURCE: Tables A-1 (col. 8) and B-3.

have produced a decline of 37 per cent; the change in the deposit-reserve ratio, a decline of 20 per cent; interaction between the two ratios, a rise of 10 per cent; these three converted the 17½ per cent rise that high-powered money would have produced into a 35 per cent decline in the stock of money.[46] For a more detailed examination of these changes, we

[46] The trough of the money stock was reached in April 1933. Although the percentage decline from Aug. 1929 to Apr. 1933 is only slightly larger than from Aug. 1929 to Mar. 1933 (35.7 rather than 35.2 per cent), the percentage changes in the money stock each determinant would have produced if it alone had changed over the longer period show larger differences: 13, —35, —19, and 9 per cent, in

consider separately each of the periods distinguished in the preceding section and marked off on our charts.

THE STOCK MARKET CRASH, OCTOBER 1929

Before the stock market crash, all three determinants of the money stock, and hence also the money stock itself, had been roughly constant. The constancy in high-powered money reflected a rough constancy in each of the categories into which we have divided the corresponding assets of the monetary authorities: the gold stock, Federal Reserve private claims, and other physical assets and fiat of the monetary authorities (see Chart 32B). However, the constancy of Federal Reserve private claims conceals a not uninteresting detail, brought out by Chart 33, which shows the components of Federal Reserve credit outstanding. The total was roughly constant because a decline in bills discounted was offset by a rise in bills bought. The reason for the divergent movements was the simultaneous rise in August 1929 of the New York Reserve Bank's discount rate from 5 to 6 per cent and the decline of its buying rate on bills (bankers' acceptances) from 5¼ to 5⅛ per cent. We analyzed the reason for these apparently inconsistent movements in the preceding chapter (section 4). Their effect was to make it profitable for banks to get funds from the Reserve System by creating acceptances and selling them to the Reserve Banks rather than by increasing their own indebtedness.

When the crash came, there were widespread attempts by holders of securities to liquidate them and by banks and other lenders outside New York to reduce their loans. As in all such cases, the position of the collection of participants is different from that of any one participant. Long-term securities cannot, on net, be liquidated in a short interval but only

---

the order shown in the text. The reason is that the return flow of currency after the banking holiday reduced high-powered money substantially and also raised the deposit-currency ratio from Mar. to Apr. 1933.

The numerical values of the contributions of the determinants during the contraction, dated as ending in Mar. and in Apr. 1933, follow.

Change in Money Stock That Would Have Been Produced by
Indicated Determinant if It Alone Had Changed

	Rate of Change Per Year (per cent)		Fraction of Total Change	
Proximate Determinant	*Aug. 1929– Mar. 1933*	*Aug. 1929– Apr. 1933*	*Aug. 1929– Mar. 1933*	*Aug. 1929– Apr. 1933*
High-powered money	4.6	3.2	−0.37	−0.28
Deposit-reserve ratio	−6.2	−5.9	0.52	0.49
Deposit-currency ratio	−13.0	−11.8	1.07	0.98
Interaction	2.6	2.3	−0.22	−0.19
All	−12.1	−12.0	1.00	1.00

Detail may not add to total because of rounding.

334

transferred from one holder to another. The widespread attempts to liquidate simply reduced prices to a level at which intended purchases matched intended sales.

Loans on securities, especially call loans, are a somewhat more complex affair. In large measure, what is involved is also a transfer of debts from one lender to another, rather than a change in total. But, in addition, the total can be altered much more rapidly. Aside from default, one way is by a transfer of other assets, as most directly when a borrower transfers money to a creditor and reduces his own money balance, or more indirectly when a borrower acquires cash by selling the security serving as collateral to someone else who draws down a money balance to acquire it. Another way is by what is in effect mutual cancellation of reciprocal debts. The most obvious but clearly insignificant example involves the cancellation by two borrowers of loans they have made to one another. A less obvious but more important example involves a longer chain, say, a corporation lending on call in the stock market and simultaneously borrowing from a bank. If the bank takes over the call loan in discharge of its loan to the corporation, the total of the two kinds of debt outstanding is reduced. The total can also be altered by creation of debts; for example, if a corporation lending on call in the market is willing to accept a note from a bank or—more realistically—a deposit in that bank in return for the corporation's claim. In that case, the total of the two kinds of debt is increased.

The essential point for our purpose is that the demand for liquidation of security loans involves one of three arrangements: (1) finding someone willing to take over the loans which, as for securities, can be done by a change of price, that is, a rise in interest rates; (2) finding someone willing to acquire assets for money to be used by the borrower to repay his loan, which can be done by lowering the price of the assets; or (3) arranging for more or less roundabout mutual cancellation or creation of debts, which involves changes in the relative prices of the various assets. The pressure on interest rates and on security prices can be eased by any measure that enhances the supply of funds in one of these forms to facilitate the liquidation of loans in one of these ways.

The situation was eased greatly at the time of the stock market crash by the willingness of New York banks to take over the loans. In the first week after the crash, those banks increased their loans to brokers and dealers by $1 billion and the rest of their loans by $300 million.[47] In large measure, this involved a creation of debts. The former lenders, the "others" for the accounts of whom the New York banks had been making loans, accepted deposits in New York banks as repaying their loans, and the New York banks in turn took over the claims on the bor-

[47] For sources, see footnote 5, above.

CHART 32

High-Powered Money, by Assets and Liabilities of the Treasury
and Federal Reserve Banks, Monthly, 1929–March 1933

A. Liabilities

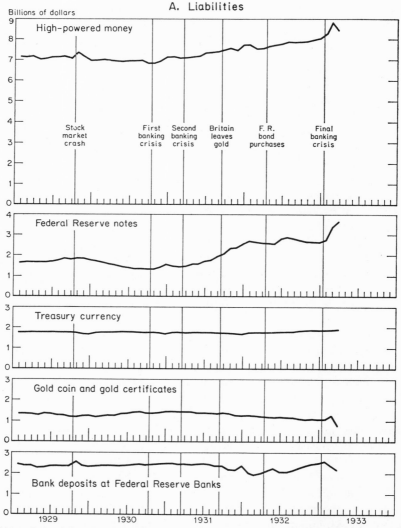

NOTE: Federal Reserve notes, Treasury currency, and gold coin and certificates are outside
the Treasury and Federal Reserve Banks.
SOURCE: Same as for Chart 19.

CHART 32 (Concluded)

B. Assets

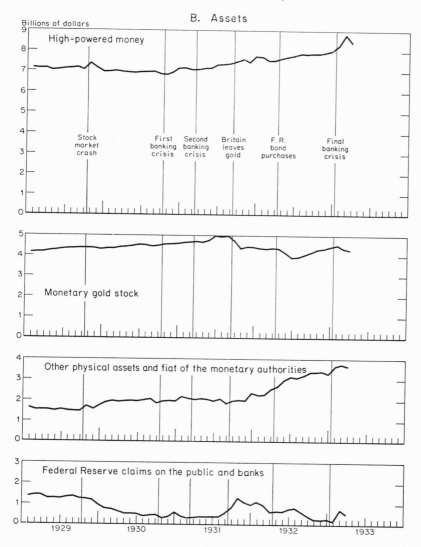

Billions of dollars

rowers without pressing for their immediate payment. That is the reason the monetary effect of the crash shows up in our money stock series as a sharp increase in demand deposits and the reason the increase was in New York City. Indeed, the increase in our estimates understates the magnitude of the action of the New York banks. Some of the loans taken over

337

CHART 33

Federal Reserve Credit Outstanding, by Types, Monthly,
1929–March 1933

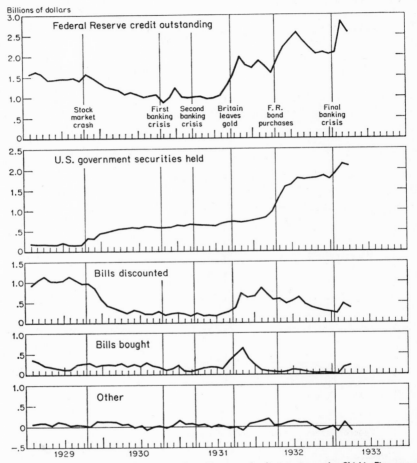

SOURCE: Same as for Chart 22, except that all seasonal adjustments are by Shiskin-Eisenpress
method (reference given in source for Chart 21).

were for the accounts of out-of-town banks and were matched by an increase in interbank deposits of $510 million in New York City weekly reporting member banks. But our money stock estimates exclude interbank deposits.

To be able to expand deposits, the New York banks had to be able either to raise the ratio of deposits to reserves or to acquire additional reserves. The first was impossible because New York banks had no excess reserves. Indeed, the ratio of deposits to high-powered reserves was lower in New York than in the rest of the country because of the higher legal reserve requirements imposed on banks in central reserve cities. Therefore the increase in deposits in New York relative to deposits in the rest of the country in October 1929 produced a decline in the average deposit-reserve ratio for the country as a whole. Accordingly, the New York banks had to and did acquire additional reserves, as the bulge in high-powered money shows. They did so in the week of the crash partly by borrowing from the Federal Reserve Bank of New York, which, in Harrison's words, kept its "discount window wide open and let it be known that member banks might borrow freely to establish the reserves required against the large increase in deposits resulting from the taking over of loans called by others;"[48] and partly by virtue of the purchase by the New York Bank of about $160 million of government securities. That purchase was far in excess of the amount the System's Open Market Investment Committee had been authorized to purchase for System account. It was made by the New York Bank on its own initiative for its own account without consulting either the Open Market Investment Committee or the Board. Though subsequently ratified, it was, as we shall see in more detail in section 5, below, the occasion for another battle in the struggle between the Bank and the Board, which had important effects on Federal Reserve policy during the rest of the contraction.

The actions taken by the New York Reserve Bank were timely and effective. Despite the stock market crash, there were no panic increases in money market rates such as those in past market crises, and no indirect effects on confidence in banks which might have arisen if there had been any sizable defaults on security loans. Harrison himself expressed the view that "it is not at all unlikely that had we not bought governments so freely, thus supplementing the reserves built up by large additional discounts, the stock exchange might have had to yield to the tremendous pressure brought to bear upon it to close on some one of those very bad days the last part of October."[49] Harrison may have overstated the case— he was, after all, writing in defense of the actions the New York Bank had taken—but that is by no means certain.

In the month following the crash, there was a reversal. Deposits declined, as more lasting arrangements for the transfer and reduction of stock market loans replaced the temporary shift of many of those loans to New York banks. The changes in deposits produced a decline in the deposit-currency ratio, following the rise in October, and a decline in

---

[48] Harrison, Miscellaneous, Vol. I, letter, dated Nov. 27, 1929, Harrison to all governors. During the week ending Oct. 30, 1929, discounts increased $200 million at all Reserve Banks, of which $130 million was the increase in New York City weekly reporting member bank borrowings from the New York Reserve Bank.

[49] Ibid., letter, dated Nov. 27, 1929, Harrison to all governors.

the deposit-reserve ratio milder than that in October. High-powered money also declined as a result of a reduction in bills discounted and in the gold stock, generally attributed to the withdrawal by foreigners of funds from the New York money market.[50] The net effect was to leave the stock of money after the crash at a lower level than before. At the end of November 1929, the stock of money was $1.3 billion, or 3 per cent, less than it had been at the end of September. By the end of December, most of the loss had been made up; the stock of money was about $0.5 billion, or 1 per cent, less than in September. These changes were concentrated in demand deposits. From December 1929 to October 1930, the stock of money fluctuated around a roughly constant level though with a mild downward trend. In October 1930, the stock of money was almost the same as it had been in November 1929 and nearly 2 per cent below its level at the end of December 1929.

For the period from August 1929 to October 1930 as a whole, the money stock declined by 2.6 per cent. High-powered money alone declined by 5 per cent. However, the deposit-currency ratio rose by about 7 per cent, enough to offset a minor decline in the deposit-reserve ratio as well as half the decline in high-powered money. In October 1930, the deposit-currency ratio stood at the highest level reached at any time in the 93 years covered by our data, except only for a fractionally higher peak reached in the month of the stock market crash (see Charts 31 and 64, and Table B-3). As we noted earlier, the public was clearly not greatly concerned at the time about the safety of bank deposits. But the high ratio made the System peculiarly vulnerable to the development of any such concern, as the following years were to demonstrate so tragically.

The decline in high-powered money occurred despite an increase of $210 million in the gold stock and of $470 million in the fiat of the monetary authorities. The latter increase reflected mostly a rise in government securities held by the System, i.e., the substitution of noninterest-bearing for interest-bearing government debt. Those expansionary factors were more than offset by a decline in Federal Reserve private claims of $1,020 million—$100 million in bills bought and $920 million in bills discounted and other claims (see Chart 32B). Ultimately then, it was the failure of the Reserve System to replace the decline in discounts by other

---

[50] The return flow of foreign funds gave temporary relief to the foreign exchanges, which had been under pressure during the period of speculation. Foreign currencies had depreciated vis-à-vis the dollar, while foreigners were remitting funds to the security markets here. Before the peak in stock prices in 1929, the prices of those currencies had declined to the United States' gold import point. After the crash, the return flow of funds raised their prices to the gold export point. For example, the pound was as low as $4.845857 in Sept. 1929 and in Dec. was as high as $4.882010 (the figures are noon buying rates for cable transfers to New York, from *Commercial and Financial Chronicle*, Sept. 21, 1929, p. 1969; Dec. 27, 1929, p. 4017).

credit outstanding that was responsible for the decline in the stock of money.

The decline in discounts took place despite sharp reductions in discount rates—at the New York Bank, from 6 per cent to 2½ per cent in June 1930 (Chart 29). The successive declines in discount rates—the first of which came in November 1929, three months after the date set by the National Bureau as the reference cycle peak—though sharp and rapid by earlier standards, took place during a time when there was a sharp decline in the demand for loans and an increase in the demand for assets regarded as safe. Both made for a sharp decline in market interest rates. Though the discount rate fell absolutely, it probably rose relative to the relevant market interest rates, namely, those on short-term securities with essentially zero risk of default. Hence, discounting became less attractive. It is perhaps worth noting that this is not merely a retrospective judgment. The New York Reserve Bank favored more rapid reductions in the rate than those made. Harrison said in May 1931 that "if there had been no Federal Reserve System in October, 1929, money rates would probably have come down more rapidly than they had . . . ." In September 1930, Adolph Miller of the Federal Reserve Board said at a meeting with all the governors, "Money is not really cheap nor easy." In mid-1930, Harold L. Reed, in the second of his two excellent books on the Federal Reserve System said: "In the writer's opinion, however, there was much stronger ground for holding that the rate reductions had been too gradual and long delayed" than that they had been too rapid.[51]

As the near-constancy of the deposit-reserve ratio indicates, there was no tendency of banks to accumulate excess reserves. It has been contended with respect to later years (particularly during the period after 1934, when large excess reserves accumulated) that increases in high-powered money, through expansion of Federal Reserve credit or other means, would simply have been added to bank reserves and would not have been used to increase the money stock. In other words, a rise in high-powered money would have been offset by a decline in the deposit-reserve ratio. We shall argue later that the contention is invalid even for the later period. It is clearly not relevant to the period from August 1929 to October 1930. During that period, additional reserves would almost certainly have been put to use promptly. Hence, the decline in the stock

[51] See sect. 5 below for the New York Bank's position. The quotation from Harrison is from Harrison, Notes, Vol. I, May 21, 1931; from Miller, Charles S. Hamlin, Hamlin Papers, Manuscript Division, Library of Congress, Diary, Vol. 18, Sept. 25, 1930, p. 86; from Reed, *Federal Reserve Policy, 1921–1930*, New York, McGraw-Hill, 1930, p. 191. This may not have been Miller's view earlier in the year. In May, Hamlin reported, "Miller said the Federal Reserve Bank of New York was obsessed with the idea that easy money would help the business recession" (Hamlin, Diary, Vol. 17, May 9, 1930, p. 151).

of money is not only arithmetically attributable to the decline in Federal Reserve credit outstanding; it is economically a direct result of that decline.

ONSET OF FIRST BANKING CRISIS, OCTOBER 1930

The onset of the banking crisis is clearly marked in all three proximate determinants but particularly in the deposit ratios (Chart 31). From a peak of 11.5 in October 1930, the ratio of deposits to currency declined sharply—a decline that was to carry the ratio, with only minor interruptions along the way, to a low of 4.4 in March 1933. The deposit-reserve ratio likewise began a decline that was to carry it from a level of 12.9 in October 1930—the all-time high was 13.4 in April 1929—to a level of 8.4 in March 1933. These declines brought the deposit-currency ratio back to its level at the turn of the century and the deposit-reserve ratio to its level in 1912. They thus wiped out the whole of the much heralded spread in the use of deposits and "economy" in reserves achieved under the Reserve System.

The decline in the stock of money as a result of the banking crisis— a decline of slightly more than 3 per cent from October 1930 to January 1931, or more than in the preceding fourteen months—was clearly a result of the declines in the two deposit ratios, since high-powered money rose by 5 per cent. As Charts 32B and 33 show, the rise of $340 million in high-powered money, seasonally adjusted, was produced partly by an inflow of $84 million of gold[52]—the source that had always been the major reliance in pre-Federal Reserve crises—partly by an increase of $117 million in Federal Reserve credit outstanding. The increase in Federal Reserve credit consisted partly of a rise of $41 million in government securities, the balance of a rise in float. A rise in discounts just about offset a decline in bills bought. There was a brief spurt of roughly $200 million in bills discounted in the two weeks after the failure of the Bank of United States, but it does not show up in the seasonally adjusted end-of-month figures plotted in Chart 33.

The rise in Federal Reserve credit certainly helped to offset some of the immediate effects of the banking crisis. But the movement was minor in magnitude. Many an earlier year-end shows rises of comparable magnitude and, even at its peak in December 1930, seasonally adjusted Federal Reserve credit was only 84 per cent of its level in the summer of 1929 when the System was seeking to curb speculation. The one other measure taken by the System in reaction to the banking crisis was a re-

[52] The gold inflows reflected partly the Hawley-Smoot Tariff Act passed in June 1930, which raised the tariff to the highest level up to that time in U.S. history; partly the reduction of U.S. lending abroad, and the continuance at a high level of interest and dividends on investments abroad and of war debt payments; partly the consequence of U.S. deflation on imports and exports. See sect. 4, below.

duction in late December 1930 in the New York Reserve Bank's discount rate to 2 per cent—to reassure the public.[53]

The rise in Federal Reserve Bank credit was temporary. After December 1930, discounts declined, bills bought were allowed to run off without replacement, while government security holdings increased by only a small fraction of the combined decline in discounts and bills bought. High-powered money rose in January 1931, only because a continued gold inflow offset the decline in Federal Reserve credit. It declined in February despite continued gold inflow, and rose slightly in March along with a minor rise in Federal Reserve credit and the gold stock. The decline in Federal Reserve credit from December 1930 to March 1931 was greater than the gold inflow. In effect, the System was not only sterilizing the gold inflow, but exerting a contractionary influence greater than the expansionary influence of the gold inflow.

Despite the reduction in high-powered money in February 1931, the money stock rose a bit because of a rise in both deposit ratios, as the wave of bank failures died down and confidence in banks was somewhat restored. As suggested earlier, if the rises in the deposit ratios had been reinforced by a vigorous expansion in high-powered money, instead of being offset by a reduction, the ground gained might have been consolidated and extended.

ONSET OF SECOND BANKING CRISIS, MARCH 1931

The onset of the second banking crisis is clearly marked in Chart 31 by the renewed decline in the deposit ratios and the beginning of a decline in the money stock at the fastest rate so far in the contraction. In the five months from March to August, to exclude wholly the effects of Britain's departure from gold in September, the stock of money fell by 5¼ per cent, or by almost exactly the same percentage as in all the preceding nineteen months of the contraction. This was at the phenomenal annual rate of 13 per cent, yet the rate was soon to rise still higher.

As after the first banking crisis, the decline in the stock of money was entirely a consequence of the fall in the deposit ratios. High-powered money rose, this time by 4 per cent from March to August, and so offset nearly half the contractionary effect of the declining deposit ratios. There were, however, two differences between the second banking crisis and the first one some six months earlier.

---

[53] Governor Harrison wrote, "he had been urged from many quarters to make a reassuring statement which might aid in quieting the banking situation. Such a statement was practically impossible because to be strong enough to do any good it would run the risk of being contradicted by any small bank failure which might thereafter occur. The rate reduction, apart from other reasons, served as a method of stating to the public that money was freely available" (Harrison, Open Market, Vol. II, Jan. 21, 1931).

(1) This time, the rise in high-powered money was produced almost entirely by the continued gold inflow, whereas earlier there had been at least a temporary increase in Federal Reserve credit, which helped to absorb some of the initial effects of the crisis. Federal Reserve credit remained almost perfectly stable, rising slightly only in July and August 1931. Despite the unprecedented liquidation of the commercial banking system, the books of the "lender of last resort" show a decline in bills discounted from the end of February to the end of April—a period when the usual seasonal movement is upward—and a rise from April to the end of August that made the whole increase from February to August less than th usual seasonal increase; they show irregular increases and decreases in bills bought, with the total at the end of August $75 million higher than at the end of February, but still below its level at the turn of the year; and they show an increase of $130 million in government securities purchased, the whole of the increase beginning late in June. Of this increase, $50 million was a purely technical move rather than a reaction to domestic financial difficulties: it simply offset other reductions in credit outstanding. The remaining $80 million represented a deliberate, if timid, move to contribute ease.[54]

(2) The second crisis lasted longer. In late 1930, there were signs of improvement after two or three months. On this occasion, as Chart 31 shows, the deposit-currency ratio—the most sensitive indicator of the public's attitude toward banks—not only continued to fall, but fell at an increasing rate. There was no sign that the crisis was drawing to an end when Britain's departure from gold intensified it.

Aside from the modest open market purchases in July and August, the only other domestic action of the System relevant to the money stock was a further reduction in the discount rate of the New York Reserve Bank to 1½ per cent in May—before the sharp June increase in bank failures. As we have seen, the reduction did not stimulate borrowing. On a different front, potentially of great consequence for the domestic money stock, the System participated in loans to foreign banks as part of an international effort to avert financial catastrophe abroad.[55]

[54] Federal Reserve Board, *Annual Report* for 1931, pp. 7–8. These figures are all as of Wednesdays. Of the $130 million of government securities purchased, $80 million was for System account and $50 million for the New York Bank's own account (Harrison, Open Market, Vol. II, minutes of June 22 and Aug. 11, 1931, Open Market Policy Conference meetings; Miscellaneous, Vol. I, letter, dated July 9, 1931, Harrison to Seay; Notes, Vol. I, July 16, 1931, and Vol. II, Aug. 4, 1931). The latter purchase was made to offset the effect of the transfer of foreign-held balances from the acceptance market to Federal Reserve Banks.

[55] During the second and third quarters of 1931, the Federal Reserve Bank of New York in association with other Federal Reserve Banks purchased prime commercial bills with guaranteed repayment in gold from the Austrian National Bank, the National Bank of Hungary, the Reichsbank, and the Bank of England. The credit agreements with the Federal Reserve Banks at their separate maximums

BRITAIN'S DEPARTURE FROM GOLD, SEPTEMBER 1931

In the few months after the departure of Britain from the gold standard, the proximate determinants of the money stock plotted in Chart 31 continued the pattern of the preceding five months, but the pattern was even more emphatic. The stock of money fell still faster: in the five months from August 1931 to January 1932, it fell by 12 per cent—compared with 5 per cent in the preceding five months—or at the annual rate of 31 per cent—compared with 13 per cent. High-powered money again rose, this time by about 4½ per cent, and again offset only part, and this time a smaller part, of the effect of the declines in the deposit ratios, particularly the deposit-currency ratio. The banks were so hard pressed to meet the demands of their depositors that, try though they did, they were able to do little to lower the ratio of their deposit liabilities to their reserves. That had to wait for a more propitious time, which is why the most rapid decline in the deposit-reserve ratio came later when the decline in the deposit-currency ratio had tapered off, and the slowest decline came earlier when the deposit-currency ratio was declining fastest. As we shall see in later chapters, much of the adjustment on the part of the banks did not come until after the end of the business contraction and the beginning of recovery. The timing relations between changes in the two deposit ratios during the 1931–32 segment of the contraction repeated the tendencies we have observed in each earlier banking crisis.

The major difference, aside from scale, between the five-month period, August 1931–January 1932, and the preceding five months is the source of the rise in high-powered money, which does not show up in Chart 31 but does in Charts 32B and 33. Up to August 1931, high-powered money had risen chiefly as a result of gold inflows. As noted in section 1 above, the period after Britain's departure from gold saw a sharp outflow, particularly in September and October 1931, large enough to offset

---

aggregated about $156 million and were renewed several times. Reserve Bank holdings of bills payable in foreign currencies increased from $1 million at the end of March to $145 million in August (Federal Reserve Board, *Annual Report* for 1931, pp. 12–13).

See also Harrison, Miscellaneous, Vol. I, letter, dated July 9, 1931, Harrison to McDougal; Open Market, Vol. II, minutes of meeting, Aug. 11, 1931; and Notes, Vol. I, June 1, 15, 22; July 13, 16, 1931; Vol. II, July 28, 30; Aug. 4; Sept. 24, 28, 1931, for discussion of the foreign credits. One of the directors of the New York Reserve Bank, Charles E. Mitchell, was quoted as saying, "In all of these cases, he was concerned about the soundness of the operation to be undertaken by the Federal reserve banks which, in their domestic business, take as few chances as possible," and "the thing which bothered him with regard to these foreign credits was the risk involved when, at home, the Federal reserve banks take no risks" (Harrison, Notes, Vol. I, June 22, 1931).

the gold inflows during the earlier segments of the contraction. High-powered money rose because Federal Reserve credit outstanding rose. Federal Reserve credit rose primarily because of the sharp rise in discounts as banks, having no other recourse open to them, were driven to borrowing from the Reserve System, despite the unprecedentedly sharp rises in discount rates in October 1931. Bills bought increased substantially in September and October, but then were allowed to run off so that, by January 1932, they had fallen below their level at the end of August 1931. All told, from August 1931 to January 1932, the rise of $330 million in high-powered money was accounted for by a rise of $560 million in discounts, $80 million in government securities, $270 million in other assets of the monetary authorities, offset by a decline of $580 million in the gold stock.

During those five months when high-powered money rose by $330 million, currency held by the public increased by $720 million. The extra $390 million had to come from bank reserves. Since banks were unwilling and unable to draw down reserves relative to their deposits,[56] the $390 million, amounting to 12 per cent of their total reserves in August 1931, could be freed for currency use only by a multiple contraction of deposits. The multiple worked out to roughly 14, so deposits fell by $5,727 million or by 15 per cent of their level in August 1931. It was the necessity of reducing deposits by $14 in order to make $1 available for the public to hold as currency that made the loss of confidence in banks so cumulative and so disastrous. Here was the famous multiple expansion process of the banking system in vicious reverse. That phenomenon, too, explains how seemingly minor measures had such major effects. The provision of $400 million of additional high-powered money to meet the currency drain without a decline in bank reserves could have prevented a decline of nearly $6 billion in deposits.

In discussing the 1907 crisis, we showed how the rise in deposit ratios had made the banking system more vulnerable to an attempted conversion of deposits to currency. The situation in 1931 was even more extreme. At no time in 1907 did the public hold more than $6 in deposits for every $1 it held in currency; in March 1931, when the second banking crisis began, it held over $10 in deposits for every $1 of currency, an amount it succeeded in reducing to under $7 by January 1932. In 1907, the banks owed less than $9 in deposits for every $1 of high-powered money they held as reserves; in March 1931, they owed more than $12. The more extensive use of deposits—widely regarded during the twenties as a sign of the great progress and refinement of the American financial structure—and the higher ratio of deposits to reserves—widely regarded as a sign of the effectiveness of the new Reserve System in promoting

[56] At the end of Jan. 1932, their excess reserves totaled $40 million.

"economy" in the use of reserves—made the monetary system much more vulnerable to a widespread loss of confidence in banks. The defenses deliberately constructed against such an eventuality turned out in practice to be far less effective than those that had grown up in the earlier era.

When bank failures tapered off in February and March 1932, the deposit-currency ratio temporarily stopped falling. However, high-powered money declined by $160 million in those two months, despite a dwindling of gold outflows, mainly as a result of changes in Reserve Bank credit: a decline of $280 million in discounts, and a continued decline of $50 million in bills bought, while government security holdings rose by about $180 million. Discounts declined because banks took advantage of the pause in the demands on them to repay some of their borrowings. They followed that course despite a reduction in the New York Bank's discount rate to 3 per cent in February. The banks took advantage of the pause also to strengthen their reserve position somewhat, so the deposit-reserve ratio fell slightly from January to March 1932. The result was that the stock of money continued to decline though at a slower pace. In these two months it fell by another 2 per cent, an annual rate of 13 per cent, which can be described as moderate only by comparison with the preceding 31 per cent annual rate of decline.

The beginning of the purchase of government securities on a large scale by the Federal Reserve System in April 1932, involving purchase of $350 million during that month (see Chart 33 for seasonally adjusted end-of-the-month figures), had no immediate effect on the behavior of the stock of money. It declined another 4½ per cent for another four months, or at an annual rate of 14 per cent. The decline then slowed up sharply, the money stock falling one-half of 1 per cent in the two months from July to September 1932, or at the annual rate of 3 per cent. From September on, it rose mildly until January 1933, when the money stock was one-half of 1 per cent higher than in September 1932, implying an average rate of growth of about 1¾ per cent per year.

The reason the bond purchases had no greater effect to begin with is that they were offset in part by a renewed outflow of gold and the rest was more than offset by continued declines in the deposit ratios. From April to July 1932, when Reserve System holdings of government securities went up by roughly $1 billion, the gold stock fell by about half that amount, most of the outflow going to France. At the same time, a renewed flurry of bank failures in June produced a further appreciable decline in the deposit-currency ratio, and the continued efforts of the banks to strengthen their position produced a further decline in the deposit-reserve ratio.

The gold drain ceased in mid-June and was replaced by an inflow.

Over the rest of the year, the gold stock rose by $600 million, bringing the gold stock in January 1933 above its level a year earlier. Reserve System bond purchases ceased in August 1932. Discounts and bills bought fell from July on, so that total Federal Reserve credit outstanding reached a peak in that month and fell by $500 million from then to January 1933. Nonetheless, high-powered money continued to rise at roughly a constant rate from April 1932 to January 1933 because of the reversal of the gold flow, plus an increase of $140 million in national bank notes. The latter increase was due to an amendment attached to the Home Loan Bank Act of July 1932, which broadened the range of government bonds eligible as security for national bank notes.[57] Once the deposit-currency ratio reached its trough in July 1932, the rise in high-powered money plus the rise in the deposit-currency ratio were enough to offset the continued fall in the deposit-reserve ratio and produce the pattern of change in the money stock already described.

The form taken by the improvement in the banking position, recorded in the deposit-reserve ratio, is worth noting because it presaged a development that was to be important in the next few years. Banks began to accumulate substantial reserves in excess of legal requirements. Since the Reserve System regarded the so-called "excess reserves" as a sign of monetary ease, their accumulation contributed to adoption of the policy of keeping total government securities at the level reached in early August. Excess reserves were interpreted by many as a sign of lack of demand for bank funds, as meaning that monetary authorities could make "credit" available but could not guarantee its use, a position most succinctly conveyed by the saying, "monetary policy is like a string; you can pull on it but you can't push on it." In our view, this interpretation is wrong. The reserves were excess only in a strictly legal sense. The banks had discovered in the course of two traumatic years that neither legal reserves nor the presumed availability of a "lender of last resort" was of much avail in time of trouble, and this lesson was shortly to be driven home yet again. Little wonder that the reserves they found it prudent to hold exceeded substantially the reserves they were legally required to hold.[58] As noted above, their reaction was the same as in

[57] The amendment permitted use for a period of three years of all government bonds bearing interest at 3⅜ per cent or less, including future bond issues during the period. From August 1929 up to July 1932 there was a slight increase—$60 million—in national bank notes in circulation, as national banks exercised somewhat more fully their right to issue on the security of three government bond issues bearing interest at 2 per cent, which had the circulation privilege.

[58] See Chap. 8, sect. 1, for evidence on this view. In Dec. 1932, Governor Meyer said that "if the banks knew that there was going to be a constant amount of excess reserves over a long period, that amount could be relatively small and still be more effective than a much larger but uncertain amount . . . . We have not obtained the full effect of recent large excess reserves because of uncertainty as to our future policy" (Harrison, Notes, Vol. III, Dec. 22, 1932).

earlier crises, only greater in magnitude in response to the greater severity of the crisis.

The final banking crisis, which terminated in the banking holiday early in March 1933, was in most essential respects a duplicate of the two preceding ones but still more drastic. The money stock fell 12 per cent in the two months from January to March 1933, or at an annual rate of decline of 78 per cent. For reasons we discuss in detail in the next chapter, our estimates overstate the decline in the stock of money, but hardly any reasonable allowance for error could cut the rate of decline to less than the 31 per cent rate of decline from August 1931 to January 1932. As in the earlier crises, high-powered money rose, primarily as a result of a rise in discounts and a lesser rise in bills bought. Chart 33 shows an appreciable rise in government securities. This rise is produced by the seasonal adjustment. There is no rise in the original figures. The early months of the years before 1933 were generally characterized by a decline in the Reserve portfolio of government securities in response to the return flow of currency from circulation usual at that season. In 1933, there was, of course, a drain of currency rather than a return flow: government securities were nevertheless reduced in January by $90 million, but then raised in February by $70 million, to a level at which they also stood at the end of March. Seasonal adjustment of the figures converted the decline in January and the modest rise in February to appreciable increases, and raised the original March figure only slightly less.

The banking holiday in March renders all the money figures noncomparable with earlier ones, so we consider the change from January to February alone, as an approximation of the decline up to the bank holiday. In that one month the money stock fell $4\frac{1}{2}$ per cent, or at an annual rate of 56 per cent. Currency held by the public rose by over $600 million, high-powered money by $535 million—almost the same. But even the remaining $65 million which had to be supplied from bank reserves, plus the scramble by banks for reserves, produced a decline in deposits of over $2 billion in that one month, or nearly $7\frac{1}{2}$ per cent of the already shrunken total. This time the multiplier was not 14 but 29.

The major monetary difference between the final banking crisis and the earlier ones was that for the first time the internal drain in part clearly took the form of a drain of gold coin and certificates. As Chart 32A shows, the volume of gold coin and certificates had risen mildly in 1930 but then had been constant or declining until the onset of the final crisis. In January 1933, the amount of gold coin and gold certificates outside the Treasury and Federal Reserve Banks was $420 million less than at its peak in December 1930, $340 million less than at its previous

January peak in 1931. The decline was apparently in some measure the result of a deliberate policy on the part of the Federal Reserve System of adding to its gold reserves by paying out Federal Reserve notes instead of gold certificates where feasible, a reversal of the policy adopted during the twenties to keep down the apparent reserve ratio (see Chapter 6, section 4).[59] Though the total of gold coin and gold certificates declined, the amount of gold coin alone increased by nearly $120 million, from $65 million in April 1931 to $181 million in December 1932. That increase may have reflected a preference for gold coin in the earlier period, though to some extent it must reflect the growth of all forms of currency as opposed to deposits. But if it does reflect a preference for gold, that preference was not sufficiently widespread or dramatic to attract much attention. In February and March 1933, the situation was entirely different, as shown by the sharp spurt in gold coin and certificates in early 1933 in Chart 32A. Fears of devaluation were widespread and the public's preference for gold was unmistakable. On February 23, 1933, Harrison told the directors of the New York Reserve Bank, "there is little that foreigners can do to hurt our gold position, . . . the real danger comes from domestic sources."[60]

[59] Gold certificates in circulation declined in all but three months in 1931 and 1932—when the certificates may have been paid out partly because of a shortage of other forms of currency, as in Feb. and Mar. 1933 before the bank holiday— for a net change of $460 million. Although there is no acknowledgment in the *Annual Report* for 1931 and 1932 that such a retirement policy was in effect, it is significant that the *Federal Reserve Bulletin* (Nov. 1931, p. 604) contains the following comment:

> In considering the gold position of the country, it should be noted also that there are $1,000,000,000 of gold certificates in circulation, a large part of which can be retired by the Federal reserve banks by substituting an equivalent amount of Federal [reserve] notes. The retirement of gold certificates would increase the gold holdings of the reserve banks, and of this increase 40 per cent would be required as reserves against the additional Federal reserve notes and 60 per cent would be added to the system's excess reserves.

[60] He went on to say, "During the last ten days out-payments of gold coin at this bank, and, probably, at all of the Federal reserve banks have been heavier than in any recent similar period. This movement represents something more than the hoarding of currency, which reflects a distrust of banks; it represents in addition a distrust of the currency itself and it is inspired by talk of devaluation of the dollar and inflation of the currency" (Harrison, Notes, Vol. III).
Harrison made efforts to get banks to discourage hoarding. He suggested that they refuse to provide facilities for storage of gold and to grant loans against the collateral of an equivalent amount of gold. With respect to the first, he suggested that banks impose no obstacles to the acquisition of gold but make no offer of safe-keeping facilities; with respect to the second, he advised banks to decline a loan to buy gold on the ground that it was a loan for a capital purpose. He said, "I saw no occasion for a member bank, in these times particularly when so many people who needed credit for business purposes could not obtain the credit, to make loans to their customers for the purpose of buying gold to hoard. It was nothing but a speculative loan gambling on our going off the gold standard" (Conversations, Vol. II, Feb. 9, 1933). Direct pressure had come full circle.

3. *Bank Failures*

The preceding account gives a prominent place in the sequence of events during the contraction to the successive waves of bank failures. Three questions about those failures deserve further attention: Why were the bank failures important? What was the origin of the bank failures? What was the attitude of the Federal Reserve System toward the bank failures?

ROLE OF BANK FAILURES

The bank failures had two different aspects. First, they involved capital losses to both their owners and their depositors, just as the failure of any other group of business enterprises involved losses to their owners and creditors. Second, given the policy followed by the Reserve System, the failures were the mechanism through which a drastic decline was produced in the stock of money. Which aspect was the more important for the course of business?

For the United States, the two aspects were so closely related that it may seem impossible to distinguish them and to judge their separate effects. But even for the United States alone, a few figures serve to show that the second was vastly more important than the first. Regarded solely in their first aspect, the failures imposed losses totaling about $2.5 billion on stockholders, depositors and other creditors of the more than 9,000 banks that suspended operations during the four years from 1930 through 1933. Slightly more than half the loss fell on depositors, the rest on other creditors and stockholders.[61] A loss of $2.5 billion is certainly sizable, yet by itself it would not entitle bank failures to the amount of attention we and other students of the period have devoted to them. By comparison, over the same four years, the value of all preferred and common stock in all enterprises in the United States is estimated to have declined by $85 billion. Or, to make a different comparison, the decline in the total value of all shares listed on the New York Stock Exchange in October 1929 is estimated to have been nearly $15½ billion.[62] As a fraction of total wealth, the losses produced by bank failures were minor and would deserve no more attention than losses of a comparable amount in, say, real estate.

---

[61] Loss to depositors, estimated at $1.3 billion (unpublished FDIC estimates; see source notes to Table 16, part 1); loss to other creditors is a rough guess; loss to stockholders, estimated at $0.9 billion (*Federal Reserve Bulletin*, Sept. 1937, p. 897). A sizable fraction of the losses was not realized until after the end of the banking holiday. Of the more than 9,000 banks that suspended in the years from 1930 through 1933, more than 3,500 suspended after Mar. 15, 1933.

[62] *Historical Statistics of the United States, Colonial Times to 1957*, Bureau of the Census, 1960, Series F-175, p. 150; *Business Statistics*, 1932 Supplement, p. 104.

In the second aspect, the situation is entirely different. The total stock of money fell by over one-third from 1929 to 1933; commercial bank deposits fell by over 42 per cent; in absolute amount, they fell $18 billion. Total deposits in suspended banks alone were much larger than losses, close to $7 billion in the same four years. If the bank failures deserve special attention, it is clearly because they were the mechanism through which the drastic decline in the stock of money was produced, and because the stock of money plays an important role in economic developments. The bank failures were important not primarily in their own right, but because of their indirect effect. If they had occurred to precisely the same extent without producing a drastic decline in the stock of money, they would have been notable but not crucial. If they had not occurred, but a correspondingly sharp decline had been produced in the stock of money by some other means, the contraction would have been at least equally severe and probably even more so.

Persuasive evidence for this final statement is provided by Canadian experience. Canada had no bank failures at all during the depression; its 10 banks with 3,000-odd branches throughout the country did not even experience any runs, although, presumably as a preventive measure, an eleventh chartered bank with a small number of branches was merged with a larger bank in May 1931. But because Canada kept its exchange rate with the United States fixed until Britain left the gold standard in September 1931 and then maintained its exchange rate at a new level involving a smaller depreciation than that undergone by the pound sterling, its internal level of income and its stock of money had to adjust to maintain external equilibrium. Though the required fall in both prices and income was sharp, the depreciation of the Canadian exchange rate permitted the percentage fall to be somewhat smaller than that in the United States. The stock of money fell sharply also, but by a much smaller percentage than in the United States. Even the smaller fall was, however, nearly one and a half times as large as the fall in any contraction in U.S. history since the Civil War except only the 1929–33 contraction. So it can hardly be regarded as minor. The relevant figures are as follows:[63]

Percentage Decline, 1929–33	United States	Canada
Stock of money	33	13
Net national product	53	49
Velocity	29	41

[63] Except for the Canadian currency component, which is an uncentered annual average of monthly data, money stock figures are annual averages of monthly data, centered on June 30. Canadian data are sums of demand, notice, and provincial government deposits in chartered banks, minus duplications (*Canada Gazette*, Dominion of Canada, Jan. 1929–Jan. 1934), plus currency held by the public (*Canada Year Book*, 1947, Dominion Bureau of Statistics, p. 1023). Net national income at factor cost, for Canada, from *Canadian Statistical Review*, 1953 Supplement, Dominion Bureau of Statistics, p. 15.

Why was the decline in the stock of money so much sharper in the United States relative to the decline in income than it was in Canada? Or, alternatively, why did not the stock of money in Canada have to fall much more sharply than it did to be consistent with so sharp a decline in income? The reason for the difference is, we believe, primarily the effect of the U.S. bank failures themselves. The bank failures made deposits a much less satisfactory form in which to hold assets than they had been before in the United States or than they remained in Canada. That, of course, is the reason they produced such a shift in the deposit-currency ratio in the United States. While currency was an alternative, it was not a fully satisfactory alternative, otherwise deposits would never have constituted so large a fraction of the total stock of money. Hence the demand for the sum of deposits and currency was reduced by the diminished attractiveness of deposits—an effect of the bank failures not heretofore considered. Of course, that effect was not strong enough to offset completely the increased demand for money relative to income as a result of the other factors associated with the contraction, such as the great increase in uncertainty, the decline in attractiveness of equities and real goods, and so on (see Chapter 12). If it had been, the amount of money would have fallen by a larger percentage than income fell, i.e., velocity would have risen rather than have fallen as it did. But the effect was strong enough to make the decline in velocity decidedly smaller in the United States than in Canada, where the same effect was not present. In Canada, deposits remained as attractive as they had ever been, and there was accordingly no reduction in the demand for money from this source. The other factors increasing the demand for money had full scope.

Paradoxically, therefore, the bank failures, by their effect on the demand for money, offset some of the harm they did by their effect on the supply of money. That is why we say that, if the same reduction in the stock of money had been produced in some other way, it would probably have involved an even larger fall in income than the catastrophic fall that did occur.

ORIGIN OF BANK FAILURES

The issue that has perhaps received the most attention centers on the reasons for the bank failures. Did they arise primarily from the financial practices of the preceding years? Or were they produced by the developments of the early thirties? Even if the first view were correct, the indirect monetary consequences of the failures are separable from the failures as such and need not have been also the near-inevitable consequences of the developments of the twenties. As we have just seen, it was the indirect consequences that were the most important effect of the bank failures.

353

As noted in Chapter 6, there is some evidence that the quality of loans and investments made by individuals, banks, and other financial institutions deteriorated in the late twenties relative to the early twenties in the ex ante sense that, had the later loans and investments been subject to the same economic environment as the earlier ones, they would have displayed a higher ratio of losses through default. The evidence for such deterioration is fully satisfactory only for foreign lending. For the rest, the studies made have not satisfactorily separated, and some have not even recognized, the difference between the ex ante deterioration, in the sense just specified, and the ex post deterioration that occurred because the loans and investments came to fruition and had to be repaid in the midst of a major depression. Loans and investments, identical in every respect except the year made, would have fared worse if made in the later than if made in the earlier twenties. By their concentration on ex post experience, authors of most of the studies unquestionably exaggerate whatever difference in ex ante quality there was. Indeed, many of the results are consistent with no deterioration at all in ex ante quality.

If the evidence is unsatisfactory for loans and investments in general, it is even sparser and more unsatisfactory for the loans and investments of commercial banks in particular. And there is some reason to believe that the experience of banks may have been different from that of other lenders. During the later years of the twenties, particularly in 1928 and 1929, banks were under steady reserve pressure. As we have seen, their total deposits were roughly constant from early 1928 to after the cyclical peak in August 1929. Whatever they might have done in the generally optimistic and exuberant environment of the time if they had been more plentifully supplied with reserves, they had no choice but to be highly selective in their loans and investments.

If there was any deterioration at all in the ex ante quality of loans and investments of banks, it must have been minor, to judge from the slowness with which it manifested itself. As we have seen, the contraction in business during the first fourteen months from the peak in August 1929 to October 1930 and particularly during the twelve months after the stock market crash was extremely severe. One reason may have been that banks were being forced to contract by a reduction in high-powered money, so that their deposits fell by 2 per cent in the course of the fourteen months. Yet, in that fourteen-month period, deposits in banks that suspended operations were only one-fifth to one-third higher than they were in the fourteen months beginning with either the cyclical peak of May 1923 or of October 1926: the amounts are $263 million for 1923–24, $281 million for 1926–27, and $347 million for 1929–30. In both earlier contractions, the decline in general economic activity, and hence the pressure on borrowers, was milder than from 1929 to 1930;

and, in addition, deposits in commercial banks rose by 5 to 6 per cent rather than falling as they did from 1929 to 1930.

The great surge in bank failures that characterized the first banking crisis after October 1930 may possibly have resulted from poor loans and investments made in the twenties. After the failure of the Bank of United States in December 1930, Governor Harrison told his board of directors that "the Reserve Bank had been working for a year or more to improve conditions in the Bank of United States, although there was no evidence that the condition of the bank was impaired," and J. H. Case, chairman of the board, said the bank's condition was probably not satisfactory in July 1929.[64] However, the subsequent pay-out record during the liquidation of the Bank of United States suggests that, if there was any permanent impairment of assets at the time the bank failed, it could not have been great.

Whatever may have been true of the initial bank failures in the first banking crisis, any ex ante deterioration in the quality of loans and investments in the later twenties or simply the acquisition of low-quality loans and investments in that period, even if no different in quality than in earlier periods, was a minor factor in the subsequent bank failures. As we have seen, the banking system as a whole was in a position to meet the demands of depositors for currency only by a multiple contraction of deposits, hence of assets. Under such circumstances, any runs on banks for whatever reason became to some extent self-justifying, whatever the quality of assets held by banks. Banks had to dump their assets on the market, which inevitably forced a decline in the market value of those assets and hence of the remaining assets they held. The impairment in the market value of assets held by banks, particularly in their bond portfolios, was the most important source of impairment of capital leading to bank suspensions, rather than the default of specific loans or of specific bond issues.[65] As W. R. Burgess, at the time a deputy governor of the

[64] Harrison, Notes, Vol. I, Dec. 18, 1930.
[65] The president of Federation Bank and Trust Company, closed by the New York State Superintendent of Banks on Oct. 30, 1931, explained that the bank had prospered for many years "and as a matter of fact right up to the past few months, when due to the nationwide rapid and unforeseen depreciation in bonds and other securities, the falling away in values of the bonds and securities owned by the company impaired the bank's capital structure" (*Commercial and Financial Chronicle*, Nov. 7, 1931, p. 3038).
In his contemporary account of the American banking system, R. W. Goldsmith wrote: "The depression of bond values, which started as far back as 1929 in the field of urban real estate bonds and reached foreign bonds and land bank bonds in the course of 1931, began to endanger the whole banking structure and notably the large city banks the moment first-grade bonds were affected in a most drastic way: From the middle of 1931 to the middle of 1932, railroad bonds lost nearly 36 per cent of their market value, public utility bonds 27 per cent, industrial bonds 22 per cent, foreign bonds 45 per cent, and even United States Government securities 10 per cent" (R. W. Goldschmidt [Goldsmith], *The Changing Structure*

New York Reserve Bank, told the Bank's board of directors in February 1931, the chief problem confronting many banks was the severe depreciation in their bond accounts; "given a better bond market and rising bond prices, . . . the condition of banks now jeopardized by depreciation in their bond accounts would, in many cases, improve automatically beyond the point of immediate danger."[66] Because there was an active market for bonds and continuous quotation of their prices, a bank's capital was more likely to be impaired, in the judgment of bank examiners, when it held bonds that were expected to be and were honored in full when due than when it held bonds for which there was no good market and few quotations. So long as the latter did not come due, they were likely to be carried on the books at face value; only actual defaults or postponements of payment would reduce the examiners' evaluation. Paradoxically, therefore, assets regarded by the banks as particularly liquid and as providing them with a secondary reserve turned out to offer the most serious threat to their solvency.

The most extreme example of the process we have been describing is the experience after Britain left the gold standard. The decline of 10 per cent in the price of government bonds and of 20 per cent in the price of high-grade corporate bonds (noted in the preliminary memorandum for the January 11, 1932, meeting of the Open Market Policy Conference, cited earlier) clearly did not reflect any deterioration in the quality of credit in the twenties or "bad" banking in any meaningful sense of the term. It reflected the inevitable effect of the enforced dumping of bonds by banks to reduce the volume of their assets by a large multiple of the amount of additional currency supplied to depositors.

If deterioration of credit quality or bad banking was the trigger, which it may to some extent have been, the damaging bullet it discharged was the inability of the banking system to acquire additional high-powered money to meet the resulting demands of depositors for currency, without a multiple contraction of deposits. That inability was responsible alike for the extent and importance of bank failures and for the indirect effect bank failures had on the stock of money. In the absence of the provision of additional high-powered money, banks that suffered runs as a result

---

of *American Banking*, London, Routledge, 1933, p. 106). We are indebted to Manuel Gottlieb for this reference.

Commenting on bank suspensions in 1932, Bray Hammond wrote: "The situation had worked to the point where the stronger banks were being dragged down by the weaker banks, partly because the latter drew on the former for reserves and partly because the forced liquidation of portfolios by banks in difficulties impaired the value of portfolios of all other banks" ("Historical Introduction," *Banking Studies*, Board of Governors of the Federal Reserve System, 1941, p. 29).

[66] Harrison, Notes, Vol. I, Feb. 26, 1931. See also footnote 12, above.

of the initial failure of "bad" banks would not have been helped by holding solely U.S. government securities in addition to required reserves. If the composition of their assets did not stop the runs simply by its effect on depositors' confidence, the banks would still have had to dump their government securities on the market to acquire needed high-powered money, and many would have failed.[67] Alternatively, the composition of assets held by banks would hardly have mattered if additional high-powered money had been made available from whatever source to meet the demands of depositors for currency without requiring a multiple contraction of deposits and assets. The trigger would have discharged only a blank cartridge. The banks would have been under no necessity to dump their assets. There would have been no major decline in the market prices of the assets and no impairment in the capital accounts of banks. The failure of a few bad banks would not have caused the insolvency of many other banks any more than during the twenties when a large number of banks failed. And even if an abnormally large number of banks had failed because they were bad, imposing losses on depositors, other creditors, and stockholders, comparable to those actually imposed, that would have been only a regrettable occurrence and not a catastrophe if it had not been accompanied by a major decline in the stock of money.

FEDERAL RESERVE SYSTEM'S ATTITUDE

The failure of the Bank of United States provoked much soul searching by the directors of the New York Reserve Bank. They devoted meeting after meeting from mid-December 1930 to April 1931 to discussions of the responsibilities of the Reserve Bank with respect to member bank suspensions and of the actions it could take to prevent them. They were well aware of the serious shock the failures had administered to confidence not only in commercial banks but also in the Federal Reserve System. Owen D. Young, then deputy chairman of the board of directors of the New York Bank, repeated to his fellow directors the remark of an upstate New York banker that the failure of the Bank of United States "had shaken confidence in the Federal Reserve System more than any other occurrence in recent years."[68] At the first joint meeting of the Federal Reserve Board and the Open Market Policy Conference after the banking difficulties had developed, Adolph Miller, a member of the Board, commented that "the banking situation was now more important than the credit situa-

[67] Of course, had banks held only U.S. government securities in addition to their required reserves, the Reserve System would have been under much greater pressure than it was to intervene by providing additional high-powered money to support the prices of those securities. But that is an aspect of the problem wholly different from the effect of the possible deterioration of credit quality.
[68] Harrison, Notes, Vol. II, Aug. 13, 1931.

tion, and asked what the governors were planning to do in different districts if further banking trouble started."[69] The minutes of directors' meetings of the New York Bank and memoranda prepared for meetings of the Open Market Policy Conference reveal that the technical personnel of the Bank and the Board were fully aware of the interconnection between the banking and the credit situations, and of the effects of the liquidation of securities to meet the demands of depositors.[70] Repeatedly during the next two years, the problem of bank failures and bank supervision was discussed at meetings within the System.

Despite the attention to the problem after 1930, the only System actions directed specifically at the problem of bank failures were the proposals noted above for measures that others might take, with particular emphasis on proposals designed to permit assets to be valued more liberally in bank examinations. The general tenor of System comments, both inside and out, was defensive, stressing that bank failures were a problem of bank management which was not the System's responsibility.

The major reason the System was so belated in showing concern about bank failures and so inactive in responding to them was undoubtedly limited understanding of the connection between bank failures, runs on banks, contraction of deposits, and weakness of the bond markets— connections we have tried to spell out earlier in this chapter. The technical personnel of the New York Bank understood these connections, as undoubtedly many other individuals in the System did also; but most of the governors of the Banks, members of the Board, and other administrative officials of the System did not. They tended to regard bank failures as regrettable consequences of bad management and bad banking practices, or as inevitable reactions to prior speculative excesses, or as a consequence but hardly a cause of the financial and economic collapse in process. As implied in Miller's comment quoted above, they regarded the banking situation as something different from the credit situation.

Four additional circumstances may help to explain the System's failure both to develop concern over bank closings at an earlier date and to undertake more positive measures when concern did develop. (1) Federal Reserve officials had no feeling of responsibility for nonmember banks. In 1921–29 and the first ten months of 1930, most failed banks were nonmembers, and nonmembers held a high percentage of the deposits involved. (2) The failures for that period were concentrated among smaller banks and, since the most influential figures in the System were big-city bankers who deplored the existence of smaller banks, their disappearance may have been viewed with complacency. (3) Even in November and December 1930, when the number of failures increased sharply, over 80

[69] Harrison, Open Market, Vol. II, minutes of meeting, Jan. 21, 1931, p. 7.
[70] See, for example, quotations in footnote 12, above.

per cent were nonmembers. (4) The relatively few large member banks that failed at the end of 1930 were regarded by many Reserve officials as unfortunate cases of bad management and therefore not subject to correction by central bank action.[71]

In September 1931, when Governor Harrison convened a meeting of commercial bankers to discuss means of making deposits in closed banks available, he recalled that "at one time it was the feeling of many of us down town that the effects of the failure of . . . small banks in the community could be isolated," but "it was clear that the continued closing of institutions in the city is now having serious repercussions. . . ."[72]

4. *International Character of the Contraction*

In 1929, most countries of the Western world had returned to a monetary standard involving fixed exchange rates between different national currencies. The standard was widely known as the gold-exchange standard because many countries kept their monetary reserves in the form of balances of other currencies convertible into gold at fixed prices, notably sterling and dollars, rather than in the form of gold itself. Official agencies in such countries, usually the central banks, often fixed exchange rates directly by standing ready to buy or sell the national currency at fixed rates in terms of other currencies, rather than indirectly by standing ready to buy or sell gold at fixed prices in terms of the national currency.

Since the gold-exchange standard, like the gold standard, involved fixed exchange rates, it also meant that, so long as the standard was maintained, prices and incomes in different countries were intimately connected. They had to behave so as to preserve a rough equilibrium in the balance of payments among the countries. The use of the gold-exchange standard did mean, however, that there was less leeway in the adjustments among countries—the rough equilibrium could not be quite so rough as under the full gold standard. The gold-exchange standard rendered the international financial system more vulnerable to disturbances for the same reason that the rise in the deposit-reserve ratio rendered the domestic monetary system more vulnerable: because it raised the ratio of claims on the relevant high-powered money—in this case, ultimately, gold—to the amount of high-powered money available to meet those claims.

The links forged by the fixed rates of exchange ensured a worldwide decline in income and prices after 1929, just as the links forged by the less rigidly fixed exchange rates in 1920 ensured a worldwide decline then. No major contraction involving a substantial fall in prices could develop in any one country without those links enforcing its trans-

---

[71] We are indebted to Clark Warburton for this paragraph.
[72] Harrison, Office, Vol. II, Sept. 11, 1931.

mission and spread to other countries. There was sufficient play in the links to permit minor uncoordinated movements but not to permit major ones.

As in 1920, the worldwide scope of the contraction once it got under way does not mean that it did not originate in the United States. Ever since World War I at the latest, the United States has been a sufficiently important participant in world trade and in world capital and financial markets and has held a sufficiently large fraction of the world's gold stock to be capable of initiating worldwide movements and not merely of reacting to them. Of course, if it did initiate a worldwide disturbance, it would inevitably be affected in turn by reflex influences from the rest of the world.

We saw in Chapter 5 that there is good reason to regard the 1920–21 contraction as having been initiated primarily in the United States. The initial step—the sharp rise in discount rates in January 1920—was indeed a consequence of the prior gold outflow, but that in turn reflected the United States inflation in 1919. The rise in discount rates produced a reversal of the gold movement in May. The second step—the rise in discount rates in June 1920 to the highest level in Federal Reserve history before or since—was a deliberate act of policy involving a reaction stronger than was needed, since a gold inflow had already begun. It was succeeded by a heavy gold inflow, proof positive that the other countries were being forced to adapt to United States action in order to check their loss of gold, rather than the reverse.

The situation in 1929 was not dissimilar. Again, the initial climactic event—the stock market crash—occurred in the United States. The series of developments which started the stock of money on its accelerated downward course in late 1930 was again predominantly domestic in origin. It would be difficult indeed to attribute the sequence of bank failures to any major current influence from abroad. And again, the clinching evidence that the United States was in the van of the movement and not a follower is the flow of gold. If declines elsewhere were being transmitted to the United States, the transmission mechanism would be a balance of payments deficit in the United States as a result of a decline in prices and incomes elsewhere relative to prices and incomes in the United States. That decline would lead to a gold outflow from the United States which, in turn, would tend—if the United States followed gold-standard rules—to lower the stock of money and thereby income and prices in the United States. However, the U.S. gold stock rose during the first two years of the contraction and did not decline, demonstrating as in 1920 that other countries were being forced to adapt to our monetary policies rather than the reverse.

The international effects were severe and the transmission rapid, not only because the gold-exchange standard had rendered the international financial system more vulnerable to disturbances, but also because the United States did not follow gold-standard rules. We did not permit the inflow of gold to expand the U.S. money stock. We not only sterilized it, we went much further. Our money stock moved perversely, going down as the gold stock went up. In August 1929, our money stock was 10.6 times our gold stock; by August 1931, it was 8.3 times the gold stock. The result was that other countries not only had to bear the whole burden of adjustment but also were faced with continued additional disturbances in the same direction, to which they had to adjust. As Harrison noted in early 1931, foreign commentators were particularly critical of the monetary policy of the United States because

the gold as it came into the country has been used by member banks to repay Federal reserve credit in one form or another, with the result that in this period the total volume of Federal reserve credit had declined by an amount equal to the gold imports. Thus it may be said that the United States has prevented the usual or normal effect of gold which has come to it . . . . The evils to the world of continued gold sterilization . . . are so great as to make desirable a careful scrutiny of Federal reserve open market policy.[73]

The effects first became severe in those countries that had returned to gold with the smallest actual gold reserves, and whose financial structures had been most seriously weakened by World War I—Austria, Germany, Hungary, and Rumania. To shore up the financial systems of those countries, international loans, in which the Reserve System participated, were arranged. But so long as either the basic pressure on those countries deriving from deflation in the United States was not relieved, or the fixed exchange-rate link which bound them to the U.S. dollar was not severed, such assistance was at best a temporary palliative. In country after country, that is what it proved to be. As they experienced financial difficulties, the United States, as we have seen, was in turn affected by the reflex influence of the events it had set in train.

The key role of fixed exchange rates in the international transmission mechanism is cogently illustrated by the case of China. China was on a silver rather than a gold standard. As a result, it had the equivalent of a floating exchange rate with respect to gold-standard countries. A decline in the gold price of silver had the same effect as a depreciation in the foreign exchange value of the Chinese yuan. The effect was to insulate Chinese internal economic conditions from the worldwide depression. As world prices fell in terms of gold, so did the gold price of silver. Hence the prices of goods in terms of silver could remain approximately the same. China could continue to maintain external balance without undergoing an internal deflation. And that is what happened. From 1929

[73] Harrison, Open Market, Vol. II, Apr. 27, 1931.

to 1931, China was hardly affected internally by the holocaust that was sweeping the gold-standard world,[74] just as in 1920–21, Germany had been insulated by her hyperinflation and associated floating exchange rate.[75]

The first major country to cut the link was Britain, when she left the gold standard in 1931. The trough of the depression in Britain and in other countries that accompanied Britain in leaving gold was reached in the third quarter of 1932. In the countries that remained on the gold standard or, like Canada, that went only part way with Britain, the depression dragged on. In China, whose currency appreciated relative to the pound as a result of the sharp depreciation of the pound relative to gold, the depression set in for the first time in 1931.

Of course, the country in the vanguard of such an international movement need not stay there. France, which had accumulated a large stock of gold as a result of returning to the gold standard in 1928 at an exchange rate that undervalued the franc, and therefore had much leeway, at some point passed the United States and not only began to add to its gold stock but also, after late 1931, to drain gold from the United States. The link between the franc and the dollar was cut when the United States suspended gold payments in March 1933, which proved to be the business cycle trough for the United States and countries closely linked to it. In France, which stayed on gold for a further interval, the contraction dragged on still longer. Although there was an upturn from July 1932 to July 1933, the low point of the interwar years was not reached until April 1935.

5. *Development of Monetary Policy*

The course of monetary policy in the difficult and critical years of the contraction was greatly influenced by the struggle for power within the Federal Reserve System, the beginnings of which were described in the preceding chapter. At the time of the stock market crash, the New York Reserve Bank acted in the tradition of its earlier dominance, moving rapidly, decisively, and on its own. The adverse reaction of the Board greatly inhibited further independent measures by New York.

In 1930, New York strongly favored expansionary open market operations, but after the middle of the year was unable to persuade either the other Bank governors—all of whom by this time had become members of the reorganized Open Market Policy Conference, which replaced the earlier Open Market Investment Committee—or the Board in Washington. The same was true in 1931, except that New York was less

[74] Arthur Salter, *China and Silver*, New York, Economic Forum, 1934, pp. 3–6, 15–17.
[75] Frank D. Graham, *Exchange, Prices, and Production in Hyperinflation: Germany, 1920–23*, Princeton University Press, 1931, pp. 287–288.

vigorous in pressing for expansionary action, though it was now supported by the new governor (Eugene Meyer) of the Federal Reserve Board.

The reaction to Britain's departure from gold did not provoke a flare-up of those conflicts. The measures adopted at that time were favored by almost all affiliated with the System. The agreement reflected the dominant importance then attached to the preservation of the gold standard and the greater significance attached to external than to internal stability, by both the System and the community at large. Not long after, the differences within the System that had been submerged in the fall of 1931 re-emerged, New York generally pressing for expansionary open market operations, supported by the governor and some other members of the Board and by a few Bank governors, and opposed by most of the Bank governors.

The open market operation of 1932 was acceded to largely under Congressional pressure and with the new Glass-Steagall Act ostensibly permitting release of the System's expansionary powers. The operation was terminated in August, shortly after Congress adjourned, because so many Bank governors remained unenthusiastic about the policy and reluctant or unwilling to pursue it. The deadlock persisted through the rest of the contraction.

THE STOCK MARKET CRASH, OCTOBER 1929

At the time of the stock market crash, the Open Market Investment Committee consisted of five Bank governors with the New York governor as chairman. It was operating under its recommendation to the Board, September 4, which had been approved by the Board on October 1, to purchase "not to exceed $25,000,000 a week" of short-term government securities if needed to supplement purchases of acceptances, "for the purpose of avoiding any increase and, if possible, facilitating some further reduction in the total volume of member bank discounts . . . ." Up to the week ending October 23, the Committee had not made any government security purchases because bills had been available. The System's holdings had declined by $16 million, while its bill holdings had increased by $115 million.[76]

When the crash came, the New York Bank had no doubt about what steps should be taken and proceeded to take them. It purchased $160 million of government securities in addition to encouraging New York banks to discount freely. The amount purchased was far in excess of the amount that the Open Market Investment Committee was authorized to purchase, but the New York Bank did not claim to be operating for the Committee. It contended it had the right to purchase government secu-

[76] Harrison, Open Market, Vol. I, minutes, Sept. 24, 1929, and letter, dated Oct. 1, 1929, Young to Harrison.

rities for its own account, as a matter of general credit policy, without the Board's approval.[77] Harrison informed Governor Young of the Federal Reserve Board that his directors had authorized him to purchase government securities without limitation as to amount, and that on October 29, before the call loan rate was announced, a purchase had been arranged.

Members of the Board regarded the New York Bank's failure to seek the authorization of the Board before taking action as smacking of insubordination, though some regarded the action itself as desirable. As a legal matter, the New York Bank seemed clearly within its rights. Under the 1923 agreement setting up the Open Market Investment Committee, each Reserve Bank retained the right to purchase and hold government securities for its own account. Young and most Board members acknowledged the legal right yet felt that the challenge to the Board's authority was insupportable. After much discussion, the Board finally authorized Young to tell Harrison that, if New York should request approval of a reduction of its rate to 5 per cent, the Board would consent on condition that no further purchases of government securities be made except with approval of the Board.[78] On November 1, the discount rate at the New York Bank was so reduced. To the New York directors it was clear that the System ought to proceed immediately with further purchases for "unless this is done, after the events of the past weeks, there may be greater danger of a recession in business with consequent depression and unemployment, which we should do all in our power to prevent," as they declared in a resolution they adopted on November 7.[79] Under the leadership of Harrison, the Open Market Investment Committee, meeting November 12, recommended that "the present limit of $25,000,000 per week on the purchase of government securities be removed and that the Committee be authorized in lieu thereof to purchase not to exceed $200,000,000 of government securities for account of such banks as care to participate . . . ," having in mind also the fact "that present conditions may possibly develop to the point where, as an emergency measure, in the interest of maintaining banking and business stability, it may be necessary quickly to purchase large amounts of Government securities in order to avoid any undue stringency in credit."[80]

[77] Of the $160 million government securities purchased by New York in the week ending Oct. 30, $75 million was transferred to System account. During the following two weeks, the New York Bank bought an additional $25 million directly for System account.

[78] Hamlin, Diary, Vol. 16, Oct. 29, 30, 1929, pp. 187–196. Miller did not consider the purchase desirable. He suggested a resolution to the effect that the Board would not have approved the purchase, had it been consulted; that New York was more concerned about the stock market than the general credit situation; that forcing the banks to come to the discount window would have been the proper response.

[79] For the resolution, see Harrison, Miscellaneous, Vol. I.

[80] Open Market, Vol. I, minutes of meeting, Nov. 12, 1929.

The next day, the Board notified the Committee that "the general situation was not sufficiently clarified for the System to formulate and adopt a permanent open market policy at that time," but conceded that if "an emergency should arise with such suddenness and be so acute that it is not practicable to confer with the Governor, the Board will interpose no objection to a purchase operation being undertaken, with the understanding, however, that prompt advice of such purchase be furnished the Board."[81]

On November 15, Governor Young of the Federal Reserve Board was in New York, and Harrison had an exchange of views with him: "I told him," Harrison wrote in recording the interview, "that I wanted a very frank and complete conversation with him regarding our present differences in the matter of the purchase of government securities . . . that it had become obvious that the Federal Reserve Board and the directors of the Federal Reserve Bank of New York were reaching a point in their views regarding their respective powers where it might have very serious consequences unless we could come to some sort of a workable understanding or agreement . . . I told him that more and more the Board had taken to itself not supervisory powers but the equivalent of operating functions and the responsibility for the detailed transactions of the various Federal reserve banks. . . ." Harrison then reviewed the Board's veto, earlier in 1929 for a period of four months, of the increase in the discount rate the directors of the New York Bank had repeatedly voted; the Board's decision that year to fix the spread above the minimum buying rate for acceptances within which the Bank might operate, although it had never done so earlier, and, during the fall of the year, its actual determination of the minimum rate, which had always been the Bank's prerogative; and finally, its stand

that we should go to the Federal Reserve Board in advance for a prior approval of any transactions in government securities . . . I told him that the logical consequence of his point of view, which was that the Federal Reserve Board should approve of all these things in advance, was that the Federal Reserve Board would become a central bank operating in Washington . . . [H]is only comment was that the Federal Reserve Board had been given most extraordinarily wide powers, that as long as the Board had those powers, they would feel free to exercise them and Congress could determine whether they objected to having a central bank operating in Washington.[82]

Neither side was prepared to make any concessions until Governor Young had a meeting with Owen D. Young, deputy chairman of the board of directors of the New York Bank, in the office of Secretary of the Treasury Mellon, the ex-officio chairman of the Reserve Board, on November 22 to discuss the Board's power over transactions in govern-

[81] *Ibid.*, letter, dated Nov. 13, 1929, Young to Harrison.
[82] Harrison, Conversations, Vol. I, Nov. 15, 1929.

ment securities. Secretary Mellon said he was willing to give the New York directors the widest discretion, but he realized that the Board had rights and duties in the matter. Owen D. Young said he saw no reason—apart from sudden critical emergencies, about which there was no dispute—his directors could not obtain the consent of the Board to all major transactions. Governor Young replied that was just what the Board wanted.[83]

The next day, November 23, Governor Young and Secretary Mellon met with Harrison, who stated that "we in New York were willing and prepared to operate any policy agreed upon either for our own account or for the System account." Young answered that he was prepared to approve without reservation the Open Market Investment Committee's recommendation of November 12, but first wanted to know

> where this would leave the debated question of the New York bank's operating for its own account. I [Harrison] told him that I felt that this involved a matter of procedure and jurisdiction which I would like to leave for determination sometime later on when we were through this critical period and when we could work out some mutually satisfactory procedure when conditions and peoples' emotions were in a quieter and more normal state. I then made this proposition: That if the Federal Reserve Board would approve the Open Market Investment Committee's report without qualification, leaving it to the committee to execute, I would recommend to our directors on next Wednesday [November 27] that the Federal Reserve Bank of New York refrain, until such time as it and the Federal Reserve Board might formulate some mutually satisfactory procedure, from purchasing government securities for its own account as a matter of general credit policy without the Board's approval.

As a result of this understanding, the Board reconsidered, November 25, and voted to approve the Committee's recommendation and the policy outlined in the resolution of the directors of the New York Bank.[84] Although authorized to purchase $200 million, the Committee purchased only $155 million between November 27, 1929, and January 1, 1930.

In response to inquiries from other Banks about the New York purchases during the week of the stock market crash, Harrison wrote a long letter to all governors on November 27, describing the situation in New York at the time, explaining the reasons for the measures the Bank took, and defending them. Some governors supported the action and ex-

[83] Hamlin, Diary, Vol. 17, Nov. 12, 13, 22, 1929, pp. 13, 17, 20–22, 31–32.

[84] The motion to approve was passed 5 to 3, the Secretary of the Treasury and the Comptroller voting with Governor Young, Vice-Governor Platt, and Hamlin. Miller objected on the ground that "money was now cheap and would be made cheaper by the purchase of Government securities" and that it would be bad Federal Reserve policy—"abdication in favor of the Federal Reserve Bank of New York." The two other negative votes were cast by Board members Edward Cunningham, an Iowa farmer, and George James, a Memphis merchant (see section 7, below). Harrison, Miscellaneous, Vol. I, letter, dated Nov. 25, 1929, Young to Harrison; Office, Vol. II, memorandum of Nov. 25, 1929; Hamlin, Diary, Vol. 17, Nov. 24, 25, 1929, pp. 35–36, 38–40.

pressed willingness to participate in the purchases. Others criticized the action on the ground that it merely delayed "natural liquidation" and hence recovery.[85]

The situation which confronted the New York Bank during the first few weeks after the crash was to recur during the succeeding years of the contraction: it had a policy, which the Board or the other Banks would not approve, or would approve only reluctantly after protracted discussion. At the time of the crash, New York went ahead on its own. Though the Bank then yielded to the Board in November 1929, later on it again considered but, as we shall see, did not adopt, the alternative of ignoring the System account and purchasing for its own account, as it had in October 1929.

FROM THE STOCK MARKET CRASH TO BRITAIN'S
DEPARTURE FROM GOLD, 1929–31

From the time of the crash on, the New York Bank favored the reduction of discount rates and purchase of bills and securities in sufficiently large amounts to offset reductions in discounts. The directors of the New York Bank apparently voted to reduce the discount rate from 5 per cent to 4½ per cent for the first time on November 14, 1929, and the Board gave its approval. On January 30, 1930, the directors voted to reduce the rate to 4 per cent; the Board disapproved by a tie vote. On February 7, the reduction was again voted by the directors and on the first vote by the Board again lost on a tie vote. One member then changed his vote to affirmative, not because he approved the rate reduction, but because he disapproved defeat of a motion on a tie vote; so the reduction was approved. The reduction of the rate to 3½ per cent on March 14 was apparently approved by the Board the first time the directors voted it. On April 24, the directors voted to reduce the discount rate to 3 per cent; the reduction was disapproved by the Board. It was voted again on May 1, with the directors this time even considering but deciding against a public statement if the Board should again disapprove. However, the Board approved it. Similar repeated delays were encountered in getting Board approval of reductions in buying rates on bills.[86]

[85] Harrison, Miscellaneous, Vol. I, Nov. 27, 1929; for criticism, see Notes, Vol. I, meeting of executive committee, June 9, 1930.

[86] For the time before Apr. 17, 1930, the first date of minutes of directors' meetings of the New York Reserve Bank in the Harrison Papers, we have relied mainly on Hamlin's Diary for statements about delays in Board approval of New York's requests for reductions in discount rates. Hamlin simply notes the Board's approval on Nov. 14, 1929, without indicating whether the motion to reduce was before the Board for the first time. He does not refer to the reduction in the rate, effective Mar. 14, 1930. (See Hamlin, Diary, Vol. 17, Nov. 14, 1929; Jan. 30, Feb. 6, Apr. 24, May 1, 1930, pp. 23, 87, 97, 139–141, 145–146; also Harrison, Miscellaneous, Vol. I, letter, dated Feb. 5, 1930, Harrison to all governors; another letter,

New York had even less success in winning approval of its recommendations for open market purchases. After the purchases in the final months of 1929, which were in accord with the usual seasonal pattern of increase in Federal Reserve credit outstanding, the Open Market Investment Committee was most reluctant to engage in further purchases. Some members were in favor of selling government securities in the usual pattern of the post-Christmas season. The final recommendation of the January meeting of the Committee was that "no open market operations in Government securities [were] necessary at this time either to halt or to expedite the present trend of credit."[87]

In early March, concerned about the worsening of the economic situation and the inability of the New York Bank to maintain its bill portfolio, the directors of the Bank voted to authorize purchase of $50 million of government securities. The purchases were carried out after approval by the Board and a circular letter to all Bank governors asking whether they wanted to participate. When the Open Market Committee met formally at the end of March, it concluded that "at present there is no occasion for further purchases of Government securities."[88]

That was the final meeting of the Open Market Investment Committee. It was replaced by the Open Market Policy Conference of all twelve Bank governors, with an executive committee consisting initially of the same five governors who had constituted the Committee (New York, Boston, Chicago, Cleveland, Philadelphia). But the executive committee was in a different position from the former Committee. It was entrusted with executing policy decisions of the Conference; it did not, like the earlier Committee, both initiate and execute policy. The Conference itself remained a voluntary organization of equals. Each Bank was free to decide whether it would or would not participate in a purchase or sale recommended by the Conference, though dissenters were required to acquaint the Federal Reserve Board and the chairman of the executive committee with the reasons for not participating. Each Bank also reserved the option to withdraw from the Conference. New York was not at all happy about the change and consented to it reluctantly and only with the explicit proviso that the Conference had no authority over transactions in

dated Mar. 17, 1930, Case to Governor Young; and a letter, dated Apr. 29, 1930, Harrison to Platt; Notes, Vol. I, Apr. 24, May 1, 1930.)

At the Open Market Policy Conference meeting on May 21–22, 1930, Governor Harrison reported that "in a number of recent weeks the Federal Reserve Board had failed to approve without delay applications of the Federal Reserve Bank of New York for a lower minimum buying rate on bills, and that for considerable periods the New York bank had therefore been without any downward flexibility in its bill buying rate as was the case at that very time" (Open Market, Vol. I).

[87] *Ibid.*, minutes of meeting, Jan. 28–29, 1930.
[88] Miscellaneous, Vol. I, letter, dated Mar. 7, 1930, Case to all governors; Open Market, Vol. I, minutes of meeting, Mar. 24–25, 1930.

bankers' acceptances.[89] As in 1929, New York hoped to be able to accomplish through the purchase of bills what it might not be able to persuade the rest of the System to do through transactions in government securities. Unfortunately, New York was not successful with its alternative.

At its first meeting in May 1930, the Open Market Policy Conference made no recommendation but left limited authority in the hands of the executive committee. Early in June, Harrison recommended that the System undertake the purchase of $25 million a week for a two-week trial period, arguing that "small purchases of Government securities at this time could do no harm . . . and might be desirable," and, as in earlier years, suggesting that security purchases be resorted to only if easing through the acceptance market failed. The recommendation to purchase was much milder than the statements at the meetings of the New York directors, and the amount recommended was much smaller than they thought desirable. Indeed, "there was some reluctance" on the part of the New York directors "to accept this program on the grounds that our difficulties of credit administration have grown largely out of our disposition to postpone action and to administer remedies in homeopathic doses." Apparently, however, Harrison felt that a bold program was certain to be rejected and preferred agreement on a small program to rejection of a large one. A majority of the executive committee and of governors agreed (after being consulted by telephone or telegram), the Board approved, and the purchase was made. A decline in the System's bill holdings during the two weeks largely offset the effect of the purchase of government securities, so, on June 23, Harrison suggested that purchases continue in the amount of about $25 million a week. This time, the executive committee rejected the recommendation by a vote of 4 to 1.[90]

Faced with a clear rejection of its leadership, the New York Bank considered three alternatives: (1) simply to accede without further action in the hope that its views would eventually prevail; (2) to "withdraw from the . . . Conference and, assuming that the approval of the Federal Reserve Board either can be or need not be secured, purchase Government securities for the account of this bank"; (3) to conduct a campaign of persuasion. The Bank adopted the third alternative, perhaps partly because Harrison had lingering doubts about the validity of New York's

[89] Commenting the following year on the change, Harrison was recorded by Hamlin as saying that "he had always felt it was a mistake to put all the Governors on the Open Market Policy Conference; that the Governors came instructed by their directors; that under the former System the Executive Committee were never so instructed" (Hamlin, Diary, Vol. 19, Aug. 1931, p. 123). See also Harrison, Open Market, Vol. I, minutes of meeting, Mar. 24–25, 1930; Notes, Vol. I, May 1, 1930; Open Market, Vol. I, letter, dated May 15, 1930, Case to Young.

[90] Harrison, Open Market, Vol. I, minutes of meeting, May 21–22, 1930; Miscellaneous, Vol. I, telegram, dated June 3, 1930, Harrison to Young; Notes, Vol. I, June 5, 1930; Open Market, Vol. I, June 23, 1930.

position. As the report on the relevant directors' meeting has it, the decision to adopt the third alternative was influenced by the existence of a "real difference of opinion among those deemed capable of forming a judgment, as to the power of cheap and abundant credit, alone, to bring about improvement in business and in commodity prices."[91]

In July 1930, Harrison accordingly wrote a long letter to all governors, telling them his directors "felt so earnestly the need of continuing purchases of government securities that they have suggested that I write to you outlining some of the reasons why the Federal Reserve Bank of New York has for so many months favored having the Federal Reserve System do everything possible and within its power to facilitate a recovery of business." There followed a closely reasoned, informed, and well documented analysis of the economic situation and the problem of monetary policy. Harrison stressed the seriousness of the recession, indicated that while there were many other causes of the recession, tight money of the preceding two years had contributed to it, and placed greatest importance on the depressed state of the bond market and the limited availability of funds for long-term financing. "In previous business depressions," he wrote, "recovery has never taken place until there has been a strong bond market." Harrison acknowledged that there was little demand for short-term funds, and that "when the System buys securities, short-time money becomes more plentiful and cheaper." However, "it has been demonstrated in the past that in such circumstances, through a further increase in the reserves of member banks money will be made available for the bond market or shifted to the bond market from the short time market or from other investments less profitable than bonds." He pointed out that Federal Reserve credit had declined and that banks were sensitive to borrowing. "[A]n even small amount of borrowing under present conditions is as effective a restraint as substantially a greater amount was a year ago." He concluded that "while there may be no definite assurance that open market operations in government securities will of themselves promote any immediate recovery, we cannot foresee any appreciable harm that can result from such a policy and believe that the seriousness of the present depression is so great as to justify taking every possible step to facilitate improvement."[92]

One notable omission from Harrison's letter was reference to the stock of money, as such. Like almost every other document on monetary policy

[91] Harrison, Notes, Vol. I, June 26, 1930. On several occasions, Harrison revealed doubts (Notes, Vol. I, July 17, Sept. 17, 1930). It is clear from internal documents of the Bank that the technical personnel, notably W. R. Burgess and Carl Snyder, were the most consistent supporters of expansionary measures on a large scale. Perhaps because of these doubts, perhaps because of his overriding desire to secure consensus, Harrison continued to present to the rest of the System purchase proposals scaled down well below the level that some of the directors and technical personnel of the Bank regarded as desirable.

[92] Miscellaneous, Vol. I, letter, dated July 3, 1930, Harrison to all governors.

within the System until the 1950's, the emphasis was exclusively on credit conditions rather than the stock of money. However, the omission did not affect the policy conclusion; it only altered the line of argument through which it was reached. Consideration of the behavior of the stock of money would have led to precisely the same conclusion: that the System should act so as to prevent a reduction in the amount of high-powered money available and indeed so as to increase it. Moreover, as we saw in section 3, there was a particularly close connection at the time between the bond market and the money stock. Improvement in the bond market would have done much to avert the subsequent bank failures. And though this connection was not explicit in the letter, it was implicit.[93] Harrison's letter and the replies to it provide an extraordinarily illuminating and comprehensive picture of attitudes toward monetary matters within the System. Only two governors—Eugene Black of Atlanta and George Seay of Richmond—clearly and unambiguously agreed with Harrison's analysis and supported his policy recommendations. The rest disagreed, most of them sharply.

James McDougal of Chicago wrote that it seemed to him there was "an abundance of funds in the market, and under these circumstances, as a matter of prudence . . . it should be the policy of the Federal Reserve System to maintain a position of strength, in readiness to meet future demands, as and when they arise, rather than to put reserve funds into the market when not needed." He went on to stress the danger that "speculation might easily arise in some other direction" than in the stock market. McDougal had all along been the most outspoken opponent of the New York policy and was to remain for the rest of the contraction a consistent proponent of selling government securities on almost any occasion. The demands for which the System should husband its resources remained in the future. McDougal's outlook was particularly influential because Chicago was next only to New York in importance as a financial center, and because he had been with the System so long. McDougal had been appointed governor of the Chicago Bank at its founding in 1914, at the same time Strong was appointed governor in New York. He had had disagreements with New York on earlier occasions.[94]

[93] One important advantage of explicit attention to the stock of money, both on that occasion and later, would have been provision of a clearly defined indicator by which to judge in quantitative terms the needs and effects of policy. The outsider is struck, in reading the reports of discussions within the System, by the vagueness and imprecision of the criteria used. For example, with the "needs of business" undefined, one participant regarded "credit," also undefined, as "redundant," another as "tight." Lack of a common universe of discourse and inability to reduce differences of opinion to quantitative terms were probably important factors enabling differences to persist for so long with no approach to a meeting of minds.

[94] Harrison, Miscellaneous, Vol. I, letter, dated July 10, 1930, McDougal to Harrison; Lester V. Chandler, *Benjamin Strong, Central Banker*, Brookings, 1958, pp. 79, 445.

John U. Calkins of San Francisco was no less explicit than McDougal was. In an earlier letter to Governor Young explaining why San Francisco had not participated in the June open market purchases, he had stated that "with credit cheap and redundant we do not believe that business recovery will be accelerated by making credit cheaper and more redundant." In his reply to Harrison's letter, he repeated the sentiment, expressed the view that "the creation, promotion, or encouragement of a bond market" is not "within the province of the Federal Reserve System," and that "no encouragement of the market for foreign bonds can counterbalance the destructive effect upon our foreign trade of the tariff bill recently approved." He went on to say, "We believe that the volume of credit forcibly fed to the market up to this time has had no considerable good effect, certainly no discernible effect in the last few months. We also believe that every time we inject further credit without appreciable effort, we diminish the probable advantage of feeding more to the market at an opportune moment which may come."[95]

Lynn P. Talley of Dallas wrote that his directors were not "inclined to countenance much interference with economic trends through artificial methods to compose situations that in themselves grow out of events recognized at the time as being fallacious"—a reference to the stock market speculation of 1928–29. Talley's letter, like some others, reveals resentment at New York's failure to carry the day in 1929 and the feeling that existing difficulties were the proper punishment for the System's past misdeeds in not checking the bull market. "If a physician," wrote Talley, "either neglects a patient, or even though he does all he can for the patient within the limits of his professional skill according to his best judgment, and the patient dies, it is conceded to be quite impossible to bring the patient back to life through the use of artificial respiration or injections of adrenalin."[96]

W. B. Geery of Minneapolis wrote that "there is danger of stimulating financing which will lead to still more overproduction while attempting to make it easy to do financing which will increase consumption."[97]

George W. Norris of Philadelphia replied that discussions with an insurance company executive and with a private banker in Philadelphia had confirmed him in his own view "of the fruitlessness and unwisdom of attempting to depress still further the abnormally low interest rates now prevailing." Later in the year, at a meeting of the Open Market Policy Conference in September, Norris, in strong disagreement with what he regarded as the current policy of the System, read a lengthy memorandum summarizing the Philadelphia view. The Philadelphia Bank objected to

[95] Miscellaneous, Vol. I, letter, dated June 16, 1930, Calkins to Young; letter, dated July 10, 1930, Calkins to Harrison.
[96] Miscellaneous, Vol. I, letter, dated July 15, 1930, Talley to Harrison.
[97] *Ibid.*, letter, dated July 7, 1930, Geery to Harrison.

"the present abnormally low rates for money" as an interference "with the operation of the natural law of supply and demand in the money market . . ." and concluded, "this is a complete and literal reversal of the policy stated in the Board's Tenth Annual Report . . . We have been putting out credit in a period of depression, when it was not wanted and could not be used, and will have to withdraw credit when it is wanted and can be used."[98]

These views, which seem to us confused and misguided, were by no means restricted to the Reserve System. The Federal Advisory Council, whose members were leading bankers throughout the country, consistently adopted recommendations expressing the same point of view, using phrases such as, "the present situation will be best served if the natural flow of credit is unhampered by open-market operations."[99] However, even in the financial community, the New York Reserve Bank was not alone in its view of the situation. The July 1930 monthly letter of the Royal

[98] Harrison, Miscellaneous, Vol. I, letter, dated July 8, Norris to Harrison; Open Market, Vol. I, memorandum read by Norris at Sept. 25, 1930, meeting. The memorandum is such a remarkably clear statement of the real bills doctrine that was so widely accepted at the time and earlier that it is worth quoting at greater length. The policy which had

> created artificially low interest rates, and artificially high prices for government securities . . . is an injustice to our member banks. It had resulted in making open market operations usurp the discount function, and tends to foster the regrettable impression that there is some element of impropriety in borrowing by member banks . . . [A]s the result of injecting a large amount of unasked and unneeded Federal Reserve credit into an already glutted money market, we find ourselves with over 600 millions of governments on hand, the bulk of which must ultimately be disposed of . . . We do not undertake to say how much Federal Reserve credit should be in use today, but we do hold to the belief that a substantial part of it should be the result of a demand expressed in borrowing by member banks, and used in cooperation with those banks. Less than one-sixth of it is of this character today.

In addition to the letters quoted, and the two from Black and Seay, a brief letter was sent to Harrison by O. M. Attebery, deputy governor at St. Louis, on behalf of Governor Martin, on vacation, expressing doubts and stating that conditions in the Eighth District provided no justification for further open market purchases (Miscellaneous, Vol. I, letter, dated July 9, 1930). Frederic H. Curtiss, chairman of the Boston Bank, sent a lengthy letter dated July 9 (the Boston Bank at the time had no governor, Harding having died in April, and Young, still governor of the Board, not yet having been appointed to fill the Boston Bank vacancy). Curtiss' letter expressed strong opposition to further purchases on the ground that they were likely to feed the stock market rather than the bond market. Only the Federal Reserve Bank of Cleveland did not reply, but its governor acknowledged the letter by telephone. In a letter to Governor Young, Harrison summarized the views expressed by Governor Fancher of Cleveland on his own behalf and as spokesman for a majority of his directors, "that continued purchases of government securities would not contribute substantially to . . . recovery and that, therefore, they would not . . . favor further purchases" (Miscellaneous, Vol. I, letter, dated July 23, 1930, Harrison to Young).

[99] Quoted from recommendation, dated Nov. 18, 1930 (Federal Reserve Board, *Annual Report* for 1930, p. 228).

Bank of Canada concluded that "immediate and decisive action on the part of the Federal Reserve Banks in putting new funds into the market in large volume is what is necessary to arrest the present serious and protracted price decline and to change the present psychology of business."

One cannot read the correspondence with Harrison just reviewed, the minutes of open market meetings, and similar Reserve System documents without being impressed with the extraordinary differences between New York and most of the other Banks in the level of sophistication and understanding about monetary matters. Years of primary and direct responsibility for the conduct of monetary policy in the central money market of the country and of cooperation with men similarly placed in the other leading money markets of the world had developed in the technical personnel, officers, and directors of the New York Bank a profound awareness of monetary relations and a sensitive recognition of the effects of monetary policy actions. Those qualities were clearly absent at most other Reserve Banks, which had of necessity been concerned primarily with local and regional matters, or at the Federal Reserve Board, which had played only a minor role in the general conduct of policy and had had no important operating functions.

The largely negative response evoked by Harrison's letter induced New York on several occasions during July to consider again engaging in open market purchases on its own but with the approval of the Board, and Harrison sounded out the sentiment of the Board about such action. The results were sufficiently unfavorable to deter any attempt.[100]

By September, 1930, some of the Banks were even opposed to seasonal easing. As Harrison told his directors,

Some of the other Federal Reserve Banks, including perhaps a majority of the banks whose governors form the executive committee of the System Open Market Policy Conference, advocate a policy of correction rather than of anticipation. They would allow tightening of the money market and hardening of rates of interest to develop, and then would move to correct the situation through the purchase of Government securities.

A few days later, when Carl Snyder, at a meeting of the officers' council of the New York Bank, suggested that "this deflation should now be aggressively combatted by additional purchases of Government securities . . . ," Harrison replied that "from a System standpoint it is a practical impossibility to embark on such a program at the present time—to do so would mean an active division of System policy."[101]

Despite the decline in Federal Reserve credit outstanding, the Board described its policy for the year 1930 as one of "monetary ease . . . expressed through the purchase at intervals of additional United States

[100] Harrison, Notes, Vol. I, July 10, 24, 1930; and Office, Vol. II, June 5, 1930.
[101] Notes, Vol. I, Sept. 11, 17, 1930.

Government securities and in progressive reductions of reserve bank discount and acceptance rates."[102] This is a striking illustration of the ambiguity of the terms "monetary ease" and "tightness" and of the need stressed above (p. 272) to interpret Federal Reserve actions in the light of all the forces affecting the stock of money and credit conditions. It seems paradoxical to describe as "monetary ease" a policy which permitted the stock of money to decline in fourteen months by a percentage exceeded only four times in the preceding fifty-four years and then only during extremely severe business-cycle contractions. And those words seem especially paradoxical when other factors were tending to expand the money stock, so that a potential expansion was converted into an actual contraction entirely by the decline in Federal Reserve credit outstanding.

In the context of the changes then occurring in the economy and in the money markets, the policy followed should be regarded as one of monetary "tightness" not "ease." During a period of severe economic contraction extending over more than a year, the System was content to let its discounts decline by nearly twice its net purchases of government securities, and to let its total credit outstanding decline by almost three times the increase in the gold stock. Through early 1932, the most striking feature of the System's portfolio of government securities and bills bought is the usual seasonal pattern of contraction during the first half of the year and expansion during the second. From August 1929 to October 1930, the whole increase in government securities plus bills bought came in the second half of 1929. The System's holdings of government securities plus bills bought were nearly $200 million lower at the end of July 1930 than they were at the end of December 1929. Even a mechanical continuation of the System's earlier gold sterilization program, by which it had quite explicitly recognized the need to determine its actions in light of other factors outside its control, would have called for more vigorous expansionary action from August 1929 to October 1930. Such action would have limited the decline in Federal Reserve credit outstanding to $210 million, the magnitude of the rise in the gold stock, instead of allowing the actual seasonally adjusted decline of $590 million. As we read the earlier policy statements of the Board, they called for going beyond mechanical gold sterilization in view of contemporary economic conditions. Since the bull market in stocks had collapsed and there were no signs of anything approaching speculation in commodities, any expansion in credit would be likely to be, in the words of the *Tenth Annual Report* (for 1923), "restricted to productive uses."[103]

[102] Federal Reserve Board, *Annual Report* for 1930, p. 1.

[103] It should be noted, however, that the possibility that easy money conditions might stimulate speculative excesses in the stock market was a recurrent theme in

The stalemate within the System continued, with only minor variations, throughout the next year. Harrison was pressed on the one side by his officers and directors—though less consistently by the directors than in the preceding year—to work for greater easing and larger purchases. On the other side, he felt strongly his responsibilities, as chairman of the Open Market Policy Conference, to carry out loyally the policy adopted by the Conference. The one major difference in the situation was the replacement of Roy Young by Eugene Meyer as governor of the Federal Reserve Board. Young became governor of the Boston Bank in September 1930 and, as such, was a member of the executive committee of the Conference, where he joined McDougal in consistently opposing purchases and favoring sales.[104] Meyer was generally favorable toward purchases and, not having gone through Harrison's frustrating experience of 1930, inclined to press strongly for them.

The January 1931 meeting of the Open Market Policy Conference brought out clearly the changes in the situation. From October to mid-December 1930, there had been virtually no change in the System's holdings of government securities. The banking difficulties in New York following the failure of the Bank of United States in the second week of December necessitated purchase of $45 million of government securities by the New York Reserve Bank for its own account. They were bought from two banks undergoing heavy withdrawals of currency in order to enable them to avoid borrowing. In addition, $80 million of government securities were purchased for System account, as Harrison explained, "in order to avoid too great tightening of credit due to an unusual amount of 'window dressing'." The purchases were made in accordance with the authorization by the Conference meeting on September 25, 1930, as a compromise between the advocates of "anticipation" and "correction," of purchases up to $100 million for seasonal ease.[105] At its January 1931

---

the deliberations of the period, e.g., Harrison, Miscellaneous, Vol. I, letter, dated Mar. 17, 1930, J. H. Case (chairman of the New York Bank) to Governor Young; Notes, Vol. I, Apr. 24, 1930; Miscellaneous, Vol. I, letter, dated Apr. 29, Harrison to Platt; *ibid.*, letter, dated July 10, 1930, J. B. McDougal to Harrison.

[104] According to Hamlin, Young was eased out of his position on the Board because of the administration's disappointment with his leadership. If so, the result could hardly have been the one intended. As governor of the Boston Bank and a member of the executive committee of the Conference, he may well have been in a position to exercise a stronger influence on open market operations, the key area in which policy had been and continued to be unsatisfactory, than he could have exercised as governor of the Federal Reserve Board (see Hamlin, Diary, Vol. 18, Sept. 4, 6, 24; Oct. 3, 10; Nov. 24, 1930, pp. 67, 70, 84, 89, 91–93, 118–119).

[105] See Harrison, Open Market, Vol. I, minutes of meeting, Jan. 21, 1931, in which Harrison reviewed changes in the money market since the Sept. 25, 1930, meeting. See also a memorandum, prepared for Harrison by W. R. Burgess, dated Dec. 19, 1930, referring to the absence of change in the System account between Sept. 25, 1930, and the date of the memorandum. The purchases by New York up

meeting, the Open Market Policy Conference recommended that "it would be desirable to dispose of some of the System holdings of government securities as and when opportunity affords itself to do this without disturbance or any tightening of the money position."[106] When the members of the Reserve Board met subsequently with the governors, both Adolph Miller and Eugene Meyer objected. Harrison, in his capacity as chairman of the Conference, defended the recommendation on the ground that it "represented a compromise since some of those present were in favor of considerable sales of securities, while others were only in favor of such moderate sales as might be necessary to take up the slack." Meyer, sensitive to political repercussions, stated that

a reduction of bills and discounts of the System did not involve the launching of any major policy, whereas the sale of governments is commonly interpreted as a major move in Federal reserve policy. The Reserve System has been accused in a number of quarters of pursuing a deflationary policy in the past year, and a sale of government securities at this time is likely to draw fire. In this situation it would appear most desirable to avoid a move which appears to present a major change in policy when there is no necessity for doing it.

Despite Meyer's reservations, the Board approved the Conference's recommendation and, by February 1931, security holdings had fallen by $130 million, although there was concern about the associated tightening of the bond market.[107]

---

to that date were only $40 million from one large bank. The purchases for System account after Dec. 20 were made by New York at its own discretion, the executive committee at a meeting on that day in Washington with Governor Meyer and several Board members having agreed "to leave it to the judgment of the Federal Reserve Bank of New York whether some additional amount of government securities should be purchased within the $100,000,000 authority with the understanding that the New York bank would keep in close communication with the members of the committee" (*ibid.*, minutes of executive committee meeting, Dec. 20, 1930).

[106] The original resolution as passed had the word "undue" (later deleted) before "tightening."

[107] Harrison, Open Market, Vol. II, minutes of meeting, Jan. 21, 1931, and letter, dated Jan. 29, 1931, McClelland (for Board) to Harrison, approving the recommendation; Notes, Vol. I, Jan. 15, 19, 22, 1931.

A memorandum on the Open Market Policy Conference meeting of Jan. 21, 1931, written by E. A. Goldenweiser, the Federal Reserve System's director of research, stated:

Meyer strongly opposes sales of securities beyond the amount bought in December for seasonal and special purposes . . . . The rest of the governors did not change their minds, but were impressed by Meyer's sincerity and force. It appears to have been his first bout with the intrenched hard-money crowd of the Federal reserve system.

The memorandum is part of the Goldenweiser Papers in the Manuscript Division of the Library of Congress (Container 1, folder of Confidential Memoranda,

377

In April 1931, Harrison, as chairman of the Open Market Policy Conference, presented a report to the Governors Conference. He expressed great concern about the gold inflow and the dangers to the world of continued gold sterilization by the United States.[108] As to the domestic situation, he noted:

> While it is commonly stated that money conditions have been exceedingly easy in recent months, and while indeed money rates have been at very low levels there has not been over a period of months any consistent surplus of Federal reserve funds pressing for use upon the market . . . . Furthermore, apart from the relatively easy position of the banks in the larger cities, credit cannot be said to be very cheap or very plentiful generally throughout the country.[109]

Harrison's report was discussed at the Open Market Policy Conference, which approved, at his urging, a three-part program to make gold imports more effective and credit more active: maintenance of the bill portfolio, if possible; reduction of buying rates on bills and, less definitely, of discount rates; and—as a last resort, if bills purchased did not enable earning assets to be maintained—authority for the executive committee to purchase up to $100 million of government securities. The resolution including the final part of this mild program—the only part within the Conference's exclusive jurisdiction—was adopted with four reluctant supporters, three of the four, members of the executive committee.[110]

No purchases were made under that recommendation until after a June 22 meeting of the executive committee, at which Harrison urged purchases of $50 million. Meyer, who was present at the meeting, strongly supported Harrison, saying that "the Federal Reserve Board would . . . have some preference for a larger program of purchases . . . ." The authorization was granted with only one negative vote (Young of Boston), because Norris of Philadelphia abstained and McDougal of Chicago voted against his convictions out of deference to President Hoover's proposal, announced two days earlier, of a moratorium on intergovernmental debts ("purchases of governments would be received by the public as supporting the President's announcement"). On July 9, the executive

---

1922–33). Of the seven cardboard letter files (described as containers in the Division's records), only six are open to readers; the seventh may be opened before 1965 only upon written permission from Mrs. Goldenweiser. Only a small fraction of the open collection contains current analyses of Federal Reserve policy in 1919–45, the period of Goldenweiser's service with the Board. The Goldenweiser Papers are meager in coverage compared to the Harrison Papers and provide a far less comprehensive view from within the Federal Reserve System than the Hamlin Diary does. Consequently, we have made only minor use of them.

[108] See quotation from his report in sect. 4, above.
[109] Open Market, Vol. II, Apr. 27, 1931.
[110] Norris of Philadelphia, Young of Boston, and McDougal of Chicago. The fourth was Calkins of San Francisco (*ibid.*, minutes of meeting, Apr. 29, 1931).

committee agreed to a further purchase of $50 million to complete the $100 million authorized in April, but buying was stopped on July 16 at only $30 million because of Harrison's concern over foreign developments and despite the remonstrances of Meyer.[111]

By early August, Harrison and Meyer again pressed for purchases. In discussing the situation with the executive committee of directors of the New York Bank, Meyer presented figures showing that between November 1, 1930, and August 5, 1931, there had been "a total increase of $421,000,000 in the gold stock of the United States; that currency circulation had increased $350,000,000 instead of showing a normal seasonal decline of at least $100,000,000; and that the Bank of France had withdrawn about $125,000,000 from the market" (presumably the acceptance market). He then pointed out that "while there had been no intentional contraction of the base on which credit could be extended, the sterilization of an amount larger than the gain of gold had been passively permitted." He said that, "if we had been asked last November whether we would favor, or even permit, the sterilization of $400,000,000 of gold, undoubtedly we would have answered in the negative."[112]

When a majority of the executive committee of the Open Market Policy Conference proved to be unwilling to support further purchases, a meeting of the full Conference was called for August 11. Harrison proposed a program, to be put into effect when desirable, authorizing the executive committee to buy up to $300 million of government securities. Other governors, except Black of Atlanta who joined Harrison in favor of it, were entirely negative in their reaction, and the Conference voted instead an authorization for the executive committee to buy or sell $120 million.[113]

So far as we can discover, that was the first Conference meeting at which there was explicit reference to a problem later to be cited as a major reason for the Reserve System's failure to make any extensive security purchases—the problem of free gold. However, the free gold problem, to be discussed in the next section, played no role in the outcome.

When the Conference met the same day with members of the Board, Harrison was again in the position of having to present and defend a recommendation he did not favor. He explained that the Conference opposed immediate purchases of large amounts of government securities, because banks would not employ excess reserves. The banks' reason:

[111] Harrison, Open Market, Vol. II, minutes of executive meeting, June 22, 1931; Miscellaneous, Vol. I, letter, dated July 9, 1931, Harrison to Seay; Notes, Vol. I, July 16, 23, 1931.

[112] Notes, Vol. II, Aug. 10, 1931.

[113] Open Market, Vol. II, minutes of executive committee meeting, Aug. 4, 1931; minutes of meeting, Aug. 11, 1931. The $120 million included the usual $100 million plus the $20 million authorized in April but not used.

"most prime investments are selling on a very low yield basis, while secondary bonds consist largely of railroad issues, of which a considerable proportion may in a short time become ineligible for investment by savings banks, insurance companies, and trust funds, due to the provisions of various state laws. In addition the bond market has been uncertain because of pressure on the market, due to forced liquidation of bond portfolios of closed banks." Governor Meyer and other members of the Board expressed disappointment at the action taken by the Conference, "in that it limited possible purchases to an ineffective amount." However, the only consequence of their disappointment was a change in the timing of the Board's session with the Conference. Thereafter, the two bodies discussed policy actions before rather than after the Conference adopted its recommendation. Later, when the Board formally considered the recommendation, it did not approve it outright but delegated to Governor Meyer the authority to approve purchases but not sales.[114] In the event, not even the $120 million authorization was carried out.

BRITAIN'S DEPARTURE FROM GOLD, SEPTEMBER 1931

Britain's departure from gold and the resulting gold outflow from the United States changed the focus of policy-making from the Open Market Policy Conference back to the New York Bank. New York had always had, and continued to have, primary responsibility for international monetary relations. The Bank of England, the Bank of France, and other central banks had always treated the New York Bank as their counterpart and had conducted negotiations and consultations with it. The Board had been kept informed, consulted in the process, and its approval obtained

[114] Harrison, Open Market, Vol. II, minutes of meetings, Aug. 11, Nov. 30, 1931; and letter, dated Aug. 18, 1931, Meyer to Harrison.
   Though Harrison was in agreement with Meyer on the substance of the policy issue, he was disturbed by the Board's response to the Conference recommendation, and complained to Meyer that it was contrary to the rules adopted when the Conference was established. To his own board of directors, Harrison stated:

. . . the whole situation emphasized the inherent difficulties of existing open market procedure. Direction of system policies by a conference of twelve men who must also consult the Federal Reserve Board means . . . that . . . we run a real risk of having no policy at all. Some of the Federal reserve bank governors . . . attended the Conference with preconceived ideas which would not admit of argument, and others in spite of, or perhaps because of, the fact that their banks would not be able to participate in further purchases of government securities, looked at the whole question from the narrow standpoint of their individual position (Notes, Vol. II, Aug. 20, 1931).

   Commenting on the results of that meeting of the Conference, Governor Meyer said, according to Hamlin, that "Governor Harrison could present a matter very gracefully, but could not sell it; that if the Board had taken part in the conference, he believed the Governors would have followed the Board and the New York bank" (Hamlin, Diary, Vol. 19, Aug. 11, 1931, p. 129). He may have been right on this occasion, but later experience suggests that he was unduly sanguine.

before final action, but it had never had a major voice in forming policy. The other Reserve Banks had for the most part simply been kept informed. That had been the practice while Strong was alive and had remained the practice. The most recent instance during the contraction had been the negotiations in the summer of 1931 in connection with loans to foreign banks.

New York had little doubt about what action to take. At its October 8 meeting, the board of directors voted to raise the discount rate from $1\frac{1}{2}$ to $2\frac{1}{2}$ per cent. The arguments given at the meeting were, first, the gold outflow itself, and second, "advices from France, where foreign fears concerning the dollar appear to have concentrated, which indicated that an increase in the rate would be interpreted there more favorably than otherwise." Some fear was expressed that the rise in rates might have adverse domestic effects, particularly by interfering with Hoover's efforts to organize a National Credit Corporation, but that fear was belittled. Harrison noted that any unfavorable effect on the bond market could be offset by security purchases, since the executive committee of the Open Market Policy Conference still had authority, under the recommendation of the August 11 meeting, to buy up to $120 million of government securities.[115] The only discordant note was a cablegram from Burgess, who was in Europe on a mission for the Bank, recommending no action that would bring about higher money rates in the United States.[116] The cablegram was read at the meeting, then disregarded. The Reserve Board promptly approved the rise in discount rates, several of its members having been strongly in favor of a rise ever since the beginning of the gold drain.[117]

A week later, Eugene Meyer attended the directors' meeting at the New York Bank. Harrison proposed a further increase in the discount rate to $3\frac{1}{2}$ per cent, giving as the technical reason the continued gold outflow. One director, Charles E. Mitchell, expressed serious doubts about the domestic effects. Meyer replied that "an advance in the rate was called

[115] However, three days earlier, at a meeting of the executive committee of the board of directors, Harrison said that "he considered the gold position of the System paramount at this time and on that account would not be inclined to purchase Government securities" (Harrison, Notes, Vol. II, Oct. 5, 1931).

[116] Burgess had arrived in Europe on Oct. 9 to attend a regular monthly meeting at Basle of the Bank for International Settlements. It was the first time a Federal Reserve official had formally participated in discussions of European central bankers at the world bank. The New York Bank was not a member, because it had been forbidden by the State Department to subscribe to shares of the BIS when the latter was formed in 1930. However, there were unofficial ties between the two institutions, strengthened by the fact that Gates W. McGarrah, president of the BIS, had formerly been chairman of the New York Bank.

[117] Hamlin and Miller, at least, strongly favored an increase in discount rates and considered a possible effect on the bond market as no valid reason for delay (Hamlin, Diary, Vol. 19, Oct. 1, 1931, p. 148).

for by every known rule, and that . . . foreigners would regard it as a lack of courage if the rate were not advanced." He expressed the opinion that "the bond market was already adjusted to a higher level of interest rates, and therefore it would be but little affected."[118] A month later, Owen D. Young pressed the desirability of purchasing government securities to offset unfavorable domestic effects. Harrison was exceedingly hesitant to accede.[119]

The sharp rises in discount rates were widely supported not only within the System but also outside.[120] The maintenance of the gold standard was accepted as an objective in support of which men of a broad range of views were ready to rally. The drain of gold was a dramatic event for which there were many precedents.[121] Thus both the problem and its solution seemed clear and straightforward. Indeed, one gets the impression that after grappling with unfamiliar, elusive, and subtle problems, the System greeted with almost a sense of relief the emergence of a problem that could be put in black-and-white terms.

Less than two weeks after the second rise in discount rates, the executive committee of the Open Market Policy Conference met. The preliminary memorandum for the meeting outlined the drastic change that had occurred in currency in circulation, pointed out that internal developments had been more important than the gold outflows in their effects on domestic business, and noted that the decline in deposits "constitutes by far the most rapid shrinkage in member bank deposits during the life of the System." Nevertheless, McDougal continued to recommend that the System should reduce its security holdings, although—in addition to the unprecedented pressure on commercial banks at the time—it was the beginning of the season when the System typically expanded its security holdings. The final outcome was a vote against sales but in favor of requesting the Federal Reserve Board to give the committee the same leeway for sales that the Board had given it for purchases under the Conference recommendation of August 11.[122]

[118] Harrison, Notes, Vol. II, Oct. 15, 1931.

[119] *Ibid.*, Nov. 25, 1931.

[120] "We think the really constructive event of the week has been . . . the action of the New York Federal Reserve Bank in raising its rediscount rate . . . . This step should have been taken long ago, and, indeed, it was a sad error of judgment to put such a fantastically low rate as that at New York in force. . ." (*Commercial and Financial Chronicle*, Oct. 10, 1931, p. 2305). ". . . [T]he Federal Reserve Bank of New York has been driven into making another advance of a full 1% in its rediscount rate . . . , a decidedly wise move. . . " (*ibid.*, Oct. 17, 1931, p. 3460). The New York *Times* reported that the rise was "welcomed by almost all bankers" (Oct. 11, 1931); that the rise was "hailed with enthusiasm in banking circles" (Oct. 16, 1931).

[121] See, however, further discussion in sect. 6, below.

[122] Harrison, Open Market, Vol. II, memorandum and minutes of executive committee meeting, Oct. 26, 1931. In the course of the meeting, Harrison noted that "the free gold position . . . was not a consideration at this time. . . ."

The preliminary memorandum for a meeting of the full Conference at the end of November noted with satisfaction that the "foreign and domestic drains upon bank reserves were met in the classic way by increases in discount rates combined with a policy of free lending." It recorded that "one result" of the rise in discount rates and the associated rise in other market rates "was certainly to make bankers and others more timid and reluctant in contemplating new uses of funds or new enterprises." It stressed the sharp decline in bond prices and the resulting worsening of the position of the banks. It discussed the year-end seasonal problem, suggesting that purchases "similar to those made last year" should be provided for, and proposed deferring the longer-term policy decisions until after the first of the year. The Conference adopted a resolution giving the executive committee authority to purchase up to $200 million of governments for seasonal needs.[123] Only part of that authority was in fact exercised. Government security holdings were raised by $75 million to the end of December 1931 and then lowered by $50 million in January 1932.

During those months, it is not clear that Harrison was as unhappy with the policy followed as he had been before and was to be again. His concern about gold inhibited his desire to expand Federal Reserve credit. New York still had control over the buying rate on bills, subject only to the approval of the Board. As we have seen, New York had repeatedly tried to use bill purchases to enable it to accomplish on its own what it could not accomplish through the System open market account. Yet the bill buying rate, which had been raised from $1\frac{1}{4}$ per cent to $3\frac{1}{8}$ per cent in October along with the discount rate, was reduced only slowly and moderately, to 3 per cent on November 20, and to $2\frac{3}{4}$ per cent on January 12, 1932. Both reductions left the rate above the market rate and therefore did not lead to an increase in bill holdings.

Early in January 1932, partly under pressure from his staff and directors, Harrison resumed his advocacy of a program of further substantial purchases as part of a broader national program which he outlined to the meeting of the Open Market Policy Conference that month. The main features of the program were: passage of an act establishing the Reconstruction Finance Corporation, then under consideration by Congress; organized support of the bond market, predicated on an agreement between the railroads and the unions to cut wage rates; cooperation of Federal Reserve Banks and member banks with the Treasury in its financing program; purchase of bills by the Reserve System when possible; reductions in discount rates; and, as a final step, "buying of Governments, if necessary, facilitated by an alleviation of the free gold position," the

[123] Governor McDougal asked assurance at the meeting that no purchases would be made immediately. Governors Norris and Fancher said "they were not disposed to approve of the purchase of government securities solely for the purpose of enabling the New York and Chicago banks to keep out of debt at the end of the year" (*ibid.*, memorandum and minutes of meeting, Nov. 30, 1931).

final phrase being a reference to proposals then under consideration which were finally embodied in the Glass-Steagall Act. The Conference authorized the executive committee to purchase up to $200 million, "if necessary," over three negative votes.[124] That authorization was not exercised at all. Between the January 11 and February 24, 1932, meetings of the Conference, government security holdings declined by $11 million, bill holdings by $80 million, while discounts rose $20 million. Federal Reserve credit outstanding fell by $100 million over the six-week period.

The February meeting of the Open Market Policy Conference was largely a repetition of the January meeting, although the pending passage of the Glass-Steagall Act removed the problem of free gold. At the joint meeting with the Board preceding the formal business session, Meyer, who continued as governor of the Board though he had by then been named chairman of the RFC as well, asserted that "it seemed unnecessary for the banking position to be subjected to severe strain because of the funds withdrawn for hoarding." Miller stated that "he believed there was never a safer time to operate boldly than at present." He indicated that "he would approve purchases on an even larger scale than the amounts being discussed." McDougal continued to argue that "on general principles he preferred to see the banks borrowing to secure funds." The upshot was a mild expansion in the authority of the executive committee. It was authorized to buy up to $250 million at the approximate rate of $25 million a week, McDougal and Young voting in the negative. Immediately after the general meeting, the executive committee voted 3 to 2 to start the program.[125]

OPEN MARKET PURCHASE PROGRAM OF 1932

That modest program would very likely never have been expanded into a major one, or perhaps even carried out, if it had not been for direct and indirect pressure from Congress. Harrison told the executive committee of his directors on April 4 that apparently "the only way to forestall some sort of radical financial legislation by Congress, is to go further and faster with our own program." When Harrison reported to a full meeting of his directors on April 7 that the executive committee of the Open Market Policy Conference was deeply divided about the wisdom of accelerating the purchase program, and had voted to continue the existing program, one of the directors asked "if a more vigorous program

---

[124] Harrison, Open Market, Vol. II, minutes of meeting, Jan. 11, 1932. McDougal of Chicago, Seay of Richmond, and Deputy Governor Day, representing Governor Calkins of San Francisco, were the three who voted in the negative. Neither Governor Young nor any other representative of the Boston Bank attended the meeting. The Kansas City Bank was represented by a director who was not present at the session when the resolution was adopted.

[125] *Ibid.*, minutes of meeting, Feb. 24, 1932.

on the part of the Federal Reserve System would not be helpful in defeating the Thomas bonus bill and other similar legislation. Governor Harrison said that Senator Thomas had indicated to him that he might be satisfied not to press for Congressional action if the System would proceed more vigorously." The Bank directors accordingly voted to have the Bank, subject to the approval of the Board, buy for its own account up to $50 million of government securities, outside the System account and before the meeting of the Conference, which was set for April 12.[126]

In opening the joint meeting of the Conference and the Reserve Board, preceding the business meeting of the Conference, Governor Meyer "called attention, merely as a matter of information, to the fact that a resolution had been offered in the Senate asking the Federal Reserve Board to state its program . . . . Consideration of this resolution had been postponed. He stated that the Reserve System could now undertake to do more toward aiding in the recovery than it had yet done, and that he believed the time had come when the System might be expected to use its powers more fully in an effort to stop the credit decline." Other members of the Board supported Meyer. Ogden L. Mills, since February 13, 1932, Secretary of the Treasury, who had all along been in favor of more extensive action, stated: "For a great central banking system to stand by with a 70% gold reserve without taking active steps in such a situation was almost inconceivable and almost unforgivable. The resources of the System should be put to work on a scale commensurate with the existing emergency."

After the Board left, the Conference voted 10 to 1 to approve a resolution offered by Harrison authorizing the executive committee to purchase up to $500 million of government securities in addition to the unexpired authority granted at the February 24 meeting. The purchases were to be made as rapidly as practicable and, if possible, to be no less than $100 million in the current statement week ending next day, April 13.[127] The

---

[126] Notes, Vol. II, Apr. 4, 7, 1932.

[127] The lone dissenter was Governor Young of the Boston Bank, who had said at the joint session with the Board that he

questioned whether purchases of governments which piled up reserves in the centers would result in the distribution of these funds to other parts of the country. He was skeptical of getting the cooperation of the banks without which success appeared difficult, and was apprehensive that a program of this sort would develop the animosity of many bankers, and was apprehensive also that an extensive program of purchases of government securities would impair the confidence of the public in the Reserve banks. He cited the experience of 1931 as an indication of the futility of government purchases.

Governor McDougal of Chicago asked whether the Reserve System "could retain the confidence of the public after inaugurating a policy of this sort, which was in some measure inflationary, particularly since it involved the use of government securities as collateral for Federal reserve notes" (Harrison, Open Market, Vol. II, minutes of meeting, Apr. 12, 1932).

final proviso was inserted after Harrison had informed the Conference he was scheduled to testify the next day before a subcommittee of the House on a bill that in effect would have directed the Reserve System to purchase in the open market until wholesale prices had risen to their 1926 level. He said that "it would probably be necessary for him to make some reference to the program at that time."[128]

After the initial program was voted on April 12, the System bought $100 million of government securities per week for five weeks. At the May 17 meeting, the Conference again voted another $500 million open market purchase, McDougal joining Young in dissenting. At the suggestion of Meyer, the weekly rate of purchases after that meeting was reduced. Harrison deplored the reduction: "The temper of Congress is not improving, and the danger of unsound credit proposals is still great. It might, therefore, be unwise to give unnecessary substance to the argument now being used, that the Federal Reserve System intends soon to abandon its open market program." Yet in June, partly no doubt in the hope of conciliating McDougal and Young, he suggested to the executive committee of the Conference that the purchases each week be geared to the maintenance of member bank excess reserves at a figure somewhere between $250 and $300 million, the purchases to be as small as possible to preserve the desired level, but with some increase from week to week in the System's holdings, "to avoid the creation of a feeling that the policy of the system had been changed."[129]

By the end of June, as Burgess summarized the results of the program for the New York directors, total purchases of $1 billion had offset a loss of $500 million in gold and a reduction of $400 million in discounts and bills bought, leaving a net increase of $100 million in Federal Reserve credit outstanding. To Owen D. Young, this meant that "most of our efforts had, in reality, served to check a contraction of credit rather than to stimulate an expansion of credit. We have been clearing the way for action, rather than taking action. . . ." A week later, in discussing the pressure from Chicago and Boston to stop the program, he said,

As it is, we are asked to stop when we are just half way through our program, when we are just at the point where further purchases of Government securities

---

[128] The hearings, which threatened to develop into a full-scale investigation of the System, were held by the House Subcommittee on Banking and Currency on H.R. 10517 (a bill to stabilize commodity prices, introduced by Rep. T. Alan Goldsborough). Governor Harrison testified that the Federal Reserve "began to really utilize the" Glass-Steagall Act only two days before he appeared before the committee (*Congressional Record*, House, June 8, 1932, p. 12354, remarks of Mr. Goldsborough). See also *Stabilization of Commodity Prices*, Hearings before the House Subcommittee on Banking and Currency, 72d Cong., 1st sess., part 2, pp. 477–478, 500–501.

[129] Harrison, Open Market, Vol. II, minutes of meetings, May 17 and June 16, 1932; Notes, Vol. II, May 26, 1932.

will bring actual and affirmative pressure to bear upon the member banks . . . .
To stop just when you have reached the place where you are able to put on the
pressure the program was designed to produce, would be a ridiculous thing to
do. We shall have no policy left if we do this.[130]

Chicago and Boston took those same facts as evidence in favor of
their opposition to the program, as evidence that it had only substituted
an undesirable form of credit for a desirable form. McDougal, reported
Harrison, "does not see what the purchases have done anyway, and is in
favor of stopping." Governor Young felt "that there are going to be a
lot more banks closed, that there will be a large increase in borrowing at
the Federal reserve banks and that, therefore, we are wasting our resources buying Government securities."[131]

Some officers of the New York Bank, notably Burgess, and some directors favored continuing the program, with the approval of the Board,
even if that meant New York would have to proceed without Chicago and
Boston. Since the Reserve Board was in favor of continuing the program,
it doubtless would have approved. But Harrison was unwilling to follow
that course. The gold reserve ratio of the New York Bank was only 50
per cent, of the System 58 per cent, of Chicago 75 per cent. Yet Chicago
was reluctant to participate. His own feeling, Harrison said, "is that
we should continue with our open market program, and perhaps step it up
a bit, but on one condition—that the program be made a real System program and that the Federal Reserve Banks of Boston and Chicago, in particular, give it their affirmative support." When the comment was made
that the Board had the legal power to require other Banks to rediscount
for New York, if its ratio fell below 50 per cent, Harrison replied "that
it would be most undesirable for us to go ahead in defiance of the wishes
of the other Federal reserve banks and then to have those banks bale us
out under compulsion. System policy and the system Open Market Policy
Conference might just as well be thrown out the window under such circumstances."[132]

At that juncture, Harrison made a final effort to secure the cooperation
of Boston and Chicago. He pleaded the case not only with the governors
and directors of the two Banks but also with commercial bankers and businessmen in the two cities. Owen D. Young made a trip to Chicago to

[130] Notes, Vol. II, June 30, July 5, 1932.

[131] Office, Vol. III, July 5, 1932; Notes, Vol. II, June 30, 1932.

[132] Notes, Vol. II, June 30, July 5, 1932. Harrison was at first attracted by the
proposal that the Reserve Board bring pressure on the other Banks to participate
in the purchase program. The Board's authority to compel one Reserve Bank to
rediscount paper for another Reserve Bank, it was suggested, would apply also to
purchases of government securities, when the reserve position of several Banks was
involved (*ibid.*, June 30, 1932). On reconsideration, he decided that the Board
had no power to bring such pressure, and that, "furthermore, this bank would be
the first to object to such action by the Board, in other circumstances" (*ibid.*,
July 5, 1932; see also July 11, 1932).

attempt to persuade the directors of the Chicago Bank. But all to no avail.[133]

In an attempt to decide the issue, the full Open Market Policy Conference met on July 14. At the joint meeting with the Board, Governor Meyer suggested that "in determining future policy it was important to consider that the public effect of any discontinuance of the policy which had been pursued would be unfortunate, and also that in future policy every effort should be made to secure an effective united system policy." He pointed out that "there existed a trend in Congress toward giving the System more centralization, and that the open market program offered a test of the capacity of the System to function effectively in its present form."[134] The Conference voted that excess reserves should be maintained

---

[133] Notes, Vol. II, July 7, 14, 1932; Office, Vol. III, letter, dated July 8, 1932, Harrison to Owen D. Young.

[134] Harrison, Open Market, Vol. II. Meyer was referring to the series of bills introduced by Senator Glass (see footnote 29, above), the most recent on Mar. 17, 1932, predecessors of the Banking Act of 1933. The latest bill was the occasion for a bitter exchange of letters between Glass and Harrison. With the approval of the New York Bank's directors, Harrison wrote to Senator Peter Norbeck, chairman of the Senate Banking and Currency Committee, enclosing a letter he had sent Glass, Feb. 6, about an earlier draft of the bill, which read in part as follows:

Many provisions of this bill are designed further to limit the autonomy of the individual Federal reserve banks and to concentrate more and more power in the Federal Reserve Board . . . . [T]he provisions of your bill relating to the open market committee which is given jurisdiction over operations in bills as well as government securities are so cumbersome as to be inimical to the best interest of Federal reserve operation . . . . The bill requires approval not only of the Federal Reserve Board but of a committee of 12 representatives of the several Federal reserve banks . . . . Under the proposed bill no operations in securities or bankers bills, even the day to day transactions, can be effected, even in cases of emergency, without approval of the committee . . . .
To the extent that your bill further shifts power and authority from the Federal reserve banks to the Federal Reserve Board, to that extent, I believe it aims towards centralized operation and control through a politically constituted body in Washington.

On Apr. 9, Glass answered Harrison's letter to Norbeck, writing:

In my considered view it constitutes a challenge to statutory authority and an unyielding antagonism to any restraining influence whatsoever.
. . . you and your board have thus stated in unequivocal terms the misconception of the Federal Reserve banking act which so long has been reflected in the extraordinary policies pursued by the New York bank with respect to both domestic and foreign transactions.

The "extraordinary policies" referred to by Glass, who was an undeviating follower of the real bills doctrine, included the use of open market operations in government securities and the failure to restrict loans to real bills only. In his eyes, the failure was responsible for both the boom and the bust.

Harrison's reply of Apr. 18 concluded the exchange:

The officers and directors of this bank have been just as desirous to do their part in checking the use of bank credit for excessive speculation as you or anyone

at approximately $200 million by purchases limited in total to the amount previously authorized by the Conference but not executed—$207 million. For the guidance of the executive committee, the Conference recommended purchases not to exceed $15 million a week—except in unusual or unforeseen circumstances—but not less than $5 million a week for the next four weeks. McDougal, Young, and Seay of Richmond voted against even this resolution.[135]

Freed from Congressional pressure—Congress adjourned on July 16—the Conference lapsed into its earlier pattern.[136] The program adopted was a minimum face-saving program, and was carried out at nearly the minimum level consistent with the letter of the recommendation. McDougal and Young refused to participate in further purchases. Harrison was unwilling to proceed on his own. As a consequence, in the four weeks after the Conference met, total purchases amounted to $30 million ($15 million the first week, then $5 million a week). From August 10 until the close of the year, the System's holdings remained almost precisely constant.

THE BANKING PANIC OF 1933

The preliminary memorandum for the January 4, 1933, meeting of the Open Market Policy Conference said of the existing situation, "that a good start was made toward recovery, that this movement has been interrupted, and is now hesitant and uncertain." At the meeting, both Governor Meyer and Secretary of the Treasury Mills stressed that any slackening in Federal Reserve open market policy might provide an excuse for the adoption of inflationary measures by Congress. Governor Harrison listed the Congressional situation as one of three reasons for holding the System portfolio of government securities intact; the second was that a reduction "might operate as a check to the bond market thus retarding business recovery and further injuring bond portfolios of banks;" the third

---

else. From their practical experience in operating a bank in this money center, they feel that in the long run there is only one really effective method of bringing about this result, and that is the traditional method of the vigorous use of discount rate and open market operations . . . . The tragedy of the experience of 1928 and 1929 lay, in our opinion, in the failure of the Reserve System promptly and vigorously to use the instruments for credit control which decades of experience have proved to be powerful and effective (Miscellaneous, Vol. II).

[135] Open Market, Vol. II, minutes of meeting, July 14, 1932.

[136] To the executive committee of the New York Bank's board of directors Harrison reported on July 11, 1932, a discussion he had had with Meyer in which "Governor Meyer agreed as to desirability of going ahead with the System open market program saying that, if for no other reason, it is politically impossible for us to stop at this particular time. The program was begun at about the time the Goldsborough Bill was introduced in Congress and if it were terminated just as Congress adjourned we would be crucified next winter" (Notes, Vol. II, July 11, 1932).

was that larger excess reserves might lead to the elimination of interest on deposits in principal centers, thus distributing "the pressure for putting money to work more widely." Against those three reasons, Harrison listed three others in favor of some reduction of the portfolio: first, the "System open market policy had not been one to accumulate any definite amount of securities but rather to check deflation through the reduction of bank debt and the creation of substantial excess reserves, which had been accomplished;" second, any further substantial increase in excess reserves might not increase pressure on the banks to lend and invest but would serve only to minimize control when necessary; third, the open market purchases had enabled the Treasury to borrow cheaply and "so in some measure has encouraged the continuance of an unbalanced budget."

The sentiment of most governors was clearly in favor of reducing the portfolio, and the final motion reflected that sentiment. It gave the executive committee authority to reduce the System's holdings of Treasury bills, the reduction in January not to exceed $125 million and not to bring excess reserves below $500 million. The committee was authorized to purchase securities if necessary to prevent excess reserves from falling below the existing level, but not if such purchases would do more than make up for declines in holdings. Before any increase in security holdings above the existing level was made, a new meeting of the Conference was to be convened.[137]

The policy recommendation was followed, and security holdings reduced by $90 million in January, despite the concern of Burgess and Treasury officials about the weakness of the bond market, and despite renewed banking difficulties. By February 1, 1933, excess reserves had fallen below $500 million, and the purchases made were not enough to restore that level. From the last week in January to February 15, the System increased its security holdings by $45 million, and permitted total Reserve credit to rise by $70 million. Yet, in those three weeks alone, member bank reserve balances at Federal Reserve Banks declined by $280 million.

The state to which open market operations—the most potent monetary tool of the System—had fallen was graphically revealed when, as the banking difficulties mounted in February, Harrison ruled out a meeting of the Conference on grounds that it would be "difficult, if not impossible, to hold a meeting of the system Open Market Policy Conference at this time." Instead, New York turned to bills as an alternative. On February 16, New York requested, and the Board approved, a reduction in its minimum buying rates on bills to ½ of 1 per cent. It acquired $350 million in

<hr>

[137] Harrison, Open Market, Vol. II, preliminary memorandum, dated Dec. 31, 1932, and minutes of meeting, Jan. 4–5, 1933.

bills the following two weeks, though at the end of the second the Bank raised the bill rate twice, to 1 per cent on February 27, and to 1½ per cent on March 1, in consonance with rises in the discount rate. It also acquired $25 million of government securities in the first of the two weeks and $2 million in the second, primarily to enable banks to liquidate by selling government securities instead of borrowing on them.[138]

In the final two months prior to the banking holiday, there was nothing that could be called a System policy. The System was demoralized. Each Bank was operating on its own. All participated in the general atmosphere of panic that was spreading in the financial community and the community at large. The leadership which an independent central banking system was supposed to give the market and the ability to withstand the pressures of politics and of profit alike and to act counter to the market as a whole, these—the justification for establishing a quasi-governmental institution with broad powers—were conspicuous by their absence.

6. *Alternative Policies*

It is clear that the monetary policies followed from 1929 to 1933 were not the inevitable result of external pressure. At all times, alternative policies were available and were being seriously proposed for adoption by leading figures in the System. At all times, the System was technically in a position to adopt the alternative policies.

To give a clearer idea of the consequences of the policies actually followed, we consider explicitly the alternatives available at three critical periods and what their effects might have been. The periods are: (1) the first ten months of 1930; (2) the first eight months of 1931; (3) the four months following Britain's departure from gold in September 1931. This is followed by an evaluation of the chief justification that has been offered by writers on Federal Reserve history for the policy actually pursued in late 1931 and early 1932, namely, that a shortage of "free gold" greatly inhibited use of the policy alternatives available to the System until the passage of the Glass-Steagall Act at the end of February 1932.

The successive banking crises which followed the first period and occurred during the other two were, as we saw in section 2, each more severe than the preceding. Measures that might have been adequate to cope with the earlier ones would have been inadequate for the later ones. On the other hand, as we shall see, the bond purchases actually made in the spring and summer of 1932, which did halt the decline in the stock of money but were inadequate to prevent a subsequent relapse some months after, would have been more than adequate to cope with the earlier crises. As so often in human affairs, a stitch in time saves nine.

[138] Notes, Vol. III, Jan. 16; Feb. 2, 6, 16, 27, 1933; Conversations, Vol. II, Jan. 18, 1933. Quotation from Notes, Vol. III, Feb. 16, 1933.

JANUARY 1930 TO END OF OCTOBER 1930

None of the arguments later advanced in support of the view that expansionary monetary measures by the Federal Reserve System might have been ineffective or undesirable applies to this period, as noted above. There was no sign of lack of confidence in banks by the public, or of unusual concern by banks about their own safety. Banks were using reserves to the full. Any increase in reserves probably would have been put to use in expanding the assets of banks. Expansionary measures offered no threat to the gold standard. On the contrary, the gold reserve was high and gold inflows persisted. Throughout the twenties, the System had been concerned that it held too large a fraction of the world's gold stock; the only problem about gold that evoked discussion in 1930 within the System was how to repel the flow. Finally, no serious monetary difficulties had yet arisen abroad.

To evaluate the possible quantitative effect of an alternative policy, let us consider what the effect would have been if the purchase program actually carried out in 1932 had been carried out in 1930 instead; that is, if the System had embarked on a program to raise its security holdings by $1 billion during the first ten months of 1930. From December 1929 to October 1930, if we adjust for seasonal effects, government security holdings actually rose by $150 million. If some $850 million additional government securities had been purchased, high-powered money, instead of declining by $160 million, would have risen by $690 million, all of which would have increased reserves, since during the first ten months of 1930 the public reduced its currency holdings. However, changes in other forms of Reserve Bank credit might have reduced the impact of the hypothetical additional purchase. From December 1929 to October 1930, bills bought fell by $110 million—from $240 million to $130 million—and bills discounted fell by $390 million—from $590 million to $200 million. The purchase of $850 million additional government securities would doubtless have produced an even larger decline in bills discounted and less certainly in bills bought, since banks would have used some of the funds to repay borrowings and there might have been a larger demand for bankers' acceptances. To make rather extreme allowance for such an effect, let us suppose that discounts and bills bought had each been reduced to $50 million. Even then, the effect of the purchases would have been a rise in Federal Reserve credit outstanding by $130 million instead of the actual decline of $490 million, and a rise in high-powered money by $460 million.

If the deposit ratios had behaved as in fact they did, the change from a decline in high-powered money of 2½ per cent to a rise of 6½ per cent would have converted the actual 2 per cent decline in the stock of money into a rise of 7 per cent. Under those circumstances, the deposit ratios might have altered in a direction to offset some of the hypothetical rise in high-powered money. But even very large allowances on this score would hardly change the general conclusion: a rise in the System's security holdings by $1 billion instead of $150 million in the first ten months of 1930 would have changed the monetary situation drastically, so drastically that such an operation was almost surely decidedly larger than was required to convert the decline in the stock of money into an appreciable rise.

The change in the monetary situation might have affected the gold movement, reducing the gold inflow or even converting it into a gold outflow. But it would have done that only by its effects on the trend of economic activity and on the state of the capital markets. Only if the change in the monetary climate had lessened the severity of the economic contraction and made the capital markets easier, would it have affected gold flows. But it is precisely the achievement of such results that would have been the aim of the alternative policies. Hence, a reduction in the gold inflow would have been a sign of the success of the alternative policy, not an offset to it.

The hypothetical purchase of government securities would have reduced in two ways the likelihood of a banking crisis like the one in the fall of 1930: indirectly, through its effect on the severity of the contraction; and directly, through its effect on the balance sheets of banks. The indirect effect would have improved the ability of borrowers to repay loans; the direct effect would have meant that bank reserves were rising sharply instead of staying roughly stable. It is impossible to say with any assurance that these effects would have prevented a banking crisis from occurring—though they might have—but it is certain they would have reduced the magnitude of any crisis that did occur and hence the magnitude of its aftereffects.

The effects on the capital markets and the reduction in the drain of gold from the rest of the world would have had desirable effects abroad. Again, these might not have prevented the later financial difficulties entirely, but they certainly would have eased them.

JANUARY 1931 TO END OF AUGUST 1931

The early months of 1931 were the next crucial time for monetary policy. The banking crisis had died down, there were signs of returning confidence in banks and of improving conditions in business. We have already suggested (section 2) that a vigorous monetary push at that time might have converted the faint signs of recovery into sustained revival.

Let us suppose that actual policy to the end of 1930, including the first banking crisis, had been what it was, but that in the first eight months of 1931 the System had raised its security holdings by $1 billion instead of $80 million, after allowing for seasonal changes. During those eight months, currency held by the public rose by $370 million as a result of the internal drain on the banking system; bank reserves fell by $120 million. The difference between the rise in currency and the decline in bank reserves, or $250 million, is the amount by which high-powered money rose. The purchase of $920 million additional government securities, with no change in bills discounted or bills bought, would have raised high-powered money by $1,170 million instead, enough to meet the drain of currency that actually occurred and at the same time to increase bank reserves by $800 million. With such a sizable increase in their reserves, instead of a decrease of $120 million, banks would have been freed from the necessity of liquidating securities, and could have reduced their borrowing from the Reserve System, instead of increasing it by $40 million. The bond market would accordingly have been far stronger, bank failures would have been notably fewer, and hence the runs on banks milder if at all appreciable. In consequence, the drain of currency into circulation would have been smaller than it was and the increase in bank reserves would have been even larger than these figures suggest.

To put the matter as before, in terms of the effect on Federal Reserve credit—again assuming that bills discounted and bills bought would each have been reduced to $50 million—had the System bought an additional $920 million of government securities during the first eight months of 1931, Federal Reserve credit outstanding would have risen by $470 million instead of $40 million. High-powered money, under these circumstances, would have risen by $680 million or by 10 per cent instead of by 3½ per cent. Even if both the deposit ratios had fallen by as much as they did, the result would have been no change in the stock of money, instead of a decrease of 5½ per cent.

On this occasion, however, effects of the change in the monetary climate on the deposit ratios would clearly have enhanced rather than offset the expansionary effect of the hypothetical open market purchases. Depositors would have been far less eager to convert deposits into currency and banks, to strengthen still further their reserve position. Both deposit ratios would therefore have fallen less than they did. The second banking crisis might indeed never have occurred at all in such a changed monetary environment. Once again a $1 billion purchase program would have been much greater than needed to change drastically the monetary situation. But even if the second banking crisis had occurred, and even if it had been as severe as it was, the hypothetical open market operation would have completely eliminated its effect on the stock of money.

Again, the change would have produced a reduction in the inflow of gold and might have converted it into an outflow with a resulting easing of the financial difficulties in Europe. And again, this must be counted an achievement of the hypothetical purchase program and not an offset.

SEPTEMBER 1931 TO END OF JANUARY 1932

We cited earlier the statement in a System memorandum written in November 1931 that the "foreign and domestic drain upon bank reserves [after Britain's departure from gold] were met in the classic way by increases in discount rates combined with a policy of free lending." The memorandum included a quotation from the *locus classicus* of central bank policy, Bagehot's *Lombard Street*. In fact, however, the System followed Bagehot's policy only with respect to the external drain, not the internal drain. To meet an external drain, Bagehot prescribed a high Bank rate, the part of his prescription the System followed. To meet an internal drain, he prescribed lending freely. "A panic," he wrote, "in a word, is a species of neuralgia, and according to the rules of science you must not starve it. The holders of the cash reserve must be ready not only to keep it for their own liabilities, but to advance it most freely for the liabilities of others."[139] Despite the assertion to the contrary in the memorandum, the System gave little more than lip service to this part of Bagehot's prescription, either before the external drain or after it ended. True, during the height of the internal and external drain in October, it permitted its discounts and its bills bought to rise sharply. But this was at the initiative of the member banks, in spite of sharp rises in the rates on both, and was a result of the desperate situation of member banks because of the double drain. As we have seen, even after the height of the crisis, the New York Bank reduced bill buying rates only gradually and kept them above market rates, so bills bought declined rapidly. The System took no active measures to ease the internal drain, as it could have done through open market purchases. Contrast its behavior with that reported approvingly by Bagehot:

The way in which the panic of 1825 was stopped by advancing money has been described in so broad and graphic a way that the passage has become classical. "We lent it," said Mr. Harman on behalf of the Bank of England, "by every possible means and in modes we have never adopted before; we took in stock on security, we purchased Exchequer bills, we made advances on Exchequer bills, we not only discounted outright, but we made advances on the deposit of bills of exchange to an immense amount, in short, by every possible means consistent with the safety of the Bank, and we were not on some occasions over-nice."[140]

Though the response of the System to the external drain was "classic," it was sharply at variance with the alternative policy the System had de-

---

[139] Walter Bagehot, *Lombard Street*, London, Henry S. King, 1873, p. 51.
[140] *Lombard Street*, pp. 51–52.

veloped during the 1920's, the gold sterilization policy. That policy called not for tightness but for ease to counter the gold drain and, even more clearly, for ease in the period before and after the gold drain to counter the internal drain.[141]

The System had sterilized inflows and outflows of gold during the twenties. It had more than sterilized inflows from August 1929 to August 1931. Consistent policy called for sterilizing the outflow after September 1931 as well. And the System was in an extraordinarily strong technical position to follow such a policy. Just before Britain's departure from the gold standard, the U.S. gold stock was at its highest level in history, over $4.7 billion, and amounted to about 40 per cent of the world's monetary gold stock. The System's reserve percentage—the ratio of its gold holdings to its note and deposit liabilities—exceeded 80 per cent in July, averaged 74.7 in September, and never fell below 56.6 in October. At the lowest point, toward the end of October, its gold reserves exceeded legal requirements for cover by more than $1 billion.[142] And this sum could have been expanded under pressure by $80 million to $200 million by simple bookkeeping adjustments.[143] Further, the Reserve Board had the legal power to suspend gold reserve requirements with negligible sanctions, a power it did in fact invoke in early 1933.

The major short-term balances subject to withdrawal were held by France. French short-term balances, which had been declining since 1929, amounted to $780 million in January 1931 (out of a total of $1.8

[141] For example, see the memorandum by Benjamin Strong, listing the reasons for the Federal Reserve easy-money policy of 1924, one of which was, "To check the pressure on the banking situation in the West and Northwest and the resulting failures and disasters. . ." (*Stabilization,* Hearings before the House Banking and Currency Committee, 69th Cong., 1st sess., Mar.–June 1926; Feb. 1927, pp. 335–336). One of the tests of Federal Reserve policy, 1922–26, that Strong proposed was the number of bank failures (p. 476). See also Adolph Miller of the Federal Reserve Board on the role of the System in lending to "banks that are in distressed communities" and supplying emergency currency needs (pp. 861, 898–899); and W. R. Burgess, then assistant Federal Reserve agent of the New York Bank, on the powers of the System for stabilization, including "desperate remedies for a desperate emergency" (p. 1019).

[142] In contrast, the System's gold reserve ratio was only 53 per cent at its maximum in 1919 when it permitted inflation to proceed unchecked, and it did not take contractionary action in 1920 until the ratio had fallen to less than 43 per cent.

[143] Federal Reserve notes in vaults of issuing Federal Reserve Banks were subject to the same collateral and reserve requirements as notes in circulation. On Oct. 31, 1931, there were about $320 million of such notes in vaults of issuing Banks. According to an internal System memorandum, about $120 million in vault would have been adequate (Harrison, Miscellaneous, Vol. I, enclosure, dated Aug. 20, 1931, in letter, dated Aug. 21, Harrison to McDougal). A reduction of $200 million would have released $80 million in required gold reserves held against the notes. If, instead of 60 per cent eligible paper, gold were held as collateral against the notes, an additional $120 million in gold would have been released from legal requirements.

billion held by European countries) and by September were around $700 million.[144] France was strongly committed to staying on gold, and the French financial community, the Bank of France included, expressed the greatest concern about the United States' ability and intention to stay on the gold standard. That accounted for the special volatility of the French balances. As it happened, though the French balances were not withdrawn in October 1931,[145] they were almost entirely withdrawn in the

---

[144] *Banking and Monetary Statistics*, p. 574. These are estimates of short-term balances held by France and all of Europe in reporting New York banks on Jan. 31, 1931. The peak figures a year earlier were $890 million and $2.0 billion, respectively.

[145] Harrison informed the Bank of France in Oct. that, if it did not want to invest its funds in the U.S. money market, he preferred not to hold French deposits in excess of $200 million. He suggested that it buy gold which would be either earmarked for the Bank of France or exported to France. The French representatives expressed surprise at Harrison's willingness to part with gold, but were not eager to withdraw it at the time because of their fears of possible inflationary effects of gold imports on the French economy and because of the loss of earnings to the Bank of France. It was agreed, however, that the Bank of France would effect a gradual repatriation of a substantial fraction of its balances in New York (Harrison, Notes, Vol. II, Oct. 15 and 26, 1931).

Rumors about Harrison's conversations with the French misrepresented their substance: he was said to have requested them not to take more gold from this country and they had not agreed; and he was said to have committed himself to maintain a firm money policy. He denied these rumors in a letter to Governor Meyer:

> I have reviewed these matters in some detail only because of the continued and repeated reports of an agreement in the nature of a "bargain" whereby the Federal Reserve Bank of New York surrendered its freedom of action regarding credit or discount rate policies in exchange for a promise from the Bank of France that it would not withdraw its funds from the market. There was not any such agreement, nor any such bargain. The Bank of France is perfectly free at any time it chooses to withdraw its dollar funds. The Federal Reserve Bank of New York is equally free in its credit and discount policies. In fact, there has never been a time in any of my conversations with any central bank when there was any request or even any suggestion that they or we should in any way make a commitment as to any future policy that would in any way destroy or limit our complete freedom of action in our own self-interest.

These statements by Harrison are not necessarily inconsistent with the assertion by E. A. Goldenweiser, who was director of the Board's Division of Research and Statistics at the time: "The Bank of France at that time had large deposits in the United States and it was understood by the authorities that, if bill rates in this country did not advance, these deposits would be withdrawn in gold."
Without France's asking for a commitment and without Harrison's entering into one, the French representatives could still have made it clear that they would regard failure of the United States to raise discount rates as a sign that the United States was not serious about its announced intention to take whatever measures were necessary to stay on the gold standard (Harrison, Miscellaneous, Vol. I, letter, dated Dec. 18, 1931, Harrison to Meyer; *ibid.*, letter, dated Dec. 22, 1931, Harrison to Calkins, who evidently had accepted the rumors as truth; E. A. Goldenweiser, *American Monetary Policy*, New York, McGraw-Hill, 1951, pp. 158–159).

spring of 1932.[146] Their withdrawal in October would have made no ultimate difference in the gold position. It would, however, have reduced the System's reserve percentage to about 49 per cent and hence might have had psychological effects somewhat different from those experienced when the balances were actually withdrawn, since the System's reserve percentage did not then fall below 58 per cent. The lowest the reserve percentage ever reached during the 1932 open market operation was 56 per cent (monthly averages of daily figures). Consequently, it seems highly likely that, if a gold sterilization policy had been adopted, gold outflows would have ceased long before the legal reserve ratio was reached, let alone before the gold stock was drastically depleted.[147]

Suppose the System had raised discount rates when it did, adopting the "classic" remedy for an external drain, but had accompanied the measure by purchase of government securities as called for by the "classic" remedy for an internal drain and by its earlier sterilization policy. Again, to be concrete, let $1 billion be the amount of the hypothetical increase in its security holdings. What would have been the consequence?

Between August 1931 and January 1932, currency held by the public rose by $720 million and bank reserves fell by $390 million, which means that, as a result of the increase in discounts and other minor changes, high-powered money had risen by $330 million despite the gold drain. Other items being the same, Reserve purchases of $1 billion of government securities would have meant an increase of $1,330 million in high-

[146] French short-term balances with reporting New York banks were, on selected dates, in millions: Sept. 16, 1931, $685; Dec. 30, 1931, $549; May 11, 1932, $304; June 15, 1932, $102; June 29, 1932, $49 (*Banking and Monetary Statistics*, pp. 574–575). The statistics include all deposits and short-term securities held by the French at reporting domestic banks and bankers, but they may not include other American short-term liabilities to French citizens, such as bills and short-term securities held for them by agents other than the reporting banks. Hence these figures may underestimate French withdrawals.

Governor Harrison denied that the ultimate withdrawal of French short-term balances reflected French dissatisfaction with the change in Federal Reserve policy in the spring of 1932, though that was widely reported. He said, "[S]ome people might argue that our policy had been responsible for the recent heavy outflow of gold, but we know that it was largely the repatriation of central bank balances which would have been withdrawn in any case" (Notes, Vol. II, June 30, 1932).

[147] Goldenweiser asserts the contrary, writing that "a full-fledged easing policy [by which he clearly means, from the context, low discount rates, rather than open market operations] . . . would have involved a suspension of reserve requirements against Federal Reserve deposits" (*American Monetary Policy*, p. 159). However, Goldenweiser gives no evidence to support his assertion. It may have been the opinion of the authorities at the time, though we have been able to find no internal document in the Goldenweiser Papers or in the Harrison Papers and no reference in the Hamlin Diary indicating that such a policy was ever seriously contemplated or its consequences for the reserve ratio explicitly considered. These documents make the rise in discount rates appear to be more nearly a conditioned reflex than a policy decision reached after full consideration of a range of feasible alternatives.

powered money. That sum would have provided the whole $720 million in currency withdrawn by the public and at the same time have enabled bank reserves to increase by $610 million instead of decreasing by $390 million, or one-eighth of their initial level. The increase in bank reserves would have permitted a multiple expansion in deposits instead of the multiple contraction that actually took place.

Of course, under these circumstances, banks would have been under far less heavy pressure than they were and would have borrowed less from the Reserve System, thereby offsetting some of the hypothetical increase in high-powered money. However, this offset would have reflected fewer bank failures and a reduction in the public's desire to convert deposits into currency. Hence, the currency held by the public would have risen less than it did. The net effect of these offsetting factors on bank reserves might have been either expansionary or contractionary.

Again, to suggest orders of magnitude, suppose that from August 1931 to January 1932, discounts and bills bought had both remained unchanged instead of the first rising from $280 million to $840 million, and the second falling from $310 million to $100 million. Even under these assumptions, a purchase of $1 billion of government securities would have meant a rise in high-powered money by $650 million more than the actual rise. Even if we couple these assumptions with the further extreme assumption that, under such greatly improved monetary conditions, the deposit ratios would have fallen as much as they did—and for the deposit-currency ratio, the fall in so short a time was the largest on record—the result would have been to cut the decline in the stock of money to less than half the actual decline from August 1931 to January 1932. Only a moderate improvement in the deposit-currency ratio—a decline from 8.95 to 7.10 instead of to 6.47—would, under these hypothetical circumstances, have enabled the stock of money to be stable instead of falling by 12 per cent.

The crises were becoming successively more severe, so this time the $1 billion we have been using as our standard is not, as in the earlier periods, clearly a multiple of the amount required to turn the monetary tide. But these calculations suggest that an open market purchase of that size would have been adequate. And with so great a change in the monetary tide, the economic situation could hardly have deteriorated so rapidly and sharply as it did.

THE PROBLEM OF FREE GOLD

In the book he published after retiring from the System, from which we quoted above, Goldenweiser analyzed briefly the System's reaction to Britain's departure from gold. After discussing the rise in discount rates in reaction to the external drain, which he terms a "brief return to orthodoxy"[148] which "had only passing and temporary effects on the banking system or on the course of the depression," he went on to say, with respect to the internal drain:

> More serious was the fact that the System did not extend sufficient aid to member banks through discounting their paper and that it failed to pursue a vigorous policy of purchases in the open market. For this failure of the System to give more help in an emergency the major blame is on the law which prescribed rigid rules for the eligibility of paper for discount and also barred government securities from collateral acceptable for Federal Reserve notes.[149]

The problem to which Goldenweiser referred is the so-called free-gold problem. The internal drain had increased the volume of Federal Reserve notes outstanding. The law specified that the System hold against notes a reserve of 40 per cent in gold and additional collateral of 60 per cent in either gold or eligible paper (which consisted of commercial, agricultural, or industrial loans, or loans secured by U.S. government securities rediscounted by member banks; loans to member banks secured by paper eligible for rediscount or by government securities; and bankers' acceptances, i.e., "bills bought" in the terminology of Federal Reserve accounts). Because the System did not have enough eligible paper to furnish 60 per cent of the collateral for Federal Reserve notes, part of the gold in excess of minimum requirements had to be pledged for this purpose. The amount of free gold not needed to meet either minimum gold requirements or collateral requirements was therefore less than the amount of excess gold reserves. The Federal Reserve System, in its *Annual Report* for 1932, and Goldenweiser, in the passage quoted above and elsewhere in his book, assert that the shortage of free gold was an important factor preventing the System from engaging in larger open market purchases, such as the hypothetical purchases discussed in the preceding subsection. Such purchases, they assert, would have reduced eligible paper holdings still further by reducing rediscounts and therefore could have been conducted only to a very limited extent without eliminating free gold entirely. The Glass-Steagall Act of February 27, 1932, disposed of that problem by permitting government bonds in the Reserve Banks' portfolios as well as eligible paper to serve as collateral against Federal Reserve notes in addition to the 40 per cent minimum gold reserve.[150]

Our own examination of the evidence leads us to a different conclu-

[148] However, while discount rates were raised at all Reserve Banks in Oct. or Nov. 1931, they were reduced a few months later only in Dallas and Richmond and New York. The reduction in New York was made more than four months after the second rise in Oct. 1931, and brought the discount rate only one-quarter of the way back to the level before the gold drain. Four months later, a second reduction was made in New York to 2½ per cent—only halfway back to the level before the gold drain—where the rate remained until raised again in March 1933.

[149] *American Monetary Policy,* pp. 159–160.

[150] See footnote 26, above, for other provisions of the Glass-Steagall Act.

sion. Despite the attention it has since received, we do not believe a shortage of free gold exerted any major influence on Federal Reserve policy, for five reasons.

(1) The earliest published full-dress discussion of free gold during the 1929–33 contraction we have found is an article by Benjamin Anderson in the *Chase Economic Bulletin* of September 29, 1930. Anderson, a firm believer in the real bills doctrine and an equally firm opponent of open market operations, warned, "There is not enough free gold to justify artificially cheap money."[151] We have found no evidence that the article exerted any influence within the Reserve System. In any event, by the time it appeared, New York had already lost its battle for expansionary open market purchases, and the general lines which were to dominate policy until the spring of 1932 had already been set.

(2) The earliest unpublished System document on free gold we have found is a memorandum by Goldenweiser, written on January 3, 1930. He refers to a Board discussion of a statement by Anderson "that free gold was down to $600,000,000 . . . " (in an address to the American Economic Association and American Statistical Association on December 30, 1929); Anderson concluded, "The Federal Reserve System is nearing the time when it must look to its own reserve . . . ." The memorandum makes clear that the Reserve System regularly kept track of free gold, and that its level was not at the time a source of concern to the Board.

The limited attention paid to free gold by the System is suggested by the fact that the earliest mention of free gold we have found in the Hamlin Diary is an entry of July 30, 1931, and in the Harrison Papers, a preliminary memorandum, August 3, 1931, for the meeting of the Open Market Policy Conference on August 11. Both noted that free gold on July 29 totaled $748 million and that internal bookkeeping adjustments, involving reduction of Federal Reserve notes in the tills of most Reserve Banks to a "reasonable minimum," would have raised the free gold on that date to $1,086 million.[152] A later memorandum of August 21, 1931, prepared at the New York Bank considered the likely effect on free gold of a variety of alternative hypothetical developments including large-scale open market purchases, internal drain of notes and gold, and an external drain and concluded that, even under rather extreme assumptions, free

[151] Anderson had referred to the significance of free gold in a Mar. 14, 1930, article (p. 13), indicating his intention to discuss the subject fully later, as he did in the Sept. 1930 *Bulletin* article, "The Free Gold of the Federal Reserve System and the Cheap Money Policy" (p. 8). W. R. Burgess told the Board that a subsequent article by Anderson on gold (*Chase Economic Bulletin*, Mar. 16, 1931) did much damage abroad to the Federal Reserve System (Hamlin, Diary, Vol. 19, Oct. 30, 1931, p. 173).

[152] See Goldenweiser Papers, Container 1, folder of Confidential Memoranda, 1922–33; New York *Times*, Dec. 31, 1929, which refers to Anderson's address; Hamlin, Diary, Vol. 19, p. 132; Harrison, Open Market, Vol. II.

gold did not constitute an important limitation on the alternatives available to the System.[153] The preliminary memorandum for the October 26 meeting of the Open Market Policy Conference noted there had been little change in free gold as a result of the gold outflow. Excess gold reserves had declined from $1.9 billion on September 16, 1931, to $1.1 billion on October 21, but free gold reserves had been roughly constant at over $0.8 billion because of a rise in eligible paper holdings. The preliminary memorandum for the November 30, 1931, meeting did not even refer to free gold, though it did note, "there is still plenty of gold left." After the first of the year, free gold may have fallen as low as $400 million during January and February 1932, which could have been raised to perhaps $525 million by bookkeeping adjustments.[154] Hence the actual amount of free gold throughout the whole period was sufficient to have permitted extensive open market operations.

(3) While free gold was alluded to from time to time at meetings of the Conference or of its executive committee or of the Federal Reserve Board or of the New York Bank directors, it was almost always mentioned as a problem by persons who had opposed open market operations all along on other grounds; it was never given as the principal argument against purchases, and the objections raised on this score almost always were immediately countered by figures showing that a shortage of free gold offered no serious limitation to policy.[155] It is impossible to read

[153] In his letter transmitting the memorandum to all governors, Harrison concluded, "apart from the position of individual Reserve banks the system as a whole has ample funds to deal with any situation within reason which may arise, and that in matters of policy we are probably in a position to do whatever seems wise for the country's economy."
The memorandum stated the immediate effect of the purchase of $300 million of government bonds would be a reduction of about $137 million in free gold, leaving the System about $600 million, which could be increased to more than $900 million by reducing Federal Reserve notes in vaults of the Reserve Banks. A large increase in the demand for Federal Reserve notes or for gold, according to the statement, would not affect the free gold position because that increase would be accompanied by an increase in Federal Reserve discounts and bill holdings, which would supply eligible paper collateral for Federal Reserve notes and release gold used for that purpose. Gold then in use as collateral, exclusive of free gold, was sufficient to provide a 40 per cent reserve for more than $3 billion of additional note circulation, or to provide $1¼ billion of gold for export (Miscellaneous, Vol. I).
[154] Open Market, Vol. II. No continuous figures on free gold during the critical period, Sept. 1931–Feb. 1932, were shown either in the *Annual Report* or *Federal Reserve Bulletin* for 1931 and 1932, and we have been able to find none in any System publication since. Our estimates for Jan. and Feb. 1932 are based on a chart in Federal Reserve Board, *Annual Report* for 1932, p. 17, plus amounts of their own notes held by issuing Banks, p. 91.
[155] At the Aug. 11, 1931, meeting of the Open Market Policy Conference, Governors Calkins and Seay said, in response to Harrison's recommendation of substantial purchases of government securities, their Banks did not hold enough free gold to permit them to participate in further purchases. Governor Harrison

402

in full the record of proceedings of the Open Market Policy Conference and of meetings of the New York Bank directors during the period from September 1931 through February 1932 and assign great significance to free gold as a factor determining policy. The closest approach to serious concern was expressed in January and February 1932, when the Glass-Steagall Act was in process of enactment and the problem was on its way to solution.[156] Concern over the gold problem during the period centered

---

cited the figures on free gold in the memorandum of Aug. 3, 1931, referred to above, and pointed out that "the question to decide was not whether individual banks could, or could not, participate, but to try to agree on a System policy which would be helpful." When the Conference met with the Board later that day, Governor Meyer asked if "there was any danger to the System" in authorizing the executive committee to purchase $200 million or $300 million of government bonds. "Mr. Goldenweiser stated that there was no danger in that direction as we have $750,000,000 free gold which can be increased to $1,000,000,000 by withdrawals from the agents" (Harrison, Open Market, Vol. II).

At a meeting of the executive committee of the directors of the New York Bank on Oct. 5, Owen D. Young asked how the purchase of government securities by the Reserve Banks "would fit into the proposed plan" for a corporation, eventually designated the National Credit Corporation. Harrison answered, "that he considered the gold position of the System paramount at this time, and on that account would not be inclined to purchase Government securities." Three days later, however, at a board meeting of the New York Bank, Harrison said "that the amount of free gold held by the System had not been materially affected by the recent loss of gold, so that there was still considerable leeway for purchases of Government securities" (Notes, Vol. II, Oct. 5, 8, 1931).

At the Oct. 26, 1931, meeting of the Conference, Harrison said that "the free gold position of the System was not a consideration at this time" (Open Market, Vol. II). On Oct. 27, Goldenweiser reported to the Board that free gold had been maintained despite the gold exports of the preceding five weeks (Hamlin, Diary, Vol. 19, pp. 169–170). No reference was made to free gold at the Nov. 30, 1931, meeting of the Conference, which authorized the executive committee to buy up to $200 million of government securities before the end of the year (Open Market, Vol. II).

The earliest mention of the free gold problem we have found in publications of the Federal Reserve Board is in the *Bulletin,* Sept. 1931, pp. 495–496. The term is defined and a chart is presented showing free gold and excess reserves of the Reserve Banks from 1925 on. It is referred to again in the *Bulletin,* Nov. 1931, p. 604. No mention of free gold is made in the *Annual Report* for 1931. In neither that report nor any earlier one is there a suggestion of legislation to meet such a problem, though it was standard procedure for the Reserve System to list legislative recommendations in its reports. The *Annual Report* for 1932, in commenting on the passage of the Glass-Steagall Act, contains the first discussion of free gold in the annual reports.

[156] On Jan. 4, 1932, Harrison told the executive committee of the New York Bank that "his only hesitancy in recommending" substantial purchases of government bonds was on account of the relatively small amount of free gold "we now have at our disposal," and for that reason the Reserve Banks should have authority to pledge all their assets as collateral for Federal Reserve notes (Notes, Vol. II, Jan. 4, 1932).

His hesitancy did not prevent his urging open market purchases at the Jan. 11, 1932, meeting of the Conference (see sect. 5, above). At the Feb. 24 meeting just before the enactment of the Glass-Steagall bill, the System's failure to pursue

not in the Federal Reserve System but in the White House and Treasury. At a conference with Congressional leaders on October 6, 1931, President Hoover presented the proposals eventually embodied in the Glass-Steagall Act.[157]

(4) If free gold had been a serious handicap to a desired policy, feasible measures fully consistent with past policies of the System were available, even during the height of the gold drain, to relieve the free gold problem. (a) The bookkeeping adjustments referred to above were apparently exploited to some extent, but by no means fully. (b) Bills could have been purchased instead of government securities, since they were eligible as collateral for Federal Reserve notes. After rising sharply during the height of the crisis (September–October, 1931), holdings declined continuously from October 1931 to February 1932, because buying rates were kept above market rates.[158] (c) Member banks could have been encouraged

---

actively bill purchases, discount rate reduction, and "buying of Government securities, if necessary, facilitated by alleviation of free gold position," recommended on Jan. 11, was explained as follows:

> Continued uncertainties in the domestic situation, as well as a large drain of gold to Europe and particularly to France, stimulated by fear of inflation in this country, have been important factors in making it seem undesirable to carry through an aggressive program of reduction in discount rates and purchases of Government securities. The relatively small amount of free gold held by the reserve system was a further major factor in limiting the possibilities of purchases of Government securities (Open Market, Vol. II, minutes of meetings, Jan. 11, and Feb. 24, 1932).

[157] Hoover, *Memoirs,* pp. 115–118; see also Benjamin Anderson, "Our Gold Standard Has Not Been in Danger for Thirty-Six Years," *Chase Economic Bulletin,* Nov. 10, 1932, p. 10.

[158] On behalf of the System it could be claimed that the decline was not its own choice, that its buying rate on acceptances was below the rediscount rate, but New York City banks, which alone had bills, were substantially out of debt to the Federal Reserve Bank of New York by Nov. 1931 and hence had no incentive to sell (H. H. Villard, "The Federal Reserve System's Monetary Policy in 1931 and 1932," *Journal of Political Economy,* Dec. 1937, p. 727). The crucial point, however, is the relation of the buying rate, not to the rediscount rate, but to the market rate. As Villard has pointed out, from Aug. 1931 through Oct. 1931, while the System's bill holdings were expanding, its buying rate was at or below the market rate; thereafter its buying rate was $\frac{1}{8}$ to $\frac{1}{4}$ percentage point above the market rate (*ibid.,* pp. 728–732). If the Reserve Bank had lowered the buying rate, the New York banks would have sold their acceptances to it. The New York Bank was fully aware that the relevant consideration was the relation of the buying rate to the market rate and not to the rediscount rate, as its actions in Aug. 1929 show. On Jan. 21, 1932, Harrison told his board of directors, "[W]e should probably have lowered our bill rates because they [are] well above the effective market rates and our portfolio of bills [is] rapidly diminishing" (Harrison, Notes, Vol. II).

Benjamin Anderson, who argued that the availability of free gold was a constraint on Federal Reserve expansionary policies (which, as we have noted, he opposed), nevertheless denied that the Glass-Steagall Act was essential to

to increase their discounts. At all times there was ample eligible paper in the portfolios of member banks.[159] Goldenweiser and others recognize this but say that the only way to increase the amount in the hands of the Federal Reserve Banks would have been to sell bonds and thereby force member banks to discount.[160] They add, quite correctly, that such a step would have been deflationary. However, that was not the only way. Failure of banks to discount was partly a consequence of the long-standing Federal Reserve pressure against continuous borrowing. In 1929, the System went beyond that and resorted to "direct pressure" to dissuade member banks from discounting for particular purposes. It would have been easier to use direct pressure to persuade member banks in 1931 or

---

relieve the constraint. He listed alternatives available for increasing the supply of free gold similar to those listed in our item 4. Concerning 4 (b) he wrote:

> Moreover, it would have been very easy to increase the volume of open-market acceptances available for purchase by the Federal Reserve Banks, by concerted policy involving the coöperation of banks and great business corporations—a proposal of this sort was actually made by important industrial leaders ("Our Gold Standard Has Not Been in Danger," p. 9).

[159] See the figures on country and reserve city member banks' holdings of eligible assets, including eligible paper and U.S. government securities not pledged against national bank note circulation, on June 30 or at call dates, June 1926 through Dec. 1932, Federal Reserve Board, *Annual Report* for 1932, p. 126.

Holdings of eligible paper, including paper under rediscount, were four times as large as member bank borrowings, when this ratio was at a low point in Dec. 1931. Of course, member bank borrowings were secured by U.S. government securities as well as by eligible paper, so the possibility of increased borrowing on the basis of eligible paper holdings in Dec. 1931 is understated.

On Mar. 24, 1932, in Hearings before the Senate Committee on Banking and Currency on S. 4115 (*National and Federal Reserve Banking. System,* 72d Cong., 1st sess., p. 109), Senator Glass remarked, "Let me say that in an interview I had with him as late as last Saturday evening, the chief of banking operations in the Federal reserve system stated to me that the banks had ample eligible paper."

Holdings of eligible paper were also widely distributed, according to figures Glass presented during the Senate debate on the Glass-Steagall bill. He said he supported the section of the bill that permitted banks without eligible paper to rediscount other security satisfactory to the Reserve Banks, not because banks no longer held adequate amounts of eligible paper, but because of the psychological effect of the measure in freeing the fear-ridden banks from their inhibition to rediscount the eligible paper they owned (*Congressional Record,* Senate, Feb. 17, 1932, p. 4137; see also H. P. Willis and J. M. Chapman, *The Banking Situation,* New York, Columbia University Press, 1934, pp. 678–679).

[160] Goldenweiser, *American Monetary Policy,* p. 160; and Federal Reserve Board, *Annual Report* for 1932, p. 18. Benjamin Anderson believed force would not have been necessary:

> They [the Federal Reserve Banks] could have done this [sold government securities] without force, by arrangement with the great banks of the country in such a way as to tighten money markets little, if at all, if it were done in concert and as a matter of general policy ("Our Gold Standard Has Not Been in Danger," p. 9).

1932 to increase their discounts, since that could have been made profitable for member banks.[161]

(5) Finally, enactment of the Glass-Steagall Act on February 27, 1932, entirely removed the problem of free gold. Yet, as we have seen, its enactment did not lead to a change in Federal Reserve policy. The large-scale open market operation of 1932 was begun six weeks later primarily because of Congressional pressure and was allowed to lapse not long after Congress adjourned.

The conclusion seems inescapable that a shortage of free gold did not in fact seriously limit the alternatives open to the System. The amount was at all times ample to support large open market purchases. A shortage was an additional reason, at most, for measures adopted primarily on other grounds. The removal of the problem did not of itself lead to change of policy. The problem of free gold was largely an ex post justification for policies followed, not an ex ante reason for them.

[161] The System need only have offered to discount member bank paper backed by government securities (which constituted acceptable collateral for Federal Reserve notes) at a rate below the market yield on government securities. Under Secretary of the Treasury Mills apparently made that recommendation to the Open Market Policy Conference meeting on Jan. 11 and 12, 1932. The Treasury, which had to raise $1½ billion by June 30, wanted to encourage bank subscriptions in the face of a severe depreciation in government securities since Sept. 1931. "The inclination of banks to subscribe would be increased by reduction of Federal reserve discount rates to give some differential between those rates and the yields on government securities. If banks can be induced to borrow and buy the net effect must be an expansion of credit" (Harrison, Open Market, Vol. II). No action was taken on the recommendation.

Suggestion of a "variation of the 'direct pressure' method, tried unsuccessfully in 1929," namely, "borrowing . . . would not be frowned upon by the Federal Reserve Banks," was made in 1930 by a New York Bank director, but it was not considered to be a practical solution of the problem (Notes, Vol. 1, May 26, 1930). Individual Reserve Banks must have differed at any given time in the encouragement to discount they gave their member banks. See, for example, Charles E. Mitchell's comments on the San Francisco Bank, which suggest that it was not liberal in its interpretation of eligibility requirements (Notes, Vol. II, Oct. 15, 1931). Even Harrison, who in Oct. 1931 recommended that New York City banks borrow freely from the System "what was necessary to meet the needs of the situation," hesitated to call bankers in to see him in this connection, because "we must be prepared to have our action construed as an invitation to come in and borrow from this bank and to do something with the funds thus obtained. This procedure would, therefore, have its responsibilities." Owen D. Young said he wanted "to stop, look, and listen," before proceeding "by calling group meetings of bankers and by issuing what will be, in effect, an invitation to the member banks to come in and borrow at this bank" (Notes, Vol. II, Oct. 26, 1931; Mar. 24, 1932).

Clark Warburton maintains that, far from encouraging discounting as a means of getting more eligible paper, "as bank failures became frequent, the Federal Reserve banks developed an extremely hard-boiled attitude toward member banks which needed to borrow to meet deposit withdrawals" ("Has Bank Supervision Been in Conflict with Monetary Policy?", *Review of Economics and Statistics*, Feb. 1952, pp. 70–71).

7. Why Was Monetary Policy So Inept?

We trust that, in light of the preceding sections of this chapter, the adjective used in the heading of this one to characterize monetary policy during the critical period from 1929 to 1933 strikes our readers, as it does us, as a plain description of fact. The monetary system collapsed, but it clearly need not have done so.

The actions required to prevent monetary collapse did not call for a level of knowledge of the operation of the banking system or of the workings of monetary forces or of economic fluctuations which was developed only later and was not available to the Reserve System. On the contrary, as we have pointed out earlier, pursuit of the policies outlined by the System itself in the 1920's, or for that matter by Bagehot in 1873, would have prevented the catastrophe. The men who established the Federal Reserve System had many misconceptions about monetary theory and banking operations. It may well be that a policy in accordance with their understanding of monetary matters would not have prevented the decline in the stock of money from 1929 to the end of 1930.[162] But they under-

[162] For example, H. Parker Willis, who played a major role in the evolution of the Federal Reserve Act, was regularly reported in the columns of the *Commercial and Financial Chronicle* in 1931 and 1932—he had resigned from the editorship of the *Journal of Commerce* in May 1931—as inveighing against open market operations and arguing that the only task of the Reserve System was to discount eligible paper. A cabled article by Willis in a French publication (*Agence Économique et Financière*) in Jan. 1932, announcing that the Federal Reserve System had adopted inflationary policies, created a sensation in European financial circles. Governor Moret of the Bank of France cabled the article to Harrison for comment. It read in part:

> Inflation is the order of the day . . . . The discount rate will probably be low-
> ered at the next meeting of the Board of Directors of the Federal Reserve Bank
> of New York. [The rate was not lowered until Feb. 26, possibly because of
> Willis' article.] The reduction of the buying rate for acceptances in the open
> market which took place on Tuesday [Jan. 12] is a preparatory measure to
> which the Federal Reserve Bank always has recourse in such cases. Financial
> circles consider it an indication of a change in monetary policy and expect heavy
> purchases of government securities, acceptances, and perhaps of other bills
> . . . . There is reason to expect that all attempts to curb inflation and hamper
> credit expansion based on long term paper will meet with general opposition.
> Inflationary ideas have seriously taken hold of many minds in financial circles
> . . . . Wall Street . . . hails inflation as assuring an upward movement of
> securities . . . . The greatest danger inheres in the risks to which the Federal
> Reserve Banks are exposed in connection with the various proposals for the
> broadening of their discount and loan operations . . . . In view of these de-
> velopments certain observers remark that the gold export which ceased some time
> ago may easily begin again, the markets which permit the free export of gold
> having everywhere become very narrow (Harrison, Miscellaneous, Vol. II,
> Willis article, dated Jan. 13, 1932, quoted in full in cable, dated Jan. 15, 1932,
> Bank of France to Harrison).

Telephone calls and cable messages were exchanged by the New York Bank and the Bank of France before the excitement over Willis' article subsided (Conver-

stood very well the problem raised by a panic attempt to convert deposits into currency, and they provided ample powers in the act to deal with such a panic. There is little doubt that a policy based solely on a thorough perusal of the hearings preceding the enactment of the Federal Reserve Act and a moderately informed understanding of them would have cut short the liquidity crisis before it had gone very far, perhaps before the end of 1930.[163]

Contemporary economic comment was hardly distinguished by the correctness or profundity of understanding of the economic forces at work in the contraction, though of course there were notable exceptions. Many

---

sations, Vol. II, Jan. 14, 1932, dictated Jan. 20; Miscellaneous, Vol. II, cable, dated Jan. 15, 1932). New York City banks also received cables from their Paris agencies inquiring about the article. On Jan. 16, Harrison asked Senator Glass to use his influence to stop "Willis' rather steady flow of disturbing and alarming articles about the American position" (Miscellaneous, Vol. II).

Willis followed his former teacher J. Laurence Laughlin in his espousal of the "real-bills" doctrine (see Chap. 5, footnote 7). He applied those criteria to the operations of Federal Reserve Banks when he helped draft the Federal Reserve Act while serving in 1912–13 as an expert on the House Banking and Currency Subcommittee of which Carter Glass was chairman. After Glass became a Senator, Willis continued to be closely associated with him.

[163] See *Banking and Currency Reform*, Hearings before a subcommittee (Carter Glass, Chairman) of the House Banking and Currency Committee, 62d Cong., 3d sess., Jan. 7–Feb. 28, 1913; and *A Bill to Provide for the Establishment of Federal Reserve Banks*, Hearings before the Senate Banking and Currency Committee (R. L. Owen, Chairman), 63d Cong., 1st sess., Sept. 2–Oct. 27, 1913, 3 vols. In the House hearings especially, many witnesses showed clear understanding of the remedy for a liquidity crisis: cf. the testimony of Leslie M. Shaw, former Secretary of the Treasury, pp. 99–101; F. J. Wade, St. Louis banker, pp. 219–221; W. A. Nash, former chairman of the New York City Clearing House Association, pp. 338–339; A. J. Frame, Wisconsin banker, pp. 415–421. Frame did not favor establishing a reserve system; he urged extension of the Aldrich-Vreeland Act to state banks so they could "obtain extra cash in time of trouble." If that were done, "we would never have a suspension of cash payments in the United States again" (p. 421). In the Senate hearings, cf. the testimony of G. M. Reynolds, Chicago banker, Vol. I, p. 228; and Nathaniel French, Iowa businessman, who testified, "We can prevent a panic such as occurred in 1907 . . . by provisions for an elastic note issue, the mobilization of reserves, and their use in time of need" (Vol. III, p. 2075).

Note also Clark Warburton's comment:

It is apparent that the Federal Reserve System could operate as intended—i.e., to provide an elastic currency without contracting member bank reserves—if and only if the Federal Reserve Banks acquired additional assets . . . to the full extent of increased currency issues in the form of Federal Reserve notes . . . . The necessity of keeping this principle in mind in the operations of the Federal Reserve System is so obvious—in view of its discussion in the literature preceding establishment of the Federal Reserve System and the provisions of the Federal Reserve Act—that the failure of Federal Reserve officials to handle the System in conformity with it in the 1930's warrants a charge of lack of adherence to the intent of the law ("Monetary Difficulties and the Structure of the Monetary System," *Journal of Finance*, Dec. 1952, p. 535).

professional economists as well as others viewed the depression as a desirable and necessary economic development required to eliminate inefficiency and weakness, took for granted that the appropriate cure was belt tightening by both private individuals and the government, and interpreted monetary changes as an incidental result rather than a contributing cause.[164]

The banking and liquidity crisis must, however, be distinguished from the contraction in general. It was a much more specific phenomenon, with far more clearly etched predecessors which had been studied and classified at length. One might therefore have expected a much better understanding of the banking and liquidity crisis and of the measures required to resolve it satisfactorily than of the contraction in general. To some extent, this expectation was fulfilled. For example, Congressman A. J. Sabath of Illinois wrote to Eugene Meyer in January 1931, after Meyer had turned down his suggestion that the proper response to the increase in bank failures was relaxation of eligibility requirements in order to encourage rediscounting: "Does the board maintain there is no emergency existing at this time? To my mind if ever there was an emergency, it is now, and this, I feel, no one can successfully deny. For while 439 banks closed their doors in 1929, during the year 1930, 934 banks were forced to suspend business." On the floor of the House, Sabath said, "I insist it is within the power of the Federal Reserve Board to relieve the financial and commercial distress."[165] Some academic people,

[164] See, for example, Alvin H. Hansen, *Economic Stabilization in an Unbalanced World*, New York, Harcourt, Brace, 1932, pp. 377–378. The repeated attempts to curb federal expenditures and the sharp tax rise in 1932 testify to the effectiveness of these views. Writing in 1932, A. B. Adams (*Trends of Business, 1922–1932*, New York, Harper, 1932, p. 68) stated:

It would be quite undesirable to have an additional inflation of bank credit in this country at the present time. There is too much of the old inflation to be gotten rid of before business can be put on a sound basis. Temporary inflation would result only in a postponement of the inevitable deflation and readjustment and thereby result only in prolonging the present depression.

[165] *Reconstruction Finance Corporation*, Hearings before the House Banking and Currency Committee, 72d Cong., 1st sess., Jan. 6, 1932, pp. 78, 102–104. See also the testimony in March 1932 of former Senator R. L. Owen of Oklahoma, a banker and lawyer before his election to the Senate in 1907, and chairman of the Senate Banking and Currency Committee when the Federal Reserve Act was passed:

The powers of the Federal Reserve Board and of the Federal reserve banks were abundantly great to have checked the collapse of values if they had had the vision to employ the authority given by law.

Instead of expanding their credit when credit was being contracted and correcting the dangerous evil they contracted their own credits from December, 1929, to June, 1930, about $700,000,000 and only expanded it by Federal reserve notes when the depositors in banks were driven by fear to wholesale hoarding in August, 1930. Since January, 1932, they are again contracting credit.

Clearly what the authorities of the Federal Reserve System should have done was to buy United States bonds and bills in the open market and emit Federal

such as Harold Reed, Irving Fisher, J. W. Angell, and Karl Bopp expressed similar views.[166]

Despite these important exceptions, the literature, and particularly the academic literature, on the banking and liquidity crisis is almost as depressing as that on the contraction in general. Most surprisingly, some of those whose work had done most to lay the groundwork for the Federal

---

reserve notes to the extent necessary to stop the depression as far as it was due to the contraction of credit and currency. They were so advised by the experts of the Royal Bank of Canada and by others. They should have needed no advice for a remedy so self-evident (*Stabilization of Commodity Prices*, Hearings before the House Subcommittee on Banking and Currency, 72d Cong., 1st sess., part 1, p. 136).

See also testimony of D. H. Fisher, a director of the largest national farm loan association in the U.S., and of an Indiana county bankers' association (*ibid.*, pp. 289–293).

The monthly letter of the Royal Bank of Canada noted in July 1932:

. . . [I]t is obvious that the attitude of the Reserve System during 1930 and 1931 to credit contraction was passive . . . When hoarding set in [dated October 1930 by the letter], this further contraction of credit was only partly offset by the purchase of securities . . . [I]t is necessary for large surplus reserves to accumulate in order that the banks should feel that it is safe for them to pursue a more liberal policy with their clients. It is noteworthy that in relation to the violence of the great depression, there has been much less of an accumulation of surplus reserves than in previous periods.

[166] See footnote 51 above; also H. L. Reed, "Reserve Bank Policy and Economic Planning," *American Economic Review*, Mar. 1933 Supplement, pp. 114, 117 (he subsequently qualified his argument, on the ground that quantitative controls need to be supplemented by qualitative controls, in "The Stabilization Doctrines of Carl Snyder," *Quarterly Journal of Economics*, Aug. 1935, pp. 618–620); Irving Fisher, *Booms and Depressions*, New York, Adelphi, 1932, pp. 96, 106, 126–134, 148–152; and J. H. Rogers, who wrote, "For the failure to create . . . a basis for much-needed credit and price expansion, the Federal Reserve System is by many capable students of its policy being held directly responsible. It is contended with much force that in periods like the present one, these central institutions must either use their great 'open-market' powers to arrest damaging price declines, or else must face highly deserved criticism" (*America Weighs Her Gold*, Yale University Press, 1931, pp. 206–209); W. I. King, who wrote, "Suppose . . . that in 1930, when prices began to plunge downward precipitously, the proper Federal authorities had begun vigorously to pump new money into circulation. Would not this process have started prices upward, restored confidence, or optimism, and brought business back to normal by the middle of 1931? The most probable answer . . . seems to be 'Yes!'" ("The Immediate Cause of the Business Cycle," *Journal of the American Statistical Association*, Mar. 1932 Supplement, p. 229); J. W. Angell, "Monetary Prerequisites for Employment Stabilization," in *Stabilization of Employment*, C. F. Roos, ed., Bloomington, Principia, 1933, pp. 207–214, 222–226; Karl Bopp, who wrote, ". . . Mr. A. C. Miller, who seems to be the dominant figure in the Board, has stated that he is opposed to open-market operations—the only effective method of stimulating revival from a severe depression—except as a 'surgical operation.' Even through 1932 he was not of the opinion that such a 'surgical operation' was necessary" ("Two Notes on the Federal Reserve System," *Journal of Political Economy*, June 1932, p. 390).

Reserve Act or who had been most intimately associated with its formulation—for example, O. M. W. Sprague, E. W. Kemmerer, and H. Parker Willis—were least perceptive, perhaps because they had so strong an intellectual commitment to the view that the Federal Reserve System had once and for all solved problems of liquidity. One can read through the annual *Proceedings* of the American Economic Association or of the Academy of Political Science and find only an occasional sign that the academic world even knew about the unprecedented banking collapse in process, let alone that it understood the cause and the remedy.

That climate of intellectual opinion helps to explain why the behavior of the Federal Reserve System from 1929 to 1933 was not checked or reversed by vigorous and informed outside criticism. But neither the climate of opinion nor external financial pressures nor lack of power explains why the Federal Reserve System acted as it did. None of them can explain why an active, vigorous, self-confident policy in the 1920's was followed by a passive, defensive, hesitant policy from 1929 to 1933, least of all why the System failed to meet an internal drain in the way intended by its founders. Economic contraction from 1929 to the fall of 1930, before the onset of the liquidity crisis, was more severe than it was from 1923 to 1924 or from 1926 to 1927. Yet, in reaction to those earlier recessions, the Reserve System raised its holdings of government securities by over $500 million from December 1923 to September 1924 and by over $400 million from November 1926 to November 1927 (all figures as of the last Wednesday of the month). By contrast, its security holdings in September 1930 were less than $500 million above the lowest level at any time in 1929 and more than four-fifths of the increase had occurred before the end of 1929 in response to the stock market crash. In the financially turbulent years, 1930 and 1931, the System's holdings of government securities varied over a narrower range than in all but two of the relatively tranquil years from 1922 through 1928—1925 and 1926.

The explanation for the contrast between Federal Reserve policy before 1929 and after, and hence for the inept policy after 1929, that emerges from the account in the earlier sections of this chapter is the shift of power within the System and the lack of understanding and experience of the individuals to whom the power shifted. Until 1928, the New York Bank was the prime mover in Federal Reserve policy both at home and abroad, and Benjamin Strong, its governor from its inception, was the dominant figure in the Federal Reserve System. Strong represented the System in its dealings with central banks abroad in a period when each of the great central banks seemed to be personified by a single outstanding individual—the Bank of England by Montagu Norman, the Bank of France by Émile Moreau, the German Reichsbank by Hjalmar Schacht. In the early years of the System, Strong was chairman and the

411

dominant figure of the Governors Conference, a group composed of the chief executive officers of the twelve Reserve Banks. Later, in 1922, when the Conference established a Governors Committee on open market operations, out of which developed the Open Market Investment Committee, he was named permanent chairman.[167]

Strong began his career as a commercial banker. He had been deeply involved in the 1907 banking crisis, as secretary of the Bankers Trust Company, something of a "bankers' bank," and as head of a committee set up by the New York financial leaders "to determine which institutions could be saved and to appraise the collateral offered for loans."[168] That experience had greatly impressed him, as it did the banking community in general, and had given him a strong interest in the reform of banking and currency. It had much to do with his becoming the first governor of the New York Bank.

Strong, more than any other individual, had the confidence and backing of other financial leaders inside and outside the System, the personal force to make his own views prevail, and also the courage to act upon them. In one of his last letters on System policy, to Walter Stewart on August 3, 1928, he spoke of the necessity of an easy money policy to anticipate the approach of the "breaking point" Stewart feared, and commented:

> Here is where I fear the consequences of hesitation or differences of opinion within the System . . . . If the System is unwilling to do it, then I presume the New York Bank must do it alone, despite the tradition which we have helped to create and maintain, that no extensive open-market operations should be conducted by individual banks. An emergency presents the possible need for emergency measures.[169]

One of the directors of the New York Bank recalled in April 1932, when the System finally began large-scale open market purchases, that he had once asked Strong, "why the authority for Federal reserve banks to purchase Government securities had been inserted in the Federal Reserve Act and that Governor Strong had replied that it was in there to use. Governor Strong had said further that if this power were used in a big way, it would stop any panic which might confront us."[170] If Strong had still been alive and head of the New York Bank in the fall of 1930, he

[167] See Chandler, *Benjamin Strong*, pp. 41–53, 69–70, 214–215, and Chaps. VII–XI.

[168] Chandler, *Benjamin Strong*, pp. 27–28.

[169] Chandler, *Benjamin Strong*, p. 460.

[170] Harrison, Notes, Vol. II, Apr. 4, 1932. The director, Clarence A. Woolley, then asked why the open market purchases "could not have been done sooner." He said, "the national nervous system has now been subject to strain for 29 months whereas, in former periods of business depression, 5 or 6 months have sufficed to clear up the worst of the wreckage. Is the Federal Reserve System responsible for cutting off the dog's tail by inches?" Burgess pointed out that "the presence

would very likely have recognized the oncoming liquidity crisis for what it was, would have been prepared by experience and conviction to take strenuous and appropriate measures to head it off, and would have had the standing to carry the System with him. Strong, knowing that monetary measures could not be expected to produce immediate effects, would not have been put off the expansionary course by a temporary persistence of the decline in business activity.[171]

Strong became inactive in August 1928 and died in October of that year. Once he was removed from the scene, neither the Board nor the other Reserve Banks, as we have seen, were prepared to accept the leadership of the New York Bank.[172] Chandler says in his biography,

---

of the Federal Reserve System tended to extend both the period of stimulation and of depression of business activity" (*ibid.*).

[171] See the copy of a letter, dated at Colorado Springs, Aug. 26, 1923, from Strong to Adolph Miller, in the Goldenweiser Papers (Container 3, folder of Open Market Committee, 1923–52). Strong wrote in part:

> The phenomena of credit somewhat resemble some of the phenomena of tuberculosis, concerning which I can speak with some certainty. Any imprudence or excess by a T. B. sufferer will not show ill results often for weeks or months. Some unusual mental or physical effort starts a slight inflammation which gradually develops, causes a lesion, then later comes the temperature, pulse, cough, etc. In our operations, suppose the imprudence consists in selling 50 or 100 millions of our Section 14 investments in the New York market . . . . [W]e can if we are ignorant or careless pull down the credit structure at a rapid and dangerous rate, by a sale of investments, which shortly causes pressure to liquidate a much greater volume of bank loans. That process is at maximum— (with rapid pulse and high temperature)—at some indefinite period following our sale, and we may fail to detect the cause on account of the lag I mention.

Irving Fisher said, "Governor Strong died in 1928. I thoroughly believe that if he had lived and his policies had been continued, we might have had the stock market crash in a milder form, but after the crash there would not have been the great industrial depression" (*Annals of the American Academy of Political and Social Science*, Philadelphia, 1934, p. 151). See also Carl Snyder, *Capitalism the Creator*, New York, Macmillan, 1940, p. 203.

[172] An episode in the struggle between the Board and the Banks, still earlier than the dispute about how to deal with the stock market boom, occurred in the fall of 1927, when the Chicago Reserve Bank was unwilling to reduce its discount rate in line with the easy-money policy originated by Strong and adopted by the Board. The Board finally ordered the Chicago Bank (by a 4 to 3 vote) to reduce its rate— an unprecedented action. The "action aroused bitter controversy both within and without the System . . . . Most of the critics questioned the legality of the action; all denied the wisdom of this assertion of power in the absence of an emergency." Though Strong himself wanted a reduction in the Chicago rate, he "was quite unhappy about the Board's action and sought to prevent, or at least to delay it" (Chandler, *Benjamin Strong*, pp. 447–448). Presumably, he saw the preservation of the Banks' independence and indeed dominance in the System as more important than the specific substantive action of the moment.

Governor Crissinger's resignation may have been related to that incident. The Board met on Sept. 9 to impose the rate without being informed by Crissinger that Strong had telephoned him earlier in the day asking him to delay the meeting until Secretary of the Treasury Mellon, who had conferred with Strong in New

Strong's death left the System with no center of enterprising and acceptable leadership. The Federal Reserve Board was determined that the New York Bank should no longer play that role. But the Board itself could not play the role in an enterprising way. It was still weak and divided despite the substitution of Young for Crissinger in 1927. Moreover, most of the other Reserve Banks, as well as that in New York, were reluctant to follow the leadership of the Board, partly because of the Board's personnel, partly because they still thought of it as primarily a supervisory and review body. Thus it was easy for the System to slide into indecision and deadlock.[173]

The Banks outside New York, seeking a larger share in the determination of open market policy, obtained the diffusion of power through the broadening of the membership of the Open Market Investment Committee in March 1930 to include the governors of all the Banks. Open market operations now depended upon a majority of twelve rather than of five governors and the twelve "came instructed by their directors" rather than ready to follow the leadership of New York as the five had been when Strong was governor.

The shift in the locus of power, which almost surely would not have occurred when it did if Strong had lived, had important and far-reaching consequences. Harrison, Strong's successor at New York, was a lawyer who had acted as counsel to the Federal Reserve Board from 1914 to 1920 before coming to the New York Bank as one of Strong's deputies. In 1929 and 1930, he operated in the aura of Strong's legacy and sought to exercise comparable leadership. As time went on, however, he reverted to his natural character, that of an extremely competent lawyer and excellent administrator, who wanted to see all sides of an issue and placed great value on conciliating opposing points of view and achieving harmony. He was persuasive yet too reasonable to be truly single minded and dominant. Nevertheless, if the composition of the Open Market Committee had not been changed, his policies might have prevailed in June 1930—though that change probably was partly a reaction to New York's independent actions to meet the stock market crash. As it was, he had neither the standing in the System nor the prestige outside the System nor the personal force to get his policy views accepted in the face of active opposition or even plain inertia. His proposals were repeatedly voted down by the other Bank governors. When they finally agreed to a large open market operation in the spring of 1932, they were halfhearted and only

---

York, upon his return from a trip abroad, would arrive in Washington the next day. Presumably Mellon would have tried to dissuade the Board from taking action, and in any case would have tied the vote (Hamlin, Diary, Vol. 14, Sept. 15, 1927, p. 38). Crissinger resigned Sept. 15.

[173] *Benjamin Strong*, p. 465. Hamlin, who resented the dominance of the New York Bank (see his Diary, Vol. 19, Aug. 10, 1931, p. 126), nevertheless wrote of Strong, "He was a genius—a Hamilton among bankers. His place will be almost impossible to fill" (Diary, Vol. 16, Oct. 18, 1928, p. 60).

too eager to discontinue it. On January 20, 1933, Harrison told Hamlin that a majority of the governors really favored a complete reversal of open market policy by letting government securities run off.[174]

We commented earlier on the difference in the level of understanding and sophistication about monetary matters displayed by New York and the other Reserve Banks. The difference is understandable in view of the circumstances in which the several Banks operated and of their responsibilities. New York was the active financial center of the country. The securities market in general and the government securities market in particular were concentrated there. So also were international financial transactions. New York was the only U.S. money market that was also a world market. Despite the attempt of the Federal Reserve Act to reduce the dominance of New York in the banking structure, the demands of banks in the rest of the country for funds continued to be channeled through the other Reserve Bank cities into New York, and banks in the rest of the country continued to maintain correspondent relations with New York banks, especially after the stock market boom got under way. The New York Federal Reserve Bank was therefore acutely sensitive to the state of the financial markets and to the liquidity pressure not only on banks there but also on their correspondent banks throughout the country. Among Reserve Banks, the New York Bank alone was effectively national in scope and accustomed to regard itself as shaping, not merely reacting to, conditions in the credit market. The other Banks were much more parochial in both situation and outlook, more in the position of reacting to financial currents originating elsewhere, more concerned with their immediate regional problems, and hence more likely to believe that the Reserve System must adjust to other forces than that it could and should take the lead. They had no background of leadership and of national responsibility. Moreover, they tended to be jealous of New York and predisposed to question what New York proposed.

The form which the shift of power took—from New York as dominant head of a five-man committee to New York as the head of an executive committee administering policies adopted by the twelve governors—also had an important effect. A committee of twelve men, each regarding himself as an equal of all the others and each the chief administrator of an institution established to strengthen regional independence, could much more easily agree on a policy of drift and inaction than on a coordinated policy involving the public assumption of responsibility for decisive and large-scale action.[175] There is more than a little element of truth in the jocular description of a committee as a group of people, no one of whom knows what should be done, who jointly decide that

---

[174] Diary, Vol. 22, p. 61.
[175] Compare statements by Harrison in footnotes 89 and 114 above.

nothing can be done. And this is especially likely to be true of a group like the Open Market Policy Conference, consisting of independent persons from widely separated cities, who share none of that common outlook on detailed problems or responsibilities which evolves in the course of long-time daily collaboration. Such a committee is likely to be able to take decisive action only if it happens to include a man who is deferred to by all the rest and is accustomed to dominate. Strong might have played such a role. Harrison could not.

The shift of power from New York to the other Banks might not have been decisive, if there had been sufficiently vigorous and informed intellectual leadership in the Board to have joined with Harrison in overcoming the resistance of some of the other Banks. However, no tradition of leadership existed within the Board. It had not played a key role in determining the policy of the System throughout the twenties. Instead, it had been primarily a supervisory and review body.[176] It had its way in early 1929 about the use of "direct pressure" instead of quantitative measures in dealing with speculation, because it had a veto power over discount rate changes, not because it was able to win the Banks to its views.

There was no individual Board member with Strong's stature in the financial community or in the Reserve System, or with comparable experience, personal force, or demonstrated courage. Roy Young, governor of the Reserve Board until September 1, 1930, was apparently an able administrator, and Strong supported his appointment. However, he took a leading role in the conflict between the Bank and the Board and strongly opposed open market operations in government securities. He left the Board to become governor of the Reserve Bank of Boston, a position which enabled him to continue to exert his influence against the policy favored by New York—and perhaps not less effectively than before. Young was succeeded by Eugene Meyer, who had left his Wall Street brokerage firm in 1917 to serve with a war agency, became head of the War Finance Corporation, and then served with a number of government agencies, including the Federal Farm Loan Board, before coming to the Reserve Board in 1930. Meyer was appointed just after Harrison had failed in his

---

[176] The salary structure in the System at that time is some indication of the relative position of the Banks and the Board and of their ability to attract able people. Board members received $12,000 a year until 1935. Though equal to the salary of cabinet members, those salaries were drastically lower than those of Bank governors (later presidents). Strong at New York received $50,000 a year from 1919 until his death, and Harrison the same. The salaries of other Bank governors ranged from a low of $20,000 (six southern and western Banks) to $35,000 (Chicago) during the twenties. The relative differentials were only slightly narrower in 1960: Board members, $20,000 (the chairman $500 more); the highest paid Bank president, $60,000 (New York); the lowest, $35,000 (all other Banks except Chicago and San Francisco).

attempt to persuade the other governors to engage in open market purchases and just before the onset of the first liquidity crisis—on both grounds a difficult time to get the System to change course sharply. Perhaps, if he had had more time to develop his leadership of the System, he might have been able to lead the System along a different route.[177] In the initial months at his post, he was in favor of expansionary measures and, through most of 1931, he tried unsuccessfully to persuade the Conference to approve larger open market purchases. During his six months as chairman of the RFC, February–July 1932, members of the Board felt he slighted his duties as governor. None of the other full-time members of the Board or staff had the personal qualities and the standing within the System to exercise the required leadership.[178]

[177] During Meyer's term of office, two committees of the Reserve System (including officials of several Reserve Banks), appointed to study problems of branch, chain, and group banking, and of reserves, submitted reports but no action was taken on their recommendations (see Report of the Federal Reserve Committee on Branch, Group, and Chain Banking, mimeographed, 1932; and "Member Bank Reserves—Report of the Committee on Bank Reserves of the Federal Reserve System," Federal Reserve Board, *Annual Report* for 1932, pp. 260–285). Meyer recommended to the Senate Committee on Banking and Currency a unified commercial banking system for the United States to be implemented by limiting banking privileges to institutions with national charters. He obtained the opinion of the Board's general counsel in support of the constitutionality of such legislation (*ibid.*, pp. 229–259), but no further steps were taken.

[178] Harrison opposed Meyer's acceptance of the chairmanship of the RFC (Notes, Vol. II, Jan. 21, 1932).

The remaining members of the Board from 1929 to 1933 consisted of Edmund Platt (who served as vice-governor until he left the Board on Sept. 15, 1930), Adolph Miller, Charles S. Hamlin, George R. James, Edward Cunningham (until Nov. 28, 1930), and Wayland W. Magee (after May 5, 1931). Platt had studied law, had been a newspaper editor, then a member of Congress (where he served on the Banking and Currency Committee) before he was appointed to the Board in 1920. Miller and Hamlin were members of the original Board appointed in 1914. Miller, an economist of considerable scholarly ability, had written some good articles on monetary matters. But he, and Hamlin as well, had already demonstrated just after World War I an incapacity to exert leadership and to take an independent course. In Chandler's words, Miller, "undoubtedly the most able of the appointed members of the Board, was the eternal consultant and critic, never the imaginative and bold enterpriser" (*Benjamin Strong*, p. 257, and also pp. 44–45). If any credence can be put in Hamlin's repeated comments on Miller, this is a generous evaluation. Hamlin's Diary makes Miller out to be a self-centered person, with little hesitancy in using his public position for personal advantage, and capable of shifting position on important issues for trivial reasons (see Vol. 4, Aug. 6, 1918, pp. 180–181; Vol. 6, May 6, 1921, p. 90; Vol. 14, Jan. 6, June 9, 1928, pp. 105, 106, 180; Vol. 16, Oct. 30, 1929, p. 194).

Hamlin was a lawyer, described by Chandler as "intelligent, . . . but . . . as one of his associates put it, 'an amanuensis sort of fellow unlikely to undertake anything on his own'" (*Benjamin Strong*, pp. 256–257). His Diary confirms this view. He was shrewd, particularly about political issues and details of administration, public spirited in a self-righteous way, dependable and honest, if inclined to be partisan, and, fortunately for our purposes, an inveterate and, so far as we can judge, an accurate gossip. But the Diary shows exceedingly limited under-

417

The detailed story of every banking crisis in our history shows how much depends on the presence of one or more outstanding individuals willing to assume responsibility and leadership.[179] It was a defect of the financial system that it was susceptible to crises resolvable only with such leadership. The existence of such a financial system is, of course, the ultimate explanation for the financial collapse, rather than the shift of power from New York to the other Federal Reserve Banks and the weakness of the Reserve Board, since it permitted those circumstances to have such far-reaching consequences. Nonetheless, given the financial system that existed, the shift of power and the weakness of the Board greatly reduced the likelihood that the immediate decisive action would be taken, which was required to nip the liquidity crisis in the bud.

In the absence of vigorous intellectual leadership by the Board or of a consensus on the correct policy in the community at large or of Reserve Bank governors willing and able to assume responsibility for an independent course, the tendencies of drift and indecision had full scope. Moreover, as time went on, their force cumulated. Each failure to act made another such failure more likely. Men are far readier to plead—to themselves as to others—lack of power than lack of judgment as an explanation for failure. We have already seen this tendency expressed in the

standing of the broader issues of monetary policy and no sign of venturesomeness in thought or action. James was a small merchant and manufacturer from Tennessee and, for a few years, had been president of a commercial bank; Cunningham, a farmer; Magee, also a farmer and rancher, who had been a member of the board of the Omaha branch of the Reserve Bank of Kansas City and then a director of the Bank of Kansas City (see Chandler's comments, *Benjamin Strong*, pp. 256–257).

Of the staff, E. A. Goldenweiser, director of research and statistics from 1926 to 1945, was perhaps the most influential, but he was primarily a technician. His predecessor, Walter W. Stewart, had been close to Strong, had influenced him greatly, and continued their relationship after leaving the Board in 1926. Goldenweiser was a gentle person who could not match Stewart's influence on policy.

The ex officio members of the Reserve Board were the Comptroller of the Currency, and the Secretary of the Treasury, who served as chairman—from 1921 to February 1932, Andrew W. Mellon, a well-known financier and industrialist at the time of his appoinment; thereafter, until March 1933, Ogden L. Mills. Mills, a lawyer, tax expert, and Congressman, before becoming Under Secretary of the Treasury in 1927, was an able and forceful man. As mentioned above, he gave active support to the Glass-Steagall bill because he saw lack of free gold limiting Federal Reserve action. Mills apparently contributed the chief ideas embodied in the Emergency Banking Act of Mar. 9, 1933 (see Chapter 8).

J. W. Pole, formerly chief U.S. national bank examiner, and Comptroller of the Currency from 1928 to September 1932, advocated as a bank reform measure branch banking limited to "trade areas" or regions around important cities. But he had no influence of record on bank legislation or Federal Reserve policy during that period (see Comptroller of the Currency, *Annual Report*, 1929, p. 5; 1930, p. 5; 1931, p. 1). Hamlin referred to him as "on the whole, a good but not very strong man" (Diary, Vol. 21, Sept. 1, 1932, pp. 105–106).

[179] See Sprague, *History of Crises, passim.*

Federal Reserve System's reaction to the criticism of its policies during 1919–21. It was expressed again in 1930–33 as the Board explained economic decline and then banking failures as occurring despite its own actions and as the product of forces over which it had no control. And no doubt the Board persuaded itself as well as others that its reasoning was true. Hence, as events proceeded, it was increasingly inclined to look elsewhere for the solution, at first to hope that matters would right themselves, then increasingly to accept the view that crisis and doom were the inescapable product of forces in the private business community that were developing beyond the System's control. Having failed to act vigorously to stem the first liquidity crisis in the fall of 1930, the System was even less likely to act the next time. It was only great pressure from Congressional critics that induced the System to reverse itself temporarily in early 1932 by undertaking the large-scale securities purchases it should have made much earlier. When the operation failed to bring immediate dramatic improvement, the System promptly relapsed into its earlier passivity.

The foregoing explanation of the financial collapse as resulting so largely from the shift of power from New York to the other Federal Reserve Banks and from personal backgrounds and characteristics of the men nominally in power may seem farfetched. It is a sound general principle that great events have great origins, and hence that something more than the characteristics of the specific persons or official agencies that happened to be in power is required to explain such a major event as the financial catastrophe in the United States from 1929 to 1933.

Yet it is also true that small events at times have large consequences, that there are such things as chain reactions and cumulative forces. It happens that a liquidity crisis in a unit fractional reserve banking system is precisely the kind of event that can trigger—and often has triggered—a chain reaction. And economic collapse often has the character of a cumulative process. Let it go beyond a certain point, and it will tend for a time to gain strength from its own development as its effects spread and return to intensify the process of collapse. Because no great strength would be required to hold back the rock that starts a landslide, it does not follow that the landslide will not be of major proportions.

419

CHAPTER 8

New Deal Changes in the Banking Structure and Monetary Standard

THE New Deal period offers a striking contrast in monetary and banking matters. On the one hand, monetary policy was accorded little importance in affecting the course of economic affairs and the policy actually followed was hesitant and almost entirely passive. On the other hand, the foundations of the American financial structure and the character of the monetary standard were profoundly modified. Both developments were direct outgrowths of the dramatic experiences of the preceding years. The apparent failure of monetary policy to stem the depression led to the relegation of money to a minor role in affecting the course of economic events. At the same time, the collapse of the banking system produced a demand for remedial legislation that led to the enactment of federal deposit insurance, to changes in the powers of the Federal Reserve System, and to closer regulation of banks and other financial institutions. The depressed state of the economy, the large preceding fall in prices and, despite those conditions, the poor competitive position of our exports thanks to the depreciation of the pound and other currencies, all combined with the New Deal atmosphere to foster experimentation with the monetary standard. The experiments involved temporary departure from gold, a period of flexible and depreciating exchange rates, silver purchases, subsequent nominal return to gold at a higher price for gold, and drastic changes in the terms and conditions under which gold could be held and obtained by private parties.

This chapter describes the changes that were made in the banking structure (section 1) and in the monetary standard (section 2). The next chapter discusses the monetary policies followed during the New Deal period.

1. *Changes in the Banking Structure*

Three kinds of legislative measures were enacted after the 1933 banking panic: emergency measures designed to reopen closed banks and to strengthen banks permitted to open; measures that effected a more lasting alteration in the commercial banking structure—the most important being federal deposit insurance—and, more generally, in the financial structure; measures that altered the structure and powers of the Federal Reserve System. In addition, the banking system was affected in important

420

ways by the reaction of the banks themselves, independently of legislation, to their experiences during the prior contraction.

EMERGENCY MEASURES

We have already had occasion to refer to the Emergency Banking Act of March 9, 1933. Title I of the act approved and confirmed the action taken by President Roosevelt in proclaiming a nationwide bank holiday from March 6 to March 9, inclusive, under the wartime measure of October 6, 1917, which conferred broad powers over banking and currency upon the President of the United States.[1] Title I, further, amended the wartime measure to empower the President in time of national emergency to regulate or prohibit the payment of deposits by all banking institutions. During the period of emergency proclaimed by the President, member banks were forbidden to transact any banking business unless authorized by the Secretary of the Treasury with the approval of the President.

Title II of the act provided for the reopening and operation on a restricted basis of certain national banks with impaired assets, which under existing laws would have been placed in receivership and liquidated. Conservators were to be appointed for those banks by the Comptroller of the Currency. The Comptroller could direct the conservators to make available for immediate withdrawal amounts of existing deposits he deemed it safe to release; and the conservators, subject to his approval, could receive new deposits, available for immediate withdrawal without restriction and segregated from other liabilities of the bank. The conservators were also to be charged with the duty of preparing plans of reorganization, subject to the Comptroller's approval, which could be put into effect with the consent of 75 per cent of a bank's depositors and other creditors or of two-thirds of the stockholders.

Title III provided for issues of nonassessable preferred stock by national banks to be sold to the general public, or the Reconstruction Finance Corporation (RFC), which might also buy similar issues from state banks.

Title IV provided for emergency issues of Federal Reserve Bank notes up to the face value of direct obligations of the United States deposited as security, or up to 90 per cent of the estimated value of eligible paper and bankers' acceptances acquired under the provisions of the Emergency Banking Act. After the emergency recognized by the Presidential proclamation of March 6, 1933, had terminated, Federal Reserve Bank notes could be issued only on the security of direct obligations of the United States. Over $200 million of Federal Reserve Bank notes were issued

---

[1] By a proclamation issued on Dec. 30, 1933, the President relinquished jurisdiction over nonmember banks assumed by the federal government at the time of his proclamation of a banking holiday.

in 1933. Thereafter until the war, they were retired as fast as returned from circulation. The liability for those notes was assumed by the Treasury in March 1935.

Under Title IV, Federal Reserve Banks were also authorized, until March 3, 1934, to make advances in exceptional and exigent circumstances to member banks on their own notes on the security of any acceptable assets. That provision superseded the one regarding advances to member banks in the Glass-Steagall Act (see Chapter 7, footnote 26). The provision was extended by Presidential proclamation until March 3, 1935, when it expired. The provision adopted in the Banking Act of 1935 omitted the requirement that advances be made only in exceptional and exigent circumstances and to member banks whose other means of obtaining accommodation from Federal Reserve Banks were exhausted (see below, pp. 447–448).

Opening of Banks

Under the authority of the Emergency Banking Act, President Roosevelt issued a proclamation on March 9 continuing the banking holiday, and an executive order on March 10 empowering the Secretary of the Treasury to issue licenses to member banks to reopen. Every member bank was directed to make application for a license to the Federal Reserve Bank of its district, which would serve as an agent of the Secretary in granting licenses. The executive order also empowered state banking authorities to reopen their sound banks that were not members of the Federal Reserve System. Another executive order dated March 18 granted state banking authorities permission to appoint conservators for unlicensed state member banks when consistent with state law.

In a statement to the press on March 11 and a radio address on March 12, the President announced the program for reopening licensed banks on March 13, 14, and 15. Member banks licensed by the Secretary of the Treasury as well as nonmember banks licensed by state banking authorities "opened for normal business on an unrestricted basis, except so far as affected by legal contracts between the banks and depositors with respect to withdrawals or notice of withdrawals"[2] on March 13, in the twelve Federal Reserve Bank cities; on March 14, in some 250 cities having active, recognized clearing house associations; and on March 15, elsewhere.

Effect on Number and Deposits of Banks

At the turn of the year, two months before the banking holiday, there had been nearly 17,800 commercial banks in operation, by the definition of banks then in use (Table 13). When the banking holiday was ter-

[2] Statement by the Secretary of the Treasury to the superintendent of banks of each state, Mar. 11, 1933, *Federal Reserve Bulletin*, Mar. 1933, p. 128.

TABLE 13

NUMBER AND DEPOSITS OF COMMERCIAL BANKS BEFORE
AND AFTER BANKING HOLIDAY

		Deposits (billions of dollars)		
Definition of Banks and Class of Banks	Number (1)	Adjusted Demand Plus Time, Seasonally Adjusted (2)	Total Demand Plus Time, Unadjusted for Seasonal (3)	Ratio (3) ÷ (2) (4)
As defined in:		DEC. 31, 1932		
All-Bank Statistics				
1. Active commercial banks	18,074	29.2	36.1	1.24
2. Not classified as banks by 1932 definition	278	1.0		
Federal Reserve Bulletin, 1932				
3. Active commercial banks	17,796	28.2		
		MAR. 15, 1933		
4. Suspended, merged, or liquidated between Dec. 31, 1932, and Mar. 15, 1933	447		0.2	
5. Total commercial banks (line 3 minus line 4)	17,349			
6. Licensed	11,878	23.3	27.4	1.18
7. Unlicensed	5,430	3.4	4.0	
8. Licensed plus unlicensed (line 6 plus line 7)	17,308	26.7	31.4	
9. Discrepancy (line 5 minus line 8)	41			

NOTE: Where reported figures are not available, estimates are shown only for items useful in deriving line 8, as described in source notes.

SOURCE, BY LINE

1. Col. 1: Interpolation between June 1932 and June 1933 figures, shown in *All-Bank Statistics*, p. 37; the interpolation was based on June and Dec. 1932 and June 1933 figures on number of banks in *Banking and Monetary Statistics*, p. 19. The difference between the latter and former series at June dates was interpolated along a straight line and added to the Dec. figure in *ibid*.

   Col. 2: Table A-1.

   Col. 3: Interpolation between June 1932 and June 1933 figures, shown in *All-Bank Statistics*, p. 36; the interpolation was based on June and Dec. 1932 and June 1933 figures on deposits of banks in *Banking and Monetary Statistics*, p. 19. The ratio of the Dec. figure to its own inter-June straight-line trend value was multiplied by the straight-line trend value computed at the end of Dec. between the June figures in *All-Bank Statistics*.

2. Col. 1: Line 1 minus line 3.

   Col. 2: The excess of demand deposits adjusted plus time deposits for June dates, 1932–33, in *All-Bank Statistics* (pp. 60 and 36), over the corresponding sums in *Banking and Monetary Statistics* (p. 34) was obtained; an estimate of the excess was interpolated for Dec. along a straight line. An estimate was then added for deposits

(continued)

NOTES to TABLE 13 (continued)

in commercial banks included in the *Banking and Monetary Statistics* series but not included in the *Federal Reserve Bulletin* (*FRB*) series for 1932 (referred to in the table as defined in *FRB*, 1932,). *FRB* in 1932 did not show adjusted deposits, so only a comparison of total deposits excluding interbank deposits in this source (Dec. 1933, p. 746) and in *Banking and Monetary Statistics* (p. 19) is possible. A rough conversion to adjusted deposits was made of excess of total deposits in *ibid.* over the *FRB* figure, and added to the excess of adjusted deposits in *All-Bank Statistics* over the series in *Banking and Monetary Statistics*.

3. Col. 1: *FRB*, Dec. 1933, p. 746.
    Col. 2: Line 1 minus line 2.

4. Cols. 1, 3: *FRB*, Sept. 1937, p. 867.

6. Col. 1: Sum of figures for licensed member banks on Mar. 15, 1933 (*FRB*, June 1935, p. 404), and for licensed nonmember banks on Mar. 22, 1933 (*Annual Report of the Secretary of the Treasury*, 1933, p. 24).
    Col. 2: Figure for end of Mar. from Table A-1: (a) adjusted to Mar. 15, by multiplying by ratio of total deposits of licensed member banks on Mar. 15 to corresponding figure for Mar. 29 (25,554/25,850, *FRB*, June 1935, p. 404 and Apr. 1933, p. 216); and (b) adjusted to 1932 definition of banks by subtracting line 2, col. 2, reduced 10 per cent for assumed change in deposits, Dec. 31, 1932–Mar. 15, 1933.
    Col. 3: Sum of figures for licensed member banks on Mar. 15, 1933 (*FRB*, June 1935, p. 404), for licensed nonmember banks on Apr. 12, 1933 (*FRB*), minus an estimate of the deposits in nonmember banks that were licensed between Mar. 15 and Apr. 12. The figures are deposits as of Dec. 31, 1932, scaled down 10 per cent for assumed change in deposits, Dec. 31, 1932–Mar. 15, 1933.

7. Cols. 1, 3: Derived as the sum of:

	Number	Deposits ($ millions)
(a) Unlicensed member banks on Mar. 15, 1933 (*Federal Reserve Bulletin*)	1,621	2,867
(b) Unlicensed nonmember banks on Apr. 12, 1933 (*FRB*)	2,959	1,321
(c) Fall in unlicensed nonmember banks, Mar. 15–Apr. 12, 1933	850	325
	5,430	4,513

For item c, the changes, Mar. 15–Apr. 12, 1933, were estimated as follows:

	Number
(1) Licensed nonmember banks, Mar. 22 (*Annual Report*, Treasury, 1933, p. 24)	6,800
(2) Licensed nonmember banks, Apr. 12 (*FRB*, June 1935, p. 404)	7,392
(3) Liquidations of licensed and unlicensed nonmember banks, Mar. 16–Apr. 30 (*FRB*, Apr. 1934, p. 251)	258
Change in number, (2) + (3) − (1)	850

We had no information on deposits corresponding to numbers shown above. We arbitrarily assumed that the change in deposits in licensed nonmember banks, Mar. 22–Apr. 12, 1933, on a per-bank basis, approximated the change in deposits of licensed member banks, on a per-bank basis, Mar. 15–Apr. 12, 1933. The ratio for member banks between those two dates was 105.0. We used 104.0 for nonmember banks, multiplied average deposits on Apr. 12 by this ratio to get the

(continued)

average on Mar. 22, and multiplied again by the number of licensed nonmember banks to get estimated deposits in licensed nonmember banks on Mar. 22.

		Deposits ($ millions)
(1)	Licensed nonmember banks, Mar. 22 (as above)	4,803
(2)	Licensed nonmember banks, Apr. 12 (*FRB*, June 1935, p. 404)	5,020
(3)	Liquidations of licensed and unlicensed nonmember banks, Mar. 16–Apr. 30 (*FRB*, Apr. 1934, p. 251)	108
	Change in deposits, (2) + (3) − (1)	325

The figure for number of banks needed no further adjustment. That for deposits needed to be reduced $161 million to correct for overstatement of deposits in nonmember banks; and by $321 million, for overstatement of deposits in member banks. The deposits of nonmember banks on Apr. 12, 1933, and of member banks on Mar. 15, 1933, are the deposits those banks had on Dec. 31, 1932. We have a measure of the overstatement for nonmember banks on June 30, 1933: data on number of and deposits in unlicensed member and nonmember banks in *Federal Reserve Bulletin*, June 1935, p. 404, where member bank deposits are the deposits those banks held on June 30, 1933, and nonmember bank deposits are the deposits those banks held on Dec. 31, 1932. These figures may be compared with the data in *All-Bank Statistics*, p. 72 (6 mutual savings banks with estimated $7 million in deposits have been deducted to obtain all commercial bank figures), which presumably show actual June 30, 1933, nonmember as well as member bank figures. The Dec. 1932 data for nonmember banks overstate deposits on June 30, 1933, by 12.2 per cent. Applying this percentage to line b, above, yields $161 million.

The measure of the overstatement for member banks is also based on an end-of-June 1933 comparison. For June 28, 1933, deposits in unlicensed member banks are the deposits those banks had on Dec. 31, 1932 (*FRB*, July 1933, p. 453). For June 30, 1933, we have actual deposits in those banks on this date (*FRB*, June 1935, p. 404). There is an 11.2 percentage difference between the two sets of figures. Applying this percentage to line a, above, yields $321 million.

7. Col. 2: Entry for unlicensed in col. 3 divided by ratio, line 6, col. 4.
9. Col. 1: Line 3 minus the sum of lines 4 and 8. Any of the components, lines 4, 6, and 7, may contribute to the discrepancy of 41 banks, based on the total shown in line 3. (In *Banking and Monetary Statistics*, p. 19, the total figure is 17,802, presumably because of the addition of certain private banks that did not report to state banking authorities and of institutions earlier not classified as commercial banks.) Line 4, for example, gives revised figures. Earlier sources showed the number of suspended banks, Jan. 1–Mar. 15, 1933, as 462 (see *Federal Reserve Bulletin*, Apr. 1934, p. 251). If 15 banks were excluded from the number of suspensions by the later source because they were reopened by June 30, 1933 (banks not licensed after the holiday were not considered suspensions if reopened by that date), our total of active banks in Dec. 1932 derived from lines 4, 6, and 7 would be too small by that number. Both lines 6 and 7 are partly estimated. The use of Mar. 22 figures for licensed nonmembers may slightly exaggerate the total for all banks in line 6. The figure for unlicensed nonmember banks included in line 7 was obtained indirectly and may well be too small not only by the discrepancy of 41 but also by a larger number, if line 6 is an overstatement.

minated, only 17,300 remained to be recorded in the statistics, and fewer than 12,000 of those were licensed to open and do business. The more than 5,000 unlicensed banks were left in a state of limbo, to be either reopened later—the fate of some 3,000—or to be closed for good and either liquidated or consolidated with other banks—the fate of over 2,000

TABLE 14

DISPOSITION BY DECEMBER 31, 1936, OF COMMERCIAL BANKS NOT LICENSED TO OPEN AT
TERMINATION OF BANKING HOLIDAY, MARCH 15, 1933
(deposits in millions of dollars)

Date	Number Still Unlicensed (1)	Change in Number of Banks			Deposits in Banks Still Unlicensed[a] (5)	Change in Deposits in Banks		
		Total (2)	Licensed to Reopen (3)	Suspended, Liquidated, or Merged (4)		Total (6)	Licensed to Reopen (7)	Suspended Liquidated or Merged (8)
1933								
Mar. 15	5,430				4,031			
June 30	3,078	2,352	1,964	388	2,200	1,831	642	1,189
Dec. 30	1,769	1,309	576	733	1.025	1,175	496	679
1934								
June 30[b]	622	1,147	477	670	346	679	225	454
Dec. 26	190	432	174	258	96	250	79	171
1936								
Dec. 31	0	190	107	83	0	96	67	29
Total Mar. 15, 1933, to Dec. 31, 1936		5,430	3,298	2,132		4,031	1,509	2,522

[a] Deposits are unadjusted for interbank deposits, float, or seasonal.
[b] For nonmember banks, June 27, 1934.

SOURCE, BY COLUMN

(1, 5) Sums of data for member and nonmember banks.
Mar. 15, 1933: Unrounded figures from notes to Table 13, line 7, col. 1.
June 30, 1933: *All-Bank Statistics*, p. 72 (6 mutual savings banks with estimated $7 million in deposits deducted to obtain all unlicensed commercial bank figures). Other dates: *Federal Reserve Bulletin*, Jan. 1935, p. 62. Zero is shown for Dec. 31, 1936, although there were still 10 unlicensed banks with $1,748,000 deposits, neither granted licenses to reopen nor placed in liquidation or receivership on this date (*FRB*, Sept. 1937, p. 867). These banks are treated here as if they were in receivership by this date.

(2) Change in col. 1.

(3) Col. 2 minus col. 4.

(4, 8) *Annual Report* of the Comptroller of the Currency, 1934, pp. 785–790; 1935, pp. 807–808. Figure for Dec. 31, 1936, is a residual obtained by subtracting sum of data through Dec. 30, 1934, from total for period through Dec. 31, 1936, in *FRB*, Sept. 1937, p. 867.

(6) Change in col. 5.

(7) Col. 6 minus col. 8. Deposits in banks granted licenses, July 1, 1933, to Dec. 31, 1936 (*FRB*), amounted to $716 million compared with total of $867 million shown here.

(Table 14). The changes in deposits were only slightly less drastic. From December 1932 to March 15, 1933, deposits in banks open for business fell by one-sixth. Seventy per cent of the decline was accounted for by the deposits on the books of banks not licensed to open, yet not finally disposed of (Table 13, lines 3–7, col. 2).

The banks licensed to open operated generally without restrictions, though in some cases legal contracts were in effect limiting withdrawals by depositors to a specified fraction of the amounts due them.[3] Many of the unlicensed banks, in their turn, were open for a limited range of business, with conservators authorized to receive new deposits subject to the order of the depositor and segregated from other funds. The line between licensed and unlicensed banks was therefore less sharp in practice than in the records.

Fate of Unlicensed Banks

Table 14 shows what happened to the unlicensed banks over the next several years. By the end of June 1933 over 2,300 of the banks, holding nearly half the total restricted deposits, had been disposed of—nearly 2,000 banks were licensed to reopen, 388 closed. However, the closed banks had decidedly the larger volume of deposits, and this was to remain true for the rest of the period as well, so that the three-fifths of the banks ultimately reopened held only three-eighths of the deposits.

The RFC played a major role in the restoration of the banking system as it had in the futile attempts to shore it up before the banking holiday. It invested a total of over $1 billion in bank capital—one-third of the total capital of all banks in the United States in 1933—and purchased capital issues of 6,139 banks, or almost one-half the number of banks.[4] In addition, it made loans to open banks for distribution to de-

---

[3] "Deposits in licensed banks the payment of which has been deferred beyond the time originally contemplated" amounted to $103 million in June 1933, $55 million in June 1934, and were apparently zero in June 1935 (sums of national and nonnational bank data from Comptroller of the Currency, *Annual Report,* 1933, pp. 420, 629; 1934, pp. 523, 755).

[4] The RFC was authorized to buy preferred stock and capital notes and debentures of banks by the Emergency Banking Act and an amendment to it. Most of the banks in which it invested were those originally permitted to resume operations only on a limited withdrawal basis (Jesse H. Jones [with Edward Angly], *Fifty Billion Dollars,* New York, Macmillan, 1951, p. 21). To avoid the suggestion that RFC investment signified a bank's weakness, some stronger banks which did not actually need new capital were asked to sell the Corporation a modest amount of preferred stock or capital notes. According to Jones, fewer than twenty of the more than six thousand banks into which the RFC put capital actually had no need of it (p. 34). The capital was invested on the understanding that it would be retired out of about one-half the net earnings of the banks after payment of dividends or interest on RFC capital. RFC investment permitted the banks to charge off losses. Approximately 51 per cent of its investment had been retired by February 1939 (Reconstruction Finance Corporation, *Seven-Year Report to the*

positors of $187 million and to closed banks of over $900 million, on the security of the best assets of those institutions. The loans, made after the banking panic, were in addition to loans of $951 million to open banks and of $80 million to closed banks made before the banking panic.[5] In aggregate, 5,816 open banks and 2,773 closed banks obtained RFC loans totaling more than $2 billion. RFC and other federal authorities doubtless also played a role in fostering bank mergers, particularly purchase by larger banks of smaller banks with doubtful portfolios, that served further to reduce the number of individual banks and, hopefully, to strengthen their solvency.

Effects on Money Stock Measures

The banking holiday and its aftermath make our recorded figures on the money stock even less reliable than for other times as indicators of some consistent economic magnitude meriting the label money. Before the banking holiday, many banks had imposed restrictions on the use of deposits in an attempt to avoid suspension. Those deposits are counted in full in the recorded money stock. On the other hand, after the holiday, both restricted and unrestricted deposits in unlicensed banks are excluded completely from the recorded money stock.[6] The shift in treatment, which can hardly correspond to a shift in economic significance, is the major factor behind the sharp decline in the recorded figures in March 1933. Consistent accounting would require exclusion of restricted deposits throughout or their inclusion throughout. Criteria of economic significance would call for including in the money stock a fraction of restricted deposits, the fraction fluctuating over time. Any one of these courses would eliminate the discontinuous drop in our series in March 1933 and yield a milder decline before March and a milder rise thereafter.

Unfortunately, there is no adequate statistical basis for estimating

President and the Congress of the U.S., February 2, 1932, to February 1, 1939, p. 5).

[5] RFC, Seven-Year Report, pp. 4, 6, for total loans. For RFC loans from Feb. 2, 1932, to Mar. 3, 1933, see RFC, Summaries of the Activities of the RFC and Its Condition as of December 31, 1935, GPO, Jan. 1936, p. 14. Loans for distribution to depositors in closed banks were relatively small before the banking holiday because the original RFC Act limited their aggregate amount to $200 million. An amendment June 14, 1933, removed the limit. Loans to going banks were relatively small after the banking holiday because they were superseded by RFC capital purchases.

[6] The restricted deposits in licensed banks referred to in footnote 3 above are included in Table A-1. Figures on unrestricted deposits in unlicensed banks are available only for national banks at call dates June 1933–Dec. 1934 (Comptroller of the Currency, Annual Report, 1933, p. 649; 1934, p. 776; 1935, p. 806). The largest amount of unrestricted deposits recorded was $77 million in June 1933, 8 per cent of frozen deposits. The absolute amount declined along with frozen deposits in unlicensed banks, the ratio of the first to the second remaining in the neighborhood of a tenth.

restricted deposits before March 1933;[7] hence they cannot easily be excluded. Table 15 and Chart 34 therefore bridge the discontinuity at that month by *including* restricted deposits throughout to derive an alternative estimate of the stock of money similar in construction before and after the holiday. This alternative estimate is compared with the estimate in our basic tables.

Neither of these two estimates is economically ideal. The alternative estimate may be viewed as setting an upper limit to the "ideal" estimate of the money stock, and our money stock figures in Table A-1 as setting a lower limit. We have noted that the figures in Table A-1 are not continuous from February to March 1933, since the figures for February include restricted deposits and the figures for March exclude them. That is why a dotted line is used on Chart 34 in connecting the values for February and March. The alternative estimate at the end of March, however, is also not strictly continuous with the end-of-February figure, so a dotted line again is used in connecting the two figures. At the end of March, depositors in unlicensed banks, for which neither a conservator nor a receiver had been appointed, had reason to regard deposits in such

---

[7] See *Federal Reserve Bulletin,* Dec. 1937, p. 1206, for a discussion of the extent of the restriction of withdrawals before the banking holiday.

The placing of restrictions on deposit withdrawals, a practice that had been used in 1931 in the East North Central States, became more prevalent in 1932 as a measure to cope with the steady withdrawal of funds. These restrictions on deposit withdrawals were usually imposed through 'depositors' agreements' deferring withdrawal of varying percentages of deposits over periods of time ranging up to five years, certain percentages of deposits to be released at the end of the first year and additional percentages at the end of the succeeding years. New business was conducted on an unrestricted basis. Unfortunately, comprehensive figures are not available to show the number of banks that obtained deposit deferment agreements, or the amount of deposits involved in such deferment agreements, but from what information is available it appears that the practice was followed in a number of States during 1931 and 1932.

Another type of bank moratoria that became common during this period, particularly in the East North Central States, was the reorganization of banks through the waiver or surrender of a portion of deposits by the depositors. This was accomplished in some cases through outright contributions by certain of the depositors, but usually there was a segregation of assets for the benefit of waiving depositors under a trust agreement, with a right in the bank to substitute assets during a period of time running generally from two to five years. Figures are not available at present to show the losses sustained by depositors through this type of reorganization of distressed banks. . . .

Many banks in a number of places had closed temporarily in 1932 under special 'banking holidays' declared by civil authorities. The first of a series of State-wide banking holidays was declared in Nevada at the beginning of November, 1932. Though originally for a 12-day period, it was subsequently extended. Early in 1933 more local bank holidays were declared by city authorities and many existing ones were extended, in order to permit banks to obtain deposit deferment or waiver agreements and to afford banks an opportunity to raise funds and make adjustments necessary to enable them to continue to meet their obligations.

TABLE 15

ALTERNATIVE MONEY STOCK ESTIMATES, MARCH 1933–JUNE 1935

(amounts in millions of dollars)

Date	Ratio of Total Deposits, Unlicensed to Licensed Banks (1)	Commercial Bank Deposits Adjusted (2)	Unlicensed Bank Deposits Adjusted (3)	Commercial Bank (Licensed and Unlicensed) Deposits Adjusted (4)	Currency Held by the Public (5)	Currency Plus Commercial Bank (Licensed and Unlicensed) Deposits Adjusted (6)	Recorded Money Stock (7)
1933							
Mar. 29	13.49	24,461	3,300	27,761	5,509	33,270	29,970
Apr. 12	12.84						
May 3	10.96	24,545	2,690	27,235	5,202	32,437	29,747
May 31	8.87	25,081	2,225	27,306	5,019	32,325	30,100
June 28	7.18	25,138	1,805	26,943	4,949	31,892	30,087
June 30	7.07						
Aug. 2	6.30	25,274	1,592	26,866	4,886	31,752	30,160
Aug. 30	5.71	25,342	1,447	26,789	4,850	31,639	30,192
Sept. 27	5.17	25,431	1,315	26,746	4,830	31,576	30,261
Oct. 25	4.69						
Nov. 1	4.50	25,584	1,151	26,735	4,803	31,538	30,387
Nov. 29	3.82	25,719	982	26,701	4,844	31,545	30,563
Dec. 30	3.18						
1934							
Jan. 3	3.10	25,968	805	26,773	4,839	31,612	30,807
Jan. 31	2.58	26,463	683	27,146	4,491	31,637	30,954
Feb. 28	2.15	27,101	583	27,684	4,513	32,197	31,614
Mar. 5	2.08						
Mar. 28	1.78	27,690	493	28,183	4,550	32,733	32,240
May 2	1.41	28,015	395	28,410	4,556	32,966	32,571
May 30	1.17	28,232	330	28,562	4,566	33,128	32,798
June 27	0.97	28,489	276	28,765	4,584	33,349	33,073
June 30	0.95						
July 25	0.80						

430

Date	(1)	(2)	(3)	(4)	(5)	(6)	(7)
Aug. 22	0.70						
Aug. 29	0.67	29,606	198	29,804	4,628	34,432	34,234
Sept. 26	0.57						
Oct. 3	0.53	29,470	156	29,626	4,627	34,253	34,097
Oct. 31	0.38	30,155	115	30,270	4,590	34,860	34,745
Nov. 28	0.34	30,547	104	30,651	4,631	35,282	35,178
Dec. 26	0.26						
1935							
Jan. 2	0.25	30,502	76	30,578	4,559	35,137	35,061
Jan. 30	0.20	31,414	63	31,477	4,621	36,098	36,035
Feb. 27	0.18	32,065	58	32,123	4,700	36,823	36,765
Mar. 27	0.14						
Apr. 3	0.13	32,103	42	32,145	4,714	36,859	36,817
Apr. 24	0.12						
May 1	0.12	32,669	39	32,708	4,708	37,416	37,377
May 29	0.11	32,866	36	32,902	4,715	37,617	37,581
June 30		33,341	0	33,341	4,708	38,049	38,049

SOURCE, BY COLUMN

(1) At italicized dates, data for licensed and unlicensed banks are available. Ratios for dates not in italics, corresponding to the Wed. nearest end of month in Table A-1, were interpolated on a straight line between logarithms of the ratios at italicized dates.
Data for licensed and unlicensed banks are sums for member and nonmember banks. For member banks, see *Federal Reserve Bulletin*, Apr. 1933, p. 216; and Sept. 1934–June 1935 issues. For nonmember banks: Mar. 29, 1933, estimated as in Table 13, lines 6 and 7, col. 3; Apr. 12, 1933, June 30, 1933 (licensed), and subsequent italicized dates: *FRB*, Sept. 1934–June 1935 issues; June 30, 1933 (unlicensed), *All-Bank Statistics*, p. 72.
Original figures for Mar. 29, and Apr. 12, 1933, are deposits held by the designated licensed and unlicensed banks on Dec. 31, 1932. No adjustment for shrinkage in deposits after Dec. 1932 was made, on the assumption that col. 1 would not be affected. Figures for unlicensed banks and for licensed member banks on June 30, 1933, are as of that date; original figures for licensed nonmember banks are deposits held by those banks on Dec. 31, 1932; these figures were reduced 10 per cent for comparability with data for other banks on this date. Figures for member banks on Oct. 25, 1933, are as of that date; for nonmember banks the deposits held by those banks on Dec. 31, 1932; figures for licensed nonmembers were reduced 10 per cent, for unlicensed nonmembers 12.2 per cent for comparability with member bank data. Thereafter figures were assumed to be on a current basis.

(2, 5, 7) Table A-1.
(3) Col. 1 times col. 2.
(4) Col. 2 plus col. 3.
(6) Col. 4 plus col. 5.

CHART 34

Alternative Money Stock Estimates, February 1933–June 1935

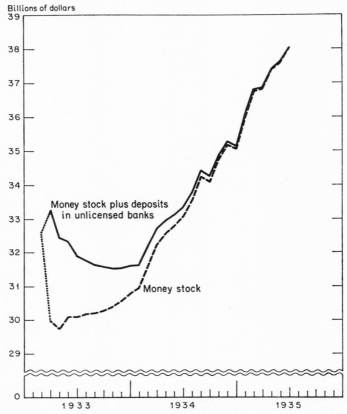

Billions of dollars

Money stock plus deposits in unlicensed banks

Money stock

SOURCE: Table 15, cols. 6 and 7, and Table A-1, col. 8.

banks as less akin to cash then they had been before the banking holiday, even though restricted then. The attempt to achieve continuity with February by including all deposits in unlicensed banks in March figures accordingly overstates the money stock even on the concept implicit in the estimates for the end of February.[8] And that concept itself overstates

[8] The figures for currency held by the public in the alternative estimate also involve an overstatement. Table A-1 treats vault cash in unlicensed banks, beginning Mar. 1933, as currency held by the public because unlicensed banks are not counted as banks. We estimate the amount of vault cash in unlicensed banks to have been about $50 million at the end of that month, and to have declined thereafter along with the reduction in deposits in unlicensed banks. Strictly, the alternative estimate of money stock including deposits in unlicensed banks should exclude from currency held by the public the vault cash in those banks.

the money stock by treating $1 of restricted deposits as strictly on a par with $1 of unrestricted deposits.

Another defect in our figures traceable to the bank holiday is their exclusion of perhaps as much as $1 billion of currency substitutes introduced in communities bereft of banking facilities before, during, and immediately after the panic.[9] To the extent currency substitutes were used because restricted deposits were unavailable to depositors, the error of their exclusion from Table A-1 before the panic is offset by the error of the inclusion of restricted deposits. To the extent they were so used after the panic, currency substitutes should be added to Table A-1, since unlicensed bank deposits are not included in that table, but not to the alternative estimates in Table 15 or Chart 34, since these include unlicensed bank deposits. To the extent currency substitutes came into use to replace deposits in failed banks and the reduction of deposits in open banks, i.e., to enable the public to raise the ratio of currency to deposits, both Table A-1 and Table 15 should include them. There seems no way now, however, of estimating the changing amounts of these currency substitutes in 1932 and 1933.

Finally, we note two minor defects in the series in Table A-1: the figures exclude unrestricted deposits in unlicensed banks; the figures for commercial bank deposits are probably too low for February 1933 and too high for March 1933.[10]

None of the several experiments we have made to take these various defects into account has been sufficiently illuminating to add much to the simple statement that an "ideal" estimate would be somewhere between the two curves in Chart 34. Almost any such intermediate curve which is plausible, in the sense that it is consistent with our qualitative knowledge of other defects and also divides the space between the two limits in proportions that do not vary erratically from month to month, implies that economic recovery in the half-year after the panic owed nothing to monetary expansion; the apparent rise in the stock of money is simply a statistical fiction. The emergency revival of the banking system contributed to recovery by restoring confidence in the monetary and economic system and thereby inducing the public to reduce money balances

[9] See Chap. 7, footnote 32.

[10] For the information available on the amount of unrestricted deposits in unlicensed banks, see footnote 6 above.

As to the second defect, the reason is that no published figures are available between the middle of Feb. and the middle of Apr. for the interpolators used to estimate nonmember bank deposits between call dates. End-of-Feb. and end-of-Mar. interpolators were obtained along a straight line between the Feb. and Apr. figures for the interpolators. This problem does not arise with the monthly member bank figures, since the gaps in this series were filled on the basis of weekly reporting member bank figures which are available throughout for Wednesdays nearest the end of the month. See our forthcoming companion volume, "Trends and Cycles in the Stock of Money in the United States, 1867–1960," a National Bureau study.

relative to income (to raise velocity) rather than by producing a growth in the stock of money.

Federal Insurance of Bank Deposits

Federal insurance of bank deposits was the most important structural change in the banking system to result from the 1933 panic, and, indeed in our view, the structural change most conducive to monetary stability since state bank note issues were taxed out of existence immediately after the Civil War. Individual states had experimented with systems of deposit insurance and numerous proposals for federal deposit insurance had been introduced into the U.S. Congress over many years. A bill providing for deposit insurance was passed by the House of Representatives in 1932 under the sponsorship of Representative Henry B Steagall, chairman of the House Banking and Currency Committee, but killed in the Senate because of intense opposition by Senator Carter Glass, an influential member of the Senate Banking and Currency Committee. Glass favored merely a liquidating corporation to advance to depositors in failed banks the estimated amount of their ultimate recovery. In 1933, Steagall and Glass agreed to combine the two proposals and incorporate them in the Banking Act of 1933. The resulting section of the act provided for a permanent deposit insurance plan with very extensive coverage to become effective July 1, 1934.[11]

It is a nice example of how institutions are developed and shaped that the actual plan which first became effective on January 1, 1934, resulted from an amendment to the Banking Act of 1933 introduced by a Senator from the minority party and at least initially opposed by President Roosevelt.[12] It was opposed also by leading bankers and by some ranking

[11] FDIC, *Annual Report,* 1950, pp. 63–67. We have also been greatly helped by a letter from Clark Warburton, which summarized the detailed origins of federal deposit insurance. See also Chap. 7, footnote 27, above.

[12] Jones (*Fifty Billion Dollars,* pp. 45–46) asserts that President Roosevelt opposed deposit insurance and requested Congress to reject the Vandenberg amendment. See also Arthur M. Schlesinger, Jr., *The Coming of the New Deal,* Boston, Houghton Mifflin, 1959, p. 443; B. N. Timmons, *Jesse H. Jones,* New York, Holt, 1956, pp. 184, 195.

Carter H. Golembe comments:

. . . it was the only important piece of legislation during the New Deal's famous 'one hundred days' which was neither requested nor supported by the new administration.

Deposit insurance was purely a creature of Congress. For almost fifty years members had been attempting to secure legislation to this end, without success; while in individual states the record of experimentation with bank-obligation insurance systems dated back more than a century. The adoption of nation-wide deposit insurance in 1933 was made possible by the times, by the perseverance

individuals in the Federal Reserve System.[13] The amendment, introduced by Senator Arthur Vandenberg, provided for a temporary system of deposit insurance, pending the adoption on July 1, 1934, of the permanent system. The period of operation of the temporary plan was extended to July 1, 1935, by an amendment in 1934 and to August 31, 1935, by a Congressional resolution signed by the President. On August 23, 1935, a permanent system in roughly its present form became effective under the provisions of Title I of the Banking Act of 1935.

The Banking Act of 1933 neither abolished nor reduced the powers of any existing government body concerned with banking. It simply superimposed an additional agency, the Federal Deposit Insurance Corporation, whose functions both supplemented and duplicated those of existing agencies. Under the terms of the act, all banks that were members of the Federal Reserve System were required to have their deposits insured by the FDIC; nonmember banks could be admitted to insurance upon application to and approval by the Corporation. Insurance was initially (January 1, 1934) limited to a maximum of $2,500 of deposits for each depositor; the limit was raised to $5,000 on July 1, 1934, and to $10,000 on September 21, 1950.[14] Insured banks were required in return to pay

---

of the Chairman of the House Committee on Banking and Currency [Henry B. Steagall], and by the fact that the legislation attracted support from two groups which formerly had divergent aims and interests—those who were determined to end destruction of circulating medium due to bank failures and those who sought to preserve the existing banking structure ("The Deposit Insurance Legislation of 1933," *Political Science Quarterly*, June 1960, pp. 181–182).

[13] Golembe, "Deposit Insurance Legislation," p. 198, footnote 23. At meetings of the board of directors of the New York Federal Reserve Bank in 1933, strong opposition to deposit insurance was expressed by Harrison, Eugene Black, then governor of the Federal Reserve Board, and members of the New York board. The chief alternative proposed was RFC loans under liberalized lending authority, possibly combined with Federal Reserve loans to member banks under sect. 10(b), the Reserve System to be guaranteed against loss on such loans by the federal government. Also proposed was a relaxation of requirements for membership by banks in the Reserve System. The alternative makes clear that opposition was not so much to the assumption by government of ultimate responsibility for deposits as to the by-passing of the Reserve System and the establishment of a potential competitor (George L. Harrison Papers on the Federal Reserve System, Columbia University Library, Harrison, Notes, Vol. III, Apr. 10, May 25, June 1, 1933, pp. 153–156, 197–200, 205–206; for a full description of the Papers, see Chap. 5, footnote 41 and the accompanying text).

[14] Despite the impression conveyed by these limits, protection of the circulating medium rather than protection of the small depositor against loss was the overriding concern of the legislators in establishing deposit insurance, as in earlier attempts to introduce it. In support of this contention, Golembe cites the fact that "under the original insurance plan, slated to go into operation on June 30, 1934, insurance coverage was to apply to all types of deposit accounts, with maximum limits for each depositor which were fairly generous . . . . Only in the temporary plan, designed to operate for six months, was coverage restricted to $2,500 for each depositor. However, the original plan never did go into effect. After several extensions of the temporary plan, during the course of which coverage

premiums calculated as a percentage of their deposits[15] and, if not members of the Federal Reserve System, to submit to examination by the FDIC. The Corporation had the right to examine national and state member banks only if it obtained the written consent either of the Comptroller of the Currency or of the Board of Governors of the Federal Reserve System. In 1950, however, the FDIC was empowered to make special examinations of member banks at its own discretion. Member banks are therefore in principle subject to examination by three agencies: the Federal Reserve System; the Comptroller of the Currency, if national banks, or their state banking commissions, if state banks; and the FDIC. Nonmember insured banks may be examined by two agencies: their state banking commissions and the FDIC. In practice, of course, agreements have been worked out among the different agencies to minimize duplicate examination.[16]

Insurance first became effective on January 1, 1934. Within six months, nearly 14,000 of the nation's 15,348 commercial banks, accounting for

---

was raised to $5,000 for each depositor . . . it was found that this provided full coverage for more than 98 per cent of the depositors." Moreover, FDIC procedures in helping a distressed insured bank, which have the effect of protecting all deposits, and the immediate payment of insured deposits rather than payment over time in the form of receivers' dividends, suggest that protection of the circulating medium from the consequences of bank failures was the primary function of deposit insurance (Golembe, "The Deposit Insurance Legislation," pp. 193–194).

[15] The premium for members of the Temporary Deposit Insurance Fund was ½ of 1 per cent of deposits eligible for insurance. Only one-half the premium was ever paid, and part of that half which was unused at the close of the temporary fund was returned to the banks. Under the permanent system, the premium was changed to $\frac{1}{12}$ of 1 per cent of total deposits, payable semiannually. The Federal Deposit Insurance Act of Sept. 21, 1950, again changed the base for deposit insurance assessment. Each semiannual assessment computation is now based on the average of reports on two dates instead of the daily average for the six-months' period; also, in determining the assessment base, other items besides cash items are deductible from deposits. In addition, the act provided that three-fifths of the premium payments by insured banks in excess of the Corporation's operating expenses, losses, and additions to the insurance fund to cover anticipated losses during the calendar year are to be credited pro rata to the banks to be applied in the following year as part payment for premiums which become due in that year. An amendment, dated July 14, 1960, raised the fraction to two-thirds.

[16] In addition numerous clearing house associations also exercise a degree of supervision over their member banks. The variety of supervisory agreements has been a perennial source of concern to the supervising bodies themselves, and one of their important activities has been coordination of examination and standards (see Board of Governors of the Federal Reserve System, *Annual Report*, 1938, pp. 11–18; and FDIC, *Annual Report*, 1938, pp. 61–79). See also Clark Warburton, "Co-ordination of Monetary, Bank Supervisory, and Loan Agencies of the Federal Government," *Journal of Finance*, June 1950, pp. 161–166. Warburton argues, correctly in our view, that the Board of Governors should be relieved of such duties as the regular examination of member banks, which should be concentrated in the agencies concerned with the affairs of individual banks, such as the Comptroller of the Currency, the state banking commissions, and the FDIC.

some 97 per cent of all commercial bank deposits, were covered by insurance. The number of uninsured commercial banks has since declined to under 400, and their deposits now amount to less than 1 per cent of total deposits in all commercial banks. Mutual savings banks, which were also eligible for insurance, found it much less attractive. In mid-1934 only 66 out of 565 banks, accounting for only a bit over one-tenth of all mutual savings deposits, were insured. The coverage of mutual savings banks rose slowly until World War II, then accelerated, so that by the end of 1945, 192 out of 542 banks accounting for two-thirds of all deposits were insured, and by the end of 1960, 325 out of 515 accounting for 87 per cent of all deposits.[17]

Federal deposit insurance has been accompanied by a dramatic change in commercial bank failures and in losses borne by depositors in banks that fail (Table 16). From 1921 through 1933, every year requires at least three digits to record the number of banks that suspended; from 1934 on, two digits suffice, and from 1943 through 1960, one digit, for both insured and noninsured banks. For the thirteen-year period 1921 to 1933, losses borne by depositors averaged $146 million a year or 45 cents per $100 of adjusted deposits in all commercial banks. For the twenty-seven years since, losses have averaged $706,000 a year, or less than two-tenths of 1 cent per $100 of adjusted deposits in all commercial banks; moreover, over half the total losses during the twenty-seven years occurred in the very first year of the period and were mostly a heritage of the pre-FDIC period.

Technically, only deposits not exceeding a specified sum (since 1950, $10,000) are insured. In 1960, insured deposits amounted to only 57 per cent of all deposits of insured banks. In practice, however, the near-absence of bank failures recorded in Table 16 means that all deposits are effectively insured. The reduction in failures is not of course attributable to any correspondingly drastic improvement in the quality of bank officials or in the effectiveness of the supervisory authorities; nor is it attributable to the addition of still another examination agency, though the addition

---

[17] The wartime increase is attributable to the admission to membership of 125 New York State mutual savings banks on July 1, 1943. They and others had withdrawn from the temporary deposit insurance plan in June 1934. They wanted a premium rate that recognized the lower factor of risk in insuring savings banks and, in addition, believed that the savings banks' own insurance agency could safeguard depositors better than any national agency. In New York the mutual savings banks created their own insurance fund on July 1, 1934. Mutual savings banks in two New England states also organized statewide insurance plans. The New York plan and the arguments for it were abandoned in favor of membership in the FDIC in 1943. It was then held that in a real emergency statewide protection would not be strong enough and federal assistance would be required (A. A. Berle, *The Bank that Banks Built: The Story of Savings Banks Trust Company, 1933–1958*, New York, Harper, 1959, pp. 65, 71–73). See also FDIC, *Annual Report*, 1960, pp. 91, 93.

TABLE 16
COMMERCIAL BANK SUSPENSIONS, 1921–60
PART I. BEFORE FDIC

Year	Number of Suspensions (1)	Deposits (2)	Losses Borne by Depositors (3)	Losses to Depositors per $100 of Deposits Adjusted in All Commercial Banks (dollars) (4)
		(thousands of dollars)		
1921	506	172,806	59,967	0.21
1922	366	91,182	38,223	0.13
1923	646	149,601	62,142	0.19
1924	775	210,150	79,381	0.23
1925	617	166,937	60,799	0.16
1926	975	260,153	83,066	0.21
1927	669	199,332	60,681	0.15
1928	498	142,386	43,813	0.10
1929	659	230,643	76,659	0.18
1930	1,350	837,096	237,359	0.57
1931	2,293	1,690,232	390,476	1.01
1932	1,453	706,187	168,302	0.57
1933	4,000	3,596,708	540,396	2.15

PART II. AFTER FDIC

ALL COMMERCIAL BANKS

Year	Number of Suspensions (1)	Deposits (2)	Losses Borne by Depositors (3)	Losses to Depositors per $100 of Deposits Adjusted in All Commercial Banks (dollars) (4)
1934	61	37,332	6,502	0.02282
1935	31	13,902	600	0.00180
1936	72	28,100	185	0.00049
1937	82	33,877	155	0.00039
1938	80	58,243	293	0.00076
1939	71	158,627	1,374	0.00329
1940	48	142,787	57	0.00012
1941	17	29,797	33	0.00006
1942	23	19,517	20	0.00003
1943	5	12,525	13	0.00002
1944	2	1,915	4	0.0
1945	1	5,695	0	0.0
1946	2	494	0	0.0
1947	6	7,207	0	0.0
1948	3	10,674	0	0.0
1949	8	8,027	69	0.00006
1950	5	5,555	0	0.0
1951	5	6,097	394	0.00031
1952	4	3,313	0	0.0
1953	3	18,652	70	0.00005
1954	4	2,948	407	0.00028
1955	5	11,953	8	0.00001
1956	3	11,689	178	0.00011
1957	2	2,418	0	0.0
1958	9	10,413	277	0.00016
1959	3	2,595	46	0.00003
1960	2	7,990	546	0.00031

(continued)

TABLE 16 (concluded)
PART II. AFTER FDIC

	BREAKDOWN OF COMMERCIAL BANKS, BY INSURED STATUS					
	Insured Banks			Noninsured Banks		
Year	Number of Suspensions	Deposits (thousands of dollars)	Losses Borne by Depositors	Number of Suspensions	Deposits^a (thousands of dollars)	Losses Borne by Depositors^b
	(1)	(2)	(3)	(1)	(2)	(3)
1934	9	1,968	19	52	35,364	6,483
1935	25	13,319	415	6	583	185
1936	69	27,508	171	3	592	14
1937	75	33,349	110	7	528	45
1938	73	57,205	33	7	1,038	260
1939	59	156,188	936	12	2,439	438
1940	43	142,429	31	5	358	26
1941	15	29,718	33	2	79	0
1942	20	19,186	5	3	331	15
1943	5	12,525	13	0	0	0
1944	2	1,915	4	0	0	0
1945	1	5,695	0	0	0	0
1946	1	347	0	1	147	0
1947	5	7,040	0	1	167	n.a.
1948	3	10,674	0	0	0	0
1949	4	5,475	0	4	2,552	69
1950	4	5,513	0	1	42	0
1951	2	3,408	0	3	2,689	394
1952	3	3,170	0	1	143	0
1953	2	18,262	0	1	390	70
1954	2	998	0	2	1,950	407
1955	5	11,953	8	0	0	0
1956	2	11,329	62	1	360	116
1957	1	1,163	0	1	1,255	n.a.
1958	4	8,240	55	5	2,173	222
1959	3	2,595	46	0	0	0
1960	1	6,955	289	1	1,035	257

SOURCE, BY COLUMN

PART I

(1–3) Unpublished estimates, Division of Research and Statistics, FDIC, used with permission of the Corporation. Number and deposits slightly revised, by FDIC, from *Federal Reserve Bulletin*, Sept. 1937, pp. 868, 873. Losses estimated by FDIC by applying to the deposits the appropriate loss percentages derived from samples (see FDIC, *Annual Report*, 1934, pp. 84, 86; 1940, pp. 70–73).

(4) Col. 3 divided by June commercial bank deposits in Table A-1.

PART II

All Commercial Banks

(1–3) Sum of corresponding cols. for insured and noninsured banks.

(4) Col. 3 divided by June commercial bank deposits in Table A-1.

Insured Banks

(1–3) FDIC, *Annual Report*, 1958, pp. 5, 27–28; 1959, p. 5; 1960, p. 5. The banks counted are those requiring disbursements by the FDIC. Two mutual savings

(continued)

NOTES TO TABLE 16 (concluded)

banks included in the published figures were deducted by us (*ibid.*, 1938, pp. 250, 256, and 1939, p. 216).

Noninsured Banks

(1–3) Unpublished estimates, Division of Research and Statistics, FDIC; for cols. 1 and 2, the estimates are revisions of figures given in FDIC, *Annual Report*, 1960, p. 181, and sources listed there.

ᵃ Deposits of noninsured suspended banks are missing in the following years for the following numbers of banks: 1938, 1; 1939, 2; 1941, 1; and 1954, 1.

ᵇ Losses borne by depositors for the following numbers of noninsured suspended banks are missing in the years marked "n.a." and in the additional years listed below.

Year	Banks	Deposits ($000's)
1934	6	341
1938	1	n.a.
1939	2	n.a.
1940	2	12
1941	1	n.a.
1942	1	101
1951	1	1,600
1954	1	n.a.
1958	3	454

n.a. = not available.

of the FDIC apparently meant closer supervision and examination of insured state banks. Rather, it reflects, in the main, two other factors. First, "bad" banks, though perhaps no less frequent than before, are seldom permitted to fail if they are insured; instead, they are reorganized under new management or merged with a good bank, with the FDIC assuming responsibility for losses in connection with depreciated assets. Second, the knowledge on the part of small depositors that they will be able to realize on their deposits even if the bank should experience financial difficulties prevents the failure of one bank from producing "runs" on other banks that in turn may force "sound" banks to suspend. Deposit insurance is thus a form of insurance that tends to reduce the contingency insured against.

Adopted as a result of the widespread losses imposed by bank failures in the early 1930's, federal deposit insurance, to 1960 at least, has succeeded in achieving what had been a major objective of banking reform for at least a century, namely, the prevention of banking panics. Such panics arose out of or were greatly intensified by a loss of confidence in the ability of banks to convert deposits into currency and a consequent desire on the part of the public to increase the fraction of its money held in the form of currency. The resulting runs on banks could be met in a fractional reserve system only if confidence were restored at an early

440

stage. Otherwise, they inevitably brought restriction of convertibility of deposits into currency.

As we have seen, the Aldrich-Vreeland Act and then the Federal Reserve System were both attempts to solve this problem by enabling banks to convert their assets into additional high-powered money for use in meeting the demands of their depositors for currency. The aim was to make it possible for runs or their equivalent, once begun, to be met without forcing banks either to suspend business individually or, by concerted action, to restrict the conversion of deposits into currency. The Aldrich-Vreeland Act succeeded on the one occasion it was used, the outbreak of World War I. The Federal Reserve System failed in the early 1930's though, as we have seen, proper use of its powers could have averted the panic. As these powers were in fact used, however, the existence of the System served only to postpone repeatedly the final crisis, which, when it finally came, was more severe and far-reaching than any earlier panic.

Federal deposit insurance attempts to solve the problem by removing the initial reason for runs—loss of confidence in the ability to convert deposits into currency. While there have been substantial changes since 1934 in the ratio of currency to deposits (see Chapters 9 to 11 below), there have been no radical changes in short periods like those before 1934, always the invariable hallmark of a liquidity crisis and a banking panic. And it is hard to believe that any are likely to occur in the foreseeable future.

True, if for any reason there should be a substantial and long-continued decline in the stock of money, such as occurred from 1929 to 1933, the effects on the value of bank assets would very likely cause so many banks to become insolvent as to exhaust existing reserve funds of the FDIC. However, the greater part of the 1929–33 decline in the stock of money was not independent of the initial bank failures. It was rather a consequence of them, because of their effect on the deposit-currency ratio and the failure of the Reserve System to offset the fall in the ratio by a sufficient increase in high-powered money. Had federal deposit insurance been in existence in 1930, it would very likely have prevented the initial fall in the deposit-currency ratio in late 1930 and hence the tragic sequence of events that fall set in train, including the drastic decline in the money stock. It may be that, today, a radical change in the deposit-currency ratio would evoke a different and more suitable response from the monetary authorities, so that, even in the absence of federal deposit insurance, a banking panic, once begun, would not be permitted to cumulate. The existence of federal deposit insurance greatly reduces, if it does not eliminate, the need to rely on such a response.

As we have seen in earlier chapters, banking panics have occurred only during severe contractions and have greatly intensified such contractions,

441

if indeed they have not been the primary factor converting what would otherwise have been mild contractions into severe ones. That is why we regard federal deposit insurance as so important a change in our banking structure and as contributing so greatly to monetary stability—in practice far more than the establishment of the Federal Reserve System.[18]

Other Changes

The other changes in the commercial and savings banking structure during the New Deal period are much less far reaching than the establishment of deposit insurance and can be noted summarily.

Conditions of membership in the Federal Reserve System were modified to make permissible the admission of Morris Plan and mutual savings banks. Rules governing the establishment of branch banks were somewhat liberalized, and double liability on stock of national banks was eliminated. Investment affiliates of commercial banks were prohibited, and interlocking directorates between commercial banks and investment companies restricted.

National bank notes were converted into a Treasury obligation and arrangements made to retire them from circulation. The provision for issuing them terminated on August 1, 1935, with the redemption of the two remaining issues of U.S. bonds bearing the circulation privilege.[19] The volume in circulation had declined to $650 million by August 1935. It has been declining steadily ever since; even so, at the end of 1960, the volume listed as still in circulation was $55 million.[20]

[18] See Milton Friedman, "Why the American Economy is Depression-Proof," *Nationalekonomiska Föreningens,* sammantrade den 28 April 1954, pp. 59–60. To avoid misunderstanding, we should note explicitly that deposit insurance is but one of several ways in which a panic-proof banking system could have been achieved. Our comments are not intended to suggest that some other method might not have been preferable to deposit insurance. For an alternative method, see Friedman, *A Program for Monetary Stability,* New York, Fordham University Press, 1960, pp. 65–76.

[19] Each national bank transferred to the Treasury the liability for its circulating notes by depositing enough funds with it over and above the 5 per cent redemption fund already held by the Treasury to cover its notes outstanding. Those deposits reduced member bank reserves, but the funds disbursed by the Treasury to redeem the called bonds restored reserves. Since 1935, as national bank notes have returned from circulation, Federal Reserve Banks have shipped them to the Treasury for retirement. Payment for these notes is made to the Federal Reserve Banks by a charge against the Treasury's account. The Treasury replenishes its account by depositing with the Reserve Banks gold certificate credits which it set aside for this purpose, drawn from part of the profit accruing to the government upon the devaluation of the dollar (see footnote 53, below).

[20] This sum includes the amount that has been lost or destroyed as well as notes that are in numismatic collections and notes that are still in use as currency. To judge from the rate at which the sum outstanding has been declining, it seems likely that perhaps half the sum outstanding will sooner or later be offered for retirement. If we ignore amounts held in numismatic collections, this implies that

442

Banks were prohibited by law or regulation from paying interest on demand deposits and from paying rates of interest on time deposits higher than those specified by the Board of Governors of the Federal Reserve System for member banks and by the FDIC for insured nonmember banks. Member banks were also prohibited from acting as agents of nonbank lenders in placing funds in the form of security loans in the stock market.[21]

Throughout American banking history, the view has recurrently been expressed that payment of interest on deposits led to "excessive" competition among banks, and "forced" them to reduce reserves to an undesirably low level and to engage in unduly risky investment and lending policies because of the necessity of earning income to pay the interest. The suggestion had frequently been made that the payment of interest be prohibited.[22] The prohibition was finally adopted for demand deposits in

---

something like $30 million of national bank notes has been lost or destroyed. Though large in absolute amount, the annual rate of loss implied is rather small. For the 97 years from 1864 through 1960, the average amount of national bank notes in circulation was $369 million. The conjectured sum lost or destroyed is roughly 10 per cent of this average or roughly one-tenth of 1 per cent per year.

These estimates imply that paper currency is lost or destroyed at the rate of $1 per year for each $1,000.

[21] In addition, the Banking Act of 1933 made member banks subject to severe reprisal for undue use of bank credit "for the speculative carrying of or trading in securities, real estate, or commodities, or for any other purposes inconsistent with the maintenance of sound credit conditions." The Reserve Banks were authorized to suspend uncooperative banks "from the use of the credit facilities of the Federal Reserve System." The Federal Reserve Board was authorized to fix for each district "the percentage of individual bank capital and surplus which may be represented by loans secured by stock or bond collateral." If, despite an official warning to curtail them, such loans by member banks were increased, Reserve Bank 90-day advances to the offending banks on their own notes became due immediately, and the banks might be suspended from rediscount privileges.

[22] L. W. Mints, *A History of Banking Theory*, University of Chicago Press, 1945, pp. 141, 185, 209, 234–235. The suggestion predated the establishment of the Federal Reserve System—when there was no general distinction between demand and time deposits—and the arguments advanced related particularly to payment of interest on bankers' balances which were, for the most part at least, withdrawable on demand. In 1933, during the discussions leading to the Banking Act of 1933, the arguments were restated against demand deposits generally, whether or not they were bankers' balances. A quotation from O. M. W. Sprague (*History of Crises Under the National Banking System,* National Monetary Commission, 1910, p. 21) provides a good summary of the general stand against payment of interest on deposits:

> The interest-paying banks were unable to maintain large reserves and at the same time realize a profit from the use of the funds thus attracted. Particularly was this the case when the accumulation of such funds was only temporary. The extra supply of money to be lent forced down rates, and, as rates fell, more and more had to be lent by the banks in order even to equal the interest which they had contracted to pay.

The argument is of course a standard one made by private groups seeking "cartel" powers: e.g., one of the arguments used in the 1930's in justifying control

member banks—in the Banking Act of 1933—and for demand deposits in other insured banks—in the Banking Act of 1935—partly because of the greater willingness after 1933 to legislate with respect to economic matters, partly because of the view—in our opinion, largely erroneous—that the banking difficulties of the early 1930's derived in considerable measure from the stock market boom and the participation of banks in the boom as direct lenders and as agents for others.[23]

One consequence of the prohibition of payment of interest on demand deposits has been a marked decline in the importance of interbank deposits—the demand deposits on which the payment of interest had been most widespread and at the highest rates. For member banks, balances at domestic banks were 76 per cent of deposits at Federal Reserve Banks at the end of 1933. They had fallen to 49 per cent by the end of 1937 and to 28 per cent by 1948. They have since risen to about 50 per cent. Beyond this, the prohibition had no great effect until recent years. The

---

over entry into medicine was that physicians whose incomes were "unduly" low would be driven to engage in "unethical" practices. See, for example, A. D. Bevain, "The Overcrowding of the Medical Profession," *Journal of the Association of Medical Colleges*, Nov. 1936, pp. 377–384; and Milton Friedman and Simon Kuznets, *Income from Independent Professional Practice*, New York, NBER, 1945, p. 12 and references there cited in footnote 18.

The payment or nonpayment of interest on demand deposits does not alter in any way the incentive to use assets so as to yield the largest return, as judged by the banker, where return is defined to include nonmonetary as well as monetary elements. The prohibition of payment of interest is simply a government enforced price-fixing agreement. If the prohibition were effective, if it initially increased returns to existing banks, and if entry into the banking industry were free, the effects would be the usual open cartel effects: more banks than would otherwise exist, each operating at partial capacity and competing away the initial extra returns until the returns to skill and capital invested in banking were the same as in other fields. Since entry is not free, thanks to the need to get a franchise from a government authority, the results would likely be intermediate between those just described and the results to be expected if entry were prohibited entirely: a higher market value of the stock of banks, and roughly the competitive return to skill and per dollar of market value of capital.

Of course, all this assumes that the prohibition is not evaded as, of course, it can be at least partly by altering the amount of services given to depositors.

[23] After the prohibition of the payment of interest on demand deposits was in effect, another reason favoring the prohibition was discovered. Under the temporary deposit insurance plan, banks were assessed on insured deposits only; under the proposed permanent plan, on total deposits. City banks complained that under the permanent plan, their assessments would subsidize small country banks, since total deposits of city banks were considerably larger than their insured deposits while total deposits of country banks were not much more than their insured deposits. It was then noted that the reduction in expenses as a result of the prohibition of the payment of interest on demand deposits—expenses mainly borne by city banks —served as an offset to their assessments for deposit insurance (*Banking Act of 1935,* Hearings before a subcommittee of the Senate Committee on Banking and Currency on S. 1715, 74th Cong., 1st sess., 1935, part 1, pp. 29–30; part 2, pp. 433, 490–492).

rate of earnings on bank assets was so low during the 1930's and 1940's that banks were led to impose service charges on depositors, that is, the rate of interest on demand deposits was essentially negative, so that the fixed price for demand deposits was, as it were, above the market price for demand deposits. Competition has taken the form of changes in these service charges and of the provision of special services to depositors.

The limitation of rates of interest paid on time deposits,[24] though initially welcomed by commercial banks, has more recently been a hindrance to them in the competition for these deposits with alternative institutions, particularly savings banks and savings and loan associations, which pay higher rates (see Chapter 12). These rates, too, have for much of the time been ineffective. Discontinuous changes in them after they have become effective have produced sizable perturbations in the rate of change of commercial bank time deposits.

The reduction in interbank deposits plus the prohibition of banks' acting as agents of nonbank lenders in placing funds on the stock market contributed to the sharp decline in security loans by banks and the dwindling in importance of the call-loan market as a means of investing secondary reserves.

CHANGES IN THE STRUCTURE AND POWERS OF THE FEDERAL RESERVE SYSTEM

The Banking Act of 1935 changed the name of the Federal Reserve Board to the Board of Governors of the Federal Reserve System; reconstituted the Board by eliminating ex officio members; raised the salaries and lengthened the terms of the Board members; and reorganized the Federal Open Market Committee to consist of the seven members of the Board plus five representatives of the Federal Reserve Banks, instead of the twelve heads of the Banks, as under the Banking Act of 1933.[25] In addi-

---

[24] Regulation Q of the Board of Governors regulating interest rates on time deposits provides that where state banking authorities have fixed maximum interest rates payable on time deposits at figures lower than those set by the Board of Governors, the lower state figures become the maximum which can be paid by member banks located in those states.

[25] The change in name was the final seal on the transfer of effective power from the Banks to the Board. Heretofore, the chief executive officers of the Banks had been governors, the title generally assigned to the operative head of central banks. Only the executive head of the Board had also been a governor and addressed as such. The other members were simply members of the Board and were addressed without title. Henceforth, the members of the Board were governors in formal title as in fact and the executive heads of the Banks were presidents.

According to Marriner Eccles, it was at Senator Glass' insistence that the Secretary of the Treasury as an ex officio member was dropped: " 'When I was Secretary of Treasury,' Glass said, . . . 'I had considerable influence with the action of the Board, and I . . . have suspected . . . that frequently since the Secretary of the Treasury had too much influence upon the Board, and I do not

tion, it completed a step begun in the Banking Act of 1933 by eliminating the power of Banks to buy and sell government securities for their own account except with the explicit permission or at the direction of the Federal Open Market Committee.[26] These measures recognized and

think he ought to be there' " (*Beckoning Frontiers*, New York, Knopf, 1951, p. 216 n.). Eccles says Senator Glass had no objection to the ex officio membership of the Comptroller of the Currency, but Secretary of the Treasury Morgenthau was piqued that a subordinate in his department and not he would serve on the Board so, to mollify him, the Comptroller was also dropped. As we shall see in Chapters 10 and 11 and as we saw in Chapter 5, the Treasury does not need actual representation on the Board of Governors to exercise considerable influence upon its actions.

The chief executive officer of each Federal Reserve Bank was designated for the first time in the Banking Act of 1935 as the president, formerly called governor, rather than the chairman of the board of directors who is also known as the Federal Reserve agent. The election of each Bank's president and first vice-president by the board of directors is subject to the approval of the Board of Governors. Since 1942, the five representatives of the Reserve Banks chosen annually to serve on the Federal Open Market Committee must be either Reserve Bank presidents or vice-presidents. The role of the Federal Reserve agents, who supervise the issue of Federal Reserve notes, has been greatly reduced since the Banking Act of 1935.

[26] The regulations governing the Federal Open Market Committee (FOMC)—organized under the Banking Act of 1933 and composed of all the Reserve Bank governors—gave the Banks permission to purchase government securities for their own account, subject to certain restrictions, in an emergency involving individual banking institutions (Federal Reserve Board, *Annual Report* for 1933, p. 302). Harrison tried but failed to persuade the FOMC organized under the Banking Act of 1935 to adopt a similar provision. On the first vote, his motion was passed 6 to 5, with all the Bank presidents and one member of the Board voting in favor (there were only six Board members at the time; a seven-man Board was not appointed until 1955). The motion finally lost by a tie vote, for the Board member changed his vote on the ground that the motion—which he still favored—ought not prevail without a larger affirmative margin (Harrison, Miscellaneous, Vol. IV, letter, dated Jan. 19, 1937, Harrison to Eccles; also Harrison, Open Market, Vol. IV, minutes of meeting, Jan. 26, 1937).

The by-laws of the FOMC under the Banking Act of 1935 also provided that members representing Banks did not serve as representatives of the particular Banks that elected them nor were they to be instructed by those Banks. Eccles said that "the open market committee should be composed entirely as a public body and . . . the banks should participate only through an advisory committee, the banks not knowing what was to be done but having a chance to be heard through a committee" (Harrison, Notes, Vol. VII, July 16, 1936; also Vol. VII, Mar. 5, 1936).

Presidents of Banks serving on the FOMC were prohibited by its by-laws from divulging to their directors actions taken at a FOMC meeting. Eccles said that "it would not be proper for directors of the Federal reserve banks affiliated with organizations owning Government securities to have any information which might benefit the organization with which they are associated" (*ibid.*, Vol. VII, July 16, 1936). He disclaimed the idea that any of the directors would take advantage of their situation, but "there is a good deal of talk in Congress about just that sort of thing." Harrison deplored the "throttling of officers and directors of reserve banks by the Board of Governors of the Federal Reserve System" (*ibid.*, Nov. 12, 1936).

446

consolidated the trend of power within the System away from the Federal Reserve Banks and toward Washington. In the same direction was the provision requiring the Board and the Federal Open Market Committee to keep and publish a complete record of all actions taken and of the considerations underlying the actions.

The broadening of the powers of the System was of greater significance than the change in its structure. The Board and the Banks naturally attributed the System's failure to stem the 1929–33 contraction and to prevent the banking panic to its inadequate powers rather than to the use it made of the powers it had. It both requested additional powers and was urged to accept them. The first measure along these lines preceded the panic: the Glass-Steagall Act, discussed earlier, which broadened acceptable collateral for Federal Reserve notes and permitted emergency advances to member banks on any asset. Other provisions of the Banking Act of 1935, all extending the System's powers, are:

(1) Enlargement of the Board's power to alter reserve requirements. First granted in 1933 by the Thomas Amendment to the Agricultural Adjustment Act of 1933 as an emergency power to be exercised only with permission of the President, the emergency power was replaced by a permanent grant of authority, not dependent on Presidential permission, to change reserve requirements between the minimum percentages specified in the act of June 1917 and twice those percentages.[27] A further change in reserve requirements prescribed reserves against government deposits. Country banks, in particular, benefited by a provision permitting "due from" items to be deducted from gross demand deposits instead of solely from "due to" items.

(2) Broadening of the lending powers of the Banks. The section of the Glass-Steagall Act which had allowed emergency advances was liberalized and made permanent. It authorized a Reserve Bank to make advances to

[27] In Aug. 1948 Congress granted the Board temporary power, terminating June 30, 1949, to raise the maximum percentages permitted under the Banking Act of 1935 by 4 points on demand deposits, by 1½ points on time deposits.

In July 1959 the Board was authorized to treat vault cash as part of a member bank's reserves. In Dec. 1959 central reserve and reserve city banks with vault cash holdings greater than 2 per cent of their demand deposits and country banks with vault cash holdings greater than 4 per cent of their demand deposits were given permission to count the excess as reserves. Effective Aug. 25, 1960, the percentage was changed to 2½ per cent for country banks and, effective Sept. 1, 1960, to 1 per cent for reserve city and central reserve city banks. Since Nov. 1960 all vault cash has been counted as part of a member bank's reserves.

Under the law passed in July 1959, the Board was also required to eliminate the central reserve city classification within three years. By Dec. 1, 1960, there was no longer any differential between central reserve and reserve city reserve requirements, and the central reserve city classification that had come into existence nearly a hundred years earlier passed into history.

The Board's authority to allow individual banks in central reserve and reserve cities to carry lower reserves was also broadened in July 1959.

its member banks on any satisfactory security whenever desired, subject only to the rules of the Board. The theory of eligibility as the basis for Federal Reserve credit was thus laid to rest.

(3) Empowering the Board to set a maximum limit to interest rates paid by member banks on time deposits. Granted by the Banking Act of 1933, that power was reaffirmed by the Banking Act of 1935 which gave the same power to the Federal Deposit Insurance Corporation with regard to insured nonmember banks.

(4) Granting of power to the Board to regulate credit advanced by bankers and brokers to their customers for purchasing and carrying registered securities. With this power, granted by the Securities Exchange Act of 1934, the Board has since set margin requirements for loans granted by member and nonmember banks on stocks (Regulation U), and by members of national security exchanges on stocks and bonds (Regulation T).[28] This grant of power was the final outcome of the concern of the Board with stock market speculation in the late twenties and of its attempt to use "direct pressure" to discriminate between stock market and other uses of credit. It was the precursor of other powers directed at the control of particular uses of credit—in particular, control over credit extended for the purchase of consumer goods and for real estate construction, both of which proved to be temporary powers. We shall have occasion to refer to credit controls later (see below, Chapters 9 and 10).

The additional powers, like the powers already possessed by the System, can be divided into three categories: those whose main role is to enable the Board to control the *quantity of money*—we may call these the instruments of monetary policy; those whose main role is to enable the Board to control the *price and use of credit*—we may call these the instruments of credit policy;[29] and those whose main role is to enable the Board to supervise the operations of banks—we may call these the instruments of *bank supervision*. Of course, as our use of the word "main" suggests, there is no hard and fast line between them, and each power may have effects on the quantity of money, the price and use of credit, and the operations of banks. Open market operations and rediscounting were the

[28] Originally margin requirements were applied only against "long" security transactions. On Nov. 1, 1937, the Board included short sales within the scope of margin regulation, with margin for short sales set at 50 per cent, for long reduced from 55 to 40 per cent. Since the war, margin requirements have been uniform for both long and short sales. Up to Apr. 1, 1936, variable percentage margins were set, the margin requirement rising within limits set with each increase in the price of the security. Since then, margin requirements have been a fixed percentage of the price.

[29] Warburton refers to the same distinction, terming it one between "monetary control" and "loan control" (see "Monetary Control under the Federal Reserve Act," *Political Science Quarterly*, Dec. 1946, pp. 513–516).

chief initial monetary powers; the banking measures under consideration added power to vary reserve requirements. Eligibility requirements were the chief initial credit powers; the powers added in this class included control of security credit and, for a time later on, consumer and real estate credit; in addition, the granting of authority to Reserve Banks to make advances to member banks on any satisfactory security rendered the initial eligibility requirements largely irrelevant. Bank examination, requirements for admission to the Federal Reserve System, and, in terms of initial views about their role, reserve requirements were the chief initial supervisory powers; the added powers included control over interest rates on time deposits, control over the percentage of bank capital and surplus that could be represented by security loans, and the policing of the prohibition of the payment of interest on demand deposits.

POLICIES OF BANKS

The banks that survived the holocaust of the early thirties probably differed from those that went under. In addition, and very likely much more important, they undoubtedly drew from the experience lessons that affected their future behavior. For both reasons, the banks that survived understandably placed far greater weight on liquidity than the banks in existence in 1929.

The pressure for liquidity is, as we shall see, the best explanation for two notable changes in the composition of bank assets. The changes are: first, a sharp rise in the fraction held in the form of cash assets (cash in vault, items in process of collection, and balances at other banks including Reserve Banks), a change commented on earlier (Chapter 7, section 2) in connection with the emergence of "excess" reserves in 1932; second, a sharp rise in investments relative to loans.

In 1929, cash assets amounted to 14 per cent of total assets, and loans were more than two and one-half times investments (Table 17). By mid-1933, cash assets had risen to 18 per cent of total assets along with a shrinkage of more than one-third in total assets, and there is little doubt that only the frozen condition of banks prevented the percentage from being still higher. At the same time loans were only slightly larger than investments. Moreover, the investments had shifted in composition, from less than 40 per cent in the form of U.S. government securities in 1929 to over 50 per cent in 1933[30] and, judging from member bank data, from nearly three-quarters of U.S. securities in the form of bonds, generally longer term, to only a bit over one-half in this form (Table 18). Those moves were all in the direction of increasing the fraction of its assets that an individual bank could convert into cash at short notice and with small capital loss—these were properties of its assets whose importance had been

[30] *All-Bank Statistics,* p. 35.

TABLE 17

COMPOSITION OF ASSETS OF COMMERCIAL BANKS, SELECTED DATES, 1929–60

Date^a	Assets (billions of dollars)					Percentage of Total Assets in:				Ratio of Loans to Investments (10)
	Loans (1)	Investments (2)	Cash Assets (3)	Other (4)	Total (5)	Loans (6)	Investments (7)	Cash Assets (8)	Other (9)	
1929	36.1	13.7	9.0	3.6	62.4	57.9	22.0	14.4	5.8	2.6
1933	16.5	14.1	7.4	2.6	40.5	40.7	34.8	18.3	6.4	1.2
1934	15.7	17.1	9.6	2.5	45.0	34.9	38.0	21.3	5.6	0.9
1935	15.0	19.7	11.8	2.4	48.9	30.7	40.3	24.1	4.9	0.8
1936	15.6	23.1	14.5	2.4	55.6	28.1	41.5	26.1	4.3	0.7
1937	17.5	22.1	15.0	2.3	56.9	30.8	38.8	26.4	4.0	0.8
1938	16.1	21.1	16.8	2.2	56.2	28.6	37.5	29.9	3.9	0.8
1939	16.4	23.0	19.9	2.2	61.4	26.7	37.5	32.4	3.6	0.7
1940	17.4	23.8	24.6	2.0	67.8	25.7	35.1	36.3	2.9	0.7
1941	20.3	27.3	25.8	1.9	75.4	26.9	36.2	34.2	2.5	0.7
1945	23.7	90.9	30.2	1.5	146.2	16.2	62.2	20.7	1.0	0.3
1948	39.9	74.0	34.2	1.8	149.8	26.6	49.4	22.8	1.2	0.5
1957	91.0	73.5	40.0	3.9	208.4	43.7	35.3	19.2	1.9	1.2
1958	95.6	84.3	43.5	4.4	227.8	42.0	37.0	19.1	1.9	1.1
1959	103.4	82.7	42.9	4.7	233.7	44.2	35.4	18.4	2.0	1.3
1960	115.3	74.8	47.1	5.3	242.5	47.5	30.8	19.4	2.2	1.5

^a June 30 or nearest available call date.

SOURCE: Cols. 1–5, from *All-Bank Statistics*, pp. 34–35; and *Federal Reserve Bulletin*.

TABLE 18
CHIEF KINDS OF UNITED STATES GOVERNMENT DIRECT OBLIGATIONS HELD BY MEMBER BANKS, 1928-41

End of:	Member Bank Holdings (millions of dollars)				Per Cent of Total Member Bank Holdings in:			Holdings as Per Cent of Total Amounts Outside Federal Reserve Banks			
	Total (1)	Bills and Certificates (2)	Notes (3)	Treasury and Liberty Bonds (4)	Bills and Certificates (5)	Notes (6)	Treasury and Liberty Bonds (7)	Total (8)	Bills and Certificates (9)	Notes (10)	Treasury and Liberty Bonds (11)
Dec. 1928	4,312	554	729	3,028	12.85	16.91	70.22	28.0	29.4	32.7	26.8
June 1929	4,155	446	704	3,005	10.73	16.94	72.32	27.6	28.3	32.7	26.6
June 1930	4,061	259	463	3,340	6.38	11.40	82.25	29.4	22.2	33.6	29.7
June 1931	5,343	901	403	4,039	16.86	7.54	75.59	36.1	47.4	94.8	32.4
June 1932	5,628	962	503	4,163	17.09	8.94	73.97	34.6	42.5	50.8	32.0
June 1933	6,887	1,113	2,049	3,725	16.16	29.75	54.09	36.2	50.2	53.4	28.7
June 1934	9,137	1,427	2,871	4,838	15.62	31.42	52.95	40.0	65.5	52.9	31.8
June 1935	9,871	1,099	4,314	4,458	11.13	43.70	45.16	41.7	75.9	50.7	32.5
June 1936	11,721	1,266	5,161	5,295	10.80	44.03	45.18	41.2	73.0	52.2	31.4
June 1937	10,870	821	4,361	5,689	7.55	40.12	52.34	35.8	48.9	46.2	29.6
June 1938	10,215	316	3,653	6,246	3.09	35.76	61.15	34.5	63.3	45.8	29.6
June 1939	10,946	441	2,720	7,786	4.03	24.85	71.13	35.1	52.2	44.8	32.0
June 1940	11,600	797	2,543	8,261	6.87	21.92	71.22	36.5	61.2	48.4	32.8
June 1941	14,238	1,127	2,631	10,481	7.92	18.48	73.61	40.3	70.3	53.9	36.3

NOTE: Details do not necessarily add to totals because of rounding.

SOURCE, BY COLUMN

(1) Sum of cols. 2–4.

(2–4) *Banking and Monetary Statistics*, p. 77.

(8) Holdings of the Federal Reserve Banks were deducted from the total of the 4 kinds of debt outstanding (*ibid.*, pp. 332, 343, 375, 509–510). All bonds held by the Federal Reserve Banks were treated as Treasury or Liberty bonds. Col. 1 was expressed as a percentage of the difference.

(9–11) Procedure similar to that for col. 8, except that in 1929–31, no June breakdown of Federal Reserve holdings was available. The percentage distribution of the 4 kinds of debt in June 1929 and 1930 was assumed the same as on the preceding Dec. 31 and in June 1931 the same as on the following Dec. 31.

impressed on commercial bankers by the experiences of the preceding few years.

As total assets increased sharply after 1933, bankers took the opportunity offered by the increase to strengthen their cash position and to expand investments, and among them, governments, more rapidly than loans. By 1940, cash assets had mounted to 36 per cent of total assets (Table 17). Loans were only about 70 per cent of investments and about 70 per cent of investments were in the form of U.S. government securities.

Unfortunately, there are no adequate data on the maturity distribution of bank investments. Beginning in late 1928, data are available on the distribution of government security holdings of all member banks among three categories: bills and certificates of indebtedness; notes; and bonds (see Table 18). The first category had a maturity of less than one year when issued, the second, of one to five years, and the third, of more than five years. However, depending on the particular security, the remaining maturity, *when purchased* or held, might be quite different from the original maturity. A bond, for example, might have a remaining maturity when purchased or held of less than a year and so be comparable in maturity to bills. In consequence, the distribution of security holdings among the indicated categories is at best a very rough index of their distribution by maturity.

The data show a decided shift in the composition of the security holdings of banks after 1928 and 1929. In 1928, 1929, and 1930, bonds constituted about 70 to 80 per cent of the total of U.S. securities held by member banks, the balance being distributed somewhat more in notes than in bills and certificates. In 1931 and 1932, bonds remained about 75 per cent of the total, but about two-thirds of the remainder was in the form of bills and certificates and one-third in notes, suggesting that under the pressure of successive liquidity crises banks shifted into shorter-term securities. After 1932, the fraction in the form of bonds fell steadily to 54 and 53 per cent in June of 1933 and 1934, 45 per cent in June of 1935 and 1936. True, after 1932, notes rose sharply relative to bills and certificates, from one-third of the three combined in 1932 to two-thirds in 1933 and 1934 and to four-fifths in 1935 and 1936. However, that shift was largely a result of a limited supply of bills and certificates. Member banks held close to 50 per cent of the bills and certificates outside the Federal Reserve Banks from 1931 to 1933, and around 70 per cent from 1934 to 1936. They held roughly 50 per cent of the notes from 1932 to 1936 and around one-third of the bonds. By contrast, in 1928 banks held about 30 per cent each of the bills and certificates and of the notes outside the Federal Reserve System and about a quarter of the bonds. The banks had absorbed so much larger a fraction of the bills, certificates, and notes

452

outside the Federal Reserve System than of the bonds that banks had become the dominant factor in the market for these short-term obligations.

No doubt changes in the demand for loans and in the supply of investments, and the large increase in available reserves produced by the gold inflows—all of which constituted changes in the supply of assets for banks to hold—played a role in the shifts in asset composition. However, the major factor was not those but rather a shift in the liquidity preferences of commercial banks, that is, a change in the demand by banks for assets, which is to say, in the portfolio composition they sought to attain for any given structure of yields. The inflow of gold—the most dramatic force operating on the supply side—in the first instance increased the cash assets of the banking system. But the banks were individually free to convert the additional assets into other forms, and collectively of course that conversion would have been and was reflected in a rise in the stock of money and in the total assets of banks. Such reactions on the part of banks could therefore have offset in full, as they did in part, the effect of the gold inflow on the *ratio* of cash assets to total assets. There was, of course, some lag in the reactions of banks, and no doubt the lag made cash assets somewhat larger relative to total assets during the periods of steady gold inflow than they otherwise would have been. Such a lag cannot, however, account for the continued increase in the ratio of cash assets to total assets, since there was no corresponding increase in the rate of gold inflow. Moreover, such a lag cannot explain the shifting composition of noncash assets.

The behavior of rates of interest is decisive evidence that the shifting composition of noncash assets cannot be explained by changes in the supply of assets available for banks to hold but only by changes in liquidity preferences on the part of the banks. Suppose the shifts in bank portfolios had reflected mainly shifts in supply without a change in the preferences of banks for different kinds of assets. The assets whose *relative* importance in the portfolio increased should then also have been the ones on which the yield rose in comparison with the yield on other assets, since the issuers of such assets would have had to raise their yield to induce banks to hold them in increased amount.[31] In fact, the structure of

[31] The wording is deliberately vague about how the yields should be compared, whether in terms of the ratio of yields or the absolute difference between them (spread). It is an open question, about which there is no general agreement, which is the more relevant for judging changes in the relative attractiveness of assets. In our view, this question cannot be given a single answer; sometimes the one and sometimes the other will be the more relevant, though on the whole, for our present purpose, the spread seems preferable. Fortunately, however, for the episode under discussion, it makes no difference how the question is answered. Except for cash assets (see footnote 32), the major movements in the spread and in the relative yield were in the same direction.

453

CHART 35
Changing Relations Among Interest Yields, 1928–39

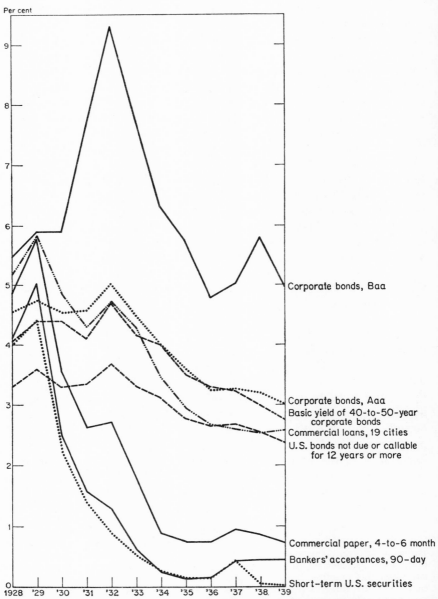

Per cent

Corporate bonds, Baa

Corporate bonds, Aaa
Basic yield of 40-to-50-year
corporate bonds
Commercial loans, 19 cities
U.S. bonds not due or callable
for 12 years or more

Commercial paper, 4-to-6 month

Bankers' acceptances, 90-day

Short-term U.S. securities

1928 '29 '30 '31 '32 '33 '34 '35 '36 '37 '38 '39

SOURCE: Baa and Aaa corporate bonds, commercial loans, bankers' acceptances, *Banking and Monetary Statistics*, pp. 448, 464, 468. Commercial loan rate, annual averages; for 1939 based on Jan.-Feb. only; monthly data unavailable thereafter on a comparable basis. Basic yield of 40- to 50-year corporate bonds, *Historical Statistics*, 1960, p. 657, Series X-347. U.S. government bonds, *Federal Reserve Bulletin*, Dec. 1938, p. 1045; Feb. 1940, p. 139. Commercial paper, *Historical Statistics*, 1949, p. 346, averaged annually. Short-term U.S. government securities, *FRB*, May 1945, p. 483: 3- to 6-month certificates and notes, 1928–30; 3- to 9-month Treasury bills, 1931–42.

454

interest rates moved the other way for assets other than cash assets.[32] Rates charged on customer loans and yields on long-term government bonds were low after 1933 by earlier standards, and customer rates had fallen more than long-term bond yields; however, rates on short-term commercial paper, bankers' acceptances, and short-term U.S. securities— the kinds of assets whose relative importance in bank portfolios had increased most—were lower still by those standards (see Chart 35).[33] Among corporate bonds, yields on lower-grade bonds had fallen decidedly less from 1929 to 1936 than yields on high-grade bonds had, again suggesting a shift of preference toward the more certain. The most notable change in the structure of rates of return from before to after the 1929–33 contraction was the sharp widening in spread among assets differing in the degree of confidence the holder could attach to their convertibility into a known cash sum at need and on short notice. It follows that the initial supposition that the change in bank portfolios reflected mainly shifts in the supply of assets is untenable. The change must have reflected shifts in demand by banks and others for different kinds of assets.[34] Moreover, the change in the distribution of government

[32] The argument from interest rates alone, which is decisive for other assets, is not decisive for cash assets. It does not, of course, follow that there was no shift in preferences for cash assets comparable to that for the other assets that rose in relative importance in bank portfolios. On the contrary, we argue below that there was such a shift, and that it reinforced a change in conditions of supply to produce a much larger rise in the relative importance of cash assets in bank portfolios than would otherwise have occurred.

For the cash assets of Table 17, the yield fell from a minor positive amount, because of interest paid on interbank balances, to zero. The ratio of the yield on other assets to the yield on cash assets therefore rose from a finite amount to infinity. However, the spread between other yields and the yield on cash assets as a whole undoubtedly fell. For an unduplicated cash total for the banking system as a whole, i.e., high-powered money holdings, the yield was zero throughout, so the ratio of yields remained unchanged, while the spread fell. The change in conditions of supply therefore fostered a rise in the fraction of assets held in the form of cash assets.

[33] It should be noted that the customer loan rate is not, like all the other rates in Chart 35, a market rate, and may for that reason be subject to a wider margin of error. In addition, other dimensions of the loan, such as collateral conditions, the size of the compensating balance borrowers are required to hold, and so on, may vary more than for market rates.

[34] The increased demand for short- relative to long-term securities was no doubt partly motivated by a belief that rates of interest were likely to rise in the future. That expectation would make long securities less attractive than short at the same rate, or at a difference in rates that prevailed earlier when such expectations were not held. David Meiselman argues persuasively that the whole of the change in spread between one-year and longer rates on corporate bonds can be explained by the shift in relative demand arising from such expectation effects (see his *The Term Structure of Interest Rates*, Englewood Cliffs, N.J., Prentice-Hall, 1962). Meiselman does not consider in detail rates for periods of less than a year, which play a crucial role in our analysis.

These expectation effects do not, of course, explain the widening of the spread between more and less risky investments of the same maturity; that must have

455

securities of varying maturity between banks and other holders could only have occurred because the change in bank preferences for liquidity was greater than any corresponding change in the preferences of other holders.

The evidence furnished by interest rates is confirmed by a study by C. O. Hardy and Jacob Viner of the availability of bank credit in the Chicago Federal Reserve District during the period from the bank holiday to September 1, 1934. The study, based mainly on interviews with bankers and brokers, was undertaken "to find out so far as possible whether, and to what extent, the small volume of bank loans was due to the desire of banks to retain or attain liquidity, to the attitude of examining officials, to the unwillingness of businessmen to assume the risk of borrowing to maintain or expand their operations, or to the impairment of the capital of many businessmen by losses incurred during the depression which made

---

reflected a shift of preference toward the less risky for other reasons. As the next sentence in the text indicates, they can explain the change in distribution of government securities among banks and others only if banks had different expectations from those of others, believing that rates would rise more rapidly in the rather short-term future than others thought they would.

While Meiselman's conclusion may be entirely justified for rates for periods of a year or longer and while its being the correct explanation for rates for shorter periods would not seriously affect the conclusions stated in the text—since they do not depend on the reason for the shift in preferences—we do not believe that his conclusion can be extended to the rates for very short periods with which we are most concerned. As we have seen, banks came to play a dominant role in the market for some of these assets, and the behavior of the corresponding rates therefore hinges critically on shifts in banks' preferences. The evidence we adduce below to explain the notable increase in bank cash assets strongly supports the view that the 1929–33 experience led banks to attach a much greater value than formerly to assets that could be converted into known cash sums at need and at short notice for reasons other than the belief that interest rates would rise. Their experience, more trying than that of other asset holders, must have impressed them with their greater need to hedge against uncertainty; and the structure of their liabilities meant that such hedging required them to shift to shorter-term securities, as they did.

A shift in bank preferences for reasons other than expectations about future rates therefore explains in a simple and straightforward manner (1) the very great increase in spread for very short-term relative not only to long-term but also to one-year rates; (2) the sharp shift in composition of bank portfolios; (3) the shift in the distribution of government securities among holders; and (4) the behavior of "excess reserves." The expectations hypothesis can then supplement this explanation for banks and be the major explanation for longer rates and other holders.

In more recent work on the cyclical behavior of the term structure of interest rates, Reuben Kessel has found that combining the expectations hypothesis with liquidity considerations gives a more satisfactory explanation of the empirical evidence than either gives alone for maturities both shorter and longer than one year. While the finding does not demonstrate that *shifts* in liquidity preference played the role we assign to them, it perhaps makes that interpretation more plausible than it would otherwise be (see his forthcoming "The Cyclical Behavior of the Term Structure of Interest Rates," an NBER study, in preparation).

them poor banking risks." The authors concluded: "That there exists a genuine unsatisfied demand for credit on the part of solvent borrowers, many of whom could make economically sound use of working capital . . . That one of the most serious aspects of this unsatisfied demand is the pressure for liquidation of old working-capital loans, even sound ones. That this pressure is partly due to a determination on the part of bankers to avoid a recurrence of the errors to which they attribute much of the responsibility for the recent wave of bank failures . . . ."[35]

The increased fraction of bank assets held in the form of cash assets, unlike the increased fraction held in short-term investments, can be partly explained by supply considerations. As noted, a lagged reaction to the gold inflow may have contributed to the increase. More important, because longer lasting, rates of interest in general fell, which made cash assets more attractive compared to other assets (or, equivalently, less costly in terms of income sacrificed). Moreover, the shift in preferences depressed particularly the yields on short-term highly liquid assets, fostering still more the shift into cash. For example, the yield on Treasury bills averaged 0.515 per cent per year in 1933, 0.256 in 1934, 0.137 in 1935, and 0.143 in 1936. After rising to 0.447 in 1937 in response to the doubling of reserve requirements (see Chapter 9 below), it fell to 0.053 in 1938, 0.023 in 1939, and 0.014 in 1940. At those yields it was hardly worthwhile to hold bills instead of cash. In consequence, while the ratio of government securities to total assets for all banks reached its peak in 1936, the ratio of cash assets to total assets continued rising until 1940.

While supply considerations explain part of the shift into cash assets, they cannot explain the whole of the shift, which was motivated also by the same desire for liquidity as the shift into investments. To begin with, cash assets were acquired along with investments to satisfy that desire; after 1936, the acquisition of cash assets became the most convenient and least costly way to achieve the desired liquidity. Indirect confirmation of these propositions is furnished by the evidence from interest rates that the shift into investments reflected a change in the liquidity preferences of banks. Such a change could clearly be expected also to affect cash assets since those assets fulfill par excellence the end desired in holding short-term investments—convertibility into known sums at need and on short notice. In addition, there are a number of other bits of evidence that together are fairly decisive.

Perhaps the most striking of these is a comparison between Canadian and United States experience made by George R. Morrison.[36] Canada's

[35] *Report on the Availability of Bank Credit in the Seventh Federal Reserve District,* submitted to the Secretary of the Treasury, GPO, 1935, pp. 3 and VI.
[36] In "Liquidity Preferences of Commercial Banks," unpublished Ph.D. dissertation, University of Chicago, 1962.

cyclical experience was almost the same as that of the United States from 1929 to 1939, except that it was spared any bank failures or widespread runs on banks. Rates of interest moved in much the same way as in the United States—to be expected from the close link between the financial markets in the two countries. Canadian banks increased their cash assets relative to their deposits, but by a very much smaller proportion than did U.S. banks.

A second bit of evidence comes from Morrison's examination of the relation in the United States between cash assets and interest rates before 1929 and after 1939. On the basis of both earlier and later experience, the increase in cash assets in the 1930's was much larger than the increase that might have been expected to be produced by the decline in yields alone.

Our analysis of the reaction of member banks to the doubling of reserve requirements in 1936 and 1937 is still another bit of evidence that they had accumulated cash assets because their demand for liquidity had risen. When the rise in reserve requirements immobilized the accumulated cash, they proceeded rather promptly to accumulate additional cash for liquidity purposes (see the more detailed discussion in Chapter 9).[37]

The form taken by the increase in cash assets was doubtless affected by the prohibition of payment of interest on demand deposits. Had the prohibition not existed, more of the growth of cash assets might have taken the form of balances at other commercial banks rather than at Federal Reserve Banks. As it was, there was no incentive to hold at other commercial banks balances desired for their liquidity. How great this effect was is by no means clear. The low yield on short-term assets would have meant a low rate of interest offered for interbank balances and perhaps even a zero rate of interest, in which case the result would have been the same.

The shift in liquidity preferences of banks was destined to be temporary. To judge by the experience of earlier episodes,[38] the passage of time without any extensive series of bank failures would have dulled the fears of bank managers, leading them to set a lower premium on liquidity. In any case, the establishment of FDIC, which was accompanied by a dramatic reduction in the rate of bank failures, provided additional assurance against the occurrence of "runs" of the kind that had produced the shift in liquidity preferences. Such assurance, while by no means clear at the start of FDIC, eventually became increasingly clear, but still it took

[37] See also Phillip Cagan's forthcoming monograph on determinants and effects of changes in the money stock in the United States since 1875, a National Bureau study, Chap. 5.

[38] See Chap. 2, sect. 4; Chap. 3, sect. 3; and Chap. 4, sect. 6. Also see Cagan's forthcoming study referred to in the preceding footnote, and Morrison's study referred to in footnote 36, above.

time for banks to adapt their behavior to that new fact It is therefore not surprising that the ratio of cash assets to total assets continued rising until 1940.

Though the ratio of cash assets to total assets fell drastically during the war and remained at an even lower level thereafter, it has remained above its 1929 level (Table 17, col. 8). The reason is not a continued higher preference on the part of banks for cash assets but rather a rise in reserve requirements. Banks have no choice about the form of their required reserves. That fraction of their assets has to be kept as cash assets—indeed, until 1959, as deposit balances at the Federal Reserve System—and, as they found out at great cost in 1930–33, can not be drawn upon for emergencies without precipitating suspension. A change in a bank's cash ratio as a result of a change in reserve requirements is, therefore, a different phenomenon from a change as a result of a shift in asset preference.

Aggregate data on required reserves are available only for member banks. Accordingly, Table 19, which eliminates required reserves from both the numerator and denominator of the cash ratio, is restricted to member banks. In 1929, member banks held 11.3 per cent of their assets in excess of required reserves in the form of cash in vault, cash items in the process of collection, and balances at banks (commercial and Federal Reserve) in excess of required reserves. That ratio rose steadily from 1933 to 1936, then fell as a result of the doubling of reserve requirements in 1936–37, then resumed its rise to a peak of nearly 30 per cent in 1940. By 1945 it was back to roughly its 1929 level, and it has fluctuated around that level since, whereas the ratio of all cash assets to total assets (column 3) has fluctuated around a level several percentage points higher than the 1929 level.

Unlike the cash ratio, the ratio of investments to loans continued to rise during the war. Although it has fallen since, it is still about twice its 1929 level. However, the divergent behavior of the cash ratio and the investment-loan ratio does not imply that the effect of the increased preference for liquidity on the demand for investments lasted longer than its effect on the demand for cash. Just as the demand for both categories expanded together from 1932 to 1940, so the demand for both could have declined together subsequently, since the divergent behavior of the actual ratios can be readily explained by differences on the supply side. During the war there was a rapid increase in the supply of government securities, and probably also a decrease in the relative demand for bank loans because many firms were financed by federal government funds. As is consistent with this interpretation, the spread in yield between highly liquid and less liquid bank assets narrowed, if anything, during the war—to an especially striking extent if government bonds whose

459

TABLE 19
RELATION OF CASH ASSETS TO REQUIRED RESERVES AND TOTAL ASSETS,
MEMBER BANKS, SELECTED DATES, 1929–60
(dollars in billions)

Date[a]	Total Assets (1)	Cash Assets (2)	Cash Assets as Percentage of Total Assets (3)	Required Reserves (4)	Required Reserves as Percentage of Total Assets (5)	Cash Assets in Excess of Required Reserves as Percentage of Total Assets in Excess of Required Reserves (6)
1929	45.5	7.2	15.8	2.3	5.1	11.3
1933	33.0	6.2	18.8	1.8	5.5	14.1
1934	37.4	8.2	21.9	2.1	5.6	17.3
1935	40.7	10.1	24.8	2.6	6.4	19.7
1936	46.5	12.5	26.9	2.9	6.2	22.0
1937	47.5	13.0	27.4	6.0	12.6	16.9
1938	47.1	14.8	31.4	5.1	10.8	23.1
1939	51.9	17.6	33.9	5.9	11.4	25.4
1940	57.8	21.8	37.7	6.9	11.9	29.3
1941	64.9	22.7	35.0	7.8	12.0	26.1
1945	126.4	25.8	20.4	13.3	10.5	11.1
1948	127.3	30.3	23.8	16.7	13.1	12.3
1957	176.5	35.3	20.0	18.3	10.4	10.7
1958	194.0	38.5	19.8	18.3	9.4	11.5
1959	197.3	37.9	19.2	18.0	9.1	11.1
1960	204.2	41.9	20.5	17.7	8.7	13.0

[a] June 30 or nearest available call date.

SOURCE, BY COLUMN

(1) *Banking and Monetary Statistics*, pp. 72 and 74, and *Member Bank Call Report*.
(2) The sum of reserves at Federal Reserve Banks, cash in vault, balances at domestic and foreign banks, and cash items in process of collection, from same source as for col. 1.
(3) Col. 2 divided by col. 1.
(4) 1929–41: *Banking and Monetary Statistics*, pp. 395–396.
   1945–59: *Member Bank Call Report*.
   1960: Average for week ending June 15, 1960, from *Federal Reserve Bulletin*, Dec. 1960, p. 1350.
(5) Col. 4 divided by col. 1.
(6) Computed from cols. 1, 2, and 4.

prices were pegged by the Federal Reserve are regarded as highly liquid assets. After the war, the supply of government securities remained high, and an increasing proportion of business firms found it possible to raise funds they required on the open market. The spread of rates of return continued to narrow through 1960. Supply conditions had reverted somewhat by that time, but not fully, to prewar conditions, hence the investment-loan ratio remained above its 1929 level.

It should be noted that our interpretation of the changes in the composition of bank assets and, in particular, of the emergence of a large volume of "excess reserves" in the 1930's runs sharply counter to an interpretation that is widely held[39]—and one that was also implicit in Federal Reserve policy in the 1930's and has been to a lesser degree since. According to that interpretation, excess reserves were primarily unneeded surplus funds held by banks, proof of easy-money conditions and of a lack of private demand for credit. Banks were, as it were, in metastable equilibrium. Additional funds acquired by banks were in the main simply added to cash balances; additional demands on banks were met by reducing balances. There was no unique desired structure of assets, corresponding to given rates of return on assets, disturbance of which would prompt banks to seek to restore that same structure; they would be content to retain the new one. On this view, changes in reserve requirements had no effect, so long as they did not absorb all excess reserves either for all banks or for any significant group of banks.[40] This was the view explicitly presented by the Board of Governors in connection with the doubling of reserve requirements in 1936–37.[41] As we have already implied and as we

[39] Woodlief Thomas, "Monetary Controls," *Banking Studies,* Board of Governors of the Federal Reserve System, 1941, reprinted 1947, pp. 341–342; Allan Sproul, "Changing Concepts of Central Banking," *Money, Trade, and Economic Growth,* in Honor of J. H. Williams, New York, Macmillan, 1951, pp. 297–298; R. A. Gordon, *Business Fluctuations,* New York, Harper, 1952, pp. 398–399. An interpretation essentially identical with ours is presented by Paul A. Samuelson, "Fiscal Policy and Income Determination," *Quarterly Journal of Economics,* Aug. 1942, p. 594.

[40] See Board of Governors of the Federal Reserve System, *Annual Report,* 1936, p. 15; 1937, p. 2; E. A. Goldenweiser, *Monetary Management,* New York, McGraw-Hill, 1949, pp. 57–59; and *idem, American Monetary Policy,* New York, McGraw-Hill, 1951, pp. 175–182.

[41] Opinions expressed within the System were less dogmatic and unqualified than official justifications for the actions taken were, though their general tenor was the same.

A series of memoranda dealing with excess reserves, prepared at the Federal Reserve Bank of New York from 1934 on, apparently provided the initial intellectual basis for doubling reserve requirements (see Chap. 9, sect. 4). These memoranda, as well as statements by Bank officials to the New York board of directors, the FOMC, and the Board of Governors, present essentially the view outlined above, when they deal with the specific subject of the large accumulation of excess reserves and the measures that should be taken to deal with them. For example, a memorandum, dated Nov. 7, 1935, "Plans for Credit Control," states, "Had there been no gold inflow the excess reserves created by the Reserve System

point out in more detail in Chapter 9 in discussing the 1937–38 contraction, the reaction to the doubling of requirements contradicts the official view and supports our interpretation.

2. Changes in the Monetary Standard

GOLD POLICY

President Roosevelt's proclamation of a bank holiday on March 6, 1933, also prohibited banks from paying out gold or dealing in foreign exchange during the bank holiday. The Emergency Banking Act of March 9, 1933, which confirmed and extended the March 6 proclamation, granted the President emergency powers over banking transactions and over foreign exchange dealings and gold and currency movements. The next day, March 10, the President issued an executive order extending the restrictions on gold and foreign exchange dealings beyond the banking holiday proper and, in effect, prohibiting gold payments by banking and non-banking institutions alike, unless permitted by the Secretary of the Treasury under license. The order also narrowly limited foreign exchange dealings. Those measures were a precursor to nearly a year of tinkering with the monetary standard which culminated in the most far-reaching alteration in its legal structure since the departure from gold during the Civil War and subsequent resumption in 1879.[42]

Despite the effective suspension of gold payments, the price of gold,

---

would now have been entirely absorbed by the increase in the required reserves [as a result of deposit expansion]"—a statement implying that deposit expansion would have been identical even if the reserves had increased at a much slower rate (Harrison, Notes, Vol. VI; also Harrison, Special, no. 9, p. 2). At the same time, this view is occasionally qualified by the recognition that the same level of excess reserves may have different effects on the willingness of member banks to expand their earning assets, and in different contexts statements are made that go even further in the direction of our intepretation. For example, President Harrison suggested, in commenting on the first rise in reserve requirements in 1936, that it "lessened to some extent the pressure upon banks to invest their surplus funds," i.e., that it had a contractionary effect (Harrison, Open Market, Vol. IV, unrevised minutes of meeting, Nov. 19, 1936). The explicit reconciliation of the two strands in System opinion rested on a distinction of magnitude.

The conclusion we draw from perusal of the Harrison Papers is that the officers of the New York Bank quite explicitly recognized the changed liquidity preferences of banks and the desirability of excess reserves to meet them from 1930 to 1934 or 1935 (see Chap. 7, sect. 5), but they could not accept excess reserves so large in magnitude as those that accumulated thereafter as a reflection of such changed preferences, hence were led to the view that they had no constructive effects.

[42] For a detailed chronology and description of the steps taken during the year, see J. D. Paris, *Monetary Policies of the United States, 1932–1938*, New York, Columbia University Press, 1938, pp. 12–32 and 118–120. For a different kind of description of the same events, see F. A. Pearson, W. I. Myers, and A. R. Gans, "Warren as Presidential Adviser," *Farm Economics*, New York State College of Agriculture, Cornell University, No. 211, Dec. 1957.

or the rate of exchange between the dollar and currencies like the French franc that remained rigidly linked to gold, hovered around "par" for over a month. The suspension was presumably regarded as part of the banking emergency and hence expected to be temporary; foreign exchange transactions were strictly controlled and limited; the administration made no official announcement that it proposed to permit the dollar to depreciate or be devalued; and after some weeks, several licenses to export gold were granted. Moreover, the technical gold position was sufficiently strong so that there was little doubt the preceding gold parity could have been maintained if desired; the ratio of the gold stock to the total stock of money was higher than at any time since 1914.

One important step, unprecedented in the United States, was taken during this period. On April 5, an executive order forbade the "hoarding" of gold and required all holders of gold, including member banks, to deliver their holdings of gold coin, bullion, or certificates to Federal Reserve Banks on or before May 1 except for rare coins, reasonable amounts for use in industry and the arts, and a maximum of $100 per person in gold coin and gold certificates.[43] The gold coin and gold certificates were exchanged for other currency or deposits at face value, and the bullion was paid for at the legal price of $20.67 per fine ounce. The "nationalization" of gold outside Federal Reserve Banks was later completed by an order of the Secretary of the Treasury, dated December 28, 1933, excepting only rare coins and a few other minor items from the requirement that all gold coin, gold bullion, and gold certificates be delivered to the Treasurer of the United States at face value corresponding to the legal price of $20.67 per fine ounce. The expiration date for the surrender of gold was later set as January 17, 1934,[44] when the market price of gold was in the neighborhood of $33 per fine ounce.[45]

[43] *Federal Reserve Bulletin,* Apr. 1933, pp. 213–214.
[44] *FRB,* Feb. 1934, p. 80.
[45] Pearson, Myers, and Gans, "Warren," p. 5647. The amount of gold coin and gold certificates outside the Treasury and the Federal Reserve Banks at the end of Feb. 1933 was estimated by contemporary Federal Reserve statistics to be $1,220 million, of which $571 million was in coin and $649 million in certificates (*FRB,* Feb. 1934, p. 95). These statistics show the amount of gold coin outside the Treasury and Federal Reserve as falling to $367 million at the end of Mar. 1933 (before the first executive order requiring the transfer of gold coin), to $335 million at the end of Apr., then declining gradually to $311 million at the end of Dec. and to $287 million at the end of Jan. 1934 (*ibid.*). The gold coin then outstanding was dropped from the monthly circulation statement as of Jan. 31, 1934. It was assumed that that amount had mainly been lost, destroyed, exported without record, or was in numismatic collections, although some unknown amount remained illegally in private hands. Since the amount turned in to the Treasury at $20.67 an ounce between June 1934 and June 1960 totaled less than $12 million, it might be concluded that the amount of gold coin outstanding after Jan. 1934 was not significant.
The experience with national bank notes analyzed in footnote 20, however, in-

463

An executive order of April 20, 1933, extending and revising the gold embargo, and comments by the President at his news conference the preceding day ended the period of stability in the price of gold. The President made it clear that the administration intended to permit the dollar to depreciate in terms of foreign currencies as a means of achieving a rise in domestic prices. The order applied the restrictions on foreign exchange transactions not only to banks licensed under the executive

---

dicates that losses could have accounted for only a small part of the $287 million still outstanding at the end of Jan. 1934. Whatever losses there were presumably occurred during the period from 1907 to 1933, since in 1907 the Director of the Mint presented revised estimates of gold coin in circulation which took into account probable losses from 1873 to 1907. The average amount of gold coin reported as in circulation from 1907 through 1933 was $490 million. The rate of loss of gold coin would presumably be substantially less than that of national bank notes. Even the rate of loss for national bank notes of roughly $1 per $1,000 per year would have meant a loss of only $12.7 million over the 26-year period.

Could unrecorded gold exports have accounted for most of the $287 million of gold coin not surrendered by the public by the end of Jan. 1934? We think not. The two main channels for export of gold without record before 1934 were immigrant remittances and travel expenditures. To estimate the probable size of such exports, we applied to the balance of payments figures for those items, 1907–33, the ratio of the gold correction for 1873–1900 to similar balance of payments figures for those years. The estimate so obtained is $80 million, but it may well be an overstatement: (1) the gold correction for the earlier period is only in part —although probably in major part—attributable to unrecorded exports; (2) travel expenditures for the earlier period are limited to passengers' transportation and travel expenses, while for the period since 1907 they also include import freight payments.

If the estimates of gold lost and gold exported without record are added to the gold coin returned to the Treasury since 1934, we are still far short of accounting for even half of the $287 million. We therefore concluded that in Jan. 1934 the bulk of the $287 million was retained illegally in private hands. For this reason we restored to the gold stock and gold circulation the $287 million which the Federal Reserve subtracted for 1914–33 from the figures as originally published. Since gold coin has not been a component of the money stock since Jan. 31, 1934, our series exclude the $287 million since that date.

Until July 14, 1954, it was lawful for U.S. citizens to hold as rare coin only two coins of each specimen minted. A regulation of the Secretary of the Treasury (*Federal Register*, XIX, No. 135, July 14, 1954, p. 4331) removed any limit on the possession of gold coin minted before Apr. 5, 1933, designating all such coins as of numismatic value.

Although it has been illegal since 1933 for the public to hold gold certificates, amounts outstanding were not dropped from the monthly circulation statement after Jan. 1934, as they were for gold coin. There has, however, been a substantial decline in gold certificates from the total of $178 million recorded as outstanding at the end of Jan. 1934. At the end of 1960 only $30 million was still reported in circulation, most of which probably may not be returned to the Treasury. Application of the loss rate for national bank notes to the average amount of gold certificates in circulation from 1880 through 1933 yields a probable loss of $24 million over the 53-year period. However, in all likelihood this is an overestimate, since gold certificates were surely subject to a decidedly smaller rate of loss. This judgment is based on the fact that, compared with national bank notes, gold certificates were of higher denominations, and a larger proportion of the amounts outstanding was held in bank vaults.

464

order of March 10, but also to all persons dealing in foreign exchange. On the same day, the Thomas amendment to the Agricultural Adjustment Act was offered in Congress. The amendment, enacted into law on May 12, and explicitly directed at achieving a price rise through expansion of the money stock, contained a provision authorizing the President to reduce the gold content of the dollar to as low as 50 per cent of its former weight. The dollar price of gold immediately started rising, which is to say that so also did the dollar price of foreign currencies, including both those like the French franc that remained on gold and those like the pound sterling that had gone off gold at an earlier date. In the next three months, the market price of gold rose to $30 an ounce, and thereafter fluctuated erratically between a low of about $27 and a high of nearly $35 until January 30, 1934, when the Gold Reserve Act was passed.[46] During that period, the United States had a floating exchange rate determined in the market from day to day, as in the period from 1862 to 1879. However, there was considerably greater government interference in the market. On September 8, 1933, an official gold price, to be fixed daily at the estimated world market figure less shipping and insurance cost, was established. The Treasury agreed to buy gold at that price to give American gold miners a price as high as they could have obtained by export in the absence of the export embargo.

Starting in October, the government intervened actively to raise the price of gold. The Reconstruction Finance Corporation was authorized to buy newly mined domestic gold from October 25 on, and a few days later, through the agency of the Federal Reserve Banks, to buy gold abroad. The purchase price was raised almost daily. For a time, the large scale of RFC purchases abroad made the announced price for newly-mined domestic gold the effective market price. From the end of November, however, until the end of January 1934, the announced price exceeded the market price abroad.[47]

The aim of the gold policy was to raise the price level of commodities, particularly farm products and raw materials, which sustained the greatest relative decline during the preceding years of deflation. That aim was pursued simultaneously through other New Deal measures, of which the National Recovery Administration's promulgation of "codes" and the Agricultural Adjustment Administration's production controls were the most notable. It was not pursued, as we have seen, through any substantial increase in the quantity of money, though the Thomas amendment provided the legal basis for an increase even without the concurrence of the Federal Reserve System. Most farm products and raw materials exported by the United States had a world market in which this country,

[46] See Pearson, Myers, and Gans, "Warren," pp. 5636, 5645–5647.
[47] Pearson, Myers, and Gans, "Warren," p. 5646.

while sometimes important as both supplier and purchaser, was seldom dominant. The prices of such commodities in foreign currencies were determined by world demand and supply and were affected by events in the United States only insofar as these, in turn, affected the amounts supplied and demanded by the United States. Even then, such prices were affected much less than in proportion to the changes in U.S. sales and purchases. Hence, the decline in the foreign exchange value of the dollar meant a roughly proportional rise in the dollar price of such commodities, which is, of course, what did happen to the dollar prices of cotton, petroleum products, leaf tobacco, wheat, and similar items. The aim of the gold policy to raise prices of farm products and raw materials was therefore largely achieved.

The decline in the foreign exchange value of the dollar was initially a product of speculative sale of dollars in the expectation of devaluation—a short-term capital outflow. The decline was sustained by shifts in the demand (by which, as always, we mean demand schedules) for imports and supply (again, supply schedules) of exports produced by the cessation of internal deflation. The resolution of the banking panic and restoration of confidence in the monetary system were accompanied by an increase in velocity, a higher rate of spending, and rising prices. As a result, prices rose in the United States relative to prices in other countries. If the exchange value of the dollar had not fallen, the price rise would have discouraged exports and encouraged imports. Those forces were subsequently reinforced by U.S. purchase of gold at home and abroad.

U.S. purchase of domestic gold involved a reduction in the supply of goods for export, since gold is a potential export good, and hence a reduction in the demand for dollars by holders of other currencies (to buy the domestically produced gold). The purchase of foreign gold involved an increase in the demand for goods for import (namely, gold) and hence in the supply of dollars offered in exchange for foreign currencies (to buy foreign gold). The combined effect was to create a potential deficit in the U.S. balance of payments at the former exchange rate. Given a flexible rate, the potential deficit was closed by a depreciation of the dollar sufficient to generate, through an increase in exports or a decline in imports or a movement of speculative funds, an amount of foreign currencies exceeding the amount demanded for other purposes by enough to pay for the gold.

These effects depended very little on the fact that gold was the commodity purchased. Given a floating exchange rate, essentially the same effects on the dollar prices of internationally traded goods would have followed from the same dollar volume of government purchase of wheat or perfume or foreign-owned art masterpieces, or from the economically equivalent program, adopted after World War II, of building up stockpiles of foreign-produced strategic goods. Of course, had one of these other commodities been used as the vehicle for the purchase program, gold would have been one of the class of domestically produced goods, export of which was stimulated by the U.S. depreciation of the dollar, and one of the class of foreign-produced goods, import of which was discouraged by the depreciation. Consequently, the hypothetical alternative purchase program would have tended to make the net inflow of gold less or the net outflow of gold more than it otherwise would have been. As it was, the use of gold as the vehicle necessarily meant an accumulation of gold, just as the use of wheat or perfume or foreign-owned masterpieces would have meant an accumulation of that commodity.

The choice of gold as the vehicle did have an important effect on the impact of the program on foreign countries. In the first place—and a corresponding effect would be present for any particular commodity— the program had a special impact on gold-producing countries. In the second place—and this effect would be present only for a commodity serving as the basis of a monetary standard—it had a special impact on gold-standard countries. Being committed to sell gold at a fixed price in terms of their own currency, those countries necessarily experienced pressure on their gold reserves, which in turn necessitated either abandonment of the gold standard or internal deflationary pressure. Entirely aside from the changes in the *relative* demands and supplies of goods they imported or exported arising out of the gold-purchase program, those countries were placed in the position of having to adjust their whole nominal price level.[48]

---

[48] It may help to put this point somewhat differently in terms of a particular example. Suppose the purchase program had been for French perfumes. Then, given the French internal monetary position, the price of such perfumes in francs would rise, the price in francs of other French exports would tend to fall (since the depreciation of the dollar would make them more expensive to Americans in dollars and hence reduce the quantity demanded at the former franc price), and the price in francs of goods imported into France from the U.S. would also tend to fall (since the depreciation of the dollar would reduce the franc equivalent of the former dollar price). Nothing can be said about the remaining prices: some might remain constant, some fall and some rise, depending on their substitutability in consumption and production for other exports and imports.

Now let the purchase program be for gold, either a program to spend a fixed number of dollars per month for gold, or to buy a fixed number of ounces per month at the market price in dollars, or to buy whatever number of ounces would be offered at a fixed dollar price higher than the prior market price, or any combination of these programs. Let France be on a gold standard and be the only country on a gold standard. Suppose, first, that France takes whatever measures are necessary to preserve her gold reserves intact and hence to force all U.S. gold purchases to be made elsewhere. This could occur through a general deflation of all French prices sufficient to make the depreciation of the dollar vis-à-vis the franc enough greater than its depreciation vis-à-vis other (nongold-standard) currencies so that the fixed franc price for gold, times the dollar price of the franc, yields a dollar price of gold above (or just equal to) the market price of gold in other

The device used to achieve a decline in the exchange value of the dollar—borrowing funds (through the issue of RFC securities) to purchase gold—was not unprecedented. The identical device was incorporated in the Resumption Act and employed before 1879 but that time for precisely the opposite purpose: to promote a rise in the exchange value of the dollar. In discussing that episode, we pointed out that the mechanical as opposed to the psychological effects of the accumulation of a gold reserve rendered resumption more rather than less difficult. The reasons are precisely those just given to explain why the gold purchases contributed to the decline in the exchange value of the dollar. In the one case as in the other, it is doubtful that the device was nearly so important as the less dramatic forces that were at work beneath the surface, but this is clearer in the 1879 episode when the device worked against the objective than it is in the 1933 episode when it fostered the objective.

A major obstacle to using gold as a vehicle for lowering the exchange value of the dollar and thereby raising prices was the existence of the so-called gold clause in many government and private obligations and in private contracts. That clause, whose use dated back to the greenback period after the Civil War, required payment either in gold proper, or in a nominal amount of currency equal to the value of a specified weight of gold. It was designed precisely to protect lenders and others against currency depreciation. The clause, if honored, would have multiplied the nominal obligations of the federal government and of many private borrowers for interest and principal of debt by the ratio of the new price of gold to the old price of gold. Also it would have reduced the stimulating

---

currencies, times the price of those currencies in dollars. It would then be cheaper for the U.S. to buy gold in those other countries than to acquire it from France at the fixed franc price. France would have avoided a reduction of her gold reserve at the cost of undergoing a general deflation. However, even if we ignore the costs of the deflationary process, this involves a greater adjustment than is appropriate. At the lower nominal price level in France, the former gold reserves would now have a greater value in terms of goods and services. Hence, it would be appropriate for France to make part of the adjustment through a reduction in gold reserves measured in ounces of gold.

This final point makes clear how the adjustment would tend to occur if all countries except the U.S. were on a gold standard. The extra gold demanded by the U.S. would be provided both from new production and by a reduction in reserves that would otherwise have been held, matched by a reduction in the price level in terms of gold in the rest of the world.

For the United States, the primary effect of the existence of some gold-standard countries or of all other countries' adherence to the gold standard would be a change in the magnitude of the depreciation of the dollar in terms of foreign currency, since the depreciation would have to be enough to offset not only the change in "real" demands and supplies produced by the purchase program but also the decline in the general level of prices in terms of gold in the rest of the world. If the program selected provided for spending a fixed number of dollars per month on gold, there would be a secondary effect arising out of the fact that the same number of dollars expended would buy different quantities of gold.

468

effects on private activity of the reduction in the ratio of debt to income which, it was hoped, would result from currency depreciation. Accordingly, a joint resolution was introduced into Congress on May 6 and passed on June 5, 1933, abrogating the gold clause in all public and private contracts, past and future. In February 1935, the Supreme Court, by a five-to-four decision, in effect upheld the constitutionality of that resolution.[49]

At the outset, the gold policy was one of two mutually inconsistent policies with respect to the monetary standard simultaneously pursued by President Roosevelt. The other was the organization of a World Monetary and Economic Conference which convened in London, June 1933. President Hoover had set in train the arrangements for the convocation of the conference in May 1932, and it was originally scheduled to be held in January 1933. The aim of the conference was to achieve cooperative action on international economic problems, and hopes were high that it would produce an agreement stabilizing foreign exchange arrangements. But the conference was nearly a complete failure. One reason was that, while it was in process, the President apparently decided definitely to adopt the path of currency depreciation. He sent a message to the conference on July 2, 1933, which dissociated the United States from any attempt to achieve what was described as a "temporary and probably an artificial stability in foreign exchange on the part of a few large countries" and was termed a "specious fallacy."[50] The message was at the time given much of the public blame for the failure of the conference. However, whatever the President might have said and however consistent U.S. policy might have been, it seems dubious that the economic preconditions existed for a viable exchange stabilization agreement. The fundamental difficulties were the probable incompatibility of the exchange rates of the sterling bloc and of the nations that still remained on gold, and the unwillingness at the time of the gold-bloc countries to change their gold parities.

The period of a variable price for gold came to an end on January 31, 1934, when the President, under the authority of the Gold Reserve Act passed the day before, specified a fixed buying and selling price of $35 an ounce for gold, thereby devaluing the gold dollar to 59.06 per cent of its former weight. Under the terms of the act, title to all gold coin and bullion was to be vested in the United States; all gold coins were to be withdrawn from circulation and melted into bullion and further gold

[49] The Court upheld the right of Congress to abrogate the gold clause in private, state, and city obligations, but not in those of the U.S. government. The Court, however, denied the claim of a plaintiff for a judgment for $16,931.25 in legal tender currency on his U.S. government bond of $10,000, on the ground that he had not shown any loss whatever in relation to purchasing power.
[50] Message reproduced in Paris, *Monetary Policies*, pp. 166–167.

coinage was to be discontinued; the Secretary of the Treasury was to control all dealings in gold; and the President was authorized to fix the weight of the gold dollar at any level between 50 and 60 per cent of its prior legal weight.[51]

Since the Treasury had formerly valued its own gold holdings at $20.67 an ounce and paid only that price for the gold it acquired from private individuals, commercial banks, and the Federal Reserve System, it realized a large "paper" profit from the revaluation of the dollar; which is to say, the Treasury could print additional paper money entitled "gold certificates" to a nominal value of nearly $3 billion without acquiring additional gold and yet conform to the legal requirement that it hold a specified weight of gold (now less than before) for each dollar printed. Those gold certificates could not legally be held by private individuals, but they could be held by Federal Reserve Banks. Accordingly, to realize its "profits," the Treasury had to turn over gold certificates to the Federal Reserve System, receiving in return a deposit credit that it could convert into Federal Reserve notes or pay out by check. Stripped of its legal trappings, the economic effect was identical with a simple grant of authority to the Treasury to print and to put in circulation nearly $3 billion of fiat currency in addition to the $3 billion in greenbacks already explicitly authorized by the Thomas Amendment to the Agricultural Adjustment Act.[52]

[51] The President requested the legislation in a message to Congress on Jan. 15, 1934. He recommended vesting title to all gold in the United States in the government for three reasons: (1) to end use of gold as a means of payment; (2) to limit transfer of gold bullion to settlement of international balances; (3) and to give the government ownership of any added dollar value of the country's gold stock as a result of a decrease in the gold content of the dollar.

On the same day an executive order regulating transactions in foreign exchange reaffirmed the regulations in the order of Apr. 20, 1933, requiring a Treasury license for every transaction in foreign exchange, for transfer of credit between banks in and outside the United States, and for export of any legal tender currency from the United States. But the order specifically excluded from the license requirement foreign exchange transactions for usual business purposes, for reasonable travel expenses, for fulfillment of contracts in existence before Mar. 9, 1933, and for transfers of credit between banks in the Continental United States and banks in its possessions. The authority of the Treasury and its agent, the Federal Reserve Banks, to require complete information on every foreign exchange transaction was reaffirmed, as was the Treasury's power to prohibit types of transactions not approved.

On Jan. 16, 1934, the function of buying gold of domestic origin was transferred from the RFC to the Federal Reserve Banks. The weight of the gold dollar, as fixed in the Presidential proclamation of Jan. 31, 1934, was 15.238+ grains of standard gold 0.900 fine (or 13.714+ grains of pure gold), which is 59.06 per cent of the weight of the old gold dollar fixed at 25.8 grains of standard gold 0.900 fine (or 23.22 grains of pure gold). An ounce troy equals 480 grains. The new price of gold, $35, is obtained by dividing 480 by 13.714+, as the old price, $20.67, is obtained by dividing 480 by 23.22.

[52] The legal trappings do raise a problem in getting an economically meaning-

Of the paper profit, $2 billion was assigned to a stabilization fund set up under the control of the Secretary of the Treasury and authorized to deal in gold, foreign exchange, securities, and other credit instruments for the purpose of stabilizing the exchange value of the dollar.[53]

Since February 1, 1934, the official price of gold has remained fixed at $35 an ounce. In this sense, that date marked the return to a gold standard. But the gold standard to which the United States returned was very different, both domestically and internationally, from the one it had left less than a year earlier. The Mint has since bought all gold offered to it at the price of $35 an ounce but sells only for the purpose of foreign payment. As noted, the holding of gold coin and bullion is forbidden to private individuals in the United States, except for use in industry and the arts and for numismatic holdings, and gold no longer circulates domestically. The Federal Reserve continues to have a gold reserve requirement, but the state of the reserve has not been a direct influence on policy at any time since 1933, though it has threatened to become one since a sharp decline in the U.S. gold stock began in 1958. For example, when, in 1945, the System was approaching the then existing requirement (40 per cent for notes and 35 per cent for deposits), the law was changed to require a uniform 25 per cent.

Fixed buying and selling prices for gold have no longer been the major reliance for maintaining rigid exchange rates with other currencies, even those of countries nominally on gold. Instead, a new central bank organ was created, the stabilization fund, with powers to engage in open market purchase and sale of foreign exchange and nonmonetary gold to influence exchange rates. During the late thirties, most of the so-called gold-bloc countries finally left gold, and nominally floating exchange rates with government speculation through stabilization funds became the rule.

---

ful breakdown of high-powered money, by assets of the monetary authorities. One division that seems economically significant is between commodity money (the monetary gold stock) and fiduciary money (the balance). So long as the price of gold is unchanged, this division is fairly clear and meaningful. The change in the price, however, raises difficulties. If all the gold is revalued at the new price, the arithmetic makes the increase in price appear as a sudden rise in the commodity component of high-powered money and a decline in the fiduciary component. Economically, there is no such change. Hence our gold stock figures, in the breakdown of high-powered money, by assets of the monetary authorities, are expressed at cost, which means that the paper profits are kept as part of the fiduciary component of high-powered money, but subsequent acquisitions at the higher price are included in full in the commodity component. See also Chap. 5, above, pp. 209–212.

[53] Of the balance of the paper profit, $645 million was used for the redemption of national bank notes, which simply substituted one form of fiduciary currency for another; $27 million was transferred to the Federal Reserve Banks for making industrial loans; $2 million was charged off to losses in melting gold coins; and $141 million remained in the General Fund cash balance (see Paris, *Monetary Policies*, p. 29).

During the war, many countries fixed "official" exchange rates but sought to maintain them by extensive control over foreign exchange transactions, imitating the devices developed by Schacht for Germany in the 1930's, rather than by free purchase or sale at fixed prices of either gold or foreign exchange. Since then, an even wider variety of actual arrangements has coexisted.

Perhaps the best description of the role of gold in the United States since 1934 is that, rather than being the basis of the monetary system, it is a commodity whose price is officially supported in the same way as the price of wheat, for example, has been under various agricultural programs. The major differences are that the support price for agricultural products is paid only to domestic producers, the gold-support price to foreign as well as domestic; the agricultural products accumulated are freely sold at the support prices to anyone, the gold only to certain foreign purchasers and not to any domestic ones. In consequence, the gold program has set a floor under the world price of gold in terms of dollars.

The substitution in January 1934 of a fixed price for gold, rather than a variable price as under the earlier purchase program, meant that the number of dollars spent on gold was no longer under the direct control of U.S. authorities. Having fixed the price, they were committed to buy all that was offered. But the effects of such purchases were the same as under the earlier program. For the United States, the purchases meant an increase in the dollar value of other exports relative to the dollar value of imports, thanks to a rise in prices of internationally traded goods relative to domestic goods through the combined effect of changes in exchange rates and in domestic price levels of the various countries. For gold-producing countries, the purchases meant an increased price for one of their products, hence an expansion in the gold industry relative to other industries and a rise in income. For gold-standard countries, the price fixed for gold by the United States determined the rate of exchange between their currencies and dollars. They either had to adjust their internal price level to that new rate—in the process presumably disposing of some of their reserves as measured in ounces of gold—or to change their own fixed price for gold. For all gold-standard and gold-producing countries except the United States and for nongold-standard and nongold-producing countries, the gold purchases meant a reshuffling of international trade in response to a decreased U.S. demand for products other than gold, and an increased demand for such products by gold-producing countries; the program meant an increased supply of products from the United States and a decreased supply from gold-producing countries. Finally, international trade had to adjust to measures adopted by gold-standard countries to meet loss of their reserves.

The price fixed for gold initially overvalued the product, of course,

472

and therefore stimulated a rapid increase in production and a rapid accumulation of government stocks. Production in the United States including its possessions rose from less than 2.6 million ounces in 1933 to 6 million in 1940; in the world, from 25 million ounces in 1933 to 41 million in 1940. The rise in prices of other commodities and services since 1940 has lowered the relative price of gold and reduced U.S. gold output (1960) below its 1933 level, though world output still exceeds the level of that year. The gold stock in the Treasury rose from 200 million ounces when the support price was fixed in early 1934 to 630 million ounces by the end of 1940, a rise that was 1¾ times as much as aggregate world output during the intervening period. The gold stock declined somewhat during the war, then rose to an all-time high in 1949. By the end of 1960 it had fallen again to about 510 million ounces, still about 2½ times its level when the fixed price was established.

In purchasing gold, as in purchasing agricultural or other commodities, the U.S. government can be said to have three proximate sources of funds:[54] tax receipts, borrowing, or creation of money.[55] The one difference is that the support program for other commodities (excepting silver, for which see below) carries with it no authorization to create money, whereas the support program for gold does, thereby automatically providing the financial means for its continuance. Treasury deposits at Federal Reserve Banks can be increased through gold purchases by gold certificate credits equal to the amount of gold purchased times the official price of gold. Except for a minor handling charge (¼ of 1 per cent), this has also been, in practice, the amount the Treasury spent by drawing a check on its deposits in acquiring gold. Gold purchases are usually financed in this way; hence, increases in the gold stockpile produce no automatic budgetary pressure. The link between gold purchases and Treasury authorization to create high-powered money is, of course, the main remnant of the historical role of gold, and still serves to give gold some special monetary significance. The one important occasion when a different method of finance was used was in 1937, when the Treasury "sterilized" gold by paying for gold with funds raised through security issues (see Chapter 9, section 3).

It is easier to describe the gold policy of the United States since 1934 than it is to describe the resulting monetary standard of the United States.

[54] The word proximate is intended as a warning of the oversimplification involved in associating particular expenditures with particular receipts.

[55] It might be more meaningful to describe the two latter as borrowing in interest-bearing form and borrowing in noninterest-bearing form. More fundamentally still, money creation may itself be either borrowing (if prices are not raised thereby) or taxation (if prices are raised). See Friedman, "Discussion of the Inflationary Gap," *Essays in Positive Economics,* University of Chicago Press, 1955, p. 257; also, above, Chap. 2, footnote 64, and Chap. 5, footnote 35.

It is not a gold standard in the sense that the volume of gold or the maintenance of the nominal value of gold at a fixed price can be said to determine directly or even at several removes the volume of money. It is conventional to term it—as President Roosevelt did—a managed standard, but that simply evades the difficult problems of definition. It is clearly a fiduciary rather than a commodity standard, but it is not possible to specify briefly who manages its quantity and on what principles. The Federal Reserve System, the Treasury, and still other agencies have affected its quantity by their actions in accordance with a wide variety of objectives. In principle, the Federal Reserve System has the power to make the quantity of money anything it wishes, within broad limits, but it has seldom stated its objectives in those terms. It has sometimes, as when it supported bond prices, explicitly relinquished its control. And it clearly is not unaffected in its actions by gold flows. So long as the exchange rate between the dollar and other currencies is kept fixed, the behavior of relative stocks of money in various countries must be close to what would be produced by gold standards yielding the same exchange rates, even though the mechanism may be quite different. Perhaps a "discretionary fiduciary standard" is the best simple term to characterize the monetary standard which has evolved. If it is vague and ambiguous, so is the standard it denotes.

The rise in the dollar price of gold-bloc currencies was at first much greater than that of currencies not linked to gold. From January 1933 to September 1934 the rise was 70 per cent for the currencies of France, Switzerland, Belgium, the Netherlands, and Italy, and less than 50 per cent for the pound sterling. The gold-standard currencies therefore appreciated not only relative to the dollar but also relative to other currencies. The differential appreciation measured the special impact of our gold price-support program on the position of the gold-standard countries. The fact that they lost gold meant that they bore, as it were, a larger part of the effect of the expansion of U.S. exports and contraction of U.S. imports other than gold than other countries did, and thereby cushioned the initial impact on those other countries.

As we have seen, had nothing else intervened, the gold-standard countries would have had to reduce their internal price levels relative to those of other countries in order to stay on gold, which is to say, in order to render something like the new structure of exchange rates consistent with no pressure on the balance of payments. In fact, something else did intervene, but it intensified rather than eased the problem of the gold-standard countries. Gold purchases under the fixed price-support program coincided with a flight of capital to the United States from Europe largely induced by political changes: first, the rise to power of Hitler in Germany which led to a large-scale attempt to transfer capital

474

out of Germany, particularly by Jews; then the increasing fears of war which led to a flight of capital from France, Britain, and other European countries.

Since the flight of capital constituted an increased demand for dollars, its effects on exchange rates and on U.S. trade in commodities and services other than gold were in precisely the opposite direction to those of the gold price-support program and tended to offset them.[56] There was simultaneously an increased offer of dollars for gold on the part of the U.S. government and an increased demand on the part of foreigners for dollars to hold. By trading assets held abroad for gold and transferring the gold to the U.S. Treasury, foreigners could acquire dollars and the Treasury could acquire gold without in any way affecting the rest of the U.S. balance of payments. To the extent that such offsetting occurred, the gold program did not affect U.S. trade currents and the relative prices of internationally traded goods in the United States in ways described earlier. Since such changes in trade currents and relative prices tended to reduce the amount of gold offered for sale to the United States at its fixed price, the capital inflow meant that this country acquired a larger amount of gold at $35 an ounce than it otherwise would have. Hence, while the capital inflow and the gold price-support program had opposite effects on U.S. exchange rates and on U.S. trade in commodities and services other than gold, both tended to raise its gold stock.

For gold-standard countries that were themselves subject to a capital

[56] If the U.S. had continued its floating exchange-rate policy of 1933 and had fixed no firm price at which it was willing to buy the world's gold, the capital flight would have produced an appreciation of the U.S. dollar relative to other currencies, which would have discouraged exports from the U.S. and encouraged imports into the U.S. That outcome would have produced the unfavorable balance of trade required as the physical side of the capital import—and incidentally, would have worked against one of the domestic objectives of New Deal policy, namely, to raise exports relative to imports as a means of stimulating employment. If, instead, the U.S. and other countries involved had all been on a gold standard of the nineteenth century variety, the attempt to transfer capital to the U.S. would have increased gold reserves in this country, even without a rise in the dollar price of gold, and decreased gold reserves abroad; it would have increased proportionately the money stock in the U.S. and thereby have promoted a rise in domestic prices and income; and it would have decreased the money stock abroad and thereby have promoted a fall in prices and income in foreign countries. These changes would have tended to produce precisely the same shift in relative prices and the same unfavorable balance of trade as the appreciation of the dollar under the hypothetical floating exchange rates would have done.
To avoid misunderstanding, we should record explicitly that the actual working out of the adjustment might be—and in our opinion would be—very different under floating and rigid rates for reasons that are outlined in a different connection in Friedman, "The Case for Flexible Exchange Rates," *Essays in Positive Economics,* pp. 157–203. Nevertheless, the character of the adjustment required would be identical; the difference—and in some contexts an essential difference—is the efficiency of the mechanism of adjustment.

outflow—that is, for all the important so-called gold-bloc countries that had remained on gold after 1933—the capital outflow reinforced rather than offset the effect of the gold price-support program. It required an additional reduction in internal price levels beyond that called for by the support program. Exports had to be still larger relative to imports if they were to finance the capital outflow without a continued outflow of gold.

The deflation that would have been required by the combined effect of the U.S. gold price-support program and the capital outflow was more than the gold-bloc countries were willing to undergo, as perhaps the effect of either alone might also have been. Accordingly, in the fall of 1936, France and Switzerland devalued their currencies in conjunction with a tripartite agreement between the United States, France, and Great Britain. Other gold-bloc countries either followed suit or abandoned the gold standard.

There is no direct way to separate the opposite effects on U.S. international trade of the capital flight and the gold-price support program; one can only record their combined effect on international trade together, of course, with the effect of still other factors, such as the changing level of business activity. On the whole, however, Table 20, which summarizes the combined effect, suggests that the gold price-support program was quantitatively more important than the flight of capital in its effects on U.S. international trade for the years 1934–39 as a whole. The evidence is, however, somewhat mixed, and this conclusion must therefore be regarded as highly tentative.

The chief ambiguity in the evidence is in the balance-of-payments figures in the first two parts of the table. As we have seen, the gold price-support program alone would have tended to produce an increase in the U.S. balance of trade in commodities and services other than gold, through either exchange rate changes, or changes in international prices sufficient to lower U.S. prices relative to foreign prices when both were expressed in a common currency.[57] The capital inflow alone would have acted in the opposite direction. Because of errors in balance of payments figures, it is by no means clear what actually happened. Lines 1 and 5 give the balance of trade estimated directly from figures on imports and exports, line 1 in absolute amounts, line 5 as a percentage of national income to adjust for both price changes and changes in the size of the economy. To judge from these statistics, the balance of trade was substantially lower for 1934–39 as a whole than for the decade of the twenties, and a trifle lower than for the depression years 1930–33. Lines 2 and 6 give the balance of trade as estimated indirectly from figures on capital and gold movements; the difference between the estimates in line 1 and line 2 is

[57] Note that this is consistent with a rise in the absolute level of U.S. prices if the exchange value of the dollar depreciates.

the item labeled "errors and omissions" in the official figures published on the balance of payments. These errors and omissions are sufficiently large to reverse the direction of difference. Lines 2 and 6 show the balance of trade as noticeably larger in 1934–39 than in either the twenties or 1930–33 (in line 2, the balance of trade is equal to that in the twenties, but since prices were lower, it was decidedly larger in real terms). Lines 1 and 5 imply that capital flows were quantitatively more important; lines 2 and 6, that the gold-purchase program was more important.

We are inclined to put more weight on the evidence from lines 2 and 6 than on that from lines 1 and 5, for two reasons. First, an examination of the sources of error in the figures suggests that the indirect estimates are likely to be more accurate than the direct estimates.[58] Second, as we shall see below, the price data rather unambiguously indicate that the gold-purchase program was the more important. As it happens, the estimates in line 6 are also the ones comparable to those we have used in our several charts showing the relation between relative prices and capital movements (Charts 9, 17, and 36).

From the estimates for the three years 1934–36, mostly before French and Swiss devaluation, and the three years thereafter, 1937–39, the dominance of the gold-purchase program appears to be clearly greater in the second period than in the first. By providing gold, as it were, from their monetary balances to exporters of capital, the gold-standard countries facilitated the direct offsetting of the capital and the gold movements described earlier. Indeed, the figures for both lines 5 and 6 indicate that, during the earlier years, the capital movement had more impact on the balance of trade than did the gold flow.

The price data in the third section of Table 20 indicate that the gold program was more important than the capital flow, despite the divergent movement of prices in different countries, mostly reflecting the impact of different dates of devaluation. Though many other forces may in principle affect relative prices, these other forces have in practice been quite minor. In the whole period from 1879 to 1914, for example, when both Britain and the United States were continually on gold, the price ratio like that in Table 20 (given annually in Table A-4, column 1, for 1871–1960) varied only between 90 and 106, and some of that variation, as we have seen, can be accounted for by capital movements. Hence, these

[58] See *Balance of Payments, 1949–1951,* Office of Business Economics, 1952, pp. 115–117. What is in question is whether errors and omissions are to be interpreted as primarily unrecorded capital items or unrecorded trade and service items. If the former, the estimates in line 1 should be more accurate; if the latter, the estimates in line 2 should be more accurate. It should be noted that our inclination to accept the latter interpretation is contrary to the most widely held view.

477

TABLE 20

United States Balance of International Payments and Ratio of Purchasing-Power Parity to Exchange Rates, 1923–39

	1923–29	1930–31	1932–33	1930–33	1934–36	1937–39	1934–39
	ANNUAL AVERAGE AMOUNT (billions of dollars)						
Balance of trade in commodities and services other than gold (exports minus imports) lines 1, 2							
1. Estimated directly	1.07	0.74	0.34	0.54	0.16	0.78	0.47
2. Estimated from capital movements	0.86	0.95	0.41	0.68	0.47	1.27	0.87
3. Capital inflow minus unilateral transfers to foreign countries	−0.84	−0.90	−0.49	−0.69	0.86	0.74	0.80
4. Gold outflow	−0.02	−0.05	0.08	0.02	−1.33	−2.01	−1.67
	AVERAGE PER CENT OF NATIONAL INCOME						
Balance of trade in commodities and services other than gold (exports minus imports) lines 5, 6							
5. Estimated directly	1.32	1.03	0.78	0.91	0.33	1.09	0.71
6. Estimated from capital movements	1.07	1.32	0.94	1.13	0.89	1.76	1.32
7. Capital inflow minus unilateral transfers to foreign countries	−1.03	−1.28	−1.13	−1.21	1.42	1.01	1.21
8. Gold outflow	−0.04	−0.04	0.19	0.08	−2.31	−2.76	−2.54

(continued)

TABLE 20 (concluded)

	1923–29	Jan. 1930 to Aug. 1931 Before Britain Abandoned Gold	Sept. 1931 to Dec. 1933 After	1930–33	Jan. 1934 to Sept. 1936 Before France and Switzerland Devalued	Oct. 1936 to Aug. 1939 After	Jan. 1934 to Aug. 1939
				MONTHLY AVERAGES (per cent)			
9. Ratio (1929 = 100) of purchasing-power parity to exchange rates, U.S. implicit price index relative to:							
a. British cost of living divided by cents per pound	98.8	97.4	108.2	103.7	87.7	85.5	86.6
b. French cost of living divided by cents per franc	112.2	86.9	71.6	78.0	52.0	80.2	66.5
c. Swiss cost of living divided by cents per franc	100.7	94.2	79.4	85.6	58.1	80.3	69.5

NOTE: Because of rounding, there may be discrepancies in the last decimal place.

SOURCE, BY LINE

1. Balance of trade in commodities and services as reported includes excess of gold production over nonmonetary gold consumption (see *Balance of Payments, 1949–1951*, Office of Business Economics, Dept. of Commerce, 1952, pp. 23, 113). Excess obtained by subtracting gold sales (*Balance of Payments, 1958*, pp. 11–12, line 8) from gold outflow (line 4 of the present table) was subtracted from the reported balance (*ibid.*, pp. 11–12, line 23).

2. Sum, with sign changed, of lines 3 and 4 of the present table. (Line 2 minus line 1 is the OBE'S "errors and omissions.")

3. *Ibid.*, pp. 11–12, sum of lines 24, plus 30, plus 41.

4. 1923–33: *Banking and Monetary Statistics*, Board of Governors of the Federal Reserve System, 1943, p. 538. 1934–39: *Federal Reserve Bulletin*, 1947–49 issues.

5–8. Same as lines 1–4, except that each item for each year was first divided by national income from same source as for Chart 62.

9. U.S. implicit price index: Same source as for Chart 62. British and Swiss cost of living: *Statistical Yearbook of the League of Nations*, 1931/32–1939/40 issues. French cost of living: 1923–June 1931, Oct. 1931–Dec. 1938, *ibid.* (data are quarterly for Paris only); July–Sept. 1931, data from *ibid.* were interpolated to months by average monthly price of 34 household commodities in *Annuaire Statistique, 1946*, France, Institut National de la Statistique, p. 199; Jan.–Aug. 1939, League of Nations data were extrapolated by a quarterly cost-of-living index in *ibid.*, *1940–45*, p. 211. Exchange rates: *Banking and Monetary Statistics*, pp. 670, 680–681.

price ratios are sensitive and accurate indicators of the effects of monetary changes and of such major factors as the gold program and the capital flow.

To judge from implicit prices in the United States and cost-of-living indexes for Britain, France, and Switzerland, U.S. prices, adjusted for changes in exchange rates, were lower relative to prices in other countries after 1933 than in either the twenties or 1930–33. This is the result to be expected if the gold price-support program had a greater effect than the capital inflow had.

The difference between British prices, on the one hand, and French and Swiss prices, on the other, before the French and Swiss devaluation in 1936 reflects the disproportionate initial impact of the gold-purchase program on France and Switzerland referred to above: their gold losses implied a large balance of payments deficit reflecting high prices internally relative to U.S. prices. Once they devalued, the differential effect was eliminated. Had the gold-purchase program alone been operating, one might have expected a decline in the ratio in the table for Britain balancing a rise in the ratios for France and Switzerland—just the reverse of the movements after the British devaluation in 1931. In fact, what happened was that the British ratio stayed roughly the same, while the French and Swiss rose sharply to meet it. The reason is that the capital outflow from those countries affected all alike and tended to raise all those ratios above the level that would have been produced by the gold price-support program alone.

To digress for a moment: in some ways the most striking feature of Table 20 is the greater similarity between the balance-of-payments figures for 1923–29 and those for 1930–33 than between either and those for 1934–39. The first two sets of figures show remarkably little trace of the economic holocaust that was sweeping the world. The United States was supposedly ceasing to lend to the world, yet it exported almost as much capital in absolute amount per year from 1930 to 1933 as from 1923 to 1929 and more as a percentage of national income. The reason is, figuratively, that, given no basic change in conditions of production, the incentives to invest in various countries, or monetary arrangements, the preservation of the general pattern of the figures in Table 20 was precisely the vehicle for the international transmission and coordination of the economic collapse, whatever its initial source. The attempt to change these figures—for example, the attempt by the United States to cease foreign lending—produced repercussions abroad that largely frustrated the attempt and forced this country, as it were, to continue lending.

Of course, had the capital flight occurred in the absence of the gold price-support program, the U.S. balance of trade in commodities and services other than gold after 1934 would have been less than it actually

480

was, and U.S. prices relative to foreign prices would have fallen less than they actually did or perhaps would have risen. This is so because the appreciation of the U.S. dollar relative to other currencies produced by the capital flow would have discouraged exports and encouraged imports. How much less would the balance of trade have been? Since the capital flight itself would have meant an import of gold, the balance of trade would certainly not have been less by more than $1.67 billion (Table 20, line 4, last column)—but this is so outside a limit that it is of little practical value. Similarly, in the absence of the capital flight, the balance of trade would have been higher, but again no useful estimate of how much higher can readily be made.

If we use the period 1923–29 as a basis of comparison, speak in terms of nominal dollar sums, and neglect other factors, we may summarize the combined impact of the gold price-support program and the capital flight as follows. For the six years 1934 through 1939, the statistics show that the U.S. government was buying some $1.7 billion per year more in gold than it and its citizens were wont to; and, at the same time, the U.S. economy was reducing the excess of its sales abroad over its purchases abroad of other commodities and services by some $0.6 billion per year— i.e., selling net that much less or buying net that much more—or holding that excess constant, depending on the treatment of the $0.6 billion consisting of errors and omissions in the recorded accounts (compare the difference between lines 1 and 2 of Table 20 for 1923–29 and the same difference for 1934–39). The foreign currency to finance that recorded $2.3 or $1.7 billion net increase in purchases was provided by a shift from net lending or acquisition of assets by U.S. citizens abroad of $0.8 billion a year to net borrowings or sale of assets of some $0.8 billion a year, or by an even larger shift in the same direction if the errors are assigned to the capital items. The shift from the net export to the net import of capital, in its turn, reflected mainly the desire on the part of many foreigners to hold assets in the form of U.S. dollars or U.S. securities rather than in the form of currencies and securities of European nations.

The same evidence is given year-by-year and over a longer period in Chart 36 which shows the relation between relative prices in the United States and other countries, adjusted for exchange rate changes, and capital movements into and gold movements out of the United States (expressed as a fraction of net national product) from 1920 to 1960.

Before 1932, the lines showing capital imports and unilateral transfers alone and this sum plus the gold outflow (or its equivalent, with the opposite sign, the balance of trade in commodities and services other than gold) differ little from one another either in level or year-to-year movements. The capital movements are so much larger in magnitude that they dominate the gold movements. Before 1929 the year-to-year movements of

CHART 36
U.S. Net International Capital Movement as a Ratio to National
Income, and Purchasing-Power Parity, 1920–60

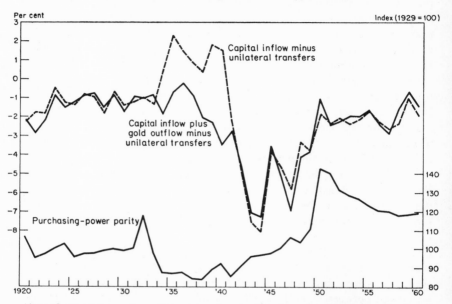

NOTE: Capital inflow, minus unilateral transfers, is plotted as plus. Gold outflow is plotted as plus.
SOURCE: Table A-4.

both capital and the payments balance show the kind of loose relation to movements in relative prices in the U.S. and Britain that we found for earlier periods (see Charts 9 and 17 above).

From 1929 to 1933, a wide divergence developed between the U.S.–British price ratio and capital movement. The price ratio rose in 1932 to a peak higher than any other value attained since 1871, the year the series starts. The payments balance shows only a mild reflection of the sharp rise in the price ratio and the capital movement alone a still milder one. The reason is that Britain's departure from gold in 1931 and the emergence of a sterling bloc and a gold bloc introduced wide diversity into the world pattern of prices. It is not possible during that period to regard movements in British prices as a reliable index of movements in world prices. This is shown in Chart 51 (p. 586) by the series expressing U.S. prices relative to Swiss prices, which is linked to the U.S.–British series in 1929. There was a sharp divergence between the two from 1929 to at least 1937, when they came fairly close together, only to diverge again after World War II began in 1939. In 1933, U.S. devaluation

482

produced the same kind of decline in U.S. prices relative to Swiss prices that British devaluation had earlier produced in British prices relative to both U.S. and Swiss prices. For the period from 1931 on, some curve intermediate between the British and the Swiss would seem the appropriate continuation of the earlier U.S.–British price ratio.

After 1932 and particularly after 1933 up to 1941, there was a dramatic divergence between capital movement figures and the figures for the balance of trade in commodities and services other than gold, a divergence of a very much larger order of magnitude than occurred before or since. That divergence represents the unprecedentedly large gold movements produced by the gold-purchase program and the flight of capital from Europe. In relation to the capital movement figures alone, U.S. prices were much lower relative to British, and even more, relative to Swiss prices than during the twenties or later during the forties and fifties. As we have seen, the difference reflects largely the effect of the gold-purchase program. The balance of trade figures alone, on the other hand, show much more nearly the same relation to the relative prices as earlier, if we use a curve intermediate between the British and Swiss.

THE SILVER-PURCHASE PROGRAM[59]

The Thomas amendment, passed on May 12, 1933, and containing a provision authorizing the President to reduce the gold content of the dollar, also gave the President sweeping powers with respect to silver. They were hardly used until December 21, 1933, when, disappointed by the effects of the gold-purchase program and under pressure from Senators from silver states as well as other proponents of currency expansion, President Roosevelt used the authority granted by the Thomas amendment to direct U.S. mints to receive all newly produced domestic silver offered to them up to December 31, 1937, at $64\frac{64}{99}$ cents an ounce (i.e., $0.6464 . . . an ounce).

The market price of silver was at that time about 44 cents an ounce, or some 75 per cent above the level at the end of 1932 and in early 1933. The rise, only slightly greater than the simultaneous depreciation of the dollar, reflected mostly the effect on all commodities with a worldwide market of the changed foreign exchange value of the dollar. But no doubt it was in part also a speculative rise promoted by expectations, raised by the Thomas amendment as well as by an agreement on silver with other countries reached at the ill-fated London Economic Conference, that the U.S. government would "do something for silver."

The nominal monetary value of silver was, and still is, $1 $2\frac{29}{99}$, or $1.2929 . . . an ounce. This value dates from 1792, when the silver dollar

---

[59] We have drawn heavily on Paris, *Monetary Policies,* in connection with this and with the preceding section.

was defined as containing 371.25 grains of pure silver.[60] But it had not been an effective market price since the gold content of the dollar had been reduced in 1834. From 1834 to 1873, the Mint ratio then established overvalued gold, hence the market value of silver was higher than $1.29+, and none was coined; the United States, though nominally bimetallic, was effectively on gold (excluding the greenback period). After 1873, when free coinage was not permitted, silver fell in value relative to gold (Chapter 3, footnote 52), a trend that though irregular was interrupted significantly only in 1889–90, thanks to the earlier silver purchase programs of 1878–90 and 1890–93, and again during World War I. Except for World War I, the market price since the turn of the century had generally been less than half the nominal mint value. Since that date, the U.S. government had made no substantial silver purchases, except after World War I to replace silver that had been shipped to India during the war (see above, Chapter 5, footnote 31). Silver had remained in a monetary limbo with respect to new acquisitions: it was used for subsidiary coin, a small volume of standard silver dollars circulated mostly in silver states, and a roughly fixed stock of silver certificates remained as a relic of the earlier silver agitation.[61] The amount of silver in use as coin or as backing for currency both inside and outside the Treasury totaled about 650 million ounces in December 1933 and had a nominal monetary value of $840 million, of which $300 million was in the form of subsidiary coin. The total market value of the stock of silver at the time the purchase program began was of course very much smaller, approximately $285 million, and that figure was some 70 per cent higher than at the end of 1932. The rather bizarre purchasing price of $64\frac{64}{99}$ cents an ounce was arrived at by adopting the fiction that silver was being accepted at its monetary value with a seigniorage charge of 50 per cent.

The President's directive to purchase newly mined silver did not stop agitation for further measures on the part either of those interested primarily in silver or of those who saw silver as a useful device for expanding the money stock. Numerous bills were introduced providing for additional action with respect to silver, many coupling that action with the use of the "seigniorage profits" for specific purposes, such as soldiers' bonus, purchase of farm products, and the like. The result was the Silver Purchase Act of June 19, 1934, which closely followed recommendations

[60] An ounce troy equals 480 grains. An ounce of silver is therefore worth 480 divided by 371.25 or $1.2929 . . . .

[61] The stock of silver dollars and certificates in and outside the Treasury increased from about $270 million in 1920, when the Treasury began to purchase silver to replace bullion shipped to India during World War I, to $540 million in 1928, at which amount it remained until the start of the silver-purchase program in Dec. 1933. Silver certificates in circulation fluctuated with changes in the public's demand for currency. The stock of subsidiary silver, as well as amounts in circulation, grew until the 1929–33 contraction.

made by the President in a message of May 22, 1934, and which directed the Secretary of the Treasury to purchase silver at home and abroad until the market price reached $1.29+ an ounce, or until the monetary value of the silver stock held by the Treasury reached one-third of the monetary value of the gold stock. The Secretary was given wide discretion in carrying out that mandate.

A purchase program under the authority of this and subsequent acts was still legally in effect in 1962, repeated efforts to repeal silver-purchase legislation having been blocked.[62] Under the authority of these acts and the initial and subsequent Presidential proclamations, the Treasury acquired some 3,200 million ounces of silver, approximately half in the four years ending December 31, 1937, and half from then to June 30, 1961.

Of the total, some 110 million ounces was silver that was "nationalized" on August 9, 1934, when the President required all holders of silver, with exceptions for silver being used in the arts and for silver coins, to turn their holdings in to the U.S. Mint at a price equivalent to 50.01 cents per fine ounce, a measure similar to the nationalization of gold and adopted for the same reason: to capture for the government profits expected to result from raising the price of silver.[63]

Another 880 million ounces was newly mined domestic silver. Since the Treasury price for newly mined domestic silver until 1955 was higher than the market price, nearly all domestic silver went to the Treasury and the demand of American silver users was met by foreign silver. From then until November 1961, when the Treasury discontinued sales, the market price approximated the support price, and silver users not only absorbed current output but also purchased from Treasury stocks. The price paid by the Treasury for the newly mined domestic silver varied between 64.64 . . . cents and 90.5050 . . . cents an ounce (corresponding to 30 per cent seigniorage). In April 1935, when the market price rose above 64.64 . . . , reaching a peak of over 81 cents at the end of April, the Treasury twice raised its price, first to a trifle over 71 cents an ounce (corresponding to 45 per cent seigniorage) then to 77.57 . . . cents (corresponding to 40 per cent seigniorage). The market price then fell, par-

[62] On Jan. 22, 1962, President Kennedy requested Congress to repeal silver-purchase legislation under which the government is required to buy all newly mined silver offered to it at the currently fixed price of 90½ cents per ounce. He also called for repeal of the silver transfer tax, under which the government takes 50 per cent of the profit from silver transactions. Legislation embodying the President's request was passed on June 4, 1963, when this book was in press.

[63] The one important difference was the recall of gold but not silver from circulation as coins. The reason for the difference, of course, is that the silver content of coins even when nominally full-bodied, as the silver dollar is, was worth less in the market than the face value, and that of subsidiary silver coins decidedly less. (The weight of silver in a silver dollar equals the face value if silver is valued at $1.2929 . . . an ounce; for smaller silver coins the weight so valued is less than their face value.)

ticularly sharply at the end of 1935, and reached a level of 45 cents in early 1936, but the Treasury price remained 77.57 . . . cents until December 1937, when it was lowered to the earlier level of 64.64. . . . After the Presidential proclamation authorizing purchases at that level expired in June 1939, an act was passed on July 6, 1939, directing the purchase of all domestic silver offered at a seigniorage charge of 45 per cent. The Treasury's silver purchases dwindled to nearly nothing soon after we entered the war. By the end of 1945 the market price had risen above 71 cents, so on July 31, 1946, an act was passed reducing seigniorage to 30 per cent—effectively establishing a buying price of 90½ cents per ounce for newly mined domestic silver—and authorizing the Secretary of the Treasury to sell nonmonetized (seigniorage or free) silver to domestic industry at not less than 90½ cents per ounce.[64] As noted above, the market price rose by 1955 to the neighborhood of the Treasury support price. From that year until November 1961, sales from Treasury stock pegged the market price at the Treasury support price. The Treasury then announced it would end sales on November 28. Once the Treasury suspended sales, the market price rose above the support price.[65]

The remaining amount purchased by the Treasury, totaling 2,210 million ounces, was silver purchased abroad at prevailing market prices. All in all, total expenditures for silver from December 31, 1933, to mid-1961 amounted to roughly $2 billion.

In spite of silver purchases of $2 billion and the accompanying sextupling of the physical quantity of silver in use as coin and currency

[64] During World War II, because of increased industrial demand for silver, some 170 million ounces were sold by the Treasury from nonmonetized silver in the General Fund, under the Green Act of July 12, 1943, for industrial uses and for Philippine coinage. The act expired on Dec. 31, 1945. In addition, over 900 million ounces were loaned temporarily to war industries for nonconsumptive electrical use. Some 410 million ounces were lend-leased to India and other countries to be returned within five years after the signing of the Japanese Peace Treaty in April 1952. All but 15 million ounces had been returned by the end of 1961.

Under the act of 1946, 138 million ounces were sold to industry, mostly after 1958. The reduction of the stock of nonmonetized silver held by the Treasury from nearly 200 million ounces at the end of 1958 to 22 million ounces when sales were suspended in 1961 reflected, in addition to sales to industry, withdrawals for subsidiary silver coinage.

[65] Within a few weeks after the order suspending sales was issued, the market price rose to $1.04¾. After declining somewhat in early 1962, the price rose to $1.09 during Aug. 1962, the highest price since Aug. 1920, when the Treasury was in the market to buy silver to retire Pittman Act certificates (see Chap. 6, footnote 60), and by June 1963, when this book was in press, to within 1½ cents of the monetary price of $1.2929. . . . When and if the market price of silver reaches the monetary price, under existing law it will be pegged close to that price by Treasury redemption of silver certificates, so long as the Treasury's silver stock holds out, and by melting down of coined silver dollars.

or held by the Treasury, the U.S. silver program never came close to achieving either of the objectives specified in the 1934 Silver Purchase Act: a market price equal to the monetary value of $1.2929 . . . , or a ratio of the monetary stocks of silver and gold of 1 to 3. The market price of silver in 1960 was about 91.4 cents an ounce and had never been much higher between 1934 and 1960.[66] The rise from 25 cents an ounce at the end of 1932 was larger than the concurrent rise in wholesale prices in general, but not by much. In 1960, the price of silver was 3.7 times the end-of-1932 level; wholesale prices, 2.9 times. The ratio of monetary silver to monetary gold stocks, both at their nominal monetary values, was just over 1 to 5 immediately before the rise in the official price of gold in January 1934; the change in the gold price reduced the ratio to 1 to 9; the heavy silver purchases restored the ratio of 1 to 5 by early 1936; until the war, continued silver purchases on the average just balanced increases in gold stock, so that the ratio fluctuated about that level. Since then the ratio has been dominated by changes in the gold stock. At the postwar peak in the gold stock in 1949, the ratio stood at 1 to 7. By the end of 1960, gold outflow had raised the ratio to 1 to 4.

In terms of its domestic effects, the silver-purchase program, like the gold-purchase program, is best regarded as a price-support program for a particular commodity, or perhaps a combination of a price-support program and a stockpiling program. In contrast with gold and as for wheat, only the price of domestic output has been effectively supported On the other hand, like gold and in contrast with wheat, purchases have been made of both domestic output and silver drawn from foreign output and stocks. Indeed, two and a half times as much has been purchased from abroad as from domestic output. Again, as with both gold and wheat, the silver program offers dramatic evidence of the high elasticity of supply of stockpiled products and the resulting difficulty of substantially altering their relative prices by a governmental purchase program, even one of very large size relative to initial output. Domestic silver output more than tripled—from under 2 million ounces a month to nearly 6 million—in the four years from the Presidential proclamation of December 21, 1933, to December 31, 1937, the period covered by that proclamation.

As with gold, the one important domestic monetary element in the silver program has been the automatic link between silver purchases and authorization to issue currency. The large so-called seigniorage charge for

[66] From 1957 to 1961 world monetary and nonmonetary consumption of silver rose at an annual rate of 4 per cent, world production at an annual rate of about 1.5 per cent. Prices and output of silver would undoubtedly have been higher in the absence of sales by the U.S. at the support price. World output may be expected to rise at a faster rate in response to the rise in the market price since the Treasury suspended sales.

newly mined silver, and the difference between the monetary value and the market price for foreign silver, have meant that silver purchases increased the authorization to issue currency by a considerably larger sum than the amount paid for the silver. In practice, the Treasury has apparently issued silver certificates equal to the amount actually paid for the silver, and has treated the excess monetary value as a miscellaneous budget receipt.

It is not easy to judge the purely domestic monetary effects of the silver-purchase program. It has involved the printing of additional silver certificates totaling over $2 billion and so in the first instance has added this much to the stock of money. However, the Federal Reserve System has always been in a position to offset this direct effect, and, as we shall see, the silver purchases to some extent reduced the gold inflow. The additional silver certificates may therefore have been simply a substitute for additional Federal Reserve notes which would otherwise have been printed. In view of the generally passive behavior of the Federal Reserve System, particularly in the period up to the end of 1937 when silver purchases were greatest, it is likely that the truth is somewhere between, and that the silver purchases led to a somewhat more rapid increase in the stock of money than would otherwise have occurred. In any event, the sums involved were small compared to either the total increase in the stock of money or the concurrent inflow of gold.

The effects on the United States other than these monetary effects were twofold. In the first place, the program involved public expenditures to stockpile a commodity and therefore increased federal government outlays—not in terms of budget accounts but in terms of economic effects. The expenditures were not large relative to the government budget. At their highest, from the end of 1933 through 1937, they averaged $220 million a year (for foreign and domestic silver combined) in comparison with federal government expenditures of the order of $7 billion a year. However, they were extremely large in comparison with the outlay of the industry they were at least partly intended to help. Total domestic silver output, even valued at the price paid by the Treasury, averaged only about $40 million a year, 1934–37,[67] and, of course, the excess of that value over the returns which the resources employed could have earned in other ways was much smaller still. Hence, viewed as a measure to "help" silver producers—including in that term not only enterprises producing silver but also persons supplying labor and other resources for production of silver—even the immediate returns from the silver-purchase program involved gross Treasury expenditures of well over $5, perhaps as much as $25 or more, for each dollar of return to silver

[67] *Historical Statistics of the United States, Colonial Times to 1957,* Bureau of the Census, 1960, p. 351, Series M-36.

producers, though, for a reason given in the next paragraph, this over-states the net cost of the program substantially.[68] And the long-run effects of the silver-purchase program have surely offset much of this immediate gain, if they have not converted it into a loss, by reducing the monetary use of silver in the rest of the world—a point to which we shall return.

The second effect on the United States, besides the direct effect on the money stock, was on the balance of international payments. Like the gold purchases, the silver purchases involved in effect the offer of dollars for foreign currencies (in order to buy foreign silver), and thereby helped finance the capital inflow into the United States. In the absence of the silver purchases, the potential U.S. payments surplus would have been larger, and hence gold inflows would have been larger as well. Given our gold policy, therefore, silver purchases were to some extent a substitute for gold purchases. This offset reduced both the net cost of the silver program and the amount by which it can be supposed to have increased the stock of money.

The most important effects of the silver program were not these domes-tic effects—which, though major in relation to the silver industry, were relatively minor in relation to the economy as a whole—but the effects on other countries. The silver program is a dramatic illustration of how a course of action, undertaken by one country for domestic reasons and relatively unimportant to that country, can yet have far-reaching consequences for other countries if it affects a monetary medium of those countries.

China was most affected. At the time, China was on a silver standard, though for minor transactions it also used local currencies of copper and nickel, whose value in silver varied from time to time.[69] Because the ex-change value of silver varied relative to gold, China was spared the initial effects of the worldwide depression. Its currency depreciated relative to other currencies, so its internal prices could remain relatively stable despite the fall in world prices. After Britain's devaluation at the end of 1931, and still more after the United States' departure from gold in 1933, the situation changed drastically. China's currency appreciated, the country was subject to the pressure of internal deflation, and it experienced widen-ing economic difficulties. The initial pressure was, of course, felt as a decline in exports relative to imports. The potential deficit in the balance of payments was met by export of silver, which in its turn tended to con-

---

[68] "Well over $5" is obtained by dividing $220 million, peak average annual Treasury expenditures for silver, by $40 million, annual value of domestic silver output. "Perhaps as much as $25 or more" is a conjecture that not more than one-fifth of the $40 million is the excess over the amount that resources employed in silver output could have earned in alternative uses.

[69] See Arthur Salter, *China and Silver*, New York, Economic Forum, 1934, pp. 46–47, 56–57.

tract the internal money supply. The pressure was somewhat eased by the availability of minor copper and nickel coinage which could change in value relative to silver, but it is doubtful that the offset was of major significance.

The U.S. silver-purchase program greatly intensified the pressure on China. As we have seen, from early 1933 to the end of the year the market price of silver rose nearly 75 per cent, and by mid-1935, under the impact of the silver-purchase program, its initial price had nearly trebled. The effect on China's international trade position can perhaps be appreciated best by expressing these figures in terms more familiar to the reader. It was as if, when Britain and the United States were both on the gold standard in the 1920's, Britain had been confronted over the course of two years with a rise in the dollar price of the pound sterling from $4.86 to nearly $15.00, resulting from changes in the U.S. gold price, without any change in the pound price at which Britain was obligated to sell gold, and without any substantial change in external or internal circumstances affecting the supply of or demand for products it purchased or sold. The result of the silver-purchase program, of course, was to drain China of silver. Its government imposed the equivalent of an export embargo on silver in an attempt to offset the appreciation of its currency. Not surprisingly, the legal obstacles to export were of no avail. Smuggling drained silver from China as rapidly as legal export had earlier.[70] Finally, in November 1935, China nationalized silver in circulation, officially abandoned the silver standard, and replaced it with a managed fiduciary standard. The new standard specified that a fractional silver reserve be held by the bank of issue, but it gave the public no right to redeem notes or deposits in silver.[71]

The owners of silver benefited, of course, from the high foreign exchange value of silver. Had silver been simply a commodity, the U.S. purchase program would have been a largely unalloyed boon, enabling the holders of silver to sell their stocks at an unexpectedly high price. Because silver served as the monetary base of China, however, students of the period are unanimous that the boon was more than offset by the economic effects of the drastic deflationary pressure imposed on China and the resulting economic disturbances. The deflationary pressure and disturbances, aside from their economic effects, certainly did not contribute to the political stability of China. Much of the limited stock of political capacity had to be devoted first to unsuccessful attempts to prevent the export of silver, then to the sweeping monetary "reform" of 1935. Furthermore, by converting China from a commodity standard effectively to a

[70] See Paris, *Monetary Policies,* p. 66.
[71] See Frank M. Tamagna, *Banking and Finance in China,* New York, Institute of Pacific Relations, 1942, pp. 142–150.

paper standard, the so-called reform rendered it both easier and more tempting to finance later war expenditures by inflationary currency issues. Under pressure of the needs of war and then revolution, China probably would in any event have departed from silver, resorted to paper money issues, and have succumbed to hyperinflation. But there can be little doubt that the effects of U.S. silver policy on China's monetary structure increased the likelihood of those events and speeded up their occurrence.

Though the Chinese experience is the most dramatic, China was by no means the only country affected by the silver-purchase program. Mexico, a major silver producer and user, was led to proclaim a bank holiday in April 1935 because the bullion value of the peso had risen above its monetary value. All coins were ordered to be exchanged for paper currency, and the export of silver money was prohibited. A year and a half later, after the world price of silver had fallen, silver coinage was restored.[72] Similar events occurred in numerous other countries throughout the world. A U.S. Treasury order in May 1935 prohibiting the import of foreign silver coins was of course ineffective. It simply meant that the coins were melted down outside the United States and the bullion shipped in instead of the melting being done, as earlier, in New York.

A policy undertaken as part of a broader program to promote adoption of "a permanent measure of value, including both gold and silver, [as] . . . a world standard," to quote from President Roosevelt's silver message of May 22, 1934,[73] had the effect of a major diminution in the worldwide monetary role of silver.

COMPOSITION OF THE CURRENCY

The effect of changes discussed in the preceding sections is in part recorded in the figures on the composition of U.S. currency, 1932–60, in Table 21. From one-sixth of the total currency in circulation, gold has declined to a negligible sum representing gold certificates lost in the course of time, held in numismatic collections, or held illegally. The figures record no coin as in circulation. However, there surely has been some in these same categories, although since 1955, there have been no limits on the possession of gold coin, all such coins having been designated rare coin (see above, footnote 45). Silver, which rose from one-eighth to one-fourth of total currency during the height of the silver-purchase program, has continued to rise in absolute amount but so much less rapidly than the total that it is back to roughly its initial proportion. National bank notes, accounting for over one-eighth of the currency in 1932, have been in the process of retirement since 1935 and are now a

[72] Paris, *Monetary Policies,* p. 71.
[73] As reproduced by Paris, pp. 187–188.

TABLE 21

COMPOSITION OF UNITED STATES CURRENCY IN CIRCULATION, OUTSIDE THE
TREASURY AND FEDERAL RESERVE BANKS, SELECTED DATES, 1932–60

End of June	Total	Gold		Silver[a]	National Bank Notes[b]	Other Treasury Currency[c]	Federal Reserve Notes
		Coin	Certifi-cates				
			MILLIONS OF DOLLARS				
1932	5,408	166	716	640	701	406	2,780
1933	5,434	34	265	647	920	508	3,061
1938	6,461	0	78	1,612	217	438	4,114
1945	26,746	0	52	2,565	120	1,142	22,867
1960	32,065	0	30	3,917	56	968	27,094
			PERCENTAGE DISTRIBUTION				
1932	100.0	3.1	13.2	11.8	13.0	7.5	51.4
1933	100.0	0.6	4.9	11.9	16.9	9.3	56.3
1938	100.0	0	1.2	24.9	3.4	6.8	63.7
1945	100.0	0	0.2	9.6	0.4	4.3	85.5
1960	100.0	0	0.1	12.2	0.2	3.0	84.5

[a] Includes standard silver dollars, silver certificates, Treasury notes of 1890, and subsidiary silver.

[b] After Aug. 1935, national bank notes became liabilities of the Treasury on a par with "other Treasury currency."

[c] Includes minor coin, U.S. notes, and Federal Reserve Bank notes. Before Mar. 1935, Federal Reserve Bank notes were liabilities of the issuing Reserve Banks.

SOURCE: *Circulation Statement of United States Money:* 1932–38, *Banking and Monetary Statistics*, p. 409; 1945, *Federal Reserve Bulletin*, Aug. 1946, p. 889; 1960, *FRB*, Aug. 1960, p. 883.

negligible fraction of the total. The variety of items under "other Treasury currency," including minor coin, U.S. notes, and Federal Reserve Bank notes, has, like silver, risen in absolute amount but fallen as a fraction of the total from over 7 per cent to 3 per cent. Evidencing the continued centralization of monetary authority, and the shift from a quasi-commodity standard to a dominantly fiduciary standard, Federal Reserve notes have taken up the slack, rising from 51 per cent of currency in circulation in 1932 to 84 per cent in 1960.[74]

[74] The Nov. 1961 order suspending silver sales from the Treasury's nonmonetized stock also directed the Treasury to use the silver cover for silver certificates for future subsidiary coinage and to replace silver certificates consequently retired by Federal Reserve notes. Only $5 and $10 denominations were affected by the order. In Jan. 1962, the President asked Congress to authorize the Federal Reserve System to issue $1 and $2 Federal Reserve notes to make possible the gradual retirement of silver certificates of those denominations. The authorization was included in the act of June 4, 1963, repealing the silver purchase acts.

CHAPTER 9

Cyclical Changes, 1933–41

As WE have seen, severe contractions tend to be succeeded by vigorous rebounds. The 1929–33 contraction was no exception. Net national product rose no less than 76 per cent in current prices and 59 per cent in constant prices from 1933 to the next cyclical peak in 1937, or at average rates of growth of 14 and 12 per cent per year, respectively (see Chart 37). These are extraordinary rates of growth. Two other four-year periods show larger rises in income in current prices, but both are wartime periods, one, terminating just after World War I, the other, during World War II. No other four-year period from the time recorded annual figures start in 1869 to 1960 shows so large a rate of rise in income in constant prices.

1. Changes in Money, Income, Prices, and Velocity

It is a measure of the severity of the preceding contraction that, despite such sharp rises, money income was 17 per cent lower in 1937 than at the preceding peak eight years earlier and real income was only 3 per cent higher. Since population had grown nearly 6 per cent in the interim, per capita output was actually lower at the cyclical peak in 1937 than at the preceding cyclical peak. There are only two earlier examples in the recorded annual figures, 1895 and 1910, when per capita output was less than it was at the preceding cyclical peaks in 1892 and 1907, respectively. Furthermore, the contraction that followed the 1937 peak, though not especially long, was unusually deep and proceeded at an extremely rapid rate, the only occasion in our record when one deep depression followed immediately on the heels of another.

In consequence, the most notable feature of the revival after 1933 was not its rapidity but its incompleteness. Throughout the revival, unemployment remained large. Even at the cyclical peak in 1937, seasonally adjusted unemployment was 5.9 million; by the trough thirteen months later, it had risen to 10.6 million out of a labor force of nearly 54 million.

The revival was initially erratic and uneven. Reopening of the banks was followed by a rapid spurt in personal income and industrial production (see Chart 37). The spurt was intensified by production in anticipation of the codes to be established under the National Industrial Recovery Act (passed June 16, 1933), which were expected to raise wage rates and

CHART 37

Money Stock, Income, Prices, and Velocity, Personal Income
and Industrial Production, in Reference Cycle Expansions
and Contractions, March 1933–December 1941

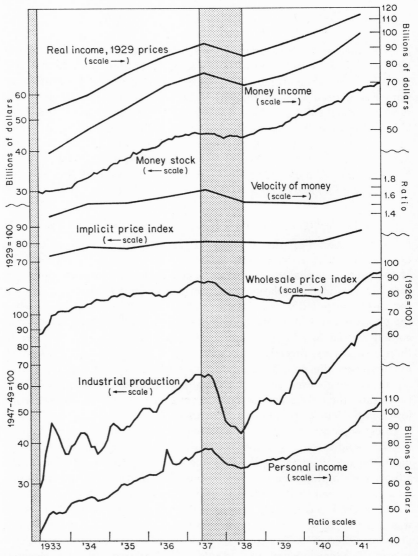

NOTE: Shaded areas represent business contractions; unshaded areas, business expansions.
SOURCE: Industrial production, same as for Chart 16. Personal income, same as for Chart 28.
Other data, same as for Chart 62.

prices, and did. A relapse in the second half of 1933 was followed by another spurt in early 1934 and then a further relapse. A sustained and reasonably continuous rise in income and production did not get under way until late 1934; and then it was disproportionately concentrated in the production of nondurable goods and services and of goods for government purchase as compared with previous and subsequent experience. At the cyclical peak in 1937, the nondurables component of the index of industrial production was more than 21 per cent above its value at the 1929 peak, whereas the durables component was some 6 per cent below its value at the 1929 peak. The difference reflected largely an unusually low level of private capital formation. Net private investment remained negative until 1936. When it became positive in 1936 and early 1937, an unusually large part consisted of additions to inventories.[1] At its highest in early 1937, private construction was only one-third of the highest level reached in the mid-twenties.

In his detailed analysis of the revival, Kenneth Roose quite plausibly attributes the unusually low level of private investment at that time mainly to the effects of governmental policies. Those policies tended to make profits relatively low. Wage rises were promoted first through the NIRA codes and then, when the codes were declared unconstitutional in 1935, through the National Labor Relations Act and the enactment of minimum wage laws. Other labor costs were raised by laws imposing a variety of new taxes, notably social security taxes, enacted in 1935 and effective in 1936–37, along with federal provision for unemployment compensation and old age security payments. The undistributed profits tax law, both enacted and effective in 1936, reduced profits net of tax. In addition, and perhaps even more important, business confidence in possibilities for future returns, already shaky because of the 1929–33 experience, was weakened still further by these and other measures: some regulating business (such as the Securities Act of 1933 and the Securities Exchange Act of 1934, the divorce of investment banking from commercial banking under the Banking Act of 1933, restrictions on public utility holding companies enacted in 1935); others expanding government activities into areas up to then reserved mostly for private enterprise (such as the creation of the Tennessee Valley Authority in 1933, the Resettlement Administration and the Rural Electrification Administration in 1935, the Social Security Board in 1935, the Home Owners Loan Corporation in 1933, and the Federal Farm Mortgage Corporation in 1934); still others seeming to threaten the sanctity of private contracts and property (such as the cancellation of gold clauses and the "nationalization" of gold and

---

[1] See K. D. Roose, *The Economics of Recession and Revival,* Yale University Press, 1954, pp. 45–47. Roose describes the inventory accumulation as unplanned (p. 186).

silver). The effects of these measures were exacerbated by the deliberate maintenance of an unbalanced budget, by attacks on "economic royalists" and "monopoly" by the President and other administration spokesmen, and by the President's proposal to reorganize the Supreme Court. Social tension was heightened by establishment of the Congress of Industrial Organizations, use of the sit-down strike, widespread labor troubles and—from the other side—establishment of the Liberty League and similar organizations by opponents of the New Deal. The result was "a highly emotional controversy as to desirable methods and goals for the political, social, and economic life," and "a bitter division of opinion over the New Deal, its measures and philosophy," hardly calculated to establish an atmosphere conducive to vigorous enterprise and confident risk taking.[2]

The unusually small demand for funds to engage in capital formation contributed to a fall in the level of long-term interest rates, and the low level of rates is in its turn an additional bit of evidence that there was, in fact, an unusually small demand. During the 1920's, high-grade corporate bonds yielded around $4\frac{1}{2}$ to 5 per cent; in the later 1930's, such bonds yielded 3 to $3\frac{1}{2}$ per cent. Lower-grade bonds also fell in yield, though the spread between lower- and higher-grade bonds widened—evidence of the unwillingness of the saver, like the entrepreneur, to undertake risk. The same phenomenon may help account for the widening spread between long- and short-term rates, which brought short-term rates to unprecedentedly low levels. The commercial paper rate fell to $\frac{3}{4}$ of 1 per cent in the second half of 1934 and remained at that level until early 1937; the Treasury bill rate fluctuated around a level of $\frac{1}{8}$ of 1 per cent from April 1934 to the end of 1936 and at even lower levels after a temporary rise in 1937. As we have seen, the desire for liquidity on the part of banks played an especially important role in bringing down the short-term rates (see Chart 35).

Interest rates were not only low; in addition, they declined during the cyclical expansion of 1933–37. The reversal of the usual cyclical pattern was probably the result of the large inflow of capital from abroad, discussed in the preceding chapter, which added sharply to the supply of loanable funds, reinforcing the effect of an unusually small demand on the level of rates and more than offsetting the cyclical expansion in demand that doubtless did occur.

Like production, wholesale prices first spurted in early 1933, partly for the same reason—in anticipation of the NIRA codes—partly under the stimulus of depreciation in the foreign exchange value of the dollar. Wholesale prices then stabilized to rise again at a more moderate pace throughout most of the period to mid-1937, interrupted only by a mild decline in 1936. All told, from the 1933 trough to the 1937 peak, wholesale

[2] Quotations from Roose, *Economics of Recession,* p. 61.

prices rose nearly 50 per cent. Cost of living rose decidedly less, by 13 per cent. The comprehensive index implicit in Kuznets' deflation of the net national product, available only on an annual basis, was only 11 per cent higher for 1937 than for 1933. While the wholesale price index generally shows a wider amplitude than the cost-of-living index or the implicit index, the differences were much wider than usual. They reflect in part the differential impact of devaluation on goods entering international trade; those goods are more important in the wholesale price index than they are in the other indexes. But it may also be that the differences reflect in part an understatement of the price rise by the cost-of-living and implicit indexes; the recorded prices of many items included in those indexes, but not in the wholesale price index, are much more stable than the actual prices of those items.

As in the other episodes we have considered, the broad movements in the stock of money correspond with those in income. From its trough in April 1933, the recorded stock of money rose 53 per cent to its subsequent peak in March 1937, or at an average annual rate of nearly 11 per cent per year. So large a rise has occurred in a four-year period only immediately after resumption (1879–83), in reaction to the deep depression of the early 90's (1897–1901), and during the two world wars. Yet the stock of money in 1933–37, like money income, did not regain its average 1929 level. The difference was, however, much smaller for money than for income. Velocity, though it rose some 20 per cent in the four years, was still some 15 per cent below its 1929 level, so a difference between 1929 and 1937 of 2 per cent in the stock of money was converted into a 17 per cent difference in money income. The 1937 peak was followed by an unusually severe contraction in money as in income. We have seen that the stock of money generally rises during contractions in general business, though at a slower pace than during the preceding expansions. It falls in absolute level primarily during unusually severe contractions. In 1937 it fell absolutely. The fall was only 3 per cent, from specific cycle peak to specific cycle trough, yet it was the first time since the 1890's that the stock of money had fallen absolutely in two successive contractions in general business.

An extremely interesting feature of the 1933 to 1937 expansion is the relation between the rise in the stock of money and the rise in prices. We may obtain a standard of comparison from two earlier cyclical expansions, which involved a reaction to deep depressions comparable in duration to the 1929–33 contraction (1879–82 in reaction to the 1873–79 contraction, and 1896– or 1897–99 in reaction to the generally depressed years 1891–96 or –97). If we rely on annual figures for all three expansions —monthly figures are available only for the third—the stock of money rose 53 per cent from 1879 to 1882, 41 per cent from 1896 to 1899, and

46 per cent from 1933 to 1937. The rise in implicit prices was also of roughly the same order of magnitude in the three expansions: 10 per cent, 6 per cent, and 11 per cent, respectively. But the rise in wholesale prices was much larger in the third expansion: in annual averages, 20 per cent in 1879-82, 12 per cent in 1896-99, and 31 per cent in 1933-37; in terms of the change from the three months centered on the specific cycle trough to the three months centered on the specific cycle peak, 28 per cent from 1879 to 1882, 26 per cent from 1897 to 1900, and 45 per cent from 1933 to 1937.[3]

What accounts for the greater rise in wholesale prices in 1933-37, despite a probably higher fraction of the labor force unemployed and of physical capacity unutilized than in the two earlier expansions? One factor, already mentioned, was devaluation with its differential effect on wholesale prices. Another was almost surely the explicit measures to raise prices and wages undertaken with government encouragement and assistance, notably, NIRA, the Guffey Coal Act, the agricultural price-support program, and National Labor Relations Act. The first two were declared unconstitutional and lapsed, but they had some effect while in operation; the third was partly negated by Court decisions and then revised, but was effective throughout the expansion; the fourth, along with the general climate of opinion it reflected, became most important toward the end of the expansion.

There has been much discussion in recent years of a wage-price spiral or price-wage spiral as an explanation of post-World War II price movements. We have grave doubts that autonomous changes in wages and prices played an important role in that period. There seems to us a much stronger case for a wage-price or price-wage spiral interpretation of 1933-37—indeed this is the only period in the near-century we cover for which such an explanation seems clearly justified. During those years there were autonomous forces raising wages and prices.[4] The wage and

---

[3] The specific cycle dates are:

Trough	Peak
June 1879	Aug. 1882
June 1897	Mar. 1900
Feb. 1933	Apr. 1937

[4] The wage-price spiral or price-wage spiral is often stated as if the existence of strong unions or strong producer monopolies were sufficient to set in motion autonomous forces raising wages and prices. This is wrong and involves the confusion between "high" and "rising" that is so common a fallacy in reasoning about economic matters. Strong unions and strong producer monopolies simply imply high wages for the unionized labor and high prices for the commodities monopolized relative to the wages of other labor and the prices of other commodities; they do not imply a continuous tendency for those wages and prices to be forced still higher. Such autonomous upward pressure is to be expected only from *increasingly* strong unions, and *increasingly* strong monopoly groups in the process

price rises occurred in an environment of rapid growth in the money stock, and so they could take place without meeting a monetary barrier or producing an absolute increase in unemployment. In what is perhaps the most common version of the wage-price spiral analysis, the monetary barrier which would block a wage-price spiral is looked upon as being removed by monetary authorities committed to a full employment policy and hence willing to increase the stock of money to prevent unemployment resulting from rises in wages and prices. That was not the sequence from 1933 to 1937; the rise in the money stock was produced not by the monetary authorities but by the gold inflow. Though accidental gold inflow served the same economic function as compliant monetary authorities would have, it occurred despite rather than because of the actions of unions, business organizations, and government in pushing up prices.

*If this analysis is right, it suggests that, in the absence of the wage and price push, the period 1933–37 would have been characterized by a smaller rise in prices and a larger rise in output than actually occurred. Moreover, that tendency would have been reinforced by its indirect effects on the stock of money. A smaller rise in domestic prices would have meant a still larger favorable balance of trade and hence a still larger gold inflow. The changed political and economic climate might well have evoked a greater demand for investment, a smaller decline in interest rates or perhaps even a rise instead of a decline, and a less rapid fall in the ratio of deposits to reserves desired by commercial banks. The rise in the stock of money would therefore probably have been greater on two scores: high-powered money would have risen more, and the ratio of the money stock to high-powered money would have declined less. The rise in output would also therefore probably have been greater on two scores: the fraction of the increase in money income accounted for by an increase in output would have been larger; and the increase in money income itself would have been larger.

2. Factors Accounting for Changes in the Money Stock

Chart 38 facilitates a more detailed examination of changes in the money stock and of the factors accounting for them. High-powered money was the major factor accounting arithmetically for the change in the money

---

of raising their wages and prices to levels consistent with their newly acquired monopoly power.

In 1933–37, this condition was clearly satisfied for unions. They experienced a major growth in numbers and strength. Union membership increased two and a half times, and just about doubled as a percentage of nonagricultural employment from 1933 to 1937 (*Historical Statistics of the United States, Colonial Times to 1957,* Bureau of the Census, 1960, Series D-743 and D-745, p. 98). For producer groups, the legislation referred to had the same effect, increasing their effective power to make prices approximate more closely the level that would be optimum for a monopoly.

CHART 38

The Stock of Money and Its Proximate Determinants,
March 1933–December 1941

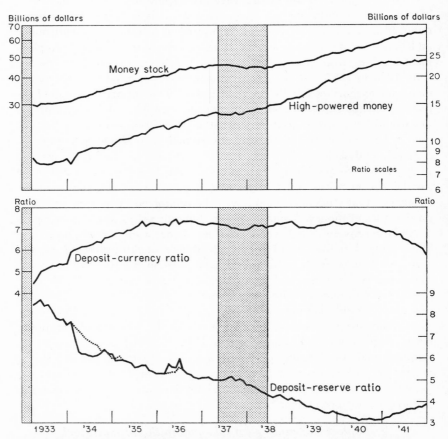

NOTE: Shaded areas represent business contractions; unshaded areas, business expansions.
SOURCE: Tables A-1 (col. 8) and B-3. Dotted section of deposit-reserve ratio smoothes deposits
and reserves (see Chart 44 and the accompanying text).

stock over the period as a whole as well as for smaller fluctuations in subperiods of 1933 to 1941. The stock of money grew by 51 per cent from
March 1933 to the reference peak in May 1937, and high-powered money,
by 60 per cent. The concurrent rise in the ratio of deposits to currency,
which alone would have made for a more rapid rise in the money stock
than in high-powered money, was more than offset by the decline in the
ratio of deposits to bank reserves. The deposit-currency ratio behaved
very smoothly, rising sharply from 1933 to 1935 and making its largest

500

contribution to the growth of the money stock in those years, then tapering off to remain roughly constant until 1940. The deposit-reserve ratio was more irregular, particularly in 1934 and in 1936. In both years, those irregularities offset corresponding irregularities in high-powered money and so left an impress on the stock of money only in much muted form.

From 1937 to mid-1940, money and high-powered money, though they have the same pattern of movement, converged sharply. The convergence resulted from the continued decline, at an accelerated pace, of the deposit-reserve ratio, this time neither offset nor intensified by movements in the deposit-currency ratio. From mid-1940 to 1945 (see Chart 46), the movements of the two deposit ratios were reversed, the deposit-currency ratio falling and the deposit-reserve ratio rising, so that they again offset one another, and the stock of money moved roughly proportionately to high-powered money.

The composition of additions to high-powered money from 1933 to 1940 differed according to whether it is viewed in terms of the liabilities of the monetary authorities—which is to say, the assets of the public and the banks holding the high-powered money—or in terms of the assets carried on the books of the monetary authorities as the counterpart of those liabilities. From the point of view of the public and the banks, the increase was primarily in Federal Reserve money (Chart 39A), most of the increase being in Federal Reserve deposits. Treasury currency rose a trifle (mostly because additions to silver currency exceeded the volume of national bank notes that were retired). Recorded gold fell to zero after it became illegal to hold, though some gold was probably held illegally. On the other hand, on the consolidated books of the monetary authorities, the increase in high-powered money was matched almost entirely by an increase in gold. Federal Reserve claims on the public and the banks fell to nearly zero, as discounting went out of fashion, and the System's holdings of acceptances became negligible. The remaining category of assets—which we designate other physical assets and fiat— fluctuated within a narrow range. The major fluctuations reflected the Treasury gold sterilization and desterilization operations in 1937 and 1938, which we consider in more detail below. Sterilization corresponded to the replacement of fiat by gold (on the liability side, of noninterest-bearing obligations by interest-bearing ones if financed by borrowing, or net reduction in obligations if financed by a budget surplus), and desterilization corresponded to the opposite.

The 1933–40 relationships were in interesting contrast with those that prevailed during both the twenties and the 1929–33 contraction. In the first place, the ratio of deposits to currency receded from an active and strategic role to a largely passive and secondary role. During the twenties, the steady rise in the deposit-currency ratio was the major factor account-

CHART 39

High-Powered Money, by Assets and Liabilities of the Treasury and Federal Reserve Banks, 1933–41

A. Liabilities

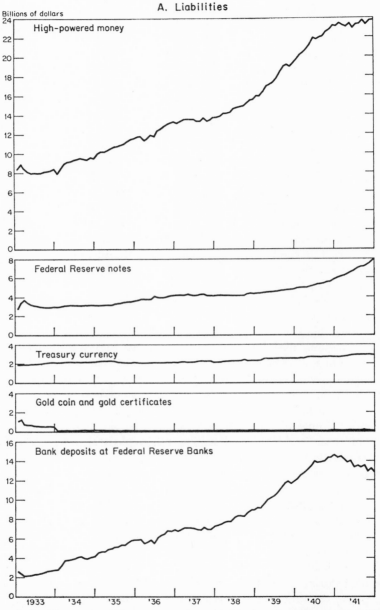

NOTE: Federal Reserve notes, Treasury currency, and gold coin and certificates are outside the Treasury and Federal Reserve Banks.

SOURCE: Same as for Chart 19, but the cumulated devaluation profit was deducted from the seasonally adjusted official gold stock. Devaluation profit as of Jan. 31, 1934, from *Banking and Monetary Statistics*, p. 538. For subsequent months, annual devaluation profit, from the *Annual Report* of the Secretary of the Treasury, 1940, pp. 634–635, and 1941, p. 428, was cumulated to the Jan. 31, 1934, figure.

CHART 39 (Concluded)

B. Assets

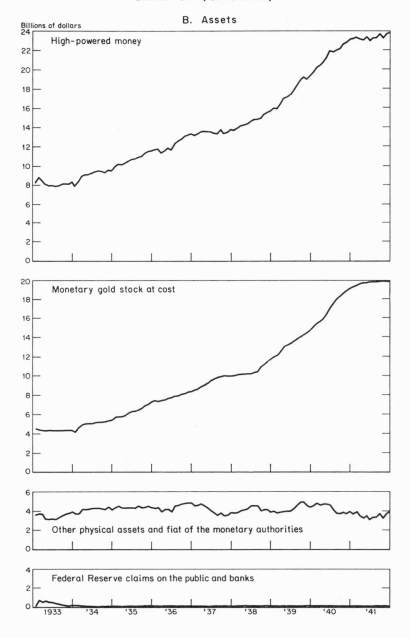

Billions of dollars

High-powered money

Monetary gold stock at cost

Other physical assets and fiat of the monetary authorities

Federal Reserve claims on the public and banks

1933   '34   '35   '36   '37   '38   '39   '40   '41

503

ing for the concurrent rise in the stock of money; from 1930 to 1933, recurrent declines in the ratio signaled renewed liquidity crises. After 1933, the initial sharp rise in the ratio is partly spurious, reflecting the defects in our money estimates analyzed in Chapter 8 (section 1) and arising from the reclassification of deposits in unlicensed banks. The reclassification had the effect of raising the ratio of deposits to currency.[5] If this effect is allowed for, there remains a gradual rise in the ratio of deposits to currency from the low point reached in 1933 to mid-1935. Thereafter, the ratio was highly stable until 1940, when it began to decline. The rise from 1933 to 1935 was clearly a reaction to the prior decline. It was a sign of renewed confidence in banks, of renewed willingness to hold deposits instead of currency, just as the 1930–33 decline had been a result of a loss of confidence in bank deposits. However, the level around which the ratio fluctuated between 1935 and 1940, about 7.20, was much lower than the peak of 11.57 attained in 1929. It was about the same as the level reached in 1921, which in turn was somewhat below the level in the years immediately before World War I. Cagan's detailed analysis of the deposit-currency ratio implies that the low level between 1935 and 1940 was primarily attributable to the cost of holding deposits, which was higher than at earlier dates—interest on demand deposits was outlawed and instead service charges were imposed.[6] The decline after 1940 we consider in connection with wartime developments (Chapter 10).

A second and more interesting contrast is found in the tools employed by the Reserve System and in the relative roles of the Reserve System and the Treasury. During the 1920's and to a lesser extent the early 1930's, there was little connection between movements in high-powered money and in the gold stock because of a clear inverse relation between movements in the gold stock and in Federal Reserve credit outstanding (see Chart 25). The Federal Reserve System used its powers, particularly during the twenties, to sterilize gold movements and to prevent erratic short-term changes in high-powered money. After 1933, on the other hand, Federal Reserve credit outstanding was almost constant and the

[5] Our estimates include currency in the vaults of unlicensed banks as part of currency held by the public. The opening of a previously unlicensed bank or its merger with a licensed bank, therefore, increased the numerator of the deposit-currency ratio and reduced the denominator. The reclassification also had a lesser effect on the deposit-reserve ratio. Our estimates treat deposits of unlicensed member banks at Federal Reserve Banks as part of total member bank reserves and therefore include them in the denominator of the deposit-reserve ratio. The opening of a previously unlicensed bank or its merger with a licensed bank increased the numerator of the deposit-reserve ratio by the full amount of the released deposits, but increased the denominator only by vault cash.

[6] Phillip Cagan, *The Demand for Currency Relative to the Total Money Supply*, New York, NBER, Occasional Paper 62, 1958, pp. 20–22.

discount rate was not altered from early 1934 to mid-1937 (see Chart 41, below). As we have seen, the changes in high-powered money reflected mainly movements in the gold stock. Such deviations as there were between the changes in high-powered money and the gold stock reflected offsetting measures by the Treasury, which altered its cash holdings and deposits at the Federal Reserve. This contrast applies not only to year-to-year movements but equally to seasonal movements. In the 1920's and early 1930's, Federal Reserve credit outstanding had a distinct seasonal movement, corresponding to the seasonal movement in currency outside the Treasury and Reserve Banks (Chart 26). After 1933, currency had the same seasonal movement as earlier, but Federal Reserve credit outstanding had essentially no seasonal movement. The System discarded almost entirely the role it had assumed in the 1920's and along with it the tools it had developed at that time. For such actions as it engaged in it used new tools acquired in 1933–35—control over margin requirements on securities and over reserve requirements of member banks.

A third and closely related contrast appears in the connection between movements in high-powered money and in the ratio of deposits to bank reserves. In the 1920's, both rose, though the rise in high-powered money had nearly stopped by 1925, while the rise in the deposit-reserve ratio continued steadily throughout the decade; and both were highly stable in their shorter-term movements. After 1930, the two began to move inversely, high-powered money rising and the ratio of deposits to bank reserves declining, as banks sought to strengthen their liquidity position. The general inverse movement continued after 1933, with addition of a much more regular tendency for the short-term irregularities in the deposit-reserve ratio to offset corresponding irregularities in high-powered money. The distinction between the general inverse movement over a period of years, and the shorter-term, month-to-month offsetting movements deserves more attention and we shall return to it. The short-term tendency is related to the preceding contrast. The Federal Reserve was no longer smoothing minor irregularities in high-powered money, hence the banks adjusted to them. The short-term irregularities in the deposit-reserve ratio can therefore correctly be interpreted as a fairly passive response on the part of banks to the short-term irregularities in high-powered money. This has fostered the view that the longer-term decline— a manifestation of the accumulation of excess reserves, discussed above— was also a passive reaction to the growth of high-powered money, a view discussed above and rejected (Chapter 8, section 1).

The first of these contrasts requires no further discussion. In connection with the other two, we shall consider factors accounting for changes in high-powered money (section 3); policy actions of the Federal Reserve (section 4); changes in the deposit-reserve ratio (section 5); and, finally,

505

by way of a summary of the rest, the role of monetary measures in the 1937–38 contraction and the subsequent recovery (section 6).

3. *Changes in High-Powered Money*

The breakdown of high-powered money by assets of the monetary authorities, presented in Chart 39B, consolidates the accounts of the Treasury and the Federal Reserve System. Though appropriate for analyzing the joint effect of the monetary authorities on the money stock, the consolidation conceals the relative roles of the two separate agencies and hence cannot be used to document our conclusion that the Treasury had become the active monetary authority. For this purpose, we need to separate out the items over which the Treasury had direct control: its cash and its deposits at Federal Reserve Banks. Since those deposits are a liability of the Banks, they cancel out when Treasury and Reserve accounts are consolidated.

When the Treasury bought gold, it paid with a check on its account at one of the Federal Reserve Banks. At the same time, however, it could print gold certificates of a corresponding amount and either add them to its cash balances or deposit them at the Reserve Banks. Such a transaction therefore meant a rise in high-powered money equal to the value of the gold purchase and no change in Treasury cash and deposits at Reserve Banks. As we have seen, transactions of this kind accounted for the major movements in high-powered money from 1933 to 1941. This point is demonstrated again in Chart 40 with a series on the monetary gold stock slightly different from that given at cost in Chart 39B. This one is expressed in official values, which changed abruptly at the end of January 1934 when the official price of gold was raised. We use official values in this chart in order to make the gold series comparable with the series on Treasury cash plus deposits at the Reserve Banks, also plotted on the chart.

The gold series is smoother than the high-powered money series. The main reason is that movements in Treasury cash and in deposits at Federal Reserve Banks altered the impact of the gold stock, and accounted almost entirely for the discrepancies between movements in high-powered money and the gold stock. Though changes in Treasury cash and deposits at Reserve Banks need not affect high-powered money, during that period they did. The Treasury can change its cash and deposits at Reserve Banks by various bookkeeping operations such as printing Treasury currency authorized but not issued, or destroying Treasury currency it holds, or selling securities to or buying them from the Reserve Banks. None of these operations will affect high-powered money. However, with one exception, no such transaction of any size was undertaken from 1933 to 1941. Other operations changing Treasury cash and deposits at Reserve Banks all

506

CHART 40

Major Factors Accounting for Changes in High-Powered Money,
1933–41

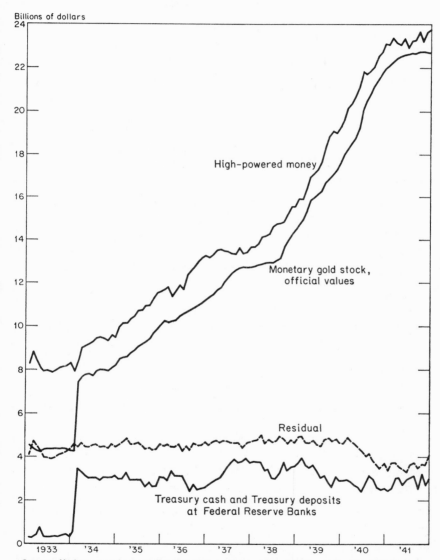

SOURCE: High-powered money, Table B-3. Monetary gold stock, same as for Chart 19. Treasury cash and deposits, Table A-3. Residual, see text.

507

change high-powered money by the same amount but in the opposite direction, since they consist of a transfer of cash or deposits at Reserve Banks from the public and banks to the Treasury, or conversely.[7]

We did not find it necessary in the preceding chapter to take explicit account of Treasury cash and deposits at Federal Reserve Banks, for two reasons. In the first place, Treasury cash and deposits at the Banks fluctuated much less in the twenties than they did later. In the second place, in the twenties and early thirties, the Reserve System deliberately undertook to offset seasonal changes in Treasury holdings as well as in other short-term factors tending to introduce irregularities into the total volume of high-powered money. After 1933, the System apparently gave up any attempt to smooth short-term movements. In consequence, high-powered money became more erratic in its month-to-month movements after 1933 than before (compare Chart 38 with Charts 23 and 31).

The extent to which the gold stock and changes in Treasury cash and deposits at the Reserve Banks jointly fail to account for movements in high-powered money is shown by the line in Chart 40 labeled "residual." It plots the excess of high-powered money over the sum of the gold stock and Treasury cash and deposits at Reserve Banks. It therefore reflects all other factors. The movements in the residual are small and even some of these are Treasury induced, reflecting bookkeeping transactions that make our series on Treasury cash and deposits at Reserve Banks an inexact index of the effects of Treasury operations on high-powered money. Only the movements in the residual in 1933 and early 1937 and the sharp decline in 1940 can be plausibly attributed to Federal Reserve rather than Treasury action. The first reflects Reserve System operations in the wake of the bank holiday; the second, operations accompanying the reserve requirement changes; and the third, reduction of Federal Reserve credit outstanding through open market sales (see Chapter 10).

Though the initial sharp jump in the gold stock from January to February 1934 is accounted for primarily by the revaluation of gold, part of it was produced by the substantial amount of gold imported, as foreigners took advantage of the higher buying price. The new gold price became official on January 31, 1934. Gold was almost immediately shipped

[7] Such operations, when they increase Treasury cash or deposits at Reserve Banks, involve the Treasury's taking in from the public and the banks, in the form of cash or checks on Reserve Banks, more from sales of securities or taxes or other receipts than it pays out in the same form to redeem securities or to meet current expenses. But this means that the public and the banks transfer part of their high-powered money to the Treasury. Since our series on high-powered money refers solely to money held outside the Treasury and the Reserve System, it follows that such a transfer reduces high-powered money by the same amount that it adds to Treasury cash and deposits at the Reserve Banks; and conversely, when the transfer is from the Treasury to the public and the banks. In practice, the initial transfer from the public is typically to Treasury accounts at commercial banks. The Treasury then transfers its deposits at commercial banks to Reserve Banks.

to the United States. In the six weeks from February 1 to March 14, more than $0.5 billion of gold (valued at the new price) was imported. At the same time, Treasury cash and deposits at Federal Reserve Banks, excluding the profit from revaluation of gold, declined. The two factors together account for the sharp rise in high-powered money from the end of January to the end of March—a rise of $1 billion or one-eighth of the initial level, much the largest percentage change in so short an interval during the whole period—1907 to 1960—for which monthly data on high-powered money are available.

Once the initial rush of gold imports was over, the gold stock continued to rise at a fairly steady rate to the end of 1937. Until France left gold in late 1936, roughly half of U.S. gold imports came from France. For the next year, France was a net importer of gold from the U.S. rather than a net exporter. During the last quarter of 1937, a large-scale withdrawal of foreign short-term balances followed rumors that further devaluation of the dollar was being considered as a possible counter-cyclical measure.[8] On net, the United States lost gold from October 1937 to February 1938. Withdrawal of European short-term funds from the United States ceased in July 1938. These counter movements roughly offset the forces making for a continued flow of gold to this country, so the total gold stock remained fairly steady from autumn 1937 to autumn 1938. Munich then led to a further flight of capital from Europe and a sudden increase in the rate of gold inflow. The outbreak of war simply maintained the rate of the gold inflow. The intensification of Britain's war effort after the fall of France in early 1940 and her attempt to tap American supplies of war material, as she had in World War I, produced a further increase. Finally, the enactment of lend-lease in early 1941, which relieved Britain and her allies of the necessity of acquiring dollars to finance war purchases, brought an end to the rapid growth of the gold stock.

Many of the minor fluctuations (Chart 40) in Treasury cash holdings

[8] The Gold Reserve Act of Jan. 30, 1934, empowered the President to establish the gold content of the dollar anywhere between 50 to 60 per cent of its former weight. The devaluation he proclaimed the following day established the gold content at about 59 per cent of the former weight. Hence he still had authority to change the purchase price of gold or the weight of the dollar. The power to devalue was allowed to expire in 1943 but *de facto* devaluation can still legally be effected by the Secretary of the Treasury under the power he acquired in the Gold Reserve Act to buy and sell gold, with the approval of the President, "at such rates and upon such conditions as he may deem advantageous to the public interest."

However, M. A. Kriz has pointed out that the Secretary of the Treasury's authority to change the market price of gold has been limited by the obligations assumed by the U.S. as a member of the International Monetary Fund and by the provision in the Bretton Woods Agreements Act of July 31, 1945, requiring legislative action by Congress before any change is made in the par value of the U.S. dollar ("Gold in World Monetary Affairs Today," *Political Science Quarterly*, Dec. 1960, p. 504 n.).

and deposits at Federal Reserve Banks, which are mirrored in corresponding fluctuations in high-powered money, probably reflect largely seasonal discrepancies between receipts and expenditures. Although the series plotted have been seasonally adjusted, both expenditures and receipts of the federal government changed so radically that the statistical adjustments probably have not succeeded in eliminating all seasonal effects.

There remain for comment a number of discrepancies of more moment.

(1) The marked irregularity in the first half of 1936 in high-powered money reflects an abnormal accumulation of Treasury deposits at Federal Reserve Banks from both March income- and gift-tax collections and, more important, from a large flotation of bonds and Treasury notes.

(2) The failure of high-powered money to reflect the growth of the gold stock in the first nine months of 1937 is a result of the gold-sterilization program adopted by the Treasury in December 1936. During that period, the Treasury paid for the gold it bought by borrowing rather than by using the cash balances it could create on the basis of the gold; the purchase of gold was therefore accompanied by a rise in its cash plus deposits at the Reserve Banks (see Chart 40).

The operation was economically identical with the sterilization actions of the Federal Reserve in the 1920's, when the System sold bonds on the open market to offset the increase in high-powered money that would otherwise have arisen from a gold inflow. The difference was that the Treasury rather than the System sold the bonds and took the initiative in sterilizing gold. As we shall see, the program became effective at about the same time as the second of two rises in reserve requirements imposed by the Federal Reserve. The sterilization program sharply reinforced the effect of the rise in reserve requirements in producing monetary tightness: the rise in reserve requirements increased the demand for high-powered money; simultaneously, the Treasury's action virtually brought to a halt an increase in the stock of high-powered money which had been proceeding with only minor interruptions since 1933.

(3) The more rapid increase in high-powered money than in the gold stock in the first half of 1938 reflected the reverse process: desterilization of gold by the Treasury, which is to say, its printing of gold certificates corresponding to some of the "inactive" gold in the Treasury; deposit of the certificates at the Reserve Banks, and drawing on those balances to pay government expenses or to redeem debt. Again, the operation was essentially an open market purchase of securities but one undertaken by the Treasury at its initiative.

A start toward desterilization was made in September 1937, when the Board of Governors of the Federal Reserve System requested the Treasury to release $300 million from the inactive gold account.[9] There was, of

[9] Board of Governors of the Federal Reserve System, *Annual Report*, 1937, p. 9.

course, no technical reason the Board itself could not have taken the economic equivalent of that step by buying $300 million of government securities. The Treasury released the amount requested by the Federal Reserve in a bookkeeping sense. However, it continued to sterilize all further gold purchases, which amounted to $174 million in that month, so that inactive gold held by the Treasury fell only $126 million in September 1937. The net effect of those actions as well as of other transactions affecting Treasury accounts was a decline of $136 million in Treasury cash and deposits at the Federal Reserve. This is the amount by which high-powered money grew in September, as a result of Treasury operations, over and above the increase in the gold stock in that month.

As of January 1, 1938, the Treasury limited the addition to the inactive gold account in any one quarter to the amount by which total gold purchases exceeded $100 million, and on April 19, 1938, discontinued the inactive gold account, which then amounted to about $1.2 billion. Once again, that was largely a bookkeeping step, the economic effect of which can be judged only by taking into account the simultaneous changes in other Treasury accounts. Initially, the inactive gold was simply moved from Treasury cash to Treasury deposits at Federal Reserve Banks, and so had no immediate monetary effect. Effective desterilization did not occur until more than a year after formal desterilization. Over that period the sum of Treasury cash holdings and deposits at Reserve Banks fell about $0.75 billion, then rose about $1 billion, and only after February 1939 began to decline toward the level that had prevailed before the sterilization program (Chart 40).

(4) The marked month-to-month irregularity in high-powered money in 1941 reflects a correspondingly increased irregularity in Treasury balances in that year, arising partly from sharper fluctuations in income-tax receipts as a result of the increased taxes imposed under the Revenue Acts of June 25 and October 8, 1940, partly from a series of bond issues which about coincided in time with the seasonal peaks in tax receipts. Again, this is an example of precisely the kind of irregularity that, by the late 1920's, the Federal Reserve System had learned to smooth with great effectiveness.

4. *Federal Reserve Policy*

In the period under consideration, the Federal Reserve System made essentially no attempt to alter the quantity of high-powered money by using either of the two instruments which had been its major reliance up to 1933: open market operations, which, as we saw in Chapter 6, had developed in the twenties from a means to acquire earnings into the major technique of monetary control; and rediscounting, which had initially been regarded as the primary instrument of Federal Reserve policy but had become one blade of the scissors of which open market operations was the other. Open market purchases and sales were made continually but, with only a few exceptions, in order to maintain the total portfolio intact or to alter its composition and thereby affect the structure of rates of return, not to alter the total amount of Federal Reserve credit outstanding. As President Harrison described it in 1939, the System had, in the course of those years, shifted its attention from "credit control" to "market control."[10]

After a decline and later rise in 1933, Federal Reserve credit outstanding was almost perfectly constant from 1934 to mid-1940. (There was then a sharp decline to a new level in 1941, discussed in Chapter 10.) The only change that shows up at all noticeably on a scale the size of Chart 41 is an increase and then a decrease on the occasion of the outbreak of World War II. Comparison of Chart 41 with Charts 25 and 33 shows how sharp the contrast with earlier experience was. In the five years 1934 through 1938, taken as a whole, Federal Reserve credit outstanding varied within a range of $177 million. In each of the seven years from 1924 through 1930, taken separately, the range is wider and in six of the seven years, more than twice as wide.

As Chart 41 shows, after a series of declines in 1933 and early 1934 following the rise in March 1933, the rediscount rate at New York remained at $1\frac{1}{2}$ per cent for nearly three and one-half years and was lowered to 1 per cent in August 1937, some three months after the cyclical peak in May. It remained at that level for over five years. The longest preceding period of constancy was nineteen months—in 1915–16 and again in 1918–19.

Even this evidence understates the contrast between the use of these instruments by the Federal Reserve System in the period under consideration and in the earlier period. Whatever fluctuation occurred in Federal Reserve credit outstanding arose largely from variation in "float" (the difference between the amounts credited and debited to member bank accounts for items in the process of collection) and in bills bought and bills discounted. From January 1934 through March 1937, government securities held at month's end fluctuated within a range of $17 million; on successive Wednesdays, within a $4 million range; and was exactly equal to $2,430 million in 133 out of 170 weeks. In early 1937, the System purchased $96 million of bonds in connection with money-market tightness and a sharp flurry in short-term rates accompanying the final rise in reserve requirements. It then kept the level fixed for half a year, bought $38 million more in November 1937 and kept the new level fixed until

[10] George Leslie Harrison Papers on the Federal Reserve System, Columbia University Library, Harrison, Notes, Vol. VII, Dec. 7, 1939. For a full description of the Papers, see Chap. 5, footnote 41 and the accompanying text.

CHART 41

Use of Tools by Federal Reserve System, March 1933–December 1941

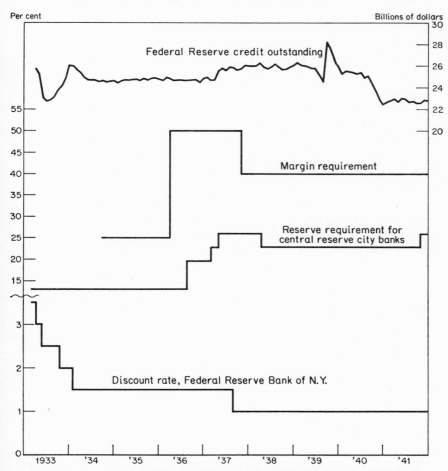

SOURCE: Federal Reserve credit outstanding, end-of-month data, from *Banking and Monetary Statistics*, pp. 376–377, seasonally adjusted by Shiskin-Eisenpress method (see source for Chart 21). Other series, *Banking and Monetary Statistics*, pp. 400, 441–442, 504.

mid-1939. Use of open market operations to influence the volume of Federal Reserve credit outstanding from day to day, week to week, and month to month ceased to be a continuous activity of the System.

Discounting, too, fell into even greater disuse than the constancy of the rate alone suggests. In the earlier period, the discount rate was seldom above short-term open market rates. For example, the New York discount rate was never above the average open market rate on 4- to 6-month

513

commercial paper in any week from 1919 through 1931. From 1934 on, the discount rate was seldom below short-term open market rates. The New York discount rate was never below the average 4- to 6-month commercial paper rate in any week in the eight years from 1934 through 1941. The result, of course, was negligible use of rediscounting facilities. From 1918 to August 1933, the average amount of bills discounted in any month never fell below the $155 million of August 1931 and was generally several times that sum; from September 1933 through August 1941, it never rose above $138 million, after June 1934, never above $24 million, and was mostly below $10 million.

The Federal Reserve System repeatedly referred to its policy as one of "monetary ease" and was inclined to take credit—and, even more, was given it—for the concurrent decline in interest rates, both long and short. It is hard to accept this view in terms of the traditional instruments of the System and, as we shall see, the new instruments it used—control over reserve requirements and over margin requirements on securities— were employed entirely as restrictive devices. As to open market operations, failure to reduce the System's portfolio was, it is true, an act of self-restraint which permitted gold inflows to have full effect on high-powered money. But there is no reason gold inflows should provide the appropriate growth in high-powered money month after month. Moreover, Federal Reserve officials expressed recurrent concern in meetings of the Federal Open Market Committee about the inflationary effect of the gold movements but were inclined to leave any offsetting open market operations to the Treasury. They used instead their new tool of changes in reserve requirements.

With respect to discount policy, the Federal Reserve was misled by the tendency, present recurrently throughout its history before and since, to put major emphasis on the absolute level of the discount rate rather than on its relation to market rates. The rate in the thirties was low in comparison with rates in earlier periods but, as we have seen, it was much higher compared with market rates than it had ever been. By relevant standards, the discount policy was abnormally tight, not easy. The System regarded the lack of discounting as a reflection of the large accumulation of excess reserves and hence as a lack of need for accommodation. That view no doubt had some validity, but the causal chain ran the other way as well. With discount rates so high relative to market rates, discounting was an expensive way to meet even temporary needs for liquidity. Banks, therefore, had an incentive to rely on other sources of liquidity, including the accumulation of larger than usual reserves.[11]

[11] As we have seen above, the System's belief that it was being "easy" in 1930 and 1931 reflected the same fallacy in the interpretation of discount rates, and, as we shall see in Chap. 11, so did the emphasis on "free reserves" in the policy

Given the large inflow of gold, a relatively tight discount policy was probably the correct policy for most of the period. The stock of money rose steadily throughout the period except for 1937, when the rise was interrupted by Treasury sterilization of gold and the doubling of reserve requirements. And, as we have seen, the rate of rise was large. It is by no means clear that a still larger rate of rise was desirable. And even if it were, given the attitudes of the commercial banks, it probably would have been preferable to provide them with more reserves through open market purchases than through encouragement of discounting. Our point therefore is not at all that the discount policy followed was a mistake, but only that it cannot be regarded as having contributed to monetary "ease."

Up to 1941 at least, whatever may have been the reasons for the low and declining levels of interest rates, Federal Reserve policy was clearly not one of them. The System's high discount rate relative to market rates and, as we shall see, increases in reserve requirements probably induced banks to resort to short-term paper rather than to discounting as a source of secondary reserves, and thereby helped to produce the abnormally low level of short-term rates relative to long-term rates that prevailed in the thirties. But the low level of long-term rates and its declining tendency must clearly be attributed to other factors. We have already expressed the view that the most important were probably the combination of a low demand for funds for private capital formation and an increase in the supply of funds arising out of the flight of capital from Europe to the United States. In addition, a gradual downward revision of expectations about the level of future short-term rates doubtless served to narrow the spread between short- and long-term interest rates after the mid-1930's.

One other piece of evidence of the radical change in Federal Reserve policy is the absence of any substantial pattern in the seasonal movement in Reserve credit outstanding (see Chart 42). As we saw, the seasonal movement in Reserve credit in the twenties—roughly similar in amplitude and pattern to that in currency outside the Treasury and Federal Reserve Banks—largely protected member bank deposits at the Reserve Banks from seasonal changes in the demand for currency (Chart 26). In the thirties, currency had about the same seasonal movement as before, and Treasury deposits at Reserve Banks, now at least ten times their former volume, had a very large seasonal movement. But the seasonal movement in Reserve credit in the thirties was negligible in amplitude and did little to offset those forces. Accordingly, member bank deposits at Reserve Banks were subject to wide seasonal variation.

The Securities Exchange Act of 1934 and the Banking Act of 1935

---

discussions of the 1950's. The fallacy is also identical with that embodied in the pegging of government security prices, which the System took so long to perceive at all fully.

CHART 42

Seasonal Patterns Affected by Federal Reserve Policy, 1933–41

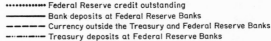

•••••••••••• Federal Reserve credit outstanding
———————— Bank deposits at Federal Reserve Banks
– – – – – Currency outside the Treasury and Federal Reserve Banks
–··—··—··— Treasury deposits at Federal Reserve Banks

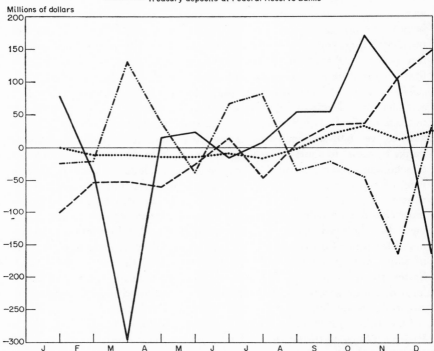

NOTE: Treasury cash is not shown because no seasonal movement was discernible after 1933.
SOURCE: Federal Reserve credit outstanding, bank deposits at Federal Reserve Banks, same as for Chart 26. Currency, same, using seasonal index computed from 1934–41 data. Treasury deposits at Federal Reserve Banks, same, using original data and 1931–43 seasonal index underlying seasonally adjusted data in Table A-3.

gave the System two permanent powers: control over margin require-ments on securities, and authority to raise or lower reserve requirements of member banks between the legal level before 1933 and twice that level.[12] Both powers were lodged in the Board alone. Chart 41 shows the use that was made of them. Margin requirements were imposed as soon as the power was granted, then raised sharply at the beginning of 1936 when the Board was increasingly concerned with potential inflation,

[12] In Aug. 1948, Congress granted the Board a temporary power, terminating June 30, 1949, to raise the maximum percentages permitted under the Banking Act of 1935 by 4 points on demand deposits and by 1½ points on time deposits.

then lowered part way in late 1937 when the recession was in process. Both the granting of that power and its use were a result of the experience during the late 1920's when the Board, among many others, was concerned with the bull market in stocks and felt constrained to check "speculation." In our view, the imposition of those requirements and their variation had negligible monetary consequences and can be ignored for our purposes. The power to alter reserve requirements is a different matter. It is an extremely potent control and was used in what seems retrospectively a drastic fashion, the requirements being doubled to the maximum level permitted in three steps within a nine-month period. The System thus abandoned its old tools—open market operations and rediscounting—and applied with vigor its new tool for the earlier purpose. Yet even so drastic a use of that new power does not contradict the view that the Federal Reserve System was following a largely passive policy. The rise in reserve requirements was not imposed primarily to affect current conditions but to enable the System to control future developments it feared might be set in train by the large excess reserves.

The Reserve System's neglect of seasonal and other short-term movements, the maintenance of a constant portfolio of government securities, the absence of change in discount rates, and the doubling of reserve requirements all had common roots in the sharp rise in member bank excess reserves and in the System's interpretation of the significance of excess reserves.

Retrospectively, the initial accumulation of excess reserves, after the banking panic of 1933 and before the devaluation of the dollar, to a level of about $800 million was welcomed in explicit recognition that the experience of prior years had altered commercial bank attitudes: a volume of reserves which would have been expansionary before 1929 might be contractionary in 1934.[13] However, as excess reserves accumulated in

[13] The retrospective view was stated in a memorandum on excess reserves, dated Dec. 13, 1935, for a Federal Open Market Committee (FOMC) meeting, and on Jan. 23, 1936, by Harrison in a meeting with his directors (Harrison, Open Market, Vol. II; Notes, Vol. VI). The open market purchase program which created the initial accumulation of excess reserves was not, however, voted primarily for that purpose. An Apr. 1933 Governors Conference, according to Harrison, "was not in favor of embarking on another excess reserve program," but the governors favored purchases of government securities if necessary to meet Treasury requirements; the New York Bank approved the Conference resolution to that effect (Notes, Vol. III, Apr. 24, 1933). A similar view had been expressed at the Apr. 22, 1933, meeting of the Open Market Policy Conference, which authorized the executive committee to purchase up to $1 billion of government securities "to meet Treasury requirements." Deputy Governor McKay of Chicago voted against the resolution. The Board thought the authorization too narrow, and approved the recommendation without the limitation "to meet Treasury requirements" (Open Market, Vol. II, minutes of meeting; telegram, dated May 12, 1933, Board—signed Chester Morrill—to Harrison). Purchases were not made until after May 23, when Governor Black—appointed the week before to replace

amounts which dwarfed any earlier levels, attitudes changed. As an internal memorandum, dated December 13, 1935, and prepared at the New York Bank, put it: "It seems very probable that with excess reserves of such extraordinary dimensions there comes a point when further increases have no constructive effects."[14] The view, always held by many, that excess reserves were idle funds serving little economic function and reflecting simply absence of demand for loans or lack of supply of investments came to be accepted and taken for granted by almost all—albeit, of course, with minor qualifications expressed from time to time.

Given this interpretation, it seemed pointless to try to offset seasonal and other short-term movements. The excess reserves could and, as we shall see, did cushion their effects to a large extent. Similarly, variation in discount rates could not be expected to affect credit conditions. If the commercial banks were passive, ready and willing to make loans or purchase securities, and were being kept from doing so only by lack of demand, there was little to be gained by making it cheaper or more expensive for them to acquire still more reserves.

This interpretation also explains the reason the System engaged in no extensive purchases of government securities after November 1933. Why add to excess reserves, which were being so rapidly expanded by gold inflows and which served no current economic function? It does not explain why the System kept its security holdings constant. Certainly, after mid-1935, gold inflows were viewed as expanding excess reserves at too rapid a rate and as raising dangers of future inflation. The obvious reaction would be to sell government securities and thereby offset the gold inflow. At first, that measure was not taken because the System was unwilling to do anything that could be interpreted as contractionary at a

---

Eugene Meyer as governor of the Board—met with the executive committee of the Open Market Policy Conference. The New York view was that an increase in excess reserves was desirable at the time but not beyond an accumulation of $500 million (Open Market, Vol. II, minutes of executive committee meeting; Notes, Vol. III, May 15, July 6, 1933).

Early in Aug., when excess reserves had reached $550 million, the executive committee of the Conference proposed to discontinue purchases, and again in Sept. and Oct., when the excess was even larger. Purchases were nevertheless continued until Nov. 15, 1933—totaling $600 million—because of administration pressure. The committee had been warned, that cessation of purchases "might . . . precipitate immediate and definite inflation through the issue of greenbacks," on the insistence of Senator Thomas and others in Congress (Conversations, Vol. II, Sept. 16, 1933, conversation with Governor Black). Owen D. Young, however, saw no merit in increasing excess reserves beyond existing levels through open market purchases in preference to the issue of greenbacks—authorized to be issued up to $3 billion by the Thomas amendment to the Agricultural Adjustment Act of May 12, 1933 (Notes, Vol. III, Sept. 7, 1933).

[14] The memorandum, a revision of an earlier version, dated Sept. 19, 1935 (Notes, Vol. VI) and Oct. 22, 1935 (Open Market, Vol. III), was circulated to the members of the FOMC before its meeting on Dec. 17–18, 1935 (ibid.).

time when economic conditions were extremely depressed, when there were repeated threats of legislative measures that many officials within the System regarded as "greenbackism," when the System felt itself in a delicate position vis-à-vis both the administration and Congress, and when the Treasury with its Stabilization Fund was in a position to off- set any action the System might take. Later, those considerations were greatly reinforced by concern about earnings. As excess reserves mounted, sales of securities large enough to reduce reserves to levels regarded as appropriate would also have reduced the income of the Reserve Banks to negligible amounts. Governor Harrison was reported to have told his directors in September 1935 "he realized that central banks cannot give primary consideration to the question of earnings, but . . . he also realized that they must have some funds with which to stay in bus- iness."[15]

The result was that the System drifted into a policy of holding a rigid portfolio of government securities. It did not want to buy and felt it could not sell. Time and again, at meetings of the New York Bank's directors and of the Federal Open Market Committee, the desirability of achieving flexibility in the System's portfolio by selling some securities or letting some run off was stressed and agreed to by almost everyone present. The System felt itself in a straitjacket from which it urgently wished to be freed. Yet the considerations mentioned in the preceding paragraph re- peatedly inhibited such action. And, of course, the longer the portfolio was held constant, the stronger the inhibitions against selling, because the constant portfolio became a public symbol in which a change might be interpreted as signaling a major change in policy. It should be empha- sized that keeping the volume of securities constant from week to week, as securities matured and had to be replaced, was no easy task. We have described the System's policy as passive—and so it was if judged by the total volume of securities held—but it took unremitting and skilled ac- tivity to keep the total constant.

While the total was kept constant, the distribution among maturities altered from time to time. Much attention was devoted to the appro-

<hr>

[15] Harrison, Notes, Vol. VI, Sept. 26, 1935. Listing of reasons for initial failure to sell government securities is based on: Office, Vol. IV, Oct. 16, 1935; Notes, Vol. V, memorandum, dated Mar. 15, 1934, another dated Mar. 16, 1935, on excess reserves; *ibid.*, minutes of directors' meetings, Jan. 24, Feb. 21, Mar. 7, 21, Sept. 26, Oct. 6, 1935; Open Market, Vol. III, minutes of meetings, Oct. 22–24, and memorandum, dated Dec. 13, 1935. Other reasons noted were the risk of starting a liquidation of government security holdings by banks and the public and the likelihood of Board disapproval of sales. Burgess apparently had some qualms because of the disastrous sequel to sales in Jan. 1933. He said, ". . . we had tried the idea of flexibility . . . in January 1933, and had made a mess of it" (Notes, Vol. IV, Mar. 8, 1934; also the same view in Notes, Vol. V, Jan. 24, 1935).

priate composition of the portfolio, and there was a persistent attempt to use changes in the composition of the portfolio to foster an "orderly market" in government securities. That objective increasingly came to the fore in the System's considerations in view of the growing importance of government securities, the large federal deficits requiring financing, and hence the growing concern of the Treasury with the bond market. Beginning in early 1935, much deliberate attention was directed toward the problem. The System uniformly agreed that it should not "rig" the market by pegging the prices of government securities; and nearly as uniformly that it should maintain an orderly market. But how to distinguish the one from the other and how to keep the one from degenerating into the other raised problems. Transactions to maintain an orderly market were of course conducted predominantly in New York, so it was the New York Bank that considered the distinction and its explicit formulation most fully. Harrison described the Bank's operating principle as "our . . . practice of putting bids in under the market just so that there would be no air pockets and no disorder," and as quite different from "putting a floor under it" or pegging.[16] As we shall see in Chapter 10, once the United States entered the war, there was a rapid transition from maintaining an orderly market to pegging the prices of government securities.

The 1936–37 increases in reserve requirements apparently had their origin in proposals made by the New York Bank. Beginning in early 1934, the Bank's staff prepared a series of internal memoranda, some circulated also to the Federal Open Market Committee, in which it examined the problem of excess reserves, emphasized potential dangers they raised, and considered alternative ways to control them. In the key memorandum (dated December 13, 1935, from which we have already quoted) it was concluded that open market operations would be an inefficient technique because of the size of the excess reserves, and that the discount rate would be inefficient because of the absence of borrowing. Hence, the appropriate tool was a change in reserve requirements, a discontinuous policy instrument poorly suited for continuous short-term adjustments but an appropriate means of immobilizing excess reserves and thereby establishing a situation in which the flexible instrument of open market operations could be used. Moreover, it was argued that accumulation of excess reserves was itself a consequence of a discontinuous

[16] Harrison, Conversations, Vol. III, Apr. 2, 1937; Office, Vol. V, memorandum, dated Mar. 16, 1938, Harrison to Burgess.

In addition to executing orders for the System account, the New York Bank continued to serve as the Treasury's agent in the government securities market. Harrison commented, ". . . the Treasury acts somewhat as a long-range investor, more or less always having funds to put into Government securities for various accounts, whereas the Open Market Committee acts as a market stabilizer" (Notes, Vol. VI, Feb. 4, 1937).

measure—the devaluation of the dollar. "Must we not," to quote the memorandum, "recognize that the devaluation of the dollar carried with it, as one of the necessary conditions of its successful operation, the need for a fundamental readjustment of reserve requirements?" Or, as Harrison put it to his directors, "the larger part of the existing excess reserves is the result of government actions, and correction by government action will be necessary before control will be back in central bank hands."[17]

In the December 1935 memorandum, the author recognized possible dangers in raising reserve requirements, and in taking that step too soon. It should not be taken "until production has returned to normal, or at least until the present trend toward a return to normal provides unmistakable evidence of continuing." The operating officials were usually less cautious. At an October 31, 1935, meeting with his directors, Harrison said that if he were a dictator, he would raise reserve requirements immediately by 25 per cent; a week later, he said he would raise them by 50 per cent in two steps.[18] The Federal Open Market Committee at a meeting on October 22 to 24, 1935, passed a resolution urging the desirability of reducing the volume of excess reserves preferably by raising reserve requirements. The resolution continued: "There are also risks incident to . . . raising reserve requirements. This method of control is new and untried and may possibly prove at this time to be an undue and restraining influence on the desirable further extension of bank credit." It included a recommendation that the Board of Governors make studies of the distribution of excess reserves and of the effects of a rise in requirements.[19]

Two months later, at the December 17–18, 1935, meeting of the Federal Open Market Committee, with the technical memorandum serving as one of the background documents, the matter again received extensive attention. A clear majority of the governors (the Federal Open Market Committee had not yet been reorganized in accordance with the Banking Act of 1935 and hence still consisted of the operating heads of all the Banks, who until March 1, 1936, retained the title governor) were in favor of action by the System to immobilize excess reserves but did not agree on the appropriate means. Some wanted to sell securities, others to

[17] The memorandum is in Harrison, Open Market, Vol. III; Harrison's remarks, in Notes, Vol. VI, Sept. 26, 1935; see also his remarks at the Sept. 19, 1935, meeting of directors. The dates of earlier memoranda on excess reserves are Mar. 15, 1934, and Mar. 6, 1935 (Harrison, Notes, Vol. V); Mar. 21, 1935 (Open Market, Vol. III); Sept. 19, 1935 (Notes, Vol. VI); Oct. 22, 1935 (Open Market, Vol. III); Nov. 7, 1935 (Notes, Vol. VI, and Special, no. 7).

[18] Harrison, Notes, Vol. VI. Interestingly enough, Owen D. Young, then chairman of the board of directors of the New York Bank, was opposed to an immediate rise in reserve requirements for what seems to us the correct reason: there was no point in taking such a step simply as a precautionary matter, with the danger that it might have adverse consequences; there would be ample time to take it when the need was clear (*ibid.*, Nov. 7, 1935).

[19] Harrison, Open Market, Vol. III.

urge the Board to raise reserve requirements. The result was that an initial resolution urging the Board to raise reserve requirements was voted down, 7 to 5. Harrison then drafted a revised resolution making clear that some who voted for the resolution favored open market sales rather than a rise in reserve requirements but favored the latter rather than no action. The resolution was passed by a vote of 8 to 4.

William McChesney Martin, governor of the St. Louis Bank, summarized in a statement to the FOMC the views of those opposed to action at that time. "It is true," he said, "that the System having an excess reserve of $3,000,000,000 affords the possibility of a run-away condition, but we should not be fooled by considering a possibility as a probability . . . . [C]onditions at present do not offer signs of an immediate probability. In any action taken at the present time there is too great danger of discouraging efforts toward recovery . . . ."[20]

The detailed record makes clear that two factors other than those cited in the technical memorandum led Harrison and other governors to favor reserve requirement changes rather than open market operations. One, already mentioned, was the problem of earnings. The other, more subtle and less clearcut, was a consequence of the continuing conflict between the Banks and the Board. The Board alone had the power to change reserve requirements. Harrison envisaged the change as a once-for-all change which would not be reversed. Let reserve requirements rise to their legal limit, and the chief monetary power the Board alone could exercise would be immobilized along with the excess reserves. Open market operations—in which the Banks shared power with the Board—and discount rates—which the Banks established subject to Board review—would then resume their place as the continuing instruments of monetary policy.[21]

Technique aside, why seek to immobilize reserves at that time? Why not, in Martin's words, wait until the possibility became a probability? Granted that the proponents of the move did not expect the rise in reserve requirements to have any significant effect and hence viewed it as immediately harmless. Why not wait until the need was clearer? One reason was strictly political and accounts for any probable difference about timing between the author of the technical memorandum and Harrison. The Board was in process of reorganizing the System in accordance with

[20] Harrison, Open Market, Vol. III, statement, read by Governor Martin at Dec. 17, 1935, meeting.

[21] Harrison told a special meeting of his directors (Dec. 16, 1935) called to discuss excess reserves and Federal Reserve policy: "If we increase reserve requirements, we shall put the Reserve Banks in the position where they will have a chance to control the situation by open market operations and changes in discount rates. If we sell government securities first, we shall put whatever control is left in the hands of the Board of Governors which alone has power to increase or decrease reserve requirements" (Harrison, Notes, Vol. VI, Dec. 16, 1935).

the Banking Act of 1935. Harrison felt that if action was not taken at the end of 1935, it probably would not be taken for a full year—in his view, too long to wait.

The technical reasons for taking action were spelled out in the December 1935 memorandum. "At such a point [when further increases in excess reserves have no further constructive effects] excess reserves may contain possibilities of positive harm . . . [1] may give rise to disproportionate bank investment in government securities . . . [2] banks may acquire government and other bonds at prices which later may not be sustained . . . [3] with money so freely available, states, municipalities, and the national government, and other borrowers as well, may be tempted to over-borrow . . . [4] general fear which many people entertain that excess reserves of the present magnitude must sooner or later set in motion inflationary forces which, if not dealt with before they get strongly under way, may prove impossible to control . . . [5] the very fact of such inordinately large excess reserves may, by causing foreign expectation of favorable conditions for speculative investment, accentuate the gold inflow which is the real source of our problem."

In this list, the technical reasons we have numbered 1, 2, and 3 are inconsistent with the literal interpretation of excess reserves as idle funds accumulating because of the absence of desirable loans and investments; they clearly involve an effect of excess reserves on bank assets and hence on the rate of expansion of total bank credit. They are not, however, inconsistent with the actual somewhat mixed Reserve System interpretation which also included recognition, either implicitly as above or explicitly, that it was an oversimplification to regard excess reserves as idle funds having literally no effect. The listed reasons correctly reflect the almost exclusive preoccupation of the System with the "credit" effects of monetary policy as opposed to its effects on the stock of money. In all the discussion between 1930 and 1940 at the New York directors' meetings, as recorded in the Harrison Papers, we have noted only one explicit discussion of the quantity of money and its velocity as relevant to monetary policy—by Marriner Eccles, appointed governor of the Federal Reserve Board, November 1934, Black having resigned in August.[22] Otherwise, changes in the volume of demand deposits were sometimes referred to because of their relation to required reserves and as a reflection of changes in commercial bank credit; changes in currency in circulation were considered because of their effect on bank reserves and as a source of demand for Federal Reserve credit. There was no consideration—systematic or unsystematic—

[22] The discussion occurred in the course of a long meeting with the New York directors on the proposed Banking Act of 1935 (Harrison, Notes, Vol. V, Feb. 18, 1935). See also Chap. 7, footnote 93, above, and Chap. 11, sect. 3.

of the total stock of money as a magnitude that either was or should be controlled by the System, nor of changes in the stock as measuring the impact of the System. The System's role was seen exclusively in terms of conditions in the money market, i.e., the market for loans and investments.

Technical reason 5 is a most curious one, since it is precisely the reverse of the view repeatedly expressed during the climactic period from 1931 to 1933. Then the view had been that fear of inflation in the United States would lead foreigners to withdraw gold; now, that it would produce an inflow. A reconciliation is possible: whereas earlier foreign balances were mostly governmental and had to be held primarily in fixed dollar form, now the capital inflow was primarily private and either was channeled into equities or could be so channeled—though we have no evidence that that explanation was either true or believed to be true. More likely, the inconsistency simply reflects the fact that different people composed the System. The natural tendency to regard the System as one individual, holding consistent or at least connected views through time, is in the main correct. There does develop a System position which impresses itself on the members of the organization and which they come to accept and, of course, also to shape—almost without knowing it. But the explanation is not correct in every detail. The System's personnel had changed since 1933, and System philosophy was not all-pervasive.

Technical reason 4 is the only one publicly stated at the time in justifying the rise in reserve requirements in August 1936 and in March and May 1937. In the words of the 1937 *Annual Report,* "the Board's action was in the nature of a precautionary measure to prevent an uncontrollable expansion of credit in the future."[23] The Board contended at the time that the action was not a reversal of the System's easy-money policy. It made extensive studies before it took that action to assure itself that excess reserves were widely distributed geographically and among banks, so that most banks could satisfy the higher reserve requirements without mechanical difficulties. It denied then—and has continued to ever since—that the measure had any significant current influence.[24]

When the rise in reserve requirements was recommended by the FOMC at the end of 1935, and even when the first rise was imposed in August 1936, there was apparently no intention to exert a contractionary influence. By January 1937, when the two later rises were scheduled, the situation was somewhat different. In his briefing of the FOMC on January 26, 1937, Goldenweiser (who had been appointed its

---

[23] Board of Governors of the Federal Reserve System, *Annual Report,* 1937, p. 2.
[24] See Board of Governors of the Federal Reserve System, *Annual Report,* 1936, pp. 2, 14–15; 1937, p. 2; M. S. Eccles, *Beckoning Frontiers,* New York, Knopf, 1951, pp. 289–293; and E. A. Goldenweiser, *American Monetary Policy,* New York, McGraw-Hill, 1951, pp. 176–179.

economist while continuing to serve as the Board's director of research) said: "the most effective time for action to prevent the development of unsound and speculative conditions is in the early stages of such a movement when the situation is still susceptible of control, and that, as present indications were that such a time had arrived, as the technical market situation is favorable for action at the present time, and as short-term rates had been abnormally low in relation to long-term rates and some stiffening of the former would be desirable, action to absorb excess reserves should be taken at this time." John H. Williams (economic adviser to the New York Bank, 1933–52, and a vice-president, 1936–47, and in 1937 associate economist of the FOMC) said of the business and economic situation, "in certain respects it was going beyond a normal state," and joined Goldenweiser in advocating a further rise in reserve requirements.[25] In discussions at meetings of the New York Bank directors in January 1937, Harrison made clear his awareness that a rise in reserve requirements would have a tightening effect and his approval of such an effect; most of the directors agreed.[26]

The desire to tighten in early 1937 is entirely understandable. Economic expansion had been proceeding irregularly for four years and steadily for two; wholesale prices had risen nearly 50 per cent since March 1933; stock market prices had roughly doubled between 1935 and the end of 1936. Harrison and others in the System felt strongly that, in the past, the System had always been late in reacting; by their criterion of the absolute level of interest rates, the money market was abnormally easy.

[25] Harrison, Open Market, Vol. IV, minutes of meeting, Jan. 26, 1937.
[26] Harrison, Notes, Vol. VI, Jan. 7, 14, 21, 28, 1937.
Clark Warburton has noted that the extensive studies of the Board regarding the ability of banks to satisfy the higher reserve requirements (see footnote 24, above) missed an important element in the impact, namely, the loss of reserves by central reserve city banks as other banks drew on their correspondent balances ("Monetary Difficulties and the Structure of the Monetary System," *Journal of Finance,* Dec. 1952, pp. 543–544). That element was discussed at a Jan. 1937 meeting of the New York Bank directors, but did not change Harrison's views. G. W. Davison, a banker, who recommended using only half the remaining power to raise reserve requirements, pointed out that "some of the central reserve and reserve city banks would feel the shock of an increase in reserve requirements 'both ways'; in addition to having their own reserve requirements increased, they would be subject to withdrawals of funds by out-of-town banks" (Harrison, Notes, Vol. VI, Jan. 21, 1937). The Board had apparently been urged to make the increase in reserve requirements applicable only to central reserve and reserve city banks. Country banks, it was suggested, would give up Federal Reserve membership if reserve requirements of state banking systems were substantially lower. Goldenweiser argued, however, that reserve requirements were not an important factor in a bank's decision regarding membership and, furthermore, country banks "as a group had a large aggregate amount of excess reserves and excess balances with correspondents and could easily meet the increased requirements" (Open Market, Vol. IV, minutes of meeting, Jan. 26, 1937). He did not mention the impact of the withdrawal of those balances on the central reserve city banks.

What rendered the action unfortunate in retrospect was, as we shall see, that the System failed to weigh the delayed effects of the rise in reserve requirements in August 1936, and employed too blunt an instrument too vigorously; this was followed by a failure to recognize promptly that the action had misfired and that a reversal of policy was called for. All those blunders were in considerable measure a consequence of the mistaken interpretation of excess reserves and their significance.

While the desire to take restrictive action in early 1937 is understandable, it is difficult to have much sympathy with the argument in the technical memorandum, and the explicit justification of its action by the Board: it was desirable to reduce excess reserves solely as "a precautionary measure to prevent an uncontrollable expansion of credit in the future." Even if the Board had been right in its opinion that the action taken would have no immediate effects, why, if no current effects were desired, take a step that could just as readily be taken when undesirable expansion of credit started to occur? What would make such future expansion "uncontrollable"? The Board's only argument was that excess reserves were larger than the System's total government security holdings, and that the increase in reserve requirements reduced excess reserves to a level below that total. Even if the comparison were relevant, a later increase in reserve requirements would have had the same effect. Harrison's earlier argument (see above) that the reorganization of the Board would force a delay was clearly a tenable reason for advance action. But by the time the Board acted, the reorganization was completed and that reason no longer had any substance.

Our conclusion, expressed above, is that the increase in reserve requirements did have important current effects. Comparison of the timing of the increases in requirements with the timing of the behavior of the money stock documents this conclusion in detail. The decision to impose the first rise in reserve requirements was announced in July 1936, and the rise was effective in August. In the next five months, from the end of July to the end of December 1936, the ratio of deposits to bank reserves declined sharply as banks sought to restore their excess reserve position. In consequence, although high-powered money grew by decidedly more in those five months than in the prior seven months, the stock of money grew by less than half as much.[27] The month-to-month figures are even more impressive. They show high rates of growth of the money stock in April, May, and June 1936, and a sharp drop in the rate of growth thereafter. The second rise in reserve requirements was announced on

[27] And even this understates the contrast, since most of the increase in high-powered money in the prior seven months came at the very end, and hence might have been expected to have delayed effects. The increase from June 1936 to July 1936 was six-sevenths of the increase from the end of Dec. 1935 to the end of July 1936.

January 30, 1937, and became effective in two steps, on March 1 and May 1. High-powered money was at the same time held roughly constant by Treasury sterilization of gold. The money stock reached an absolute peak in March and fell with only minor interruptions to the end of the year. The cyclical expansion reached its peak in May 1937.[28] The March and May rises in reserve requirements were also accompanied by a general rise in market yields. Treasury bills, longer-term governments, and many private bonds fell sharply in price and, as noted, the Federal Reserve was induced to engage in minor offsetting open market purchases.

Those minor open market operations were taken only after an extensive series of discussions, which revealed wide disagreement within the System, and partly in response to pressure from the Treasury. A meeting was called by the Board, after the March rise in reserve requirements and accompanying market disturbances, to consider whether to rescind the May rise or whether to offset the rises by purchases in the open market. Harrison and most of the other Bank presidents were opposed to any action. The System policy was to reduce excess reserves, they argued, and the flurry in the bond market was insufficient reason to alter the policy. The most that should be done, in their view, was to promote an orderly market but without pegging and without preventing a decline in the price of government securities which was on the whole desirable. Governor Eccles, almost alone among the members of the FOMC, took the opposite view. He favored large-scale purchases or rescinding of the final rise in reserve requirements. His position, as summarized in a memorandum by Williams, was that "there was no inconsistency in decreasing excess reserves by a large amount, through the relatively clumsy instrument of increasing reserve requirements, and then effecting a partial increase by the elastic and adjustable instrument of open market operations, in order to facilitate an orderly process of transition." And, of course, this is the technique the Reserve System has since come to adopt. The final compromise at the time, involving purchases of a moderate amount of securities, satisfied no one. It was acceded to by the majority, not only in deference to Eccles, but also partly because of the strong views expressed

[28] In a first draft of a memorandum, dated Jan. 27, 1938, dealing with the question, "Did the Raising of the Reserve Requirements Cause the Depression?", Williams analyzed the change in assets and liabilities of banks and reached a negative conclusion. Looking only at the absolute changes in demand deposits—which increased substantially from June 30, 1936, to Dec. 31, 1936, and declined only $300 million from Dec. 31, 1936, to June 30, 1937—and without reference to earlier changes, Williams arrived at his answer to the question. Apparently, he did not recognize that the significance of a given change might depend upon whether it represents a continuation or a radical departure from earlier trends. His emphasis throughout was on effects in the credit market. He mentioned changes in demand deposits only as evidence on the total earning assets of commercial banks (Harrison, Special, no. 22. The memorandum was prepared at the request of the FOMC).

by Secretary of the Treasury Morgenthau, who blamed the whole setback in the bond market on the increase in reserve requirements.[29]

Although the peak of the expansion is dated May 1937, and although the following contraction was one of the sharpest on record, it was apparently not until August or September that the technical staff of the System became seriously concerned about the state of business or began to suggest the desirability of expansionary action. At a September 11, 1937, FOMC meeting, Goldenweiser reported only that "there was a possibility that the uncertain situation . . . might lead to a decline in business and to a recession of indeterminable magnitude." Williams reported he was changing his mind: "there might be some recession." On the basis of these reports, the Committee decided to ask the Treasury to desterilize $200 or $300 million of gold and to direct the executive committee to purchase securities to meet seasonal needs.[30] As we have seen, the System purchased $38 million in November 1937, and then made no further changes in the total volume of securities until mid-1939.

Reserve requirements were not reduced until April 1938, some two months before the cyclical trough in June 1938, to a level that eliminated only one-quarter of the combined effect of the earlier rises. The action was taken by the Board despite opposition to it by Harrison. Reserve requirements remained unchanged at the new level until November 1, 1941.[31]

Despite the close connection in time between the reserve requirement changes, the money market disturbances, and the subsequent business contraction, Harrison and the other chief proponents of the increase in reserve requirements insisted there was no connection. They regarded assertions to the contrary by economic analysts outside the System as simply ill-informed and persistently opposed expansionary monetary policies to counter the contraction. At the September 11, 1937, FOMC meeting, Harrison "expressed himself as feeling that non-monetary measures were probably the ones to be used at this time since the adverse developments in business were of a non-monetary nature." To his directors, he pointed out in December that "most of the executives of the Reserve System do not believe that monetary action would afford relief in the present business situation, regardless of whether the causes of the recession are monetary or non-monetary but rather that it was felt that improvement

[29] Harrison, Conversations, Vol. III, memorandum, dated Apr. 14, 1937, Williams to Harrison; see also *ibid.*, Harrison's reports of conversations with Morgenthau, Eccles, and other Board members, Mar. 31, Apr. 2, 9, 14, 15, 16; another memorandum, dated Apr. 14, 1937, by Williams, and one, dated Apr. 23, 1937, by Allan Sproul; and Open Market, Vol. IV, minutes of executive committee meetings, Mar. 13, 22, and 23, and of FOMC, Apr. 3 and 4, 1937.

[30] Open Market, Vol. IV, minutes of meetings, Sept. 11 and 12, 1937.

[31] Open Market, Vol. IV, minutes of meeting, Apr. 29, 1938.

in the business situation would be more influenced by actions of the Administration."[32]

The irony is that Harrison's arguments against open market purchases at this juncture very nearly duplicated those he encountered when he urged open market purchases in 1930. He now upheld views that he then so vigorously opposed. The difference, of course, was that he was then on the offensive and was not burdened with a prior position inconsistent with purchases, whereas now he was on the defensive. For him to favor an expansion of excess reserves, when they were very large by standards he had earlier adopted, would have meant reversing a position he had espoused for years. His situation was in many respects precisely that of his opponents in 1930. His experience is a striking illustration of how difficult it is for anyone—whether in practical affairs, politics, industry, science, the arts—however able and disinterested, as Harrison was in unusual measure, to reverse a strongly held intellectual position.

In economic aspects, the years 1937–38 are strikingly reminiscent of 1920–21. On both occasions, in the course of a rapid rise in the money stock, the System took vigorous action with untried tools that produced a sharp retardation in the rate of growth of the stock, followed shortly by an absolute decline. On both occasions, the action was also accompanied by a pause in a rising tide of economic activity, followed by an exceptionally sharp but fairly brief decline. On both occasions, the System was slow to recognize the onset of contraction and, even after it did, refrained from reversing its policies for some time. On both occasions, it undertook significant expansionary action just two months before the cyclical trough, each time using the same tool it had used in its initial contractionary actions—in 1921, reducing discount rates, in 1938, reducing reserve requirements. On both occasions, it was strongly criticized for having produced or fostered a contraction, and on both it staunchly contended that the timing relation between the monetary actions and the contraction was purely coincidental and that nonmonetary factors were at fault.

The parallelism of the two periods is shown in Chart 43, which plots for both contractions the money stock, month-to-month changes in the stock, and the index of industrial production. The month of vigorous Federal Reserve restraining action in 1920 was clearly January, when discount rates were raised sharply. The counterpart in 1937 is less obvious. We have taken it to be January 1937, when the forthcoming rises in reserve requirements were announced, rather than either March or May, when they became effective. January 1937 was chosen on the grounds that the announcement gave banks an incentive to prepare for the forthcoming rises, even if not required to at once, just as the rise in discount rates in January 1920 gave banks an incentive to reduce their discounts,

[32] Notes, Vol. VII, Sept. 16, Dec. 9, 1937.

CHART 43

Money Stock, Change in Money Stock, and Industrial Production,
During Two Similar Episodes in Federal Reserve History:
1919–22 and 1936–39, Superimposed

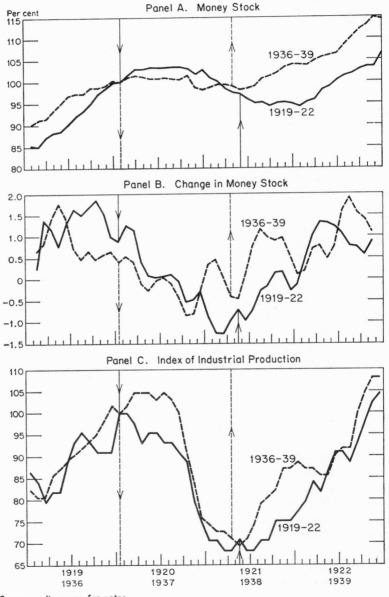

Panel A. Money Stock

Panel B. Change in Money Stock

Panel C. Index of Industrial Production

See opposite page for notes.

530

even if not required to at once. Accordingly, we have expressed the stock of money and industrial production as 100 in January 1920 for the earlier contraction and in January 1937 for the later, and have super-imposed the two months in plotting the series. The month-to-month rates of change are expressed as percentages of the money stock in the base month of January 1920 or January 1937 and are smoothed by a three-term moving average (with weights of 1,2,1). The initial downward pointing arrows mark the months of vigorous restraining action, the later upward pointing arrows, the months of reversal of monetary action.

There is certainly an extraordinary resemblance between the curves in each pair. The major difference is that the money stock was rising at a faster rate in 1919 than it was in 1936, was carried further above 100 by its momentum, and subsequently fell further and for a longer time. That difference is not reflected in the index of industrial production but is reflected in wholesale prices, which rose more rapidly in 1919 than in 1936 and fell more after 1920 than after 1937—by about 45 per cent compared with 15 per cent. In the later contraction, the initial drop in the rate of change in the money stock reflects the August 1936 rise in reserve requirements.

The 1936–37 episode is also an instructive example of how technical defects in a monetary tool may greatly enhance mistakes in policy arising from erroneous analysis and thus play an independent role.[33] Had the power to vary reserve requirements not been available, the System could have sought to reduce excess reserves by the same amount through open market operations instead. It might at first be supposed that, given its analysis of excess reserves, it would have done that and would also thereby have produced the same deflationary effects, i.e., that the key defect was in the analysis, not in the particular instrument used to im-plement the analysis. However, even a rough calculation of the orders of magnitude involved shows this supposition to be wrong, even if we put entirely to one side the System's nearly complete abandonment of open market operations as a major instrument of monetary policy. The initial reserve requirement increase, effective in August 1936, reduced

[33] For a discussion of the defects of variable reserve requirements as a tool of monetary policy, see Milton Friedman, *A Program for Monetary Stability*, New York, Fordham University Press, 1960, pp. 45–50.

Notes to Chart 43.

NOTE: In Panels A and C, monthly data are expressed as percentages of the base month, Jan. 1920 or Jan. 1937—the months marking the onset of Federal Reserve pressure.

In Panel B, month-to-month changes in the money stock are expressed as percentages of the money stock in Jan. 1920 or Jan. 1937, and the percentages averaged by a weighted 3-term moving average (weights = 1,2,1).

The solid and dashed vertical lines pointing downward mark the month in each period of the onset of F.R. pressure; pointing upward, the month in each period of the start of F.R. easing measures.

SOURCE: Money stock, Table A-1, col 8. Index of industrial production, same as for Chart 16.

excess reserves by about $1.5 billion, and the second and third increases, effective in March and May 1937, reduced them by another $1.5 billion. On the System's analysis that the reserves were excess in the economic as well as legal sense, to achieve the same result through open market operations would have required sales of those amounts on the corresponding dates. The amounts were exceedingly large relative to other magnitudes of the time. The $3 billion involved in the three steps together exceeded by one-fifth total holdings of government securities by the Federal Reserve System and amounted to nearly one-quarter of total high-powered money. Even if the System had had enough government securities in its portfolio, it is hardly conceivable that it would have sought to sell $1.5 billion of securities in the course of a few weeks and then only seven months later a further $1.5 billion in the course of two months. And even if it had begun, it would not have been committed to see the whole operation through as it virtually was, once a reserve requirement change was announced, and hence could have readily reversed course when the results became manifest. The tool used was, therefore, not simply the means whereby a defective policy was put into effect but also materially affected the outcome.

We have explained both the extreme passivity of the Federal Reserve System during the thirties and the one notable exception as resulting from its interpretation of excess reserves. But, to a large extent, this is a superficial explanation. Why was the System so ready to adopt that interpretation or, if it did, to let the interpretation condemn it to inactivity? Why, for example, did it ask the Treasury on several occasions to take actions that the System could equally well have taken?

First, the passivity reflected partly the natural tendency of individuals and, especially, official bodies to avoid responsibility for unfavorable occurrences by pleading limited power. The shattering of earlier high hopes made the tendency especially strong in the present instance. The belief that traditional instruments of monetary policy had been impotent in the decline of 1929–33—largely a rationalization of failure—strongly fostered their neglect in the later thirties.

Second, a passive policy was fostered also by the changing locus of power in the System and the changing personalities in positions of power that played such an important part in the System's performance during the contraction (see Chapter 7). In 1930, New York's commanding role in the System was reduced when the other Banks and the Board succeeded in limiting its freedom of action. The New Deal sealed the shift of power away from New York and concentrated it in Washington rather than in the other Banks. The dominant role of the Board was formalized by the Banking Act of 1935, and there were no subsequent developments to counteract the shift.

The transfer of power from a financial institution in the active financial center of the country to a political institution in the active political center fostered a shift in policy from the kind of continuous day-to-day concern with market activity, and continuous involvement in it, that is the mark of the active trader and participant in economic matters, to the discontinuous occasional pronouncement and enactment of legislation or rules, that is the mark of political activity. The difference was clearly foreshadowed in 1929 in the divergent opinions on how to deal with speculation. New York favored the quantitative impersonal technique of monetary restriction affecting directly the interests of operators in the market; Washington favored exhortation and administrative action on examination of each case by the lenders, which affected only at one remove the operators in the market. The difference, after the Board took over, is reflected more subtly in the virtual absence of continuous and day-to-day open market operations affecting the total volume of holdings, and in increased reliance on discontinuous instruments such as changes in reserve requirements and, above all, on public pronouncements.

Third, the preceding factors were reinforced by a change in the climate of intellectual and political opinion about economic matters. There developed a far readier acceptance of government intervention in the details of economic activity that fostered emphasis on such policy measures as margin requirements, bank examination and regulation, and control of security issues. More important from our point of view, emphasis shifted from monetary to fiscal measures. It was widely accepted that monetary measures had been found wanting in the twenties and the early thirties. The view that "money does not matter" became even more widely held, and intellectual study and analysis of monetary institutions and arrangements probably reached an all-time low in the study of economics as a whole. Emphasis shifted to fiscal measures, to influencing economic activity by government expenditure and taxation. Deficit spending, pump priming, and public works—not central bank policies—were widely regarded as the means to recovery. No wonder the Treasury became the active center of monetary policy as well.[34]

The Keynesian revolution in economic theory was a manifestation of that trend and helped to foster it. But certainly until 1937 and probably for some time thereafter, it played little role in the monetary developments we have described. Use of Keynesian ideas subsequently to promote "cheap-money" policies has led to the view that the Federal Reserve

[34] Harrison was critical of the Board's 1938 *Annual Report*, which stated, "Under existing conditions the Treasury's powers to influence member bank reserves outweigh those possessed by the Federal Reserve System" (p. 5). He said "he felt that the powers of the Board of Governors for credit control were belittled in the report which at the same time tended to over-emphasize the credit control powers of the Treasury" (Harrison, Notes, Vol. VII, Feb. 2, 1939).

System actively followed a cheap-money policy before 1937. We have seen that it did not. The Keynesian approach involved a shift of emphasis away from the "monetary" effects of monetary policy—that is, the effects on the stock of money—to the "credit" effects—that is, the effects on interest rates. The Federal Reserve System, as we have seen, had always emphasized interest rates and the use of credit, rather than the monetary effects. It did, however, make a different shift after 1937, from seeking to affect credit conditions indirectly through member bank reserves to seeking to affect them directly by operations in the government securities market involving changes in the composition of its portfolio.[35]

Marriner Eccles, who served as chairman of the Board of Governors (before 1936, governor of the Federal Reserve Board), November 1934 to April 1948, and as a member of the Board until July 1951, vividly documents some of these points in his memoirs. He stresses: (1) the Banking Act of 1935 and its importance in centering formal power in the Board— he regarded his shepherding of the act through the Congress as perhaps his major accomplishment and as comparable in importance to the establishment of the Federal Reserve System; (2) achievement of coordination in bank examination among the different regulatory agencies and adoption of an examination policy that would exert countercyclical influence; and (3) the importance of deficit spending for achieving recovery. He emphasizes that his support of deficit spending predated his acquaintance with Keynes' work, and that his policy position owed little to Keynes. He attributes the contraction of 1937–38 almost entirely to a change in the difference between government expenditures and receipts and ascribes little or no importance to the changes in reserve requirements and the stock of money.[36]

5. *Changes in the Deposit-Reserve Ratio*

Our view that the shorter-term movements in the deposit-reserve ratio require a different interpretation than the longer-term movements do

[35] For example, "This change [in open market policy] reflected a shift in emphasis in the use of open-market operations from their influence on member bank reserves to their direct influence on conditions in the capital market" (Board of Governors of the Federal Reserve System, *Annual Report*, 1939, p. 2).

[36] Eccles, *Beckoning Frontiers,* pp. 166–174; 202; 221–228; 266–268; 272–278; 130–132; 293–295; 309–320. Eccles claims (pp. 272–273) that it was upon his initiative that representatives of the Federal Deposit Insurance Corporation, the Comptroller of the Currency, and the Federal Reserve System were brought together to reach an agreement on a joint bank examination policy and ignores the impetus provided by the FDIC. He views the other agencies, as well as the Treasury Department and the state bank examiners, as obstructionist because they opposed Federal Reserve policies on examination procedures. The changes adopted in examination procedures did not in fact yield an examination policy that was countercyclical in influence, since the other supervisory agencies did not share the Federal Reserve view that the examination process should be subordinate to monetary policy (see Chap. 8, footnote 16).

was recorded above. The shorter-term movements are mostly temporary adaptations to short-term irregularities in high-powered money and deposits, reflecting, as it were, departures from the desired ratio which the banks tolerate, either because the irregularities are expected shortly to be reversed or because it takes time to adjust to unexpected changes. The inverse correlation between these irregularities in the deposit-reserve ratio and in high-powered money is an essential characteristic of the adjustment process. The long-term movements, on the other hand, represent mostly deliberate adaptation of the deposit-reserve ratio to a level desired by the banks in accordance with the interest rates at which they can lend and borrow and with the value they place on liquidity. That value, in its turn, depends on their confidence in their ability to raise cash at need from either the System or other banks. Such a deliberate adaptation by the banks does not occur instantaneously when there is a change in the desired level of the deposit-reserve ratio. Rather, it proceeds at a desired pace, just as an individual whose conception of the desirable pattern of his assets suddenly changes may take considerable time to readjust his portfolio. The observed inverse correlation between these longer-term movements in the deposit-reserve ratio and in high-powered money during the period under consideration is a coincidence, not an essential characteristic of the adjustment process, as the positive correlation in the twenties and again in the forties attests.

Two short-term irregularities require comment: (1) the sharp drop in the deposit-reserve ratio from January to March 1934, its mild rate of decline from March to July, and its rise from July to October; (2) the irregularities in early 1936.

The initial sharp drop in 1934, like the contemporaneous rise in high-powered money, is unprecedented in our series. There is no other two-month period since 1907, when our monthly data begin, that shows anything like so sharp a fall. The initial sharp drop seems quite clearly to reflect the large gold imports in February and March; the subsequent movements, the gradual adjustment of the banking system to that shock and the return to a desired position. Gold imports have two direct effects on the deposit-reserve ratio. First, gold raises bank deposits when it is deposited to the credit of the importer; second, it raises bank reserves when the recipient bank deposits at its Federal Reserve Bank the Treasury check it receives in payment for the gold, which it is legally required to turn over to the Treasury. The arithmetic effect of gold imports is, therefore, to raise the numerator and denominator of the deposit-reserve ratio by the same absolute amount. Since the ratio is greater than one, the numerator is raised by relatively less than the denominator and hence the ratio tends to decline. The increase in reserves encourages banks to expand. But that takes time, and the amount of time must surely depend on the size and unexpectedness of the change, and its temporal and geographic concentration.

In the 1934 instance, as we have noted, the change was unprecedentedly large and both temporally and geographically concentrated, the bulk of it occurring within the course of six weeks from January 31 to March 14 in New York City. Over the six-week period, high-powered money, affected as we have seen chiefly by changes in the gold stock and in Treasury cash holdings and deposits at Federal Reserve Banks, increased by $855 million and member bank deposits at Reserve Banks by $800 million or by 30 per cent.[37] We have weekly figures on deposits owned by the public and on their breakdown between banks in New York City and outside it only for weekly reporting member banks. In the same six-week period, deposits of all weekly reporting member banks at Reserve Banks increased $720 million and their net demand deposits $650 million. New York banks account for roughly 60 per cent of the increase both in deposits at Reserve Banks and in net demand deposits of all weekly reporting member banks, although they held initially only 46 per cent of net demand deposits and less than 40 per cent of deposits at Reserve Banks. Deposits of New York weekly reporting banks at Reserve Banks rose by 56 per cent in the course of the six-week period, and at a time of year when both deposits and reserves tend to fall seasonally. Little wonder that the first impact was on the deposit-reserve ratio, and that it took time for the banking system to adjust to the increase in reserves.

On this interpretation, the slow decline in the deposit-reserve ratio from March to July 1934 and the subsequent rise to October reflect primarily the adjustment by banks to the accession to their reserves; secondarily, the continued increase in high-powered money to July and then its rough constancy to October. This would imply an adjustment period of something like seven months, which seems not unreasonable. The level of the deposit-reserve ratio reached at the end of October was decidedly lower than the January level. However, if our interpretation is correct, the difference was not a passive reaction to the gold inflow, like the drop from January to March, but a continuation of the declining trend of 1933, representing a process of adjusting the deposit-reserve ratio to the level desired by banks.

A rough indication of the effect on the deposit-reserve ratio of the erratic movements in high-powered money can be obtained by a hypothetical calculation distributing the increment to the gold stock more evenly. The dotted line in Chart 44 is the result of such a calculation: the growth in high-powered money from January 1934 to March 1935 was assumed to have occurred by equal absolute amounts each month;

[37] Weekly figures for high-powered money were derived following the same procedures described in Table B-3 for the monthly figures.

CHART 44

Deposit-Reserve Ratio, March 1933–December 1941, and
Hypothetical Ratio, Assuming Even Growth of High-Powered Money,
January 1934–March 1935 and February–June 1936

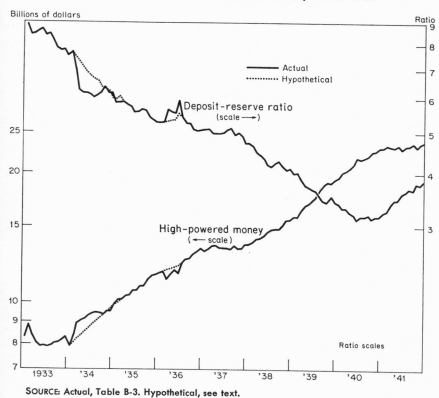

SOURCE: Actual, Table B-3. Hypothetical, see text.

the difference between actual high-powered money and this hypothetical
stock was subtracted from both deposits and bank reserves. The dotted
line is the ratio of the two resulting hypothetical figures. It will be seen
that it produces a continuation of the 1933 trend in the deposit-reserve
ratio and is fairly close to the actual ratio from October 1934 on. This
dotted line is, on our interpretation, an estimate of the longer-run deposit-
reserve ratio that banks were seeking to achieve.

The second short-term irregularity in the deposit-reserve ratio of sufficient size to merit attention occurred in the first half of 1936. We have
already noted that the fluctuation in high-powered money of which that
was a reflection arose largely from an unusual accumulation of and

537

variation in Treasury deposits at Federal Reserve Banks. If we smooth that fluctuation by the procedure followed for 1934—substituting for actual high-powered money the values interpolated along a straight line between the actual February and July values—the result is that depicted by the dotted line in Chart 44. This computation eliminates the sharp rise in March, but not a noticeable peak in June. The latter reflects an unusual outflow of currency into circulation, as does the concurrent dip in the deposit-currency ratio (Chart 38), associated with the redemption during the latter half of June of adjusted service bonds in the amount of $800 million.[38]

The longer-term movements in the deposit-reserve ratio in Chart 44 readily lend themselves to interpretation in terms of our earlier analysis (Chapter 8, section 1). In May 1933, after the immediate readjustment to the banking panic, the deposit-reserve ratio began to move downward. If the dotted lines of Chart 44 are substituted for the actual to allow for the short-term perturbations just discussed, and if attention is concentrated on the period through June 1936, the decline appears to be proceeding at a steadily decreasing rate and the ratio to have reached a fairly steady level in early 1936. In July the first increase in reserve requirements was officially announced and, coincidentally, the deposit-reserve ratio resumed its downward course but at a very mild pace. Later reserve increases left no immediate impact on the ratio, which was fairly constant to August 1937, when it started declining at a pace roughly comparable to that after mid-1933, until it leveled off again in 1940.

In our view, that behavior is to be interpreted as the result of two successive shifts in the preferences of banks for reserve funds, and the adaptation of portfolio positions to the changed preferences. The first shift occurred as a result of the experience during 1929–33, and the adaptation took about three years, from 1933 to 1936. The second occurred as a result of the successive rises in reserve requirements, reinforced by the occurrence of a severe contraction that was a stern reminder of earlier experience. The adaptation to it took about the same length of time, from 1937 to 1940.[39] In both cases, the adaptations occurred in an environment of generally declining interest rates which, even with stable preferences, would have induced banks to hold larger reserves. The 1933–

[38] Under the terms of the Adjusted Compensation Act of Jan. 27, 1936, passed over Presidential veto, more than $1.5 billion in bonus nine-year interest-bearing bonds, convertible into cash at any time, was distributed on June 15 to World War I veterans.

[39] Phillip Cagan has analyzed the reserve ratio adjusted for requirement changes —in his terminology, the usable reserve ratio. By 1938, the usable ratio had returned to its 1936 level. He is doubtful that the banks desired to hold larger usable reserves than in 1936, but offers no alternative explanation for the rise in usable reserves from 1938 to 1940 (see his forthcoming monograph on the determinants and effects of changes in the U.S. money stock, a National Bureau study).

36 shift in preferences was one factor contributing to the sharp fall in the ratio of short-term to long-term rates; the reserve increases in their turn produced a temporary rise in short-term rates, as banks sought cash instead of secondary reserves in the form of short-term securities; and the 1937–40 shift in preferences contributed to a decline, even sharper after mid-1937 than from 1933 to 1936, in the ratio of rates on short-term U.S. securities to long-term rates. Throughout, the high level of the discount rate relative to market rates reinforced the banks' reluctance (bred of their 1929–33 experience) to rely on borrowing from the Federal Reserve Banks for liquidity and led them instead to rely on cash reserves in excess of legal requirements and on short-term securities.[40]

This interpretation dates the second shift in preferences as occurring at the end of 1936 or early in 1937. In terms of the numerical behavior of the deposit-reserve ratio itself, as recorded in Chart 44, the second shift in preferences could as readily be dated as occurring at the end of 1937 or in mid-1938. If it were, it would have to be interpreted as a reaction to the 1937–38 contraction and as unrelated to the reserve re-

[40] The rise in reserve requirements in 1936 and 1937 was accompanied by a reduction in total holdings of government securities by member banks. The reduction was concentrated in bills and notes, which the banks largely replaced by deposits at the Reserve Banks. As a result, member bank holdings of government bonds rose from 45 per cent of their total holdings of government securities in 1936 to 74 per cent in 1941. The yield on 9-month Treasury bills rose from about 0.1 per cent per annum in Nov. 1936 to over 0.7 per cent on May 1, 1937, when the final rise in reserve requirements became effective, as a result of the pressure to convert from bills to cash. After the pressure subsided, banks presumably sought again to acquire bills. But the supply outside the Federal Reserve was so small that their attempt served only to reduce yields on bills to a level so close to zero— much of the time less than 0.01 per cent per annum—as to induce banks to hold cash or notes instead. Indeed, yields on Treasury bills were occasionally negative in 1940, when their price was bid up by purchasers seeking to convert cash into other assets for short periods to reduce tax liability under personal property tax laws.

At a directors' meeting of the New York Bank on Aug. 26, 1937, when the discount rate was reduced from 1½ to 1 per cent, effective the next day, Harrison reported a discussion he had had with commercial bankers, the upshot of which was agreement "that it would be better to borrow at the Federal Reserve Bank than to sell securities" if additional reserves were needed. He was interrupted by G. W. Davison, a banker, who said he "was shocked by Mr. Harrison's resumé of the views of the New York bankers because it differed so materially from his own impressions gained from contacts with certain of the bankers." Davison said bankers preferred to dispose of their holdings of bankers' acceptances and Treasury bills rather than borrow at the Reserve Bank. He had argued with the bankers that the Reserve System would not change reserve requirements every day, that they "certainly don't want the Federal Reserve to buy more Governments, and don't want the Treasury to abandon sterilization of gold, and that, consequently, borrowing at the Federal Reserve Bank was the logical way to supply needed reserves for seasonal requirements." Harrison's reply was that "if the banks want to see a return to normal banking relationships he couldn't understand why they were reluctant to conduct their affairs in such a way that borrowing at the Federal Reserve would ensue" (Harrison, Notes, Vol. VII, Aug. 26, 1937).

quirement increase. The rough constancy from late 1936 to August 1937 would have to be interpreted as the final stage of adjustment to the earlier shift in preferences. The main reason we reject this alternative interpretation is that it does not allow for the effects of the gold-sterilization program of the Treasury, which kept high-powered money roughly constant from December 1936 to late 1937. Just as the unusually rapid increase in high-powered money in early 1934 temporarily lowered the deposit-reserve ratio, with adaptation to the decline taking some seven months, the sterilization program must have had the opposite effect in 1937.

Suppose bank preferences had not been affected by the reserve changes. The abrupt cessation—as a result of gold sterilization—of a rise in high-powered money that had been proceeding for over three years would have produced a temporary bulge in the deposit-reserve ratio and a later return to the desired level. Given about the same seven-month adjustment time required in 1934, the temporary bulge would not have disappeared until about June or July of 1938, some seven months after high-powered money resumed its rise. The deposit-reserve ratio shows no such absolute bulge but it does show a flattening in 1937, such as would have been produced by the superposition of a temporary bulge lasting until mid-1938 on a declining longer-run desired level. The peak discrepancy between the bulge and the hypothetical desired level came in August 1937, when the amount of "inactive gold" in the Treasury balance reached its maximum.

Although we explain the behavior of the deposit-reserve ratio from 1937 to 1940 as an adaptation by banks to changed preferences resulting primarily from the increase in reserve requirements, and as reflecting the impact of gold sterilization, we do not exclude an effect due to the 1937–38 contraction. It must have been an additional factor inducing banks to prefer a lower deposit-reserve ratio.

If, as we argue, banks were primarily concerned about reserves in excess of legal requirements, the reduction in reserve requirements in April 1938 should have satisfied some of their desire for liquidity. But that change leaves no clear impress on the recorded deposit-reserve ratio. It is tempting to extrapolate the trend of the deposit-reserve ratio before July 1938 forward, and after September 1938 backward, and interpret the difference as a delayed reaction to the reduction in reserve requirements. But this is reading more into the data than can be justified without a much more detailed study than we have made.

The deposit-reserve ratio reached a trough in 1940 and thereafter began to rise, a rise that continued through 1946, though at a much milder pace from mid-1943 on than from 1940 to 1943. The rise from early 1942, when the Federal Reserve System officially began supporting the yield on bills and, in effect, on other government securities as well (see below, Chapter 10), raises no problem of interpretation. With fixed prices guaranteed by the Reserve System, government securities were the equivalent of cash and yielded some return, leaving no reason to hold reserves in excess of requirements for liquidity purposes. Hence "excess reserves" quickly fell to a low level which remained relatively stable.

The more interesting question is why the ratio rose from 1940 to 1942. If the 1940 level represented the attainment of a desired liquidity position, what produced the rise after 1940? One factor was doubtless the sharp change in the behavior of high-powered money. From rapid growth, it rather suddenly shifted in early 1941 to rough constancy, as a result of a sharp decline in gold imports. This constituted another short-term irregularity which banks might be expected initially to absorb and then react to only after a considerable lag. However, we are inclined to doubt that the adaptation by banks to that irregularity can account for the whole rise in the deposit-reserve ratio, since this explanation would mean that there had been essentially no adjustment at all for the whole year 1941, whereas the earlier evidence suggests a lag of about seven months.[41]

A second contributing factor might have been a rise in yields on alternative investments, which would make it more expensive to hold cash and thus induce banks to hold relatively less, even with given preferences for liquidity. However, the behavior of interest rates contradicts this view. Rates on private obligations, including commercial loans by banks, remained roughly stable from 1940 to early 1942; the yield on long-term governments fell slightly; the only rates that rose were on Treasury bills, so there was a narrowing of the spread between long-term and short-term government securities (see Table 22). But the narrowing of the spread suggests that the rise in short-term rates was a consequence of a decreased preference for liquidity rather than of a movement along an unchanged liquidity preference schedule. Just as the earlier shift in preferences of banks toward a desire for greater liquidity produced a widening in the spread, a shift in the opposite direction might be expected to produce a narrowing of the spread.

Hence, we are inclined to believe that the rise in the deposit-reserve ratio from 1940 to early 1942 reflected in part a shift in the preferences of banks in the opposite direction from the shifts in 1933 and 1937. We have already suggested why such a shift seems reasonable. The accumulation of experience under FDIC and a seven-year period without serious banking difficulties might well promote a reversal of the drive for liquidity that arose from the 1929–33 experience. A similar though less drastic sequence had followed earlier and less severe banking panics.

[41] The same percentage growth in high-powered money from Dec. 1940 to Dec. 1941 as from Dec. 1939 to Dec. 1940 would have added $4.5 billion to high-powered money. If this sum is added to both deposits and bank reserves in Dec. 1941, it yields a hypothetical deposit-reserve ratio almost identical with the actual ratio in Dec. 1940.

TABLE 22

AVERAGE RATES OR YIELDS ON SELECTED ASSETS, JUNE 1940–MARCH 1942

	Prime Commercial Paper, 4- to 6-Month NBER (1)	Prime Commercial Paper, 4- to 6-Month FRB (2)	90-Day Bankers' Acceptances (3)	Business Loans of Commercial Banks, 79 Cities Shifting Weights (4)	Constant Weights (5)	Basic Yield of 40- to 50-Year Corporate Bonds (6)	U.S. Bonds Not Due or Callable for 12 Years or More (7)	3-Month Treasury Bills (8)	(7) − (8) (9)
June 1940	0.81	0.56	0.44	2.59	1.9	2.68	2.39	0.071	2.319
June 1941	0.69	0.56	0.44	2.55	2.1	2.65	1.91	0.089	1.821
Mar. 1942	0.69	0.63	0.44	2.48	2.0	2.65	2.00	0.212	1.788

SOURCE, BY COLUMN

(1) Same source as for Chart 35.

(2–4, 7–8) Banking and Monetary Statistics, pp. 451, 460, 464; Federal Reserve Bulletin, Aug. 1942, p. 825. In col. 4 the rates charged are weighted according to the dollar volume of new loans made at each rate.

(5) FRB, Mar. 1949, p. 231. The rates charged in 4 size groups of loans are weighted according to the loans outstanding in each group on Nov. 20, 1946.

(6) Straight-line interpolation between annual (Feb.) figures in Historical Statistics, 1949, p. 279.

This analysis of the behavior of the deposit-reserve ratio yields, as a by-product, estimates of the reaction time of the banking system, of interest in their own right, especially for analysis of lags in the response to monetary policy measures taken by the Reserve System. We have suggested that it takes some seven months for banks to adjust to an unanticipated discrepancy between their actual and desired reserve positions produced by a change in their actual position, and some three years for banks to carry through a thoroughgoing revision of their actual reserve position as a result of a change in the desired position.

6. *Role of Monetary Factors in the 1937 Contraction and Subsequent Recovery*

The preceding sections have analyzed the factors accounting for the behavior of the money stock in the period 1933–41. Before we leave that period, a few explicit comments on the effect of the changes in the money stock on economic activity are in order. Extensive controversy has arisen about this issue, particularly about the 1937 contraction. Because the final increases in reserve requirements preceded the cyclical peak in May by such a short interval, many commentators have regarded them as partly or wholly responsible for the subsequent contraction. On the other hand, the Federal Reserve System has argued that those changes could not have had such an effect since they only absorbed excess reserves. Further, the much greater importance attributed by economic analysts, during the 1930's and ever since, to government fiscal operations than to monetary changes has led students to attach more importance to the contemporaneous shift in the government's budget from a deficit toward a surplus than to monetary policy measures. In his recent exhaustive study of that episode, Kenneth Roose concludes:

> In broad outline, the causation may be reduced to a relatively few important elements . . . . [N]et government contribution to income was drastically reduced in January 1937 . . . .
> [A]t the same time . . . the Federal Reserve action on excess reserves caused short-term governments to weaken and set up thereby a chain of reactions which resulted in increased costs of capital and the weakening of the securities markets to which business expectations are very sensitive, especially in the United States. The operation of the undistributed profits tax, in addition to its effects on business expectations, also reduced the cash position of even the large companies. The imperfect supply of capital funds and their increased cost made it more difficult for borrowers to obtain capital. Most important of all, however, was the reduced profitability of investment, beginning in the first quarter of 1937. This resulted from the increased costs, in which labor costs played a prominent part . . . . [T]he immediate decline in profit ratio, accompanied by the prospect of sharp declines in future profits, is adequate reason for the occurrence and timing of the recession.[42]

[42] Roose, *Economics of Recession*, pp. 238–239.

It is symptomatic of the change in intellectual outlook of which we have spoken that this judicious, eclectic statement should stress solely the "credit" aspects of monetary action and omit entirely the "monetary" aspects. Precisely the same is true of a draft of a memorandum prepared at the New York Federal Reserve Bank by John H. Williams in answer to the question whether the reserve requirement changes caused the 1937–38 depression. Williams emphasized essentially the same factors as Roose, except that he gave even less weight to Federal Reserve action on the grounds, first, that up to June 1937, "there was no contraction of bank deposits or bank assets," and, second, "if the action on reserve requirements was in any degree responsible for the business recession, it was because of its effect on interest rates," yet "at the end of the fiscal year 1937 money rates were but little changed from the rates existing at the beginning, and were throughout the year . . . at abnormally low levels."[43]

Consideration of the effects of monetary policy on the stock of money certainly strengthens the case for attributing an important role to monetary changes as a factor that significantly intensified the severity of the decline and also probably caused it to occur earlier than otherwise. As we have seen, the money stock grew at a rapid rate in the three successive years from June 1933 to June 1936—at continuous annual rates of 9.5 per cent, 14.0 per cent, and 13.0 per cent. The rapid rise was a consequence of the gold inflow produced by the revaluation of gold plus the flight of capital to the United States. It was in no way a consequence of the contemporaneous business expansion: the only way the expansion could significantly have increased the money stock would have been by inducing banks to hold smaller reserves, yet they were in fact doing the opposite. And the rapid rate of rise in the money stock certainly promoted and facilitated the concurrent economic expansion.

The combined impact of the rise in reserve requirements and—no less important—the Treasury gold-sterilization program first sharply reduced the rate of increase in the money stock and then converted it into a decline. From June 1936 to June 1937, the money stock grew at the continuous annual rate of 4.2 per cent per year and then in the following year fell at the rate of 2.4 per cent. The absolute peak in the money stock came in March 1937; the trough in May 1938, though December 1937 was almost as low.[44] The cyclical peak is dated in May 1937; the cyclical trough, in June 1938. As we have seen, neither the retardation in the rate of rise in the money stock nor the subsequent decline in the money stock

---

[43] Harrison, Special, no. 22, draft of memorandum, dated Jan. 27, 1938.

[44] If we measure the changes from June 1936 to the peak in the money stock in Mar. 1937 and then to the subsequent trough in May 1938, the resultant continuous annual rates of change are +6.3 and −2.9 per cent.

—any more than the preceding rapid rise—can be attributed to the contemporaneous course of business; they were produced by deliberate policy measures that offset the expansionary influence of the continuing gold inflow. The sharp retardation in the rate of growth of the money stock must surely have been a factor curbing expansion, and the absolute decline, a factor intensifying contraction. Though the decline may not seem large in absolute amount, it was the third largest cyclical decline recorded in our figures, exceeded only by the 1920–21 and 1929–33 declines.

Recovery came after the money stock had started to rise. It rose at continuous annual rates of 7.8, 13.1, and 12.1 per cent in the three years from June 1938 to June 1941, once again mostly as a result of the continued inflow of gold, and despite a continued decline in the deposit-reserve ratio to 1940 as an aftermath of the increases in reserve requirements. Munich and the outbreak of war in Europe were the main factors determining the U.S. money stock in those years, as Hitler and the gold miners had been in 1934 to 1936. Doubtless, other factors helped to account for the onset of recovery and for its pace, but the rapid increase in the money stock certainly at the very least facilitated their operation.

The rates of growth of the money stock during the periods of expansion from 1933 to 1936 and from 1938 to 1941 were unusually high and make more credible than otherwise widespread concern with dangers of inflation in the midst of large-scale unemployment. Yet, they were so high chiefly because of the unprecedented magnitude of the preceding decline. Averaged over the dozen years from 1929 to 1941, the rate of growth of the money stock was less than 2½ per cent per year and of real output less than 2 per cent per year—both well below the long-time average U.S. experience. In 1941, Kuznets' implicit price index was 13 per cent below its 1929 level, and even wholesale prices were some 8 per cent below their 1929 level, despite a rise of over 10 per cent from 1940 to 1941 alone under the impact of the first stage of the wartime boom. How different the history of that fateful dozen years might have been if the money stock had grown steadily at its average rate of 2½ per cent per year, let alone at the higher long-term historical rate, instead of first falling by one-third from 1929 to 1933 and then doubling from 1933 to 1941.

CHAPTER 10

World War II Inflation, September 1939–August 1948

THE OUTBREAK of war in Europe in September 1939 ushered in a period of inflation comparable to the inflations which accompanied the Civil War and World War I, though more protracted than either. By the postwar price peak nine years later (August 1948), wholesale prices had more than doubled, the implicit price deflator had somewhat less than doubled, the stock of money had nearly tripled, and money income had multiplied more than two-and-a-half-fold (see Chart 45). As this comparison indicates, velocity on net fell over the period. After an initial rise to 1942, it fell sharply to 1946 and then rose mildly to 1948. According to annual data, wholesale prices rose at the average rate of 8.2 per cent per year; the implicit price deflator, 6.5 per cent per year; the stock of money, 12.3 per cent per year; money income, 10.7 per cent per year; real income, 4.2 per cent per year; and velocity fell at the average rate of 1.7 per cent per year.[1] Substantial though these rates of change are, the rate of rise in the money stock was slightly lower than in World War I and about half the rate in the Civil War; the rate of rise in prices was less than three-fifths the rate in World War I and only one-third that in the Civil War.[2]

As in World War I, wholesale prices jumped on the outbreak of war, then stayed roughly constant for about a year before resuming their

[1] Paralleling World War I figures, our income figures for 1942–45 are modifications of Kuznets' estimates on the basis of Kendrick's "national security version" of net national product (see Chap. 5, footnote 16).

[2] For prices and money stock, the comparison between the three wars is as follows:

	World War II	World War I	Civil War
Start of war	Sept. 1939–[a]	July 1914–[b]	April 1861–
Price peak	Aug. 1948	May 1920	Jan. 1865
	RATE OF RISE, PER CENT PER YEAR		
Money stock	12.1	12.9	24.0[c]
Wholesale prices	8.7	15.3	24.5

[a] Measured from Aug. 1939, see Table 23.

[b] Measured from June 1914, see Table 16.

[c] From June 1861 through fiscal year ending June 1865. Data for those years are from Milton Friedman, "Price, Income, and Monetary Changes in Three Wartime Periods," *American Economic Review*, May 1952, p. 624.

These figures for World War II differ from those given in the text, because they are derived from monthly rather than annual data.

546

CHART 45

Money Stock, Income, Prices, and Velocity, and Industrial Production, in Reference Cycle Expansions and Contractions, 1939–48

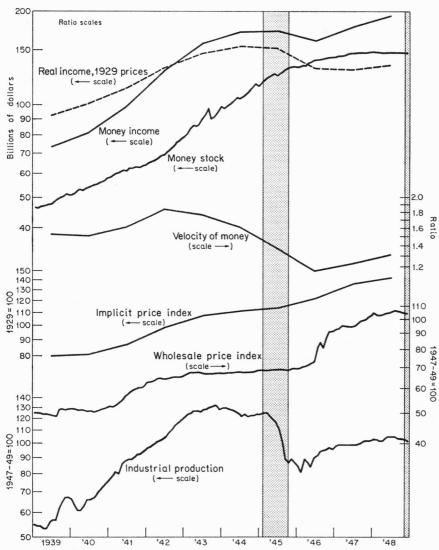

NOTE: Shaded areas represent business contractions; unshaded areas, business expansions.
SOURCE: Industrial production, same as for Chart 16. Other data, same as for Chart 62.

547

TABLE 23

CHANGES IN PRICES AND IN STOCK OF MONEY, AND SOURCE OF CHANGES IN STOCK OF MONEY, DURING THREE SEGMENTS OF THE PERIOD AUGUST 1939–AUGUST 1948

		SEGMENT				
	U.S. Neutrality Aug. 1939 Through Nov. 1941	War or Wartime Deficits		To Postwar Price Peak		Period as a Whole Aug. 1939 Through Aug. 1948
		Nov. 1941 Through Aug. 1945	Nov. 1941 Through Jan. 1946	Aug. 1945 Through Aug. 1948	Jan. 1946 Through Aug. 1948	
Number of months	27	45	50	36	31	108
Percentage change in:						
1. Wholesale prices	23	14	16	55	53	118
2. Stock of money	29	102	107	14	11	197
3. High-powered money	29	80	83	7	5	149
Per cent change per year in:						
4. Wholesale prices	9	4	4	15	16	9
5. Stock of money	11	19	18	4	4	12
6. High-powered money	11	16	15	2	2	10
Fraction of change in stock of money (total change = 1.00) attributable to change in:						
7. High-powered money	0.99	0.84	0.83	0.53	0.49	0.84
8. Ratio of commercial bank deposits to vault cash plus deposits at Federal Reserve Banks	0.16	0.39	0.38	0.01	-0.02	0.31
9. Ratio of commercial bank deposits to currency held by the public	-0.15	-0.15	-0.14	0.46	0.52	-0.09
10. Interaction of ratios	-0.01	-0.07	-0.07	0	0	-0.05

Fraction of change in high-powered money
(total change = 1.00) consisting of change in:

11. Monetary gold stock	1.15	−0.14	−0.14	1.15	1.58	0.26
12. F.R. claims on the public and banks	0.02	0.04	0.03	0	0.03	0.03
13. Other physical assets and fiat of monetary authorities	−0.17	1.10	1.11	−0.15	−0.61	0.71

NOTE: Because of rounding, components may not always add to 1.00.

SOURCE, BY LINE

1, 4.   *Continuation of Historical Statistics*, pp. 47, 78.
2–3, 5–13.   Same as for corresponding lines of Table 10, except that original data for lines 11–12 from 1942 on are from *Federal Reserve Bulletin*. Result in lines 11–13 is the same whether or not the gold stock is adjusted approximately to cost by subtracting the cumulated devaluation profit.

upward movement. As in World War I also, prices rose more rapidly before and after involvement than during the United States' active participation in the war, at least as judged from the available indexes. Again as in World War I, the sources of the rise in the stock of money were quite different in the three periods just distinguished: the period of U.S. neutrality, the period of our active participation in the war, and the postwar period. Table 23 records the changes in prices and the stock of money during those periods and the factors accounting for the changes in the stock of money.

1. *U.S. Neutrality, September 1939–November 1941*

Politically, the period of U.S. neutrality was clearly demarcated. Economically, it was not. During its early months—the so-called "phony war" period—the war had little impact on the U.S. economy. After a brief speculative movement in the final quarter of 1939, production, employment, and personal income in general declined until May 1940. The Nazi attack on the Low Countries and the subsequent fall of France brought a dramatic reversal. Britain and her remaining allies started placing large-scale orders for war material in the United States. As we saw earlier, there was a sharp increase in mid-1940 in the rate of flow of gold to the United States, as gold was shipped to pay for war material. The United States simultaneously embarked on a greatly expanded defense program. Those developments spurred a rapid expansion in industrial production, employment, and personal income. Because of the large absolute amount of unemployment and unused industrial capacity, wholesale prices at first remained stable, starting to rise only in the fall of 1940. Economically, therefore, the beginning of the war for the United States as a neutral might better be dated in the month when its effects first began to be felt—say, May 1940.

To mark the close of that phase and the active involvement of the United States in the war, the month when lend-lease began, March 1941, is probably a better date than early December when war was declared against Germany and Japan. Before lend-lease, Britain paid for war purchases by transferring over $2 billion in gold, drawing down British dollar balances by $235 million, and selling $335 million in U.S. securities —the last two requisitioned in large part by the British government from British subjects.[3] Thereafter, the U.S. government paid for much of the war material, nominally in return for services rendered in exchange to the United States. Lend-lease, under which some $50 billion was spent by the end of the war, was the counterpart in World War II of U.S.

---

[3] See *International Transactions of the United States During the War, 1940–1945*, Economic Series No. 65, Office of Business Economics, Dept. of Commerce, 1948, pp. 112–115. The figures cited cover the period Sept. 1939–Dec. 1940.

loans to its allies in World War I. Within a month after the enactment of lend-lease, the rapid rise in the gold stock that began in 1938 and accelerated after the fall of France came to an end.

Whichever pair of dates is used—whether August 1939, just before the outbreak of war in Europe, through November 1941, just before Pearl Harbor (the dates used in Table 23) or those just suggested of May 1940 through March 1941—the growth of the money stock during the period of U.S. neutrality was attributable entirely to the concomitant growth of the gold stock (see Table 23, lines 7 and 11, for the first pair of dates). The gold stock played the same role between those dates as it did during the period of neutrality in World War I, when about 80 per cent of the increase in the stock of money was attributable to the increase in the gold stock. During the neutrality period in World War II, the stock of money grew by 29 per cent, high-powered money by the same percentage, and the increase in high-powered money was less than in the gold stock, the difference being absorbed by a decline in the sum of Federal Reserve Bank private claims and the fiat of the monetary authorities.

A rise in the ratio of commercial bank deposits to reserves, as banks reduced their excess reserves, tended to increase the money stock but was about offset by a concomitant decline in the ratio of deposits to currency (Chart 46 and Table 23). These deposit ratios were to continue to move in opposite directions throughout the war, just as they had during most of World War I.

In the World War I neutrality period, the Federal Reserve System had been powerless to offset the effects of the gold inflow, since it possessed no earning assets to sell. In the World War II period, the Federal Reserve was in a much stronger technical position. It had a portfolio of over $2 billion of government securities which it could have sold at will. True, even the sale of its whole portfolio would have offset less than half the gold inflow from August 1939 to November 1941. However, the Treasury could have offset the rest—or indeed the whole or more than the whole—of the gold inflow by sterilization operations like those it had conducted in late 1936 and early 1937, when it sold securities and used the proceeds to pay for gold rather than printing gold certificates to do so. Between them, therefore, the Treasury and the Federal Reserve were technically in a position to control the changes in high-powered money (see Chart 47 for the breakdown of high-powered money, by assets and liabilities of the monetary authorities).

The behavior of prices gave reason to be concerned with the growth of the money stock. From August 1939 to November 1941, wholesale prices rose 23 per cent, or at the rate of 9 per cent per year and, as we have seen, nearly the whole of the increase occurred in the final fifteen months of

551

CHART 46
The Stock of Money and Its Proximate Determinants, Monthly, August 1939–August 1948

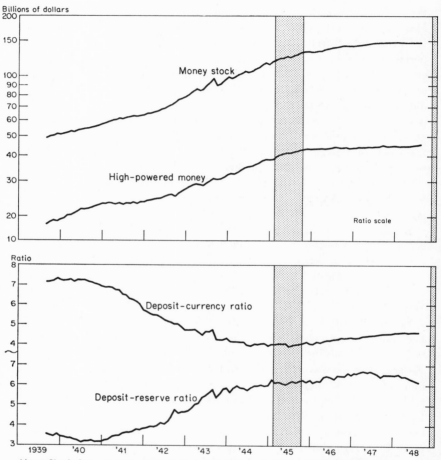

NOTE: Shaded areas represent business contractions; unshaded areas, business expansions.
SOURCE: Tables A-1 (col. 8) and B-3.

the period, when wholesale prices rose nearly 20 per cent and the stock of money over 16 per cent. Yet, as is clear from Chart 49, below, the Federal Reserve engaged in no extensive open market operations. In the three weeks after the outbreak of war in September 1939, it purchased some $400 million of government securities to offset a sharp drop in the prices of U.S. government bonds.[4] These were sold off in the next few

[4] These operations were regarded by the Board as a departure from past practice,

months so that, by the turn of the year, the System's holdings of government securities were at their prewar level. Further sales of about $300 million were made from June to December 1940; thereafter, the System's holdings of government securities were kept rigid until the United States entered the war. The System thus largely continued the policy with respect to open market operations and gold inflows that it had followed since 1933.

During the period of neutrality, the Treasury, like the Reserve System, undertook no operations to offset the gold inflow. Its weekly balances in cash and Federal Reserve deposits fluctuated considerably, from a minimum of about $2.4 billion to a maximum of about $3.4 billion. The billion-dollar range was nearly half again as wide as the range in Federal Reserve credit outstanding, so that Treasury operations were a more important factor affecting the money stock than Federal Reserve open market operations. But the fluctuations in Treasury balances were not undertaken for reasons of monetary policy and show no systematic connection with monetary factors. They were simply a largely unintended result of fluctuations in expenditures and tax receipts and of the flotation and retirement of securities.

In response to the rapid rise in prices and the stock of money, the Federal Reserve took two actions in addition to the open market sales in the latter half of 1940. Both were taken near the end of the period of neutrality and both, in line with the general policy of the thirties, involved use of new instruments of control.

On September 1, 1941, under authority of the President's executive order of August 9, 1941, the Board imposed controls on consumer credit, prescribing in Regulation W minimum down payments and maximum maturities applicable to consumer credit extended through instalment sales of certain listed articles. Because consumer durable goods shortly

---

since their object was not to affect the volume of member bank reserves and indebtedness. The operations were justified on two grounds: (1) their influence directly on the prices and yields of government obligations and indirectly on the prices and yields of corporate bonds, and hence on general economic recovery; (2) the importance of safeguarding the enlarged member bank portfolio of government securities from "unnecessarily wide and violent fluctuations in price" (Board of Governors of the Federal Reserve System, *Annual Report*, 1939, pp. 5–6). The first reference to maintaining "orderly market conditions" was made in the *Annual Report*, 1937, pp. 6–7, concerning Federal Reserve purchases in Apr. 1937, though, as pointed out in Chap. 9, concern with maintaining an "orderly market" dated from not later than 1935. Two important differences between the early enunciation of the policy of maintaining an orderly market for government securities and its later wartime character are evident: (1) in 1939, the professed aims were to protect member bank portfolios, not Treasury interests as a borrower, and to assure an orderly capital market as a condition of general economic recovery; (2) in 1939, a rigid system of support prices was not yet contemplated, but only the degree of support that would prevent wide fluctuations in the prices of government securities.

CHART 47

High-Powered Money, by Assets and Liabilities of the Treasury and Federal Reserve Banks, 1939–48

A. Liabilities

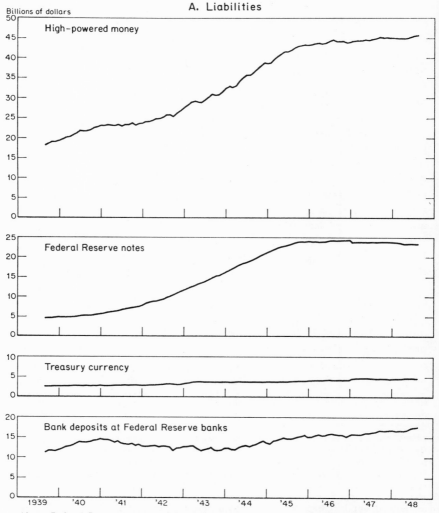

NOTE: Federal Reserve notes and Treasury currency are outside the Treasury and Federal Reserve Banks. Between $40 million and $65 million of gold certificates recalled but not turned in are included in high-powered money but not shown in its components viewed as liabilities.

SOURCE: Chart 39 was extended, using *Federal Reserve Bulletin* for Federal Reserve credit outstanding and monetary gold stock, and *Annual Report* of the Secretary of the Treasury, 1942–49, for the devaluation profit.

CHART 47 (Concluded)

B. Assets

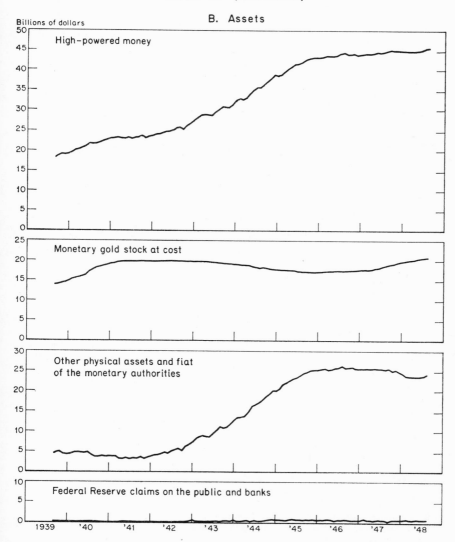

Billions of dollars

High-powered money

Monetary gold stock at cost

Other physical assets and fiat
of the monetary authorities

Federal Reserve claims on the public and banks

1939 '40 '41 '42 '43 '44 '45 '46 '47 '48

became unavailable for the duration of the war, the volume of consumer credit fell rapidly after Pearl Harbor. Consumer credit control was, in consequence, of little significance during the war. It is worth note, first, because it represented an extension to a new area of the principle, initially applied to security loans, of controlling specific types of credit, and second, because it was destined to play a somewhat more important role after the war.

555

The Board's other measure was to raise reserve requirements on November 1, 1941, to the maximum limit permitted by law, thereby rescinding the reduction made in April 1938. That measure converted $1.2 billion of the then extant $4.7 billion of excess reserves into required reserves.[5] A sign of the changed attitudes of banks is that they made no attempt to rebuild their excess reserves, as they had after the reserve increases of 1936 and 1937, but rather proceeded to continue to reduce their remaining excess reserves. The effect of the reserve requirement increase shows up only in a slackened rate of rise of the deposit-reserve ratio from October—immediately following the announcement on September 23 of the forthcoming rise—to roughly April 1942, when the Federal Reserve announced that it would peg the rate on Treasury bills. The ratio then started to rise at an even faster rate than before the reserve requirement increase. It is ironic that the increase, presumably intended to "tighten" monetary conditions and to restrain the expansion of bank liabilities, did so only to a minor extent, whereas the earlier increase, intended as a precautionary move and designed to have no immediate impact, had exercised a sharp restraining influence.

2. Period of Wartime Deficits, December 1941–January 1946

The expanded defense program initiated in 1940 and lend-lease initiated in early 1941 produced a substantial increase in government expenditures. These were offset for a time by a rise in tax rates and tax revenues. By early 1941, however, the deficit had begun to rise sharply. For calendar 1941, cash operating outgo exceeded cash operating income by $10 billion or nearly half of total expenditures.[6] Pearl Harbor brought a sharp intensification of these tendencies. Government expenditures nearly tripled from calendar 1941 to calendar 1942, and rose a further 50 per cent from 1942 to 1943, reaching a peak of nearly $95 billion in 1944. Tax re-

[5] Concern over the volume of excess reserves was expressed in a special report to the Congress dated Dec. 31, 1940, made jointly by the Board of Governors, the presidents of the Federal Reserve Banks, and the Federal Advisory Council (*Federal Reserve Bulletin,* Jan. 1941, pp. 1–2). Among other points in the program it presented, the report requested the Congress to increase the minimum statutory reserve requirements to the maximum defined in the Banking Act of 1935 and to permit the Federal Open Market Committee (not the Board of Governors) to increase requirements to double the new minimum.

The reader is reminded that, for the period after 1940, we have not had access to internal documents of the Federal Reserve System like those in the Harrison Papers, or to an insider's running account like the Hamlin Diary. Hence, our discussion of Federal Reserve policy is less informed in detail than for earlier years and it is not as well documented. The Reserve System could perform a service to students of the period by making such documents available.

[6] The cash deficit or surplus differs from the budget deficit or surplus in consolidating the accounts of the social security and other trust funds with those of other government agencies. It therefore gives a more satisfactory index for our purposes of the impact of government operations on the rest of the economy.

ceipts also rose but more slowly and in no greater ratio. As a result, the cash deficit rose to levels without precedent, either in absolute amount or as a percentage of national income: to nearly $40 billion in calendar 1942, over $50 billion in 1943, over $45 billion in 1944, and over $35 billion in 1945—sums averaging nearly 30 per cent of the contemporary net national product. Government expenditures fell rapidly after the end of hostilities while tax revenues remained high. As in World War I, within six months after the end of the war the government was taking in more than it was paying out, so that the period of wartime deficits came to an end about January 1946.

As in World War I, those changes involved a continuation and intensification of trends already in process. The transfer of economic resources from peace to war production had been going on apace since early 1940. On the physical side, intensification of trends was undoubtedly much sharper in World War II than in World War I. The period of neutrality was longer in World War I than in World War II and that of active hostilities shorter; and World War II saw a far more complete conversion to a "total war" economy than World War I did. On the financial side, the situation was reversed. Thanks to lend-lease, active war meant less of a change in the source of finance for war activity in World War II than it had in World War I.

PRICE MOVEMENTS

As in World War I, also, our entry into active war was rather surprisingly accompanied by a slowing down of the rate of rise in the available price indexes, while the termination of wartime deficits was accompanied by a sharp speeding up. As Table 23 shows, the wholesale price index rose at the rate of 4 per cent a year during the period of wartime deficits, compared with 9 per cent in the prior period and 16 per cent in the succeeding period. These figures are less reliable indicators of the behavior of prices in World War II than the corresponding figures are for World War I. General price control was instituted in early 1942 and suspended in mid-1946. During the period of price control, there was a strong tendency for price increases to take a concealed form, such as a change in quality or in the services rendered along with the sale of a commodity or the elimination of discounts on sales or the concentration of production on lines that happened to have relatively favorable price ceilings. Moreover, where price control was effective, "shortages" developed, in some cases—such as gasoline, meats, and a few other foods—accompanied by explicit government rationing. The resulting pressure on consumers to substitute less desirable but available qualities and items for more desirable but unavailable qualities and items was equivalent to a price increase not recorded in the indexes. Finally, there was undoubtedly much legal avoidance and illegal evasion of the price controls through a variety of devices of which the explicit "black market" was perhaps the least important. The result was that "prices," in any economically meaningful sense, rose by decidedly more than the "price index" during the period of price control. The jump in the price index on the elimination of price control in 1946 did not involve any corresponding jump in "prices"; rather, it reflected largely the unveiling of price increases that had occurred earlier. Allowance for the defects in the price index as a measure of price change would undoubtedly yield a decidedly higher rate of price rise during the war and a decidedly lower rate after the war than those recorded in Table 23, and hence a substantially smaller difference between the rate of price rise during the war and before and after. It seems unlikely, however, that allowance for these defects would reverse the qualitative conclusion that prices rose more slowly during the war than before or after.

In World War I, differences in the rate of price change were accompanied by corresponding differences in the rate of change of the stock of money: the stock of money also rose less rapidly during the war than before or after. In World War II, the reverse occurred: the stock of money rose much more rapidly during the war than before or after. This is the counterpart of the decline in velocity, 1942–46, and its subsequent rise— just the opposite of the behavior of velocity in 1917–18 and after.

BEHAVIOR OF VELOCITY

It is by no means clear what factors explain the behavior of velocity in World War II. Velocity rose by a fifth from 1940 to 1942—or slightly less than from 1915 to 1918—then declined by over a third to 1946. From 1946 to 1948 it rose by 13 per cent, to a level still much lower than in 1939 (see Chart 45). Quarterly data on national income and monthly data on personal income suggest that velocity reached its peak in the fourth quarter of 1942 and its trough in the final quarter of 1945 or the first quarter of 1946.

The initial rise in velocity is not surprising. Velocity, as measured, generally rises during economic expansions and falls during economic contractions. The expansion from 1940 to 1942 was vigorous and after mid-1940 was accompanied by sharp price increases which might be expected to discourage the holding of assets in the form of money.

What needs explanation is the decline in velocity after 1942. Price control inhibited increases in prices after early 1942 and kept many increases that did occur from showing up in the price index. It might be argued that the cessation of the rise in the index removed the incentive, provided by the prior price increase, to economize on the holding of money. But even if it were granted that the price index properly recorded the price movements that determined the amount of money balances the community desired to hold relative to its income, the cessation of the price rise could hardly account for more than a return of velocity to, say, the 1940 level. It could not account for the fall of velocity well below that level. Even to regard it as responsible for reducing velocity to the 1940 level would grossly overestimate its effect, since that would assume full adjustment of velocity to the prior rate of rise of prices, whereas the evidence of earlier chapters suggests that the adjustment of velocity to changes in the rate of change in prices is slow and tardy.

It seems likely that any direct effect of price control was less important than the unavailability to consumers of automobiles and other consumer durable goods, after wartime cessation of their production in 1942,[7] and than the restrictions imposed on construction and on private capital formation. Both consumers and business enterprises were prevented from using their funds to purchase kinds of goods they regard as increasing their wealth, which ordinarily absorb a large fraction of increases in income and an especially large fraction of transitory increases. The blocking of these channels of spending induced consumers and business enterprises to increase the stock of other assets—in particular, as it turned out, money and government securities—to a much higher level than otherwise, relative to income.

The counterpart on income account of the accumulation of liquid assets was an unprecedentedly high level of personal saving. Personal saving would have been large in any event because of the abnormally high level of income associated with full employment and the war boom. But saving was much larger than can readily be accounted for by income alone. One important reason is that consumers accumulated in the form of liquid assets funds that they would otherwise have spent or have tried to spend on automobiles, other durable goods, and residential construction. The recurrent bond campaigns with their appeal to patriotism may have contributed also to the high rate of saving, but we are inclined to be skeptical that they had much effect on the amount of saving. If they had any effect, it was probably on the form in which savings were held—more in government securities relative to other assets. Insofar as one of the alternatives was money, the bond campaigns tended to make the decline in velocity less than it otherwise would have been.[8]

[7] Limitation (L-) orders were first issued in the summer of 1941 by the Supply, Priority, and Allocations Board, a predecessor of the War Production Board, restricting the output of finished products and eventually prohibiting production for civilian use of automobiles, trucks, refrigerators, washing machines, electric appliances, etc. Prohibition of nonmilitary automobile production took effect Feb. 1, 1942, and of many other consumer durables by Sept. 1942.

[8] To avoid misunderstanding, it should perhaps be noted that the statements in the text are not intended to be a full analysis of the factors accounting for the high level of wartime savings. Numerous other factors doubtless played a role. See "A

Both money and government securities, of course, were fixed in value in nominal terms and so would have been poor forms in which to hold wealth if their holders had expected them to depreciate sharply in their command over real goods. Two points are relevant in this connection. First, the assets were being held to exercise command at a later time over particular kinds of goods—on the interpretation suggested above, especially over durable goods not currently available. It was entirely reasonable for the public to expect the prices of these goods to decline—in a formal sense, they had to, since their current prices were effectively infinite. And that expectation was reinforced by the sharp rise in the price of second-hand items of this kind. With respect to these goods, money holdings could be expected to be worth more after the war. Second, almost certainly the most widely-held expectation at the time was that prices would go down after the war—if this expectation seems unreasonable to us, it is only by hindsight. Memory of the sharp price decline after World War I was reinforced by the climate of opinion formed by the depressed 1930's and both were further strengthened by much-publicized predictions of "experts" that war's end would be followed by a major economic collapse.

These expectations about the postwar period were important not only because of their implications for the form in which savings were held but also because expectations of great instability in the near future enhanced the importance attached to accumulating money and other liquid assets. The expected price change meant that those assets would yield more than they would otherwise; the expected instability, that they were more desirable for any given yield. Both, therefore, worked in the direction of reducing velocity and hence also the price rise associated with any given increase in the stock of money. (See Chapter 12 for a fuller analysis of velocity and of the role of expectations about the degree of future economic instability.)

World War I differed markedly from World War II with respect to both the availability of goods and expectations about the postwar behavior of prices and income. "Shortages" and "controls" in World War I were nowhere nearly so sweeping as in World War II, and no major branch of civilian production suspended output entirely. World War I came after nearly two decades of generally rising prices, when the climate of opinion was characterized by belief in unlimited future potentialities rather than by fear of secular stagnation.

Once the war was over in 1945 and durable goods gradually became

National Survey of Liquid Assets Distribution According to Income," *Federal Reserve Bulletin*, July 1946, pp. 716–722; Michael Sapir, "Review of Economic Forecasts for the Transition Period," *Studies in Income and Wealth*, Vol. 11, New York, National Bureau of Economic Research, 1949, pp. 312–314; Lenore A. Epstein, "Consumers' Taxable Assets," *ibid.*, Vol. 12, 1950, pp. 440–453.

available again, holders of the accumulated assets tried to use them to purchase such goods. The attempt to use the accumulated assets tended to
raise prices and incomes and to reduce the ratio of such assets to income.
It is therefore entirely consistent with the preceding analysis that velocity
should have started to rise in early 1946. What is perhaps surprising is
that initially it rose so little and then subsequently rose for so long a period, but these puzzles we shall leave for later (section 3, below, and
Chapter 12).

The decline in velocity and of course also the accompanying rise in output explain why prices rose so much more slowly than the stock of
money during the period of wartime deficits. We turn now to the factors
accounting for the rise in the stock of money.

PROXIMATE DETERMINANTS OF THE RISE IN THE MONEY STOCK

As Table 23 shows, the rise in the stock of money during the war was
predominantly accounted for—in an arithmetic sense—by the concurrent
rise in high-powered money, just as it had been in the period of neutrality.
But, precisely paralleling World War I, there was a major difference in
the source of the rise in high-powered money. In both war periods,
Federal Reserve credit outstanding rather than gold accounted for the
rise in high-powered money. The Federal Reserve System again became
essentially the bond-selling window of the Treasury and used its monetary powers almost entirely for that purpose.

The Reserve System performed the same role somewhat differently in
the two wars. In World War I, the System increased its private claims by
discounting member bank bills mostly secured by government obligations;
its own holdings of government securities were small throughout. In
World War II, discounts were small throughout, and the Federal Reserve
increased its credit outstanding by buying government securities. In our
terminology, there was an increase in the fiat of the monetary authorities.
The common effect was an increase in high-powered money which was
distributed between currency and bank reserves—about equally in World
War I, about six-sevenths to currency, one-seventh to reserves in World
War II. The increment in bank reserves, of course, permitted a multiple expansion of bank deposits. The corresponding growth of commercial
bank assets largely took the form of an increase in loans in World War I;
of an increase in holdings of government securities in World War II.[9]
But again the difference was largely formal. Perhaps half the World War
I increase in loans to customers was secured by government obligations;
in World War II, the banks purchased the securities directly. Dissatis-

[9] From June 1941 to June 1945, the increase in commercial bank holdings of
U.S. government obligations was $64 billion, or 90 per cent of the increase in
commercial bank assets over the period. From June 1917 to June 1919 the increase
in total loans extended by commercial banks was $4.2 billion, or 44 per cent of the
increase in commercial bank assets over the period.

561

faction with World War I experience led to a shunning of the earlier forms. Similar political and economic pressures led to the adoption of the same substance. Some idea of the magnitudes of those operations is given by the following figures: from November 1941 to January 1946, the government debt outside the U.S. government and the Federal Reserve System grew by $178 billion, of which some $69 billion was acquired by commercial banks; currency held by the public grew by $17 billion; commercial bank deposits, by $52 billion; and Federal Reserve credit outstanding, by $22 billion.

In April 1942, the Federal Open Market Committee announced that it would keep the rate on Treasury bills,[10] mostly 90-day maturities, fixed at 3/8 of one per cent per year by buying or selling any amount offered or demanded at that rate.[11] That rate was kept fixed until the middle of 1947. No such rigid commitment was made for other government securities but an effective pattern was established for them as well—ranging from roughly 7/8 of one per cent for certificates to 0.9 per cent for 13-month notes, 1.5 per cent for 4½-year notes, and 2.5 per cent for long-term bonds.[12] The System bought whatever amount of these securities was

[10] Treasury bills are obligations issued on a discount basis with varying maturities up to 12 months. During the war they were issued weekly, usually for a term of 3 months in denominations from $1,000 to $1,000,000 at maturity.

[11] On Aug. 7, 1942, the Federal Open Market Committee directed the Federal Reserve Banks to give the seller a repurchase option at the same rate for an equal amount of bills of the same maturity, and extended the privilege of sale and repurchase to dealers in securities, corporations, and other holders of liquid funds.

[12] Certificates of indebtedness are Treasury obligations limited by law to a maturity of one year. They are sold at par plus any accrued interest, and interest on them is paid at the time of their maturity. They were offered by the Treasury in Apr. 1942 for the first time since 1934. The term of issue during the period of war deficits was usually 11 to 12 months. As many as ten issues a year were offered, usually as of the first of the month, in denominations from $1,000 to $1,000,000, at a rate, from Nov. 1942 on, of 7/8 of one per cent. Maturing issues were usually refunded into new issues of certificates of indebtedness or occasionally into 13-month notes to prevent two issues from maturing on the same date.

Treasury notes are obligations with maturity of more than one year and not over 5 years. They are sold at par plus any accrued interest. Interest rates on them during the war ranged from about 0.90 per cent on 13-month maturities to 1.25 per cent on those maturing in about 3 years, and to 1.5 per cent on those maturing in 4½ years. During the period of war deficits there were seven issues of Treasury notes exclusive of 13-month notes, which the market treats like certificates.

Treasury marketable bonds have maturities of more than 5 years. Maturities of most bonds offered during the war ranged from 10 to 25 years. They were sold at par plus any accrued interest, the interest rate varying with their maturity as shown in the tabulation.

Maturity of Bonds	Callable by Treasury (years)	Coupon Rate (per cent)
10	8	2
15	12	2¼
25	20	2½

necessary to prevent their yields from rising but did not commit itself to sell them freely in order to prevent yields from falling. The relatively fixed pattern of rates on government securities was the counterpart in World War II of the relatively fixed discount rate in World War I.

The support program converted all securities into the equivalent of money. Since the pattern of rates was carried over from the late thirties and reflected an abnormally high valuation of liquidity, the Reserve Banks tended to acquire bills and, to a smaller extent, certificates and, to a still smaller extent, notes, rather than bonds; and banks to acquire bonds, notes, and certificates, rather than bills. So long as the bill rate was kept absolutely fixed, the pattern of rates for other issues could be maintained only if (1) the Treasury adjusted its issues to provide only the relatively small amount of bills holders desired at those rates; or (2) the Federal Reserve System changed the initial composition of debt instruments issued by the Treasury to the composition holders desired, by buying bills and other securities as they approached a comparable maturity, and by selling bonds. The Treasury was not averse to a decline in long rates and, as the System's bond portfolio declined (by the end of the war, bonds constituted only $1 billion of the System's total government security holdings of $23 billion; see Chart 48), attempts by other holders to get out of short-term securities and into long-term—"playing the pattern of rates," as it was termed—produced a decline in yields on long-term securities beginning in 1944.

In late 1942, the discount rate was lowered to $\frac{1}{2}$ of one per cent on advances secured by short-term government securities (Chart 49). However, that change was of little significance since, if banks held such securities, it was generally cheaper for them to acquire any needed reserves by selling bills yielding $\frac{3}{8}$ of one per cent rather than by using them as collateral to borrow at $\frac{1}{2}$ of one per cent. In 1942 also, the System lowered reserve requirements for central reserve city banks.[13]

With government security prices supported, there was no incentive for banks to hold excess reserves. They could satisfy liquidity needs instead by holding income-yielding securities. The reduction in excess reserves, together with the reduction just noted in required reserves, produced a continued increase in the ratio of bank deposits to bank reserves, from not quite 4 to 1 in November 1941 to over 6 to 1 by January 1946. Had there been no change in the deposit-currency ratio, the increase in the deposit-reserve ratio would have made the percentage increase in the stock of money about $1\frac{3}{4}$ times the percentage increase in high-powered

[13] The initial grant of authority in the Banking Act of 1935 to vary reserve requirements specified a uniform increase or decrease for all central reserve and reserve city banks and a uniform increase or decrease for all country banks. The authority to vary requirements for the central reserve city class separately was granted in July 1942.

CHART 48

Government Securities Held by Federal Reserve Banks,
March 1941–August 1948

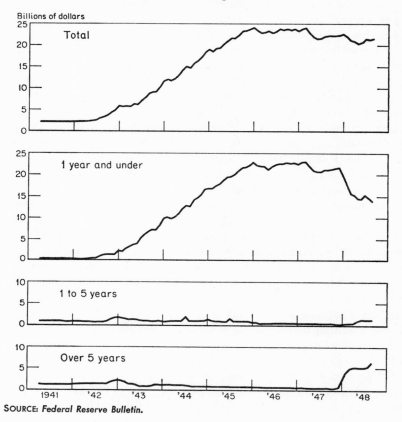

SOURCE: *Federal Reserve Bulletin.*

money. However, about half the excess of that 1¾ over unity was offset
by a continued decline in the deposit-currency ratio from 6 to 1 in
November 1941 to 4 to 1 in January 1946. In his detailed analysis of the
deposit-currency ratio, Cagan has attributed its decline during the war in
part to increased use of currency in preference to deposits as a means of
avoiding increased income tax levies, in part to black market activities,
expansion of the armed forces, and greater mobility of the civilian population.[14]

The direction of movement of both deposit ratios was the same in

---

[14] See Phillip Cagan's forthcoming volume on determinants and effects of changes
in the U.S. money stock, 1875–1955, a National Bureau study.

CHART 49
Use of Tools by Federal Reserve System, August 1939–August 1948

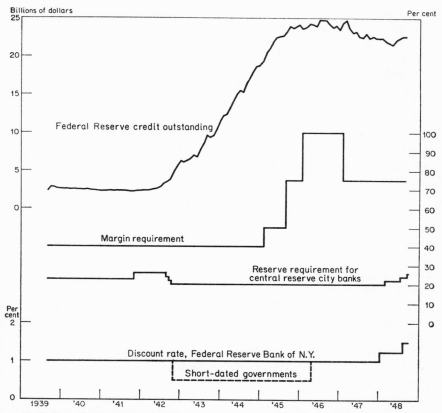

NOTE: Short-dated government securities, for which discount rate is shown, are due or callable in one year or less.

SOURCE: Same as for Chart 41, except that *FRB* is source for 1942–48 data.

World War II as in World War I. However, the relative importance of the changes differed sharply. In World War I, the decline in the deposit-currency ratio was some two to three times as important in its effect on the stock of money as the rise in the deposit-reserve ratio; in World War II, the relative importance was reversed.

The bond drives of World War II placed much emphasis on avoiding the sale of securities to commercial banks on the ground that purchases by banks were "inflationary" in a sense in which purchases by others were not. Certain issues were made ineligible for bank purchase and attempts were made to "tailor" other issues to particular classes of pur-

565

chasers. At the same time, however, contradictory policies were also followed. The Federal Reserve System encouraged banks to purchase government securities by assurance that it would make reserves available. As stated in its 1942 *Annual Report*, " . . . the Federal Reserve authorities endeavored to induce banks to make more complete use of their existing reserves and also supplied them with such reserve funds as they needed from time to time to purchase the Government securities offered to them."[15] The Treasury, moreover, offered a large percentage of its securities at rates unattractive to nonbank investors.[16]

The attempts to avoid sales to commercial banks—which, partly because of the contradictory policies followed, did not succeed—rested on a misconception based on a failure to distinguish between sales to Reserve Banks and sales to commercial banks. Sales to Reserve Banks created high-powered money. For given deposit-reserve and deposit-currency ratios, each additional dollar of high-powered money meant an increment of several additional dollars of money—the famous multiple expansion. However, for a given level of high-powered money, the identity of the purchasers of securities and, in particular, their identity as commercial banks or others could affect the stock of money only if it affected one of the deposit ratios, and it is hard to see why it should have any appreciable effect on either.[17]

Still more basically, it is necessary to distinguish here, as it was in earlier chapters, between the arithmetic of changes in the money supply, just outlined, and the economics of the changes. Given the monetary policy of supporting a nearly fixed pattern of rates on government securities, the Federal Reserve System had no effective control over the quantity of high-powered money. It had to create whatever quantity was necessary to keep rates at that level. Though it is convenient to describe the process as running from an increase in high-powered money to an increase in the stock of money through deposit-currency and deposit-reserve ratios, the chain of influence in fact ran in the opposite direction —from the increase in the stock of money consistent with the specified pattern of rates and other economic conditions to the increment in high-powered money required to produce that increase. It is an elementary economic truism, applicable to the money market as elsewhere, that one cannot simultaneously control both the price and the quantity of a good without some explicit rationing mechanism. If the price is fixed, the

[15] Board of Governors of the Federal Reserve System, *Annual Report*, 1942, p. 9.
[16] See Clark Warburton, "Monetary Policy in the United States in World War II," *American Journal of Economics and Sociology*, Apr. 1945, pp. 377–389; *idem*, "A Hedge Against Inflation," *Political Science Quarterly*, Mar. 1952, pp. 5–8.
[17] See Friedman, *A Program for Monetary Stability*, New York, Fordham University Press, 1960, pp. 53–55 and 107, footnote 1, for further discussion of the monetary effects of sales of government securities to commercial banks.

quantity must be permitted to be whatever is consistent with that price, and conversely.

Success in avoiding sales to commercial banks could have been achieved by making the securities more attractive to nonbank purchasers by offering them higher returns. That would have involved a change in the pattern of rates pegged and could therefore have had a significant influence. A smaller increase in the total stock of money, and hence in high-powered money, would have been necessary to support the alternative higher pattern of rates than the actual pattern, since the higher rates would have made holding bonds more attractive relative to holding money. One consequence would also have been a higher velocity.

BASIC DETERMINANTS OF THE RISE IN THE MONEY STOCK

Given the pattern of rates supported, what determined the amount of increase in the stock of money? It is difficult enough to answer the question in abstract terms. It is far more difficult to fill in the details or to explain why the magnitudes involved were what they were, and we shall not attempt to do so at all exhaustively. For our purposes, we may regard the physical quantity of resources to be used by government as fixed by other considerations—though, of course, still more basically, the quantity might well have been revised, if it had been associated with a very different level of inflationary pressure. The quantity of resources used by government had to be matched by a corresponding release of resources by the members of the community. They received incomes corresponding to essentially the whole of resources employed, and they had to be persuaded or induced or forced to refrain from exercising command over a fraction of those resources corresponding to the fraction employed by the government. The financial counterpart of the release of resources was the payment of taxes, or the accumulation of claims against the government in the form of either interest-bearing government securities or noninterest-bearing debt of the government, the three together being equal over any period to the expenditures of the government. The increase in the stock of money had to be whatever was necessary to render the sum of the three items equal to the expenditures of the government. Part of the increase in the stock of money took the form of government issue of money, part took the form of whatever increase in privately created money (in that period, bank deposits not matched by an increment in reserves) was necessary to provide the public with the ratio of deposits to currency it desired and the banks with the ratio of deposits to reserves they desired.

It should be emphasized that all these items were being simultaneously determined. What we have taken as fixed was the physical quantity of resources to be used by government, not government expenditures. If

567

prices (needless to say, as "correctly" measured, not as recorded in a necessarily imperfect index number) were constant during the process, any issue of money would correspond to "voluntary saving." It would mean that the public wished to add that amount to its real assets in the form of the noninterest-bearing obligations we call money.[18] And conversely, prices could remain constant only if the public did wish to add to its real assets in the form of interest- and noninterest-bearing obligations an amount equal to the excess of government expenditures at those prices over tax receipts at those prices. If prices rose during the process, the issue of money would correspond partly to "voluntary saving"— insofar as the real and not only the nominal value of the money stock rose—and partly to a tax on money balances. The nominal increment in the money stock required to keep its real value unchanged can be regarded as vouchers recording the payment of this tax on money balances.[19] In any event, the government could acquire real resources only through either taxation—consisting in part of explicit taxes, in part of an implicit tax on money balances—or borrowing, consisting in part of borrowing in a noninterest-bearing form. The distribution between taxes and borrowing was determined in part by the level of taxes imposed by legislation, in part by the preferences of the public with respect to "voluntary saving."[20]

The major government actions affecting the amount by which the money stock increased were therefore the decisions about how much real resources to devote to the war effort, the level of tax rates enacted, measures affecting voluntary saving, and measures affecting the fraction of their savings individuals wished to use to add to their holdings of money. For the period of war or wartime deficits, over 45 per cent of total federal expenditures were financed by explicit taxes. This was an impressive performance in comparison with that in World War I, but it left a much larger deficit compared with national income because of the

[18] Insofar as the issue of money was in the form of privately created money, the government was in essence sharing its monopoly of the issuance of noninterest-bearing securities with the commercial banks. From the government's point of view, it issued interest-bearing obligations corresponding to that part of the hypothetical "voluntary saving."

[19] Insofar as the issue of money was in the form of privately issued money, the government was in effect sharing the proceeds of the tax on money balances with commercial banks (see Friedman, "Price, Income, and Monetary Changes," pp. 619–625).

[20] For a fuller analysis, see Friedman, "Discussion of the Inflationary Gap," in *Essays in Positive Economics*, University of Chicago Press, 1955, pp. 251–262; also Martin Bailey, "The Welfare Cost of Inflationary Finance," *Journal of Political Economy*, Apr. 1956, pp. 93–110; Armen A. Alchian and Reuben A. Kessel, "Redistribution of Wealth through Inflation," *Science*, Sept. 4, 1959, pp. 537–539; Ralph Turvey, "Inflation as a Tax in World War II," *Journal of Political Economy*, Feb. 1961, pp. 72–73; and Friedman, "Price, Income, and Monetary Changes," *loc. cit.* See also above, Chap. 2, footnote 64, and Chap. 5, footnote 35.

larger magnitude of the war effort. We have already noted that the cessation of production of certain durable goods had the effect of raising voluntary saving. The rationing of other goods and the limited availability of still others may have had a similar effect. Aside from government measures, the widespread fear of a postwar depression worked in the same direction. The pattern of interest rates fixed on government obligations also affected the level of voluntary saving—a higher level of interest rates would have given a greater inducement to save, a lower level, a lesser inducement—but probably had its main effect on the form savings took. It seems not unlikely that the much higher level of rates paid on government securities in World War I than in World War II is one reason the nonbank public increased its holdings of government securities by about three dollars for every one dollar increase in its money stock in World War I and by only half that amount in World War II.

By comparison with World War I, the impressive difference is that despite a much larger war effort, longer continued deficits, and larger deficits relative to national income, prices rose more slowly during World War II than during World War I, both during the whole of the period from the start of the war to the postwar price peak, and apparently also during the period of wartime deficits. There appear to be two main reasons for the difference, neither having much to do with the design of government policy. The first is the much greater increase in willingness to save in World War II, the monetary counterpart of which was the decline in velocity during the war, discussed above. The second is that the tax on money balances implicit in inflationary money creation was a much more productive tax in World War II than in World War I, because of the lower velocity prevailing during World War II than during World War I (Table 24, line 3). Money balances averaged 45 per cent of one year's national income in 1914–20, 69 per cent in 1939–48. A 1 per cent tax on money balances—if we ignore the reflex influence of the tax on the amount of money balances held—therefore yielded 0.45 per cent of a year's national income in World War I, 0.69 per cent, or about 1½ times as much, in World War II.

This is the computation needed to judge the importance of the increase in the public's money stock. An additional problem is the fraction of the increase in the money stock created directly by the government and the fraction created by the banks or, to put it differently, the sharing of the tax yield between the government and the banks. The implicit sharing arrangement determines how much money the government can issue per dollar increase in the total money stock; or, alternatively, how much of its deficit it can finance by issuing money, how much by bonds, and how much of the bonds directly or indirectly must go to banks. In this respect, too, there was a substantial difference between the wars. In the World

War I inflation (1914–20), the total money stock increased $6.92 for every dollar of government-created money (high-powered money minus the gold stock), in the World War II inflation (1939–48), $4.74. The main reason for the difference was the change in the ratio of deposits to reserves. During the World War I inflation, banks added $14.16 to their deposits for every dollar increase in reserves; during the World War II

TABLE 24

COMPARISON OF MONEY CREATION IN TWO WORLD WAR PERIODS OF INFLATION

	Period of Inflation	
	World War I 1914–20	World War II 1939–48
Money created by government as a fraction of average annual net national product		
1. Total	0.050	0.146
2. Per year	0.008	0.016
Average velocity		
3. Average NNP ÷ average stock of money	2.205	1.445
Money created by government as a fraction of average stock of money		
4. Total	0.110	0.211
5. Per year	0.018	0.023
Expansion ratio of monetary system		
6. Increase in high-powered money per dollar increase in government-created money	1.377	1.357
7. Increase in stock of money per dollar increase in high-powered money	5.027	3.492
Increase in stock of money as a fraction of average stock		
8. Total	0.762	0.998
9. Per year	0.127	0.111
Increase in stock of money as a fraction of average annual NNP		
10. Total	0.346	0.690
11. Per year	0.058	0.077

NOTE: Figures for money stock, high-powered money, and gold stock are annual averages centered on June 30. Averages for each war period weight the initial and terminal years each as one-half year.

Government-created money equals high-powered money minus the gold stock.

inflation, $10.47. A subsidiary reason was a change in the relation between deposit and currency expansion—in World War I, the public added $6.91 to its deposits per dollar increase in currency; in World War II only $3.89.

For the war inflations as a whole, the effects of these differences are summarized in Table 24. As this table shows, the combined effect of the changes in the level of velocity and in the expansion ratio of the monetary system was that the government was able to acquire twice as large a fraction of average annual income (1.6 instead of 0.8 per cent, line 2) by direct money creation, yet produce only seven-eighths as large an increase in the total money stock per year (11.1 per cent instead of 12.7 per cent, line 9). This smaller increase in the total money stock was in its turn equivalent to a decidedly larger fraction of average annual income (7.7 per cent instead of 5.8 per cent, line 11) so that both directly and indirectly money creation was a more effective device for acquiring resources for government purposes.

In terms of federal government expenditures during the period of wartime deficits, 48 per cent was financed by explicit taxes; 7 per cent by direct government money creation; 14 per cent by private money issue, which can be regarded as the indirect effect of government money creation but had as its nominal counterpart interest-bearing rather than noninterest-bearing government debt; and 31 per cent by interest-bearing government securities not matched by money creation. If the wholesale price index is regarded as correctly measuring the price changes during the war, then about one-fifth of the money creation can be regarded as a tax on money balances, four-fifths as voluntary saving embodied in the form of noninterest-bearing monetary assets.[21] This would mean that, in all, slightly over half of expenditures was financed by taxes, and that about one-tenth of the taxes took the form of a tax on money balances. The defects of the price index mean that these figures probably underestimate the importance of taxes as a fraction of expenditures and of the tax on money balances as a fraction of total taxes.

EFFECT OF WAR LOAN DRIVES

One detail of the behavior of the money stock merits attention before we leave the period. In Chart 46 it will be noted that the money stock behaved in a much more irregular fashion during 1943, in particular, but also in 1944 and 1945, than it did before or after. The reason was the flotation of government securities through a series of bond drives—seven War Loan drives and a concluding Victory Loan—about five months apart, November 1942–December 1945. As it happened, three of the bond drives came in the final months of the year and two in the middle,

[21] Wholesale prices rose 14 per cent from Dec. 1941 to Dec. 1945 (roughly the initial and terminal dates of the calendar years included in our estimate of federal government expenditures during the period of wartime deficits). The nominal amount of money that would have been required to keep money balances at their initial real level was 13 per cent of the actual increase from Dec. 1941 to Dec. 1945. The amount that would have been required to maintain money balances at their terminal real level was 24 per cent of the actual increase. The correct figure, assuming the price rise to be correct, is between these two, and we have approximated it as 20 per cent.

For simplicity, we have combined direct and indirect money creation, and have neglected the assignment of part of what we have called the tax proceeds to the commercial banks. For a more refined analysis, see Ralph Turvey, "Inflation as a Tax in World War II," *Journal of Political Economy*, Feb. 1961, pp. 72–73.

CHART 50

**Member Bank Deposits During War Bond Drives, With and Without
U.S. Government War Loan Deposits, Monthly and Semimonthly
Averages, Unadjusted for Seasonal Changes, 1942–45**

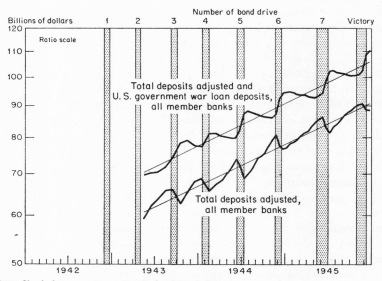

NOTE: Shaded areas represent periods of bond drives.
SOURCE: Data are monthly or semimonthly averages of daily figures, seasonally unadjusted,
from *FRB*. Total deposits adjusted are demand deposits adjusted plus time deposits. Dates of
bond drives, from *Annual Report* of the Secretary of the Treasury, 1946, p. 507.

which meant that they had some of the repetitive effects characteristic
of a seasonal movement. As a result, their effects have been to some
extent eliminated from the seasonally adjusted series plotted in Chart 46.
That is mainly why the irregularity produced by the bond drives in our
money series is much greater for 1943 than for 1944 and 1945.

Chart 50 is designed to enable us to study in some detail the effects of
the bond drives. It is restricted to deposits, since the bond drives had no
noticeable effects on currency, and to member banks only, because for
that period we have monthly or semimonthly averages of daily figures for
them but not for all commercial banks. It plots figures unadjusted for
seasonal variations to avoid inadvertent elimination of any bond drive
effects. The bottom line in the chart is for demand and time deposits
owned by the public and thus excludes U.S. government deposits. The
top line is the same total plus U.S. government deposits. The shaded
areas in the chart are the periods of the bond drives.

On the occasion of each bond drive, purchasers of securities transferred deposits to war loan accounts maintained by the Treasury at commercial banks. As the government transferred its deposits from war loan accounts to Federal Reserve Banks, and thence to the public to pay for its expenditures, government deposits were transferred back to private accounts. This process is clearly marked in the chart. On the occasion of each bond drive, the upper line rises and the lower falls. Between drives, the reverse occurs.

After April 1943, the war loan accounts maintained by the Treasury were exempt from reserve requirements, so any transfer of funds to those accounts in the first instance reduced required reserves. If reserves held had risen steadily and if banks had taken full advantage of the released reserves, so that required reserves had risen during bond drives as they did between drives, the banks could have kept the lower line in Chart 50 free from any effects of the bond drives. On the occasion of each drive, they could have expanded their total earning assets to the amount of the deposits transferred to war loan accounts and subsequently could have reduced their earning assets as the war loan accounts were reduced. Under these hypothetical circumstances, our money stock figures, like the lower line of the chart, would have been unaffected by the bond drives. The whole of the effect would have been recorded in the upper line.

Conversely, if reserves held had risen steadily and if banks had taken no advantage of the reserves released by the transfer of deposits, so that required reserves had fallen during bond drives and risen between drives, the banks could have kept the upper line of Chart 50 free from any effects of the bond drives; the full effect would have been recorded in the lower line.

The actual situation was roughly midway between these extremes, as can be seen by noting that the fluctuations about the straight lines we have drawn to indicate the trends in the two series are not much different in amplitude for the upper than for the lower series.

There are three reasons the actual situation did not correspond to the first extreme. (1) The actual behavior of reserves was not that assumed above. During some of the drives, specifically the second through the fifth (April to May 1943–July to August 1944), the Reserve System offset some of the effect of the transfer of deposits by reducing its credit outstanding. To some extent, therefore, the declines in the lower line of Chart 50 reflect changes in available reserves. (2) The full use of the released reserves would have involved substantial transaction costs, since it implied first acquiring and then disposing of assets as government war loan accounts first increased and then decreased. (3) No doubt, it took time for banks to realize the possibilities of taking measures to increase deposits in advance or coincidentally with the drive itself, rather than subsequently when its effect was manifest in excess reserves. As time

573

went on, the banks adjusted more fully to the bond drives. Visual evidence is provided by the chart, in which the fluctuations of the upper curve about its straight-line trend become wider, if anything, in amplitude, whereas fluctuations of the lower curve become a trifle narrower. And some rough calculations confirm this visual impression.[22]

3. From the End of the War to the Price Peak, August 1945–August 1948

Economic activity reached its wartime peak early in 1945 when it became clear that the end of the war was approaching. The National Bureau dates the reference peak in February 1945. Demobilization began after V-E Day (May 8, 1945), continued at an accelerated pace after V-J Day (September 2, 1945), and was accompanied by a sharp decrease in government expenditures and a rapid decline in industrial production. Nevertheless, the contraction was brief and relatively mild and the heavy unemployment that was widely feared did not develop. The trough, which the National Bureau dates in October 1945, was followed by a vigorous expansion. A decline in government purchases of goods and services from $83 billion in 1945 to $30 billion in 1946 was offset by rapid conversion from wartime to peacetime production. Seasonally adjusted unemployment in 1945 never reached 2.5 million and remained below that level thereafter until beyond the end of the expansion in November 1948.

After a brief pause in the third quarter of 1945, the wholesale price index continued rising and, as we have already noted, jumped sharply in mid-1946 when price control was dropped. The 16.4 per cent per year rate of rise in the wholesale price index from January 1946 to August

---

[22] For example, the ratio of the rise in the upper curve to the decline in the lower curve during the successive bond drives is shown in the tabulation.

Bond Drive	Ratio of Rise in Upper Curve to Decline in Lower Curve
3	1.30
4	1.28
5	1.46
6	1.68
7	1.55
8	3.51

For a more sophisticated calculation, allowance should be made for point 1 in the text. Such a more sophisticated calculation and, in general, a more detailed study of the effects of the bond drives than we have made would be of considerable interest. It might, for example, provide additional evidence on the time required for adjustment by the banking system to changes in circumstances.

We are indebted to George Morrison for pointing out to us that the use of seasonally adjusted figures in an earlier version had led us to erroneous conclusions about the reactions of banks to the bond drives.

1948 overstates substantially the rate of rise in prices during the period. Nonetheless, there was clearly a price rise of considerable magnitude. The rise in prices and in income reflected mostly the rise in velocity referred to earlier, rather than a growth of the money stock. The money stock grew only 14 per cent from the end of the war to August 1948 and only 11 per cent, or at the rate of only a little over 4 per cent per year, from January 1946 to August 1948.[23]

The rise in the money stock itself from January 1946 to August 1948 was attributable, in an arithmetic sense, mostly to growth of high-powered money. In sharp contrast with the corresponding period after World War I (when the gold stock fell and the increase in high-powered money came from a rapid expansion in Federal Reserve claims on the public and the banks), this time the increase in high-powered money was produced by a rise in the gold stock, about a third of which was offset by a decline in the fiat of the monetary authorities (see Tables 23 and 10). The gold inflow occurred despite U.S. participation in UNRRA —which was authorized even before the termination of lend-lease—the subsequent loan to Britain, and the Marshall Plan. Though these unilateral transfers satisfied many of the pressing demands of war-devastated countries, the residual demands, as well as the demands of neutral countries desiring goods not available during the war, led to a gold inflow.

A rise in the ratio of deposits to currency was as important as the increase in high-powered money in accounting for the increase in the stock of money. With the end of the war, the wartime factors affecting the demand for currency lost their influence, and the public increased its deposits relative to currency holdings. However, a minor part of the rise in the deposit-currency ratio was offset by a slight decline in the deposit-reserve ratio.

This description of postwar monetary changes needs to be supplemented by some account of events within the period. The slight decline in the deposit-reserve ratio was the net result of a rise from January 1946 to May 1947, which was more than offset by the subsequent decline to August 1948. A shift of deposits away from reserve and central reserve city banks, with higher reserve requirements, toward country banks mainly accounted for the movement in the deposit-reserve ratio from

[23] The coverage of the money stock series in 1948 is not strictly comparable to that of the series in 1945 and 1946 (see Appendix A). Currency held by the public in 1948 includes vault cash in banks in territories and the possessions, as well as in U.S. mutual savings banks; such vault cash is excluded in the earlier years. Likewise, demand balances of mutual savings banks at U.S. commercial banks are included in adjusted deposits in 1948, excluded in the earlier years. The percentage change figures in the text would not, however, be altered by revision of the 1945–46 money stock estimates to make them comparable to the later one. The excluded items totaled $165–$170 million in 1945–46, or slightly more than one-tenth of 1 per cent of the money stock excluding them.

August 1945 to April 1947; we do not know what accounts for the initial fall thereafter, but the noticeable acceleration of the fall after February 1948 clearly reflects three increases in reserve requirements imposed over the following seven months.

The expansion in high-powered money was concentrated within the 11 months from August 1945 to July 1946 ($1.9 billion) and the 15 months from May 1947 to August 1948 ($1.1 billion; see Chart 46). High-powered money was $3.1 billion higher at the end of August 1948 than at the end of August 1945, but only $1.2 billion higher than at the end of July 1946. From July 1946 to May 1947, the decline in the fiat of the monetary authorities just about offset the rise in the gold stock, so that high-powered money was roughly unchanged (see Chart 47B).

The initial and terminal expansions in high-powered money played quite different monetary roles. The first was a source of monetary expansion. The second was not; it was rather a reaction to other monetary measures.

Most of the terminal $1.1 billion increase in high-powered money from May 1947 to August 1948 was a reaction to changes in reserve requirements (Chart 49). Reserve requirements for member banks in central reserve cities were raised $1 billion by an increase of 4 points in the percentage they were required to maintain against demand deposits. The increase was imposed in two equal steps on February 27 and June 11, 1948. To acquire the added reserves, banks sold government securities which, under the support program, the Reserve System was committed to buy. Those security purchases thereby added to Reserve credit outstanding. (In September, a third increase affecting all member banks, and time as well as demand deposits, raised reserve requirements a further $2 billion. As a result, member banks sold government securities to the Federal Reserve, and Reserve Bank credit showed another increase—see the next chapter.)

In contrast, the initial increase in high-powered money from August 1945 to July 1946 provided the banks with a net addition to their reserves in excess of requirements. The money stock rose vigorously, by $11.1 billion, as compared with $5.3 billion in the period of stationary high-powered money from July 1946 to May 1947 and $1.8 billion in the terminal period of increase in high-powered money.[24] The money stock therefore grew decidedly more in the first 11 months of the three-year period than in the next 25 months. The money stock reached an absolute peak in January 1948 and declined mildly for the next 12 months, foreshadowing the approaching price peak and the recession of 1948 to 1949. This is another example of the previously observed tendency of monetary changes to precede changes in economic conditions.

[24] See footnote 23, above.

The foremost monetary puzzle of the immediate postwar period is why the money stock did not grow at a very much more rapid pace. The sharp difference from its behavior after World War I, when the most rapid rate of increase in the stock of money came after the end of the wartime deficits, does not reflect any fundamental difference in monetary policy. After both wars, the Reserve System continued the wartime policy of providing all the high-powered money demanded at a fixed rate: in World War I, through maintaining an unchanged discount rate; in World War II, through supporting the price of government securities at unchanged levels. And the reversal of the gold flows, from an outflow after World War I to an inflow after World War II, should have fostered a more rapid rate of monetary expansion after the later war.

Federal Reserve pronouncements were full of expressions of concern about the inflationary danger of the large stock of money, and about the necessity to avoid further expansion. Yet, until the middle of 1947, action was limited to requests for additional powers;[25] changes in discount rates which were of no significance (because the System continued its wartime support of the bill rate at $\frac{3}{8}$ of 1 per cent and the certificate rate at $\frac{7}{8}$ of 1 per cent, so that it continued to be cheaper for banks to meet reserve needs by selling such securities of which they held substantial amounts rather than by discounting);[26] and an increase in margin requirements on security purchases to 100 per cent in January 1946 followed by a reduction to 75 per cent in February 1947 (see Chart 49). Consumer credit controls were continued until November 1, 1947, when the Congress terminated the authority of the Board of Governors to regulate such credit. With the expansion of production of consumer durable goods, the controls became relevant as they had not been during the war. They may have limited the growth of this type of credit some-

[25] The Board of Governors suggested (*Annual Report*, 1945, pp. 7–8) that three additional powers be granted the System:

1. To limit the amount of long-term securities which any commercial bank could hold in relation to its net demand deposits
2. To require all commercial banks to maintain secondary reserves of Treasury bills and certificates in addition to their high-powered money reserves against net demand deposits
3. To raise reserve requirements, within some specified limit, against net demand deposits of any commercial bank

[26] By the end of Apr. 1946, the preferential discount rate of 1 per cent on advances to nonmember banks secured by direct obligations of the U.S. was eliminated at all Reserve Banks. Thereafter the rate in effect on loans to individuals, partnerships, and corporations (the rate ranged from 2½ to 2¾ per cent by the end of 1948) applied to advances to nonmember banks. In Apr. and May 1946 all the Reserve Banks discontinued the preferential discount rate of 0.5 per cent on advances to member banks secured by government obligations maturing or callable within a year, and the prevailing discount rate of 1 per cent became applicable to advances secured by all maturities of government obligations.

what but it is doubtful that they could have been a major factor affecting the growth of the money stock as a whole.

Yet from mid-1946 on, the rate of growth of the money stock fell sharply. The announced readiness of the Federal Reserve Banks to support the price of government securities led to no extensive monetization of the debt; on the contrary, Federal Reserve credit outstanding remained roughly constant during 1946 and then fell sharply in the spring of 1947. Yields on long-term government debt were below support levels throughout 1946 and the first part of 1947, so that the System could have sold long-term securities without violating its support policy. It did not do so, however, and indeed could not have gone far on its own in this direction, since it held less than $1 billion of such securities. Its holdings were in bills and certificates, and there was little demand for these at the support rates (see Chart 48).

During the war, the 2½ per cent interest rate on long-term securities which the Federal Reserve was committed to protect was below the level consistent with no change in the stock of money and required for its maintenance the continuous creation of high-powered money—as was the 3 to 4 per cent discount rate in the active phase of World War I, and the same or a higher rate for some eighteen months thereafter. By contrast, less than a year after the active phase of World War II, the same 2½ per cent rate was *above* the level consistent with no change in the stock of money and would have required for its rigid maintenance the destruction of high-powered money.

During the immediate postwar period and for some time thereafter, the Federal Reserve System did not question, at least officially, the desirability of supporting the price of government obligations.[27] But it did favor raising the bill and certificate support rates. On July 10, 1947, the posted ⅜ of 1 per cent buying rate on Treasury bills and the repurchase option granted to sellers of bills were terminated, though the pegged rate of ⅞ of 1 per cent on certificates was maintained. It has been reported that the Treasury, which had been reluctant to see any change in the pattern of rates, consented to the rise in the interest costs on its short-term debt because of the offset created by the adoption on April 23, 1947, by the Federal Reserve System of a policy of paying into the Treasury approximately 90 per cent of the net earnings of the Federal Reserve Banks.[28]

[27] See statements in *Annual Report*, 1945, p. 7; 1946, p. 6; 1947, p. 8; 1948, pp. 2, 4, 20; 1949, pp. 7–8; 1950, p. 2; 1951, pp. 3, 4, 95, 98.

[28] This was accomplished under the authority granted to the Board (sect. 16 of the Federal Reserve Act) to levy an interest charge on Federal Reserve notes not covered by gold certificates. Before 1933, each Federal Reserve Bank had to pay a franchise tax to the government equal to 90 per cent of its net earnings, after it had accumulated a surplus equal to its capital. That provision was repealed by

On August 8, 1947, the Federal Open Market Committee took the next step in the program of raising the support rates somewhat, by discontinuing the ⅞ per cent buying rate on certificates. The Treasury progressively raised the rate on newly issued certificates until it reached 1⅛ per cent in December 1947. At the same time, the bill rate moved up to 1 per cent. Not until the fourth quarter of 1948, after the price peak, did the Treasury increase the certificate rate to 1¼ per cent and the rate on bills to about 1⅛ per cent.

In addition to these measures, the Treasury changed the composition of the debt by increasing the amount of long-term debt relative to short, thereby achieving the same effect as the Federal Reserve could have by selling long-term securities and buying short-term, if it had had the long-term securities to sell.[29] Yields firmed, rising from 2.26 per cent in mid-October 1947 to 2.37 in mid-November. At that point the Federal Reserve and Treasury stepped in to prevent a further increase in yields, which is to say, decline in the price of bonds. The System bought $2 billion in government bonds in November and December, and Treasury investment accounts bought over $900 million. On December 24, the Federal Open Market Committee established a new lower support level for the price of government bonds and yields rose to 2.45 per cent. This was the level at which prices of long-term governments were maintained through 1948, the System buying an additional $3 billion through March 1948.

The sharp narrowing of the differential between short and long rates as a result of the rise in the rates on bills and certificates made short-term securities relatively more attractive to holders, led them to shift the composition of their portfolios, and thereby produced a reverse shift in the

---

the amendment to the Federal Reserve Act, contained in the Banking Act of 1933, providing for the establishment of the FDIC. The Congress required each Reserve Bank to subscribe to the capital stock of the FDIC an amount equal to one-half of its surplus on Jan. 1, 1933. Because of the reduction in their surplus as a result of the subscription, the Reserve Banks were relieved of the franchise tax. Earnings over the period ending 1944 were sufficient to restore the surplus only to less than 75 per cent of the Banks' subscribed capital. In 1945 and 1946, however, earnings were large enough to increase the surplus above the combined capital of the Banks.

The relationship between the action on earnings and the elimination of the posted ⅜ of 1 per cent buying rate is implied in the record of the Federal Open Market Committee, which reports discussions with representatives of the Treasury including those items on the agenda (Board of Governors of the Federal Reserve System, *Annual Report,* 1947, pp. 90–92). See *Commercial and Financial Chronicle,* July 10, 1947, p. 20 (124), for the suggestion that the transfer of Federal Reserve earnings to the Treasury was the *quid pro quo* for Treasury acquiescence in the rise in interest costs.

[29] From Apr. to Oct. 1947, the Treasury sold $1.8 billion of bonds held in its own investment accounts, and in Oct. issued a new nonmarketable 2½ per cent bond.

Federal Reserve System's portfolio (Chart 48). That shift rather than any net monetization of debt accounted for the Federal Reserve purchases just listed. The purchase of $5 billion of bonds from November 1947 through March 1948 was accompanied by a reduction of some $6 billion in the System's holdings of short-term government securities, so that Federal Reserve credit outstanding was more than $1 billion lower at the end of March 1948 than at the end of October 1947. The announced pattern of rates taken as a whole, therefore, continued to be above rather than below the level consistent with no change in the money stock. Since the pattern was then made effective, whereas before that actual rates had been below the announced rates, monetary contraction was, as we have seen, actually produced during calendar 1948.

The situation was not recognized at the time. Concern continued to focus on inflation even though, in retrospect, it is clear inflationary pressure was rapidly waning and the seeds of a contraction were being sown. In November 1947, the System tried its by now almost traditional confession of impotence—resort to moral suasion. A joint statement by bank supervisory authorities was issued to banks urging them to avoid making nonessential loans. In January 1948, discount rates at all Reserve Banks were raised to 1.25 per cent, and in August, to 1.5 per cent but, since in both cases market yields on bills and certificates were lower, neither rate was effective. More significantly, as already noted, reserve requirements were raised. Since country and reserve city bank requirements were at their prior legal maximums, the final rise—which occurred in September 1948, a month after the price peak—was applicable to all banks only because an act of Congress passed in the preceding month had authorized a temporary increase in the legal maximums, which were to revert to their former level in June 1949.[30] In August 1948, Congress also restored Federal Reserve control over consumer credit until June 1949, when control was once again permitted to terminate.

A counterpart of the relatively small rise in the money stock during the period from 1946 to 1948 was the relatively small rise in velocity. As we have seen, velocity fell by more than a third between 1942 and 1946. The rise from 1946 to 1948 offset less than a quarter of this decline, leaving velocity in 1948 at less than three-quarters its level in 1942 and at only seven-eighths its level in 1939, which itself was low by historical standards. Yet one might have expected both the attempt to "use" the wartime accumulation of liquid assets and the rising prices that rendered it costly to hold money balances to produce a sharp rise in velocity, which

[30] The new maximums against net demand deposits were 30 per cent at central reserve city banks, 24 per cent at reserve city banks, and 18 per cent at country banks, and against time deposits, 7½ per cent at all banks. The requirement imposed in September was 26, 22, 16, and 7½ per cent, respectively.

would, of course, have further intensified the price rise. To put the matter in terms of liquid asset holdings: in 1939, the year the war broke out in Europe, the public held money balances amounting to about 8 months' income, and mutual and postal savings deposits plus savings and loan association shares plus government securities amounting to an additional 5 months' income; so the total of those liquid assets amounted to 13 months' income. By 1946, money balances amounted to over 10 months of a much higher income and the broader total of liquid assets to 21 months' income. In the next two years, the public—despite its pent-up demand for goods unavailable earlier and despite vigorous economic expansion—reduced those balances only moderately: money to 9 months' income, about half-way between the prewar and immediate postwar levels; and the broader total of liquid assets to 18 months' income, or only three-eighths of the way back to the prewar level.

The connection between the changes in velocity and the public's willingness to hold liquid assets fixed in nominal amount perhaps helps to make clear why the low rate of increase in the money stock and the small rise in velocity are different aspects of essentially the same phenomenon. Both reflect a willingness on the part of the public to hold relatively large amounts of money and government securities at fairly low rates of interest. Paradoxical though it may seem, the low rate of increase in the money stock reflected the public's willingness to hold much money, as part of its willingness to hold much of its assets in liquid form. Had the public desired to dispose of more of its liquid assets, the attempt to do so would have tended to drive down prices of government securities and raise their yields, which, in turn, would have led the Federal Reserve, in pursuance of its support program, to buy government securities, thereby raising high-powered money and the total stock of money.

How was it that an interest rate of 2½ per cent on long-term government securities was above the level consistent with a stable money stock in a period of expansion and rising prices; or, equivalently, that at this rate, the public was willing to hold an abnormally high quantity of nominal dollar assets relative to its income?

One factor was the large surplus of the government in the calendar years 1946 through 1948: in 1946, which was a transitional year with respect to the money stock as well, the cash surplus was a nominal $0.04 billion; in 1947, $5.7 billion; and in 1948, $8.0 billion. The effect of the associated debt requirement on the technical monetary position has already been taken into account implicitly in our discussion of the arithmetic of the change in the money stock.[31] In any event, given the support policy of the

---

[31] In 1946, the Treasury used its unusually large General Fund balance, derived from overborrowing in the Victory Loan, to retire debt. That was a bookkeeping operation involving the simultaneous reduction of deposits in war loan accounts

Reserve System, the money stock during that period, as during the war, had to be whatever was consistent with the supported pattern of rates, and one or another of the proximate determinants—in practice primarily high-powered money—had to adapt to produce that stock. Hence, the important effects of the surplus are to be found elsewhere. Just as, during the war, any excess of federal expenditures over tax receipts had to be matched by an accumulation of government obligations—noninterest-bearing or interest-bearing—by the public at large, so after the war, an excess of federal receipts had to be matched by a reduction of government obligations. Put differently, during the war, the federal government spent more than it received in taxes, so the members of the public had to spend less than they received as income. The rise in prices was one factor inducing them to do so, and the rise in the stock of money was one form in which they accumulated their unspent receipts. After the war, the federal government took in more in taxes than it spent, so the members of the public had to spend more than they received as income. The failure of prices to rise more than they did was necessary to

---

requiring no reserves—a debt of the banks to the government—and of securities held by the banks—a debt of the government to the banks. (The exemption of war loan accounts from member bank reserve requirements expired on June 30, 1947, as a result of the Presidential proclamation, issued Dec. 31, 1946, terminating the period of hostilities of World War II.)

There has been much discussion of the monetary impact of the use of surplus revenues to retire debt, particularly of the effect of retiring debt held by different holders. This was a continuation of the wartime confusion assigning special importance to commercial bank-held debt. *Other things being the same*, retirement of Federal Reserve-held debt through the transfer of Treasury deposits at commercial banks involved a reduction in high-powered money, and therefore a contracting influence on the money stock. Retirement of debt held by commercial banks through the transfer of Treasury deposits at commercial banks requiring reserves involved initially a reduction of the same amount in deposits requiring reserves and in bank assets in the form of government securities. Given fractional reserves, the retirement released excess reserves that would tend to be used to restore the initial level of deposits and assets, and so it was neutral in its monetary effects. Retirement of nonbank-held debt with Treasury deposits requiring reserves involved simply a transfer of ownership of deposits with no direct effects on either deposits or reserves.

But other things were not the same. Given the support program, both the amount and distribution of the debt were effectively determined by the holders. Both had to be whatever was required to make the pattern of rates conform to the one being supported. For example, if the Treasury used the surplus to retire long-term securities held by the public, when, at the fixed rates, the public wished to retain the long terms and dispose of its short terms, the result would be a tendency of short-term rates to rise and long-term rates to fall. This would lead in turn to sales of long terms and purchases of short terms by the Federal Reserve in order to maintain the rate pattern, so leading to precisely the same result as if the Treasury had initially retired short-term securities. And similarly for any other pattern of Treasury operations and public preferences. Treasury operations only determined whether a particular holder acquired his securities from or disposed of them to the Treasury or the Federal Reserve or other holders.

induce them to do so, while the slow rise in the stock of money reflected the effect of the excess spending by the public.

Had the federal government not run a surplus, the public, with its accumulated liquid assets and pent-up demand, would have *tried* to spend more in the postwar period than it received—an impossibility, since one man's expenditures are another's receipts. The process of trying, however, would have tended to raise prices and incomes and so would have reduced the level of liquid assets relative to income by this inflationary route. Moreover, the process would doubtless have tended to raise interest rates and so would have produced a monetization of the debt and a still larger rise in prices. As it was, the federal surplus enabled some reduction of liquid assets relative to income to be achieved without inflation. To put the matter still differently: in terms of the market for loanable funds, the Treasury surplus constituted an increase in the supply of loanable funds and thereby reduced the interest rate that would clear the market at any given price level, just as the Treasury deficit during the war constituted an increase in the demand for loanable funds and so tended to raise the interest rate. The shift in the direction of the Treasury's influence helps explain why roughly the same level of supported interest rates was below the level consistent with no change in the money stock during the war, and above that level after 1946 or 1947.

The Treasury surplus explains how the public could reduce the ratio of its money and its liquid assets relative to its income, to a limited extent, without producing either inflationary pressure on prices or monetary expansion under the support program. It does not explain why the public sought to reduce the ratios only slightly more than by that limited extent. It is here that the second factor we believe to be important enters. That factor was a continued fear of a major contraction and a continued belief that prices were destined to fall. A rise in prices can have diametrically opposite effects on desired money balances depending on its effect on expectations. If it is interpreted as the harbinger of further rises, it raises the anticipated cost of holding money and leads people to desire lower balances relative to income than they otherwise would. In our view, that was the effect of price rises in 1950 and again in 1955 to 1957. On the other hand, if a rise in prices is interpreted as a temporary rise due to be reversed, as a harbinger of a likely subsequent decline, it lowers the anticipated cost of holding money and leads people to desire higher balances relative to income than they otherwise would. In our view, that was the effect of the price rises in 1946 to 1948. An important piece of evidence in support of this view is the behavior of yields on common stocks by comparison with bond yields. A shift in widely-held expectations toward a belief that prices are destined to rise more rapidly will tend to produce a *fall* in stock yields relative to bond yields because of the hedge

583

which stocks provide against inflation. That was precisely what happened from 1950 to 1951 and again from 1955 to 1957. A shift in widely-held expectations toward a belief that prices are destined to fall instead of rise or to fall more sharply will tend to have the opposite effect—which is precisely what happened from 1946 to 1948.[32]

Despite the extent to which the public and government officials were exercised about inflation, the public acted from 1946 to 1948 as if it expected deflation. There is no real conflict. The major source of concern about inflation at that time was not the evils of inflation per se—though no doubt these played a role—but the widespread belief that what goes up must come down and that the higher the price rise now the larger the subsequent price fall. In our view, this fear or expectation of a subsequent contraction and price decline reconciled the public to only a mild reduction in its liquid asset holdings relative to its income and induced it to hold larger real money balances than it otherwise would have been willing to. In this way, it made the postwar rise more moderate. The situation at the close of the two world wars was therefore quite different. The situation after World War II, unlike that after World War I, as noted, was one of widespread expectation of a price decline.

To avoid misunderstanding: our belief that the most puzzling feature of experience during the early postwar years is why, *given the monetary*

[32] We are indebted to David Meiselman for calling this piece of evidence to our attention. The data follow.

Quarter	Yield on Baa Corporate Bonds	Yield on 125 Industrial Common Stocks		Corporate Bond Yield Minus Yield on 125 Industrial Common Stocks	
		Dividend	Earnings	Dividend	Earnings
		FALLING PRICE EXPECTATIONS			
I 1946	2.97	3.46	2.64	−0.49	0.33
IV 1948	3.52	6.56	15.18	−3.04	−11.66
		RISING PRICE EXPECTATIONS			
III 1950	3.25	6.49	15.93	−3.24	−12.68
III 1951	3.50	6.13	8.75	−2.63	−5.25
I 1955	3.47	4.14	8.25	−0.67	−4.78
IV 1957	5.04	4.46	6.78	0.58	−1.74

SOURCE: Bond and dividend yields are quarterly averages of monthly data; no seasonal movement was discernible. Earnings yield is earnings per share divided by a quarterly average of price per share and adjusted for seasonal by us. Data are from *Business Statistics;* primary source is Moody's Investors Service.

To make the risk roughly alike as between bonds and stocks, we used Baa bonds. The use of Aaa bonds would not, however, alter the direction of change in the yield differences for the three periods. Aaa bond yield minus dividend yield is −0.96, −3.74; −3.86, −3.24; −1.16, −0.46 (next to the last col.). Aaa bond yield minus earnings yield is −0.14, −12.36; −13.30, −5.86; −5.27, −2.78 (last col.).

policies followed, prices and the money stock rose so little does not imply either approval of those policies or belief that a higher rise in prices and the money stock would have been desirable. The relatively small rise in the money stock was not a product of monetary policy designed to achieve that result but, on the contrary, the policy followed involved surrender of any possibility of explicitly controlling the money stock. The relatively small rise was a product primarily of Treasury surpluses and of widespread expectations that a severe price decline was in the offing. Those expectations were partly a product of the severe 1929–33 contraction, which fostered a belief that severe contractions were the peacetime danger if not indeed the norm; and partly a product of the 1920–21 price collapse, which fostered a belief that major wars were followed by deflation and depression. Of course, had those factors not made the monetary policy actually followed consistent with a small rise in the money stock, the policy might have been changed, as it was subsequently under the impact of the Korean War experience.

In retrospect, an even lower rate of increase in prices and the money stock would have been preferable during 1946 and 1947. A different monetary policy permitting or forcing a rise in the interest rates on government securities could have contributed to this result, though whether without an overreaction like that of 1920 is harder to say. Hindsight is far better than foresight, and the possibility of understanding the course of events after the fact is no evidence that authorities at the time could have produced precisely the "right" pattern of changes in the money stock.

4. *The Balance of Payments*

World War II, like World War I, was characterized by levels of capital export (in World War II, including unilateral transfers) unmatched in any peacetime periods either in absolute magnitude or as percentages of national income. The pattern of the capital exports is fairly similar in the two wars (see Chart 51). A very sharp increase from 1914 to 1917 matches an even sharper increase from 1940 to 1944 (these appear as decreases in the chart, which plots capital inflows and hence shows outflows as a negative item). There was then a four-year decline in the World War I period, a one-year decline in World War II. The extension of aid in one form or another to the war-devastated countries of the world after the second war resulted in an increase for two years followed by a three-year fall to a level around which capital exports fluctuated for some years thereafter. After World War I, the decline which began in 1918 continued through 1923, with capital exports subsequently varying around a rather constant level until 1933.

The peak level of capital exports, expressed as a fraction of net national

585

CHART 51

U.S. Net International Capital Movement as a Ratio to National Income, and Purchasing-Power Parity, 1914–60

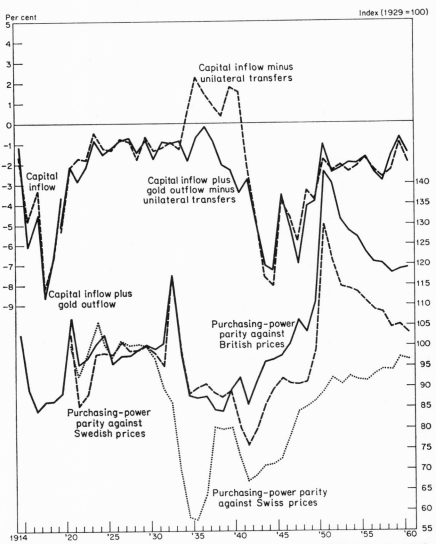

NOTE: Capital inflow, minus unilateral transfers, is plotted as plus. Gold outflow is plotted as plus.

SOURCE: Table A-4.

product, was about the same in World War II as in World War I—8.0 per cent in 1944 compared to 8.2 per cent in 1917—but the period of abnormally high capital exports was somewhat more prolonged in the later period, nine years compared to six. The similarity in level of peak capital exports is surprising in view of the greater war effort involved in World War II; the difference in the length of the period of abnormally high capital exports reflects the longer duration of the second war.

After both wars, the new level attained when capital exports had receded was higher than the prevailing level under earlier peacetime conditions. From 1907 to 1914, the United States was in approximate balance, neither importing nor exporting capital; from 1923 to 1932, the United States exported capital on balance at the rate of about 1 per cent of net national product; and from 1950 to 1960, at about 2 per cent of net national product. The source of the shift was, however, different in the two postwar periods. The higher level of capital exports plus unilateral transfers after the first World War reflected private foreign lending; the higher level after the second World War reflected government loans and grants—the British loan, Marshall Plan, and other foreign aid expenditures, and loans through the Export-Import Bank, the World Bank, and other similar agencies.

The exchange rate between the dollar and the pound sterling behaved in one respect quite differently in World War II than it did in World War I. In World War I, the pound appreciated sharply on the outbreak of war, only subsequently returning to its prewar parity and being pegged during the rest of the war at near its prewar parity; in the second war, the pound depreciated sharply on the outbreak of the war. From the time Britain left gold in 1931, the pound had no official parity. It first depreciated sharply to a monthly low of $3.28 at the end of 1932, then apreciated to a high of $5.15 in early 1934 after the United States revalued gold. From 1934 to mid-1938, the pound fluctuated around a level slightly below $5.00. Munich and the stepped-up capital outflow from Europe brought a decline to slightly over $4.60 in August 1939. On the outbreak of the war, the pound fell precipitously, first, to under $4.00, then, to as low as $3.27 after the fall of France.

From that point on, the World War I pattern was repeated. Britain fixed the pound officially at $4.035, imposed exchange controls much more extensive and detailed than in World War I, and requisitioned foreign securities and exchange holdings of British nationals. The official rate was made effective by the autumn of 1940 and maintained thereafter. After lend-lease was enacted in 1941, most of the current pressure on the pound was removed, just as it was in World War I after the United States entered the war and assumed responsibility for financing the dollar purchases of its allies.

Whereas the curve in Chart 51 recording capital exports shows the same pattern in the two wars, the curve recording relative prices in the United States and in Britain, adjusted for changes in exchange rates, does not. In World War I, U.S. prices fell sharply relative to British prices along with the sharp increase in U.S. capital exports, and the price ratio rose along with the decrease in capital exports. As we saw in Chapter 5, the relationship between price movements and capital movements in World War I seemed roughly in line with the relationships displayed in the prewar period. In World War II, the price curve in the figure displays almost the reverse relationship; it rises markedly from 1941 to 1947, with no clear response to rises or falls in capital exports.

What explains this failure of the capital movements to be reflected in relative prices, as they had been in general throughout the preceding 70 years? One factor which immediately suggests itself is the system of exchange controls which Britain adopted in World War II, much more extensive than that in World War I. However, this factor works in the wrong direction. As we pointed out in Chapter 5, the effect of foreign exchange controls was to enable Britain, for any given exchange rate, to maintain a higher price level at home than she otherwise could or, alternatively, for given price levels at home and abroad, to maintain a higher dollar price of the pound sterling than she otherwise could. But either alternative means that foreign exchange controls would make the price ratio plotted in Chart 51 lower than otherwise, since this ratio is adjusted for the exchange rate. Yet the puzzle is why this ratio is so high. Foreign exchange controls could provide an explanation only if the United States had imposed such controls to a very much greater extent than in World War I, but it did not.

The only explanation we can offer is that the abnormal behavior of the price ratio reflects not exchange controls but internal price controls, which made the price-index numbers used to compute the ratio seriously defective as measures of "prices" in some more meaningful sense. Price control and rationing were far more extensive in Britain than in the United States, and hence the British index number might be expected to deviate even more from an ideal measure of prices than the U.S. index number.[33]

---

[33] In judging the relationship between price and capital movements in Chart 51, it should be noted that the capital movement figures have had a secular downward trend relative to the price ratio ever since the beginning of the series in 1871. This means that a given level of capital imports into the United States has tended to be consistent over time with an ever higher price level in the U.S. relative to Britain; or, alternatively, that a given ratio of prices has been consistent with an ever lower level of capital imports (or higher level of capital exports). The obvious explanation of this result is a growing comparative advantage of the United States relative to Britain, a consequence that might be expected to follow from a more rapid rate of technological growth and capital accumulation in the U.S. Such a growing comparative advantage was one of the most popular

588

Some evidence bearing on this explanation is furnished by the comparisons with Swiss and Swedish prices plotted in Chart 51. Though prices were controlled in Switzerland and Sweden to a considerable extent during the war, the controls were less extensive than those in Britain or the United States. In addition, both countries were probably subject to less inflationary pressure. A comparison of U.S. prices with Swiss and Swedish prices should therefore, if anything, be biased by price control in the opposite direction from the comparison of U.S. with British prices.[34]

As we saw in Table 20, British depreciation in 1931 produced a sharp dispersion in the international structure of prices, largely eliminated by the 1936 devaluations of the gold-bloc countries. Just before the war, from 1937 to 1939, the curves for the British, Swedish, and Swiss price ratios were closer together than they had been since 1930, so those years provide a fairly uniform starting point. The only other official change in exchange rates in years close to the war years is the appreciation of the Swedish krona by about 16 per cent in the summer of 1946, which accounts for the decline in the Swedish curve in that year.

---

explanations adduced for the alleged "dollar shortage" after the war (see John R. Hicks, "An Inaugural Lecture," *Oxford Economic Papers*, June 1953, pp. 121–135).

[34] A recent study of Swedish experience during World War II provides Swedish monetary and price data for a comparison with wartime changes in similar U.S. data.

Percentage change, II 1939–II 1945, in:	Sweden	United States
1. Currency plus adjusted demand deposits	110	203
2. Money stock (item 1, plus time deposits in commercial banks)	93	163
3. Consumer price index	49	30
4. Wholesale price index	80	39

The much smaller rise in Swedish than in U.S. monetary magnitudes suggests lesser inflationary pressure in Sweden, though, for two reasons, it is not decisive evidence. (1) The wartime disruptions of trade probably had a more serious effect on the productive potential of Sweden than of the United States. (2) Sweden had a smaller fraction of its productive potential unemployed in 1939 than did the United States.

The much larger rise in Swedish than U.S. price index numbers, despite the smaller rise in monetary magnitudes, seems reasonably clear evidence of a lesser suppression of price rises by price control. However, from the third quarter of 1942 to the second quarter of 1945, a period in which price controls tightened, there was no rise in Swedish prices, yet monetary totals rose a further 30 per cent. Perhaps that is why the discrepancy between the price ratios of U.S. against British and Swedish prices narrows after 1942, whereas the discrepancy between the price ratios of U.S. against British and Swiss prices continues to widen to 1945.

For Swedish figures, see Daniel J. Edwards, "Process of Economic Adaptation in a World War II-Neutral Country: A Case Study of Sweden," unpublished Ph.D. dissertation, University of Virginia, 1961, pp. 144–145, 163–164. We are indebted to Edwards for making his dissertation available to us.

For the war years proper, the Swiss and Swedish comparisons both yield results to be expected from the earlier relationships between capital movements and unilateral transfers, on the one hand, and relative prices, on the other. U.S. prices fell relative to prices in both countries from 1939 to 1941, rose from then to 1950 for Swedish prices, to 1951 for Swiss prices. The initial fall roughly coincides with a period when U.S. capital exports and transfers were increasing, and the subsequent rise with a period of generally declining U.S. capital exports and transfers. Moreover, the magnitude of the fall and of the rise in U.S. purchasing-power parity bore roughly the same relation to the magnitude of the changes in capital exports and transfers as it did in earlier periods.[35]

[35] Disruptions of transportation and financial arrangements were so great during World War II that it may seem pointless to seek to find a continuation of peacetime relations between capital movements and relative prices. And, of course, it is not impossible that these relations might be so thoroughly distorted by the wartime effects as to alter fundamentally the peacetime relations. However, our experience in World War I, when the relationships were little affected, should give pause.

Wartime or peacetime, any discrepancy between the amount of foreign currency Americans want to acquire to spend or invest or give away or hold and the amount non-Americans want to give up to acquire dollars for corresponding purposes will have to be eliminated, since ex post the sums acquired and disposed of are equal. The differences between wartime and peacetime are two: (1) the amounts that the parties desire to acquire or dispose of are altered (demand and supply curves for foreign exchange are shifted); (2) direct controls are used much more extensively to eliminate ex ante discrepancies. Regarding (1), it is not clear what the net effect of the shifts is. One might expect that for neutral nations both demand for and supply of foreign exchange would have been reduced by the increased hazards of trade (which, as it were, increased the average price of imports and simultaneously reduced the average proceeds from exports). Regarding (2), if the exchange rates prevailing could be maintained without extensive controls, it must have been because relative prices adjusted for exchange rates were not far out of line with those required to maintain equilibrium.

What was the mechanism that maintained the relationship between relative prices and capital outflows? Part of the answer may be that during World War II capital outflows adjusted to relative prices to a greater extent than they had during peacetime. Suppose, for example, citizens of a neutral country were tending to accumulate dollar balances. In peacetime, the attempt to dispose of these actual or potential balances would set in motion forces bringing relative prices, adjusted for exchange rates, into line with desired capital movements. In wartime, this attempt may have been short-circuited, partly because neutrals might have been willing to hold more dollar balances, just as U.S. citizens were, in anticipation of being able to acquire, after the war, goods currently unavailable; partly because foreign-exchange controls by either the neutral nation or the U.S. might freeze the balances temporarily. In either case, the accumulation of dollar balances, whether desired or undesired, would constitute a capital inflow offsetting the autonomous U.S. capital outflows to its allies. But insofar as that occurred, it meant the capital outflow was adjusting to relative prices, since high relative prices in the U.S. would tend toward a large offsetting capital inflow, low relative prices, toward a small offsetting inflow.

But this is only part of the story. As neutrals accumulated dollar balances in excess of desired amounts, they sought to acquire local currency, and government agencies fixing exchange rates were required to provide them with such currency,

These comparisons with Swiss and Swedish prices therefore offer some support for the hypothesis that internal price controls and consequent defects in price index numbers account for the failure of the British price ratio to show the same relation to price movements during and after World War II as it had earlier.[36]

---

thus producing the kinds of effects internally that gold flows would have produced. The mechanism was essentially the same as that during peacetime.

Finally, changes in exchange rates were always waiting in the wings if needed. As already noted, insofar as they were not needed, it meant that the prior adjustment mechanisms were adequate.

[36] A more decisive test of this hypothesis would require computation of the Swiss and Swedish price ratios for a longer period, and an examination for the earlier periods of the quantitative relation between movements in capital and in such alternative price ratios.

More generally, it seems to us that a full and detailed study of the relationships summarized in Chart 63, below, would be exceedingly valuable. The chart is based on crude data for both price and capital movements, yet it reveals a relationship of precisely the kind that theoretical considerations suggest, and one that seems to have persisted from the post–Civil War decade until World War II, at least.

CHAPTER 11

Revival of Monetary Policy, 1948–60

THE OUTSTANDING monetary feature of the twelve years after the price peak in 1948 is the unusually steady rate of growth of the money stock (see Chart 52). The period is comparable in this respect to the three earlier periods of relative stability that we singled out above—1882–92, 1903–13, and 1923–29. As in those earlier periods, relative stability of the rate of growth of the money stock was accompanied by relative stability of the rate of growth of output and the rate of change in prices (see Chart 52 and Table 25).[1] The stability of the rate of change in the money stock during 1948–60 was, however, more striking than of the rate of change in output or in prices. The standard deviation of the year-to-year percentage change in the money stock was only three-fifths as large as the lowest value for the three other relatively stable periods: it was also lower than for any other period of similar length since 1869; such statements do not hold for output or prices. Velocity was relatively less stable during 1948–60 than during two of the three earlier periods of stability, though decidedly more stable than during any of the periods of fluctuating prices. One of the interesting questions about the period is why velocity should have been so unstable.

One purely statistical factor that probably contributes to the low standard deviation for money in the latest period is an improvement in the quality of the figures. We doubt, however, that this is *the,* or even *a,* major factor. It clearly cannot be for the comparison with 1923–29, since the main difference in quality is probably between the figures before and after 1914.

The uneventful and steady growth of the money stock contrasts sharply with the controversy and discussion about the role of monetary policy and its relation to other aspects of economic policy that marked the

---

[1] The periods in Table 25 begin and end in years of cyclical peaks, except for 1939. The exception was made in order to keep separate the World War II period. Use of periods containing a full number of cycles is intended to avoid any bias arising from cyclical forces. Use of peaks rather than troughs to mark off the periods reflects our repeated finding that a sizable contraction tends to be followed by a sizable expansion but not conversely (see our forthcoming volume, "Trends and Cycles in the Stock of Money in the United States, 1867–1960"). The peak-to-peak periods therefore have a greater degree of independence of one another than trough-to-trough periods would have.

CHART 52
Money Stock, Income, Prices, and Velocity, and Industrial Production, in Reference Cycle Expansions and Contractions, 1948–60

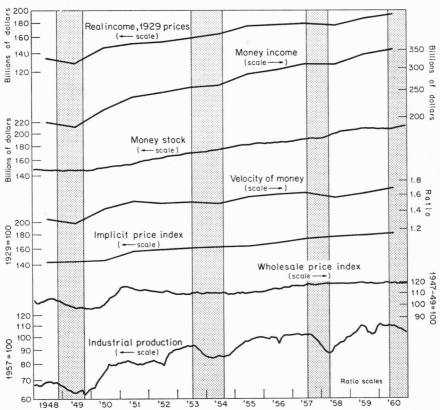

NOTE: Shaded areas represent business contractions; unshaded areas, business expansions.
SOURCE: Wholesale price index, 1948–51, *Continuation to 1952 of Historical Statistics of the United States, 1789–1945*, Bureau of the Census, 1954, p. 47; 1952–60, *Business Statistics*, 1955, 1957, 1961, Office of Business Economics. Other data, same as for Charts 16 and 62.

decade. The sharp upward surge of prices which came with the Korean War dramatized the impotence of the monetary authorities to stem inflationary pressure, so long as they were committed to support the prices of government securities. The price rise was accompanied by the semipublic controversy between the Federal Reserve System and the Treasury which terminated in the so-called "Accord" of March 1951 and was followed some two years later by the explicit abandonment of the support policy. Few episodes in American monetary history have attracted so

TABLE 25

COMPARATIVE STABILITY OF RATE OF CHANGE IN MONEY STOCK AND IN OTHER
MAGNITUDES, IN PERIODS OF RELATIVELY STABLE PRICES AND PERIODS
OF FLUCTUATING PRICES, 1869-1960

| | Standard Deviation of Year-to-Year Percentage Changes in: | | | | | |
Period	Monetary Gold Stock (1)	High-Powered Money (2)	Money Stock (3)	Velocity of Money (4)	Wholesale Prices (5)	Real Income (6)
1869–82	20.3	5.7	6.9	8.1	7.0	7.8
1882–92	**4.4**	**2.0**	**3.7**	**3.4**	**4.6**	**3.7**
1892–1903	8.8	4.6	7.1	5.6	5.5	6.9
1903–13	**3.5**	**2.7**	**3.7**	**5.3**	**4.7**	**7.4**
1913–23	10.1	8.9	6.9	9.9	20.3	8.7
1923–29	**5.5**	**1.4**	**2.8**	**4.3**	**3.7**	**2.5**
1929–39	8.6	6.2	10.6	9.4	9.6	12.1
1939–48	8.8	6.8	6.8	10.6	7.2	8.9
1948-60	**4.4**	**2.9**	**1.7**	**4.7**	**3.9**	**4.7**

NOTE: Boldface denotes periods of relative economic stability. The dates are annual reference peaks in the National Bureau chronology, except 1939, which is the initial year of World War II.

SOURCE: Figures are annual averages centered on June 30, if not given annually in the sources shown.

MONETARY GOLD STOCK

1869–78, June 30 figures from *Annual Report* of the Secretary of the Treasury, 1928, p. 552, minus gold presumed lost (estimated by us through 1872, thereafter from Director of the Mint, *Annual Report*, 1887, p. 86, and 1907, pp. 87 and 92), were interpolated by the step method. Under the step method, if an even number of months intervenes between two months having known values, the value for the first known month is carried forward halfway and the value for the second known month is carried backward halfway. If the number of months is odd, all but the center month are assigned the value at the nearer of the two known months and the center one is made the average of the known months.

After June 1878, figures are monthly—end of month through 1946, monthly average of daily figures thereafter.

July 1878–June 1907, Report of the Treasurer in *Annual Report* of the Secretary of the Treasury, 1891, pp. 159 ff.; 1898, pp. 109 ff.; 1903, pp. 205 ff.; 1909, pp. 190 ff.; and 1915, pp. 339 ff., minus gold presumed lost as estimated in Director of the Mint, *loc. cit.*

July 1907–Dec. 1913, *Circulation Statement of U.S. Money*, U.S. Treasury Dept.

1914–Jan. 1934, *Banking and Monetary Statistics*, Board of Governors of the Federal Reserve System, 1943, pp. 536–537, plus $287 million added back to restore gold assumed by the Federal Reserve, on insufficient evidence, to have been lost (*ibid.*, p. 407, and present text, Chapter 8, footnote 45).

1934–41, *Banking and Monetary Statistics*, pp. 537–538. In computing the change in the monetary gold stock from 1933 to 1934, the devaluation profit of $2,806 million was excluded from the 1934 figure, although it was included in computing the change from 1934 to 1935. The variability of the gold stock during the period 1929–39 is therefore not affected by the increment to it resulting from the devaluation.

1942–60, *Federal Reserve Bulletin*.

(continued)

HIGH-POWERED MONEY

1869–78, annual averages from figures in Table B-3 were computed by the step method.
From June 1878 on, annual averages were computed from monthly figures. June 1878–Apr. 1907, same source as for Table B-3. May 1907–Dec. 1960, Table B-3.

MONEY STOCK

1869–1907, annual averages from Table A-1, col. 8, were computed by the step method. From May 1907 on, annual averages were computed from monthly data, *ibid.*

VELOCITY OF MONEY

Table A-5.

WHOLESALE PRICES

Historical Statistics of the United States from Colonial Times to 1957, Bureau of the Census, 1960, Series E-1, E-13, and E-25, pp. 115–117; and *Business Statistics*, 1961, p. 36.

REAL INCOME

Same as for Chart 62.

much attention in the halls of Congress and in academic quarters, alike.[2] Subsequently, the decision by the Federal Open Market Committee to limit its open market operations to short-term government obligations, preferably Treasury bills (the so-called "bills only" doctrine), was op-

[2] Two Congressional investigations centered largely on Treasury–Federal Reserve relations and produced an extensive and valuable body of evidence on monetary policy. The 1949–50 inquiry of a subcommittee under the chairmanship of Senator Paul H. Douglas focused public attention on the importance of restoring "the freedom of the Federal Reserve to restrict credit and raise interest rates for general stabilization purposes" (Report, cited below, p. 2). It issued three volumes (Joint Committee on the Economic Report, Subcommittee on Monetary, Credit, and Fiscal Policies, *Monetary, Credit, and Fiscal Policies*, Statements to the subcommittee and Hearings, 81st Cong., 1st sess., 1949; and Report pursuant to S. Con. Res. 26, 81st Cong., 2d sess., S. Doc. 129, 1950). The 1951–52 inquiry of a subcommittee under the chairmanship of Representative Wright Patman covered much the same ground as the Douglas investigation, with special reference to events immediately before and after the Accord. The subcommittee issued a volume of hearings; a two-volume compendium of replies to questionnaires—the questions varying with the respondent—which it had submitted to the Treasury, the chairman of the Board of Governors and the chairman of the Federal Open Market Committee, the presidents of the Federal Reserve Banks, the Council of Economic Advisers, federal and state bank examining authorities, the Reconstruction Finance Corporation, economists, bankers, life insurance executives, and dealers in U.S. government securities; and a report, somewhat less forthright on the role of monetary policy than the Douglas subcommittee report (Joint Committee on the Economic Report, Subcommittee on General Credit Control and Debt Management, *Monetary Policy and the Management of the Public Debt*, Replies to Questions, Hearings, and Report, 82d Cong., 2d sess., 1952).
Books on the period include: Marcel Rist, *La Federal Reserve et les Difficultés Monétaires d'Après Guerre, 1945–1950*, Paris, Amand Colin, 1952; J. S. Fforde, *The Federal Reserve System, 1945–1949*, Oxford, Clarendon Press, 1954; William E. Bensel, *Federal Reserve Open Market Operations in the Postwar Period, 1946–1954*, New Brunswick, N. J., American Bankers Association, 1955; see also Lester V. Chandler, *Inflation in the United States, 1940–1948*, New York, Harper, 1951.

posed publicly by the president of the New York Federal Reserve Bank and became the object of Congressional criticism and discussion, especially after the doctrine became intertwined with the dispute over the legal ceiling on the rate of interest at which the Treasury could issue long-term securities.

The extensive discussion of monetary policy was itself part of a sharply changed climate of opinion about the role of government in economic affairs. The Great Contraction and the New Deal had bequeathed both an increased sensitivity to fluctuations in economic activity and a widespread acceptance of the view that government had a direct responsibility for the maintenance of something approximating "full employment," a view that found legislative expression in the Employment Act of 1946. Improvements in statistical information combined with greater sensitivity to produce widespread knowledge and public concern about economic movements which, in a less sophisticated day, would have passed almost without attention except as students of business cycles delved into them long after the event.

Fiscal policy—which is to say, changes in government expenditures and tax receipts—was at first viewed as the primary means whereby the government could discharge its responsibility. As time went on, however, difficulties of achieving appropriately timed countercyclical changes in government expenditures and tax receipts, beyond those resulting automatically from changes in economic activity, became all too clear, particularly when the exigencies of, first, the Korean War and, then, the cold war came to play so large a role in determining the budget. Moreover, experience at home and abroad somewhat restored confidence in the efficacy of monetary changes. The result was an increasing shift of emphasis to monetary policy as a means of promoting "full employment" and price stability.

1. *Behavior of Money, Income, Prices, and Velocity*

As Chart 52 shows, the contraction the National Bureau dates as beginning in November 1948 was brief and relatively mild, reaching a trough in October 1949. As we saw in the preceding chapter, the trough had been preceded by a mild decline in the stock of money, dating from January 1948, and in prices, dating from August 1948. Both the money stock and prices declined throughout the contraction, the trough in the money stock coming one month after the reference trough and that in prices coming three months later. The total decline in the stock of money was about $1\frac{1}{2}$ per cent, three-fifths of which came before the cyclical peak; and in prices, about 8 per cent.

The decline in the stock of money, though small, is yet atypical. Cyclical declines of greater magnitude had occurred on only six earlier occa-

596

sions (seven, including the January 1867–January 1868 decline), and each such decline had been accompanied by a severe contraction in economic activity. True, the smallest of them—the 3 per cent decline in 1937–38—was twice as large as the 1948–49 decline. Yet the usual behavior of the money stock during earlier mild contractions had been one of continued growth at a diminished rate. Why was the 1948–49 contraction an exception? Why was the 1½ per cent decline in the money stock not accompanied by a sharper decline than occurred in income and prices?

The reason is not far to seek. Throughout almost the whole period from the Civil War through World War II, velocity was subject to a generally declining trend and, in addition, tended to decline relative to its trend during the contraction phase of a cycle. Hence, even a relatively mild decline in the stock of money, such as the 3 per cent decline associated with the 1937–38 contraction, was converted into a severe decline in income. In 1948–49, the underlying trend of velocity was sharply upward, in reaction to the sizable decline during the war. As a result, the usual cyclical decline in velocity relative to its trend produced only a 3½ per cent absolute decline in velocity and permitted an absolute decline in the stock of money to occur with only a mild decline in income.

The recovery from the trough in October 1949 was vigorous. Economic activity reattained its previous peak level by about April 1950, accompanied by a rise in both velocity (as judged from monthly ratios of personal income to money stock not shown in Chart 52) and the stock of money, but with hardly any change in the level of wholesale prices. The outbreak of the Korean War in June 1950 converted a vigorous revival into a speculative boom. Wholesale prices started to rise at a rate comparable with their rate of rise in 1941—by some 16 per cent in the eight months from June 1950 to February 1951. The stock of money showed no acceleration in its rate of rise but velocity did.

We suggested earlier that, in the immediate postwar years, the public at large anticipated a substantial decline in prices at some future date. The mildness of the 1948–49 recession and the failure of prices to retreat more than slightly from their postwar highs must have weakened that expectation, and the outbreak of the Korean War gave it the *coup de grace*. In its place, there arose a fear of the renewal of wartime shortages and price rises. Producers and consumers alike sought to forestall the shortages and to increase their inventories of physical goods relative to their liquid assets.

In the two years from mid-1949 to mid-1951, the public reduced its holdings of liquid assets relative to its income by more than it had in the two years from 1946 to 1948, and that from a lower level. The public's

597

holdings of money, mutual and postal savings deposits, savings and loan shares, and government securities amounted to 13.3 months' income in 1939 and to 21.4 months' at its peak annual value after the war in 1946. It fell to 18.4 months' income in 1948, then rose to 19.3 months' in 1949, and fell to 15.8 months' by 1951. What was true of the broader total of liquid assets was also true of money alone. The stock of money fell from 10.3 months' net national product in 1946 to 9.2 months' in 1948, and from 9.5 months' in 1949 to 7.9 months' in 1951. The latter decline meant a rise in velocity of 20 per cent from 1949 to 1951.

The rapid rise in velocity in response to a changed pattern of anticipations, rather than a rapid rise in the stock of money, was the major force that produced the upsurge in prices. And the rise in prices was the major force that produced pressure on the monetary authorities leading to the March 1951 Treasury–Federal Reserve Accord, which we shall discuss further in section 3.

The Accord in its turn helped to bring to an end the rise in both wholesale prices and velocity, peaks in both coinciding roughly with the Accord. Though the boom had its origin in a rise in velocity, it could hardly have continued for long without an expansion in the money stock. The Accord prevented the expansion from occurring quasi-automatically. In addition, it also raised the public's desired level of money balances by reducing the liquidity of government securities and so induced a mild decline in velocity. Until 1950, the ratio of the public's money holdings to its income had declined from its 1946 level by about the same percentage as the ratio of its other liquid assets to its income—both by about 18 or 19 per cent. From 1950 to 1951, the money ratio declined substantially less than the other liquid asset ratio—by 6 per cent compared with 10 per cent; and from 1951 to 1952, the money ratio rose by 2 per cent while the other liquid asset ratio fell a further 2 per cent. That is why a rise in the money stock at the annual rate of 3.0 per cent from June 1950 to February 1951 was accompanied by a rapid price rise, whereas a rise at the annual rate of 5.1 per cent from February 1951 to June 1952 was accompanied by a mild price decline.

Economic activity continued at a high level for some two years after the price peak in early 1951, accompanied by mildly declining wholesale prices. The tapering off of the rapid price rise in early 1951 together with the failure of the feared shortages to occur—possibly reinforced by the announcement effects of the Accord and the controversy surrounding it— apparently undermined the widespread belief in the inevitability of sharp price rises, without however producing a return to earlier anticipations that prices were destined to fall. This conclusion is suggested by the rough stabilization of velocity from 1951 to 1953 at a level closer to the high of 1951 than to the much lower level attained in 1948 and 1949. It is supported by the behavior of the difference between the yields on bonds and on stocks. This difference, which may be interpreted as an index of the expected rate of change in prices, rose sharply from 1950 to 1951,[3] then remained at roughly the same level for the next two years (bond yield minus earnings yield) or continued its rise more slowly (bond yield minus dividend yield). It is supported also by direct responses of the public to questions about price expectations.[4] However, none of these bits of evidence is more than suggestive. Our understanding of the behavior of velocity is not sufficiently precise to enable us to rule out other possible explanations of the stability of velocity. The difference between yields on bonds and on stocks on some occasions in the past has not been a fully reliable indicator of price expectations alone. And what people say in answer to questions may not be reliable indicators of the expectations implicit in their actual behavior. Even if it were, the counting of noses is hardly the appropriate weighting of expectations for explaining the forces determining a particular aggregate economic magnitude.

At the outset of 1953 the monetary authorities became concerned about inflationary pressure and initiated a series of restrictive actions, further described below, which produced a drastic tightening of money markets and the closest thing to a money market crisis since 1933. The restrictive actions, the changed general expectations about monetary policy that accompanied them, and the final bond market crisis may well have played an important role in determining the timing of a peak in general business—in July 1953, rather than later. If so, the bond market crisis itself was probably only the final straw since, as we have seen, such events take time to produce their effect. Yet the bond market crisis came only two months before the peak in general business. It is also possible that the monetary events were not decisive but that other underlying forces were making for the culmination of the expansion in any event; and that those forces enhanced the tightening effect of the monetary measures taken. Whichever the case, the money market disturbances were responsible for a shift of monetary policy toward ease which preceded the

[3] See data in footnote 32 of Chapter 10.

[4] The Michigan Survey Research Center's surveys of the public's price anticipations, 1950–53, provide further evidence:

Expected Change in Consumer Prices	Percentage Distribution of Spending Units Early in:			
	1950	1951	1952	1953
Increase	15	76	53	17
No change	36	16	30	43
Decrease	41	4	7	31

The rest were uncertain or their response was not ascertained. See *Federal Reserve Bulletin,* July 1952, p. 742; June 1953, p. 592; also George Katona and Eva Mueller, *Consumer Attitudes and Demand, 1950–52,* Ann Arbor, University of Michigan, 1953, pp. 25–26.

downturn in general business. That shift was quite unlike the usual pattern of a substantial lag in action by the monetary authorities when faced with an economic downturn. The early reversal of monetary policy was a happy circumstance that probably contributed to the mildness of the recession.

Recovery after the trough in August 1954 was at first accompanied by relatively stable prices. Beginning in 1955, wholesale prices started rising. The rise was not large by historical standards. On the average, wholesale prices rose by 9 per cent during the expansions of nonwar cycles from December 1867 through August 1954. They rose only 7 per cent in the August 1954 to July 1957 expansion. However, the rise continued beyond the cyclical peak in July 1957 and throughout most of the brief contraction that reached its trough in April 1958. Coming as it did, after more than two decades which saw several dramatic periods of sharply rising prices and none of sharply falling prices and in an environment of acute sensitivity to economic changes, the mild price rise produced widespread concern about the dangers of secular inflation. That concern may well explain the behavior of velocity which, after falling by $2\frac{1}{2}$ per cent from 1951 to 1954, rose by 10 per cent from 1954 to 1957. That percentage rise had been exceeded in peacetime during only three preceding expansions: 1932 to 1937, in reaction to the major decline during the Great Contraction; 1946 to 1948, in reaction to the wartime decline; and 1949 to 1953, in response to the Korean speculative boom. The concern about inflation may also explain a further rise in the difference between the yields on bonds and on stocks (see footnote 32 of Chapter 10).

The monetary authorities reacted sharply, if belatedly, to the contraction that began in July 1957. The money stock reached an absolute peak during the quarter after the cyclical peak, but the pause in its growth was brief. From the end of 1957 it rose sharply, especially in the first half of 1958, and then more gently in the second half. For the calendar year 1958, as a whole, it rose at the rate of $6\frac{1}{2}$ per cent, the largest annual rate of rise since 1946. There was a rapid turnaround in economic activity when the contraction ended in April 1958. The rapid turnaround after much talk about the dangers of a severe collapse, together with a large outflow of gold, apparently led the monetary authorities to conclude that they had overdone monetary expansion and that inflation remained the major danger. The money stock reached an absolute peak in September 1959, and then fell by 1.1 per cent to June 1960, the largest fall of which we have a record in months of cyclical *expansion:* the only earlier ones occurred in 1928–29 and 1948.

The course of economic activity is more than usually difficult to read over that period because of the extended steel strike in the second half

600

of 1959. There were already some signs that the vigorous phase of expansion was past and that at least a plateau was being approached when the steel strike produced a sharp decline in industrial production (Chart 52). What is clear is that vigorous expansion was not resumed after the end of the strike in November 1959. Economic activity stayed at an approximately constant level until the cyclical peak in May 1960, eight months after the peak in the money stock—timing similar to that we have found to hold for the rate of change in the money stock for many preceding cyclical turns.

The economic expansion lasted only a month more than two years, much the shortest expansion in the postwar period. During its course, wholesale prices stayed roughly constant, though consumer prices rose 2.3 per cent. Employment rose sharply, but unemployment, though it declined from the levels reached in mid-1958, stayed relatively high. From January 1955 through November 1957, seasonally adjusted unemployment never rose above 5 per cent of the civilian labor force. In 1959 and 1960, unemployment fell below 5 per cent in only one month. Real income rose by 4.7 per cent annually from 1958 to 1960, a rate of growth that was not large compared with usual experience during a cyclical expansion. All in all, the expansion was not only brief, it was also relatively mild.

Velocity rose by 3.8 per cent annually from 1958 to 1960, a rate of rise that was moderately high for a cyclical expansion. There were no indications, however, of widespread renewed expectations of further rises in prices.

In light of earlier episodes and, in particular, of the tendency of absolute declines in the stock of money to be associated with severe contractions, it is tempting to attribute the brevity and mildness of the expansion to the early date in the expansion at which the growth of the money stock came to a halt and to the subsequent sizable absolute decline. Be that as it may, when in early 1960 it became more and more evident that a contraction rather than a resumption of vigorous expansion was the more likely prospect, the monetary authorities took measures to reverse the decline in the stock of money. From June 1960 through June 1961, the stock of money rose at an annual rate of 6½ per cent, almost as rapidly as in early 1958.

2. Factors Accounting for Changes in the Money Stock

As Chart 53 shows, the period from 1948 to 1960 was characterized by broadly opposite movements of high-powered money and the ratio of deposits to bank reserves about their net upward trends, and by a nearly continuous rise in the deposit-currency ratio. From August 1948 to May

CHART 53

The Stock of Money and Its Proximate Determinants, Monthly, 1948–60

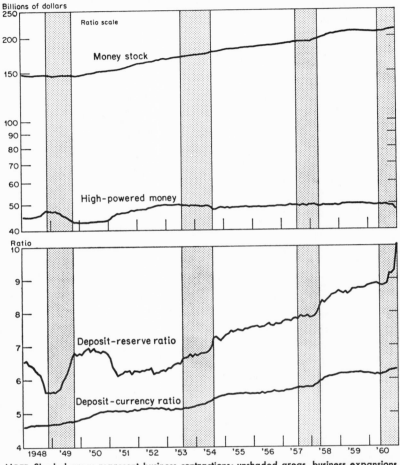

NOTE: Shaded areas represent business contractions; unshaded areas, business expansions.
SOURCE: Tables A-1 (col. 8) and B-3.

1960, 23 per cent of the increase in the stock of money was attributable to the rise in high-powered money, 40 per cent to the rise in the deposit-reserve ratio, and 30 per cent to the rise in the deposit-currency ratio.

The opposite movements in high-powered money and in the deposit-reserve ratio were for the most part the result of changes in reserve requirements for member banks. Reserve requirements were raised in 1948, lowered in 1949, raised again in 1951, lowered in 1953, 1954, 1958, 1959,

CHART 54

Interest Yields, and Use of Tools by Federal Reserve System,
1948–60

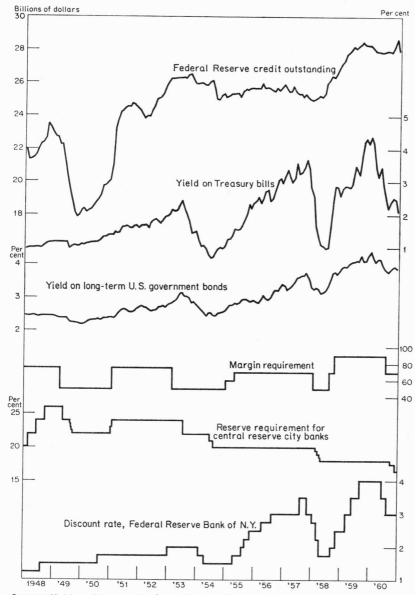

SOURCE: Yield on Treasury bills (new bills issued), from *Federal Reserve Bulletin*, seasonally
adjusted by NBER. Yield on long-term U.S. bonds (taxable bonds neither due nor callable in less
than 10 to 15 years), no seasonal adjustment needed. Other data, same as for Charts 41 and 49.

603

and 1960 (see Chart 54).[5] Banks, throughout, held little excess reserves and adjusted promptly to changes in reserve requirements, so each of these changes shows up in the recorded deposit-reserve ratio. In each case except for 1953 and 1960, the change in reserve requirements was accompanied by a change in Federal Reserve credit outstanding (monthly averages of daily figures) in the same direction, which means in a direction tending to offset the effect of the change in reserve requirements on the stock of money. Until 1951, the change in Federal Reserve credit outstanding was a consequence of the bond support program; thereafter, of a deliberate policy on the part of the System to use open market operations to spread out the effects of discontinuous changes in reserve requirements.

DECLINE IN THE MONEY STOCK, JANUARY 1948–NOVEMBER 1949

We have already noted the increases in reserve requirements in February, June, and September 1948. The first two increases applied only to banks in central reserve cities. The final increase applied to all banks and was quantitatively the most important, as may be seen from the sharper drop in the ratio of deposits to reserves it produced. Except for banks in central reserve cities, reserve requirements had been at their legal maximum since 1941, and the final increase was made possible only by legislation passed in August 1948 at a special session of Congress called by President Truman to consider measures to counter inflation—one of the few measures passed at that session. The legislation authorized increases until June 1949 in the maximum reserve requirements that could be imposed by the Board.[6] Having requested such an increase, the Board no doubt felt under some pressure to make use of its new power. Otherwise, it might well not have done so, since, as we have seen, the money stock had been declining since January 1948 and prices had reached their peak in August. Another measure passed at the special session gave the Federal Reserve System renewed power to control instalment credit, and that power too was used in September.

The immediate effect of the rise in reserve requirements was that member banks began selling government securities to replenish their reserves, the Reserve System, of course, being committed to buy them under its price-support policy for government securities. The increase in required reserves was roughly $2 billion—the amount of government securities the

[5] In 1959 for the first time since 1917 under the Federal Reserve System, member banks were permitted to count a fraction of their vault cash as satisfying legal reserve requirements. That fraction was increased in Sept. 1960. After Nov. 1960 all vault cash could be counted as reserves. Except in 1959, changes in reserve requirements in other years listed in the text pertained to the percentage of reserves to be maintained against net demand or time deposits.

[6] See Chap. 10, footnote 30.

Reserve System bought in September. The amount of high-powered money continued to be a resultant of the amount of money consistent with the yields on government securities being maintained by the System rather than an independent determinant of the stock of money under control of the System.

Insofar as the changes in reserve requirements had any effect beyond the arithmetic one of leading member banks to exchange interest-bearing obligations of the government for noninterest-bearing obligations (deposits at the Reserve Banks), it must have been to reduce the willingness of member banks to make loans or to acquire assets other than government securities. That effect reinforced the effect of increased yields on short-term governments which had taken place in 1947, and again in mid-1948 when the yield on Treasury bills was permitted to rise along with a rise in the discount rate (see Chart 54, which gives the yield on Treasury bills and long-term bonds). As we have already seen, since January 1948 the pattern of yields being maintained by the System had been consistent with a decline in the stock of money. The rise in yields in mid-1948 and in reserve requirements in September strengthened the forces that accounted for the tendency of the money stock to decli e— chiefly the effects on the demand for money of the government surplus and of expectations of a fall in prices (see the preceding chapter).

The decline in the stock of money doubtless contributed to the contraction that began in November 1948. In its turn the contraction, when it came, was one more factor making for a decline in the stock of money. Under its bond-support program, the System had been obliged to make heavy purchases of long-term government bonds during most of 1948 to keep their prices from falling below a level corresponding to a yield of 2½ per cent. In early 1949, a larger volume of bonds was demanded by non-Reserve buyers than was offered by non-Reserve sellers at this price. In the absence of Reserve intervention, prices would have risen sharply. Though the Reserve was committed only to maintain a floor under bond prices, not to peg them or prevent them from rising, it apparently felt that the reversal in the market situation was only temporary. Whether for this reason or some other, it did in fact come close to pegging prices in the first half of 1949 by selling over $3 billion of government bonds. The result was a decline in Federal Reserve credit outstanding by over $2 billion from the cyclical peak in November 1948 to the end of April 1949, just before a reduction in reserve requirements. A small gold inflow and a substantial reduction in Treasury deposits at Federal Reserve Banks offset about one-third of the contraction in Federal Reserve credit. These movements are illustrated in Chart 55, which is similar to Chart 40. The curve labeled "residual" plots high-powered money minus the sum of the gold stock and Treasury cash and deposits at the Reserve

CHART 55
Major Factors Accounting for Changes in High-Powered Money, Monthly, 1948–60

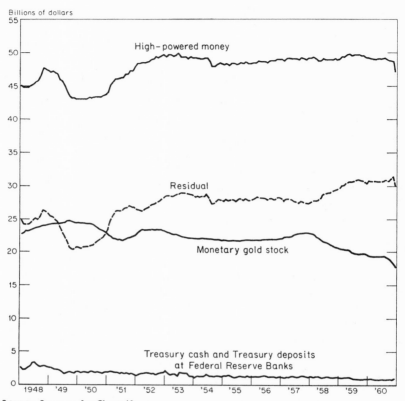

SOURCE: Same as for Chart 40.

Banks and hence isolates movements that are mainly attributable to Federal Reserve action. (The range of movement in the residual, wider in Chart 55 than in Chart 40, reflects the larger role of the Federal Reserve in the postwar period in accounting for changes in high-powered money in contrast with its role in the thirties, when the Treasury was dominant.) A rise in the deposit-currency ratio further eased the impact on bank reserves of Federal Reserve sales but, even so, member bank reserve balances fell by some $900 million from November 1948 through April 1949 (see Chart 56A, for seasonally adjusted commercial bank deposits at Federal Reserve Banks).

The Reserve System was relatively slow in reacting to the contraction, though not nearly as slow as in 1920 when its first move came sixteen

606

months after the cyclical turn. In March and April 1949, four and five months after the cyclical peak, credit controls were eased and margin requirements on security loans were reduced. More important than either, between May 1 and September 1, six successive reductions in reserve requirements reduced required reserves by nearly $4 billion.[7] Most important of all, in June the System announced, in effect, that it would no longer seek to prevent bond prices from rising. In July yields on long-term securities accordingly fell and so also did yields on bills (Chart 54). For the time being, the System regained some control over its credit outstanding, being freed from the straitjacket imposed by the pegging of yields on governments. The existence of an implied commitment to put a floor under bond prices still had an effect. Bonds were, as a result, more secure investments and therefore had a lower yield, but the System could at least determine to some extent how much to buy and sell. After the final reduction in reserve requirements on September 1, the System kept Reserve credit outstanding roughly constant for the balance of the year and through the first part of 1950, and hence refrained from offsetting the expansionary influence of the released reserves. As we have seen, the trough in the stock of money came one month after the trough in economic activity in October 1949.

In World War II, the peak in the stock of money preceded the peak in prices, in contrast with the timing in World War I when the two roughly coincided; and the World War II decline in the money stock was milder, 1½ per cent rather than 9 per cent, though more protracted, 22 months compared with 16 months. The more rapid reversal of policy by the Federal Reserve System no doubt was one factor accounting for the relative mildness of the World War II decline, but several others were probably more important.

In the first place, the 1920 decline in the money stock was preceded by and in its initial phases associated with a gold outflow which intensified the effect of the restrictive actions taken by the Federal Reserve System, whereas the 1948 decline was preceded by and associated with a gold inflow which offset the effects of restrictive Reserve actions.

In the second place, the Reserve System took vigorous restrictive action in the earlier episode: discount rates were raised from 4 to 7 per cent in the course of eight months, at a time when borrowings from the System substantially exceeded member bank reserve balances. In the later episode, Reserve action was limited to a rise in yields on Treasury

[7] The reductions lowered reserve requirements in effect since Sept. 1948 from 26, 22, and 16 per cent of net demand deposits to 22, 18, and 12 per cent for central reserve city, reserve city, and country banks, respectively, and from 7½ per cent of time deposits to 5 per cent. These were greater reductions than would have occurred automatically by the expiration on June 30, 1949, of the Board's temporary authority to raise reserve requirements.

CHART 56

High-Powered Money, by Assets and Liabilities of the Treasury and
Federal Reserve Banks, 1948–60

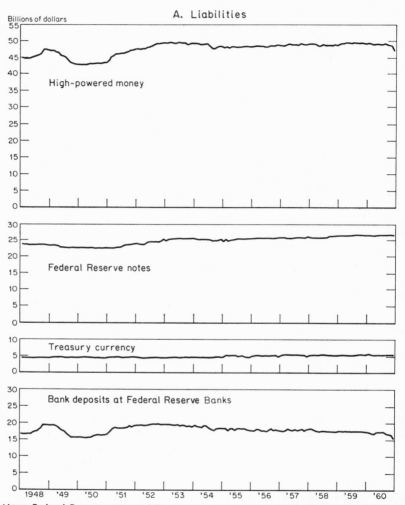

A. Liabilities

NOTE: Federal Reserve notes and Treasury currency are outside the Treasury and Federal
Reserve Banks. Between $25 million and $50 million in gold certificates recalled but not turned in
are included in high-powered money, but not shown in its components viewed as liabilities.
SOURCE: Chart 47 was extended using *Annual Report* of the Secretary of the Treasury, 1950–60,
for the devaluation profit.

CHART 56 (Concluded)

B. Assets

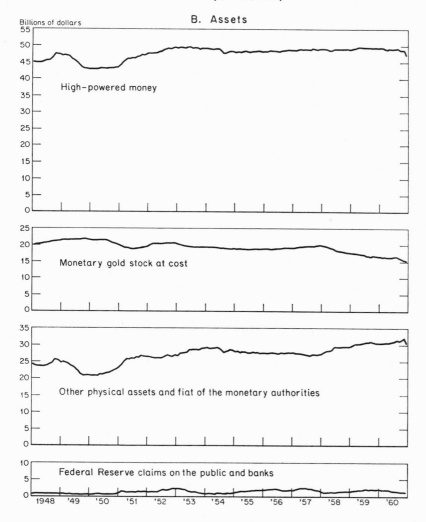

bills from ⅜ to 1 per cent and then to 1¼ per cent, on long-term government bonds from about 2¼ to about 2½ per cent, and in the discount rate, in any event ineffective, from 1 to 1½ per cent. Federal Reserve restriction in 1948–49 was so slight that the decline in the money stock may well have been produced by other forces: the change in market conditions, discussed above, that converted yields earlier consistent with inflation into yields that could be maintained only by reducing the money stock.

609

In the third place, the difference in form of Federal Reserve creation of high-powered money during and immediately after the war—while of little significance for the concurrent expansion in the stock of money—may have been of greater significance for its subsequent behavior. In World War I, the increase in Federal Reserve credit outstanding was chiefly in the form of loans to member banks, the money created being made available for government use through purchase of government securities by banks or their customers. The assets acquired by the System with the money it created were thereby almost wholly liabilities of member banks, and the cost to member banks of retaining the use of the corresponding funds was directly determined by the discount rate. The rise in discount rates therefore impinged directly and in the first instance on the banks. In World War II, the increase in Federal Reserve credit outstanding was chiefly in the form of purchases of government securities, which is to say—if we consolidate the accounts of the Federal Reserve and the Treasury and so eliminate bookkeeping fictions—in the form of direct creation of money for government use, with no private liabilities entering as an intermediate step. When banks acquired those funds to add to reserve balances, the matching liabilities were deposit liabilities of the banks to the public, the cost of which was affected directly by neither the discount rate nor the yields maintained on government securities. Federal Reserve action, permitting short-term yields on securities to rise, therefore impinged on a wider front and, in the first instance, neither forced nor even necessarily induced any contraction by banks.

THE KOREAN WAR PERIOD

The outbreak of the Korean War in June 1950, as we have already noted, drastically altered public expectations about the near-term future and unleashed a speculative boom. The accompanying rise in interest rates pushed up yields to levels at which the Reserve System was committed to support government security prices and occasioned widespread concern, within the System and outside, that the support program would become the engine for a large and uncontrollable expansion in the money stock.

In August 1950 the Board of Governors approved a rise in discount rates and an open market policy designed to permit some rise in yields on government securities. It made a public announcement to that effect.[8]

[8] In addition, in Aug. the buying rate on bankers' acceptances was raised, and bank supervisory agencies requested voluntary cooperation of lenders in restraining credit. In Nov. the banks were again requested to restrain unnecessary expansion of credit. Between Mar. 1951 and May 1951 all financing institutions were requested to participate in a program of voluntary credit restraint provided for in the Defense Production Act of Sept. 1950. Under the authority of the act, con-

REVIVAL OF MONETARY POLICY

The Treasury reacted by announcing, long in advance, that it would maintain the existing yield in its September–October 1950 refunding. The Federal Reserve purchased most of the refunding issue, though at the same time selling a small amount of other securities and permitting yields on them to advance a trifle. The episode shows up in Chart 54 in the extremely rapid rise in late 1950 in Federal Reserve credit outstanding, a large fraction of which took the form of purchases of the refunding issue. Needless to say, however, what mattered was not the details of the particular issues offered by the Treasury but the pattern of rates supported. Given the pattern with the continued assurance that it would be supported, plus the speculative boom, an expansion in the Reserve System's portfolio was inevitable.

All told, from June 1950 to the end of the year, the System's holdings of government securities rose by $2.4 billion and Reserve Bank credit outstanding by $3.5 billion. Despite the rapid rise in Reserve Bank credit outstanding, the money stock rose only moderately. It had risen at an annual rate of $4\frac{1}{2}$ per cent from December 1949 to June 1950; it rose at an annual rate of less than 3 per cent from June 1950 to December 1950. As is apparent from Chart 55, the main reason was that the increase in Reserve Bank credit outstanding was largely offset by a substantial outflow of gold, which resulted from a rapid increase in U.S. demand for imports stimulated in part by the attempt to accumulate stockpiles of raw materials. As minor contributing factors, a mild rise in the deposit-reserve ratio in the first half of the year was followed by a mild decline in the second, and the rate of rise in the deposit-currency ratio was lower in the second half of the year than in the first.

The rise in velocity associated with the speculative boom meant that even the relatively modest increase in the money stock was accompanied by a rapid rate of growth of income. Personal income had risen at an annual rate of 11 per cent from December 1949 to June 1950; it rose at about twice that rate from June to December 1950. Industrial production rose rapidly until August 1950, when capacity limitations imposed a slackening. Wholesale prices had risen at an annual rate of nearly 8 per cent in the first half of 1950; they rose at the rate of 22 per cent in the second half.

The rapid stepping up of the pace of expansion, with what seemed a threat of near-runaway inflation, evoked persistent pressure on the Reserve System to halt monetary expansion; augmented the System's desire to be freed from its commitment to support a particular pattern

---

sumer credit controls were established in Sept. and strengthened in Oct. 1950. Real estate credit for residential and certain categories of commercial construction was restricted in Oct. 1950, and Jan. and Feb. 1951. Margin requirements were raised from 50 to 75 per cent of market value in Jan. 1951.

of rates on government securities; and brought home to government officials, generally, the dangers in the existing situation. The result was the Treasury–Federal Reserve Accord of March 1951—discussed more fully in section 3 below—which ended the System's responsibility for support of government securities at pegged prices.

Just before the Accord, in January and February, reserve requirements were raised, banks acquiring over half the additional $2 billion of reserves needed by selling government securities to the System. That was the final reserve-requirement change in which the offsetting movement in high-powered money was quasi-automatic and outside the control of the System. After the Accord, long-term bond prices were permitted to decline: long-term $2\frac{1}{2}$ per cent bonds, which had been supported at $100\frac{3}{4}$ at the beginning of the year, were quoted at 97 during the last half. Active support of the short-term market was withdrawn and, as a result, short-term rates fluctuated at or below the discount rate (see Chart 54).

From March 1951, the month of the Accord, through December 1952, the month before the Eisenhower Administration took office, the money stock continued to rise fairly steadily. Indeed, it rose at a higher annual rate, 5 per cent, than it had in the sixteen months from the November 1949 trough in the money stock to the Accord, when the annual rate was $3\frac{1}{2}$ per cent. As we saw earlier, the change in the liquidity of government securities produced by abandonment of rigid support prices, plus altered expectations, made the higher rate of growth in the money stock consistent with a change from rapidly rising to mildly declining prices.

The rise in the stock of money was accounted for arithmetically by an increase in high-powered money, since both deposit ratios remained relatively constant (Chart 53). The Reserve System kept the discount rate and reserve requirements unchanged (Chart 54). The increase in high-powered money was produced partly by a rise in the gold stock—prices abroad rose more than at home and stimulated a gold inflow—and partly by an increase in the fiat of the monetary authorities (see Chart 56B). The System's holdings of government securities were $1.3 billion higher on the last Wednesday of December 1952 than at the time of the Accord, but those purchases were not large enough to prevent yields on government securities from rising substantially—on bills from nearly 1.4 per cent in early 1951 to about 2 per cent at the end of 1952, on long-term bonds from under $2\frac{1}{2}$ per cent to $2\frac{3}{4}$ per cent.

THE CRISIS IN EARLY 1953

Though wholesale prices were relatively stable during 1951–52, at the beginning of 1953 the Reserve System became concerned about inflation, presumably because of the rapid rise in bank loans, instalment credit outstanding, and mortgage debt, and also because of the rise in stock prices in the second half of 1952. In January 1953 all Federal Reserve Banks raised the discount rate from 1¾ to 2 per cent. The System also brought direct pressure on member banks to cut down their borrowings— since mid-1952 generally larger than their excess reserves—and to limit increases in the volume of their loans.[9] In March the Federal Open Market Committee formally and explicitly abandoned price support of government securities, and adopted a policy of keeping "hands off" during periods of Treasury financing.[10]

The Treasury, whose top leadership changed in January 1953, willingly accepted, if it did not suggest, the System's decision not to assist with refunding operations. The new leadership was dedicated to "sound money" and to lengthening the maturity structure of the federal debt. In April the Treasury offered a new 25–30 year 3¼ per cent bond, the longest maturity issued since October 1941; in May the rates of interest on FHA insured and VA guaranteed mortgages were raised to 4½ per cent. Chairman William McChesney Martin, Jr. of the Board of Governors suggested in a speech on May 6 that commercial banks should not look to the System to supply their fall seasonal need for reserves, but should use their own funds. The market interpreted those developments as signs of greater restraint to come. A wave of selling of governments brought their prices down to new lows, the new 3¼ per cent bond fell below par, and market interest rates rose. There was a quick change in monetary policy, when the System was confronted with more tightness than it had intended.[11] The reversal in monetary policy

[9] Margin requirements on stock purchases were, nevertheless, reduced from 75 to 50 per cent on Feb. 20, 1953, because at that time there seemed no evidence of inflationary tendencies in the stock market.
[10] In Mar. 1953, the Federal Open Market Committee approved the following changes with respect to operations for the System account (Board of Governors of the Federal Reserve System, *Annual Report,* 1953, p. 88):
"It is not now the policy of the Committee to support any pattern of prices and yields in the Government securities market, and intervention in the Government securities market is solely to effectuate the objectives of monetary and credit policy (including correction of disorderly markets).
"Pending further study and further action by the Committee, it should refrain during a period of Treasury financing from purchasing (1) any maturing issues for which an exchange is being offered, (2) when-issued securities, and (3) outstanding issues of comparable maturity to those being offered for exchange."
[11] Arthur F. Burns, who became Economic Adviser to the President at the end of Mar. 1953, argues that events in early 1953 were not "a typical response to a moderate degree of credit tightening. More than anything else, they reflected the bewilderment of a financial community that had become accustomed to stable interest rates and had forgotten how a restrictive credit policy works. Government officials could overlook the criticism that 'tight money' brought on the industrial recession which became visible around mid-1953. They knew better, as did many others. However, they could not escape the fact that they had misjudged the psychology of financial markets. The memory of this minor embarrassment under-

began in the week ending May 13, when the System began buying Treasury bills. It acquired $370 million in U.S. securities during the balance of the month and $500 million in June. It lowered reserve requirements in July, the month of the cyclical peak.

The bond market crisis was in one respect a blessing in disguise. For the first time in its history, the Reserve System was led to undertake *easing* action before or coincidentally with a peak in general business. It thereby almost surely set in motion monetary forces which helped ease the ensuing contraction in economic activity.

The reserve requirement reductions in July 1953 were allowed to have their full effect on the money stock, Federal Reserve credit outstanding being kept roughly constant when allowance is made for its seasonal movement. Further steps were taken in 1954, discount rates being lowered in February and April–May 1954, and reserve requirements being lowered again in June and July–August 1954—the latter month marking the cyclical trough.

THE PERIOD FROM 1954 TO 1960

The records of Federal Open Market Committee meetings after 1954 contain frequent shifts in the language used to describe Federal Reserve policy: from a policy of "active ease" to one of "ease" at the end of 1954, from "ease" to "restraining inflationary developments" in 1955; a qualification about "avoiding deflationary tendencies" was added in January 1956, removed in March, added again in May, and deleted again in August. The directive to the operators of the open market account was then retained unchanged during most of 1957. Despite repeated discussions in their 1957 meetings about the possibility of a downturn, it was not until November, four months after the peak in business dated by the National Bureau as occurring in July, that the Committee definitely acknowledged that a recession was in process and changed the wording of its directive.

Our various measures of monetary action show no marked changes comparable to those changes in language—labeled by some participants in the market as an "open-mouth" policy. The money stock rose 2.8 per cent from June 1953 to June 1954, and 3.9, 1.9, and 2.9 per cent in the succeeding three years, respectively. The growth of the money stock owed nothing to changes in high-powered money, though the steadiness of the growth reflected a corresponding steadiness in high-powered money. High-powered money reached a peak in mid-1953, from which it declined slowly and fairly steadily to the third quarter of

---

standably made them more cautious in the next encounter with economic excesses" (*Prosperity Without Inflation*, New York, Fordham University Press, 1957, p. 56).

1954, and then recovered by August 1957 to a level somewhat below that in June 1953. The decline in high-powered money to 1954 reflected chiefly a decline in Reserve Bank credit outstanding, the subsequent rise, chiefly an inflow of gold. All these movements, however, were fairly moderate. The source of the increase in the money stock was the steady rise in both deposit ratios. The rise in the deposit-reserve ratio reflected, on the one hand, the reserve reductions in mid-1953 and mid-1954; and, on the other, a growth of time deposits relative to demand deposits. The latter development was very similar to one which had occurred in the 1920's, likewise a period of pressure on member bank reserves. The 1953–57 growth of time deposits of commercial banks relative to demand deposits was fostered by a rise, effective January 1957, in maximum rates of interest the Board permitted to be paid on time deposits. The rise in the deposit-currency ratio was a continuation of an upward trend since the end of the war and presumably in part reflected rising income.

Federal Reserve action, other than open market purchases and sales, consisted of a series of changes in the discount rate: at New York, from $1\frac{1}{2}$ per cent to 3 per cent by six rises of $\frac{1}{4}$ percentage point each in April, August, September, and November 1955, and April and August 1956; and a final rise from 3 to $3\frac{1}{2}$ per cent in August 1957, a month after the cyclical peak. Those rises in discount rates cannot be regarded as of themselves restrictive, since they did not keep up with short-term market rates, which rose considerably throughout the period. Bill rates rose from about $\frac{3}{4}$ of 1 per cent in mid-1954 to over $3\frac{1}{2}$ per cent in late 1957. In consequence, the discount rate, which had been $\frac{3}{4}$ of 1 per cent *above* the bill rate in mid-1954, was only $\frac{3}{8}$ of 1 per cent above it in July 1956, and $\frac{1}{8}$ of 1 per cent *below* it in October 1957. That is presumably one reason the money stock rose more rapidly from 1956 to 1957 than from 1955 to 1956, when rises in discount rates kept pace with the rising market rates.[12] For although the amount of high-

---

[12] This point is particularly relevant for the period because of the importance apparently attached by the System to so-called "free reserves" as a proximate criterion in determining its open market purchases and sales. Free reserves are defined as the difference between "excess reserves" of member banks and member bank "borrowings" from the System or, equivalently, as the difference between member bank reserve balances and the sum of their required reserves and their borrowings from the System. Official and semiofficial statements by persons connected with the System suggested that free reserves could be regarded as an index of "tightness" or "ease" of monetary policy. It was widely believed that the System set its proximate objectives in terms of a free reserve position it sought to attain. Consequently, the actual level of free reserves was scrutinized from week to week as an index of the System's intentions. Free reserves were negative throughout most of 1956 and 1957, averaging —$533 million in Apr. 1956, rising irregularly to $117 million in Jan. 1957, and then declining to —$508 million in June 1957.

Arithmetically, a given level or pattern of movement of free reserves is con-

powered money was roughly constant from 1956 to 1957 and Federal Reserve credit outstanding actually fell, the relatively high market rate induced banks to raise deposits relative to reserves, partly by measures designed to render time deposits more attractive. This was the main source of the higher rate of increase of the money stock from 1956 to 1957 than in the prior year.

In November 1957, four months after the cyclical peak, the Federal Reserve System reversed its policy. Discount rates were reduced to 3 per cent, and further reductions, bringing the rate down to 1¾ per cent by April 1958, were made in January, March, and April.[13] In

---

sistent with almost any level or pattern of movement of the total money stock. For example, free reserves can remain constant at any specified number, positive or negative, and the money stock, increase at a rapid rate or decrease at a rapid rate. It is only necessary that total reserve balances minus member bank borrowings change at the same rate as required reserves.

Economically, there is presumably some level of free reserves at any given time that banks desire to maintain, a level they try neither to increase by liquidating assets nor to decrease by acquiring assets. If the System tries to maintain a higher level of free reserves than the banks desire, the banks will use the excess to increase their loans and investments and, in the process, will increase the money stock and required reserves, and so reduce free reserves. The System can frustrate the banks by creating still more high-powered money, which will produce a continued increase in the money stock. Conversely, if the System tries to maintain a lower level of free reserves than the banks desire, it can do so only by forcing a decline in the money stock. Thus, a level of free reserves above the desired level can be maintained only by expanding the money stock, and conversely. In principle, to each difference between actual free reserves and the level desired when the money stock is stable there corresponds a particular rate of change in the money stock. Whether a given level of free reserves involves monetary expansion or contraction therefore depends not only on its absolute size, but also on its relation to the level banks are, perhaps implicitly, seeking to attain. And the desired level in turn must depend critically on the relation of the discount rate to market rates. If market rates are high relative to discount rates, banks will have much incentive to use their resources to the full and to borrow from the Reserve System; they will be seeking, that is, to maintain (on the average) substantial negative free reserves. If market rates are low relative to discount rates, banks will have little incentive to be in debt to the Reserve System; they will be seeking to maintain positive free reserves. Maintenance of, say, zero free reserves by the System would in the first instance produce monetary expansion; in the second, monetary contraction.

Average free reserves were at very similar levels in the 8 months ending in Aug. 1956 and Aug. 1957 but, since discount rates were lower relative to market rates in the latter than in the former period, the same level of free reserves was "easier" or more expansionary.

For a detailed theoretical and statistical analysis of the relation of free reserves to the rate of change in the money supply, see A. J. Meigs, *Free Reserves and the Money Supply*, University of Chicago Press, 1962.

[13] The policy directive of the Federal Open Market Committee was changed in Nov. 1957 to call for open market operations with a view, among other things, to "fostering sustainable growth in the economy without inflation, by moderating the pressures on reserves"; and again in Dec., to "cushioning adjustments and mitigating recessionary tendencies in the economy." This wording continued

addition, reserve requirements were reduced in four steps in February, March, and April. Beginning in March 1958 and continuing through September 1959, open market purchases served to raise Federal Reserve credit, offsetting a sharp decline in the gold stock which began in February 1958 and continued with few interruptions for the following three years (see Charts 54 and 55). The sharp deliberate reversal in policy, probably the sharpest and most vigorous since the reaction in the opposite direction to Britain's departure from the gold standard in 1931, was no doubt prompted by two circumstances: the widening expression of concern that the recession in process would turn into a major contraction; and widespread criticism of the Reserve System for both the final rise in the discount rate—reportedly made against the advice of both the chairman of the Council of Economic Advisers and the Secretary of the Treasury—and for not reversing even sooner. Whatever its motivation, the reversal brought a sharp change in the behavior of the money stock. Whereas the money stock had been virtually unchanged in the final five months of 1957, it rose 4.1 per cent in the first six months of 1958 or at an annual rate of over 8 per cent. One must go back to 1946 to find so high a rate of rise during a six-month period. In the next six months it rose a further 2.4 per cent, making the total rise for the year 6½ per cent.

A number of developments combined to produce another sharp reversal in monetary policy and in the movement of the money stock beginning in 1959. First, the trough in economic activity was reached in April 1958 though, as usual, the fact that a trough had been reached was not clearly recognized until months later. The brevity of the contraction—confounding widespread dire predictions—and the vigorous pace of the rise in industrial production after April made the magnitude of the monetary reaction seem greater, if anything, than had been required, and produced renewed emphasis by the Federal Reserve System upon the dangers of inflation rather than of contraction. Second, the large outflow of gold during 1958, which, as noted above, continued for several years, produced widespread concern inside and outside the government. The asymmetrical reaction to gold movements which proved so disastrous in the early 1930's—willingness to accept inflows of gold without letting them affect internal policy, but much greater sensitivity to outflows—was again manifest, though in much muted form and under circumstances in which the financial system was in a much stronger position to resist shocks. Third, retrospective examination of its earlier policy

---

in effect until Mar. 1958, when the final phrase was changed to "contributing further by monetary ease to resumption of stable growth of the economy" (Board of Governors of the Federal Reserve System, *Annual Report,* 1957 and 1958).

persuaded the Reserve System that it had erred during the 1954–57 expansion by continuing "ease" for too long; that, while an easy-money policy was justified in 1954 and perhaps early 1955, the System should have taken severely restrictive measures in mid-1955 at the latest.[14] It was determined not to repeat the error.

The results of these developments are clearly reflected in Federal Reserve action. During 1958 and the first nine months of 1959, the Reserve System had completely offset the large outflow of gold and had kept total high-powered money roughly constant (see Chart 55). The rapid expansion of the money stock was produced by a rise in the two deposit ratios, the rise in the deposit-reserve ratio being largely a response to reductions in reserve requirements allowed in February–April 1958; the rise in the deposit-currency ratio, to a rise in the rate of interest offered on time deposits (see Chart 53). In September 1958 the discount rate at the Reserve Bank of New York was raised in response to the sharp rise in market rates,[15] and it was raised further at four subsequent dates in 1958 and 1959, to a level of 4 per cent in September 1959. After September 1959, Reserve Bank credit outstanding declined, reinforcing the effect on high-powered money of the continuing gold outflow; the deposit-currency ratio declined mildly; and the rise in the deposit-reserve ratio tapered off. As a result, the rate of growth of the money stock slackened and the money stock reached an absolute peak in September 1959.

The steel strike, as noted earlier, produced a sharp drop in industrial production beginning July 1959. It was widely believed that the drop was purely temporary and that, once the strike was settled, economic expansion would continue at something like the vigorous pace it had displayed from 1958 to 1959. Those expectations were disappointed. The recovery after the termination of the steel strike in November 1959 brought industrial production back to a level in January 1960 only slightly higher than the level in June 1959; thereafter, industrial production moved around a roughly horizontal level until midyear.

Perhaps the most striking sign of unfulfilled expectations and one of the most unusual features of the expansion was the behavior of interest

[14] See the testimony of Chairman Martin, *Employment, Growth, and Price Levels,* Hearings, part 6A, Joint Economic Committee, 86th Cong., 1st sess., July 24–30, 1959, pp. 1309–1310; also Ascher Achinstein, *Federal Reserve Policy and Economic Stability, 1951–57,* Senate Committee on Banking and Currency, 85th Cong., 2d sess., S. Rept. 2500, Oct. 10, 1958, pp. 52–55.

[15] The sharp turnaround in market rates in July 1958 followed a large Treasury financing in mid-June and gave rise to outcries against speculation in government securities. The result was an extensive investigation by the Federal Reserve System and the Treasury. See *Treasury-Federal Reserve Study of the Government Securities Market,* part I, July 1959, parts II and III, Feb. 1960. See also footnote 38, below.

rates (see Chart 54). Interest rates typically rise throughout expansion: in cycles from 1857 to World War II they frequently turned down some months after the peak in business; since World War II their cyclical turns have coincided with the turns in business. In the 1958–60 expansion, after rising from mid-1958 through 1959 to levels not exceeded since late 1929 or early 1930, they started to decline sharply in early 1960, four or five months *before* the cyclical peak in May. Short-term rates fell particularly sharply: e.g., 4- to 6-month commercial paper rates from a high of 5.12 per cent in January 1960 to a low of 3.58 per cent in August; the yield on newly-issued 3-month Treasury bills from 4.19 per cent in December 1959 to 2.47 per cent in July 1960. There is no other expansion period in our record during which commercial paper rates led the reference cycle peak by so many months; in only two other cycles since 1857 did the turn in this series precede the cyclical peak and then only by one month in each instance. This is the first expansion for which we have figures when the standing at the three months centered on the peak was lower than that of the last third of the expansion.

The behavior of interest rates was clearly not a response to monetary policy. On the contrary, discount rates at the New York Bank were raised three times during 1959, the final rise coming in September, and the Reserve System permitted high-powered money to decline from September 1959 through April 1960—the last third of the expansion—both of which might be expected to work in the direction of higher, rather than lower, interest rates. The behavior of interest rates, or rather the decline in the demand for loanable funds which produced it, did however have an influence on monetary developments. It meant that Federal Reserve policy was tighter than intended; that, unlike the period from 1956 to 1957, when rises in the discount rate did not keep pace with rises in market rates, so that steps intended to tighten monetary conditions produced relative ease, this time, the peak discount rate of September 1959 was continued for a half-year after the decline in market rates, making the steps taken by the Reserve System even tighter than intended.

The result of those developments was a decline in the stock of money of 1.1 per cent from its highest level in September 1959 to its lowest level in June 1960. The final decline came despite attempts by the System to reverse the movement. Beginning in early March and continuing through November 1960, the System supplied reserves to member banks through open market purchases of government securities. The discount rate at the Reserve Bank of New York was reduced in June 1960 and again in August. In the week ending September 1, reserve requirements were reduced on net by $600 million and in the week ending December 1 by $1,300 million. The reductions were a result of a narrowing of the difference between central reserve and reserve city bank requirements against net demand deposits and a result of increases in vault cash allowable as reserves.[16]

The decline in the money stock from September 1959 to June 1960 was sizable in terms of past experience, exceeded appreciably only by declines during past major contractions in business (counting 1893–97 as one contraction) and just barely by the decline from January 1948 to November 1949. Moreover, the general trend of velocity was no longer so sharply upward as it had been during the 1948–49 decline in the stock of money. The decline therefore was potentially more serious.

The attempt by the System to reverse the movement came early, about two months before the cyclical peak—the second time in its history the System had eased before a peak. There is some similarity to the earlier occasion in 1953, in that both times the early reversal of policy reflected in part the realization that a greater degree of tightness had developed than the System had intended to produce by its actions. But there was also an important difference. On the later occasion, the System was much more clearly aware of the desirability of moving early and had been criticized much more extensively for maintaining what was widely regarded as an unduly tight policy during the latter part of 1959. A much better case can therefore be made for 1959 than for 1953 that the System was deliberately seeking to move in advance of the cyclical turn.

3. Developments in Monetary Policy

During the war and early postwar period, the Federal Reserve System recognized the limitations imposed on monetary policy by a commitment to fix the price of government securities, yet nonetheless strongly favored the support policy—certainly in all official statements and, so far as we can determine, unofficially as well. After all, the Treasury had been the active maker of monetary policy since 1933. The use of mone-

[16] For country member banks, there was (Nov. 24, 1960) an increase in required reserves against net demand deposits, which partially offset the additional reserve funds made available to them by the authorization to count all their vault cash as reserves. However, to avoid misunderstanding, it should be noted that the authorization to count vault cash as reserves cannot, without further evidence, be taken as equivalent in its effects on banks to either a reduction of reserve requirements of the kind formerly in effect by the same number of dollars or to an increase in reserve funds by the same number of dollars. See footnote 12 above; sects. 4 and 5 of Chap. 9; and Milton Friedman, "Vault Cash and Free Reserves," *Journal of Political Economy*, Apr. 1961, pp. 181–182. Haskel Benishay's criticism of Friedman's conclusion stated there is irrelevant ("Free Reserves Up or Level," *ibid.*, Aug. 1962, p. 403). While total required reserves did not change, authorization to count vault cash as reserves lowered required reserves at Federal Reserve Banks, and it is from that reduction that Friedman's conclusion—desired free reserves will increase—follows correctly.

tary powers primarily to facilitate government financing was a natural continuation. Moreover, it was a course of action the System had adopted in World War I, and that central banks the world over and ever since their rise to importance had found desirable in wartime. In its annual reports, the *Federal Reserve Bulletin,* and speeches and articles by Board members and employees and Bank officials, the System repeatedly defended its acceptance of responsibility for "the orderliness and stability of the Government securities market," and painted in dark tones the "widespread repercussions throughout the economy" that would result from "disorderly conditions in the market for Government securities," to quote from the *Annual Report* for 1947.[17] No doubt, the System wanted a somewhat different pattern of rates after the war— higher yields on bills and certificates than the yields prevailing during the war. As a result, differences arose with the Treasury. But the System's main aim was to devise some means whereby support of the government securities market would be rendered consistent with control over monetary conditions. It made repeated suggestions for legislation designed to render the two consistent, though it is doubtful that adoption of any or all the suggestions would, in fact, have accomplished it.[18]

An announcement in June 1949 by the Federal Open Market Committee, issued after consultation with the Treasury, that its operations in the future would be conducted "with primary regard to the general business and credit situation" while continuing the "policy of maintaining orderly conditions in the Government security market, and the confidence of investors in Government bonds," was interpreted by some to mean a fundamental change in Federal Reserve policy, though the announcement was subject to a different interpretation.[19] Late in 1949, the System and the Treasury began to work increasingly at cross-purposes, though again the conflict reflected not so much a fundamental

[17] Pp. 3 and 8. See also references in Chap. 10, footnote 27.

[18] See Board of Governors of the Federal Reserve System, *Annual Report,* 1945, pp. 7–8; 1946, pp. 6–7; 1947, pp. 7–11; 1948, pp. 4–7. See also footnote 25, Chap. 10.

[19] To Senator Paul H. Douglas, the June 1949 announcement was no indication that in the future the Treasury would consent to flexibility in Federal Reserve open market operations. See the examination of Chairman Thomas B. McCabe of the Federal Reserve System by Senator Douglas on Dec. 3, 1949 (*Monetary, Credit, and Fiscal Policies,* Hearings, pp. 493–494).

"Senator Douglas: This is my point: Did not that announcement or decision mean at the time it was issued [June 1949]—namely, one of recession or inventory adjustment—that securities would not be sold and did it not, therefore, tend to keep down or to depress interest rates and, therefore, of course, would it not be acceptable to the Treasury? But does it follow that, because the Treasury agreed at this time that the Treasury will go along with primary regard to the general business and credit situations in other periods?

"If we were in a period of inflation and were to carry out this policy, it might

difference in belief about the role the System should play, but rather lack of agreement on the detailed yields on government securities it should support.[20]

---

mean—it would mean to the degree that the Federal Reserve Board exercised its powers—the sale of securities, a rise in the interest rate, and a fall in the prices of Government securities.

"In other words, the instance of cooperation which you choose was one which was very happy from the Treasury point of view, when there was no conflict between the two purposes in a period of depression. But would this cooperation necessarily continue in a period of inflation?

"Mr. McCabe: The acid test of relationships and even of partnerships, Senator, comes when you have to meet a critical situation in the future. I am going on the assumption that this was an agreement made by men of understanding and good will and that it means what it says.

"Senator Douglas: This is not a statement of policy for an indefinite period of time. I think it is somewhat indefinite in language; but certainly, whatever it means, it does not mean the two bodies are bound forever.

"Mr. McCabe: To the Federal Reserve, it means flexibility.

"Senator Douglas: That in periods of inflation the interest rate will be increased and, if necessary, the prices of Government securities depressed?

"Mr. McCabe: That the open-market operations will be flexible—

"Senator Douglas: Flexible both ways?

"Mr. McCabe: And that we will conform to the economic situation with which we are confronted.

"Senator Douglas: You will have flexibility both ways?

"Mr. McCabe: Both ways.

"Senator Douglas: Do you think the Treasury so understands it?"

[20] At the end of 1949, the Federal Open Market Committee decided to increase short-term rates as an indication that a policy of monetary ease had shifted to a policy of mild restriction. The Treasury's version of the situation that followed is given in its reply, dated Feb. 12, 1952, to the questionnaire, circulated by the Joint Committee on the Economic Report, on the role of monetary and debt management:

The Federal Reserve thought it should act at once to meet the changing economic situation. In early January of 1950 it recommended that short-term rates be moved up once again—from the $1\frac{1}{8}$ per cent 1-year rate to $1\frac{1}{4}$ per cent on a 14-month note. The Treasury was not sure that this was desirable so soon and felt that caution was called for. It might be unwise to clamp down immediately upon the upturn in business which had barely started. The Treasury agreed, however, to go along with a gradual raising of the certificate rate. The first step toward this was taken with the issue dated February 1.

The Treasury also had some doubts about the wisdom of putting pressure on the long-term bond market during this period, such as was resulting from Federal Reserve selling. The Federal Reserve had reduced its Government bond holdings by $3¾ billion during 1949. Now in early 1950, the Treasury was uncertain as to how much additional selling pressure the long-term market could stand. Our analyses in the first half of the year showed that there was no substantial net demand for Government securities on the part of long-term institutional investors. The bonds sold by the Federal Reserve were acquired by nonbank investors primarily by switches from short-term issues. Nevertheless, the Federal Reserve sold $1.6 billion of bonds during the first half of 1950. It increased its holdings of short issues by over $1 billion, however, with the result that the total portfolio of the System declined by less than $600 million (*Mone-*

THE TREASURY—FEDERAL RESERVE ACCORD

The conflict was sharply intensified by the outbreak of the Korean War in 1950: the war brought, on the one hand, a speculative boom which raised market rates and so once again meant that support of government securities at prior levels would lead to an expansion in the money stock the Reserve System could not control; and, on the other, a possibility of large government deficits, which made the Treasury exceedingly sensitive to the state of the market for government securities.

As we have seen, despite a rapid rise in the System's holdings of government securities, the money stock did not rise drastically. Furthermore, no substantial government deficit emerged; tax receipts rose at as rapid a rate as expenditures could be increased. But neither fact was clear at the time; the pace of economic expansion and the rise in prices, both dramatically accelerated, were far more visible features of the economic landscape.

The episode involving the September-October refunding, when the Reserve System despite earlier announcements had to buy a large part of the issue to prevent its utter failure, brought matters to a temporary head. A compromise was reached: the System agreed to forego further increases in the short-term rate and in member bank reserve requirements until completion of Treasury refunding on December 15, 1950, and January 1, 1951; and the Treasury consented to offer in exchange for maturing obligations a five-year 1¾ per cent note, one of the two longest government obligations issued since the 1945 Victory Loan (the other was a five-year 1½ per cent note issued in March 1950). The new issue was not a success. A large fraction of the maturing issues was either bought by the Federal Reserve or had to be redeemed by the Treasury for cash.

The Treasury viewed the result as an indication of lack of Reserve cooperation. Conferences followed in January and February, attended by President Truman, Treasury and Reserve officials, the chairmen of the two banking committees of Congress, and the chairman of the Joint

---

tary Policy and the Management of the Public Debt, Replies to Questions, Part 1, pp. 65–66).

President Allan Sproul of the Reserve Bank of New York, commented:

The Treasury evidently thought that our arguments for credit restraint were being made known to the market and were resulting in downward pressure on prices and upward pressure on yields of Government securities. We observed, on the other hand, that the Treasury was adopting the practice of announcing forthcoming offerings of securities weeks instead of days in advance of the actual offering date, thus in effect committing us to continuous support of existing market conditions if the offerings were to be successful (*Monetary Policy,* Hearings, p. 519).

Committee on the Economic Report. Early in March an agreement was reached, by the terms of which the Federal Reserve was relieved of responsibility for supporting the government security market at pegged prices. Under the terms of the Accord, the Treasury in April exchanged a 2½ per cent bond for a 2¾ per cent bond. During the exchange, the System continued support purchases but at declining prices; after the exchange, only modest purchases were made through June to prevent disorderly conditions; and during the last half of the year practically no long-term bonds were bought, and active support of the short-term market was withdrawn.

The dire consequences the System had earlier predicted would follow abandonment of support at rigid prices, and which some unofficial commentators continued to predict, up to and beyond the Accord itself, did not follow.[21] The market quickly adapted itself to fluctuations in the prices

[21] In Jan. 1950 the Douglas subcommittee report summarized official views as follows:

> Treasury and Federal Reserve officials have advanced a number of reasons for the policy of holding down the yields and supporting the prices of Governments in the face of inflation. (1) Such a policy holds down service charges on the Federal debt . . . . (2) The maintenance of relatively stable prices on Governments helps to maintain confidence in the public credit and facilitates Treasury sales of securities for both new financing and refunding purposes . . . . (3) The maintenance of stable security prices protects investors against capital depreciation and prevents any loss of public confidence in financial institutions, including banks, that might result from a serious decline of these prices. (4) Any marked decline in the price of Governments would be communicated to other parts of the credit market and might bring about unemployment and deflation by interfering with the flotation of new private securities. And (5) any feasible rise of the yields on Governments would be so ineffective as an anti-inflationary measure as not to be worth its cost (*Monetary, Credit, and Fiscal Policies*, Report, p. 26).

Predictions of unofficial commentators were based on one or another of the above objections to the removal of support prices. For example, Seymour E. Harris: "A rise of rates of 2–4 per cent might achieve a great deal; but it is dubious that one of ¼–½ per cent would result in much beyond a partial demoralization of the securities market, with investors awaiting further declines in prices and rises in rates" ("The Controversy over Monetary Policy," *Review of Economics and Statistics*, Aug. 1951, p. 181). Alvin H. Hansen: "If the Reserve System should abandon altogether its support of an 'orderly market,' long-term bonds might then fall to a very low figure. A drastic decline in security values opens, however, a prospect sufficiently frightening so that we can be quite sure that in fact no responsible monetary authority (Federal Reserve and Treasury combined) would stand by and allow it to happen" (*ibid.*, p. 192). James Tobin: "It may well be, therefore, that effective monetary policy would require such a large and rapid increase in interest rates that the accompanying capital losses would be almost as unpalatable to holders of liquid assets as inflation itself" (*ibid.*, p. 198). Roy Blough (then a member of the Council of Economic Advisers): "Over the longer run, in my opinion, this is a high-saving economy and a low-interest-rate economy . . . . But why is this situation a matter of any concern? Why not have high interest rates now and low interest rates when we need them? The difficulty is that interest rates in the past have not adjusted downward with sufficient rapidity

of government securities without any financial crisis. The abandonment of support at rigid prices did, of course, change the character of government securities, rendering them a less close substitute for money. As a result, there was a shift in the composition of the public's assets, government securities declining slightly relative to money, as we have already noted.

The public and personal character of the events leading up to the Accord has given the episode the appearance of a straight conflict between agencies, each impressed with its own special responsibilities and problems. From this point of view, the Federal Reserve System finally succeeded in freeing itself from the shackles with which the Treasury had earlier bound it and reattained its long desired former independence. This melodramatic view misrepresents the situation fundamentally, though it contains an element of truth. The Federal Reserve could not fail to be impressed in the course of its day-to-day operations by the limitations the support program imposed on its monetary actions and to desire a greater degree of leeway. The Treasury, in its turn, under the day-to-day exigencies of debt management and the need to raise funds to refinance debt issues as they became due and, in addition, faced with the possibility of having to finance a deficit, could not fail to be impressed by the advantages of a ready residual buyer and of low interest charges. Yet, as we have seen, the bond-support program originated partly in the Reserve System, which wholeheartedly supported it. A few years after the Accord, the Treasury was to become a strong advocate of an unsupported government bond market and of the desirability of paying whatever interest rate was required, rather than holding down the rate when the cost might be an inflationary expansion of the money stock. Moreover, even up to and beyond the Accord, it is by no means clear that the Reserve System sought abandonment of the support program rather than achievement of minor flexibility in support levels. Not until two years after the Accord did the System explicitly forswear support of the prices of government securities as an aim of policy.[22] The internal logic of events, more than principles espoused

to meet the changing needs . . . . Another reason for avoiding high-interest rates is that the continually rising interest rate which might be necessary for the Government to outbid the market might result in placing actually less securities in the hands of the public than if a lower interest rate had been maintained . . ." (testimony, Mar. 14, 1952, *Monetary Policy*, Hearings, p. 253).

[22] See footnote 10, above. That action was taken some two years after the Accord and is the first official statement for the record of the abandonment of a support policy. It is therefore further evidence that it is neither what the Accord necessarily signified nor what the Reserve System interpreted it as signifying at the time.

Chairman Martin stated on Jan. 27, 1956, that it was not until Sept. 24, 1953 (when the second provision in footnote 10, above, was re-enacted, after having been rescinded by the Federal Open Market Committee on June 11, 1953) that "we had arrived at the point where we hoped we did not have to ever again

by the System, made the Accord the first step in the abandonment of the support program.

The unfolding of a similar sequence throughout most of the world is further evidence that the forces leading to the change in the role of monetary policy symbolized by the Accord were much more basic than a conflict between agencies. At the end of the war, dominant intellectual opinion in the United States and abroad assigned a minor role to monetary policy. As a result of the Great Contraction, of the widespread success of the Keynesian revolution in academic economic thought, and of the experience with wartime controls which succeeded in suppressing some of the manifestations of the accumulation of money balances, the view was accepted that "money does not matter," that the stock of money adapted itself passively to economic changes and played a negligible independent role. Further, the major postwar problem was widely assumed to be prevention of deflation and depression, not inflation. The wartime accumulation of liquidity was regarded as providing a highly desirable source of postwar purchasing power. The sole role assigned to monetary policy was to keep interest rates low and thereby to facilitate or perhaps, rather, not to hinder investment. This was the view not only within the Federal Reserve System in this country but also in most western countries.[23] It led throughout the world, as it did in the United States, to postwar monetary policies stressing low interest rates—to "cheap-money policies"—though the exact form of the policy differed from country to country.

Events belied expectations. Country after country was bedeviled by inflation, the United States to a much smaller extent than most. Under the pressure of inflation, both ideas and policies changed. The countries that maintained cheap-money policies continued to be plagued by inflation; at least some that abandoned such policies—notably Italy in 1947 and Germany in 1948—succeeded in stemming it. Monetary

---

directly support Treasury securities;" that from the time of the Accord, until Sept. 1953, "we gradually worked in that direction. You see, it was an evolutionary process" (Senate Committee on Banking and Currency, *Nomination of William McChesney Martin, Jr.,* Hearings, 84th Cong., 2nd sess., p. 15).

[23] A particularly clear statement of this view was given by E. A. Goldenweiser, then director of research for the Board of Governors, in a speech on postwar problems and policies, printed in the Feb. 1945 *Federal Reserve Bulletin* (pp. 112–121). Goldenweiser dismissed inflation as something "we are likely to escape in this postwar period," and said, "A much more serious and lasting problem . . . will be the problem of finding jobs for people released from the services and from war industries." With respect to monetary policy, he said, ". . . we must in the first place maintain the value of Government bonds . . . . This will have to be one of the financial cornerstones. . . . This country will have to adjust itself to a 2½ per cent interest rate as the return on safe, long-time money, because the time has come when returns on pioneering capital can no longer be unlimited as they were in the past."

policy came to be assigned a more important role and cheap-money policies to lose their attractiveness. The tendency was further fostered by developments in economic thinking which raised doubts about some of the more extreme conclusions drawn from Keynesian analysis.[24] In the United States, renewed interest in monetary policy was fostered also by failure of the 1948–49 recession to develop into a serious decline and then received a sharp fillip from the apparent impotence of the Reserve System, so long as prices of government obligations were supported, to take effective action to stem the inflation associated with the Korean War. The subsequent subsidence of the price rise and the failure of serious consequences to follow from termination of the support of government bond prices further enhanced the prestige of monetary policy and encouraged a continued shift toward assigning it a greater role.

POLICY CRITERIA TO REPLACE SUPPORT OF GOVERNMENT BOND PRICES

Rigid support of prices of government securities was clearly a defective criterion for monetary policy. But it had the operational advantage of being definite and precise, of specifying fairly narrowly the actions required to conform to it, and of leaving little leeway for discretion. Its abandonment required the Reserve System to formulate, explicitly or implicitly, the criterion or criteria to be adopted in its place to guide policy actions. The heightened importance attached to monetary policy gave the task increased urgency. In many ways the System was in the same position as in the early twenties. Now, as then, the dominance of Treasury financing considerations had been overthrown. Now, as then, the gold position gave much leeway and seemed an almost irrelevant consideration for short-term policy.

On the basis of the sometimes slight hints garnered from the System's annual reports, from Congressional testimony, and other published documents, we infer that two criteria were more or less explicitly considered and that an amalgam constituted the main guide to policy

[24] In particular, the developments leading to recognition of the so-called "Pigou effect." See G. Haberler, *Prosperity and Depression*, 3rd ed., Geneva, League of Nations, 1941, pp. 242, 403, 491–502, and *idem*, "The Pigou Effect Once More," *Journal of Political Economy*, June 1952, pp. 240–246; A. C. Pigou, "The Classical Stationary State," *Economic Journal*, Dec. 1943, pp. 343–351, and *idem*, "Economic Progress in a Stable Environment," *Economica*, n.s., Aug. 1947, pp. 180–188; J. Tobin, "Money Wage Rates and Employment," in *The New Economics*, Seymour Harris, ed., New York, Knopf, 1947, pp. 572–587, esp. 584–585, and *idem*, "Asset Holdings and Spending Decisions," *American Economic Review*, Papers and Proceedings, May 1952, pp. 109–123; D. Patinkin, "Price Flexibility and Full Employment," *American Economic Review*, Sept. 1948, pp. 543–564, reprinted in a revised version in *Readings in Monetary Theory*, F. A. Lutz and L. W. Mints, eds., Philadelphia, Blakiston for American Economic Association, 1951.

627

for most of the fifties until, toward the end of the decade, the problem of gold began to come to the fore, and prevention of gold outflows to compete with both.

One criterion was that of providing for the appropriate secular growth of the stock of money. In the *Annual Report* for 1952, the Board of Governors defined the System's objective as follows: "to restrict bank credit and monetary expansion to the growth needs of the economy." Again, from the same *Annual Report:* "Federal Reserve credit policy in 1952 was designed to limit bank credit expansion to amounts consistent with the requirements of a growing economy operating at a high level without inflation." The principle is echoed in the January 1954 *Economic Report of the President:* "Also required is a supply of money in keeping with the increase in the physical volume of production and trade. Such a growing money supply is necessary to prevent the development of deflationary pressures, to maintain equity values, and to keep the purchasing power of the dollar reasonably stable."[25]

These statements may seem innocuous or trite. They are neither. They represent a near-revolutionary change. So far as we have been able to learn from either published documents, the Hamlin Diary, the Goldenweiser Papers, or the Harrison Papers, the System had never officially or unofficially regarded the behavior of the money stock, as such, as a relevant immediate criterion of policy, though of course individuals within the System no doubt did. As we have repeatedly noted, the System had been concerned almost exclusively with the credit aspects of its operations—in the sense of their effects on interest rates, availability of funds in the market, the cost and availability of credit—not with changes in the stock of money. From this point of view, the support policy was cut from the same cloth: it differed from the historical policy of the System primarily in its rigidity. The earlier position had been that appropriate rates of interest and conditions in the credit market varied from time to time, in accordance with a host of factors whose net effect could only be determined by "judgment."

The System had been concerned with changes in demand deposits and in currency outstanding, primarily because of their effects on the demand for Reserve Bank credit or on the reserve position of member banks, and because these in turn affected the ease or tightness of the money market, i.e., the market for loans and investments. It had been dismayed during the two wars at the enormous expansion in the money stock and had persistently opposed "greenbackism." So it had clearly recognized in those contexts the link between the stock of money and

[25] Board of Governors of the Federal Reserve System, *Annual Report,* 1952, pp. 1, 2; *Economic Report of the President,* 1954, p. 6.

prices. Yet those considerations are all very different from taking the change in the money stock as a relevant immediate criterion of policy. They are all consistent with what we take to have been the central principle of the System: if the "money market" is properly managed so as to avoid the nonproductive use of credit and to assure the availability of credit for productive use, then the money stock will behave correctly and can be left to take care of itself.[26]

A striking bit of evidence on the minor role assigned by the Federal Reserve System to changes in the stock of money is its neglect until relatively recently of statistical data on the stock of money. Despite the mass of monthly and even weekly data on production, prices, interest rates, and the like published by the System since its establishment, reasonably comprehensive figures on the stock of money at intervals so short as a month were first published in 1944, and figures adjusted for seasonal variation, not until 1955.[27]

To the best of our knowledge, the first explicit reference in the System's annual reports to changes in the money stock occurred in 1948. The references can be interpreted as meaning that quantitative changes in the money stock are relevant to Federal Reserve policy in their own right, and not simply as indirect reflections of conditions in credit markets.[28] Statements like those quoted above from the 1952 *Annual Report* have been made fairly regularly since then by Chairman William McChesney Martin, Jr. They give the impression that providing an average rate of growth of the money stock matching or appropriate to the secular rate of growth of output, though not dominant in short-term policy, has become a background aim of the System.[29]

In referring to the stock of money, the System has generally used

[26] See also Chap. 9, sect. 4, discussion of this point.
[27] *Banking and Monetary Statistics*, published in 1943, made available comprehensive figures for two dates a year, 1923–41, for June dates, 1892–1922 (see pp. 34–35). But even these were only retrospective; they had not been published periodically before.
[28] Board of Governors of the Federal Reserve System, *Annual Report*, 1948, pp. 18–20; 1949, pp. 22–24; 1950, pp. 21–23; 1951, pp. 19–21.
[29] For example, see various statements of Chairman Martin of the Board of Governors in testifying before Congressional committees.
On Feb. 3, 1954, he said ". . . there are certain factors in the money supply that have to be adjusted at every point . . . . There is . . . the growth factor in the economy, and as to 'growth' there has been a lot of talk about 3 per cent or 4 per cent as being an approximate growth figure . . . . [T]here has been some publicity given to us because we did use in our spring projection a figure of 3 per cent, which got out to the press. There is no harm in its getting out, but that does not mean that we will follow that particular percentage at another time" (Joint Committee on the Economic Report, *January 1954 Economic Report of the President*, Hearings, 83d Cong., 2d sess., pp. 122–123).
On Jan. 20, 1956, in hearings on his nomination for a full term of 14 years,

a concept—the sum of currency held by the public and demand deposits adjusted—narrower than the one we designate by that term. That narrower total was the only one it regularly published in seasonally adjusted form from March 1955 to August 1962. In the latter month, it began publishing also time deposits adjusted at commercial banks in seasonally adjusted form. While the *Federal Reserve Bulletin* through 1962 had not presented a seasonally adjusted total of currency held by the public plus demand and time deposits adjusted in commercial banks—which is our concept of money stock—it is now obtainable directly from that source.[30]

The references to achieving the appropriate secular rate of growth of the money stock have not usually been accompanied by a specific statement of what that rate is, or how it is to be determined. Chairman Martin once expressed himself as favoring a 3 per cent rate of increase

---

he said: "We have to have an expanding money supply generally with a growing country" (*Nomination of William McChesney Martin, Jr.*, p. 3).

On Dec. 11, 1956, he was questioned by Senator Joseph C. O'Mahoney (Joint Economic Committee, Subcommittee on Economic Stabilization, *Monetary Policy: 1955-56*, Hearings, 84th Cong., 2d sess., p. 127).

"Senator O'Mahoney. What I have been trying to find out, unfortunately without ‑success, all day long is: What is the yardstick by which you measure the amount of money that ought to be created?

"Mr. Martin. Well, the yardstick—there is no firm yardstick, but we have looked on the normal growth of the country in terms of perhaps 2, 3, 4 per cent, no fixed formula, and we have added to the money supply generally for that purpose."

On Aug. 14, 1957, Martin told the Senate Committee on Finance, "I think we have a responsibility for [economic] growth. We should increase the money supply to provide for that growth" (Senate Committee on Finance, *Investigation of the Financial Condition of the United States*, Hearings, part 3, 85th Cong., 1st sess., p. 1301).

In an opening statement to the Joint Economic Committee on July 29, 1959, he said: "In this review [of Federal Reserve experience and of the effects of its operations upon the market and the banking system], we were naturally mindful of the specific tasks of the System: namely, to regulate the growth of the money supply in accordance with the economy's needs. . . ." (*Employment, Growth, and Price Levels*, Hearings, part 6A, p. 1235).

[30] The *Bulletin* also presented regularly a total and its separate components broader than our concept of money—including time deposits in mutual savings banks and in the Postal Savings System, in addition to the components in our concept—but only in seasonally unadjusted form. That total has not been shown since Aug. 1962, at the time of writing, but only a still broader total—in addition to the items just listed, foreign bank deposits and U.S. government balances (similar to column headings in Table A-3)—also in seasonally unadjusted form only. The number of variants possibly reflects the following comment by Martin: ". . . I live with the money supply, our staff lives with the money supply, and I find it very difficult to know what the components of it really [last two words transposed in source] are and how they will change. I think all of us have to study a great deal more before we can say positively and precisely that this is what constitutes the money supply" (Joint Economic Committee, *January 1961 Economic Report of the President and the Economic Situation and Outlook*, Hearings, 87th Cong., 1st sess., Mar. 7, 1961, p. 483).

in the narrow money total the System designated the money supply, but later testified that it was unwise to have used that figure.[31]

The second criterion, which came to dominate short-term policy, was that the System should aim at producing countercyclical variation in credit conditions and, explicitly, in the money stock: that it should "lean against the wind" by taking restrictive action during periods of economic expansion, and expansionary action during periods of economic contraction. That criterion was much more traditional; it was one of the themes of the *Tenth Annual Report* and had always been recognized as precept despite its frequent violation in practice. Now it was given far more prominence than ever before, almost completely burying the "needs of trade" doctrine with which it had been so uneasily harnessed in the *Tenth Annual Report*.[32] The countercyclical theme in the fifties was generally described in terms of avoiding either inflation or deflation, and explicit attention was given to changes in the stock of money, unlike earlier versions which emphasized exclusively changes in the credit market.[33]

Despite numerous public statements indicating that the policy of the System was to "lean against the wind," there was little discussion of the precise content of the policy. For example, there was essentially no discussion of how to determine which way the relevant wind was blowing. Yet, the System explicitly recognized that the relevant wind was not the current one, but the wind that would be blowing when the policy measures adopted now affected the course of events which, as we have repeatedly seen, is generally months later. Neither was there any discussion of when to start leaning against the wind. Yet, when the wind first changes direction, certainly from declining to expanding business, the System would want to help it along rather than counter it. There was

[31] See House Ways and Means Committee, *Public Debt Ceiling and Interest Rate Ceiling on Bonds*, Hearings, 86th Cong., 1st sess., June 10–12, 1959, p. 173; and *Employment, Growth, and Price Levels*, Hearings, part 6A, p. 1330.

[32] About the only relic of the needs of trade doctrine was the occasional expression of concern with "speculation" and "use of bank credit for speculative purposes." See *January 1954 Economic Report of the President*, Hearings, p. 125; Board of Governors of the Federal Reserve System, *Annual Report*, 1961, p. 5.

[33] For example, Martin was asked in Aug. 1957 what the System was doing currently to curb inflation. He answered: "We are looking at a growth factor in the economy, and we think that growth factor should normally be in the neighborhood of 3 or 4 per cent. In excess of that is, we think, too much. We have let the money supply—of course, these figures sometimes are changed, because you add time deposits to demand deposits, but we usually eliminate time deposits from these figures—we have let the growth of the money supply slow down to about 1 per cent. We have let the balance of the 2 per cent on our 3 per cent growth take place out of the velocity of money, the turnover of money, and we have felt that that was about right, though I think sometimes we felt that perhaps we have erred a bit on the side of letting the velocity accumulate faster—it is very difficult to measure—than the situation warranted" (*Investigation of the Financial Condition of the United States*, Hearings, part 3, pp. 1306–1307).

more comment, but hardly any of it specific about how hard to lean against the wind. The System's policy measures were all quantitative and could be applied in greater or lesser measure. In straight descent from the *Tenth Annual Report,* the System regarded the decision as one that had to be based on the balancing of numerous imponderables, which had best be left to the informed "judgment" of the men in charge and could not be explicitly formalized.[34]

After the gold stock began to decline in 1958, and especially after the decline assumed the proportions of a major flight in late 1960, there was, as noted above in section 2, something of a repetition of earlier experience: great concern with preventing further outflows and a tendency to subordinate other objectives to that end, as in 1920 and in 1931. However, the other objectives were given far more weight this time and, perhaps equally important, the System's autonomy from general political influences was much weaker. Both reflected the same phenomenon: the acceptance of full employment as a major goal of general economic policy and the assumption of responsibility by government for its achievement.

"BILLS ONLY" OR "BILLS PREFERABLY"

In the course of 1953, a dispute arose between the Board of Governors and the Federal Reserve Banks, particularly the New York Bank, about open market tactics. At the meeting of the Federal Open Market Committee in March, a number of changes in operating procedure were adopted, including the provision that "under present conditions, operations for the System account should be confined to the short end of the market (not including correction of disorderly markets)."[35] At the June meeting, that provision was stricken from the operating rules by a vote of five Federal Reserve Bank presidents to four members of the Board, the other two members of the Board being absent.[36] In September, the provision was re-enacted,[37] only two Bank presidents voting against the action, one being Allan Sproul of New York.

---

[34] See statements by Chairman Martin: "Our purpose is to lean against the winds of deflation or inflation, whichever way they are blowing . . ." (*Nomination of William McChesney Martin, Jr.,* p. 5); "We have to lean against the wind, whichever way the wind is blowing" (Senate Committee on Finance, *Investigation of the Financial Condition of the United States,* Hearings, part 6, 85th Cong., 2d sess., Apr. 23, 1958, p. 1929). On recognition of the time lag in application of Reserve policies, see *ibid.,* p. 1949. On the importance of judgment, see *ibid.,* part 3, p. 1261 ("The work of the System requires a continuous study and exercise of judgment in order to be alert to the way the economy is trending . . .").

[35] Board of Governors of the Federal Reserve System, *Annual Report,* 1953, p. 88. For two other changes in operating procedure adopted at that meeting, see footnote 10, above.

[36] The provision in the second paragraph, quoted in footnote 10, above, was also stricken.

[37] Also the one referred to in preceding footnote.

632

The policy then adopted was adhered to until February 1961 and came to be known as the "bills only" policy, although in 1960 Federal Reserve spokesmen emphasized that it was actually a "bills preferably" policy.[38] The System's justification for the policy was that bills have a broader, more nearly perfect market than other government securities and hence that, in restricting its operations to this market, the System interferes least with the operation of the securities market. By restricting its purchases and sales to one type of security, the System need decide only "how much," not also "what kind." It argued that decisions on the kind of securities to purchase would involve it in determining the structure of rates, a type of activity closely akin to the maintenance of a pattern during the war. It defended itself against the charge that restricting its operations to bills implicitly determines the structure of rates by arguing that the securities market is so fluid and interconnected that the effects of purchases or sales in any part of the market are transmitted very rapidly to all other parts. But, of course, this also means that the structure of rates would not be affected by departure from the "bills only" doctrine and hence removes an argument for as well as one against that doctrine. It argued further that the major effect of its actions is on bank reserves and thence on the total stock of money, and that the pattern of rates is affected much less by the

---

[38] See R. A. Young and C. A. Yager, "The Economics of Bills Preferably," *Quarterly Journal of Economics,* Aug. 1960, pp. 341–373. The Federal Reserve System departed from its "bills only" policy for the first time in Nov. 1955, again in July 1958, and again in Nov. 1960. In 1955 it bought $167 million 12-month Treasury certificates and could have bought twice as much again, under the authorization issued by the Federal Open Market Committee. "The specific occasion for an acquisition of certificates rather than bills was to facilitate a large-scale Treasury refunding operation at a time of stringent money market conditions not foreseen when the terms of the Treasury refunding were decided upon" (Board of Governors of the Federal Reserve System, *Annual Report,* 1955, p. 8).

Incidentally, see Senator Paul H. Douglas' cross-examination of Chairman Martin on the episode (*Nomination of William McChesney Martin, Jr.,* pp. 6–25). Douglas, who was concerned with the fact that there had been an acquisition—not with its maturity—was critical of Martin and the eight other Federal Open Market Committee members who voted for the purchase—in response to Treasury requests—although monetary policy at the time was restrictive.

In July 1958 the Open Market Committee "concluded that the market situation had become disorderly and decided to intervene temporarily in the medium- and long-term sectors of the Government securities market" (*Annual Report,* 1958, p. 7). The intervention followed the collapse of speculative activity connected with the issue in June 1958 of the 2⅝ per cent bonds of 1965. The System then bought $1.1 billion of 1⅝ per cent 12-month Treasury certificates—in a $16.3 billion refunding operation of three called issues of Aug. 1958—$110 million of "rights" of maturing securities, and in addition some securities other than Treasury bills.

In the two weeks ending Nov. 9, 1960, the System added $1.2 billion of government securities to its portfolio, including securities other than bills with maturities no longer than 13 months (see also *ibid.,* 1960, pp. 5, 69).

kinds of securities the System purchases or sells, in the first instance, than by the assets banks acquire or dispose of in reacting to the gain or loss in their reserves.[39]

From the point of view of the effect of Federal Reserve action on the stock of money, what matters, in the first instance, as the System quite properly stated, is only the amount of high-powered money created, which is determined by the size of open market operations, not by the kind of securities bought or sold. The kind of securities bought or sold can have an effect on the stock of money only through the effect, if any, of changes in the market structure of interest rates on the deposit-reserve ratio banks seek to attain. If the bills only policy has nonetheless aroused considerable controversy, it is largely because of the tendency we have noted on the part of economists and others to emphasize the "credit" effects of monetary policy rather than the "monetary" effects, which is to say, the effects on the structure of interest rates rather than on the stock of money. The major criticism levied against the bills only policy was that the System was denying itself an instrument, considered potent by the critics, for affecting economic activity, namely, affecting the relative yields on long- and short-term securities.

The central issue raised by bills only is really the internal division of responsibility among different government authorities, and it arises only because of the largely arbitrary—which does not mean unimportant —division of responsibility for debt management between the Federal Reserve and the Treasury. In the absence of any restrictions on the terms at which the Treasury can issue securities, bills only does not limit at all what the Treasury and Federal Reserve System can do jointly. Suppose the authorities desire to add to high-powered money by reducing the amount of long-term securities in the hands of the public. Given the bills only policy, the System cannot do this alone simply by buying long-term securities; instead it buys bills; the Treasury then sells the same amount of bills and uses the proceeds to retire long-term securities. Alternatively, suppose the authorities desire to reduce high-powered money by increasing the amount of long-term securities in the hands of the public. Under the bills only doctrine, the Reserve System does not sell such securities to the public directly; it sells bills instead. The Treasury sells the same amount of long-term securities and uses the proceeds to retire bills. In each case, the consolidated

[39] Deane Carson, "Recent Open Market Committee Policy and Technique," *Quarterly Journal of Economics,* Aug. 1955, pp. 335–341; W. L. Smith, "Debt Management in the United States," Study Paper no. 19, *Employment, Growth, and Price Levels,* Joint Economic Committee, 86th Cong., 2d sess., Jan. 28, 1960, pp. 118–134. See also W. W. Riefler, "Open Market Operations in Long-Term Securities," *Federal Reserve Bulletin,* Nov. 1958, pp. 1260–1274.

634

balance sheets of the Federal Reserve System and the Treasury, on the one hand, and of the public at large—including commercial banks and other financial institutions—on the other, will be identical, whether the operation is conducted by the Reserve System alone without the bills only policy, or by the Reserve System and the Treasury together with that policy. In these terms, the bills only policy consists of assigning responsibility for the maturity distribution of the debt to the Treasury— an allocation of responsibility that seems eminently reasonable.

Of course, there are restrictions on the terms at which the Treasury can issue securities. The most important, dating from legislation in 1918, and the one that was the source of extensive controversy is the legal ceiling of $4\frac{1}{4}$ per cent on the rate of interest at which the Treasury can issue marketable securities with a maturity of more than five years. That restriction was the fundamental reason for the bitterness and extent of the controversy over bills only, although some of the participants may not have seen the connection. The legal ceiling was well above the market rate and hence of no practical significance in the first decade after World War II. The rapid rise in interest rates after 1956, however, changed the situation. By September 1959, the market rate on long-term government securities exceeded the legal ceiling on the interest coupon. The Treasury repeatedly requested Congress to remove the limit and Congress repeatedly refused.[40] After February 1960, market rates of interest declined, and the pressure to raise or remove the legal ceiling on the interest coupon abated. Later in the year, however, bills only became a political issue in the Presidential campaign. Shortly after the change of administration, the Federal Reserve abandoned the policy, and the Treasury announced that, if necessary, it would abolish the interest rate ceiling by offering at a discount new Treasury securities of more than five years' maturity bearing a coupon at the legal rate.[41]

[40] It is ironic that Senator Douglas, who played such an important role in the termination of the support program through the investigation he headed in 1949–50 and who was so consistent and vigorous an opponent of that program, should in 1959 have been foremost among those opposed to the removal of the limitation on the interest rate at which the Treasury could sell long-term securities, a limitation that is logically equivalent to a support policy. Douglas rationalized his position by arguing that while there was no logical justification for the interest rate ceiling, market interest rates were in fact at or above the legal ceiling only because of inept monetary policies, of which he regarded bills only as one, and that failure to consent to removal of the ceiling was an effective political expedient to bring pressure on the monetary authorities to revise their policies. See *Congressional Digest*, Nov. 1959, pp. 267, 269, 271, for Senator Douglas' speech, made on the floor of the Senate on June 8, 1959, opposing the administration's request that the interest rate ceiling on long-term U.S. debt be raised.

[41] A statement in opposition to bills only was made by John F. Kennedy during his Presidential campaign. The Federal Reserve abandoned the rule in Feb. 1961. The decision to resume dealing in issues of various maturities was made, according

In the absence of bills only, the legal ceiling on the interest rate on long-term Treasury securities could readily have been evaded through joint action by the Federal Reserve System and the Treasury, without resort to selling securities at a discount. Suppose the monetary authorities desired to float a long-term issue but could not without paying a higher yield than the 4¼ per cent interest coupon permitted by law. The Treasury could issue the security at terms permitted by law, sell it to the Federal Reserve at par, either directly or indirectly via market intermediaries, and the Federal Reserve could then resell the security or sell a comparable security from its portfolio at the market price. The capital loss recorded by the System would be simply a bookkeeping entry serving to reduce the amount the System pays the Treasury out of Federal Reserve earnings; the consolidated books of the Federal Reserve and the Treasury would be the same with respect both to the balance sheet and the income account as if the Treasury had been able to conduct the operation directly.

The Federal Reserve and the Treasury were understandably loath to use that device in face of the unwillingness of Congress to repeal the interest rate ceiling. Bills only was therefore, in effect, a policy that, by explicitly ruling out such a cooperative evasion, made effective a legally imposed limitation on debt management—the precise reason the policy was so much criticized.

The abandonment of bills only in 1961 was linked to fears about the gold outflow. Stemming the gold outflow called for high interest rates to induce foreigners to hold dollar balances; the domestic business contraction called for expansionary monetary action. One policy the Board hoped would reconcile the two contradictory objectives was to alter the structure of rates: to keep bill rates high in order to foster the holding of dollar balances, and to keep long-term rates low in order to foster domestic business expansion. The bills only policy was abandoned to enable the System to pursue its new policy by buying long-term securities and selling, or not buying, short-term securities. The Treasury, on its part, adjusted the maturity structure of the obligations it issued to foster the same result.

---

to the announcement, "in the light of conditions that have developed in the domestic economy and in the U.S. balance of payments with other countries," and the determination as to which offerings of securities to buy would be "governed by the prices that appear most advantageous, i.e., the lowest prices" (New York Times, Feb. 21, 1961, pp. 49, 58, and Board of Governors of the Federal Reserve System, Annual Report, 1961, p. 43).

The Treasury cited an interpretation by the Attorney General as authority that it was lawful to use the device of advance refunding as a means of issuing new Treasury bonds at yields in excess of 4¼ per cent. The device had been used by the Treasury in the Eisenhower Administration, but no bond had been offered at yields in excess of the nominal ceiling.

4. Why the Stable Rate of Growth of the Money Stock?

This detailed examination of the trees leaves unanswered the question about the forest raised at the outset of this chapter. Why is it that the rate of change in the money stock was so highly stable? Was it purely coincidence?

While we are not prepared to deny coincidence a role, and perhaps an important one, two other factors may have contributed to the result, though we are most uncertain that they provide a fully satisfactory answer. One such factor may well have been the availability since 1944 of monthly data on the money stock itself, referred to earlier. It has meant that changes in the stock of money *could* be taken into account, though quite clearly the money stock has been only one of many factors the System has taken into account.

It could be argued that, in the interval between adoption of the bond-support program in 1942 and the Accord in 1951, the money stock was outside the control of the System, and hence the availability of figures on its behavior was irrelevant for at least that period. However, this view seems unduly superficial. Had large changes in the money stock, in prices, or in other economic indicators occurred sooner than they did, strong pressure to abandon the rigid bond-support program would also have arisen sooner than it did. It may be coincidence that such pressure did not arise until 1950. It does not follow that the stable behavior of the stock of money before 1951 is also attributable to coincidence. Suppose the kinds of pressure that arose in 1950 had arisen in 1948 or 1949. The main result might have been simply an earlier abandonment of the rigid bond-support program, with roughly the same degree of stability as that experienced in the behavior of the stock of money. Whatever forces account for the relative stability from 1951 on would have started operating sooner.

Another factor which may have played a role was the combination of uncertainty on the part of the monetary authorities about their role and about the consequences of their actions, together with unmatched public attention to the course of economic events. That meant that the monetary and other economic authorities were being subjected to constant scrutiny and held to high—perhaps impossibly high—standards. The combination induced a tendency to move slowly in either direction, to be more vigorous in pronouncements than in actions. At the same time, together with the greater availability of data, it meant that sharp movements in the money stock figures would not long go unnoticed or unattended to, as they had on occasion in the past.

The importance of this factor is attested to by developments in the later years of the period. Progressively, the Reserve System and the informed public came to attribute more significance to monetary changes, and the Reserve System came to have more confidence in being able to predict the consequences of its own actions. As a result, it began to move more vigorously. There are signs in the money stock series in Chart 52 of growing variability in the amplitude of change as the period wore on. Our figures show that the slowing up of the rate of growth of the money stock in 1956–57 was almost as great as in 1952–53, and in 1959–60 it was greater than in 1952–53; the expansion in 1958 was greater than in 1954, and in 1960 almost as great as in 1958. There are therefore some signs that the period of high stability in the rate of change in the money stock may be a passing phase.

Though the growing variability has primarily reflected the greater confidence of the System in the efficacy of monetary changes, it may also have reflected partly an unintended and cumulative element arising from the lag between monetary action and effect. The stepping up of the rate of monetary growth in 1954 probably did not have its full effects until 1955 and 1956. When those effects were manifest in the form of price rises, the Reserve System was led to counteract the rises by slowing up the rate of growth of the money stock. Having perhaps overreacted in the first instance, it was led to overreact still more in the second. But again, these effects were not manifest until 1957 and 1958, and in their turn produced a still larger reaction in the form of an exceedingly rapid rate of growth of the money stock in 1958. That growth once again led to a sharp reaction in 1959 on the part of the Reserve System, which itself contributed to the brevity of the business cycle expansion. The halting pace of the expansion, in its turn, produced the sharp reversal of monetary policy in March 1960. These Reserve System actions helped to prevent a protracted contraction following upon the unduly early termination of the 1958–60 expansion. Instead, the contraction was extremely brief and mild, running from May 1960 only to February 1961.

If this interpretation has any validity, it leads to the somewhat paradoxical conclusion that confidence in the efficacy of monetary policy in the 1950's was inversely related to monetary stability. As that confidence has grown, it has produced a growing instability in the stock of money. Hopefully, the process is not explosive but self-limiting.

CHAPTER 12

The Postwar Rise in Velocity

FOR THE student of money, the most distinctive feature of the postwar period and the one that has attracted most discussion and comment is the sharply rising trend in the velocity of money noted in section 1 of Chapter 11 and recorded in Chart 52. From an all-time low of 1.16 in 1946, velocity of money rose to a postwar high of 1.69 in 1960, a level that had not been equaled since 1930 except for the early war years 1942 and 1943. The contrast with earlier experience is sharp. As far back as our figures go, the general tendency is for velocity of money to decline secularly at a rate that has averaged slightly more than 1 per cent per year over the nine decades from 1869 to 1960 (Chart 57). We are inclined to attribute the secular decline to the associated rise in per capita real income, that is, to view the services rendered by money balances as a "luxury" of which the amount demanded rises more than in proportion to the rise in income.[1] But incomes have continued to rise in the postwar period, hence there is no reason on this score why the long-term trend should not have continued.

Viewed in the long-term perspective provided by Chart 57, the postwar rise is the second of two surprisingly similar episodes, both at variance with earlier behavior. The unprecedented collapse in the velocity of money from 1929 to 1932 is roughly matched by the corresponding collapse from 1942 to 1946; the rise from 1932 to 1942, interrupted from 1937 to 1940, is roughly matched by the rise from 1946 to 1960, interrupted from 1951 to 1954. As Chart 58 demonstrates, though the second movement has persisted for a somewhat longer period than the first, the two episodes are alike not only in general pattern and in the magnitude of the total rise and fall, but even in some of their minor

[1] The secular trends in velocity of money and real income alone are not strong evidence for that interpretation, because the trends have been predominantly in a single direction and hence constitute, as it were, only a single observation. The two trends might have independent explanations and their movement in opposite directions be a coincidence. Our confidence in the statement in the text derives from the conformity of the relation suggested by the trends with other evidence, notably the relation between per capita deposits and per capita income from state to state in individual years, as analyzed in detail by Edward Feige in a doctoral dissertation in process at the University of Chicago, and the relation between velocity and income between countries and over time for countries other than the U.S.

639

CHART 57
Interest Rates and Two Measures of Velocity, Annually, 1869–1960

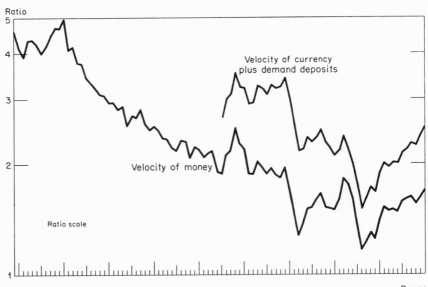

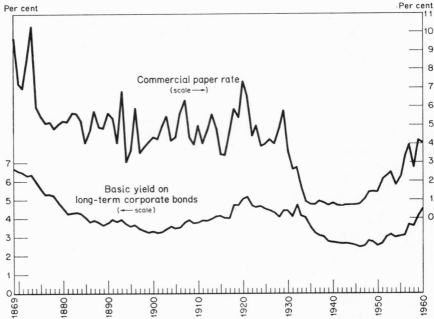

SOURCE: Velocity, Table A-5. Commercial paper rate, averaged annually from monthly data, through Jan. 1937 from F. R. Macaulay, *Some Theoretical Problems Suggested by the Movements of*

CHART 58

Velocity of Money, 1929–42 and 1942–60, Superimposed

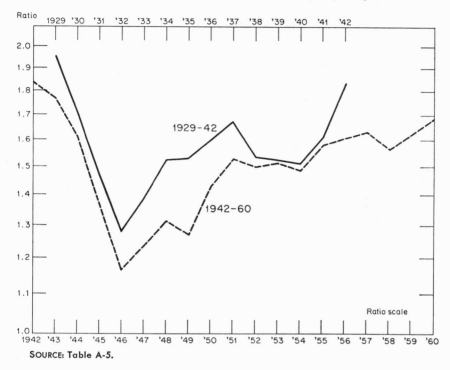

SOURCE: Table A-5.

movements. As befits episodes superimposed on a declining trend, the second movement occurs around a lower level than the first.

In this perspective, the postwar rise appears to be largely a reaction to the prior fall, just as the rise from 1932 to 1937 or 1942 appears to be a reaction to the fall from 1929 to 1932. But why did the velocity of money fall so sharply from 1929 to 1932 and again from 1942 to 1946,

Interest Rates, Bond Yields and Stock Prices in the United States since 1856 (New York, NBER, 1938), pp. A145–A161; thereafter, from monthly averages of weekly figures from Bank and Quotation Record of *Commercial and Financial Chronicle.*

Long-term interest rate, through 1899, averaged annually from monthly data for railroad bond yields from Macaulay, pp. A145–A152, col. 5, with 0.114 per cent arithmetic addition to raise averages to the level of the following segment. From 1900 on, basic yields of corporate bonds to 30-year maturity: 1900–42, David Durand, *Basic Yields of Corporate Bonds, 1900–1942* (NBER, Technical Paper 3, 1942); 1943–47, Durand and W. J. Winn, *Basic Yields of Bonds, 1926–1947: Their Measurement and Pattern* (NBER, T.P. 6, 1947); 1948–51, *The Economic Almanac, 1953–1954* (National Industrial Conference Board), p. 119; 1952–58, Durand, "A Quarterly Series of Corporate Basic Yields, 1952–57..." (*Journal of Finance,* Sept. 1958), p. 349; 1959–60, unpublished estimates by Scudder, Stevens & Clark.

and why did the recovery take so long? In these terms, the puzzle is less why the velocity of money was "so high" in 1955 to 1960 than why it was so low and so variable during the preceding twenty-five years.

Though the unusual behavior of the velocity of money during that quarter-century had its inception in the sharp response to the cyclical contraction of 1929–33, there is little unusual in the behavior of the velocity of money in the course of subsequent business cycles; what is unusual is its behavior over periods encompassing several cycles. As we have seen for earlier periods, velocity generally rises during business expansions and falls during business contractions. The sharp downward secular trend in the velocity of money before 1929 meant that the fall during business contraction tended to be larger than the rise during business expansion, and that business expansion frequently was characterized by a lower than average rate of decline rather than by an actual rise. The same pattern of a rise relative to trend during business expansions and a fall relative to trend during business contractions is observable for the period since 1932, except for the sharp decline during the final years of the wartime expansion, 1942–45. For the rest, the main difference from earlier periods is only that the cyclical reaction was superimposed on a strong upward longer-term movement, so the rises were decidedly larger than the declines. Velocity reached absolute peaks in 1937, 1948, 1953, 1957, and 1960, along with business, and in each case declined subsequently during the business contraction. Annual data like those in Charts 57 and 58 are, of course, crude instruments for judging cyclical movements. However, the conclusion they suggest—that the cyclical movements in velocity since 1932, both before and after the war, are not dissimilar to earlier movements—is confirmed by the available quarterly and monthly data.

Aside from the postwar period, the velocity of money has apparently borne precisely the opposite relation to real income over cycles as over secular periods. Over cycles, velocity has moved in the same direction as per capita real income; over secular periods—at least until World War II—in the opposite direction. In a study reported on elsewhere, one of us has shown that the difference between the cyclical and secular relation can be explained by supposing that the amount of money the public wishes to hold is determined by the longer-term expected or permanent levels of income and prices, rather than by current income and prices, as measured by statisticians.[2] According to this interpretation, the secular decline in the velocity of money has been a reaction to a rise in longer-term expected or permanent per capita real income. The cyclical rises and falls have reflected fluctuations in current income and prices,

[2] Milton Friedman, *The Demand for Money: Some Theoretical and Empirical Results,* National Bureau of Economic Research, Occasional Paper 68, 1959.

as measured by statisticians, around their long-term expected levels, rather than cyclical changes in the longer-term magnitudes themselves.

Suppose holders of money, whether individuals or business enterprises, adjust their holdings not to their current receipts or to current prices but to the receipts and prices they expect to prevail over a somewhat longer future period. This difference will be of little significance for long-period data; over decades the expected or permanent magnitudes will move in the same direction as the measured magnitudes. But the difference will be important over cycles. In a cyclical expansion, measured income will presumably rise decidedly more than permanent income. The stock of money might therefore rise more than in proportion to permanent income, as it does over longer periods, yet less than in proportion to measured income, as it does over cycles.

A statistical relation embodying this distinction between measured and permanent magnitudes, which was computed for the period 1870–1954, was highly successful in reproducing both cyclical and longer-term movements in the velocity of money. As the discussion of Chart 58 suggests, it has been as successful in reproducing postwar cyclical movements as it has in earlier periods, but it has failed to reproduce the general postwar trend of velocity. The statistical relation, extended to 1960, shows a continuation of the long-term downward trend, not the clear upward trend of the actual velocity figures. That discrepancy poses the problem of the present chapter.

In our discussion of the wartime period, we cited a number of special circumstances of the time as contributing to the wartime decline in the velocity of money. The unavailability of consumer durable goods during the later war years induced individuals to accumulate liquid assets instead. With respect to these goods, effective prices were certain to fall after the war, since their current prices were essentially infinite. There was, therefore, an incentive to accumulate money and other liquid assets to be used later to purchase goods not currently available. The expectation of a postwar general price decline and the fear of a severe postwar depression worked in the same direction. The high wartime mobility of people and the frequent difficulty of acquiring goods when and as desired made high money balances more desirable than they would be in ordinary times for current purposes and not only as a store of value intended for future purchases. And presumably other factors were at work as well. Given that wartime phenomenon, an immediate postwar reaction involving the working down of excess balances of liquid assets in general and of money in particular was only to be expected (see Chapter 10, above). What is puzzling is why the reaction should have taken so long. The rise in the velocity of money to 1948, or perhaps even to 1951, might be explainable along these lines, but surely not the failure of the long-term downward trend in the velocity of money to reassert itself thereafter. Why should velocity instead have continued to rise? Or, equivalently, why should money balances, expressed in terms of the number of months' income to which they correspond, have continued to fall?

The holding of money balances sometimes involves direct costs: for currency—accidental loss, theft, safe-deposit fees; for deposits—service charges and losses through default by banks. Money balances may also yield direct returns in monetary form or in forms capable of being easily expressed in monetary terms: interest,[3] and services rendered by banks to depositors—such as clearing checks, or implicit or explicit assurance that a loan will be available on demand, or the encouraging of borrowers to purchase the depositors' products. The algebraic sum of these items per dollar of money, where returns are regarded as positive and costs as negative, is the net direct return to money. It may be positive—when money may be said to yield a monetary return on the average—or negative—when money may be said to involve a monetary cost on the average. In addition to these direct costs and returns, money yields nonpecuniary services—the reason individuals and business firms are willing to hold money instead of other assets that yield a higher direct return. The amount of money (in real terms) individuals and business firms will want to hold, i.e., the volume of monetary services they will choose to buy, will depend on the value they attach to the monetary services, on the one hand, and on the cost of such services, on the other, including both the direct cost— if the sum of returns and cost is negative—and the indirect cost incurred by the sacrifice of higher returns which could be obtained by holding assets in other forms.

Most students attempting to explain the continued postwar rise in velocity have attributed it to either of two circumstances: (1) a greater rise in the return on alternative assets than in the net direct return on money, and hence a rise in the amount sacrificed to acquire monetary services; or (2) a reduction in the value attached to monetary services because of institutional changes which have created closer substitutes for money than formerly existed or have widened the availability of such near-moneys, with special emphasis on savings and loan association shares and short-term government securities. As we shall see, while these factors may be capable of rationalizing the postwar movement, they cannot explain the similar upward movement in velocity from

---

[3] Some demand deposits paid interest before 1933; time deposits have throughout; even currency has at times paid interest, as did the 5 per cent Treasury notes issued during the Civil War (W. C. Mitchell, *A History of the Greenbacks*, University of Chicago Press, 1903, pp. 174–175).

1932 to 1942. Furthermore, that explanation for the postwar period would require attributing to the factors listed a far greater importance than they seem to have exerted in earlier decades. As a consequence, we are inclined to regard them as explaining at best only a minor part of the postwar movement and to accept instead an alternative interpretation that emphasizes (3) a decline in the value attached to monetary services because of changed expectations of holders of money about the likely degree of future economic stability.

1. *Changes in the Return on Alternative Assets*

The relation between the return on wealth held in the form of money and held in the form of other assets depends, of course, on the particular other assets considered. Two broad classes must be distinguished: assets fixed in nominal amount, such as government interest-bearing securities or private fixed-dollar obligations; "real assets," such as real property or commodities or corporate equities. For both classes, the return consists of two parts: (1) the direct money yield in the form of interest on securities, dividends on equities, rent on real property; and (2) the rate of change in the price of the assets, which may, of course, be positive or negative. The second part is not significant for many fixed-dollar securities; it is significant mostly for long-term securities or for lower-grade securities on which risk of default is fairly large. The rate of change in price may, however, be much the more important of the two parts of the return to real assets, particularly during periods of rapid changes in the general price level. The returns relevant for asset choices are, of course, not actual but expected returns. Actual returns are relevant only insofar as they affect expectations. In the postwar period, the returns on both alternative classes of assets have clearly risen more than the direct return on money has.[4] Rates of interest on fixed-dollar

---

[4] It has become customary to refer to the algebraic difference between the return on some alternative asset and the return (positive or negative) on money as the "cost of holding money" or the "cost of monetary services." That sense is quite different from the ordinary use of the term cost. When we speak of the cost of automobile travel, we refer to the absolute expenditures per mile of travel, not to the difference between such expenditures and the cost of traveling a mile by some other means. In the usual sense of the term, the cost of monetary services is the negative of what we have been calling the net direct return on money. The returns on other assets are comparable to what, in speaking of the demand for most goods and services, we would refer to as the costs or prices of other goods and services which might be substitutes or complements or neither.

The reasons for the special usage with respect to money are twofold. First, it is common to neglect the direct returns and direct costs, and hence to regard the direct price of monetary services or return from money as zero. The cost of money in the usual sense, then, is a constant throughout and disappears from the analysis. Second, there has been a widespread tendency to use theoretical models in which all assets are classified into either two categories—money and bonds—or three categories—money, bonds, and real assets—with only one price or two prices of

obligations have risen sharply. At the same time, the legal prohibition on payment of interest on demand deposits and the legal restrictions on the maximum rate that may be paid on time deposits in commercial banks—both dating from the Banking Act of 1933, for member banks, and from regulations of the Federal Deposit Insurance Corporation in 1934 and the Banking Act of 1935, for insured nonmember banks—have prevented any fully offsetting rise in interest received on money. As noted in section 1 of Chapter 11, the postwar period has seen a shift from a widespread expectation that prices would fall sharply to an equally widespread expectation that they would continue to rise. These two changes are of course not independent. The sharp rise in interest rates on fixed-dollar obligations relative to the net current yield on equities presumably reflects directly the shift in expectations about likely movements in commodity prices.

Chart 59 plots for the period 1929 to 1960: the yield on long-term securities; the commercial paper rate; the difference between the yield on bonds and the yield on equities, which may be regarded as a rough index of the expected rate of change in prices;[5] velocity of money; and the velocity of currency plus adjusted demand deposits alone—a concept to which we shall return.

For the postwar period alone, the evidence summarized in this chart is entirely consistent with the view expressed by a number of writers that the rise in yields on alternative assets, by inducing holders of money to economize on money balances, was the major factor accounting for the postwar rise in velocity.[6] Since 1946, the rise in the velocity of money has been accompanied by a sharp rise in both long- and short-term interest rates and since 1950 in the difference between bond and equity yields.

Even for the postwar period, however, this interpretation has a serious

---

other relevant assets. The second tendency is the counterpart of the tendency to speak of "the" interest rate.

To avoid confusion, we shall use "alternative cost" to refer to the difference between the returns on other assets and on money.

[5] See comment in Chapter 11, p. 599.

[6] See H. A. Latané, "Cash Balances and the Interest Rate—A Pragmatic Approach," *Review of Economics and Statistics,* Nov. 1954, pp. 456–460; also "Income Velocity and Interest Rates—A Pragmatic Approach," *Employment, Growth, and Price Levels,* Joint Economic Committee, Hearings, part 10, 86th Cong., 1st sess., pp. 3435–3443 (reprinted with minor changes in the *Review of Economics and Statistics,* Nov. 1960, pp. 445–449); J. G. Gurley, "Liquidity and Financial Institutions in the Postwar Period," Study Paper No. 14, Study of *Employment, Growth, and Price Levels,* Joint Economic Committee, 86th Cong., 1st sess., Jan. 25, 1960, GPO, 1960, pp. 3–57; James Tobin, "The Interest-Elasticity of Transactions Demand for Cash," *Review of Economics and Statistics,* Aug. 1956, pp. 241–247.

CHART 59
Yields on Selected Assets Alternative to Money Holdings, and Two Measures of Velocity, 1929–60

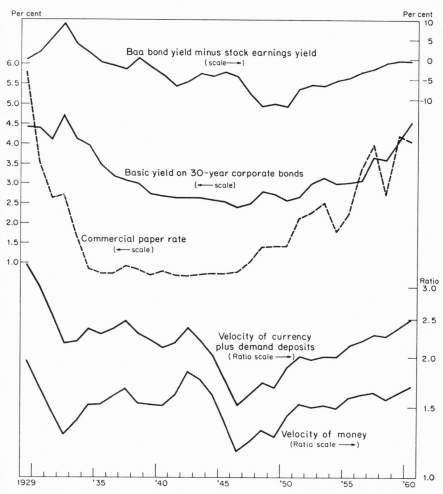

SOURCE: Bond yield minus stock earnings yield, i.e., earnings-price ratio for 125 industrial common stocks computed from data in Moody's *Industrial Manual, 1961* (New York, Moody's Investors Service, 1961), p. a26, subtracted from the annual yield on Baa industrial bonds, *ibid.*, p. a21. Other data, same source as for Chart 57.

defect; it explains too much. If interest rates account for the later postwar rise in the velocity of money, presumably they had a similar effect in the earlier postwar period. But the velocity rise in the earlier postwar years, as we have seen, can be accounted for as simply a recovery from abnormally low wartime values, so the interest rate explanation is superfluous.

For the period as a whole, the interpretation has the opposite defect. It does not explain the earlier rise in the velocity of money, from 1932 to 1942, since interest rates remained low or were falling during that period and, while there was some rise in commodity prices, the difference between the bond and equity yields shows no close relation to the movement in velocity. Interest rates might be regarded as explaining the initial decline in velocity from 1929 to 1932, but they clearly play no part in the decline from 1942 to 1946. In consequence, if the rate of return on alternative assets is accepted as explaining the postwar movement in the velocity of money, some other explanation will have to be found for the earlier movements.

We turn now to a more detailed analysis of the relation between the postwar rise in the velocity of money and changes in the rate of return on alternative assets. In this analysis we shall examine separately interest rates and the rate of change in prices.

INTEREST RATES

If the postwar movement in the velocity of money has been primarily a response to changed interest rates, then velocity or, equivalently, the quantity of money demanded must be highly sensitive to the rate of interest. From 1946 to 1960, velocity rose by 45 per cent; yields on long-term governments, from a bit above 2 to a bit above 4 per cent or by about 2 percentage points; basic yields on long-term corporate bonds, by about the same amount; and the commercial paper rate, from under 1 per cent to over 4 per cent, or by about 3.5 percentage points. If the velocity change was a response to the interest rate change, then each percentage-point rise in the long-term rate of interest produced a rise of about 22½ per cent in the velocity of money and each percentage-point rise in the short-term rate of interest, a rise of about 13 per cent in the velocity of money. These may, of course, be overestimates because they make no allowance at all for the postwar reaction to the wartime decline in velocity; on the other hand, they may be underestimates because they make no allowance for the postwar increase in income that, in light of earlier evidence, presumably tended to produce a decline in the velocity of money. That decline, in terms of the interpretation under consideration, was more than offset by the coincidental rise in interest rates.

648

No such sensitive relation between interest rates and velocity is evident for the longer period for which we have data, as is clear even from the time series of interest rates and velocity plotted in Chart 57. More systematic evidence is furnished by multiple correlations we have computed between the amount of money demanded, expressed in constant prices, real income, and various rates of interest, for both cycle averages and annual data extending over periods up to more than ninety years in length. In some correlations the long-term bond yield displays the most consistent statistical connection, in others, the short-term rate on commercial paper. However, the estimated effect of either is much too small in magnitude to explain the postwar rise in velocity. A 1 percentage-point rise in the bond yield or in the commercial paper rate has been associated, on the average of the longer period, with a 3 to 4 per cent decline in the amount of money demanded, rather than with the 13 to 22½ per cent change required to rationalize postwar behavior. This conclusion is also suggested by Selden's work on the determinants of velocity.[7]

A study by Latané[8] is the only one we know that not only attributes the postwar movement in velocity to interest rate changes but also presents empirical evidence to support the conclusion that the postwar relation is the same as the prewar. Latané analyzes the velocity of a narrower monetary total than the one we have termed "money." For the narrower monetary total, including only currency and adjusted demand deposits, and for the period from 1909 to 1958, he finds a very close relation between velocity and interest rates, a relation that seems not to have changed over the period. He finds no need to introduce the level of real income as an additional variable. Interest rates alone suffice to account for a large fraction of the variation in the velocity of currency plus demand deposits adjusted.

In order to facilitate a reconciliation of Latané's results with ours, we have plotted in Charts 57 and 59 velocity figures calculated for the narrower total of currency and adjusted demand deposits.[9] We have

---

[7] Richard T. Selden, "Monetary Velocity in the United States," *Studies in the Quantity Theory of Money,* Milton Friedman, ed., University of Chicago Press, 1956, pp. 195–205.

In a more recent study (*The Postwar Rise in the Velocity of Money,* New York, NBER, Occasional Paper 78, 1962, reprinted from the *Journal of Finance,* Dec. 1961, pp. 506, 522), Selden advances the hypothesis that the cost of borrowed funds is the proper measure of the alternative cost of holding money, and that changes in the rates charged by banks on short-term loans to business from 1951 to 1957 are "fully adequate to account for velocity rises of the order actually experienced." However, Selden does not present any evidence for that period or for a longer one to support his assertion.

[8] See footnote 6, above.

[9] Use of the narrower total is often defended on the grounds that only the items it contains are a medium of exchange, that time deposits in commercial banks can be used to make payments only if they are first converted into either

made separate estimates of demand and time deposits only beginning June 1914, which is why the velocity of currency plus demand deposits adjusted is plotted in Chart 57 only from 1915 on. It is clear from Chart 57 that both the major and the cyclical movements of velocity of currency plus demand deposits adjusted parallel the corresponding movements of the velocity of money. With respect to these movements, the behavior of the two concepts is interchangeable, and any explanation offered for the velocity of money is equally relevant for the velocity of currency and demand deposits adjusted. In particular, insofar as the distinction between measured and permanent income serves to explain the cyclical movements of the velocity of money, it explains equally the cyclical movements of the velocity of currency plus demand deposits adjusted. The major difference between the two velocities is in intermediate movements during the twenties, the thirties, and the fifties. In the twenties, the velocity of currency plus demand deposits adjusted had a rising trend, the velocity of money, a declining trend. In the thirties, after 1932, the reverse was true: the velocity of currency plus demand deposits adjusted had a horizontal or falling trend, the velocity of money, a rising trend. After 1946, both had a rising trend, but the rise of velocity of currency plus demand deposits adjusted was somewhat steeper.

All the divergences are readily accounted for. The divergence during

---

currency or demand deposits. Two points need to be made about such statements. (1) The implicit criterion for choosing the total to which to apply the term "money" is by no means clearly appropriate. Money is a term that has been used to refer not solely to a medium of exchange but also and, in our view more basically, to a temporary abode of purchasing power enabling the act of purchase to be separated from the act of sale. Just where the line should be drawn between assets regarded as money and those regarded as near-moneys or simply as "other assets" is not something that can or should be decided either once for all or on the basis of verbal considerations. It must depend on the purpose and on the empirical relevance of a particular distinction for that purpose under specific circumstances, which is to say, on the empirical stability and regularity of relationships between the chosen total and other variables. (2) While broadly correct, the distinction asserted is not strictly accurate in fact. What are called time deposits have on many occasions been subject to transfer by check. Some components of currency cannot in fact be used as a medium of exchange without first being converted into either other currency or demand deposits, for example, $10,000 bills. Items not included in either total are used as a medium of exchange, for example, American Express travelers' checks, debit balances of stock market brokers (see Chap. 6, p. 277, above).

Our own view is that the question of definition is not a matter of principle but of expediency, and that the basic problem is to avoid confusion and misunderstanding which inevitably arise because the same word is used in different senses. Relations that hold for one total called money may not hold for another total called by the same name. The difference may reflect no conflict of substance, only a difference of terminology. That is why we have tried to use the word money to refer to the same concept throughout this volume, and to use different language to refer to any other concept.

the twenties was the result of changed conditions of supply of deposits introduced by the Federal Reserve System, which for the first time imposed lower legal reserve requirements against time deposits than against demand deposits. Banks were thereby induced to increase the attractiveness of time deposits, with the result that member bank time deposits grew appreciably relative to member bank demand deposits. That development was a cause of concern to the System, as we saw in Chapter 6, particularly because one of the techniques used by the banks was to reduce the operational difference between demand and time deposits.

The divergence during the thirties had the same explanation operating in the opposite direction. Legal reserve requirements declined in importance to banks in comparison with the prudential reserves they desired to maintain, as reflected in the extraordinary accumulation of so-called excess reserves. At the same time, interest rates the banks could earn on their assets declined. Both led banks to reduce the relative attractiveness of time deposits by gradually lowering throughout the thirties the average interest they paid on them. True, prohibition of payment of explicit interest on demand deposits after 1933 worked in the opposite direction, but such payments had earlier been made largely on interbank balances, which are excluded from demand deposits held by the public, as we measure them. The prohibition was accompanied by a ceiling on interest payable on time deposits. Since a large fraction, if not most deposits held by banks had never paid explicit interest, it continued to be a possible and common practice to pay interest on demand deposits in the form of services rendered free of charge.

Since 1946, the chief factor accounting for the divergence between the slope of the upward trend in the velocity of money and that in the velocity of currency plus demand deposits adjusted has been the sharp rise in interest rates, accompanied by a change in bank reserve preferences. The interest rate rise has again made the different legal reserve requirements for demand and time deposits important to banks. Banks have had an incentive to offer a higher return on deposits, both demand and time, but the incentive has been greater for time deposits. Moreover, for the first time, prohibition of payment of interest on demand deposits has been economically effective, limiting the capacity of banks to attract demand deposits of that restricted class on which they might have been ready to pay explicit interest. Though the ceiling rates payable on time deposits imposed a similar limit, they were at first sufficiently high to be ineffective and later were raised (see section 2, below). Consequently, rates paid on commercial bank time deposits have risen sharply in the postwar period (see Chart 61, below). The result has been a sharp rise in the ratio of commercial bank time deposits to commercial bank demand deposits, and hence a slower rise in the velocity of money than in the velocity of currency plus demand deposits adjusted.[10]

As these latter comments suggest, the velocity of currency plus demand deposits adjusted, at least in the postwar period, may be more sensitive to interest-rate changes than the velocity of money is. A change in rates of return on other assets is likely to be reflected more fully in the rate of interest paid on time deposits than in the largely implicit rate paid on demand deposits, and will not be reflected in the return on currency at all. A similar phenomenon may well have been true even before prohibition of payment of interest on demand deposits, since most demand deposits other than interbank deposits, as noted above, did not bear explicit interest. It is therefore plausible that, both since the war and earlier, rising interest rates have induced a shift toward time deposits and falling rates an opposite shift. Latané's finding of a closer relation between interest rates and the velocity of currency plus demand deposits adjusted than we have found between interest rates and the velocity of money need therefore involve no conflict of results, but simply consistent answers to different questions.

Latané goes further. He argues that interest rates alone can account for all the changes in the velocity of currency plus demand deposits adjusted—random perturbations aside—since 1909 and, in particular, for the whole of the postwar rise. And this does conflict with our findings. In the first place, as Chart 57 indicates, from 1915 on the longer-term movement in the velocity of currency plus demand deposits adjusted is much the same as that in the velocity of money. We have attributed the latter primarily to changes in real income; Latané attributes the former entirely to changes in interest rates. In the second place, since about 1951, time deposits alone have risen relative to income and thereby have made for a decline in the velocity of money; hence the whole of the rise in velocity of money is attributable to the rise in the velocity of currency plus demand deposits adjusted. If the latter rise can be fully accounted for by interest rates, so can the former; but our separate analysis of it suggested that it could not be. Let us take up these two points in reverse order.

We cited two major reasons for considering the postwar rise in interest rates unsatisfactory as a full explanation of the postwar rise in velocity of money: failure of interest-rate changes to account for the other major movements in the velocity of money since 1929; and absence of any

[10] Our interest in the total we call money derives chiefly from the side of the demand for such assets on the part of holders of wealth. We conjecture that it is partly because the division between demand and time deposits has been so much affected by the kind of changes in supply conditions discussed in this and the two preceding text paragraphs that we find a generally more stable relation between the total we call money and other economic magnitudes than between the sum of currency and demand deposits adjusted and the same economic magnitudes.

sufficiently strong influence of interest rates over the longer period covered by Chart 57. Do these reasons hold also for the velocity of currency plus demand deposits adjusted?

The answer given by Chart 59 for the period since 1929 is less clear and decisive for that velocity than it is for the velocity of money, yet on balance the same. Interest rates cannot explain the sharp decline in the velocity of currency plus demand deposits adjusted from 1942 to 1946, or the rise from 1932 to 1937. One contradiction for the velocity of money in 1935–42 is not present for the velocity of currency plus demand deposits adjusted, for in those years the latter velocity has roughly the same horizontal trend as the commercial paper rate. Nevertheless, it is true for both velocities, 1929–60, that only the initial decline and the terminal rise clearly parallel corresponding movements in interest rates. These are sizable movements for both velocities, yet they constitute, at most, two observations to set against the erratic inverse relation for the rest of the period covered by Chart 59.

For the longer period, we have no estimates of the velocity of currency plus demand deposits adjusted before 1915. However, we know enough to demonstrate rather conclusively that that velocity must have declined sharply from 1880 to World War I, and hence must have experienced the same long-term movement as the velocity of money did.[11] Interest

[11] In 1914, commercial bank time deposits amounted to less than 30 per cent of the money stock. Velocity of currency plus demand deposits adjusted was therefore $\frac{3}{7}$, or 43 per cent, higher than was the velocity of money. Suppose—to take the extreme possibility which produces the maximum discrepancy between movements of the two velocities—that commercial bank time deposits were zero in the years 1875–80. Then the velocity of currency plus demand deposits adjusted at that date would have been the same as the velocity of money. Even by this extreme supposition, the velocity of currency plus demand deposits adjusted would have been over 4 from 1875 to 1880, and about 3 from, say, 1910 to 1914, and so would have declined by about $\frac{1}{3}$.

In discussing long-period movements, Latané refers to Kuznets' reservations about the year-to-year accuracy of his annual net national product figures, 1869–89, which are the numerator of the ratio constituting the velocity of money figures ("Income Velocity and Interest Rates," *Review of Economics and Statistics*, Nov. 1960, pp. 447–448). The year-to-year inaccuracies, however, are clearly irrelevant as a possible explanation of the secular decline in velocity. If the decline in velocity of roughly 50 per cent from 1869 to 1899 is to be accounted for by the use of faulty net national product data, this would imply that Kuznets' figure for 1869 is twice as large as it should be. Not only is such a large magnitude of error implausible, but also, as we argued in section 2 of Chapter 2, any error is almost surely in the opposite direction. The defects of the statistics made for an underestimate of income in 1869, and the pattern of Kuznets' figures from 1869 to 1879 indicates strongly that the 1869 estimate is an underestimate (worksheets underlying Simon Kuznets, *Capital in the American Economy: Its Formation and Financing*, Princeton for NBER, 1961). In consequence, our judgment is that the series in Chart 57 understates the magnitude of the decline in the velocity of money over the period as a whole.

Upward adjustment of the net national product figures in the early years would improve the consistency of the figures with Latané's interpretation in one respect,

rates, especially the commercial paper rate, and the velocity of currency plus demand deposits adjusted and also the velocity of money display the same general long-term movement since 1915. This relation, how-ever, does not hold for the velocity of money from 1880 to 1915 and equally would not hold for the velocity of currency plus demand deposits adjusted if figures for that concept could be plotted on the chart. We therefore conclude that for the velocity of currency plus demand deposits adjusted, as for the velocity of money, the broad range of evidence does not support a sufficiently elastic response of the corresponding money balances to interest-rate changes to make the whole of the postwar rise in the velocity of currency plus demand deposits adjusted attributable to the postwar rise in interest rates.

With respect to the role of income, the longer-period comparison seems decisive. We have just noted that the behavior of interest rates cannot account for the decline from 1880 to 1915 in either the velocity of money or the velocity of currency plus demand deposits adjusted. But if a rise in real per capita income accounts for these declines, as we have suggested it does, there is no reason to suppose that real income suddenly stopped having any effect in 1915 or thereabouts. It seems much more reasonable that, after 1915 as before, the rise in per capita real income tended independently to produce a more than proportional rise in the real amount that wealth holders demanded of both currency plus demand deposits adjusted and the broader total we term money; that that effect was more than offset during the twenties for the narrower total by the increasing spread between the attractiveness of time deposits and demand deposits, referred to earlier; that the effect of per capita real income was intensified in the thirties by the sharp decline in rates of interest; and that it has been offset to some extent in the period since the end of World War II by the rise in interest rates.[12]

---

however. As it stands, the velocity of money was roughly stable from 1869 to 1879, the decade when long-term interest rates fell most sharply. Adjusted for an under-estimate of income, the velocity of money figures would presumably decline during that period, though it would take an adjustment larger than seems at all plausible to produce a decline in the velocity of money in that decade as large as in subsequent decades.

See section 4 below for an alternative explanation of the low actual level of the velocity of money in the 1870's relative to the backward extrapolation of later trends.

[12] Selden suggests in his article on velocity by sectors that the operation of the income effect is limited to households only. This may be so. However, it is not at all clear that it is. Money balances may be a factor of production, the marginal productivity of which rises relative to other factors with an expansion of scale of both the individual enterprise and the economy. Selden's own cross-section data on firms of different sizes suggest that money balances have this property (see Selden, *Postwar Rise in the Velocity*, pp. 500–502, and 524, footnote 24. See also Fried-man, *The Demand for Money*, p. 8).

Income, like interest rates, may have an effect of different magnitude on each of the monetary totals. It is conceivable that the services rendered by time deposits are more of a "luxury" than those rendered by currency and demand deposits, and hence that the income elasticity of demand for the services of money is greater than that for the services of currency plus demand deposits alone. It is conceivable, too, that any such difference has been more important since 1915 than before. On the basis of the evidence to date, however, we remain skeptical that any such difference is so great as to justify regarding the velocity of currency plus demand deposits adjusted as independent of the level of per capita real income.

All in all, there is no irreconcilable conflict between Latané's results and ours. The appearance of conflict arises primarily from the different span of time covered by the two analyses and only secondarily from use of two different monetary totals. Had we analyzed solely the time period Latané covered, we too would have been led to assign greater importance to interest-rate changes and less importance to income changes than we have. Conversely, we conjecture that, had the relevant data been available to enable Latané to analyze the period we cover, he would have been led to assign greater importance to income changes and less importance to interest-rate changes than he does. These differences are intensified by the difference in monetary totals. It is plausible, though not yet demonstrated that: (1) the elasticity of demand for currency plus demand deposits adjusted with respect to rates of interest on other assets is higher in absolute value than the corresponding elasticity of demand for this total plus time deposits in commercial banks; and (2) the elasticity of demand for currency plus demand deposits adjusted with respect to real per capita income is smaller than the corresponding elasticity for time deposits, and hence than the corresponding elasticity for money.[13] Consequently, for either period, interest rates might well play more of a role and income changes less of a role in explaining movements in the velocity of currency plus demand deposits adjusted than in explaining movements in the velocity of money.

If a single explanation is to be used for the whole period, then, whether the analysis is concerned with currency plus demand deposits adjusted or with our concept of money, the movements in income and interest rates alone cannot explain the postwar rise in velocity. The postwar rise in both velocities is contrary to the first, and more rapid than the other variable alone could have been expected to produce.

There remains the possibility that the demand for money became more sensitive to movements in interest rates after World War II than it had

[13] In line with our analysis, the relevant concept of income is permanent rather than measured income.

been before. Two reasons have been cited why this might be so. (1) The prohibition of interest payments on demand deposits plus restrictions on rates commercial banks could pay on time deposits prevented them from passing higher interest rates on directly to depositors. That meant, it might be argued, that the rise in interest rates produced a larger differential between the rates paid on deposits and on other assets than a comparable rise would have produced at an earlier date. (2) An institutional change, it is said, occurred in corporate cash management, with corporations paying much greater attention than they had formerly to economizing on money balances. One reason cited for such a change is a factor we consider again in the next section: emergence of closer substitutes for money in the form of Treasury bills and other short-term securities, substitutes which have highly flexible rates and are outstanding in much greater volume and with a broader and better market than ever before. Their availability has, it is said, not only reduced the amount of money demanded at any given interest rate—the effect considered in the next section—but also increased the sensitivity of reaction to changed interest rates.

It may well be that these factors have worked in the direction of increased sensitivity to interest rate changes. However, it seems highly doubtful that they alone could have produced the great increase required to account for the postwar rise in the velocity of money, for two reasons. (1) In some studies of earlier periods, attempts have been made to take into account the interest paid on deposits by using as a variable, to measure the alternative cost of money, the difference between the rate earned on other assets and the rate paid on money. In the studies we know of, allowance for interest on deposits has generally produced a poorer rather than a closer relation, indicating that the effect of interest paid on deposits was sufficiently small to be swamped by the error in the estimates of its amount.[14] These results are not decisive, since the studies are for the period after 1919, and hence cover only a few years when banks were free to vary the rates paid. Conceivably, before 1919, interest rates on deposits varied more widely and responded more rapidly to changes in market rates. Such qualitative evidence as we have, however, gives no reason to suppose that this was the case; it suggests rather that, then as later, rates paid on deposits changed only very sluggishly relative to market rates. Moreover, in the post–World War II period, banks have been able to pass on to holders of demand deposits rises in the interest rate earned on their assets, to some extent through alterations in service charges, including no rise in service charges

[14] See Selden, "Monetary Velocity," pp. 199–203. James Ford has also computed correlations of the type referred to with similar results (in a study presented before the Money and Banking Workshop, University of Chicago, 1961).

656

as costs in general rose. Further, much of the rise in the velocity of money occurred before the date at which the legal limit on time-deposit rates became economically relevant or effective. (2) A decisive piece of evidence relevant to the role of institutional changes in corporate cash management is furnished by Selden's estimates of velocities for separate economic sectors. According to these estimates, based on flow-of-funds data, the rise in velocity was larger for the consumer sector than for the corporate sector, yet institutional changes suggesting greater sensitivity of money balances to interest rates seem restricted to the corporate sector.[15]

To summarize this discussion of interest rates: The postwar rise in interest rates could account at most for something like a 6 to 8 per cent increase in the velocity of money, if the pre–World War II relation between interest rates and the velocity of money held for the postwar period as well. There is no persuasive evidence of a decided increase in the sensitivity of the velocity of money to interest rates. In consequence, the postwar rise in interest rates can account at most for only a small part of the 45 per cent rise in velocity from 1946 to 1960.

RATES OF CHANGE IN PRICES

Failure has marked every attempt we know of to find a systematic relation between the quantity of money demanded in the United States and either the current rate of change in commodity prices or a weighted average of the past rates of change in prices, taken as an estimate of the rate of change expected to prevail in the future.[16] Yet Cagan has found a close relation for other countries for periods marked by substantial price movements.[17] The most plausible reason for the difference, in our view, is the small size of price changes in the United States except in wartime periods. As a result, while a significant relation may well be present in the United States, changes in other variables affecting the demand for money may readily have hidden it. The looked-for effect may have been too small in magnitude to be revealed by such blunt tools as multiple correlation analysis and the simple expectational model involved in taking a weighted average of past occurrences as an

[15] See Selden, *Postwar Rise in the Velocity,* pp. 488, 492. Selden notes that high-income households and personal trusts may be sensitive to yields on long-term tax-exempt securities and Treasury bills; high- and middle-income households, to yields on liquid fixed claims; and middle- and low-income households, to costs of consumer and mortgage credit (pp. 527–528).

[16] See Selden, "Monetary Velocity," pp. 202–203. In our work, we have experimented with such variables without success and so has James Ford.

[17] See Phillip Cagan, "The Monetary Dynamics of Hyperinflation," *Studies in the Quantity Theory of Money,* Milton Friedman, ed., pp. 25–117. Similarly striking results were obtained by John Deaver, "The Chilean Inflation and the Demand for Money," unpublished Ph.D. dissertation, University of Chicago, 1961.

indicator of the future. We expressed the view in Chapter 4 that different expected price trends may well have been one reason velocity fell less rapidly from 1902 to 1907 than from 1885 to 1891 (see Table 6 and the accompanying discussion).

The shift after World War II in expectations about price movements may well have been larger than shifts at any earlier period covered by our data.[18] Hence we cannot rule out the possibility that it played an important role. In order to get some idea about the possible magnitude of its effect, we may draw on Cagan's results for other countries. One way is to ask how large a change in expectations about price movements would be required to account for the observed change in the velocity of money, given the relation between velocity and expected price change that Cagan found for other countries. The answer, using Cagan's estimates for seven hyperinflations as a group, is that the expected rate of change in prices, expressed as an instantaneous annual rate, would have had to change by 95 percentage points—e.g., from an expected fall at the rate, say, of 45 per cent per year to an expected rise at the rate of 50 per cent per year—to account for the rise in the velocity of money from 1946 to 1960.[19] This is almost certainly an overestimate of the re-

---

[18] Cagan was unable to find any close relation between price movements and the quantity of money demanded in wartime periods preceding the seven hyperinflations in European countries he studied ("Monetary Dynamics of Hyperinflation," p. 61), yet these periods displayed in general much higher rates of price rise than those experienced in the United States. His evidence suggests that there is a long lag between the occurrence of substantial price rises and the development of widespread expectations of further price rises.

The reason for supposing that there may have been a sizable shift in expectations in the United States is therefore not that the community extrapolated war and postwar experience. It is rather the point made in the preceding chapter, that post–World War I experience plus the Great Contraction produced a widespread expectation of a price decline after the war which gave way to the opposite expectation when prices rose instead of declining.

[19] Cagan uses the following demand curve for money:

$$\log_e \frac{M}{P} = -\alpha E - \gamma,$$

where M is the nominal stock of money, P is the price level, E is the expected instantaneous rate of change in prices, and α and γ are parameters. Suppose two points for different dates (designated, say, by subscripts 0 and 1) are regarded as satisfying this equation. Then

$$\log_e \left(\frac{M}{P_1} \right) - \log_e \left(\frac{M}{P_0} \right) = -\alpha(E_1 - E_0) = -\alpha\Delta E.$$

To suppose this equation to account for the rise in the velocity of money from 1946 to 1960 implies a value of 0.37 for the left hand side of the equation (the natural logarithm of the ratio of velocities). Cagan estimates α as 4.68 months for all seven hyperinflations combined when E is rate of change per month ("Monetary Dynamics of Hyperinflation," p. 45), which is equivalent to 0.39 years when E is rate of change per year. This gives 0.37/0.39 or 0.95 for the required value of ΔE. The smallest and largest values of α for individual hyperinflations are 2.30 and 8.70 months (*ibid.*, p. 43), which would give 1.93 and 0.51 respectively as extreme values for ΔE.

quired change in expectations, since there is strong reason to believe that the demand for money is more sensitive to very low expected rates of price change than Cagan's equation indicates.[20] However, no reasonable correction on this score would bring the estimate of the change required to account for the velocity movement to a level at all plausible as a description of the change in expectations from, say, 1946 to 1960.

We are therefore led to conclude that, like changes in interest rates, changes in the expected rate of change in prices can at most account for only a minor part of the postwar rise in velocity. Furthermore, the effects of these two factors may not be additive. Insofar as the postwar change in interest rates reflects the change in price expectations, and insofar as this was also true for the periods from which we infer the effect of interest rates, the indicated effect of interest rate changes includes the effect of changed price-rise expectations. Similarly, the changes in the rate of change in prices used to compute Cagan's equation were probably accompanied by corresponding changes in interest rates, so his estimates implicitly include their effect as well.

2. Development of Money Substitutes

A second major factor cited as an explanation of the postwar rise in velocity is the development of closer substitutes for money, noted above, which is said to have produced a decline in the demand for money itself. The major specific items generally cited are short-term government securities and shares in savings and loan associations, both of which have grown in volume much more rapidly than the stock of money has.[21]

In evaluating this argument, we must distinguish among four different reasons for the postwar increase in holdings of money substitutes. One reason is a rise in rates of return yielded by the substitutes which makes holding money more costly and hence leads individuals and businesses to hold a larger part of their assets in interest-bearing form. A reduction in the amount of money held on this score is simply a movement along a demand schedule relating the desired stock of money to interest rates. This has been taken fully into account in the preceding section, and there is nothing to add.

[20] Martin J. Bailey shows in "The Welfare Cost of Inflationary Finance" (*Journal of Political Economy,* Apr. 1956, pp. 98–99) that, if Cagan's equation is extrapolated to values of $E = 0$, it yields stocks of money much smaller than were actually held in earlier "normal" years when prices were and had been relatively stable, which implies the conclusion stated in the text.

[21] Another item sometimes cited is the growth of term insurance (see Walter Williams, "The Availability of Term Life and of Health Insurance as Factors Affecting the Demand for Money," *Journal of Political Economy,* Apr. 1961, pp. 187–191).

The second reason is a change in some other variable affecting the demand for money, such as expectations about economic stability, considered in section 4 below, which leads individuals to desire to hold a smaller fraction of their assets in the form of money. This, too, is a movement along an appropriately defined demand schedule for money. Its counterpart will be an increase in holdings of assets other than money, including among them the money substitutes under consideration and also a wide variety of other assets. Here, too, the increased holding of money substitutes is a consequence, not a cause, of the increased velocity.

The third reason is a change in the attractiveness of money substitutes relative to other assets rather than relative to money. This reason is worth noting explicitly, because it seems likely that it is not specifically a postwar development, but has occurred over a rather long period and is a major part of the explanation of the rapid secular growth of financial intermediaries. As agriculture, and perhaps also independent nonfarm business, have declined in importance relative to industry and trade and corporate enterprise, so also has the direct ownership of real assets by individuals relative to their total wealth. Wealth holders have consequently come to hold a larger part of their wealth in the form of claims of great variety.

The fourth possible reason for the increase in holdings of money substitutes is that institutional changes produce new types of money substitutes not formerly available, or new patterns of adjustment involving the more extensive use of money substitutes. These developments lead to a shift in the demand schedule for money, so that the desired stock of money is less than it was formerly at the same rate of interest on assets formerly available, and at the same value of other variables affecting the quantity of money demanded. This is the one reason that is relevant to the present section. For corporate and other business holders of money, the main changes suggested have been a greater availability of short-term government securities and institutional changes in the market for them. Perhaps such changes have been important, but we doubt it. Short-term government securities have been available for a long time. In addition, in the 1920's and earlier, call money provided an equally safe and convenient means of investing funds for short periods. Insofar as such short-term investment of funds fell into disuse and then later revived in the form of investment in governments, it seems more plausible to interpret these shifts as reactions to the decline and then subsequent rise in interest rates, rather than to the emergence of any new financial instrument. The growth in the volume of short-term government securities has not been a net addition to government debt but rather a substitution for long-term debt. The substitution has been accompanied by a rise in short-term yields relative to long-term, which suggests that asset holders have simply been induced by greater yields to hold the one instead of the other; that what has occurred has been largely a shift within the category of government securities and that any shift from money to government securities has simply been a reaction to higher interest rates.

Available estimates of business holdings of various types of assets cast further doubt on the significance of new financial instruments or adjustment patterns for the postwar rise in velocity. The holdings of government securities by the corporate nonfinancial business sector dropped sharply after the end of the war, from some $22 billion at the end of 1945 to $14 billion at the end of 1947. They rose sharply in the next few years, reaching nearly $21 billion in 1951. For the next few years, holdings were highly volatile, reaching as high as $23.5 billion in 1955 and falling to $19 billion in 1954 and 1956–57, but showing no steady tendency to rise. By contrast, this sector's balances of currency and demand deposits have risen at a much steadier pace throughout the period. More important for the present argument, there is no tendency for changes in securities to move in the opposite direction from changes in currency and deposits, a movement that might be expected if they were close substitutes. On the contrary, the two categories tend, if anything, to move together.[22] Despite the attention lavished in the financial literature on the alleged substitution of Treasury bills for corporate money balances, we are therefore inclined to regard this factor as playing no appreciable role in the postwar rise in velocity.[23]

For noncorporate holders of money, two developments require attention: the emergence of United States savings bonds and the growth of savings and loan shares. United States savings bonds, first introduced in 1935, provided individuals with a form of assets that had many of the characteristics of money and especially of savings deposits: redeemability on demand at a stated nominal value specified in advance. However, this financial instrument clearly did not contribute to the postwar rise in velocity; if it had any effect, it was to restrain the rise in velocity. The major growth in holdings of savings bonds came during the war.

[22] *Federal Reserve Bulletin*, Aug. 1959, p. 1058; 1960, p. 942; 1961, p. 996, Table 8: Sector Statements of Financial Assets and Liabilities. Selden also notes that velocity increases in the corporate sector from 1951 to 1957 did not result from shifts from money to governments (*Postwar Rise in the Velocity*, pp. 518–519); see also Clay Anderson, "Managing the Corporate Money Position," *Business Review* of the Federal Reserve Bank of Philadelphia, Mar. 1961.

[23] *Employment, Growth, and Price Levels*, Joint Economic Committee, Staff Report, Dec. 24, 1959, 86th Cong., 1st sess., GPO, 1959, pp. 349–351; George Garvy, *Deposit Velocity and Its Significance*, Federal Reserve Bank of New York, Nov. 1959, pp. 62, 68–72; C. E. Silberman, "The Big Corporate Lenders," *Fortune*, Aug. 1956, pp. 111–114.

The peak of holdings was reached in 1950, and since then there has been a substantial decline. The return on savings bonds was practically constant for most of the period,[24] while the return on other assets rose, including the return on commercial bank time deposits. Before 1952, briefly in 1956, and again in 1959–60, the rate of interest paid on commercial bank time deposits actually exceeded the yield on E bonds held one year; though yields on E bonds held to maturity have, throughout, substantially exceeded the commercial bank time deposit rate.[25] Hence, there may have been some shift out of savings bonds into commercial bank time deposits. If so, this would have restrained the rise in velocity.

Savings and loan shares are a different matter. As Chart 60 shows, the growth of savings and loan shares has been far more rapid than of any other form of savings deposits, although all forms of savings deposits have grown more rapidly than currency plus demand deposits. From over $7 billion at the end of 1945, savings and loan shares had multiplied more than eightfold to over $60 billion at the end of 1960. In 1945, the volume of savings and loan shares was only a little more than one-twentieth the total stock of money and less than one-half total mutual savings deposits; in 1960, the volume of savings and loan shares was more than one-quarter the stock of money and almost one and three-quarters times mutual savings deposits.

The rapid growth of all forms of savings deposits presumably reflects the rise in rates of return on them. But it is clear from Chart 61 that the more rapid growth of savings and loan shares than of the other forms of deposits cannot be explained by a rise in the relative rate of return. Though the return on savings and loan shares has throughout been higher than that on the other forms of savings deposits, the differential has narrowed, if anything, over the period.

The differential between the interest rates paid on savings and loan shares and on mutual savings deposits has narrowed more than the differential between the savings and loan rate and the rate on commercial bank time deposits. The latter has narrowed also despite the much stricter limitations on commercial bank interest rates than on mutual

[24] Yield to Maturity of Series E Bonds, 1945–60

Period	Yield (per cent)
8/45–4/52	2.9
5/52–1/57	3.0
2/57–5/59	3.25
6/59–	3.75

SOURCE: *Annual Report* of the Secretary of the Treasury, 1959, p. 226. If not held to maturity, yields on savings bonds were lower than the figures shown above.

[25] See George Hanc, *The United States Savings Bond Program in the Postwar Period*, NBER, Occasional Paper 81, 1962, Chart 3, p. 27.

CHART 60

Money Stock Components and Selected Near-Moneys, 1945–60

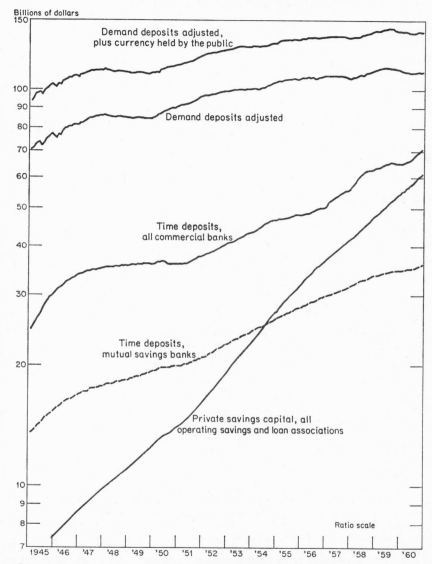

SOURCE: Deposits and currency, Table A-1. Savings and loan associations, private savings capital, original Dec. data, 1945–58, from *Trends in the Savings and Loan Field, 1958* (Federal Home Loan Bank Board, Nov. 1959); original data for other months from Table 1 in *Selected Balance Sheet Data, All Operating Savings and Loan Associations* (attached to 1955–59 Dec. issues of FHLBB release, *Savings, Mortgage Financing and Housing Data*) and from the Dec. 1960 and Sept. 1961 issues of the same table published separately, all seasonally adjusted by ratio-to-moving-total method.

663

CHART 61
Interest or Dividend Rates Paid on Time Deposits and Savings and Loan Association Shares, 1945–60

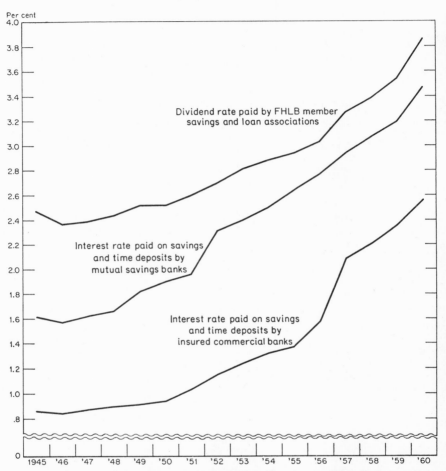

SOURCE: Savings and loan associations, dividends divided by averages of Dec. 31 share capital, both from *Combined Financial Statements* (Federal Home Loan Bank Board), 1948, 1954, 1955, 1958, and 1959 issues; and from "Advance Highlights–1960: Combined Financial Statements, Member Savings and Loan Associations" (FHLBB, Washington, no date). Mutual savings banks, 1945–59, *Mutual Savings Banking: Basic Characteristics and Role in the National Economy*, National Association of Mutual Savings Banks, Prentice-Hall for Commission on Money and Credit, 1962, p. 87. 1960 (preliminary) figure, NAMSB, personal communication. Commercial banks, interest divided by average savings and time deposits, all from *Annual Report*, FDIC, 1953–58 and 1960 issues.

savings bank interest rates.[26] Apparently, in the early postwar years, the maximum rate of 2½ per cent permitted on commercial bank savings deposits[27] was sufficiently above the relevant market rate to make it of no economic significance. To judge from the relative behavior of time deposits at commercial and mutual savings banks, the interest limitation first became significant in late 1954. Before then, these two classes of deposits had risen at roughly similar rates (see Chart 60). Beginning in late 1954, commercial bank time deposits rose at a decidedly lower rate than mutual savings deposits. When the maximum interest rate payable on commercial bank time deposits was raised to 3 per cent effective January 1, 1957, there was an immediate reaction. Commercial bank time deposits began to rise at a much more rapid rate and by mid-1958 had more than regained their position relative to mutual savings deposits. The failure of commercial bank time deposits to grow rapidly from mid-1959 to mid-1960 apparently was a reflection of the prevailing Federal Reserve tight money policy, rather than an indication that the interest rate limitation was again becoming effective. Be that as it may, commercial bank time deposits resumed a rapid growth rate in the second half of 1960.

The 1954–58 episode is interesting for our purpose, not only because it reveals so clearly the effect of the interest rate limitation, but also because it gives some evidence on the substitutability of different classes of deposits. The rapid growth of savings and loan shares—the reasons for which we have yet to determine—can be a major reason for the

[26] As noted in Chap. 8, sect. 2, the Federal Reserve System establishes maximum rates of interest payable by member banks on savings and time deposits under the provisions of Regulation Q. Maximum rates that may be paid by insured nonmember banks are established by the FDIC and are the same as those in effect for member banks. In setting their dividend rates, mutual savings banks may require the approval of state banking authorities under whose supervision they operate, as in New York. In other states a statutory maximum is fixed, in some cases so high as to be ineffective. All insured savings and loan associations are required by law to accumulate reserves for losses until such reserves and undivided profits are the equivalent of 10 or 15 per cent of assets, depending upon the state or federal laws under which they operate. The balance of net income is available for distribution to shareholders, without maximum limits on dividend rates.

[27] Also on time deposits payable in 6 months or more. The maximum was 2 per cent on time deposits payable in 90 days to 6 months, and 1 per cent on time deposits payable in less than 90 days. Time deposits are classified as regular savings deposits or time deposits, including certificates of deposit and open-account time deposits. Open-account time deposits are held mainly by corporations, institutions, and foreigners; only individuals and nonprofit institutions are permitted to hold regular savings deposits at commercial banks. At four of the five call dates for which a breakdown is available of time deposits of individuals, partnerships, and corporations at all member banks (June 1940, 1957, 1958, and 1960), regular savings deposits were between 85 and 90 per cent of that total. At the remaining (wartime) call date the comparable percentage was 95 (see *Federal Reserve Bulletin*, Apr. 1958, pp. 422–426, and *Member Bank Call Report*, June 15, 1960).

postwar rise in velocity only if such assets are a close substitute, from the point of view of asset holders, for what we label money. However, the behavior of deposits from 1954 to 1958 suggests that neither mutual savings deposits nor savings and loan shares are very close substitutes for commercial bank time deposits, at least for short periods. The noticeable slackening off in the growth of commercial bank time deposits from the end of 1954 to the end of 1956 and subsequent rapid rise from early 1957 to mid-1958 leave no detectable imprint on either mutual savings deposits or savings and loan shares (see Chart 60). Demand deposits show more movement over that period, growing more rapidly 1954–56 than from early 1957 to mid-1958, when they resumed a more rapid rate of growth. Some of this movement can perhaps be interpreted as reflecting substitution, on the part of asset holders, of demand deposits for commercial bank time deposits. Even on demand deposits, however, the imprint is slight, and the mild effect during this period can be explained as a result of supply relations rather than of demand relations. The clear implication is that the growth of commercial bank time deposits after the lifting of the interest rate ceiling was mostly at the expense of a wide variety of other types of asset holdings.[28] But substitution relations are symmetrical. If commercial

[28] To illustrate the magnitudes, consider the changes in various types of deposits and in currency held by the public over the period before and after the change in the interest ceiling:

	Annual per cent change from:		(2) minus (1)	Absolute annual change corresponding to difference in rate of growth
	Dec. 1954 to Dec. 1956 (1)	Dec. 1956 to June 1958 (2)	(3)	($ billions) (4)
Commercial bank time deposits	3.6	13.0	+9.4	+4.4
Mutual savings bank deposits	6.6	6.2	−0.4	−0.1
Savings and loan shares	15.6	12.5	−3.2	−0.9
Demand deposits adjusted	1.8	0.9	−0.8	−0.9
Currency held by the public	1.4	0.5	−1.0	−0.3

For savings and loan association shares, the differential rate of growth appears from Chart 60 to reflect simply the concave downward trend rather than reflecting the more rapid rate of growth of commercial bank time deposits in the later period. However, even if all these differences in rates of growth were regarded as a result of substitution by asset holders in favor of commercial bank time deposits, they would account for only half the absolute magnitude of the change in the latter.

For currency and demand deposits adjusted, these changes cannot be regarded as a result solely of substitution by asset holders. The conditions of supply link the nominal amount of currency and demand deposits to the nominal

bank time deposits are not a close substitute for savings and loan shares, then neither are savings and loan shares for commercial bank time deposits. Hence this evidence suggests that the postwar expansion of savings and loan shares was predominantly at the expense of assets other than money in the portfolios of wealth holders.

That episode provides of course only a single piece of evidence on

---

amount of time deposits in such a way that a higher rate of rise in the amount of the latter, for whatever reason, must mean a smaller rate of rise in the former for given conditions of supply (i.e., given high-powered money and bank reserve ratios). For example, suppose asset holders desired to substitute commercial bank time deposits for their holdings of government securities. To short-circuit a complicated process, let us suppose they transfer government securities directly to commercial banks and receive in return time deposit credits of equal value. The commercial banks would then have less reserves in relation to liabilities than before. To repair their reserve position, they would sell off assets and set in train a sequence that would lead to a reduction in the amount of currency and demand deposits held by the public. Again, in order to short-circuit the whole process, so that the initial acquisition of additional time deposits will have no further repercussions, the time deposits would have to be acquired in small part by reduction of currency and demand deposit holdings in addition to the transfer of government securities. (For conditions prevailing in Dec. 1954, each additional dollar in time deposits would require a reduction of 3 cents in currency held by the public and 11 cents in demand deposits. The 3 cents of currency plus the roughly 2 cents reserves released by the reduction in demand deposits would provide the 5 cents required as reserve for each dollar of time deposits, and these proportions would leave the ratio of demand deposits to currency held by the public unchanged.)

In consequence of the mechanical supply relations, an analysis of nominal figures like those in the tabulation just above is not a satisfactory indicator of substitution in demand. For this purpose, we should look at real magnitudes. For if the opposite movement of commercial bank time deposits and currency plus demand deposits adjusted were solely the result of the mechanical supply relations, the effect would be a differential behavior of prices, so that the movement in the real amount of currency plus demand deposits would show no impact of the changed movement of time deposits. Unfortunately, such an analysis would require much more satisfactory procedures than we possess for converting nominal magnitudes into real magnitudes.

An alternative indication might be provided by a differential movement of currency and demand deposits. Insofar as the mechanical supply relation only is involved, the effect should be the same on currency and demand deposits. Insofar as a substitution on the demand side is involved, if time deposits were a closer substitute for demand deposits than currency is, the effect would be greater on demand deposits than on currency. The figures in the above tabulation do not show such a greater effect: the annual rate of growth of demand deposits fell by 0.8 percentage points, of currency by 1.0 percentage points. On the basis of these figures, currency is a closer substitute for time deposits than demand deposits are, though the difference is small, and the whole of the percentage decline in the growth of demand deposits may be attributable to the mechanical supply relation. A zero estimate of substitution of time deposits for demand deposits serves as a lower limit, just as the 20 per cent figure obtained from the entries in col. 4 of the tabulation serves as an upper limit.

We are indebted to John R. Culbertson for calling to our attention the importance of the mechanical supply relation.

the substitutability of various forms of deposits.[29] It certainly does not rule out the possibility that the growth of savings and loan shares has, in the longer run, been partly at the expense of a growth that would otherwise have taken place in the volume of money, as we define it, relative to income.

The spectacular growth of savings and loan shares raises questions of interpretation on both the demand and supply side. On the demand side, the question is why asset holders have been willing to hold so much larger a volume of such shares despite the apparent decline in the differential return on them suggested by Chart 61.[30] On the supply side, the question is how savings and loan associations have continued to be able to pay higher rates than other savings institutions have paid despite so large an expansion in their liabilities. Apparently both the demand curve for savings and loan shares and the supply curve of such shares have shifted drastically to the right.

On the demand side, the most plausible explanation seems to be the change in the character of savings and loan association shares as a result of their insurance by the federal government. The Federal Savings and Loan Insurance Corporation was established in 1934,[31] the same year that the Federal Deposit Insurance Corporation began to insure banks. In subsequent years, total shares in all savings and loan associations, which had fallen from $6.3 billion in 1930 to $4.8 billion in 1933, continued to fall to roughly $4.1 billion by the end of the decade.[32] Although a rapidly increasing fraction of associations joined FSLIC, so that accounts in insured associations rose from less than $0.5 billion at the end of 1935 to $1.8 billion by the end of 1939, less than half of savings and loan shares were then in insured associations. During the war, the rise in total savings and loan shares accelerated, and the proportion insured continued to grow so that, by the end of 1945, the volume of total shares was over $7 billion, and roughly 70 per cent of that total was in insured associations. In the next five years, total shares nearly doubled, reaching $14.0 billion, and the proportion insured rose to 81 per cent.

Insurance of savings and loan association shares by a federal corporation clearly reduced the risk attached to ownership of such shares—a

[29] The change in the interest rate ceiling on commercial bank time deposits, effective Jan. 1, 1962—from 3 to 4 per cent on deposits held 1 year or more, and from 3 to 3½ per cent on deposits held less than one year—will in time provide evidence on another episode.

[30] The data plotted in the chart are national averages. Mutual savings banks are geographically concentrated, so it may be that a fuller study comparing rates in the same geographical areas might yield different results.

[31] In the National Housing Act of June 27, 1934 (P.L. 479).

[32] *Trends in the Savings and Loan Field,* 1958, Home Loan Bank Board, Washington, Nov. 1959.

consideration of some importance in view of a fairly high rate of failure and considerable losses to shareholders during the Great Contraction.[33] Just as insurance increased the confidence of individuals in commercial bank deposits, so it unquestionably made savings and loan shares a more attractive asset to hold, and somewhat more like "money" as an asset. However, until 1950, the insurance provisions were less liberal for savings and loan associations than for commercial banks, making it rather more likely that, in the event of default, the saver might have to wait one to three years for cash repayment of much of his claim.[34] Presumably this difference reduced the attractiveness of savings and loan shares relative to commercial bank deposits or currency, as well as the degree of substitutability between them.

In 1950, the insurance provisions in the event of default were changed and made identical with those applicable to commercial bank deposits insured by the FDIC.[35] There are still some differences between FSLIC and FDIC, with respect to the definition of a default and the financial resources and ultimate recourse of the two corporations,[36] but they seem

[33] For the four years 1930–33, losses averaged roughly one-half of 1 per cent of total savings and loan shares per year, whereas in the preceding ten years they had been negligible, about 1 one-hundreth of 1 per cent. For the period 1930–33 alone, savings and loan losses were less than half as large relative to share accounts as losses in commercial banks relative to deposits. However, that was mainly because liquidation of defaulting savings and loan associations was spread over a longer period. For the decade 1930–39, relative losses per year were roughly the same in savings and loan associations as in commercial banks. The slower liquidation of savings and loan associations than that of commercial banks may help to account for the apparently slower recovery of confidence of savings and loan shareholders than of commercial bank depositors. (Losses on savings and loan shares, from Savings and Loan Annuals, U.S. Savings and Loan League, 1946, p. 187; computed as a percentage of savings and loan shares, from sources listed in notes to Chart 60; for losses on commercial bank deposits, see Table 16.)

[34] Sect. 405 of Title IV of the National Housing Act of 1934 provided that, in the event of a default by an insured savings and loan association, FSLIC make available to insured shareholders either a new insured account in an institution not in default equal in amount to the insured account so transferred, or, at the option of the shareholder, 10 per cent of his account in cash, 50 per cent of the remainder in negotiable noninterest-bearing debentures of the corporation, within one year, and the balance in the same form, within three years from the date of the default.

[35] Sect. 5 of An Act to Amend the Federal Deposit Insurance Corporation Act, passed Sept. 21, 1950 (P. L. 797), provided that in the event of default of an insured association, payment of each insured account shall be made by FSLIC as soon as possible either in cash or by making available in another insured institution an account equal in amount to the insured account in the defaulting institution. This provision is identical with that governing FDIC. Accounts are insured up to $10,000 by both corporations.

[36] The failure of a savings and loan association to pay accounts at the end of a 30- or 60-day waiting period, after notice of withdrawal had been given by the shareholder, does not constitute a default, as would failure by a commercial bank to pay its deposits on demand. The insured institution must be declared in default by the proper public supervisory authority or by a court of

of little practical importance. The result of the 1950 changes was clearly to make savings and loan shares more like commercial bank deposits and currency.

A still more rapid rate of increase in savings and loan shares followed the change in insurance provisions. From 1945 to 1950, those shares rose at the rate of 13 per cent per year; from 1950 to 1955, at 16 per cent per year; and, although the rate of growth has tapered off since then, it still averaged 13 per cent per year from 1955 to 1960. In the meantime, the fraction of savings and loan shares in insured associations continued to rise to over 90 per cent by the end of 1960, with total savings and loan shares more than $60 billion.

Improved quality of savings and loan shares as a result of insurance, plus the time it takes for asset holders to adjust on the demand side and savings and loan associations on the supply side, seem to us to explain in large part the willingness of asset holders to hold so rapidly growing an amount of savings and loan shares, despite a narrowing of the differential between the yield on them and on time and savings deposits.

On the supply side, the explanation seems clear for the growth of savings and loan shares without a sharp reduction in the rate of return offered. These associations specialize in housing loans—particularly on residential construction—and the postwar period has been a period of high residential construction and of rapid growth of home ownership. Accordingly there has been a strong and expanding market for their wares. A similarly rapid growth occurred during the housing boom of the 1920's.

For interpretation of the postwar behavior of the velocity of money, the crucial question is the extent to which savings and loan shares can be regarded as having grown at the expense of "money," not because they yielded higher interest than formerly, but because they had become closer substitutes for money. Pending some additional independent evidence on the sensitivity of both money balances and savings and loan shares to interest rates, and on changes in the substitutability of savings and loan shares for money, there is no fully satisfactory answer. But it is possible to get at least some idea of the orders of magnitude involved.[37]

---

competent jurisdiction, depending upon the source of the association's charter, before federal savings and loan insurance becomes operative.

Until recent years, the ratio of FSLIC assets to the volume of shares in insured savings and loan associations was considerably higher than that of FDIC assets to deposits in insured banks. The ratio has been declining for FSLIC, but has been fairly constant for FDIC, 1934–60. As a result, since 1956, the ratio has been somewhat lower for FSLIC than for FDIC.

[37] We know of only one study directed at quantitative estimates of the substitutability between savings deposits and demand deposits, by Roy Elliott ("Savings Deposits as Money," unpublished paper prepared for the Workshop in Money and Banking, University of Chicago, 1960). Elliott used cross-section data for

The first requisite is an estimate of that part of the growth of savings and loan shares regarded as reflecting an improvement in their quality, and hence not taken into account in allowing for interest rate or other changes. This part might be regarded as shifting to some extent the demand function for money rather than as a manifestation of a movement along it. Our first idea was that we might get a rough estimate by comparing the postwar period with the 1920's, as the nearest reasonably comparable period of no change in the quality of savings and loan shares. But insofar as this comparison has any relevance, it is to suggest that the rapid postwar growth raises no problems at all: during the nine years from 1920 to 1929, savings and loan shares per capita in constant prices rose at a rate of 14 per cent per year or at more than one and one-half times the annual rate of rise of the comparable figure from 1945 to 1960. Yet during the 1920's, there was no sign of markedly unusual behavior of velocity. To get a more modest estimate of the rate of growth of savings and loan shares in the absence of any quality change, we computed their average per capita level in constant prices for the decade of the 1920's and for the decade of the 1930's. The rate of growth from the 1920's to the 1930's was 4.9 per cent per year.

Accordingly, we used this figure as an estimate of the hypothetical "normal" rate of growth after the war, beginning with the level of 1945 which, as it happens, was some 10 per cent below the average level of savings and loan shares per capita in constant prices for the decade of the 1930's. We then attributed the whole excess of the rate of growth of savings and loan association shares since World War II over that from the decade of the 1920's to the decade of the 1930's to improvement in quality—admittedly a highly arbitrary procedure. Our only justification is that some such estimate of the normal rate of growth is required, and that much experimentation with alternative extrapolations persuades us that our estimate of the normal rate of growth is on the low side, if anything, and therefore will tend to overstate the increase in savings and loan capital that can be attributed to improved quality. According to this estimate, some $29 billion of the 1960 annual average of $58 billion of savings and loan shares can be regarded as the amount attributable to improvement in quality.

---

states to estimate a relation between (1) demand deposits per capita plus a fraction s of savings deposits per capita and (2) real income per capita. He shows that the reciprocal of the value of s that gives the best fit can be regarded as an estimate of the number of dollars of savings deposits equivalent to $1 of demand deposits in providing monetary services. His estimated value of s varies from about 0.25 to about 0.6 in different years. Since this estimate is for all savings accounts together (commercial bank time, plus mutual savings bank deposits, plus savings and loan shares), it overestimates the relevant multiple for savings and loan shares alone, presumably a less close substitute for demand deposits than are commercial bank time deposits.

The next question is by how much the accumulation of the $29 billion of savings and loan shares reduced the demand for money. At the most, of course, it could have reduced it dollar for dollar, since $1 of savings and loan shares is clearly not fully equivalent, as a source of monetary qualities, to $1 of currency or commercial bank deposits. Or to put it differently, at least some of the increased holding of savings and loan shares must have been at the expense of assets other than money—such as U.S. savings bonds, mutual savings deposits, and the like. At this extreme limit, the effect of substituting $29 billion of savings and loan shares for $29 billion of money would have been to raise velocity in 1960 by about 14 per cent; at that limit, therefore, the growth of savings and loan shares could account at most for one-third of the postwar rise in velocity. And this extreme estimate is probably at least four or five times its actual influence.[38]

3. Combined Effect of Factors So Far Considered

If we put together the items considered to this point, it seems unlikely that, even all together, they can account for as much as half of the 45 per cent postwar rise in the velocity of money. Perhaps the most important factor is the postwar reaction to wartime accumulation induced by the unavailability of durable goods. The other factors—the rise in interest rates, shifts in price expectations, and improvement in quality of savings and loan association shares—seem of much less importance. Moreover, the growth of income might have been expected to produce a decline in velocity, and so might some other factors, of which two are: (1) the declining relative attractiveness of U.S. savings bonds, which may have had about as large an effect as the increased attractiveness of savings and loan shares had—but in the opposite direction; and (2) termination of Federal Reserve support of yields on marketable government bonds, which may have had as large an effect as the rise in interest rates had—but in the opposite direction. Such bonds were a much closer substitute for money when they were supported than when their prices were freely determined in the market, hence the termination of support increased the demand for money and so tended to reduce velocity.[39] It follows that the major part of the postwar movement remains to be explained.

---

[38] The upper limit of the effect discussed in footnote 28, above, is 20 per cent. Elliott's analysis (footnote 37) is also consistent with such an upper limit.

[39] The money stock rose some 6 per cent in the year following the Accord without a price rise, whereas about 3 to 4 per cent per year has been, historically, the percentage increase consistent with stable prices. This implies that the demand for money increased about 2 or 3 per cent as a result of the termination of support (see Friedman, *A Program for Monetary Stability*, New York, Fordham University Press, 1959, pp. 107–108, footnote 5).

In one respect, the conclusion is highly satisfactory intellectually. The factors so far considered apply especially to the postwar period. They have little relevance to the 1929–42 gyrations of velocity and hence, if they fully explained the postwar behavior, we should be driven to seek some further *ad hoc* explanations of the earlier episode. It is much more appealing to find common roots of two such similar episodes.

4. *Expectations About Stability*

One possible common root of the two episodes is changing patterns of expectations about economic stability. Other things being the same, it is highly plausible that the fraction of their assets individuals and business enterprises wish to hold in the form of money, and also in the form of close substitutes for money, will be smaller when they look forward to a period of stable economic conditions than when they anticipate disturbed and uncertain conditions. After all, the major virtue of cash as an asset is its versatility. It involves a minimum of commitment and provides a maximum of flexibility to meet emergencies and to take advantage of opportunities. The more uncertain the future, the greater the value of such flexibility and hence the greater the demand for money is likely to be. In a qualitative sense, an explanation of the movement of the velocity of money in these terms is consistent with both the 1929 to 1942 and the 1942 to 1960 movements in velocity.

The contraction after 1929 clearly shattered beliefs in a "new era," in the likelihood of long-continued stability which, in the present view, had served to raise velocity in the later 1920's above the level it would otherwise have reached. The contraction instilled instead an exaggerated fear of continued economic instability, of the danger of stagnation, of the possibility of recurrent unemployment. The result, from this point of view, was a sharp increase in the demand for money, accounting for the magnitude of the decline in velocity from 1929 to 1932. Some decline was to be expected in any event, since the velocity of money usually declines during a cyclical contraction, reflecting—or so our studies suggest —the tendency of holders of money to adjust their balances to their longer-term or permanent income rather than their current income as measured by statisticians. But the actual decline was greater than can be accounted for in this way.[40]

---

[40] Moreover, the bank failures during 1931–32 by themselves were a factor that might have been expected to raise velocity. They made deposits in commercial banks less attractive as a form in which to hold wealth. The reduced attractiveness of deposits was, of course, reflected in the attempted shift to currency, and possibly to other assets. Evidence on the behavior of velocity in Canada, 1929–33, supports this view (see Chap. 7, sect. 3). Had it not been for bank failures in the U.S., there might have been a more drastic fall in velocity, and hence even more to be explained by increased uncertainty.

673

The reaction in observed velocity after 1932 was smaller than might have been expected from the usual cyclical effect of the rise in current income. Throughout the rest of the 1930's, the velocity of money, though it recovered somewhat from the trough of 1932, remained relatively low. Presumably there was some return of confidence by 1937 as a result of the rapid, though incomplete, recovery from 1933 to 1937 which, along with the usual cyclical forces, helps to explain the rise in velocity. However, the sharp contraction from 1937 to 1938 apparently revived fears of instability. While the decline in velocity from 1937 to 1938 was a usual cyclical reaction, the continued decline from 1938 to 1940 was not. It occurred despite business expansion, when velocity typically rises. Only after war in Europe broke out and a war boom began, did velocity really revive and return to anything like the level that might have been expected on the basis of the long past.

After the United States entered the war, and particularly after the tide seemed to be turning and the end of the war to be approaching, a high degree of uncertainty arose about postwar prospects. Obvious necessity for much reshuffling of economic activity in the course of reconversion to peacetime pursuits was compounded by extensive talk—a legacy of the depression—of the dangers of a postwar collapse. The mild decline in velocity from 1942 to 1943 and the sharp decline from 1943 to 1946 can be regarded as one consequence. The recovery from 1946 to 1948 and decline from 1948 to 1949 were both usual cyclical reactions, but the subsequent rise from 1949 to 1951 was much sharper than could be accounted for by a cyclical reaction alone. According to our present interpretation, it reflected a decline in fears of a postwar collapse and a growing confidence in future economic stability, arising from the failure of the 1948–49 recession to develop into a major contraction and receiving a further fillip from the Korean War. The rise in velocity was interrupted from 1951 to 1954, though a continued high level of economic activity from 1951 to 1953 should have increased the public's confidence in future stability. We are inclined to attribute the interruption from 1951 to 1953 to two special factors: first, the end of the bond-support program which increased the demand for money; second, the end of the rapid price rise associated with the early stages of the Korean War. The decline from 1953 to 1954 was the usual cyclical decline.

The mildness and brevity of the 1953–54 recession must have strongly reinforced the lesson of the 1948–49 recession and reduced still further the fears of great economic instability. The sharp rise in the velocity of money from 1954 to 1957—much sharper than could be expected on cyclical grounds alone—can be regarded as a direct reflection of the growth of confidence in future economic stability. The brevity of the

1957–58 recession presumably further reinforced confidence in stability but, clearly, each such episode in the same direction must have less and less effect, so one might suppose that by 1960 expectations were approaching a plateau. If this be so, if the present interpretation is right, and if the experienced degree of economic instability shows no drastic change, one might expect the rise in velocity to end and the long-term downward trend to emerge once more.

This qualitative account is plausible but alone can hardly be convincing. It needs to be complemented by a quantitative analysis showing that changing views about economic stability can account for the magnitude of the changes in the velocity of money. Though we have made some attempts at such analysis, we have not so far obtained results worth presenting; our preliminary findings neither clearly support nor clearly contradict the qualitative analysis. They are simply inadequate.

If this explanation should prove to be valid, it would have implications for assets other than money. In the first place, a decline in demand for money as a result of expectations of lesser economic instability should imply that funds, otherwise held in the form of money, would be distributed among a wide variety of other assets; there seems no reason for their concentration in close substitutes for money. In the second place, similar considerations should apply to other highly liquid assets desired mainly for precautionary purposes. Hence, one might expect that the ratio of near-moneys to other assets, as well as the ratio of money to other assets, would have declined relative to their long-term trends, or to the value that might be expected on other grounds. We have not explored this implication of our analysis.

The conclusions in this section are highly tentative. Full confidence in them must await further evidence. Nevertheless, changing expectations about economic stability seem at the moment a more plausible explanation of postwar movements in the velocity of money than any of the other factors we have examined.

CHAPTER 13

A Summing Up

THE MONETARY history of the United States during the century since the Civil War has been colorful and varied. In tracing its tortuous course, we have found it necessary to delve into domestic politics, international economic arrangements, the functioning of large administrative organizations, the role of personality in shaping events, and other matters seemingly far removed from the counting house. The varied character of U.S. monetary history renders this century of experience particularly valuable to the student of economic change. He cannot control the experiment, but he can observe monetary experience under sufficiently disparate conditions to sort out what is common from what is adventitious and to acquire considerable confidence that what is common can be counted on to hold under still other circumstances.

Throughout the near-century examined in detail we have found that:

1. Changes in the behavior of the money stock have been closely associated with changes in economic activity, money income, and prices.
2. The interrelation between monetary and economic change has been highly stable.
3. Monetary changes have often had an independent origin; they have not been simply a reflection of changes in economic activity.

These common elements of monetary experience can be expected to characterize our future as they have our past. In addition, we can expect the future like the past to give further examples of the less specific generalization that:

4. In monetary matters, appearances are deceiving; the important relationships are often precisely the reverse of those that strike the eye.

1. *Relation Between the Stock of Money and Other Economic Variables*

From 1867 to 1960, the 93 years for which we have estimates of the money stock, there have been two major price inflations: a more than doubling of prices from 1914 to 1920 and again from 1939 to 1948, the periods during and after each of the two world wars. In both

676

wars, there was also a more than doubling in the money stock. So large a rise in the money stock in a correspondingly brief time did not occur in any other period.

A substantial and fairly long-continued peacetime rise in prices occurred during only one period: from 1897 to 1914, when prices rose by 40 to 50 per cent. The average annual rate of rise in the stock of money from 1897 to 1914 was higher than during any other period of comparable length that excludes the two world wars. It is widely feared that the post–World War II period may ultimately turn out to be another such period of long-continued rise in prices. However, as of 1960 it clearly was not. The major price rises since 1945 have been either a carry-over from World War II or connected with the Korean War.

We have characterized four segments of the 93 years as displaying a relatively high degree of economic stability: 1882–92, 1903–13, 1923–29, 1948–60. Each has also displayed a high degree of stability of the year-to-year change in the stock of money; the remaining periods have shown appreciably greater instability of the year-to-year change in both money and income.

In 93 years, there have been six periods of severe economic contraction that produced widespread distress and unemployment. Historians of business cycles classify those contractions as of a different order of magnitude if not of a different species than the milder contractions that have come on the average some four years apart (see Chart 62). The most severe contraction was the one from 1929 to 1933. The others were 1873–79, 1893–94—or better, perhaps, the whole period 1893 to 1897, which contained two business cycle contractions separated by a brief and incomplete expansion—1907–08, 1920–21, and 1937–38. Each of those severe contractions was accompanied by an appreciable decline in the stock of money, the most severe decline accompanying the 1929–33 contraction. The only other decline at all comparable in magnitude to the six was in the first year of the series, 1867 to 1868, the final stage of the liquidation of some of the Civil War monetary expedients. There have been only two other periods in the whole 93 years in which the stock of money has declined appreciably for more than an isolated few months, 1948–49 and 1959–60, and the declines in both those periods were decidedly smaller in magnitude than in any of the six severe contractions. The remaining contractions have left their impress in the form of a slower rate of growth of the stock of money during contractions than during expansions, rather than in an absolute decline.

Of the six severe contractions, four were characterized by major banking or monetary disturbances: 1873–79, by controversy over the greenbacks and resumption of specie payments and by a banking crisis in 1873; the 1890's, by controversy over the role of silver, a banking crisis in 1890, and a more severe banking crisis in 1893 involving concerted restriction by the banks of the convertibility of deposits into currency; 1907–08, by a banking panic also involving restriction; and 1929–33, by collapse of the banking system involving the disappearance through failure or merger of one-third of the banks and terminating in a nationwide banking holiday and complete cessation of banking activities for a week. Only one other banking crisis at all comparable in severity to the four has occurred during the whole period: the banking crisis of 1884, an episode in the course of the third longest contraction in our period (1882 to 1885), which is on the borderline for inclusion in our list of severe contractions.

In the two other severe contractions, 1920–21 and 1937–38, the decline in the money stock was a consequence of policy actions of the Federal Reserve System: in 1920–21, a sharp rise in the discount rate in early 1920 followed by another such rise some four and a half months later; in 1937–38, a doubling of reserve requirements in 1936 and early 1937. In both cases, the subsequent decline in the money stock was associated with a severe economic decline, but in neither did it lead to a banking crisis.

Of relationships revealed by our evidence, the closest are between, on the one hand, secular and cyclical movements in the stock of money and, on the other, corresponding movements in money income and prices. Since real income tends to vary over the cycle in the same direction as money income does, we have also observed a close relation between cyclical movements in the money stock and in real income or business activity. The relation between secular movements in the money stock and in real income is much less close. Real income grew at much the same rate during each of the four periods of stability listed earlier. Yet the money stock and prices grew at quite different rates, prices declining by 1 per cent a year in one period, rising by 2 per cent a year in another. Apparently, the forces determining the long-run rate of growth of real income are largely independent of the long-run rate of growth of the stock of money, so long as both proceed fairly smoothly. But marked instability of money is accompanied by instability of economic growth.

2. *Stability of Monetary Relations*

The relation between money and other economic variables has been not only close but also highly stable in form and character. One striking example of the stability of basic economic relations is the behavior of relative prices in the United States and Great Britain adjusted for changes in the exchange rate between the dollar and the pound. We have a reasonably continuous series from 1871 on (Chart 63). In the 79 years from 1871 to 1949, vast changes occurred in the economic structure and development of the United States, the place of Britain in the world economy, the internal monetary structures of both the United States and Britain, and the international monetary arrangements linking them. Yet, despite these changes, despite two world wars, and despite the statistical errors in the price-index numbers, the adjusted price ratio expressed on a base which makes 1929 = 100 was between 84 and 111 in all but one of the 79 years. The exception was 1932. It reflected the disruption of international monetary relations that followed Britain's devaluation in the fall of 1931, which made Britain temporarily unrepresentative of the world outside the sterling area with which the United States traded. Within a year, the ratio was back in the earlier range. Moreover, almost the extremes of the range were experienced in the very first decade, during which the ratio ranged from 111 in 1871 to 86 in 1876. In 1950, after Britain had again devalued in the fall of 1949, the ratio, as in 1932, shot outside the prior range, this time by a much more sizable amount, to 143. That deviation was longer lasting, partly because of the smaller role Britain had come to play in the world economy, but even more, we believe, because of the development of more effective techniques for suppressing the expression of price rises or their equivalent in computed price-index numbers. Yet, year by year, the ratio declined until 1958, when it reached 118, only slightly outside the earlier range; it remained at roughly that level through 1960.

Even though we are accustomed to regard the United States as nearly self-sufficient, the economic integration of the Western world has been sufficiently close to leave U.S. prices little leeway relative to external prices when both are expressed in a common currency. There has been more leeway in how the price relation was achieved—whether through changes in internal prices or in exchange rates—than in what relation could be achieved. Wide variations in tariffs, a major gold-purchase program, vast shifts in the direction of capital movements (see Chart 63), or imposition by our trading partners of extensive exchange controls—none of these has altered radically the price relationships required to yield some measure of equilibrium in international payments.

The velocity of money, which reflects the money-holding propensities of the community, offers another example of the stability of basic monetary relations. As the real income of the people of the United States rose, and perhaps also as deposits were made more convenient by the spread of banking facilities, the community came to hold a decidedly larger amount of money relative to its income, which is to say, the velocity

CHART 63

U.S. Net International Capital Movement as a Ratio to National Income, and Purchasing-Power Parity, 1871–1960

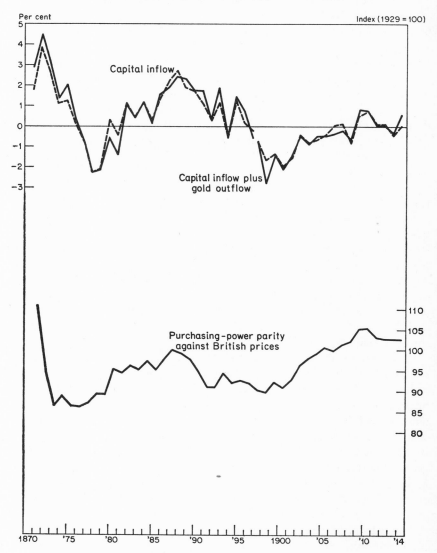

NOTE: Calendar years are shown. Movements in a fiscal year are plotted at the beginning of the calendar year. Capital inflow, minus unilateral transfers to foreign countries, is plotted as plus. Gold outflow is plotted as plus. Both are for fiscal years 1871–97, calendar years 1897–1960. Capital movements are in gold values, 1871–78. Unilateral transfers are not subtracted

CHART 63 (Concluded)

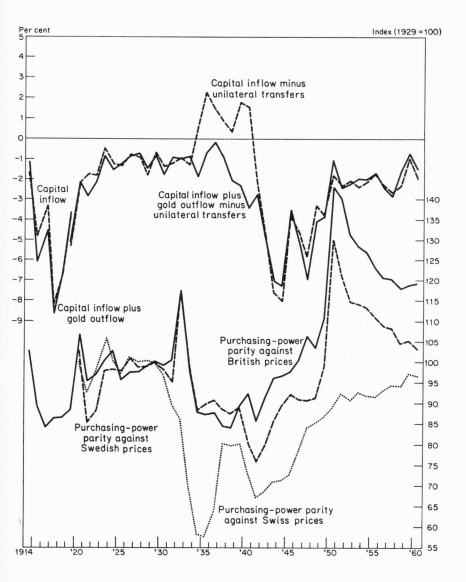

from capital inflow before 1919, because they were small and hence departure from the usual
treatment of the balance of payments did not seem worthwhile.
SOURCE: Table A-4.

681

of money declined. In 1869, the stock of money amounted to less than three months' income; in 1960, to more than seven months' income. The numerical value of velocity therefore changed considerably. However, the change occurred rather steadily: somewhat more rapidly when prices were falling during the 1880's and early 1890's and so making the holding of money more attractive; and somewhat more slowly when prices were rising from 1897 to 1914. The only major exceptions were during and after the great contraction of the 1930's, which saw a major fall in velocity and then a rebound, and during and after World War II, which also saw a major fall in velocity and then a postwar rebound. In response to cyclical fluctuations, velocity has shown a systematic and stable movement about its trend, rising during expansion and falling during contraction. Even the large movement accompanying the Great Contraction partly fits this pattern; it was so large partly because the cyclical movement was so large.

During the nine decades ending in 1960, the velocity of money fell by an average of slightly over 1 per cent a year. During business expansions it either rose or declined at less than this rate; during contractions it declined at more than this rate. The amplitudes of the cyclical rise and fall tended to vary with the amplitude of the cyclical movements in economic activity. Since many of the cyclical movements in economic activity had approximately the same amplitude, so did many of the cyclical movements in velocity. Despite the secular trend, the consistent cyclical pattern, and the sizable margin of error in our estimates, the observed year-to-year change in velocity was less than 10 per cent in 78 out of the 91 year-to-year changes from 1869, when our velocity figures start, to 1960. Of the 13 larger changes, more than half came during either the Great Contraction or the two world wars, and the largest change was 17 per cent. Expressed as a percentage of a secular trend, velocity was within the range 90 to 110 in 53 years, 85 to 115 in 66 years. Of the remaining 26 years, 12 were during the first 15 years, for which the income figures are seriously defective, and 7 during the Great Contraction and the two world wars.

One other monetary relation that has been highly stable is the relation between changes in the stock of money and cyclical movements in economic activity. On the average, the stock of money rose at a higher rate than money income; this is the other side of the secular decline in velocity. The rise was more rapid than usual during cyclical expansions and less rapid than usual during cyclical contractions. The rate of rise tended to slow down well before the peak in business and to speed up well before the trough. This pattern prevails throughout the period, in the very earliest cycle our data cover and also in the most recent.

The careful reader of our narrative will have come across many another detailed example of stable monetary relations to supplement these very broad ones: the similar effects of the gold-purchase programs undertaken in 1878 to prepare for resumption and after 1933 to raise domestic prices; the reliability of the deposit-currency ratio as a signal of a liquidity problem; the similar initial movements of U.S. wholesale prices following the outbreak of World Wars I and II—in both cases in a direction opposite to that which prevailed later; and so on.

These uniformities have persisted despite radical changes in monetary arrangements. From 1862 to 1879, the United States had an independent national money, convertible into neither gold nor silver nor the money of any other country at any fixed ratio. The stock of money could therefore be determined internally. From 1879 to 1914, U.S. money was convertible into gold at a fixed ratio specified by law and maintained in practice. The stock of money and internal prices had to be at levels that would produce a rough balance in international payments without abnormal gold movements. The stock of money was a dependent, not an independent variable, though, of course, there was some leeway in short periods. Both before and after 1879, until the Reserve System was established, the U.S. unit banking system was divided between national and nonnational banks, each having roughly half of total deposits, and neither subject to any central control except as the Treasury from time to time undertook central banking functions.

From 1914 to 1933, U.S. money continued to be rigidly linked to gold, but the number of other national moneys so linked had diminished. The United States had achieved a far more important role in the world economy, and foreign trade had become a smaller part of U.S. economic activity. The links between U.S. money and international trade were therefore far looser than in earlier years. In addition, the Federal Reserve Act not only established central control over most of the banking system but also provided an agency that could deliberately intervene to alter or even to reverse the relation between international payments and the domestic stock of money.

In early 1933, the rigid link between U.S. money and gold was severed. A year later, a rigid link was re-established at a different ratio. However, the gold standard then re-established and legally prevailing ever since was very different from the pre-1933 standard. Gold was eliminated from circulation, and ownership of monetary gold by private citizens was made illegal, so that the national money was no longer freely convertible into gold at a fixed ratio. The loosening of the links between money and gold and, consequently, between money and international trade was completed by other countries, many of which went even further in severing all connection between the national money and gold. Today gold is primarily a commodity whose price is pegged rather than the keystone of the world or the U.S. monetary system. However, the legacy of history and the use of gold as a vehicle for fixing exchange rates still give it a monetary significance possessed by no other commodity subject to government price-fixing.

A major change occurred in the banking system in 1934 as a result of the inception of federal insurance of bank deposits. It appears to have succeeded, as the Federal Reserve Act did not, in making impossible the mushrooming of a loss of public confidence in some banks into a banking panic arising out of a widespread attempt on the part of the public to convert deposits into currency.

These changes in monetary arrangements have altered markedly the forces determining the stock of money. As a result, they have altered also the behavior of the stock of money. For example, in the 46 years from 1914 to 1960, when a government agency had explicit responsibility for the behavior of the stock of money, the year-to-year change in the stock was a more variable magnitude than in the prior 35 years, when it was determined by the quasi-automatic mechanism of the gold standard. On the other hand, in the period since the end of World War II, it has been a much less variable magnitude than it was in any earlier period of comparable length (Table 25).

The changing monetary arrangements have affected in diverse ways the three variables we have found useful to regard as the arithmetic determinants of the stock of money: the stock of high-powered money; the ratio of the public's deposits to its currency holdings; and the ratio of the deposit liabilities of the commercial banking system to its reserves, which we have defined as equal to its total holdings of high-powered money (Chart 64).

The stock of high-powered money was the major factor accounting arithmetically for changes in the stock of money. Changes in high-powered money were, however, produced by different forces at different times: in the greenback period, mainly by changes in government fiduciary issues; from 1879 to 1914, mainly by gold flows, though to some extent also by changes in national bank notes and currency issued in exchange for silver; from 1914 to 1960, mainly by changes in Federal Reserve credit outstanding, with the notable exception of the years from 1934 to 1940 when gold flows dominated.

The deposit-currency ratio has been of major importance primarily during periods of financial difficulties. In each such period, the public's loss of confidence in banks led to an attempt to convert deposits into currency which produced a sharp decline in the ratio of deposits to currency and strong downward pressure on the stock of money. The establishment of the Federal Reserve System was expected to deprive such shifts in the deposit-currency ratio of monetary significance by providing a means of increasing the absolute volume of currency available for the public to hold, when the public desired to substitute currency for deposits, without requiring a multiple contraction of deposits. In practice, it did not succeed in achieving that objective. The most notable shift in the deposit-currency ratio in the 93 years from 1867 to 1960 occurred from 1930 to 1933, when the ratio fell to less than half its initial value and in three years erased the secular rise of three decades. Though the absolute volume of currency held by the public rose, it did so only at the expense of a very much larger decline in deposits, the combined effect being a decline of one-third in the total stock of money. The inception of federal insurance of bank deposits in 1934 finally changed decisively the behavior of the deposit-currency ratio. Since then it has not been subject to drastic changes in short periods, and it is not likely to be in the future.

The ratio of deposits to reserves, like the deposit-currency ratio, has been of major importance at times of financial difficulties, though it has played a more consistent minor role by generally rising during business expansions and falling during business contractions. Whenever the public has shown distrust of banks by seeking to lower the deposit-currency ratio, banks have reacted by seeking to strengthen their reserves. After a brief interval, they have succeeded in doing so, which is to say, in lowering the deposit-reserve ratio, thereby adding further to the downward pressure on the stock of money.

The deposit-reserve ratio has also varied over longer periods in response to changes in monetary arrangements. It rose notably in the greenback period as a result of the maturing of national banks and an increase in the relative importance of nonnational banks. It rose again in the decade from 1897 to 1907, partly as a result of the assumption by the Treasury of wider central-banking functions. It rose again after establishment of the Federal Reserve System, which both lowered legal requirements and gave banks confidence that, in case of need, they had a ready "lender of last resort" to fall back on. The monetary collapse from 1930 to 1933 changed the picture profoundly. It produced a decline in the deposit-reserve ratio from its all-time high in 1929 to a level, a decade later, not much above the level at the start of our series in 1867. The 1930–33 experience taught banks not to rely on the Federal Reserve System for liquidity; it took them some three years to adjust their reserves to the associated shift in their preferences for liquidity. Successive increases in reserve requirements in 1936–37 produced another shift in their preferences; again it took the banks some three years to adjust. Since then, the deposit-reserve ratio has risen as the role of deposit insurance in eliminating the danger of runs on banks has been recognized, and the effects of the earlier experiences have worn off. If adjustment is made for changes in legal requirements, the ratio is back to its level of the late twenties.

Despite these marked alterations in the forces affecting the stock of money, there has been, as we have seen, little alteration in the relation between the changes, once determined, in the stock of money and other economic variables. The external forces impinging on the stock of money have changed radically. At the same time, the impact of changes in the stock of money on the rest of the economy appears to have been highly stable.

3. *Independence of Monetary Changes*

The close relation between changes in the stock of money and changes in other economic variables, alone, tells nothing about the origin of either or the direction of influence. The monetary changes might be dancing to the tune called by independently originating changes in the other economic variables; the changes in income and prices might be dancing to the tune called by independently originating monetary changes; the two might be mutually interacting, each having some elements of independence; or both might be dancing to the common tune of still a third set of influences. A great merit of the examination of a wide range of qualitative evidence, so essential in a monetary history, is that it provides a basis for discriminating between these possible explanations of the observed statistical covariation. We can go beyond the numbers alone and, at least on some occasions, discern the antecedent circumstances whence arose the particular movements that become so anonymous when we feed the statistics into the computer.

One thing is abundantly clear from our narrative. Monetary changes have in fact often been independent, in the sense that they have often not been an immediate or necessary consequence of contemporaneous changes in business conditions.

The clearest example is perhaps the monetary expansion from 1897 to 1914, which was worldwide and reflected an increased output of gold. The increased output of gold was partly a consequence of earlier decades of declining prices, which encouraged gold production, and so speaks also for a mutual interaction between monetary and economic changes. But clearly the monetary expansion cannot be attributed to the contemporary rise in money income and prices. By itself, the rise in money income and prices made for a reduced output of gold in the world at large and for an outflow of gold from any single country in a gold-standard world. If the common movement of money and income was not purely coincidental, the direction of influence must run from money to income.

686

The two major rises in the stock of money during World Wars I and II are about equally clear. In the early stages of both wars, the rise reflected an inflow of gold into the United States, as belligerent nations used the resources they could readily mobilize to purchase war material in the United States. The inflows of gold were not by-products of contemporary changes in economic activity in this country or abroad, as gold flows had been in the years before 1914. They were a consequence of the outbreak of the two wars and the deliberate policy decisions of the political authorities in the countries at war. In the later stages of both wars, the rise reflected political decisions of U.S. authorities about the financing of war expenditures. Those decisions involved a major expansion in high-powered money which continued the work begun by gold inflows. Again, if the common movement of the stock of money and of money income and prices is not coincidental or the consequence of a common cause, the direction of influence must run from money to income.

The resumption and silver episodes display a substantial independence in the monetary changes that occurred and also a rather complex action and interaction between monetary and business changes. The pressures for and against resumption in the 1870's and the drive for free silver in the 1890's were major elements that shaped the course of events. Both were in some measure independent of the contemporary course of economic activity, though not of course of longer-run economic developments. Both were also much affected by the course of events, the pressures against resumption and for free silver being greatly strengthened by a slowing down or decline in the pace of business activity or a decline in agricultural prices. More important, such contemporaneous events as the state of the harvests at home and abroad, developments in the railroad industry in the 1870's and in the London money market in the 1890's had important effects on the particular dates at which those political pressures produced monetary disturbances, which in their turn reacted on business conditions and political attitudes.

The establishment of the Federal Reserve System provides the student of money a closer substitute for the controlled experiment to determine the direction of influence than the social scientist can generally obtain. The System was at times simply a means through which other forces operated—as during the two world wars, and much of the thirties when it followed a largely passive course, and after World War II when its policy of supporting the prices of government securities left it little independent initiative. But the establishment of the System gave a small body of individuals the power, which they exercised from time to time, to alter the course of events in significant and identifiable ways through a deliberative process—a sequence parallel with the conduct of a controlled experiment. True, the actions of the monetary authorities were greatly affected by the climate of opinion and knowledge in which they operated. Their attitudes, the experiments they undertook, and the interpretation they placed on the results were to a large extent determined by the contemporary course of events and the contemporary state of knowledge about monetary phenomena. This has also been true of physical scientists in deciding what experiments to undertake and in interpreting the results in light of preceding experiments and the contemporary body of knowledge. In either case, such dependence on the existing state of knowledge does not alter the scientific independence from the prior or contemporary course of events of the changes introduced into the controlled variables. What it means in both cases is simply that later students may reinterpret the results of the experiments in light of the changed body of knowledge and draw conclusions that are different from those drawn by the original experimenters.

True, also, it is often impossible and always difficult to identify accurately the effects of the actions of the monetary authorities. Their actions are taken amidst many other circumstances, and it may not be at all clear whether their actions or some of the other circumstances produced the results observed. This is equally true of the experiments of physical scientists. No experiment is completely controlled, and most experiments add little to tested and confirmed knowledge about the subject of experiment. It is the rare crucial experiment that throws a flood of light on its subject—a light that blinds us to many less important experiments that were necessary before the one crucial experiment could be made.

Three counterparts of such crucial experiments stand out in the monetary record since the establishment of the Federal Reserve System. On three occasions the System deliberately took policy steps of major magnitude which cannot be regarded as necessary or inevitable economic consequences of contemporary changes in money income and prices. Like the crucial experiments of the physical scientist, the results are so consistent and sharp as to leave little doubt about their interpretation. The dates are January–June 1920, October 1931, and July 1936–January 1937. These are the three occasions—and the only three—when the Reserve System engaged in acts of commission that were sharply restrictive: in January 1920, by raising the rediscount rate from 4¾ per cent to 6 per cent and then in June 1920, to 7 per cent, at a time when member banks were borrowing from the Reserve Banks more than the total of their reserve balances; in October 1931, by raising the rediscount rate from 1½ per cent to 3½ per cent within a two-week period, at a time when a wave of failures was engulfing commercial banks, as in the preceding year, and indebtedness to the System was growing; in July 1936 and January 1937, by announcing the doubling of reserve requirements in three stages, the last effective on May 1, 1937, at a time when the Treasury was engaged in gold sterilization, which was the equivalent of a large-scale restrictive open market operation. There is no other occasion in Federal Reserve history when it has taken explicit restrictive measures of comparable magnitude—we cannot even suggest possible parallels.

The strictly monetary changes associated with those actions were equally sharp and distinctive. The actions were followed after some months in 1920 and 1936–37, immediately in 1931, by sharp declines in the stock of money, the three sharpest declines within a twelve-month period in the history of the Reserve System: declines of 9 per cent (1920), 14 per cent (1931), and 3 per cent (1937), respectively. And for the first and third declines, the numbers understate the severity of the monetary reaction. In 1919 and again in 1936, the money stock was growing at a rapid rate, so the subsequent declines represented a deceleration from an unusually high rate of growth to an unusually high rate of decline. The 1931 decline—the severest absolute decline of the three—was the mildest in terms of deceleration; the money stock in the preceding year had been falling at a slightly lower rate, so the increase in the rate of decline in the year beginning October 1931 was only about one percentage point.

The economic changes associated with those monetary actions were equally sharp and equally distinctive. Each was followed by sharp contractions in industrial production, after some months in 1920 and 1936–37, and immediately in 1931: declines within a twelve-month period of 30 per cent (1920), 24 per cent (1931), and 34 per cent (1937), respectively. There are only two other comparably severe declines in industrial production: during 1929–31, dealt with further below; and 1945, when the sharp decline represented a shift in the composition of output away from military products after the end of the war, rather than a general contraction in economic activity, as at the other four dates. Other indicators confirm the story told by industrial production. Whether one looks at wholesale prices, freight car loadings, common stock prices, or department stores sales, the downturns that followed the three monetary actions are the severest by a wide margin in the history of the Federal Reserve System, except only the 1929 to 1931 decline.[1]

The strength of the evidence furnished by those three quasi-controlled experiments can perhaps be made clearer by an analogy. Suppose we had medical records of 42 married couples (to match the 42 years of Federal Reserve history from 1919 to 1960, excluding World War I because the System was not effectively in control). Suppose 3 men and 4 women were found to have a specified illness; suppose that 3 of the 4 women turned out to be the wives of the 3 men with the same illness. The

[1] In addition to the three restrictive actions, three expansionary actions by

689

presumption that the illness was contagious would certainly be very strong—especially so, if it were discovered that the husband of the fourth woman was the only remaining man to have a biologically related but not identical illness. Similarly, the three episodes described above establish a comparably strong presumption that the economic changes were the consequence of the deliberately undertaken monetary actions, and hence that our finding of a close covariation between the stock of money and income reflects the existence of an influence running from money to income. Indeed, in one respect the analogy seriously understates the strength of the evidence. It takes no account of the time sequence of events.[2]

---

the Reserve System—apart from those it took in the two world wars—were associated with correspondingly sharp monetary and economic changes.

Monetary Action	Associated Change in Money Stock	Associated Change in Industrial Production
Dec. 1923–Oct. 1924 F. R. purchase of $0.5 billion of govern-_ments	Feb. 1924–Feb. 1925 19 per cent increase	July 1924–July 1925 22½ per cent increase
Apr.–Aug. 1932 F. R. purchase of $1 billion of governments	Apr. 1932–Jan. 1933 Shift from 14 per cent annual rate of decline to 1¾ per cent annual rate of rise	July–Nov. 1932 14 per cent increase
Mar.–Dec. 1958 F. R. purchase of $3 billion of governments; $4.6 billion increase in F. R. credit	Dec. 1957–Dec. 1958 6.6 per cent increase	Apr. 1958–Apr. 1959 23 per cent increase

We regard these episodes as less striking and decisive than the three cited in the text, because the associated monetary and economic changes are less distinctive: e.g., from June 1933 to June 1936, there was no Federal Reserve action, yet the stock of money rose by 44 per cent and industrial production by 31 per cent.

[2] This reflects the one respect in which the analogy is inexact. Time is continuous. There is no particular reason for taking the year instead of the quarter or the biennium as the unit of analysis, and for regarding 42 discrete observations as containing the same information as our time series covering 42 years. It is not at all clear whether the appropriate number is larger or smaller than 42. Serial correlation among successive years points toward a smaller number: say, 10, the number of complete reference cycles in the period from Mar. 1919 to Feb. 1961. The possibility of identifying turns and timing relations monthly argues for a larger number, since the continuous data give information not available from the discrete unordered data.

If the 4 ill wives and 3 ill husbands were distributed at random among 42 wives and 42 husbands, the probability that the 3 husbands would be married to 3 of the wives is 1 in 2,870. The corresponding probability for the same number of ill wives and husbands distributed among a total of 10 couples is 1 in 30.

The presumption that the economic changes were the consequence of the monetary changes is greatly strengthened by examination of the one sharp economic contraction not associated with explicit restrictive measures by the Federal Reserve System—the 1929 to 1931 contraction, which was the first part of the great contraction from 1929 to 1933. That contraction has served perhaps more than any other experience to strengthen the view that money dances to the tune of business. The reason is that the Reserve System did not, in fact, stem the decline of one-third in the stock of money—by far the largest in the course of a cyclical contraction at least since 1893–43—or the accompanying contraction in economic activity. The System pleaded impotence, arguing explicitly that the nonmonetary forces making for contraction were so strong and violent that it was powerless to stem the tide, and implicitly that the depth of the decline in the money stock was due to the depth of the decline in business activity, rather than, as the evidence cited above suggests, the reverse. Many others, recognizing the good intentions of the monetary authorities and the ability of many individuals in the System, while independently holding a wide variety of views about the role of money in economic affairs, accepted the System's plea. In addition, a revolution in economic theory, having quite different origins and by no means necessarily implying the impotence of monetary policy, offered a theoretical structure that at one and the same time could rationalize the impotence of monetary policy and provide an intellectually satisfying alternative explanation of the economic debacle.

There is one sense—and, so far as we can see, only one—in which a case can be made for the proposition that the monetary decline was a consequence of the economic decline. That sense is not relevant to our main task of seeking to understand economic interrelations, since it involves relying primarily on psychological and political factors. The System was operating in a climate of opinion that in the main regarded recessions and depressions as curative episodes, necessary in order to purge the body economic of the aftereffects of its earlier excesses. The prevailing opinion also confused money and credit; confused the elasticity of one component of the money stock relative to another with the elasticity of the total stock; regarded it as desirable that the stock of money should respond to the "needs of trade," rising in expansions and falling in contractions; and attached much greater importance to the maintenance of the gold standard and the stability of exchanges than to the maintenance of internal stability. Most of those attitudes characterized the public at large and not merely the financial community or the Reserve System in particular. Given that milieu, it can be argued that the System followed an inevitable policy; that it could not have been expected to prevent the appreciable decline in the stock of money during

691

1930, because it and others as well regarded the decline as a desirable offset to earlier speculative excess; and that its failure to react vigorously, after banks began failing on a large scale in late 1930 and the public sought to convert deposits into currency, reflected the attitude that it was desirable to liquidate "bad" banks, to let "nature take its course" rather than to support the financial system "artificially." Certainly, the assignment of priority to the maintenance of the gold standard was in a proximate sense the reason for the sharp rise in discount rates in October 1931 following Britain's departure from gold and a gold outflow from the United States—the restrictive action described above as one of the System's crucial experiments.

This account portrays accurately an important part of the situation. It helps to explain how able and public-spirited men could have acted in a manner which in retrospect appears misguided, why there was so notable an absence of economic statesmanship outside the System and hence no steady informed pressure on the System for different action. But even on that level, the account is seriously incomplete. We are inclined to believe that the particular course of action followed by the Reserve System owed less to the climate of opinion—though it was certainly a necessary condition—than to a sequence of more or less accidental events and the running conflict for power within the System. Benjamin Strong's death in 1928 unleashed an active phase of conflict which dominated policy throughout 1929, producing a deadlock between the Board and the New York Bank—acting as leader of all the Banks —about the proper policy to adopt in face of the stock market boom. The result was a policy that, in our view, was too easy to break the bull market and too tight to permit vigorous business expansion. The conflict plus the reaction by the rest of the System to the New York Bank's independent (and effective) operations in the wake of the stock market crash in October 1929 indirectly led to a shift of power over open market operations. A 5-man committee, dominated by the New York Bank, was replaced by a 12-man committee of the 12 Federal Reserve Bank governors in which New York played a less important role. That shift stacked the cards heavily in favor of a policy of inaction and drift.

We share the view expressed by Carl Snyder, for many years associated with the New York Bank as a statistician and economist, that if Benjamin Strong could "have had twelve months more of vigorous health, we might have ended the depression in 1930, and with this the long drawn out world crisis that so profoundly affected the ensuing political developments."[3] As it was, Strong's successor at New York, George L. Harrison, vigorously advocated expansionary action in 1930, but was unable to

[3] Carl Snyder, *Capitalism the Creator*, New York, Macmillan, 1940, p. 203.

prevail over the combined opposition of the Board and the other Bank governors. Harrison was in favor of expansionary action in 1931, that time with the support of the new governor of the Board, Eugene Meyer, but the pattern of deadlock and inaction had been set, to be broken only temporarily in 1932 under the pressure of Congressional prodding. Despite the general climate of opinion, the technical personnel of the New York Bank—and it must be recalled that under Strong the New York Bank dominated System policy almost completely—were consistently in favor of the policies which seem to us in retrospect the ones that should have been followed.

In any event, what is relevant to our present purpose is neither praise nor blame, nor even a full understanding of the reasons for the System's behavior under the difficult and trying circumstances it faced. Even if its behavior was psychologically or politically inevitable under the circumstances, that would explain only why the quasi-controlled experiment was conducted. It would not explain the results of the experiment. The question would remain whether the monetary changes were the inevitable result of the economic changes, so that, if the System had not been the intermediary, some other mechanism would have enforced the same monetary changes; or whether the monetary changes can be regarded as an economically independent factor which accounted in substantial measure for the economic changes. There is little doubt about the answer. At all times throughout the 1929–33 contraction, alternative policies were available to the System by which it could have kept the stock of money from falling, and indeed could have increased it at almost any desired rate. Those policies did not involve radical innovations. They involved measures of a kind the System had taken in earlier years, of a kind explicitly contemplated by the founders of the System to meet precisely the kind of banking crisis that developed in late 1930 and persisted thereafter. They involved measures that were actually proposed and very likely would have been adopted under a slightly different bureaucratic structure or distribution of power, or even if the men in power had had somewhat different personalities. Until late 1931—and we believe not even then—the alternative policies involved no conflict with the maintenance of the gold standard. Until September 1931, the problem that recurrently troubled the System was how to keep the gold inflows under control, not the reverse.

To consider still another alternative: if the pre-1914 banking system rather than the Federal Reserve System had been in existence in 1929, the money stock almost certainly would not have undergone a decline comparable to the one that occurred. Comparison of the 1907 banking panic under the earlier system and the closely similar liquidity crisis which began in late 1930 offers strong evidence for this judgment. If the earlier system had been in operation, and if everything else had proceeded as it did up to December 1930, the experience of 1907 strongly suggests that there would have been a more severe initial reaction to the bank failures than there was in 1930, probably involving concerted restriction by banks of the convertibility of deposits into currency. The restriction might have had more severe initial effects toward deepening the economic contraction than the persistent pressure on the banking system that characterized late 1930 and early 1931 had. But it also would have cut short the spread of the crisis, would have prevented cumulation of bank failures, and would have made possible, as it did in 1908, economic recovery after a few months.

While, therefore, the actions of the Reserve System in 1929–33 may be understandable under the circumstances, even psychologically and politically inevitable, the contraction is additional strong evidence for the economic independence of monetary changes from the contemporary course of income and prices, even during the early phase of the contraction, from 1929 to 1931, when the decline in the stock of money was not the result of explicit restrictive measures taken by the System. It can indeed be regarded as a fourth crucial experiment, making the matching of independent monetary decline and subsequent economic decline 4 to 4.[4]

The existence of an important independent influence running from money to income explains the contrast we have noted between the variability in monetary arrangements during the near-century we have studied and the stability of the relation between changes in money and in other economic variables. The variability of monetary arrangements has produced, as we have seen, a corresponding variation in the movements of money itself. But, given that the major channel of influence is from money to business, there is no reason the changes in monetary arrangements should have altered the relation between movements in money and in business. That relation is determined primarily by the channels through which money affects business. So long as they remain the same, as apparently they have, so also should the relation between money and business.

Suppose, however, the major channel of influence had been from business to money. Changes in monetary institutions would then have

[4] For 42 married couples, the probability that 4 ill husbands and 4 ill wives chosen at random would constitute 4 married couples is 1 in 111,930. For the alternative of 10 (see footnote 2, above) as the total number of couples, 1929–31 and October 1931 cannot be regarded as two separate observations, since both fall within a single reference cycle. It is therefore necessary to change the number of ill individuals. The simplest counterpart is to suppose 10 married couples, 3 ill husbands and 3 ill wives. The probability that the ill husbands and wives would constitute 3 married couples if chosen at random is then 1 in 120.

affected not only the behavior of money but also the relation between money and other economic variables, since a change in business would have had different effects on the stock of money under the different monetary arrangements. Under the pre-1914 gold standard, for example, a business expansion in the United States tended to generate a deficit in the balance of payments, which in turn tended to produce an outflow of gold and hence downward pressure on the stock of money. That particular link in the sequence was largely severed by the gold-sterilization policy followed by the Federal Reserve in the 1920's and by the Treasury in part of the 1930's, and was greatly weakened by the change in the character of the gold standard during the rest of the period after 1914. Both before and after 1914, business expansion raised interest rates and stimulated banks to expand. However, before 1914 a rise in interest rates could raise the stock of money only through a rise in the deposit-reserve ratio or through the attraction of capital and thereby gold from abroad. After 1914, a rise in interest rates could also raise the stock of money by inducing banks to borrow more heavily from the Federal Reserve System. If the predominant direction of influence had been from business to money, these and other changes in the links between business and money would very likely have produced an appreciably different relation between movements in the two before and after 1914, and perhaps also for further subdivisions of those periods.

While the influence running from money to economic activity has been predominant, there have clearly also been influences running the other way, particularly during the shorter-run movements associated with the business cycle. The cyclical pattern of the deposit-reserve ratio is one example. The resumption and silver episodes, the 1919 inflation, and the 1929–33 contraction reveal clearly other aspects of the reflex influence of business on money. Changes in the money stock are therefore a consequence as well as an independent source of change in money income and prices, though, once they occur, they produce in their turn still further effects on income and prices. Mutual interaction, but with money rather clearly the senior partner in longer-run movements and in major cyclical movements, and more nearly an equal partner with money income and prices in shorter-run and milder movements—this is the generalization suggested by our evidence.

4. Deceptiveness of Appearances

Money is a fascinating subject of study because it is so full of mystery and paradox. The piece of green paper with printing on it is little different, as paper, from a piece of the same size torn from a newspaper or magazine, yet the one will enable its bearer to command some measure of food, drink, clothing, and the remaining goods of life; the other is fit only to light the fire. Whence the difference? The piece of green paper reads, "The United States of America will pay to the bearer on demand . . . dollars," or words to that effect, plus an assertion that it is "legal tender." But under current circumstances, the promise amounts only to a commitment to exchange one piece of green paper for one or several other pieces of green paper or for coins which, if melted down, will sell on the market as metal for less than the amount of paper money they serve to redeem. The legal-tender quality means only that the government will accept the pieces of paper in discharge of debts due to itself, and that the courts will regard them as discharging debts stated in dollars. Why should they also be accepted by private persons in private transactions for goods and services?

The short answer—yet the right answer—is that each accepts them because he is confident others will. The pieces of green paper have value because everybody thinks they have value, and everybody thinks they have value because in his experience they have had value. Our economy could not operate at more than a small fraction of its present level of productivity without a common and widely accepted medium of exchange; yet that common and widely accepted medium of exchange is, at bottom, a social convention which owes its very existence to the mutual acceptance of what from one point of view is a fiction.

The social convention or the fiction or what you will is no fragile thing. On the contrary, the social value of a common money is so great that people will stick to the fiction even under extreme provocation— whence, of course, comes part of the gains that can be obtained from inflation by the issuers of the money and hence also the temptation to inflate. But neither is the fiction indestructible: extreme variation in the quantity of the green paper—as in the U.S. Revolutionary War or in the hyperinflations in various countries after World Wars I and II—or moderate variation in its quantity plus legally and effectively enforced ceilings on nominal prices—as in Germany after World War II—can render the paper formerly serving as money worthless and induce people to seek substitutes—like the cigarettes and cognac which for a time became the medium of exchange in Germany after World War II.

Money is a veil. The "real" forces are the capacities of the people, their industry and ingenuity, the resources they command, their mode of economic and political organization, and the like. As John Stuart Mill wrote more than a century ago:

There cannot, in short, be intrinsically a more insignificant thing, in the economy of society, than money; except in the character of a contrivance for sparing time and labour. It is a machine for doing quickly and commodiously, what would be done, though less quickly and commodiously, without it: and like many other kinds of machinery, it only exerts a distinct and independent influence of its own when it gets out of order.[5]

Perfectly true. Yet also somewhat misleading, unless we recognize that there is hardly a contrivance man possesses which can do more damage to a society when it goes amiss.

Each man believes he can determine how much of his wealth he will hold in money; yet the total amount of money available for all to hold is outside the control of all holders of money taken together. Each bank thinks it can determine how much of its assets it will hold in the form of currency, plus deposits at Federal Reserve Banks, to meet legal reserve requirements and for precautionary purposes. Yet the total amount available for all banks to hold is outside the control of all banks together. If any one bank receives an accession to its cash, it can therewith acquire additional noncash assets equal at most to that accession; yet if all banks together receive an accession to cash, the banking system can therewith acquire additional assets equal to a multiple of that accession.

This deceptiveness of appearances has recurred again and again in the course of our narrative. The price of gold in terms of greenbacks during the Civil War may have fluctuated from day to day in accordance with the changing fortunes of war; but the fortunes of war affected to only a minor extent the level about which the fluctuations occurred— only as they affected the willingness of foreigners to hold greenbacks or securities expressed in terms of greenbacks. The level reflected rather the drastic decline in cotton exports and the rising internal prices in the North as money was issued to help finance the war.

One measure taken to foster resumption, which is to say, to raise the value of the dollar in terms of foreign currencies, was identical with a measure taken by Franklin D. Roosevelt to achieve precisely the opposite purpose, to lower the value of the dollar in terms of foreign currency. In both cases, the Treasury undertook to buy gold abroad. The New Deal's economics was correct, at least in this respect; so the adoption of the same measure during the greenback period meant that the mechanical effects of the purchase of gold abroad made resumption more rather than less difficult.

Although resumption was a major political issue for a decade and a half, its successful achievement owed little to the measures taken in its name. The main governmental contribution was a minor reduction in high-powered money—granted, no mean achievement on a purely political level, in view of the pressure to expand the issue of greenbacks. Resumption succeeded because the rapid growth of output brought a halving of the price level despite a mild rise in the stock of money.

[5] *Principles of Political Economy* (1848), Ashley Ed., New York, 1929, p. 488.

The governmental measures that had the greatest effect on resumption were not the explicitly monetary measures but the acts of omission and commission that contributed to the rapid growth of output.

The proponents of free silver were attacked by "sound money" forces on the ground that free silver would produce an unduly rapid expansion in the money stock and thereby breed price inflation. The limited purchases of silver made by the Treasury were deplored because it was believed they raised unduly the stock of money and were thus harbingers of the inflation that would be unleashed by unlimited purchases. In fact, given that the gold standard was not abandoned, the main economic harm done by the silver agitation was that it enforced an unduly slow rate of increase in the money stock and thereby produced deflation. It did so because the fear that the United States would abandon gold reduced capital inflows which would otherwise have been larger, or fostered capital flights. In turn, these required lower prices in the United States than would otherwise have been necessary in order to balance international payments at the exchange rates fixed by official prices of gold in the United States and abroad.

Bryan's defeat in 1896 marked the crest of the silver agitation. It was the crest, not because Bryan lost his silver tongue, nor because the advocates of "sound money" persuaded the advocates of free silver by their arguments, but because gold discoveries and improvements in gold mining and refining made gold the effective vehicle for the inflation that Bryan and his followers had sought to achieve with silver.

The banking panic of 1907 produced apparently irresistible pressure for banking reform. Yet we have found reason to believe that at least the final step of that panic, the concerted restriction by banks of the convertibility of deposits into currency, was a therapeutic measure which cut short the liquidity crisis, prevented good banks from failing in droves as victims of mass hysteria and, at the cost of severe but brief difficulties, enabled recovery and expansion to come after a short-lived contraction.

The reform measure finally enacted—the Federal Reserve System— with the aim of preventing any such panics or any such restriction of convertibility in the future did not in fact stem the worst panic in American economic history and the severest restrictions of convertibility, the collapse of the banking system from 1930 to 1933 terminating in the banking holiday of March 1933. That same reform, intended to promote monetary stability, was followed by about thirty years of relatively greater instability in the money stock than any experienced in the pre-Federal Reserve period our data cover, and possibly than any experienced in the whole of U.S. history, the Revolutionary War alone excepted.

The stock market boom and the afterglow of concern with World War I inflation have led to a widespread belief that the 1920's were a period of inflation and that the collapse from 1929 to 1933 was a reaction to that. In fact, the 1920's were, if anything, a time of relative deflation: from 1923 to 1929—to compare peak years of business cycles and so avoid distortion from cyclical influences—wholesale prices fell at the rate of 1 per cent per year and the stock of money rose at the annual rate of 4 per cent per year, which is roughly the rate required to match expansion of output. The business cycle expansion from 1927 to 1929 was the first since 1891–93 during which wholesale prices fell, even if only a trifle, and there has been none since.

The monetary collapse from 1929 to 1933 was not an inevitable consequence of what had gone before. It was a result of the policies followed during those years. As already noted, alternative policies that could have halted the monetary debacle were available throughout those years. Though the Reserve System proclaimed that it was following an easy-money policy, in fact it followed an exceedingly tight policy.

The proponents of the New Deal were strongly in favor of easy money. And there was rapid monetary expansion during the later thirties, produced primarily by two things: the rise in the price of gold and the rise of Hitler to power, which stimulated a capital flow to the United States. The rapid monetary expansion owed nothing to monetary actions other than the rise in the price of gold. Though that rise had the direct effect intended, some of the measures accompanying it—in particular the nationalization of gold, the abrogation of gold clauses, and the New Deal's program aside from monetary policy—had the opposite effects by discouraging business investment. The one major monetary action of the Federal Reserve during that period was the doubling of reserve requirements in 1936 and 1937 under newly acquired powers. The action was not intended to have significant contemporary deflationary effects; it was taken primarily as a "precautionary" step; the Reserve System satisfied itself that excess reserves were ample and widely distributed. In the event, in combination with Treasury gold sterilization, it had a serious deflationary impact.

The silver-purchase program of the 1930's was undertaken with the ostensible objective of raising the proportion of silver in the nation's monetary reserves from one-sixth to one-third, in large part to aid silver miners. The program involved aggregate expenditures of $2 billion from 1933 to 1960, amounting to at least $5 for each dollar of benefit to U.S. silver miners. Yet the increase in the proportion of silver to one-third was never achieved. But the silver-purchase program in the thirties did impose several years of drastic deflation on China, drove China permanently and Mexico temporarily off the silver standard.

and must be counted as a major factor weakening China both economically and politically.

World War II was widely expected to be followed by severe unemployment. The Reserve System girded itself for the possibility and welcomed the bond-support program, because the System thought it would be consistent with easy-money policies which would be required after the war. In the event, inflation rather than deflation loomed as the greater danger and, under the added impetus to inflation given by the Korean War, the Federal Reserve was finally led to divest itself of the self-imposed chains of the bond-support program.

What happened in the United States happened also abroad. The quantity of money, it had come to be widely believed, was of little economic significance except as control over it might be the means of keeping long-term interest rates lower than otherwise, which, in turn, might contribute a mite to the level of aggregate demand, which would otherwise be deficient. Easy money was the near-uniform prescription. Inflation was the near-uniform result. It was stemmed only as easy money was given up. One result has been to restore a healthy respect for the role of money in economic affairs.

Velocity has been rising throughout almost the whole of the postwar period in contrast to its decline in the preceding three-quarters of a century. A large part of the rise was clearly a reaction to the wartime decline. But the rise has been too large and too long continued to be accounted for in this way alone. Numerous explanations have been offered, ranging from the wider availability and better quality of substitutes for money to the rise in interest rates, to fear of inflation. We are inclined to believe that, while these may all have played a part, the rise over and above the reaction to the wartime decline has been mainly produced by increasing confidence on the part of the public at large in the stability of the economy. In accordance with this interpretation, we expect the secular decline to be resumed. But we are still too close to the appearances to be at all sure in what way they are deceptive. We shall have to wait for experience to unfold before discriminating finally among the alternative explanations.

One thing of which we are confident is that the history of money will continue to have surprises in store for those who follow its future course—surprises that the student of money and the statesman alike will ignore at their peril.

APPENDIXES

APPENDIX A
Basic Tables

For greater detail on estimates in Tables A-1, A-2, and A-3, see our forthcoming "Trends and Cycles in the Stock of Money in the United States, 1867–1960," Part Two, a National Bureau study. For an analysis of our interpolation procedures, see Milton Friedman, *The Interpolation of Time Series by Related Series,* New York, National Bureau of Economic Research, Technical Paper 16, 1962.

TABLE A-1

CURRENCY HELD BY THE PUBLIC AND DEPOSITS, SEASONALLY ADJUSTED, 1867–1960
(millions of dollars)

DATE	Currency Held by the Public (1)	Commercial Banks Demand (2)	Commercial Banks Time (3)	Total (4)	Mutual Savings Banks (5)	Postal Savings System (6)	Cols. 1 and 2 (7)	Cols. 1 and 4 (8)	Cols 1, 4 5 and (9)
1867									
Jan.	585			729	276			1,314	1,59⬤
1868									
Jan.	531			713	324			1,244	1,56⬤
1869									
Jan.	529			735	374			1,264	1,638
1870									
Jan.	510			779	436			1,289	1,72⬤
1871									
Jan.	546			844	521			1,390	1,911
1872									
Jan.	542			1,041	612			1,583	2,19⬤
1873									
Feb.	552			1,070	684			1,622	2,30⬤
1874									
Feb.	526			1,066	745			1,592	2,337
1875									
Feb.	544			1,151	795			1,695	2,49C
Aug.	510			1,185	837			1,695	2,532
1876									
Feb.	516			1,158	842			1,674	2,51⬤
Aug.	506			1,152	847			1,658	2,505
1877									
Feb.	514			1,166	841			1,680	2,521
Aug.	525			1,092	818			1,617	2,435
1878									
Feb.	526			1,053	797			1,579	2,376
Aug.	529			1,026	772			1,555	2,327
1879									
Feb.	520			1,023	751			1,543	2,294
Aug.	574			1,201	744			1,775	2,519
1880									
Feb.	624			1,295	787			1,919	2,706
Aug.	662			1,380	829			2,042	2,871
1881									
Feb.	714			1,545	867			2,259	3,126
Aug.	797			1,702	957			2,499	3,456
1882									
June	807			1,787	951			2,594	3,545
1883									
June	856			1,955	1,004			2,811	3,814
1884									
June	842			1,922	1,034			2,764	3,798

(continued)

TABLE A-1 (continued)

| DATE | Currency Held by the Public (1) | DEPOSITS ADJUSTED | | | | | Summations | | |
| | | Commercial Banks | | | Mutual Savings Banks (5) | Postal Savings System (6) | | | |
		Demand (2)	Time (3)	Total (4)			Cols. 1 and 2 (7)	Cols. 1 and 4 (8)	Cols. 1, 4, 5 and 6 (9)
1885									
June	780			2,057	1,067			2,837	3,904
1886									
June	753			2,330	1,125			3,083	4,208
1887									
June	793			2,486	1,183			3,279	4,463
1888									
June	821			2,541	1,237			3,362	4,599
1889									
June	819			2,724	1,300			3,543	4,843
1890									
June	888			3,020	1,373			3,908	5,282
1891									
June	921			3,098	1,427			4,019	5,446
1892									
June	929			3,541	1,517			4,470	5,987
1893									
June	985			3,203	1,546			4,188	5,734
1894									
June	883			3,341	1,571			4,224	5,796
1895									
June	881			3,596	1,650			4,477	6,128
1896									
June	832			3,434	1,693			4,266	5,959
1897									
June	873			3,609	1,784			4,482	6,266
1898									
June	1,017			4,120	1,869			5,137	7,007
1899									
June	1,068			4,966	1,999			6,034	8,033
1900									
June	1,191			5,187	2,128			6,378	8,506
1901									
June	1,232			6,104	2,260			7,336	9,596
1902									
June	1,280			6,729	2,389			8,009	10,398
1903									
June	1,399			7,123	2,504			8,522	11,026
1904									
June	1,404			7,580	2,601			8,984	11,585
1905									
June	1,476			8,596	2,743			10,072	12,815
1906									
June	1,586			9,278	2,911			10,864	13,775

(continued)

TABLE A-1 (continued)

DATE	Currency Held by the Public (1)	Commercial Banks			Mutual Savings Banks (5)	Postal Savings System (6)	Cols. 1 and 2 (7)	Cols. 1 and 4 (8)	Cols 1, 4, 5 and (9)
		Demand (2)	Time (3)	Total (4)					
1907									
May	1,715			9,942	3,019			11,657	14,67
June	1,697			9,918	3,011			11,615	14,62
July	1,662			9,941	3,017			11,603	14,62
Aug.	1,654			9,898	3,027			11,552	14,57
Sept.	1,631			9,743	3,030			11,374	14,4C
Oct.	1,730			9,540	3,023			11,270	14,29
Nov.	1,784			9,373	3,021			11,157	14,17
Dec.	1,861			9,183	3,017			11,044	14,06
1908									
Jan.	1,893			9,018	3,021			10,911	13,93
Feb.	1,814			8,990	3,021			10,804	13,82
Mar.	1,757			9,133	3,018			10,890	13,90
Apr.	1,744			9,227	3,018			10,971	13,98
May	1,707			9,384	3,019			11,091	14,11
June	1,719			9,503	3,000			11,222	14,22
July	1,712			9,637	3,010			11,349	14,35
Aug.	1,668			9,799	3,024			11,467	14,49
Sept.	1,676			9,908	3,032			11,584	14,61
Oct.	1,698			10,042	3,036			11,740	14,77
Nov.	1,684			10,221	3,044			11,905	14,94
Dec.	1,714			10,271	3,055			11,985	15,04
1909									
Jan.	1,678			10,405	3,068			12,083	15,15
Feb.	1,682			10,459	3,079			12,141	15,22
Mar.	1,672			10,549	3,086			12,221	15,30
Apr.	1,683			10,654	3,096			12,337	15,43
May	1,677			10,773	3,124			12,450	15,57
June	1,687			10,889	3,133			12,576	15,70
July	1,672			10,970	3,149			12,642	15,79
Aug.	1,687			11,049	3,168			12,736	15,90
Sept.	1,708			11,120	3,181			12,828	16,00
Oct.	1,704			11,179	3,195			12,883	16,07
Nov.	1,703			11,204	3,208			12,907	16,11
Dec.	1,709			11,292	3,221			13,001	16,22
1910									
Jan.	1,719			11,272	3,239			12,991	16,23
Feb.	1,704			11,355	3,253			13,059	16,31
Mar.	1,695			11,458	3,265			13,153	16,41
Apr.	1,690			11,419	3,280			13,109	16,38
May	1,702			11,385	3,295			13,087	16,38
June	1,716			11,404	3,290			13,120	16,41
July	1,710			11,383	3,302			13,093	16,39

(continued)

TABLE A-1 (continued)

DATE	Currency Held by the Public (1)	DEPOSITS ADJUSTED					Summations		
		Commercial Banks			Mutual Savings Banks (5)	Postal Savings System (6)	Cols. 1 and 2 (7)	Cols. 1 and 4 (8)	Cols. 1, 4, 5 and 6 (9)
		Demand (2)	Time (3)	Total (4)					
910									
Aug.	1,728			11,417	3,318			13,145	16,463
Sept.	1,758			11,530	3,328			13,288	16,619
Oct.	1,774			11,642	3,339			13,416	16,755
Nov.	1,743			11,706	3,347			13,449	16,796
Dec.	1,734			11,756	3,356			13,490	16,846
911									
Jan.	1,735			11,816	3,370	*		13,551	16,921
Feb.	1,730			11,879	3,381			13,609	16,990
Mar.	1,743			11,931	3,389			13,674	17,063
Apr.	1,776			12,074	3,400			13,850	17,250
May	1,781			12,151	3,411			13,932	17,343
June	1,743			12,219	3,429	1		13,962	17,392
July	1,751			12,285	3,444	1		14,036	17,481
Aug.	1,775			12,270	3,463	2		14,045	17,510
Sept.	1,756			12,373	3,474	4		14,129	17,607
Oct.	1,750			12,527	3,479	6		14,277	17,762
Nov.	1,745			12,659	3,490	9		14,404	17,903
Dec.	1,698			12,760	3,501	11		14,458	17,970
912									
Jan.	1,706			12,862	3,516	13		14,568	18,097
Feb.	1,738			12,913	3,527	14		14,651	18,192
Mar.	1,750			12,997	3,535	16		14,747	18,298
Apr.	1,787			13,025	3,547	17		14,812	18,376
May	1,827			13,068	3,557	19		14,895	18,471
June	1,831			13,170	3,587	20		15,001	18,608
July	1,827			13,212	3,598	22		15,039	18,659
Aug.	1,830			13,268	3,613	23		15,098	18,734
Sept.	1,831			13,305	3,621	24		15,136	18,781
Oct.	1,857			13,397	3,633	26		15,254	18,913
Nov.	1,825			13,496	3,645	27		15,321	18,993
Dec.	1,817			13,513	3,658	28		15,330	19,016
913									
Jan.	1,831			13,553	3,674	28		15,384	19,086
Feb.	1,842			13,621	3,685	30		15,463	19,178
Mar.	1,833			13,588	3,693	31		15,421	19,145
Apr.	1,870			13,611	3,704	32		15,481	19,217
May	1,888			13,555	3,716	33		15,443	19,192
June	1,881			13,519	3,732	34		15,400	19,166
July	1,869			13,513	3,739	35		15,382	19,156
Aug.	1,872			13,641	3,749	36		15,513	19,298
Sept.	1,896			13,787	3,763	36		15,683	19,482

* Less than one-half million dollars, Jan.–May 1911.

(continued)

TABLE A-1 (continued)

DATE	Currency Held by the Public (1)	Commercial Banks Demand (2)	Time (3)	Total (4)	Mutual Savings Banks (5)	Postal Savings System (6)	Cols. 1 and 2 (7)	Cols. 1 and 4 (8)	Cols 1, 4 5 and (9)
1913									
Oct.	1,909			13,866	3,766	37		15,775	19,5
Nov.	1,886			13,901	3,776	38		15,787	19,6
Dec.	1,870			13,949	3,786	39		15,819	19,6
1914									
Jan.	1,847			14,009	3,805	40		15,856	19,7
Feb.	1,871			14,034	3,817	41		15,905	19,7
Mar.	1,854			14,140	3,826	42		15,994	19,8
Apr.	1,764			14,228	3,839	43		15,992	19,8
May	1,843			14,347	3,851	43		16,190	20,08
June	1,830	9,674	4,642	14,316	3,841	44	11,504	16,146	20,0
July	1,819	9,670	4,646	14,316	3,849	45	11,489	16,135	20,0
Aug.	1,909	9,657	4,638	14,295	3,856	48	11,566	16,204	20,1
Sept.	2,066	9,719	4,728	14,447	3,859	51	11,785	16,513	20,4
Oct.	2,080	9,644	4,808	14,452	3,858	54	11,724	16,532	20,4
Nov.	1,891	9,699	4,774	14,473	3,860	57	11,590	16,364	20,28
Dec.	1,874	9,717	4,728	14,445	3,862	58	11,591	16,319	20,2
1915									
Jan.	1,901	9,785	4,778	14,563	3,875	60	11,686	16,464	20,3
Feb.	1,855	9,947	4,807	14,754	3,879	61	11,802	16,609	20,54
Mar.	1,875	9,975	4,862	14,837	3,881	62	11,850	16,712	20,6
Apr.	1,905	10,011	4,892	14,903	3,886	64	11,916	16,808	20,75
May	1,887	10,097	4,997	15,094	3,891	65	11,984	16,981	20,93
June	1,894	10,225	5,025	15,250	3,873	67	12,119	17,144	21,08
July	1,897	10,318	5,038	15,356	3,895	68	12,215	17,253	21,21
Aug.	1,874	10,416	5,066	15,482	3,921	68	12,290	17,356	21,34
Sept.	1,903	10,688	5,187	15,875	3,940	69	12,591	17,778	21,78
Oct.	1,942	11,168	5,343	16,511	3,949	71	13,110	18,453	22,47
Nov.	1,917	11,309	5,427	16,736	3,967	72	13,226	18,653	22,69
Dec.	1,975	11,422	5,584	17,006	3,986	73	13,397	18,981	23,04
1916									
Jan.	2,045	11,648	5,617	17,265	4,013	75	13,693	19,310	23,39
Feb.	2,014	11,875	5,702	17,577	4,037	76	13,889	19,591	23,70
Mar.	2,061	11,921	5,735	17,656	4,057	78	13,982	19,717	23,85
Apr.	2,122	12,019	5,866	17,885	4,080	80	14,141	20,007	24,16
May	2,128	12,117	6,009	18,126	4,104	83	14,245	20,254	24,44
June	2,178	12,170	6,003	18,173	4,103	87	14,348	20,351	24,54
July	2,174	12,307	6,138	18,445	4,136	92	14,481	20,619	24,84
Aug.	2,169	12,569	6,137	18,706	4,173	95	14,738	20,875	25,14
Sept.	2,190	12,786	6,291	19,077	4,203	99	14,976	21,267	25,56
Oct.	2,216	13,001	6,427	19,428	4,230	103	15,217	21,644	25,97
Nov.	2,255	13,196	6,599	19,795	4,251	107	15,451	22,050	26,40
Dec.	2,241	13,362	6,895	20,257	4,277	110	15,603	22,498	26,88

(continued)

TABLE A-1 (continued)

| | | DEPOSITS ADJUSTED | | | | | Summations | | |
| | Currency Held by the Public (1) | Commercial Banks | | | Mutual Savings Banks (5) | Postal Savings System (6) | Cols. 1 and 2 (7) | Cols. 1 and 4 (8) | Cols. 1, 4, 5 and 6 (9) |
DATE		Demand (2)	Time (3)	Total (4)					
17									
Jan.	2,351	13,633	6,970	20,603	4,292	115	15,984	22,954	27,361
Feb.	2,422	13,798	6,920	20,718	4,299	119	16,220	23,140	27,558
Mar.	2,509	13,917	7,005	20,922	4,309	124	16,426	23,431	27,864
Apr.	2,582	13,988	7,094	21,082	4,320	128	16,570	23,664	28,112
May	2,640	14,146	7,192	21,338	4,331	132	16,786	23,978	28,441
June	2,678	14,197	7,067	21,264	4,342	134	16,875	23,942	28,418
July	2,744	14,461	7,246	21,707	4,347	139	17,205	24,451	28,937
Aug.	2,829	14,566	7,242	21,808	4,356	141	17,395	24,637	29,134
Sept.	2,922	14,369	7,245	21,614	4,367	143	17,291	24,536	29,046
Oct.	2,959	14,142	7,404	21,546	4,361	140	17,101	24,505	29,006
Nov.	3,070	14,224	7,434	21,658	4,359	141	17,294	24,728	29,228
Dec.	3,159	15,156	7,422	22,578	4,359	141	18,315	25,737	30,237
18									
Jan.	3,092	15,000	7,453	22,453	4,358	142	18,092	25,545	30,045
Feb.	3,258	14,547	7,497	22,044	4,352	144	17,805	25,302	29,798
Mar.	3,331	15,117	7,499	22,616	4,351	146	18,448	25,947	30,444
Apr.	3,385	15,141	7,527	22,668	4,350	147	18,526	26,053	30,550
May	3,422	14,499	7,491	21,990	4,347	148	17,921	25,412	29,907
June	3,523	14,764	7,552	22,316	4,344	151	18,287	25,839	30,334
July	3,699	14,850	7,628	22,478	4,368	155	18,549	26,177	30,700
Aug.	3,887	15,001	7,698	22,699	4,397	157	18,888	26,586	31,140
Sept.	4,027	15,790	7,743	23,533	4,422	158	19,817	27,560	32,140
Oct.	4,106	15,157	7,774	22,931	4,444	151	19,263	27,037	31,632
Nov.	4,091	15,615	7,901	23,516	4,471	161	19,706	27,607	32,239
Dec.	4,096	16,686	8,165	24,851	4,498	165	20,782	28,947	33,610
19									
Jan.	3,962	16,390	8,338	24,728	4,534	170	20,352	28,690	33,394
Feb.	3,954	16,131	8,489	24,620	4,564	173	20,085	28,574	33,311
Mar.	3,944	16,843	8,596	25,439	4,599	174	20,787	29,383	34,156
Apr.	3,962	17,089	8,669	25,758	4,639	175	21,051	29,720	34,534
May	3,936	17,099	8,768	25,867	4,678	171	21,035	29,803	34,652
June	3,888	17,502	8,930	26,432	4,715	170	21,390	30,320	35,205
July	3,958	17,790	9,204	26,994	4,750	169	21,748	30,952	35,871
Aug.	3,963	18,071	9,349	27,420	4,789	165	22,034	31,383	36,337
Sept.	4,002	18,361	9,536	27,897	4,823	162	22,363	31,899	36,884
Oct.	4,053	18,719	9,912	28,631	4,858	159	22,772	32,684	37,701
Nov.	4,121	18,917	10,065	28,982	4,892	159	23,038	33,103	38,154
Dec.	4,213	19,252	10,042	29,294	4,926	159	23,465	33,507	38,592
20									
Jan.	4,179	19,077	10,365	29,442	4,963	159	23,256	33,621	38,743
Feb.	4,309	19,317	10,535	29,852	4,994	158	23,626	34,161	39,313
Mar.	4,372	19,534	10,745	30,279	5,029	157	23,906	34,651	39,837

(continued)

TABLE A-1 (continued)

		DEPOSITS ADJUSTED					Summations		
DATE	Currency Held by the Public (1)	Commercial Banks			Mutual Savings Banks (5)	Postal Savings System (6)	Cols. 1 and 2 (7)	Cols. 1 and 4 (8)	Cols. 1, 4, 5 and (9)
		Demand (2)	Time (3)	Total (4)					
1920									
Apr.	4,418	19,365	10,880	30,245	5,069	158	23,783	34,663	39,89
May	4,414	19,331	10,973	30,304	5,108	159	23,745	34,718	39,98
June	4,463	19,129	11,116	30,245	5,146	159	23,592	34,708	40,01
July	4,500	19,093	11,122	30,215	5,180	161	23,593	34,715	40,05
Aug.	4,574	18,971	11,227	30,198	5,220	160	23,545	34,772	40,15
Sept.	4,624	18,884	11,268	30,152	5,269	160	23,508	34,776	40,20
Oct.	4,657	18,685	11,284	29,969	5,297	160	23,342	34,626	40,08
Nov.	4,534	18,380	11,315	29,695	5,330	160	22,914	34,229	39,71
Dec.	4,487	18,661	11,370	30,031	5,362	161	23,148	34,518	40,04
1921									
Jan.	4,317	18,157	11,440	29,597	5,388	163	22,474	33,914	39,46
Feb.	4,278	17,990	11,374	29,364	5,408	161	22,268	33,642	39,21
Mar.	4,220	17,532	11,343	28,875	5,433	159	21,752	33,095	38,68
Apr.	4,160	17,270	11,318	28,588	5,452	157	21,430	32,748	38,35
May	4,129	17,250	11,286	28,536	5,472	155	21,379	32,665	38,29
June	4,047	16,908	11,257	28,165	5,492	153	20,955	32,212	37,85
July	3,987	16,742	11,171	27,913	5,504	152	20,729	31,900	37,55
Aug.	3,938	16,848	11,204	28,052	5,521	151	20,786	31,990	37,66
Sept.	3,905	16,645	11,185	27,830	5,533	150	20,550	31,735	37,41
Oct.	3,805	16,852	11,275	28,127	5,545	148	20,657	31,932	37,62
Nov.	3,744	16,961	11,275	28,236	5,558	146	20,705	31,980	37,68
Dec.	3,735	16,910	11,258	28,168	5,572	145	20,645	31,903	37,62
1922									
Jan.	3,614	16,837	11,212	28,049	5,599	144	20,451	31,663	37,40
Feb.	3,614	17,034	11,390	28,424	5,619	143	20,648	32,038	37,80
Mar.	3,632	17,052	11,490	28,542	5,646	142	20,684	32,174	37,96
Apr.	3,626	17,593	11,647	29,240	5,659	141	21,219	32,866	38,66
May	3,606	17,794	11,736	29,530	5,671	139	21,400	33,136	38,94
June	3,625	17,993	12,028	30,021	5,683	138	21,618	33,646	39,46
July	3,608	18,115	12,287	30,402	5,720	136	21,723	34,010	39,86
Aug.	3,657	18,074	12,475	30,549	5,763	135	21,731	34,206	40,10
Sept.	3,717	18,321	12,455	30,776	5,801	134	22,038	34,493	40,42
Oct.	3,725	18,401	12,611	31,012	5,849	132	22,126	34,737	40,71
Nov.	3,742	18,342	12,646	30,988	5,885	132	22,084	34,730	40,74
Dec.	3,778	19,060	12,860	31,920	5,919	131	22,838	35,698	41,74
1923									
Jan.	3,730	18,968	12,894	31,862	5,968	130	22,698	35,592	41,69
Feb.	3,793	18,995	13,042	32,037	6,011	130	22,788	35,830	41,97
Mar.	3,854	18,544	13,417	31,961	6,060	130	22,398	35,815	42,00
Apr.	3,894	18,794	13,507	32,301	6,103	131	22,688	36,195	42,42
May	3,956	18,865	13,638	32,503	6,146	131	22,821	36,459	42,73
June	3,988	18,665	13,758	32,423	6,189	132	22,653	36,411	42,73

(continued)

TABLE A-1 (continued)

		DEPOSITS ADJUSTED					Summations		
	Currency Held by the Public (1)	Commercial Banks			Mutual Savings Banks (5)	Postal Savings System (6)	Cols. 1 and 2 (7)	Cols. 1 and 4 (8)	Cols. 1, 4, 5 and 6 (9)
ATE		Demand (2)	Time (3)	Total (4)					
23									
July	3,982	18,652	13,745	32,397	6,226	132	22,634	36,379	42,737
Aug.	3,999	18,589	13,832	32,421	6,270	132	22,588	36,420	42,822
Sept.	3,999	18,715	13,881	32,596	6,307	133	22,714	36,595	43,035
Oct.	3,966	18,852	13,971	32,823	6,335	132	22,818	36,789	43,256
Nov.	4,018	18,831	14,051	32,882	6,373	132	22,849	36,900	43,405
Dec.	3,978	18,959	14,131	33,090	6,403	131	22,937	37,068	43,602
24									
Jan.	3,897	18,864	14,155	33,019	6,440	129	22,761	36,916	43,485
Feb.	3,955	18,735	14,355	33,090	6,460	130	22,690	37,045	43,635
Mar.	3,978	18,755	14,451	33,206	6,506	131	22,733	37,184	43,821
Apr.	3,969	18,862	14,591	33,453	6,507	132	22,831	37,422	44,061
May	3,991	19,006	14,634	33,640	6,534	133	22,997	37,631	44,298
June	3,944	19,282	14,766	34,048	6,589	133	23,226	37,992	44,714
July	3,911	19,614	14,911	34,525	6,625	133	23,525	38,436	45,194
Aug.	3,904	19,943	15,031	34,974	6,638	133	23,847	38,878	45,649
Sept.	3,854	20,257	15,209	35,466	6,682	133	24,111	39,320	46,135
Oct.	3,905	20,312	15,388	35,700	6,726	134	24,217	39,605	46,465
Nov.	3,927	20,680	15,480	36,160	6,778	133	24,607	40,087	46,998
Dec.	3,915	20,487	15,559	36,046	6,839	133	24,402	39,961	46,933
25									
Jan.	3,930	20,794	15,711	36,505	6,864	133	24,724	40,435	47,432
Feb.	3,936	20,978	15,845	36,823	6,896	132	24,914	40,759	47,787
Mar.	3,943	20,857	15,975	36,832	6,924	132	24,800	40,775	47,831
Apr.	3,926	21,011	16,030	37,041	6,963	132	24,937	40,967	48,062
May	3,931	21,194	16,189	37,383	6,987	132	25,125	41,314	48,433
June	3,926	21,436	16,329	37,765	7,040	132	25,362	41,691	48,863
July	3,943	21,525	16,402	37,927	7,056	131	25,468	41,870	49,057
Aug.	3,917	22,024	16,516	38,540	7,083	131	25,941	42,457	49,671
Sept.	3,908	22,333	16,645	38,978	7,057	132	26,241	42,886	50,075
Oct.	3,938	22,292	16,753	39,045	7,143	132	26,230	42,983	50,258
Nov.	3,921	22,222	16,856	39,078	7,191	132	26,143	42,999	50,322
Dec.	3,964	22,123	16,940	39,063	7,240	133	26,087	43,027	50,400
26									
Jan.	3,960	22,136	17,091	39,227	7,232	133	26,096	43,187	50,552
Feb.	3,980	22,221	17,144	39,365	7,290	134	26,201	43,345	50,769
Mar.	3,954	22,150	17,163	39,313	7,317	134	26,104	43,267	50,718
Apr.	4,014	21,865	17,259	39,124	7,345	134	25,879	43,138	50,617
May	3,972	22,156	17,369	39,525	7,376	134	26,128	43,497	51,007
June	3,978	22,104	17,457	39,561	7,431	134	26,082	43,539	51,104
July	4,024	21,833	17,510	39,343	7,464	135	25,857	43,367	50,966
Aug.	3,987	21,981	17,591	39,572	7,496	135	25,968	43,559	51,190
Sept.	3,974	21,918	17,587	39,505	7,549	135	25,892	43,479	51,163

(continued)

TABLE A-1 (continued)

		DEPOSITS ADJUSTED					Summations		
	Currency Held by	*Commercial Banks*			Mutual Savings	Postal Savings	Cols.	Cols.	Cols 1, 4
DATE	the Public (1)	Demand (2)	Time (3)	Total (4)	Banks (5)	System (6)	1 and 2 (7)	1 and 4 (8)	5 and (9)
1926									
Oct.	3,976	21,711	17,631	39,342	7,591	136	25,687	43,318	51,0
Nov.	3,955	21,773	17,628	39,401	7,694	137	25,728	43,356	51,1
Dec.	3,983	21,456	17,573	39,029	7,701	139	25,439	43,012	50,8
1927									
Jan.	3,991	21,535	17,815	39,350	7,743	140	25,526	43,341	51,2
Feb.	3,996	21,667	18,127	39,794	7,783	142	25,663	43,790	51,7
Mar.	4,008	21,823	18,156	39,979	7,839	144	25,831	43,987	51,9
Apr.	4,015	21,709	18,282	39,991	7,864	146	25,724	44,006	52,0
May	3,980	22,184	18,456	40,640	7,914	147	26,164	44,620	52,6
June	3,951	21,845	18,588	40,433	7,961	147	25,796	44,384	52,4
July	3,964	21,866	18,694	40,560	8,006	147	25,830	44,524	52,6
Aug.	3,906	22,071	18,740	40,811	8,047	147	25,977	44,717	52,9
Sept.	3,942	21,880	18,824	40,704	8,110	148	25,822	44,646	52,9
Oct.	3,905	22,025	18,900	40,925	8,168	148	25,930	44,830	53,1
Nov.	3,850	22,538	19,211	41,749	8,242	148	26,388	45,599	53,9
Dec.	3,859	21,882	19,224	41,106	8,289	148	25,741	44,965	53,4
1928									
Jan.	3,825	22,312	19,513	41,825	8,336	148	26,137	45,650	54,1
Feb.	3,802	22,409	19,619	42,028	8,375	149	26,211	45,830	54,3
Mar.	3,871	22,352	19,880	42,232	8,404	150	26,223	46,103	54,6
Apr.	3,878	22,701	19,969	42,670	8,459	151	26,579	46,548	55,1
May	3,875	22,508	20,087	42,595	8,490	151	26,383	46,470	55,1
June	3,925	21,836	20,100	41,936	8,517	152	25,761	45,861	54,5
July	3,881	22,094	19,999	42,093	8,553	152	25,975	45,974	54,6
Aug.	3,903	21,906	20,007	41,913	8,600	151	25,809	45,816	54,5
Sept.	3,870	22,171	19,943	42,114	8,656	152	26,041	45,984	54,7
Oct.	3,819	22,390	20,127	42,517	8,702	152	26,209	46,336	55,1
Nov.	3,913	22,489	20,044	42,533	8,738	153	26,402	46,446	55,3
Dec.	3,834	22,602	20,138	42,740	8,778	153	26,436	46,574	55,5
1929									
Jan.	3,828	22,281	20,080	42,361	8,778	152	26,109	46,189	55,11
Feb.	3,849	22,409	20,034	42,443	8,808	153	26,258	46,292	55,25
Mar.	3,902	22,384	19,927	42,311	8,813	153	26,286	46,213	55,17
Apr.	3,866	22,480	19,767	42,247	8,816	153	26,346	46,113	55,08
May	3,883	22,183	19,748	41,931	8,828	153	26,066	45,814	54,79
June	3,911	22,278	19,729	42,007	8,845	154	26,189	45,918	54,91
July	3,887	22,796	19,717	42,513	8,858	158	26,683	46,400	55,41
Aug.	3,919	22,552	19,807	42,359	8,866	159	26,471	46,278	55,30
Sept.	3,822	22,593	19,912	42,505	8,882	160	26,415	46,327	55,36
Oct.	3,832	24,432	19,891	44,323	8,842	161	28,264	48,155	57,15
Nov.	3,852	21,651	19,535	41,186	8,822	163	25,503	45,038	54,02
Dec.	3,800	22,634	19,433	42,067	8,820	163	26,434	45,867	54,85

(continued)

TABLE A-1 (continued)

| | Currency Held by the Public (1) | DEPOSITS ADJUSTED | | | | | Summations | | |
| | | Commercial Banks | | | Mutual Savings Banks (5) | Postal Savings System (6) | Cols. 1 and 2 (7) | Cols. 1 and 4 (8) | Cols. 1, 4, 5 and 6 (9) |
ᴅATE		Demand (2)	Time (3)	Total (4)					
30									
Jan.	3,752	21,925	19,618	41,543	8,861	164	25,677	45,295	54,320
Feb.	3,748	22,190	19,520	41,710	8,907	166	25,938	45,458	54,531
Mar.	3,717	22,619	19,817	42,436	8,956	167	26,336	46,153	55,276
Apr.	3,670	22,265	19,705	41,970	8,990	169	25,935	45,640	54,799
May	3,694	21,631	19,848	41,479	9,025	171	25,325	45,173	54,369
June	3,681	21,612	20,010	41,622	9,059	176	25,293	45,303	54,538
July	3,669	21,731	19,943	41,674	9,121	181	25,400	45,343	54,645
Aug.	3,704	21,357	20,033	41,390	9,164	186	25,061	45,094	54,444
Sept.	3,634	21,408	20,038	41,446	9,233	189	25,042	45,080	54,502
Oct.	3,594	21,392	20,068	41,460	9,285	192	24,986	45,054	54,531
Nov.	3,674	21,353	19,713	41,066	9,330	200	25,027	44,740	54,270
Dec.	3,809	21,113	19,132	40,245	9,416	244	24,922	44,054	53,714
31									
Jan.	3,818	20,743	19,092	39,835	9,534	277	24,561	43,653	53,464
Feb.	3,823	20,890	19,229	40,119	9,598	291	24,713	43,942	53,831
Mar.	3,861	20,897	19,124	40,021	9,655	302	24,758	43,882	53,839
Apr.	3,897	20,353	19,210	39,563	9,747	313	24,250	43,460	53,520
May	3,897	19,993	19,026	39,019	9,816	324	23,890	42,916	53,056
June	3,995	19,888	18,715	38,603	9,864	346	23,883	42,598	52,808
July	4,058	19,744	18,508	38,252	9,900	371	23,802	42,310	52,581
Aug.	4,177	19,252	18,145	37,397	9,944	422	23,429	41,574	51,940
Sept.	4,289	19,080	17,564	36,644	9,984	469	23,369	40,933	51,386
Oct.	4,537	18,173	16,645	34,818	10,009	537	22,710	39,355	49,901
Nov.	4,503	17,852	16,099	33,951	10,020	564	22,355	38,454	49,038
Dec.	4,604	17,290	15,445	32,735	9,970	604	21,894	37,339	47,913
32									
Jan.	4,896	16,611	15,059	31,670	9,897	665	21,507	36,566	47,128
Feb.	4,824	16,486	14,803	31,289	9,905	691	21,310	36,113	46,709
Mar.	4,743	16,367	14,652	31,019	9,942	705	21,110	35,762	46,409
Apr.	4,751	16,131	14,543	30,674	9,924	721	20,882	35,425	46,070
May	4,746	15,785	14,360	30,145	9,894	741	20,531	34,891	45,526
June	4,959	15,490	14,031	29,521	9,890	783	20,449	34,480	45,153
July	5,048	15,104	13,979	29,083	9,874	828	20,152	34,131	44,833
Aug.	4,988	15,201	13,853	29,054	9,854	847	20,189	34,042	44,743
Sept.	4,941	15,270	13,746	29,016	9,863	857	20,211	33,957	44,677
Oct.	4,863	15,393	13,844	29,237	9,860	870	20,256	34,100	44,830
Nov.	4,842	15,713	13,756	29,469	9,876	883	20,555	34,311	45,070
Dec.	4,830	15,511	13,690	29,201	9,901	900	20,341	34,031	44,832
33									
Jan.	4,979	15,648	13,527	29,175	9,899	941	20,627	34,154	44,994
Feb.	5,588	14,394	12,625	27,019	9,837	1,005	19,982	32,607	43,449
Mar.	5,509	13,543	10,918	24,461	9,740	1,112	19,052	29,970	40,822

(continued)

TABLE A-1 (continued)

		DEPOSITS ADJUSTED					Summations		
DATE	Currency Held by the Public (1)	Commercial Banks			Mutual Savings Banks (5)	Postal Savings System (6)	Cols. 1 and 2 (7)	Cols. 1 and 4 (8)	Cols. 1, 4, 5 and (9)
		Demand (2)	Time (3)	Total (4)					
1933									
Apr.	5,202	13,837	10,708	24,545	9,688	1,158	19,039	29,747	40,5
May	5,019	14,430	10,651	25,081	9,616	1,178	19,449	30,100	40,8
June	4,949	14,283	10,855	25,138	9,586	1,185	19,232	30,087	40,8
July	4,886	14,201	11,073	25,274	9,561	1,176	19,087	30,160	40,8
Aug.	4,850	14,265	11,077	25,342	9,534	1,177	19,115	30,192	40,9
Sept.	4,830	14,341	11,090	25,431	9,534	1,179	19,171	30,261	40,9
Oct.	4,803	14,510	11,074	25,584	9,516	1,187	19,313	30,387	41,0
Nov.	4,844	14,714	11,005	25,719	9,520	1,196	19,558	30,563	41,2
Dec.	4,839	14,920	11,048	25,968	9,532	1,206	19,759	30,807	41,5
1934									
Jan.	4,491	15,229	11,234	26,463	9,549	1,198	19,720	30,954	41,7
Feb.	4,513	15,785	11,316	27,101	9,575	1,198	20,298	31,614	42,3
Mar.	4,550	16,198	11,492	27,690	9,610	1,197	20,748	32,240	43,0
Apr.	4,556	16,324	11,691	28,015	9,622	1,195	20,880	32,571	43,3
May	4,566	16,431	11,801	28,232	9,631	1,194	20,997	32,798	43,6
June	4,584	16,484	12,005	28,489	9,648	1,195	21,068	33,073	43,9
July	4,609	16,930	12,027	28,957	9,657	1,188	21,539	33,566	44,4
Aug.	4,628	17,499	12,107	29,606	9,590	1,190	22,127	34,234	45,0
Sept.	4,627	17,397	12,073	29,470	9,684	1,190	22,024	34,097	44,9
Oct.	4,590	17,967	12,188	30,155	9,681	1,196	22,557	34,745	45,6
Nov.	4,631	18,386	12,161	30,547	9,698	1,201	23,017	35,178	46,0
Dec.	4,559	18,215	12,287	30,502	9,704	1,205	22,774	35,061	45,9
1935									
Jan.	4,621	19,027	12,387	31,414	9,710	1,198	23,648	36,035	46,9
Feb.	4,700	19,653	12,412	32,065	9,740	1,203	24,353	36,765	47,7
Mar.	4,714	19,545	12,558	32,103	9,763	1,200	24,259	36,817	47,7
Apr.	4,708	19,878	12,791	32,669	9,769	1,198	24,586	37,377	48,3
May	4,715	20,058	12,808	32,866	9,775	1,203	24,773	37,581	48,5
June	4,708	20,491	12,850	33,341	9,787	1,202	25,199	38,049	49,0
July	4,687	20,747	12,865	33,612	9,793	1,187	25,434	38,299	49,2
Aug.	4,752	22,052	12,854	34,906	9,796	1,189	26,804	39,658	50,6
Sept.	4,805	21,576	12,971	34,547	9,810	1,189	26,381	39,352	50,3
Oct.	4,838	21,876	13,035	34,911	9,817	1,194	26,714	39,749	50,7
Nov.	4,875	22,393	13,083	35,476	9,836	1,196	27,268	40,351	51,3
Dec.	4,879	22,153	13,306	35,459	9,841	1,198	27,032	40,338	51,3
1936									
Jan.	4,924	22,138	13,325	35,463	9,849	1,205	27,062	40,387	51,4
Feb.	4,982	22,557	13,365	35,922	9,870	1,211	27,539	40,904	51,9
Mar.	5,016	22,565	13,385	35,950	9,893	1,213	27,581	40,966	52,0
Apr.	5,005	23,132	13,653	36,785	9,897	1,212	28,137	41,790	52,8
May	5,030	23,915	13,651	37,566	9,901	1,211	28,945	42,596	53,7
June	5,250	24,380	13,711	38,091	9,928	1,229	29,630	43,341	54,4

(continued)

TABLE A-1 (continued)

| | | DEPOSITS ADJUSTED | | | | | Summations | | |
DATE	Currency Held by the Public (1)	Commercial Banks Demand (2)	Time (3)	Total (4)	Mutual Savings Banks (5)	Postal Savings System (6)	Cols. 1 and 2 (7)	Cols. 1 and 4 (8)	Cols. 1, 4, 5 and 6 (9)
1936									
July	5,222	24,567	13,835	38,402	9,949	1,241	29,789	43,624	54,814
Aug.	5,225	24,466	13,922	38,388	9,963	1,246	29,691	43,613	54,822
Sept.	5,278	24,918	14,000	38,918	9,976	1,248	30,196	44,196	55,420
Oct.	5,316	24,842	14,052	38,894	9,988	1,252	30,158	44,210	55,450
Nov.	5,378	25,040	14,025	39,065	10,002	1,253	30,418	44,443	55,698
Dec.	5,466	25,386	14,128	39,514	10,018	1,257	30,852	44,980	56,255
1937									
Jan.	5,469	25,133	14,230	39,363	10,042	1,263	30,602	44,832	56,137
Feb.	5,490	25,387	14,429	39,816	10,072	1,266	30,877	45,306	56,644
Mar.	5,480	25,591	14,381	39,972	10,099	1,268	31,071	45,452	56,819
Apr.	5,521	25,456	14,414	39,870	10,106	1,267	30,977	45,391	56,764
May	5,501	25,100	14,563	39,663	10,113	1,264	30,601	45,164	56,541
June	5,512	25,075	14,608	39,683	10,104	1,264	30,587	45,195	56,563
July	5,547	24,972	14,743	39,715	10,143	1,268	30,519	45,262	56,673
Aug.	5,616	24,695	14,841	39,536	10,154	1,269	30,311	45,152	56,575
Sept.	5,608	24,545	14,968	39,513	10,154	1,266	30,153	45,121	56,541
Oct.	5,589	23,974	14,953	38,927	10,125	1,266	29,563	44,516	55,907
Nov.	5,573	23,766	14,887	38,653	10,130	1,266	29,339	44,226	55,622
Dec.	5,524	23,565	14,875	38,440	10,129	1,266	29,089	43,964	55,359
1938									
Jan.	5,485	23,825	14,939	38,764	10,138	1,269	29,310	44,249	55,656
Feb.	5,451	24,062	15,001	39,063	10,159	1,268	29,513	44,514	55,941
Mar.	5,460	24,143	14,899	39,042	10,176	1,265	29,603	44,502	55,943
Apr.	5,433	23,988	14,916	38,904	10,172	1,258	29,421	44,337	55,767
May	5,451	23,606	14,881	38,487	10,179	1,252	29,057	43,938	55,369
June	5,428	23,745	14,927	38,672	10,165	1,248	29,173	44,100	55,513
July	5,453	24,026	14,838	38,864	10,191	1,248	29,479	44,317	55,756
Aug.	5,455	24,770	14,879	39,649	10,196	1,249	30,225	45,104	56,549
Sept.	5,531	25,039	14,816	39,855	10,202	1,245	30,570	45,386	56,833
Oct.	5,553	25,391	14,837	40,228	10,227	1,247	30,944	45,781	57,255
Nov.	5,582	25,960	14,769	40,729	10,235	1,247	31,542	46,311	57,793
Dec.	5,598	26,131	14,847	40,978	10,238	1,249	31,729	46,576	58,063
1939									
Jan.	5,682	25,986	14,908	40,894	10,271	1,255	31,668	46,576	58,102
Feb.	5,749	25,804	14,935	40,739	10,309	1,260	31,553	46,488	58,057
Mar.	5,807	26,209	14,978	41,187	10,350	1,263	32,016	46,994	58,607
Apr.	5,900	26,401	15,055	41,456	10,364	1,261	32,301	47,356	58,981
May	5,904	26,581	15,042	41,623	10,380	1,258	32,485	47,527	59,165
June	5,946	26,640	15,095	41,735	10,387	1,259	32,586	47,681	59,327
July	5,980	27,475	15,119	42,594	10,428	1,265	33,455	48,574	60,267
Aug.	6,073	28,268	15,122	43,390	10,441	1,267	34,341	49,463	61,171
Sept.	6,136	28,948	15,091	44,039	10,441	1,263	35,084	50,175	61,879

(continued)

TABLE A-1 (continued)

DATE	Currency Held by the Public (1)	Commercial Banks Demand (2)	Time (3)	Total (4)	Mutual Savings Banks (5)	Postal Savings System (6)	Cols. 1 and 2 (7)	Cols. 1 and 4 (8)	Cols. 1, 4, 5 and 6 (9)
1939									
Oct.	6,169	29,298	15,161	44,459	10,467	1,267	35,467	50,628	62,362
Nov.	6,201	30,193	15,124	45,317	10,472	1,271	36,394	51,518	63,261
Dec.	6,214	29,797	15,239	45,036	10,481	1,275	36,011	51,250	63,006
1940									
Jan.	6,291	30,249	15,247	45,496	10,520	1,286	36,540	51,787	63,593
Feb.	6,359	30,689	15,343	46,032	10,558	1,294	37,048	52,391	64,243
Mar.	6,414	31,148	15,475	46,623	10,596	1,298	37,562	53,037	64,931
Apr.	6,449	30,951	15,422	46,373	10,612	1,299	37,400	52,822	64,733
May	6,505	31,665	15,491	47,156	10,601	1,295	38,170	53,661	65,557
June	6,610	32,153	15,565	47,718	10,584	1,290	38,763	54,328	66,202
July	6,664	32,562	15,544	48,106	10,579	1,293	39,226	54,770	66,642
Aug.	6,748	32,634	15,588	48,222	10,585	1,294	39,382	54,970	66,849
Sept.	6,841	33,041	15,639	48,680	10,593	1,292	39,882	55,521	67,406
Oct.	6,966	33,596	15,621	49,217	10,595	1,292	40,562	56,183	68,070
Nov.	7,069	34,089	15,644	49,733	10,613	1,295	41,158	56,802	68,710
Dec.	7,278	34,633	15,765	50,398	10,615	1,300	41,911	57,676	69,591
1941									
Jan.	7,401	35,214	15,815	51,029	10,613	1,310	42,615	58,430	70,353
Feb.	7,561	36,236	15,901	52,137	10,624	1,314	43,797	59,698	71,636
Mar.	7,705	36,755	15,945	52,700	10,627	1,316	44,460	60,405	72,348
Apr.	7,830	36,841	16,014	52,855	10,620	1,313	44,671	60,685	72,618
May	7,968	37,599	15,971	53,570	10,599	1,306	45,567	61,538	73,443
June	8,174	37,175	15,947	53,122	10,606	1,300	45,349	61,296	73,202
July	8,389	38,208	15,952	54,160	10,557	1,303	46,597	62,549	74,409
Aug.	8,586	38,120	15,981	54,101	10,542	1,305	46,706	62,687	74,534
Sept.	8,734	38,517	16,018	54,535	10,516	1,307	47,251	63,269	75,092
Oct.	8,867	38,251	16,100	54,351	10,528	1,313	47,118	63,218	75,059
Nov.	9,101	38,783	16,008	54,791	10,531	1,319	47,884	63,892	75,742
Dec.	9,544	38,615	15,928	54,543	10,500	1,310	48,159	64,087	75,897
1942									
Jan.	9,787	39,620	15,692	55,312	10,354	1,305	49,407	65,099	76,758
Feb.	10,026	40,115	15,578	55,693	10,325	1,302	50,141	65,719	77,346
Mar.	10,227	40,526	15,448	55,974	10,288	1,300	50,753	66,201	77,789
Apr.	10,447	41,497	15,490	56,987	10,301	1,301	51,944	67,434	79,036
May	10,742	42,259	15,503	57,762	10,311	1,302	53,001	68,504	80,117
June	11,067	42,315	15,616	57,931	10,354	1,310	53,382	68,998	80,662
July	11,495	43,826	15,707	59,533	10,376	1,324	55,321	71,028	82,728
Aug.	11,860	44,773	15,865	60,638	10,424	1,339	56,633	72,498	84,261
Sept.	12,285	45,703	15,988	61,691	10,446	1,352	57,988	73,976	85,774
Oct.	12,649	47,385	16,135	63,520	10,500	1,371	60,034	76,169	88,040
Nov.	13,173	47,997	16,193	64,190	10,572	1,390	61,170	77,363	89,325
Dec.	13,744	48,861	16,262	65,123	10,637	1,411	62,605	78,867	90,915

(continued)

TABLE A-1 (continued)

		DEPOSITS ADJUSTED					Summations		
DATE	Currency Held by the Public (1)	Commercial Banks			Mutual Savings Banks (5)	Postal Savings System (6)	Cols. 1 and 2 (7)	Cols. 1 and 4 (8)	Cols. 1, 4, 5 and 6 (9)
		Demand (2)	Time (3)	Total (4)					
1943									
Jan.	14,100	50,297	16,642	66,939	10,700	1,400	64,397	81,039	93,139
Feb.	14,600	52,546	16,795	69,341	10,773	1,500	67,146	83,941	96,214
Mar.	14,900	54,241	16,857	71,098	10,828	1,500	69,141	85,998	98,326
Apr.	15,200	53,073	17,013	70,086	10,905	1,500	68,273	85,286	97,691
May	15,700	53,380	17,320	70,700	10,998	1,500	69,080	86,400	98,898
June	15,900	56,926	17,534	74,460	11,103	1,600	72,826	90,360	103,063
July	16,500	59,121	17,959	77,080	11,219	1,600	75,621	93,580	106,399
Aug.	16,900	62,380	18,348	80,728	11,325	1,700	79,280	97,628	110,653
Sept.	17,200	54,745	18,308	73,053	11,351	1,700	71,945	90,253	103,304
Oct.	17,500	55,607	18,618	74,225	11,452	1,700	73,107	91,725	104,877
Nov.	18,100	58,421	18,856	77,277	11,589	1,700	76,521	95,377	108,666
Dec.	18,600	61,263	19,140	80,403	11,713	1,800	79,863	99,003	112,516
1944									
Jan.	18,900	59,453	19,538	78,991	11,821	1,800	78,353	97,891	111,512
Feb.	19,200	60,168	19,737	79,905	11,914	1,900	79,368	99,105	112,919
Mar.	19,600	61,110	20,075	81,185	12,006	1,900	80,710	100,785	114,691
Apr.	20,100	62,317	20,540	82,857	12,149	1,900	82,417	102,957	117,006
May	20,600	63,882	20,979	84,861	12,288	2,000	84,482	105,461	119,749
June	21,000	62,324	21,244	83,568	12,427	2,000	83,324	104,568	118,995
July	21,300	62,788	21,684	84,472	12,551	2,100	84,088	105,772	120,423
Aug.	21,700	64,943	22,184	87,127	12,710	2,100	86,643	108,827	123,637
Sept.	22,200	66,212	22,729	88,941	12,844	2,200	88,412	111,141	126,185
Oct.	22,700	68,266	23,505	91,771	13,024	2,200	90,966	114,471	129,695
Nov.	23,100	70,189	23,739	93,928	13,184	2,300	93,289	117,028	132,512
Dec.	23,300	67,443	24,210	91,653	13,337	2,300	90,743	114,953	130,590
1945									
Jan.	23,700	70,077	24,654	94,731	13,501	2,400	93,777	118,431	134,332
Feb.	24,100	71,225	25,255	96,480	13,674	2,400	95,325	120,580	136,654
Mar.	24,400	72,805	25,788	98,593	13,827	2,500	97,205	122,993	139,320
Apr.	24,700	73,304	26,354	99,658	14,036	2,600	98,004	124,358	140,994
May	24,900	73,729	26,776	100,505	14,188	2,600	98,629	125,405	142,193
June	25,300	72,167	27,204	99,371	14,374	2,600	97,467	124,671	141,645
July	25,600	73,478	27,919	101,397	14,539	2,700	99,078	126,997	144,236
Aug.	25,800	74,510	28,617	103,127	14,729	2,800	100,310	128,927	146,456
Sept.	26,100	75,672	29,217	104,889	14,876	2,800	101,772	130,989	148,665
Oct.	26,200	76,326	29,739	106,065	15,037	2,900	102,526	132,265	150,202
Nov.	26,000	77,114	29,894	107,008	15,188	2,900	103,114	133,008	151,096
Dec.	26,200	76,216	30,247	106,463	15,341	2,900	102,416	132,663	150,904
1946									
Jan.	26,200	75,700	30,600	106,300	15,484	3,000	101,900	132,500	150,984
Feb.	26,200	76,900	31,100	108,000	15,620	3,000	103,100	134,200	152,820
Mar.	26,300	76,500	31,400	107,900	15,735	3,000	102,800	134,200	152,935

(continued)

TABLE A-1 (continued)

| | | DEPOSITS ADJUSTED | | | | | Summations[a] | | |
| | Currency Held by the Public (1) | Commercial Banks | | | Mutual Savings Banks (5) | Postal Savings System (6) | Cols. 1 and 2 (7) | Cols. 1 and 4 (8) | Cols. 1, 4, 5 and (9) |
DATE		Demand (2)	Time (3)	Total (4)					
1946									
Apr.	26,400	78,600	31,700	110,300	15,902	3,100	105,000	136,700	155,7(
May	26,400	79,700	32,000	111,700	16,048	3,100	106,100	138,100	157,24
June	26,700	80,100	32,500	112,600	16,241	3,100	106,800	139,300	158;64
July	26,500	80,800	32,700	113,500	16,341	3,100	107,300	140,000	159,44
Aug.	26,500	80,800	32,900	113,700	16,438	3,200	107,300	140,200	159,83
Sept.	26,400	81,300	33,200	114,500	16,472	3,200	107,700	140,900	160,57
Oct.	26,400	81,500	33,300	114,800	16,589	3,200	107,900	141,200	160,98
Nov.	26,400	81,500	33,600	115,100	16,695	3,200	107,900	141,500	161,39
Dec.	26,300	81,300	33,900	115,200	16,819	3,300	107,600	141,500	161,61
1947									
Jan.	26,600	82,000	34,000	116,000	16,900	3,300	108,700	142,700	162,9(
Feb.	26,700	82,200	34,000	116,200	17,000	3,300	109,000	143,000	163,3(
Mar.	26,700	83,000	34,200	117,200	17,200	3,400	109,600	143,800	164,4(
Apr.	26,700	83,600	34,400	118,000	17,200	3,400	110,300	144,700	165,3(
May	26,700	84,200	34,500	118,700	17,200	3,400	110,800	145,300	165,9(
June⁻	26,600	84,700	34,600	119,300	17,400	3,400	111,400	146,000	166,8(
July	26,600	85,000	34,800	119,800	17,500	3,400	111,600	146,400	167,3(
Aug.	26,600	85,200	34,800	120,000	17,500	3,400	111,800	146,600	167,5(
Sept.	26,500	85,400	34,800	120,200	17,600	3,400	112,000	146,800	167,8(
Oct.	26,500	85,600	35,000	120,600	17,600	3,400	112,000	147,000	168,0(
Nov	26,500	85,800	35,000	120,800	17,700	3,400	112,300	147,300	168,4(
Dec.	26,400	85,800	35,200	121,000	17,700	3,400	112,200	147,400	168,5(
1948									
Jan.	26,400	86,200	35,300	121,500	17,800	3,400	112,600	147,900	169,1(
Feb.	26,400	86,000	35,400	121,400	17,900	3,400	112,300	147,700	169,0(
Mar.	26,200	85,600	35,400	121,000	18,000	3,400	112,000	147,400	168,8(
Apr.	26,100	85,400	35,400	120,800	18,000	3,400	111,600	147,000	168,4(
May	26,100	85,200	35,400	120,600	18,000	3,400	111,200	146,600	168,0(
June	26,000	85,200	35,600	120,800	18,100	3,400	111,300	146,900	168,4(
July	26,000	85,400	35,600	121,000	18,200	3,400	111,400	147,000	168,6(
Aug.	26,000	85,400	35,600	121,000	18,200	3,400	111,500	147,100	168,7(
Sept.	26,000	85,300	35,700	121,000	18,200	3,300	111,300	147,000	168,5(
Oct.	26,000	85,200	35,700	120,900	18,300	3,300	111,200	146,900	168,5(
Nov.	26,000	85,000	35,800	120,800	18,300	3,300	110,900	146,700	168,3(
Dec.	25,800	84,900	35,700	120,600	18,400	3,300	110,700	146,400	168,1(
1949									
Jan.	25,700	84,500	35,800	120,300	18,400	3,300	110,200	146,000	167,7(
Feb.	25,700	84,400	35,900	120,300	18,600	3,300	110,200	146,100	168,0(
Mar.	25,700	84,500	35,900	120,400	18,600	3,300	110,200	146,100	168,0(
Apr.	25,700	84,600	36,000	120,600	18,700	3,300	110,300	146,300	168,3(
May	25,600	84,800	36,000	120,800	18,800	3,300	110,500	146,500	168,6(
June	25,600	84,800	36,000	120,800	18,800	3,300	110,400	146,400	168,5(

(continued)

TABLE A-1 (continued)

		DEPOSITS ADJUSTED					Summations[a]		
DATE	Currency Held by the Public (1)	Commercial Banks			Mutual Savings Banks (5)	Postal Savings System (6)	Cols. 1 and 2 (7)	Cols. 1 and 4 (8)	Cols. 1, 4, 5 and 6 (9)
		Demand (2)	Time (3)	Total (4)					
1949									
July	25,500	84,800	36,000	120,800	18,900	3,300	110,400	146,400	168,600
Aug.	25,400	84,700	36,100	120,800	19,000	3,200	110,100	146,200	168,400
Sept.	25,400	84,600	36,100	120,700	19,000	3,200	110,000	146,100	168,300
Oct.	25,300	84,600	36,100	120,700	19,100	3,200	109,900	146,000	168,300
Nov.	25,200	84,600	36,100	120,700	19,200	3,200	109,800	145,900	168,300
Dec.	25,200	85,000	36,000	121,000	19,300	3,200	110,100	146,100	168,600
1950									
Jan.	25,100	85,200	36,000	121,200	19,400	3,200	110,300	146,300	168,900
Feb.	25,200	85,700	36,200	121,900	19,400	3,200	110,800	147,000	169,600
Mar.	25,200	86,200	36,400	122,600	19,600	3,200	111,400	147,800	170,600
Apr.	25,200	86,800	36,400	123,200	19,700	3,200	112,100	148,500	171,400
May	25,200	87,300	36,600	123,900	19,800	3,100	112,500	149,100	172,000
June	25,100	87,800	36,600	124,400	19,800	3,100	112,800	149,400	172,300
July	25,000	88,400	36,400	124,800	19,800	3,000	113,400	149,800	172,600
Aug.	25,000	89,000	36,200	125,200	19,800	3,000	114,000	150,200	173,000
Sept.	24,900	89,200	36,200	125,400	19,800	3,000	114,200	150,400	173,200
Oct.	25,000	89,600	36,200	125,800	19,900	3,000	114,600	150,800	173,700
Nov.	25,000	89,800	36,200	126,000	20,000	3,000	114,800	151,000	174,000
Dec.	25,000	90,200	36,200	126,400	20,000	2,900	115,300	151,500	174,400
1951									
Jan.	25,100	90,800	36,200	127,000	20,000	2,900	115,800	152,000	174,900
Feb.	25,200	91,000	36,200	127,200	20,000	2,900	116,200	152,400	175,300
Mar.	25,200	91,500	36,100	127,600	20,000	2,800	116,700	152,800	175,600
Apr.	25,200	91,600	36,200	127,800	20,200	2,800	116,800	153,000	176,000
May	25,400	91,800	36,200	128,000	20,200	2,800	117,200	153,400	176,400
June	25,400	92,200	36,400	128,600	20,200	2,800	117,600	154,000	177,000
July	25,600	92,300	36,600	128,900	20,400	2,800	118,000	154,600	177,800
Aug.	25,800	93,000	36,900	129,900	20,400	2,800	118,800	155,700	178,900
Sept.	25,800	93,600	37,200	130,800	20,600	2,700	119,400	156,600	179,900
Oct.	26,000	94,200	37,400	131,600	20,600	2,700	120,200	157,600	180,900
Nov.	26,000	95,200	37,600	132,800	20,800	2,700	121,300	158,900	182,400
Dec.	26,200	95,800	37,600	133,400	20,800	2,700	122,000	159,600	183,100
1952									
Jan.	26,300	96,200	37,800	134,000	21,000	2,700	122,500	160,300	184,000
Feb.	26,300	96,700	38,200	134,900	21,000	2,700	123,000	161,200	184,900
Mar.	26,400	96,800	38,300	135,100	21,200	2,700	123,200	161,500	185,400
Apr.	26,400	96,900	38,400	135,300	21,400	2,600	123,400	161,800	185,800
May	26,500	97,300	38,700	136,000	21,500	2,600	123,800	162,500	186,600
June	26,600	97,600	38,900	136,500	21,600	2,600	124,300	163,200	187,400
July	26,700	97,700	39,100	136,800	21,800	2,600	124,400	163,500	187,900
Aug.	26,800	98,000	39,400	137,400	22,000	2,600	124,800	164,200	188,800
Sept.	27,000	98,500	39,700	138,200	22,100	2,600	125,400	165,100	189,800

(continued)

TABLE A-1 (continued)

DATE	Currency Held by the Public (1)	Commercial Banks Demand (2)	Time (3)	Total (4)	Mutual Savings Banks (5)	Postal Savings System (6)	Cols. 1 and 2 (7)	Cols. 1 and 4 (8)	Cols. 1, 4, 5 and 6 (9)
1952									
Oct.	27,000	98,700	40,000	138,700	22,200	2,600	125,800	165,800	190,600
Nov.	27,200	99,000	40,200	139,200	22,400	2,600	126,200	166,400	191,400
Dec.	27,400	99,100	40,600	139,700	22,600	2,500	126,400	167,000	192,100
1953									
Jan.	27,400	99,100	40,800	139,900	22,700	2,500	126,600	167,400	192,600
Feb.	27,500	99,200	40,900	140,100	22,800	2,500	126,700	167,600	192,900
Mar.	27,600	99,800	41,000	140,800	23,000	2,500	127,400	168,400	193,900
Apr.	27,600	100,000	41,200	141,200	23,200	2,500	127,600	168,800	194,500
May	27,700	100,000	41,600	141,600	23,400	2,500	127,700	169,300	195,200
June	27,800	100,100	41,800	141,900	23,400	2,400	127,800	169,600	195,400
July	27,800	100,100	42,000	142,100	23,600	2,400	127,900	169,900	195,900
Aug.	27,800	100,200	42,400	142,600	23,800	2,400	128,000	170,400	196,600
Sept.	27,800	100,100	42,600	142,700	23,900	2,400	127,900	170,500	196,800
Oct.	27,800	100,200	43,000	143,200	24,000	2,400	128,000	171,000	197,400
Nov.	27,800	100,200	43,200	143,400	24,200	2,400	128,000	171,200	197,800
Dec.	27,800	100,400	43,400	143,800	24,300	2,400	128,200	171,600	198,300
1954									
Jan.	27,700	100,600	43,600	144,200	24,500	2,300	128,400	172,000	198,800
Feb.	27,700	100,800	43,900	144,700	24,600	2,300	128,400	172,300	199,200
Mar.	27,600	100,900	44,200	145,100	24,800	2,300	128,600	172,800	199,900
Apr.	27,600	100,600	44,500	145,100	25,000	2,300	128,200	172,700	200,000
May	27,600	101,400	44,800	146,200	25,100	2,300	129,000	173,800	201,200
June	27,600	101,600	45,200	146,800	25,200	2,200	129,200	174,400	201,800
July	27,500	102,000	45,700	147,700	25,400	2,200	129,500	175,200	202,800
Aug.	27,400	102,500	46,000	148,500	25,500	2,200	130,000	176,000	203,700
Sept.	27,400	102,800	46,300	149,100	25,700	2,200	130,200	176,500	204,400
Oct.	27,400	103,400	46,600	150,000	25,800	2,200	130,800	177,400	205,400
Nov.	27,400	104,000	46,700	150,700	26,000	2,200	131,400	178,100	206,300
Dec.	27,400	104,400	46,700	151,100	26,200	2,100	131,800	178,500	206,800
1955									
Jan.	27,400	104,900	46,800	151,700	26,400	2,100	132,400	179,200	207,700
Feb.	27,500	105,800	47,000	152,800	26,600	2,100	133,200	180,200	208,900
Mar.	27,500	105,500	47,000	152,500	26,700	2,000	133,000	180,000	208,700
Apr.	27,600	106,000	47,100	153,100	26,800	2,000	133,600	180,700	209,500
May	27,600	106,300	47,200	153,500	27,000	2,000	133,900	181,100	210,100
June	27,600	106,300	47,400	153,700	27,200	2,000	133,900	181,300	210,500
July	27,600	106,600	47,500	154,100	27,200	2,000	134,200	181,700	210,900
Aug.	27,700	106,600	47,800	154,400	27,400	2,000	134,300	182,100	211,500
Sept.	27,700	106,800	48,000	154,800	27,600	1,900	134,600	182,600	212,100
Oct.	27,800	106,800	48,200	155,000	27,800	1,900	134,600	182,800	212,500
Nov.	27,800	106,500	48,200	154,700	27,900	1,900	134,300	182,500	212,300
Dec.	27,800	106,800	48,100	154,900	28,000	1,900	134,600	182,700	212,600

(continued)

TABLE A-1 (continued)

DATE	Currency Held by the Public (1)	Commercial Banks Demand (2)	Time (3)	Total (4)	Mutual Savings Banks (5)	Postal Savings System (6)	Cols. 1 and 2 (7)	Cols. 1 and 4 (8)	Cols. 1, 4, 5 and 6 (9)
1956									
Jan.	27,900	107,200	48,200	155,400	28,200	1,900	135,100	183,300	213,400
Feb.	27,900	107,200	48,400	155,600	28,400	1,800	135,000	183,400	213,600
Mar.	28,000	107,400	48,600	156,000	28,400	1,800	135,400	184,000	214,200
Apr.	27,900	107,700	48,700	156,400	28,600	1,800	135,600	184,300	214,700
May	28,000	107,400	48,800	156,200	28,800	1,800	135,400	184,200	214,800
June	28,000	107,700	49,100	156,800	29,000	1,800	135,600	184,700	215,500
July	28,000	107,500	49,400	156,900	29,000	1,800	135,400	184,800	215,600
Aug.	28,000	107,200	49,800	157,000	29,200	1,700	135,200	185,000	215,900
Sept.	28,000	107,600	50,000	157,600	29,400	1,700	135,700	185,700	216,800
Oct.	28,100	107,700	50,200	157,900	29,600	1,700	135,800	186,000	217,300
Nov.	28,200	108,000	50,200	158,200	29,700	1,700	136,000	186,200	217,600
Dec.	28,200	108,200	50,200	158,400	29,900	1,600	136,500	186,700	218,200
1957									
Jan.	28,300	108,200	50,800	159,000	30,000	1,600	136,400	187,200	218,800
Feb.	28,200	108,200	51,600	159,800	30,200	1,600	136,400	188,000	219,800
Mar.	28,300	108,200	52,200	160,400	30,200	1,600	136,500	188,700	220,500
Apr.	28,300	108,200	52,600	160,800	30,400	1,600	136,400	189,000	221,000
May	28,300	108,200	53,200	161,400	30,500	1,500	136,600	189,800	221,800
June	28,300	108,100	53,600	161,700	30,700	1,500	136,400	190,000	222,200
July	28,300	108,100	54,000	162,100	30,800	1,400	136,400	190,400	222,600
Aug.	28,300	108,200	54,500	162,700	30,900	1,400	136,600	191,100	223,400
Sept.	28,400	107,900	54,900	162,800	31,100	1,400	136,200	191,100	223,600
Oct.	28,300	107,600	55,300	162,900	31,200	1,400	136,000	191,300	223,900
Nov.	28,300	107,400	55,500	162,900	31,400	1,400	135,700	191,200	224,000
Dec.	28,300	107,200	55,600	162,800	31,600	1,300	135,500	191,100	224,000
1958									
Jan.	28,300	107,000	56,200	163,200	31,800	1,300	135,300	191,500	224,600
Feb.	28,300	107,600	57,200	164,800	32,000	1,300	135,800	193,000	226,300
Mar.	28,300	107,700	58,200	165,900	32,200	1,300	136,000	194,200	227,700
Apr.	28,300	108,200	59,200	167,400	32,400	1,200	136,500	195,700	229,300
May	28,400	108,700	60,200	168,900	32,600	1,200	137,000	197,200	231,000
June	28,400	109,700	61,000	170,700	32,800	1,200	138,000	199,000	233,000
July	28,400	109,400	61,800	171,200	32,800	1,200	137,800	199,600	233,600
Aug.	28,400	110,200	62,400	172,600	33,000	1,200	138,600	201,000	235,200
Sept.	28,500	110,600	62,700	173,300	33,200	1,200	139,200	201,900	236,300
Oct.	28,500	111,100	62,800	173,900	33,400	1,200	139,600	202,400	237,000
Nov.	28,600	111,900	62,800	174,700	33,600	1,200	140,400	203,200	238,000
Dec.	28,600	112,200	63,000	175,200	33,900	1,100	140,800	203,800	238,800
1959									
Jan.	28,600	112,600	63,400	176,000	33,900	1,100	141,200	204,600	239,600
Feb.	28,700	112,800	63,600	176,400	33,800	1,100	141,600	205,200	240,100
Mar.	28,800	113,200	63,800	177,000	34,000	1,100	142,000	205,800	240,900

(continued)

TABLE A-1 (concluded)

		DEPOSITS ADJUSTED					*Summations*[a]		
	Currency Held by the Public (1)	Commercial Banks			Mutual Savings Banks (5)	Postal Savings System (6)	Cols. 1 and 2 (7)	Cols. 1 and 4 (8)	Cols. 1, 4, 5 and 6 (9)
DATE		Demand (2)	Time (3)	Total (4)					
1959									
Apr.	28,800	113,300	64,200	177,500	34,200	1,100	142,200	206,400	241,700
May	28,900	113,700	64,700	178,400	34,400	1,100	142,600	207,300	242,800
June	29,000	113,800	65,000	178,800	34,400	1,100	142,800	207,800	243,300
July	29,000	114,200	65,100	179,300	34,400	1,000	143,300	208,400	243,800
Aug.	29,000	113,700	65,400	179,100	34,500	1,000	142,800	208,200	243,700
Sept.	29,000	113,800	65,600	179,400	34,700	1,000	142,800	208,400	244,100
Oct.	29,000	113,400	65,600	179,000	34,700	1,000	142,400	208,000	243,700
Nov.	29,000	113,200	65,400	178,600	34,800	1,000	142,200	207,600	243,400
Dec.	28,900	112,600	65,400	178,000	34,900	1,000	141,500	206,900	242,800
1960									
Jan.	29,000	112,400	65,400	177,800	34,900	900	141,300	206,700	242,500
Feb.	29,000	112,000	65,400	177,400	34,900	900	141,000	206,400	242,200
Mar.	29,000	111,600	65,600	177,200	35,000	900	140,600	206,200	242,100
Apr.	29,000	111,400	66,000	177,400	35,200	900	140,500	206,500	242,600
May	29,000	110,900	66,300	177,200	35,200	900	139,900	206,200	242,300
June	28,900	110,500	66,800	177,300	35,200	800	139,400	206,200	242,200
July	28,900	110,700	67,400	178,100	35,400	800	139,600	207,000	243,200
Aug.	28,900	110,800	68,400	179,200	35,500	800	139,700	208,100	244,400
Sept.	29,000	111,500	69,200	180,700	35,700	800	140,400	209,600	246,100
Oct.	29,000	111,600	69,800	181,400	35,800	800	140,600	210,400	247,000
Nov.	29,000	111,200	70,400	181,600	36,000	800	140,200	210,600	247,400
Dec.	29,000	111,400	70,800	182,200	36,200	800	140,400	211,200	248,200

[a] Beginning Jan. 1947, figures in col. 7 are *FRB* totals of unrounded figures corresponding to those shown in cols. 1 and 2; col. 8 is the sum of cols. 7 and 3; col. 9 is the sum of cols. 8, 5, and 6.

SOURCE, BY COLUMN

Column 1, Currency Held by the Public

This series is a residual derived by subtracting vault cash (Table A-2, col. 1) from currency outside the Treasury and (beginning Nov. 1914) Federal Reserve Banks. The dating of the vault cash series determined the dating of the currency series.

I. 1867–1942: Published figures for the components of currency outside the Treasury and Federal Reserve Banks were corrected for discontinuities. By straight-line interpolation the components or their totals were shifted from end-of-June dates to the end-of-month dates shown in col. 1, 1867–78. Beginning June 1878, monthly data were available.

The components were added together. A rough seasonal correction was made Aug. 1878–Aug. 1881. No correction was made June 1882–June 1906. From May 1907 through Dec. 1942 the series was seasonally adjusted in two stages:

Each end-of-month day was corrected by a combined intraweekly and monthly seasonal factor derived from a two-way analysis of variance with disproportionate frequencies.

(continued)

722

Repetitive movements that still remained, May 1907–Dec. 1913, June 1924–June 1932, and June 1935–June 1941, were corrected by the method of ratio to moving average. By straight-line interpolation beginning May 1907 the end-of-month data were shifted to Wed. or Fri. nearest end of month, to make dating of this series correspond with that of vault cash. The latter series was then subtracted to get the figures shown in col. 1, 1867–1942.

A list of the components, noting cases in which corrections of the published figures were required, follows:

A. GOLD COIN

1. Jan. 1867–Feb. 1878: Gold outside the Treasury, from *Banking and Monetary Statistics* (Board of Governors of the Federal Reserve System, 1943), p. 408, minus gold presumed lost, estimated 1866–72 by us, 1873–78 in *Annual Report* (Director of the Mint), 1887, p. 86; 1907, pp. 87 and 92.
2. Aug. 1878–May 1907: Gold outside the Treasury was obtained by subtracting the amount in the Treasury from corrected figures of the stock. The uncorrected gold stock is in "Report of the Treasurer," *Annual Report* of the Secretary of the Treasury, 1898, pp. 109 ff.; 1903, pp. 205 ff.; 1909, pp. 190 ff. Gold in the Treasury is from *ibid.*, 1898, pp. 59 ff.; 1903, p. 173; 1909, pp. 190 ff. Correction for the amount of gold presumed lost is an arithmetic interpolation of June estimates, 1878–79; of Dec. estimates, 1879–1907, in *Annual Report* (Mint), as in I.A.1.
3. June 1907–Dec. 1913: Stock of gold in "Report of the Treasurer," *Annual Report* (Treasury), 1909, pp. 190 ff.; 1915, pp. 339 ff., minus gold in the Treasury, *ibid.*
4. Jan. 1914–Dec. 1933: Gold outside the Treasury and Federal Reserve Banks, *ibid.*, pp. 409–412, plus $287 million added back to restore gold, assumed by the Federal Reserve on insufficient evidence to have been lost (*Banking and Monetary Statistics*, p. 407). See Chap. 8, footnote 45, above.
5. Jan. 1934–Dec. 1942: *Ibid.*, pp. 412–413; *Circulation Statement of U.S. Money* (Treasury Department, published monthly since March 1887).

B. GOLD CERTIFICATES, SILVER CERTIFICATES, U.S. NOTES, CURRENCY NOTES, AND TREASURY NOTES OF 1890

1. Jan. 1867–Feb. 1878: *Banking and Monetary Statistics*, p. 408.
2. Aug. 1878–Dec. 1913: "Report of the Treasurer," 1898, pp. 131 ff., 128 ff.; 1903, pp. 219 ff., 217 ff.; *Circulation Statement of U.S. Money.*
3. Jan. 1914–Dec. 1942: *Banking and Monetary Statistics*, pp. 409–413; *Circulation Statement of U.S. Money.*

C. STANDARD SILVER DOLLARS

1. Jan. 1867–Feb. 1878: *Banking and Monetary Statistics*, p. 408, plus $6 million of trade dollars for 1877; see *Annual Report* (Treasury), 1887, p. 87.
2. Aug. 1878–Dec. 1913: "Report of the Treasurer," 1898, pp. 125 ff.; 1903, pp. 215 ff.; *Circulation Statement of U.S. Money.*
3. Jan. 1914–Dec. 1942: *Banking and Monetary Statistics*, pp. 409–413; *Circulation Statement of U.S. Money.*

D. SUBSIDIARY SILVER

1. Jan. 1867–Feb. 1878: *Banking and Monetary Statistics*, p. 408.
2. Aug. 1878–June 1880: "Report of the Treasurer," 1898, pp. 124 ff.
3. June 1881–June 1910: In June 1910 the Director of the Mint deducted $9.7 million from the estimate of the stock of subsidiary silver at that date, to adjust "for the excess of imports over exports for the fiscal years 1881–1910" (*ibid.*, 1910, p. 290). This error was distributed on a straight line over the period 1881–1910 and was deducted along with subsidiary silver in the Treasury from the stock as reported by the Treasurer, *ibid.*, 1898, pp. 112 and 68; 1903, pp. 207 and 174; 1909, pp. 195 and 194; 1915, p. 343.

(continued)

NOTES TO TABLE A-1 (continued)

4. July 1910–Dec. 1913: *Circulation Statement of U.S. Money.*
5. Jan. 1914–Dec. 1942: *Banking and Monetary Statistics,* pp. 409–413; *Circulation Statement of U.S. Money.*

E. FRACTIONAL CURRENCY

1. Jan. 1867–Aug. 1878: All but $1 million of the fractional paper currency still outstanding June 30, 1878 (*Banking and Monetary Statistics,* p. 408), was assumed to have been lost. The loss was distributed over the period 1863–78 and was deducted from the published figures. Fractional currency was assumed to have been $1 million in Aug. 1878 and zero thereafter (it is not shown in the published monthly data beginning June 1878).

F. OTHER U.S. CURRENCY

1. Jan. 1867–Feb. 1876: *Banking and Monetary Statistics,* p. 408. This item is a total of various Civil War issues, retirement of which was substantially achieved by 1868.

G. STATE BANK NOTES

1. Jan. 1867–Feb. 1878: *Ibid.*

H. NATIONAL BANK NOTES

1. Jan. 1867–June 1935: These are (a) published figures, minus (b) estimates of national bank notes in vaults of issuing banks and in transit.
   a. *Published Figures of National Bank Notes*
      (1) Jan. 1867–Feb. 1878: *Ibid.,* p. 408.
      (2) Aug. 1878–Feb. 1887: Total outstanding, from *Annual Report,* Comptroller of the Currency, 1891, p. 125, minus amount in Treasury, from "Report of the Treasurer," 1898, p. 44.
      (3) Mar. 1887–Dec. 1913: *Circulation Statement of U.S. Money.*
      (4) Jan. 1914–June 1935: *Banking and Monetary Statistics,* pp. 409–412.
   b. *Estimates of National Bank Notes in Vaults of Issuing Banks and in Transit*
      (1) Jan. 1867–June 1906: For the call date nearest the end of each of these months, national bank note liabilities, from *Annual Report* (Comptroller), 1916, Vol. II, pp. 329–355, were subtracted from:
         (a) 1866–69: National bank notes outstanding, from A. P. Andrew, *Statistics for the United States, 1867–1909* (National Monetary Commission, 1910, S. Doc. 570, 61st Cong., 2d sess.), p. 43.
         (b) 1870–1906: Circulation of national bank notes secured by U.S. bonds, from *Annual Report* (Comptroller), 1891, Vol. I, p. 125; 1904, Vol. I, pp. 99–101; 1908, pp. 124–129.
      (2) May 1907–June 1928: Notes in vaults of issuing banks are straight-line monthly interpolations between call date figures of circulating notes of national banks received from the Comptroller and on hand (*Annual Report,* annual issues). Notes in transit are straight-line monthly interpolations between mid- and end-of-year estimates of the transit item, obtained by deducting national bank call date figures of national bank notes received from the Comptroller (*ibid.*) from circulation of national bank notes secured by U.S. bonds (*ibid.,* 1918, Vol. II, pp. 19–21; 1924, pp. 158–160; 1928, pp. 222–223).
      (3) July 1928–June 1935: Notes in vaults of issuing banks and in transit are straight-line monthly interpolations between mid- and end-of-year estimates, obtained by deducting national bank call date figures of national bank note liabilities (*ibid.,* annual issues) from circulation of national bank notes secured by U.S. bonds (*ibid.,* 1931, pp. 178–179; 1935, pp. 183–184).
2. July 1935–Dec. 1942: *Banking and Monetary Statistics,* pp. 412–413; *Circulation Statement of U.S. Money.*

(continued)

J. MINOR COIN

1. Before 1900 no data are available.
2. June 1900–Dec. 1913: Straight-line monthly interpolation between June figures, *Banking and Monetary Statistics*, pp. 408–409.
3. Jan. 1914–Dec. 1942: *Ibid.*, pp. 409–413; *Circulation Statement of U.S. Money.*

K. FEDERAL RESERVE NOTES AND FEDERAL RESERVE BANK NOTES

1. Nov. 1914–Dec. 1942: *Banking and Monetary Statistics*, pp. 409–413; *Circulation Statement of U.S. Money.*

II. 1943–60: Federal Reserve estimates of currency held by the public (published as "currency outside banks") are directly available in monthly issues of the *Federal Reserve Bulletin*, beginning Feb. 1944. They are end-of-month figures, Jan. 1943–Dec. 1946, adjusted by us, 1943–45, for monthly but not intraweekly seasonal variations; thereafter, with a seasonal adjustment by the Federal Reserve System. For Jan. 1947–June 1960 (monthly averages of semimonthly averages of daily figures, *ibid.*, Oct. 1960, p. 1115) and July–Dec. 1960 (monthly averages of daily figures, *ibid.*, Aug. 1961, p. 937), the Federal Reserve System provides seasonally adjusted figures. For a later version of Federal Reserve seasonally adjusted figures since 1947 for currency held by the public than that shown in Table A-1, see *Supplement to Banking and Monetary Statistics*, Sect. 1, Board of Governors of the Federal Reserve System, Oct. 1962, pp. 20–22.

Column 2, Demand Deposits Adjusted, All Commercial Banks

I. June 1914–June 1919: These are sums of estimates for (A) New York State national banks; (B) New York State nonnational and all commercial banks in 9 urbanized states (Cal., Conn., Ill., Mass., Mich., N.J., Ohio, Pa., R.I.) and D.C.; and (C) all commercial banks in 38 rural states; minus (D) U.S. government deposits, June 1917–June 1919.

A. NEW YORK STATE NATIONAL BANKS

Call date figures from *Abstract of Reports of Condition of National Banks*, Comptroller of the Currency (published at national bank call dates since 1897), with estimated breakdown of demand and time deposits, June–Oct. 1914, were seasonally adjusted by us.

1. June 1914–Dec. 1914: Call date ratios of demand to time deposits were computed and interpolated to Wed. nearest end of month. Next, a monthly series of total deposits adjusted of New York State national banks was obtained by interpolating between the call date figures to Wed. nearest end of month on the basis of an estimating equation derived from the correlation of these figures and average net deposits of member banks of the N.Y.C. Clearing House, *Commercial and Financial Chronicle* (weekly issues for designated period, figures seasonally adjusted by us). Total deposits adjusted divided by the sum of 1 and the demand-time ratio yielded estimates of time deposits; demand deposits were computed as residuals.
2. Jan. 1915–June 1919: Weekly average net demand deposits of N.Y.C. Clearing House member and nonmember banks (*ibid.*) served as the monthly interpolator of the call date figures for demand deposits.

B. N.Y. STATE NONNATIONAL BANKS AND ALL COMMERCIAL BANKS IN 9 URBANIZED STATES AND D.C.

Call date figures for each class of banks in this subtotal were obtained separately, summed, and interpolated to Wed. nearest end of month, as follows.

1. *Call Date Figures*
   Total deposits adjusted of N.Y. nonnational banks from *Annual Report on Banks of Discount and Deposit*, N.Y. State Superintendent of Banks, for designated period, seasonally corrected by us, and of private banks from *All-Bank Statistics, United*

(continued)

NOTES TO TABLE A-1 (continued)

States, 1896–1955 (Board of Governors, FRS, 1959), pp. 747–748, were shifted to national bank call dates by straight-line interpolation, and broken down into demand and time deposits on the basis of the breakdown shown in *Annual Report* (Comptroller) at selected June dates, 1914–30.

Call date figures for national banks in the 9 urbanized states and D.C. from *Abstract . . . National Banks* (Comptroller), with estimated breakdown of demand and time deposits, June–Oct. 1914, were seasonally adjusted by us.

Report date figures for nonnational banks in 10 urbanized units from annual reports of the respective state banking departments were treated as comparable to national bank call date figures, if the report dates were not more than two weeks from a national bank call date.

For June dates, figures were available for all 11 urbanized units; for intermediate call dates, for a varying number of these units. Estimates for all call dates for the 9 urbanized states and D.C. and N.Y. nonnational banks were computed by multiplying the trend value for all 11 units, interpolated between June dates to a given call date, by the ratio of the actual value for the reporting urbanized units at that call date to the trend value for these units. No seasonal movement was observed in the final series.

2. *Monthly Figures*
   a. June 1914–Dec. 1914: Call date ratios of demand to time deposits were computed and interpolated to Wed. nearest end of month. Next, a monthly series of total deposits adjusted of N.Y. State nonnational banks and all commercial banks in the 9 urbanized states and D.C. was obtained by interpolating between the call date figures on the basis of an estimating equation derived from the correlation of these figures and a composite series, seasonally adjusted, of weekly average gross deposits of N.Y. nonnational banks from *Annual Report* (N.Y. State Supt.), 1914, and Boston and Phila. Clearing House banks (*Commercial and Financial Chronicle*). Total deposits adjusted, divided by the ratios plus 1, yielded estimates of time deposits; demand deposits were computed as residuals.
   b. Jan. 1915–June 1919: Weekly average demand deposits, less float, but including U.S. government deposits at Boston Clearing House banks and, beginning Sept. 1917, at Phila. Clearing House banks (*ibid.*), served as the monthly interpolator of the call date figures for demand deposits.

C. ALL COMMERCIAL BANKS IN 38 RURAL STATES

Figures at June dates for the 38 rural states were obtained by subtracting from demand deposits adjusted of all commercial banks in the U.S. (*All-Bank Statistics*, pp. 35–36), the sum of I.A and I.B above. For 9 of these states (Ala., Ariz., Ark., Col., Del., Fla., Ga., Idaho, Ind.) report date information from the annual reports of the respective state banking departments was added to figures for the rest of the 38 states derived by straight-line interpolation between the June figures. No seasonal movement was observed in the final series. Monthly figures are interpolations along a straight line between the call date figures.

D. U.S. GOVERNMENT DEPOSITS

See Table A-3, col. 2.

II. July 1919–Dec. 1945: These are sums of estimates for member banks and non-member banks.

A. MEMBER BANKS

1. June 1919–Mar. 1923: An estimate of net demand deposits of nonweekly reporting member banks was computed from an estimating equation derived from the correlation of figures for these banks, Apr. 1923–Dec. 1928 (all member bank figures, Federal Reserve Board, *Annual Report*, 1927, p. 108; 1928, p. 116, minus

(continued)

weekly reporting member bank figures, *Banking and Monetary Statistics*, pp. 136–140) and figures for net demand deposits of weekly reporting member banks outside N.Y. City (*ibid.*, pp. 200–205). The estimate was added to net demand deposits of weekly reporting member banks to get totals for all member banks (*ibid.*, pp. 132–136).

Net demand deposits are larger than demand deposits adjusted. The difference between these two measures of deposits is known for all member banks at call dates (*ibid.*, p. 73). By straight-line interpolation between the call date differences, June 1919–Apr. 1920, to Fri. nearest end of month, a monthly difference series was computed. For May 1920–Mar. 1923, the call date differences were interpolated to Fri. nearest end of month (Wed., beginning May 1921) on the basis of a seasonally adjusted interpolator: interbank balances of weekly reporting member banks (in the 12 Reserve Bank cities only), minus their balances at domestic banks (*Banking and Monetary Statistics*, pp. 133–136). The monthly differences were then subtracted from the monthly estimates of net demand deposits of all member banks to obtain demand deposits adjusted.

2. Apr. 1923–Dec. 1935: Net demand deposits of all member banks (*Annual Report*, Fed. Res. Bd., 1927, p. 108; 1928, p. 116; 1933, p. 168; 1934, p. 154; 1935, p. 153), variously dated as of a certain day of the month or as monthly averages of daily figures, were adjusted to represent the Wed. closest to end of month. A call date difference series of net demand deposits minus demand deposits adjusted (*Banking and Monetary Statistics*, pp. 73–75), seasonally adjusted, was interpolated to Wed. nearest end of month on the basis of a seasonally adjusted interpolator: interbank balances minus balances at domestic banks of reporting member banks (*ibid.*, pp. 136–151). The monthly differences were then subtracted from the monthly estimates of net demand deposits of all member banks to obtain demand deposits adjusted.

3. Jan. 1936–Apr. 1943: Gross demand deposits of all member banks (*ibid.*, p. 42; *FRB*, monthly issues, 1942–43), in the form of monthly averages of daily figures, were adjusted to represent the Wed. closest to end of month. Gross demand deposits are larger than demand deposits adjusted. The difference between these two measures of deposits is known for all member banks at call dates (*Banking and Monetary Statistics*, p. 75, and *Member Bank Call Report*, 1942–43) and for weekly reporting member banks (*Banking and Monetary Statistics*, pp. 152–163, and *FRB*, monthly issues, 1942–43). An estimate of the difference series for nonweekly reporting member banks, interpolated along a straight line to Wed. nearest end of month between call date estimates (the call date difference series for all member banks, minus the weekly reporting member bank difference series at Wednesdays nearest call dates, both seasonally adjusted), was added to the difference series for weekly reporting member banks to get a monthly difference series for all member banks, monthly. The monthly differences were then subtracted from the monthly estimates of gross demand deposits of all member banks to get demand deposits adjusted.

4. May 1943–Dec. 1945: Demand deposits adjusted, in the form of monthly averages of daily figures, May 1943–Mar. 1944, thereafter semimonthly averages of daily figures (*FRB*), were adjusted to represent the Wed. closest to end of month.

B. NONMEMBER BANKS

1. Call date estimates were derived as the sum of nonmember banks in (a) New York, (b) 9 urbanized states and D.C., and (c) 38 rural states; minus (d) U.S. government deposits, as follows:

a. *Call Date Figures for New York State*

Total deposits of N.Y. nonnational banks (*Annual Report*, N.Y. State Supt., seasonally corrected by us) and of private banks (*All-Bank Statistics*, pp. 747–748) were shifted to member bank call dates by straight-line interpolation, and broken down into demand and time deposits on the basis of the breakdown

(continued)

NOTES TO TABLE A-1 (continued)

shown in *Annual Report* (Comptroller) at selected June dates, 1914–30. From these nonnational bank figures, demand deposits less duplications of N.Y. state member banks (*Member Bank Call Report*) were subtracted, after seasonal correction, to get demand deposits less duplications of nonmember banks.

b. *Call Date Figures for 9 Urbanized States and D.C.*

Report date figures for nonnational banks in these units, from annual reports of the state banking departments, were treated as comparable to member bank call date figures if the report dates were not more than two weeks from a member bank call date. From these nonnational bank figures, demand deposits less duplications of state member banks in these 10 units were deducted. For June dates, figures were available for all 10 units, for intermediate call dates for a varying number of these units. Estimates for all call dates for the 9 urbanized states and D.C. were computed by multiplying the trend value for all 10 units, interpolated between June dates to a given call date, by the ratio of the actual value for the reporting urbanized units at that call date to the trend value for these units. No seasonal movement was observed in the final series.

c. *Call Date Figures for 38 Rural States*

Demand deposits, less float but including U.S. government deposits, were obtained for June dates by subtracting from figures for all commercial banks (*All-Bank Statistics*, pp. 35–36) member bank data and the sum of subsections II.B.1.a and II.B.1.b. For 9 rural states (see this col., June 1914–June 1919, subhead I.C), report date information on nonnational banks was obtained from annual reports of the respective state banking departments, and state member bank figures for these states were deducted to obtain a nonmember bank sample. Inter-June call date estimates are based on the movements of the data for the changing sample of 9 rural states and a presumed relationship between the sample and the nonsample, calculated from member bank data for sample and nonsample similar in composition to the nonmember bank data. The total for the 38 states is the sum of the sample and the estimated nonsample.

d. *Call Date Figures for U.S. Government Deposits*

Table A-3, col. 2.

2. *Monthly Figures*

a. June 1919–June 1923: Straight-line interpolations to Fri. (beginning May 1921, Wed.) nearest end of month between the call date estimates for all nonmember banks.

b. June 1923–Dec. 1945: The call date series, obtained as described above, was interpolated to Wed. nearest end of month on the basis of the following interpolators:

(1) June 1923–Dec. 1935: Demand deposits of member banks in smaller places (*Annual Report*, Fed. Res. Bd., 1927, p. 108; 1928, p. 116; 1933, p. 168; 1934, p. 154; 1935, p. 153), variously dated as of a certain day of the month or a monthly average of daily figures. The dating was adjusted to represent the Wed. closest to end of month, and the data were adjusted for changes from 1920 to 1930 in Census classification of cities as smaller or larger centers.

(2) Jan. 1936–June 1943: Gross demand deposits of member banks in smaller places from *Banking and Monetary Statistics*, p. 42, and *FRB* (monthly issues, 1942–43), in the form of monthly averages of daily figures. The dating was adjusted to represent the Wed. closest to end of month and the data were adjusted for changes from 1930 to 1940 in Census classification of cities as smaller or larger centers.

(3) July 1943–Dec. 1945: Demand deposits adjusted of country member banks, in the form of monthly averages of daily figures, July 1943–Mar. 1944, thereafter semimonthly averages of daily figures (*FRB*). The dating was adjusted to represent the Wed. closest to end of month.

(continued)

III. Jan. 1946–Dec. 1946: Federal Reserve seasonally adjusted estimates for last Wed. of the month (*FRB*, Feb. 1960, p. 135).

IV. Jan. 1947–June 1960: Monthly averages of Federal Reserve seasonally adjusted semimonthly averages of daily figures (*FRB*, Oct. 1960, p. 1115).

V. July 1960–Dec. 1960: Federal Reserve seasonally adjusted monthly averages of daily figures (*FRB*, Aug. 1961, p. 937). For a later version of Federal Reserve seasonally adjusted figures since 1947 for demand deposits adjusted than that shown in Table A-1, see *Supplement to Banking and Monetary Statistics*, Sect. 1, Board of Governors of the Federal Reserve System, Oct. 1962, pp. 20–22.

Column 3, Time Deposits Adjusted, All Commercial Banks

I. June 1914–June 1919: These are sums of estimates for the same 3 classes of banks used to get demand deposits in this period.

A. N.Y. STATE NATIONAL BANKS

1. June 1914–Dec. 1914: For procedure used in estimating data for these banks, see description under col. 2.
2. Jan. 1915–June 1919: Weekly average net time deposits of N.Y.C. Clearing House member and nonmember banks (*Commercial and Financial Chronicle*) served as the monthly interpolator of the call date figures for time deposits.

B. N.Y. STATE NONNATIONAL BANKS AND ALL COMMERCIAL BANKS IN 9 URBANIZED STATES AND D.C.

1. June 1914–Dec. 1914: For procedure used in estimating data for these banks, see description under col. 2.
2. Jan. 1915–June 1919: Total deposits minus demand deposits (both as described for these banks under col. 2).

C. IN 38 RURAL STATES

1. Time deposits of the 38 rural states at June dates and intermediate call dates were derived as described above for these banks under col. 2. Monthly figures are interpolations along a straight line between the call date figures.

II. July 1919–Dec. 1945: These are sums of estimates for member banks and nonmember banks.

A. MEMBER BANKS

1. June 1919–Mar. 1923: Estimated figures for net time deposits of nonweekly reporting member banks were computed from an estimating equation derived from the correlation of figures for these banks, Apr. 1923–Dec. 1928 (all member bank figures, Federal Reserve Board, *Annual Report*, 1927, p. 108; 1928, p. 116, minus weekly reporting member bank figures, *Banking and Monetary Statistics*, pp. 138–140) and figures for net time deposits of weekly reporting member banks. The estimated figures were added to net time deposits of weekly reporting member banks to get totals for all member banks.
Net time deposits include Postal Savings System deposits at member banks. Call date figures of Postal Savings at member banks (*ibid.*, p. 73) were interpolated along a straight line to Fri. nearest end of month (Wed., beginning May 1921) and deducted from total net time deposits.
2. Apr. 1923–Dec. 1945: Net time deposits of all member banks (*Annual Report*, Fed. Res. Bd., 1927, p. 108; 1928, p. 116; 1933, p. 168; 1934, p. 154; 1935, p. 153; *Banking and Monetary Statistics*, p. 42; *Federal Reserve Bulletin*, monthly issues, 1942–46)—variously dated as of a certain day of the week, as monthly averages of daily figures and semimonthly averages of daily figures—were adjusted to

(continued)

NOTES TO TABLE A-1 (continued)

represent the Wed. closest to end of month. Monthly estimates of Postal Savings redeposited at member banks and, beginning Feb. 1939, U.S. government time deposits and, beginning Sept. 1928, interbank time deposits, obtained as follows, were then deducted from the monthly net time deposits series to obtain time deposits adjusted.

a. *Postal Savings Redeposited at Member Banks*

    (1) Apr. 1923–Feb. 1938: Figures are straight-line interpolations between call dates to Wed. nearest end of month.

    (2) Mar. 1938–Jan. 1939: These are sums of Postal Savings redeposited at weekly reporting member banks (*Banking and Monetary Statistics*, pp. 157–163, and *FRB*, monthly issues, 1942–46) and estimates of Postal Savings in nonweekly reporting member banks (the call date series minus the weekly reporting member bank series at Wednesdays closest to call dates, with straight-line interpolations for intervening months).

b. *Postal Savings Redeposited at Member Banks, Plus U.S. Government Time Deposits at Member Banks*

    (1) Feb. 1939–Dec. 1945: Same procedure as above, except that weekly reporting member bank figures combine Postal Savings System deposits with U.S. government time deposits at those banks; hence, member bank call date figures for the two classes of deposits were combined, beginning Dec. 1938 (*Banking and Monetary Statistics*, p. 75, and *Member Bank Call Report*). The nonweekly reporting monthly series was derived as above for Mar. 1938–Jan. 1939.

c. *Interbank Time Deposits*

    (1) Sept. 1928–Sept. 1934: Figures are straight-line interpolations between call dates (*Banking and Monetary Statistics*, p. 78) to Wed. nearest end of month.

    (2) Oct. 1934–Dec. 1945: Sums of interbank time deposits of weekly reporting member banks (*ibid.*, pp. 149–163; and *FRB*, monthly issues, 1942–46) and estimates of interbank time deposits of nonweekly reporting member banks (the call date series, minus the weekly reporting member bank series, at Wed. closest to call dates, with straight-line interpolations for intervening months).

B. NONMEMBER BANKS

1. June 1919–Mar. 1923: Straight-line interpolations to Wed. nearest end of month between call date estimates for all nonmember banks, parallel with the demand deposit estimates for these banks, June 1919–June 1923 (see source notes for col. 2). Postal Savings System deposits at nonnational banks and state member banks were deducted from their reported time deposits; then the residual time deposits of state member banks were deducted from those of nonnational banks to get nonmember bank time deposits.

2. July 1923–Dec. 1945: The call date series obtained as for col. 2 above, subperiod June 1919–June 1923, was interpolated to Wed. nearest end of month with the following interpolators.

    a. June 1923–Mar. 1943: Net time deposits of member banks in smaller places (Federal Reserve Board, *Annual Report*, 1927, p. 108; 1928, p. 116; 1933, p. 168; 1934, p. 154; 1935, p. 153; *Banking and Monetary Statistics*, p. 42; *Federal Reserve Bulletin*, monthly issues, 1942–43)—variously dated as of a certain day of the month or as a monthly average of daily figures—were adjusted for changes from 1920 to 1940 in Census classification of cities as smaller or larger centers. The dating was adjusted to represent the Wed. nearest end of month.

    b. Apr. 1943–Dec. 1945: Net time deposits of country member banks in smaller places (*ibid.*, 1943–46), in the form of semimonthly averages of daily figures, were adjusted to represent the Wed. nearest end of month.

(continued)

III. Jan. 1946–Dec. 1960: Federal Reserve estimates for last Wed. of the month from *FRB*, monthly issues, seasonally adjusted by us. Beginning Jan. 1947, we averaged pairs of last-Wed.-of-month figures to get figures centered at mid-month. For Federal Reserve seasonally adjusted figures since 1947 for commercial bank time deposits—not previously available—see *Supplement to Banking and Monetary Statistics*, Sect. 1,[4] Board of Governors of the Federal Reserve System, Oct. 1962, pp. 20–22.

Column 4, Total Deposits Adjusted, All Commercial Banks

I. Jan. 1867–June 1906: These are sums of figures for national and nonnational banks.

A. NATIONAL BANKS

Call date figures closest to ends of months shown in col. of dates of this table, from *Annual Report* (Comptroller), 1916, Vol. II, pp. 328–335.

B. NONNATIONAL BANKS

1. Jan. 1867–Feb. 1875: Estimates from James K. Kindahl, "The Period of the Resumption in the United States, 1865–1879" (unpublished Ph.D. dissertation, U. of Chicago, 1958). The figures, available with a description of their derivation in *Historical Statistics of the United States, Colonial Times to 1957* (Bureau of the Census, 1960, Series V-88), were attributed by us to the ends of the months shown in this table.
2. Aug. 1875–June 1895: From David Fand, "Estimates of Deposits and Vault Cash in the Nonnational Banks in the Post-Civil War Period in the United States" (unpublished Ph.D. dissertation, U. of Chicago, 1954). The figures, available with a description of their derivation in *Historical Statistics*, 1960, Series V-89–90, were adjusted for seasonal variations by us.
3. June 1896–June 1906: From *All-Bank Statistics*, pp. 43–44, adjusted for seasonal variations by us.

II. May 1907–May 1914: These are sums of estimates for three classes of banks: (A) New York State national banks; (B) New York State nonnational and all commercial banks in 9 urbanized states (see col. 3 above) and D.C.; and (C) all commercial banks in 38 rural states.

A. N.Y. STATE NATIONAL BANKS

Total deposits adjusted of N.Y. State national banks, from *Abstract . . . National Banks* (Comptroller), for designated period (figures seasonally adjusted by us) were interpolated between call dates to Wed. nearest end of month on the basis of an estimating equation derived from the correlation of these figures and average net deposits of member banks of the N.Y.C. Clearing House, from *Commercial and Financial Chronicle* figures (seasonally adjusted by us).

B. N.Y. STATE NONNATIONAL BANKS AND ALL COMMERCIAL BANKS IN 9 URBANIZED STATES AND D.C.

A monthly series of total deposits adjusted was obtained by interpolating to Wed. nearest end of month between call date figures.
The interpolator of the call date series was a seasonally adjusted composite series of weekly average gross deposits of N.Y. nonnational banks from *Annual Report* (N.Y. State Supt.), and of the Clearing House banks of the following cities: Chicago, May 1907–Dec. 1908 only (Andrew, *Statistics for the United States*, pp. 149–150); St. Louis, New Orleans, and San Francisco, May 1907–Dec. 1908 only (E. W. Kemmerer, *Seasonal Variations in the Relative Demand for Money and Capital in the United States*, National Monetary Commission, S. Doc. 588, 61st Cong., 2d sess., 1910, pp. 269, 274, 275); and Boston and Philadelphia (*Commercial and Financial Chronicle*).

(continued)

NOTES TO TABLE A-1 (continued)

The call date figures were obtained as follows for each class of banks in subtotal II.B.

1. *N.Y. Nonnational Banks*

   Total deposits adjusted of these banks, from *Annual Report* (N.Y. State Supt.), seasonally corrected, and of private banks, from *All-Bank Statistics* (pp. 747–748), were shifted to national bank call dates by straight-line interpolation.

2. *National Banks in 9 Urbanized States and D.C.*

   Call date figures, from *Abstract . . . National Banks* (Comptroller), were seasonally adjusted by us.

3. *Nonnational Banks in 9 Urbanized States and D.C.*

   Report date figures, from annual reports of the respective state banking departments, were treated as comparable to national bank call date figures, if report dates were not more than two weeks from a national bank call date.

For June dates, figures were available for all 11 units, for intermediate call dates for a varying number of these units. Estimates for all call dates for banks in the 9 urbanized states and D.C. and for N.Y. nonnational banks were computed by multiplying the trend value for all urbanized units, interpolated between June dates to a given call date, by the ratio of the actual value for the urbanized units reporting at that call date to the trend value for these units. No seasonal movement was observed in the final series.

C. ALL COMMERCIAL BANKS IN 38 RURAL STATES

Figures at June dates for the 38 rural states were obtained by subtracting from total deposits adjusted of all commercial banks in the U.S. (*All-Bank Statistics*, pp. 35–36) the sum of subsections II.A and II.B above. For 9 of these states (listed with rural states under col. 2, June 1914–June 1919), report date information from the annual reports of the respective state banking departments was added to figures for the rest of the 38 states, derived by straight-line interpolation between the June figures. No seasonal movement was observed in the final series. Monthly figures are interpolations along a straight line to Wed. nearest end of month between the call date figures.

III. June 1914–Dec. 1960: Col. 2 plus col. 3.

Column 5, Mutual Savings Bank Deposits

I. Jan. 1867–Feb. 1875: Emerson W. Keyes, *A History of Savings Banks in the United States* (New York, 1878), table facing p. 532, sum of all cols. except for Cal., Iowa, Chicago, and D.C. Deposit figures in latter cols. are for stock savings banks, according to present definition, while cols. used omit deposits of such banks. Data were interpolated on a straight line to the end of each month.

II. Aug. 1875–June 1895: Fand, "Estimates of Deposits and Vault Cash," corrected for seasonal variations by us as required.

III. June 1896–June 1906: *All-Bank Statistics*, p. 48.

IV. May 1907–Nov. 1923: These are seasonally adjusted sums of estimates for four groups of states.

A. 6 NEW ENGLAND STATES (CONN., ME., MASS., N.H., R.I., VT.)

Total deposits, minus interbank deposits, of mutual savings banks of the 6 N.E. states were compiled from the reports of state banking departments. The report dates were treated as end-of-month dates, with dates falling between the 16th of a given month and the 15th of the following month considered as the end of the given month. Benchmark dates, with some exceptions, were end-of-June dates. If no figure was reported for a state at a bench-mark date, one was estimated by straight-line interpolation between closest report dates.

(continued)

For bench-mark dates, figures were thus available for all 6 states; for certain other end-of-month dates, for a scattering of these states. By an estimating formula, a figure was derived for each N.E. state at each end-of-month date for which there was at least one reported observation. For these dates, the sum of known and estimated figures was obtained. For end-of-month dates for which there was no reported observation, we interpolated along a straight line between the closest dates for which aggregate figures for the 6 states were computed as described above.

B. 9 OTHER STATES (DEL., IND., MD., MINN., N.J., OHIO, WASH. BEGINNING SEPT. 1917, W. VA. INCLUDED THROUGH MAR. 1922, WIS.)

Total deposits, minus interbank deposits, of mutual savings banks of this group of states was compiled as described in IV.A above. Gaps were filled in by straight-line interpolation between the closest dates for which there were reported figures.

C. NEW YORK STATE

Jan. 1 and July 1 figures, from *Annual Report* (N.Y. State Supt.), Part II; bench-mark dates for other than end of June, from *Annual Report* (Comptroller), 1907, 1909, 1911–13. Gaps were filled in by straight-line interpolation between the closest dates for which there were reported figures.

D. PENNSYLVANIA

Estimates of deposits of a Pa. stock savings bank were deducted from figures for mutual and stock savings banks combined, available for 2 report dates yearly, 1907–17 (*Annual Report*, Pa. Commissioner of Banking), and for 4 report dates, 1918–23 (unpublished figures from the Pa. Department of Banking). For one report date a year, the stock savings bank figure was obtained by subtracting from the combined figures for Pa. mutual and stock savings banks (*All-Bank Statistics*, p. 890) the figures for Pa. mutual savings banks alone. Estimates for the stock savings banks at other dates were obtained by straight-line interpolation. The residual mutual savings bank figures were seasonally adjusted. End-of-month figures were obtained by straight-line interpolation between the residuals.

V. Dec. 1923–Dec. 1946: These are seasonally adjusted sums of estimates for four groups of states.

A. 6 NEW ENGLAND, AS IN IV.A, ABOVE AND 3 EASTERN STATES (DEL., MD., N.J.)

The procedure was the same as described above for this col., subperiod May 1907–Nov. 1923, IV.A, except that, for end-of-month dates for which there was no reported observation for any of the 9 states in this group, estimates were derived from an estimating equation based on the correlation of the data for this group with a seasonally adjusted monthly series of deposits of mutual savings banks in New York State (see V.C below).

B. 6 OTHER STATES (IND., MINN., OHIO, ORE. BEGINNING JAN. 1932, WASH., WIS.)

The procedure was the same as described above for this col., subperiod May 1907–Nov. 1923, IV.B.

C. NEW YORK STATE

End-of-month dates other than June and Dec., from *Survey of Current Business*, Supplement, 1932, pp. 76–77; 1936, p. 47; 1938, p. 56; 1940, p. 52; 1942, p. 65; 1947, p. 75. June and Dec. figures, from *Annual Report* (N.Y. State Supt.), Part II. The series was adjusted for seasonal variations.

(continued)

NOTES TO TABLE A-1 (concluded)

D. PENNSYLVANIA

Same procedure as for May 1907–Nov. 1923, IV.D.

VI. Jan. 1947–Dec. 1960: Federal Reserve estimates for last Wed. of month, from *Federal Reserve Bulletin* (monthly issues), seasonally adjusted by us. We averaged pairs of the last-Wed.-of-month figures to get figures centered at mid-month.

Column 6, Deposits at Postal Savings System

The Postal Savings System opened for business January 1911.

I. Jan. 1911–Oct. 1955: Depositors' balances including principal of outstanding and unclaimed deposits, monthly, from its *Annual Report of Operations*, minus monthly estimates of depositors' balances at banks in the U.S. possessions. The series was seasonally adjusted by us, Jan. 1913–July 1930.

II. Nov. 1955–Dec. 1960: Federal Reserve estimates for last Wed. of month, from *FRB* (monthly issues), without seasonal adjustment. We averaged pairs of the last-Wed.-of-month figures to get figures centered at mid-month.

TABLE A-2
BANK RESERVES, SEASONALLY ADJUSTED, 1867–1960
(billions of dollars)

Date	Vault Cash (1)	Bank Deposits at Federal Reserve Banks (2)	Bank Reserves (3)	Date	Vault Cash (1)	Bank Deposits at Federal Reserve Banks (2)	Bank Reserves (3)
1867				1885			
Jan.	0.267		0.267	June	0.453		0.453
1868				1886			
Jan.	0.244		0.244	June	0.442		0.442
1869				1887			
Jan.	0.232		0.232	June	0.464		0.464
1870				1888			
Jan.	0.248		0.248	June	0.488		0.488
1871				1889			
Jan.	0.230		0.230	June	0.499		0.499
1872				1890			
Jan.	0.240		0.240	June	0.478		0.478
1873				1891			
Feb.	0.231		0.231	June	0.512		0.512
1874				1892			
Feb.	0.275		0.275	June	0.600		0.600
1875				1893			
Feb.	0.239		0.239	June	0.529		0.529
Aug.	0.257		0.257	1894			
1876				June	0.686		0.686
Feb.	0.242		0.242	1895			
Aug.	0.245		0.245	June	0.621		0.621
1877				1896			
Feb.	0.243		0.243	June	0.567		0.567
Aug.	0.234		0.234	1897			
1878				June	0.651		0.651
Feb.	0.237		0 237	1898			
Aug.	0.238		0.238	June	0.704		0.704
1879				1899			
Feb.	0.232		0.232	June	0.738		0.738
Aug.	0.241		0.241	1900			
1880				June	0.763		0.763
Feb.	0.273		0.273	1901			
Aug.	0.310		0.310	June	0.838		0.838
1881				1902			
Feb.	0.291		0.291	June	0.863		0.863
Aug.	0.316		0.316	1903			
1882				June	0.858		0.858
June	0.317		0.317	1904			
1883				June	1.002		1.002
June	0.328		0.328	1905			
1884				June	0.994		0.994
				1906			
June	0.347		0.347	June	1.042		1.042

(continued)

TABLE A-2 (continued)

Date	Vault Cash (1)	Bank Deposits at Federal Reserve Banks (2)	Bank Reserves (3)	Date	Vault Cash (1)	Bank Deposits at Federal Reserve Banks (2)	Bank Reserves (3)
1907				**1910**			
May	1.126		1.126	July	1.476		1.476
June	1.118		1.118	Aug.	1.478		1.478
July	1.161		1.161	Sept.	1.453		1.453
Aug.	1.164		1.164	Oct.	1.423		1.423
Sept.	1.184		1.184	Nov.	1.473		1.473
Oct.	1.155		1.155	Dec.	1.484		1.484
Nov.	1.205		1.205				
Dec.	1.208		1.208	**1911**			
				Jan.	1.506		1.506
1908				Feb.	1.530		1.530
Jan.	1.200		1.200	Mar.	1.523		1.523
Feb.	1.281		1.281	Apr.	1.500		1.500
Mar.	1.328		1.328	May	1.522		1.522
Apr.	1.365		1.365	June	1.539		1.539
May	1.353		1.353	July	1.509		1.509
June	1.362		1.362	Aug.	1.517		1.517
July	1.385		1.385	Sept.	1.527		1.527
Aug.	1.429		1.429	Oct.	1.536		1.536
Sept.	1.423		1.423	Nov.	1.561		1.561
Oct.	1.406		1.406	Dec.	1.600		1.600
Nov.	1.420		1.420				
Dec.	1.391		1.391	**1912**			
				Jan.	1.610		1.610
1909				Feb.	1.592		1.592
Jan.	1.413		1.413	Mar.	1.564		1.564
Feb.	1.409		1.409	Apr.	1.547		1.547
Mar.	1.419		1.419	May	1.531		1.531
Apr.	1.429		1.429	June	1.501		1.501
May	1.443		1.443	July	1.525		1.525
June	1.456		1.456	Aug.	1.523		1.523
July	1.463		1.463	Sept.	1.514		1.514
Aug.	1.442		1.442	Oct.	1.518		1.518
Sept.	1.444		1.444	Nov.	1.540		1.540
Oct.	1.432		1.432	Dec.	1.566		1.566
Nov.	1.437		1.437				
Dec.	1.429		1.429	**1913**			
				Jan.	1.562		1.562
1910				Feb.	1.546		1.546
Jan.	1.410		1.410	Mar.	1.528		1.528
Feb.	1.438		1.438	Apr.	1.522		1.522
Mar.	1.469		1.469	May	1.514		1.514
Apr.	1.442		1.442	June	1.534		1.534
May	1.453		1.453	July	1.567		1.567
June	1.455		1.455	Aug.	1.552		1.552

(continued)

TABLE A-2 (continued)

Date	Vault Cash (1)	Bank Deposits at Federal Reserve Banks (2)	Bank Reserves (3)	Date	Vault Cash (1)	Bank Deposits at Federal Reserve Banks (2)	Bank Reserves (3)
1913				1916			
Sept.	1.553		1.553	Nov.	1.567	0.588	2.155
Oct.	1.544		1.544	Dec.	1.646	0.630	2.276
Nov.	1.576		1.576				
Dec.	1.606		1.606	1917			
				Jan.	1.661	0.629	2.290
1914				Feb.	1.686	0.651	2.337
Jan.	1.624		1.624	Mar.	1.660	0.693	2.353
Feb.	1.613		1.613	Apr.	1.618	0.672	2.290
Mar.	1.630		1.630	May	1.632	0.688	2.320
Apr.	1.664		1.664	June	1.425	0.983	2.408
May	1.686		1.686	July	1.281	1.087	2.368
June	1.652		1.652	Aug.	1.175	0.994	2.169
July	1.654		1.654	Sept.	1.115	1.139	2.254
Aug.	1.630		1.630	Oct.	1.106	1.168	2.274
Sept.	1.662		1.662	Nov.	1.111	1.271	2.382
Oct.	1.642		1.642	Dec.	1.093	1.301	2.394
Nov.	1.452	0.228	1.680				
Dec.	1.351	0.244	1.595	1918			
				Jan.	1.085	1.336	2.421
1915				Feb.	1.064	1.386	2.450
Jan.	1.349	0.268	1.617	Mar.	1.067	1.415	2.482
Feb.	1.370	0.284	1.654	Apr.	1.066	1.441	2.507
Mar.	1.385	0.291	1.676	May	1.013	1.420	2.433
Apr.	1.390	0.318	1.708	June	0.972	1.397	2.369
May	1.426	0.312	1.738	July	0.935	1.348	2.283
June	1.441	0.320	1.761	Aug.	0.905	1.426	2.331
July	1.464	0.313	1.777	Sept.	0.947	1.444	2.391
Aug.	1.544	0.325	1.869	Oct.	1.010	1.555	2.565
Sept.	1.551	0.334	1.885	Nov.	1.015	1.337	2.352
Oct.	1.544	0.344	1.888	Dec.	1.008	1.425	2.433
Nov.	1.572	0.356	1.928				
Dec.	1.536	0.370	1.906	1919			
				Jan.	0.997	1.502	2.499
1916				Feb.	0.966	1.507	2.473
Jan.	1.554	0.407	1.961	Mar.	0.992	1.526	2.518
Feb.	1.579	0.410	1.989	Apr.	1.001	1.606	2.607
Mar.	1.558	0.424	1.982	May	0.993	1.634	2.627
Apr.	1.507	0.441	1.948	June	0.996	1.633	2.629
May	1.461	0.509	1.970	July	0.997	1.638	2.635
June	1.482	0.469	1.951	Aug.	1.006	1.666	2.672
July	1.518	0.501	2.019	Sept.	1.025	1.644	2.669
Aug.	1.591	0.514	2.105	Oct.	1.035	1.705	2.740
Sept.	1.608	0.528	2.136	Nov.	1.053	1.700	2.753
Oct.	1.619	0.548	2.167	Dec.	1.041	1.620	2.661

(continued)

737

TABLE A-2 (continued)

Date	Vault Cash (1)	Bank Deposits at Federal Reserve Banks (2)	Bank Reserves (3)	Date	Vault Cash (1)	Bank Deposits at Federal Reserve Banks (2)	Bank Reserves (3)
1920				1923			
Jan.	1.030	1.700	2.730	Mar.	0.894	1.876	2.770
Feb.	1.032	1.718	2.750	Apr.	0.874	1.839	2.713
Mar.	1.032	1.730	2.762	May	0.868	1.856	2.724
Apr.	1.028	1.756	2.784	June	0.860	1.834	2.694
May	1.035	1.746	2.781	July	0.879	1.809	2.688
June	1.038	1.713	2.751	Aug.	0.908	1.827	2.735
July	1.032	1.721	2.753	Sept.	0.921	1.827	2.748
Aug.	1.009	1.721	2.730	Oct.	0.912	1.862	2.774
Sept.	0.997	1.674	2.671	Nov.	0.918	1.866	2.784
Oct.	0.990	1.683	2.673	Dec.	0.920	1.850	2.770
Nov.	1.019	1.628	2.647				
Dec.	1.013	1.673	2.686	1924			
				Jan.	0.917	1.900	2.817
1921				Feb.	0.917	1.901	2.818
Jan.	1.021	1.617	2.638	Mar.	0.900	1.909	2.809
Feb.	0.975	1.635	2.610	Apr.	0.897	1.936	2.833
Mar.	0.931	1.602	2.533	May	0.909	1.927	2.836
Apr.	0.945	1.620	2.565	June	0.915	1.992	2.907
May	0.894	1.615	2.509	July	0.928	2.074	3.002
June	0.905	1.597	2.502	Aug.	0.939	2.077	3.016
July	0.861	1.622	2.483	Sept.	0.938	2.094	3.032
Aug.	0.821	1.617	2.438	Oct.	0.950	2.135	3.085
Sept.	0.833	1.648	2.481	Nov.	0.955	2.126	3.081
Oct.	0.822	1.635	2.457	Dec.	0.939	2.165	3.104
Nov.	0.828	1.643	2.471				
Dec.	0.847	1.664	2.511	1925			
				Jan.	0.945	2.132	3.077
1922				Feb.	0.954	2.187	3.141
Jan.	0.854	1.617	2.471	Mar.	0.925	2.106	3.031
Feb.	0.867	1.661	2.528	Apr.	0.933	2.121	3.054
Mar.	0.878	1.716	2.594	May	0.920	2.137	3.057
Apr.	0.858	1.737	2.595	June	0.919	2.106	3.025
May	0.860	1.796	2.656	July	0.926	2.148	3.074
June	0.863	1.833	2.696	Aug.	0.924	2.177	3.101
July	0.858	1.787	2:645	Sept.	0.939	2.189	3.128
Aug.	0.855	1.783	2.638	Oct.	0.937	2.179	3.116
Sept.	0.861	1.780	2.641	Nov.	0.945	2.188	3.133
Oct.	0.873	1.741	2.614	Dec.	0.965	2.232	3.197
Nov.	0.892	1.789	2.681				
Dec.	0.919	1.779	2.698	1926			
				Jan.	0.962	2.185	3.147
1923				Feb.	0.967	2.184	3.151
Jan.	0.910	1.892	2.802	Mar.	0.967	2.203	3.170
Feb.	0.899	1.853	2.752	Apr.	0.963	2.189	3.152

(continued)

TABLE A-2 (continued)

Date	Vault Cash (1)	Bank Deposits at Federal Reserve Banks (2)	Bank Reserves (3)	Date	Vault Cash (1)	Bank Deposits at Federal Reserve Banks (2)	Bank Reserves (3)
1926				**1929**			
May	0.955	2.199	3.154	July	0.891	2.345	3.236
June	0.943	2.209	3.152	Aug.	0.906	2.330	3.236
July	0.947	2.202	3.149	Sept.	0.909	2.344	3.253
Aug.	0.937	2.206	3.143	Oct.	0.931	2.582	3.513
Sept.	0.946	2.228	3.174	Nov.	0.909	2.391	3.300
Oct.	0.946	2.171	3.117	Dec.	0.874	2.304	3.178
Nov.	0.921	2.180	3.101				
Dec.	0.922	2.188	3.110	**1930**			
				Jan.	0.888	2.340	3.228
1927				Feb.	0.875	2.376	3.251
Jan.	0.915	2.186	3.101	Mar.	0.861	2.385	3.246
Feb.	0.915	2.173	3.088	Apr.	0.858	2.380	3.238
Mar.	0.929	2.273	3.202	May	0.866	2.345	3.211
Apr.	0.937	2.259	3.196	June	0.850	2.377	3.227
May	0.938	2.278	3.216	July	0.831	2.425	3.256
June	0.956	2.331	3.287	Aug.	0.807	2.442	3.249
July	0.943	2.291	3.234	Sept.	0.793	2.402	3.195
Aug.	0.940	2.315	3.255	Oct.	0.816	2.407	3.223
Sept.	0.939	2.319	3.258	Nov.	0.841	2.420	3.261
Oct.	0.928	2.313	3.241	Dec.	0.883	2.433	3.316
Nov.	0.939	2.357	3.296				
Dec.	0.951	2.373	3.324	**1931**			
				Jan.	0.852	2.482	3.334
1928				Feb.	0.827	2.426	3.253
Jan.	0.927	2.357	3.284	Mar.	0.789	2.440	3.229
Feb.	0.931	2.381	3.312	Apr.	0.817	2.405	3.222
Mar.	0.927	2.366	3.293	May	0.819	2.414	3.233
Apr.	0.912	2.421	3.333	June	0.846	2.461	3.307
May	0.905	2.379	3.284	July	0.839	2.424	3.263
June	0.900	2.325	3.225	Aug.	0.841	2.357	3.198
July	0.890	2.300	3.190	Sept.	0.862	2.347	3.209
Aug.	0.901	2.287	3.188	Oct.	0.856	2.177	3.033
Sept.	0.897	2.299	3.196	Nov.	0.815	2.140	2.955
Oct.	0.898	2.325	3.223	Dec.	0.819	2.312	3.131
Nov.	0.919	2.353	3.272				
Dec.	0.930	2.354	3.284	**1932**			
				Jan.	0.806	2.002	2.808
1929				Feb.	0.787	1.926	2.713
Jan.	0.919	2.408	3.327	Mar.	0.791	2.005	2.796
Feb.	0.908	2.382	3.290	Apr.	0.775	2.118	2.893
Mar.	0.893	2.357	3.250	May	0.759	2.205	2.964
Apr.	0.869	2.284	3.153	June	0.788	2.041	2.829
May	0.879	2.286	3.165	July	0.738	2.072	2.810
June	0.865	2.326	3.191	Aug.	0.723	2.139	2.862

(continued)

TABLE A-2 (continued)

Date	Vault Cash (1)	Bank Deposits at Federal Reserve Banks (2)	Bank Reserves (3)	Date	Vault Cash (1)	Bank Deposits at Federal Reserve Banks (2)	Bank Reserves (3)
1932				**1935**			
Sept.	0.705	2.251	2.956	Nov.	0.862	5.787	6.649
Oct.	0.686	2.347	3.033	Dec.	0.870	5.829	6.699
Nov.	0.706	2.430	3.136				
Dec.	0.716	2.482	3.198	**1936**			
				Jan.	0.902	5.846	6.748
1933				Feb.	0.915	5.881	6.796
Jan.	0.711	2.582	3.293	Mar.	0.928	5.428	6.356
Feb.	0.897	2.322	3.219	Apr.	0.958	5.630	6.588
Mar.	0.787	2.118	2.905	May	0.963	5.832	6.795
Apr.	0.729	2.143	2.872	June	0.991	5.457	6.448
May	0.712	2.184	2.896	July	0.992	6.108	7.100
June	0.699	2.296	2.995	Aug.	0.973	6.366	7.339
July	0.680	2.325	3.005	Sept.	0.963	6.488	7.451
Aug.	0.698	2.413	3.111	Oct.	0.973	6.705	7.678
Sept.	0.691	2.568	3.259	Nov.	0.955	6.795	7.750
Oct.	0.675	2.638	3.313	Dec.	0.952	6.839	7.791
Nov.	0.715	2.606	3.321				
Dec.	0.731	2.732	3.463	**1937**			
				Jan.	0.967	6.761	7.728
1934				Feb.	0.973	6.839	7.812
Jan.	0.745	2.711	3.456	Mar.	0.969	7.062	8.031
Feb.	0.753	3.145	3.898	Apr.	0.974	7.042	8.016
Mar.	0.783	3.665	4.448	May	0.954	7.041	7.995
Apr.	0.767	3.771	4.538	June	0.935	7.038	7.973
May	0.784	3.808	4.592	July	0.942	6.896	7.838
June	0.787	3.889	4.676	Aug.	0.903	6.825	7.728
July	0.764	4.049	4.813	Sept.	0.927	7.093	8.020
Aug.	0.781	4.082	4.863	Oct.	0.905	6.882	7.787
Sept.	0.780	3.995	4.775	Nov.	0.879	6.955	7.834
Oct.	0.788	3.952	4.740	Dec.	0.894	7.234	8.128
Nov.	0.810	4.129	4.939				
Dec.	0.813	4.133	4.946	**1938**			
				Jan.	0.898	7.297	8.195
1935				Feb.	0.926	7.441	8.367
Jan.	0.829	4.548	5.377	Mar.	0.990	7.661	8.651
Feb.	0.826	4.633	5.459	Apr.	1.021	7.723	8.744
Mar.	0.825	4.624	5.449	May	1.035	7.798	8.833
Apr.	0.815	4.814	5.629	June	1.057	8.124	9.181
May	0.846	4.907	5.753	July	1.033	8.292	9.325
June	0.858	5.127	5.985	Aug.	1.041	8.298	9.339
July	0.859	5.161	6.020	Sept.	1.070	8.231	9.301
Aug.	0.863	5.321	6.184	Oct.	1.064	8.607	9.671
Sept.	0.835	5.328	6.163	Nov.	1.084	8.874	9.958
Oct.	0.844	5.606	6.450	Dec.	1.101	8.869	9.970

(continued)

TABLE A-2 (continued)

Date	Vault Cash (1)	Bank Deposits at Federal Reserve Banks (2)	Bank Reserves (3)	Date	Vault Cash (1)	Bank Deposits at Federal Reserve Banks (2)	Bank Reserves (3)
1939				**1942**			
Jan.	1.067	9.154	10.221	Mar.	1.383	12.867	14.250
Feb.	1.053	9.099	10.152	Apr.	1.429	12.964	14.393
Mar.	1.093	9.493	10.586	May	1.404	12.623	14.027
Apr.	1.070	9.956	11.026	June	1.407	12.759	14.166
May	1.084	10.115	11.199	July	1.443	12.715	14.158
June	1.111	10.241	11.352	Aug.	1.395	12.586	13.981
July	1.084	10.610	11.694	Sept.	1.391	11.711	13.102
Aug.	1.116	11.137	12.253	Oct.	1.396	12.403	13.799
Sept.	1.114	11.607	12.721	Nov.	1.367	12.452	13.819
Oct.	1.111	11.803	12.914	Dec.	1.359	12.595	13.954
Nov.	1.176	11.619	12.795				
Dec.	1.207	11.872	13.079	**1943**			
				Jan.	1.5	12.730	14.2
1940				Feb.	1.5	12.815	14.3
Jan.	1.188	12.143	13.331	Mar.	1.4	12.763	14.2
Feb.	1.197	12.599	13.796	Apr.	1.6	12.162	13.8
Mar.	1.183	12.768	13.951	May	1.5	11.637	13.1
Apr.	1.183	13.063	14.246	June	1.6	11.983	13.6
May	1.236	13.374	14.610	July	1.7	12.122	13.8
June	1.244	13.960	15.204	Aug.	1.6	12.490	14.1
July	1.260	13.812	15.072	Sept.	1.6	11.980	13.6
Aug.	1.291	13.842	15.133	Oct.	1.6	11.825	13.4
Sept.	1.257	13.921	15.178	Nov.	1.5	11.878	13.4
Oct.	1.288	14.274	15.562	Dec.	1.5	12.268	13.8
Nov.	1.293	14.363	15.656				
Dec.	1.257	14.571	15.828	**1944**			
				Jan.	1.6	12.446	14.0
1941				Feb.	1.6	11.991	13.6
Jan.	1.318	14.360	15.678	Mar.	1.6	12.027	13.6
Feb.	1.315	14.520	15.835	Apr.	1.7	12.442	14.1
Mar.	1.293	14.158	15.451	May	1.7	12.787	14.5
Apr.	1.323	13.889	15.212	June	1.6	13.008	14.6
May	1.386	14.005	15.391	July	1.6	12.842	14.4
June	1.416	13.382	14.798	Aug.	1.6	13.041	14.6
July	1.425	13.444	14.869	Sept.	1.6	13.286	14.9
Aug.	1.411	13.271	14.682	Oct.	1.6	13.653	15.3
Sept.	1.393	13.504	14.897	Nov.	1.6	14.100	15.7
Oct.	1.414	12.935	14.349	Dec.	1.7	13.609	15.3
Nov.	1.396	13.156	14.552				
Dec.	1.364	12.830	14.194	**1945**			
				Jan.	1.6	13.459	15.1
1942				Feb.	1.7	14.104	15.8
Jan.	1.433	12.886	14.319	Mar.	1.7	14.385	16.1
Feb.	1.423	12.696	14.119	Apr.	1.7	14.660	16.4

(continued)

TABLE A-2 (continued)

Date	Vault Cash (1)	Bank Deposits at Federal Reserve Banks (2)	Bank Reserves (3)	Date	Vault Cash (1)	Bank Deposits at Federal Reserve Banks (2)	Bank Reserves (3)
1945				**1948**			
May	1.7	15.020	16.7	July	1.990	17.496	19.486
June	1.6	14.695	16.3	Aug.	2.001	17.663	19.664
July	1.7	14.707	16.4	Sept.	2.011	18.491	20.502
Aug.	1.8	14.970	16.8	Oct.	2.026	19.445	21.471
Sept.	1.7	15.182	16.9	Nov.	2.035	19.412	21.447
Oct.	1.7	15.338	17.0	Dec.	2.042	19.426	21.468
Nov.	1.8	15.569	17.4				
Dec.	1.9	15.162	17.1	**1949**			
				Jan.	2.044	19.218	21.262
				Feb.	2.042	19.358	21.400
1946				Mar.	2.035	19.120	21.155
Jan.	1.8	15.368	17.2	Apr.	2.032	19.005	21.037
Feb.	1.9	15.535	17.4	May	2.026	18.293	20.319
Mar.	1.8	15.584	17.4	June	2.010	17.962	19.972
Apr.	1.7	15.498	17.2	July	2.012	17.477	19.489
May	1.8	15.547	17.3	Aug.	2.010	16.858	18.868
June	1.8	15.841	17.6	Sept.	2.002	16.029	18.031
July	2.0	16.023	18.0	Oct.	2.004	15.748	17.752
Aug.	1.8	15.807	17.6	Nov.	2.010	15.893	17.903
Sept.	2.0	15.680	17.7	Dec.	2.013	15.825	17.838
Oct.	2.1	15.671	17.8				
Nov.	2.1	15.425	17.5	**1950**			
Dec.	2.1	15.550	17.6	Jan.	2.021	15.896	17.917
				Feb.	2.029	15.781	17.810
1947				Mar.	2.053	15.718	17.771
Jan.	1.797	15.752	17.549	Apr.	2.065	15.693	17.758
Feb.	1.801	15.828	17.629	May	2.074	15.910	17.984
Mar.	1.811	15.778	17.589	June	2.116	15.888	18.004
Apr.	1.819	15.848	17.667	July	2.127	16.028	18.155
May	1.818	16.071	17.889	Aug.	2.127	16.140	18.267
June	1.825	16.063	17.888	Sept.	2.141	16.300	18.441
July	1.833	16.301	18.134	Oct.	2.152	16.183	18.335
Aug.	1.846	16.440	18.286	Nov.	2.156	16.311	18.467
Sept.	1.865	16.827	18.692	Dec.	2.165	16.468	18.633
Oct.	1.875	16.582	18.457				
Nov.	1.889	16.603	18.492	**1951**			
Dec.	1.903	16.634	18.537	Jan.	2.174	16.944	19.118
				Feb.	2.181	17.768	19.949
1948				Mar.	2.200	18.214	20.414
Jan.	1.922	16.703	18.625	Apr.	2.216	18.717	20.933
Feb.	1.932	16.582	18.514	May	2.241	18.465	20.706
Mar.	1.938	16.787	18.725	June	2.260	18.500	20.760
Apr.	1.945	16.808	18.753	July	2.266	18.378	20.644
May	1.967	16.956	18.923	Aug.	2.280	18.587	20.867
June	1.979	17.243	19.222	Sept.	2.289	18.674	20.963

(continued)

TABLE A-2 (continued)

Date	Vault Cash (1)	Bank Deposits at Federal Reserve Banks (2)	Bank Reserves (3)	Date	Vault Cash (1)	Bank Deposits at Federal Reserve Banks (2)	Bank Reserves (3)
1951				**1955**			
Oct.	2.276	19.021	21.297	Jan.	2.570	18.151	20.721
Nov.	2.278	18.931	21.209	Feb.	2.570	18.197	20.767
Dec.	2.283	19.076	21.359	Mar.	2.571	17.917	20.488
				Apr.	2.574	18.085	20.659
1952				May	2.575	18.080	20.655
Jan.	2.295	19.216	21.511	June	2.584	17.952	20.536
Feb.	2.313	19.153	21.466	July	2.599	18.041	20.640
Mar.	2.314	19.229	21.543	Aug.	2.610	18.127	20.737
Apr.	2.324	19.148	21.472	Sept.	2.612	18.024	20.636
May	2.337	19.254	21.591	Oct.	2.618	18.055	20.673
June	2.330	19.260	21.590	Nov.	2.620	17.910	20.530
July	2.336	19.762	22.098	Dec.	2.630	17.878	20.508
Aug.	2.347	19.811	22.158				
Sept.	2.359	19.915	22.274	**1956**			
Oct.	2.375	19.815	22.190	Jan.	2.629	17.876	20.505
Nov.	2.387	19.859	22.246	Feb.	2.636	17.875	20.511
Dec.	2.397	19.946	22.343	Mar.	2.649	18.007	20.656
				Apr.	2.658	18.011	20.669
1953				May	2.683	17.956	20.639
Jan.	2.404	19.645	22.049	June	2.708	17.880	20.588
Feb.	2.413	19.668	22.081	July	2.700	17.699	20.399
Mar.	2.417	19.534	21.951	Aug.	2.700	17.966	20.666
Apr.	2.416	19.432	21.848	Sept.	2.708	18.021	20.729
May	2.422	19.389	21.811	Oct.	2.709	17.878	20.587
June	2.426	19.532	21.958	Nov.	2.709	17.963	20.672
July	2.414	19.069	21.483	Dec.	2.702	17.954	20.656
Aug.	2.428	19.103	21.531				
Sept.	2.441	19.062	21.503	**1957**			
Oct.	2.447	18.874	21.321	Jan.	2.694	17.865	20.559
Nov.	2.449	19.005	21.454	Feb.	2.702	17.839	20.541
Dec.	2.454	18.917	21.371	Mar.	2.710	17.942	20.652
				Apr.	2.709	18.055	20.764
1954				May	2.716	17.949	20.665
Jan.	2.457	19.072	21.529	June	2.713	17.976	20.689
Feb.	2.458	18.933	21.391	July	2.716	18.031	20.747
Mar.	2.459	18.941	21.400	Aug.	2.719	17.880	20.599
Apr.	2.466	18.921	21.387	Sept.	2.724	17.962	20.686
May	2.457	19.066	21.523	Oct.	2.703	18.006	20.709
June	2.460	19.008	21.468	Nov.	2.694	17.920	20.614
July	2.487	18.629	21.116	Dec.	2.732	18.025	20.757
Aug.	2.497	18.023	20.520				
Sept.	2.507	17.946	20.453				
Oct.	2.525	18.302	20.827	**1958**			
Nov.	2.550	18.461	21.011	Jan.	2.720	18.050	20.770
Dec.	2.563	18.294	20.857	Feb.	2.728	18.190	20.918

(continued)

743

TABLE A-2 (concluded)

Date	Vault Cash (1)	Bank Deposits at Federal Reserve Banks (2)	Bank Reserves (3)	Date	Vault Cash (1)	Bank Deposits at Federal Reserve Banks (2)	Bank Reserves (3)
1958				**1959**			
Mar.	2.729	17.957	20.686	Aug.	2.905	17.665	20.570
Apr.	2.735	17.647	20.382	Sept.	2.933	17.655	20.588
May	2.740	17.542	20.282	Oct.	2.944	17.602	20.546
June	2.758	17.837	20.595	Nov.	2.929	17.509	20.438
July	2.760	17.708	20.468	Dec.	2.982	17.247	20.229
Aug.	2.773	17.698	20.471				
Sept.	2.798	17.578	20.376	**1960**			
Oct.	2.837	17.548	20.385	Jan.	3.052	17.101	20.153
Nov.	2.870	17.536	20.406	Feb.	3.031	17.027	20.058
Dec.	2.815	17.458	20.273	Mar.	3.055	16.969	20.024
				Apr.	3.050	16.968	20.018
1959				May	3.054	17.060	20.114
Jan.	2.848	17.592	20.440	June	3.074	17.069	20.143
Feb.	2.855	17.704	20.559	July	3.077	17.106	20.183
Mar.	2.860	17.683	20.543	Aug.	3.138	17.134	20.272
Apr.	2.896	17.860	20.756	Sept.	3.088	16.666	19.754
May	2.927	17.787	20.714	Oct.	3.094	16.720	19.814
June	2.903	17.644	20.547	Nov.	3.155	16.500	19.655
July	2.922	17.688	20.610	Dec.	3.128	15.045	18.173

SOURCE, BY COLUMN

Column 1, Vault Cash

I. Jan. 1867–Feb. 1875: Sums of figures for (A) national banks, (B) nonnational commercial banks, and (C) mutual savings banks, treated as end-of-month data. No seasonal adjustment was attempted.

 A. Vault cash in national banks is the sum of bills of national banks, bills of other banks, fractional currency, specie, legal tender notes, compound interest notes, 3 per cent certificates, and U.S. certificates of deposit, from *Annual Report* of the Comptroller of the Currency, 1918, Vol. II, pp. 248–255, at the call dates nearest ends of months shown in this table.

 B. Vault cash in nonnational commercial banks, from J. K. Kindahl, "The Period of the Resumption in the United States, 1865–1879" (unpublished Ph.D. dissertation, U. of Chicago, 1958). See description in *Historical Statistics of the United States, Colonial Times to 1957*, 1960, under Series V-88.

 C. Vault cash in mutual savings banks was estimated as follows. The Feb. 1876 ratio of the vault cash in all mutual savings banks (see below) to that in the mutual savings banks of N.Y. State, from *Annual Report* of the Banking Department Relative to Savings Banks and Trust Companies, and Mass., from *Annual Report* of the Massachusetts Savings Bank Commissioners, was extrapolated back to 1867 by the ratio of the deposits of all mutual savings banks to those of N.Y. and Mass., from E. W. Keyes, *A History of Savings Banks in the United States* (New York, 1878), Vol. II, p. 532. Vault cash in N.Y. and Mass. mutual savings

(continued)

banks was divided by the extrapolated ratios to obtain vault cash in all mutual savings banks.

II. Aug. 1875–June 1906: Sums of figures for (A) national banks, and (B) nonnational commercial and mutual savings banks, treated as end-of-month data.
   A. Vault cash of national banks is the sum of bills of other banks, fractional currency, specie, legal tender notes, trade dollars, and U.S. certificates of deposit, from *Annual Report* (Comptroller), 1918, Vol. II, pp. 254–267, and *All-Bank Statistics, 1896–1955* (Board of Governors, FRS, 1959), p. 39. From Aug. 1875 to Aug. 1881, the figures were interpolated on a straight line between closest call dates to the end of Feb. and Aug. From 1882 to 1906, the call date figure nearest June 30 was used.
   B. Vault cash of nonnational commercial and mutual savings banks was obtained as follows.
      1. Aug. 1875–June 1895: David Fand, "Estimates of Deposits and Vault Cash in the Nonnational Banks in the Post-Civil War Period in the United States" (unpublished Ph.D. dissertation, U. of Chicago, 1954). See description in *Historical Statistics*, 1960, under Series V-89–90.
      2. June 1896–June 1906: *All-Bank Statistics*, pp. 43, 47.

III. May 1907–Dec. 1917: These are sums of estimates for (A) Clearing House banks of selected cities; (B) other reporting banks including mutual savings banks; and (C) nonreporting banks.
   A. These are seasonally adjusted sums of vault cash in the Clearing House banks of the following cities for the following periods: Chicago, 1907–08, from A. P. Andrew, *Statistics for the United States, 1867–1909* (National Monetary Commission, 1910, S. Doc. 570, 61st Cong., 2d sess.), pp. 149–150; St. Louis, New Orleans, San Francisco, 1907–08, from E. W. Kemmerer, *Seasonal Variations in the Relative Demand for Money and Capital in the United States* (National Monetary Commission, 1910, S. Doc. 588, 61st Cong., 2d sess.), pp. 269, 274–275; Philadelphia, 1907–17, *American Banker* (monthly issues); Boston, 1907–16, from *Statement of the Associated Banks* (Boston Clearing House Assn., weekly issues); New York, 1907–17 (including nonmembers of the Clearing House, May–Sept. 1907, and all N.Y. City banks not in the Clearing House, Feb. 1908–Dec. 1917), from *Commercial and Financial Chronicle*. Weekly data are dated Wed., mid-point of week nearest end of month. The New York series was seasonally adjusted separately, the remaining cities as a group. Since neither the data for New York nor for the other 6 cities were continuous, a hypothetical continuous series was constructed for each of these totals for the purpose of deriving the seasonal factors, by raising the level of the less inclusive to that of the more inclusive segment. The seasonal factors were then applied to the discontinuous data.
   B. These are residual vault cash figures for other reporting banks, including mutual savings banks, reporting to state agencies but not in the clearing house group of banks. From call date figures for all reporting banks (described in III. B.2, below), call date figures for the 7-city total of Clearing House banks were deducted.
      1. To obtain the call date series for the Clearing House banks, the weekly series for N.Y. banks and for banks in the 6 other cities were used. For a call date that fell on a Wed., the weekly figures were corrected for seasonal by the index for the month nearest to the week of the call date, and were totaled. For a call date that fell on another day of the week, such deseasonalized totals were taken for the preceding and following Wed. and interpolated to the call date on a straight line.
      When the composition of the clearing house total changed from one call date to the next, the totals were first made continuous by including or excluding the cities that created the discontinuity in order to obtain comparable residuals. We interpolated along a straight line between the call date residuals to Wed.

(continued)

nearest end of month and restored the actual discontinuity to the monthly interpolations.

2. Call date vault cash figures for all reporting banks are seasonally adjusted sums of vault cash in national and nonnational banks. Vault cash in national banks, from *Annual Report* (Comptroller), was adjusted simultaneously for the intra-weekly and for monthly seasonal changes, 1874–1917 and 1917–49. The original data for vault cash in nonnational banks were obtained at midyear dates from *ibid.*, and at report dates from the reports of state banking departments. A hypothetical continuous series of vault cash in nonnational banks in 16 states, 1907–16, dated entirely as of national bank call dates, was constructed for the purpose of deriving combined daily and monthly seasonal factors. These factors were applied to nonnational bank cash in all states except New York. For vault cash in nonnational banks of N.Y. State, combined daily and monthly seasonal factors were calculated, 1897–1917. This separate index was computed because vault cash in these banks, which did not usually report at national bank call dates, averaged 40 per cent of all nonnational bank vault cash, 1907–17. Seasonal factors for June 1917–June 1919 were obtained by averaging the daily-monthly indexes for nonmember banks (described below) and for state member banks, weighted by the estimated per cent of all nonnational bank vault cash comprised by nonmember and state member bank vault cash, respectively. This index was also used to adjust New York nonnational bank figures, 1917–19.

For each state, we seasonally adjusted the vault cash reported, whether dated identically with national bank call dates or not. If not dated identically, the seasonally adjusted figures were interpolated on a straight line to national bank call dates between closest report dates. When each nonidentically dated report date figure had been used once for interpolation, we had to fill in remaining gaps between June dates. To do so, we first classified the 48 states and D.C. and the possessions into four groups: N.Y.; all other units with mutual savings banks; states in the South and Southeast without mutual savings banks; and all other states without mutual savings banks. We filled in the gaps in each of the series in these groups on the basis of estimating equations derived from data for random pairs of states in each group. For each call date we thus obtained a published, seasonally adjusted, observation or an estimated value of vault cash for each of the 50 units. The entries were summed to get vault cash in all reporting banks at national bank call dates.

C. Vault cash in nonreporting private banks in Mass., N.J., Pa., Md., Va., Ga., Tex., Ohio, Ill., Mich., Iowa, Mont., Wash.—states that did not require reports from this class of banks—was obtained at June dates from *All-Bank Statistics* and interpolated on a straight line to Wed. nearest end of month.

IV. Jan. 1918–June 1919: These are sums of estimates for (A) weekly reporting member banks; (B) other reporting banks including mutual savings banks; and (C) nonreporting banks.

A. The Fri. nearest end-of-month figures on vault cash in weekly reporting member banks, from *Federal Reserve Bulletin* (monthly issues), were seasonally adjusted by us with combined monthly and daily correction factors.

B. Estimates of vault cash in other reporting banks, including mutual savings banks, were derived as follows. From the call date figures for all reporting banks, obtained as described in III.B.2, call date figures for weekly reporting member banks were deducted. For call dates that fell on a Fri., the deseasonalized Fri. figure for weekly reporting member banks was used; for call dates that fell on another day of the week, a figure was interpolated along a straight line between deseasonalized Fri. figures for the week immediately preceding and for the week immediately following the call date. We interpolated along a straight line between the call date residuals to Fri. nearest end of month.

(continued)

C. Nonreporting bank June figures on vault cash by states, as for May 1907–Dec. 1917, were interpolated on a straight line to Fri. nearest end of month.

V. July 1919–Dec. 1942: These are sums of estimates for (A) weekly reporting member banks; (B) nonweekly reporting member banks; (C) reporting nonmember banks including mutual savings banks; (D) nonreporting nonmember banks.

A. Estimates of vault cash in weekly reporting member banks are the same as for Jan. 1918–June 1919, except that beginning May 1921 the figures are Wed. data. The source for the original series through 1941 is *Banking and Monetary Statistics*, pp. 132–162; thereafter, *FRB*.

B. Estimates of vault cash in nonweekly reporting member banks are residual figures, obtained as described in IV.B (except that, beginning May 1921, Wed. call dates were used), from seasonally adjusted call date figures for all member banks. The latter series is a sum of vault cash in national banks and in state member banks. Vault cash in national banks, from *Annual Report* (Comptroller), was adjusted simultaneously for intraweekly and monthly seasonal variations, applying seasonal factors based on the years 1917–49. Vault cash in state member banks, from *Member Bank Call Report* (June 1917–Mar. 1929), thereafter obtained as a residual by subtracting national bank figures from member bank figures (*ibid.*) was also adjusted for daily and monthly seasonal changes. At national bank call dates that were not also state member bank call dates, 1919–22, state member bank figures are straight-line interpolations.

C. Estimates of vault cash in reporting nonmember banks, including mutual savings banks, are straight-line interpolations to Fri. (beginning May 1921, Wed.) nearest end of month between call date estimates. The latter were derived as follows. Vault cash in nonnational banks, by states, was obtained at report dates from reports of state banking departments and at mid- and some end-of-year dates from *Annual Report* (Comptroller). For state report dates coinciding with member bank call dates, vault cash in state member banks was deducted from that in nonnational banks to get nonmember bank vault cash. A hypothetical continuous series of vault cash in nonmember banks in all states with identically dated observations yielded daily and monthly seasonal factors. For state report dates that did not coincide with member bank call dates, seasonal factors for nonnational banks were obtained by combining seasonal factors for state member banks (see V.B) with the nonmember bank factors, weighting the two factors with the share of nonnational bank vault cash held by each of these two constituent classes of banks. The nonidentically dated, seasonally corrected nonnational bank figures were then converted into nonidentically dated nonmember bank figures by reading from a freehand curve, plotting for each state the smoothed ratio of corrected nonmember to nonnational bank data derived from the dates for which identically dated figures were available. Identically dated nonmember bank figures were obtained by straight-line interpolation between two such estimated nonmember bank nonidentically dated figures closest to the call date, or between one such nonidentically dated and a preceding or following identically dated nonmember bank figure.

We had figures for nonmember banks in 48 states, D.C., and the possessions, with gaps in each series for some inter-June call dates. The states were classified into three groups: all states, including N.Y., with mutual savings banks; states in the South and Southeast without mutual savings banks; and all other states. We filled in the gaps in each of the series in these groups on the basis of estimating equations derived from data for random pairs of states in each group. For each call date we summed the published, seasonally adjusted, observations and the estimated values of vault cash obtained for each of the 50 units to get vault cash in all reporting nonmember banks at call dates.

D. Estimates of vault cash in nonreporting nonmember banks are June figures for states, as for nonreporting banks, May 1907–Dec. 1917, interpolated on a straight line to Fri. (beginning May 1921, Wed.) nearest end of month.

(continued)

747

Notes to Table A-2 (concluded)

VI. Jan. 1943–Dec. 1946: Seasonally unadjusted end-of-month figures for currency outside banks were subtracted from similar figures for currency outside the Treasury and Federal Reserve Banks, from *FRB* (monthly issues), and the residuals, which include mutual savings bank vault cash, were seasonally adjusted by us.

VII. Jan. 1947–Dec. 1960: Monthly averages of semimonthly averages of daily figures for commercial banks only (*ibid.*, Oct. 1960, pp. 1116–1121, and an unpublished Federal Reserve table for 1960), seasonally adjusted by Shiskin-Eisenpress method (see Julius Shiskin and Harry Eisenpress, *Seasonal Adjustments by Electronic Computer Methods*, NBER, Technical Paper 12, 1958).

Column 2, Bank Deposits at Federal Reserve Banks

This series is a sum of (A) member bank deposits, *minus* (B) float, *plus* (C) nonmember bank clearing account, seasonally adjusted by Shiskin-Eisenpress method.
  A. Member bank deposits at Federal Reserve Banks were estimated as follows.
    1. 1914–21: *Annual Report*, Federal Reserve Board. Figures are end-of-month. Dec. 1914, last Fri. of month, Nov. 1914 and Jan. 1915–Apr. 1921, last Wed. of month thereafter.
    2. 1922–60: *Banking and Monetary Statistics*, pp. 378–394; *FRB* (monthly issues, 1942–61). Last Wed.-of-month figures, 1914–46; monthly averages of daily figures, 1947–60. Negligible deposits of member mutual savings banks since 1934 were not deducted, for lack of data.
  B. Float was derived as follows.
    1. 1914–16: Unavailable.
    2. Jan. 1917–Apr. 1929: Uncollected items less deferred availability items, from Federal Reserve Board, *Annual Report* (1917–26); *FRB* (1927–29); and *Commercial and Financial Chronicle* (1929), were adjusted to the level of float shown for the end of those years, from *Annual Report*, Board of Governors of the Federal Reserve System, 1955, p. 70. From 1924 on, the adjustment was made by subtracting Federal Reserve notes of other Federal Reserve Banks (interpolated 1924–26 between end-of-Dec. figures, *Banking and Monetary Statistics*, pp. 330–331; thereafter available monthly in Federal Reserve Board, *Annual Report*). May 1929–Feb. 1952: Uncollected items less deferred availability items, from *FRB*.
    3. Mar. 1952—Dec. 1960: Float, obtained directly from *ibid.*, with same dating as member bank deposits at Federal Reserve Banks.
  C. Nonmember bank clearing account monthly figures, except in 1917, are interpolations along a straight line between end-of-Dec. figures. June 1917 is the July 6 figure; July–Nov. 1917 are last Fri. of the month, *FRB*. End-of-Dec. figures are from the following sources:
    1. 1914–21, 1926–43, 1945–60: *Annual Report* (Fed. Res. Bd. and Bd. of Governors of the FRS).
    2. 1922–25: "Other" deposits at Federal Reserve Banks minus nonmember bank clearing account were interpolated on a straight line between 1921 and 1926 figures. The interpolations were subtracted from figures for those years for total "other" deposits (other deposits on Federal Reserve balance sheets are other than member bank, Treasury, and foreign).
    3. 1944: Straight-line interpolation between end-of-Dec. figures for 1943 and 1945.

Column 3, Bank Reserves

Col. 1 plus col. 2.

TABLE A-3
U.S. GOVERNMENT BALANCES, SEASONALLY ADJUSTED, 1867–1960
(millions of dollars)

Date	Treasury Cash (1)	At Commercial and Savings Banks (2)	At Federal Reserve Banks (3)
1867 Jan.	148	30	
1868 Jan.	135	28	
1869 Jan.	126	16	
1870 Jan.	128	10	
1871 Jan.	111	11	
1872 Jan.	83	15	
1873 Feb.	67	13	
1874 Feb.	79	12	
1875 Feb.	90	13	
Aug.	93	11	
1876 Feb.	96	11	
Aug.	99	11	
1877 Feb.	101	10	
Aug.	113	10	
1878 Feb.	144	10	
Aug.	176	40	
1879 Feb.	196	237	
Aug.	212	43	
1880 Feb.	209	11	
Aug.	209	11	
1881 Feb.	228	11	
Aug.	235	12	
1882 June	231	13	
1883 June	236	14	
1884 June	240	14	
1885 June	240	14	
1886 June	306	17	
1887 June	305	23	
1888 June	308	58	
1889 June	268	47	
1890 June	245	31	
1891 June	173	26	
1892 June	147	14	
1893 June	138	14	
1894 June	142	14	
1895 June	215	15	
1896 June	288	17	
1897 June	261	16	
1898 June	231	49	
1899 June	273	76	
1900 June	280	99	
1901 June	307	99	
1902 June	312	124	

(continued)

749

TABLE A-3 (continued)

Date	Treasury Cash (1)	U.S. Government Balances At Commercial and Savings Banks (2)	At Federal Reserve Banks (3)
1903 June	311	147	
1904 June	281	110	
1905 June	288	71	
1906 June	326	91	
1907 May	343	190	
June	341	179	
July	326	167	
Aug.	327	161	
Sept.	330	169	
Oct.	278	198	
Nov.	262	211	
Dec.	269	237	
1908 Jan.	293	241	
Feb.	303	243	
Mar.	318	219	
Apr.	315	209	
May	355	168	
June	336	148	
July	323	130	
Aug.	307	134	
Sept.	305	135	
Oct.	290	130	
Nov.	277	123	
Dec.	307	120	
1909 Jan.	312	111	
Feb.	327	97	
Mar.	312	83	
Apr.	315	69	
May	314	69	
June	299	67	
July	297	60	
Aug.	304	52	
Sept.	305	51	
Oct.	310	49	
Nov.	298	48	
Dec.	303	47	
1910 Jan.	310	46	
Feb.	302	47	
Mar.	302	47	
Apr.	309	48	
May	312	49	
June	312	50	

(continued)

TABLE A-3 (continued)

| Date | Treasury Cash (1) | U.S. Government Balances | |
		At Commercial and Savings Banks (2)	At Federal Reserve Banks (3)
1910 July	295	52	
Aug.	301	54	
Sept.	311	51	
Oct.	315	48	
Nov.	308	46	
Dec.	315	45	
1911 Jan.	314	45	
Feb.	309	45	
Mar.	308	45	
Apr.	312	45	
May	314	44	
June	333	46	
July	347	49	
Aug.	352	52	
Sept.	357	50	
Oct.	359	48	
Nov.	348	46	
Dec.	349	51	
1912 Jan.	346	56	
Feb.	343	59	
Mar.	340	54	
Apr.	346	53	
May	356	54	
June	369	56	
July	350	60	
Aug.	361	63	
Sept.	366	58	
Oct.	373	51	
Nov.	370	45	
Dec.	366	48	
1913 Jan.	369	50	
Feb.	369	48	
Mar.	358	45	
Apr.	360	45	
May	367	46	
June	351	50	
July	348	55	
Aug.	361	68	
Sept.	345	81	
Oct.	345	89	
Nov.	334	85	
Dec.	326	82	

(continued)

TABLE A-3 (continued)

Date	Treasury Cash (1)	U.S. Government Balances At Commercial and Savings Banks (2)	At Federal Reserve Banks (3)
1914 Jan.	331	76	
Feb.	324	68	
Mar.	322	65	
Apr.	318	64	
May	314	62	
June	323	61	
July	350	67	
Aug.	335	73	
Sept.	345	73	
Oct.	347	69	
Nov.	403	65	
Dec.	425	62	
1915 Jan.	401	60	
Feb.	411	59	
Mar.	398	55	
Apr.	386	50	
May	359	47	
June	359	45	
July	356	46	
Aug.	335	48	
Sept.	311	45	15
Oct.	293	41	15
Nov.	301	36	15
Dec.	297	31	17
1916 Jan.	238	32	28
Feb.	283	32	35
Mar.	270	34	38
Apr.	288	37	41
May	303	37	48
June	299	36	101
July	354	36	53
Aug.	330	37	51
Sept.	311	36	39
Oct.	309	35	30
Nov.	306	33	27
Dec.	290	31	28
1917 Jan.	239	32	25
Feb.	239	34	13
Mar.	251	35	50
Apr.	253	39	112
May	237	87	92

(continued)

TABLE A-3 (continued)

Date	Treasury Cash (1)	U.S. Government Balances At Commercial and Savings Banks (2)	At Federal Reserve Banks (3)
1917 June	245	284	268
July	215	295	214
Aug.	262	355	156
Sept.	245	918	61
Oct.	246	1,821	291
Nov.	209	2,257	224
Dec.	230	632	101
1918 Jan.	335	856	198
Feb.	274	1,454	107
Mar.	275	1,045	121
Apr.	270	1,218	125
May	286	1,951	152
June	292	1,562	95
July	305	1,506	86
Aug.	264	1,374	81
Sept.	270	990	88
Oct.	262	2,133	189
Nov.	276	1,462	177
Dec.	294	411	56
1919 Jan.	303	991	77
Feb.	355	1,452	158
Mar.	361	989	146
Apr.	369	1,074	88
May	366	1,171	120
June	393	978	73
July	378	858	66
Aug.	391	975	49
Sept.	410	670	77
Oct.	418	612	79
Nov.	414	536	86
Dec.	393	592	34
1920 Jan.	382	403	79
Feb.	331	148	80
Mar.	266	175	25
Apr.	257	199	40
May	249	193	29
June	242	191	36
July	212	239	17
Aug.	212	214	40
Sept.	221	337	39
Oct.	219	246	15
Nov.	231	135	19
Dec.	223	264	62

(continued)

TABLE A-3 (continued)

Date	Treasury Cash (1)	U.S. Government Balances At Commercial and Savings Banks (2)	At Federal Reserve Banks (3)
1921 Jan.	212	204	23
Feb.	220	223	46
Mar.	253	317	88
Apr.	239	277	33
May	238	168	39
June	205	387	37
July	205	488	41
Aug.	205	289	53
Sept.	216	451	84
Oct.	223	350	48
Nov.	221	295	44
Dec.	219	268	103
1922 Jan.	224	446	93
Feb.	219	502	55
Mar.	224	273	54
Apr.	226	257	75
May	223	263	54
June	233	153	49
July	219	266	21
Aug.	225	295	58
Sept.	220	164	17
Oct.	224	308	40
Nov.	235	369	32
Dec.	223	342	7
1923 Jan.	211	235	37
Feb.	218	236	38
Mar.	232	385	81
Apr.	219	330	51
May	213	383	41
June	220	310	49
July	214	222	52
Aug.	218	199	43
Sept.	211	210	25
Oct.	222	165	45
Nov.	208	158	33
Dec.	212	214	61
1924 Jan.	213	221	33
Feb.	212	245	34
Mar.	218	265	105
Apr.	214	257	34
May	223	204	40
June	222	181	36

(continued)

TABLE A-3 (continued)

Date	Treasury Cash (1)	U.S. Government Balances At Commercial and Savings Banks (2)	At Federal Reserve Banks (3)
1924 July	222	185	56
Aug.	221	205	39
Sept.	222	261	48
Oct.	220	315	31
Nov.	221	328	22
Dec.	214	224	54
1925 Jan.	230	245	42
Feb.	209	278	24
Mar.	210	401	33
Apr.	213	314	28
May	220	304	39
June	212	180	26
July	214	168	26
Aug.	211	169	28
Sept.	205	241	26
Oct.	219	204	44
Nov.	218	192	42
Dec.	209	287	16
1926 Jan.	223	316	35
Feb.	232	390	46
Mar.	219	362	82
Apr.	215	330	17
May	214	380	16
June	206	228	12
July	207	246	41
Aug.	206	204	27
Sept.	218	276	44
Oct.	213	239	37
Nov.	211	222	34
Dec.	215	217	42
1927 Jan.	207	252	27
Feb.	216	279	31
Mar.	203	229	31
Apr.	211	224	25
May	207	203	26
June	213	184	30
July	208	203	17
Aug.	204	240	15
Sept.	206	335	21
Oct.	205	311	7
Nov.	201	156	2
Dec.	209	261	18

(continued)

TABLE A-3 (continued)

Date	Treasury Cash (1)	U.S. Government Balances At Commercial and Savings Banks (2)	At Federal Reserve Banks (3)
1928 Jan.	206	214	19
Feb.	203	170	25
Mar.	198	239	24
Apr.	203	196	21
May	209	164	23
June	203	235	12
July	205	394	37
Aug.	207	468	30
Sept.	203	122	28
Oct.	207	220	22
Nov.	205	281	23
Dec.	206	237	33
1929 Jan.	203	219	15
Feb.	204	169	19
Mar.	201	234	16
Apr.	211	237	36
May	211	297	15
June	211	322	55
July	214	240	17
Aug.	203	245	19
Sept.	211	244	38
Oct.	205	235	21
Nov.	220	261	34
Dec.	219	136	31
1930 Jan.	210	122	28
Feb.	215	84	33
Mar.	205	178	37
Apr.	213	164	24
May	211	173	50
June	221	224	28
July	214	227	32
Aug.	217	138	38
Sept.	205	190	31
Oct.	208	202	30
Nov.	212	85	40
Dec.	214	240	20
1931 Jan.	206	209	37
Feb.	215	188	27
Mar.	215	244	22
Apr.	217	281	28
May	217	115	65
June	222	313	35

(continued)

756

TABLE A-3 (continued)

Date	Treasury Cash (1)	U.S. Government Balances At Commercial and Savings Banks (2)	At Federal Reserve Banks (3)
1931 July	220	357	11
Aug.	226	273	44
Sept.	224	372	23
Oct.	223	305	44
Nov.	223	318	37
Dec.	226	376	47
1932 Jan.	224	553	34
Feb.	225	351	39
Mar.	223	517	40
Apr.	231	305	45
May	232	409	14
June	224	430	24
July	247	509	46
Aug.	248	339	65
Sept.	266	691	51
Oct.	247	674	35
Nov.	249	620	41
Dec.	267	506	39
1933 Jan.	279	453	39
Feb.	272	265	30
Mar.	349	445	54
Apr.	346	496	131
May	275	477	80
June	269	837	47
July	280	836	46
Aug.	272	1,159	75
Sept.	271	1,021	59
Oct.	271	1,279	130
Nov.	285	1,175	139
Dec.	292	872	21
1934 Jan.	355	1,272	258
Feb.	3,395	1,992	47
Mar.	3,262	1,650	42
Apr.	2,934	1,535	222
May	2,999	1,538	58
June	2,943	1,649	115
July	2,914	1,692	133
Aug.	2,914	1,534	33
Sept.	2,912	1,207	165
Oct.	2,939	1,063	103
Nov.	2,931	1,098	146
Dec.	3,038	1,548	116

(continued)

757

TABLE A-3 (continued)

Date	Treasury Cash (1)	U.S. Government Balances At Commercial and Savings Banks (2)	At Federal Reserve Banks (3)
1935 Jan.	2,950	1,561	61
Feb.	2,907	1,474	104
Mar.	2,930	1,273	357
Apr.	2,902	1,417	69
May	2,896	1,239	82
June	2,911	956	69
July	2,865	808	105
Aug.	2,633	770	55
Sept.	2,723	785	96
Oct.	2,605	668	67
Nov.	2,571	714	92
Dec.	2,566	812	503
1936 Jan.	2,553	760	510
Feb.	2,516	703	456
Mar.	2,528	884	818
Apr.	2,529	1,054	620
May	2,579	1,178	560
June	2,501	1,077	627
July	2,441	1,130	387
Aug.	2,375	1,095	117
Sept.	2,458	977	268
Oct.	2,390	924	112
Nov.	2,353	736	186
Dec.	2,368	869	213
1937 Jan.	2,529	650	188
Feb.	2,620	505	228
Mar.	2,753	409	234
Apr.	2,956	400	87
May	3,182	282	128
June	3,445	631	80
July	3,576	559	189
Aug.	3,719	710	171
Sept.	3,575	660	148
Oct.	3,662	540	125
Nov.	3,627	570	300
Dec.	3,620	736	129
1938 Jan.	3,648	744	152
Feb.	3,579	844	195
Mar.	3,551	744	220
Apr.	2,192	764	1,205
May	2,254	768	1,213
June	2,299	543	741

(continued)

TABLE A-3 (continued)

Date	Treasury Cash (1)	U.S. Government Balances At Commercial and Savings Banks (2)	At Federal Reserve Banks (3)
1938 July	2,357	574	643
Aug.	2,480	553	790
Sept.	2,816	644	914
Oct.	2,751	685	648
Nov.	2,689	770	820
Dec.	2,707	774	870
1939 Jan.	2,770	825	946
Feb.	2,716	888	1,231
Mar.	2,722	769	904
Apr.	2,691	889	854
May	2,636	896	1,021
June	2,559	732	825
July	2,370	762	716
Aug.	2,327	730	778
Sept.	2,260	635	584
Oct.	2,250	703	393
Nov.	2,359	788	747
Dec.	2,367	747	602
1940 Jan.	2,359	782	585
Feb.	2,374	834	591
Mar.	2,372	738	521
Apr.	2,293	864	447
May	2,200	945	420
June	2,186	792	258
July	2,250	781	576
Aug.	2,291	766	892
Sept.	2,294	681	717
Oct.	2,187	729	423
Nov.	2,182	801	337
Dec.	2,213	645	340
1941 Jan.	2,200	391	275
Feb.	2,204	514	388
Mar.	2,251	588	787
Apr.	2,283	595	789
May	2,221	677	513
June	2,276	678	718
July	2,330	727	764
Aug.	2,400	970	777
Sept.	2,259	997	327
Oct.	2,209	1,016	1,029
Nov.	2,180	1,278	544
Dec.	2,215	1,487	801

(continued)

TABLE A-3 (continued)

Date	Treasury Cash (1)	U.S. Government Balances At Commercial and Savings Banks (2)	At Federal Reserve Banks (3)
1942 Jan.	2,196	1,476	322
Feb.	2,189	1,944	841
Mar.	2,187	2,363	273
Apr.	2,186	2,015	117
May	2,188	2,005	122
June	2,195	1,848	416
July	2,224	2,408	152
Aug.	2,216	2,559	160
Sept.	2,222	3,362	699
Oct.	2,249	4,013	418
Nov.	2,243	4,854	159
Dec.	2,194	8,400	750
1943 Jan.	2,200	6,600	52
Feb.	2,212	4,200	15
Mar.	2,224	3,000	41
Apr.	2,234	10,800	404
May	2,272	11,400	7
June	2,268	8,000	390
July	2,272	7,100	464
Aug.	2,279	4,700	234
Sept.	2,274	16,300	722
Oct.	2,298	17,900	376
Nov.	2,299	13,300	466
Dec.	2,316	10,400	706
1944 Jan.	2,322	10,700	144
Feb.	2,350	17,600	150
Mar.	2,329	14,700	623
Apr.	2,334	10,900	256
May	2,310	7,100	344
June	2,314	19,500	548
July	2,339	20,300	276
Aug.	2,407	16,100	339
Sept.	2,373	13,500	427
Oct.	2,372	8,700	242
Nov.	2,334	8,200	287
Dec.	2,368	20,800	653
1945 Jan.	2,371	18,300	532
Feb.	2,355	15,600	493
Mar.	2,356	13,400	257
Apr.	2,382	9,800	474
May	2,315	8,200	477
June	2,314	24,400	671

(continued)

TABLE A-3 (continued)

Date	Treasury Cash (1)	*U.S. Government Balances* At Commercial and Savings Banks (2)	At Federal Reserve Banks (3)
1945 July	2,260	20,800	717
Aug.	2,262	17,300	423
Sept.	2,268	14,300	573
Oct.	2,244	11,700	481
Nov.	2,269	13,100	547
Dec.	2,306	24,600	851
1946 Jan.	2,295	24,600	626
Feb.	2,317	25,000	884
Mar.	2,271	22,400	441
Apr.	2,267	20,000	458
May	2,265	17,400	763
June	2,262	13,400	947
July	2,250	11,600	543
Aug.	2,274	10,700	660
Sept.	2,301	9,300	316
Oct.	2,285	7,900	519
Nov.	2,271	6,400	653
Dec.	2,272	3,100	434
1947 Jan.	2,215	3,889	932
Feb.	2,149	3,367	1,495
Mar.	1,403	3,123	1,285
Apr.	1,347	2,586	748
May	1,358	2,106	677
June	1,334	1,398	684
July	1,320	1,433	730
Aug.	1,322	1,468	821
Sept.	1,320	1,574	648
Oct.	1,328	2,082	895
Nov.	1,326	1,672	1,210
Dec.	1,325	1,536	950
1948 Jan.	1,294	1,469	1,385
Feb.	1,287	1,792	1,051
Mar.	1,378	1,960	1,054
Apr.	1,337	2,109	1,226
May	1,337	2,488	1,480
June	1,321	2,720	1,916
July	1,320	2,463	1,927
Aug.	1,320	2,356	1,622
Sept.	1,324	2,280	1,380
Oct.	1,320	2,230	1,513
Nov.	1,318	2,411	1,509
Dec.	1,317	2,530	1,361

(continued)

761

TABLE A-3 (continued)

Date	Treasury Cash (1)	U.S. Government Balances At Commercial and Savings Banks (2)	At Federal Reserve Banks (3)
1949 Jan.	1,305	2,528	1,270
Feb.	1,303	2,848	1,252
Mar.	1,353	2,776	1,002
Apr.	1,323	2,390	1,070
May	1,319	1,909	893
June	1,309	1,839	560
July	1,303	1,704	436
Aug.	1,308	2,686	473
Sept.	1,312	3,034	619
Oct.	1,306	3,307	524
Nov.	1,311	3,546	449
Dec.	1,309	3,753	667
1950 Jan.	1,304	4,340	624
Feb.	1,301	3,884	489
Mar.	1,323	3,407	652
Apr.	1,313	3,168	644
May	1,304	3,157	519
June	1,298	3,680	718
July	1,304	3,595	644
Aug.	1,302	3,213	610
Sept.	1,301	3,412	663
Oct.	1,302	2,922	550
Nov.	1,295	3,169	446
Dec.	1,300	3,151	596
1951 Jan.	1,302	3,288	522
Feb.	1,286	3,646	722
Mar.	1,291	4,435	628
Apr.	1,286	5,759	566
May	1,286	5,393	577
June	1,284	5,260	401
July	1,290	4,688	482
Aug.	1,280	3,960	436
Sept.	1,280	3,771	495
Oct.	1,276	4,037	413
Nov.	1,296	3,319	430
Dec.	1,299	3,545	264
1952 Jan.	1,296	3,616	169
Feb.	1,288	3,859	309
Mar.	1,276	4,128	344
Apr.	1,270	4,563	485
May	1,273	4,775	506
June	1,277	5,076	483

(continued)

TABLE A-3 (continued)

Date	Treasury Cash (1)	U.S. Government Balances At Commercial and Savings Banks (2)	At Federal Reserve Banks (3)
1952 July	1,268	7,733	354
Aug.	1,266	5,732	437
Sept.	1,270	5,443	278
Oct.	1,268	5,410	493
Nov.	1,293	5,369	570
Dec.	1,298	5,961	564
1953 Jan.	1,302	5,906	890
Feb.	1,290	5,457	453
Mar.	1,286	4,744	248
Apr.	1,270	3,959	350
May	1,266	3,164	336
June	1,265	3,238	74
July	1,263	4,745	601
Aug.	1,264	6,033	561
Sept.	1,269	5,996	470
Oct.	1,268	4,313	494
Nov.	929	4,999	469
Dec.	785	4,676	605
1954 Jan.	791	4,846	321
Feb.	802	4,679	541
Mar.	804	4,475	492
Apr.	817	4,217	528
May	821	4,099	466
June	809	4,420	804
July	812	4,001	522
Aug.	803	4,493	503
Sept.	796	4,431	477
Oct.	796	5,826	543
Nov.	812	6,139	462
Dec.	823	5,884	453
1955 Jan.	828	5,052	508
Feb.	815	4,943	475
Mar.	809	4,382	684
Apr.	805	5,082	463
May	806	4,878	410
June	820	4,433	403
July	807	4,382	464
Aug.	804	4,594	491
Sept.	803	4,342	482
Oct.	785	4,412	461
Nov.	788	4,324	514
Dec.	791	4,044	448

(continued)

763

TABLE A-3 (continued)

Date	Treasury Cash (1)	U.S. Government Balances At Commercial and Savings Banks (2)	At Federal Reserve Banks (3)
1956 Jan.	787	3,811	481
Feb.	782	3,971	505
Mar.	764	4,771	521
Apr.	767	4,356	517
May	770	4,840	540
June	773	4,366	552
July	784	3,712	509
Aug.	786	4,245	443
Sept.	787	4,873	469
Oct.	788	3,911	453
Nov.	782	4,231	447
Dec.	783	3,995	485
1957 Jan.	784	3,365	408
Feb.	796	2,928	367
Mar.	783	3,531	418
Apr.	780	4,525	412
May	769	3,826	499
June	776	3,897	522
July	793	4,291	466
Aug.	786	3,016	441
Sept.	790	3,772	500
Oct.	802	4,105	475
Nov.	800	3,234	470
Dec.	780	4,030	400
1958 Jan.	760	3,748	577
Feb.	689	3,719	472
Mar.	713	5,182	461
Apr.	699	4,463	475
May	702	4,884	437
June	694	5,691	450
July	722	5,306	484
Aug.	724	4,997	497
Sept.	727	4,378	412
Oct.	712	4,307	441
Nov.	694	4,388	428
Dec.	707	4,562	484
1959 Jan.	690	5,027	444
Feb.	691	6,050	462
Mar.	672	4,566	492
Apr.	673	4,927	482
May	671	4,630	497
June	623	3,800	496

(continued)

TABLE A-3 (concluded)

Date	Treasury Cash (1)	U.S. Government Balances At Commercial and Savings Banks (2)	At Federal Reserve Banks (3)
1959 July	438	4,306	480
Aug.	421	4,817	509
Sept.	420	5,391	512
Oct.	411	4,996	511
Nov.	418	5,031	520
Dec.	409	5,581	529
1960 Jan.	408	5,884	560
Feb.	417	5,561	564
Mar.	410	5,337	500
Apr.	395	4,123	526
May	389	5,562	500
June	406	5,781	496
July	439	5,835	488
Aug.	429	5,700	460
Sept.	432	5,510	488
Oct.	431	5,761	491
Nov.	410	6,031	499
Dec.	425	5,312	522

SOURCE, BY COLUMN

Column 1, Treasury Cash

I. Jan. 1867–Feb. 1878: Money held in Treasury on June 30, 1866–78, less amounts held in trust against gold and silver certificates, from *Annual Report* of the Secretary of the Treasury, 1928, p. 550, was interpolated on a straight line to the ends of the months shown.

II. Aug. 1878–June 1906: Sums of the following components of Treasury cash, reported the first of each month (treated as end-of-preceding-month figures), with revisions of the published data as indicated. Source for the later years, *Circulation Statement of U.S. Money*, Treasury Department (published monthly since March 1887), used for all but subsidiary silver, plus the following for the earlier years.

A. GOLD. "Report of the Treasurer," *Annual Report* (Treasury), 1898, pp. 59 ff.; 1903, p. 172.

B. SILVER (excluding silver bullion held by the Treasury and Mint). *Ibid.*, 1891, pp. 75 ff; 1903, pp. 207–208, 174–175, 215–216, 219–220. Revised, 1890–1903, to exclude the cover for Treasury notes of 1890.

C. TREASURY NOTES OF 1890. *Ibid.*, 1898, pp. 45 ff.; 1903, pp. 176 ff.

D. NATIONAL BANK NOTES. *Ibid.*, 1898, pp. 44–45; 1903, p. 172.

E. UNITED STATES NOTES. *Ibid.*, 1898, pp. 68 ff.; 1903, pp. 176 ff. Revised, 1890–1901, to exclude the cover for currency certificates.

F. SUBSIDIARY SILVER. *Ibid.*, 1898, pp. 68 ff.; 1903, p. 174; 1909, p. 194. Minor coin is not included.

(continued)

NOTES TO TABLE A-3 (continued)

III. May 1907–Oct. 1914: Seasonally adjusted sums of first-of-month data, treated as end-of-preceding-month figures: for cash, excluding minor coin, from *Circulation Statement of U.S. Money;* and for minor coin, from the Treasury *Daily Statement* (available in printed form for every Treasury business day since Jan. 3, 1895, in handwritten form for earlier dates back to Jan. 1, 1877, in the files of the Treasury Department).

IV. Nov. 1914–Dec. 1921: End-of-month figures from *Banking and Monetary Statistics,* Board of Governors of the Federal Reserve System, 1943, pp. 373–374, seasonally adjusted by us.

V. Jan. 1922–Dec. 1946: Wed. figures nearest end of month, *ibid.,* pp. 378 ff. and *Federal Reserve Bulletin,* seasonally corrected by us through 1933.

VI. Jan. 1947–Dec. 1960: Monthly averages of daily figures, *ibid.,* seasonally adjusted by Shiskin-Eisenpress method (see Julius Shiskin and Harry Eisenpress, *Seasonal Adjustments by Electronic Computer Methods,* NBER, Technical Paper 12, 1958).

Column 2, U.S. Government Balances at Commercial and Savings Banks

I. Jan. 1867–June 1906: Call date figures for the sum of U.S. deposits and deposits of U.S. disbursing officers (*Annual Report,* Comptroller of the Currency, 1918, Vol. II, pp. 249–275) were interpolated by the step method to middle of month; no seasonal movement was observed; two-month averages of middle-of-month data were obtained to convert to an end-of-month basis. Step-method interpolation of call date figures involves two procedures.

A. The number of days intervening between a given call date and the following one is divided in half. This half-way date usually falls in the month following the given call date. The number of days in the month up to this half-way date is then expressed as a fraction of the total number of days in that month, the balance as 1.00 minus that fraction. For example, there are call dates on Jan. 7 and Apr. 1, 1867. The mid-point date is Feb. 17.5, 1867. Since there are 28 days in the month, 17.5 represents 0.625, the balance of 10.5 days, 0.375. The value for Feb. is 0.625 of the Jan. call date figure plus 0.375 of the Apr. call date figure.

B. The months for which no figures were derived as above were assigned the value of the nearest call date. Here, the value for Mar. was the call date figure for Apr.

II. May 1907–Dec. 1908: This is a sum of seasonally adjusted monthly data for Clearing House banks in N.Y. City (*Commercial and Financial Chronicle,* weekly issues for designated period) and Boston (Boston Clearing House Assn., *Statement of the Associated Banks of Boston as Returned to the Clearing House*), plus interpolations along a straight line to Wed. nearest end of month between seasonally adjusted call date figures of government deposits at all other national banks (government deposits at national banks on call dates, from *Abstract of Reports of Condition of National Banks,* Comptroller of the Currency, published at national bank call dates since 1897), minus the Clearing House data.

III. Jan. 1909–May 1917: Interpolations along a straight line to Wed. nearest end of month between the seasonally adjusted call date figures of government deposits at national banks (*ibid.*).

IV. June 1917–Nov. 1917: This is a sum of seasonally adjusted monthly data for Clearing House member and nonmember banks in N.Y. City (*Commercial and Financial Chronicle*) and, beginning Sept., Phila. Clearing House banks (*ibid.*), plus interpolations along a straight line to Wed. nearest end of month between seasonally adjusted call date figures of government deposits at all other national

(continued)

766

and nonnational banks. The call date figures for all national banks were obtained from the source listed in II, above; for all nonnational banks, from an estimating equation derived from FDIC data for insured banks, 1934–46, which related the ratio of demand deposits adjusted to U.S. government demand deposits at national banks to the same ratio for nonnational banks. The call date figures for all banks less the Clearing House data at call dates served as the call date figures for the banks not in the above Clearing Houses.

V. Dec. 1917–Nov. 1938: This is a sum of government demand deposits on Fri. (Wed., beginning May 1921) nearest end of month at (A) weekly reporting member banks; (B) nonweekly reporting member banks; (C) nonmember banks.
A. Government demand deposits at weekly reporting member banks from *FRB* and *Banking and Monetary Statistics*, pp. 132 ff., seasonally adjusted by us.
B. Government demand deposits at nonweekly reporting member banks were estimated as follows. Weekly reporting member bank figures interpolated to call dates along a straight line between the weekly data closest to a call date were subtracted from all member bank call date figures of government deposits (*Banking and Monetary Statistics*, p. 73). The residuals were expressed as ratios to the weekly reporting member bank figures at call dates, and the ratios applied to seasonally adjusted weekly reporting member bank figures for the Fri. (or Wed.) nearest end of month that was closest to each call date. Intervening months were filled in by straight-line interpolation.
C. Government demand deposits at nonmember banks were estimated as follows. A call date series was computed from an estimating equation derived from FDIC data for insured banks, 1934–46, which related the ratio of demand deposits adjusted to U.S. government demand deposits at national banks to the same ratio for nonmember banks. By straight-line interpolation to the Fri. (or Wed.) nearest the end of the month between the call date figures, a monthly series was obtained.

VI. Dec. 1938–Nov. 1942: The series was derived in the same way as for Dec. 1917–Nov. 1938, with the addition of government time deposits at all banks. Government time deposits at call dates beginning Dec. 1938 are a sum of data for member banks and estimates for nonmember banks. Data for member banks were obtained as a residual through Dec. 1941 by subtracting U.S. government demand deposits (*Member Bank Call Report*, Board of Governors of the Federal Reserve System, for designated period) from U.S. government demand and time deposits (*Banking and Monetary Statistics*, p. 75); data were estimated for Apr. 1942 on the basis of U.S. government time deposits at national banks (*Abstract . . . National Banks*, Comptroller); and thereafter were obtained from *Member Bank Call Report*. Estimates for nonmember banks at June and Dec. dates are either data for all nonnational banks (*Annual Report*, Comptroller), minus state member bank data (member bank data, minus national bank data), or estimates based on insured nonmember bank data (*Assets and Liabilities of Operating Insured Banks*, FDIC, semi-annual call reports since June 1934). Other call date estimates were obtained by rough interpolation. A monthly series was interpolated between the call date figures to Wed. nearest end of month.

VII. Dec. 1942–Dec. 1946: End-of-month figures from *Federal Reserve Bulletin*, seasonally unadjusted, because tentative adjustments were unsatisfactory.

VIII. Jan. 1947–Dec. 1960: Sums of figures for government demand deposits at (A) member banks, (B) all other banks, and (C) government time deposits at all banks.
A. Government demand deposits at member banks are monthly averages of semi-monthly averages of daily figures (*ibid.*, Oct. 1960, pp. 1116–1121) and an unpub-

(continued)

767

NOTES TO TABLE A-3 (concluded)

lished Federal Reserve table for 1960, seasonally adjusted by Shiskin-Eisenpress method.

B. Government demand deposits at all other banks, 1947–53, are straight-line interpolations between semiannual data for all banks (*Annual Report*, FDIC), minus data for member banks (*Member Bank Call Report*); 1954–60, last-Wed.-of-month figures obtained by subtracting member bank from all bank figures (*FRB*, monthly issues), shifted to center of month by straight-line interpolation.

C. Government time deposits at all banks are straight-line interpolations between semiannual data (*Annual Report*, FDIC).

Column 3, U.S. Government Balances at Federal Reserve Banks

I. Nov. 1914–Dec. 1921: End-of-month data from *Banking and Monetary Statistics*, pp. 373–374.

II. Jan. 1922–Dec. 1946: Data for Wed. nearest end of month (*ibid.*, pp. 378 ff., and *FRB*, monthly issues), seasonally adjusted by us.

I II. Jan. 1947–Dec. 1960: Monthly averages of daily figures (*ibid.*), seasonally adjusted by Shiskin-Eisenpress method.

TABLE A-4

PURCHASING-POWER PARITY AND INTERNATIONAL CAPITAL MOVEMENTS, 1871–1960

Year	Purchasing-Power Parity (1929 = 100) Against: British Prices (1)	Swedish Prices (2)	Swiss Prices (3)	Net Capital Inflow to U.S. Minus Unilateral Transfers (outflow from U.S. is minus)[a] As Per Cent of NNP (4)	Plus Gold Outflow or Minus Inflow as Per Cent of NNP (5)
1871	110.6			1.80	2.86
1872	94.5			3.83	4.47
1873	86.4			2.62	3.14
1874	88.7			1.18	1.39
1875	86.3			1.27	2.06
1876	86.0			0.03	0.36
1877	86.9			−0.80	−0.79
1878	89.1			−2.20	−2.26
1879	89.1			−2.10	−2.11
1880	95.2			0.33	−0.53
1881	94.3			−0.41	−1.40
1882	96.1			1.06	1.04
1883	95.1			0.48	0.42
1884	97.1			1.01	1.18
1885	95.1			0.33	0.16
1886	97.7			1.37	1.60
1887	100.0			2.22	1.90
1888	99.1			2.72	2.49
1889	97.9			1.90	2.37
1890	94.7			1.73	1.77
1891	91.0			1.16	1.76
1892	91.0			0.33	0.34
1893	94.4			1.18	1.90
1894	92.0			−0.58	−0.54
1895	92.6			1.20	1.46
1896	91.9			0.24	0.71
1897	90.1			−0.19	−0.56
1897	90.1			−0.71	−0.71
1898	89.7			−1.63	−2.71
1899	92.2			−1.34	−1.38
1900	90.8			−1.99	−2.07
1901	92.8			−1.51	−1.49
1902	96.3			−0.44	−0.48
1903	98.0			−0.77	−0.88
1904	99.1			−0.64	−0.46
1905	100.7			−0.43	−0.44
1906	99.9			0.09	−0.34

(continued)

TABLE A-4 (continued)

Year	Purchasing-Power Parity (1929 = 100) Against: British Prices (1)	Swedish Prices (2)	Swiss Prices (3)	Net Capital Inflow to U.S. Minus Unilateral Transfers (outflow from U.S. is minus)[a] As Per Cent of NNP (4)	Plus Gold Outflow or Minus Inflow as Per Cent of NNP (5)
1907	101.3			0.13	−0.20
1908	102.1			−0.81	−0.68
1909	105.2			0.51	0.83
1910	105.5			0.79	0.79
1911	103.1			0.14	0.07
1912	102.9			0.11	0.05
1913	102.7			−0.42	−0.34
1914	102.6			0.05	0.58
1914	102.6			−1.69	−1.16
1915	89.1			−4.81	−6.09
1916	84.1			−3.34	−4.55
1917	86.3			−8.19	−8.63
1918	86.5			−6.69	−6.65
1919	88.5			−3.88	−3.65
1919	88.5			−5.38	−5.14
1920	106.5	102.8	99.8	−2.23	−2.16
1921	95.4	85.4	92.8	−1.73	−2.84
1922	97.0	88.0	97.8	−1.80	−2.18
1923	100.4	97.8	105.7	−0.48	−0.87
1924	102.7	98.2	100.4	−1.22	−1.51
1925	95.8	97.9	97.1	−1.34	−1.21
1926	97.4	101.0	101.3	−0.78	−0.86
1927	97.5	98.7	100.1	−0.92	−0.73
1928	99.0	98.9	100.2	−1.78	−1.46
1929	100.0	100.0	100.0	−0.69	−0.82
1930	99.2	98.1	96.8	−1.36	−1.72
1931	100.5	95.3	89.6	−1.21	−0.93
1932	117.5	116.6	86.1	−0.97	−0.99
1933	98.0	98.4	69.9	−1.29	−0.88
1934	87.8	88.3	58.1	0.50	−1.84
1935	87.2	89.3	57.5	2.29	−0.67
1936	87.6	90.7	63.5	1.47	−0.22
1937	84.4	88.6	80.2	0.86	−0.84
1938	84.1	87.7	79.8	0.38	−2.03
1939	89.3	89.3	79.9	1.79	−2.30
1940	92.1	80.1	73.4	1.52	−3.48

(continued)

TABLE A-4 (concluded)

Year	Purchasing-Power Parity (1929 = 100) Against:			Net Capital Inflow to U.S. Minus Unilateral Transfers (outflow from U.S. is minus)[a]	
	British Prices (1)	Swedish Prices (2)	Swiss Prices (3)	As Per Cent of NNP (4)	Plus Gold Outflow or Minus Inflow as Per Cent of NNP (5)
1941	85.6	75.8	67.1	−2.19	−2.77
1942	91.1	79.6	68.1	−4.97	−4.86
1943	95.8	85.5	70.6	−7.51	−7.04
1944	96.6	89.3	71.1	−8.03	−7.27
1945	97.6	92.0	72.5	−3.81	−3.55
1946	100.3	90.9	78.4	−4.60	−5.09
1947	106.2	90.7	83.9	−5.78	−6.94
1948	103.4	91.2	85.1	−3.31	−4.10
1949	110.6	98.9	86.7	−3.76	−3.86
1950	142.9	129.9	89.0	−1.90	−1.09
1951	140.3	121.5	92.3	−2.37	−2.40
1952	131.5	114.8	90.8	−2.07	−2.22
1953	128.5	114.2	92.5	−2.39	−1.94
1954	126.9	113.4	91.8	−2.11	−1.99
1955	123.2	110.9	91.5	−1.70	−1.69
1956	120.6	108.8	93.2	−2.29	−2.43
1957	120.3	108.4	94.3	−2.64	−2.87
1958	118.1	104.7	94.2	−2.32	−1.59
1959	118.8	105.2	97.1	−1.01	−0.71
1960	119.2	103.1	96.6	−1.94	−1.47

[a] Fiscal years through 1897, calendar years thereafter. Before 1914, includes errors and omissions; before 1919, excludes unilateral transfers. Figures for the years marking the changes are computed in two ways.

SOURCE, BY COLUMN

Column 1, Purchasing-Power Parity Against British Prices

U.S. implicit price index was divided by U.K. prices, and the quotient was divided by the exchange rate in cents per pound; 1929 was taken as 100.
A. U.S. implicit price index: Same source as for Chart 62.
B. U.K. prices:
  1. 1879–1913, furnished by Phyllis Deane; based on Board of Trade wholesale price indexes plus allowances for rents and wages.
  2. 1914–18, Ministry of Labour cost-of-living index from J. B. Jefferys and Dorothy Walters, "National Income and Expenditure of the United Kingdom, 1870–1952" (*Income and Wealth*, Series V, London, Bowes and Bowes, 1955), p. 40.
  3. 1919–56, Ministry of Labour retail price index furnished by Phyllis Deane.
  4. 1957–60, same, extrapolated by *Annual Abstract of Statistics* (U.K. Central Statistical Office), 1959, p. 293; and *Economic Trends*, June 1961, p. 23.

(continued)

771

NOTES TO TABLE A-4 (continued)

C. U.K. exchange rate:
1. 1871–78, par of $4.8665 was multiplied by price of gold in greenbacks shown in Chart 5.
2. 1879–1913, $4.8665 was assumed.
3. 1914–41, *Banking and Monetary Statistics* (Board of Governors of the Federal Reserve System, 1943), p. 681.
4. 1942–60, *Federal Reserve Bulletin.*

Column 2, Purchasing-Power Parity Against Swedish Prices

U.S. implicit price index was divided by Swedish prices, and the quotient divided by the exchange rate in cents per krona; 1929 was taken as 100.
A. U.S. implicit price index: Same source as for Chart 62.
B. Swedish prices (a cost-of-living index):
1. 1920–36, *Statistical Yearbook of the League of Nations*, 1932/33–1934/35, 1937/38–1938/39, 1940/41 issues.
2. 1937–60, *Statistical Yearbook*, United Nations, 1954, 1956, 1958–61 issues.
C. Swedish exchange rates:
1. 1920–41, *Banking and Monetary Statistics*, p. 679.
2. 1942–45, *Statistical Yearbook*, United Nations, 1948, p. 375.
3. 1946–60, *FRB.*

Column 3, Purchasing-Power Parity Against Swiss Prices

U.S. implicit price index was divided by Swiss prices, and the quotient divided by the exchange rate in cents per franc; 1929 was taken as 100.
A. U.S. implicit price index: Same source as for Chart 62.
B. Swiss prices (a cost-of-living index):
1. 1920–44, *Statistical Yearbook of the League of Nations*, 1932/33–1936/37, 1938/39, 1942/44 issues.
2. 1945–60, *Statistical Yearbook*, United Nations, 1955, 1958–61 issues.
C. Swiss exchange rates:
1. 1920–41, *Banking and Monetary Statistics*, p. 680.
2. 1942–45, *Statistical Yearbook*, United Nations, 1948, p. 375.
3. 1946–60, *FRB.*

Column 4, Net Capital Inflow Minus Unilateral Transfers as Per Cent of NNP

A. Capital inflow:
1. 1871–97, Matthew Simon, "The United States Balance of Payments, 1861–1900" (*Trends in the American Economy in the Nineteenth Century*, Studies in Income and Wealth, Vol. 24, Princeton for NBER, 1960), Table 27, line 30.
2. 1897–1914, R. W. Goldsmith, *A Study of Saving in the United States*, Vol. II, Princeton, 1955, Table K-1, col. 7, minus Table K-3, col. 9. Goldsmith cites P. D. Dickens, "The Transition Period in American International Financing, 1897–1914" (unpublished Ph.D. dissertation, George Washington Univ., 1933). Capital movement includes short-term capital movement and errors and omissions.
3. 1914–19, capital movement, minus both short-term capital movement and errors and omissions, from R. E. Lipsey, "A Summary of the Available Statistics" (NBER Capital Requirements Study, Work Memorandum No. 31, unpublished, NBER, no date), pp. 62, 71, citing Goldsmith.
4. 1919–55, *Balance of Payments* (Dept. of Commerce, Office of Business Economics) 1958, pp. 10–13.
5. 1956–60, *Survey of Current Business*, July 1961, p. 24.
B. Unilateral transfers (see footnote a, above): Same as for capital inflow, 1919–60. Unilateral transfers include military supplies and services.
C. National income: Money income as for Chart 62.

(continued)

Column 5, Net Capital Inflow Minus Unilateral Transfers
Plus Gold Outflows as Per Cent of NNP

A. Gold outflow:
1. 1871–97, Simon, *loc. cit.*, Table 27, line 28.
2. 1897–1913, *Monthly Summary of Commerce and Finance* (Dept. of Commerce [and Labor, Bureau of Statistics]), Dec. 1910, pp. 1127–1129; Dec. 1911, pp. 1068–1070; (Bureau of Foreign and Domestic Commerce), Dec. 1914, p. 514.
3. 1914–18, 1941, *Banking and Monetary Statistics*, p. 536, net gold export, plus increase in gold under earmark.
4. 1919–40, *ibid.*, p. 538.
5. 1942–60, *FRB*.
B. Other items: Same as for col. 4.

Fiscal year 1898 figure, used in calculation on p. 203, above, is −2.977.

TABLE A-5
VELOCITY OF MONEY, 1869–1960, AND OF CURRENCY PLUS DEMAND DEPOSITS, 1915–60

Year	Velocity of Money (1)	Year	Velocity of Money (1)	Velocity of Currency Plus Demand Deposits (2)	Year	Velocity of Money (1)	Velocity of Currency Plus Demand Deposits (2)
1869	4.57						
1870	4.12						
1871	3.91	1901	2.47		1931	1.47	2.60
1872	4.34	1902	2.35		1932	1.28	2.16
1873	4.35	1903	2.34		1933	1.38	2.19
1874	4.23	1904	2.21		1934	1.52	2.36
1875	3.99	1905	2.18		1935	1.52	2.29
1876	4.19	1906	2.32		1936	1.60	2.35
1877	4.48	1907	2.30		1937	1.67	2.47
1878	4.70	1908	2.08		1938	1.53	2.30
1879	4.67	1909	2.23		1939	1.52	2.21
1880	4.97	1910	2.20		1940	1.51	2.11
1881	4.10	1911	2.09		1941	1.61	2.17
1882	4.16	1912	2.15		1942	1.84	2.37
1883	3.76	1913	2.17		1943	1.77	2.20
1884	3.75	1914	1.91		1944	1.61	2.02
1885	3.43	1915	1.90	2.68	1945	1.37	1.75
1886	3.30	1916	2.12	3.01	1946	1.16	1.52
1887	3.22	1917	2.18	3.11	1947	1.23	1.62
1888	3.10	1918	2.51	3.53	1948	1.31	1.73
1889	3.06	1919	2.28	3.24	1949	1.27	1.68
1890	2.93	1920	2.20	3.22	1950	1.43	1.89
1891	2.94	1921	1.90	2.90	1951	1.53	2.00
1892	2.81	1922	1.88	2.94	1952	1.50	1.97
1893	2.87	1923	2.04	3.26	1953	1.51	2.01
1894	2.55	1924	1.97	3.21	1954	1.49	2.01
1895	2.71	1925	1.88	3.09	1955	1.58	2.14
1896	2.67	1926	1.95	3.26	1956	1.61	2.19
1897	2.81	1927	1.87	3.21	1957	1.63	2.28
1898	2.55	1928	1.84	3.25	1958	1.56	2.26
1899	2.48	1929	1.95	3.42	1959	1.63	2.36
1900	2.53	1930	1.70	3.02	1960	1.69	2.50

SOURCE: Money income was divided by the money stock, or by the sum of currency plus demand deposits.

A. Money stock: Figures in col. 8 of Table A-1 were averaged annually to center on June 30. For 1867–1907, annual averages were constructed from monthly figures obtained by step interpolation (see notes to Table 25, above, for explanation of step interpolation).

B. Currency plus demand deposits: Figures in col. 7 of Table A-1 were averaged to center on June 30.

(continued)

774

APPENDIX A: BASIC TABLES

C. Money income:
1. 1869–1916, 1920–41, 1946–55: Net national product, current prices, variant III, component method, from worksheets underlying Simon Kuznets, *Capital in the American Economy* (Princeton for NBER, 1961).
2. 1917–19, 1942–45: Values of Kuznets' money income for each year were interpolated arithmetically along a straight line connecting the estimates for the terminal years; these trend values were multiplied by the ratios to corresponding trend values of Kendrick's national security version (J. W. Kendrick, *Productivity Trends in the United States*, Princeton for NBER, 1961); see footnote 16, Chap. 5, above.
3. 1956–60: Series ends in 1955, accordingly the linear relationship between Kuznets' estimates and Department of Commerce national income estimates, 1946–55, was used to extrapolate Kuznets' series, 1956–60.

APPENDIX B

Proximate Determinants of the Nominal Stock of Money

1. *Classification of Types of Money, by Holders*

IN ANALYZING the proximate determinants of the nominal stock of money in the United States, it is useful to distinguish between several kinds of things that might be designated as part of the stock of money. Historically, the most important distinction has been between specie or warehouse receipts for the monetary commodity (for the United States in the period we cover, gold) and fiduciary claims. Fiduciary claims may be obligations of private institutions (banks) or of government monetary authorities, including quasi-government bodies such as the Federal Reserve System in this country or the Bank of England before 1946 in Great Britain. Fiduciary claims may be in the form of currency (bank notes, silver dollars, silver certificates, subsidiary silver, minor coin)[1] or deposits (commercial bank deposits, Federal Reserve deposits). This gives five kinds of money or potential money to be considered:

1. Specie
2. Obligations of banks: currency
3. Obligations of banks: deposits
4. Obligations of monetary authorities: currency
5. Obligations of monetary authorities: deposits

Each of these may in turn be held by any of three categories of holders:

    a. Public
    b. Banks
    c. Monetary authorities

NOTE: This appendix was prepared as a result of Clark Warburton's penetrating criticisms of the omission in an early draft of any justification of our analysis of the determinants of the money stock.

[1] Silver dollars, subsidiary silver, and silver certificates could be treated as corresponding partly to a monetary commodity or to warehouse receipts for a monetary commodity, and partly to fiduciary claims: as a monetary commodity or warehouse receipts up to the market value of the amount of silver in the coins or the amount of silver treated as equal to the face value of certificates for monetary purposes; as fiduciary claims for the balance. However, unless there is a dual standard with a variable rate of exchange between silver and gold, it seems better to regard as "specie" only that commodity whose market value equals its monetary value, and to regard coins made from any other supposedly monetary commodity or certificates for such a commodity as fiduciary currency claims issued to finance a stockpiling program of the commodity in question. Of course, under a nominally bimetallic standard, this may involve a shift from time to time in the commodity regarded as money, as occurred in the U.S. in 1834.

The distinction between holders is in terms of the role as an issuer of claims that might be designated as money. For example, local or state government units that have no money-issuing powers are for this purpose to be regarded as part of the "public" (see Chapter 1, footnote 2). Similarly, if feasible, it is desirable to include the money balances federal agencies hold for purposes connected with ordinary operations of the government as part of the public's holdings of money rather than as part of the operations of the monetary authorities. We have accordingly included in the public's holdings the balances of government corporations and credit agencies. We have not included any part of the U.S. Treasury's balances—though in principle some should be—because of the near-impossibility of separating operating balances from monetary authority balances. Government monetary authorities include the government bodies that have ultimate monetary authority whether so labeled or not (currently, primarily the Federal Reserve System and the Treasury). Similarly, private institutions that issue claims regarded as money are to be regarded as "banks" whether generally so termed or not.[2]

In a fully consolidated statement, liabilities of some banks held by other banks will cancel; similarly, monetary authority liabilities held by the monetary authorities will cancel. Moreover, under current conditions in the United States, deposit liabilities of monetary authorities may not be held by the public, with some minor exceptions,[3] but this situation need not prevail.[4] For our purposes, we shall treat the banks on a consolidated basis throughout. We shall not, however, fully consolidate

[2] For example, "George Smith's" money, issued by the Wisconsin Marine and Fire Insurance Company, was widely used in the 1840's and readily acceptable at par with specie. For this purpose, that company is to be regarded as a bank (see J. J. Knox, *A History of Banking in the United States,* New York, Bradford Rhodes, 1900, pp. 726–728, 740–742).

Currently, it would be eminently plausible to regard travelers' checks issued by the American Express Company as "money" and the American Express Company, or the division of the company that issues such checks, as a bank. The only reason we have not done so in our estimates is that the cost of getting adequate data did not seem justified by the amounts involved. Incidentally, the American Express Company and other nonbank issuers of travelers' checks are, to the best of our knowledge, the only private institutions in the U.S. issuing currency. They are also one of a very small class of private institutions issuing fiduciary money, including deposits, subject to no legal reserve requirements. This class includes, in addition, the few remaining unincorporated banks and Illinois state banks that are not members of the Federal Reserve System. Travelers' checks issued by banks are treated as part of their reported deposits.

For the definition of a bank used in our estimates, see Chap. 1, footnote 4.

[3] For example, we treat mutual savings banks as part of the public, but they may have deposits with the Federal Reserve System (see footnote 13, below). We do not, however, include these deposits in our estimates of the money stock, though the logic of our procedure would call for our doing so. The omission was initially inadvertent, and we have not corrected it because the amounts involved are trivial and the cost of estimating them monthly would be substantial.

[4] For example, the Bank of England has long held private deposits (U. K.,

the accounts of the monetary authorities at all points in our analysis. The reasons are entirely practical. In the first place, the accounts we regard as those of the monetary authorities (in the earlier period the U.S. Treasury accounts, later, the Treasury and the Federal Reserve accounts) are a mixture of monetary authority accounts proper and working balances of government agencies. In the second place, legislative distinctions have frequently made the total of a particular kind of obligation inside and outside the Treasury meaningful independently of the intramonetary authority division (as, for example, legal limits on the amount of U.S. notes outstanding) or have made the division itself meaningful (as, for example, the legislative distinction between the Treasury and the Federal Reserve). The failure to consolidate can, however, introduce a largely arbitrary element into any intramonetary authority accounts (for examples, see below).

We thus have the 5×3 classification of Table B-1. The blank items

TABLE B-1
SYMBOLIC REPRESENTATION OF TYPES OF MONEY, CROSS-CLASSIFIED BY HOLDER

	Class of Holder			
Type of Money	Public	Banks	Monetary Authorities	Total
1. Specie	S	S_b	S_t	S'
2. Obligations of banks: currency	N		N_t	N'
3. Obligations of banks: deposits	D		D_t	D'
4. Obligations of monetary authorities: currency	U	U_b	U_t	U'
5. Obligations of monetary authorities: deposits	F	F_b	F_t	F'
Total	M	R	T	

in this table correspond to intrasector obligations that cancel out in a consolidated statement. Foreign banks and foreign monetary authorities are excluded from the second and third columns although, to the extent that they are holders of U.S. specie and currency, they are included in our estimates of the first column. Nonbank foreigners who are holders of U.S. specie, currency, and deposits are also included in our estimates of the first column. In principle, the first column should be restricted to holdings of United States money by its nationals, with the holdings of foreigners and foreign banks excluded.

The total of the first column, labeled M, is the total we have designated as "the stock of money held by the public" or, in general,

Committee on the Working of the Monetary System [Radcliffe Committee], *Report,* Cmnd. 827, Aug. 1959, pp. 123–124, paragraph 364).

simply the stock of money. It is the total in which we are primarily interested and the determinants of which we seek to analyze.[5]

The total of the second column consists of the unduplicated cash assets of the banking system taken as a whole, which we refer to here as their high-powered reserves or simply as their reserves, R. This meaning of "reserves" must be distinguished sharply from other meanings often attributed to the term. It does not correspond with funds that can be used to satisfy legal reserve requirements, which is one way the term is sometimes used. For example, until recently, bank vault cash could not be used to meet reserve requirements of member banks of the Federal Reserve System, so neither S_b nor U_b qualified as legal reserves, although they are always included in our total of reserves. Prior to the Federal Reserve System, under the National Banking Act, banks could use deposits at other banks to satisfy part of their legal reserve requirements. These cancel out in the above consolidated statement and hence are not included in our total of reserves. Reserves, in our sense, do not correspond, either, with the total the individual bank is likely to regard as its reserves. The individual bank will generally include deposits at other banks and cash items in the process of collection, both of which cancel out in a consolidated statement. We have chosen to use the term reserves as we do in order to have a concept as free as possible from the effects of the legislative provisions of a particular time and place or of the particular institutional structure of the banking system. In our view, the legal provisions and institutional structure can most fruitfully be taken into account as factors affecting the value of R that the banking system will seek to achieve for a given structure of liabilities or, more rarely, as affecting the composition of R.

The total of the third column consists of the cash balances of the monetary authorities (designated T, for U.S. Treasury, which was the chief monetary authority until the Reserve System was established and continues to possess important monetary powers). Generally, the separate items in this total have had different significance. Specie has generally been held as "backing" or "reserves" for the currency issued by the government (U, for U.S. currency).[6] It is therefore included indirectly

[5] There are, however, four minor deviations between this total and our actual estimates. Our actual estimates exclude: (1) some travelers' checks mentioned in footnote 2 above; (2) deposits at the Federal Reserve Banks to the credit of the public mentioned in footnote 13 below and to the credit of mutual savings banks mentioned in footnote 3 above; (3) vault cash held by mutual savings banks, excluded for the reasons cited in footnote 3 with respect to item 2; (4) operating balances of the U.S. government which we have not separated from Treasury balances. All four items should in principle be included.

[6] Specie corresponding to warehouse certificates in circulation, that is, in the hands of the public or the banks (e.g., gold certificates for which the Treasury holds an amount of gold equal in monetary value to the face amount of the certificates) has been included in S or S_b, not in S_t.

779

in U. Only the excess of U' over S_t represents fiduciary currency. Bank obligations held by the monetary authorities are quite different. They are either working balances or balances held for monetary policy purposes. For example, a major monetary technique of the Treasury before the Reserve System existed was to increase or decrease D_t at the expense of S_t (or through creating currency). The total of S_t, N_t, and D_t is an unduplicated total, logically comparable to R. The remaining items, U_t and F_t, are intrasector items that acquire meaning only because, as it were, the left hand may not know what the right hand is doing. The items are largely arbitrary. For example, the Treasury has at times had unutilized authority to issue currency. Had it utilized the authority but simply added the currency to its balances, U_t would be increased with no economic effect. Similarly, the Treasury can currently acquire additional balances at the Federal Reserve (F_t) by creating interest-bearing obligations and transferring them to the Federal Reserve with no economic effect. In the main, for the period after the Federal Reserve, we have consolidated the monetary authority accounts and treated U_t and F_t as zero. We retain them here because during the earlier period we have at times found it useful to refer to the division of total currency between the amounts inside and outside the Treasury: $(S_t + N_t + U_t)/(S' + N' + U')$ and $(S + S_b + N + U + U_b)/(S' + N' + U')$.

No symbol has been used for the total of the final column because this total has no clear meaning. From an economic point of view, it clearly involves double counting. The reserves held by the banks and the specie held by the monetary authorities duplicate corresponding parts of what the public considers its money holdings. If such duplications were eliminated, M could be regarded as divided into a specie component equal to S' and a fiduciary component equal to $M - S'$. The total $M + N_t + D_t$ is for some purposes a meaningful total, since it includes all the unduplicated obligations of the banks and since $N_t + D_t$ may have been inappropriately assigned to the monetary authorities when N_t and D_t are, in practice, simply working balances of governmental agencies.

2. Simplified Cross-Classification

Since 1935, item 2, currency issued by banks, has been zero, because banks are prohibited from issuing notes.[7] For the rest of our period, this item consisted of national bank notes, except for the first few years, when it included a small and declining amount of state bank notes. Though nominally an obligation of the banks, national bank notes were specifically guaranteed by and were also indirectly an

---

[7] As mentioned above, in an economic sense there is an exception, namely, travelers' checks, which, however, are omitted from our estimates.

obligation of the Treasury, because they had to be matched (before 1900, more than matched) by U.S. bonds as security. After 1874, they were issued under conditions that essentially gave the Treasury control over the amount outstanding, through its decisions about the volume of bonds bearing the circulation privilege and the interest coupon on them.[8] So far as the public was concerned, national bank notes were accepted throughout as interchangeable with currency issued directly as an obligation of the U.S. government.[9] For most state banks also, that was apparently true: national bank notes were acceptable along with other currency as satisfying legal reserve requirements.[10] For national banks there was a difference. Other government-

[8] See Chap. 2, sect. 1. Before 1874, an upper limit to the volume of national bank notes was fixed by statute and the Treasury had no control over it. The requirement of a 5 per cent redemption fund in lawful money from 1874 on did not affect Treasury control. The banks could treat that fund as part of the reserves legally required for deposits. On the other hand, this description is inapplicable to the period before 1874, when the legal reserve requirements of national banks applied to deposits plus circulating notes, so that notes were more nearly identical with deposits than with the notes issued by the Treasury.

[9] In fact, in connection with the exemption from taxation "by or under state or municipal authority" of "all bonds, treasury notes and other obligations of the United States," "obligation or other security of the United States" was defined by statute to include national bank notes. See act of June 30, 1864 (13 Stat. L., 222), sects. 1 and 13, and the codification of the latter section, Mar. 4, 1909, in sect. 147 of the Penal Code of the United States (35 Stat. L., 1115):

> The words "obligation or other security of the United States" shall be held to mean all bonds, certificates of indebtedness, national-bank currency, coupons, United States notes, Treasury notes, gold certificates, fractional notes, certificates of deposit, bills, checks, or drafts for money, drawn by or upon authorized officers of the United States, stamps and other representatives of value, of whatever denomination, which have been or may be issued under any Act of Congress (National Monetary Commission, *Laws of the United States Concerning Money, Banking, and Loans, 1778–1909*, GPO, 1910, pp. 183–184, 187, 675).

[10] G. E. Barnett (*State Banks and Trust Companies Since the Passage of the National-Bank Act*, National Monetary Commission, Vol. VII, 1911, p. 116) notes:

> Under the national bank-act, the cash-in-bank reserve must consist of "lawful money" (i.e., gold coin of the United States, silver dollars, fractional silver coin, legal-tender notes, treasury notes of July 14, 1890, and United States gold and silver certificates). No special importance appears to have been attached to the phraseology employed in most of the state banking laws in defining the cash-in-bank reserve. In some of them the phrase used is "cash on hand," in a large number it is "lawful money," and in still others the several varieties of currency which may be counted are enumerated. Such enumerations usually include national-bank notes.

Barnett's summary of the frequency of the provision that cash-in-bank reserve consist of lawful money is, however, misleading. An examination of *Digest of State Banking Statutes* (National Monetary Commission, Vol. III, 1910, compiled by S. A. Welldon) reveals that only 7 states—Ariz., Fla., La., Mich., Nev., N.M., W.Va.—of the 48 covered specifically limited cash-in-bank reserve to lawful money and, even in those cases, it is not clear from the language of the

issued currency was "lawful money,"[11] whereas national bank notes were not, and only lawful money was acceptable as satisfying legal reserve requirements. However, we known of no banking episode after 1874 in which this distinction played any significant role. Because the public regarded national bank notes as interchangeable with lawful money, banks could always readily convert one into the other, so the proportion of one or the other in their vault cash was of little significance. Moreover, for reasons already cited, we have found it most useful to define reserves of the banking system in a way that is independent of legal reserve requirements.

These considerations (and the discussion in Chapter 2, section 1) suggest that for our period we can treat national bank notes as part of the currency obligations of the monetary authorities, including them as part of U, U_b, U_t, and U', and in this way eliminate item 2 from explicit consideration. It should be emphasized that this simplification is justified only by the special character of the national bank notes and would not be appropriate in general for bank issues of currency. For example, it almost surely would be undesirable for the period before the Civil War, when state bank notes were significant and in no way an obligation of the monetary authorities.[12] The framework of analysis developed below would accordingly have to be altered to make it fully applicable to such other periods.

It should be emphasized that, in terms of conditions of issue and hence the determinants of the amount outstanding, the combination of items 2 and 4 cannot be regarded as a single homogeneous total, not only because of the difference between 2 and 4, but also because of differences among such components of 4 as U.S. notes, silver dollars, silver certificates, subsidiary silver, minor coin, etc.

A further simplification possible for our period without any appreciable loss in the analytical value of the classification is to combine

---

statute that currency other than lawful money would not satisfy the reserve requirement: e.g., Arizona required banks to "keep on hand in lawful money of the United States 15 per cent of the aggregate amount of their deposits; of this reserve two-fifths must be in *cash* and three-fifths on deposit with other banks approved by the comptroller" (*ibid.*, p. 51); Nebraska defined cash as including lawful money of the U.S. and exchanges for any clearing-house association (p. 386). The majority of statutes specified that cash-in-bank reserve consist simply of cash, or lawful money and national bank notes. All classes of banks, moreover, under the jurisdiction of the 7 states listed were not necessarily subject to the lawful money reserve requirement—mainly, it was restricted to so-called state banks, not commercial savings banks or trust companies.

[11] Nevertheless, for the period Dec. 1879–July 1882 the Comptroller of the Currency did not count silver certificates as lawful money. Sect. 12 of the act of July 12, 1882, established the lawful money character of silver certificates. Subsidiary silver and minor coin never qualified as lawful money.

[12] For reasons indicated in footnote 8, it is of questionable appropriateness for the first few years covered by our series.

items 4 and 5, the currency and deposit obligations of the monetary authorities. Before creation of the Federal Reserve System, deposit obligations were nonexistent. Since then, the amount held by the public (item F) has been comparatively small and data on it difficult to obtain.[13] For banks, the distinction has been important, and comparable with the distinction between national bank notes and lawful money, discussed above. From 1917 to 1959, only deposits at the Federal Reserve Banks satisfied the legal reserve requirements of member banks; currency obligations of the monetary authorities did not. However, currency issued by the monetary authorities has always been readily and very promptly convertible into deposits and, with minor exceptions,[14] deposits have been readily convertible into currency. The fact that the legal reserve requirements could be satisfied only by deposits doubtless affected the total amount of reserves—in our meaning of the term—that banks sought to hold under other given conditions; and in consequence the recent change permitting currency to be counted as satisfying legal reserve requirements has doubtless shifted the demand for reserves by banks.[15] However, it seems better to take into account the changing legal status of currency and deposits at the monetary

[13] For example, on Dec. 31, 1960, mutual savings banks held $0.8 million in deposits at Federal Reserve Banks, whereas commercial banks held $16.8 billion of such deposits (see FDIC, *Annual Report*, 1960, p. 142, for mutual savings and member commercial bank figures; Board of Governors of the Federal Reserve System, *Annual Report*, 1960, p. 111, for nonmember bank figure; sum of two latter figures is the commercial bank figure cited). The public on that date presumably held a large fraction of the $8.2 million outstanding officers' and certified checks, drawn on the Reserve Banks—possibly paid out for open market purchases, and one of the sources of federal funds for nonbank participants in the federal funds market. The reserves of corporations engaged in foreign banking or financing under the Edge Act, held by Federal Reserve Banks, totaled $19.1 million and in principle should be included in the public's deposit holdings (FRS, *Annual Report*, 1960, p. 111). "All other deposits" shown in the latter source totaled $343 million on Dec. 31, 1960, and consisted mainly of interest on Federal Reserve notes, set up on Federal Reserve accounts as due the U.S. Treasurer but not yet taken into the Treasurer's account. On other dates, a residual miscellany of other items, which varied from Bank to Bank, would have constituted more important components of "all other deposits." Those items, including noncash collection items, foreign deposits, payroll deductions for U.S. savings bond subscriptions, are ultimately credited to member bank reserves, foreign deposits, and the U.S. Treasurer. The miscellaneous accounts included in "all other deposits," which in principle should also be included in the public's deposit holdings, are negligible.

[14] On some occasions and in some parts of the country during the final stages of the banking panic of 1933, some Federal Reserve Banks or branches ran short of Federal Reserve currency. In February, for example, the Chicago Reserve Bank paid out gold certificates during the run on the banks in the district because it did not have on hand emergency stocks of Federal Reserve notes. In Seattle in early 1933, banks were unable to convert their Federal Reserve deposits into currency. So far as we know, these are the only exceptions.

[15] See Milton Friedman, "Vault Cash and Free Reserves," *Journal of Political Economy*, Apr. 1961, pp. 181–182.

authorities as one factor affecting banks' actions rather than as a reason for retaining the distinction between U_b and F_b. The conditions of issue of F' have differed at times from those of the note liabilities of the Federal Reserve System. However, as we have seen, different components of U' already have different conditions of issue, so combining U' and F' does not introduce any new source of heterogeneity.

Again, it should be emphasized that this simplification would not be justified under all conditions. For example, suppose the monetary authorities issued deposits held by the public in appreciable magnitude, the public regarded these deposits as near-perfect substitutes for commercial bank deposits, and the public regarded monetary authority currency as a near-perfect substitute for specie. It would then be most undesirable to combine monetary authority currency and deposits into one category since that would confound categories relevant to analyzing the money-holding behavior of the public.

With these simplifications, Table B-1 reduces to the simpler 3×3 classification of Table B-2.

TABLE B-2
SIMPLIFIED SYMBOLIC REPRESENTATION OF TYPES OF MONEY,
CROSS-CLASSIFIED BY HOLDER

Type of Money	Public	Class of Holder Banks	Monetary Authorities	Total
Specie	S	S_b	S_t	S'
Obligations of banks: deposits	D		D_t	D'
Obligations of monetary authorities	A	A_b	$A_t(O)$	$A*(A')$
Total	M	R	$T(T')$	

NOTE: The symbols in parentheses represent the situation in which the accounts of the monetary authorities are fully consolidated.

A = currency obligations of monetary authorities. A_b = currency plus deposit obligations of monetary authorities.

3. *Specie Standard with No Money Issued by Monetary Authorities*

Under an effective specie standard, that is to say, one in which specie or warehouse certificates for specie are held by the public ($S \neq 0$), and other forms of money exchange at fixed terms for specie, all other forms of money are promises to pay specie. The simplest version of such a system that includes deposits is one in which banks issue only deposits; the government monetary authorities issue no claims of their own and hold no specie or bank deposits (though of course government agencies do hold working balances); if a government monetary authority

784

exists at all, it limits its activities to warehousing and minting and assuring the weight and fineness of specie. In this simplified version, the third column and third line of Table B-2 would be suppressed, reducing it to a 2×2 table.

In such a specie standard, the total amount of money can be regarded as determined, in a way yet to be defined precisely, by three factors:

1. The total amount of specie in the community, S'
2. The amount of deposits that the banks create per dollar of specie they hold, D/S_b, which in this case also equals D/R or, more generally, the behavior patterns of the banking system
3. The proportion in which the public divides its money balances between specie and deposits, expressed by the amount of deposits per dollar of specie, D/S, which in this case also equals $D/(M - D)$, or, more generally, the behavior patterns of the public with respect to their money holdings

We choose this particular set of three "determinants" because they correspond to economically meaningful categories of influences largely independent of one another.

1. For the world as a whole or a closed economy, the stock of specie depends on current and past conditions of production of gold or other monetary commodity. At any time, it is largely a legacy of the past and all other factors must adjust to it. For a single country that is a small part of the set of economically linked economies using the same commodity as a monetary standard, the relation is almost reversed. In the main, the conditions of international trade determine the amount of money in the community consistent with international financial balance, and the monetary structure (i.e., items 2 and 3) will determine the amount of gold required to permit that stock of money (see discussion in Chapter 3).

2. In the special monetary standard under consideration, the reserves of the banking system, as we have defined reserves, consist entirely of specie. The amount of specie the banks wish to hold relative to their deposit liabilities depends on two major sets of factors: legal reserve requirements, if any, and desired "precautionary reserves." Legal reserve requirements include requirements about the form (e.g., specie vs. deposits at other banks) in which the legally required reserves must be held. Desired precautionary reserves reflect each bank's own judgment of the amount of specie it should hold in its own interest to assure its ability to meet any demands for redemption of its liabilities. The amount of precautionary reserves desired by a bank, in turn, depends mainly on the rate of return the bank can get on assets other than

785

specie reserves, which measures the incentive to economize on reserves, and on the likelihood that it will be subjected to demands for specie.

In the short run, individual banks generally regard their deposits as being more or less given and their specie reserves as under their own control. Hence it would be more directly in accord with their attitudes to use as a determinant the ratio of reserves to deposits rather than, as we do, the ratio of deposits to reserves. The reasons we use D/R instead of its reciprocal are, first, in order to have the determinant in a form in which it is positively rather than inversely related to the money stock and, second, because as explained in the next paragraph, the situation of the banking system as a whole is largely the reverse of the situation of an individual bank.

It appears to each individual bank that it can determine the amount of specie it possesses. If it wishes to add to its specie, for example, it can simply sell assets for specie. But any gain of specie by one bank is likely to be largely at the expense of specie held by other banks. The total amount the banking system can acquire is limited by the total available in the community. If many banks jointly seek to add to their specie, their sales of assets will produce a reduction in deposit liabilities through the familiar deposit contraction process. The banks may or may not add to their absolute holdings of specie but, in the process of trying to do so, they will certainly produce a fall in the *ratio* of deposits to specie. The fall in the ratio will sooner or later satisfy the banking system's desire for liquidity, whether or not the absolute amount of specie rises. A corresponding sequence of statements applies to a desire by banks to reduce their specie holdings. Hence, what the banking system as a whole controls is neither deposits nor reserves alone but rather the *ratio* of deposits to reserves.

Generally speaking, banks can fairly rapidly achieve any desired ratio of deposits to reserves. However, sometimes they may not be able to. On such occasions, the actual ratio may differ from the desired ratio and will depend on whatever circumstances prevent the banks from satisfying their desires[16]—historically, chiefly banking panics, when runs on banks have reduced specie holdings below the amount desired. As our text shows, one effect after a panic has subsided has almost invariably been a fall of the desired ratio of deposits to reserves below the pre-panic level.

3. In the special monetary standard under consideration, the public's money holdings consist entirely of specie and deposits. All currency is

---

[16] A warning is perhaps in order that this is an oversimplified statement. The "desired" ratio may differ between the short and long run, and one factor that determines the short-run "desired" ratio is the rate at which a discrepancy between the actual short- and long-run desired ratio is being eliminated or created. For a fuller analysis of a logically similiar problem, see A. J. Meigs, *Free Reserves and the Money Supply,* University of Chicago Press, 1962.

specie or warehouse certificates for specie. The public will, of course, have preferences about the form of its currency holdings—denominations, coin vs. notes, etc. However, we may regard the various forms of currency as in perfectly elastic supply relative to one another, so the public's preferences can always be satisfied and currency can be regarded as a single homogeneous whole.[17] Deposits may similarly be of various types—at different banks, demand vs. time, etc. Again, however, we may regard them for present purposes as in perfectly elastic supply relative to one another from the point of view of the holder. This supposition would require more modification in a full analysis than the corresponding supposition for specie does. Banks can alter the attractiveness of different types of deposits by the rates of interest they offer to pay on them or by the services they offer.[18] And conversely, if the different kinds of deposit services are not produced under conditions of constant cost, any widespread shift in public preferences for different types of deposits may alter the relative terms which banks offer on such deposits. However, these effects are clearly of the second order of importance compared with the relation between deposits and currency.

The public's choice of the proportion in which it holds deposits and currency depends on the relative usefulness of the two media, on the costs of holding them, and perhaps on income. The higher the rate of return on deposits in the form of interest or services rendered without charge, or the lower the net service charges if service charges exceed interest paid on deposits, the higher will be the fraction of its money holdings the public will desire to keep in the form of deposits. As with the different kinds of deposits considered in the previous paragraph, this is one way banks can affect the public's division of its money stock. Another and more subtle way is through actions that affect the public's attitudes about the convertibility of deposits into specie. These actions include changes in the ratio of specie to deposits banks hold, as well as other actions affecting public confidence. Hence, while the present and preceding "determinants" are under the proximate control of different economic units and while there are many variables affecting them independently, there are also some important links between them.

[17] It could, of course, also be so regarded if various types of currency were in inelastic supply with respect to one another but were regarded as perfect substitutes by holders of money. This point is of no significance for our case of a specie standard, but it is for cases considered later, when on these grounds we treat different types of currency such as U.S. notes and national bank notes as part of a homogeneous total.

[18] For example, the differential reserves on demand and time deposits specified by the Federal Reserve Act lowered the relative cost to banks of providing time deposits. As a result, banks were led to make time deposits more attractive by paying higher rates of interest and by endowing them more fully with the properties of demand deposits, in particular, making them in fact payable on demand. As a result, time deposits rose relative to demand deposits (see Chap. 6).

We use the ratio of deposits to currency rather than its reciprocal to allow the determinant to be positively rather than inversely related to the money stock. And we express the public's desires in terms of the *ratio* of deposits to currency rather than in terms of the absolute magnitudes of the components, because it is the ratio that the public as a whole controls. It appears to each holder of money that he can determine the absolute amount he holds in currency and in deposits. If he wishes, for example, to convert deposits into currency, he simply asks the bank to redeem his deposit in currency. However, the bank thereby weakens its reserve position and, by the familiar process, puts pressure on other banks to contract as it seeks to restore its reserves. The result is that, in a fractional reserve system, for a given total amount of specie (item 1) and given reserve behavior by the banks (item 2), the attempt to convert deposits into currency reduces the sum of the two for the public as a whole. If the public as a whole seeks to convert deposits into currency, the attempt reduces deposits by a larger amount than it raises currency, and thereby reduces the *ratio* of deposits to currency, which, sooner or later, will satisfy the public's desire for currency instead of deposits. Similar statements apply to an attempt by the public to convert currency into deposits.

Generally speaking, the public like the banks can fairly rapidly achieve any desired ratio of deposits to currency. However, sometimes it may not be able to. On such occasions, the actual ratio may differ from the desired ratio and will depend on whatever circumstances prevent the public from satisfying its desires—again, historically, chiefly banking panics.

The arithmetical relation between the stock of money and the three determinants can be set forth simply. In the special monetary standard under consideration:

$$(1) \qquad M = S + D,$$
$$(2) \qquad S' = S + S_b = S + R,$$
$$(3) \qquad \frac{M}{S'} = \frac{S + D}{S + R}.$$

Divide numerator and denominator by S:

$$\frac{1 + \dfrac{D}{S}}{1 + \dfrac{R}{S}} = \frac{1 + \dfrac{D}{S}}{1 + \left(\dfrac{R}{D} \cdot \dfrac{D}{S}\right)}.$$

Multiply numerator and denominator by $\dfrac{D}{R}$:

788

(4)
$$\frac{M}{S'} = \frac{\dfrac{D}{R}\left(1 + \dfrac{D}{S}\right)}{\dfrac{D}{R} + \dfrac{D}{S}}.$$

Hence

(5)
$$M = S' \cdot \frac{\dfrac{D}{R}\left(1 + \dfrac{D}{S}\right)}{\dfrac{D}{R} + \dfrac{D}{S}}.$$

4. A Pure Fiduciary Standard

A monetary standard in which there is no commodity serving as money, no specie, but in which all currency is purely fiduciary currency issued by the monetary authorities is in one sense at the opposite pole, yet in another sense logically identical with the standard just considered. The U.S. standard from 1862 to 1878 approximated such a standard and so has the U.S. standard since 1934—though gold was held by the public or banks or monetary authorities in both cases. In the earlier example, it was held only because there was wide expectation that the standard would be changed; in the later, gold is held only by the monetary authorities.

Under this standard, the first line of Table B-2 is suppressed. If, for simplicity, we suppose the monetary authorities to hold no deposits at banks, and we consolidate their accounts, the third column is suppressed also, and we have again a 2 × 2 table identical with that for the preceding standard except that A replaces S, A_b replaces S_b, and A' replaces S'. The currency issued by the monetary authorities serves the same economic function as specie. The determinants remain the same with this change. Our prior discussion of the factors affecting item 2, the ratio of deposits to reserves, and item 3, the ratio of deposits to currency, applies in full. However, our discussion of the determinants of S' will apply to A' only if the monetary authorities seek to peg at a fixed value the rate of exchange between the currency of the country in question and the currencies of other countries, and succeed in doing so. If rates of exchange are variable, the volume of currency, A', can be determined by the monetary authorities independently of the flow of international payments.

Monetary powers may of course be split, in which case A' may be composed of obligations issued by different agencies which jointly constitute the monetary authorities or, what is equivalent, of obligations issued under different legislative provisions. For example, from 1862 to 1878, A' included U.S. notes, national bank notes, fractional silver currency, etc. Since 1934, A' has included silver certificates, subsidiary silver, Federal Reserve notes, Federal Reserve deposits, etc. However, so long as these different obligations are either in perfectly elastic supply relative to one another (e.g., coins of different denominations, or Federal Reserve notes of different denominations) or regarded as perfect substitutes for one another by holders of money (e.g., U.S. notes and national bank notes, U.S. notes and Federal Reserve notes), this division has no economic effect in and of itself. Only the total matters, and the division of authority is important only as it affects the total.

The arithmetical relation among the determinants of this standard can be derived directly from equation 5 by substituting A' for S' and A for S to give:

$$(6) \qquad M = A' \cdot \frac{\dfrac{D}{R}\left(1 + \dfrac{D}{A}\right)}{\dfrac{D}{R} + \dfrac{D}{A}}.$$

5. A Mixed Specie and Fiduciary Standard: A Special Case

The penultimate paragraph suggests one way to extend the analysis for these special standards to the more general standard described by Table B-2, in which there are both specie and fiduciary obligations issued by monetary authorities. Suppose the monetary authorities under a specie standard succeed so well in maintaining their obligations uniformly redeemable at fixed terms in specie that holders of money regard the obligations of the monetary authorities as perfect substitutes for specie. The banks will then desire to maintain some ratio of D to R but will be indifferent about the proportions in which R consists of specie, S_b, or obligations of the monetary authorities, A_b. Similarly, the public will desire to maintain some ratio between deposits, D, and currency, $S + A$, but will be indifferent about the proportions in which currency consists of specie, S, or obligations of the monetary authorities, A. The total of specie and obligations of the monetary authorities held by the public and the banks will then play the same role each played separately in the previously described standards.

Let us continue to suppose the authorities hold no deposits at banks, so that we can continue to neglect D_t. Call the composite total of specie and the consolidated obligations of the monetary authorities, just referred to, high-powered money, H, or more fully, high-powered money outside the monetary authorities, so that

$$(7) \qquad H = S + S_b + A + A_b,$$

or the total of kinds of money that can be used for currency or as reserves. Let C designate the amount of currency held by the public, so that

$$(8) \qquad C = S + A.$$

We then have:

(9) $M = C + D,$

(10) $H = C + R,$

(11) $$\frac{M}{H} = \frac{C + D}{C + R} = \frac{\frac{D}{R}\left(1 + \frac{D}{C}\right)}{\frac{D}{R} + \frac{D}{C}},$$

or

(12) $$M = H \cdot \frac{\frac{D}{R}\left(1 + \frac{D}{C}\right)}{\frac{D}{R} + \frac{D}{C}}.$$

Equation 12 is, of course, identical with equations 5 and 6 except that H replaces S' and A', respectively, and C replaces S and A, respectively. Alternatively, equations 5 and 6 can be considered special cases of 12 when obligations of the monetary authorities and specie respectively are set equal to zero.

Granted its assumptions, equation 12 enables us to view the money stock in the same way for the whole of our period as a result of three sets of factors: those that determine the total of H, those that determine the deposit-currency ratio, and those that determine the deposit-reserve ratio. Institutional changes may change each of the sets of factors, but we can express their effects throughout by the same summary figures, which, for simplicity, we call the proximate determinants of the stock of money.

The numerical values of H, D/C, and D/R are given, for the whole of our period, in Table B-3 at the end of this appendix.

Equation 12 is the basic equation that we have used in most of our analysis of the factors affecting the money stock. A variant of it, which we have not used, allows for a fourth set of factors, those that determine the amount of high-powered money held by the monetary authorities relative to the amount held by the banks and the public. This involves considering the amount of high-powered money as a result of two factors: the amount of a broader total, $H + T$, and the fraction of the broader total held by the monetary authorities $T/H + T$. It is an identity that

(13) $$H = (H + T)\left(1 - \frac{T}{H + T}\right).$$

Substituting equation 13 in equation 12 gives:

(14) $$M = \frac{(H + T)\left(1 - \frac{T}{H + T}\right) \cdot \frac{D}{R}\left(1 + \frac{D}{C}\right)}{\frac{D}{R} + \frac{D}{C}}.$$

791

However, this equation is a crude expedient. Under some circumstances, $H + T$ may be a meaningful total. However, it is inconsistent with our treatment of banks and the public to regard the monetary authorities as determining $T/H + T$. By the reasoning we used to analyze the roles of the public and the banks, the authorities should be regarded as determining the ratio of their obligations to whatever they promise to give in redemption for them—under a specie standard, the ratio of their obligations to their specie. But that would require a subdivision of H into its parts and would render unfeasible the simplification of this section. To put the point differently, unless there is some problem about the redeemability of the authorities' claims, the authorities' balances of high-powered money are meaningless or irrelevant: the authorities can make them whatever they want simply by printing claims and storing them. The necessity of separating out the authorities' balances therefore must mean that specie and claims on the monetary authorities are not perfect substitutes for money holders, and that a full analysis requires the recognition of three types of money, as set forth in the next section.

Before turning to that section, a word is needed about one other point, the treatment of the authorities' deposits at banks. These are left out of all our formulas and we have so far assumed them to be zero. In fact, they are not zero. The problem they raise is that, on the one hand, they affect the reserves of banks but, on the other, they cannot be regarded as being determined by any behavioral relation to the extent that they really are an instrument of monetary policy rather than working balances of one of the monetary authorities, i.e., the Treasury. We have chosen to take them into account as a factor that may affect D/R rather than explicitly in our formula. One practical justification for this procedure is that the only times U.S. Treasury deposits at banks have been sizable have been during periods of war financing, when special provisions have exempted such deposits from the legal reserve requirements applicable to other deposits. Hence, the effect of Treasury deposits on D/R, as we define the ratio, has almost surely been minor throughout our period. One alternative would be to include Treasury deposits in the formula as follows:

$$(15) \qquad M = H \cdot \frac{\left(\dfrac{D + D_t}{R}\right)\left(1 + \dfrac{D}{C}\right)}{\dfrac{D + D_t}{R} + \dfrac{D}{C} + \dfrac{D_t}{C}},$$

which is identically equivalent to equation 12. However, while it is possible to attribute behavioral significance to $(D + D_t)/R$, it is hard to attribute any to D_t/C or to any easy modification.

6. A More General Case of a Mixed Specie and Fiduciary Standard

For a more general case, in which the monetary authorities are to be regarded as concerned with the convertibility of claims on them, the relevant basic factors are presumably:

1. The total amount of specie
2. The ratio the authorities maintain between their specie holdings and the claims on them[19]
3. The ratios the banks maintain between their liabilities and specie and between their liabilities and claims on the monetary authorities, separately, since in this case the two are not perfect substitutes
4. The ratios the public maintains between deposits and currency of the authorities, and between deposits and specie, separately, since again the two latter are not perfect substitutes

An arithmetical expression for the money stock in terms of these factors can be derived as before.

$$(16) \qquad M = S + D + A,$$

$$(17) \qquad S' = S + S_b + S_t,$$

$$(18) \qquad \frac{M}{S'} = \frac{S + D + A}{S + S_b + S_t} = \frac{1 + \dfrac{D}{S} + \dfrac{A}{S}}{1 + \dfrac{S_b}{S} + \dfrac{S_t}{S}}$$

$$= \frac{1 + \dfrac{D}{S} + \dfrac{A}{S}}{1 + \dfrac{S_b}{D} \cdot \dfrac{D}{S} + \dfrac{S_t}{A + A_b} \cdot \dfrac{A + A_b}{S}}$$

$$= \frac{1 + \dfrac{D}{S} + \dfrac{A}{S}}{1 + \dfrac{S_b}{D} \cdot \dfrac{D}{S} + \dfrac{S_t}{A + A_b} \left(\dfrac{A}{S} + \dfrac{D}{S} \cdot \dfrac{A_b}{D} \right)}$$

$$= \frac{\dfrac{D}{S_b} \left(1 + \dfrac{D}{S} + \dfrac{A}{S} \right)}{\dfrac{D}{S_b} + \dfrac{D}{S} + \dfrac{D}{S_b} \cdot \dfrac{S_t}{A + A_b} \left(\dfrac{A}{S} + \dfrac{D}{S} \cdot \dfrac{A_b}{D} \right)},$$

[19] We are here treating the claims on the monetary authorities as a single homogeneous total. A still more general case would distinguish between different categories of claims, for example, deposits and notes. The distinction is important if, for example, one type of claim (deposits) satisfies legal reserve requirements and the other does not. This distinction, of course, existed under the Federal Reserve from 1917 until 1959, when vault cash, including Federal Reserve notes, again became eligible to satisfy legal reserve requirements.

or

(19) $$M = S' \cdot \frac{\frac{D}{S_b}\left(1 + \frac{D}{S} + \frac{A}{S}\right)}{\frac{D}{S_b} + \frac{D}{S} + \frac{D}{S_b} \cdot \frac{S_t}{A + A_b}\left(\frac{A}{S} + \frac{D}{S} \cdot \frac{A_b}{D}\right)}.$$

This expression, while it gives a formal statement in terms of the factors relevant to the more general case, is so complex we have not used it.

7. Contribution of the Determinants to Changes in the Stock of Money

Given that the stock of money can be regarded as an arithmetical result of H, D/R, and D/C, according to equation 12, a change in the stock of money is likewise attributable to a change in the three determinants, and it would be desirable to be able to determine the fraction of any given change attributable to the change in each of the determinants. To simplify notation, we replace D/R by b (for the banks' ratio) and D/C by p (for the public's) in equation 12, so that

$$M = H \cdot b(1 + p)/(b + p).$$

Since our interest is mostly in relative rather than absolute changes, we begin by taking the logarithm of equation 12 in this form:

(20) $\log M = \log H + \log b + \log (1 + p) - \log (b + p)$.

For continuous changes, there is of course no problem. We simply write the total derivative of $\log M$ as

(21) $$\frac{d \log M}{dt} = \frac{\partial \log M}{\partial H}\frac{dH}{dt} + \frac{\partial \log M}{\partial b}\frac{db}{dt} + \frac{\partial \log M}{\partial p}\frac{dp}{dt},$$

(22) $$= \frac{1}{H}\frac{dH}{dt} + \frac{p}{b(b + p)}\frac{db}{dt} + \frac{b - 1}{(1 + p)(b + p)}\frac{dp}{dt}.$$

The ratio of each of the right-hand terms to $d \log M/dt$ then gives the fraction of the percentage change in M attributable to each determinant.

However, our observations are at discrete intervals. More important, we shall want to talk about changes in M over much longer intervals than those between successive observations. This raises no problem for H, because it enters as a separable term in equation 20 (i.e., because neither b nor p enters into the partial derivative of $\log M$ with respect to H). However, it does raise a problem for the two deposit ratios because they enter jointly into the final term of $\log M$ (i.e., because each is a variable in the partial derivative of $\log M$ with respect to the other). This means that over any discrete period there will be an interaction between the effects of changes in b and p, so there is no unique way to divide the change in $\log M$ into fractions attributable to each determinant separately. This is the usual index number problem and, as usual, we resolve it by taking one point in time as the base. Consider time points t_0 and t_1.

The total change in log M between these time points is:

$$(23) \qquad \Delta \log M = \log M_1 - \log M_0.$$

Let us consider the hypothetical changes in M that would have occurred if each of the determinants in turn had changed as it did, while the others had remained at their initial values. This gives:

$$(24) \quad \text{(Effect of } \Delta H) = \Delta \log M \ (b = b_0, p = p_0) = \log H_1 - \log H_0,$$
$$(25) \quad \text{(Effect of } \Delta b) = \Delta \log M \ (H = H_0, p = p_0) = \log b_1 - \log b_0$$
$$- \log(b_1 + p_0) + \log (b_0 + p_0),$$
$$(26) \quad \text{(Effect of } \Delta p) = \Delta \log M(H = H_0, b = b_0) = \log (1 + p_1)$$
$$- \log (1 + p_0) - \log (b_0 + p_1) + \log (b_0 + p_0).$$

Equation 24 is an estimate of the separate effect of the change in H, and equations 25 and 26 approximate estimates of the separate effects of changes in b and p respectively. Each divided by equation 23 is an estimate of the fraction of the percentage change in M attributable to the corresponding determinant. However, the sum of equations 24, 25, and 26 need not be equal to 23. The difference between equation 23 and the sum of 24, 25, and 26 is the interaction, and is equal to:

$$(27) \quad \text{(Interaction)} = - \log (b_1 + p_1) + \log (b_1 + p_0) + \log (b_0 + p_1)$$
$$- \log (b_0 + p_0).$$

Its ratio to equation 23 is the fraction of the change that cannot by this device be attributed to b and p separately.

The breakdown that would be obtained by starting with time point 1 as the base and considering hypothetical changes from then back to 0 would, of course, be different. However, it is clear from equations 23 to 27, and the corresponding equations obtained by interchanging the subscripts 0 and 1, that (1) the fraction attributed to H is the same; (2) the numerical value of interaction is the same but, expressed as a fraction of the total change in M, opposite in sign; (3) the fraction attributed to b is equal to its prior value plus the prior fraction attributed to interaction; (4) the fraction attributed to p is also equal to its prior value plus the prior fraction attributed to interaction. Hence, if interaction is small, as it generally is in our applications of these formulas, so is the arbitrary element involved in the use of a particular time point as the basis for the calculation.

Particularly with respect to high-powered money, this breakdown of the change in M can be readily confused with a very different breakdown. We can regard the total stock of money as equal to high-powered money plus the fiduciary element in bank deposits, or

(28)
$$M = H + D_f,$$

where

(29)
$$D_f = D - R.$$

We can then ask what fraction of the change in M *consists of* a change in high-powered money. The answer is given directly by

(30)
$$\frac{\Delta H}{\Delta M}.$$

This answer is very different from that obtained from the ratio of equation 24 to 23. The reason is clear. If b and p are constant, a 10 per cent increase in H, say, will mean a 10 per cent increase in M. The ratio of equation 24 to 23 would be unity and we would say that 100 per cent of the change in M is *attributable* to the change in H. However, if the fiduciary element in deposits accounted for, say, 85 per cent of the money stock, then only 15 per cent of the change in M would *consist of* the change in H, as given by formula 30.

8. *Contribution of Components to Changes in High-Powered Money*

High-powered money is itself a sum of separable components. For example, in the model of section 5,

(7)
$$H = S + S_b + A + A_b.$$

In the period after 1914, $A + A_b$ can be separated into Treasury obligations and Federal Reserve obligations. This breakdown classifies high-powered money by the form in which it is held by the public or the banks:

1. Gold coins and certificates
2. Treasury currency including silver dollars, silver certificates, subsidiary silver, minor coins, and national bank notes
3. Federal Reserve notes
4. Federal Reserve deposits

This is essentially the breakdown we use before 1914, limited, of course, to items 1 and 2.

The difficulty with this breakdown is that it does not distinguish fully between the fiduciary and nonfiduciary elements in the total, since items 2 to 4 may be in part nonfiduciary, the Treasury and the Federal Reserve System holding gold as "backing." Another way to view high-powered money is therefore in terms of the assets that correspond to it on the books of the monetary authorities. The variant of this alternative we have adopted treats all gold, valued at cost to the Treasury, as if it corresponded dollar-for-dollar to high-powered money in the hands of the public and the banks, as it would if gold certificates had been issued to them in exchange for gold and all gold had been acquired solely in exchange for such gold certificates. It treats the remainder of high-powered money as a contribution of the Federal Reserve System through its claims on the public and the banks—bills discounted, bills bought, and other Federal Reserve credit not including holdings of government securities; as a contribution of both the Reserve System and the Treasury based on their holdings of physical assets—bank premises for the Reserve System, silver stocks for the Treasury; and finally as a fiduciary contribution of the Treasury based on its fiat.

The derivation of this asset breakdown requires the consolidation of the accounts of the Treasury and Federal Reserve System, and the consolidation of their balance sheets in order to match particular liabilities against particular assets. To illustrate in schematic form, let us set up balance sheets for the Federal Reserve System and the Treasury.

ASSETS   LIABILITIES

Federal Reserve System

1. Gold certificates
2. Treasury currency
3. Discounts, advances, acceptances,
   cash items in process of collection
   (i.e., private claims)
4. U.S. government securities
5. Bank premises and other assets
6. TOTAL ASSETS

7. Federal Reserve notes held by the
   Treasury and public
8. Deposits due to U.S. Treasury
9. Other Federal Reserve deposits
10. Deferred availability items
11. Other liabilities
12. Capital accounts
13. TOTAL LIABILITIES

Treasury

14. Gold matching gold certificates
15. Free gold
16. Silver at cost
17. Federal Reserve notes
18. Federal Reserve deposits
19. Book entry to balance (comparable
    to a firm's "good will")
20. TOTAL ASSETS

21. Gold certificates
22. Treasury currency

23. TOTAL LIABILITIES

Federal Reserve System plus Treasury

24. Gold matching gold
    certificates = 14 − 1
25. Free gold = 15 + 1
26. Silver = 16
27. Private claims = 3
28. Bank premises and other assets = 5
29. Book entry to
    balance = 4 + 19 − 12

30. TOTAL ASSETS

31. Federal Reserve notes in
    circulation = 7 − 17
32. Other Federal Reserve deposits = 9
33. Gold certificates in
    circulation = 21 − 1
34. Treasury currency in
    circulation = 22 − 2
35. Deferred availability items = 10
36. Other liabilities = 11
37. TOTAL LIABILITIES

Items 31, 32, 33, and 34, plus gold coins in circulation, give the breakdown of high-powered money by the forms in which it is held. A matching asset breakdown can be obtained by transferring items 35 and 36 to the left-hand side of the balance sheet, as follows:

Federal Reserve System plus Treasury

24 + 25 = gold	31 = Federal Reserve notes in circulation
27 = Federal Reserve private claims	32 = other Federal Reserve deposits
26 + 28 = physical assets	33 = gold certificates in circulation
29 − 35 − 36 = "good will" or fiat	34 = Treasury currency in circulation

Hence we show the change in high-powered money as consisting of changes in:

1. The gold stock, valued at its cost to the Treasury—this means we exclude the excess valuation of gold appropriated by the Treasury upon the devaluation of gold in January 1934, since this is a fiduciary element
2. Federal Reserve private claims
3. Physical assets and fiat of the Treasury and the Federal Reserve System

For the years after 1914 we thus present a twofold breakdown of high-powered money, by the liabilities and by the matching assets of the monetary authorities.

Because these components enter additively into an equation like 7 in absolute amounts, the absolute change in H can most easily be broken down into the part contributed by each component by simply dividing the change in a component by the change in H. The sum of such fractions necessarily adds to unity, so interaction is zero and the time point taken as the base is irrelevant. Hence, we have followed this procedure, even though it is inconsistent with the procedure followed for money, which subdivides the percentage rather than the absolute change. Of course, the two approach the same thing as the period of change approaches zero so, for a finite time interval, they can be regarded as approximations of one another.

TABLE B-3
PROXIMATE DETERMINANTS OF THE MONEY STOCK, SEASONALLY ADJUSTED,
1867–1960
(dollar amounts in billions)

DATE	High-Powered Money (1)	RATIO OF DEPOSITS ADJUSTED *All Commercial Banks* To Bank Reserves (2)	To Currency Held by the Public (3)	DATE	High-Powered Money (1)	RATIO OF DEPOSITS ADJUSTED *All Commercial Banks* To Bank Reserves (2)	To Currency Held by the Public (3)
1867				1886			
Jan.	0.852	2.73	1.25	June	1.195	5.27	3.09
1868				1887			
Jan.	0.775	2.92	1.34	June	1.257	5.36	3.13
1869				1888			
Jan.	0.761	3.17	1.39	June	1.309	5.21	3.10
1870				1889			
Jan.	0.758	3.14	1.53	June	1.318	5.46	3.33
1871				1890			
Jan.	0.776	3.67	1.55	June	1.366	6.32	3.40
1872				1891			
Jan.	0.782	4.34	1.92	June	1.433	6.05	3.36
1873				1892			
Feb.	0.783	4.63	1.94	June	1.529	5.90	3.81
1874				1893			
Feb.	0.801	3.88	2.03	June	1.514	6.05	3.25
1875				1894			
Feb.	0.783	4.82	2.12	June	1.569	4.87	3.78
Aug.	0.767	4.61	2.32	1895			
1876				June	1.502	5.79	4.08
Feb.	0.758	4.79	2.24	1896			
Aug.	0.751	4.70	2.28	June	1.399	6.06	4.13
1877				1897			
Feb.	0.757	4.80	2.27	June	1.524	5.54	4.13
Aug.	0.759	4.67	2.08	1898			
1878				June	1.721	5.85	4.05
Feb.	0.763	4.44	2.00	1899			
Aug.	0.767	4.31	1.94	June	1.806	6.73	4.65
1879				1900			
Feb.	0.752	4.41	1.97	June	1.954	6.80	4.36
Aug.	0.815	4.98	2.09	1901			
1880				June	2.070	7.28	4.95
Feb.	0.897	4.74	2.08	1902			
Aug.	0.972	4.45	2.08	June	2.143	7.80	5.26
1881				1903			
Feb.	1.005	5.31	2.16	June	2.257	8.30	5.09
Aug.	1.113	5.39	2.14	1904			
1882				June	2.406	7.56	5.40
June	1.124	5.64	2.21	1905			
1883				June	2.470	8.65	5.82
June	1.184	5.96	2.28	1906			
1884				June	2.628	8.90	5.85
June	1.189	5.54	2.28				
1885							
June	1.233	4.54	2.64				

(continued)

TABLE B-3 (continued)

DATE	High-Powered Money (1)	RATIO OF DEPOSITS ADJUSTED All Commercial Banks To Bank Reserves (2)	To Currency Held by the Public (3)	DATE	High-Powered Money (1)	RATIO OF DEPOSITS ADJUSTED All Commercial Banks To Bank Reserves (2)	To Currency Held by the Public (3)
1907				**1910**			
May	2.841	8.83	5.80	July	3.186	7.71	6.66
June	2.815	8.87	5.84	Aug.	3.206	7.72	6.61
July	2.823	8.56	5.98	Sept.	3.211	7.94	6.56
Aug.	2.818	8.50	5.98	Oct.	3.197	8.18	6.56
Sept.	2.815	8.23	5.97	Nov.	3.216	7.95	6.72
Oct.	2.885	8.26	5.51	Dec.	3.218	7.92	6.78
Nov.	2.889	7.78	5.25				
Dec.	3.069	7.60	4.93	**1911**			
				Jan.	3.241	7.85	6.81
1908				Feb.	3.260	7.76	6.87
Jan.	3.093	7.52	4.76	Mar.	3.266	7.83	6.85
Feb.	3.095	7.02	4.96	Apr.	3.276	8.05	6.80
Mar.	3.085	6.88	5.20	May	3.303	7.98	6.82
Apr.	3.109	6.76	5.29	June	3.282	7.94	7.01
May	3.060	6.94	5.50	July	3.260	8.14	7.02
June	3.081	6.98	5.53	Aug.	3.292	8.09	6.91
July	3.097	6.96	5.63	Sept.	3.283	8.10	7.05
Aug.	3.097	6.86	5.87	Oct.	3.286	8.16	7.16
Sept.	3.099	6.96	5.91	Nov.	3.306	8.11	7.25
Oct.	3.104	7.14	5.91	Dec.	3.298	7.98	7.51
Nov.	3.104	7.20	6.07				
Dec.	3.105	7.38	5.99	**1912**			
				Jan.	3.316	7.99	7.54
1909				Feb.	3.330	8.11	7.43
Jan.	3.091	7.36	6.20	Mar.	3.314	8.31	7.43
Feb.	3.091	7.42	6.22	Apr.	3.334	8.42	7.29
Mar.	3.091	7.43	6.31	May	3.358	8.54	7.15
Apr.	3.112	7.46	6.33	June	3.332	8.77	7.19
May	3.120	7.47	6.42	July	3.352	8.66	7.23
June	3.143	7.48	6.45	Aug.	3.353	8.71	7.25
July	3.135	7.50	6.56	Sept.	3.345	8.79	7.27
Aug.	3.129	7.66	6.55	Oct.	3.375	8.83	7.21
Sept.	3.152	7.70	6.51	Nov.	3.365	8.76	7.40
Oct.	3.136	7.81	6.56	Dec.	3.383	8.63	7.44
Nov.	3.140	7.80	6.58				
Dec.	3.138	7.90	6.61	**1913**			
				Jan.	3.393	8.68	7.40
1910				Feb.	3.388	8.81	7.39
Jan.	3.129	7.99	6.56	Mar.	3.361	8.89	7.41
Feb.	3.142	7.90	6.66	Apr.	3.392	8.94	7.28
Mar.	3.164	7.80	6.76	May	3.402	8.95	7.18
Apr.	3.132	7.92	6.76	June	3.415	8.81	7.19
May	3.155	7.84	6.69	July	3.436	8.62	7.23
June	3.171	7.84	6.65	Aug.	3.424	8.79	7.29

(continued)

TABLE B-3 (continued)

DATE	High-Powered Money (1)	RATIO OF DEPOSITS ADJUSTED *All Commercial Banks* To Bank Reserves (2)	To Currency Held by the Public (3)	DATE	High-Powered Money (1)	RATIO OF DEPOSITS ADJUSTED *All Commercial Banks* To Bank Reserves (2)	To Currency Held by the Public (3)
1913				**1916**			
Sept.	3.449	8.88	7.27	Nov.	4.410	9.19	8.78
Oct.	3.453	8.98	7.26	Dec.	4.517	8.90	9.04
Nov.	3.462	8.82	7.37				
Dec.	3.476	8.69	7.46	**1917**			
				Jan.	4.641	9.00	8.76
1914				Feb.	4.759	8.87	8.55
Jan.	3.471	8.63	7.58	Mar.	4.862	8.89	8.34
Feb.	3.484	8.70	7.50	Apr.	4.872	9.21	8.16
Mar.	3.484	8.67	7.63	May	4.960	9.20	8.08
Apr.	3.428	8.55	8.07	June	5.086	8.83	7.94
May	3.529	8.51	7.78	July	5.112	9.17	7.91
June	3.482	8.67	7.82	Aug.	4.998	10.05	7.71
July	3.473	8.66	7.87	Sept.	5.176	9.59	7.40
Aug.	3.539	8.77	7.49	Oct.	5.233	9.47	7.28
Sept.	3.728	8.69	6.99	Nov.	5.452	9.09	7.05
Oct.	3.722	8.80	6.95	Dec.	5.553	9.43	7.15
Nov.	3.571	8.61	7.65				
Dec.	3.469	9.06	7.71	**1918**			
				Jan.	5.513	9.27	7.26
1915				Feb.	5.708	9.00	6.77
Jan.	3.518	9.01	7.66	Mar.	5.813	9.11	6.79
Feb.	3.509	8.92	7.95	Apr.	5.892	9.04	6.70
Mar.	3.551	8.85	7.91	May	5.855	9.04	6.43
Apr.	3.613	8.73	7.82	June	5.892	9.42	6.33
May	3.625	8.68	8.00	July	5.982	9.85	6.08
June	3.655	8.66	8.05	Aug.	6.218	9.74	5.84
July	3.674	8.64	8.09	Sept.	6.418	9.84	5.84
Aug.	3.743	8.28	8.26	Oct.	6.671	8.94	5.58
Sept.	3.788	8.42	8.34	Nov.	6.443	10.00	5.75
Oct.	3.830	8.75	8.50	Dec.	6.529	10.21	6.07
Nov.	3.845	8.68	8.73				
Dec.	3.881	8.92	8.61	**1919**			
				Jan.	6.461	9.90	6.24
1916				Feb.	6.427	9.96	6.23
Jan.	4.006	8.80	8.44	Mar.	6.462	10.10	6.45
Feb.	4.003	8.84	8.73	Apr.	6.569	9.88	6.50
Mar.	4.043	8.91	8.57	May	6.563	9.85	6.57
Apr.	4.070	9.18	8.43	June	6.517	10.05	6.80
May	4.098	9.20	8.52	July	6.593	10.24	6.82
June	4.129	9.31	8.34	Aug.	6.635	10.26	6.92
July	4.193	9.14	8.48	Sept.	6.671	10.45	6.97
Aug.	4.274	8.89	8.62	Oct.	6.793	10.45	7.06
Sept.	4.326	8.93	8.71	Nov.	6.874	10.53	7.03
Oct.	4.383	8.97	8.77	Dec.	6.874	11.01	6.95

(continued)

TABLE B-3 (continued)

DATE	High-Powered Money (1)	RATIO OF DEPOSITS ADJUSTED All Commercial Banks To Bank Reserves (2)	To Currency Held by the Public (3)	DATE	High-Powered Money (1)	RATIO OF DEPOSITS ADJUSTED All Commercial Banks To Bank Reserves (2)	To Currency Held by the Public (3)
1920				1923			
Jan.	6.909	10.78	7.05	Mar.	6.624	11.54	8.29
Feb.	7.059	10.86	6.93	Apr.	6.607	11.91	8.30
Mar.	7.134	10.96	6.93	May	6.680	11.93	8.22
Apr.	7.202	10.86	6.85	June	6.682	12.04	8.13
May	7.195	10.90	6.87	July	6.670	12.05	8.14
June	7.214	10.99	6.78	Aug.	6.734	11.85	8.11
July	7.253	10.98	6.71	Sept.	6.747	11.86	8.15
Aug.	7.304	11.06	6.60	Oct.	6.740	11.83	8.28
Sept.	7.295	11.29	6.52	Nov.	6.802	11.81	8.18
Oct.	7.330	11.21	6.44	Dec.	6.748	11.95	8.32
Nov.	7.181	11.22	6.55				
Dec.	7.173	11.18	6.69	1924			
				Jan.	6.714	11.72	8.47
1921				Feb.	6.773	11.74	8.37
Jan.	6.955	11.22	6.86	Mar.	6.787	11.82	8.35
Feb.	6.888	11.25	6.86	Apr.	6.802	11.81	8.43
Mar.	6.753	11.40	6.84	May	6.827	11.86	8.43
Apr.	6.725	11.15	6.87	June	6.851	11.71	8.63
May	6.638	11.37	6.91	July	6.913	11.50	8.83
June	6.549	11.26	6.96	Aug.	6.920	11.60	8.96
July	6.470	11.24	7.00	Sept.	6.886	11.70	9.20
Aug.	6.376	11.51	7.12	Oct.	6.990	11.57	9.14
Sept.	6.386	11.22	7.13	Nov.	7.008	11.74	9.21
Oct.	6.262	11.45	7.39	Dec.	7.019	11.61	9.21
Nov.	6.215	11.43	7.54				
Dec.	6.246	11.22	7.54	1925			
				Jan.	7.007	11.86	9.29
1922				Feb.	7.077	11.72	9.36
Jan.	6.085	11.35	7.76	Mar.	6.974	12.15	9.34
Feb.	6.142	11.24	7.86	Apr.	6.980	12.13	9.43
Mar.	6.226	11.00	7.86	May	6.988	12.23	9.51
Apr.	6.221	11.27	8.06	June	6.951	12.48	9.62
May	6.262	11.12	8.19	July	7.017	12.34	9.62
June	6.321	11.14	8.28	Aug.	7.018	12.43	9.84
July	6.253	11.49	8.43	Sept.	7.036	12.46	9.97
Aug.	6.295	11.58	8.35	Oct.	7.054	12.53	9.91
Sept.	6.358	11.65	8.28	Nov.	7.054	12.47	9.97
Oct.	6.339	11.86	8.33	Dec.	7.161	12.22	9.85
Nov.	6.423	11.56	8.28				
Dec.	6.476	11.83	8.45	1926			
				Jan.	7.107	12.46	9.91
1923				Feb.	7.131	12.49	9.89
Jan.	6.532	11.37	8.54	Mar.	7.124	12.40	9.94
Feb.	6.545	11.64	8.45	Apr.	7.166	12.41	9.75

(continued)

TABLE B-3 (continued)

DATE	High-Powered Money (1)	RATIO OF DEPOSITS ADJUSTED *All Commercial Banks* To Bank Reserves (2)	To Currency Held by the Public (3)	DATE	High-Powered Money (1)	RATIO OF DEPOSITS ADJUSTED *All Commercial Banks* To Bank Reserves (2)	To Currency Held by the Public (3)
1926				**1929**			
May	7.126	12.53	9.95	July	7.123	13.14	10.94
June	7.130	12.55	9.94	Aug.	7.155	13.09	10.81
July	7.173	12.49	9.78	Sept.	7.075	13.07	11.12
Aug.	7.130	12.59	9.93	Oct.	7.345	12.62	11.57
Sept.	7.148	12.45	9.94	Nov.	7.152	12.48	10.69
Oct.	7.093	12.62	9.89	Dec.	6.978	13.24	11.07
Nov.	7.056	12.71	9.96				
Dec.	7.093	12.55	9.80	**1930**			
				Jan.	6.980	12.87	11.07
1927				Feb.	6.999	12.83	11.13
Jan.	7.092	12.69	9.86	Mar.	6.963	13.07	11.42
Feb.	7.084	12.89	9.96	Apr.	6.908	12.96	11.44
Mar.	7.210	12.49	9.97	May	6.905	12.92	11.23
Apr.	7.211	12.51	9.96	June	6.908	12.90	11.31
May	7.196	12.64	10.21	July	6.925	12.80	11.36
June	7.238	12.30	10.23	Aug.	6.953	12.74	11.17
July	7.198	12.54	10.23	Sept.	6.829	12.97	11.41
Aug.	7.161	12.54	10.45	Oct.	6.817	12.86	11.54
Sept.	7.200	12.49	10.33	Nov.	6.935	12.32	10.93
Oct.	7.146	12.63	10.48	Dec.	7.125	12.14	10.57
Nov.	7.146	12.67	10.84				
Dec.	7.183	12.37	10.65	**1931**			
				Jan.	7.152	11.95	10.43
1928				Feb.	7.076	12.33	10.49
Jan.	7.109	12.74	10.93	Mar.	7.090	12.39	10.37
Feb.	7.114	12.69	11.05	Apr.	7.119	12.28	10.15
Mar.	7.164	12.82	10.91	May	7.130	12.07	10.01
Apr.	7.211	12.80	11.00	June	7.302	11.67	9.66
May	7.159	12.97	10.99	July	7.321	11.72	9.43
June	7.150	13.00	10.68	Aug.	7.375	11.69	8.95
July	7.071	13.20	10.85	Sept.	7.498	11.42	8.54
Aug.	7.091	13.15	10.74	Oct.	7.570	11.48	7.67
Sept.	7.066	13.18	10.88	Nov.	7.458	11.49	7.54
Oct.	7.042	13.19	11.13	Dec.	7.735	10.46	7.11
Nov.	7.185	13.00	10.87				
Dec.	7.118	13.01	11.15	**1932**			
				Jan.	7.704	11.28	6.47
1929				Feb.	7.537	11.53	6.49
Jan.	7.155	12.73	11.07	Mar.	7.539	11.09	6.54
Feb.	7.139	12.90	11.03	Apr.	7.644	10.60	6.46
Mar.	7.152	13.02	10.84	May	7.710	10.17	6.35
Apr.	7.019	13.40	10.93	June	7.788	10.44	5.95
May	7.048	13.25	10.80	July	7.858	10.35	5.76
June	7.102	13.16	10.74	Aug.	7.850	10.15	5.82

(continued)

803

TABLE B-3 (continued)

DATE	High-Powered Money (1)	RATIO OF DEPOSITS ADJUSTED *All Commercial Banks* To Bank Reserves (2)	To Currency Held by the Public (3)	DATE	High-Powered Money (1)	RATIO OF DEPOSITS ADJUSTED *All Commercial Banks* To Bank Reserves (2)	To Currency Held by the Public (3)
1932				**1935**			
Sept.	7.897	9.82	5.87	Nov.	11.524	5.34	7.28
Oct.	7.896	9.64	6.01	Dec.	11.578	5.29	7.27
Nov.	7.978	9.40	6.09				
Dec.	8.028	9.13	6.05	**1936**			
				Jan.	11.672	5.26	7.20
1933				Feb.	11.778	5.29	7.21
Jan.	8.272	8.86	5.86	Mar.	11.372	5.66	7.17
Feb.	8.807	8.39	4.84	Apr.	11.593	5.58	7.35
Mar.	8.414	8.42	4.44	May	11.825	5.53	7.47
Apr.	8.074	8.55	4.72	June	11.698	5.91	7.26
May	7.915	8.66	5.00	July	12.322	5.41	7.35
June	7.944	8.39	5.08	Aug.	12.564	5.23	7.35
July	7.891	8.41	5.17	Sept.	12.729	5.22	7.37
Aug.	7.961	8.15	5.23	Oct.	12.994	5.07	7.32
Sept.	8.089	7.80	5.27	Nov.	13.128	5.04	7.26
Oct.	8.116	7.72	5.33	Dec.	13.257	5.07	7.23
Nov.	8.165	7.74	5.31				
Dec.	8.302	7.50	5.37	**1937**			
				Jan.	13.197	5.09	7.20
1934				Feb.	13.302	5.10	7.25
Jan.	7.947	7.66	5.89	Mar.	13.511	4.98	7.29
Feb.	8.411	6.95	6.00	Apr.	13.537	4.97	7.22
Mar.	8.998	6.23	6.09	May	13.496	4.96	7.21
Apr.	9.094	6.17	6.15	June	13.485	4.98	7.20
May	9.158	6.15	6.18	July	13.385	5.07	7.16
June	9.260	6.09	6.21	Aug.	13.344	5.12	7.04
July	9.422	6.02	6.28	Sept.	13.628	4.93	7.05
Aug.	9.491	6.09	6.40	Oct.	13.376	5.00	6.96
Sept.	9.402	6.17	6.37	Nov.	13.407	4.93	6.94
Oct.	9.330	6.36	6.57	Dec.	13.652	4.73	6.96
Nov.	9.570	6.18	6.60				
Dec.	9.505	6.17	6.69	**1938**			
				Jan.	13.680	4.73	7.07
1935				Feb.	13.818	4.67	7.17
Jan.	9.998	5.84	6.80	Mar.	14.111	4.51	7.15
Feb.	10.159	5.87	6.82	Apr.	14.177	4.45	7.16
Mar.	10.163	5.89	6.81	May	14.284	4.36	7.06
Apr.	10.337	5.80	6.94	June	14.609	4.21	7.12
May	10.468	5.71	6.97	July	14.778	4.17	7.13
June	10.693	5.57	7.08	Aug.	14.794	4.25	7.27
July	10.707	5.58	7.17	Sept.	14.832	4.29	7.21
Aug.	10.936	5.64	7.35	Oct.	15.224	4.16	7.24
Sept.	10.968	5.61	7.19	Nov.	15.540	4.09	7.30
Oct.	11.288	5.41	7.22	Dec.	15.568	4.11	7.32

(continued)

TABLE B-3 (continued)

DATE	High-Powered Money (1)	RATIO OF DEPOSITS ADJUSTED All Commercial Banks To Bank Reserves (2)	To Currency Held by the Public (3)	DATE	High-Powered Money (1)	RATIO OF DEPOSITS ADJUSTED All Commercial Banks To Bank Reserves (2)	To Currency Held by the Public (3)
1939				1942			
Jan.	15.903	4.00	7.20	Mar.	24.477	3.93	5.47
Feb.	15.901	4.01	7.09	Apr.	24.840	3.96	5.45
Mar.	16.393	3.89	7.09	May	24.769	4.12	5.38
Apr.	16.926	3.76	7.03	June	25.233	4.09	5.23
May	17.103	3.72	7.05	July	25.653	4.20	5.18
June	17.298	3.68	7.02	Aug.	25.841	4.34	5.11
July	17.674	3.64	7.12	Sept.	25.387	4.71	5.02
Aug.	18.326	3.54	7.14	Oct.	26.448	4.60	5.02
Sept.	18.857	3.46	7.18	Nov.	26.992	4.65	4.87
Oct.	19.083	3.44	7.21	Dec.	27.698	4.67	4.74
Nov.	18.996	3.54	7.31	1943			
Dec.	19.293	3.44	7.25	Jan.	28.3	4.71	4.75
1940				Feb.	28.9	4.85	4.75
Jan.	19.622	3.41	7.23	Mar.	29.1	5.01	4.77
Feb.	20.155	3.34	7.24	Apr.	29.0	5.08	4.61
Mar.	20.365	3.34	7.27	May	28.8	5.40	4.50
Apr.	20.695	3.26	7.19	June	29.5	5.48	4.68
May	21.115	3.23	7.25	July	30.3	5.59	4.67
June	21.814	3.14	7.22	Aug.	31.0	5.73	4.78
July	21.736	3.19	7.22	Sept.	30.8	5.37	4.25
Aug.	21.881	3.19	7.15	Oct.	30.9	5.54	4.24
Sept.	22.019	3.21	7.12	Nov.	31.5	5.77	4.27
Oct.	22.528	3.16	7.07	Dec.	32.4	5.83	4.32
Nov.	22.725	3.18	7.04	1944			
Dec.	23.106	3.18	6.92	Jan.	32.9	5.64	4.18
1941				Feb.	32.8	5.88	4.16
Jan.	23.079	3.25	6.89	Mar.	33.2	5.97	4.14
Feb.	23.396	3.29	6.90	Apr.	34.2	5.88	4.12
Mar.	23.156	3.41	6.84	May	35.1	5.85	4.12
Apr.	23.042	3.47	6.75	June	35.6	5.72	3.98
May	23.359	3.48	6.72	July	35.7	5.87	3.97
June	22.972	3.59	6.50	Aug.	36.3	5.97	4.02
July	23.258	3.64	6.46	Sept.	37.1	5.97	4.01
Aug.	23.268	3.68	6.30	Oct.	38.0	6.00	4.04
Sept.	23.631	3.66	6.24	Nov.	38.8	5.98	4.07
Oct.	23.216	3.79	6.13	Dec.	38.6	5.99	3.93
Nov.	23.653	3.77	6.02	1945			
Dec.	23.738	3.84	5.71	Jan.	38.8	6.27	4.00
1942				Feb.	39.9	6.11	4.00
Jan.	24.106	3.86	5.65	Mar.	40.5	6.12	4.04
Feb.	24.145	3.94	5.55	Apr.	41.1	6.08	4.03

(continued)

TABLE B-3 (continued)

DATE	High-Powered Money (1)	RATIO OF DEPOSITS ADJUSTED All Commercial Banks To Bank Reserves (2)	To Currency Held by the Public (3)	DATE	High-Powered Money (1)	RATIO OF DEPOSITS ADJUSTED All Commercial Banks To Bank Reserves (2)	To Currency Held by the Public (3)
1945				**1948**			
May	41.6	6.02	4.04	July	45.5	6.21	4.65
June	41.6	6.10	3.93	Aug.	45.7	6.15	4.65
July	42.0	6.18	3.96	Sept.	46.5	5.90	4.65
Aug.	42.6	6.14	4.00	Oct.	47.5	5.63	4.65
Sept.	43.0	6.21	4.02	Nov.	47.4	5.63	4.65
Oct.	43.2	6.24	4.05	Dec.	47.3	5.62	4.67
Nov.	43.4	6.15	4.12				
Dec.	43.3	6.23	4.06	**1949**			
				Jan.	47.0	5.66	4.68
1946				Feb.	47.1	5.62	4.68
Jan.	43.4	6.18	4.06	Mar.	46.9	5.69	4.68
Feb.	43.6	6.21	4.12	Apr.	46.7	5.73	4.69
Mar.	43.7	6.20	4.10	May	45.9	5.95	4.72
Apr.	43.6	6.41	4.18	June	45.6	6.05	4.72
May	43.7	6.46	4.23	July	45.0	6.20	4.74
June	44.3	6.40	4.22	Aug.	44.3	6.40	4.76
July	44.5	6.31	4.28	Sept.	43.4	6.69	4.75
Aug.	44.1	6.46	4.29	Oct.	43.1	6.80	4.77
Sept.	44.1	6.47	4.34	Nov.	43.1	6.74	4.79
Oct.	44.2	6.45	4.35	Dec.	43.0	6.78	4.80
Nov.	43.9	6.58	4.36				
Dec.	44.0	6.55	4.38	**1950**			
				Jan.	43.0	6.76	4.83
1947				Feb.	43.0	6.84	4.84
Jan.	44.1	6.61	4.36	Mar.	43.0	6.90	4.86
Feb.	44.3	6.59	4.35	Apr.	43.0	6.94	4.89
Mar.	44.3	6.66	4.39	May	43.2	6.89	4.92
Apr.	44.4	6.68	4.42	June	43.1	6.91	4.96
May	44.6	6.64	4.45	July	43.2	6.87	4.99
June	44.5	6.67	4.48	Aug.	43.3	6.85	5.01
July	44.7	6.61	4.50	Sept.	43.3	6.80	5.04
Aug.	44.9	6.56	4.51	Oct.	43.3	6.86	5.03
Sept.	45.2	6.43	4.54	Nov.	43.5	6.82	5.04
Oct.	45.0	6.53	4.55	Dec.	43.6	6.78	5.06
Nov.	45.0	6.53	4.56				
Dec.	44.9	6.53	4.58	**1951**			
				Jan.	44.2	6.64	5.06
1948				Feb.	45.1	6.38	5.05
Jan.	45.0	6.52	4.60	Mar.	45.6	6.25	5.06
Feb.	44.9	6.56	4.60	Apr.	46.1	6.11	5.07
Mar.	44.9	6.46	4.62	May	46.1	6.18	5.04
Apr.	44.9	6.44	4.63	June	46.2	6.19	5.06
May	45.0	6.37	4.62	July	46.2	6.24	5.04
June	45.2	6.28	4.65	Aug.	46.7	6.23	5.03

(continued)

TABLE B-3 (continued)

DATE	High-Powered Money (1)	RATIO OF DEPOSITS ADJUSTED *All Commercial Banks* To Bank Reserves (2)	RATIO OF DEPOSITS ADJUSTED *All Commercial Banks* To Currency Held by the Public (3)	DATE	High-Powered Money (1)	RATIO OF DEPOSITS ADJUSTED *All Commercial Banks* To Bank Reserves (2)	RATIO OF DEPOSITS ADJUSTED *All Commercial Banks* To Currency Held by the Public (3)
1951				**1954**			
Sept.	46.8	6.24	5.07	Nov.	48.4	7.17	5.50
Oct.	47.3	6.18	5.06	Dec.	48.3	7.24	5.51
Nov.	47.2	6.26	5.11				
Dec.	47.6	6.25	5.09	**1955**			
				Jan.	48.1	7.32	5.54
1952				Feb.	48.3	7.36	5.56
Jan.	47.8	6.23	5.10	Mar.	48.0	7.44	5.55
Feb.	47.8	6.28	5.13	Apr.	48.3	7.41	5.55
Mar.	47.9	6.27	5.12	May	48.3	7.43	5.56
Apr.	47.9	6.30	5.12	June	48.1	7.48	5.57
May	48.1	6.30	5.13	July	48.2	7.47	5.58
June	48.2	6.32	5.13	Aug.	48.4	7.45	5.57
July	48.8	6.19	5.12	Sept.	48.3	7.50	5.59
Aug.	49.0	6.20	5.13	Oct.	48.5	7.50	5.58
Sept.	49.3	6.20	5.12	Nov.	48.3	7.54	5.56
Oct.	49.2	6.25	5.14	Dec.	48.3	7.55	5.57
Nov.	49.4	6.26	5.12				
Dec.	49.7	6.25	5.10	**1956**			
				Jan.	48.4	7.58	5.57
1953				Feb.	48.4	7.59	5.58
Jan.	49.4	6.34	5.11	Mar.	48.7	7.55	5.57
Feb.	49.6	6.34	5.09	Apr.	48.6	7.57	5.61
Mar.	49.6	6.41	5.10	May	48.6	7.57	5.58
Apr.	49.4	6.46	5.12	June	48.6	7.62	5.60
May	49.5	6.49	5.11	July	48.4	7.69	5.60
June	49.8	6.46	5.10	Aug.	48.7	7.60	5.61
July	49.3	6.61	5.11	Sept.	48.7	7.60	5.63
Aug.	49.3	6.62	5.13	Oct.	48.7	7.67	5.62
Sept.	49.3	6.64	5.13	Nov.	48.9	7.65	5.61
Oct.	49.1	6.72	5.15	Dec.	48.9	7.67	5.62
Nov.	49.3	6.68	5.16				
Dec.	49.2	6.73	5.17	**1957**			
				Jan.	48.9	7.73	5.62
1954				Feb.	48.7	7.78	5.67
Jan.	49.2	6.70	5.21	Mar.	49.0	7.77	5.67
Feb.	49.1	6.76	5.22	Apr.	49.1	7.74	5.68
Mar.	49.0	6.78	5.26	May	49.0	7.81	5.70
Apr.	49.0	6.78	5.26	June	49.0	7.82	5.71
May	49.1	6.79	5.30	July	49.0	7.81	5.73
June	49.1	6.84	5.32	Aug.	48.9	7.90	5.75
July	48.6	6.99	5.37	Sept.	49.1	7.87	5.73
Aug.	47.9	7.24	5.42	Oct.	49.0	7.87	5.76
Sept.	47.9	7.29	5.44	Nov.	48.9	7.90	5.76
Oct.	48.2	7.20	5.47	Dec.	49.1	7.84	5.75

(continued)

TABLE B-3 (concluded)

DATE	High-Powered Money (1)	RATIO OF DEPOSITS ADJUSTED All Commercial Banks		DATE	High-Powered Money (1)	RATIO OF DEPOSITS ADJUSTED All Commercial Banks	
		To Bank Reserves (2)	To Currency Held by the Public (3)			To Bank Reserves (2)	To Currency Held by the Public (3)
1958				1959			
Jan.	49.1	7.86	5.77	July	49.6	8.70	6.18
Feb.	49.2	7.88	5.82	Aug.	49.6	8.71	6.18
Mar.	49.0	8.02	5.86	Sept.	49.6	8.71	6.19
Apr.	48.7	8.21	5.92	Oct.	49.5	8.71	6.17
May	48.7	8.33	5.95	Nov.	49.4	8.74	6.16
June	49.0	8.29	6.01	Dec.	49.4	8.80	6.16
July	48.9	8.36	6.03				
Aug.	48.9	8.43	6.08	1960			
Sept.	48.9	8.51	6.08	Jan.	49.2	8.82	6.13
Oct.	48.9	8.53	6.10	Feb.	49.1	8.84	6.12
Nov.	49.0	8.56	6.11	Mar.	49.0	8.85	6.11
Dec.	48.9	8.64	6.13	Apr.	49.0	8.86	6.12
				May	49.1	8.81	6.11
1959				June	49.0	8.80	6.13
Jan.	49.0	8.61	6.15	July	49.1	8.82	6.16
Feb.	49.3	8.58	6.15	Aug.	49.2	8.84	6.20
Mar.	49.3	8.62	6.15	Sept.	48.8	9.15	6.23
Apr.	49.6	8.55	6.16	Oct.	48.8	9.15	6.25
May	49.6	8.61	6.17	Nov.	48.7	9.23	6.26
June	49.5	8.70	6.17	Dec.	47.2	10.03	6.28

SOURCE, BY COLUMN

Column 1, High-Powered Money

Jan. 1867–Oct. 1914: Currency held by the public (Table A-1, col. 1), plus bank vault cash (Table A-2, col. 1).

Nov. 1914–Dec. 1960: Same components as above, plus bank deposits at Federal Reserve Banks (see Table A-2, col. 2).

Column 2, Ratio of Deposits to Reserves

Commercial bank deposits (Table A-1, col. 4) divided by bank reserves (Table A-2, col. 3).

Column 3, Ratio of Deposits to Currency

Commercial bank deposits (Table A-1, col. 4) divided by currency held by the public (Table A-1, col. 1).

Director's Comment

ALBERT J. HETTINGER, JR.

PARTNER, LAZARD FRÈRES AND COMPANY

THE National Bureau affords its directors the privilege of submitting a "memorandum of dissent or reservation" to a manuscript accepted for publication. What I am submitting are neither dissents nor reservations, but a questioning comment. I have read the manuscript twice, in original draft and in final galley proof. I eagerly await the more pleasant reading afforded by a published volume, where tables appear in context and charts, by their presence, remove that need for faith, defined by St. Paul as "the substance of things hoped for, the evidence of things not seen." This volume, if my judgment is sound, is one of the truly great ones published by the National Bureau. Its breadth of scope, its penetrating use of analytical tools to set forth, dissect, and in a sense reconstitute, as it might have been, nearly a century of the monetary history of the United States, has created a finished product that I will reread more than once with enjoyment coupled with a conviction that time so spent is profitably employed. My questioning is not of the logic of a brilliant presentation, but of an underlying assumption. My brief comments will be based largely upon the period 1929–33. The authors state, in their summation of the period, "There is one sense—and, so far as we can see, only one—in which a case can be made for the proposition that the monetary decline was a consequence of the economic decline. That sense is not relevant to our main task of seeking to understand economic relations, since it involves relying primarily on psychological and political factors" (p. 691).

We are inevitably, in varying degrees, influenced by our background and environment. Mine compels me to place much greater weight upon these "psychological and political factors" than the authors would be willing to concede. I am a businessman by profession, an amateur economist by avocation. My doctor's degree in economics regrettably lies nearly half a century in the past; my few years of university teaching are almost as remote; competitive business, a combination of industry and finance, has been my profession since 1926. To me, business is simply decision making and calculated risk taking. Decisions are not always easy, and the risk taking is real; I survive by virtue of my competitors' mistakes—if they did not make about as many as I do, I would be an ex-businessman. It has been burned in upon me that monetary policy, in final analysis, acts on men whose conduct is not predictable; it neither operates in vacuum nor in a world in which all other factors can be taken as constant.

The difficulty of predicting the impact of economic measures was faced in the *Third Report* of the British Council on Prices, Productivity and Incomes, generally assumed to have been written by Sir Dennis Robertson.[1] After some 72 sections attempting to analyze the situation and weigh the probabilities, there follows: "But no precise judgment of the balance of all these factors is possible; economic restraints and incentives operate on men's minds where it is not possible to forecast their precise effects; they operate also in circumstances which are constantly changing." And Lord Keynes, here a "decision maker," told the 1931 annual meeting of the investment trust of which he was chairman: "I have reluctantly reached the conclusion that nothing is more suicidal than a rational investment policy in an irrational world" (quoted from memory, without verification of exact phraseology). He also states in his *Treatise on Money:* "To diagnose the position precisely at every stage and to achieve this exact balance may sometimes be, however, beyond the wits of man."[2] One final example: Sir Henry Clay's biography of Lord Norman[3] tells of the head of the Bank of England, physically exhausted but feeling that the international monetary system was temporarily under control, yielding to doctors' orders and taking a brief cruise on the Mediterranean—to be greeted when the ship put into port with the news that Britain had gone off gold!

The authors of this volume in discussing the silver situation (1893–97) recognize the importance of psychological and political factors when they say, "the entire silver episode is a fascinating example of how important what people think about money can sometimes be. The fear that silver would produce an inflation sufficient to force the United States off the gold standard made it necessary to have a severe deflation in order to stay on the gold standard" (p. 133).

I have often wished that Professor Taussig had included, in the economic text I studied, a chapter on the force of momentum. Value, I was taught, was the determining long-run factor, and deviations in price from value, short term and self-correcting. I learned the force of a spiraling downward momentum, feeding on emotional fear, during the 1929–33 period, and experienced a replay during the confidence crisis and stock market debacle of the spring of 1962. A nonstatistical view

[1] London, H.M. Stationery Office, July 1959, p. 25, paragraph 73.
[2] New York, Harcourt, Brace, 1930, Vol. I, p. 255.
[3] *Lord Norman,* London, Macmillan, 1957.

of the psychology of the 1929–33 period was presented in a paper delivered by J. M. Barker (university teacher, banker, and senior official of Sears, Roebuck & Co.) before a midwestern conference of bankers in 1936, from which I quote:

> Whenever you have a group of people thinking the same thing at the same time you have one of the hardest emotional causes in the world to control. The more people that are thinking the same thing the more surely you are at the mercy of unreasoning, emotional mob psychology as a cause, with sometimes dire economic effects. . . . If you consider the universality of the speculative mania of the later days of the last boom, you will see how completely the people of this country, to say nothing of the world, were under the influence of the mob psychology of unreasoning, emotional cupidity. When the break came, cupidity turned into unreasoning, emotional, universal fear. . . . In every city of this country, business men, hard hit or already wiped out in the stock market in the earlier part of the crash, were still watching the quotations every day to see how things were going. They saw the market dropping, dropping, dropping. Is there any doubt they made their decisions from day to day under the influence of the emotional backgrounds formed by their observations of the falling security prices?

The authors are highly critical of Federal Reserve policies. The continuing conflicts within the system are convincingly documented: Board, Open Market Committee, and individual Reserve Banks—they call to mind the line from one of Ibsen's plays that runs: "When the devil decided that nothing be accomplished, he appointed the first committee." The authors' diagnosis: "The bull market brought the objective of promoting business activity into conflict with the desire to restrain stock market speculation. The conflict was resolved in 1928 and 1929 by adoption of a monetary policy, not restrictive enough to halt the bull market yet too restrictive to foster vigorous business expansion" (pp. 297–298). Their conclusion that "the Board should not have made itself an 'arbiter of security speculation or values' and should have paid no direct attention to the stock market boom" (p. 291) is one I am not sure I can accept. With holding company superimposed on holding company, call loans for "others" mounting by the billion, and momentum feeding on itself, the monetary ease that would have "fostered vigorous expansion" might well have cumulated economic maladjustments whose correction was merely postponed. As it was, when the break came, "as in pre-Federal Reserve times, J. P. Morgan and Company assumed leadership of an effort to restore an orderly market by organizing a pool of funds"—yet "by the second week after the crash the phase of organized support of the market was over" (p. 305). This was a different kind of depression.

With possibly unjustifiable oversimplification in description on my part, the basic weapon in the authors' arsenal may be termed their

811

concept of high-powered money. Their treatment of its role is consistent and brilliantly analytical in depth. One point only disturbs me. There is no question as to the mathematical demonstration. If high-powered money could be increased by the Federal Reserve without that very move setting other forces in motion, unpredictable both as to source and intensity, I would have no reservations. I lack competence to pass judgment. This is not a controlled experiment, with high-powered money increased, and all other factors remaining constant. Depositors were watching their banks. "One of the reasons New York City banks were said to be reluctant to borrow from the Reserve Bank was the fear that Europeans would interpret borrowing as an indication of weakness" (p. 317). "The aversion to borrowing by banks . . . was still greater at a time when depositors were fearful of the safety of every bank and were scrutinizing balance sheets with great care to see which banks were likely to be next to go" (p. 318). To borrow from the RFC was the kiss of death: "the inclusion of a bank's name on the list was correctly interpreted as a sign of weakness, and hence frequently led to runs on the bank" (p. 325). It is difficult today to recall "the dominant importance then attached to the preservation of the gold standard and the greater significance attached to external than to internal stability, by both the System and the community at large" (p. 363). Summarizing, in the words of Lord Keynes: "If we are dealing with a closed system, so that there is only the condition of internal equilibrium to fulfill, an appropriate banking policy is always capable of preventing any serious disturbance to the *status quo* from developing at all. . . . But when the condition of external equilibrium must also be fulfilled, then there will be no banking policy capable of avoiding disturbance to the internal system."[4] A parallel reading of Professor Chandler's biography of Benjamin Strong[5] and that of Lord Norman by Sir Henry Clay should leave no doubt that we were dealing with no closed system; the extent of the erosion of newly created high-powered money would be one measure of the "disturbance to the internal system" that I (with what justification I am not capable of answering) would not treat lightly.

The authors ask, "Why was monetary policy so inept?" and answer, "We trust that, in light of the preceding sections of this chapter, the adjective used . . . to characterize monetary policy during the critical period from 1929 to 1933 strikes our readers, as it does us, as a plain description of the fact. The monetary system collapsed, but it clearly need not have done so" (p. 407). The monetary policy certainly was unsuccessful, and probably the characterization of "inept" is justified. With respect to the final statement that the collapse of the monetary

[4] *A Treatise on Money*, Vol. I, p. 349.
[5] Lester V. Chandler, *Benjamin Strong*, Washington, D.C., Brookings, 1958.

system was unnecessary, this I cannot feel has been proved. To me, each move in the high-powered-money arsenal involves a calculated risk. If its impact on men's minds is favorable, possibly even if it is neutral, the arithmetical results postulated by the authors follow as night after day. I merely cite at this point the earlier quotation from the report of the British Council on Prices, Productivity and Incomes. If those moves were deemed inflationary and "unsound," the results could have been other than those desired. In that day a citizen fearing devaluation could choose gold rather than paper, and the international flow of gold, seeking safety, was as unpredictable as that of a gun loose on a battleship pitching in heavy seas. The authors may well be right; they are outstanding monetary economists—but I would prefer the terms "possibly" or conceivably "probably" rather than "clearly" need not have happened.

If my recollection is correct, the most striking illustration of the potentialities of high-powered money are those cited in connection with the five-month period ended January 1932, in which deposits fell by $5,727 million. "The provision of $400 million of additional high-powered money to meet the currency drain without a decline in bank reserves could have prevented a decline of nearly $6 billion in deposits" (p. 346). Mathematically this was possible. Reviewing the economy in the United States at that time, and the situation in both Britain and Central Europe, I cannot believe that what in theory "could" have happened, in actuality "would" have happened.

There is a well-documented analysis of what would have happened had one billion dollars of additional high-powered money been introduced into the economy during any one of three strategic periods in the great depression: (1) January 1930 to end of October 1930, (2) January 1931 to end of August 1931, and (3) September 1931 to end of January 1932. Were a Lloyds to underwrite the assumed potential turning of the tide, I could rest more easily. If it be permitted to lapse into the terminology of the market place, there is a vast difference between gross income and net income. This would be determined by the reaction on men's minds, not only in this country, but in every monetary center of the world. Had it been favorable, the authors' assumptions are tenable; had it, for instance, been deemed an inflationary threat to the gold standard, the "cost" (in erosion of those high-powered dollars) could have reduced the "net" to such an extent as would have precluded the results confidently anticipated by the authors. Again, I don't know; I am merely questioning.

In Kerrville, Texas, the "Bank of the Charles E. Schreiner Estate" is run by Louis Schreiner, aged about 90, and was founded by his father, old Captain Schreiner, as he is termed in those parts. The old Captain laid down the rule: "The time to call your loan is before you make it," and in almost a century, good times and bad, that bank has never called a loan. High-powered money, intelligently administered by a regulatory body, can, as the authors point out, accomplish much. It cannot accomplish the impossible—there seems to me an analogy in Lord Keynes' rueful remark: "Nothing is more suicidal than a rational investment policy in an irrational world." I would have more hope of its keeping us out of trouble than in its ability to turn an emotional tidal wave after we got into trouble.

I claim no validity for my "questioning comment." During my university days I would have placed little emphasis upon the psychological and political factors: a long life in business has changed my views. The story is told that Bismarck in council, after his staff had scoffed at certain factors which they termed imponderable, reached his decision: "Gentlemen, the Imponderables have it." I have no idea whether his decision was correct, and similarly I have no idea whether the weight I attach to imponderables has validity. My comments are set forth with humility, because I have made too many mistakes to do otherwise.

Over all, my admiration for *A Monetary History of the United States, 1867–1960* is unrestrained.

Author Index

817

Subject Index

(Page numbers in **boldface** refer to tables and charts)

Acceptances, bankers' (bills), 193n
bought by F.R., **215, 271, 388**
buying rate on, of N.Y. F.R. Bank,
227n
above market rates, and decline in
F.R. holdings, 404
Board control over, question of,
256
Board delay in approving lowering
of, 1930, 367
changes in, Feb.–Mar. 1933, 390–
391
if below market rates, effect on free
gold, 404n
inadequate declines in, after Oct.
1931, 383
preferential, proposed, 227n, 264n
raised, Jan.–Mar. 1929, Mar.
1933, 289, 326
reduced, Aug. 1927, Aug. 1928,
264, 288, 290, 344
rise in F.R. holdings and, 289–
290, 344
changes in F.R. holdings, 1931–32,
346
decline in F.R. holdings, 1933–40, 501
Adjusted Compensation Act, 538n
Agricultural Adjustment Act, 1933:
Thomas amendment to, 447, 465,
470, 518n
authorized President to devalue
dollar, 465
granted President powers over
silver, 483
Agricultural Credits Act, 233n
Aldrich, Nelson W., 171
Aldrich-Vreeland Act, 9, 170, 172
amendments and provisions of, 170–
171
currency:
device to increase high-powered
money, 441
success of 1914 issue, 192, 196
success of, probable, if issued in
1930, 172
pattern for National Credit Corporation, 320

"Alliances," 116
American Bankers Association, 117,
170
American Bimetallic League, 117
Assets, fixed-dollar vs. real, direct
return on, postwar rise in, 645
Austria, failure of Kreditanstalt and
standstill agreement with, 314

Bagehot, Walter, 227, 235n
Baker, George F., 261n
Balance of payments:
China, pressure of U.S. silver purchases on, 489
gold-bloc countries, and U.S. gold
purchases and capital flight to
U.S., 474–476
U.S., 58, 66, 85, 101, 140, 198,
478, 481, 585, 679, 683, 694,
785
active vs. passive gold flows and,
98–99, 141
deficit tendency as result of Treasury gold purchases, 124, 466
forces underlying, 58
purchasing-power parity and, 98,
100
similarity of, 1923–29 and 1930–
33, 480
under gold standard, 141–142
U.S. prices consistent with equilibrium in, 78, 98, 100, 140, 588n
Balance of trade, U.S.:
and capital flight to U.S., 1934–40,
475, 476–477, 480–481
estimated directly, accuracy of, 476,
478
as per cent of national income,
478
estimated indirectly from capital
movements, accuracy of, 476,
478
as per cent of national income,
478
gold purchases, 1934–40, increased,
475–477, 480–481

opposed to seasonal easing, 1930, 374
passive, hesitant, 1929–33, 411
passive under New Deal, but banking structure and monetary standard greatly changed, 420, 465–466
principles of, in 1921, 1923 *Annual Reports*, 249–254
to promote economic stability, 1921–29, 240, 241
of providing unlimited high-powered money at fixed rate:
abandoned after Accord, 593, 625, 700
committed System to buy securities from banks, 1948, 1951, 604, 612
differences with Treasury over details, 611, 621, 625
if not offset by earlier change in surplus and expectations of price decline, 1946–48, 585
F.R. attempts to limit during Korean War, 610
and high-powered money, 578, 583
offset by public's desire to hold money and not spend, 1946–48, 581
relative to changing market conditions, 578
same after both world wars, 577
unquestioned by F.R., 1945–51, 578, 620–21, 625
of purchasing earning assets, 1914–17, 213–214
of restoring its reserve ratio, 1920–21, 229–230, 332–334
of restraint, 1923, 1926, 287
of restriction, 289, 317, 600
after gold drain, 1931, 317
decline in bond prices and rise in bank failures, 383
wide support for, 363, 382
contribution to severity of 1920–21 contraction, 237, 360, 419, 607
F.R. disclaimer of effect on 1920–21 U.S. decline, 236–237, 419
international aspects of 1920–21 decline, 236–237, 360
opposed by Treasury, 1928, 289n
sharp reversal of earlier policy, 1959, 619
timing of peak and, early 1953, 599
with new tools, 1936–37, 514

role of foreign vs. domestic factors in, 269
of seasonal adjustment, 294
of sterilizing gold flows:
1923–29, 282–283, 297
burden on rest of world of, 1929–31, 360–361
synchronous with cycle turns:
1923–27, 296
effect on 1923 *Annual Report*, 288
tight, 1930, 375
too easy to stem bull market, 1929, 265, 290, 298, 692
too tight for business expansion, 1929, 265–266, 290, 298, 692
tools of, refinement in 1920's, 296
Treasury domination after 1933, 12, 505
Monetary standard:
changes in U.S., 420, 683–684
dual, 27
during panics, 15n, 110
fiduciary:
money stock independent variable under, 89
U.S., 1862–78 vs. 1934–60, 7, 15, 85, 789
mixed fiduciary and specie, 790ff.
specie, 784ff.
uncertainty about, 7, 8, 44, 87, 91, 107, 132n, 184
banking holiday of 1933 and, 331
capital outflows and, 102, 107, 143, 146n
dating of periods, 184
decline in, and price rise, 1900–02, 148
end of, 1897 vs. 1879, 139, 184
public's preference for gold in 1933 and, 350
rebound from, 185, 242
reduction in, 146
U.S. since 1934, as discretionary fiduciary, 474
See also Gold standard
Money:
change in ideas about, after 1933, 12
fiscal policy assumed superior to, 533, 543
greater importance assigned to direct credit controls, 533
public interest in, as result of support policy, 596, 626
worldwide changes in ideas about, after 1948, 596, 626, 700

857

Young, Owen D., 365, 382, 403n
efforts to secure Chicago participation, 1932, 387–388
favored purchases with Oct. 1931 discount rate rise, 382
hesitation to encourage member bank borrowing, 406n
on open market purchases vs. greenback issues, 518n
opposed immediate rise in reserve requirements, 1935, 521n
Young, Roy A., 255n, 256, 258, 259, 261n, 265, 267, 365, 376, 384n, 385n, 386, 389, 416
conflict with Harrison, 364ff.
power of on O.M.P.C. executive committee, 376
opposed:
direct pressure, 256, 265, 267
open market purchases, 387
purchase program, 1932, 385n
pressure to stop 1932 purchases, 377
real bills advocate, 267
transfer to Boston Reserve Bank, 229n